TEXAS ALMANAC

2026-2027

TEXAS STATE HISTORICAL ASSOCIATION 73RD EDITION

TEXAS ALMANAC

2026-2027

BRETT REGAN
Managing Editor

SOFIA TREVIÑO
Assistant Editor

LAUREN C. KERRIGAN
Book Designer

JOEL A. PHILLIPS
Cover Designer

ISBN (Paperback): 978-1-62511-084-8
ISBN (Hardback): 978-1-62511-085-5
ISBN (Digital): 978-1-62511-086-2

Library of Congress ISSN: 2378-2188 (Print)
Library of Congress ISSN: 2378-2234 (Digital)

TEXAS STATE HISTORICAL ASSOCIATION

The University of Texas at Austin
3001 Lake Austin Blvd., Suite 3.116
Austin, TX 78703

Printed by Prisma Austin
Bound in San Antonio by Universal Bookbindery Inc.

For permission requests and additional inquiries:
Brett Regan (brett.regan@tshaonline.org)

Distributed by Texas A&M University Press and the Texas Book Consortium
John H. Lindsey Building, Lewis Street
4354 TAMU
College Station, TX 77843

Welcome to the Texas Almanac!

The state's most popular reference book is back, but the 73rd edition looks and feels different.

The *Texas Almanac* is now the official State Book of Texas. Our team is thrilled with the designation and the support from Representative Will Metcalf and Senator Mayes Middleton that made it possible.

You learn a lot by putting a book together, and this one is undoubtedly a great teacher.

Whether it's the impressive feature articles, fun lists, unbelievable photo galleries, the revamped county section, or updated tables, there's so much packed into these pages. We have spent the last year looking to honor the past, present, and future of the Lone Star State with something new, and we are incredibly proud of the result.

The special feel of the 2026-2027 version would not have been possible without the creativity and dedication of Sofia Treviño and Lauren C. Kerrigan. Their attention to detail, efficiency, and passion brought these chapters to life. It's truly amazing to see their talents shine from start to finish.

We appreciate the wonderful work and contributions from Joel Phillips (cover designer), Jay Knarr (indexer), Kaiya Little (editorial assistant), Anthony Head (writer), Robert Goodwin (writer), Carolyn Barta (writer), John Robinson (Texas A&M AgriLife Extension Service), John Nielsen-Gammon (Texas State Climatologist), Barkley Edwards (from Prisma), and so many more.

This book is built on history, and it's been a pleasure keeping this storied tradition alive.

Brett Regan
Managing Editor, *Texas Almanac*

Founded in 1897, the Texas State Historical Association (TSHA) is an independent nonprofit and the state's longest-running historical organization, dedicated to fostering the appreciation, understanding, and teaching of Texas history. Through its publications (*Texas Almanac, Southwestern Historical Quarterly, Handbook of Texas*), research programs, and educational initiatives, TSHA — housed at the University of Texas at Austin — promotes the rich and diverse heritage of Texas.

Greetings,

As the 48th Governor of the great state of Texas, it is my honor to welcome you to the 2026-2027 edition of the *Texas Almanac,* now recognized as the official State Book of Texas.

Texas is the Lone Star State for a reason: We stand apart as a model for the nation. Jobs are growing here, businesses are expanding here, and families are flocking here. In fact, Texas is growing faster than the nation, and more than eight in 10 who are born here stay here.

Now the eighth-largest economy when compared to the nations of the world, the Texas of today was built on the bold ideas of those who came before us. Men and women who dared to explore the vast new frontier made a living from the natural resources the land offers. They innovated, invested, and persevered, building an even bigger Texas of tomorrow for the generations yet to come.

I invite you to explore the pages of the official State Book of Texas to learn more about the rich and storied heritage of the Lone Star State and its people, government, economics, natural resources, holidays, diverse cultures, education, recreation, the arts, and so much more. Texas is big, and each of our 254 counties has something unique to offer — as do the featured articles in this edition.

If you're not in Texas right now, we invite you to come visit for a while. We're making history every day.

First Lady Cecilia Abbott joins me in thanking the Texas State Historical Association for their dedication to sharing the history and blessings of Texas and for producing this invaluable *Texas Almanac* preserving the past and present for the future of this great state.

Greg Abbott

Greg Abbott
Governor of Texas

People from all over the world admire Texas for our sweeping landscapes, booming economy, deep-rooted values, and rich heritage.

Texas' story is one of liberty, perseverance, and a fierce determination to thrive. Our independence was secured with the blood, sweat, and sacrifice of our forefathers. From early settlers and native peoples to immigrants, freedmen, outlaws, and pioneers, generations of Texans have built a state defined by grit, courage, and hope. Every Texan, past and present, plays a role in shaping our future, which is brighter than ever.

Our enduring commitment to God-given freedoms, personal responsibility, and the right to self-determination has empowered countless Texans to achieve happiness and prosperity.

The *Texas Almanac* has long been a trusted source for understanding our state's history, culture, and people. This past legislative session, in recognition of its importance, the Texas Legislature officially declared it the State Book of Texas.

Join me in celebrating this iconic publication as we continue to honor and learn about the greatest state God ever made: Texas.

Dan Patrick

Dan Patrick
Lt. Governor of Texas

Thank you!

The Texas State Historical Association and *Texas Almanac* team would like to thank everyone listed below for their generosity and participation in the **Great Texas Land Rush** program.

3sa4veterans (Eldorado)
Actress LaKira Patton (Crockett)
Alecia Carver (Serbin)
Andrew & Trina Barlow (Paige)
Andrew Sanchez (Eskota)
Anthony John Herrera (Losoya)
Ashton Miller (League City)
Becky Isbell (Ding Dong)
Bennett Farm & Ranch (Shafter)
Berryman Family Cemetery Association (Cherokee County)
Beverly Vanderpool Gartner (Vanderpool)
Blyth Swartsfager (Gregory)
Boshwynn Middleton (Middleton)
Bradley (Live Oak County)
Campbell Family (Abilene)
Carla Frances Garcia (Cotulla)
Charles Alloway (Brazoria)
Cheryl Smith (Gober)
Chris Gilbert (West Columbia)
Christopher Burge (Farmers Branch)
Chuck Preddy (Noxville)
Cleta Newsom Bramlet Stapp (Cleta)
Collins Family (Hitchcock)
Connie Hagler Jones (Hallettsville)
Curtis Family Estates (Joe Pool Lake)
David Martinez (Thurber)
David Wilson (Cheapside)
Dawson Forward Group, LLC (Dawson)
Delmar Lee Coward Jr. (Raywood, Rock Island)
Demetria Anderson (Lincoln)
Denise Lancaster (Somerset)
Dodie Juarez Scott (Mount Sharp)
Donna Carhart (Goliad County)
Dr. Guylene Rogers Robertson (Dumont)
Elizabeth Martinez-Dvorak (San Bernardo)
Erika Arnold (Ben Arnold)
Frances Moore (Mount Gillion)
Friends in Volente (Volente)
Friends of Gillespie County Country Schools, Inc. (Gillespie County)
G A P Groesbeck (Groesbeck)
Gayle Clemons Newkirk (Holland)
Golda Marie Foster (Pasche)
Hailey Koock (Koockville)
Halle Olson (Coesfield)
Henry D. Hall Jr. (Ad Hall, Milam County)
Her Tribe (Fort Bend County)
Hoytt R. Runnels (Runnels)
Ivy Deaette Frances Easterly (Easterly)
Ivy Easterly (South Padre Island)
Jack Trawick (Trawick)
Jacqueline Grounds Parks (Dodge)
James and Elizabeth Dvorak (Oyster Creek)
Jason Bludworth (Rocksprings)
Jay Wiener (Lufkin, Angelina County)
Jean and Robert Campbell (Lohn)
Jennifer Mraz (Little River-Academy, Abercrombie)
John and Andrea Alford (Shelbyville)
John L. Lemke (Double Header)
John M. Pritchard Jr. (Lavaca County)
John Misner (Anneville)
Johnny & Amber Matsoukas (Gary)
Joy Beavers-Paprskar (Cleburne)
Julie K. Staffel (Cheetham)
Karen Bishop Davis (Bishop)
Kathryn SchwauSch Branson (Harrison)
Kelly Renae Crabb (Crabb)
Kimberly Roe Yuhasz (Mansfield, Quanah)
Kyle Kristopher Duncan (Kyle)
Larry Glen Malin/Malin Custom (Channing)
Laurie Beal Cook (Lueders)
Leopoldo Serna Jr. (Seven Sisters)
Leslie V. Hitt (Papalote)
Margaret Montgomery Chapter, NSDAR (Lake Conroe, Conroe)
Maria Elena Rieck-Telles (Lytton Springs)
Marisa Watkins Jimenez (Watkins)
Markiet Sion (Sion)
Mary (Libby) Bursby (Buckner)
Michael Pittmon (Alto, Old Palestine)
Michelle M. McCoy (Tyler)
Nancy and Ken Rice (Toyah)
Nancy D. Henderson (Sterley)
Norvella Smith (Flaccus)
Officials of TuckerLand-Anderson County (Tucker)
Panola County Judge Rodger G. McLane (Deadwood)
People for Pound Town (Dripping Springs)
Peter Sanford (Peniel)
Rachel Mae Cooper-Anderson (Doak Springs)
Rancho Viesca + Mark M. Ellison (Sarahville de Viesca)
Rebeca Nicholson + Lighthouse Creates LLC (Puerto Rico)
Renee Joy Duhon (Concord)
Rhonda Reynolds Baulch (Cloverhill)
Rio Grande Lodge No. 81 AF & AM (McAllen)
Robert D. Minshew (Crecy)
Roger and Cecelia Motzko (Florence)
Rowena Fojtasek (Rowena)
Royce David James (Jamestown)
Sami (Hoard)
Samuel Collins III (Galveston County)
Shawnee Schaeferling (Shawnee)
Sister Lisa Yvette Patterson (Patterson Settlement)
Steve Denmark (Sabinal)
Symphony Tarbutton (Quitman)
TFR Bronzes (Bolivar, Byers, Clay County)
The Family of LaDonna Lavine Archer (Deweyville)
The Grand Crew (Dog Ridge)
The Johnson & Burns Family (Gonzales County)
The Lanks (Ding Dong)
Tom Gill (Tom Gill)
Tom Jackson (Lynn Grove)
UHAUL Allens Creek Storage (Bovine Bend)
Urban Cookhouse (Prosper)
Veronica and Lonnie Espinoza (Cove)
Whiteside Museum of Natural History (Baylor County)
Wild Lion Productions (Galveston)
Woods Family (White City)

Donors from August 1, 2024 through September 19, 2025.

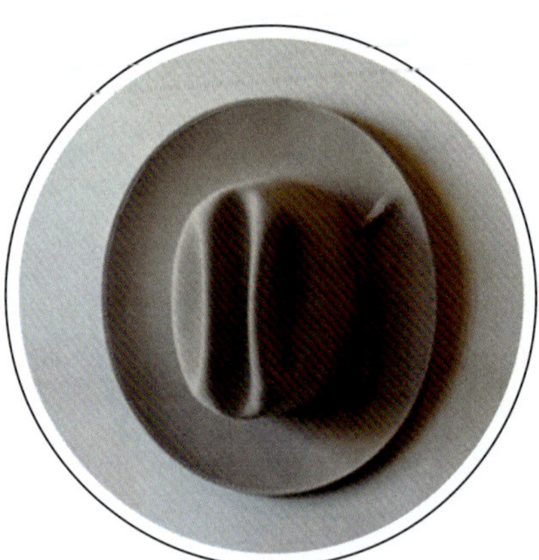

TABLE OF CONTENTS

UNSPLASH/MEGAN BUCKNALL

UNSPLASH/TANELI LAHTINEN

The SPACE AGE in Texas

BY ANTHONY HEAD

UNSPLASH/ALEXANDER ANDREWS

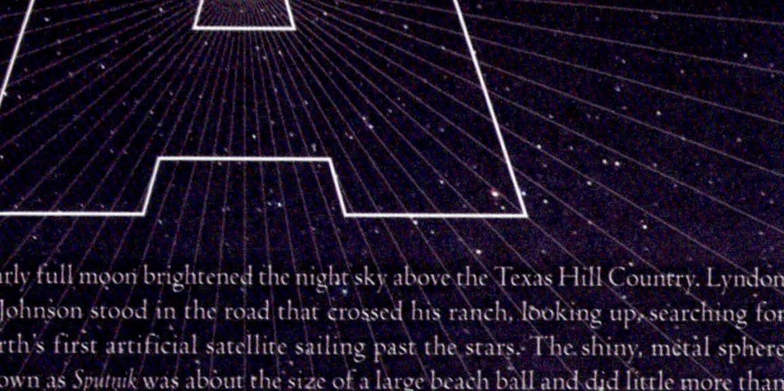

nearly full moon brightened the night sky above the Texas Hill Country. Lyndon B. Johnson stood in the road that crossed his ranch, looking up, searching for Earth's first artificial satellite sailing past the stars. The shiny, metal sphere known as *Sputnik* was about the size of a large beach ball and did little more than orbit Earth every 98 minutes, emitting a constant *beep-beep, beep-beep* from a one-watt radio transmitter. But it was up there — *in space* — and it wasn't made in America. Such thoughts were unsettling to the U.S. Senator from Texas.

From a wider perspective, the Space Age dawned brightly on that moonlit Friday night, October 4, 1957, when the Soviet Union (USSR; now Russia) launched its *Sputnik 1* satellite. Humanity was taking one small step on its way to becoming spacefaring people — ready to chart courses to the Moon, the planets, and the unknowns of our galaxy. As news of the achievement spread, people around the world looked for the tiny point of light silently speeding across the sky, and they felt fascination and awe as well as, like Johnson, fear and uncertainty about the future.

Space was being called the "new frontier" and once Texas got involved, two major American goals — putting people into space and on the Moon — were achieved within a decade.

Today, having earned its singular role in space operations, Texas is a global aerospace leader and mission critical for human spaceflight. After building America's space program in the 1960s, the Lone Star State is one of only a few places in the world that boasts Earth-to-orbit capability.

At the end of 2025 the Space Age remains youthful, relatively speaking, and robust with Texas glowing like the brightest star in the sky.

UNSPLASH/ALEX MOLISKI

THE AMERICAN SPACE AGE DAWNS IN TEXAS

"Our sole hope was the Vanguard rocket, which was to carry our own four-pound satellite into orbit. Then came the final blow. On December 6, 1957, the Vanguard rocket blew up on its launching pad."

LYNDON B. JOHNSON ON THE UNITED STATE'S FIRST ATTEMPT TO LAUNCH A SATELLITE AFTER SPUTNIK.

Beginning in 1944, military rockets could briefly travel beyond the Kármán Line, which is 62 miles above sea level and the generally accepted altitude where Earth's atmosphere ends. It's all space after that. *Sputnik* soared 500 miles past that mark and then stayed in orbit for three months.

Senator Johnson's immediate concern was the country's newly revealed military vulnerabilities. The ongoing Cold War with the USSR pressured both countries into developing ever-more-capable nuclear and thermonuclear weapons; Johnson worried the Soviets intended — or at least threatened — to launch nukes from space and build military bases on the Moon.

The National Aeronautics and Space Act of 1958 declared it a U.S. policy that "activities in space should be devoted to peaceful purposes for the benefit of all mankind." It also established the National Aeronautics and Space Administration (NASA), a civilian-led agency tasked to "plan, direct, and conduct aeronautical and space activities" of a scientific and peaceful nature. Johnson supported the legislation because it didn't prevent the Department of Defense from developing weapons systems for the new frontier above the Kármán Line.

Three years later, as John F. Kennedy's vice president, Johnson strongly backed his boss' commitment to "landing a man on the Moon and returning him safely to the Earth," setting up a high-stakes Space Race with the USSR and its moon-landing ambitions.

Johnson and a coalition of powerful Texas politicians, such as Houston congressman Albert L. Thomas, the chairman of the House Appropriations Committee's Subcommittee on Defense (with outsized control of NASA's budget), and influential Houstonians including Morgan J. Davis, chairman of Humble Oil and Refining Company (now EXXON); George R. Brown, owner of Brown & Root construction company (now KBR); and Kenneth S. Pitzer (president of Rice University), maneuvered the Texas Gulf Coast into position to make Kennedy's moon shot a reality.

In September 1961, Houston was chosen from 23 sites across the country for NASA's Manned Spacecraft Center (MSC). American pride and global leadership would be developed in the laboratories, research centers, and testing facilities of a 1,620-acre campus located south of Houston in an area called Clear Lake City.

Already the country's seventh-largest city and growing with its energy-sector economy, Houston embraced its unique place in the universe by cultivating the kind of aerospace ecosystem needed to execute the world's first human moon landing. Corresponding with the buildup of the commercial aerospace industry, NASA recruited thousands of highly skilled engineers, designers, flight directors, instructors, and scientists for the MSC.

Then came the astronauts — Alan B. Shepard Jr., Virgil I. "Gus" Grissom, and other test pilots — fresh off the thrilling Mercury Program, where they had trained to fly and function in microgravity. Houston welcomed them as heroes-in-the-making in 1962 with a Fourth of July parade and barbecue. The original space cowboys were so enormously popular they were offered free houses, although NASA insisted that went a bit too far.

A full seven years before the world heard Neil A. Armstrong's historic status update, "Houston, Tranquility Base here. The Eagle has landed," the Bayou City entered an exciting era as Space City and never looked back. Perhaps nothing characterized these changing times better than when the Houston Colt .45s became the Astros in 1964 and began playing Major League Baseball in an enormous new air-conditioned stadium that came to be called the Astrodome.

It took three years to construct the MSC, including Building 30, which houses Mission Control, the critical operations and communications link between astronauts and Earth. Crews trained on new Gemini spacecraft at nearby Ellington Field and rigorously conditioned themselves to work and survive under extremely challenging conditions.

Like most everyone else, astronauts and rocket scientists like to live close to the office. Several communities like Clear Lake City and Nassau Bay developed around

ABOVE: Apollo 1 astronauts Gus Grissom, Ed White and Roger B. Chaffee, 1966.

WIKIMEDIA COMMONS

the MSC, while existing towns such as El Lago, Seabrook, and Webster, for example, began attracting NASA employees, aerospace professionals, contractors, and others carrying out the new Space Age work.

The Apollo Program — NASA's official name for the moon-landing missions — included increasingly difficult rocket launches, test flights, and orbital missions taking astronauts ever closer to the lunar surface. The country's morale suffered an early blow on January 27, 1967, when a fire broke out during a launch-rehearsal test of Apollo 1, killing Gus Grissom, Roger B. Chaffee, and Edward H. "Ed" White II.

Only a year and a half earlier, San Antonio celebrated "Ed White Day" to honor its native son becoming the country's first spacewalking astronaut. White made American history on June 3, 1965, spending 23 minutes outside his Gemini 4 spacecraft, afloat in space, more than 100 miles high.

This was NASA's maiden EVA — or extravehicular activity — and when a jubilant White was ordered back into the capsule, he replied, "I'm coming back in, and it's the saddest moment of my life."

President Johnson was in office for all of Apollo's heavy lifting, doing his best to ensure NASA's shrinking budgets didn't stifle missions or momentum, especially when the escalating war in Vietnam and domestic clashes over civil rights required so much energy and so many resources and were impacting so many lives. Across the country, Americans openly questioned the economics of the Space Race — if not the entire space program — threatening to impede Johnson's "Great Society" vision.

The financial and time pressures created by the Space Race were eased somewhat in October 1967, when the U.S. and USSR signed the Treaty on Principles Governing the Activities of States in the Exploration and Use of Outer Space, including the Moon and Other Celestial Bodies. Known as the "Outer Space Treaty," it stated that no country could own the Moon, and so whoever got there first gained serious bragging rights but only a limited advantage for exploiting whatever waited to be exploited.

In late December 1968, the U.S. surpassed the USSR's technical capabilities when Apollo 8 and its crew first orbited the Moon, flying 70 miles above its surface before returning to Earth. A few weeks later, when Johnson left office, NASA was about six months from winning the Space Race. Along with his wife, Lady Bird, Johnson attended the enormously significant and historic Apollo 11 launch on July 16, 1969.

Alan L. Bean, Prime Crew Lunar Module Pilot of the Apollo 12 Lunar Landing Mission, in his space suit minus the helmet. He is standing outside beside a mock-up of the Lunar Lander.

Four days later, science-fiction became reality.

Apollo continued for three more years and six missions, including Apollo 12 with Alan L. Bean, the fourth person and first Texan (from Wheeler) to set boots on the Moon; and Apollo 14 with Edgar D. "Ed" Mitchell (from Hereford) as lunar module pilot.

On July 31, 1971, San Antonio's David R. Scott stepped out of Apollo 15's lunar lander, scanned the Moon's surface to the horizon, and said, "As I stand out here in the wonders of the unknown at Hadley, I sort of realize there's a fundamental truth to our nature. Man *must* explore. And this is exploration at its greatest."

Kennedy is forever remembered for issuing the "hard" challenge that sent two men to the Moon's surface. President Richard M. Nixon enjoyed the "most historic telephone call ever made from the White House" on July 29, 1969, when he dialed up Armstrong and Edwin E. "Buzz" Aldrin Jr. after they hopped around for a while on the dusty Moon. Nixon also hosted them and colleague Michael Collins, who had remained in orbit during the landing, at the White House four months after they returned safely to Earth.

When Johnson died in January 1973, the moon missions were over, the U.S. led the planet in space exploration, and Houston would continue building its legacy in humanity's great space achievements.

At the end of the year, NASA renamed MSC as the Lyndon B. Johnson Space Center (JSC).

WIKIMEDIA COMMONS

President Nixon meets the Apollo 11 astronauts, Neil A. Armstrong, Edwin E. Aldrin,Jr., and Michael Collins, on the lawn of the White House on their return from their Global Goodwill Tour.

WIKIMEDIA COMMONS

TRANSFORMING OUR UNDERSTANDING

"Perhaps the most important and lasting impact on the entire space effort in the United States is and will continue to be in the field of education, the field from which the Space Age was born."

FROM A 1972 CONGRESSIONAL REPORT ON SPACE AGE EDUCATION.

Sputnik ignited a crisis of confidence in American education. Students needed *a lot* more instruction in science, technology, engineering, and mathematics (STEM). The National Defense Education Act (NDEA) of 1958 was a course correction in school curriculums to introduce and amplify subjects critical to the burgeoning fields of space operations.

The nation's first dedicated Department of Space Science opened in 1963 at Rice University, which had donated the Clear Lake City acreage for the JSC. With 16 faculty and alumni already having traveled to space, Rice and NASA continue working closely. The Rice Space Institute opened in 2000 as a collaborative research and education hub for space science and technology.

The University of Houston (UH) was another early NASA partner, notably training the space agency's engineers and technicians in computer programming when the MSC was under construction. In 1987, the Sasakawa International Center for Space Architecture opened within UH's Cullen College of Engineering, offering the world's only master's degree in space architecture.

Among several UH alumni-astronauts are mission specialist Guion S. Bluford Jr., who compiled 688 total hours off the planet, and Bruce McCandless II, who used a nitrogen-propelled Manned Maneuvering Unit in 1984 to perform the first untethered spacewalk and saying, "It may have been one small step for Neil but it's a heck of a big leap for me."

Along with an ongoing need for specialty training in heavy industry and manufacturing, the Space Age requires highly educated, critically thinking people constantly dreaming up, researching, devising, and carrying out ever-more-complex activities. And just as the aerospace industry concentrated around and then expanded beyond its Houston base, specialized STEM-heavy fields of education did the same with Texas schools of every academic level.

With intensifying global competition in space activities, Texas universities, like the following, continue making a lasting educational impact for the future:

- **Center for Space Medicine,** Baylor University
- **Center for Space Research,** Cockrell School of Engineering, University of Texas at Austin
- **South Texas Space Science Institute,** University of Texas Rio Grande Valley
- **Space Force University Partnership Program,** University of Texas at El Paso (and other UT system schools)
- **Space Institute,** Texas A&M University in College Station
- **William B. Hanson Center for Space Sciences,** University of Texas at Dallas

KNOWN AS THE "OUTER SPACE TREATY," IT STATED THAT NO COUNTRY COULD OWN THE MOON, AND SO WHOEVER GOT THERE FIRST GAINED SERIOUS BRAGGING RIGHTS BUT ONLY A LIMITED ADVANTAGE FOR EXPLOITING WHATEVER WAITED TO BE EXPLOITED.

LEFT: Skylab Orbital Workshop.
BELOW: Apollo-Soyuz Test Project Flown Silver Robbins Medallion.

MORE GIANT LEAPS (AND SOME WITH GIANT COSTS)

"The Lord has blessed us with a beautiful day here. We appreciate all of the hard work everyone has put into this and we are ready to go."

AMARILLO NATIVE AND SPACE SHUTTLE COLUMBIA COMMANDER RICHARD D. "RICK" HUSBAND MOMENTS BEFORE LIFTOFF ON JANUARY 16, 2003. THE MISSION ENDED FATALLY FOR THE ENTIRE CREW 15 DAYS LATER.

Apollo provided a boost to American pride and valuable lessons for launching the next phase of crewed space missions: extended periods living and working in low-Earth orbit. Crews had walked in space. With America's first orbiting space laboratory, Skylab (May 14, 1973 to February 8, 1974), the time had come to get to work in space.

It wasn't huge, but once deployed approximately 270 miles above Earth, the roughly cylindrical Skylab housed three-person crews conducting science experiments while simultaneously being studied for the effects of prolonged exposure to microgravity. Crews rendezvoused with and departed the station via Apollo Command and Service Modules (CSM), with the first mission lasting 28 days racing through the realm of satellites and leftover spacecraft components.

The second astronaut group included Texan Alan Bean and more than doubled the duration to 59 days. "After 25 days or so we seemed to stabilize physically up there," Bean said after his return. "We seemed to hit a groove and felt we could have stayed there indefinitely."

When Skylab's final crew departed after 84 days in space, NASA expected to reuse the lab once the space shuttles began flying. Extreme solar activity, however, impacted Skylab's orbit and the 170,000-pound scientific outpost gradually descended from its orbit. On July 11, 1979, much of Skylab burned up re-entering Earth's atmosphere, although remaining debris fell into the Indian Ocean and populated areas of western Australia.

The Apollo-Soyuz Test Project (July 15–24, 1975) was NASA's second crewed program after beating the USSR to the Moon, and it became a significant achievement of Cold War cooperation. Three American astronauts aboard an

WIKIMEDIA COMMONS

Columbia Space Shuttle.

Apollo CSM rendezvoused in orbit with two cosmonauts in a Soyuz capsule. After docking the spacecraft together and opening the adjoining hatches, Americans and Soviets shook hands about 140 miles above the Earth.

Both countries were inching toward improved geopolitical relations, making the moment a poignant gesture. More than a symbolic photo-op, however, the mission marked a significant turning point for international space relations. The crews previously trained together in the U.S. and USSR, and in space they performed joint scientific and technical experiments, establishing a working relationship for the future International Space Station (ISS).

Low -Earth-orbit transportation became a priority in the late 1970s and early 1980s, although concepts for a reusable spaceplane for shuttling humans between Earth and orbiting space stations were devised even before the Apollo missions. When NASA decided to construct a long-term space station, it needed big, reliable, and reusable vehicles for the job.

The new orbiters resembled futuristic jets (for that time, at least) with massive cargo bays. Launched from Earth with huge fuel tanks and reusable boosters, Space Shuttles, as they were known, were aerodynamically designed for hypersonic, supersonic, sub-sonic, and landing-speed environments. They touched down on aircraft runways and launched again after a short period of servicing.

Every crewmember of every shuttle mission trained at the JSC. They lived nearby or in Houston, often for years that sometimes stretched into decades, raising families, coaching Little League, shuttling the drill team, cheering on the Astros and the NBA's Houston Rockets — participating in all the typical rhythms and routines of life on Earth. Until launch day. Until liftoff.

Robert L. Crippen of Beaumont piloted Space Shuttle *Columbia* on the program's maiden flight, April 12, 1981. After orbiting Earth 37 times and returning, *Columbia* launched again exactly seven months later. As with every crewed operation above the Kármán Line, JSC's Mission Control managed both flights.

Packed with space-station components, satellites, and other payloads, the shuttle program spanned 135 missions over 30 years. It suffered two tragic and fatal setbacks: in January 1986, *Challenger* exploded 73 seconds after liftoff; and *Columbia* was destroyed during its re-entry in February 2003. Both crews were lost. Following the second disaster, President George W. Bush ordered all shuttles permanently grounded upon completion of the ISS.

THE SPACE SHUTTLE FLEET

ENTERPRISE

Dates of Operation: August 12, 1977 – October 26, 1977

Not intended for spaceflight, this orbiter test model helped determine the shuttle-frame's flight-worthiness and landing capabilities.

COLUMBIA

Dates of Operation: April 12, 1981 – February 1, 2003

Number of Missions: 28

Deployed satellites as well as the Chandra X-ray-detecting space telescope. Columbia's final mission ended tragically on February 1, 2003, when the orbiter burned up during its re-entry. All seven crewmembers died. Debris from the shuttle was discovered in Texas and Louisiana.

CHALLENGER

Dates of Operation: April 4, 1983 – January 28, 1986

Number of Missions: 10

Deployed commercial satellites and carried the European Space Agency's Spacelab. Challenger's final mission on January 28, 1986, ended in an explosion shortly after launching from Kennedy Space Center in Florida, killing all seven crewmembers.

DISCOVERY

Dates of Operation: August 30, 1984 – March 9, 2011

Number of Missions: 39

Deployed several ISS components and the Hubble Space Telescope. It was the final shuttle to dock with Russia's space station Mir.

ATLANTIS

Dates of Operation: October 3, 1985 – July 21, 2011

Number of Missions: 33

Delivered components for the ISS, conducted missions with the Russian space station Mir, and carried aboard the European Space Agency's Spacelab. Atlantis' final flight marked the end of the Shuttle Program.

ENDEAVOUR

Dates of Operation: May 7, 1992 – June 1, 2011

Number of Missions: 25

In addition to delivering the first U.S.-built component to the ISS and repairing the Hubble Space Telescope, a crew aboard the Endeavour spacewalked to retrieve — with their gloved hands — a wayward satellite and guide it into the cargo bay.

ISS-56, International Space Station.

THE INTERNATIONAL SPACE STATION

In June 2024, the news cycle began lighting up with reports of two American astronauts "stranded" 250 miles above Earth at the ISS. NASA's Sunita L. "Suni" Williams and Barry E. "Butch" Wilmore arrived for an eight-day mission aboard a Boeing Starliner capsule, which did not perform as expected and subsequently returned to Earth without its crew aboard.

Williams and Wilmore spent 286 days in space before a SpaceX Dragon Capsule retrieved them in March 2025. The ordeal was a setback for one legacy aerospace company and a triumph for a relatively new one, but the ISS performed exactly as expected. Williams told a reporter a couple of weeks before returning to Earth, "You know, we've got food, we've got clothes. We have great crew members up here."

In addition to being well-supplied, the ISS is a truly magnificent flying machine: a microgravity research laboratory moving at nearly five miles every second. Including its large solar arrays, the ISS spans almost the length of a football field with end zones, and there's habitable space comparable to a five-bedroom house. It's been continuously occupied since November 2, 2000, usually with rotating six- and seven-member international crews, and the JSC's Mission Control stays in touch around the clock every day of the year.

Among its many purposes, the ISS is where prolonged exposure to weightlessness is continuously studied in preparation for setting up long-term habitation on the Moon. Williams and Wilmore contributed greatly to this research, although NASA's Francisco "Frank" Rubio stayed aboard the ISS for 371 days in 2022-2023. Cosmonaut Valeri Polyakov spent 437 continuous days in 1994-1995 aboard Mir, the most so far.

President Ronald Reagan originally directed NASA to build a continuously crewed orbiting lab in 1984, but Space Station Freedom (as it would have been called) languished with delays. In the 1990s, following the dissolution of the USSR, the U.S. continued cooperation with the Russian Federation's space program, Roscosmos, and sent space shuttles to its space station, Mir. The ISS was eventually completed with Russia and space agencies from Canada, Japan, and Europe.

Since its inception, the ISS has certainly had its share of technical issues — air leaks, coolant leaks, equipment failures — but it continues as a critical information bridge to the rest of the spacefaring 21st century while contributing to the development of life on Earth.

Even without a telescope, Earthlings can see the ISS sailing past the stars in the night sky, but only until sometime in 2030, when it's expected to meet its operational lifespan. Current NASA plans include deorbiting the ISS to burn up on re-entry over an ocean.

WIKIMEDIA COMMONS

THE DAWNING OF TEXAS' NEW SPACE AGE

"We believe we can fire rocket engines, build our drones and spaceplanes, and still allow people to be present with their families, and I am so proud of that."

SARAH A. "SASSIE" DUGGLEBY, CEO AND CO-FOUNDER OF VENUS AEROSPACE IN HOUSTON.

From a private launch pad on Matagorda Island, approximately 23 miles due east of Rockport (as the ruby-throated hummingbird flies), the *Conestoga I* lifted off on September 9, 1982, and into history as the world's first nongovernmental-agency rocket to reach sub-orbital space. The uncrewed *Conestoga I* was privately financed, built, and launched by Houston's Space Services, and it climbed to about 160 miles above Earth.

Although that sounds like a rather mild achievement from a time that feels light years in the past, it was an unprecedented civilian success. During the following 43 years — a blink of time — the private industry built upon that single flight to earn its dominance in the new frontier.

For example, Blue Origin Enterprises (established in 2000) and Space Exploration Technologies Corp. (SpaceX, established in 2002), started with ambitious visions of returning people to the Moon, traveling to Mars, and establishing deep-space colonies. Their immediate goals, however, were driving down manufacturing and operating costs associated with Earth-to-orbit payload delivery. In other words, better transportation solutions.

After the shuttles retired in 2011, people and things still needed rides to space. Domestic and international demand for those rides, even just for satellite deployment, already exceeded NASA's capabilities. SpaceX's Dragon made the first commercial cargo mission to the ISS in 2012, which was followed by Cygnus spacecraft from Orbital Sciences (now Northrop Grumman) in 2014.

Russian Soyuz, launched from Baikonur Cosmodrome in Kazakhstan, were the primary transportation to the ISS for all crews, no matter their nation of origin, until 2020. A SpaceX Crew Dragon arrived at the station on November 17 with four crewmembers aboard, including NASA mission specialist Shannon Walker, a native of Houston.

"Space Station in so many ways felt exactly the same when I was there the second time as I was the first time. The difference, however, was there is so much more *stuff* on the space station," Walker said in 2022. "And so it's a more crowded space, but a very familiar space to live."

FROM TEXAS TO THE MOON: THE NEW SPACE RACE

"Starship is so big that the concept of how we put things in space, how people will travel in space, is totally different."

GWYNNE R. SHOTWELL, SPACE X PRESIDENT AND CEO, DISCUSSING SPACE LOGISTICS IN NOVEMBER 2024.

When President Donald J. Trump signed Space Directive-1 on December 11, 2017, he refocused America's space program for using the Moon as the likely launch site for human travel to deep space and Mars. Project Artemis is NASA's collaboration with international and commercial partners to execute a new, long-lasting moonshot. In November 2024, the uncrewed *Artemis 1* Space Launch System (SLS) completed a successful test flight around the Moon.

Right now, women and men are training at the JSC's facilities for future crewed lunar missions, and just as vital, many of the world's most innovative technology-driven companies are driving the state's growing, diversified space economy. There are also four FAA-licensed spaceports and launch sites that helped take Texas from being the home of Space City to being America's Space State .

On July 20, 2021, Blue Origin's reusable New Shepard Rocket and Crew Capsule System launched the first humans into space *from Texas soil.* Although Blue Origin's goals for human spaceflight include establishing critical infrastructure for a multiplanetary future, its launch pad at Corn Ranch, near Van Horn in West Texas, is also becoming well-known for its role in the state's growing appeal for astrotourism.

Blue Origin M7. New Shepard Crew Capsule.

WIKIMEDIA COMMONS

SpaceX is headquartered near Brownsville at the newly incorporated company town of Starbase (formerly Boca Chica Village), where it develops fully reusable, heavy lift launch vehicles, including Starship, and conducts regular test launches. Additionally, the SpaceX Rocket Development and Test Facility is located in McGregor, and Bastrop is home to its Starlink satellite manufacturing facility.

The Austin region is growing with future-facing businesses, including Firefly Aerospace, which was originally formed in 2014 and is headquartered in Cedar Park. Firefly is the second commercial company to achieve a soft landing of an unmanned craft on the Moon with its Blue Ghost lander in March 2025. Houston-based Intuitive Machines' Odysseus accomplished the feat first in February 2024.

There is so much to learn about the Moon, including how to extract its helium, gold, water, and other elements and return them to Earth, or incorporate them into long-term lunar infrastructure needed for machines and humans to function. A whole bunch of heavy-lift rockets, orbiters, cargo containers, and landers need to be built. A colony's worth of oxygen and water has to be supplied. And what about food?

While those and countless more critical issues get worked out, the future uncertainties of being spacefaring people contribute greatly to the urgency of today's Space Race, one with many more participants, like the European Space Union, China, India, Brazil, and Japan, and with many lunar prizes for the taking.

Some old thorny issues are still in play. Even in the vastness of space tensions are brewing over future claimed and unclaimed lunar territory. In July 2022, during the Russia-Ukraine war, Russia announced its withdrawal from the ISS to build its own orbital space stations. Like the U.S., China, and other countries, Russia's plans include permanent lunar colonies, some of which, undoubtedly, are destined for the far side of the Moon, always facing away from Earth due to its synchronous rotation. Its communication and observation challenges make it something of a shadowy destination.

Illustration of a SpaceX Crew Dragon spacecraft.

Lyndon B. Johnson agonized over space becoming a war zone. Although there has not (officially) been active cosmic military engagement, President Trump established the U.S. Space Force within the Department of the Air Force in December 2019. Military assets, including satellites, are essential tools for America's defense above and below the Kármán Line.

Texas-based Firefly develops rapid space access systems for Space Force and is, along with other companies, improving space domain awareness and providing tactical response capabilities.

Not surprisingly, satellites from several nations already orbit the Moon. Although the U.S.-drafted Artemis Accords of 2020 specify principles for "peaceful, sustainable, and transparent cooperation in space," they are not accepted by every country who signed the Outer Space Treaty, which leaves Earth's only natural satellite virtually unregulated and lawless ahead of humanity's settlement. Without long-term international — and perhaps intergalactic — lunar agreements, the Moon's future colonization could make the settlement of the American Frontier appear positively peaceful by comparison.

THE EARTH-SPACE DYNAMIC

"A lot of what we do is tied to what you can see in the sky."

DAMOND BENNINGFIELD, WRITER AND PRODUCER OF STARDATE RADIO PROGRAM BY THE UNIVERSITY OF TEXAS MCDONALD OBSERVATORY, ON HOW HE CHOOSES CONTENT.

In the time it takes a length of damaged wire to short out, Apollo 13's mission became solely about survival and no longer about landing men on the Moon. After the short led to an oxygen tank explosion on April 13, 1970, the crew traveled approximately 248,655 miles from Earth during their perilous return. No one has piloted a spacecraft any deeper into space.

Probes, orbiters, landers, and rovers, however, have been sent to distant planets and their moons, the Sun, asteroids, and elsewhere since 1959. In the case of *Voyager 1* and *Voyager 2* — built with Texas Instruments' integrated circuits and launched in 1977 — both craft are more than 20 billion miles from Earth, still probing their way over 30,000 miles an hour through interstellar space.

More than two dozen orbiting telescopes focus on deep space and capture awe-inspiring images of streaking comets, black holes, and galaxies far, far away. Locations for terrestrial-based telescopes hardly get better than Mount Locke, between Big Bend National Park and El Paso, beneath some of the darkest skies in the country.

When the University of Texas McDonald Observatory opened near Fort Davis in 1939, it boasted the world's second-largest telescope. Today, it operates five, including one of the world's most powerful: the Hobby-Eberly Telescope.

ETHAN TWEEDIE PHOTOGRAPHYCOURTESY OF MCDONALDOBSERVATORY.ORG

The observatory is located among more than 15,000 square miles called the Big Bend Dark Sky Reserve, working to protect and preserve views of Texas' night sky. Since 2010, the observatory has promoted the Dark Skies Initiative to raise awareness of the detrimental effects of light pollution on human health and wildlife. Misdirected nighttime lighting also blocks much of the universe from the world's eyes and telescopes.

Looking up from so many points in Texas, the views often include satellites as tiny points of light sailing past the stars. They are quite useful for everything wireless, such as communication, navigation, missile guidance systems, cell phone apps, streaming movies, weather forecasts, monitoring crop growth, credit card transactions, rescue-and-recovery operations, printing and distributing the *Texas Almanac*, and so much more.

With the desire and need for global interconnectivity surging — by one estimate, there may be more than 43,000 active satellites in Earth's orbit by 2032 — Texas remains strategically positioned with Earth-to-orbit capabilities. Companies like AST SpaceMobile in Midland are part of the state's still-growing satellite-manufacturing sector.

PIONEERS OF THE FUTURE

"There are no rules of the road, so to speak, in space."

DR. MORIBA K. JAH, PROFESSOR OF AEROSPACE ENGINEERING AND ENGINEERING MECHANICS, UNIVERSITY OF TEXAS AT AUSTIN, ON THE LOGISTICAL CHALLENGE OF DEALING WITH ORBITING SPACE DEBRIS.

There is not enough space in the entire *Texas Almanac* to thoroughly document how much space-age knowledge and technology have advanced life on Earth. Nor is this article sufficient to account for every Texas company, organization, and individual making noteworthy contributions. But since the 1960s, Texas has proven to have the right stuff to be one of the world's most important space regions.

In 2023, the Texas Legislature re-established the Texas Space Commission, which originally operated between 1987 and 2003, and established the Texas Aerospace Research and

Mission Control Center minutes after the launch of the Apollo 15 lunar landing mission, 1971.

Space Economy Consortium to both work with and promote the state's commercial aerospace and related technology industries, academic institutions, and numerous economic interests. With more people and more stuff needing to go to space, there are more expectations for Texas to make it happen.

Fueled in part by artificial intelligence (AI), the expanding fields of space operations must also tackle the problems of abundant orbiting space junk; locate asteroids on collision courses with Earth and then find solutions for survival; negotiate cosmic real estate developments; establish safe corridors between here and the Moon (because somehow there *will* be traffic jams in space); get to the bottom of Unidentified Anomalous Phenomena (UAPs, formerly UFOs); and discover and perhaps make contact with other life in the universe.

The first human birth in space has yet to occur, but it's coming. Death, too, remains inevitable, and in 1994 Space Services (which launched *Conestoga 1* in 1982) founded Celestis to offer memorial spaceflight services. The Houston-based company facilitates the launch of cremated ashes and DNA samples to Earth's orbit, the Moon, and forever into deep space.

THE FINAL FRONTIER

The American Frontier was declared closed in 1890, with no remaining land regions left to settle, including within the boundaries of Texas, and it wasn't until the 1950s that the expression "new frontier" began increasingly to imply that everywhere in the universe would someday be humanity's realm to roam.

We have begun to roam.

The Space Age didn't really begin with *Sputnik*, or with the conception of the "new frontier," or when World War II's rockets crossed the Kármán Line. It was already here 15,000 years ago, during the Paleoindian period, when people looked up from where Spring Lake in San Marcos is today in order to navigate by the stars. That's also just 37 miles from where Lyndon B. Johnson would someday stare at that same sky, looking for a tiny satellite.

In fact, for most of human history, wherever we intended to go, we always looked up to the sky first.

Obviously, the Space Age began when space itself started, and no human gets back to that point. But that doesn't mean we're all lost in space. We are now navigating *through* space, charting courses to what will inevitably be our final frontier. Yet, the deeper we travel, the more we realize how precious Earth is. After all, there is one planet in the universe that's home to Texas. ★

HOUSTON: AMERICA'S MISSION CONTROL

"Houston" is the radio call sign known around the world for NASA's mission control operations rooms inside the JSC. Since 1965, mission control has facilitated every aspect of crewed missions from the time the rockets clear the launch tower until the astronauts return to Earth. Its oversight includes tracking and communicating with spacecraft and managing operations for American crews aboard the International Space Station.

In October 1985, the control rooms used during Project Apollo were listed in the National Register of Historic Places as the "Apollo Mission Control Center." A two-year restoration (2017-2019) returned the appearance of the rooms to the night of July 20, 1969, when Apollo 11 landed on the Moon.

During that renovation, just after Holly E. Ridings was named the JSC's Chief Flight Director in 2018, she made a point to spend some time alone inside the historic control center, contemplating the legacy of human achievement surrounding her, and she told herself, "You're part of the unbroken chain. You have this responsibility for whatever time you're given. Don't screw it up."

The public can view these decommissioned rooms as part of the "Historic Mission Control" tram tour offered at Space Center Houston, the JSC's Official Visitor Center.

WIKIMEDIA COMMONS

Texas
THE LONE STAR STATE
UNSPLASH/DAVID ESTRADAHCLIFIELD

CAPITAL
Austin

GOVERNMENT
Bicameral Legislature

28TH STATE TO ENTER THE UNION
Dec. 29, 1845

PRESENT CONSTITUTION ADOPTED
1876

STATE SENATORS
31

STATE REPRESENTATIVES
150

POPULATION

Population, 2024 (est.)	**31,290,831**
Population, 2020 U.S. Census	29,145,505
Population increase, 2020-2024	7.3%
Population, 2010 U.S. Census	25,145,561
Population increase, 2010-2024	24.4%

Ethnicity, 2024	**Percent**
Hispanic	39.8%
White	39.6%
Black	13.6%
Asian	6.0%
Other	1.3%

10 Largest Cities

Houston (Harris Co.)	2,390,125
San Antonio (Bexar Co.)	1,526,656
Dallas (Dallas Co.)	1,326,087
Fort Worth (Tarrant Co.)	1,008,106
Austin (Travis Co.)	993,588
El Paso (El Paso Co.)	681,723
Arlington (Tarrant Co.)	403,672
Corpus Christi (Nueces Co.)	317,317
Plano (Collin Co.)	293,286
Lubbock (Lubbock Co.)	272,086

Number of Counties	**254**
Largest population: Harris Co.	5,009,302
Smallest population: Loving Co.	48

Number of Incorporated Cities	**1,226**
Number of cities of 100,000 pop. or more	43
Number of cities of 50,000 pop. or more	73
Number of cities of 10,000 pop. or more	251

(Population and Race: U.S. Census Estimates for 2024)

NATURAL ENVIRONMENT

Area	268,599 sq. miles
Land Area	261,258.6 sq. miles
Water Area	7,340.4 sq. miles

Geographic Center
Approximately 15 miles northeast of Brady in northern McCulloch County.

Highest Point
Guadalupe Peak (8,751 ft.) in Culberson County in far West Texas.

Lowest Point
Gulf of Mexico (sea level).

UNSPLASH/JERRY KAVAN

UNSPLASH/JUDAH ESTRADA

Normal Average Annual Precipitation Range
From 55.41 inches in Newton County on the Louisiana border to 8.79 inches in El Paso County in far West Texas.

Record Highest Temperature
Seymour, Baylor Co. . . . . . Aug. 12, 1936, 120°F
Monahans, Ward Co.. . . . . June 28, 1994, 120°F

Record Lowest Temperature
Tulia, Swisher Co. . . . . Feb. 12, 1899, -23°F
Seminole, Gaines Co. . . . . . Feb. 8, 1933, -23°F

BUSINESS & ECONOMY

Per Capita Personal Income (2023) $66,252

Per Capita Consumption (2023) $52,299
Housing and utilities $9,428
Health care $7,411

Non-Farm Employment (2024) 14,318,700

Employment by Select Industries
Trade, transportation, utilities 2,803,400
Professional & business services. . . . 2,165,300
Government 2,114,800
Goods producing 2,064,200
Education & health services 1,972,400
Leisure & hospitality 1,532,900
(Per capita income/consumption: U.S. Bureau of Economic Analysis. Employment: Texas Workforce Commission)

Manufactures: Chemicals & allied products, petroleum & coal products, food & kindred products, transportation equipment.

Farm Products: Cattle, cotton, vegetables, fruits, nursery & greenhouse, dairy products.

Minerals: Petroleum, natural gas, & natural gas liquids.

Top 5 Industries by Contribution to GDP, 2024
Financial Activities . . . . $519.4 billion
Trade, Trans., & Utilities . . . . $517.1 billion
Professional & Bus. Services. . . . . $331.3 billion
Manufacturing. . . . . $312.3 billion
Natural Resources & Mining . . . . $199.2 billion
(2024 Comprehensive Annual Financial Report for the State of Texas)

Top Oil- and Gas-Producing Counties, 2024
Oil: Martin County, 245,104,438 bbl
Gas: Reeves County, 1,137,566,056 mcf
(Texas Railroad Commission)

Agriculture (2023)
Total cash receipts . . . . $29.9 billion
Animals & products . . . . $22.3 billion
All crops. . . . . $7.6 billion
Total exports. . . . . $6.6 billion
Number of farms (estimate) 231,000
Total net farm income. . . . . $15.4 billion
(U.S. Department of Agriculture, National Agricultural Statistics Service Farm Numbers)

*Honor the Texas flag;
I pledge allegiance
to thee, Texas,
one state under God,
one and indivisible.*

PLEDGE TO THE TEXAS FLAG

FLAGS OF TEXAS

Texas is called the **Lone Star State** because of its state flag with a single star. The state flag was also the **flag of the Republic of Texas**.

SIX FLAGS OF TEXAS

Six different flags have flown over Texas during eight changes of sovereignty. The accepted sequence of these flags follows:

Spain: 1519-1685, 1690-1821
France: 1685-1690
Mexico: 1821-1836
Republic of Texas: 1836-1845
Confederate States of America: 1861-1865
United States of America: 1845-1861, 1865-Present

EVOLUTION OF THE LONE STAR FLAG

The Convention at Washington-on-the-Brazos in March 1836 allegedly adopted a flag for the Republic that was designed by **Lorenzo de Zavala.** The design of de Zavala's flag is unknown, but the convention journals state that a "Rainbow and star of five points above the western horizon; and a star of six points sinking below" was added to de Zavala's flag.

There was a suggestion the letters "T E X A S" be placed around the star in the flag, but there is no evidence that the Convention ever approved a final flag design. Probably because of the hasty dispersion of the Convention and the loss of part of the Convention notes, nothing further was done with the Convention's proposals for a national flag.

A **so-called "Zavala flag"** is sometimes flown in Texas today that consists of a blue field with a white five-pointed star in the center and the letters "T E X A S" between the star points, but there is no historical evidence to support this flag's design.

The **first official flag of the Republic,** known as the **National Standard of Texas** or **David G. Burnet's flag,** was adopted by the Texas Congress and approved by President Sam Houston on December 10, 1836. The design **"shall be an azure ground with a large golden star central."**

THE LONE STAR FLAG

On January 25, 1839, President Mirabeau B. Lamar approved the adoption by Congress of a new national flag. This flag consisted of "a blue perpendicular stripe of the width of one third of the whole length of the flag, with a white star of five points in the centre thereof, and two horizontal stripes of equal breadth, the upper stripe white, the lower red, of the length of two thirds of the length of the whole flag." This is the **Lone Star Flag,** which later became the state flag.

Although Senator William H. Wharton proposed the adoption of the Lone Star Flag in 1838, no one knows who actually designed the flag. The Legislature in 1879 inadvertently repealed the law establishing the state flag, but the legislature adopted a new law in 1933 that legally re-established the flag's design.

The red, white, and blue of the state flag stand, respectively, for bravery, purity, and loyalty. The proper **finial for use with** the state flag is either **a star or a spearhead.** Texas is one of only two states that has a flag that formerly served as the flag of an independent nation. The other is Hawaii.

DISPLAYING THE STATE FLAG

The Texas Flag Code was first adopted in 1933 and completely revised in 1993. Laws governing display of the state flag are found in sections 3100.002 through 3100.152 of the Texas Government Code.

Here is a summary of those rules:

★ The Texas flag should be **displayed on state and national holidays** and on special occasions of historical significance. It should also be displayed at every school on regular school-days. **When flown out of doors,** the Texas flag should not be flown earlier than sunrise nor later than sunset unless properly illuminated. It should not be left out in inclement weather unless a weather-proof flag is used. It should be flown with the white stripe uppermost **except in case of distress.**

★ **No flag other than the United States flag should be placed above or, if on the same level,** to the state flag's right (observer's left). The state flag should be underneath the national flag when the two are flown from the same halyard. **When flown from adjacent flagpoles,** the national flag and the state flag should be of approximately the same size and on flagpoles of equal height; the national flag should be on the flag's own right (observer's left).

★ **If the state flag is displayed with the flag of another U.S. state, a nation other than the United States, or an international organization,** the state flag should be, from an observer's perspective, to the left of the other flag on a separate flagpole or flagstaff, and the state flag should not be above the other flag on the same flagpole or flagstaff or on a taller flagpole or flagstaff. If the state flag and the U.S. flag are **displayed from crossed flagstaffs,** the state flag should be, from an observer's perspective, to the right of the U.S. flag and the state flag's flagstaff should be behind the U.S. flag's flagstaff.

★ **When the flag is displayed horizontally,** the white stripe should be above the red stripe and, from an observer's perspective, to the right of the blue stripe. **When the flag is displayed vertically,** the blue stripe should be uppermost and the white stripe should be to the state flag's right (observer's left).

★ If the state and national flags are both **carried in a procession,** the national flag should be on the marching right and state flag should be on the national flag's left (observer's right).

★ **On Memorial Day,** the state flag should be displayed at half-staff until noon and then completely raised. **On Peace Officers Memorial Day** (May 15), the state flag should be displayed at half-staff all day, unless that day is also Armed Forces Day.

★ The state flag should not touch anything beneath it or be dipped to any person or thing except the U.S. flag. Advertising should not be fastened to a flagpole, flagstaff, or halyard on which the state flag is displayed.

★ If a state flag is no longer used or useful as an emblem for display, it should be destroyed, preferably by burning. A **flag retirement ceremony** is set out in the Texas Government Code mentioned earlier.

PLEDGE TO THE TEXAS FLAG

A pledge to the Texas flag was adopted in 1933 by the 43rd Legislature. It contained a phrase, "Flag of 1836," which inadvertently referred to the **David G. Burnet flag** instead of the Lone Star Flag adopted in 1839. In 2007, the 80th Legislature changed the pledge to its current form:

A person reciting the pledge to the state flag should face the flag, place the right hand over the heart, and remove any easily removable hat.

The pledge to the Texas flag may be recited at all public and private meetings at which the Pledge of Allegiance to the national flag is recited and at state historical events and celebrations.

The pledge to the Texas flag should be recited after the Pledge of Allegiance to the United States flag, if both are recited.

UNSPLASH/LUCAS BECK

STATE SYMBOLS

STATE MOTTO

"Friendship"

The word Texas, or Tejas, was the Spanish pronunciation of a Caddo Indian word meaning "friends" or "allies." It was designated by the 41st Legislature in 1930.

Yee Haw!

STATE CITIZENSHIP DESIGNATION

The people of Texas usually call themselves Texans. However, Texian was generally used in the early period of the state's history.

STATE SEAL

The design of the obverse (front) of the State Seal consists of "a star of five points encircled by olive and live oak branches, and the words, 'The State of Texas.' " (State Constitution, Art. IV, Sec. 19.) This design is a slight modification of the Great Seal of the Republic of Texas, adopted by the Congress of the Republic, December 10, 1836, and readopted with modifications in 1839.

An official design for the reverse (back) of the seal was adopted by the 57th Legislature in 1961, but there were discrepancies between the written description and the artistic rendering that was adopted at the same time. To resolve the problems, the 72nd Legislature in 1991 adopted an official design.

The 73rd Legislature in 1993 finally adopted the reverse by law. The current description is in the Texas Government Code, section 3101.001:

"(b) The reverse side of the state seal contains a shield displaying a depiction of:

(1) the Alamo; (2) the cannon of the Battle of Gonzales; and (3) Vince's Bridge.

(c) The shield on the reverse side of the state seal is encircled by:

(1) live oak and olive branches; and (2) the unfurled flags of: (A) the Kingdom of France; (B) the Kingdom of Spain; (C) the United Mexican States; (D) the Republic of Texas; (E) the Confederate States of America; and (F) the United States of America.

(d) Above the shield is emblazoned the motto, 'REMEMBER THE ALAMO,' and beneath are the words, 'TEXAS ONE AND INDIVISIBLE.'

(e) A white five-pointed star hangs over the shield, centered between the flags."

FRONT OF SEAL

BACK OF SEAL

UNSPLASH/CLARISSE MEYER; PATTY BRITO

State Song

The state song of Texas is "Texas, Our Texas." The music was written by the late William J. Marsh (who died February 1, 1971, in Fort Worth at age 90), and the words by Marsh and Gladys Yoakum Wright, also of Fort Worth. It was the winner of a state song contest sponsored by the 41st Legislature and was adopted in 1929. The wording has been changed once: Shortly after Alaska became a state in January 1959, the word "Largest" in the third line was changed by Mr. Marsh to "Boldest."

TEXAS, OUR TEXAS

Texas, our Texas! All hail the mighty State!
Texas, our Texas! So wonderful, so great!
Boldest and grandest, Withstanding ev'ry test;
O Empire wide and glorious, You stand
supremely blest.

CHORUS

God bless you Texas!
And keep you brave and strong,
That you may grow in power and worth,
Thro'out the ages long.

REFRAIN

Texas, O Texas! Your freeborn single star,
Sends out its radiance to nations near and far.
Emblem of freedom! It sets our hearts aglow,
With thoughts of San Jacinto and glorious Alamo.
Texas, dear Texas! From tyrant grip now free,
Shines forth in splendor your star of destiny!
Mother of heroes! We come your children true,
Proclaiming our allegiance, our faith, our love for you.

UNSPLASH/ANISH LAKKAPRAGADA

TEXAS STATE SYMBOLS

STATE BIRD: The mockingbird (*Mimus polyglottos*) is the state bird of Texas, adopted by the 40th Legislature of 1927 at the request of the Texas Federation of Women's Clubs.

STATE FLOWER: The state flower of Texas is the bluebonnet, also called buffalo clover, wolf flower, and el conejo (the rabbit). The bluebonnet was adopted as the state flower, at the request of the Society of Colonial Dames in Texas, by the 27th Legislature in 1901. The original resolution made Lupinus subcarnosus the state flower, but a resolution by the 62nd Legislature in 1971 provided legal status as the state flower of Texas for "Lupinus Texensis and any other variety of bluebonnet."

STATE TREE: The pecan tree (*Carya illinoinensis*) was adopted as the state tree of Texas by the 36th Legislature in 1919. The sentiment that led to its adoption probably grew out of the request of Gov. James Stephen Hogg that a pecan tree be planted at his grave.

OTHER STATE SYMBOLS

In 2001, the Texas Legislature placed restrictions on the adoption of future symbols by requiring that a joint resolution to designate a symbol must specify the item's historical or cultural significance to the state.

STATE AIR FORCE: The Commemorative Air Force (formerly known as the Confederate Air Force), based in Midland at Midland International Airport, was proclaimed the state air force of Texas by the 71st Legislature in 1989.

STATE AMPHIBIAN: The Texas toad was named the state amphibian by the 81st Legislature in 2009.

STATE AQUARIUM: The Texas State Aquarium in Corpus Christi was designated the state aquarium of Texas by the 69th Legislature in 1985.

STATE BISON HERD: The bison herd at Caprock Canyons State Park was named the official Texas State Bison Herd by the 82nd Legislature in 2011.

STATE BLUEBONNET CITY: The city of Ennis in Ellis County was designated the state bluebonnet city by the 75th Legislature in 1997.

STATE BLUEBONNET FESTIVAL: The Chappell Hill Bluebonnet Festival, held in April, was named state bluebonnet festival by the 75th Legislature in 1997.

STATE BLUEBONNET TRAIL: The city of Ennis was proclaimed the official state bluebonnet trail by the 75th Legislature in 1997.

STATE BOOK: The *Texas Almanac* was designated the official state book by the 89th Legislature in 2025.

STATE BOTANICAL GARDEN: The Lady Bird Johnson Wildflower Center, in southwest Austin, was named the State Botanic Garden and Arboretum by the 85th Legislature in 2017. Encompassing 279 acres, it is the largest all-native garden in the state and features more than 800 native plant species.

STATE BREAD: Pan de campo, translated "camp bread" and often called cowboy bread, was named the state bread by the 79th Legislature in 2005. It is a simple baking-powder bread that was a staple of early Texans and often baked in a Dutch oven.

STATE COBBLER: Peach cobbler was named the state cobbler of Texas by the 83rd Legislature in 2013.

STATE COOKING IMPLEMENT: The cast iron Dutch oven was named the cooking implement of Texas by the 79th Legislature in 2005.

STATE CRUSTACEAN: Texas Gulf Shrimp was designated the state crustacean by the 84th Legislature in 2015.

STATE DINOSAUR: *Paluxysaurus jonesi* was proclaimed the state dinosaur by the 81st Legislature in 2009, after it was discovered that the previous state dinosaur, the Brachiosaur Sauropod, Pleurocoelus, (75th Legislature in 1997) had been a misidentification.

STATE DISH: Chili was proclaimed the Texas state dish by the 65th Legislature in 1977.

STATE DOG BREED: The Blue Lacy was designated the state dog breed by the 79th Legislature in 2005. The Blue Lacy is a herding and hunting breed descended from greyhound, scent-hound, and coyote stock and developed by the Lacy brothers, who left Kentucky and settled near Marble Falls in 1858.

STATE DOMINO GAME: "42" was named the state domino game by the 82nd Legislature in 2011.

STATE EPIC POEM: "The Legend of Old Stone Ranch," written by John Worth Cloud, was named the epic poem of Texas by the 61st Legislature in 1969. The work is a 400-page history of the Albany–Fort Griffin area written in verse form.

STATE FIBER AND FABRIC: Cotton was designated the state fiber and fabric of Texas by the 75th Legislature in 1997.

STATE FISH: The Guadalupe bass, a member of the genus *Micropterus* within the sunfish family, was named the state fish of Texas by the 71st Legislature in 1989. It is one of a group of fish collectively known as black bass.

STATE FLOWER SONG: "Bluebonnets," written by Julia D. Booth and Lora C. Crockett, was named the state flower song by the 43rd Legislature in 1933.

STATE FOLK DANCE: The square dance was designated the state folk dance by the 72nd Legislature in 1991.

STATE FOOTWEAR: The cowboy boot was named the state footwear by the 80th Legislature in 2007.

STATE FRUIT: Texas red grapefruit was designated the state fruit by the 73rd Legislature in 1993.

STATE GEM: Texas blue topaz is found in the Llano uplift area in Central Texas, especially west to northwest of Mason. It was designated by the 61st Legislature in 1969.

STATE GEMSTONE CUT: The Lone Star Cut was named the state gemstone cut by the 65th Legislature in 1977.

STATE GRASS: Sideoats grama (*Bouteloua curtipendula*), a native grass found on many different Texas soils, was designated the state grass of Texas by the 62nd Legislature in 1971.

STATE GUN: The cannon was named the state gun by the 89th Legislature in 2025.

STATE HANDGUN: The 1847 Colt Walker pistol was named the state handgun by the 87th Legislature in 2021.

STATE HASHTAGS: #Texas (state), #TexasToDo (tourism), and #txlege (legislature) were all proclaimed state hashtags by the 84th Legislature in 2015.

STATE HAT: The cowboy hat was named the state hat of Texas by the 84th Legislature in 2015.

STATE HEALTH NUT: The pecan was designated the state health nut by the 77th Legislature in 2001.

STATE HORSE: The American Quarter Horse was named state horse by the 81st Legislature in 2009.

STATE INSECT: The Monarch butterfly (*Danaus plexippus*) was designated the state insect by the 74th Legislature in 1995.

STATE KNIFE: The 87th Legislature designated the Bowie knife our official state knife in 2021.

UNSPLASH/CHANTAL LIM; FARES HAMOUCHE; SIMEON JACOBSON

STATE LONGHORN HERD: The longhorn herd at Fort Griffin State Historic Site was named the state longhorn herd by the 61st Legislature in 1969.

STATE MAMMALS: The state mammals were all designated by the 74th Legislature in 1995:

- **FLYING:** Mexican free-tailed bat (*Tadarida brasiliensis*)
- **LARGE:** Longhorn (*Bos Texanus*)
- **SMALL:** Armadillo (*Dasypus novemcinctus*)

STATE MARITIME MUSEUM: The Texas Maritime Museum in Rockport was named the state maritime museum by the 70th Legislature in 1987.

STATE MUSHROOM: The Texas Star Mushroom (*Chorioactis geaster*) was named the official state mushroom by the 87th Legislature in 2021.

STATE MUSIC: Western swing was named the state's official music by the 82nd Legislature in 2011.

STATE MUSICAL INSTRUMENT: The guitar was designated the state musical instrument by the 75th Legislature in 1997.

STATE NATIVE PEPPER: The chiltepin (*Capsicum annuum* var. *glabriusculum*) was named the native pepper of Texas by the 75th Legislature in 1997.

STATE NATIVE SHRUB: Texas purple sage (*Leucophyllum frutescens*) was designated the state native shrub by the 79th Legislature in 2005.

STATE NICKNAME: "The Lone Star State" was designated the state nickname of Texas by the 84th Legislature in 2015.

STATE PASTRIES: Both the sopaipilla and strudel were named the state pastries of Texas by the 78th Legislature in 2003.

STATE PEPPER: The jalapeño pepper (*Capsicum annuum*) was designated the state pepper by the 74th Legislature in 1995.

STATE PIE: Pecan pie was named the state pie by the 83rd Legislature in 2013.

STATE PLANT: The prickly pear cactus (*Genus Opuntia*) was named the state plant by the 74th Legislature in 1995.

STATE PLAYS: There are four official state plays that were designated by the 66th Legislature in 1979:

- The Lone Star
- Texas
- Beyond the Sundown
- Fandangle

STATE POLLINATOR: The Western Honey Bee (*Apis mellifera*) was designated the official pollinator of Texas by the 84th Legislature in 2015.

STATE PRECIOUS METAL: Silver was named the official precious metal by the 80th Legislature in 2007.

STATE RAILROAD: The Texas State Railroad was designated the state railroad by the 78th Legislature in 2003. It is a steam-powered tourist excursion train that runs between the towns of Rusk and Palestine.

STATE REPTILE: The Texas horned lizard (*Phrynosoma cornutum*) was named the state reptile by the 73rd Legislature in 1993.

STATE RODEO DRILL TEAM: Ghostriders were named the official rodeo drill team of Texas by the 80th Legislature in 2007.

STATE SALTWATER FISH: Red Drum (*Sciaenops ocellatus*) was named the state's saltwater fish by the 82nd Legislature in 2011.

STATE SEA TURTLE: Kemp's Ridley Sea Turtle was named the state sea turtle of Texas by the 83rd Legislature in 2013.

STATE SEASHELL: The lightning whelk (*Busycon perversum pulleyi*) was named the state seashell by the 70th Legislature in 1987. One of the few shells that open on the left side, the lightning whelk is named for its colored stripes and is found only on the Gulf Coast.

STATE SHIP: The battleship *USS Texas* was designated the state ship by the 74th Legislature in 1995. The *USS Texas* was launched on May 18, 1912, from Newport News, Virginia, and commissioned on March 12, 1914. In 1919, it became the first U.S. battleship to launch an aircraft, and in 1939, it received the first commercial radar in the U.S. Navy. In 1940, the *Texas* was designated flagship of the U.S. Atlantic Fleet and was the last of the battleships to participate in both World Wars I and II. It was decommissioned on April 21, 1948, and is a State Historic Site, a National Historic Landmark, and a National Mechanical Engineering Landmark. It is docked along the Houston Ship Channel within the San Jacinto Battleground State Historic Site. (Undergoing repairs in drydock in Galveston as of time of publication.)

UNSPLASH/THOMAS M. EVANS; RAUL NAJERA; DOGAN ALPASLAN;

STATE SHRUB: The crape myrtle (*Lagerstroemia indica*) was designated the official state shrub by the 75th Legislature in 1997.

STATE SNACK: Tortilla chips and salsa was named the state snack by the 78th Legislature in 2003.

STATE SPORT: Rodeo was named the state sport of Texas by the 75th Legislature in 1997.

STATE SQUASH: Pumpkin was designated the state squash of Texas by the 83rd Legislature in 2013.

STATE STONE: Petrified palmwood, found in Texas principally near the Gulf Coast, was designated the state stone by the 61st Legislature in 1969.

STATE TALL SHIP: The *Elissa* was named the state tall ship by the 79th Legislature in 2005. The 1877 ship makes its home at the Texas Seaport Museum at the port of Galveston.

STATE TARTAN: The Texas Bluebonnet Tartan was named the official state tartan by the 71st Texas Legislature in 1989.

STATE 10K: The Texas Roundup 10K was named the official state 10K by the 79th Legislature in 2005 to encourage Texans to exercise and incorporate physical activity into their daily lives.

STATE TIE: The bolo tie was designated the state tie by the 80th Legislature in 2007.

STATE VEGETABLE: The Texas sweet onion was designated the state vegetable by the 75th Legislature in 1997.

STATE VEHICLE: The chuck wagon was named the state vehicle by the 79th Legislature in 2005. Texas rancher Charles Goodnight is credited with inventing the chuck wagon to carry food and supplies for the cowboys on trail drives.

STATE WATERLILY: The Nymphaea "Texas Dawn" was named the state waterlily by the 82nd Legislature in 2011.

UNSPLASH/XAVIER MCLAREN, AESTHETES EVAN WISE

Texas

ARTS & CULTURE

UNSPLASH/MEGAN BUCKNALL

Texans IN MUSIC

Ruthie Foster (Gause)
Best Contemporary Blues Album
"Mileage" (Grammys, 2025)

Cody Johnson
(Sebastapool)
Won Song of the Year
(CMA, 2025).

Willie Nelson's 154th album,
"Oh What A Beautiful World" (2025)

Kacey Musgraves (Golden) won Best Country Song for "The Architect" (Grammys, 2025).

Beyoncé (Houston) took home Album of the Year for "Cowboy Carter" (Grammys, 2025).

Post Malone (Grapevine) "F-1 Trillion" (2024)

Norah Jones (Grapevine) Best Traditional Pop Vocal Album "Visions" (2025)

Texas IN FILM & TV

"Landman" Season 2 (2025) was filmed in Fort Worth.

Jennifer Garner (Houston) "Deadpool & Wolverine" (2024)

Woody Harrelson (Midland) "Now You See Me: Now You Don't" (2025)

Pedro Pascal ("The Last of Us") grew up in San Antonio.

"Yellowstone" was filmed at 6666 Ranch in Guthrie.

Sadie Sink (Brenham) "Stranger Things" (S5, 2025)

Glen Powell (Austin) starred in "Twisters" (2024).

Wes Anderson (Houston) won his first Oscar for Best Live Action Short Film for "The Wonderful Story of Henry Sugar" (2024) .

FAMOUS TEXAS MUSEUMS

ABILENE
- Frontier Texas!
- The Grace Museum
- National Center for Children's Illustrated Literature

ALBANY
- Old Jail Art Center

ALPINE
- Museum of the Big Bend

AMARILLO
- Amarillo Museum of Art
- American Quarter Horse Hall of Fame & Museum
- Don Harrington Discovery Center
- Texas Pharmacy Museum

ANGLETON
- Brazoria County Historical Museum

AUSTIN
- Blanton Museum of Art
- Bullock Texas State History Museum
- The Contemporary Austin
- Elisabet Ney Museum
- French Legation Museum
- Harry Ransom Center
- Lady Bird Johnson Wildflower Center
- Lyndon B. Johnson Presidential Library
- Mexic-Arte Museum
- O. Henry Museum
- Pioneer Farms
- Texas Capitol Visitors Center
- Texas Memorial Museum
- Texas Military Forces Museum
- Texas Music Museum
- Thinkery
- Umlauf Sculpture Garden & Museum
- Wild Basin Wilderness Preserve
- Women & Their Work

BAY CITY
- Matagorda County Museum

BEAUMONT
- Art Museum of Southeast Texas
- Edison Museum
- Fire Museum of Texas
- Spindletop/Gladys City Boomtown
- Texas Energy Museum

BEEVILLE
- Beeville Art Museum

BELLVILLE
- Austin County Jail Museum

BELTON
- Bell County Museum

BIG SPRING
- Heritage Museum of Big Spring

BONHAM
- Fannin County Museum of History
- Fort Inglish Village
- Sam Rayburn Library & Museum

BORGER
- Hutchinson County Historical Museum

BROWNSVILLE
- Brownsville Heritage Museum
- Brownsville Museum of Fine Art
- Children's Museum of Brownsville
- Costumes of the Americas Museum
- RGV Commemorative Air Force Museum
- Stillman House Museum

BROWNWOOD
- Brown County Museum of History
- Lehnis Railroad Museum

BRYAN-COLLEGE STATION
- Brazos Valley African American Museum
- Brazos Valley Museum of Natural History
- Children's Museum of the Brazos Valley
- George H.W. Bush Presidential Library
- University Art Galleries

BUFFALO GAP
- Taylor County History Center

BURTON
- Texas Cotton Gin Museum

CANADIAN
- The Citadelle Art Museum
- River Valley Pioneer Museum

CANYON
- Panhandle-Plains Historical Museum

UNSPLASH/ERIC FRANCIS

CARTHAGE
- Texas Country Music Hall of Fame & the Tex Ritter Museum

CLARENDON
- Saints' Roost Museum

CLIFTON
- Bosque Museum

CONROE
- Heritage Museum of Montgomery County

CORPUS CHRISTI
- Art Museum of South Texas
- Corpus Christi Museum of Science & History
- Texas State Aquarium
- Texas State Museum of Asian Cultures
- USS Lexington Museum

CORSICANA
- The Pearce Museum

COTULLA
- Brush Country Museum

DALHART
- XIT Museum

DALLAS
- African American Museum
- Crow Museum of Asian Art
- Dallas Heritage Village
- Dallas Historical Society (Fair Park)
- Dallas Museum of Art
- Frontiers of Flight Museum
- George W. Bush Presidential Library
- Meadows Museum
- Nasher Sculpture Center
- Perot Museum of Nature & Science
- The Sixth Floor Museum

DENISON
- Red River Railroad Museum

DENTON
- Courthouse-on-the-Square Museum
- Denton Firefighters' Museum
- University of North Texas Art Galleries

DUBLIN
- Dublin Bottling Works
- Dublin Rodeo Heritage Museum

DUMAS
- Window on the Plains Museum

EDGEWOOD
- Heritage Park Museum of East Texas

EDINBURG
- Museum of South Texas History

EL CAMPO
- El Campo Museum of Natural History

EL PASO
- Centennial Museum/Chihuahuan Desert Gardens
- El Paso Museum of Archaeology
- El Paso Museum of Art
- El Paso Museum of History

FORT DAVIS
- Chihuahuan Desert Research Institute

FORT STOCKTON
- Annie Riggs Museum

FORT WORTH
- Amon Carter Museum of American Art
- Cattle Raisers Museum
- Fort Worth Museum of Science & History
- Kimbell Art Museum
- Log Cabin Village
- Modern Art Museum of Fort Worth
- National Cowgirl Museum & Hall of Fame
- Sid Richardson Museum
- Texas Civil War Museum
- Fredericksburg
- National Museum of the Pacific War
- Pioneer Museum of Fredericksburg

FRISCO
- Museum of the American Railroad
- National Videogame Museum

GALVESTON
- The Bryan Museum
- Galveston Children's Museum
- Moody Mansion
- Offshore Energy Center/Ocean Star
- Texas Seaport Museum & Tall Ship *Elissa*

GILMER
- Flight of Phoenix Aviation Museum

GREENVILLE
- Audie Murphy/American Cotton Museum

HENDERSON
- Depot Museum

HOUSTON
- Blaffer Art Museum, University of Houston
- Children's Museum of Houston
- Contemporary Arts Museum Houston
- Czech Center Museum Houston
- The Health Museum
- Houston Center for Contemporary Craft
- Houston Center for Photography
- Houston Fire Museum
- Houston Museum of Natural Science
- Lawndale Art Center
- Lone Star Flight Museum
- The Menil Collection
- Museum of Fine Arts, Houston
- San Jacinto Museum of History
- Space Center Houston

HUNTSVILLE
- Sam Houston Memorial Museum & Republic of Texas Presidential Library
- Texas Prison Museum

KERRVILLE
- The Museum of Western Art

KILGORE
- East Texas Oil Museum

LAKE JACKSON
- Lake Jackson Historical Museum

LAREDO
- Lamar Bruni Vergara Planetarium
- Republic of the Rio Grande Museum

LEAGUE CITY
- Butler Longhorn Museum
- West Bay Common School Children's Museum

LONGVIEW
- Longview Museum of Fine Arts

LUBBOCK
- FiberMax Center for Discovery: Agriculture

- Buddy Holly Center
- Museum of Texas Tech University
- National Ranching Heritage Center
- Science Spectrum

LUFKIN
- Naranjo Museum of Natural History
- Texas Forestry Museum

MARFA
- The Chinati Foundation

MARSHALL
- Harrison County Historical Museum
- Michelson Museum of Art

MCALLEN
- International Museum of Art & Science

MCKINNEY
- Heard Natural Science Museum & Wildlife Sanctuary

MIDLAND
- Museum of the Southwest
- Petroleum Museum

NACOGDOCHES
- Millard's Crossing Historic Village

NEW BRAUNFELS
- McKenna Children's Museum
- Sophienburg Museum & Archives

ODESSA
- Ellen Noël Art Museum
- The Presidential Archives & Leadership Library

ORANGE
- Stark Museum of Art

PANHANDLE
- Carson County Square House Museum

PERRYTON
- Museum of the Plains

PLANO
- Heritage Farmstead Museum

PORT ARTHUR
- Museum of the Gulf Coast

PORT LAVACA
- Calhoun County Museum

RICHMOND
- George Ranch Historical Park

ROCKPORT
- Texas Maritime Museum

ROSENBERG
- The Black Cowboy Museum
- Rosenberg Railroad Museum

ROUND TOP
- Henkel Square Market
- Winedale Historical Complex

SAN ANGELO
- Miss Hattie's Bordello Museum
- San Angelo Museum of Fine Arts

SAN ANTONIO
- The Alamo
- Briscoe Western Art Museum
- Holocaust Memorial Museum of San Antonio
- Institute of Texan Cultures
- McNay Art Museum
- San Antonio Art League & Museum
- San Antonio Museum of Art
- The Witte Museum

SAN MARCOS
- LBJ Museum San Marcos
- The Wittliff Collections

SARITA
- Kenedy Ranch Museum of South Texas

SCHULENBURG
- Stanzel Model Aircraft Museum

SERBIN
- Texas Wendish Heritage Museum

SHERMAN
- Sherman Jazz Museum
- The Sherman Museum

SNYDER
- Scurry County Museum

SULPHUR SPRINGS
- Southwest Dairy Museum & Education Center

TEAGUE
- The Burlington-Rock Island Railroad Museum

TEMPLE
- Czech Heritage Museum
- Railroad & Heritage Museum

TEXARKANA
- Museum of Regional History
- The Woodlands
- The Woodlands Children's Museum

THURBER
- W.K. Gordon Museum & Research Center for Industrial History of Texas

TYLER
- Discovery Science Place
- Historic Aviation Memorial Museum
- Smith County Historical Museum
- Tyler Museum of Art

VICTORIA
- Children's Discovery Museum
- Museum of the Coastal Bend
- The Nave Museum

WACO
- Dr Pepper Museum
- Martin Museum of Art
- Mayborn Museum
- Texas Ranger Hall of Fame & Museum
- Texas Sports Hall of Fame

WASHINGTON
- Star of the Republic Museum

WEATHERFORD
- Doss Heritage and Culture Center
- Museum of the Americas
- The National Vietnam War Museum

WHARTON
- 20th Century Technology Museum

WHITE SETTLEMENT
- White Settlement Historical Museum

WICHITA FALLS
- Kell House Museum
- Museum of North Texas History
- Wichita Falls Museum of Art

YOAKUM
- Yoakum Heritage Museum

TEXAS INSTITUTE OF LETTERS AWARDS

Each year since 1939, the Texas Institute of Letters has honored outstanding literature and journalism that is either by Texans or about Texas subjects.

Awards have been made for fiction, nonfiction, Southwest history, general information, magazine and newspaper journalism, children's books, translation, poetry, and book design.

The awards for book design and translation are awarded biyearly.

2024

Best Book of Fiction: Dominic Smith, *Return to Valetto*
Best First Book of Fiction: Drew Buxton, *So Much Heart*
Best Book of Nonfiction: Deborah D.E.E.P. Mouton, *Black Chameleon: Memory, Womanhood, and Myth*
Best Book of Poetry: Jennifer Grotz, *Still Falling: Poems*
Best First Book of Poetry: KB Brookins, *Freedom House*
Most Significant Scholarly Book: Whitney Nell Stewart, *This Is Our Home: Slavery and Struggle on Southern Plantations*
Best Young Adult Book: Laekan Zea Kemp, *An Appetite for Miracles*
Best Middle Grade Book: Diana López, *Los Monstruos: Felice and the Wailing Woman*
Best Picture Book: Xelena González, Adriana M. Garcia, *Remembering*
Best Translation of a Book: Cyrus Cassells, translator of *To The Cypress Again and Again: Tribute to Salvador Espriu* by Salvador Espriu and J.D. Pluecker, translator of *Trash* by Sylvia Aguilar-Zéleny
Best Short Story: Selena Gambrell Anderson, "Jewel of the Gulf of Mexico" in *McSweeney's*
Best Short Nonfiction: Skip Hollandsworth, "Amor Eterno" in *Texas Monthly*
Lon Tinkle Award (for career): Carmen Tafolla

2023

Best Book of Fiction: Rudy Ruiz, *Valley of Shadows*
Best First Book of Fiction: Ramona Reeves, *It Falls Gently All Around and Other Stories*
Best Book of Nonfiction: Kirk Wallace Johnson, *The Fishermen and the Dragon*
Best Book of Poetry: Jasminne Mendez, *City Without Altar*
Best First Book of Poetry: Laura Villareal, *Girl's Guide to Leaving*
Most Significant Scholarly Book: Sam W. Haynes, *Unsettled Land: From Revolution to Republic, the Struggle for Texas*
Best Young Adult Book: Guadalupe García McCall, *Echoes of Grace*
Best Middle Grade Book: Rebecca Balcárcel, *Shine On, Luz Véliz!*
Best Picture Book: Xelena Gonzalez, Adriana M. Garcia, *Where Wonder Grows*
Best Design of a Trade Book: Jennifer Sperry Steinorth, *Her Read* (found poetry of *The Meaning of Art* by Herbert Read)
Best Short Story: Bret Anthony Johnston, "Playing the Ghost" in *Texas Monthly*
Best Short Nonfiction: Gus Bova, "Uvalde Vive" in the *Texas Observer*
Lon Tinkle Award (for career): Beverly Lowry

PUBLIC LIBRARIES IN TEXAS

Texas public libraries continue to strive to meet the education and information needs of Texans by providing library services of high quality with oftentimes-limited resources.

There are currently more than 500 public libraries listed throughout the state.

The challenges facing public libraries in Texas are many and varied. The costs for providing electronic and online sources, in addition to traditional services, are growing faster than budgets.

Urban libraries are trying to serve growing populations, while libraries in rural areas are trying to serve remote populations and provide distance learning where possible.

Source: Library Development Division of the Texas State Library and Archives in Austin.

UNSPLASH/ED ROBERTSON

2022

Best Book of Fiction: Heath Dollar, *Old Country Fiddle: Stories*

Best First Book of Fiction: Babette Fraser Hale, *A Wall of Bright Dead Feathers*

Best Book of Nonfiction: Lise Olsen, *Code of Silence*

Best Book of Poetry: Rodney Gomez, *Arsenal with Praise Song*

Best First Book of Poetry: César Leonardo de León, *Speaking with Grackles by Soapberry Trees*

Most Significant Scholarly Book: Nicholas Keefauver Roland, *Violence in the Hill Country: The Texas Frontier in the Civil War Era*

Best Young Adult Book: David Bowles & Raúl the Third, *The Witch Owl Parliament (Clockwork Curandera)*

Best Middle Grade Book: Varian Johnson, *Playing the Cards You're Dealt*

Best Picture Book: Divya Srinivasan, *What I Am*

Best Translation of a Book: David Bowles, translator of *The Sea-Ringed World: Sacred Stories of the Americas* by María García Esperón

Best Short Story: Dagoberto Gilb, "Two Red Foxes" in *ZYZZYVA*

Best Short Nonfiction: Skip Hollandsworth, "The Notorious Mrs. Mossler" in *Texas Monthly*

Lon Tinkle Award (for career): Celeste Bedford Walker

2021

Best Book of Fiction: Bryan Washington, *Memorial: A Novel*

Best First Book of Fiction: Marisol Cortez, *Luz at Midnight*

Best Book of Nonfiction: Joe Holley, *Sutherland Springs*

Best Book of Poetry: Chera Hammons, *Maps of Injury*

Best First Book of Poetry: David Meischen, *Anyone's Son*

Most Significant Scholarly Book: Miguel Angel González-Quiroga, *War and Peace on the Rio Grande Frontier: 1830-1880*

Best Young Adult Book: Darcie Little Badger, *Elatsoe* and Francisco Stork, *Illegal*

Best Middle Grade Book: Christina Soontornvat, *A Wish in the Dark*

Best Picture Book: Jerome Pumphrey and Jarrett Pumphrey, *The Old Truck*

Best Design of a Trade Book: Mary Ann Jacob, designer of *Daddy-O's Book of Big-Ass Art*, by Bob "Daddy-O" Wade

Best Short Story: David Meischen, "Crossing the Light," in *Storylandia*

Best Short Nonfiction: ire'ne lara silva, "A Place Before Words," in *Texas Highways*

Lon Tinkle Award (for career): Benjamin Alire Sáenz

2020

Best Book of Fiction: Oscar Cásares, *Where We Come From*

Best First Book of Fiction: Bryan Washington, *Lot: Stories*

Best Book of Nonfiction: Holly George-Warren, *Janis: Her Life and Music*

Best Book of Poetry: Naomi Shihab Nye, *The Tiny Journalist*

Best First Book of Poetry: Lupe Mendez, *Why I Am Like Tequila*

Most Significant Scholarly Book: Ron Tyler, *The Art of Texas: 250 Years*

Best Young Adult Book: Rubén Degollado, *Throw: A Novel*

Best Middle Grade Book: Rebecca Balcárcel, *The Other Half of Happy*

Best Picture Book: José M. Hernández, *The Boy Who Touched the Stars*

Best Short Story: Sergio Troncoso, "Rosary on the Border" in *A Peculiar Kind of Immigrant's Son*

Best Translation: Cyrus Cassells, translator of *Still Life with Children: Selected Poems of Francesc Parcerisas*

Best Short Nonfiction: Skip Hollandsworth, "Sabika's Story," in *Texas Monthly*

Lon Tinkle Award (for career): John Rechy

2019

Best Book of Fiction: Natalia Sylvester, *Everyone Knows You Go Home*

Best First Book of Fiction: Stephen Markley, *Ohio*

Best Book of Nonfiction: Ben Fountain, *Beautiful Country Burn Again: Democracy, Rebellion, and Revolution*

Best Book of Poetry: Tarfia Faizullah, *Registers of Illuminated Villages*

Best First Book of Poetry: Megan Peak, *Girldom*

Most Significant Scholarly Book: Brent Nongbri, *God's Library: The Archaeology of the Earliest Christian Manuscripts*

Best Young Adult Book: David Bowles, *The Feathered Serpent, Dark Heart of Sky: Myths of Mexico* and *They Call Me Güero*

Best Middle Grade Book: David Bowles, *They Call Me Güero* and Varian Johnson, *The Parker Inheritance*

Best Picture Book: Chris Barton, *What Can You Do with a Voice Like That?*

Best Short Story: Clay Reynolds, "Autumn Moon," in *New Texas*

Best Short Nonfiction: Clay Reynolds, "Railroad Man," in *New Madrid*

Lon Tinkle Award (for career): Naomi Shihab Nye

2018

Best Book of Fiction: Jan Reid, *Sins of the Younger Sons*

Best First Book of Fiction: Chanelle Benz, *The Man Who Shot Out My Eye is Dead*

Best Book of Nonfiction: Roger D. Hodge, *Texas Blood: Seven Generations Among the Outlaws, Ranchers, Indians, Missionaries, Soldiers, and Smugglers of the Borderlands*

Best Book of Poetry: Sasha Pimentel, *For Want of Water: and other poems*

Best First Book of Poetry: Vanessa Villarreal, *Beast Meridian*

Most Significant Scholarly Book: Jerry D. Thompson, *Tejano Tiger: José de los Santos Benavides and the Texas-Mexico Borderlands, 1823–1891*

Best Young Adult Book: Francisco X. Stork, *Disappeared*

Best Middle Grade Book: Michael Merschel, *Revenge of the Star Survivors*

Best Picture Book: Xelena González and Adriana M. Garcia, *All Around Us*

Best Design of a Trade Book: Mary Ann Jacob, designer, *The Nueces River, Rio Escondido*, by Margie Crisp and William B. Montgomery

Best Translation of a Book: Philip Boehm, translator of *Chasing the King of Hearts,* by Hanna Krall
Best Short Story: Bret Anthony Johnston, "Miss McElroy," in *Ecotone*
Best Short Nonfiction: Rose Cahalan, "Ride Like a Girl," in *Texas Observer*
Lon Tinkle Award (for career): Sandra Cisneros

2017

Best Book of Fiction: Paulette Jiles, *News of the World*
Best First Book of Fiction: Amy Gentry, *Good as Gone*
Best Book of Nonfiction: Skip Hollandsworth, *The Midnight Assassin*
Best Book of Poetry: Bruce Bond, *Gold Bee*
Best First Book of Poetry: Miriam Bird Greenberg, *In the Volcano's Mouth*
Most Significant Scholarly Book: Max Krochmal, *Blue Texas: The Making of a Multiracial Democratic Coalition in the Civil Rights Era*
Best Young Adult Book: Phillippe Diederich, *Playing for the Devil's Fire*
Best Middle Grade Book: Kathi Appelt and Alison McGhee, *Maybe a Fox*
Best Picture Book: Dianna Hutts Aston, *A Beetle Is Shy*
Best Design of a Trade Book: Kristie Lee, *From Tea Cakes to Tamales*
Best Short Story: David Meischen, "Cicada Song," in *Salamander*
Best Short Nonfiction: Stephen Harrigan, "Off Course," in *Texas Monthly*
Lon Tinkle Award (for career): Pat Mora

2016

Best Book of Fiction: Antonio Ruiz–Camacho, *Barefoot Dogs*
Best First Book of Fiction: Mary Helen Specht, *Migratory Animals*
Best Book of Nonfiction: Jan Jarboe Russell, *The Train to Crystal City*
Best Book of Poetry: Laurie Ann Guerrero, *A Crown for Gumecindo*
Best First Book of Poetry: J. Scott Brownlee, *Requiem for Used Ignition Cap*
Most Significant Scholarly Book: Andrew Torget III, *Seeds of Empire*
Best Young Adult Book: Brian Yansky, *Utopia, Iowa*
Best Children's Book: Don Tate, *The Remarkable Story of George Moses Horton: Poet*
Best Picture Book: Pat Mora, *The Remembering Day/El dia de los muertos*
Best Design of a Trade Book: Andrea Caillouet, *The Luck Archive: Exploring Belief, Superstition, and Tradition*
Best Translation of a Book: Marian Schwartz, translator of *Anna Karenina,* by Leo Tolstoy
Best Short Story: Brian Van Reet, "The Chaff," in *Iowa Review*
Best Short Nonfiction: W.K. Stratton, "My Brother's Secret," in *Texas Monthly*
Lon Tinkle Award (for career): Sarah Bird

2015

Best Book of Fiction: Elizabeth Crook, *Monday, Monday*
Best First Book of Fiction: Merritt Tierce, *Love Me Back*
Best Book of Nonfiction: Michael Morton, *Getting Life: An Innocent Man's 25-Year Journey from Prison to Peace*
Best Book of Poetry: Katherine Hoerth, *Goddess Wears Cowboy Boots*
Best First Book of Poetry: Chloe Honum, *The Tulip-Flame*
Most Significant Scholarly Book: Lawrence T. Jones, *Lens on the Texas Frontier*
Best Young Adult Book: Claudia Guadalupe Martinez, *Pig Park*
Best Children's Book: Nikki Lofton, *Nightingale's Nest*
Best Picture Book: Pat Mora and Libby Martinez, *I Pledge Allegiance*
Best Design of a Trade Book: Bill Wittliff and Ellen McKie, *The Devil's Backbone,* written by Bill Wittliff, illustrated by Jack Unruh
Best Short Story: Brian Van Reet, "Eat the Spoil," in *Missouri Review*
Best Short Nonfiction: Pamela Colloff, "The Witness," in *Texas Monthly*

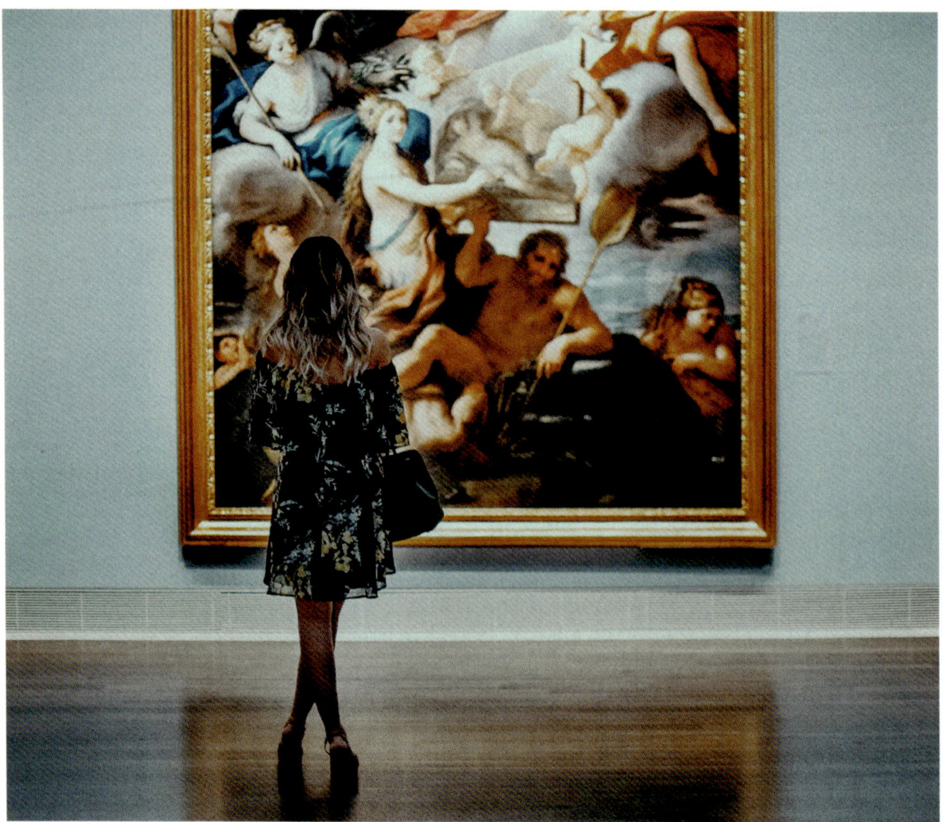

UNSPLASH/DANI MARROQUIN

STATE CULTURAL AGENCIES ASSISTING THE ARTS

Culture in Texas, as in any market, is a mixture of activity generated by both the commercial and the nonprofit sectors. The commercial sector encompasses Texas-based profit-making businesses, including commercial recording artists, nightclubs, record companies, private galleries, assorted boutiques that carry fine art collectibles, and private dance and music halls.

Texas also has extensive cultural resources offered by nonprofit organizations that are engaged in charitable, educational, and humanitarian activities.

The Texas Legislature has authorized five state agencies to administer cultural services and funds for the public good:

- Texas Commission on the Arts
- Texas Film Commission
- Texas Historical Commission
- Texas State Library and Archives Commission
- Texas State Preservation Board

Although not a state agency, another organization that provides cultural services to citizens is Humanities Texas.

The Commission on the Arts was established in 1965 to develop a receptive climate for the arts through the conservation and advancement of Texas' rich and diverse arts and cultural industries.

The Texas Commission on the Arts' goals are:

- Provide grants for the arts and cultural industries in Texas.
- Provide the financial, human, and technical resources necessary to ensure viable arts and cultural communities.
- Promote widespread attendance at arts and cultural performances and exhibitions in Texas.
- Ensure access to arts in Texas through marketing, fundraising, and cultural tourism.

The commission is responsible for several initiatives including:

- **Arts Education:** programs that serve the curricular and training needs of the state's school districts, private schools, and home schools.
- **Marketing and Public Relations:** marketing and fundraising expertise to generate funds for agency operations and increase visibility of the arts in Texas.
- **Cultural Tourism:** programs that develop and promote tourism destinations featuring the arts.

Source: Texas Commission on the Arts..

TEXAS MEDAL OF THE ARTS AWARDS

The Texas Medal of the Arts Awards are presented to artists and arts patrons with Texas ties. The awards are administered by the Texas Cultural Trust Council.

The council was established to raise money and awareness for the Texas Cultural Trust Fund, which was created by the Texas Legislature in 1993 to support cultural arts in Texas.

The medals, awarded every two years, were first presented in 2001. A concurrent proclamation by the state Senate and House of Representatives honors the recipients, and the Governor of Texas presents the awards in Austin.

2025

Multimedia: Terry Allen, *Lubbock* (Artist & Songwriter)
Music/Songwriter: Gary Clark Jr., *Austin*
Literary Arts: Elizabeth Crook, *Austin* (Author)
Musical Theatre: Sandy Duncan, *New London*
Film/Director: Richard Linklater, *Houston/Huntsville*
Arts Education: Texas Music Educators Association
Film/Actor: Dennis Quaid, *Houston*
Visual Arts: Donald Moffett, *San Antonio*
Arts Patron/Foundation: Moody Foundation, *Galveston*
Arts Patron/Individual: Mercedes T. Bass, *Fort Worth*

2023

Lifetime Achievement Award: Carole Cook, *Abilene* (Musical Theater)
Architecture: Miró Rivera Architects: Juan Miró and Miguel Rivera, *Austin*
Arts in Health: Center for Performing Arts Medicine, Houston Methodist
Dance: Septime Webre, *Brownsville*
Fashion: Lela Rose, *Dallas*
Film/Actor: Luke Wilson, *Dallas*
Film/Producer: Taylor Sheridan, *Fort Worth*
Literary Arts: Benjamin Alire Sáenz, *El Paso*
Music: Christopher Cross, *San Antonio*
Music/Songwriter: Miranda Lambert, *Lindale*
Visual Arts: Deborah Roberts, *Austin*

2021

Canceled due to COVID-19.

2019

Design: Brandon Maxwell, *Longview* (Fashion & Photography)
Music: Boz Scaggs, *Plano* (Singer & Songwriter)
Visual Arts: Trenton Doyle Hancock, *Houston and Paris, TX* (Artist)
Music Ensemble: Conspirare, *Austin* (Choral Ensemble)
Literary: Stephen Harrigan, *Austin, Abilene, and Corpus Christi* (Author & Journalist)
Film: Matthew McConaughey, *Austin, Uvalde, and Longview* (Actor)
Multimedia: Mark Seliger, *Amarillo and Houston* (Photographer)
Theater: Jennifer Holliday, *Houston* (Singer & Actor)
Arts Education: Vidal M. Treviño School of Communications and Fine Arts, *Laredo*
Architecture: Elaine Molinar, *El Paso*, and Craig Dykers, *San Antonio*

2017

Lifetime Achievement Award: Kenny Rogers, *Houston*
Multimedia: Kris Kristofferson, *Brownsville*
Music: Yolanda Adams, *Houston*
Visual Arts: Leo Villareal, *El Paso* (Artist)
Dance: Lauren Anderson, *Houston*
Literary: John Phillip Santos, *San Antonio*
Film: Janine Turner, *Euless* (Actor)
Journalism: Scott Pelley, *San Antonio* (News Broadcaster)
Television: Jaclyn Smith, *Houston* (Actor)
Theater: Renée Elise Goldsberry, *Houston*
Arts Education: Dallas Black Dance Theatre
Architecture: Frank Welch, *Dallas*
Individual Arts Patron: Lynn Wyatt, *Houston*
Corporate Arts Patrons: John Paul and Eloise DeJoria, *Austin*
Foundation Arts Patron: Tobin Endowment, *San Antonio*

2015

Lifetime Achievement Award: The Gatlin Brothers of Seminole, *Abilene and Odessa*
Multimedia: Emilio Nicolas Sr., *San Antonio* (Broadcaster)
Music: T. Bone Burnett, *Fort Worth*
Visual Arts: Rick Lowe, *Houston* (Artist)
Dance: Kilgore Rangerettes
Literary: Lawrence Wright, *Austin and Dallas*
Film: Jamie Foxx, *Terrell* (Actor)
Television: Dan Rather, *Wharton* (News Broadcaster)
Television: Chandra Wilson, *Houston* (Actor)
Theater: Robert Schenkkan, *Austin*
Arts Education: Booker T. Washington High School for the Performing and Visual Arts, *Dallas*
Architecture: Charles Renfro, *Houston*
Individual Arts Patron: Margaret McDermott, *Dallas*
Corporate Arts Patron: Dr Pepper Snapple Group, *Plano*
Standing Ovation Award: Ruth Altshuler, *Dallas*

Source: Texas Commission on the Arts.

STATE ARTISTS OF TEXAS

Since 2001, a committee of seven members appointed by the governor, lieutenant governor, and speaker of the House of Representatives selects the poet laureate, state artists, and state musician based on recommendations from the Texas Commission on the Arts.

Previously, the Texas Legislature made the nominations.

The state historian is appointed by the governor and is recommended by both the Texas State Historical Association and the Texas Historical Commission.

Year	Artist, Hometown/Residence	
	Two-dimensional	Three-dimensional
2026	Letitia Huckaby, *Benbrook*	Linda Ridgway, *Dallas*
2025	Angelbert Metoyer, *Houston*	Steve Parker, *Austin*
2024	Michael Ray Charles, *Houston*	Diana Kersey, *Lubbock, San Antonio*
2023	Gaspar Enriquez, *El Paso*	James Watkins, *Lubbock*
2022	Celia Álvarez Muñoz, *El Paso, Arlington*	Jesse Lott, *Houston*
2021	Annette Lawrence, *Denton*	Jennifer Ling Datchuk, *San Antonio*
2020	Earlie Hudnall Jr., *Houston*	Gabriel Dawe, *Dallas*
2019	Mary McCleary, *Nacogdoches*	Rick Lowe, *Houston*
2018	Sedrick Huckaby, *Fort Worth*	Beili Liu, *Austin*
2017	Kermit Oliver, *Refugio, Houston, Waco*	Beverly Penn, *San Marcos*
2016	Dornith Doherty, *Houston, Southlake*	Dario Robleto, *San Antonio, Houston*
2015	Vincent Valdez, *San Antonio*	Margo Sawyer, *Houston, Elgin*
2014	Julie Speed, *Austin, Marfa*	Ken Little, *Canyon, San Antonio*
2013	Jim Woodson, *Waco, Fort Worth*	Joseph Havel, *Houston*
2012	Karl Umlauf, *Waco*	Bill FitzGibbons, *San Antonio*
2011	Melissa Miller, *Austin*	Jesús Moroles, *Rockport*
2010	Marc Burckhardt, *Austin*	John Bennett, *Fredericksburg*
2009	René Alvarado, *San Angelo*	Eliseo Garcia, *Farmers Branch*
2008	Janet Eager Krueger, *Encinal*	Damian Priour, *Austin*
2007	Lee Herring, *Rockwall*	David Keens, *Arlington*
2006	George Boutwell, *Bosque County*	James Surls, *Athens*
2005	Kathy Vargas, *San Antonio*	Sharon Kopriva, *Houston*
2004	Sam Caldwell, *Houston*	David Hickman, *Dallas*
2003	Ralph White, *Austin*	Dixie Friend Gay, *Houston*
2000-02	Vacant	
1998-99	Carl Rice Embrey, *San Antonio*	Edd Hayes, *Humble*
1994-95	Frederick Carter, *El Paso*	Garland A. Weeks, *Wichita Falls*
1993-94	Roy Lee Ward, *Hunt*	James Eddleman, *Lubbock*
1991-92	Woodrow Foster, *Center*	Kent Ullberg, *Corpus Christi*
1990-91	Mondel Rogers, *Sweetwater*	Ron Wells, *Cleveland*

Sources: Texas State Library and Archives; Texas Commission on the Arts; The Dallas Morning News.

Years	Artist, Hometown/Residence
1988-89	George Hallmark, *Walnut Springs*
1987-88	Neil Caldwell, *Angleton*
1986-87	Chuck DeHaan, *Graford*
1984-85	Covelle Jones, *Lubbock*
1983-84	Raul Gutierrez, *San Antonio*
1981-82	Jerry Newman, *Beaumont*
1980-81	Harry Ahysen, *Huntsville*
1979-80	Dalhart Windberg, *Travis County*
1978-79	Jack Cowan, *Rockport*
1977-78	Edward "Buck" Schiwetz, *DeWitt County*
1976-77	James Boren, *Clifton*
1975-1976	Robert Summers, *Glen Rose*, Bicentennial Artist
1975-76	Jack White, *New Braunfels*
1974-75	Joe Rader Roberts, *Dripping Springs*
1973-74	Ronald Thomason, *Weatherford*
1972-73	Melvin C. Warren, *Clifton*
1971-72	Joe Ruiz Grandee, *Arlington*

LETITIA HUCKABY

STATE MUSICIANS: CLASSICAL

Year	Artist, Hometown/Residence
2026	Ana Maria Martinez, *Houston*
2025	Alecia Lawyer, *Houston*

NORAH JONES

STATE MUSICIANS: NONCLASSICAL

Year	Artist, Hometown/Residence
2026	Norah Jones, *Grapevine*
2025	Miranda Lambert, *Austin*
2024	Kelly Clarkson, *Fort Worth, Burleson*
2023	Gary Clark Jr., *Austin*
2022	Eva Ybarra, *San Antonio*
2021	Leon Bridges, *Fort Worth*
2020	Emily Gimble, *Austin*
2019	Little Joe Hernandez, *Temple/San Antonio*
2018	Marcia Ball, *Orange/Austin*
2017	George Strait, *Poteet/San Antonio*
2016	Joe Ely, *Lubbock, Austin*
2015	Jimmie Vaughn, *Dallas/Austin*
2014	Flaco Jiménez, *San Antonio*
2013	Craig Hella Johnson, *Austin*
2012	Billy Gibbons (ZZ Top), *Houston*
2011	Lyle Lovett, *Klein*
2010	Sara Hickman, *Austin*
2009	Willie Nelson, *Abbott/Austin*
2008	Shelley King, *Austin*
2007	Dale Watson, *Pasadena/Austin*
2006	Billy Joe Shaver, *Waco*
2005	Johnny Gimble, *Tyler*
2004	Ray Benson, *Austin*
2003	James Dick, *Round Top*

LEON BRIDGES

COURTESY OF LETITIA HUCKABY; COURTESY OF CHUFFMEDIA; COURTESY OF MICH MUSIC

STATE HISTORIANS OF TEXAS

Year	Historian
2025	Rick McCaslin (Nominated in 2025)
2018-24	Monte Monroe
2016-18	Vacant
2012-16	Bill O'Neal
2009-12	Light Cummins
2007-09	Jesús de la Teja

POETS LAUREATE OF TEXAS

Years	Poet, Hometown/Residence
2026	Kevin Prufer, *Houston*
2025	Octavio Quintanilla, *San Antonio*
2024	Amanda Johnston, *Austin*
2023	ire'ne lara silva, *Edinburg*
2022	Lupe Mendez, *Galveston, Houston, Rio Grande Valley*
2021	Cyrus Cassells, *Austin*
2020	Emmy Pérez, *McAllen*
2019	Carrie Fountain, *Austin*
2018	Carol Coffee Reposa, *San Antonio*
2017	Jenny Browne, *San Antonio*
2016	Laurie Ann Guerrero, *San Antonio*
2015	Carmen Tafolla, *San Antonio*
2014	Dean Young, *Austin*
2013	Rosemary Catacalos, *San Antonio*
2012	Jan Seale, *McAllen*
2011	David M. Parsons, *Conroe*
2010	Karla K. Morton, *Denton, Fort Worth*
2009	Paul Ruffin, *Huntsville*
2008	Larry Thomas, *Houston*
2007	Steven Fromholz, *Kopperl, Sugar Land*
2006	Red Steagall, *Fort Worth*
2005	Alan Birkelbach, *Plano*
2004	Cleatus Rattan, *Cisco*
2003	Jack Myers, *Mesquite*
2002	Vacant
2001	Walter McDonald, *Lubbock*
2000	James Hoggard, *Wichita Falls*
1994-99	Vacant
1993-94	Mildred Baass, *Victoria*
1989-93	Vacant
1988-89	Vassar Miller, *Houston*
1987-88	Ruth E. Reuther, *Wichita Falls*
1983-87	Vacant
1982-83	William D. Barney, *Fort Worth*
1981-82	Vacant
1980-81	Weems S. Dykes, *McCamey*
1979-80	Dorothy B. Elfstroman, *Galveston*
1978-79	Patsy Stodghill, *Dallas*
1977-78	Ruth Carruth, *Vernon*
1976-77	Florice Stripling Jeffers, *Burkburnett*
1975-76	Ethel Osborn Hill, *Port Arthur*
1974-75	Lila Todd O'Neil, *Port Arthur*
1973-74	Violette Newton, *Beaumont*
1972-73	Mrs. Clark Gresham, *Burkburnett*
1971-72	Terry Fontenot, *Port Arthur*
1970-71	Mrs. Robby K. Mitchell, *McKinney*
1969-70	Anne B. Marely, *Austin*
1968	Kathryn Henry Harris, *Waco*
1967	William E. Bard, *Dallas*
1966	Bessie Maas Rowe, *Port Arthur*
1964-65	Jenny Lind Porter, *Austin*
1963	Gwendolyn Bennett Pappas, *Houston*
1962	Marvin Davis Winsett, *Dallas*

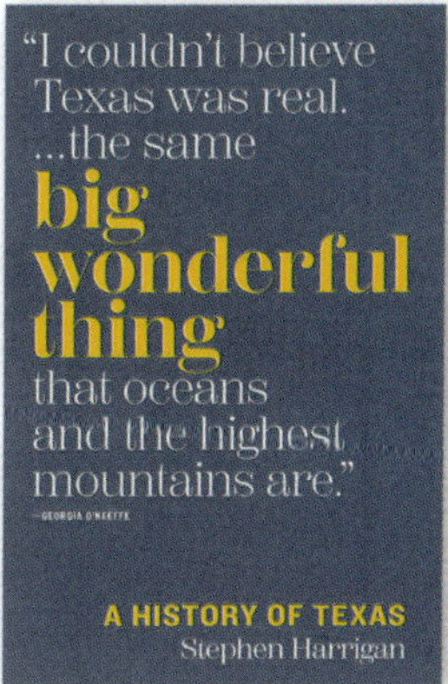

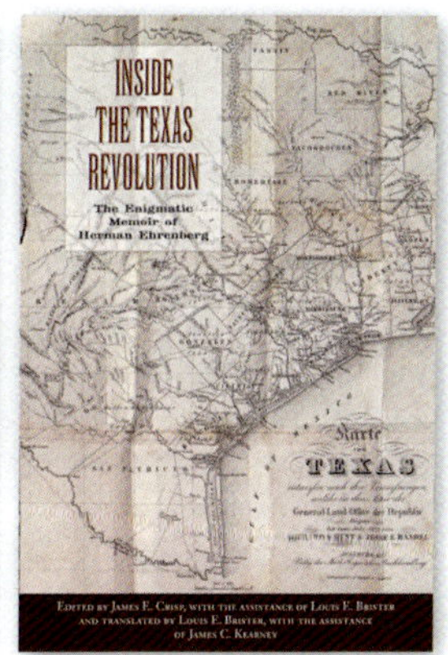

PHILOSOPHICAL SOCIETY OF TEXAS AWARDS OF MERIT

The Philosophical Society of Texas established the Award of Merit in 2000.

The categories were expanded in 2012 to separate categories, one for fiction and one for nonfiction.

In 2015, an award for poetry was introduced.

The book must be about Texas or the author must have been born in or have resided within the boundaries claimed by the Republic of Texas in 1836.

Year	Category	Winner
2024	Fiction	Elizabeth Crook, *The Madstone*, 2023.
	Nonfiction	Ron Tyler, *Texas Lithographs, A Century of History in Images*, 2023.
	Poetry	Ray Gonzalez, *Suggest Paradise*, 2023.
2023	Fiction	Stephen Harrigan, *The Leopard is Loose*, 2022.
	Nonfiction	Sam W. Haynes, *Unsettled Land: From Revolution to Republic, the Struggle for Texas*, 2022.
	Poetry	Rebecca Aronson, *Anchor*, 2022.
2022	Fiction	Jan Reid, *The Song Leader*, 2021.
	Nonfiction	James E. Crisp, *Inside the Texas Revolution: The Enigmatic Memoir of Herman Ehrenberg*, 2021.
	Poetry	César Leonardo de León, *Speaking with Grackles by Soapberry Trees*, 2021.
2021	Fiction	Paulette Jiles, *Simon the Fiddler*, 2020.
	Nonfiction	Gregg Cantrell, *The People's Revolt: Texas Populists and the Roots of American Liberalism*, 2020.
	Poetry	Matt Morton, *Improvisation Without Accompaniment*, 2020.
2020	Fiction	Leila Meachan, *Dragonfly*, 2019.
	Nonfiction	Stephen Harrigan, *Big Wonderful Thing: A History of Texas*, 2019.
	Poetry	Edward Vidaurre, *JazzHouse*, 2019.
2019	Fiction	Elizabeth Crook, *The Which Way Tree*, 2018.
	Nonfiction	Andrew Saansom, *Seasons at Selah: The Legacy of the Bamberger Ranch Preserve*, 2018.
	Poetry	Megan Peak, *Girldom*, 2018.
2018	Fiction	Chanelle Benz, *The Man Who Shot Out My Eye Is Dead*, 2017.
	Nonfiction	Andrew Sansom and William E. Reaves, *Of Texas Rivers and Texas Art*, 2017.
	Poetry	Dan Williams, *Past Purgatory, A Distant Paradise*, 2017.
2017	Fiction	Dominic Smith, *The Last Painting of Sara de Vos*, 2016.
	Nonfiction	Kenneth Hafertepe, *The Material Culture of German Texans*, 2016.
	Poetry	Jonathan Fink, *Barbarossa*, 2016.
2016	Fiction	Sanderia Faye, *Mourner's Bench*, 2015.
	Nonfiction	Ron J. Jackson Jr. and Lee Spencer White, *Joe: The Slave Who Became an Alamo Legend*, 2015.
	Poetry	James Hoggard, *New and Selected Poems*, 2015.
2015	Fiction	Sara Bird, *Above the East China Sea*, 2014.
	Fiction	James Magnuson, *Famous Writers I have Known: A Novel*, 2014.
	Nonfiction	Katie Robinson Edwards, *Midcentury Modern Art in Texas*, 2014.
	Poetry	Christian Wiman, *Once in the West*, 2014.

FILM AND TELEVISION WORK IN TEXAS

For almost a century, Texas has been one of the nation's top filmmaking states, after California and New York. Thousands of films have been made in Texas since 1910, including *Wings* — the first film to win an Academy Award for Best Picture — which was made in San Antonio in 1927.

Texas' attractions to filmmakers include its diverse locations, abundant sunshine and moderate winter weather, and a variety of support services. In 2020, the film and television industry was responsible for more than 54,730 jobs in Texas, with $4.04 billion in wages, according to the Motion Picture Association.

Besides salaries paid to locally hired technicians and actors, as well as fees paid to location owners, the production companies do business with hotels, car rental agencies, lumberyards, restaurants, grocery stores, utilities, security services, and florists.

All types of projects come to Texas besides films, including television features and news organizations, commercials, corporate films, and video games.

Many projects made in Texas originate in California studios, but Texas is also the home of many independent filmmakers who make films outside the studio system. Some films and television shows made in Texas have become icons. *Giant*, John Wayne's *The Alamo*, and the long-running TV series *Dallas* all made their mark on the world's perception of Texas.

The Texas Film Commission (TFC), a division of the Office of the Governor, markets to Hollywood Texas' locations, support services, and workforce availability. In 2007, the 80th Texas Legislature created the Texas Moving Image Industry Incentive Program (TMIIIP), administered by the TFC, to help provide grants to film, television, commercial, and video game productions.

Senate Bill 22, which passed in the 2025 89th Texas Legislature, increased funding for the TMIIIP. Every two years until 2035, the comptroller will contribute $300 million to the incentive fund, as opposed to the previous $200 million every two years. By boosting money going into the film industry in Texas, the government hopes to attract more studios to film in the state.

REGIONAL COMMISSIONS

Amarillo Film Commission
Sherman Bass, Film Commissioner

Austin Film Commission
Brian Gannon, Director

Brownsville Border Film Commission
Eva Millan, Film Commissioner

Conroe Film Commission
Ashley Shaw, Visitor Experience Specialist

Corpus Christi Film Commission
Lydia Garza, Film & Music Commissioner

Dallas Film & Creative Industries Office
Katie Schuck, Commissioner

El Paso Film and Creative Industries Commission
Drew Mayer-Oakes, Commissioner

Fort Worth Film Commission
Taylor Hardy, Film & Marketing Director

Houston Film Commission
Alfred Cervantes, Executive Director

San Antonio Film Commission
Christine Hill, Film & Music Project Manager

South Padre Island Film Commission
Blake Henry, Director

Source: Texas Film Commission and Texas Comptroller.

UNSPLASH/FELIX MOONEERAM

HOLIDAYS, ANNIVERSARIES, AND FESTIVALS (2026–2027)

Below are listed the principal federal and state government holidays; Christian, Jewish, and Islamic holidays and festivals; and special recognition days for 2026 and 2027.

Technically, the United States does not observe national holidays. Each state has jurisdiction over its holidays, which are usually designated by its legislature.

This list was compiled partially from the Texas Government Code and the U.S. Office of Personnel Management.

2026	
New Year's Day §	**Thu., Jan. 1**
Epiphany	Tue., Jan. 6
Sam Rayburn Day ‡	Tue., Jan. 6
Martin Luther King Jr. Day §	**Mon., Jan. 19**
Confederate Heroes' Day §	Mon., Jan. 19
Valentine's Day	Sat., Feb. 14
Presidents' Day §	**Mon., Feb. 16**
Ramadan, first day of	Tue., Feb. 17
Ash Wednesday	Wed., Feb. 18
Texas Independence Day §	Mon., Mar. 2
Palm Sunday	Sun., Mar. 29
César Chávez Day §	Tue., Mar. 31
Passover (Pesach), first day of	Wed., Apr. 1
Good Friday §	Fri., Apr. 3
Easter Day	Sun., Apr. 5
Former Prisoners of War Day ‡	Thurs., Apr. 9
San Jacinto Day §	Tue., Apr. 21
Mother's Day	Sun., May 10
Ascension Day	Thu., May 14
Armed Forces Day	Sat., May 16
Shavuot (Feast of Weeks)	Thu., May 21
Whit Sunday — Pentecost	Sun., May 24
Memorial Day §	**Mon., May 25**
Trinity Sunday	Sun., May 31
Flag Day (U.S.)	Sun., June 14
Islamic New Year	Tue., June 16
Emancipation Day in Texas (Juneteenth) §	**Fri., June 19**
Father's Day	Sun., June 21
Independence Day §	**Sat., July 4**
Lyndon Baines Johnson Day §	Thu., Aug. 27
Labor Day §	**Mon., Sep. 7**
Rosh Hashanah (Jewish New Year)	Fri., Sept. 11
Grandparents Day	Sun., Sept. 13
Yom Kippur (Day of Atonement)	Mon., Sept. 21
Sukkot (Tabernacles), first day of	Fri., Sept. 25
Columbus Day ‡	**Mon., Oct. 12**
Halloween	Sat., Oct. 31
Father of Texas Day ‡	Tues., Nov. 3
General Election Day §	Tue., Nov. 3
Veterans Day §	**Wed., Nov. 11**
Thanksgiving Day §	**Thu., Nov. 26**
First Sunday in Advent	Sun., Nov. 29
Hanukkah, first day of	Fri., Dec. 4
Christmas Day §	**Fri., Dec. 25**

2027	
New Year's Day §	**Fri., Jan. 1**
Epiphany	Wed., Jan. 6
Sam Rayburn Day ‡	Wed., Jan. 6
Martin Luther King Jr. Day §	**Mon., Jan. 18**
Confederate Heroes' Day §	Tue., Jan. 19
Ramadan, first day of	Sun., Feb. 7
Valentine's Day	Sun., Feb. 14
Presidents' Day §	**Mon., Feb. 15**
Texas Independence Day §	Tue., Mar. 2
Ash Wednesday	Wed., Mar. 10
Palm Sunday	Sun., Mar. 21
Good Friday §	Fri., Mar. 26
Easter Day	Sun., Mar. 28
César Chávez Day §	Wed., Mar. 31
Former Prisoners of War Day ‡	Fri., Apr. 9
San Jacinto Day §	Wed., Apr. 21
Passover (Pesach), first day of	Wed., Apr. 21
Ascension Day	Thu., May 6
Mother's Day	Sun., May 9
Armed Forces Day	Sat., May 15
Whit Sunday — Pentecost	Sun., May 16
Trinity Sunday	Sun., May 23
Memorial Day §	**Mon., May 31**
Islamic New Year	Sun., June 6
Shavuot (Feast of Weeks)	Thu., June 10
Flag Day (U.S.)	Mon., June 14
Emancipation Day in Texas (Juneteenth) §	**Sat., June 19**
Father's Day	Sun., June 20
Independence Day §	**Sun., July 4**
Lyndon Baines Johnson Day §	Fri., Aug. 27
Labor Day §	**Mon., Sept. 6**
Grandparents Day	Sun., Sept. 12
Rosh Hashanah (Jewish New Year)	Fri., Oct. 1
Yom Kippur (Day of Atonement)	Mon., Oct. 11
Columbus Day ‡	**Mon., Oct. 11**
Sukkot (Tabernacles), first day of	Fri., Oct. 15
Halloween	Sun., Oct. 31
General Election Day §	Tue., Nov. 2
Father of Texas Day ‡	Wed., Nov. 3
Veterans Day §	**Thu., Nov. 11**
Thanksgiving Day §	**Thu., Nov. 25**
First Sunday in Advent	Sun., Nov. 28
Hanukkah, first day of	Fri., Dec. 24
Christmas Day §	**Sat., Dec. 25**

Federal legal public holidays are shown in bold. If the holiday falls on a Sunday, the following Monday may be treated as a holiday. If the holiday falls on a Saturday, the preceding Friday may be treated as a holiday.

§ **State holiday in Texas.** For state employees, the Friday after Thanksgiving Day, Dec. 24, and Dec. 26 are also holidays. **Optional holidays** are César Chávez Day, Good Friday, Rosh Hashanah, and Yom Kippur. **Partial-staffing holidays** are Confederate Heroes Day, Texas Independence Day, San Jacinto Day, Emancipation Day in Texas, and Lyndon Baines Johnson Day. State offices will be open on optional holidays and partial-staffing holidays.

‡ **State Recognition Days**, as designated by the Texas Legislature.

Notes on holidays:

- Confederate Heroes Day combines the birthdays of Robert E. Lee (Jan. 19) and Jefferson Davis (June 3).
- Presidents' Day combines the birthdays of George Washington (Feb. 22) and Abraham Lincoln (Feb. 12).
- Jewish and Islamic holidays are tabular, meaning they begin at sunset on the previous evening.
- Between 1939 and 1957, Texas observed Thanksgiving Day on the last Thursday in November. As a result, in a November having five Thursdays, Texas celebrated national Thanksgiving on the fourth Thursday and Texas Thanksgiving on the fifth Thursday. In 1957, Texas changed the state observance to coincide with the national holiday.

OUT OF THIS WORLD TEXANS

There's a bright constellation of talent in the Lone Star State's pop culture universe.

BY ANTHONY HEAD

"Some people call me the space cowboy . . ." It's one of the most recognizable opening lines to any classic rock song. Steve Miller, who was raised in Dallas, wrote that lyric for 1973's hit single "The Joker" — paying homage to the "Space Cowboy" song from his band's 1969 album, *Brave New World*. Like so many other Texans, Miller often found Space Age inspiration for his work.

Just as "Sputnik moment" remains a common idiom when something suddenly changes *everything*, the Space Age amplified the cosmic character of an already larger-than-life Texas.

The candle was lit during the "Atomic Age" and the detonation of nuclear weapons in 1945, introducing a profound shift in American popular culture. Aesthetically, flying saucers, boldly colored planets, swooping rockets, and starbursts were suddenly everywhere.

Like the second stage of a rocket, the Space Age came and took everything further. Houston became "Space City" when NASA arrived in 1961, and it remains indelibly linked to America's space program. Opened in 1965 as the "Eighth Wonder of the World," the Astrodome was listed in the National Register of Historic Places in 2014. Three years later, it was designated a state antiquity landmark.

Fifty-one years after Apollo 11 made solar system history, Nassau Bay dedicated an outdoor art installation near the Johnson Space Center. Natalia Beard's 53-foot-tall illuminated steel arc commemorates the first moments of that great human achievement and shines as a beacon to the future.

Just about every American who could ever write about having been to space first spent time in Texas. So, pick any astronaut memoir or autobiography and there's no doubt Texas plays a part in their story. Texas authors have also chronicled the Space Age, building out the complete and fascinating history with each new book.

Rice University professor of history Douglas Brinkley details the geopolitical storm of the new frontier's early decades in *American Moonshot: John F. Kennedy and the Great Space Race*; former JSC historian Jennifer M. Ross-Nazzal covers the JSC's first five decades in *Making Space for Women: Stories from Trailblazing Women of NASA's Johnson Space Center*; and Austin-based Bruce McCandless III, son of astronaut Bruce McCandless II, co-wrote (with Emily Carney) *Star Bound: A Beginner's Guide to the American Space Program* to cover extremely complicated outer space topics in a decidedly Earth-friendly approach.

Long before Aline B. Carter of San Antonio became Poet Laureate of Texas (1947-1949), she built an observatory with a four-inch telescope atop her downtown house. With the heavens as her constant source of inspiration — and just as the Apollo Program began accelerating with promise for humanity's future — she wrote: "Fly on, awakening man, beyond the suns/Beyond the wheeling galaxies of space/Touch the limitless" (*Beyond the Wheeling Galaxies*, 1966).

When author L. Whitley Strieber was growing up in San Antonio, he attended astronomy lessons provided by Carter at her home observatory. In addition to being a noted horror novelist, Strieber authored several nonfiction books about encounters with some form of sentient but non-human creature, beginning with 1987's *Communion*.

In Stephen Harrigan's 2006 novel *Challenger Park*, the Austin-based writer weaves authentic drama from the space shuttle era into life's everyday fabric for the JSC's women, men, and their families. The story is set at the turn of the Millennium and lucidly shows the Earth-space dynamic on a very human scale.

Albert J. "Al" Reinert also brought humanity to his 1989 documentary *For All Mankind*. As its director, the longtime Houston-based space reporter celebrated the Apollo Program through original footage and his interviews with the people who got the job done. Reinert then co-wrote the screenplay of 1995's blockbuster *Apollo 13* with William D. Broyles Jr., a Baytown native and the founding editor of *Texas Monthly*.

Cinema auteur Richard S. Linklater encapsulates the energy, promise, and wonder of growing up in his hometown of Houston during the 1960s in *Apollo 10 ½: A Space Age Childhood*.

"It's both a kid's perspective — kind of a fantasy of the excitement of what it was to be like to be in Houston at that era — and then also, through the kid's fantasy, you get kind of an exacting recreation of the first moon landing. So the film kind of covers it from various angles, kid and adult, " Linklater told the *Texas Standard* in 2022.

Space Age dreams spread throughout Texas because of mass media, an almost antiquated term reflecting how the slow, daily drip of news from a few sources became a 24-hour, seven-day a week gusher of newspapers, magazines, television, radio, blogs, vlogs, and especially content courtesy of the telecommunications revolution and the Internet.

Roger "Roky" Erickson and his Austin band, the 13th Floor Elevators, became notable standouts for their innovative and distinct sonic output.

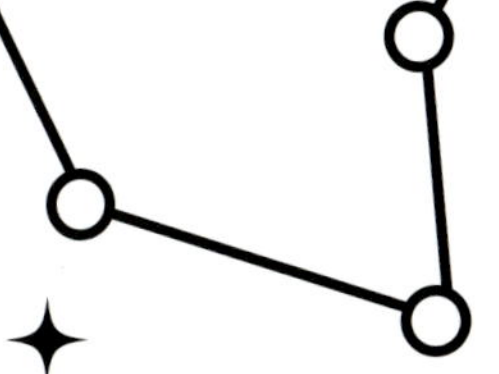

Then, of course, in 1981, the launch of an around-the-clock music video channel, MTV, on cable television famously used footage from 1969's Apollo 11 liftoff to signify the new frontier of music. It was one of those Sputnik moments that changed everything in American life.

As for Texas music, there have been songs sung about the stars and the sky above for a long, long time. It was Lubbock's Norman Carl Odam — better known as the Legendary Stardust Cowboy — who helped pioneer a style of Space Age music, later to be called "psychobilly," which sometimes coalesced with the 1960's psychedelic rock and sometimes rocketed it to another orbit entirely.

In July 1975, for instance, Fort Worth children watched live coverage of the Apollo-Soyuz mission on *KDFW* before "Captain Kangaroo" came on. By 1978, the University of Texas at Austin's McDonald Observatory was producing daily two-minute radio episodes about astronomy and Earth's place in the universe. That same program continues airing today as "StarDate" — America's longest-running national radio show dedicated to really cool stuff in the universe.

With southern rock and blues along for the ride, Houston-based Moving Sidewalks, headed by Billy Gibbons, took some not-too-small steps toward futuristic music beginning in 1966. Gibbons later traveled to space with the rest of ZZ Top in a series of music videos produced for their 1985 album *Afterburner*. ZZ Top's music literally went to space with astronaut Michael E. Fossum (current vice president of Texas A&M University), who took a digital pre-release copy of the single "Flyin' High" to the International Space Station in June 2011.

UNSPLASH/GREG RAKOZY

RELIGIOUS AFFILIATION

The 2020 U.S. Religion Census had the participation of more than 161 million individuals and 350,000 congregations, making it the most inclusive report of its kind to date. Texas continues to be one of the nation's more "religious" states, with 55.1% of the population adherents to a religion. For the population of the U.S. as a whole, 48.7% are adherents to a religion.

The census, sponsored by the Association of Statisticians of American Religious Bodies, is the only U.S. survey to report religious membership down to the county level, as well as at the state level. The Census relies on self-reports from congregations for membership numbers.

According to the survey: "Exact definitions of 'congregations' and 'adherents' vary by religious body. Congregations may be parishes, churches, synagogues, mosques, temples, or another site where a religious body has regularly scheduled worship services. Adherents generally are members, children who are not members, and others who are not members but are considered participants in the congregation."

The populations of both adherents and non-adherents in Texas have grown since the 2010 survey. Adherents in 2020 totaled 16,045,479, a 14.7% increase over 2010 adherents of 13,994,564. Those unclaimed by any faith in 2020 grew 17.5% to 13,100,026 from the 2010 total of 11,150,997.

According to the 2020 U.S. Religion Census, Texas ranks:

FIRST in number of Baptists (3,836,478)
FIRST in number belonging to nondenominational Christian churches (2,405,786)
THIRD in number of Catholics (behind California and New York)
FOURTH in number of Hindus
FOURTH in number of Buddhists
FIFTH in number of Muslims
FIFTH in number of Mormons

Largest Religious Bodies	Adherents	Share of Texas Population	Share of Texas' Adherents
Catholic Church	5,905,142	20.26%	36.80%
Southern Baptist Convention	3,319,962	11.39%	20.69%
Non-denominational Christian Churches	2,405,786	8.25%	14.99%
United Methodist Church	938,399	3.22%	5.85%
Church of Jesus Christ of Latter-day Saints	362,037	1.24%	2.26%
Jehovah's Witnesses	317,698	1.09%	1.98%
Muslim (Estimate)	313,209	1.07%	1.95%
Churches of Christ	312,132	1.07%	1.95%
Assemblies of God	296,826	1.02%	1.85%
National Missionary Baptist Convention, Inc.	294,954	1.01%	1.84%
Episcopal Church	134,318	0.46%	0.84%
Lutheran Church–Missouri Synod	112,900	0.39%	0.70%
Unclaimed by any faith	13,100,026	44.94%	—

Source: U.S. Religion Census, 2020 and U.S. Religion Census, 2010, both conducted by the Association of Statisticians of American Religious Bodies.

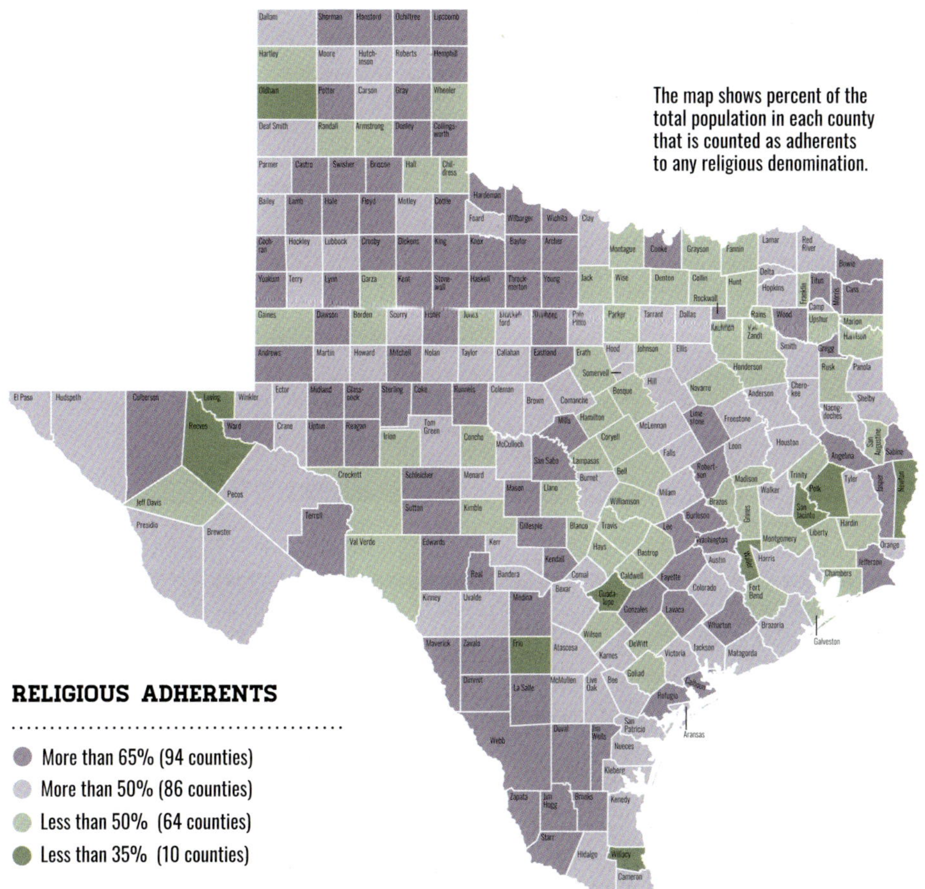

NUMBERS OF MEMBERS STATEWIDE BY DENOMINATION

	Adherents 2010	Change	Adherents 2020
Adventist	**74,120**	**+ 25,881**	**100,001**
Advent Christian Church (2 congregations)	—		95
Church of God General Conference (1 congregation)	65		38
General Conference of the Church of God (Seventh Day) (64 congregations)	—		—
Seventh–day Adventist Church (412 congregations)	74,055		99,868
United Church of God (12 congregations)	—		—
Anglican/Episcopal	**148,439**	**–14,121**	**134,318**
Anglican Catholic Church (4 congregations)	—		—
Anglican Church in North America (104 congregations)	—		—
Episcopal Church (353 congregations)	148,439		134,318
Intl Communion of the Charismatic Episcopal Church (1 congregation)	—		—
Reformed Episcopal Church (13 congregations)	—		—
Baha'i Faith (67 congregations)	**13,235**	**+ 1,169**	**14,404**
Baptist	**3,961,657**	**–125,179**	**3,836,478**
Alliance of Baptists (11 congregations)	—		—
American Baptist Association (147 congregations)	39,354		27,422
American Baptist Churches in the U.S.A. (14 congregations)	7,172		4,537
Association of Reformed Baptist Churches of America (6 congregations)	—		—
Baptist Missionary Association of America (394 congregations)	—		—
Converge Worldwide (18 congregations)	1,320		—
Full Gospel Baptist Church Fellowship (157 congregations)	—		27,088

	Adherents 2010	Change	Adherents 2020
General Association of General Baptists (6 congregations)	—		4,060
General Association of Regular Baptist Churches (5 congregations)	—		—
International Churches of Christ (11 congregations)	2,857		4,020
National Association of Free Will Baptists (42 congregations)	3,111		1,449
National Baptist Convention of America Intl, Inc. (104 congregations)	89,050		66,790
National Baptist Convention, USA, Inc (94 congregations)	59,529		79,088
National Missionary Baptist Convention of America (875 congregations)	34,039		294,954
North American Baptist Conference (13 congregations)	1,157		—
Primitive Baptists Associations (49 congregations)	—		4,291
Progressive National Baptist Convention, Inc. (9 congregations)	2,683		2,778
Seventh Day Baptist General Conf. of the U.S. and Canada (2 congregations)	67		39
Southern Baptist Convention (7,935 congregations)	3,721,318		3,319,962
Sovereign Grace Churches (8 congregations)	—		—
Buddhism	**66,116**	**– 5,234**	**60,882**
Buddhism, Mahayana (41 congregations)	49,874		26,714
Buddhism, Theravada (41 congregations)	13,461		23,373
Buddhism, Vajrayana (16 congregations)	2,781		10,795
(Catholic Liturgical) Catholic Church (1,342 congregations)	**4,673,500**	**+ 1,231,642**	**5,905,142**
(Christian Scientist) Church of Christ, Scientist (10 congregations)	**—**		**—**
(Churches of Christ) United Church of Christ (54 congregations)	**17,464**	**– 7,314**	**10,150**
Hinduism	**60,725**	**+ 16,351**	**77,076**
Hindu, Traditional Temples (37 congregations)	—		77,076
Hinduism: Hindu Post Renaissance	968		—
Hinduism: Hindu Renaissance	98		—
Hinduism: Indian–American Hindu Temple Associations	36,550		—
Hinduism: Traditional Hindu Temples	23,109		—
Holiness	**85,204**	**– 13,068**	**72,136**
Bible Methodist Connection of Churches (4 congregations)	—		—
Christian and Missionary Alliance (46 congregations)	5,465		4,731
Church of Christ (Holiness) U.S.A (5 congregations)	—		—
Church of God (Anderson, Indiana) (66 congregations)	3,990		8,860
Church of the Nazarene (323 congregations)	44,836		44,112
Churches of Christ in Christian Union (4 congregations)	—		—
Free Methodist Church–USA (18 congregations)	1,864		751
Missionary Church, The (26 congregations)	3,119		4,057
Salvation Army (55 congregations)	23,761		8,137
Wesleyan Church (19 congregations)	2,169		1,488
(Islam) Muslim Estimate (225 congregations)	**421,972**	**– 108,763**	**313,209**
Jain (4 congregations)	**—**		**—**
Jehovah's Witnesses (1,191 congregations)	**—**	**+ 317,698**	**317,698**
Judaism	**60,645**	**– 3,504**	**57,141**
Conservative Judaism (15 congregations)	17,889		17,513
Orthodox Judaism (18 congregations)	8,410		8,110
Reconstructionist Judaism (2 congregations)	356		140
Reform Judaism (29 congregations)	33,990		31,378
Latter-day Saints (Mormonism)	**300,591**	**+ 61,446**	**362,037**
Church of Jesus Christ (Bickertonite) (1 congregation)	—		—
Church of Jesus Christ of Latter–day Saints (731 congregations)	296,141		362,037
Community of Christ (31 congregations)	4,450		—
Liberal	**8,107**	**+ 2,520**	**10,627**
American Ethical Union (1 congregation)	—		—
Unitarian Universalist Association (46 congregations)	8,107		10,627
Lutheran	**272,066**	**– 61,960**	**210,106**
Association of Free Lutheran Congregations (6 congregations)	—		281
Church of the Lutheran Brethren of America	72		—
Church of the Lutheran Confession (2 congregations)	—		—
Evangelical Lutheran Church in America (308 congregations)	111,647		77,170
Evangelical Lutheran Synod (4 congregations)	75		247

	Adherents 2010	Change	Adherents 2020
Lutheran Church–Missouri Synod (LCMS) (371 congregations)	132,508		112,900
Lutheran Congregations in Mission for Christ (53 congregations)	20,936		11,382
North American Lutheran Church (35 congregations)	—		—
Wisconsin Evangelical Lutheran Synod (39 congregations)	6,828		8,126
Mennonite/Amish	**3,436**	**+ 1,853**	**5,289**
Amish Groups, undifferentiated (1 congregation)	52		59
Beachy Amish Mennonite Churches (2 congregations)	265		152
Church of God in Christ, Mennonite (11 congregations)	1,068		1,495
Conservative Mennonite Conference (2 congregations)	106		71
Eastern Pennsylvania Mennonite Church (2 congregations)	—		1,221
Maranatha Amish Mennonite (1 congregation)	—		141
Mennonite Brethren Churches, U.S. Conference of (11 congregations)	403		588
Mennonite Church, USA (25 congregations)	1,233		1,259
Unaffiliated Amish–Mennonite (Conservative) (2 congregations)	309		303
Methodist	**1,135,595**	**– 107,848**	**1,027,747**
African Methodist Episcopal Church (227 congregations)	43,839		47,550
African Methodist Episcopal Zion Church (8 congregations)	1,327		1,108
Christian Methodist Episcopal Church (212 congregations)	37,986		38,645
Congregational Methodist Church (39 congregations)	2,396		—
Evangelical Covenant Church (18 congregations)	1,393		2,045
Evangelical Free Church of America (70 congregations)	13,486		—
Evangelical Methodist Church (14 congregations)	—		—
United Methodist Church (1,758 congregations)	1,035,168		938,399
Unity of the Brethren (24 congregations)	—		—
Orthodox	**32,453**	**+ 23,325**	**55,778**
America, Canada and Europe Reg. Malankara Syriac Knanaya Arch. (3 congregations)	—		810
Antiochian Orthodox Christian Archdiocese of North America (22 congregations)	5,348		6,093
Armenian Apostolic Orthodox Church (C. of Etchmiadzin) (4 congregations)	515		1,030
Coptic Orthodox Church in North America (24 congregations)	3,866		10,519
Eritrean Orthodox Churches (7 congregations)	1,000		4,042
Ethiopian Orthodox Church in the United States of America (17 congregations)	—		8,087
Greek Orthodox Archdiocese of America (16 congregations)	12,167		11,904
Malankara Archdiocese of the Syrian Orthodox Church in N. A. (6 congregations)	1,260		1,838
Malankara Orthodox Syrian Church (17 congregations)	2,433		5,461
Orthodox Church in America, The (18 congregations)	2,657		2,557
Russian Orthodox Church Outside of Russia, The (8 congregations)	1,022		1,673
Serbian Orthodox Church in North and South America (4 congregations)	1,375		1,214
Syrian (Syriac) Orthodox Church of Antioch (3 congregations)	210		180
The Romanian Orthodox Metropolia of the Americas (3 congregations)	600		370
Pentecostal	**454,628**	**+ 42,038**	**496,666**
Apostolic Faith Mission of Portland, Oregon (3 congregations)	135		—
Assemblies of God, General Council of the (1,432 congregations)	275,565		296,826
Association of Vineyard Churches (29 congregations)	8,527		5,998
Bible Way Church of Our Lord Jesus Christ World Wide, Inc. (3 congregations)	—		340
Calvary Chapel (11 congregations)	—		—
Christian Congregation in North America (6 congregations)	—		—
Church of God (Cleveland, Tennessee) (254 congregations)	47,709		35,397
Church of God in Christ (373 congregations)	77,545		92,815
Church of God of Prophecy (86 congregations)	3,610		—
Church of God of the Apostolic Faith, Inc. (17 congregations)	—		—
Church of Our Lord Jesus Christ of the Apostolic Faith (33 congregations)	—		4,246
Church of the Living God (Christian Workers for Fellowship) (25 congregations)	—		—
Congregational Holiness Church (5 congregations)	1,280		—
Elim Fellowship (3 congregations)	—		—
Full Gospel Christian Assemblies International (72 congregations)	—		37,080
International Church of the Foursquare Gospel (71 congregations)	11,047		21,366
International Pentecostal Holiness Church	15,576		—
Open Bible Churches (3 congregations)	148		142

	Adherents 2010	Change	Adherents 2020
Pentecostal Assemblies of the World (7 congregations)	—		2,456
Pentecostal Church of God (116 congregations)	13,486		—
United Pentecostal Church International (735 congregations)	—		—
Presbyterian/Reformed	**183,290**	**– 71,309**	**111,981**
Associate Reformed Presbyterian Church (General Synod) (3 congregations)	223		—
Cumberland Presbyterian Church (37 congregations)	6,355		7,173
Cumberland Presbyterian Church in America (19 congregations)	—		2,236
ECO: A Covenant Order of Evangelical Presbyterians (37 congregations)	—		—
Evangelical Presbyterian Church (1981) (25 congregations)	2,883		—
Orthodox Presbyterian Church (21 congregations)	824		—
Presbyterian Church (U.S.A.) (417 congregations)	155,046		81,282
Presbyterian Church in America (100 congregations)	17,959		21,290
Reformed Presbyterian Church of North America (Covenanters) (3 congregations)	—		95
Quakers	**2,892**	**– 1,151**	**1,741**
Charis Fellowship (2 congregations)	—		—
Church of the Brethren (1 congregation)	118		26
Evangelical Friends Church International (9 congregations)	1,845		985
Friends General Conference (18 congregations)	929		718
Friends United Meeting (1 congregation)	—		11
Old German Baptist Brethren Church, New Conference	—		1
Reformed/Congregational	**1,957**	**+ 240**	**2,197**
Christian Reformed Church in North America (19 congregations)	1,416		1,386
Communion of Reformed Evangelical Churches (3 congregations)	—		—
Conservative Congregational Christian Conference (2 congregations)	29		230
Evangelical Association of Reformed and Congr. Christian Churches (7 congregations)	—		—
Reformed Church in America (14 congregations)	512		581
Restorationists	**466,024**	**– 47,807**	**418,217**
Christian Church (Disciples of Christ) (357 congregations)	74,817		65,650
Christian Churches and Churches of Christ (118 congregations)	40,078		40,435
Churches of Christ (1897 congregations)	351,129		312,132
(Sikh) American Sikh Council (20 congregations)	**—**		**—**
Unity Churches, Association of (41 congregations)	**—**		**—**
(Zoroastrian) Federation of Zoroastrian Associations of North America (3 congregations)	**1,095**	**– 1,095**	**—**
Unclassified	**—**		**—**
Agape Christian Fellowship (1 congregation)	—		30
Apostolic Christian Church of America (4 congregations)	46		79
Apostolic Christian Faith (2 congregations)	—		12
Biblical Mennonite Alliance (1 congregation)	—		43
Chabad Judaism (43 congregations)	—		—
Christadelphians (16 congregations)	—		—
Christian Brethren (Plymouth Brethren) (42 congregations)	—		—
Grace Gospel Fellowship (4 congregations)	—		—
Hindu Yoga and Meditation (81 congregations)	—		35,077
Independent Judaism (1 congregation)	—		20
Malankara Mar Thoma Church (8 congregations)	—		1,391
Nationwide Fellowship Mennonite Churches (2 congregations)	—		157
New Apostolic Church USA (8 congregations)	—		—
Non-denominational Christian Churches (4,212 congregations)	1,546,542	859,244	2,405,786
Unaffiliated Conservative Mennonite (1 congregation)	—		30
Unaffiliated Conservative Mennonite (Grandview fellowship) (2 congregations)	—		140
United House of Prayer (1 congregation)	—		100
Universal Fellowship of Metropolitan Community Churches (13 congregations)	2,765		1,498
Vedanta Society (3 congregations)	—		—
Statewide Totals	**13,994,564**	**+ 2,050,915**	**16,045,479**
Unclaimed (not counted as adherent to religion)	**11,150,997**	**+ 1,949,029**	**13,100,026**

Note: Some religious bodies with no adherents in Texas have been omitted from this table due to space limitations.

Source: U.S. Religion Census, 2020 and U.S. Religion Census, 2010, both conducted by the Association of Statisticians of American Religious Bodies.

FIRST UNITED METHODIST CHURCH, DALLAS

UNSPLASH/THOMAS WAVID JOHNS

the BEST of Texas

AS VOTED BY TSHA MEMBERSHIP AND FRIENDS

UNSPLASH/MEGAN BUCKNALL

Best Texas BBQ

Rudy's (Multiple Locations)
Hard Eight BBQ (Multiple Locations)
Truth BBQ (Multiple Locations)
The Original Black's BBQ (Multiple Locations)
Terry Black's Barbecue (Multiple Locations)

Favorite Texas Winery or Distillery

Becker Vineyards (Fredericksburg)
Grape Creek Vineyards (Fredericksburg)
Spoetzl Brewery (Shiner)
Augusta Vin (Fredericksburg)
Messina Hof Winery (Multiple Locations)

Favorite Texas Bar

Billy Bob's (Fort Worth)
Menger Bar (San Antonio)
Gruene Hall (Gruene)
Broken Spoke (Austin)
Scholz Garten (Austin)

Best Chicken Fried Steak

Mary's Cafe (Strawn)
The Cotton Patch Cafe (Multiple Locations)
Jim's Restaurant (Multiple Locations)
Babe's Chicken Dinner House (Multiple Locations)
Jake & Dorothy's Cafe (Stephenville)

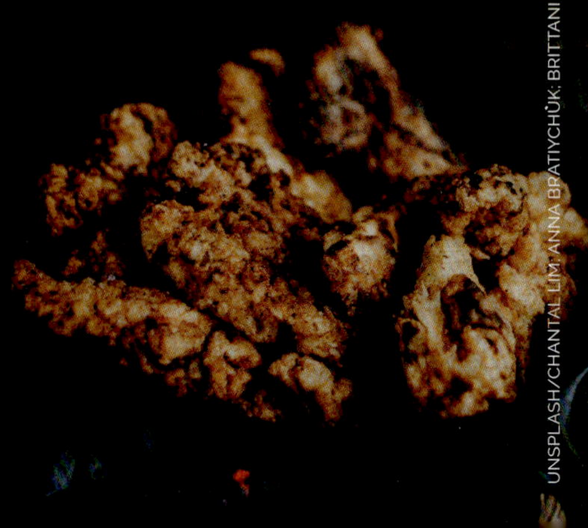

UNSPLASH/CHANTAL LIM; ANNA BRATIYCHUK; BRITTANI BURNS; IVANA CAJINA

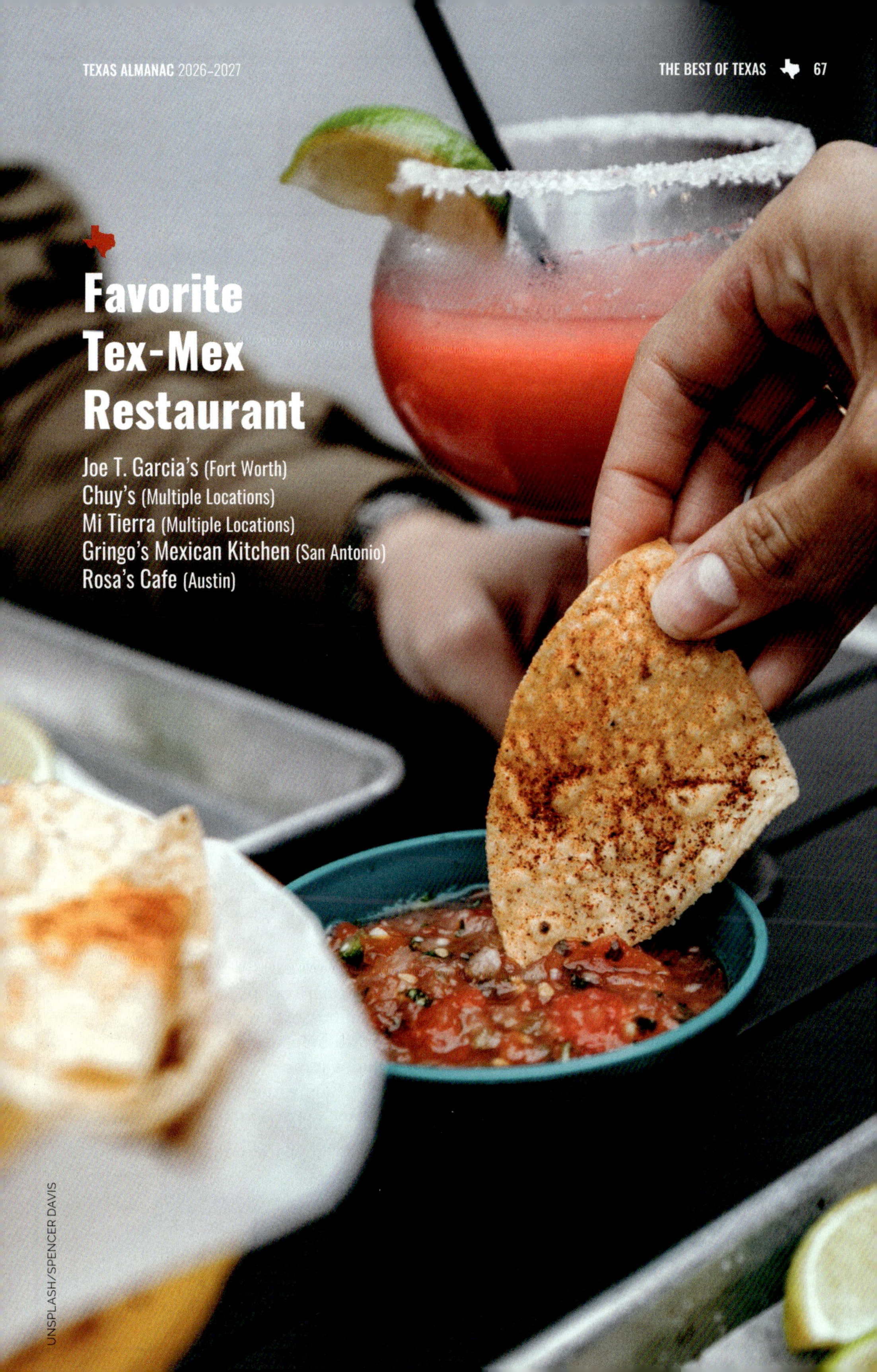

Favorite Tex-Mex Restaurant

Joe T. Garcia's (Fort Worth)
Chuy's (Multiple Locations)
Mi Tierra (Multiple Locations)
Gringo's Mexican Kitchen (San Antonio)
Rosa's Cafe (Austin)

UNSPLASH/SPENCER DAVIS

Texas

BUSINESS

UNSPLASH/COSMIC TIMETRAVELER

THE TEXAS JOB MARKET

The Texas economy added 302,400 nonfarm jobs from August 2023 to August 2024, an increase of 2.20%, to reach 14,239,200 at the end of fiscal year 2024. Texas added more new jobs than any other state over those 12 months. Private-sector employment rose by 2.10%, while government employment (federal, state, and local) grew by 2.50%. The state's rate of job growth was the seventh highest among all 50 states.

Texas Industry Performance

Employment in the goods-producing industries increased by 2.80% in fiscal 2024, while employment in the service-providing industries grew by 2.10%. Employment increased in two of three of the goods-producing industries (mining and logging, manufacturing, and construction), with mining and logging seeing a 2.10% loss.

Mining and Logging

Out of the 11 major industries, mining and logging was the only one to lose employment, decreasing by 2.10% from August 2023 to August 2024. Oil production slightly increased by 0.70% over the year to a record 1,673 million barrels led by new horizontal drilling technology.

Manufacturing

The Texas manufacturing industry gained 23,900 jobs over the past year, an increase of 2.50%. Durable goods employment was up 20,400, with the largest increase in the fabricated metals manufacturing sector (141,500). That sector is closely associated with oil and natural gas exploration and production, and employment in the sector usually follows closely to the mining industry. However, the fabricated metal manufacturing sector employment increased by 6.80% even while mining employment decreased.

Overall, durable goods employment increased by 3.30%. Nondurable-goods manufacturing employment grew by 3,500 (1.00%), with the largest increase in the food manufacturing sector (3,000 or 2.70%). Total manufacturing employment in August 2024 was 982,500.

The value of Texas exports in calendar year 2022 was a record $485 billion, an increase of 29.40% from 2021. In 2023, however, the value of Texas exports fell by 8.40%, hurt by falling oil prices. Beginning in January 2024, Texas exports began to increase again on a year-over-year basis. Through July 2024, the value of Texas exports was up by 8.20% from the corresponding period of 2023. Texas remains the nation's leading exporting state, as it has been for more than a decade. Texas exports comprised 22.00% of total U.S. exports in 2023.

Construction

Construction employment increased by 36,600 (4.40%) in fiscal 2024 to reach 860,900 in August 2024. Employment in the specialty trade contractors sector increased by 16,500 (3.60%), and heavy and civil engineering construction employment grew by 18,700 (10.70%).

Total housing construction activity in 2024 was down slightly from 2023. Single-family building permits issued in the year ending in July 2024, at 158,340, were up 17.00% from the same period one year earlier; building permits for multifamily units (5+), however, were down by 31.80%. Combined single-family and multifamily permits were down by 1.90%. According to Multiple Listing Service data from the Texas A&M Real Estate Center, the median sales price for an existing Texas single-family home was $340,000 in August of both 2024 and 2023. In August 2024, Texas had a 4.8-month inventory of existing homes for sale, up from a 3.2-month inventory in August 2023.

Professional and Business Services

Employment in the professional and business services industry increased by 23,600 (1.10%) in fiscal 2024. Employment changes varied considerably among industry sectors, with the largest increases in employment services (4.40%) and architectural, engineering, and related services (3.40%). Total professional and business services employment was 2,141,800 in August 2024.

Education and Health Services

The education and health services industry, composed of the educational services and health care and social assistance sectors, gained 56,800 jobs in fiscal 2024, an increase of 3.00%. The relatively small educational services sector saw an increase of 3,200 jobs (1.30%). Employment in the much larger health care and social assistance sector grew by 3.20% (53,600 jobs). In all, Texas education and health services employment increased to 1,955,300 in August 2024.

Financial Activities

In fiscal year 2024, overall employment in the financial activities industry grew by 2.40% (21,300 jobs). The finance and insurance sector grew by 13,100 (2.00%) while the real estate and rental and leasing sector grew by 8,200 (3.20%). Credit intermediation, which includes financial institutions such as banks, is the industry's largest sector. It employed 288,200 as of August 2024 but saw a slight decline in 2024. Total Texas financial activities industry employment reached 927,100 in that month.

Trade, Transportation, and Utilities

The trade, transportation, and utilities industry, the state's largest employer with 20.00% of total nonfarm jobs in August 2024, gained 30,800 jobs (1.10%) over the year. Employment in all three industry sectors — retail trade, wholesale trade, and transportation, warehousing, and utilities — increased during fiscal 2024. Wholesale trade employment was up 13,300 (2.00%); transportation, warehousing, and utilities employment grew by 13,900 (2.00%); and employment in the retail trade sector increased by 3,600 (0.30%). In all, the trade, transportation, and utilities industry provided 2,796,200 Texas jobs in August 2024.

Information

The information industry is a collection of diverse sectors, representing established sectors of the economy (newspaper publishing, data processing, television broadcasting, and wired telephone services) as well as some newer sectors (cell phone service providers, internet providers, and software). The computing infrastructure providers and web hosting sector saw the largest percentage increase in employment over the year (700 jobs, or 1.50%). Total industry employment grew by 2,300 (1.00%) to reach 235,300 in August 2024.

Leisure and Hospitality

Employment in the leisure and hospitality industry increased by 43,000 (2.90%) over the fiscal year. The majority of the industry's job gains occurred in the food services and drinking places sector, which added 24,100 jobs (2.00%). The largest percentage gain was in the accommodation sector, which grew by 4,300 (3.30%). Total leisure and hospitality employment in August 2024 was 1,527,600, representing about 11.00% of total Texas employment.

Other Services

The other services industry is a varied mix of business activities including repair and maintenance services; laundry services; organizations; religious organizations; political and civic organizations; funeral services; parking garages; beauty salons; and a wide range of personal services. Repair and maintenance services employment increased by 4.40%, the highest rate among other services sectors. In all, other services industry employment grew by 17,500 to reach 492,600 in August 2024.

Government Employment

Government employment grew by 51,000 (2.50%) over the year. Federal government employment increased by 6,300; local government employment increased by 35,000; and state government employment grew by 9,700. Total government employment in Texas was 2,110,400 in August 2024, or 15.00% of total employment.

CONSUMER SPENDING

Consumer spending is a major component of the Texas economy. Growth in the sales tax collections slowed significantly in fiscal 2024, up by only 1.20% ($47.2 billion) from 2023. In comparison, fiscal 2022 grew by 19.30% and 2023 grew by 8.40%.

Receipts from the retail trade sector, the sector that emits by far the most sales and use tax receipts, were essentially flat in fiscal year 2024. Collections finished 0.20% above fiscal 2023 remittances from that sector. The largest increases in receipts in major sectors compared to the previous year's collections came from the construction and services sectors.

The Consumer Confidence Index is a monthly measure of consumer optimism, an important factor affecting the sales of housing, automobiles, and other major purchases. The index for the four-state West South Central (WSC) Region, which includes Texas, was up by 5.40% in fiscal 2024. The index for the nation as a whole was up 5.00%.

Source: Excerpt from the State of Texas Annual Cash Report 2024, Comptroller of Public Accounts.

Gross Domestic Product in Current Dollars

Location	Millions of Dollars			Percent of U.S. Total			GDP* 2024 (in billions of U.S. dollars)	
	2024	2023	2022	2024	2023	2022	United States	$29,168
United States	29,184,890	27,720,709	25,744,108	100%	100%	100%	China	18,273
1. California	4,103,124	3,870,379	3,641,643	14.06%	13.96%	14.15%	Germany	4,710
2. Texas	2,709,393	2,583,866	2,402,137	9.28%	9.32%	9.33%	Japan	4,070
3. New York	2,297,028	2,172,010	2,048,403	7.87%	7.84%	7.96%	India	3,889
4. Florida	1,600,811	1,600,811	1,439,065	5.49%	5.77%	5.59%	United Kingdom	3,588
5. Illinois	1,137,244	1,098,346	1,025,667	3.90%	3.96%	3.98%	France	3,174
6. Pennsylvania	1,024,206	976,361	911,813	3.51%	3.52%	3.54%	Italy	2,377
7. Ohio	927,740	884,834	825,990	3.18%	3.19%	3.21%	Canada	2,215
8. Georgia	882,535	831,828	767,378	3.02%	3.00%	2.98%	Brazil	2,188
9. New Jersey	846,587	806,665	754,948	2.90%	2.91%	2.93%	Russia	2,184
10. North Carolina	839,122	788,103	715,968	2.88%	2.84%	2.78%	South Korea	1,870

Source: Bureau of Economic Analysis. *Source: International Monetary Fund.*

Texas Gross Domestic Product by Industry (in Millions)

Industry	2024	2023	2022	2021	2020	2015
Agriculture, Forestry, Fishing/Hunting	$12,890	$10,614	$11,217	$12,057	$8,047	$11,953
% change*	21.40	-5.40	-7.00	49.80	-2.80	15.60
Natural Resources and Mining	199,217	203,691	235,643	161,923	87,983	122,983
% change	-2.20	-13.60	45.50	84.00	-39.40	-40.30
Construction	133,467	121,727	110,223	101,495	97,280	81,284
% change	9.60	10.40	8.60	4.30	-0.40	7.70
Manufacturing	312,268	296,403	268,988	221,364	184,458	201,786
% change	5.40	10.20	21.50	20.00	-13.20	2.90
Trade, Transportation, Utilities	517,107	494,658	467,964	409,915	359,237	311,002
% change	4.50	5.70	14.20	14.10	0.00	5.90
Information	110,991	102,676	94,384	85,103	75,730	59,755
% change	8.10	8.80	10.90	12.40	2.80	10.60
Financial Activities	519,438	477,796	430,804	385,300	344,481	250,610
% change	8.70	10.90	11.80	11.80	11.40	4.20
Professional and Business Services	331,306	314,107	286,515	252,048	220,040	180,692
% change	5.50	9.60	13.70	14.50	-3.10	5.30
Educational and Health Services	177,962	166,010	149,295	138,034	126,109	106,619
% change	7.20	11.20	8.20	9.50	-1.80	6.90
Leisure and Hospitality Services	93,378	88,609	79,004	67,406	53,205	56,625
% change	5.40	12.20	17.20	26.70	-19.90	10.90
Other Private Services	53,752	50,396	45,693	40,134	36,879	33,206
% change	6.70	10.30	13.80	8.80	-5.80	3.90
Government and Schools	253,432	236,822	222,406	212,711	205,148	169,472
% change	7.00	6.50	4.60	3.70	6.00	4.70
TOTAL	$1,515,196	$1,579,299	$1,573,498	$1,579,015	$1,673,234	$1,809,397
% change	6.60	4.20	-0.40	0.40	6.00	2.70
TOTAL	$2,715,208	$2,563,509	$2,402,136	$2,087,490	$1,798,597	$1,585,987
% change	5.90	6.70	15.10	16.10	-3.30	-0.40

Percent change from the previous year. Source: 2024 Comprehensive Annual Financial Report for the State of Texas.

Average Work Hours and Earnings

The following table compares the average weekly earnings, hours worked per week, and average hourly wage in Texas for production workers in selected industries in 2023 and 2024.

Industry	Average Weekly Earnings 2024	Average Weekly Earnings 2023	Average Weekly Hours 2024	Average Weekly Hours 2023	Average Hourly Earnings 2024	Average Hourly Earnings 2023
Mining and Logging	$1,750.32	$1,592.80	52.00	49.10	$33.66	$32.44
Manufacturing	1,320.23	1,248.89	43.40	43.50	30.42	28.71
Durable Goods	1,415.62	1,408.05	43.80	44.70	32.32	31.50
Fabricated Metal Product Manufacturing	1,046.92	963.43	45.40	43.30	23.06	22.25
Nondurable Goods	1,167.42	989.36	42.70	41.50	27.34	23.84
Trade, Transportation, Utilities	—	—	—	—	—	—
Wholesale Trade	1,230.10	1,204.50	39.20	39.70	31.38	30.34
Machinery, Equipment, Supplies	1,351.23	1,198.70	43.80	40.80	30.85	29.38
Retail Trade	—	—	—	—	—	—
Motor Vehicle/Parts Dealers	870.84	1,063.31	36.30	37.80	23.99	28.13
Building Material/Garden Equipment	580.89	573.92	32.80	34.00	17.71	16.88
Gasoline Stations	491.13	475.71	32.10	31.40	15.30	15.15

Source: Texas Workforce Commission.

UNSPLASH/COLTON JONES

Employment in Texas by Industry

Texas reached 14,318,700 nonfarm jobs as of January 2025, adding 284,200 jobs from December 2023 to December 2024. This increase brought the annual nonfarm growth rate to 2.0 percent, outpacing the U.S. growth rate by 0.6 percentage points.

The following table shows Texas Workforce Commission estimates of the nonagricultural labor force by industry for December 2024 and the percent change during the year in the number employed.

Industry	Employment Dec. 2024	Monthly Change	Annual Change	Annual % Change
Total Nonagricultural	14,318,700	37,500	284,200	2.00%
Private	12,203,900	35,500	247,400	2.10%
Goods-Producing	2,064,200	2,100	50,000	2.50%
Mining & Logging (Oil, Gas)	211,200	500	-3,100	-1.40%
Construction	869,400	2,300	31,500	3.80%
Manufacturing	983,600	-700	21,600	2.20%
Service-Providing	12,254,500	35,400	234,200	1.90%
Trade, Transportation, Utilities	2,803,400	10,400	26,200	0.90%
Information	237,900	-600	5,500	2.40%
Financial Activities	941,100	1,100	32,700	3.60%
Professional & Business Services	2,165,300	17,800	43,200	2.00%
Education & Health Services	1,972,400	2,000	50,700	2.60%
Leisure & Hospitality	1,532,900	3,700	35,500	2.40%
Other Services	486,700	-1,000	3,600	0.70%
Government	2,114,800	2,000	36,800	1.80%

Source: Texas Workforce Commission.

Largest Banks Operating in Texas by Asset Size

Abbreviations: N.A. National Association.

	Name	City	Class	Assets	Loans
				(thousands of dollars)	
1	Charles Schwab Bank, SSB	Westlake	State	275,425,000	44,184,000
2	JP Morgan Chase Bank	New York City, NY	National	263,460,737	—
3	Bank of America	Charlotte, NC	National	172,792,694	—
4	Wells Fargo Bank	San Francisco, CA	National	82,854,201	—
5	Comerica Bank	Dallas	State	79,332,000	50,539,000
6	Frost Bank	San Antonio	State	52,580,731	20,754,825
7	Prosperity Bank	El Campo	National	39,595,132	22,138,519
8	Citibank	Sioux, SD	National	30,773,000	—
9	Texas Capital Bank	Dallas	National	30,621,656	22,450,066
10	Charles Schwab Premier Bank, SSB	Westlake	State	26,472,000	1,254,000
11	PNC Bank	Wilmington, DE	National	—	24,747,030
12	Zions Bancorporation, N.A.	Salt Lake City, UT	National	14,577,116	—
13	Nexbank	Dallas	National	13,943,020	8,922,256
14	First Financial Bank	Abilene	State	13,925,288	7,913,098
15	PlainsCapital Bank	University Park	State	13,329,161	7,586,833
16	Veritex Community Bank	Dallas	State	12,717,697	9,504,544
17	Stellar Bank	Houston	National	10,891,351	7,439,854
18	Cadence Bank	Birmingham, AL	National	10,825,301	—
19	Charles Schwab Trust Bank	Westlake	State	10,104,057	0
20	Amarillo National Bank	Amarillo	National	9,557,608	7,326,856
21	International Bank of Commerce	Laredo	National	9,257,828	6,427,504
22	Truist Bank	Charlotte, NC	National	8,875,215	—
23	Woodforest National Bank	The Woodlands	National	8,842,472	6,524,099
24	BOK Financial	Tulsa, OK	National	8,650,738	—
25	Southside Bank	Tyler	National	8,512,453	4,661,597
26	Capital One	New Orleans, LA	National	7,959,278	—
27	Beal Bank	Plano	National	6,619,890	947,324
28	Regions Bank	Birmingham, AL	State	6,184,176	—
29	TBK Bank, SSB	Dallas	State	5,946,055	4,546,960
30	Broadway National Bank	San Antonio	National	5,706,056	3,489,639
31	First United Bank & Trust	Durant, OK	National	5,591,023	—
32	The American National Bank of Texas	Terrell	National	5,515,169	3,150,981
33	Third Coast Bank	Humble	State	4,936,896	3,966,425
34	Vantage Bank Texas	San Antonio	State	4,553,595	3,300,789
35	Inwood National Bank	Dallas	National	4,515,18	2,467,703
36	Wells Fargo Bank South Central, N. A.	Houston	National	4,465,163	2,158,296
37	Texas Exchange Bank	Crowley	National	4,430,627	1,143,188
38	Texas Bank and Trust Company	Longview	National	4,367,018	3,493,889
39	VeraBank, N. A.	Henderson	National	4,297,154	2,825,105
40	City Bank	Lubbock	National	4,230,555	3,055,054
41	First National Bank Texas	Killeen	National	4,123,442	2,053,736
42	International Bank of Commerce	Brownsville	National	4,111,484	1,421,102
43	Simmons Bank	Pine Bluff, AR	State	4,053,722	—
44	Centennial Bank	Conway, AR	State	4,039,720	—
45	WestStar Bank	El Paso	State	3,205,734	3,205,734
46	Lone Star National Bank	Pharr	National	3,162,233	1,611,207
47	Guaranty Bank & Trust, N. A.	Mount Pleasant	National	3,112,902	2,130,855
48	Bank of the Ozarks	Little Rock, AR	National	3,044,272	—
49	TIB N.A.	Farmers Branch	National	2,955,684	1,803,193
50	Austin Bank, Texas N. A.	Jacksonville	National	2,923,289	2,360,410

Source: Texas Department of Banking, as of December 31, 2024.

UNSPLASH/JOEY CHACON

INSURANCE IN TEXAS

The Texas Department of Insurance reported that on August 31, 2024, there were 3,477 entities licensed to handle insurance business in Texas and 944,761 agents and adjusters.

Under reforms in 1993-94, a three-member State Board of Insurance was replaced by the department, with a Commissioner of Insurance appointed by the governor for a two-year term in each odd-numbered year and confirmed by the Texas Senate.

On September 1, 2005, legislation passed by the 79th Legislature took effect, transferring functions of the Texas Workers' Compensation Commission to the department and creating within it the Division of Workers' Compensation.

Also established was the office of Commissioner of Workers' Compensation, appointed by the governor, to enforce and implement the Texas Workers' Compensation Act.

Premium Rates Compared

AUTO INSURANCE
Average for Coverage by State (2025)

The U.S. average is $1,895.
Maine has the least expensive at $1,175.

State	Average
1. Louisiana	$2,883
2. Florida	$2,694
3. California	$2,416
4. Michigan	$2,352
5. Colorado	$2,337
6. South Dakota	$2,280
7. Kentucky	$2,228
8. Montana	$2,193
9. D.C.	$2,157
10. Oklahoma	$2,138
15. Texas	**$2,043**

In dollars, twelve-month rates. Information not available from some states. *Source: carinsurance.com.*

HOMEOWNERS INSURANCE
Average Premiums by State (2025)

The national average rate was $2,601.
Hawaii has the lowest home insurance rate at $613.

State	Average
1. Oklahoma	$5,858
2. Kansas	$4,843
3. Nebraska	$4,800
4. Florida	$4,419
5. Colorado	$4,099
6. Arkansas	$3,958
7. Texas	**$3,851**
8. Louisiana	$3,594
9. Missouri	$3,543
10. South Dakota	$3,390

In dollars, twelve-month rates. Coverage includes $300,000 dwelling with $1,000 deductible and $100,000 liability. *Source: insurance.com.*

Texas Insurance Premiums, Payments

Year	Total Premiums	Claim Payments	Payments as a % of Premium
2023	$265.70 billion	$161.90 billion	61.00%
2022	$243.10 billion	$182.20 billion	75.00%
2021	$212.40 billion	$164.60 billion	78.00%
2020	$193.80 billion	$141.80 billion	73.00%

Source: 2024 Annual Report, Texas Department of Insurance.

Top 5 Auto Insurers (Texas, 2023)		
Group	Premiums	% of market
Progressive	$5,851,596,768	18.30%
State Farm	$5,592,383,798	17.50%
Allstate Insurance	$3,409,214,696	10.70%
Berkshire Hathaway	$3,099,657,819	9.70%
USAA	$2,818,543,235	8.80%
Top 5 Homeowners (Texas, 2023)		
State Farm	$3,037,553,899	19.00%
Allstate Insurance	$2,393,598,165	15.00%
USAA	$1,646,792,463	10.30%
Liberty Mutual	$1,356,593,441	8.50%
Farmers Insurance	$1,180,808,785	7.40%
Top 5 Health Insurers (Texas, 2023)		
UnitedHealth	$32,944,972,688	25.20%
Health Care Service Corp.	$22,484,283,247	17.20%
Centene Corp.	$16,988,438,004	13.00%
Elevance Health Inc.	$8,378,228,089	6.40%
Humana	$7,478,382,793	5.70%
Top 5 Life Insurers (Texas, 2023)		
New York Life	$1,057,565,539	6.90%
Northwestern Mutual	$910,210,237	5.90%
Metropolitan	$859,766,748	5.60%
Prudential of America	$689,850,445	4.50%
Lincoln National	$644,120,389	4.20%

TEXAS ELECTRIC GRIDS

- The Electric Reliability Council of Texas (ERCOT) operates the electric grid for 75% of the state.
- Part of the Panhandle, part of the South Plains, and a corner of Northeast Texas are under the Southwest Power Pool (SPP).
- El Paso and the far western corner of the Trans Pecos are under the Western Electric Coordinating Council (WECC).
- The southeast corner of Texas is under the SERC Reliability Corporation.
- The councils were first formed in 1968 to ensure adequate bulk power supply.

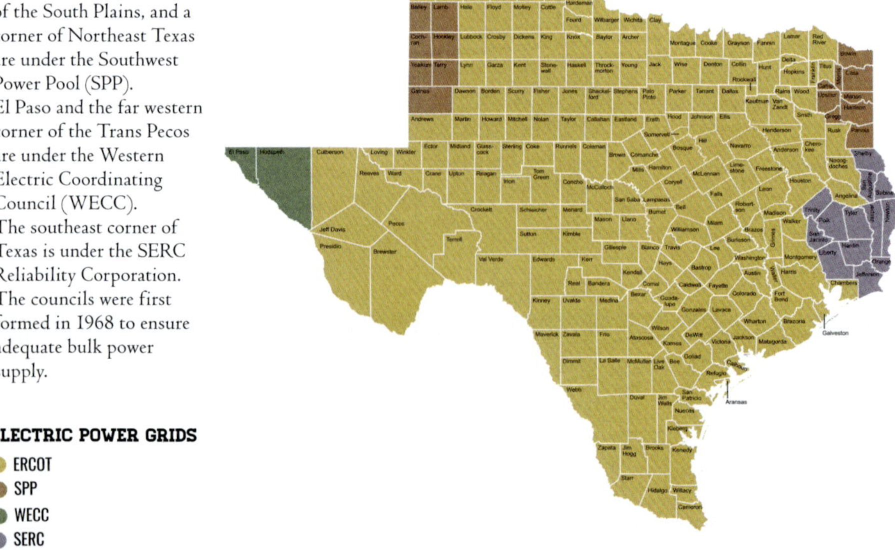

Texas' Installed Wind Capacity (MW)

	2023	2022	2021	2020	2015	2010
U.S.	147,445	141,402	132,753	118,379	66,008	40,267
Texas	40,327	39,344	34,370	30,107	14,208	10,089
Share of U.S. Total	27.35%	27.82%	25.90%	25.40%	21.50%	25.10%

Sources: U.S. Energy Information Administration and the American Wind Energy Association.

ERCOT Net Energy for Load (MWh)

	2024 Energy	Forecasted Energy	Difference	2023 Energy	Change from 2023	% Change from 2023
Jan	38,184,181	37,655,103	1.41%	32,164,147	6,020,034	18.72%
Feb	30,628,455	34,656,254	-11.62%	30,227,600	400,855	1.33%
Mar	32,205,070	34,835,027	-7.55%	31,763,108	441,962	1.39%
Apr	33,462,692	34,471,815	-2.93%	30,697,934	2,764,758	9.01%
May	39,973,544	39,583,265	0.99%	36,461,577	3,511,967	9.63%
Jun	44,374,814	43,691,178	1.56%	42,649,474	1,725,340	4.05%
Jul	44,556,097	47,028,660	-5.26%	47,428,812	-2,872,715	-6.06%
Aug	49,282,923	47,671,517	3.38%	50,250,257	-967,334	-1.93%
Sep	41,002,544	41,342,885	-0.82%	42,978,963	-1,976,419	-4.60%
Oct	39,228,005	38,361,365	2.26%	35,408,445	3,819,560	10.79%
Nov	33,761,214	35,083,182	-3.77%	31,379,259	2,381,955	7.59%
Dec	34,890,419	37,738,534	-7.55%	33,274,438	1,615,981	4.86%
Annual	461,549,959	472,118,783	-2.24%	444,684,012	16,865,947	3.79%

Source: ERCOT 2024 Demand and Energy Report.

ERCOT Max 1-Hour Demand (MWh)

	2024 Demand	Forecasted Demand	Difference	2023 Demand	Change from 2023	% Change from 2023	Max All Time	Max All Time Date
Jan	78,349	65,914	18.87%	65,632	12,717	19.38%	78,349	01/16/2024
Feb	55,860	69,258	-19.35%	63,508	-7,648	-12.04%	69,812	02/14/2021
Mar	55,306	59,517	-7.08%	53,094	2,212	4.17%	60,756	03/05/2019
Apr	64,003	62,729	2.03%	60,995	3,008	4.93%	64,003	04/30/2024
May	77,139	73,200	5.38%	68,159	8,980	13.18%	77,139	05/27/2024
Jun	79,697	77,570	2.74%	80,826	-1,129	-1.40%	80,826	06/27/2023
Jul	81,045	79,306	2.19%	82,964	-1,919	-2.31%	82,964	07/31/2023
Aug	85,245	82,239	3.66%	85,508	-263	-0.31%	85,508	08/10/2023
Sep	77,813	77,046	1.00%	84,470	-6,657	-7.88%	84,470	09/08/2023
Oct	72,550	70,993	2.19%	71,234	1,316	1.85%	72,550	10/03/2024
Nov	60,174	61,355	-1.92%	56,535	3,639	6.44%	60,174	11/04/2024
Dec	60,235	65,429	-7.94%	56,976	3,259	5.72%	74,525	12/23/2022
Annual	85,245	82,239	3.66%	85,508	—	—	—	—

Source: ERCOT 2024 Demand and Energy Report.

OIL AND GAS

Texas ranks first in oil and gas production in the United States. In 2024, Texas produced more than two billion barrels of oil and 12.7 billion cubic feet of natural gas. According to the Texas Oil and Gas Association, Texas crude oil production makes up 44.00% of the nation's total.

The industry also paid $27.3 billion in state and local taxes and state royalties in fiscal year 2024 and employed more than 492,000 Texans with an average yearly salary of $128,255.

Source: Texas Oil & Gas Association, 2024 Annual Energy & Economic Impact Report.

Top Oil-Producing Counties

The top 20 oil-producing counties are ranked below. The column on the right right lists the number of regular producing oil wells in the county as of February 2024.

Rank	County	Barrels	Oil Wells
1	Martin	245,104,438	5,821
2	Midland	230,420,338	6,293
3	Reeves	180,828,560	2,694
4	Loving	168,835,983	1,821
5	Howard	109,837,704	5,285
6	Upton	102,054,953	4,693
7	Karnes	92,527,440	3,699
8	Glasscock	68,951,464	3,880
9	Reagan	68,399,009	4,312
10	Ward	63,342,139	3,254
11	Andrews	55,961,687	9,334
12	La Salle	47,212,832	3,096
13	De Witt	44,513,976	1,227
14	Culberson	43,323,324	88
15	Dimmit	38,491,803	2,271
16	Gonzales	30,645,877	1,909
17	Atascosa	30,281,672	2,081
18	McMullen	29,617,589	2,182
19	Yoakum	26,981,437	3,780
20	Pecos	26,191,621	3,313

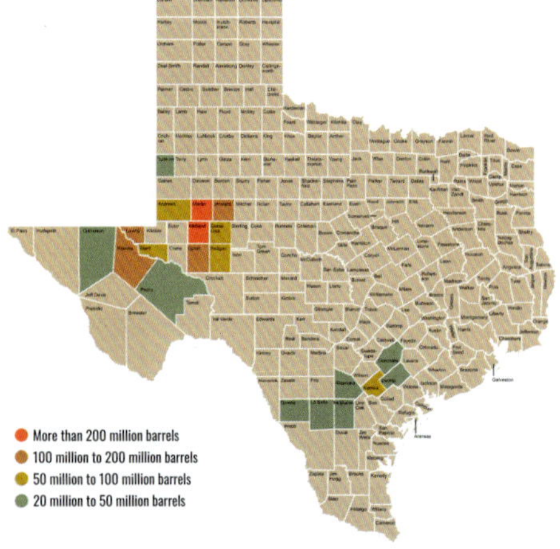

Top Gas-Producing Counties

The top 20 natural gas-producing counties are ranked below. The fourth column on the right lists the number of producing gas wells in the county as of February 2024. MCF is thousand cubic feet.

Rank	County	Gas (MCF)	Gas Wells
1	Reeves	1,137,566,056	2,337
2	Webb	1,024,156,919	6,496
3	Midland	908,581,064	73
4	Martin	651,221,179	2
5	Panola	639,185,611	4,868
6	Loving	620,241,653	1,259
7	Harrison	492,383,485	2,117
8	Culberson	490,067,173	872
9	Reagan	452,823,138	41
10	Upton	440,999,894	224
11	Howard	391,027,030	29
12	La Salle	330,538,498	1,340
13	Glasscock	320,262,225	95
14	Karnes	305,296,536	1,225
15	Tarrant	291,009,286	3,989
16	San Augustine	279,702,112	381
17	De Witt	240,141,517	1,070
18	Dimmit	224,174,686	1,904
19	Nacogdoches	205,142,792	1,235
20	Ward	199,511,154	380

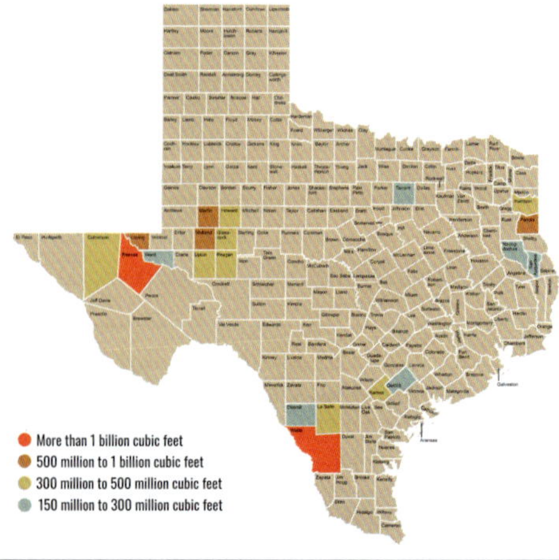

Source: Texas Railroad Commission.

OFFSHORE PRODUCTION HISTORY (OIL AND GAS)

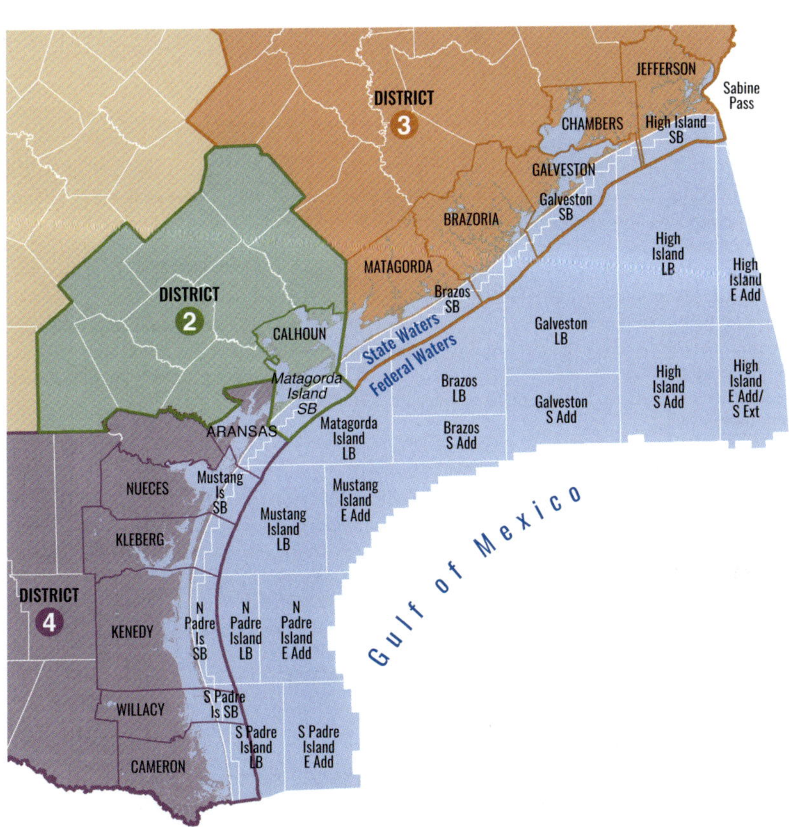

Production in Recent Years				
Year	Crude Oil BBL	Casinghead MCF	Gas Well Gas MCF	Condensate BBL
2024	31,739	24,357	1,135,114	70,719
2023	33,931	27,417	1,194,973	94,509
2022	54,617	52,978	2,003,560	70,876
2021	73,946	244,494	1,293,487	95,175
2020	105,514	56,486	2,338,343	126,695
2015	291,428	233,094	9,674,259	281,510
2010	477,303	1,160,607	27,190,112	866,959
2005	450,378	389,301	38,088,633	451,692
2000	548,046	335,415	43,843,903	220,309

2024 Production by Area				
Offshore Area	Crude Oil BBL	Casinghead MCF	Gas Well Gas MCF	Condensate BBL
Brazos-LB	0	0	0	0
Brazos-SB	0	0	0	0
Galveston-LB	31,263	23,913	51,674	43,665
Galveston-SB	—	—	—	—
High Island-LB	0	0	587,408	0
High Island-SB	0	0	0	0
Matagrda Is.-LB	92	117	0	6
Matagrda Is.-SB	0	0	0	0
Mustang Is.-LB	0	0	117,518	3,154
Mustang Is.-SB	384	327	378,514	23,894
Total	**31,739**	**24,357**	**1,135,114**	**70,719**

NONPETROLEUM MINERALS

There are many nonpetroleum, or nonfuel, minerals found in Texas. Although they are overshadowed by production of petroleum, natural gas, and natural gas liquids, many are important to the economy.

In 2024, Texas nonfuel mineral production was valued at $9.72 billion, compared to the $9.75 billion in total value for 2023, and accounted for 9.2% of the total U.S. nonfuel mineral production value of $106 billion. Among all 50 states, Texas ranked second in nonfuel mineral production, behind Nevada ($9.9 billion in 2024).

The nonfuel mineral commodities produced in Texas in 2024 include: cement, lime, sand and gravel (both construction and industrial), and stone (crushed).

In 2024, Texas was the leader in crushed stone production as well as cement, and second to California in sand and gravel (construction). Texas is one of only two states that produced tellurium (Utah). The amount and value has been withheld to avoid disclosing proprietary data for the companies involved.

ALUMINUM: Texas plants process aluminum materials in one or more ways. Plants in San Patricio and Calhoun counties produce aluminum oxide (alumina) from imported raw ore (bauxite), and a plant in Milam County reduces the oxide to aluminum.

ASBESTOS: Small occurrences of amphibole-type asbestos have been found in the state. In West Texas, richterite, a white, long-fibered amphibole, is associated with some of the talc deposits northwest of Allamoore in Hudspeth County. Another type, tremolite, has been found in the Llano Uplift of Central Texas where it is associated with serpentinite in eastern Gillespie and western Blanco counties. No asbestos is mined in Texas.

ASPHALT (NATIVE): Asphalt-bearing Cretaceous limestones crop out in Burnet, Kinney, Pecos, Reeves, Uvalde, and other counties. The most significant deposit is in southwestern Uvalde County, where asphalt occurs naturally in pore spaces of the Anacacho Limestone. The material is quarried and used extensively as road-paving material. Asphalt-bearing sandstones occur in Anderson, Angelina, Cooke, Jasper, Maverick, Montague, Nacogdoches, Uvalde, Zavala, and other counties.

BARITE: Deposits of a heavy, nonmetallic mineral, barite (barium sulphate), have been found in many localities, including Baylor, Brown, Brewster, Culberson, Gillespie, Howard, Hudspeth, Jeff Davis, Kinney, Llano, Live Oak, Taylor, Val Verde, and Webb counties. During the 1960s, there was small, intermittent production in the Seven Heart Gap area of the Apache Mountains in Culberson County, where barite was mined from open pits. Most of the deposits are known to be relatively small, but the Webb County deposit has not been evaluated. Grinding plants, which prepare barite mined outside of Texas to use as a weighting agent in well-drilling muds and as a filler, are located in Brownsville, Corpus Christi, El Paso, Galena Park, Galveston, and Houston.

BASALT (TRAP ROCK): Masses of basalt — a hard, dark-colored, fine-grained igneous rock — crop out in Kinney, Travis, Uvalde, and several other counties along the Balcones Fault Zone, and in the Trans-Pecos area of West Texas. Basalt is quarried near Knippa in Uvalde County for use as road-building material, railroad ballast, and other aggregate.

BENTONITE (SEE CLAYS).

BERYLLIUM: Occurrences of beryllium minerals at several Trans-Pecos localities have been recognized for several years.

BRINE (SEE ALSO SALT, SODIUM CHLORIDE): Many wells in Texas produce brine by solution mining of subsurface salt deposits, mostly in West Texas counties such as Andrews, Crane, Ector, Loving, Midland, Pecos, Reeves, Ward, and others. These wells in the Permian Basin dissolve salt from the Salado Formation, an enormous salt deposit that extends in the subsurface from north of the Big Bend northward to Kansas, has an east-west width of 150 to 200 miles, and may have several hundred feet of net salt thickness. The majority of the brine is used in the petroleum industry, but it also is used in water softening, the chemical industry, and other uses. Three Gulf Coast counties, Fort Bend, Duval, and Jefferson, have brine stations that produce from salt domes.

BUILDING STONE (DIMENSION STONE): Granite and limestone currently are quarried for use as dimension stone. The granite quarries are located in Burnet, Gillespie, Llano, and Mason counties; the limestone quarries are in Shackelford and Williamson counties. Past production of limestone for use as dimension stone has been reported in Burnet, Gillespie, Jones, Tarrant, Travis, and several other counties. There also has been production of sandstone in various counties for use as dimension stone.

CEMENT MATERIALS: Cement is currently manufactured in Bexar, Comal, Dallas, Ector, Ellis, Hays, McLennan,

Sources: U.S. Geological Survey's mineral industry surveys; Bureau of Economic Geology, The University of Texas at Austin.

COAL MINING LOCATIONS

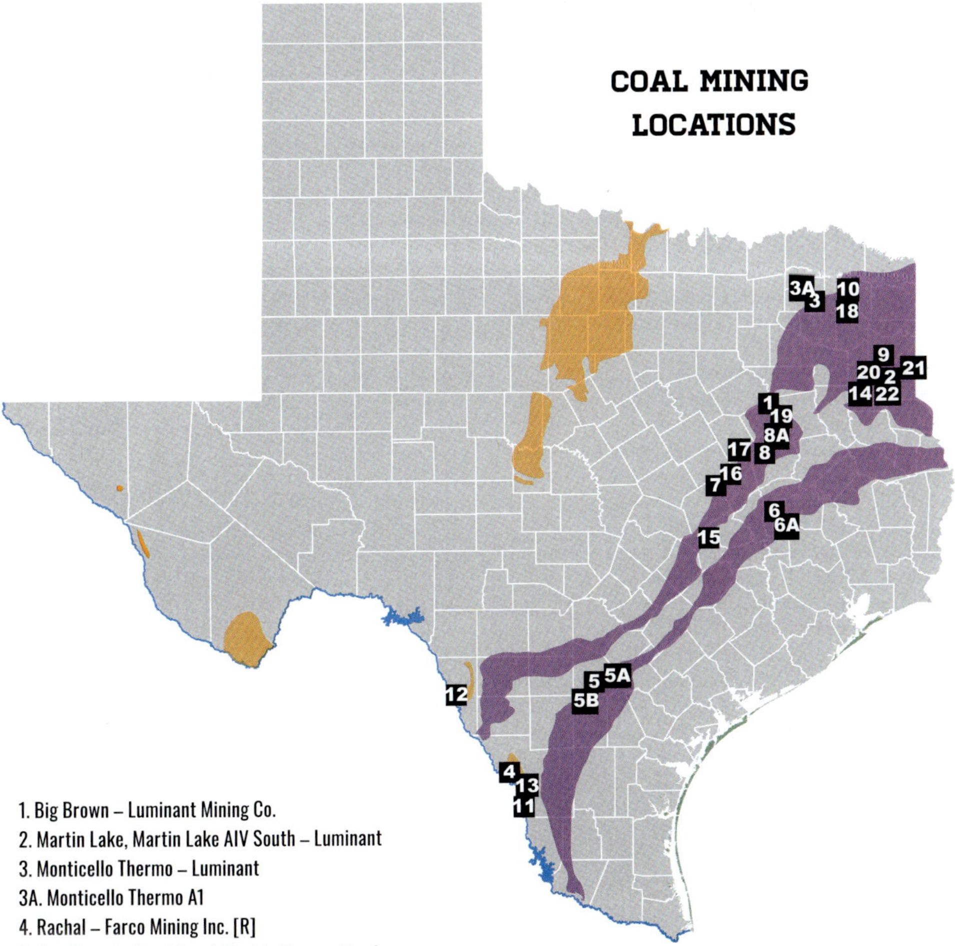

1. Big Brown – Luminant Mining Co.
2. Martin Lake, Martin Lake AIV South – Luminant
3. Monticello Thermo – Luminant
3A. Monticello Thermo A1
4. Rachal – Farco Mining Inc. [R]
5. San Miguel – San Miguel Electric Cooperative Inc.
5A. San Miguel Area C
5B. San Miguel F, G & H
6. Gibbons Creek – Texas Municipal Power Agency [R]
6A. Gibbons V
7. Calvert – Walnut Creek Mining Co.
8. Jewett – Texas Westmoreland Coal Co.
8A. Jewett E/F
9. South Hallsville No. 1 – Sabine Mining Co.
10. Monticello Winfield – Luminant
11. Palafox – Farco Mining Inc. [R]
12. Eagle Pass – Dos Repúblicas Resources Co. Inc.
13. Treviño – Farco [R]
14. Oak Hill – Luminant
15. Three Oaks – Alcoa
16. Bremond – Luminant
17. Kosse – Luminant
18. Leesburg – Luminant
19. Turlington – Luminant
20. Rusk — Sabine
21. Marshall
22. Liberty

Areas of Geologic Conditions Relating to Occurrence of Coal

Areas of Geologic Conditions Relating to Occurrence of Lignite

6 Permitted Coal Mine

[R] Reclamation Only

Nolan, and Potter counties. Many of these plants utilize Cretaceous limestones and shales or clays as raw materials for the cement. On the Texas High Plains, a cement plant near Amarillo uses impure caliche as the chief raw material. Iron oxide, also a constituent of cement, is available from the iron ore deposits of East Texas and from smelter slag. Gypsum, added to the cement as a retarder, is found chiefly in the North-Central, Central, and Trans-Pecos areas.

CHROMIUM: Chromite-bearing rock has been found in several small deposits around the margin of the Coal Creek serpentinite mass in northeastern Gillespie County and northwestern Blanco County. Exploration has not revealed significant deposits.

CLAYS: Texas has an abundance and variety of ceramic and non-ceramic clays and is one of the country's leading producers of clay products.

Almost any kind of clay — ranging from common clay used to make brick and tile to clays suitable for manufacture of specialty whitewares — can be used for ceramic purposes. Fire clay suitable for use as refractories occurs chiefly in East and North-Central Texas. Ball clay, a high-quality plastic ceramic clay, is found in East Texas.

Ceramic clay suitable for quality structural clay products, such as structural building brick, paving brick, and drain tile, is especially abundant in East and North-Central Texas. Common clay suitable for use in the manufacture of cement and ordinary brick is found in most counties of the state. Many of the Texas clays will expand or bloat upon rapid firing and are suitable for the manufacture of lightweight aggregate, which is used mainly in concrete blocks and highway surfacing.

Nonceramic clays are utilized without firing. They are used primarily as bleaching and absorbent clays, fillers, coaters, additives, bonding clays, drilling muds, catalysts, and potentially as sources of alumina. Most of the nonceramic clays in Texas are bentonites and fuller's earth. These occur extensively in the Coastal Plain and locally in the High Plains and Big Bend areas. Kaolin clays in parts of East Texas are potential sources of such nonceramic products as paper coaters and fillers, rubber fillers, and drilling agents. Relatively high in alumina, these clays also are a potential source of metallic aluminum.

COAL (SEE ALSO LIGNITE): Bituminous coal, which occurs in North-Central, South, and West Texas, was a significant energy source in Texas prior to the large-scale development of oil and gas. During the period from 1895 to 1943, Texas mines produced more than 25 million tons of coal. The mines were inactive for many years, but the renewed interest in coal as a major energy source prompted a revaluation of Texas' coal deposits. In the late 1970s, bituminous coal production resumed in the state on a limited scale when mines were opened in Coleman, Erath, and Webb counties.

Much of the state's bituminous coal occurs in North-Central Texas. Deposits are found there in Pennsylvanian rocks within a large area that includes Coleman, Eastland, Erath, Jack, McCulloch, Montague, Palo Pinto, Parker, Throckmorton, Wise, Young, and other counties. Before the general availability of oil and gas, underground coal mines near Thurber, Bridgeport, Newcastle, Strawn, and other points annually produced significant coal tonnages. Preliminary evaluations indicate substantial amounts of coal may remain in the North-Central Texas area. The coal seams there are generally no more than 30 inches thick and are commonly covered by well-consolidated overburden. Ash and sulphur content are high.

In South Texas, bituminous coal occurs in the Eagle Pass district of Maverick County, and bituminous cannel coal is present in the Santo Tomas district of Webb County. The Eagle Pass area was a leading coal-producing district in Texas during the late 1800s and early 1900s. The bituminous coal in that area, which occurs in the Upper Cretaceous Olmos Formation, has a high ash content and a moderate moisture and sulfur content. According to reports, Maverick County coal beds range from four to seven feet thick.

The cannel coals of western Webb County occur near the Rio Grande in middle Eocene strata. They were mined for more than 50 years and used primarily as boiler fuel. Mining ceased from 1939 until 1978, when a surface mine was opened 30 miles northwest of Laredo to produce cannel coal for use as fuel in the cement industry and for export. An additional mine has since been opened in that county. Tests show that the coals of the Webb County Santo Tomas district have a high hydrogen content and yield significant amounts of gas and oil when distilled. They also have a high sulfur content.

Coal deposits in the Trans-Pecos country of West Texas include those in the Cretaceous rocks of the Terlingua area of Brewster County, the Eagle Spring area of Hudspeth County, and the San Carlos area of Presidio County. The coal deposits in these areas are believed to have relatively little potential for development as a fuel. They have been sold in the past as a soil amendment **(see LEONARDITE)**.

COPPER: Copper minerals have been found in the Trans-Pecos area of West Texas, in the Llano Uplift area of Central Texas, and in redbed deposits of North Texas. No copper has been mined in Texas during recent years, and the total copper produced in the state has been relatively small. Past attempts to mine the North Texas and Llano Uplift copper deposits resulted in small shipments.

Practically all the copper production in the state has been from the Van Horn–Allamoore district of Culberson and Hudspeth counties in the Trans-Pecos area. Chief output was from the Hazel copper-silver mine of Culberson County that yielded over 1 million pounds of copper during 1891–1947. Copper ores and concentrates from outside of Texas are processed at smelters in El Paso and Amarillo.

CRUSHED STONE: Texas is among the leading states in the production of crushed stone. Most production consists of limestone; other kinds of crushed stone produced in the state include basalt (trap rock), dolomite, granite, marble, rhyolite, sandstone, and serpentinite. Large tonnages of crushed stone are used as aggregate in concrete, as road material, and in the manufacture of cement and lime. Some crushed stone is used as riprap, terrazzo, roofing chips, filter material, fillers, as well as other purposes.

DIATOMITE (DIATOMACEOUS EARTH): Diatomite is a very lightweight siliceous material consisting of the remains of microscopic aquatic plants (diatoms). It is used chiefly as a filter and filler; other uses are for thermal insulation, as an abrasive, as an insecticide carrier, as a lightweight aggregate, and for other purposes. The diatomite was deposited in shallow, fresh-water lakes that were present in the High Plains during portions of the Pliocene and Pleistocene epochs. Deposits have been found in Armstrong, Crosby, Dickens, Ector, Hartley, and Lamb counties. No diatomite is mined in Texas.

DOLOMITE ROCK: Dolomite rock, which consists largely of the mineral dolomite (calcium-magnesium carbonate), commonly is associated with limestone in Texas. Areas in which dolomite rock occurs include Central Texas, the Callahan Divide, and parts of the Edwards Plateau, High Plains, and West Texas. Some of the principal deposits of dolomite rock are found in Bell, Brown, Burnet, Comanche, Edwards, El Paso, Gillespie, Lampasas, Mills, Nolan, Taylor, and Williamson counties. Dolomite rock can be used as crushed stone (although much of Texas dolomite is soft and not a good aggregate material), in the manufacture of lime, and as a source of magnesium.

FELDSPAR: Large crystals and crystal fragments of feldspar minerals occur in the Precambrian pegmatite rocks that crop out in the Llano Uplift area of Central Texas including Blanco, Burnet, Gillespie, Llano, and Mason counties, and in the Van Horn area of Culberson and Hudspeth counties in West Texas. Feldspar has been mined in Llano County for use as roofing granules and as a ceramic material. Feldspar is currently mined in Burnet County for use as an aggregate.

FLUORSPAR: The mineral fluorite (calcium fluoride), which is known commercially as fluorspar, occurs in both Central and West Texas. In Central Texas, the deposits that have been found in Burnet, Gillespie, and Mason counties are not considered adequate to sustain mining operations. In West Texas, deposits have been found in Brewster, El Paso, Hudspeth, Jeff Davis, and Presidio counties. Fluorspar has been mined in the Christmas Mountains of Brewster County and processed in Marathon. Former West Texas mining activity in the Eagle Mountains district of Hudspeth County resulted in the production of approximately 15,000 short tons of fluorspar during the peak years of 1942 to 1950. No production has been reported in Hudspeth County since that period. Imported fluorspar is processed in Brownsville, Eagle Pass, El Paso, and Houston. Fluorspar is used in the steel, chemical, aluminum, magnesium, ceramics, and glass industries, and for various other purposes.

FULLER'S EARTH (SEE CLAY).

GOLD: No major deposits of gold are known in Texas. Small amounts have been found in the Llano Uplift region of Central Texas and in West Texas; minor occurrences have been reported on the Edwards Plateau and the Gulf Coastal Plain of Texas. Nearly all of the gold produced in the state came as a by-product of silver and lead mining at Presidio mine, near Shafter in Presidio County. Additional small quantities were produced as a by-product of copper mining in Culberson County and from residual soils developed from gold-bearing quartz stringers in metamorphic rocks in Llano County. No gold mining has been reported in Texas since 1952. Total gold production in the state from 1889–1952 amounted to more than 8,419 troy ounces, according to U.S. Bureau of Mines figures. At least 73% of all production, and probably more, came from the Presidio mine.

GRANITE: Granites in shades of red and gray and related intrusive igneous rocks occur in the Llano Uplift of Central Texas and in the Trans-Pecos country of West Texas. Deposits are found in Blanco, Brewster, Burnet, El Paso, Gillespie, Hudspeth, Llano, McCulloch, Mason, Presidio, and other counties. Quarries in Burnet, Gillespie, Llano, and Mason counties produce Precambrian granite for a variety of uses as dimension stone and crushed stone.

GRAPHITE: Graphite, a soft, dark-gray mineral, is a form of very high-grade carbon. It occurs in Precambrian schist rocks of the Llano Uplift of Central Texas, notably in Burnet and Llano counties. Crystalline-flake graphite ore formerly was mined from open pits in the Clear Creek area of western Burnet County and processed at a plant near the mine. The mill now occasionally grinds imported material. Uses of natural crystalline graphite are refractories, steel production, pencil leads, lubricants, foundry facings, and crucibles, as well as other purposes.

GRINDING PEBBLES (ABRASIVE STONES): Flint pebbles, suitable for use in tube-mill grinding, are found in the Gulf Coastal Plain, where they occur in gravel deposits along rivers and in upland areas. Grinding pebbles are produced from Frio River terrace deposits near the McMullen–Live Oak county line, but the area is now part of the Choke Canyon Reservoir area.

GYPSUM: Gypsum is widely distributed in Texas. Chief deposits are bedded gypsum in the area east of the High Plains, in the Trans-Pecos country, and in Central Texas. It also occurs in salt-dome caprocks of the Gulf Coast. The massive, granular variety, which is known as rock gypsum, is the kind most commonly used by industry. Other varieties include alabaster, satin spar, and selenite.

Bedded gypsum is produced from surface mines in Culberson, Fisher, Gillespie, Hardeman, Hudspeth, Kimble, Nolan, and Stonewall counties. Gypsum was formerly mined at Gyp Hill salt dome in Brooks County and at Hockley salt dome in Harris County. Most of the gypsum is calcined and used in the manufacture of gypsum wallboard, plaster, joint compounds, and other construction products. Crude gypsum is used chiefly as a retarder in portland cement and as a soil conditioner.

HELIUM: Helium is a very light, nonflammable, chemically inert gas. The U.S. Interior Department has ended its helium operation near Masterson in the Panhandle. The storage facility at Cliffside gas field near Amarillo and the

425-mile pipeline system will remain in operation until the government sells its remaining unrefined, crude helium. Helium is used in cryogenics, welding, pressurizing and purging, leak detection, synthetic breathing mixtures, and for other purposes.

IRON: Iron oxide (limonite, goethite, and hematite) and iron carbonate (siderite) deposits occur widely in East Texas, notably in Cass, Cherokee, Marion, and Morris counties, and also in Anderson, Camp, Harrison, Henderson, Nacogdoches, Smith, Upshur, and other counties. Magnetite (magnetic, black iron oxide) occurs in Central Texas, including a deposit at Iron Mountain in Llano County. Hematite occurs in the Trans-Pecos area and in the Llano Uplift of Central Texas. The extensive deposits of glauconite (a complex silicate containing iron) that occur in East Texas and the hematite and goethite Cambrian sandstone that crops out in the northwestern Llano Uplift region are potential sources of low-grade iron ore.

Limonite and other East Texas iron ores are mined from open pits in Cherokee and Henderson counties for use in the preparation of portland cement, as a weighting agent in well-drilling fluids, as an animal feed supplement, and for other purposes. East Texas iron ores also were mined in the past for use in the iron-steel industry.

KAOLIN (SEE CLAY).

LEAD AND ZINC: The lead mineral galena (lead sulfide) commonly is associated with zinc and silver. It formerly was produced as a by-product of West Texas silver mining, chiefly from the Presidio mine at Shafter in Presidio County, although lesser amounts were obtained at several other mines and prospects. Deposits of galena also are known to occur in Blanco, Brewster, Burnet, Gillespie, and Hudspeth counties.

Zinc, primarily from the mineral sphalerite (zinc sulphide), was produced chiefly from the Bonanza and Alice Ray mines in the Quitman Mountains of Hudspeth County. In addition, small production was reported from several other areas, including the Chinati and Montezuma mines of Presidio County and the Buck Prospect in the Apache Mountains of Culberson County. Zinc mineralization also occurs in association with the lead deposits in Cambrian rocks of Central Texas.

LEONARDITE: Deposits of weathered (oxidized) low-Btu value bituminous coals, generally referred to as "leonardite," occur in Brewster County. The name leonardite is used for a mixture of chemical compounds that is high in humic acids. In the past, material from these deposits was sold as soil conditioner. Other uses of leonardite include modification of viscosity of drill fluids and as sorbants in water-treatment.

LIGHTWEIGHT AGGREGATE (SEE CLAY, DIATOMITE, PERLITE, VERMICULITE).

LIGNITE: Almost all current coal production in Texas is located in the Tertiary-aged lignite belts that extend across the Texas Gulf Coastal Plain from the Rio Grande in South Texas to the Arkansas and Louisiana borders in East Texas.

The near-surface lignite resources, occurring at depths of less than 200 feet in seams of three feet or thicker, are estimated at 23 billion short tons. Recoverable reserves of strippable lignite, those that can be economically mined under current conditions of price and technology, are estimated by the EIA to be 722 million short tons.

Additional lignite resources of the Texas Gulf Coastal Plain occur as deep-basin deposits. Deep-basin resources, those that occur at depths of 200 to 2,000 feet in seams of five feet or thicker, are comparable in magnitude to near-surface resources. The deep-basin lignites are a potential energy resource that could conceivably be utilized by in situ (in place) recovery methods such as underground gasification.

As with bituminous coal, lignite production was significant prior to the general availability of oil and gas. Remnants of old underground mines are common throughout the area of lignite occurrence. Large strip mines produce lignite that is burned for mine-mouth electric-power generation. Mines are located in Atascosa, Franklin, Freestone, Harrison, Hopkins, Leon, Limestone, McMullen, Milam, Panola, Robertson, Rusk, and Titus counties.

LIME MATERIAL: Limestones, which are abundant in some areas of Texas, are heated to produce lime (calcium oxide) at a number of plants in the state. High-magnesium limestone and dolomite are used to prepare lime at a plant in Burnet County. Other lime plants are located in Bexar, Bosque, Comal, Hill, Johnson, and Travis counties. Lime production captive to the kiln's operator occurs in several Texas counties. Lime is used in soil stabilization, water purification, paper and pulp manufacture, metallurgy, sugar refining, agriculture, construction, removal of sulfur from stack gases, and for many other purposes.

LIMESTONE (SEE ALSO BUILDING STONE): Texas is one of the nation's leading producers of limestone, which is quarried in more than 60 counties. Limestone occurs in nearly all areas of the state with the exception of most of the Gulf Coastal Plain and High Plains. Although some of the limestone is quarried for use as dimension stone, most of the output is crushed for uses such as bulk building materials (crushed stone, road base, concrete aggregate), chemical raw materials, fillers or extenders, lime and portland cement raw materials, agricultural limestone, and removal of sulfur from stack gases.

MAGNESITE: Small deposits of magnesite (natural magnesium carbonate) have been found in Precambrian rocks in Llano and Mason counties of Central Texas. At one time, there was small-scale mining of magnesite in the area; some of the material was used as agricultural stone and as terrazzo chips. Magnesite also can be calcined to form magnesia, which is used in metallurgical furnace refractories and other products.

MAGNESIUM: On the Texas Gulf Coast in Brazoria County, magnesium chloride is extracted from sea water at a plant in Freeport and used to produce magnesium compounds and magnesium metal. During World War II, high-magnesium

Ellenburger dolomite rock from Burnet County was used as magnesium ore at a plant near Austin.

MANGANESE: Deposits of manganese minerals, such as braunite, hollandite, and pyrolusite, have been found in several areas, including Jeff Davis, Llano, Mason, Presidio, and Val Verde counties. Known deposits are not large. Small shipments have been made from Jeff Davis, Mason, and Val Verde counties, but no manganese mining has been reported in Texas since 1954.

MARBLE: Metamorphic and sedimentary marbles suitable for monument and building stone are found in the Llano Uplift and nearby areas of Central Texas and the Trans-Pecos area of West Texas. Gray, white, black, greenish black, light green, brown, and cream-colored marbles occur in Central Texas in Burnet, Gillespie, Llano, and Mason counties. West Texas metamorphic marbles include the bluish-white and the black marbles found southwest of Alpine in Brewster County and the white marble from Marble Canyon north of Van Horn in Culberson County. Marble can be used as dimension stone, terrazzo, and roofing aggregate, and for other purposes.

MERCURY (QUICKSILVER): Mercury minerals, chiefly cinnabar, occur in the Terlingua district and nearby districts of southern Brewster and southeastern Presidio counties. Mining began there about 1894, and from 1905 to 1935, Texas was one of the nation's leading producers of quicksilver. Following World War II, a sharp drop in demand and price, along with depletion of developed ore reserves, caused abandonment of all the Texas mercury mines.

With a rise in the price, sporadic mining took place between 1951 and 1960. In 1965, when the price of mercury moved to a record high, renewed interest in the Texas mercury districts resulted in the reopening of several mines and the discovery of new ore reserves. By April 1972, however, the price had declined and the mines have reported no production since 1973.

MICA: Large crystals of flexible, transparent mica minerals in igneous pegmatite rocks and mica flakes in metamorphic schist rocks are found in the Llano Uplift area of Central Texas and the Van Horn area of West Texas. Most Central Texas deposits do not meet specifications for sheet mica, and although several attempts have been made to produce West Texas sheet mica in Culberson and Hudspeth counties, sustained production has not been achieved. A mica quarry operated for a short time in the early 1980s in the Van Horn Mountains of Culberson and Hudspeth counties to mine mica schist for use as an additive in rotary drilling fluids.

MOLYBDENUM: Small occurrences of molybdenite have been found in Burnet and Llano counties, and wulfenite, another molybdenum mineral, has been noted in rocks in the Quitman Mountains of Hudspeth County. Molybdenum minerals also occur at Cave Peak north of Van Horn in Culberson County, in the Altuda Mountain area of northwestern Brewster County, and in association with uranium ores of the Gulf Coastal Plain.

PEAT: This spongy organic substance forms in bogs from plant remains. It has been found in the Gulf Coastal Plain in several localities including Gonzales, Guadalupe, Lee, Milam, Polk, and San Jacinto counties. There has been intermittent, small-scale production of some of the peat for use as a soil conditioner.

PERLITE: Perlite, a glassy igneous rock, expands to a lightweight, porous mass when heated. It can be used as a lightweight aggregate, filter aid, horticultural aggregate, and for other purposes. Perlite occurs in Presidio County, where it has been mined in the Pinto Canyon area north of the Chinati Mountains. No perlite is currently mined in Texas, but perlite mined outside of Texas is expanded at plants in Bexar, Dallas, El Paso, Guadalupe, Harris, and Nolan counties.

PHOSPHATE: Rock phosphate is present in Paleozoic rocks in several areas of Brewster and Presidio counties in West Texas and in Central Texas, but the known deposits are not large. In Northeast Texas, sedimentary rock phosphate occurs in thin conglomerate lenses in Upper Cretaceous and Tertiary rock units; possibly some of these low-grade phosphorites could be processed on a small scale for local use as a fertilizer. Imported phosphate rock is processed at a plant in Brownsville.

POTASH: The potassium mineral polyhalite is widely distributed in the subsurface Permian Basin of West Texas and has been found in many wells in that area. During 1927 to 1931, the federal government drilled a series of potash-test wells in Crane, Crockett, Ector, Glasscock, Loving, Reagan, Upton, and Winkler counties. In addition to polyhalite, which was found in all of the counties, these wells revealed the presence of the potassium minerals carnallite and sylvite in Loving County and carnallite in Winkler County. The known Texas potash deposits are not as rich as those in the New Mexico portion of the Permian Basin and have not been developed.

PUMICITE (VOLCANIC ASH): Deposits of volcanic ash occur in Brazos, Fayette, Gonzales, Karnes, Polk, Starr, and other counties of the Texas Coastal Plain. Deposits also have been found in the Trans-Pecos area, High Plains, and in several counties east of the High Plains. Volcanic ash is used to prepare pozzolan cement, cleansing and scouring compounds, and soaps and sweeping compounds; as a carrier for insecticides, and for other purposes. It has been mined in Dickens, Lynn, Scurry, Starr, and other counties.

QUICKSILVER (SEE MERCURY).

RARE-EARTH ELEMENTS AND METALS: The term, "rare-earth elements," is commonly applied to elements of the lanthanide group (atomic numbers 57 through 71) plus yttrium. Yttrium, atomic number 39 and not a member of the lanthanide group, is included as a rare-earth element because it has similar properties to members of that group and usually occurs in nature with them. The metals thorium and scandium are sometimes termed "rare metals" because their occurrence is often associated with the rare-earth elements.

The majority of rare-earth elements are consumed as catalysts in petroleum cracking and other chemical industries. Rare earths are widely used in the glass industry for tableware, specialty glasses, optics, and fiber optics.

Cerium oxide has growing use as a polishing compound for glass, gemstones, cathode-ray tube faceplates, and other polishing. Rare earths are alloyed with various metals to produce materials used in the aeronautic, space, and electronics industries. The addition of rare-earth elements may improve resistance to metal fatigue at high temperatures, reduce potential for corrosion, and selectively increase conductivity and magnetism of the metal.

Various members of this group, including thorium, have anomalous concentrations in the rhyolitic and related igneous rocks of the Quitman Mountains and the Sierra Blanca area of Trans-Pecos.

SALT (SODIUM CHLORIDE) (SEE ALSO BRINES): Salt resources of Texas are virtually inexhaustible. Enormous deposits occur in the subsurface Permian Basin of West Texas and in the salt domes of the Gulf Coastal Plain. Salt also is found in the alkali playa lakes of the High Plains, the alkali flats or salt lakes in the Salt Basin of Culberson and Hudspeth counties, and along some of the bays and lagoons of the South Texas Gulf Coast.

Texas is one of the leading salt-producing states. Rock salt is obtained from underground mines in salt domes at Grand Saline in Van Zandt County and Hockley Dome in Harris County. Salt is produced from rock salt and by solution mining as brines from wells drilled into the underground salt deposits.

SAND (INDUSTRIAL): Sands used for special purposes, due to high silica content or to unique physical properties, command higher prices than common sand. Industrial sands in Texas occur mainly in the Central Gulf Coastal Plain and in North-Central Texas. They include abrasive, blast, chemical, engine, filtration, foundry, glass, hydraulic-fracturing (propant), molding, and pottery sands. Recent production of industrial sands has been from Atascosa, Colorado, Hardin, Harris, Liberty, Limestone, McCulloch, Newton, Smith, Somervell, and Upshur counties.

SAND AND GRAVEL (CONSTRUCTION): Sand and gravel are among the most extensively utilized resources in Texas. Principal occurrence is along the major streams and in stream terraces. Sand and gravel are important bulk construction materials, used as railroad ballast, base materials, and for other purposes. In 2024, Texas was second only to California in production of sand and gravel (construction).

SANDSTONE: Sandstones of a variety of colors and textures are widely distributed in a number of geologic formations in Texas. Some of the sandstones have been quarried for use as dimension stone in El Paso, Parker, Terrell, Ward, and other counties. Crushed sandstone is produced in Freestone, Gaines, Jasper, McMullen, Motley, and other counties for use as road-building material, terrazzo stone, and aggregate.

SERPENTINITE: Several masses of serpentinite, which formed from the alteration of basic igneous rocks, are associated with other Precambrian metamorphic rocks of the Llano Uplift. The largest deposit is the Coal Creek serpentinite mass in northern Blanco and Gillespie counties from which terrazzo chips have been produced. Other deposits are present in Gillespie and Llano counties. (The features that are associated with surface and subsurface Cretaceous rocks in several counties in or near the Balcones Fault Zone and that are commonly known as "serpentine plugs" are not serpentine at all, but are altered igneous volcanic necks and pipes, and mounds of altered volcanic ash, palagonite, that accumulated around the former submarine volcanic pipes.)

SHELL: Oyster shells and other shells in shallow coastal waters and in deposits along the Texas Gulf Coast have been produced in the past chiefly by dredging. They were used to a limited extent as raw material in the manufacture of cement, as concrete aggregate and road base, and for other purposes. No shell has been produced in Texas since 1981.

SILVER: During the period 1885 to 1952, the production of silver in Texas, as reported by the U.S. Bureau of Mines, totaled about 33 million troy ounces. For about 70 years, silver was the most consistently produced metal in Texas, although always in moderate quantities. All of the production came from the Trans-Pecos country of West Texas, where the silver was mined in Brewster County (Altuda Mountain), Culberson and Hudspeth counties (Van Horn Mountains and Van Horn–Allamoore district), Hudspeth County (Quitman Mountains and Eagle Mountains), and Presidio County (Chinati Mountains area, Loma Plata mine, and Shafter district).

Chief producer was the Presidio mine in the Shafter district, which began operations in the late 1800s, and, through September 1942, produced more than 30 million ounces of silver: more than 92 percent of Texas' total silver production. Water in the lower mine levels, lean ores, and low price of silver resulted in the closing of the mine in 1942. Another important silver producer was the Hazel copper-silver mine in the Van Horn–Allamoore district in Culberson County, which accounted for more than 2 million ounces.

An increase in the price of silver in the late 1970s stimulated prospecting for new reserves, and exploration began near the old Presidio mine, near the old Plata Verde mine in the Van Horn Mountains district, at the Bonanza mine in the Quitman Mountains district, and at the old Hazel mine. A decline in the price of silver in the early 1980s, however, resulted in reduction of exploration and mine development in the region. The recent rise in the value of silver has sparked new interest in the Shafter mining district of West Texas.

SOAPSTONE (SEE TALC AND SOAPSTONE).

SODIUM SULFATE (SALT CAKE): Sodium sulfate minerals occur in salt beds and brines of the alkali playa lakes of the High Plains in West Texas. In some lakes, the sodium sulfate minerals are present in deposits a few feet beneath the lake beds. Sodium sulfate also is found in underground brines in the Permian Basin. Current production is from brines and dry salt beds at alkali lakes in Gaines and Terry counties. Past production was reported in Lynn and Ward counties. Sodium sulfate is used chiefly by the detergent, paper, and pulp industries. Other uses are in the preparation of glass and other products.

STONE (SEE BUILDING STONE AND CRUSHED STONE).

STRONTIUM: Deposits of the mineral celestite (strontium sulfate) have been found in a number of places, including localities in Brown, Coke, Comanche, Fisher, Lampasas, Mills, Nolan, Real, Taylor, Travis, and Williamson counties. Most of the occurrences are very minor, and no strontium is currently produced in the state.

SULFUR: Texas is one of the world's principal sulfur-producing areas. The sulfur is mined from deposits of native sulfur, and it is extracted from sour (sulfur-bearing) natural gas and petroleum. Recovered sulfur is a growing industry and accounted for approximately 60 percent of all 1987 sulfur production in the United States, but only approximately 40 percent of Texas production. Native sulfur is found in large deposits in the caprock of some of the salt domes along the Texas Gulf Coast and in some of the surface and subsurface Permian strata of West Texas, notably in Culberson and Pecos counties.

Native sulfur obtained from the underground deposits is known as Frasch sulfur, so-called because of Herman Frasch, the chemist who devised the method of drilling wells into the deposits, melting the sulfur with superheated water, and forcing the molten sulfur to the surface. Most of the production now goes to the users in molten form.

Frasch sulfur is produced from only one Gulf Coast salt dome in Wharton County and from West Texas underground Permian strata in Culberson County. Operations at several Gulf Coast domes have been closed in recent years. During the 1940s, acidic sulfur earth was produced in the Rustler Springs district in Culberson County for use as a fertilizer and soil conditioner. Sulfur is recovered from sour natural gas and petroleum at plants in numerous Texas counties.

Sulfur is used in the preparation of fertilizers and organic and inorganic chemicals, in petroleum refining, and for many other purposes.

TALC AND SOAPSTONE: Deposits of talc are found in the Precambrian metamorphic rocks of the Allamoore area of eastern Hudspeth and western Culberson counties. Soapstone, containing talc, occurs in the Precambrian metamorphic rocks of the Llano Uplift area, notably in Blanco, Gillespie, and Llano counties. Current production is from surface mines in the Allamoore area. Talc is used in ceramic, roofing, paint, paper, plastic, synthetic rubber, and other products.

TIN: Tin minerals have been found in El Paso and Mason counties. Small quantities were produced during the early 1900s in the Franklin Mountains north of El Paso. Cassiterite (tin dioxide) occurrences in Mason County are believed to be very minor. The only tin smelter in the United States, built at Texas City by the federal government during World War II and later sold to a private company, processes tin concentrates from ores mined outside of Texas, tin residues, and secondary tin-bearing materials.

TITANIUM: The titanium mineral rutile has been found in small amounts at the Mueller prospect in Jeff Davis County. Another titanium mineral, ilmenite, occurs in sandstones in Burleson, Fayette, Lee, Starr, and several other counties. Deposits that would be considered commercial under present conditions have not been found.

TRAP ROCK (SEE BASALT).

TUNGSTEN: The tungsten mineral scheelite has been found in small deposits in Gillespie and Llano counties and in the Quitman Mountains in Hudspeth County. Small deposits of other tungsten minerals have been prospected in the Cave Peak area north of Van Horn in Culberson County.

URANIUM: Uranium deposits were discovered in the Texas Coastal Plain in 1954 when abnormal radioactivity was detected in the Karnes County area. A number of uranium deposits have since been discovered within a belt of strata extending more than 250 miles from the middle Coastal Plain southwestward to the Rio Grande.

Various uranium minerals also have been found in other areas of Texas, including the Trans-Pecos, the Llano Uplift, and the High Plains. With the exception of small shipments from the High Plains during the 1950s, all the uranium production in Texas has been from the Coastal Plain. Uranium has been obtained from surface mines extending from northern Live Oak County, southeastern Atascosa County, across northern Karnes County, and into southern Gonzales County. Uranium is produced by in-situ leaching, brought to the surface through wells, and stripped from the solution at recovery operations.

In 1999, uranium mining shut down because of decreased value and demand. Production resumed in Texas in late 2004, when inventories were depleted and market prices rose to economic levels that allowed resumption of production.

VERMICULITE: Vermiculite, a mica-like mineral that expands when heated, occurs in Burnet, Gillespie, Llano, Mason, and other counties in the Llano Uplift region. It has been produced at a surface mine in Llano County. Vermiculite, mined outside of Texas, is exfoliated (expanded) at plants in Dallas, Houston, and San Antonio. Exfoliated vermiculite is used for lightweight concrete aggregate, horticulture, insulation, and other purposes.

VOLCANIC ASH (SEE PUMICITE).

ZEOLITES: The zeolite minerals clinoptilolite and analcime occur in Tertiary lavas and tuffs in Brewster, Jeff Davis, and Presidio counties in West Texas. Clinoptilolite also is found associated with Tertiary tuffs in the southern Texas Coastal Plain, including deposits in Karnes, McMullen, and Webb counties, and currently is produced in McMullen County. Zeolites, sometimes called "molecular sieves," can be used in ion-exchange processes to reduce pollution, as a catalyst in oil cracking, in obtaining high-purity oxygen and nitrogen from air, in water purification, and for many other purposes.

ZINC (SEE LEAD AND ZINC).

TEXAS NEWSPAPERS, RADIO, AND TELEVISION STATIONS

Texas is rich with newspapers and broadcast media, many of which have long histories. In the following list, only printed, subscription newspapers appear, and their frequency of publication is indicated by the following codes: (D) daily or at least four days a week, (TW) triweekly, (S) semiweekly, (SM) semimonthly, and (M) monthly. All others are weekly publications.

Radio and digital TV stations are those with valid operating licenses as of May 2025. Not included are those with construction permits or pending applications.

A

ABERNATHY: Newspaper: *Abernathy Advocate.*

ABILENE: Newspaper: *Abilene Reporter-News (D).* **Radio-AM:** KSLI, 1280 kHz; KWKC, 1340; KYYW, 1470; KZQQ, 1560. **Radio-FM:** KGNZ, 88.1 MHz; KACU, 89.5; KAGT, 90.5; KAQD, 91.3; KMWX, 92.5; KULL, 100.7; KEAN, 105.1; KTJK, 106.3; KEYJ, 107.9. **TV Stations:** KXVA-Ch. 15; KRBC-Ch. 29; KTAB-Ch. 30.

AGUA DULCE: Radio-FM: KOUL, 107.7 MHz.

ALAMO: Radio-FM: KJAV, 104.9 MHz.

ALBANY: Newspaper: *Albany News.* **Radio-FM:** KQOS, 91.7 MHz.

ALEDO: Newspaper: *The Community News.*

ALICE: Newspaper: *Alice Echo-News Journal (S).* **Radio-AM:** KOPY, 1070 kHz. **Radio-FM:** KAWV, 88.3 MHz; KOPY, 92.1; KNDA, 102.9.

ALLEN: Newspaper: *Allen American.* **Radio-FM:** KVDT, 103.3 MHz.

ALPINE: Newspaper: *Alpine Avalanche.* **Radio-AM:** KVLF, 1240 kHz. **Radio-FM:** KRTP, 91.7 MHz; KALP, 92.7.

ALVIN: Newspaper: *Alvin Sun.* **Radio-AM:** KTEK, 1110 kHz. **Radio-FM:** KACC, 89.7 MHz. **TV Station:** KFTH-Ch. 36.

UNSPLASH/DAWID ZAWILA

Sources: 2025 Texas Newspaper Directory and Federal Communications Commission.

AMARILLO: **Newspaper:** *Amarillo Globe-News (D).* **Radio-AM:** KGNC, 710 kHz; KIXZ, 940; KDJW, 1010; KZIP, 1310; KTNZ, 1360; KPUR, 1440. **Radio-FM:** KJRT, 88.3 MHz; KXLV, 89.1; KACV, 89.9; KAVW, 90.7; KXRI, 91.9; KQIZ, 93.1; KMXJ, 94.1; KXSS, 96.9; KGNC, 97.9; KPRF, 98.7; KBZD, 99.7; KXGL, 100.9; KATP, 101.9; KVWE, 102.9; KJJP, 105.7. **TV Stations:** KACV-Ch. 9; KFDA-Ch. 10; KCIT-Ch. 15; KAMR-Ch. 19; KVII-Ch. 20.

ANAHUAC: **Newspaper:** *The Progress.*

ANDREWS: **Newspaper:** *Andrews County News (S).* **Radio-AM:** KACT, 1360 kHz. **Radio-FM:** KACT, 105.5 MHz.

ANSON: **Newspaper:** *Western Observer.* **Radio-FM:** KTLT, 98.1 MHz.

ARANSAS PASS: **Newspaper:** *Aransas Pass Progress.* **Radio-FM:** KKWV, 88.1 MHz.

ARCHER CITY: **Newspaper:** *Archer County News.* **Radio-FM:** KPMA, 91.9 MHz.

ARLINGTON: **Radio-FM:** KLTY, 94.9 MHz. **TV Station:** KPXD-Ch. 25.

ARROYO: **Radio-FM:** KVJS, 88.1 MHz.

ATHENS: **Newspaper:** *Athens Daily Review (TW).* **Radio-AM:** KLVQ, 1410 kHz.

ATLANTA: **Newspaper:** *Cass County Citizen's Journal-Sun.* **Radio-AM:** KPYN, 900 kHz. **Radio-FM:** KNRB, 100.1 MHz.

AUSTIN: **Newspapers:** *Austin American-Statesman (D); Austin Business Journal; West Austin News (M).* **Radio-AM:** KLBJ, 590 kHz; KVET, 1300; KJFK, 1490. **Radio-FM:** KAZI, 88.7 MHz; KMFA, 89.5; KUT, 90.5; KVRX, 91.7; KLBJ, 93.7; KKMJ, 95.5; KVET, 98.1; KASE, 100.7; KPEZ, 102.3; KBPA, 103.5. **TV Stations:** KTBC-Ch. 7; KXAN-Ch. 21; KLRU-Ch. 22; KNVA-Ch. 23; KVUE-Ch. 33; KEYE-Ch. 34.

AZLE: **Newspaper:** *The Azle News.* **Radio-FM:** KYDA,101.7 MHz.

B

BAIRD: **Newspaper:** *Baird Banner.* **Radio-FM:** KABW, 95.1 MHz.

BALCH SPRINGS: **Radio-AM:** KSKY, 660 kHz.

BALCONES HEIGHTS: **Radio-FM:** KZAI, 103.7 MHz.

BALLINGER: **Newspaper:** *Runnels County Register (SM).* **Radio-AM:** KRUN, 1400 kHz. **Radio-FM:** KKCN, 103.1 MHz.

BANDERA: **Newspaper:** *Bandera Bulletin.* **Radio-FM:** KEEP, 103.1 MHz.

BANGS: **Radio-FM:** KBNX, 97.9 MHz.

BARTLETT: **Newspaper:** *Tribune-Progress.*

BASTROP: **Newspaper:** *Bastrop Advertiser (S).* **Radio-FM:** KHIB, 88.5 MHz; KLZT, 107.1.

BATESVILLE: **Radio-FM:** KRZU, 90.7 MHz; KQSA, 97.9.

BAY CITY: **Newspaper:** *The Bay City Tribune (S).* **Radio-FM:** KQUE, 88.1 MHz; KVUD, 89.5; KNTE, 101.7; KBBB, 102.5.

BAYTOWN: **Newspaper:** *Baytown Sun (TW).* **Radio-AM:** KWWJ, 1360. **TV Station:** KUBE-Ch. 31.

BEAUMONT: **Newspaper:** *The Beaumont Enterprise (D).* **Radio-AM:** KLVI, 560 kHz; KZZB, 990; KIKR, 1450. **Radio-FM:** KLBT, 88.1 MHz; KGHY, 88.5; KTXB, 89.7; KVLU, 91.3; KQXY, 94.1; KYKR, 95.1; KTCX, 102.5; KQQK, 107.9. **TV Stations:** KBMT-Ch. 12; KFDM-Ch. 15; KITU-Ch. 29.

BEE CAVE: **Radio-FM:** KTXX, 104.9 MHz.

BEEVILLE: **Newspaper:** *Beeville Bee-Picayune.* **Radio-AM:** KIBL, 1490 kHz. **Radio-FM:** KVFM, 91.3 MHz; KTKO, 105.7; KRXB, 107.1.

BELLAIRE: **Radio-AM:** KGOW, 1560 kHz.

BELLMEAD: **Radio-FM:** KRMX, 104.9 MHz.

BELLS: **Radio-FM:** KMKT, 93.1 MHz.

BELLVILLE: **Newspaper:** *The Bellville Times.*

BELTON: **Newspaper:** *The Belton Journal.* **Radio-FM:** KOOC, 106.3 MHz. **TV Station:** KNCT-Ch. 17.

BENAVIDES: **Radio-FM:** KXTM, 94.3 MHz.

BENBROOK: **Radio-AM:** KFLC, 1270 kHz. **Radio-FM:** KESS, 107.1 MHz.

BIG LAKE: **Newspaper:** *Big Lake Wildcat.*

BIG SANDY: **Newspaper:** *Big Sandy–Hawkins Journal.* **Radio-FM:** KTAA, 90.7 MHz.

BIG SPRING: **Newspaper:** *Big Spring Herald (D).* **Radio-AM:** KBYG, 1400 kHz; KBST, 1490. **Radio-FM:** KBCX, 91.5 MHz; KBTS, 94.3; KBST, 95.7; KBUG, 100.9. **TV Station:** KCWO-Ch. 33.

BIG WELLS: **Radio-FM:** KHBE, 102.1 MHz.

BISHOP: **Radio-FM:** KMZZ, 98.3 MHz.

BLANCO: **Newspaper:** *Blanco County News.* **TV Station:** KNIC-Ch. 18.

BLANKET: **Radio-FM:** KQMJ, 104.7 MHz

BLOOMINGTON: **Radio-FM:** KHVT, 91.5 MHz; KLUB, 106.9.

BLOSSOM: **Radio-FM:** KBXP, 88.5 MHz; KISY, 92.7.

BLOWOUT: **Radio-FM:** KTSN, 88.9 MHz.

BOERNE: **Newspaper:** *The Boerne Star.* **Radio-AM:** KBRN, 1500 kHz.

BONHAM: **Newspaper:** *The Fannin County Leader.* **Radio-AM:** KFYN, 1420 kHz.

BOOKER: **Newspaper:** *The Booker News.*

BORGER: **Newspaper:** *Borger News-Herald (TW).* **Radio-FM:** KWAS, 88.1 MHz; KQFX, 104.3; KQTY, 106.7. **TV Station:** KEYU-Ch. 31.

BOVINA: **Radio-FM:** KKNM, 96.5 MHz.

BOWIE: **Newspaper:** *The Bowie News.* **Radio-AM:** KNTX, 1410 kHz.

BRACKETTVILLE: **Newspaper:** *Kinney County Post.* **Radio-FM:** KEDV, 90.3 MHz.

BRADY: **Newspaper:** *Brady Standard-Herald.* **Radio-AM:** KNEL, 1490 kHz. **Radio-FM:** KNEL, 95.3 MHz.

BRECKENRIDGE: **Newspaper:** *Breckenridge American.* **Radio-FM:** KQXB, 89.9 MHz; KLXK, 93.5.

BRENHAM: **Newspaper:** *The Banner-Press.* **Radio-AM:** KWHI, 1280 kHz. **Radio-FM:** KUBJ, 89.7 MHz; KLTR, 94.1; KTTX, 106.1.

BRIDGEPORT: **Radio-FM:** KBOC, 98.3 MHz.

BROOKSHIRE: **Radio-AM:** KCHN, 1050 kHz.

BROWNFIELD: **Newspaper:** *Brownfield News (S).* **Radio-AM:** KKUB, 1300 kHz. **Radio-FM:** KLTB, 89.7 MHz; KHLK, 104.3.

BROWNSVILLE: Newspapers: *The Brownsville Herald (D); El Nuevo Heraldo (D).* Radio-AM: KVNS, 1700 kHz. Radio-FM: KBNR, 88.3 MHz; KKPS, 99.5. TV Station: KVEO-Ch. 24.

BROWNWOOD: Newspaper: *Brownwood Bulletin.* Radio-AM: KXYL, 1240 kHz; KBWD, 1380. Radio-FM: KBUB, 90.3 MHz; KHBW , 91.7; KQBZ, 96.9; KPSM, 99.3; KOXE, 101.3.

BRYAN: Newspaper: *The Eagle (TW).* Radio-AM: KTAM, 1240 kHz; KAGC, 1510. Radio-FM: KORA, 98.3 MHz; KNFX, 99.5; KKYS, 104.7. TV Stations: KBTX-Ch. 16; KYLE-Ch. 29.

BUDA: Radio-FM: KROX, 101.5 MHz.

BUFFALO: Newspaper: *Buffalo Express.* Radio-FM: WTA, 103.5 MHz.

BUFFALO GAP: Radio-FM: KBGT, 93.3 MHz.

BULLARD: Radio-FM: KZWL, 94.3 MHz.

BURKBURNETT: Newspaper: *Burkburnett Informer Star.* Radio-FM: KYYI, 104.7 MHz.

BURKE: Radio-FM: KGFZ, 97.7 MHz.

BURLESON: Radio-AM: KCLE, 1460 kHz.

BURNET: Newspapers: *Burnet Bulletin; Citizens Gazette.* Radio-FM: KMPN 95.9 MHz; KBEY, 103.9.

BUSHLAND: Radio-FM: KTXP, 91.5 MHz.

C

CALDWELL: Newspaper: *Burleson County Tribune.* Radio-FM: KALD, 91.9 MHz; KAPN, 107.3.

CALLISBURG: Radio-FM: KPFC, 91.9 MHz.

CAMERON: Newspaper: *The Cameron Herald.* Radio-AM: KTON, 1330 kHz. Radio-FM: KMIL, 105.1 MHz.

CAMPBELL: Radio-FM: KRVA, 107.1 MHz.

CANADIAN: Radio-FM: KHHC, 91.9 MHz; KWWD, 91.9 MHz.

CANTON: Newspapers: *Canton Herald; Van Zandt News.* Radio-AM: KWJB, 1510 kHz.

CANYON: Newspaper: *The Canyon News (S).* Radio-FM: KWTS, 91.1 MHz; KARX, 107.1; KZRK, 107.9.

CARBON: Radio-FM: KJDE, 100.1 MHz.

CARRIZO SPRINGS: Newspaper: *The Carrizo Springs Javelin.* Radio-FM: KCZO, 92.1 MHz; KMIK, 93.5.

CARROLLTON: Newspaper: *Carrollton Leader.* Radio-AM: KJON, 850 kHz.

CARTHAGE: Newspaper: *The Panola Watchman (S).* Radio-AM: KGAS, 1590 kHz. Radio-FM: KRTG, 88.3 MHz; KTUX, 98.9; KGAS, 104.3.

CEDAR LAKE: Radio-FM: KQVI, 89.9 MHz.

CEDAR PARK: Newspaper: *Hill Country News.* Radio-FM: KGSR, 93.3 MHz.

CELINA: Newspaper: *Celina Record.*

CENTER: Newspaper: *The Light and Champion.* Radio-AM: KDET, 930 kHz. Radio-FM: KQBB, 100.5 MHz.

CENTERVILLE: Newspaper: *Centerville News.* Radio-FM: KKEE, 101.3 MHz; KUZN, 105.9.

CHANNING: Radio-FM: KAMT, 105.1 MHz.

CHARLOTTE: Radio-FM: KSAQ, 102.3 MHz.

CHILDRESS: Newspaper: *The Red River Sun.* Radio-AM: KCTX, 1510 kHz. Radio-FM: KLCN, 90.1 MHz; KRGD, 91.1; KCTX, 96.1; KCHT 99.7.

CHILLICOTHE: Radio-FM: KVRG, 89.7 MHz.

CHRISTINE: Radio-FM: KWYU, 96.9 MHz.

CHRISTOVAL: Radio-FM: KQTC, 99.5 MHz.

CLARENDON: Newspaper: *The Clarendon Enterprise.* Radio-FM: KYCL, 88.9 MHz; KEFH, 99.3.

CLARKSVILLE: Radio-AM: KHDY, 1350 kHz. Radio-FM: KXQJ, 90.1 MHz; KHDY, 98.5.

CLAUDE: Newspaper: *The Claude News.* Radio-FM: KPUR, 95.7 MHz.

CLEBURNE: Newspaper: *Cleburne Times-Review (TW).* Radio-AM: KCPP, 1140 kHz.

CLEVELAND: Radio-FM: KLVH, 97.1 MHz; KTHT, 97.1.

CLIFTON: Newspaper: *Bosque County Record-Tribune.* Radio-FM: KWOW , 104.1 MHz.

CLUTE: Newspaper: *The Facts (D).*

CLYDE: Newspaper: *Clyde Journal.*

COAHOMA: Radio-FM: KXCS, 105.5 MHz.

COCKRELL HILL: Radio-AM: KRVA, 1600 kHz.

COLEMAN: Newspaper: *Chronicle & Democrat-Voice.* Radio-AM: KSTA, 1000 kHz. Radio-FM: KXYL, 102.3 MHz.

COLLEGE STATION: Radio-AM: KZNE, 1150 kHz; KWBC, 1550; WTAW , 1620. Radio-FM: KEOS, 89.1 MHz; KLGS, 89.9; KAMU, 90.9; KNDE, 95.1. TV Station: KAMU-Ch. 12.

COLORADO CITY: Newspaper: *Colorado City Record.* Radio-AM: KVMC, 1320 kHz. Radio-FM: KEHM, 99.3 MHz; KAUM, 107.1.

COLUMBUS: Newspapers: *The Banner-Press Newspaper; The Colorado County Citizen.* Radio-FM: KULM, 98.3 MHz.

COMANCHE: Newspaper: *The Comanche Chief.* Radio-AM: KCOM, 1550 kHz. Radio-FM: KYOX, 94.3 MHz; KCXX 103.9.

COMFORT: Newspaper: *The Comfort News.* Radio-FM: KMYO, 95.1 MHz.

COMMERCE: Radio-FM: KETR, 88.9 MHz; KYJC, 91.3.

COMSTOCK: Radio-FM: KDER, 99.3 MHz.

CONCAN: Radio-FM: KHCU, 93.1 MHz.

CONROE: Newspaper: *The Courier (D).* Radio-AM: KJOZ, 880 kHz; KYOK, 1140. Radio-FM: KHPT, 106.9 MHz. TV Stations: KPXB-Ch. 32; KTBU-Ch. 33.

CONVERSE: Radio-AM: KTMR, 1130 kHz.

COOPER: Newspaper: *Cooper Review.* Radio-FM: KPCO, 89.9 MHz; KIKT, 93.5.

COPPELL: Newspaper: *Coppell Gazette.*

COPPERAS COVE: Newspaper: *Copperas Cove Leader-Press (S).* Radio-FM: KSSM, 103.1 MHz.

CORPUS CHRISTI: Newspapers: *Corpus Christi Caller-Times (D); Coastal Bend Daily Legal & Business News (D).* Radio-AM: KCTA, 1030 kHz; KCCT, 1150; KSIX, 1230; KKTX, 1360; KUNO, 1400; KEYS, 1440. Radio-FM: KPLV, 88.7 MHz; KEDT, 90.3; KBNJ, 91.7; KMXR, 93.9; KBSO, 94.7; KZFM, 95.5; KLTG, 96.5; KRYS, 99.1. TV Stations: KIII-Ch. 8; KZTV-Ch. 10; KSCC, Ch. 19; KEDT-Ch. 23; KRIS-Ch. 26; KORO-Ch. 27.

CORRIGAN: Radio-FM: KYTM, 99.3 MHz.
CORSICANA: Newspaper: *Corsicana Daily Sun (S)*. Radio-AM: KAND, 1340 kHz.
COTULLA: Radio-FM: KCOT, 96.3 MHz; KWMJ, 100.7.
CRANE: Newspaper: *Crane News*. Radio-AM: KXOI, 810 kHz. Radio-FM: KMMZ, 101.3 MHz.
CREEDMOOR: Radio-AM: KZNX, 1530 kHz.
CROCKETT: Newspaper: *The Messenger (S)*. Radio-AM: KIVY, 1290 kHz. Radio-FM: KCKT, 88.5 MHz; KIVY, 92.7; KDVY, 93.5.
CROSBYTON: Radio-FM: KEVQ, 100.7 MHz.
CROSS PLAINS: Newspaper: *Cross Plains Review*.
CROWELL: Newspaper: *Foard County News*. Radio-FM: KTUT, 98.9 MHz.
CRYSTAL CITY: Newspaper: *Zavala County Sentinel*. Radio-FM: KHER, 94.3 MHz.
CUERO: Newspaper: *Cuero Record*. Radio-FM: KTLZ, 89.9 MHz.
CUNEY: Radio-FM: KFRO, 99.7 MHz.
CYPRESS: Radio-AM: KYND, 1520 kHz.

D

DAINGERFIELD: Newspaper: *The Steel Country Bee*.
DALHART: Newspaper: *The Dalhart Texan (S)*. Radio-AM: KXIT, 1240 kHz. Radio-FM: KWGD, 88.7 MHZ; KTDH, 89.3; KTDA, 91.7; DKBEX 96.1.
DALLAS: Newspapers: *The Dallas Morning News (D); Daily Commercial Record (D); Dallas Business Journal; The Dallas Examiner; Texas Jewish Post*. Radio-AM: KLIF, 570 kHz; KGGR, 1040; KRLD, 1080; KFXR, 1190; KTCK, 1310; KNGO, 1480. Radio-FM: KNON, 89.3 MHz; KERA, 90.1; KCBI, 90.9; KKXT, 91.7; KZPS, 92.5; KBFB, 97.9; KSPF, 98.7; KJKK, 100.3; WRR, 101.1; KDMX, 102.9; KKDA, 104.5; KRLD, 105.3. TV Stations: WFAA-Ch. 8; KERA-Ch. 14; KDTX-Ch. 21; KDFI-Ch. 27; KDAF-Ch. 32; KDFW-Ch. 35; KXTX-Ch. 36.
DECATUR: Newspaper: *Wise County Messenger (S)*. Radio-FM: KDKR, 91.3 MHz; KRNB, 105.7. TV Station: KFAA-Ch. 30.
DEER PARK: Radio-FM: KAMA, 104.9 MHz.
DE LEON: Newspaper: *De Leon Free Press*.
DELL CITY: Newspaper: *Hudspeth County Herald*.
DEL MAR HILLS: Radio-AM: KVOZ, 890 kHz.
DEL RIO: Newspaper: *The 830 Times*. Radio-AM: KDRN, 1230 kHz; KWMC, 1490. Radio-FM: KVFE, 88.5 MHz; KTPD, 89.3; KDLI, 89.9; KTDR, 96.3. TV Station: KYVV-Ch. 28.
DEL VALLE: Radio-AM: KIXL, 970 kHz.
DENISON: Radio-FM: KYFB, 91.5 MHz.
DENTON: Newspaper: *Denton Record-Chronicle*. Radio-FM: KFZO, 99.1 MHz; KHKS, 106.1.
DENVER CITY: Newspaper: *Denver City Press*.
DESOTO: Newspaper: *Focus Daily News (D)*.
DETROIT: Radio-FM: KFYN, 104.3 MHz.
DEVINE: Newspaper: *The Devine News*. Radio-FM: KRPT, 92.5 MHz.
DIBOLL: Radio-AM: KSML, 1260 kHz. Radio-FM: KAFX, 95.5 MHz.
DILLEY: Radio-FM: KKDL, 93.7 MHz; KVWG, 95.3; KLMO, 98.9.
DIMMITT: Newspaper: *The Castro County News*. Radio-AM: KDHN, 1470 kHz. Radio-FM: KNNK, 100.5 MHz.
DOSS: Radio-FM: KGKV, 88.1 MHz.
DRIPPING SPRINGS: Newspapers: *Dripping Springs Century News; News-Dispatch*. Radio-FM: KLLR, 91.9 MHz.
DRISCOLL: Radio-FM: KUKA, 105.9 MHz.
DUBLIN: Newspaper: *The Dublin Citizen*. Radio-FM: KSTV, 93.1 MHz.
DUMAS: Newspaper: *Moore County News-Press*. Radio-AM: KDDD, 800 kHz. Radio-FM: KDDD, 95.3 MHz.

E

EAGLE LAKE: Radio-FM: KJJB, 95.3 MHz.
EAGLE PASS: Radio-FM: KEPX, 89.5 MHz; KINL, 92.7. TV Station: KVAW-Ch. 18.
EARLY: Radio-FM: KJKB, 106.7 MHz.
EAST BERNARD: Newspaper: *East Bernard Express*.
EASTLAND: Newspaper: *Eastland County Today*. Radio-FM: KQXE, 91.1 MHz; KATX, 97.7.
EDEN: Newspaper: *Eden Echo*. Radio-FM: KPDE, 91.5 MHz.
EDINBURG: Radio-AM: KURV, 710 kHz. Radio-FM: KOIR, 88.5 MHz; KBFM, 104.1; KVLY, 107.9.
EDNA: Newspaper: *Jackson County Herald-Tribune*. Radio-FM: KIOX, 96.1 MHz.
EL CAMPO: Newspaper: *Wharton County Leader-Journal (S)*. Radio-AM: KULP, 1390 kHz. Radio-FM: KXBJ, 96.9 MHz.
ELDORADO: Newspaper: *Eldorado Success*. Radio-FM: KLDE, 104.9 MHz; KPEP, 106.5.
ELECTRA: Newspaper: *Electra Star-News*. Radio-FM: KOLI, 94.9 MHz.
ELGIN: Newspaper: *Elgin Courier*. Radio-AM: KTAE, 1260 kHz.
ELKHART: Radio-FM: KATG, 88.1 MHz.
ELLINGER: Radio-FM: KTIM, 89.1 MHz.
EL PASO: Newspaper: *El Paso Times (D)*. Radio-AM: KROD, 600 kHz; KTSM, 690; KAMA, 750; KQBU, 920; KHRO, 1150; KVIV, 1340; KHEY, 1380; KELP, 1590; KSVE, 1650. Radio-FM: KTEP, 88.5 MHz; KKLY, 89.5; KVER, 91.1; KLPS, 91.5; KOFX, 92.3; KSII, 93.1; KINT, 93.9; KYSE, 94.7; KLAQ, 95.5; KHEY, 96.3; KBNA, 97.5; KTSM, 99.9; KPRR, 102.1. TV Stations: KCOS-Ch. 13; KFOX-Ch. 15; KTSM-Ch. 16; KVIA-Ch. 17; KDBC-Ch. 18; KTFN-Ch. 20; KSCE-Ch. 21; KINT-Ch. 25.
EMORY: Newspaper: *Rains County Leader*.
ENCINAL: Radio-FM: KQBI, 91.7 MHz; KYLQ, 99.7; KELT, 102.5; KZPL, 105.1.
ENCINO: Radio-FM: KZTX, 91.1 MHz.
ENNIS: Newspaper: *The Ennis News*.
ESCOBARES: Radio-FM: KERG, 104.7 MHz.
ESTELLINE: Radio-FM: KZES, 91.3 MHz.

F

FAIRFIELD: Newspapers: *Freestone County Times; Freestone County Recorder-Chronicle.* Radio-FM: KNES, 99.1 MHz.

FALFURRIAS: Newspaper: *Falfurrias Facts.* Radio-AM: KLDS, 1260 kHz. Radio-FM: KRVP, 91.5 MHz; KDFM, 103.3; KPSO, 106.3.

FANNETT: Radio-FM: KZFT, 90.5 MHz.

FARMERSVILLE: Newspaper: *The Farmersville Times.* Radio-AM: KFCD, 990 kHz.

FARWELL: Newspaper: *The State Line Tribune.* Radio-AM: KIJN, 1060 kHz. Radio-FM: KIJN, 92.3 MHz. TV Station: KPTF-Ch. 18.

FERRIS: Newspaper: *The Ellis County Press.* Radio-AM: KDFT, 540 kHz.

FLATONIA: Newspaper: *The Flatonia Argus.*

FLORESVILLE: Newspaper: *Wilson County News.* Radio-FM: KJMA, 89.7 MHz; KTFM, 94.1.

FLOWER MOUND: Radio-FM: KTCK, 96.7 MHz.

FLOYDADA: Newspaper: *The Floyd County Hesperian-Beacon.* Radio-AM: KFLP, 900 kHz. Radio-FM: KFLP, 106.1 MHz.

FOLLETT: Radio-FM: KHRG, 88.7 MHz.

FORNEY: Newspaper: *Forney Messenger.*

FORT DAVIS: Newspaper: *Jeff Davis County Mountain Dispatch.*

FORT HANCOCK: Newspaper: *Hudspeth County Herald.*

FORT STOCKTON: Newspaper: *Fort Stockton Pioneer.* Radio-AM: KFST, 860 kHz. Radio-FM: KRAF, 88.3 MHz; KFST, 94.3.

FORT WORTH: Newspapers: *Fort Worth Star-Telegram (D); Commercial Recorder (D); Tarrant County Commercial Record (S); The Business Press (M).* Radio-AM: WBAP, 820 kHz; KFJZ, 870; KHVN, 970; KKGM, 1630. Radio-FM: KTCU, 88.7 MHz; KLNO, 94.1; KSCS, 96.3; KEGL, 97.1; KPLX, 99.5; KDGE, 102.1; KMVK, 107.5. TV Stations: KFWD-Ch. 9; KTXA-Ch. 18; KTVT-Ch. 19; KXAS-Ch. 24.

FRANKLIN: Newspaper: *Franklin News Weekly.* Radio-FM: KVLX, 103.9 MHz.

FRANKSTON: Radio-FM: KOYE, 96.7 MHz.

FREDERICKSBURG: Newspaper: *Fredericksburg Standard-Radio Post.* Radio-AM: KNAF, 910 kHz. Radio-FM: KIVM, 91.1 MHz; KBLC, 91.5; KNAF, 105.7. TV Station: KCWX-Ch. 5.

FREER: Radio-FM: KBTD, 89.1 MHz; KQCI, 91.5; KBRA, 95.9.

FRIENDSWOOD: Newspaper: *Friendswood Reporter News.*

FRIONA: Newspaper: *Friona Star.* Radio-FM: KGRW , 94.7 MHz.

FRISCO: Radio-AM: KATH, 910 kHz.

FRITCH: Newspaper: *The Eagle Press.*

FULTON: Radio-FM: KCBG, 89.9 MHz.

G

GAIL: Newspaper: *Borden Star.*

GAINESVILLE: Newspaper: *Gainesville Daily Register (S).* Radio-AM: KGAF, 1580 kHz. Radio-FM: KZMJ, 94.5 MHz.

GALVESTON: Newspaper: *The Daily News (D).* Radio-AM: KGBC, 1540 kHz. Radio-FM: KOVE, 106.5 MHz. TV Stations: KTMD-Ch. 22; KLTJ-Ch. 23.

GANADO: Radio-FM: KEON, 94.9 MHz.

GARDENDALE: Radio-FM: KFZX, 102.1 MHz.

GARLAND: Radio-AM: KAAM, 770 kHz. TV Station: KUVN-Ch. 33.

GARWOOD: Radio-FM: KPUY, 97.3 MHz.

GATESVILLE: Newspaper: *The Gatesville Messenger.* Radio-FM: KVLW , 88.1 MHz.

GEORGETOWN: Newspaper: *The Williamson County Sun.* Radio-FM: KHFI, 96.7 MHz; KLJA, 107.7.

GEORGE WEST: Radio-FM: KGWT, 93.5 MHz; KXAF 97.9.

GIDDINGS: Newspaper: *Giddings Times & News.* Radio-FM: KANJ, 91.1 MHz; KGID 96.3.

GILMER: Newspaper: *Gilmer Mirror.* Radio-FM: KWLL, 95.3 MHz.

GINGER: Radio-FM: KYFA, 91.5 MHz.

GLADEWATER: Newspaper: *Gladewater Mirror.* Radio-AM: KEES, 1430 kHz.

GLEN ROSE: Newspaper: *Glen Rose Reporter.* Radio-FM: KTFW , 92.1 MHz.

GOLDSMITH: Radio-FM: KTXO, 94.7 MHz.

GOLDTHWAITE: Newspaper: *The Goldthwaite Eagle.* Radio-FM: KRNR, 92.7 MHz.

GOLIAD: Newspaper: *Goliad Advance-Guard.* Radio-FM: KHMC, 95.9 MHz; KPQG 104.3.

GONZALES: Newspaper: *The Gonzales Inquirer.* Radio-AM: KCTI, 1450 kHz. Radio-FM: KCTI, 88.1 MHz; KMLR, 106.3.

GRAHAM: Newspaper: *The Graham Leader (S).* Radio-FM: KVNZ, 90.7 MHz; KWKQ, 94.7.

GRANBURY: Newspaper: *Hood County News.* Radio-AM: KPIR, 1420 kHz.

GRAND PRAIRIE: Radio-AM: KKDA, 730 kHz.

GRAND SALINE: Newspaper: *Grand Saline Sun.*

GRANITE SHOALS: Radio-FM: KHUK, 106.5 MHz.

GRAPE CREEK: Radio-FM: KPTJ 104.5 MHz.

GRAPELAND: Newspaper: *The Messenger (S).*

GREENVILLE: Newspaper: *Herald-Banner (TW).* Radio-AM: KGVL, 1400 kHz. Radio-FM: KTXG, 90.5 MHz. TV Station: KTXD-Ch. 23.

GREENWOOD: Radio-FM: KAGP 89.1 MHz.

GREGORY: Radio-FM: KPUS, 104.5 MHz.

GROESBECK: Newspaper: *Groesbeck Journal.*

GROOM: Newspaper: *The Groom News.*

GROVES: Radio-FM: KCOL, 92.5 MHz.

GROVETON: Newspaper: *Trinity County News-Standard.* Radio-FM: KDDM, 93.9 MHz.

GUTHRIE: Radio-FM: KJAG, 107.7 MHz.

H

HALLETTSVILLE: Newspaper: *Hallettsville Tribune-Herald.* Radio-FM: KTXM, 99.9 MHz.

HALLSVILLE: Radio-FM: KTLH, 107.9 MHz.

HALTOM CITY: Radio-FM: WBAP, 93.3 MHz.

HAMILTON: Newspaper: *Hamilton Herald-News.* Radio-AM: KCLW , 900 kHz.

HAMLIN: Newspaper: *The Hamlin Herald.* Radio-FM: KSAY, 88.5 MHz; KCDD, 103.7.

HARDIN: Radio-FM: KGBV, 90.7 MHz.

HARKER HEIGHTS: Radio-FM: KUSJ, 105.5 MHz.

HARLINGEN: Newspaper: *The Valley Morning Star (D).* Radio-AM: KYWW, 1530 kHz. Radio-FM: KJJF, 88.9 MHz; KFRQ, 94.5; KBTQ, 96.1. TV Stations: KFVX-Ch.16; KGBT-Ch. 18; KLUJ-Ch. 21.

HARPER: Radio-FM: KZAH, 99.1 MHz.

HARTLEY: Radio-FM: KOGW, 90.5 MHz.

HASKELL: Radio-FM: KVRP, 97.1 MHz.

HAWLEY: Radio-FM: KABT, 101.7 MHz.

HEARNE: Newspaper: *Robertson County News.* Radio-FM: KEDC, 88.5 MHz; KVJM, 103.1.

HEBBRONVILLE: Newspaper: *The Enterprise.* Radio-FM: KXAV, 98.7 MHz; KEKO, 101.7; KUFA, 104.3.

HELOTES: Radio-FM: KONO, 101.1 MHz.

HEMPHILL: Newspaper: *The Sabine County Reporter.* Radio-FM: KTHP, 103.9 MHz.

HEMPSTEAD: The Waller County Express. Radio-FM: KTWL, 105.3 MHz.

HENDERSON: Newspaper: *The Henderson News (S).* Radio-AM: KWRD, 1470 kHz.

HENRIETTA: Newspaper: *Clay County Leader.*

HEREFORD: Newspaper: *Hereford Brand (S).* Radio-AM: KPAN, 860 kHz. Radio-FM: KRLH, 90.9 MHz; KPAN, 106.3.

HEWITT: Radio-FM: KIXT, 106.7 MHz.

HICO: Newspaper: *The Hico News Review.* Radio-FM: KCBN, 107.7.

HIGHLAND PARK: Radio-AM: KBDT, 1160 kHz. Radio-FM: KVIL, 103.7 MHz.

HIGHLANDS: Newspaper: *Highlands Star-Crosby Courier.*

HIGHLAND VILLAGE: Radio-FM: KWRD, 100.7 MHz.

HILLSBORO: Newspaper: *Hillsboro Reporter.* Radio-AM: KHBR, 1560 kHz. Radio-FM: KBRQ, 102.5 MHz.

HOLLIDAY: Radio-FM: KRGH, 90.0 MHz; KWFB, 100.9.

HONDO: Newspaper: *Hondo Anvil Herald.* Radio-AM: KCWM, 1460 kHz. Radio-FM: KZTC, 89.9 MHz; KAHL, 105.9.

HOOKS: Radio-FM: KTRG, 94.1 MHz; KPWW, 95.9.

HORIZON CITY: Newspaper: *West Texas County Courier.*

HORNSBY: Radio-FM: KOOP, 91.7 MHz.

HOUSTON: Newspapers: *Houston Chronicle (D); Daily Court Review (D); Houston Business Journal; Jewish Herald-Voice.* Radio-AM: KILT, 610 kHz; KTRH, 740; KBME, 790; KEYH, 850; KPRC, 950; KLAT, 1010; KNTH, 1070; KCOH, 1230; KXYZ, 1320; KSHJ, 1430; KMIC, 1590. Radio-FM: KUHF, 88.7 MHz; KPFT, 90.1; KTSU, 90.9; KHVU, 91.7; KQBT, 93.7; KTBZ, 94.5; KKHH, 95.7; KHMX, 96.5; KBXX, 97.9; KODA, 99.1; KILT, 100.3; KLOL, 101.1; KMJQ, 102.1; KLTN, 102.9; KRBE, 104.1; KHCB, 105.7. TV Stations: KUHT-Ch. 8; KHOU-Ch. 11; KTRK-Ch. 13; KTXH-Ch. 19; KZJL-Ch. 21; KETH-Ch. 24; KRIV-Ch. 26; KIAH-Ch. 34; KPRC-Ch. 35.

HOWE: Radio-FM: KHYI, 95.3 MHz.

HUDSON: Radio-FM: KZXL, 96.3 MHz.

HUMBLE: Radio-AM: KGOL, 1180 kHz. Radio-FM: KSBJ, 89.3 MHz.

HUNT: Radio-FM: KYRT, 97.9 MHz; KLKV, 99.9.

HUNTINGTON: Radio-FM: KSML, 101.9 MHz.

HUNTSVILLE: Newspaper: *The Huntsville Item (TW).* Radio-AM: KHCH, 1410 kHz; KHVL, 1490. Radio-FM: KSHU, 90.5 MHz; KVST, 99.7; KSAM, 101.7.

HURST: Radio-AM: KMNY, 1360 kHz.

HUTTO: Radio-FM: KYLR, 92.1 MHz.

I

IDALOU: Newspaper: *Idalou Beacon.* Radio-FM: KLZK, 105.7 MHz; KRBL, 107.7.

INGLESIDE: Newspaper: *The Ingleside Index.* Radio-FM: KAJE, 107.3 MHz.

INGRAM: Newspaper: *West Kerr Current.* Radio-FM: KTXI, 90.1 MHz; KFXE, 96.5.

IOWA PARK: Newspaper: *Iowa Park Journal.* Radio-FM: KXXN, 97.5 MHz.

IRVING: Newspaper: *The Irving Rambler.* TV Station: KSTR-Ch. 34.

J

JACKSBORO: Newspaper: *Jacksboro Herald-Gazette.* Radio-FM: KKSH, 90.3 MHz; KFWR, 95.9.

JACKSONVILLE: Newspaper: *Jacksonville Progress (S).* Radio-AM: KEBE, 1400 kHz. Radio-FM: KBJS, 90.3 MHz; KKGT, 95.1; KLFZ, 102.3; KOOI, 106.5. TV Station: KETK-Ch. 22.

JASPER: Newspaper: *The Jasper Newsboy.* Radio-AM: KCOX, 1350 kHz. Radio-FM: KTXJ, 102.7 MHz; KJAS, 107.3.

JEFFERSON: Newspaper: *Jefferson Jimplecute.* Radio-FM: KHCJ, 91.9 MHz; KJTX, 104.5.

JOHNSON CITY: Newspaper: *Johnson City Record-Courier.* Radio-FM: KFAN, 107.9 MHz.

JOURDANTON: Radio-FM: KLEY, 95.7 MHz.

JUNCTION: Newspaper: *Junction Eagle.* Radio-AM: KMBL, 1450 kHz. Radio-FM: KYKK, 93.5 MHz.

K

KARNES CITY: Newspaper: *The Karnes Countywide.* Radio-FM: KZKV, 103.1 MHz.

KATY: Newspaper: *Katy Times.* TV Station: KYAZ-Ch. 25.

KAUFMAN: Newspaper: *The Kaufman Herald.*

KEENE: Radio-FM: KJRN, 88.3 MHz.

KEMPNER: Radio-FM: KOOV, 106.9 MHz.

KENEDY: Radio-AM: KAML, 990 kHz. Radio-FM: KCAF, 92.1 MHz.

KERENS: Radio-FM: KRVF, 106.9 MHz.

KERMIT: Radio-FM: KDCJ, 91.5 MHz.

KERRVILLE: Newspapers: *The Kerrville Daily Times (TW); Hill Country Community Journal.* Radio-AM: KERV, 1230 kHz. Radio-FM: KKER, 88.7 MHz; KHKV, 91.1; KRNH, 92.3; KRVL, 94.3; KKVR, 106.1. TV Station: KMYS-Ch. 32.

KILGORE: Newspaper: *Kilgore News Herald.* Radio-AM: KDOK, 1240 kHz. Radio-FM: KZLO, 88.7 MHz; KKTX, 96.1.

KILLEEN: Newspaper: *Killeen Daily Herald (D)*. Radio-FM: KNCT, 91.3 MHz; KIIZ, 92.3. TV Station: KAKW-Ch. 13.
KINGSLAND: Radio-FM: KHSB, 104.7 MHz.
KINGSVILLE: Newspaper: *The Kingsville Record*. Radio-AM: KINE, 1330 kHz. Radio-FM: KTAI, 91.1 MHz; KKBA, 92.7; KFTX, 97.5.
KNIPPA: Radio-FM: KUVG, 91.5 MHz.
KRUM: Radio-FM: KNOR, 93.7 MHz.
KURTEN: Radio-FM: KPWJ, 107.7 MHz.
KYLE: Newspaper: *Hays Free Press*.

L

LA FERIA: Newspaper: *La Feria News*.
LA GRANGE: Newspaper: *The Fayette County Record (S)*. Radio-AM: KVLG, 1570 kHz. Radio-FM: KBUK, 104.9 MHz.
LAKE DALLAS: TV Station: KAZD-Ch. 31.
LAKE JACKSON: Radio-FM: KVUJ, 91.1 MHz; KGLK, 107.5.
LAKEWAY: Newspaper: *Lake Travis View*.
LAMESA: Newspaper: *Lamesa Press Reporter (S)*. Radio-AM: KPET, 690 kHz. Radio-FM: KLMH, 88.5 MHZ; KBKN, 91.3.
LAMPASAS: Newspaper: *Lampasas Dispatch Record (S)*. Radio-AM: KCYL, 1450 kHz.
LA PORTE: Newspaper: *Bay Area Observer*. Radio-FM: KHJK, 103.7 MHz.
LAREDO: Newspaper: *Laredo Morning Times (D)*. Radio-AM: KLAR, 1300 kHz; KLNT, 1490. Radio-FM: KHOY, 88.1 MHz; KBNL, 89.9; KJBZ, 92.7; KQUR, 94.9; KRRG, 98.1; KNEX, 106.1. TV Stations: KGNS-Ch. 8; KLDO-Ch. 19.
LAUGHLIN AFB: Radio-FM: KDRX, 106.9 MHz.
LEAGUE CITY: Radio-AM: KHCB, 1400 kHz.
LEANDER: Radio-FM: KUTX, 98.9 MHz.
LEFORS: Radio-FM: KHNZ, 101.3 MHz.
LEONARD: Newspaper: *The Leonard Graphic*.
LEVELLAND: Newspaper: *Levelland & Hockley County News-Press (S)*. Radio-AM: KLVT, 1230 kHz. Radio-FM: KJDL, 105.3 MHz.
LEWISVILLE: Newspaper: *Lewisville Leader*. Radio-FM: KDXX, 107.9 MHz.
LEXINGTON: Newspaper: *Lexington Leader*.
LIBERTY: Newspaper: *The Vindicator*. Radio-FM: KHIH, 99.9 MHz.
LIBERTY HILL: Newspaper: *Liberty Hill Monthly (M)*.
LINDALE: Newspaper: *Lindale News & Times*.
LINDSAY: Newspaper: *Lindsay Letter*.
LITTLE ELM: Newspaper: *The Lakeside Journal*.
LITTLEFIELD: Newspaper: *The Lamb County Leader-News (S)*. Radio-AM: KZZN, 1490 kHz.
LIVINGSTON: Newspaper: *Polk County Enterprise (S)*. Radio-AM: KETX, 1440 kHz. Radio-FM: KEHH, 92.3 MHz.
LLANO: Newspaper: *The Llano News*. Radio-FM: KVHL, 91.7 MHz; KJFK, 96.3; KITY, 102.9. TV Station: KBVO-Ch. 27.
LOCKHART: Newspaper: *Lockhart Post-Register*. Radio-AM: KTSN, 1060 kHz.
LOMETA: Radio-FM: KACQ, 101.9 MHz.
LONGVIEW: Newspaper: *Longview News-Journal (TW)*. Radio-AM: KFRO, 1370 kHz. Radio-FM: KYKX, 105.7 MHz. TV Stations: KFXK-Ch. 20; KCEB-Ch. 35.
LORENA: Radio-FM: KYAR, 98.3 MHz.
LORENZO: Radio-FM: KKCL, 98.1 MHz.
LOUISE: Radio-FM: KABA, 90.3 MHz.
LOVELADY: Radio-FM: KHMR, 104.3 MHz.
LUBBOCK: Newspaper: *Lubbock Avalanche-Journal (D)*. Radio-AM: KRFE, 580 kHz; KFYO, 790; KKAM, 1340; KWBF, 1420; KBZO, 1460; KDAV, 1590; KTTU, 950. Radio-FM: KTXT, 88.1 MHz; KTTZ, 89.1; KAMY, 90.1; KKLU, 90.9; KLBB, 93.7; KFMX, 94.5; KLLL, 96.3; KQBR, 99.5; KONE, 101.1; KZII, 102.5; KXTQ, 106.5. TV Stations: KCBD-Ch. 35; KPTB-Ch. 16; KTTZ-Ch. 25; KAMC-Ch. 27; KLBK-Ch. 31; KJTV-Ch. 11.
LUFKIN: Newspaper: *The Lufkin Daily News (TW)*. Radio-AM: KRBA, 1340 kHz. Radio-FM: KLDN, 88.9 MHz; KSWP, 90.9; KAVX, 91.9; KYBI, 100.1; KYKS, 105.1. TV Station: KTRE-Ch. 9.
LULING: Newspaper: *Luling Newsboy and Signal*. Radio-FM: KAMX, 94.7 MHz.
LUMBERTON: Radio-AM: KHTW , 1300 kHz. Radio-FM: KKHT, 100.7 MHz.
LYTLE: Radio-FM: KZLV, 91.3 MHz.

M

MABANK: Newspaper: *The Monitor (S)*. Radio-AM: KTXV, 890 kHz.
MADISONVILLE: Newspaper: *Madisonville Meteor*. Radio-AM: KMVL, 1220 kHz. Radio-FM: KHML, 91.5 MHz; KAGG, 96.1; KMVL, 100.5.
MALAKOFF: Radio-FM: KCKL, 95.9 MHz.
MANOR: Radio-AM: KTXW , 1120 kHz; KELG, 1440.
MARBLE FALLS: Newspaper: *The Highlander (S)*. Radio-FM: KBMD, 88.5 MHz.
MARATHON: Radio-FM: KDKY, 91.5 MHz.
MARFA: Newspaper: *The Big Bend Sentinel*. Radio-FM: KMKB, 88.5 MHz; KRTS, 93.5.
MARION: Radio-AM: KBIB, 1000 kHz.
MARKHAM: Radio-FM: KKHA, 92.5 MHz; KBYC, 104.5.
MARLIN: Newspaper: *The Marlin Democrat*. Radio-FM: KRMX, 92.9 MHz.
MARSHALL: Newspaper: *Marshall News Messenger (TW)*. Radio-AM: KMHT, 1450 kHz. Radio-FM: KBWC, 91.1 MHz; KDPM, 92.3; KMHT, 103.9.
MART: Radio-FM: KWAA, 88.9 MHz.
MASON: Newspaper: *Mason County News*. Radio-FM: KZZM, 101.7 MHz; KHLB, 102.5; KMSN, 104.1.
MATAGORDA: Radio-FM: KPYM, 106.1 MHz.
MAYDELLE: Radio-FM: KKJX, 91.7 MHz.
MCALLEN: Newspaper: *The Monitor (S)*. Radio-AM: KRIO, 910 kHz. Radio-FM: KHID, 88.1 MHz; KVMV, 96.9; KGBT, 98.5. TV Station: KNVO-Ch. 17.

MCCOOK: Radio-FM: KCAS, 91.5 MHz.
MCGREGOR: Newspaper: *McGregor Mirror & Crawford Sun.*
MCKINNEY: Newspapers: *Collin County Commercial Record (S); McKinney Courier-Gazette.* Radio-FM: KNTU, 88.1 MHz.
MCLEAN: Radio-FM: KMCL, 91.5 MHz.
MCQUEENEY: Radio-FM: KZAR, 97.7 MHz.
MEMPHIS: Radio-FM: KLSR, 105.3 MHz.
MENARD: Newspaper: *Menard News and Messenger.* Radio-FM: KTCY, 105.3 MHz.
MERCEDES: Newspaper: *The Mercedes Enterprise.* Radio-FM: KTEX, 100.3 MHz.
MERIDIAN: Newspaper: *Meridian Tribune.* Radio-FM: KITT, 106.5 MHz.
MERKEL: Radio-AM: KMXO, 1500 kHz. Radio-FM: KHXS, 102.7 MHz.
MERTZON: Radio-FM: KMEO, 91.9 MHz; KBTP, 101.1; KBJX, 103.5.
MESQUITE: Radio-FM: KEOM, 88.5 MHz.
MEXIA: Newspaper: *The Mexia News (S).* Radio-AM: KBHT, 1590 kHz.
MEYERSVILLE: Radio-FM: KQBQ, 100.1 MHz.
MIAMI: Newspaper: *Miami Chief.*
MIDLAND: Newspaper: *Greenwood Ranger; Midland Reporter-Telegram (D).* Radio-AM: KCRS, 550 kHz; KWEL, 1070; KLPF, 1180; KMND, 1510. Radio-FM: KVDG, 90.9 MHz; KNFM, 92.3; KZBT, 93.3; KQRX, 95.1; KCRS, 103.3; KCHX, 106.7. TV Stations: KUPB-Ch. 18; KMID-Ch. 26.
MIDLOTHIAN: Newspaper: *Midlothian Mirror.*
MILES: Newspaper: Radio-FM: *KMLS,* 95.5 MHz.
MINEOLA: Newspaper: *Wood County Monitor.* Radio-FM: KMOO, 99.9 MHz.
MINERAL WELLS: Newspaper: *Palo Pinto Press.* Radio-AM: KVTT, 1110 kHz. Radio-FM: KYQX, 89.3 MHz.
MIRANDO CITY: Radio-FM: KBDR, 100.5 MHz.
MISSION: Newspaper: *Progress Times.*
MISSOURI CITY: Radio-AM: KBRZ, 1460 kHz.
MONAHANS: Newspaper: *The Monahans News.* Radio-AM: KCKM, 1330 kHz. Radio-FM: KMRA, 91.1 MHz; KBAT, 99.9.
MONT BELVIEU: Radio-FM: KFNC, 97.5 MHz.
MOODY: Radio-FM: KLTO, 99.1 MHz.
MORAN: Radio-FM: KCKB, 104.1 MHz.
MORTON: Radio-FM: KQOA, 91.1 MHz; KPGA, 91.9.
MOULTON: Newspaper: *Moulton Eagle.*
MOUNTAIN HOME: Radio-FM: KAXA, 103.7 MHz.
MOUNT PLEASANT: Newspaper: *Mount Pleasant Tribune.* Radio-AM: KIMP, 960 kHz. Radio-FM: KOUI, 88.3 MHz; KQYR, 90.1.
MUENSTER: Newspaper: *Muenster Enterprise.* Radio-FM: KTMU, 88.7 MHz; KZZA, 106.7.
MULESHOE: Newspaper: *Muleshoe Journal.* Radio-FM: KIXV, 91.5 MHz; KRWD, 93.3.
MUNDAY: Newspaper: *The Knox County News-Courier.*
MURPHY: Newspaper: *Murphy Monitor.*

N

NACOGDOCHES: Newspaper: *The Daily Sentinel (S).* Radio-AM: KSFA, 860 kHz. Radio-FM: KAXM, 90.1 MHz; KJCS, 103.3; KTBQ, 107.7. TV Station: KYTX-Ch. 15.
NAPLES: Newspaper: *The Monitor.*
NATALIA: Radio-FM: KYRQ, 90.3 MHz.
NAVASOTA: Newspaper: *The Navasota Examiner.* Radio-FM: KWUP, 92.5 MHz.
NEDERLAND: Radio-AM: KBED, 1510 kHz.
NEW BOSTON: Newspaper: *Bowie County Citizens Tribune.* Radio-FM: KEWL, 95.1 MHz; KZRB, 103.5; KTTY, 105.1.
NEW BRAUNFELS: Newspaper: *New Braunfels Herald-Zeitung (D).* Radio-AM: KGNB, 1420 kHz. Radio-FM: KNBT, 92.1 MHz.
NEWCASTLE: Radio-FM: KBLY, 100.5 MHz.
NEW DEAL: Radio-FM: KTTU, 97.3 MHz.
NEW ULM: Newspaper: *New Ulm Enterprise.* Radio-FM: KNRG, 92.3 MHz.
NEW WAVERLY: Radio-FM: KNLY, 91.1 MHz.
NOCONA: Newspaper: *Nocona News.*
NOLANVILLE: Radio-FM: KLFX, 107.3 MHz.
NORMANGEE: Newspaper: *The Normangee Star.*

O

ODEM: Radio-FM: KXAI, 103.7 MHz.
ODESSA: Newspaper: *Odessa American (S).* Radio-FM: KBMM, 89.5 MHz; KLVW, 90.5; KXWT, 91.3; KMRK, 96.1; KMCM, 96.9; KODM, 97.9; KHKX, 99.1; KQLM, 107.9. TV Stations: KOSA-Ch. 7; KWES-Ch. 9; KMLM-Ch. 15; KPEJ-Ch. 23; KPBT-Ch. 28; KWWT-Ch. 30.
OLNEY: Newspaper: *Olney Enterprise.* Radio-FM: KBVP, 104.3 MHz.
ORANGE: Newspaper: *The Orange Leader (S).* Radio-FM: KKMY, 104.5 MHz; KIOC, 106.1.
ORE CITY: Radio-FM: KAZE, 106.9 MHz.
OVERTON: Radio-FM: KTYK, 100.7 MHz.
OZONA: Newspaper: *Ozona Stockman.* Radio-FM: KYXX, 94.3 MHz; KCMZ, 105.5.

P

PADUCAH: Newspaper: *Paducah Post.* Radio-FM: KPZX, 94.7 MHz.
PALACIOS: Newspaper: *Palacios Beacon.* Radio-FM: KPAL, 91.3 MHz; KPLU, 100.7.
PALESTINE: Newspaper: *Palestine Herald-Press (TW).* Radio-AM: KNET, 1450 kHz. Radio-FM: KYFP, 89.1 MHz; KYYK, 98.3.
PAMPA: Newspaper: *The Pampa News (TW).* Radio-AM: KGRO, 1230 kHz. Radio-FM: KWGP, 88.5 MHz; KAVO, 90.9; KLCP, 91.7; KOMX, 100.3; KRWP, 103.3.
PANHANDLE: Newspaper: *Panhandle Herald & White Deer News.* Radio-FM: KPQP, 94.9 MHz.

PARIS: Newspaper: *The Paris News (TW).* Radio-AM: KZHN, 1250 kHz; KPLT, 1490. Radio-FM: KHCP, 89.3 MHz; KYBP, 90.1; KQPA, 91.9; KOYN, 93.9; KBUS, 101.9; KPLT, 107.7.

PASADENA: Radio-AM: KIKK, 650 kHz; KLVL, 1480. Radio-FM: KFTG, 88.1 MHz; KKBQ, 92.9.

PEARLAND: Newspaper: *Pearland Reporter News.*

PEARSALL: Newspaper: *Frio-Nueces Current.* Radio-AM: KMFR, 1280 kHz. Radio-FM: DKSAG, 103.3 MHz; KSAH, 104.1.

PECAN GROVE: Radio-AM: KREH, 900 kHz.

PECOS: Newspaper: *Pecos Enterprise.* Radio-AM: KIUN, 1400 kHz. Radio-FM: KPKO, 91.3 MHz; KDNZ, 97.3; KPTX, 98.3.

PERRYTON: Newspaper: *Perryton Herald.* Radio-AM: KEYE, 1400 kHz. Radio-FM: KJJL, 88.5 MHz; KEYE, 93.7.

PFLUGERVILLE: Radio-AM: KOKE, 1600 kHz.

PHARR: Newspaper: *The Advance News Journal.* Radio-AM: KVJY, 840 kHz.

PILOT POINT: Newspaper: *Pilot Point Post-Signal.* Radio-FM: KZMP, 104.9 MHz.

PINELAND: Radio-FM: KFAH, 99.1 MHz.

PITTSBURG: Newspaper: *The Pittsburg Gazette.* Radio-FM: KGWP, 91.1 MHz; KPIT, 91.7; KSCN, 96.9; KHFZ, 103.1.

PLAINVIEW: Newspaper: *Plainview Herald (TW).* Radio-AM: KVOP, 1090 kHz; KREW, 1400. Radio-FM: KPMB, 88.5 MHz; KBAH, 90.5; KWLD, 91.5; KRIA, 103.9; KKYN, 106.9.

PLANO: Newspaper: *Plano Star Courier.* Radio-AM: KTNO, 620 kHz.

PLEASANTON: Newspaper: *Pleasanton Express.* Radio-AM: KWMF, 1380 kHz.

PLEASANT VALLEY: Radio-FM: KZAM, 98.7 MHz.

POINT COMFORT: Radio-FM: KJAZ, 94.1 MHz.

PORT ARANSAS: Newspaper: *Port Aransas South Jetty.*

PORT ARTHUR: Newspaper: *The Port Arthur News (S).* Radio-AM: KDEI, 1250 kHz; KOLE, 1340. Radio-FM: KQBU, 93.3 MHz; KTJM, 98.5. TV Station: KBTV-Ch. 27.

PORT ISABEL: Newspaper: *Port Isabel-South Padre Press.* Radio-FM: KRIX, 95.3 MHz; KNVO, 101.1.

PORTLAND: Newspaper: *The News of San Patricio.* Radio-FM: KSGR, 91.1 MHz; KLHB, 105.5.

PORT LAVACA: Newspaper: *Port Lavaca Wave.* Radio-FM: KNAL, 93.3 MHz.

PORT NECHES: Radio-AM: KBPO, 1150 kHz.

PORT O'CONNOR: Radio-FM: KHPO, 91.9 MHz.

POST: NEWSPAPER: *The Post Dispatch.* Radio-FM: KSSL, 107.3 MHz.

PRAIRIE VIEW: Radio-FM: KPVU, 91.3 MHz.

PREMONT: Radio-FM: KLBD, 88.1 MHz.

PRESIDIO: Newspaper: *The Presidio International.* Radio-FM: KRBP, 88.1 MHz; KOJP, 95.3.

PRINCETON: Newspaper: *Princeton Herald.* Radio-FM: KXEZ, 92.1 MHz.

Q

QUANAH: Newspaper: *Quanah Tribune-Chief.* Radio-AM: KOLJ, 1150 kHz. Radio-FM: KQWD, 90.5 MHz; KQTX, 98.1.

QUEMADO: Radio-FM: KQMD, 88.1 MHz.

QUITAQUE: Newspaper: *Valley Tribune.*

R

RALLS: Newspaper: *Crosby County News.*

RANCHITOS LAS LOMAS: Radio-FM: KLIT, 93.3 MHz.

RANGER: Radio-FM: KWBY, 98.5 MHz.

RANKIN: Radio-FM: KXFS, 93.7 MHz.

RAYMONDVILLE: Newspaper: *Raymondville Chronicle & Willacy County News.* Radio-AM: KSOX, 1240 kHz. Radio-FM: KVHI, 88.7 MHz; KBUC, 102.1; KBIC, 105.7.

REFUGIO: Newspaper: *Refugio County Press.* Radio-FM: KRIK, 100.5 MHz; KXHM, 106.1.

RENO: Radio-FM: KLOW, 98.9 MHz.

RICHARDSON: Radio-AM: KKLF, 1700 kHz.

RIESEL: Newspaper: *Riesel Rustler.*

RIO GRANDE CITY: Radio-FM: KXJT, 88.3 MHz; KRGC, 95.1; KQBO, 107.5. TV Station: KTLM-Ch. 14.

ROBERT LEE: Newspaper: *Observer/Enterprise.* Radio-FM: KJVI, 105.7 MHz.

ROBINSON: Radio-FM: KWPW, 107.9 MHz.

ROBSTOWN: Radio-AM: KROB, 1510 kHz. Radio-FM: KLUX, 89.5 MHz; KSAB, 99.9; KMIQ, 104.9.

ROCKDALE: Newspaper: *Rockdale Reporter.* Radio-FM: KRXT, 98.5 MHz.

ROCKPORT: Newspaper: *The Rockport Pilot (S).* Radio-FM: KKPN, 102.3 MHz.

ROLLINGWOOD: Radio-AM: KJCE, 1370 kHz.

ROMA: Radio-FM: KRIO, 97.7 MHz.

ROSCOE: Radio-FM: KKHR, 93.5 MHz.

ROSEBUD: Newspaper: *The Rosebud News.*

ROSENBERG: Newspaper: *The Fort Bend Herald (TW).* Radio-AM: KQUE, 980 kHz. TV Station: KXLN-Ch. 30.

ROTAN: Newspaper: *Double Mountain Chronicle.*

ROUND ROCK: Newspaper: *Round Rock Leader (S).* Radio-FM: KNLE, 88.1 MHz; KFMK, 105.9.

ROXTON: Newspaper: *Roxton Progress (SM).*

ROYSE CITY: Newspaper: *Royse City Herald Banner.*

RULE: Radio-FM: KTJO, 98.5 MHz.

RUSK: Newspaper: *Cherokeean Herald.*

S

SABINAL: Radio-FM: KHAV, 107.1 MHz.

SACHSE: Newspaper: *The Sachse News.*

SAINT JO: Newspaper: *The Saint Jo Tribune.*

SALADO: Newspaper: *Salado Village Voice.*

SAN ANGELO: Newspaper: *San Angelo Standard-Times (D); Livestock Weekly.* Radio-AM: KGKL, 960 kHz; KKSA, 1260; KCCE, 1340. Radio-FM: KLRW, 88.5 MHz; KNAR, 89.3; KNCH, 90.1; KLTP, 90.9; KDCD, 92.9; KSAO, 93.9; KIXY, 94.7; KGKL, 97.5; KELI, 98.7;

KCLL, 100.1; KWFR, 101.9; KMDX, 106.1. **TV Stations:** KLST-Ch. 11; KSAN-Ch. 16; KIDY-Ch. 19.

SAN ANTONIO: Newspapers: *San Antonio Express-News (D); The Hart Beat (TW); San Antonio Business Journal.* **Radio-AM:** KTSA, 550 kHz; KSLR, 630; KKYX, 680; KTKR, 760; KONO, 860; KRDY, 1160; WOAI, 1200; KZDC, 1250; KAHL, 1310; KXTN, 1350; KCHL, 1480; KEDA, 1540. **Radio-FM:** KPAC, 88.3 MHz; KSTX, 89.1; KSYM, 90.1; KYFS, 90.9; KRTU, 91.7; KROM, 92.9; KXXM, 96.1; KAJA, 97.3; KISS, 99.5; KCYY, 100.3; KQXT, 101.9; KJXK, 102.7; KZEP, 104.5; KVBH, 107.5. **TV Stations:** KLRN-Ch. 9; KSAT-Ch. 12; KVDA-Ch. 15; KHCE-Ch. 16; KWEX-Ch. 24; WOAI-Ch. 28; KENS-Ch. 29; KABB-Ch. 30.

SAN AUGUSTINE: Newspaper: *San Augustine Tribune.* **Radio-FM:** KXXE, 92.5 MHz.

SAN BENITO: Newspaper: *San Benito News.* **Radio-FM:** KHKZ, 106.3 MHz.

SANDERSON: **Radio-FM:** KEVK, 105.1 MHz.

SAN DIEGO: **Radio-FM:** KXAM, 102.5 MHz.

SANGER: **Radio-FM:** KAWA, 89.7 MHz; KTCG, 104.1.

SAN ISIDRO: **Radio-FM:** KXYC, 97.3 MHz.

SAN JUAN: **Radio-AM:** KUBR, 1210 kHz.

SAN MARCOS: Newspaper: *San Marcos Daily Record (TW).* **Radio-FM:** KTSW , 89.9 MHz.

SAN SABA: Newspaper: *San Saba News & Star.* **Radio-AM:** KROY, 1410 kHz. **Radio-FM:** KNUZ, 106.1 MHz.

SANTA ANNA: **Radio-FM:** KXXU, 104.3 MHz; KSZX, 105.5.

SANTA FE: **Radio-FM:** KJIC, 90.5 MHz.

SAVOY: **Radio-FM:** KQDR, 107.3 MHz.

SCHERTZ: **Radio-FM:** KBBT, 98.5 MHz.

SCHULENBURG: Newspaper: *Schulenburg Sticker.*

SCOTLAND: **Radio-FM:** KTWF, 95.5 MHz.

SEABROOK: **Radio-FM:** KROI, 92.1 MHz.

SEADRIFT: **Radio-FM:** KMAT, 105.1 MHz.

SEALY: Newspaper: *The Sealy News.* **Radio-FM:** KQLC, 90.7 MHz.

SEGUIN: Newspaper: *The Seguin Gazette (S).* **Radio-AM:** KWED, 1580 kHz. **Radio-FM:** KSMG, 105.3 MHz.

SEMINOLE: Newspaper: *Seminole Sentinel (S).* **Radio-AM:** KIKZ, 1250 kHz. **Radio-FM:** KRGO, 91.5 MHz; KSEM, 106.3.

SEYMOUR: Newspaper: *The Baylor County Banner.*

SHAMROCK: Newspaper: *County Star-News.* **Radio-FM:** KJWD, 91.1 MHz; KSNZ, 92.9.

SHEPHERD: Newspaper: *San Jacinto News-Times.*

SHENANDOAH: **Radio-AM:** KRCM, 1380 kHz.

SHERMAN: Newspaper: *Herald Democrat (D).* **Radio-AM:** KJIM, 1500 kHz. **TV Station:** KXII-Ch. 12.

SHINER: Newspaper: *The Shiner Gazette.*

SIERRA BLANCA: **Radio-FM:** KNOO, 88.1 MHz.

SILSBEE: Newspaper: *The Silsbee Bee.* **Radio-FM:** KAYD, 101.7 MHz.

SILVERTON: Newspaper: *The Caprock Courier.*

SINTON: Newspaper: *The News of San Patricio.* **Radio-AM:** KDAE, 1590 kHz. **Radio-FM:** KNCN, 101.3 MHz.

SLATON: Newspaper: *The Slatonite.* **Radio-FM:** KVCE, 92.7 MHz.

SMILEY: **Radio-FM:** KSXT, 90.3 MHz; KBQQ, 103.9.

SMITHVILLE: Newspaper: *Smithville Times.*

SNYDER: Newspaper: *The Snyder News (S).* **Radio-AM:** KSNY, 1450 kHz. **Radio-FM:** KJNZ, 90.3 MHz; KGWB, 91.1; KHMZ 94.9; KLYD, 98.9; KSNY, 101.5. **TV Station:** KPCB-Ch. 17.

SOMERSET: **Radio-AM:** KYTY, 810 kHz.

SOMERVILLE: **Radio-FM:** KXBT, 88.1 MHz.

SONORA: Newspaper: *The Devil's River News.* **Radio-FM:** KHOS, 92.1 MHz.

SOUTH PADRE ISLAND: **Radio-FM:** KESO, 92.7 MHz.

SPEARMAN: Newspaper: *The Hansford County Reporter-Statesman.* **Radio-FM:** KTOT, 89.5 MHz; KXDJ, 98.3.

SPRINGTOWN: Newspaper: *Springtown Epigraph.* **Radio-FM:** KSQX, 89.1 MHz.

SPUR: Newspaper: *The Texas Spur.*

STAMFORD: Newspapers: *The Stamford American; The Stamford Star.* **Radio-AM:** KVRP, 1400 kHz. **Radio-FM:** KLGD, 106.9 MHz.

STANTON: Newspapers: *Martin County Messenger.* **Radio-FM:** KFLB, 88.1 MHz; KTPR, 89.9; KXQT, 105.9.

STEPHENVILLE: Newspaper: *Stephenville Empire Tribune.* **Radio-AM:** KSTV, 1510 kHz. **Radio-FM:** KQXS, 89.1 MHz; KEQX, 89.5; KTRL, 90.5.

STERLING CITY: **Radio-FM:** KNRX, 96.5 MHz.

STINNETT: **Radio-FM:** KZWD, 88.7 MHZ; KPWD, 91.7.

STOCKDALE: **Radio-AM:** KQQB, 1520 kHz.

STRATFORD: Newspaper: *Sherman County Gazette.* **Radio-FM:** KUHC, 91.5 MHz.

SULPHUR BLUFF: **Radio-FM:** KETE, 99.7 MHz.

SULPHUR SPRINGS: Newspaper: *Sulphur Springs News-Telegram (S).* **Radio-AM:** KSST, 1230 kHz. **Radio-FM:** KGPF, 91.1 MHz; KZRF, 91.9; KSCH, 95.9.

SUNSET VALLEY: **Radio-FM:** KVLR, 92.5 MHz.

SWEETWATER: Newspaper: *Sweetwater Reporter (TW).* **Radio-AM:** KXOX, 1240 kHz. **Radio-FM:** KRGK, 88.9 MHz; KXOX, 96.7. **TV Station:** KTXS-Ch. 20.

T

TAFT: **Radio-FM:** KYRK, 106.5 MHz.

TAHOKA: Newspaper: *Lynn County News.* **Radio-FM:** KMMX, 100.3 MHz; KAMZ, 103.5.

TATUM: **Radio-FM:** KZQX, 100.3 MHz.

TAYLOR: Newspaper: *Taylor Press (S).* **Radio-FM:** KLQB, 104.3 MHz.

TEAGUE: Newspaper: *Teague Chronicle.*

TEMPLE: Newspaper: *Temple Daily Telegram (D).* **Radio-AM:** KTEM, 1400 kHz. **Radio-FM:** KVLT, 88.5 MHz; KBDE, 89.9; KLTD, 101.7. **TV Station:** KCEN-Ch. 9.

TERLINGUA: Radio FM: KTLG, 88.5 MHz.

TERRELL: Newspaper: *The Terrell Tribune.* **Radio-AM:** KPYK, 1570 kHz.

TERRELL HILLS: **Radio-AM:** KLUP, 930 kHz. **Radio-FM:** KTKX, 106.7 MHz.

TEXARKANA: Newspaper: *Texarkana Gazette (D).* **Radio-AM:** KCMC, 740 kHz; KTFS, 940; KKTK, 1400. **Radio-FM:** KTXK, 91.5 MHz; KTAL, 98.1; KKYR, 102.5. **TV Station:** KTAL-Ch. 26.

TEXAS CITY: Newspaper: *The Post Newspaper (S)*. Radio-AM: KYST, 920 kHz.

THORNDALE: Newspaper: *Thorndale Champion*. Radio-FM: KOKE, 99.3 MHz.

THREE RIVERS: Newspaper: *The Progress*. Radio-FM: KEMA, 94.5 MHz.

THROCKMORTON: Newspaper: *Throckmorton Tribune*.

TOLAR: Radio-FM: KOME, 95.5 MHz.

TOMBALL: Radio-AM: KSEV, 700 kHz.

TOM BEAN: Radio-FM: KLAK, 97.5 MHz.

TRENT: Radio-FM: KGDI, 92.1 MHz.

TRINITY: Radio-FM: KTYR, 89.7 MHz.

TROUP: Radio-FM: KTBB, 97.5 MHz.

TULIA: Newspaper: *Swisher County News*. Radio-FM: KBTE, 104.9 MHz.

TURKEY: Radio-FM: KYLB, 96.7 MHz.

TYE: Radio-FM: KBCY, 99.7 MHz.

TYLER: Newspaper: *Tyler Morning Telegraph (TW)*. Radio-AM: KTBB, 600 kHz; KGLD, 1330; KYZS, 1490. Radio-FM: KVNE, 89.5 MHz; KGLY, 91.3; KRWR, 92.1; KTYL, 93.1; KNUE, 101.5; KKUS, 104.1. TV STATION: KLTV-Ch. 7.

U

UMBARGER: Radio-FM: KRBG, 88.7 MHz.

UNIVERSAL CITY: Radio-AM: KSAH, 720 kHz.

UNIVERSITY PARK: Radio-AM: KEXB, 1440 kHz; KAMM, 1540.

UVALDE: Newspaper: *Uvalde Leader-News (S)*. Radio-AM: KGWU, 1400 kHz. Radio-FM: KHPS, 88.9 MHz; KBNU, 93.9; KUVA, 102.3; KVOU, 104.9. TV Station: KPXL-Ch. 26.

UVALDE ESTATES: Radio-FM: KEWP, 103.5 MHz.

V

VALLEY MILLS: Newspaper: *Valley Mills Progress (SM)*.

VALLEY VIEW: Radio-FM: KQFZ, 89.1 MHz.

VAN HORN: Newspaper: *The Van Horn Advocate*. Radio-FM: KVHR, 91.5 MHz.

VEGA: Newspaper: *Vega Enterprise*.

VERNON: Newspaper: *Vernon Record*. Radio-AM: KVWC, 1490 kHz. Radio-FM: KVED, 88.1 MHz.

VICTORIA: Newspaper: *Victoria Advocate (TW)*. Radio-AM: KVNN, 1340 kHz; KITE, 1410. Radio-FM: KAYK, 88.5 MHz; KBRZ, 89.3; KVRT, 90.7; KQVT, 92.3; KTXN, 98.7; KBAR, 100.9; KVIC, 104.7; KIXS, 107.9. TV Stations: KVCT-Ch. 11; KAVU-Ch. 20.

VIDOR: Newspaper: *Vidor Vidorian*.

W

WACO: Newspaper: *Waco Tribune-Herald (TW)*. Radio-AM: KBBW , 1010 kHz; KWTX, 1230; KRZI, 1660. Radio-FM: KWBT, 94.5 MHz; KBGO, 95.7; KWTX, 97.5; WACO, 99.9; KWBU, 103.3. TV Stations: KWTX-Ch. 10; KXXV-Ch. 26; KWKT-Ch. 28.

WAKE VILLAGE: Radio-FM: KHTA, 92.5 MHz.

WASKOM: Radio-FM: KQHN, 97.3 MHz.

WAXAHACHIE: Newspapers: *Waxahachie Daily Light; The Waxahachie Sun*. Radio-AM: KBEC, 1390 kHz.

WEATHERFORD: Newspaper: *Weatherford Democrat (S)*. Radio-AM: KZEE, 1220 kHz. Radio-FM: KMQX, 88.5 MHz.

WEIMAR: Newspaper: *Weimar Mercury*.

WELLINGTON: Radio-FM: KSIF 91.7 MHz.

WELLS: Radio-FM: KVLL, 94.7 MHz.

WESLACO: Radio-AM: KRGE, 1290 kHz. TV Station: KRGV-Ch. 13.

WEST: Newspaper: *The West News*.

WEST LAKE HILLS: Radio-AM: KTXZ, 1560 kHz.

WEST ODESSA: Radio-FM: KFRI, 88.7 MHz.

WHARTON: Newspaper: *Wharton Journal-Spectator (S)*. Radio-AM: KANI, 1500 kHz.

WHEELER: Newspaper: *The Wheeler Times*. Radio-FM: KPDR, 90.3 MHz; KXNZ, 98.9.

WHEELOCK: Radio-FM: KVMK 100.9 MHz.

WHITEHOUSE: Radio-FM: KISX, 107.3 MHz.

WHITE OAK: Newspaper: *White Oak Independent*. Radio-FM: KAPW , 99.3 MHz.

WHITESBORO: Newspaper: *Whitesboro News-Record*. Radio-FM: KMAD, 102.5 MHz.

WHITEWRIGHT: Newspaper: *The Whitewright Sun*.

WICHITA FALLS: Newspaper: *Times Record News (D)*. Radio-AM: KWFS, 1290. Radio-FM: KMCU, 88.7 MHz; KMOC, 89.5; KZKL, 90.5; KNIN, 92.9; KLUR, 99.9; KWFS, 102.3; KQXC, 103.9; KBZS, 106.3. TV Stations: KJTL-Ch. 15; KAUZ-Ch. 22; KFDX-Ch. 28.

WILLIS: Radio-FM: KAFR, 88.3 MHz.

WILLS POINT: Newspaper: *Wills Point Chronicle*.

WIMBERLEY: Newspaper: *Wimberley View*.

WINFIELD: Radio-FM: KALK, 97.7 MHz.

WINNIE: Newspapers: *The Hometown Press; The Seabreeze Beacon*. Radio-FM: KLTW 105.3 MHz.

WINNSBORO: Newspaper: *Winnsboro News*. Radio-FM: KWNS, 104.7 MHz.

WINONA: Radio-FM: KBLZ, 102.7 MHz.

WINTERS: Radio-FM: KORQ, 96.1 MHz.

WIXON VALLEY: Radio-FM: KBXT, 101.9 MHz.

WOLFFORTH: Radio-FM: KAIQ, 95.5 MHz. TV Station: KLCW-Ch. 23.

WOODVILLE: Newspaper: *Tyler County Booster*.

WYLIE: Newspaper: *The Wylie News*. Radio-AM: KHSE, 700 kHz.

Y

YOAKUM: Newspaper: *Yoakum Herald-Times*. Radio-FM: KYKM, 94.3 MHz.

YORKTOWN: Newspaper: *Yorktown News-View*. Radio-FM: KGGB, 96.3 MHz.

Z

ZAPATA: Newspaper: *Zapata County News*. Radio-FM: KHEM, 89.3 MHz; KQHM 102.7.

Texas

AGRICULTURE

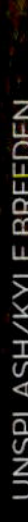

UNSPLASH/KYLE BREEDEN

AGRICULTURE IN TEXAS

History

Texas agriculture dates to the arrival of the first Paleo-Indian hunters, around 20,000 years ago. As the post-Pleistocene climate became more temperate, successive populations of Archaic, Woodland, and Late Prehistoric Texans developed hunter-gatherer and cropping cultures. In the mid-1700s, Spanish colonists established a scrappy but enduring ranching economy in the lower to mid-Rio Grande basin. Then in the 1800s, Texas was dominated by expanding crop and livestock enterprises suitable to the state's varied geography and climate.

Scope

Texas remains a major agricultural state owing to its extensive land and water resources, relatively mild climate, transportation networks, other infrastructure, agribusiness investment, and public investment in agricultural research and extension.

The agricultural economy of Texas is a part of an extended food and fiber system that represents 9% of the State's gross domestic product. It is not surprising then that Texas also has a relatively large share of the country's cropland, woodland, and rangeland. This resource base puts Texas in the top five states for agricultural cash receipts. Texas normally leads all other states in cash receipts from livestock marketings, farms and ranches, cattle on feed, cotton production, goats and mohair, sheep and lambs, cattle and calves, and beef cows.

Economic Structure

The natural resource, business, technological, and human capital investment in modern Texas agriculture reflects an ongoing substitution of labor out of agriculture and into other economic pursuits. In 1940, for example, about 23% of Texans were producers on farms and ranches, and about 17% were input suppliers or were engaged in assembly, processing, and distribution of agricultural products. But by 2008, fewer than 2% of Texans work on farms and ranches, with about 15% of the labor force providing production or marketing supplies and services, as well as retailing food and fiber products.

This capital-for-labor substitution is also reflected in the changing structure of farm operations. The number of farms in Texas decreased from 420,000 in 1940 to 231,000 in 2024 with an average size of 541 acres. The number of small farms is actually increasing, but these are operated by part-time farmers and ranchers as a lifestyle choice. Full-time, commercial farming and ranching is conducted by fewer, larger, capital-intensive operations to take advantage of economies of scale. Mechanization of farming continues as new and larger machines replace workforce and smaller equipment. Adoption of precision agriculture through the use of satellites, computers, global positioning systems, and other high-tech tools help producers manage inputs such as genetically-engineered seed, fertilizers, selective pesticides, and water.

Supply Chains

Modern agriculture operates in a global, high-tech, consumer-driven environment. Agricultural production is associated with considerable upstream and downstream economic activity. Many businesses, financial institutions, and individuals are involved in providing supplies, technology, information, credit, and other services to farmers and ranchers. Texas farmers and ranchers have developed considerable dependence upon agribusinesses. On the input side, they rely on suppliers of various inputs and services, and on the output side they need assembly and logistics services, processors, and distributors. The latter is particularly true for accessing export markets, upon which major crops like cotton, sorghum, and wheat are dependent.

Land Use

Changing rural land use is an ongoing issue as traditional crop and livestock industries compete for land with new/alternative crops or industries, recreational uses, conservation, urban and suburban development, solar and wind energy generation, etc. Many of these alternative uses are themselves a result of population growth in urban and suburban areas, implying increasing demand for space, energy, and recreational land uses.

In Texas, most land use outcomes are ultimately decided by market forces. The implication is that agricultural land will become increasingly scarce and expensive, especially in closer proximity to more profitable competing uses. The possible losers in this scenario are traditional agricultural producers who rent land. These may be part of the recently estimated 17,000 working Texas farms and ranches that have ceased operating due to land use changes. On the other hand, some operations stand to benefit from alternative land uses such as farm owner-operators who adopt joint uses, e.g., ranching and hunting leases, or agrovoltaics — agricultural use combined with solar power generation.

Water Use

Agriculture is the largest annual consumer of fresh water in Texas. Irrigation is an important factor in the State's agricultural productivity. The value of crop production from irrigated acreage is 50% to 60% of the total value of all crop production,

Sources: John Robinson, Professor and Extension Economist-Cotton Marketing, and Mark Welch, Professor and Extension Economist-Grain Marketing, Texas A&M AgriLife Extension Service, Texas A&M University System.

UNSPLASH/LUMINOSITY

although only about a third of the state's total harvested cropland acreage is irrigated. Over half of the irrigated acreage in Texas is in the High Plains region. Other concentrated areas of irrigation are the Upper Gulf Coast rice-producing area, the Lower Rio Grande Valley, the Winter Garden area of South Texas, and the Trans-Pecos area of West Texas.

Changing water resource use is an ongoing response to both natural and societal changes. For example, agricultural irrigation in Texas peaked in 1974 at 8.6 million acres of irrigated land. At that time, irrigation accounted for 75% of total estimated water use. Over the next 20 years, irrigation declined due to many factors including poor farm economics, falling aquifer levels in certain regions, higher energy costs for irrigation pumping, and the movement of much of the vegetable production from South Texas to Mexico.

By 1999, irrigation accounted for 60% of total estimated water use. For the past 15 years, total irrigated area has stabilized around six million acres. This puts Texas third in the nation, behind California and Nebraska in agricultural irrigation. As of 2022, irrigation's share of total water use in Texas had declined to 50%.

However, both the supply of and demand for irrigation water is variable. Texas is subject to periodic droughts which reduce water supplies from surface water sources (rivers, reservoirs). This, in turn, stimulates more drilling of groundwater wells, and more pumping from existing wells. As a result, there are currently declining water levels in important aquifers like the Ogallala Aquifer in the Texas High Plains, and the southern portion of the Carrizo-Wilcox formation.

The effects of Texas' expanding urban population has similar implications for the demand for water as it does for land use. To meet future water demand for growing cities and industries, several regions of the state are looking at water transfers from agricultural regions and/or individual water rights holders. Texas water planning documents further estimate that as much as 30% of future water demand could be met through agricultural irrigation conservation. To the extent that this results in more rainfed agriculture, it implies changing land use with different crop and livestock enterprises.

Future Outlook

The caloric and protein needs of a growing world population will likely increase the demand for certain crops and livestock. Responding to market signals, the Texas food and fiber system remains poised to profitably satisfy this demand. Some innovations and trends we might expect along the way include:

- Exacerbated drought issues from hotter and drier climate conditions
- Disappearance of certain industries, the most recent example of which is sugar cane production and processing in the Lower Rio Grande Valley
- Expansion/concentration of industries such as the northwestern Texas dairy shed

- Unexpected biological and market disruptions from epizootics or plant disease outbreaks (e.g., highly pathogenic avian influenza and high egg prices)
- Unexpected biological and market disruptions from destructive, invasive species (e.g., re-emergence of the new world screwworm)
- Continued development of data gathering technology via aerial drones and satellites and/or automated ground machines with "machine vision," and increasingly linked to more automated field operations
- Labor-saving and input optimizing robotics, increasingly linked to more automated field operations
- Adoption of more drought tolerant cropping systems for dryland or deficit irrigation
- Crop and livestock products with elevated nutrient levels or nutraceutical properties

Cash Receipts

Farm and ranch cash receipts in 2023 totaled $29.9 billion, with estimates of $1.2 billion for direct government payments. Realized gross farm income totaled $40.3 billion, with farm production expenses of $25 billion and net farm income totaling $15.4 billion.

Texas' Rank Among States

Measured by cash receipts from crops and livestock, Texas ranked fourth in 2023. California ranked first, Iowa ranked second, and Nebraska ranked third.

Texas normally leads all other states in cotton production, numbers of farms and ranches, cattle on feed, calf births, sheep and lambs, goats, cash receipts from livestock marketings, cattle and calves, beef cows, mohair production, and exports of fats, oils, and greases.

Cash Receipts by Commodities

COMMODITIES	2023	2022	2021	2020	2019	Percent of 2023
	(All values in thousands of dollars)					
All Commodities	**$29,857,961**	**$30,637,412**	**$25,331,155**	**$21,093,090**	**$21,245,793**	**100.00%**
Animals and products	**22,262,146**	**22,237,110**	**16,897,997**	**14,466,233**	**14,417,707**	**74.56%**
Meat animals	13,734,733	11,892,675	10,411,573	9,015,746	8,718,650	46.00%
Cattle and calves	13,374,298	11,557,144	10,053,767	8,794,871	8,469,663	44.79%
Hogs	360,435	335,531	357,806	220,875	248,987	1.21%
Dairy products, milk	3,357,214	4,225,536	2,833,922	2,757,636	2,640,193	11.24%
Poultry and eggs	4,568,769	5,479,818	3,104,592	2,189,743	2,605,939	15.30%
Broilers	3,435,591	4,180,640	2,518,594	1,659,867	2,165,130	11.51%
Misc. livestock †	601,430	639,081	547,910	503,108	452,925	2.01%
Crops	**7,595,815**	**8,400,302**	**8,433,158**	**6,626,856**	**6,828,086**	**25.44%**
Food grains	778,322	489,334	672,464	433,677	472,865	2.61%
Rice	208,849	187,351	189,008	161,145	171,385	0.70%
Wheat	565,414	297,498	479,401	269,081	298,252	1.89%
Feed crops	2,607,292	2,211,356	2,874,667	1,862,743	1,831,467	8.73%
Corn	1,348,927	1,154,451	1,486,278	901,148	1,102,881	4.52%
Sorghum	373,804	380,008	601,700	394,310	308,846	1.25%
Hay	872,331	669,100	781,512	557,493	411,260	2.92%
Cotton	1,564,897	3,064,159	2,440,722	2,038,567	2,465,937	5.24%
Oil crops	212,054	209,346	192,266	201,455	147,164	0.71%
Vegetables and melons	378,929	428,771	370,498	367,022	288,379	1.27%
Fruits and nuts	112,661	90,725	145,445	135,329	169,230	0.38%
All other crops ‡	1,941,659	1,906,611	1,737,096	1,588,065	1,453,042	6.50%

†The source data from USDA, National Agricultural Statistics Service (NASS) is confidential, so the names of commodities under this category aren't listed.

‡Includes miscellaneous vegetables and other field crops. Values are rounded to the nearest thousand. Sub-categories may not sum to total because not all sub-categories are reported.

Source: USDA/ERS Farm Income and Wealth Statistics.

UNSPLASH/KARL WIGGERS

Export Shares of Commodities

Commodity	2023	2022	2021	2020	2023 % of U.S. Total*
	(All values in millions of dollars)				
Beef and veal	1,319.3	1,568.0	1,453.7	1,060.8	13.2%
Pork	108.3	84.3	103.7	89	1.3%
Hides and skins	105	113.1	120.8	89.3	10.7%
Other livestock products [1]	322.4	368.8	358.2	286.7	7.2%
Dairy products	584.5	704.7	515.5	440.6	7.3%
Broiler meat	333.1	353.6	299.9	238.9	8.1%
Other poultry products [2]	115.1	133.7	100.8	78.1	4.6%
Vegetables, fresh	34.6	40.7	42.6	32	1.3%
Vegetables, processed	67.4	69.9	72.3	52.8	1.3%
Fruits, fresh	26	22.9	30.4	40.7	0.6%
Fruits, processed	22.5	23.1	26.7	33.8	0.6%
Tree nuts	50.7	73.2	68.1	62.6	0.6%
Rice	122.5	96.8	113.4	106	6.0%
Wheat	287.3	187.8	290.9	191.7	4.7%
Corn	233.3	246.6	386.3	175.4	1.8%
Feeds and other feed grains [3]	334.7	287.3	397.9	307.5	2.9%
Grain products, processed	156.5	106.5	142.9	130	3.3%
Soybeans	11.7	17.5	20.7	19.8	0.04%
Soybean meal	3.1	3.1	4.2	3.7	0.04%
Vegetable oils	10.1	13.9	14.8	15.1	0.4%
Other oilseeds and products[4]	108.6	104.2	109	143.3	5.6%
Cotton	1,311.5	3,353.7	1,939.8	1,799.4	21.9%
Other plant products [5]	909.5	899.8	875.9	807.2	4.7%
Total agricultural exports*	**6,577.7**	**8,873.1**	**7,488.8**	**6,204.3**	3.9%
Total animal products*	**2,887.7**	**3,326.2**	**2,952.7**	**2,283.3**	7.6%
Total plant products*	**3,690.0**	**5,547.0**	**4,536.0**	**3,921.0**	2.9%

* Totals may not add due to rounding.
1 Includes other nonpoultry meats, animal fat, live farm animals, and other animal parts.
2 Includes turkey meat, eggs, and other fowl products.
3 Includes processed feeds, fodder, barley, oats, rye, and sorghum.
4 Includes peanuts (oilstock), other oil crops, corn meal, other oilcake and meal, protein substances, bran, and residues.
5 Includes sweeteners and products, other horticulture products, planting seeds, cocoa, coffee, and other processed foods.
Source: USDA, Economic Research Service; USDA, Foreign Agricultural Service, Global Agricultural Trade System.

MAIN CROPS

In 2023, the value of crop production in Texas was 25.4% of the total value of the state's agricultural output. Cash receipts from farm sales of crops are reduced somewhat because some grain and roughage is fed to livestock on farms where produced. Drought has reduced receipts in recent years.

Receipts from all Texas crops totaled $7.6 billion in 2023, $8.4 billion in 2022, and $8.4 billion in 2021.

Cotton, corn, hay, and wheat account for a large part of the total crop receipts. In 2023, cotton contributed about 20.6% of the crop total; corn, 17.8%; and hay, 11.5%. Grain sorghum, cottonseed, vegetables, peanuts, rice, and soybeans are other important cash crops.

Cotton

Cotton has been a major crop in Texas for more than a century. Since 1880, Texas has led all states in cotton production in most years, and today the annual Texas all cotton harvest amounts to around 22.7% of total production in the United States.

Value of upland cotton produced in Texas in 2023 was $958.2 million. Cottonseed value in 2023 was $197.2 million — making the value of the Texas crop around $1.2 billion. Upland cotton was harvested from 2.1 million acres in 2023 and American-Pima from 24,000 acres, for a total of 2.12 million acres. Texas faced a historic severe drought in 2022, which impacted cotton production in recent years.

Cotton is the raw material for processing operations at gins, oil mills, compresses, and a small number of textile mills in Texas. Cotton in Texas is machine harvested. Field storage of harvested seed cotton has become common practice as gins decline in number.

Most of the Texas cotton crop is exported. China, Turkey, Mexico, and various Pacific Rim countries are major buyers. With the continuing development of fiber spinning technology and the improved quality of Texas cotton, the export demand for Texas cotton has grown.

UNSPLASH/URS LENDERMANN

Value of Cotton and Cottonseed				
Crop Year	Upland Cotton		Cottonseed	
	Production (Bales)	Value	Production (Tons)	Value
	(All figures in thousands)			
2023	2,705	$958,219	815	$197,230
2022	3,060	1,153,008	940	360,020
2021	7,700	3,444,672	2,403	600,750
2020	4,570	1,366,613	1,448	270,776
2019	6,320	1,762,522	1,902	317,634
2018	6,850	2,232,552	2,088	331,992
2017	9,270	2,950,085	2,852	393,576
2016	8,100	2,593,296	2,528	490,432
2015	5,720	1,564,992	1,844	413,056
2014	6,175	1,739,868	1,959	354,579
2013	4,170	1,493,194	1,368	347,472
2012	5,000	1,675,200	1,669	442,285
2011	3,500	1,375,920	1,228	354,892
2010	7,840	3,006,797	2,685	413,490
2009	4,620	1,328,342	1,634	254,904
2008	4,450	935,568	1,547	351,192
2007	8,250	2,391,840	2,861	443,409
2006	5,800	1,288,992	2,066	243,776
2005	8,440	1,879,757	2,869	289,739
2004	7,740	1,493,510	2,895	301,080
2003	4,330	1,199,237	1,616	202,000
2002	5,040	967,680	1,855	191,065
2001	4,260	580,723	1,724	159,470
2000	3,940	868,061	1,589	162,078
1999	5,050	993,840	1,987	160,947
1998	3,600	969,408	1,558	204,098
1997	5,140	1,482,787	1,983	226,062
1996	4,345	1,368,154	1,784	230,136
1995	4,460	1,597,037	1,828	201,080
1994	4,915	1,642,003	2,111	215,322
1993	5,095	1,308,396	2,147	255,493
1992	3,265	769,495	1,346	145,368
1991	4,710	1,211,789	1,903	134,162
1990	4,965	1,506,182	1,943	225,388
1989	2,870	812,784	1,189	141,491
1988	5,215	1,291,651	2,131	238,672
1987	4,635	1,325,981	1,915	157,971
1986	2,535	560,945	1,053	82,118
1985	3,910	968,429	1,635	102,156
1984	3,680	962,688	1,563	157,863

Source: Texas Agricultural Facts, USDA/NASS Crop Production Annual Summary, January; and Crop Values Annual Summary, February. USDA/NASS Quick Stats data system.

Grain Sorghum

Texas grain sorghum, in 2023, ranked number two in value of production in the U.S., with Kansas being number one. Much of the grain is exported, as well as used in livestock and poultry feed throughout the state. Ethanol production is a more recent demand source for Texas sorghum.

Total production of grain sorghum in 2023 was 76 million bushels from 1.6 million acres harvested. The total value reached $415.1 million, compared to 2022's $310 million total value of grain sorghum. In 2022, 950,000 acres of grain sorghum were harvested, for a total production of 50.4 million bushels.

Although grown to some extent in all counties where crops are important, the largest concentrations are in the High Plains, Coastal Bend, and the Lower Rio Grande Valley areas.

Research to develop high-yielding hybrids resistant to diseases and insect damage continues.

Rice

The Texas Rice Belt, mostly located in the upper Texas coast, covers the Wharton, Matagorda, and Colorado counties and contributes most of the state's rice production. Texas farmers grow long- and medium-grain rice only.

In 1904, the Houston Chamber of Commerce and the Southern Pacific Railroad invited Japanese farmers to the state to work with Texan rice producers. The emperor of Japan gifted seed rice, which established a turning point in Texas' rice industry.

Growing from 110 acres in 1850 to a high of 642,000 planted acres in 1954, rice production in Texas has been marked by significant yield increases and improved varieties. Record production was in 1981, with 27.2 million cwt. harvested. Highest yield was 8,370 pounds per acre in 2012.

Texas rice production in 2023 totaled 11 million cwt. from 143,000 harvested acres, with a yield of 7,670

Realized Gross Income and Net Income from Farming					
Year	Gross Farm Income	Farm Production Expenses	†Net Change In Farm Inventories	Total Net Farm Income	Total Net Income Per Farm
	(Values in millions of dollars)				(dollars)
2023	$40,315.00	$24,957.00	$– 812.3	$15,357.60	$66,483.10
2022	39,170.30	26,214.50	– 2,294.7	12,955.70	56,085.30
2021	30,956.00	22,449.60	– 494.3	8,506.10	34,437.70
2020	27,109.00	20,579.30	–928.6	6,529.70	26,436.00
2019	25,959.00	20,535.60	– 1,176.9	5,423.10	21,955.90
2018	24,432.10	21,489.50	– 1,183.2	4,215.40	17,066.40
2017	26,374.20	22,201.40	– 789.1	4,172.60	16,791.10
2016	24,629.30	22,105.50	– 77.5	2,523.90	10,450.90
2015	29,218.70	23,186.30	– 416.4	6,032.40	24,927.30
2014	30,319.80	26,512.70	407.2	3,807.10	15,507.50
2013	29,303.20	24,202.80	– 171.2	5,100.40	20,524.70
2012	27,430.80	23,842.10	– 1,075.4	3,588.80	14,412.90
2011	26,004.30	21,429.70	– 2,494.0	4,574.70	18,672.20
2010	23,474.00	18,807.40	46.6	4,666.60	18,946.80
2009	20,648.60	18,562.90	– 980.9	2,085.80	8,427.50
2008	22,523.20	19,674.00	– 1,174.8	2,849.30	11,512.30
2007	24,738.00	19,800.20	948.6	4,937.70	19,950.30
2006	20,329.60	16,010.90	– 753.8	4,318.70	18,777.00
2005	21,928.50	15,371.60	306.7	6,556.80	28,507.90
2004	21,826.40	14,343.80	539	7,482.50	32,674.70
2003	20,105.70	13,687.60	– 137.7	6,418.10	28,026.60
2002	16,567.90	11,372.80	436.8	5,195.10	22,686.00
2001	18,089.00	13,106.60	113.4	4,982.50	21,795.70
2000	16,810.10	12,707.80	– 50.2	4,102.30	18,151.80
1999	17,469.50	12,441.90	196	5,027.60	22,148.00
1998	15,506.00	12,047.40	– 817.1	3,458.60	15,303.50
1997	16,430.70	12,718.50	709.2	3,712.30	16,499.10
1996	15,025.00	12,006.60	– 290.1	3,018.40	13,475.00
1995	15,679.00	12,537.30	243.7	3,141.60	15,552.50
1994	15,394.50	11,134.70	107.7	4,259.90	21,300.00
1993	15,817.00	11,294.60	197	4,522.50	22,613.00
1992	14,482.50	10,617.60	464.1	3,864.90	21,119.70
1991	14,376.40	11,270.30	150	3,106.10	16,789.70
1990	14,421.50	11,012.90	343.9	3,408.60	18,325.80
1989	12,843.10	10,328.40	– 798.6	2,514.70	13,519.90
1988	12,842.30	10,331.70	– 128.4	2,510.60	13,425.70

† A positive value of inventory change represents current-year production not sold by December 31. A negative value is an offset to production from prior years included in current-year sales.

Source: "Economic Indicators of the Farm Sector, State Financial Summary," USDA/ERS; "Farm Income and Wealth Statistics," USDA/ERS.

pounds per acre. The crop value totaled $193.8 million. Rice production was 12.1 million cwt. in 2022 on 186,000 harvested acres, yielding 6,510 pounds per acre. The total value in 2022 was $210.6 million.

The United States produces less than two percent of the world's total rice, but it is one of the major exporters. Five percent of the yearly volume of global rice trade comes from the United States. American rice is popular abroad and is exported to more than 100 foreign countries.

Wheat

Wheat for grain is one of the state's most valuable cash crops. Wheat pastures provide considerable winter forage for cattle that is reflected in the value of livestock produced.

Texas wheat production totaled 77.7 million bushels in 2023 as yield averaged 37.0 bushels per acre. Planted acreage totaled 6.4 million acres and 2.1 million acres were harvested. The 2023 wheat value totaled $558.7 million. In 2022, Texas wheat growers planted 5.3 million acres and harvested 1.3 million acres. The yield was 30.0 bushels per acre for 2022 with total production of 39.0 million bushels at $9.15 per bushel valued at $356.9 million.

Wheat was first grown commercially in Texas near Sherman in about 1833. The acreage expanded greatly in North Central Texas after 1850 because of rapid settlement of the state and introduction of the well-adapted Mediterranean strain of wheat. A major family flour industry was developed in the Fort Worth/Dallas/Sherman area between 1875 and 1900. Now, around half of the state's acreage is planted on the High Plains and about a third of this is irrigated. Most of the Texas wheat acreage is of the hard red winter class. Because of the development of varieties with improved disease resistance and the use of wheat for winter pasture, there has been a sizable expansion of acreage in Central and South Texas.

Most wheat harvested for grain is used in some phase of the milling industry. The better-quality hard red winter wheat is used in the production of commercial bakery flour. Lower grades and varieties of soft red winter wheat are used in family flours. Byproducts of milled wheat are used for feed.

Corn

Interest in corn production throughout the state has increased since the 1970s as yields improved with new varieties. Once the principal grain crop, corn acreage declined as plantings of grain sorghum increased. Only 500,000 acres were harvested annually until the mid-1970s when development of new hybrids occurred.

Harvested acreage was 2.1 million in 2023 and 1.6 million in 2022. Yields were 122 for 2023 and 95 for 2022. Corn was valued at $1.4 billion in 2023 and $1.1 billion in 2022.

Most of the acreage and yield increase has occurred in Central and South Texas. The grain is largely used for livestock feed, but other important uses are in ethanol and food products.

Oats

Oats are grown extensively in Texas for winter pasture, hay, silage, and greenchop feeding, and some acreage is harvested for grain.

In 2023, 390,000 acres of oats were planted. From the plantings, 70,000 acres were harvested, with an average yield of 54 bushels per acre for a total production of 3.8 million bushels. Average price per bushel was $5.20 and total production value was $19.7 million.

Of the 450,000 acres planted to oats in 2022, 32,000 acres were harvested. The average yield was 55 bushels per acre. Production totaled 1.9 million bushels with a value of $10.9 million, or $6.22 per bushel.

Almost all oat grain produced in Texas is utilized as feed for livestock within the state. A small acreage is grown exclusively for planting seed.

Sugarcane, Sugar, and Seed

Sugarcane is grown from seed cane planted in late summer or fall. It is harvested 12 months later and milled to produce raw sugar and molasses. Raw sugar requires additional refining into its final form and is offered to consumers.

The sugarcane grinding mill operated at Santa Rosa in Cameron County is considered one of the most modern mills in the United States. Texas sugarcane-producing counties include Cameron, Hidalgo, and Willacy.

At a yield of 23 tons per acre, sugarcane, sugar, and seed production in 2023 totaled 432,000 tons from 18,800 harvested acres. The total value in 2023 was $14 million. In 2022, 31,200 acres were harvested for total production of 705,000 tons valued at $23.4 million. The yield was 22.6 tons per acre.

Hay, Silage, and Other Forage Crops

A large proportion of Texas' agricultural land is devoted to forage crop production. This acreage produces much of the feed requirements for the state's large domestic livestock population as well as game animals.

Approximately 100 million acres of pasture and rangeland, which are primarily in the western half of Texas, provide grazing for beef cattle, sheep, goats, horses, and game animals. The average annual acreage of forage land used for hay, silage, and other forms of machine-harvested forage is around five million acres.

All hay accounts for a large amount of this production with some corn and sorghum silage being produced. The most important hay crops are annual and perennial grasses and alfalfa. Production in 2023 totaled 8.7 million tons of hay from 4.7 million harvested acres at a yield of 1.9 tons per acre. Value of hay was $1.8 billion, or $229.00 per ton. In 2022, 6 million tons of hay were produced from 3.9 million harvested acres at a yield of 1.6 tons per acre. The value in 2022 was $1.1 billion, or $194.00 per ton.

Alfalfa hay production in 2023 totaled 468,000 tons with 85,000 acres harvested with a yield of 5.5 tons per acre. At a value of $269.00 per ton, the total value was $125.9 million. In 2022, 378,000 tons of alfalfa hay were harvested from 90,000 acres at a yield of 4.2 tons per acre. The value was $97.5 million, or $258.00 per ton.

Alfalfa, sweet corn, vetch, arrowleaf clover, grasses, and other forage plants also provide income as seed crops.

Peanuts

Well over three-fourths of the annual peanut production is from irrigated acreage. In 2023, Texas ranked second nationally in production of peanuts.

Until 1973, essentially all of the Texas acreage was planted to the Spanish type, which was favored because of its earlier maturity and better drought tolerance than other types. The Spanish variety is also preferred for some uses due to its distinctive flavor. The Florunner variety, a runner market type, is now planted on a sizable proportion of the acreage where soil moisture is favorable. The variety is later maturing but better yielding than Spanish varieties under good growing conditions. Florunner peanuts have acceptable quality to compete with the Spanish variety in most products.

In 2023, peanut production totaled 468.0 million pounds from 225,000 acres planted and 180,000 harvested,

UNSPLASH/CINDY STUNTZ

yielding 2,600 pounds per acre. At 41.0 cents per pound, the value of the crop was estimated at $187.6 million. In 2022, peanut production amounted to 327.2 million pounds from 157,000 acres planted and 114,000 harvested. With an average yield of 2,870 pounds per acre and average price of 34.0 cents per pound, the 2022 value of production was $128.6 million.

Soybeans

Soybean production is located in the areas of the Upper Coast, irrigated High Plains, and Red River Valley of Northeast Texas. Soybeans are adapted to the same general soil climate conditions as corn, cotton, or grain sorghum, provided moisture, disease, and insects are not limiting factors.

In low-rainfall areas, yields have been too low or inconsistent for profitable production under dryland conditions. Soybeans' need for moisture in late summer minimizes economic crop possibilities in the Blacklands and Rolling Plains. In the Blacklands, cotton root rot seriously hinders soybean production. Limited moisture at critical growth stages may occasionally prevent economical yields, even in high-rainfall areas of Northeast Texas and the Coastal Prairie.

Because of day length sensitivity, soybeans should be planted in Texas during the long days of May and June to obtain sufficient vegetative growth for optimum yields. Varieties planted during this period usually cease vegetative development and initiate reproductive processes during the hot, dry months of July and August. When moisture is insufficient during the blooming and fruiting period, yields are drastically reduced. In most areas of the state, July and August rainfall is insufficient to permit economical dryland production. The risk of dryland soybean production in the Coastal Prairie and Northeast Texas is considerably less when compared to other dryland areas because moisture is available more often during the critical fruiting period.

The 2023 soybean crop totaled 2.1 million bushels and was valued at $26.6 million, or $12.50 per bushel. Of the 125,000 acres planted, 85,000 were harvested with an average yield of 25.0 bushels per acre. In 2022, the Texas soybean crop averaged 20.0 bushels per acre from 85,000 acres harvested. Total production of 1.7 million bushels was valued at $22.3 million, or $13.10 per bushel.

Sunflowers

Sunflowers constitute one of the most important annual oilseed crops in the world. The cultivated types, which are thought to be descendants of the common wild sunflower native to Texas, have been successfully grown in several countries including Russia, Argentina, Romania, Bulgaria, Uruguay, Western Canada, and portions of the northern United States. Extensive trial plantings conducted in the Cotton Belt states since 1968 showed sunflowers have considerable potential as an oilseed crop in much of this area including Texas. This crop exhibits good cold and drought tolerance, is adapted to a wide range of soil and climate conditions, and tolerates higher levels of hail, wind, and sand abrasion than other crops normally grown in the state.

In 2023, sunflower production totaled 61.3 million pounds and was harvested from 45,000 acres at a yield of 1,361 pounds per acre. With an average price of $27.40 per

Texas Crop Production (2023)					
Crop	Harvested Acres	Yield Per Acre	Unit	Total Production (thousands)	Cash Value (thousands of dollars)
Corn, grain	2,100,000	122	Bushels	256,200	$1,398,852
Corn, silage	280,000	18	Ton	5,040	—
Cotton, American-Pima	24,000	500	Lb:Bale	25	—
Cotton, Upland	2,100,000	618	Lb:Bale	2,705.00	958,219
Cottonseed	—	—	Ton	815	197,230
Grapefruit*	—	250	Box	2,250	—
Hay, Alfalfa	85,000	5.5	Ton	468	125,892
Hay, excluding Alfalfa	4,600,000	1.8	Ton	8,280	1,622,880
Hay, All	**4,685,000**	**1.87**	**Ton**	**8,748**	**1,775,564**
Oats	70,000	54	Bushels	3, 780	19,656
Onions (fresh market)	9,000	280	Cwt.	2,520	85,680
Oranges*	—	185	Box	—	—
Peanuts	180,000	2,600	Lb.	468,000	187,608
Pecans*	—	257	Lb.	30,800	47,302
Potatoes	14,600	460	Cwt.	6,716	104,770
Rice	143,000	7,670	Lb:cwt.	10,972	193,824
Sorghum, Grain	1,550,000	49	Bushels:cwt.	75,950	415,112
Sorghum, Silage	185,000	13	Ton	2,405	—
Soybeans	85,000	25	Bushels	2,125	26,563
Sugarcane for sugar & seed	18,800	23	Ton	432	14,098
Sunflowers	45,000	1,361	Lb.	61,250	16,026
Wheat, Winter	2,100,000	37	Bushels	77,700	558,663
Total of Listed Crops	**16,104,400**	—	—	—	**7,747,939**

*Grapefruit, Texas 80-lb./box; Oranges, Texas 85-lb./box; Pecan production and value are utilized in-shell basis.
Source: USDA/NASS, annual crop production; annual crop values.

cwt., the crop was valued at $16 million. In 2022, 44,000 of the 52,000 acres planted to sunflowers were harvested with an average yield of 1,359 pounds per acre. Total production of 59.8 million pounds was valued at $16.1 million, or $27.00 per cwt.

Reasons for growing sunflowers include the need for an additional cash crop with low water and plant nutrient requirements, the development of sunflower hybrids, and interest by food processors in Texas sunflower oil which has high oleic acid content. Commercial users have found many advantages in this high oleic oil, including excellent cooking stability particularly for use as a deep-frying medium for potato chips, corn chips, and similar products.

Sunflower meal is a high-quality protein source free of nutritional toxins that can be included in rations for swine, poultry, and ruminants. The hulls constitute a source of roughage, which can also be included in livestock rations.

Nursery Crops

The trend to increase production of nursery crops continues to rise as transportation costs on long-distance hauling increases. This has resulted in a marked increase in the production of container-grown plants within the state. This increase is noted especially in the production of bedding plants, foliage plants, sod, and the woody landscape plants.

Plant rental services have become a multimillion-dollar business. This relatively new service provides the plants and maintains them in office buildings, shopping malls, public buildings, and even in some homes for a fee. The response has been good as evidenced by the growth of companies providing these services.

The interest in plants for interior landscapes is confined to no specific age group as both retail nurseries and florist shops report that people of all ages are buying their plants — from the elderly in retirement homes to high school and college students in dormitory rooms and apartments.

Texas Vegetable Production (2023)				
Crop	Harvested Acres	Yield Per Acre Cwt.	Production Cwt. (thousands)	Value (thousands)
Cabbage	4,400	180	792	$25,898
Cucumbers	4,800	120	576	10,298
Onions	9,000	280	2,520	85,680
Potatoes	14,600	460	6,176	104,770
Watermelons	18,800	230	4,324	66,889
Total	**51,600**	**1,270**	**14,388**	**$293,535**

Numbers may not add due to rounding.
Source: USDA/NASS, Annual Vegetable Summary, February 2025; "2023 State Agriculture Overview, Texas."

LIVESTOCK AND ANIMAL PRODUCTS

Livestock and animal products accounted for about 74.56% of Texas' agricultural cash receipts in 2023. The state ranks first nationally in all cattle, beef cattle, cattle on feed, sheep and lambs, and goats. Sales of livestock and animal products in 2023 totaled $22.3 billion, slightly up from $22.2 billion in 2022.

Cattle and calves dominate livestock production in Texas, contributing around 60.1% of cash receipts from livestock and animal products. The January 1, 2024 inventory of beef cattle and calves in Texas totaled 12 million head, valued at $16 billion, compared to 12.5 million as of January 1, 2023, which was valued at $13.9 billion.

Beef Cattle

Raising beef cattle is the most extensive agricultural operation in Texas. In 2023, cattle and calves were 44.8% of total cash receipts — $13.4 million of $29.9 million, compared with $11.6 million of $30.6 million in 2022 (37.7%).

Nearly all of the 254 counties in Texas derive more revenue from cattle than from any other agricultural commodity. The number of beef cattle and calves in Texas on January 1, 2024 totaled 12 million, compared with 12.5 million on January 1, 2023.

Calves born on Texas farms and ranches on January 1, 2023 totaled 4.3 million, compared with 4.6 million in 2022.

Dairy Product Manufacturing

The major dairy products manufactured in Texas include condensed, evaporated and dry milk, creamer, butter, and cheese. However, specifics of production and value are not available because of the small number of manufacturing plants producing these products.

Dairying

All cows' milk sold by Texas dairy farmers is marketed under the terms of Federal Marketing Orders. Most Texas dairy farmers join milk marketing cooperatives for resources and aid with processing and distribution.

Texas dairy farmers received an average price for milk of $20.30 per hundred pounds in 2023 and $25.60 in 2022. A total of 16.54 billion pounds of milk was sold to plants and dealers in 2023, bringing in cash receipts from milk to dairy farmers of $3.4 billion. This compared with 16.51 billion pounds sold in 2022 that brought in $4.2 billion in cash receipts.

UNSPLASH/ALEX HUDSON

UNSPLASH/CHRISTIN HUME

The annual average number of milk cows in Texas was 635,000 head as of January 1, 2024 inventory. This compared with 650,000 head as of January 1, 2023. Average milk production per cow in the state has increased steadily over the past several decades. The average milk production per cow in 2023 was 25,802 pounds. Milk per cow in 2022 was 25,590 pounds. Total milk production in Texas was 16.57 billion pounds in 2023 and 16.53 billion pounds in 2022. There were 479 farms reporting milk cows in Texas in 2022, as compared to the last time the number was reported in 2017, at 467.

Swine

Texas had 1.1 million head of swine on hand in December 2023. Although the number of farms producing hogs has steadily decreased, the size of production units has increased substantially. There is favorable potential for increased production.

In 2023, 615 million head of hogs were marketed in Texas, producing 597.7 million pounds of pork valued at $362.5 million. In 2022, 455.9 million head of hogs were marketed, producing 450.2 million pounds of pork valued at $338.7 million.

Goats and Mohair

All goats in Texas numbered 786,000 on January 1, 2024. This compares with 812,000 on January 1, 2023. Though data for the all-goat inventory is limited, the goat herd consists of Angora goats for mohair production. Angora goats totaled 60,000 as of January 1, 2024 and 59,000 as of 2023.

Mohair production during 2024 totaled 325,000 pounds. This compares with 329,000 in 2022. Average price per pound in 2024 was $8.90 from 56,000 goats clipped for a total value of $2.9 million. In 2023, producers received $8.60 per pound from 58,000 goats clipped for a total value of $2.8 million.

Sheep and Wool

Most sheep and lambs in Texas are concentrated in the Edwards Plateau area of West Central Texas and nearby counties. San Angelo has long been the largest sheep and wool market in the state and the center for wool and mohair warehouses, scouring plants, and slaughterhouses.

Sheep and lambs in Texas numbered 655,000 head on January 1, 2024, compared to 680,000 as of 2023. All sheep were valued at $144.1 million on January 1, 2024, compared with $146.9 million as of January 1, 2023.

Texas wool production in 2023 was 1.3 million pounds from 205,000 sheep. The value totaled $2.4 million, or $1.9 per pound. This compared with 1.6 million pounds of wool from 240,000 sheep valued at $2.6 million, or $1.7 per pound, in 2022.

Poultry and Eggs

Texas ranked fifth among the states in 2023 for cash receipts for poultry and eggs at a value of $4.6 million. The value was $5.5 billion in 2022.

Production for eggs came out to 6.4 million in 2023 and 6.6 million in 2022. Broiler production in 2023 totaled 708.6 million birds, compared with 723.3 million in 2022.

Horses

Nationally, Texas ranks as one of the leading states in horse numbers and is the headquarters for many national horse organizations. The largest single breed registry in America, the American Quarter Horse Association, has its headquarters in Amarillo. The National Cutting Horse Association and the American Paint Horse Association are both located in Fort Worth. In addition to these national associations, Texas also has active state associations that include Palominos, Arabians, Thoroughbreds, Appaloosas, and ponies.

Horses support the state's giant beef cattle and sheep industries. However, the largest horse numbers within the state are near urban and suburban areas such as the Denton and Dallas counties where they are mostly used for recreation activities. Horses are most abundant in the heavily populated areas of the state. State participation activities consist of horse shows, trail rides, play days, rodeos, polo, and horse racing. Residential subdivisions have been developed within the state to provide facilities for urban and suburban horse owners.

Hog Production

Year	Production (thousand lbs.)	Gross Income (thousands)
2023	597,747	$362,451
2022	450,161	338,748
2021	520,917	360,643
2020	505,317	222,635
2019	507,235	251,040
2018	500,566	251,220
2017	366,121	197,572
2016	365,980	191,892
2015	376,691	224,328
2014	305,146	248,928
2013	285,822	240,322
2012	414,904	288,652
2011	168,718	153,517
2010	149,934	96,676
2009	286,069	135,077
2008	328,356	143,249
2007	273,213	95,581
2006	257,644	108,844
2005	223,375	105,989
2004	202,199	90,349
2003	197,876	67,998
2002	224,441	67,255
2001	260,875	105,217
2000	328,732	115,105
1999	274,572	71,604
1998	271,444	86,349
1997	224,131	103,050
1996	204,476	94,962
1995	221,323	81,509
1994	224,397	78,394
1993	221,230	90,571
1992	217,554	79,436
1991	207,023	97,398
1990	196,225	92,222
1989	224,229	93,178
1988	236,658	100,029
1987	216,834	103,983

NA = Not Available

Source: Texas Ag Facts (various years); USDA/NASS Quick Stats. Numbers from previous years revised.

Cattle Production (Including Calves)

Year	Production (thousand lbs.)	Gross Income (thousands)
2024	6,165,812	$13,662,965
2023	6,151,115	13,403,962
2022	6,648,586	11,580,962
2021	6,684,582	10,072,700
2020	6,857,409	8,809,992
2019	6,161,133	8,485,709
2018	6,408,238	8,490,741
2017	6,302,869	8,925,006
2016	6,110,726	8,492,249
2015	6,298,675	11,492,018
2014	5,961,807	10,972,826
2013	6,147,073	10,121,953
2012	6,219,102	9,908,567
2011	7,156,677	11,076,097
2010	6,787,918	7,669,846
2009	6,923,911	6,957,343
2008	7,279,997	7,250,479
2007	6,728,348	7,651,492,
2006	6,694,200	7,347,861
2005	6,943,084	7,364,037
2004	7,412,986	8,062,320
2003	7,749,611	7,890,683
2002	7,183,427	5,878,422
2001	7,734,268	6,829,784
2000	7,469,430	6,831,902
1999	7,416,721	6,138,673
1998	7,442,737	5,788,528
1997	7,005,489	5,898,731
1996	7,027,586	5,246,456
1995	7,836,079	6,274,014
1994	7,045,620	5,859,022
1993	6,762,836	6,200,720
1992	6,391,150	5,663,799
1991	6,541,175	6,056,299
1990	5,891,200	5,878,658
1989	5,580,450	5,081,917
1988	5,711,800	5,166,656

NA = Not Available

Source: January 31, 2025; NASS Quick Stats.

Goats and Mohair Production

Year	Goats		Angora Goats		Mohair	
	Number	Farm Value	Number	Value	Production (lbs.)	Value
2024	786,000	NA	60,000	$9,000,000	325,000	$2,893,000
2023	812,000	NA	59,000	8,260,000	329,000	2,829,000
2022	839,000	NA	59,000	8,260,000	315,000	2,835,000
2021	837,000	NA	65,000	7,800,000	335,000	2,580,000
2020	869,000	NA	75,000	10,500,000	370,000	2,664,000
2019	842,000	NA	75,000	10,500,000	470,000	3,760,000
2018	869,000	NA	75,000	9,750,000	465,000	3,348,000
2017	866,000	NA	80,000	12,000,000	470,000	3,102,000
2016	847,000	NA	78,000	10,140,000	510,000	3,060,000
2015	906,000	NA	83,000	12,035,000	480,000	3,408,000
2014	906,000	NA	76,000	9,196,000	535,000	3,371,000
2013	872,000	NA	74,000	9,028,000	490,000	2,695,000
2012	905,000	NA	85,000	7,565,000	470,000	2,256,000
2011	980,000	NA	110,000	11,000,000	530,000	2,703,000
2010	1,020,000	$108,290,000	100,000	7,500,000	730,000	3,066,000
2009	1,090,000	129,920,000	120,000	10,080,000	700,000	2,170,000
2008	1,185,000	120,870,000	134,000	11,250,000	820,000	3,116,000
2007	1,272,000	147,552,000	159,000	14,220,000	960,000	3,840,000
2006	1,284,000	137,388,000	178,000	15,200,000	1,100,000	4,400,000
2005	1,250,000	138,430,000	190,000	14,070,000	1,250,000	3,750,000
2004	1,200,000	115,200,000	210,000	13,860,000	1,620,000	3,402,000
2003	1,200,000	110,400,000	240,000	NA	1,680,000	2,856,000
2002	1,250,000	106,250,000	250,000	NA	1,944,000	3,110,400
2001	1,400,000	105,000,000	300,000	NA	1,716,000	3,775,000
2000	1,300,000	74,100,000	370,000	NA	2,346,000	10,088,000
1999	1,350,000	71,550,000	550,000	NA	2,550,000	9,384,000
1998	1,400,000	71,400,000	750,000	NA	4,650,000	12,044,000
1997	1,650,000	70,950,000	1,000,000	NA	6,384,000	14,556,000
1996	1,900,000	89,300,000	1,250,000	NA	7,490,000	14,606,000
1995	1,850,000	81,400,000	1,250,000	NA	11,319,000	20,940,000
1994	1,960,000	74,480,000	1,490,000	NA	11,680,000	30,602,000
1993	1,960,000	84,280,000	1,560,000	NA	13,490,000	11,197,000
1992	2,000,000	84,000,000	1,620,000	NA	14,200,000	12,354,000
1991	1,830,000	73,200,000	NA	NA	14,800,000	19,388,000
1990	1,900,000	93,100,000	NA	NA	14,500,000	13,775,000
1989	1,850,000	100,270,000	NA	NA	15,400,000	24,794,000
1988	1,800,000	108,180,000	NA	NA	15,400,000	29,876,000
1987	1,780,000	82,592,000	NA	NA	16,200,000	42,606,000
1986	1,770,000	70,977,000	NA	NA	16,000,000	40,160,000
1985	1,590,000	76,797,000	NA	NA	13,300,000	45,885,000
1984	1,450,000	82,215,000	NA	NA	10,600,000	48,160,000
1983	1,420,000	53,250,000	NA	NA	10,600,000	42,930,000
1982	1,410,000	57,810,000	NA	NA	10,000,000	25,500,000
1981	1,380,000	53,130,000	NA	NA	10,100,000	35,350,000

NA = Not Available

Sources: "1985 Texas Livestock, Dairy and Poultry Statistics," USDA Bulletin 235, June 1986. Texas Ag Facts (various years). USDA/TASS Texas Goat and Mohair, January 31, 2025; NASS Quick Stats.

Sheep and Wool Production

Year	Sheep		Wool	
	Number	Value	Production (lbs.)	Value
2024	655,000	$144,100,000	1,200,000	$2,340,000
2023	680,000	146,880,000	1,250,000	2,375,000
2022	700,000	137,900,000	1,550,000	2,635,000
2021	730,000	132,860,000	1,400,000	3,220,000
2020	735,000	134,505,000	1,530,000	2,754,000
2019	750,000	135,750,000	1,690,000	3,211,000
2018	750,000	138,750,000	1,750,000	3,150,000
2017	710,000	129,220,000	1,800,000	2,934,000
2016	725,000	131,950,000	1,800,000	3,150,000
2015	720,000	126,000,000	1,950,000	3,198,000
2014	730,000	118,990,000	2,100,000	3,297,000
2013	680,000	96,560,000	2,300,000	4,048,000
2012	670,000	102,510,000	2,100,000	3,507,000
2011	850,000	109,650,000	2,600,000	5,746,000
2010	830,000	83,000,000	3,450,000	5,451,000
2009	870,000	87,870,000	3,500,000	3,640,000
2008	960,000	97,920,000	4,200,000	4,872,000
2007	1,050,000	111,300,000	4,500,000	5,445,000
2006	1,070,000	121,980,000	4,900,000	4,459,000
2005	1,070,000	112,350,000	5,550,000	5,328,000
2004	1,090,000	104,640,000	5,600,000	5,712,000
2003	1,040,000	82,160,000	5,600,000	5,040,000
2002	1,130,000	88,140,000	5,950,000	4,046,000
2001	1,150,000	92,000,000	6,003,000	3,122,000
2000	1,200,000	94,800,000	7,506,000	3,678,000
1999	1,350,000	95,850,000	7,956,000	3,898,000
1998	1,530,000	122,400,000	9,230,000	5,815,000
1997	1,400,000	100,800,000	10,950,000	11,607,000
1996	1,650,000	108,900,000	9,900,000	8,316,000
1995	1,700,000	100,300,000	13,468,000	15,488,000
1994	1,895,000	106,120,000	14,840,000	15,582,000
1993	2,040,000	118,320,000	17,000,000	11,050,000
1992	2,140,000	111,280,000	17,600,000	16,896,000
1991	2,000,000	108,000,000	16,700,000	13,861,000
1990	2,090,000	133,760,000	17,400,000	19,662,000
1989	1,870,000	133,445,000	18,000,000	27,180,000
1988	2,040,000	155,040,000	18,200,000	27,482,000
1987	2,050,000	133,250,000	16,400,000	19,844,000
1986	1,850,000	107,300,000	16,400,000	13,284,000
1985	1,930,000	110,975,000	16,200,000	13,284,000
1984	1,970,000	76,830,000	17,500,000	16,100,000
1983	2,225,000	86,775,000	18,600,000	15,438,000
1982	2,400,000	100,800,000	19,300,000	16,212,000
1981	2,360,000	116,820,000	20,500,000	24,600,000
1980	2,400,000	138,000,000	18,300,000	17,751,000
1979	2,415,000	152,145,000	19,075,000	18,503,000

NA = Not Available *Source: Texas Ag Facts (various years); Texas Sheep and Wool report, January 31, 2025; NASS/TASS Quick Stats.*

UNSPLASH/ROD LONG

UNSPLASH/HEATHER NEWSOME

Texas

WEATHER

UNSPLASH / NIKOLAS NOONAN

TEXAS WEATHER TRENDS

TEMPERATURE: Over the past several decades, temperatures in Texas have generally increased by about half a degree Fahrenheit per decade. Temperature increases are larger within major metropolitan areas due to the growth of the urban heat island. Similar trends are expected to continue for the next several decades. Heat extremes will generally become more frequent and intense, while cold extremes will generally become less frequent and intense.

PRECIPITATION: Over the past century, rainfall in Texas has increased by about 1-2% per decade in central and eastern Texas, while it has remained flat or declined slightly in western Texas. In addition to that long-term trend, there is considerable variability from year to year and decade to decade due to El Niño and other factors. The natural variability is expected to overwhelm and obscure any long-term trends over the next several decades.

SEVERE THUNDERSTORMS AND TORNADOES: Due to variations in data quality over the years, long-term trends in severe thunderstorms and tornadoes are unclear, and future prospects are likewise not well known.

FLOODING: Flooding involves a combination of extreme precipitation, flood control measures, and land surface characteristics. Extreme precipitation in general is increasing across Texas and the rest of the central and eastern United States. The most likely increase in flooding is within urban areas where runoff is rapid and it is difficult to install additional flood control measures.

DROUGHT: As with precipitation, interannual and decadal variability plays a major role. On top of that, rising temperatures will make evaporation more rapid, meaning that droughts will tend to develop more rapidly and have greater impacts under a given set of circumstances.

HURRICANES: The total number of hurricanes is primarily affected by natural variability. The maximum possible intensity of hurricanes is probably increasing, and due to sea level rise, the potential for large storm surges is also increasing. Finally, intense rainfall is probably becoming stronger with hurricanes as it is with other rainfall-producing systems.

UNSPLASH/REMI JACQUAINT

Sources: Unless otherwise noted, this information is provided by Texas A&M University graduate research assistants Victoria Elliott Ford, William Baule, and Alison Tarter, and Texas State Climatologist John W. Nielsen-Gammon (Office of the State Climatologist). EF Scale and Saffir-Simpson Hurricane Wind Scale supplied by the National Weather Service.

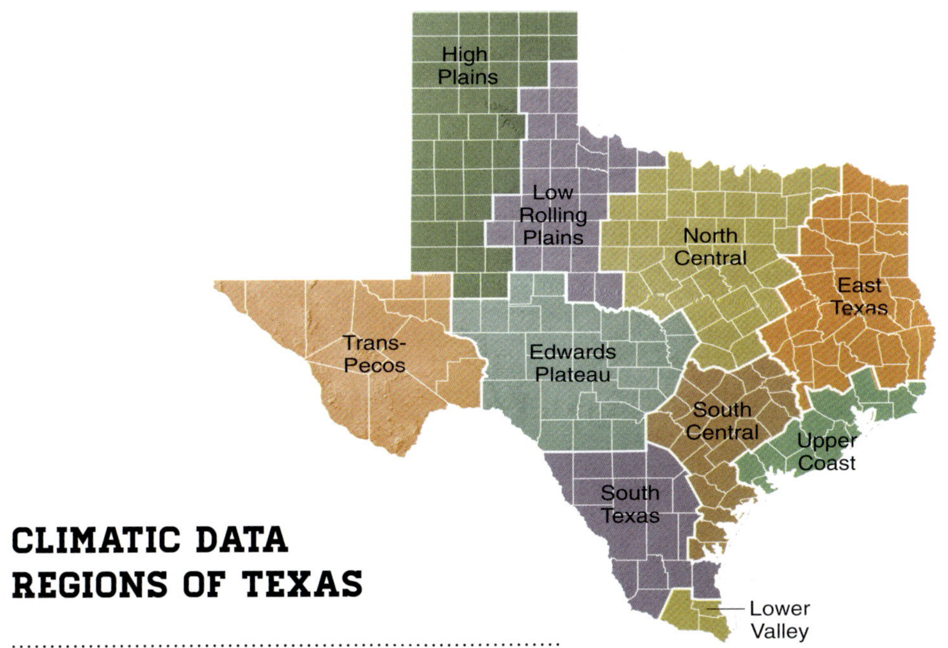

CLIMATIC DATA REGIONS OF TEXAS

Enhanced Fujita Scale: Tornado Strength	
EF Rating	3-Second Gust
0	65–85
1	86–110
2	111–135
3	136–165
4	166–200
5	Over 200

Saffir-Simpson Hurricane Wind Scale	
Category	Sustained Winds
1	86–110
2	111–135
3 (Major)	136–165
4 (Major)	166–200
5 (Major)	Over 200

2023 WEATHER SUMMARY

	Average Temperatures (2023)										Precipitation in Inches (2023)									
	High Plains	Low Plains	North Central	East Texas	Trans-Pecos	Edwards Plateau	South Central	Upper Coast	South Texas	Lower Valley	High Plains	Low Plains	North Central	East Texas	Trans-Pecos	Edwards Plateau	South Central	Upper Coast	South Texas	Lower Valley
Jan.	42	47.6	50.6	53.4	49.6	52.4	57.8	59.4	61.6	67.1	0.34	0.65	1.23	4.9	0.14	0.46	2.06	3.13	0.39	0.12
Feb.	43.3	47.1	50.5	55.2	49.9	52	58.6	60.6	62.1	66.5	0.26	0.84	2.76	3.5	0.31	0.54	1.23	3.6	0.27	0.13
Mar.	51	55.3	59.3	61.7	58.4	62.2	67.3	67.4	71.3	74.1	0.14	0.8	2.7	3.3	0.38	0.71	1.29	4.35	1.03	1.94
April	57.9	61.8	63.3	64.2	64.5	66.7	69	69.3	72.4	74.5	0.71	1.13	2.62	6.76	0.02	1.09	6.24	3.27	3.36	3.64
May	68.8	72.6	73.2	73.5	73.3	74.8	76.8	77.1	78.8	80.7	5.09	5.36	4.39	4.21	1.18	4.71	5.46	0.3	3.97	4.92
June	75.9	80.3	82.1	81.5	83.4	84.5	85.4	84.1	87.8	87.4	3.1	2.6	2.4	3.51	0.6	1.25	1.16	1.81	0.68	1.02
July	82	85.9	87.1	85.7	86.4	87.1	88.4	87.1	89.3	88.4	2.4	2.43	1.35	1.61	0.37	0.6	0.5	2.04	0.53	1.01
Aug.	82.4	88	90	88.9	84.6	88.2	90	89.1	89.6	89.2	0.95	0.46	0.34	0.61	1.68	0.68	0.88	5.53	2.49	1.11
Sep.	76.1	80.8	82.6	81	81	82.7	86.1	84.7	86.6	87.4	2.03	2.56	2.42	3.17	0.78	2.67	1.41	5.85	1.15	0.97
Oct.	61.9	66	67.8	68.4	67.9	69.2	73.2	72.6	75.2	77.4	1.8	3.76	7.4	5.22	1.19	3.55	4.17	1.49	2.53	1.97
Nov.	50.5	54.1	56.2	56.7	55.3	56.7	61.2	61.3	62.8	65.8	0.28	0.21	0.68	2.01	0.86	1.02	2.07	1.18	2.45	4.29
Dec.	44.3	48.6	51.2	51.7	50.4	52.6	57.9	58	60.3	64.4	1.82	2.58	2.62	2.81	0.19	1.31	1.17	4.31	0.73	0.81
Ann.	61.3	65.7	67.8	68.5	67.1	69.1	72.6	72.6	74.8	76.9	18.92	23.38	30.91	41.61	7.70	18.59	27.64	36.86	19.58	21.93

SIGNIFICANT AND DESTRUCTIVE WEATHER IN 2023

January 24, 2023: Tornadoes; Upper Coast
An upper-level atmospheric disturbance led to a small tornado outbreak in the upper coastal region. Eight tornadoes touched down: three EF-0s, two EF-1s, two EF-2s, and one EF-3. The whole event resulted in only two people being injured and about $8 million in damages.

January 30-February 2, 2023: Ice Storm; Statewide
An Arctic cold front swept across the state, triggering widespread winter weather and extreme cold. Freezing rain and sleet coated surfaces with ice, including roads, power lines, and trees. This led to hazardous travel conditions, widespread power outages, and extensive property damage. In total, there were seven fatalities, 45 injuries, and an estimated $87 million in economic losses.

June 12-15, 2023: Tornadoes, Strong Wind, and Hail; Statewide
A meandering low-pressure system triggered several days of severe storms across the state. Seven tornadoes touched down, including an EF-3 in Ochiltree County that killed three people and injured 100 others during its 1.5-mile trek. The multi-day event also included one EF-Unknown, two EF-0s, one EF-1, and two EF-2s. In addition to tornadoes, the state experienced destructive straight-line winds with gusts up to 90 mph and hail up to 5.9 inches in diameter (a record size for North Texas). Damages totaled over $18 million.

June 21-23, 2023: Tornado; Statewide
A slow-moving frontal boundary resulted in severe storms for a few days across the state. The worst of the storms produced an EF-3 tornado in Motley County that reached a third of a mile wide in size and was responsible for four deaths and 15 injuries. This same supercell also dropped hail as large as 4.5 inches. The multi-day event also included five EF-Unknowns, one EF-1, and straight-line winds as strong as 109 mph. There was an economic loss of $55 million.

August 22, 2023: Tropical Storm; South Texas and Lower Valley
Tropical Storm Harold made landfall near South Padre Island with winds around 50 mph and 1-3 feet of storm surge along the coast. The cyclone brought much-needed rain to the southern part of the state with totals up to seven inches in some places. More than 35,000 people in the region lost power, two EF-0 tornadoes spawned, and there was an economic loss of around $500,000.

September 24, 2023: Hail; Statewide
A cold front advancing across the state was responsible for widespread thunderstorms producing severe hail. Travis and Williamson Counties experienced the largest hailstones with sizes up to 4.0 inches. The swath across just these two counties resulted in $700 million in damages, and the whole storm complex across the state totaled up to $1.3 billion in damages.

WEATHER EXTREMES

Lowest Temperature
Canyon, Randall Co., February 1 . . . . –2°

Highest Temperature
Rio Grande Village, Brewster Co., June 24 . . . . .119°

24-Hour Precipitation
Ferris, Ellis Co., October 27 . . . . 11.28"

Monthly Precipitation
Rosser, Kaufman Co., October. . . . . 18.76"

Least Annual Precipitation
Anthony 1.0 ENE, El Paso Co.. . . . . 2.67"

Greatest Annual Precipitation
Nacogdoches Arbor Oaks, Nacogdoches Co. . . . . .61.10"

Days Warming to 100° or Higher (2023)

City	Number of Days
Houston	45
San Antonio	75
Dallas/Fort Worth	55
Austin	80
El Paso	70
Corpus Christi	42
Lubbock	46
Laredo	104
Amarillo	26
Brownsville	40

Days Cooling to 32° or Lower (2023)

City	Number of Days
Houston	0
San Antonio	5
Dallas/Fort Worth	14
Austin	8
El Paso	30
Corpus Christi	1
Lubbock	70
Laredo	0
Amarillo	89
Brownsville	0

UNSPLASH/ANNIE SPRATT

2024 WEATHER SUMMARY

	Average Temperatures (2024)										Precipitation in Inches (2024)									
	High Plains	Low Plains	North Central	East Texas	Trans-Pecos	Edwards Plateau	South Central	Upper Coast	South Texas	Lower Valley	High Plains	Low Plains	North Central	East Texas	Trans-Pecos	Edwards Plateau	South Central	Upper Coast	South Texas	Lower Valley
Jan.	36.1	39.2	41.7	44.3	45.4	44.6	50.2	51.3	53.5	59.2	0.7	1.55	0.33	9.03	0.2	0.86	6.11	8.85	1.97	1.71
Feb.	48	53.1	56.1	57.4	54.3	57.1	61.1	61.4	64.6	66.8	0.49	1.07	1.71	3.09	0.48	0.97	1.87	2.49	1.06	0.55
Mar.	52.6	56.6	60.2	61.1	58.2	61.8	66.1	66.2	69.3	72	0.43	1.27	1.68	4.67	0.13	1.08	2.01	3.28	1.12	2.06
April	60.7	64.7	67	68.2	66.7	69.8	72.5	72	76	77.3	1.27	2.5	2.72	9.04	0.1	1.32	2.42	3.68	1.01	6.29
May	70.2	74	75.4	75.9	77.7	79.2	80.9	79.6	84.7	86.3	1.94	4.57	3.44	10.96	0.31	3.54	3.29	7.54	1.91	0.81
June	80.6	83	82.4	81	84.7	84.1	84.9	83.5	87	87.5	2.78	2.82	1.62	4.37	0.62	1.76	4.09	5.18	4.18	5.73
July	80.5	83.8	83.3	81.5	82.1	83.2	84.2	83.2	85.7	85.4	2.07	1.64	0.46	8.92	1.48	3.09	5.49	12.97	2.95	4.62
Aug.	82.9	88	87.1	84.4	84.5	86.4	86.5	85.8	88.3	87.8	1.84	0.56	4.05	1.03	1.16	1.04	1.25	2.18	0.4	1.35
Sep.	73.3	76.2	77.4	77.5	75.6	76.9	82	81.1	82.8	83.8	2.15	4.02	1.18	2.69	1.33	3.16	1.69	2.86	3.17	0.42
Oct.	67.3	71.9	73.4	71.7	71.5	73.3	77.2	75.6	78.2	78.7	0.17	0.01	3.57	0.43	0.06	0.01	0.1	0.67	0.5	1.52
Nov.	51.1	56.2	60.1	62.8	58.4	61.7	68.4	68.9	70.8	74.3	3.62	5.2	3.76	5.22	0.72	1.71	1.44	3.18	0.6	1.72
Dec.	46.2	49.9	53	54.2	52.8	55.5	61	61.5	62.7	68	0.02	0.17	1.48	6.84	0	0.3	1.84	3.37	0.52	1.13
Ann.	62.5	66.4	68.1	68.3	67.7	69.5	72.9	72.5	75.3	77.3	17.48	25.38	26.00	66.29	6.59	18.84	31.60	56.25	19.39	27.91

SIGNIFICANT AND DESTRUCTIVE WEATHER IN 2024

February 26-March 16, 2024: Wildfire; High Plains and Low Rolling Plains
Downed power lines sparked a fire in Hutchinson County and rapidly grew out of control due to dry, windy conditions. This fire, referred to as the Smokehouse Creek Fire, destroyed more than 100 homes, burned over one million acres, killed thousands of livestock, and killed two people. It broke the record for the largest fire in Texas history, and economic losses exceeded $1 billion.

May 8-10, 2024: Hail; Statewide
A low-pressure system triggered numerous severe thunderstorms that hammered many portions of the state with large hail. Blanco County saw the largest hailstones with a maximum size of 6.12 inches. In total, 141 hail reports were made over the multi-day event, and property damage totaled more than $20 million.

May 25, 2024: Tornadoes; North Central
An upper-level disturbance triggered a severe weather outbreak that dropped several tornadoes in the region. Seven tornadoes touched down: four EF-1s, one EF-2, and two EF-3s. The deadliest tornado occurred in Cooke County, killing seven people and injuring over 100 others. It was estimated to be between two thirds to three quarters of a mile wide, and stayed on the ground for over 1.5 hours as a nocturnal tornado. This tornado alone resulted in about $20 million in damages.

June 1-3, 2024: Hail; Statewide
An upper-level disturbance pushed across the state and initiated many hail-producing supercells during the multi-day event. Swisher and Briscoe Counties saw the largest hailstones, with maximum estimated sizes of 7.02 inches and 6.00 inches, respectively. As of 2025, the Swisher County hailstone had yet to be confirmed as the largest recorded hailstone in Texas. Property damage as a result of hail impacts totaled around $72,000.

July 8-9, 2024: Hurricane; Upper Coast and East Texas
Hurricane Beryl made landfall as a Category 1 hurricane near Matagorda Bay with winds around 90 mph and 5-7 feet of storm surge along the coast. The cyclone was responsible for massive power outages, flooding due to heavy rains with totals up to 15 inches in some places, 16 tornadoes in Texas alone, and 11 direct and 34 indirect deaths of Texans. Fourteen of these indirect deaths were caused by overheating due to the lack of power to cool homes. In total, property damage totals were estimated to be $7.2 billion.

December 28, 2024: Tornadoes; East Texas and Upper Coast
An upper-level disturbance was responsible for initiating severe weather across these regions. Tornadoes were the primary threat with five in total: two EF-1s, one EF-2, and two EF-3s. The tornadoes were responsible for one death, 17 injuries, and an economic loss of $500,000.

WEATHER EXTREMES

Lowest Temperature
Bravo, Hartley Co., January 16 . . . . –4°

Highest Temperature
San Saba 7 NW , San Saba Co., August 23 . . . . .117°

24-hour Precipitation
Huntsville 1.3 SSE, Walker Co., May 2 . . . . .12.51"

Monthly Precipitation
Montgomery 4.0 N, Montgomery Co., May . . . . .30.99"

Least Annual Precipitation
Terlingua 6.1 NNW , Brewster Co... . . . . 1.91"

Greatest Annual Precipitation
Kountze, Hardin Co. . . . . .97.72"

Days Warming to 100° or Higher (2024)

City	Number of Days
Houston	9
San Antonio	27
Dallas/Fort Worth	23
Austin	32
El Paso	55
Corpus Christi	8
Lubbock	28
Laredo	80
Amarillo	36
Brownsville	7

Days Cooling to 32° or Lower (2024)

City	Number of Days
Houston	5
San Antonio	9
Dallas/Fort Worth	14
Austin	7
El Paso	14
Corpus Christi	3
Lubbock	48
Laredo	3
Amarillo	78
Brownsville	2

UNSPLASH/GREG JOHNSON

EXTREME WEATHER RECORDS IN TEXAS

TEMPERATURE

Lowest	-23°F	Tulia	Feb. 12, 1899
	-23°F	Seminole	Feb. 8, 1933
Highest	120°F	Seymour	Aug. 12, 1936
	120°F	Monahans	June 28, 1994
Coldest Winter	41.3°F average		1898–1899
Hottest Summer	86.8°F average		2011

WIND VELOCITY

Highest Sustained Wind		
145 mph SE	Matagorda	Sept. 11, 1961
145 mph NE	Port Lavaca	Sept. 11, 1961
Highest Peak Gust		
180 mph SW	Aransas Pass	Aug. 3, 1970
180 mph WSW	Robstown	Aug. 3, 1970

These winds occurred during Hurricane Carla in 1961 and Hurricane Celia in 1970.

RAINFALL

Wettest Year Statewide		2015	41.23 in.
Driest Year Statewide		1917	14.06 in.
Most Annual	Bridge City	2017	109.42 in.
Least Annual	Terlingua	2011	1.30 in.
Most in 24 Hours†	Alvin	July 25–26, 1979	†42.00 in.
Most in 18 Hours	Thrall	Sept. 9, 1921	36.40 in.

†Unofficial estimate of rainfall during Tropical Storm Claudette. Greatest 24-hour rainfall at an official site occurred at Albany, Shackelford County, on Aug. 4, 1978: 29.05 inches.

HAIL

Hailstones six inches or greater, since 1950		
7.02 in.	Swisher County	June 2, 2024
7.00 in.	Winkler County	May 31, 1960
6.42 in.	Medina County	*April 28, 2021
6.12 in.	Blanco County	May 9, 2024
6.00 in.	Briscoe County	June 2, 2024
6.00 in.	Medina County	April 28, 2021
6.00 in.	Moore County	June 12, 2010
6.00 in.	Ward County	May 10, 1991

*Largest documented official hailstone.

TORNADOES

Since 1950, there have been six tornadoes of the F-5 category (with winds between 261–318 mph).

Waco	McLennan County	May 11, 1953
Wichita Falls	Wichita County	April 3, 1964
Lubbock	Lubbock County	May 11, 1970
Valley Mills	McLennan County	May 6, 1973
Brownwood	Brown County	April 19, 1976
Jarrell	Williamson County	May 27, 1997

SNOWFALL

Season	65.0 in.	Romero*	1923–1924
Month	61.0 in.	Vega	Feb. 1956
Single storm	61.0 in.	Vega	Feb. 1–8, 1956
24 Hours	26.0 in.	Hillsboro	Dec. 20–21, 1929
Annual Avg.	24.2 in	Vega, Oldham County	

*Romero was in southwestern Hartley County.

Source: Office of the State Climatologist.

TEXAS DROUGHTS

Palmer Drought Severity Index										
	High Plains	Low Rolling Plains	North Central	East Texas	Trans–Pecos	Edwards Plateau	South Central	Upper Coast	South Texas	Lower Valley
FREQUENCY	40	38	40	38	43	43	41	38	42	40
1901	-2.00	-2.55	-4.58	-2.39	-2.27	-3.14	-3.84	-2.77	-3.21	-5.04
1910	-3.47	-3.89	-5.04	-3.99	-4.21	-4.49	-3.63	-2.51	-3.25	-3.43
1911	-3.69	-4.10	-5.96	-5.02	-4.02	-4.03	-4.21	-4.31	-4.39	-3.04
1917	-3.90	-4.66	-4.53	-4.90	-4.59	-4.88	-6.00	-6.03	-4.56	-3.91
1918	-3.88	-5.97	-6.12	-6.42	-3.75	-5.61	-6.13	-7.00	-4.51	-4.09
1925	-2.96	-3.26	-6.41	-6.20	-3.08	-3.95	-6.09	-5.20	-3.78	-2.51
1934	-4.66	-4.41	-4.84	-3.56	-4.88	-4.51	-2.82	-2.27	-1.54	-1.33
1935	-4.57	-3.83	-0.58	0.19	-4.68	-3.99	0.66	-0.39	0.10	-1.76
1951	-1.65	-3.36	-4.25	-3.84	-4.15	-4.67	-4.65	-4.37	-3.91	-4.10
1952	-4.23	-5.38	-5.52	-3.72	-4.28	-5.10	-4.53	-4.48	-4.45	-3.71
1953	-5.33	-5.40	-3.12	-1.27	-5.67	-4.63	-2.58	-2.21	-5.26	-4.45
1954	-4.46	-4.24	-4.29	-4.28	-4.59	-5.09	-4.87	-3.89	-3.59	-3.38
1955	-4.13	-3.77	-3.81	-3.18	-3.36	-4.79	-4.95	-3.75	-4.59	-3.60
1956	-5.62	-6.25	-6.82	-5.09	-5.47	-6.16	-6.68	-5.72	-4.78	-3.81
1957	-4.93	-5.02	-5.07	-4.92	-4.86	-5.10	-5.81	-5.64	-4.29	-4.12
1963	-2.38	-2.91	-3.95	-3.77	-2.07	-4.29	-4.80	-4.16	-3.71	-3.57
1967	-3.32	-3.42	-4.61	-3.34	-2.55	-4.11	-4.73	-2.99	-3.62	-2.44
1971	-3.33	-4.18	-4.41	-3.11	-2.80	-3.46	-5.01	-3.27	-3.68	-2.70
1974	-4.43	-4.20	-2.44	1.60	-3.44	-3.09	1.26	1.95	-1.29	-1.97
1996	-3.83	-3.58	-4.28	-3.63	-3.77	-3.88	-4.51	-2.59	-3.64	-3.04
2000	-3.87	-3.97	-3.76	-4.35	-4.93	-4.78	-4.39	-5.17	-4.12	-3.73
2006	-4.56	-4.80	-4.93	-4.16	-3.72	-4.14	-5.23	-4.32	-4.72	-4.77
2009	-2.24	-2.97	-3.88	-2.43	-2.35	-3.82	-6.36	-4.23	-5.19	-4.09
2010	-1.13	-1.20	-1.27	-3.67	-2.08	-2.02	-1.49	-1.19	-1.59	-1.68
2011	-6.98	-7.00	-5.99	-6.86	-6.52	-6.39	-6.21	-5.70	-5.45	-4.87
2012	-5.12	-4.75	-3.70	-4.36	-4.93	-3.74	-4.37	-4.72	-4.17	-4.69
2013	-4.15	-4.26	-3.43	-2.94	-3.03	-3.40	-4.47	-3.48	-4.33	-4.94
2014	-3.45	-3.29	-2.56	-1.34	-2.85	-2.93	-3.29	-2.49	-2.72	-1.23
2015	0.69	0.39	0.38	0.84	1.74	0.33	0.41	-0.59	-1.14	-0.56
2016	1.30	2.57	2.85	-2.04	-1.15	1.98	-0.47	-1.63	-1.50	-2.86
2017	-1.15	-1.43	-1.31	-2.40	-1.82	-1.47	-1.72	0.59	-1.97	-3.72
2018	-3.84	-4.33	-3.30	-2.15	-3.18	-3.69	-2.23	0.79	-2.72	-4.14
2020	-3.57	-0.58	1.41	1.63	-4.94	-3.15	-3.70	-0.40	-3.08	-3.36
2021	-3.44	-2.54	-2.16	-2.04	-4.05	-2.64	-3.95	-1.10	-3.50	-2.70
2022	-5.23	-5.53	-6.01	-3.77	-4.61	-5.93	-4.66	-3.71	-4.39	-2.00
2023	-4.48	-3.63	-3.68	-2.85	-4.85	-5.14	-4.13	-3.54	-3.58	-2.61
2024	-3.77	-2.49			-6.08	-4.41	-3.64	-2.09	-3.73	
PDSI Table Indicators	Moderate drought, PDSI between –2 and –4			Severe drought, PDSI between –4 and –6			Extreme drought, PDSI below –6			

Source: Office of the State Climatologist.

TORNADOES IN TEXAS

Texas Tornadoes by Year and Month													
Year	Jan.	Feb.	March	April	May	June	July	Aug.	Sept.	Oct.	Nov.	Dec.	TOTAL
2024	1	1	8	26	60	13	24	1	1	0	3	12	150
2023	8	2	11	11	13	25	1	4	2	6	0	0	83
2022	6	0	53	10	32	0	1	5	0	2	11	21	141
2021	1	0	32	11	43	5	1	2	0	5	2	1	103
2020	14	0	18	17	24	3	8	2	1	0	2	3	92
2019	0	0	12	39	104	13	1	0	2	13	0	0	184
2018	5	0	9	4	6	3	3	2	1	22	1	2	58
2017	22	17	36	29	43	3	3	25	1	1	0	3	183
2016	0	1	14	33	43	4	1	1	5	0	0	0	102
2015	0	0	0	48	130	3	0	0	2	20	23	22	248
2014	0	0	0	6	15	15	5	0	0	2	0	3	46
2013	1	16	0	8	41	3	0	6	0	6	0	3	84
2012	22	3	9	36	31	3	0	1	2	3	0	5	115
2011	1	1	3	57	20	6	1	4	1	2	8	0	104
2010	10	0	0	19	34	23	3	1	12	10	0	0	112
2009	0	5	4	48	18	32	2	4	1	4	1	12	131
2008	0	3	15	48	33	9	5	1	2	3	1	3	123
2007	2	1	56	61	43	21	8	4	14	2	1	3	216
2006	0	1	4	20	43	7	3	3	0	9	0	27	117
2005	0	0	6	7	27	46	15	4	2	0	0	2	109
2004	1	1	27	25	29	34	1	5	0	4	55	2	184
2003	0	0	4	31	50	29	6	1	4	12	29	0	166
2002	0	0	44	25	61	5	1	4	13	8	0	22	183
2001	0	0	4	12	36	12	0	7	15	24	27	5	142
2000	0	7	49	33	23	8	3	0	0	10	20	1	154
1999	22	0	22	23	70	26	3	8	0	0	0	4	178
1998	24	15	4	9	11	6	3	5	3	28	1	0	109
1997	0	6	7	31	59	50	2	2	1	16	3	0	177
1996	7	1	2	21	33	9	3	8	33	8	4	1	130
1995	6	0	13	36	66	75	11	3	2	1	0	10	223
1994	0	1	1	48	88	2	1	4	3	9	8	0	165
1993	1	4	5	17	39	4	4	0	12	23	8	0	117
1992	0	5	13	22	43	66	4	4	4	7	21	0	189
1991	20	5	2	39	72	36	1	2	3	8	4	0	192
1990	3	3	4	56	62	20	5	2	3	0	0	0	158
1989	3	0	5	3	70	63	0	6	3	6	1	0	160
1988	0	0	0	11	7	7	6	2	42	4	10	0	89
1987	1	1	7	0	54	19	11	3	8	0	16	4	124
1986	0	12	4	21	50	24	3	5	4	7	1	0	131
1985	0	0	5	41	28	5	3	1	1	3	1	2	90
1984	0	13	9	18	19	19	0	4	1	5	2	5	95
1983	5	7	24	1	62	35	4	22	5	0	7	14	186
1982	0	0	6	27	123	36	4	0	3	0	3	1	203
1981	0	7	7	9	71	26	5	20	5	23	3	0	176
1980	0	2	7	26	44	21	2	34	10	5	0	2	153
1979	1	2	24	33	39	14	12	10	4	15	3	0	157
1978	0	0	0	34	65	10	13	6	6	1	2	0	137
1977	0	0	3	34	50	4	5	5	12	0	6	4	123
1976	1	1	8	53	63	11	16	6	13	4	0	0	176
1975	5	2	9	12	50	18	10	3	3	3	1	1	117
1974	2	1	8	19	18	26	3	9	6	22	2	0	116
1973	14	1	29	25	21	24	4	8	5	3	9	4	147
1972	1	0	19	13	43	12	19	13	8	9	7	0	144
1971	0	20	10	24	27	33	7	20	7	16	4	23	191
1970	1	3	5	23	23	9	5	20	9	20	0	3	121
1969	0	1	1	16	65	16	6	7	6	8	1	0	127
1968	2	1	3	13	47	21	4	8	5	8	11	16	139
1967	0	2	11	17	34	22	10	5	124	2	0	5	232
1966	0	4	1	21	22	15	3	8	3	0	0	0	77
1951-65	8	22	100	204	328	252	79	70	48	51	41	11	1,214
Total	221	197	795	1,643	2,946	1,346	364	412	483	483	364	262	9,516
Average	3	3	11	23	40	18	5	6	7	7	5	4	130
Max	24	20	56	69	130	75	24	34	124	28	55	27	248

Source: Office of the State Climatologist.

TEXAS CLIMATOLOGICAL NORMALS AND EXTREME WEATHER RECORDS BY COUNTY

The Climatological Normals include Mean Maximum July Temperature, Mean Minimum January Temperature, Average Freeze Dates, Growing Season, and Mean Precipitation. They are calculated every 10 years and are based on the previous 30-year period, which is 1991–2020.

Data for counties where a weather station has not been maintained long enough to establish a reliable mean are interpolated from isoline charts prepared from mean values from stations with long-established records.

Mean Maximum for July is computed from the sum of the daily maxima. Mean Minimum for January is computed from the sum of the daily minima.

Extreme Weather Records include Record High Temperature, Record Low Temperature, and Record Rainfall; they are compiled yearly and are current through 2024.

The far left column lists Texas' 254 counties and identifies the town or landmark nearest to the National Weather Service station used to calculate Climatological Normals. Extreme Weather Records may have occurred at any weather station in that county and are identified only for Record Rainfall.

An asterisk (*) preceding an Extreme Weather Record means it also occurred on a previous date.

Sources: Texas A&M University graduate research assistants Victoria Elliott Ford, William Baule, and Alison Tarter, and Texas State Climatologist John W. Nielsen-Gammon.

County, Town or Landmark Closest to Station for Normals	Temperature								Average Freeze Dates			
	Mean Max. July	No. at or Above 100°	Mean Min. January	No. at or Below 32°	Record Highest	Record High Date	Record Lowest	Record Low Date	Last in Spring		First in Fall	
	F.	Days	F.	Days	F.	M-D-Y	F.	M-D-Y	Mo.	Day	Mo.	Day
Anderson, Palestine	92.8	8	36.9	38	114	7-26-1954	–6	2-12-1899	Mar.	23	Nov.	9
Andrews, Andrews	95.2	20	33.0	59	113	6-27-1994	–1	2-2-1985	Mar.	18	Nov.	14
Angelina, County Airport	92.4	9	39.4	28	*111	8-27-2023	–2	2-2-1951	Mar.	11	Nov.	15
Aransas, Rockport	91.6	1	48.3	4	107	9-5-2000	9	12-23-1989	Jan.	31	Dec.	25
Archer, Archer City	95.5	29	32.6	57	114	6-28-1980	*–10	12-23-1989	Mar.	25	Nov.	10
Armstrong, Claude	91.2	9	26.0	108	*108	6-28-1980	–16	2-13-1905	Apr.	13	Oct.	27
Atascosa, Pleasanton	96.0	38	42.1	19	*113	8-22-1917	–1	1-31-1949	Feb.	27	Nov.	28
Austin, Sealy	93.4	11	42.9	14	*111	9-4-2000	0	12-23-1989	Feb.	28	Dec.	2
Bailey, Muleshoe NWR	91.6	12	22.1	123	*112	6-28-1994	–21	2-8-1933	Apr.	25	Oct.	19
Bandera, Medina	93.9	13	37.0	44	*110	7-9-1939	*–5	2-2-1951	Mar.	16	Nov.	15
Bastrop, Elgin	94.3	17	41.0	18	*111	9-5-2000	–3	12-23-1989	Mar.	4	Nov.	24
Baylor, Seymour	95.5	31	29.7	69	120	8-12-1936	–14	1-4-1947	Mar.	30	Nov.	6
Bee, Beeville	93.8	14	45.5	9	114	6-22-1990	5	2-12-1899	Feb.	17	Dec.	8
Bell, Stillhouse Hollow Dam	94.1	20	37.7	33	*112	8-11-1947	–5	12-23-1989	Mar.	14	Nov.	20
Bexar, San Antonio Intl. Airport	94.4	18	42.8	14	*113	8-28-2011	*0	1-31-1949	Feb.	26	Nov.	28
Blanco, Blanco	92.4	9	37.2	44	110	9-6-2000	*–6	1-31-1949	Mar.	20	Nov.	10
Borden, Gail	92.6	22	33.7	56	116	6-27-1994	–1	12-23-1989	Mar.	27	Nov.	8
Bosque, Lake Whitney Dam	94.1	28	36.3	43	113	9-5-2000	*–3	12-23-1989	Mar.	15	Nov.	14
Bowie, Texarkana	92.0	10	35.2	46	*112	8-5-2011	–9	2-12-1899	Mar.	15	Nov.	17
Brazoria, Angleton	91.1	0	48.3	4	109	9-4-2000	6	2-12-1899	Jan.	27	Jan.	1
Brazos, College Station	94.7	18	43.1	16	112	9-4-2000	–3	1-31-1949	Feb.	27	Nov.	30
Brewster, Alpine	90.9	8	32.5	56	*119	6-24-2023	*–6	1-12-1962	Apr.	2	Nov.	3
Briscoe, Silverton	90.6	9	25.2	111	112	7-15-2020	–10	12-25-2004	Apr.	13	Oct.	28
Brooks, Falfurrias	97.2	41	45.3	10	116	7-13-2016	9	1-12-1962	Feb.	25	Dec.	1
Brown, Brownwood	95.4	30	33.9	55	113	7-19-1925	–6	12-23-1989	Mar.	22	Nov.	10
Burleson, Somerville Dam	95.9	27	36.8	37	114	9-5-2000	3	12-23-1989	Mar.	18	Nov.	9
Burnet, Burnet Muni. Airport	94.1	12	39.7	26	*114	7-11-1917	*–4	12-23-1989	Mar.	6	Nov.	23
Caldwell, Luling	96.2	24	41.2	29	111	8-28-2011	–3	1-31-1949	Mar.	5	Nov.	23
Calhoun, Port O'Connor	91.1	0	47.2	5	*109	8-29-2011	9	12-23-1989	Jan.	30	Dec.	27
Callahan, Putnam	94.0	23	33.6	53	*111	8-23-2024	–8	12-23-1989	Mar.	27	Nov.	7
Cameron, Brownsville	95.1	2	54.9	1	108	8-18-1915	12	2-13-1899	Jan.	6	Jan.	2
Camp, Daingerfield	91.4	14	36.8	34	111	8-3-2011	*10	12-9-2005	Mar.	8	Nov.	22
Carson, Panhandle	91.3	14	25.2	122	112	6-27-2011	*–10	1-12-1963	Apr.	15	Oct.	29
Cass, Wright Patman Dam	90.9	6	37.1	44	*111	8-5-2011	*–4	2-17-2021	Mar.	4	Nov.	21

UNSPLASH/MATTI JOHNSON

Growing Season	Mean Precipitation													Record Rainfall Highest Daily Total		
	January	February	March	April	May	June	July	August	September	October	November	December	Annual			
Days	In.	In.	In.	In.	In.	In.	In.	In.	In.	In.	In.	In.	In.	Location	In.	M-D-Y
234	4.05	3.87	4.11	4.13	4.32	4.50	2.57	3.66	3.31	4.23	3.85	4.20	46.80	Palestine	9.10	8-14-1991
240	0.63	0.62	0.72	0.56	1.32	2.38	1.71	1.55	1.93	1.31	0.55	0.69	13.97	Andrews	7.60	7-2-1914
247	4.66	3.88	4.21	3.69	4.64	4.22	3.34	3.75	3.94	4.73	4.53	4.68	50.27	Zavalla	11.68	8-23-2022
328	2.58	2.01	2.77	2.11	3.40	3.66	3.00	2.37	5.65	3.96	3.01	1.89	36.41	Aransas NWR	14.25	11-1-1974
231	1.68	2.02	2.01	2.43	4.75	3.39	2.51	2.90	2.77	3.77	2.03	2.20	32.46	Olney	8.45	5-15-1989
195	0.71	0.53	1.27	1.45	2.27	2.85	2.82	2.86	1.69	1.75	0.75	0.71	19.66	Claude	6.42	5-16-1951
274	1.98	1.76	2.26	2.36	3.89	3.79	2.63	2.46	3.58	2.72	2.19	1.91	31.53	Rossville	9.09	9-15-1919
279	3.35	2.69	3.36	3.47	5.21	4.20	2.37	3.65	3.93	4.30	3.92	3.45	43.90	San Felipe	12.25	4-18-2016
177	0.51	0.46	0.92	0.73	2.28	2.34	2.31	2.75	2.56	1.68	0.73	0.61	17.88	Muleshoe	5.25	5-16-1951
244	2.23	1.84	3.00	2.54	5.53	3.89	2.51	2.26	4.48	3.29	2.34	2.36	36.27	Vanderpool	11.53	8-1-1978
264	2.96	2.06	3.15	2.73	4.86	2.98	1.97	2.32	2.97	4.02	3.07	3.00	36.09	Smithville	16.05	6-30-1940
222	1.17	1.50	1.93	1.78	3.81	3.84	2.88	2.94	3.23	2.80	1.87	1.24	28.99	Lake Kemp	6.25	9-1-1986
299	1.77	1.56	2.47	2.34	3.08	3.49	3.16	2.82	4.10	2.89	2.47	1.80	31.95	Chase Field	11.55	7-16-1990
251	2.55	2.29	3.26	3.10	4.85	3.43	1.85	2.46	3.74	4.00	2.64	2.80	36.97	Killeen	11.43	9-8-2010
277	1.96	1.74	2.31	2.42	4.40	3.28	2.41	2.15	3.88	3.75	2.08	2.00	32.38	San Antonio	14.33	10-18-1998
236	2.32	1.93	2.86	2.77	4.95	3.21	1.84	2.12	3.72	3.96	2.90	2.23	34.81	Hye	20.70	9-11-1952
226	0.55	0.69	1.08	1.36	2.52	2.39	2.00	2.69	2.54	1.78	1.26	0.59	19.45	Gail	10.79	9-20-2014
243	2.51	2.42	3.49	3.55	4.60	3.85	1.68	2.03	3.83	4.37	2.56	2.69	37.58	Kopperl	11.87	6-23-2014
249	4.26	4.58	4.70	4.88	5.25	4.39	3.40	2.77	3.89	4.78	4.33	5.18	52.41	Texarkana	10.76	10-15-2023
338	4.02	2.44	2.91	2.87	3.87	4.74	4.18	4.98	7.06	4.37	4.69	3.80	49.93	Alvin	25.75	7-26-1979
278	3.43	2.90	3.41	2.87	4.60	4.01	1.98	3.10	3.50	4.93	3.31	3.71	41.75	College Station	13.39	10-16-1994
216	0.49	0.42	0.40	0.51	1.01	2.31	2.95	3.04	2.43	1.32	0.58	0.59	16.05	O2 Ranch	7.80	8-6-1920
197	0.69	0.76	1.26	1.64	2.87	3.65	2.42	2.64	2.31	1.82	0.85	0.78	21.69	Quitaque	8.58	6-1-1957
285	1.10	0.92	1.31	1.74	4.42	2.81	2.82	2.24	4.36	3.00	1.42	1.25	27.39	Falfurrias	10.00	9-20-1967
233	1.60	2.20	2.39	2.38	4.25	3.75	2.04	2.63	2.88	3.43	1.72	1.37	30.64	Winchell	8.20	9-23-1955
238	3.17	2.92	3.22	3.33	4.73	3.94	1.88	2.81	3.41	4.34	3.55	3.65	40.95	Somerville Dam	15.25	10-17-1994
262	1.65	1.63	2.66	2.12	3.67	2.85	1.79	1.76	2.89	3.18	2.25	1.93	28.38	Marble Falls	11.00	9-10-1921
263	2.40	2.16	2.74	2.94	4.20	3.55	1.85	2.60	3.42	4.20	2.57	2.76	35.39	Lockhart	13.38	10-18-1998
333	2.84	1.89	2.96	2.41	5.05	4.15	3.80	3.77	4.73	3.84	3.89	2.56	41.89	Point Comfort	14.65	6-26-1960
225	1.20	1.77	2.23	2.08	3.89	3.66	2.36	2.42	2.92	2.87	2.15	1.43	28.98	Baird	10.29	8-3-1978
365	1.08	1.03	1.45	1.47	2.22	2.86	1.98	2.16	5.73	3.83	1.76	1.21	26.78	San Benito	12.67	9-5-1933
259	3.46	4.05	4.62	4.16	4.74	3.85	3.07	2.72	3.66	4.25	3.82	4.68	47.08	Pittsburg	8.11	4-27-1958
196	0.53	0.50	1.24	1.60	2.74	3.22	2.57	3.07	1.91	1.97	0.80	0.91	21.06	Panhandle	8.05	5-16-1951
261	4.10	4.46	4.61	4.24	5.24	4.38	3.64	3.20	3.29	4.28	4.39	4.78	50.61	Linden	8.45	3-28-1989

County, Town or Landmark Closest to Station for Normals	Temperature								Average Freeze Dates			
	Mean Max. July	No. at or Above 100°	Mean Min. January	No. at or Below 32°	Record Highest	Record High Date	Record Lowest	Record Low Date	Last in Spring		First in Fall	
	F.	Days	F.	Days	F.	M-D-Y	F.	M-D-Y	Mo.	Day	Mo.	Day
Castro, Dimmitt	90.6	8	23.5	131	111	7-4-1983	*–12	2-16-2021	Apr.	22	Oct.	23
Chambers, Anahuac	90.3	1	44.8	11	106	7-9-1939	8	12-23-1989	Feb.	12	Dec.	6
Cherokee, Rusk	89.8	6	39.2	27	*111	8-20-1925	–6	2-17-2021	Mar.	7	Nov.	25
Childress, Childress	94.3	30	28.8	76	*117	6-26-2011	–13	1-17-1930	Apr.	3	Nov.	5
Clay, Henrietta	94.7	22	30.8	70	*116	8-7-1951	*–8	12-24-1989	Apr.	1	Nov.	8
Cochran, Morton	92.2	11	25.8	102	111	6-26-2011	–12	1-13-1963	Apr.	11	Oct.	31
Coke, Robert Lee	94.4	25	31.9	63	114	5-25-2000	–9	2-15-2021	Mar.	26	Nov.	7
Coleman, Coleman	95.4	23	36.4	42	114	8-3-1943	–9	12-23-1989	Mar.	14	Nov.	20
Collin, McKinney	91.3	15	36.1	44	115	8-4-2001	–11	12-23-1989	Mar.	10	Nov.	19
Collingsworth, Wellington	96.9	37	29.7	79	117	6-26-2011	–6	12-23-1989	Apr.	1	Nov.	4
Colorado, Columbus	95.7	26	40.7	30	116	9-4-2000	*4	12-24-1989	Mar.	9	Nov.	20
Comal, Canyon Dam	93.6	13	41.6	18	*112	8-4-2011	*2	12-23-1989	Mar.	1	Dec.	1
Comanche, Proctor Reservoir	95.1	23	36.2	56	116	8-22-2024	–8	12-23-1989	Mar.	12	Nov.	18
Concho, Paint Rock	95.1	29	32.1	61	*112	8-11-2023	–8	2-2-1985	Mar.	30	Nov.	5
Cooke, Gainesville	92.1	18	33.8	50	114	8-10-1936	–12	2-12-1899	Mar.	19	Nov.	14
Coryell, Gatesville	94.1	22	37.1	43	*112	9-5-2000	–8	2-16-2021	Mar.	19	Nov.	9
Cottle, Paducah	95.5	39	29.0	71	*118	6-27-2011	*–7	12-24-1989	Mar.	30	Nov.	7
Crane, Crane	95.1	26	33.6	49	115	6-27-1994	–6	2-2-1985	Mar.	16	Nov.	16
Crockett, Ozona	93.7	12	31.9	67	113	8-3-2015	–8	2-2-1951	Mar.	21	Nov.	6
Crosby, Crosbyton	91.5	13	27.6	89	113	6-28-1994	–14	2-12-1899	Apr.	5	Nov.	5
Culberson, Van Horn	93.1	12	31.6	70	112	6-25-1969	–14	2-3-2011	Mar.	21	Nov.	11
Dallam, Dalhart (6 mi. SW)	91.6	11	22.4	131	110	6-26-2011	–21	1-4-1959	Apr.	21	Oct.	20
Dallas, Dallas Love Field	95.5	22	39.9	23	115	8-18-1909	–10	2-12-1899	Mar.	2	Nov.	29
Dawson, Lamesa	93.3	17	27.6	93	114	6-28-1994	–12	2-8-1933	Apr.	4	Nov.	4
Deaf Smith, Hereford	91.1	9	23.9	118	111	6-8-1910	–17	2-1-1951	Apr.	17	Oct.	25
Delta, Cooper Dam	92.5	14	36.1	45	110		–1		Mar.	18	Nov.	13
Denton, Denton	94.3	19	35.9	38	*113	7-25-1954	–6	2-16-2021	Mar.	13	Nov.	20
DeWitt, Cuero	96.4	28	43.7	21	114	8-29-2011	2	1-31-1949	Mar.	2	Nov.	27
Dickens, Spur	93.5	23	28.0	89	117	6-28-1994	*–17	2-8-1933	Apr.	6	Nov.	4
Dimmit, Carrizo Springs	98.9	54	39.4	25	*114	6-11-1942	8	12-24-1989	Mar.	5	Nov.	22
Donley, Clarendon	92.8	22	25.3	105	117	8-12-1936	*–13	1-19-1984	Apr.	14	Oct.	26
Duval, Freer	96.8	48	45.5	9	116	6-15-1998	*12	1-24-1963	Feb.	10	Dec.	7
Eastland, Eastland	94.4	17	31.6	68	*115	8-11-1936	–8	12-24-1989	Mar.	30	Nov.	4
Ector, Penwell	93.6	18	33.9	44	116	6-28-1994	–12	2-2-1985	Mar.	15	Nov.	16
Edwards, Rocksprings	90.1	3	38.8	31	110	6-9-1988	0	12-22-1929	Mar.	8	Nov.	25
Ellis, Waxahachie	93.5	15	35.8	33	*115	8-18-2002	*–13	2-5-2011	Mar.	16	Nov.	16
El Paso, El Paso Intl. Airport	92.5	7	33.3	59	115	8-18-1909	–9	2-12-1899	Mar.	24	Nov.	11
Erath, Stephenville	96.0	19	32.9	54	114	8-11-1936	–9	2-12-1899	Mar.	29	Nov.	8
Falls, Marlin	93.6	17	35.3	38	*112	8-11-1969	*–7	1-31-1949	Mar.	21	Nov.	9
Fannin, Bonham	92.1	11	34.5	55	115	8-10-1936	–7	2-16-2021	Mar.	16	Nov.	13
Fayette, La Grange	95.4	29	41.8	19	111	8-23-1917	3	12-23-1989	Mar.	4	Nov.	25
Fisher, Rotan	94.4	27	35.4	55	116	6-27-1994	–12	2-12-1899	Mar.	17	Nov.	15
Floyd, Floydada	91.0	8	26.8	97	111	6-28-1994	–9	1-13-1963	Apr.	7	Nov.	3
Foard, Truscott	95.6	38	31.0	66	114		–7		Mar.	28	Nov.	9
Fort Bend, Sugar Land	93.4	8	45.3	7	*109	8-27-2023	8	12-23-1989	Feb.	9	Dec.	13
Franklin, Mount Vernon	93.0	14	36.0	41	112	8-3-2011	*–5	12-23-1989	Mar.	15	Nov.	16
Freestone, Fairfield	92.5	10	37.9	32	*110	9-4-2000	–2	12-23-1989	Mar.	16	Nov.	14
Frio, Dilley	96.7	29	43.4	10	113	9-6-2000	7	12-23-1989	Feb.	16	Dec.	6
Gaines, Seminole	93.4	16	29.1	82	114	6-28-1994	*–23	2-8-1933	Apr.	2	Nov.	6
Galveston, Galveston	90.9	0	50.9	2	107	8-7-2023	7	2-12-1899	Jan.	18	Jan.	7
Garza, Lake Alan Henry	93.6	23	31.6	65	116	6-28-1994	–5	2-15-2021	Mar.	29	Nov.	10
Gillespie, Fredericksburg	92.6	10	36.2	42	*109	9-5-2000	–5	1-31-1949	Mar.	18	Nov.	10
Glasscock, Garden City	92.5	17	31.5	72	114	6-27-1994	*–3	12-22-1989	Mar.	31	Nov.	6
Goliad, Goliad	94.1	20	45.0	13	*112	6-14-1998	7	1-12-1962	Feb.	25	Dec.	1
Gonzales, Gonzales	93.9	14	41.8	19	*114	8-10-1962	1	1-31-1949	Feb.	26	Nov.	28

Growing Season	Mean Precipitation													Record Rainfall Highest Daily Total		
	January	February	March	April	May	June	July	August	September	October	November	December	Annual			
Days	In.	In.	In.	In.	In.	In.	In.	In.	In.	In.	In.	In.	In.	Location	In.	M-D-Y
182	0.57	0.54	1.03	1.25	2.64	3.59	2.35	3.10	2.41	2.10	0.70	0.72	21.00	Hart	5.17	6-11-1965
302	4.59	3.07	3.63	4.41	5.39	5.84	5.68	7.02	7.02	4.75	3.85	4.47	59.72	Anahuac	15.87	8-28-1945
263	4.36	4.26	4.46	4.04	4.58	4.51	3.38	3.35	3.67	4.65	3.98	4.88	50.12	Jacksonville	11.00	11-22-1940
217	0.84	1.03	1.52	2.72	3.91	4.04	2.32	2.92	2.49	1.93	1.40	0.98	26.10	Childress Airport	5.32	10-20-1983
221	1.69	1.84	2.59	2.71	4.69	3.59	1.80	3.07	2.59	3.55	2.24	1.67	32.03	Henrietta	6.07	6-23-1959
199	0.62	0.61	1.11	0.87	1.94	2.27	2.36	2.53	2.32	1.48	0.85	0.63	17.59	Morton	4.69	7-7-1960
226	1.06	1.11	1.30	1.65	2.60	2.60	1.54	2.63	2.65	2.11	1.23	0.95	21.43	Robert Lee	8.40	10-13-1957
249	1.31	1.87	2.17	1.96	3.68	3.65	2.09	2.53	2.46	2.69	2.09	1.38	27.88	Burkett	9.47	7-5-2002
254	2.58	2.71	3.54	3.68	4.74	4.13	1.87	2.15	3.10	4.42	3.42	3.45	39.79	Gunter	11.03	5-13-1982
215	0.73	0.86	1.34	1.86	3.24	3.32	2.15	1.92	2.35	2.25	1.19	0.87	22.08	Wellington	9.50	10-3-1986
255	3.67	2.81	3.32	3.77	4.78	5.11	2.93	3.30	3.26	4.69	4.02	3.38	45.04	New Ulm	12.13	4-18-2016
276	2.44	1.98	2.78	2.87	4.46	4.08	2.70	2.43	3.88	4.91	2.88	2.43	37.84	New Braunfels	18.35	10-18-1998
249	1.72	2.08	2.54	2.45	4.43	3.98	1.78	2.32	3.03	3.58	2.09	1.78	31.78	Comanche	8.86	8-19-2004
222	1.06	1.57	1.78	1.51	3.04	3.50	2.05	2.39	2.33	2.36	1.81	1.17	24.57	Paint Rock	8.25	9-9-1980
242	2.21	2.56	3.65	3.92	5.64	4.64	2.91	2.83	3.90	4.36	3.02	3.11	42.75	Gainesville	10.07	7-2-1903
236	2.32	2.54	3.22	3.19	4.14	3.39	2.97	2.97	2.94	4.18	2.63	2.53	37.02	Gatesville	8.67	9-8-2010
223	0.84	0.88	1.62	2.36	3.32	3.54	1.89	2.20	2.93	1.91	1.35	1.04	23.88	Paducah	7.00	6-2-1991
243	0.74	0.53	0.54	0.69	1.32	1.20	0.96	1.39	1.74	1.55	0.84	0.63	12.13	Crane	5.55	8-11-1986
227	0.96	0.88	1.96	1.78	2.81	1.95	1.25	1.81	2.14	2.24	1.26	0.80	19.84	Ozona (22 mi. SE)	8.02	8-18-2007
213	0.79	0.86	1.40	1.82	2.88	2.98	2.40	2.01	2.73	1.73	1.12	0.98	21.70	Crosbyton	5.78	6-30-1913
234	0.47	0.44	0.25	0.22	0.49	1.10	2.05	1.95	1.50	0.94	0.42	0.49	10.32	Pine Springs	9.42	9-12-2014
181	0.47	0.35	0.93	1.25	1.69	2.24	2.51	2.16	1.29	1.64	0.53	0.54	15.60	Bunker Hill	5.25	7-11-1959
272	2.59	2.78	3.45	3.15	4.57	3.83	1.71	2.19	3.10	4.79	2.93	3.23	38.32	Joe Pool Lake	12.05	7-29-2004
212	0.60	0.71	1.01	0.88	2.09	2.36	1.45	1.60	2.89	1.41	1.04	0.80	16.84	Lamesa	6.24	10-10-1985
189	0.64	0.45	1.22	1.09	2.09	3.34	2.34	3.04	1.86	1.85	0.69	0.72	19.33	Hereford	*5.30	8-3-1976
241	3.32	3.45	4.31	4.16	4.91	4.17	3.42	3.04	3.25	5.75	5.01	4.46	49.25	Cooper	8.46	5-13-1982
251	2.20	2.83	3.36	3.67	4.86	3.58	2.29	2.44	2.96	4.64	2.94	2.67	38.44	Isle Du Bois SP	13.00	5-13-1982
270	2.33	1.54	2.76	2.77	4.41	3.92	2.44	2.59	3.57	3.27	2.35	2.27	34.22	Cuero	12.40	6-30-1940
209	0.74	0.84	1.31	1.93	2.77	3.31	2.36	2.39	2.46	2.10	1.21	1.07	22.49	Pitchfork Ranch	7.60	9-18-1996
265	0.98	0.76	1.33	1.15	2.92	1.83	1.74	1.41	3.28	2.05	1.15	0.97	19.57	Carrizo Springs	11.48	10-14-2013
194	0.79	0.66	1.35	2.11	3.45	3.03	2.05	2.90	2.42	2.14	0.92	0.84	22.66	Clarendon	9.25	5-4-2001
304	1.25	1.31	1.92	2.08	2.80	3.07	2.44	2.45	3.35	1.82	1.42	1.24	25.15	Benavides	9.60	9-12-1971
222	1.24	2.01	2.42	1.83	3.76	3.38	1.95	3.12	2.78	3.00	1.92	1.76	29.17	Rising Star	9.45	5-5-2024
243	0.68	0.54	0.67	0.70	1.62	1.00	1.47	1.61	1.53	1.27	0.61	0.58	12.28	Pleasant Farms	4.57	8-01-2017
258	1.03	0.93	1.81	1.66	3.35	2.50	1.95	3.10	3.38	3.05	1.66	1.62	26.04	Carta Valley	10.75	8-24-1998
230	0.40	0.48	0.32	0.25	0.30	0.78	1.80	1.76	1.57	1.06	0.51	0.79	10.02	Ferris	11.28	10-27-2023
245	2.61	2.72	3.99	3.48	4.31	4.22	2.48	2.91	3.27	4.73	2.93	3.15	40.80	El Paso	6.50	7-9-1881
226	1.84	2.16	2.82	2.91	4.97	3.33	1.99	2.96	3.32	3.32	2.33	2.18	34.13	Huckabay	10.21	4-26-1990
234	3.32	2.87	3.74	3.35	4.97	3.01	1.84	2.23	3.05	4.34	2.94	3.44	39.10	Marlin	11.90	7-31-1903
242	2.81	3.10	4.30	4.01	4.94	4.46	3.21	2.89	4.07	4.58	3.48	3.66	45.51	Bonham	13.30	7-3-1903
267	3.22	2.66	3.23	2.95	4.41	3.61	2.06	2.55	3.61	4.27	3.67	3.39	39.63	La Grange	14.69	8-27-2017
243	0.95	1.33	1.68	1.77	3.15	2.94	1.96	2.18	2.72	2.27	1.53	1.06	23.54	Rotan	6.85	8-13-1972
208	0.71	0.69	1.33	1.47	3.11	3.41	1.82	1.98	2.62	1.45	0.75	0.85	20.19	Floydada	7.75	9-12-2008
227	1.09	1.45	1.71	2.18	3.48	3.43	2.07	2.05	2.89	2.41	1.54	1.13	25.43	Crowell	8.25	9-19-1965
305	3.94	3.03	3.64	3.62	4.30	5.67	3.76	4.95	5.30	5.21	4.42	3.27	51.11	Katy	16.43	8-28-2017
245	3.41	3.73	4.52	4.13	5.07	4.17	3.18	3.10	3.58	4.74	3.86	4.70	48.19	Winfield	10.44	9-15-1913
243	3.65	3.46	3.81	3.29	4.70	4.50	1.77	2.88	3.18	4.23	3.91	4.11	43.49	Oakfield	9.08	6-1-2021
296	1.15	1.24	1.98	1.47	4.02	2.46	2.22	1.96	3.70	2.16	1.42	1.23	25.01	Derby	12.80	5-16-1980
219	0.69	0.72	1.01	1.05	2.23	1.92	2.05	1.78	2.75	1.33	1.00	0.68	17.21	Loop	6.35	10-19-1983
365	4.30	2.14	3.02	2.06	3.04	4.23	3.41	4.71	6.65	5.15	4.28	4.23	47.22	Bacliff	21.62	8-27-2017
225	0.81	0.86	1.37	1.66	2.52	2.99	2.04	1.93	2.13	1.85	1.26	0.80	20.22	Polar	9.00	9-25-1955
235	1.56	1.84	2.50	2.55	4.26	2.98	1.88	2.42	3.25	3.10	2.18	2.04	30.56	Gold	13.80	9-10-1952
219	0.95	0.97	1.27	1.32	2.75	2.06	1.68	2.42	2.45	2.46	1.20	0.87	20.40	Garden City	8.75	7-7-1945
280	2.71	1.73	2.74	2.67	4.54	3.90	2.95	3.41	4.69	3.41	2.33	2.13	37.21	Goliad	12.15	7-16-1990
272	2.37	2.07	2.80	2.82	4.68	3.41	1.95	2.92	3.58	3.94	2.73	2.66	35.93	Gonzales	16.31	8-31-1981

County, Town or Landmark Closest to Station for Normals	Temperature								Average Freeze Dates			
	Mean Max. July	No. at or Above 100°	Mean Min. January	No. at or Below 32°	Record Highest	Record High Date	Record Lowest	Record Low Date	Last in Spring		First in Fall	
	F.	Days	F.	Days	F.	M-D-Y	F.	M-D-Y	Mo.	Day	Mo.	Day
Gray, Pampa	90.8	10	24.5	110	113	6-27-2011	–12	1-11-1962	Apr.	14	Oct.	28
Grayson, Sherman	91.1	6	35.7	43	113	8-10-1936	–4	2-16-2021	Mar.	14	Nov.	19
Gregg, Longview	92.7	10	36.1	44	113	8-10-1936	–7	2-12-1899	Mar.	16	Nov.	14
Grimes, Washington St. Park	94.1	23	40.3	31	108	8-11-1969	14	1-7-1970	Mar.	7	Nov.	19
Guadalupe, New Braunfels	92.8	11	39.1	32	112	9-5-2000	0	1-30-1949	Mar.	8	Nov.	18
Hale, Plainview	91.2	9	27.5	92	112	6-27-2011	–8	2-8-1933	Apr.	6	Nov.	2
Hall, Memphis	94.3	29	27.0	89	*117	8-3-1944	–11	1-18-1930	Apr.	1	Nov.	3
Hamilton, Hico	93.6	11	33.2	54	113	8-11-1936	–11	1-31-1949	Mar.	24	Nov.	7
Hansford, Spearman	91.0	12	21.5	131	111	8-13-1936	–22	1-4-1959	Apr.	21	Oct.	23
Hardeman, Quanah	94.9	23	28.3	78	*119	6-27-1994	–15	12-23-1989	Apr.	4	Nov.	1
Hardin, Evadale	92.1	6	41.3	24	111	8-28-2023	12	2-16-2021	Feb.	25	Nov.	30
Harris, Houston Hobby Airport	92.5	3	48.1	4	111	9-4-2000	5	1-18-1930	Jan.	30	Dec.	28
Harrison, Marshall	92.8	9	34.9	39	*112	8-18-1909	–13	2-16-2021	Mar.	20	Nov.	11
Hartley, Channing	89.4	5	21.9	135	110	9-7-1907	*–20	2-8-1933	Apr.	22	Oct.	24
Haskell, Haskell	93.8	28	30.8	63	115	6-27-1994	*–6	12-23-1989	Mar.	28	Nov.	7
Hays, Dripping Springs	93.5	16	40.8	29	111	9-5-2000	–2	1-31-1949	Mar.	17	Nov.	13
Hemphill, Canadian	92.3	20	19.1	136	*112	6-26-1994	–14	1-5-1942	Apr.	27	Oct.	15
Henderson, Athens	93.1	9	36.5	41	*109	9-5-2000	–6	2-2-1985	Mar.	18	Nov.	12
Hidalgo, McAllen Intl. Airport	98.5	40	54.6	1	113	6-16-1998	10	1-12-1962	Jan.	9	Jan	3
Hill, Hillsboro	94.9	18	35.9	37	113	7-10-1917	–6	12-23-1989	Mar.	21	Nov.	10
Hockley, Levelland	91.4	13	26.7	98	115	6-28-1994	–16	1-13-1963	Apr.	9	Nov.	1
Hood, Cresson	94.7	25	33.1	58	114	8-5-2022	–8	2-16-2021	Mar.	24	Nov.	9
Hopkins, Sulphur Springs	93.0	14	36.0	49	*115	8-10-1969	–10	2-12-1899	Mar.	15	Nov.	14
Houston, Crockett	93.6	19	38.0	31	114	8-18-1909	0	2-1-1951	Mar.	13	Nov.	17
Howard, Big Spring	94.8	25	32.9	54	114	6-28-1994	–7	1-11-1962	Mar.	20	Nov.	13
Hudspeth, Sierra Blanca	96.3	33	28.7	93	115	6-28-1994	–10	2-2-1985	Mar.	29	Nov.	6
Hunt, Greenville	96.0	21	35.3	50	116	8-10-1936	*–4	1-18-1930	Mar.	18	Nov.	16
Hutchinson, Borger	93.7	14	27.6	93	116	7-11-2020	–19	1-8-1912	Apr.	12	Oct.	28
Irion, Cope Ranch	95.3	29	29.8	79	*111	6-22-2023	*–4	2-16-2021	Apr.	9	Oct.	31
Jack, Jacksboro	94.2	20	31.8	56	*113	8-29-2011	–11	2-16-2021	Mar.	28	Nov.	7
Jackson, Point Comfort	91.0	1	47.7	5	107	7-27-1954	8	1-31-1949	Feb.	1	Dec.	21
Jasper, Sam Rayburn Dam	93.2	6	42.9	30	109	9-5-2000	*2	2-2-1951	Feb.	24	Dec.	1
Jeff Davis, Fort Davis	90.2	4	32.4	72	*108	6-27-1994	*–10	1-11-1962	Apr.	5	Nov.	1
Jefferson, Port Arthur / Airport	92.2	1	45.8	8	*111	8-27-2023	4	2-12-1899	Feb.	14	Dec.	7
Jim Hogg, Hebbronville	98.5	35	47.9	8	118	7-9-2009	12	12-23-1989	Feb.	4	Dec.	12
Jim Wells, Alice	96.7	23	49.5	4	*114	7-6-1997	11	12-25-1989	Jan.	29	Dec.	29
Johnson, Cleburne	93.5	20	35.3	41	114	9-2-1939	–6	12-23-1989	Mar.	17	Nov.	12
Jones, Anson	94.5	27	31.2	56	118	6-28-1994	*–12	12-23-1989	Mar.	31	Nov.	6
Karnes, Karnes City	95.7	24	40.9	27	112	7-27-1954	6	2-12-1899	Mar.	6	Nov.	20
Kaufman, Kaufman	93.1	17	37.7	39	113	8-10-1936	–7	2-16-2021	Mar.	8	Nov.	21
Kendall, Boerne	92.1	5	38.4	40	112	8-23-1925	–4	1-31-1949	Mar.	15	Nov.	13
Kenedy, Port Mansfield	93.8	11	47.1	12	111	6-22-2023	14	1-13-1975	Feb.	17	Dec.	8
Kent, Jayton	95.1	26	29.4	82	116	6-28-1994	–6	2-3-1985	Apr.	1	Nov.	5
Kerr, Kerrville	91.0	9	35.8	46	110	7-27-1954	–7	1-31-1949	Mar.	27	Nov.	7
Kimble, Junction / Co. Airport	94.5	22	35.5	52	114	5-26-2024	–11	12-22-1929	Mar.	25	Nov.	7
King, Guthrie	96.2	33	28.8	87	119	6-28-1994	–10	12-23-1989	Apr.	4	Nov.	3
Kinney, Brackettville	93.2	19	37.9	31	113	6-21-2023	4	1-12-1962	Mar.	11	Nov.	21
Kleberg, Kingsville Air Station	95.7	19	48.4	5	115	6-15-1998	10	12-24-1989	Feb.	3	Dec.	14
Knox, Munday	95.8	31	33.1	56	*118	6-20-2011	–11	1-4-1947	Mar.	26	Nov.	11
Lamar, Paris	94.4	21	35.4	46	112	6-28-1994	*–14	1-13-1963	Mar.	14	Nov.	16
Lamb, Littlefield	91.4	12	24.3	109	*112	7-11-1917	–12	1-31-1949	Apr.	14	Oct.	26
Lampasas, Lampasas	94.9	16	35.5	55	*116	9-8-1893	9	1-12-1962	Mar.	22	Nov.	12
La Salle, Fowlerton	98.3	44	41.1	25	115	8-10-1936	–13	2-12-1899	Mar.	3	Nov.	25
Lavaca, Hallettsville	95.7	13	46.4	13	112	8-29-2011	5	12-23-1989	Feb.	17	Dec.	4
Lee, Lexington	94.2	15	40.5	27	111	9-6-2000	*2	12-23-1989	Mar.	5	Nov.	21

Growing Season	Mean Precipitation													Record Rainfall Highest Daily Total		
	January	February	March	April	May	June	July	August	September	October	November	December	Annual			
Days	In.	In.	In.	In.	In.	In.	In.	In.	In.	In.	In.	In.	In.	Location	In.	M-D-Y
194	0.79	0.63	1.46	2.21	2.84	3.19	2.50	3.09	1.93	2.22	0.98	0.95	22.79	McLean	7.60	4-3-1997
250	2.52	2.76	3.96	3.87	5.54	4.54	2.90	2.88	3.43	4.77	3.50	3.62	44.29	Van Alstyne	9.30	9-22-2018
244	4.27	4.07	4.68	4.34	4.92	4.33	2.50	2.84	3.48	4.33	3.78	4.64	48.18	Longview	12.03	3-9-2016
259	3.53	3.00	3.31	3.35	4.70	4.59	2.23	3.31	3.82	4.69	3.98	3.64	44.15	Richards	11.98	10-16-1994
253	2.31	1.89	2.74	2.46	3.63	3.56	2.98	2.37	3.53	3.16	2.38	2.56	33.57	Kingsbury	9.25	10-9-2002
209	0.68	0.60	1.25	1.52	2.86	2.74	2.38	2.12	1.99	1.63	0.83	0.73	19.33	Plainview	7.00	7-8-1960
215	0.78	0.84	1.38	2.00	3.49	2.92	2.35	2.46	2.44	1.78	1.01	0.83	22.28	Memphis	8.80	6-7-1960
229	2.40	2.81	3.02	3.12	4.39	4.77	2.06	2.73	2.72	3.81	2.20	2.14	36.17	Evant	8.35	5-5-2024
182	0.61	0.46	1.25	1.80	2.50	3.32	2.67	2.67	1.71	1.84	0.81	0.97	20.61	Gruver	9.72	6-13-2010
210	0.88	1.19	1.66	1.98	3.52	3.46	2.15	3.03	2.90	2.04	1.58	1.19	25.58	Quanah	8.03	8-2-1995
281	5.23	4.05	3.67	4.49	5.03	6.92	5.23	6.01	5.57	6.05	5.39	5.59	63.23	Kountze	15.50	8-30-2017
330	4.09	2.85	3.28	4.08	5.42	6.09	4.59	5.44	5.76	5.78	3.90	4.34	55.62	Houston-South	20.84	8-27-2017
233	4.20	3.98	5.07	4.78	4.62	4.66	3.65	3.05	3.50	4.67	4.25	4.91	51.34	Harleton	10.50	3-29-1989
183	0.54	0.43	1.12	1.38	1.77	2.64	2.56	2.40	1.55	1.94	0.48	0.88	17.69	Romero	8.27	5-17-1914
225	1.19	1.49	1.98	2.07	3.35	3.78	1.80	2.52	3.25	2.53	1.74	1.25	26.95	Haskell	14.29	8-4-1978
242	2.65	2.10	2.86	2.61	4.29	3.68	2.10	2.11	3.65	3.97	2.94	2.74	35.70	San Marcos	15.78	10-17-1998
170	0.62	0.61	1.41	1.89	3.07	3.46	2.40	2.92	1.78	2.30	0.94	1.16	22.56	Canadian	7.00	6-8-2008
242	3.54	3.88	4.08	3.82	4.30	4.09	2.53	2.64	2.97	5.09	3.49	4.32	44.75	Payne Springs	11.28	10-25-2015
365	0.77	0.72	1.38	1.43	2.03	3.05	2.03	1.81	4.61	2.10	1.17	1.06	22.16	Santa Rosa	15.49	7-28-2020
235	2.74	2.77	3.57	3.68	4.51	3.61	1.65	2.18	3.15	5.05	2.73	3.10	38.74	Aquilla	11.49	10-24-2015
205	0.66	0.60	1.12	1.00	2.40	2.67	2.06	2.29	2.29	1.53	0.87	0.78	18.27	Ropesville	5.06	9-12-2008
228	2.25	2.38	3.28	3.03	4.23	3.82	1.91	2.59	3.01	3.82	2.61	2.29	35.22	Cresson	11.08	6-4-2000
245	3.30	3.63	4.43	4.31	4.30	4.27	3.03	2.92	2.96	4.90	3.98	4.47	46.50	Cumby	8.64	4-11-2017
251	4.13	3.80	3.44	3.68	4.79	5.05	2.53	3.44	3.64	4.45	3.81	4.56	47.32	Crockett	9.11	6-8-2001
239	0.73	0.80	1.15	1.55	2.54	2.49	1.58	2.40	2.39	1.84	1.35	0.78	19.60	Big Spring	7.80	9-3-2024
221	0.57	0.33	0.20	0.21	0.38	0.68	1.58	1.36	1.18	0.87	0.38	0.58	8.32	Dell City	7.10	9-12-2013
244	3.16	3.46	4.42	4.12	5.79	4.16	3.15	2.39	3.84	4.96	3.58	3.98	47.01	Commerce	12.00	8-13-2017
198	0.73	0.57	1.33	2.01	2.71	2.84	2.98	3.73	1.78	1.99	0.93	0.86	22.46	Borger	6.27	9-22-2004
202	0.91	0.90	1.07	1.24	1.81	2.65	1.61	2.60	2.31	1.96	1.10	0.89	19.05	Mertzon	8.35	8-12-1971
225	1.49	2.26	2.95	2.84	4.29	4.01	1.85	2.18	3.14	3.85	1.86	1.94	32.66	Antelope	11.18	5-16-1989
321	3.11	1.84	3.20	2.61	4.25	4.85	3.15	3.42	4.82	3.65	3.57	2.92	41.39	Maurbro	14.80	6-26-1960
280	5.59	4.76	5.44	4.63	4.53	5.54	3.52	4.98	4.44	5.22	5.29	6.09	60.03	Evadale	14.52	9-18-1963
209	0.53	0.41	0.40	0.54	1.19	2.28	2.99	2.65	2.08	1.28	0.57	0.59	15.51	Jasper	8.05	3-29-2018
301	5.32	3.09	3.63	3.92	4.70	6.70	6.85	6.89	6.69	5.47	3.89	4.98	62.13	Port Arthur Reg AP	26.03	8-29-2017
320	1.24	1.17	1.28	1.18	2.42	2.36	2.37	1.45	4.05	2.43	1.27	1.49	22.71	Kaffie Ranch	21.02	9-12-1971
337	1.27	1.35	1.69	0.98	3.49	2.32	2.48	2.62	5.26	2.72	1.58	1.30	27.06	Alice Intl. Airport	13.21	9-13-1951
240	2.61	2.52	3.47	3.08	4.27	3.90	2.11	2.83	3.02	4.43	2.92	2.53	37.69	Lillian	9.30	5-17-1989
221	1.03	1.41	1.53	1.95	3.32	3.56	2.46	2.58	2.26	2.50	1.46	1.37	25.43	Stamford	8.22	8-4-1978
261	1.64	1.61	2.28	2.41	4.38	2.95	2.32	2.66	4.06	3.16	2.32	1.84	31.63	Cibolo Creek	13.75	9-21-1967
256	2.91	3.03	3.48	3.68	4.36	3.57	1.86	2.75	3.41	4.66	3.06	3.40	40.17	Terrell	10.59	10-28-2023
243	2.28	2.22	2.79	2.52	5.28	3.78	2.83	2.80	3.90	3.88	2.92	2.32	37.52	Kendalia	12.32	5-24-2015
300	1.26	1.44	1.93	1.48	3.05	3.22	2.41	2.72	6.16	3.27	1.81	1.58	30.33	Sarita	9.30	10-12-1973
220	0.87	1.12	1.38	1.77	3.12	3.28	2.46	2.13	2.63	2.12	1.42	0.98	23.28	Jayton	*6.50	7-29-2004
226	1.66	1.63	2.35	2.27	4.29	3.31	2.09	1.93	3.73	3.20	2.16	1.94	30.56	Lynxhaven Ranch	15.20	8-2-1978
229	0.89	1.12	2.02	1.82	3.16	2.83	1.48	2.03	2.41	2.15	1.52	1.03	22.46	Junction	8.56	10-08-2018
213	0.95	1.19	1.48	2.04	3.18	3.28	2.05	2.83	2.46	2.00	1.38	0.97	23.81	Guthrie	8.85	7-4-1986
255	0.90	0.95	1.81	1.38	3.27	2.51	1.86	2.61	3.71	2.61	1.35	1.09	24.05	Fort Clark	18.00	6-15-1899
314	1.16	1.17	1.77	1.78	3.50	3.18	1.37	2.30	4.75	2.91	1.43	1.69	27.01	Ricardo	11.30	6-21-1924
232	1.31	1.41	1.87	1.77	3.94	3.61	2.88	2.55	2.12	1.85	1.16	1.23	25.70	Munday	8.00	6-14-1930
266	1.47	1.08	2.11	1.82	3.43	2.65	2.80	1.97	3.86	2.30	1.32	1.45	26.26	Arthur City	10.50	5-12-1920
247	3.08	3.34	4.35	4.70	5.63	4.26	3.51	2.95	3.95	4.62	4.21	4.28	48.88	Olton	6.30	6-4-1985
192	0.65	0.61	1.15	1.05	2.01	2.87	2.22	2.35	2.28	1.31	0.74	0.77	18.01	Lometa	9.50	10-4-1959
238	2.24	2.19	2.96	2.53	4.58	3.53	1.88	2.34	2.45	3.02	2.25	2.20	32.17	Fowlerton	12.80	9-9-2002
297	3.06	2.30	2.99	3.51	4.40	4.54	2.50	3.18	3.67	4.28	3.25	2.74	40.42	Halletsville	20.60	8-27-2017
262	3.08	2.24	2.94	2.61	4.68	3.21	2.11	2.62	3.07	4.59	3.34	3.23	37.72	Fedor	13.00	10-17-1994

County, Town or Landmark Closest to Station for Normals	Temperature								Average Freeze Dates			
	Mean Max. July	No. at or Above 100°	Mean Min. January	No. at or Below 32°	Record Highest	Record High Date	Record Lowest	Record Low Date	Last in Spring		First in Fall	
	F.	Days	F.	Days	F.	M-D-Y	F.	M-D-Y	Mo.	Day	Mo.	Day
Leon, Centerville	93.1	10	36.9	46	113	8-18-1909	–1	12-24-2022	Mar.	20	Nov.	12
Liberty, Liberty	92.9	3	43.0	14	112	8-9-1962	5	12-24-1989	Feb.	21	Dec.	1
Limestone, Mexia	92.5	10	37.9	32	112	8-18-1909	–5	12-23-1989	Mar.	16	Nov.	14
Lipscomb, Lipscomb	92.3	20	19.1	136	*114	6-27-2011	–19	1-19-1984	Apr.	27	Oct.	15
Live Oak, Choke Canyon Dam	95.0	33	44.7	9	112	9-6-2000	11	12-26-1983	Feb.	8	Dec.	6
Llano, Llano	95.3	27	35.9	50	115	7-14-1933	–7	12-22-1929	Mar.	20	Nov.	10
Loving, Red Bluff Dam	97.7	50	31.5	69	*112	7-30-1944	0	1-5-1947	Mar.	18	Nov.	10
Lubbock, Lubbock	92.4	13	28.7	84	114	6-27-1994	–17	2-8-1933	Apr.	4	Nov.	2
Lynn, Tahoka	92.2	11	29.8	80	111	6-28-1994	–15	2-8-1933	Apr.	2	Nov.	8
Madison, Madisonville	94.1	13	38.4	35	112	9-5-2000	*–2	1-31-1949	Mar.	16	Nov.	11
Marion, Jefferson	93.0	12	35.5	55	*112	8-5-2011	*–5	12-23-1989	Mar.	18	Nov.	8
Martin, Lenorah	94.8	28	32.7	54	109		*–8		Mar.	26	Nov.	9
Mason, Mason	94.6	19	35.6	51	111	7-12-2022	*3	2-2-1985	Mar.	18	Nov.	13
Matagorda, Bay City	90.2	2	45.0	7	112	8-27-2023	7	12-23-1989	Feb.	20	Dec.	3
Maverick, Eagle Pass	97.4	53	41.0	13	*115	7-25-1944	7	2-12-1899	Feb.	19	Dec.	1
McCulloch, Brady	92.3	15	37.0	43	110	6-29-1980	*–2	1-18-1930	Mar.	14	Nov.	15
McLennan, Waco Reg. Airport	95.5	24	37.9	34	*114	7-23-2018	*–7	1-31-1949	Mar.	15	Nov.	15
McMullen, Tilden	97.2	42	45.3	12	119	7-2-1910	5	12-22-1989	Feb.	13	Dec.	3
Medina, Hondo Muni. Airport	96.1	25	40.7	25	*112	9-5-2000	4	2-1-1949	Mar.	6	Nov.	20
Menard, Menard	93.8	17	31.2	64	114	5-29-1927	–6	1-9-1879	Apr.	7	Oct.	30
Midland, Midland	95.2	24	34.3	58	*116	6-27-1994	*–12	1-11-1962	Mar.	18	Nov.	14
Milam, Cameron	93.1	9	41.0	28	114	7-10-1917	–7	1-17-1930	Mar.	6	Nov.	23
Mills, Goldthwaite	91.8	8	35.3	37	110	8-6-1964	–7	12-23-1989	Mar.	23	Nov.	11
Mitchell, Lake Colorado City	95.1	23	29.5	76	115	6-30-1907	*–7	1-4-1947	Apr.	4	Nov.	5
Montague, Bowie	92.0	13	32.0	64	115	6-28-1980	–12	2-12-1899	Mar.	27	Nov.	9
Montgomery, Conroe	94.4	9	43.8	17	113	9-4-2000	1	2-16-2021	Feb.	24	Dec.	2
Moore, Dumas	90.5	9	23.1	124	*109	6-28-1980	–18	1-5-1959	Apr.	21	Oct.	24
Morris, Daingerfield	91.4	14	36.8	34	112	8-4-1998	–5	2-16-2021	Mar.	8	Nov.	22
Motley, Matador	91.9	18	29.6	72	116	6-28-1994	–6	2-15-2021	Apr.	5	Nov.	4
Nacogdoches, Nacogdoches	91.7	13	37.9	41	*113	9-3-2000	–4	1-18-1930	Mar.	13	Nov.	17
Navarro, Corsicana	93.5	17	36.8	38	*113	7-26-1954	–7	2-12-1899	Mar.	14	Nov.	16
Newton, Toledo Bend Dam	92.9	8	39.0	39	112	8-24-2023	4	1-19-1930	Mar.	9	Nov.	18
Nolan, Roscoe	93.1	18	32.7	57	113	6-27-1994	–11	1-5-1947	Mar.	30	Nov.	8
Nueces, Corpus Christi	93.4	4	49.9	4	113	8-31-1983	*7	2-12-1899	Jan.	28	Dec.	21
Ochiltree, Perryton	93.2	14	24.9	131	*113	6-10-1981	–17	1-7-1988	Apr.	14	Oct.	30
Oldham, Vega	91.5	12	22.7	122	110	7-27-1982	*–17	2-1-1951	Apr.	19	Oct.	23
Orange, Orange	89.4	1	42.1	19	107	9-1-2000	10	12-25-1989	Feb.	28	Nov.	23
Palo Pinto, Mineral Wells	94.6	26	34.8	48	115	8-14-1999	–8	12-23-1989	Mar.	24	Nov.	10
Panola, Carthage	91.6	9	37.9	39	109	9-5-2000	1	12-24-1989	Mar.	8	Nov.	19
Parker, Weatherford	93.1	13	33.7	61	119	6-26-1980	*–11	2-12-1899	Mar.	25	Nov.	8
Parmer, Friona	90.2	6	23.7	118	109	6-19-2017	–15	1-13-1963	Apr.	22	Oct.	23
Pecos, Fort Stockton	94.4	24	37.3	40	117	6-29-1994	–7	1-3-1911	Mar.	8	Nov.	20
Polk, Livingston	93.9	11	41.7	36	116	8-3-2016	*3	12-24-1989	Mar.	1	Nov.	24
Potter, Amarillo	91.2	9	26.0	108	111	6-26-2011	–16	2-12-1899	Apr.	13	Oct.	27
Presidio, Presidio	101.4	96	36.4	25	*117	6-18-1960	–2	1-5-1972	Feb.	23	Nov.	26
Rains, Emory	90.6	10	34.4	54	112	9-5-2000	–5	12-25-1989	Mar.	20	Nov.	12
Randall, Canyon	91.4	10	23.7	107	*109	6-27-2011	–14	2-1-1951	Apr.	15	Oct.	25
Reagan, Big Lake	94.0	14	35.1	56	116	6-26-2023	–9	2-2-1985	Mar.	20	Nov.	14
Real, Camp Wood	93.3	10	36.7	48	*110	6-21-2023	0	11-29-1976	Mar.	12	Nov.	14
Red River, DeKalb	92.1	13	33.3	49	115	8-10-1936	*–7	1-18-1930	Mar.	26	Nov.	6
Reeves, Balmorhea	93.8	21	32.1	65	118	6-29-1968	–14	1-11-1962	Mar.	29	Nov.	9
Refugio, Refugio	93.3	6	46.2	11	112	9-5-2000	8	1-12-1962	Feb.	27	Dec.	2
Roberts, Miami	90.5	9	23.3	116	114	6-11-1917	–15	1-5-1942	Apr.	16	Oct.	26
Robertson, Franklin	94.3	16	41.3	24	112	9-4-2000	–1	12-23-1989	Feb.	28	Nov.	28
Rockwall, Lavon Dam	91.3	15	36.1	44	*109	7-25-1954	–1	2-16-2021	Mar.	10	Nov.	19

Growing Season	Mean Precipitation													Record Rainfall Highest Daily Total		
	January	February	March	April	May	June	July	August	September	October	November	December	Annual			
Days	In.	In.	In.	In.	In.	In.	In.	In.	In.	In.	In.	In.	In.	Location	In.	M-D-Y
239	3.47	3.22	3.90	3.11	4.65	4.00	2.47	2.71	3.22	4.22	3.63	3.81	42.41	Buffalo	9.19	10-14-1957
286	5.12	3.90	3.98	4.60	5.54	6.05	5.02	5.52	6.85	6.34	4.72	5.18	62.82	Dayton	25.00	8-27-2017
243	3.65	3.46	3.81	3.29	4.70	4.50	1.77	2.88	3.18	4.23	3.91	4.11	43.49	Mexia	9.16	5-2-2024
170	0.62	0.61	1.41	1.89	3.07	3.46	2.40	2.92	1.78	2.30	0.94	1.16	22.56	Booker	7.76	6-9-1997
302	1.51	1.41	2.38	2.01	2.98	2.68	2.76	1.69	3.62	2.33	1.49	1.65	26.51	Whitsett	15.69	9-22-1967
235	1.50	1.67	2.43	2.14	3.86	3.27	1.82	1.59	2.34	3.00	2.07	1.88	27.57	Moss Ranch	13.53	9-11-1952
239	0.80	0.33	0.48	0.22	1.01	0.93	1.48	1.05	1.94	0.97	0.52	0.35	10.08	Mentone	3.79	9-24-1955
210	0.65	0.65	1.10	1.33	2.69	2.58	1.96	1.74	2.55	1.53	0.80	0.75	18.33	Lubbock	7.81	9-12-2008
220	0.76	0.74	1.07	1.34	2.93	2.83	2.29	2.23	2.93	1.66	1.12	0.78	20.68	Tahoka	9.10	5-5-2015
240	4.36	3.35	3.38	3.40	4.86	3.76	2.91	3.42	3.87	4.72	4.34	4.40	46.77	Madisonville	8.89	10-16-2018
236	4.08	4.23	4.83	4.74	5.11	5.10	2.96	2.42	3.77	4.47	3.61	4.42	49.74	Jefferson	9.10	4-26-1921
226	0.77	0.54	0.75	0.85	1.70	1.55	1.45	1.58	1.87	1.18	0.86	0.45	13.55	Tarzan	6.54	9-20-2014
241	1.32	1.88	2.15	2.30	4.21	3.80	2.30	2.01	3.03	2.58	1.94	1.38	28.90	Mason	7.80	10-16-2018
290	3.76	2.53	3.03	3.24	4.44	5.69	4.51	4.27	5.79	4.24	4.00	3.56	49.06	Matagorda	12.20	5-7-1951
287	0.74	0.74	1.18	2.02	2.80	2.20	2.10	1.68	3.29	2.14	1.13	0.81	20.83	Eagle Pass	15.60	6-29-1936
244	1.33	1.71	2.33	2.05	3.79	2.88	2.11	2.21	2.76	2.71	1.87	1.63	27.38	Brady	9.13	7-8-2015
245	2.59	2.68	3.31	3.30	4.44	3.35	1.82	2.05	2.87	4.41	2.71	2.87	36.40	McGregor	13.08	6-16-1964
299	1.09	1.09	2.25	2.12	3.17	2.46	2.87	2.06	3.57	1.92	1.46	1.54	25.60	Calliham	12.00	4-17-2010
263	1.21	1.27	1.88	2.10	3.43	2.94	2.06	1.93	2.76	2.59	1.56	1.18	24.91	Natalia	11.47	9-27-1973
204	1.11	1.35	2.10	2.00	3.40	3.07	1.58	2.00	2.20	2.50	1.80	1.21	24.32	Callan	7.67	10-10-1961
239	0.66	0.58	0.68	0.70	1.57	1.80	1.62	1.72	1.66	1.21	0.72	0.59	13.51	Midland	7.20	5-9-1968
261	2.60	2.35	2.90	2.32	5.28	3.61	2.61	2.51	3.89	4.29	3.11	3.13	38.60	Cameron	12.45	9-10-1921
234	1.70	2.23	2.42	2.23	4.21	4.16	1.82	2.01	2.51	3.49	2.06	1.60	30.44	Mullin	9.18	5-5-2024
216	0.90	1.32	1.68	1.54	2.15	3.05	1.96	2.96	1.90	2.31	1.19	1.04	22.00	Colorado City	8.65	4-6-1900
228	1.64	2.29	3.00	3.04	5.22	4.00	2.63	2.47	3.23	3.62	2.10	2.08	35.32	Bonita	12.47	4-30-2009
285	4.38	3.32	3.46	3.39	5.46	5.21	3.32	4.53	3.69	5.39	4.77	4.10	51.02	Roman Forest	18.88	2019-9-19
183	0.39	0.40	0.98	1.38	1.91	2.27	2.72	2.99	1.66	1.80	0.52	0.68	17.70	Sunray	4.49	10-16-1968
259	3.46	4.05	4.62	4.16	4.74	3.85	3.07	2.72	3.66	4.25	3.82	4.68	47.08	Daingerfield	7.50	7-28-2009
213	0.81	0.89	1.45	1.96	2.77	3.44	2.03	2.68	2.99	1.89	1.08	0.99	22.98	Flomot	7.08	7-9-1994
248	4.46	4.21	4.47	4.01	4.53	4.09	2.88	3.66	4.07	4.34	4.44	4.78	49.94	Nacogdoches	14.22	6-28-1902
246	3.14	3.27	4.01	3.99	4.28	3.77	2.11	2.48	3.28	5.02	3.16	3.61	42.12	Corsicana	18.95	10-24-2015
253	5.30	4.50	5.12	4.68	4.30	4.94	4.66	3.43	3.95	4.23	4.78	5.77	55.66	Deweyville	20.60	9-18-1963
223	0.98	0.99	1.39	1.49	2.79	3.12	1.77	2.20	2.13	2.22	1.15	0.98	21.21	Roscoe	8.28	9-9-1980
331	1.39	1.29	2.28	2.04	3.38	3.56	2.54	2.75	5.42	3.13	2.03	1.93	31.74	Port Aransas	13.89	8-22-1999
197	0.69	0.58	1.51	1.90	2.80	3.20	3.48	2.96	1.86	2.04	0.83	0.97	22.82	Perryton	7.11	5-17-1989
183	0.56	0.40	1.09	1.28	1.83	2.66	2.72	3.26	1.57	2.09	0.64	0.72	18.82	Vega	6.07	5-16-1951
273	5.65	4.18	3.52	4.18	5.14	6.84	5.82	6.71	6.44	5.96	4.71	5.26	64.41	Bridge City	23.82	8-30-2017
231	1.59	2.19	2.98	2.63	4.00	3.55	2.13	2.49	2.66	3.28	2.41	1.89	31.80	Gordon	8.20	5-8-1997
255	4.66	4.23	4.92	4.72	4.35	4.04	3.64	3.44	3.67	4.54	4.44	5.63	52.28	Carthage	9.25	4-14-1991
230	1.96	2.55	3.03	2.69	4.42	3.93	1.86	2.59	3.19	3.76	2.95	2.25	35.18	Weatherford	8.57	8-20-2016
182	0.70	0.48	1.15	1.00	2.14	2.49	2.64	3.13	2.03	1.98	0.75	0.80	19.29	Bovina	4.73	7-21-1918
254	0.65	0.46	0.58	0.79	1.41	1.85	1.79	1.76	1.97	1.29	0.62	0.49	13.66	Bakersfield	7.10	4-30-2007
269	4.53	3.75	3.67	4.33	4.47	5.07	3.22	3.41	4.42	4.56	4.54	5.01	50.98	Corrigan	14.69	10-17-1994
195	0.71	0.53	1.27	1.45	2.27	2.85	2.82	2.86	1.69	1.75	0.75	0.71	19.66	Amarillo	5.89	10-08-2018
275	0.48	0.43	0.52	0.17	0.41	1.04	1.84	1.42	0.95	0.70	0.48	0.48	8.92	Bunton Ranch	5.50	8-23-1944
238	3.10	3.46	4.56	4.11	4.64	4.05	3.05	2.77	3.28	4.84	3.37	4.21	45.44	Lake Tawakoni	10.05	10-25-2015
192	0.59	0.40	1.06	0.99	2.25	2.68	2.26	3.03	1.90	1.98	0.68	0.63	18.45	Canyon	7.87	8-29-1968
238	1.03	0.79	0.97	1.47	1.84	2.05	2.10	1.77	2.34	1.60	1.35	0.87	18.18	Big Lake	5.87	8-15-2005
248	1.14	0.99	2.01	1.93	3.46	3.00	2.18	2.94	3.94	2.68	2.10	1.31	27.68	Leakey	11.95	9-26-2016
225	4.13	4.20	4.91	5.40	4.91	4.01	3.25	3.03	4.14	5.32	4.54	4.98	52.82	Avery	9.29	12-28-2015
228	0.66	0.41	0.38	0.50	1.05	1.13	1.82	1.87	2.02	1.09	0.60	0.57	12.10	Red Bluff Dam	7.24	6-19-1984
283	2.25	2.02	3.19	2.25	3.47	3.25	2.11	3.61	3.84	4.04	2.55	2.20	34.78	Austwell	15.96	8-26-2017
192	0.87	0.59	1.35	2.17	3.49	2.91	2.58	3.18	2.08	2.92	0.88	1.13	24.15	Miami	5.58	10-10-1985
277	3.50	2.84	3.75	2.68	4.71	3.68	1.63	3.04	3.03	4.68	3.29	3.78	40.61	Bremond	8.49	8-19-2008
254	2.58	2.71	3.54	3.68	4.74	4.13	1.87	2.15	3.10	4.42	3.42	3.45	39.79	Rockwall	7.08	9-22-2018

County, Town or Landmark Closest to Station for Normals	Temperature								Average Freeze Dates			
	Mean Max. July	No. at or Above 100°	Mean Min. January	No. at or Below 32°	Record Highest	Record High Date	Record Lowest	Record Low Date	Last in Spring		First in Fall	
	F.	Days	F.	Days	F.	M-D-Y	F.	M-D-Y	Mo.	Day	Mo.	Day
Runnels, Ballinger	94.2	26	33.1	52	116	6-30-1907	–6	1-31-1949	Mar.	22	Nov.	10
Rusk, Henderson	93.0	11	37.3	41	*111	9-2-2000	–7	2-16-2021	Mar.	15	Nov.	16
Sabine, Toledo Bend Dam	92.9	8	39.0	39	114	8-9-1947	6	2-2-1951	Mar.	9	Nov.	18
San Augustine, Broaddus	92.7	8	37.0	37	112	8-18-1909	1	2-16-2021	Mar.	18	Nov.	13
San Jacinto, Coldspring	94.4	9	43.8	17	110	8-2-1998	3	12-24-1989	Feb.	24	Dec.	2
San Patricio, Sinton	92.8	3	46.9	7	111	9-6-2000	2	2-14-2021	Feb.	1	Dec.	17
San Saba, San Saba	94.1	23	34.8	51	117	8-23-2024	–1	12-23-1989	Mar.	16	Nov.	13
Schleicher, Fort McKavett	92.1	8	34.0	56	*111	6-21-2023	–7	2-2-1985	Mar.	22	Nov.	10
Scurry, Snyder	94.1	19	30.5	71	115	8-12-1936	–11	2-2-1985	Mar.	27	Nov.	10
Shackelford, Albany	93.4	23	33.3	57	115	6-27-1972	–13	2-16-2021	Mar.	30	Nov.	8
Shelby, Center	92.9	11	37.3	42	112	9-2-2000	0	2-2-1951	Mar.	13	Nov.	15
Sherman, Stratford	91.3	9	22.0	137	108	6-24-1953	–20	2-9-1933	Apr.	21	Oct.	21
Smith, Tyler	92.2	9	40.3	29	*110	8-3-2011	–8	2-12-1899	Mar.	7	Nov.	21
Somervell, Glen Rose	94.7	25	33.4	63	115	8-19-1984	–15	12-23-1989	Mar.	28	Nov.	7
Starr, Rio Grande City	98.9	63	47.2	6	*117	6-18-2023	7	2-13-1899	Jan.	31	Dec.	17
Stephens, Breckenridge	94.5	25	30.4	70	114	8-12-1936	–8	2-16-2021	Apr.	4	Nov.	3
Sterling, Sterling City	92.5	17	31.5	72	112	6-27-1994	–13	2-2-1985	Mar.	31	Nov.	6
Stonewall, Aspermont	95.2	34	31.0	73	117	6-28-1994	–10	12-23-1989	Mar.	29	Nov.	7
Sutton, Sonora	95.0	16	32.6	70	109	6-28-1980	–8	2-2-1951	Apr.	1	Nov.	6
Swisher, Tulia	89.7	9	24.2	119	111	6-27-2011	*–23	2-12-1899	Apr.	18	Oct.	26
Tarrant, Benbrook Dam	95.8	22	35.4	43	115	8-18-1909	*–12	2-12-1899	Mar.	14	Nov.	16
Taylor, Abilene Reg. Airport	95.1	19	35.5	48	*113	8-21-2024	–9	1-4-1947	Mar.	20	Nov.	10
Terrell, Sanderson	94.2	11	34.1	49	120	6-14-2008	1	12-22-1989	Mar.	11	Nov.	11
Terry, Brownfield	92.8	14	28.1	89	111	6-28-1994	–8	1-14-1963	Apr.	3	Nov.	4
Throckmorton, Throckmorton	95.2	32	31.4	71	119	8-30-1947	–11	12-23-1989	Mar.	29	Nov.	7
Titus, Mount Pleasant	92.3	16	33.9	61	112	7-21-2022	–12	2-2-1951	Mar.	24	Nov.	7
Tom Green, San Angelo	96.1	30	35.4	49	114	6-21-2023	–6	1-18-1930	Mar.	20	Nov.	10
Travis, Austin-Camp Mabry	95.9	29	43.7	12	112	9-5-2000	*–5	1-31-1949	Feb.	20	Dec.	3
Trinity, Groveton	91.3	6	41.0	17	111	9-4-2000	1	12-23-1989	Mar.	1	Nov.	28
Tyler, Town Bluff Dam	90.6	4	39.9	28	*112	8-20-2023	*2	1-31-1949	Mar.	9	Nov.	22
Upshur, Gilmer	91.1	12	34.0	54	114	8-10-1936	–5	2-16-2021	Mar.	26	Nov.	8
Upton, McCamey	95.9	31	34.7	46	*113	6-27-1994	*–2	1-11-1962	Mar.	12	Nov.	16
Uvalde, Uvalde	96.1	25	40.7	25	114	6-9-1910	*6	2-3-1951	Mar.	6	Nov.	20
Val Verde, Del Rio Intl. Airport	97.9	41	42.6	12	*115	6-21-2023	*2	2-3-1985	Feb.	16	Dec.	3
Van Zandt, Wills Point	93.2	13	36.7	41	115	8-18-1909	*–3	2-17-2021	Mar.	11	Nov.	21
Victoria, Victoria Reg. Airport	94.1	10	45.5	9	*111	9-5-2000	*9	1-18-1930	Feb.	18	Dec.	4
Walker, Huntsville	91.3	6	41.0	17	112	8-27-2023	*–2	2-12-1899	Mar.	1	Nov.	28
Waller, Sealy	93.4	11	42.9	14	107	8-12-1969	13	1-30-1966	Feb.	28	Dec.	2
Ward, Monahans	97.3	51	28.8	74	120	6-28-1994	–9	1-11-1962	Apr.	3	Nov.	6
Washington, Brenham	93.2	13	41.3	18	113	9-5-2000	–2	1-19-1930	Mar.	2	Nov.	30
Webb, Laredo	100.1	74	48.8	5	116	6-17-1998	5	2-12-1899	Jan.	25	Dec.	17
Wharton, Pierce	94.5	13	44.5	11	112	9-5-2000	3	2-12-1899	Feb.	23	Dec.	5
Wheeler, Shamrock	91.9	16	25.3	97	117	7-12-2011	*–13	1-19-1984	Apr.	9	Oct.	30
Wichita, Wichita Falls Airport	95.3	30	31.8	59	117	6-28-1980	–15	1-4-1947	Mar.	26	Nov.	9
Wilbarger, Lake Kemp	95.4	28	30.2	71	119	8-3-1943	–9	12-23-1989	Mar.	27	Nov.	9
Willacy, Raymondville	96.8	21	49.9	3	109	6-6-1916	14	1-13-1962	Jan.	21	Dec.	26
Williamson, Taylor	94.9	21	38.1	28	113	7-11-1917	*–5	1-31-1949	Mar.	6	Nov.	24
Wilson, Floresville	95.7	24	40.9	27	*114	7-6-1984	5	1-21-1985	Mar.	6	Nov.	20
Winkler, County Airport	97.1	51	31.5	65	117	6-27-1994	*–14	1-11-1962	Mar.	26	Nov.	6
Wise, Bridgeport	94.1	23	32.8	61	*115	6-29-1980	*–8	12-23-1989	Mar.	29	Nov.	7
Wood, Mineola	91.9	16	35.3	52	114	6-18-1996	–8	2-16-2021	Mar.	20	Nov.	11
Yoakum, Plains	91.9	13	26.2	99	113	6-27-1994	–12	2-1-1951	Apr.	11	Nov.	1
Young, Olney	95.4	33	31.8	56	*120	6-3-1998	–8	12-23-1989	Mar.	31	Nov.	8
Zapata, Zapata	98.5	59	48.6	4	116	6-16-1998	13	1-4-1911	Jan.	19	Dec.	22
Zavala, Crystal City	97.6	43	45.9	8	115	9-5-2000	6	1-12-1962	Feb.	10	Dec.	10

Growing Season	Mean Precipitation													Record Rainfall Highest Daily Total		
	January	February	March	April	May	June	July	August	September	October	November	December	Annual			
Days	In.	In.	In.	In.	In.	In.	In.	In.	In.	In.	In.	In.	In.	Location	In.	M-D-Y
233	1.01	1.52	1.79	1.56	3.08	3.07	1.67	2.41	2.57	2.20	1.45	1.04	23.37	Wingate	7.68	6-19-1982
247	4.11	4.10	4.63	4.40	4.67	4.76	3.39	3.62	3.82	4.22	4.06	4.63	50.41	Henderson	11.05	3-29-1989
253	5.30	1.50	5.12	4.68	4.30	4.94	4.66	3.43	3.95	4.23	4.78	5.77	55.66	Hemphill	11.70	3-10-2018
240	4.95	5.11	5.22	4.65	4.30	4.80	3.22	4.28	4.18	4.75	1.70	5.40	55.56	San Augustine	10.60	8-18-1915
285	4.38	3.32	3.46	3.39	5.46	5.21	3.32	4.53	3.69	5.39	4.77	4.10	51.02	Oakhurst	16.30	8-28-2017
324	1.65	1.85	2.44	1.83	3.26	3.41	2.80	2.47	5.28	3.86	2.41	1.70	32.96	Welder Wildlife	14.40	9-13-1974
239	1.68	1.98	2.58	1.87	3.93	3.48	2.02	2.02	2.53	3.08	1.80	1.59	28.56	San Saba	11.20	10-5-1969
234	0.84	1.14	1.43	1.49	2.89	2.15	1.74	2.56	2.56	2.76	1.23	1.11	21.90	D. Wilson Ranch	9.51	7-16-1990
227	0.77	1.05	1.56	1.40	2.68	3.14	1.91	2.09	2.75	2.17	1.19	1.06	21.77	Knapp	5.93	5-15-1980
225	1.22	1.73	2.36	2.81	3.39	3.87	2.27	2.11	2.97	2.72	1.93	1.54	28.92	Albany	29.05	8-4-1978
248	5.18	4.81	5.26	4.96	4.46	4.96	3.65	4.18	3.57	4.95	4.89	5.62	56.49	Neuville	10.20	10-30-1941
181	0.51	0.36	1.08	1.41	2.07	2.48	2.53	2.73	1.02	1.70	0.60	0.58	17.07	Stratford	5.60	8-17-1992
257	3.95	4.26	4.25	3.99	4.32	4.78	2.72	2.92	3.23	4.72	3.84	4.68	47.66	Eads	8.24	6-7-1943
225	2.13	2.34	3.00	3.02	4.21	3.78	1.79	2.73	3.01	3.77	2.24	2.23	34.25	Glen Rose	10.73	6-22-2014
321	0.78	0.95	1.25	1.02	2.85	2.76	2.04	1.34	5.12	2.46	1.10	0.80	22.47	Rio Grande City	12.51	9-22-1967
213	1.57	1.89	2.35	2.33	3.92	3.68	2.25	2.53	2.64	2.88	1.88	1.78	29.70	Breckenridge	15.70	10-13-1981
219	0.95	0.97	1.27	1.32	2.75	2.06	1.68	2.42	2.45	2.46	1.20	0.87	20.40	Case Ranch	6.79	9-21-1972
223	0.98	1.22	1.65	1.70	3.07	3.39	2.06	2.71	2.48	1.89	1.33	1.12	23.60	Aspermont	6.92	4-28-1930
221	1.01	1.24	1.55	1.69	2.37	2.62	2.28	2.60	3.21	2.15	1.20	0.74	22.66	Humble Pump Stn	8.60	7-11-1988
189	0.70	0.69	1.36	1.46	2.70	2.94	2.41	2.65	1.99	1.91	0.96	0.77	20.54	Tulia	6.01	10-21-1918
245	2.15	2.38	3.20	3.23	4.54	3.52	1.87	2.45	3.40	4.27	2.71	2.43	36.15	Blue Mound	11.30	8-22-2022
236	1.10	1.29	1.73	1.86	3.21	3.44	1.92	2.53	2.67	2.83	1.40	1.26	25.24	Lawn	9.19	8-4-1978
243	0.56	0.52	0.78	0.62	1.68	2.30	2.02	1.61	1.84	1.15	0.52	0.68	14.28	Dryden	6.30	9-23-1990
215	0.69	0.62	1.07	1.31	2.20	2.67	1.94	1.80	2.56	1.57	0.88	0.74	18.05	Brownfield	7.85	9-21-1936
223	1.24	1.67	2.08	2.16	4.37	3.99	2.37	2.26	3.00	3.06	1.75	1.55	29.50	Throckmorton	6.53	8-4-1978
230	3.56	4.18	4.36	4.55	5.24	4.32	2.90	2.66	3.62	4.61	3.78	4.79	48.57	Mount Pleasant	8.06	11-5-1994
232	0.92	1.20	1.48	1.47	3.05	2.31	1.10	2.42	2.51	2.42	1.16	0.89	20.93	Miles	12.0	9-3-2024
291	2.64	1.89	2.88	2.42	5.04	3.68	1.96	2.74	3.45	3.91	2.92	2.72	36.25	Hill's Ranch	16.02	9-10-1921
272	4.57	3.38	3.85	3.89	4.47	5.45	3.06	4.14	4.47	4.63	4.68	4.73	51.32	Groveton	12.10	10-17-1994
258	4.98	4.85	4.62	4.45	4.68	5.15	4.17	5.03	5.26	4.99	5.12	5.80	59.10	Town Bluff	12.31	4-10-2024
229	3.76	4.09	4.22	4.66	4.49	4.07	3.05	3.01	3.68	4.57	3.81	4.51	47.92	Gilmer	7.88	4-23-1966
247	0.69	0.55	0.86	1.08	1.26	2.11	1.69	1.88	1.81	1.42	0.82	0.65	14.82	McCamey	9.13	10-4-1986
263	1.21	1.27	1.88	2.10	3.43	2.94	2.06	1.93	2.76	2.59	1.56	1.18	24.91	Montell	20.05	6-29-1913
293	0.61	0.63	1.18	1.50	3.06	2.32	1.50	2.69	2.63	2.08	0.91	0.71	19.82	Del Rio Intl. AP	17.03	8-23-1998
252	3.40	3.59	4.24	3.67	4.85	3.88	2.25	2.64	3.29	4.79	3.94	4.09	44.63	S. County Line	11.55	10-24-2015
291	2.67	1.96	2.99	3.01	5.23	4.21	3.46	3.11	4.53	3.97	2.93	2.34	40.41	Victoria	10.96	5-19-2021
272	4.57	3.38	3.85	3.89	4.47	5.45	3.06	4.14	4.47	4.63	4.68	4.73	51.32	Huntsville	14.75	8-28-2017
279	3.35	2.69	3.36	3.47	5.21	4.20	2.37	3.65	3.93	4.30	3.92	3.45	43.90	Brookshire	16.75	8-28-2017
216	0.67	0.45	0.63	0.44	1.30	1.63	1.87	1.85	2.19	1.52	0.49	0.77	13.81	Grandfalls	5.87	9-4-1986
273	3.66	3.36	3.63	3.56	5.39	4.46	2.58	3.83	4.59	5.07	4.21	3.69	48.03	Brenham	21.46	5-27-2016
329	0.77	0.65	1.34	1.30	2.82	1.81	1.86	1.58	3.87	1.66	0.97	1.05	19.68	Laredo	9.90	8-16-2022
287	3.13	1.95	2.81	3.09	4.79	4.89	4.30	3.92	5.71	5.59	5.69	3.73	49.60	New Gulf	14.00	6-26-1960
202	0.84	0.90	1.70	2.50	3.36	3.73	2.41	2.80	2.42	2.31	1.29	1.03	25.29	Shamrock	8.24	6-4-1995
228	1.20	1.40	2.02	2.50	3.81	3.35	2.02	2.53	2.99	2.88	1.63	1.56	27.89	Wichita V. Farm	8.00	8-15-1971
225	1.15	1.18	2.09	2.57	3.67	4.10	2.37	2.80	3.04	2.53	1.60	1.26	28.36	Vernon	14.82	8-2-1995
340	1.01	1.02	1.40	1.35	3.03	2.58	2.47	2.09	5.56	2.97	0.87	1.12	25.47	Port Mansfield	14.50	7-26-2020
259	2.50	2.24	3.09	3.02	4.25	3.97	2.19	2.64	3.96	3.92	2.71	2.59	37.08	Taylor	16.11	9-10-1921
261	1.64	1.61	2.28	2.41	4.38	2.95	2.32	2.66	4.06	3.16	2.32	1.84	31.63	Falls City	8.83	9-15-1968
222	0.49	0.40	0.72	0.47	1.40	1.27	1.53	1.38	1.55	1.18	0.49	0.50	11.38	Andrews	3.80	9-20-2014
222	1.67	2.21	2.84	3.04	4.55	3.73	2.07	2.18	3.04	3.91	2.19	1.91	33.34	Boyd	9.15	10-31-1981
235	3.67	4.01	4.15	3.80	4.68	3.53	2.67	2.71	3.73	4.99	3.47	5.06	46.47	Mineola	9.50	10-24-2015
200	0.52	0.59	1.04	0.91	1.56	1.99	2.10	2.10	2.48	1.43	0.70	0.77	16.19	Plains	6.11	7-5-1960
222	1.41	1.49	2.58	2.03	3.92	3.41	2.34	2.20	2.53	3.86	1.89	1.59	29.25	Olney	8.74	7-28-2004
341	0.81	0.45	0.66	1.23	2.64	2.61	2.83	1.52	4.37	1.38	1.23	0.67	20.40	Zapata	6.10	4-14-1966
307	1.04	0.85	1.70	1.31	2.23	2.07	2.07	1.92	2.43	2.00	1.00	0.84	19.46	Crystal City	13.88	10-14-2013

UNSPLASH/PETE ALEXOPOULOS

UNSPLASH/AVI WERDE

STATE GOVERNMENT OFFICIALS

The Texas state government is divided into executive, legislative, and judicial branches under the Texas Constitution, which was adopted in 1876.

The chief executive is the Governor, whose term is for four years. Other elected state officials with executive responsibilities include the Lieutenant Governor, Attorney General, Comptroller of Public Accounts, Commissioner of the General Land Office, and Commissioner of Agriculture. The terms of those officials are also four years.

The Secretary of State and the Commissioner of Education are appointed by the Governor.

Except for making numerous appointments and calling special sessions of the Texas Legislature, the Governor's powers are limited in comparison to those in most states.

Governor Greg Abbott

Lt. Governor Dan Patrick

Attorney General Ken Paxton

Comptroller of Public Accounts Kelly Hancock

Texas Land Commissioner Dawn Buckingham, M.D.

Agriculture Commissioner Sidney C. Miller

Secretary of State Jane Nelson

Education Commissioner Michael H. Morath

The 89th Texas Legislature Report

BY CAROLYN BARTA

In a session free of the political fireworks featured in their last meeting, Texas lawmakers in 2025 passed a long-stalled school voucher plan, approved a record $338 billion budget, and delivered the first meaningful boost in public school funding since 2019. The 89th Legislature also pushed the state further right on cultural issues, continuing Texas' conservative trajectory under Republican control.

The $1 billion voucher plan, launching subsidies for students to attend private schools, was folded into the largest two-year budget in state history. The cost of offering taxpayer money for private schools was offset by $8.5 billion in new public education funding, including long-overdue teacher raises and help for districts facing rising costs.

Unlike the contentious 88th session — marked by intraparty feuds and House-Senate clashes, followed by four special sessions and an impeachment trial — the 89th seemed calm. Led by the Senate, the two chambers worked in tandem to pass $51 billion in property tax relief and invest in infrastructure, including water supply, the energy grid, and highways.

Guadalupe River Flood Tragedy

Legislative accomplishments from the 140-day session faded from view over the Fourth of July weekend, when a violent flash flood on the Guadalupe River swept through the Texas Hill Country, leaving at least 130 dead, others missing, and a state in mourning.

Kerr County was the focal point. Among the dead were 27 children and counselors from Camp Mystic — a beloved summer camp near Hunt that, for generations, had drawn girls from across Texas. Rescue teams scoured debris-choked riverbanks for days, searching for the missing. The swiftly rising waters gave many no chance to escape.

The scale of the tragedy shocked the state. Neighborhoods were submerged; bridges and roadways crumbled. Communication lines failed. As communities grieved, leaders demanded answers — and action — to ensure no future flood would catch the state so unprepared.

Just weeks earlier, lawmakers had declined to pass House Bill 13, a proposal to strengthen Texas' disaster response system. The bill would have funded a statewide alert network and helped counties upgrade emergency communication tools, including outdoor warning sirens common in tornado-prone areas.

Governor Greg Abbott, who originally called a July 21 special session to deal with regulating hemp-derived THC (tetrahydrocannabinol) products after his veto of an outright ban, quickly expanded the agenda.

Flood response, preparedness, and recovery were added to the call, along with an unexpected mid-decade redistricting effort — part of a national strategy to protect the slim Republican U.S. House majority in the 2026 mid-term elections. Four Democratic-held seats in Texas were expected to be GOP targets.

President Donald J. Trump issued a major disaster declaration for the flood region, unlocking federal grants and loans, and Texas lawmakers were expected to move swiftly on emergency funding for affected counties. Early estimates pegged the economic toll at $18 to $22 billion, including damage to homes and businesses, tourism losses, and rebuilding costs.

For many Texans, though, the cost could not be counted in dollars. It was measured in lives cut short, communities shattered, and a summer marked by sorrow in a scenic and normally tranquil setting.

Historic Legislative Session

The 89th session of the Texas Legislature, which ended just a month before the Guadalupe River disaster, will be remembered largely for its impact on schools, property taxes, and investment in infrastructure. Lawmakers made historic changes to public school policy by mandating classroom posting of the Ten Commandments (quickly challenged in court) and banned cell phone use during school hours. They extended bans on diversity, equity, and inclusion (DEI) programs to K–12 schools and gave parents more power to challenge school library materials.

They also tightened bail laws, expanded immigration enforcement, restricted foreign land ownership to individuals and business from countries designated national security threats, and ordered that state records use only male and female gender terms — moves reinforcing the session's ideological tilt.

Oversight of the state lottery was shifted to a new agency amid fairness concerns, though the games remained as a revenue source.

In all, the Legislature sent more than 1,200 bills to Governor Abbott. He vetoed 26 — most notably scrapping a strict ban on intoxicating consumables derived from the cannabis plant that contain less than 0.3% of THC, which is found in marijuana at higher concentrations.

Under pressure from an industry grown to $8 billion and some 50,000 jobs with 8,000 retailers selling THC-laced consumables, Abbott asked legislators to design a bill in special session to regulate THC-infused items, like gummies, drinks, and vapes, instead of banning the products.

In a concession to veterans and patients with chronic conditions, lawmakers in regular session passed a bill expanding the state's medical marijuana program.

Private School Vouchers

The centerpiece of the 89th was Abbott's long-sought private school voucher program.

Known as Education Savings Accounts, the proposal allows families to receive up to $10,000 annually per student — more for children with disabilities — to move from public to private or religious schools. The plan repeatedly failed in past sessions, blocked by a coalition of Democrats and rural Republicans who feared the impact on local public schools.

Abbott overcame previous opposition by targeting anti-voucher Republicans in the 2024 primaries. With more than $6 million in campaign spending, he helped defeat several incumbents; others chose not to seek re-election.

The result was 26 new GOP House members, who were more reflective of the party's pro-voucher wing. The voucher measure passed, aided by the 88-to-62 GOP House majority and a new House Speaker, Dustin Burrows, who was more aligned with the governor and Lieutenant Governor Dan Patrick than his predecessor.

Burrows had replaced House Speaker Dade Phelan, whose downfall followed a series of decisions that alienated conservatives, including appointing Democrats to committee chairs, allowing the House to impeach Attorney General Ken Paxton, and resisting pressure to push vouchers.

Though hardliners backed another candidate, Burrows won with support from 49 Democrats and 36 Republicans as the session began in January 2025. Critics feared he would cater to Democrats, but he ended the session with a solid conservative record.

Some Democrats felt shortchanged for their support, after they were denied any committee chairmanships — a bipartisan tradition since the 1970s. Others said Burrows gave them vice-chairs and allowed them to be heard and advocate for their districts.

At "sine die" on June 2, Burrows said the House, which had started "in a bit of uncertainty" ended "in a much more unified and solid place."

Abbott And Patrick: Combined Power

Though the House saw leadership turnover, Abbott and Patrick were the dominant forces in the 89th Legislature.

Patrick, the Senate's presiding officer long regarded as the Capitol's most influential figure, maintained strict control over the Senate agenda and passed 90% of his priority bills with a 19-11 GOP majority.

Abbott, meanwhile, showed a more assertive style than in previous sessions. He influenced legislator elections, declared emergency items early, and used his bully pulpit to push priorities. He called the 89th the best session of his 10-year tenure, describing it as "transformative" and a "monumental" success.

All of Abbott's emergency items passed, including bail reform, teacher pay raises, water infrastructure investment, and $51 billion in property tax relief. Patrick's influence was visible in symbolic low-numbered Senate bills: SB1 (budget), SB 2 (vouchers), SB 3 (THC ban), SB 4 (homestead exemption), SB 9 (bail reform), SB 10 (Ten Commandments), SB 8 (immigration enforcement), and infrastructure bills SB 6 (electric grid) and SB 7 (water supply). He hailed the session as the best in modern Senate history.

The only public rift between Patrick and Abbott came when Abbott vetoed the THC ban that Patrick had championed. The lieutenant governor, who staged a press conference showcasing a table full of objectionable THC-laced products, said he was "stunned" by Abbott's late-hour veto and accused the governor of siding with recreational marijuana advocates after remaining silent during the session.

Throughout the session, Democrats were forced into a largely defensive posture as Republicans advanced their agenda. House leaders occasionally chafed at the power of the Senate, objecting that House initiatives were stalled by Senate dominance.

Policy Highlights From The 89th Session

Budget and spending: The $338 billion budget — $17 billion more than two years ago — was fueled by a population explosion, record sales tax collections, and leftover pandemic relief funds, factors creating an extraordinary surplus. Spending highlights included tax relief, school funding, infrastructure, health care, and border security, along with more funds for childcare, state troopers, university research, and in-state film production.

Abbott used his budget line-item veto to whack a $60-million expense for Texas to participate in a federally backed summer food program for low-income children, resulting in the rejection of an estimated $400–$450 million in federal aid.

School finance: With education funding neglected since 2019, school districts across the state were closing schools, hiring uncertified teachers, and reducing staff as they sought to keep up with rising operational costs and a teacher shortage. Two years before, public school funding was held hostage to the passage of private school vouchers. In the 2025 session, lawmakers vowed to approve both vouchers and public-school funding as part of a "Texas two-step."

Once vouchers became law, the Senate and House negotiated how to add money for the state's 1,200-plus school districts with an estimated enrollment of 5.5 million students in 2023-24.

The House wanted a steep increase in the basic per-student allotment to allow districts flexibility in spending on local priorities. The Senate pressed for a modest per-student bump while channeling most of the $8.5 billion package into targeted allocations like teacher pay, special education, early learning, safety measures, and other fixed costs.

The Senate's approach prevailed. The basic allotment, the fundamental building block of school finance, was raised from $6,160 per student to $6,215 for the year. School leaders complained that funding restricted to specified uses would cause loss of a district's independence.

More than $4 billion of the proposal's overall funding was earmarked for teacher pay raises, with a teacher's raise dependent on years of experience and district demographics. Larger increases were designed to retain veteran teachers and address needs of rural districts.

Property taxes: Buoyed by the surplus, lawmakers approved a second round of property tax cuts that began in 2023, raising the homestead exemption for school district property taxes from $100,000 to $140,000, and to $200,000 for homeowners over 65 or with disabilities, all pending voter approval. They also sought voter approval to raise the personal property tax exemption for businesses from $2,500 to $125,000.

Immigration: The Legislature approved $3.4 billion for border security, down from an earlier allocation of $6.5 billion for border initiatives. Lawmakers cited lower illegal crossings after President Trump took office and incoming federal aid for the reduction. No new money was allocated for building a border wall. The state has completed 65 wall miles and had funds to complete 85 more along the 1,200-mile Texas-Mexican border. The $3 billion saved was applied to property tax relief.

Infrastructure: Lawmakers created a $5 billion Energy Fund to spur gas-fueled power plant construction and approved $2.5 billion for water system improvements. They also proposed a 20-year, $20 billion water fund requiring voter approval.

Lottery: Faced with concerns about online third-party services known as "couriers" buying huge quantities of lottery tickets, thus skewing odds, lawmakers abolished the Lottery Commission and transferred oversight to the Texas Department of Licensing and Regulation. A Sunset review in 2029 could determine the future of the games.

Bail reform: A constitutional amendment was sent to voters to require judges to deny bail to a defendant charged with the most heinous crimes (rape, murder, human trafficking, indecency with a child) when the state proves the defendant is a threat to public safety.

Other changes restrict nonelected magistrates from setting bail in serious cases, require judges to justify why they dismiss charges, and prohibit people who plead guilty to first- or second-degree felonies from being released before sentencing. Abbott said reforms address a "revolving door" bail system for defendants, while critics warned of due process concerns and jail overcrowding.

Transgender and abortion policy: LGBTQ+ student clubs and classroom discussions on gender identity were banned in public schools. Teachers are prohibited from using transgender students' chosen names or pronouns.

On abortion, lawmakers clarified medical exceptions under the state's near-total ban after multiple women were denied emergency care, leading to a national outcry. Under the new law, doctors will be allowed to use their judgment in emergencies to protect a pregnant patient's life or major bodily function.

Starbase: Lawmakers sanctioned the formation of "Starbase," a town incorporated around Elon Musk's SpaceX facilities in Cameron County, by authorizing beach and highway closures during rocket launches. In May 2025, a local vote — largely by SpaceX employees living on-site — authorized incorporation of the town and governance by a three-member commission. Critics of the "company town" raised concerns about beach access, environmental risks, and private control of public land.

Texas Dream Act: Texas became the first state to offer in-state tuition to undocumented students in 2001. A federal lawsuit led to a court decision in 2025 blocking the tuition benefit. In response, Texas ordered colleges to begin charging undocumented students out-of-state tuition starting in Fall 2025. Legal challenges followed.

Failed legislation: Measures that failed included banning abortion pills from out-of-state; requiring proof of citizenship to vote; legalization of fentanyl test strips; denying bail to undocumented immigrants charged with violent crimes; and mandatory prison air conditioning by 2032.

Special Session: Abbott included 18 items in his call for a special session, highlighted by response to the Guadalupe flood, regulation of THC products similar to alcohol regulation, and congressional redistricting. The last mid-term redistricting in 2003 produced a GOP-dominant congressional delegation, which stood at 25 Republicans to 12 Democrats in 2025, but Trump hoped to grow that by up to five more members, placing Texas in the national political spotlight for the 2026 mid-terms.

Elections And Politics

Governor Abbott left the regular session on a political high, signing major bills in symbolic locations around the state, surrounded by supporters. Re-election to a fourth full term in 2026 would make him Texas' longest-serving governor. Patrick, running again with Trump's endorsement, was expected to easily win another term. Speaker Burrows also appeared poised for re-election by his House colleagues.

The marquee statewide race in 2026 is for the U.S. Senate, where Attorney General Paxton is challenging veteran Senator John Cornyn in the GOP primary. Though backed by Trump loyalists, Paxton acquired a polarizing profile as he survived impeachment and scandals.

Analysts say Democrats could have a rare opening in the general election if Paxton is the Republican Senate nominee. But Democrats face a steep climb. The party hasn't won statewide office since 1994. Trump carried the state in the 2024 presidential election by 56 percent to Democrat Kamala Harris' 42 percent.

Carolyn Barta is a former political writer for The *Dallas Morning News* and a retired journalism professor at Southern Methodist University.

The 89th Texas Legislature Special Session

The summer special sessions of 2025 will be remembered for two defining events: a partisan showdown over congressional redistricting that sent Democrats fleeing the state to deny a House quorum, and belated passage of flood safety laws following the Texas Hill Country disaster that killed more than 130 people.

Together they underscored how political warfare and natural catastrophe collided to shape one of the most turbulent interludes in recent legislative history.

Quorum Break Over Redistricting

Whatever harmony the 89th Legislature had managed in its regular session was shattered when more than 50 House Democrats broke quorum in the first special session of Summer 2025, temporarily halting passage of a President Trump-desired mid-decade redistricting bill and delaying action on the response to the deadly July 4 flood.

The Democrats fled to Illinois, New York, Massachusetts, and California after Governor Greg Abbott placed redistricting at the top of the session's agenda — before flood relief legislation. The redistricting proposal was designed to add five more Texas Republican seats and help the GOP maintain control of a razor-thin majority in Congress in the 2026 mid-term elections.

The Democrats met with Democratic governors and other party leaders, focusing national media attention on what they called a partisan power grab. Their absence forced an early adjournment of the first special session, but Abbott immediately called another, vowing to keep lawmakers in Austin for "special session after special session" until a new map was drawn.

Once House Democrats returned to the chamber on August 18 after their two-week absence, Republicans pushed through a plan that dismantled three minority districts in urban areas — in Houston, North Texas, and Austin-San Antonio — and reworked two South Texas swing districts to favor Republicans.

Democrats argued the maps violated the Voting Rights Act by diluting Black and Hispanic voting strength and pledged to take their fight to the courts. Republicans countered that a 2019 Supreme Court ruling upheld partisan gerrymandering.

Texas redistricting produced a bitter political fight with national implications. Congressional seats are normally redrawn each decade following the U.S. Census. But the party in the White House historically loses ground in mid-term elections and, with a slim 219-212 majority, President Trump and his allies thought continued Republican control in jeopardy. In Texas, Republicans owned 25 of 38 congressional seats before the 2026 mid-terms and stood to add seats with more favorably drawn maps.

National implications included a potential redistricting "arms race" as other states — both red and blue — considered mid-decade remaps, with California leading the way.

In Austin, the exodus resulted in frayed relations between the two parties, as Abbott and other top Republican officeholders used aggressive tactics to pressure absent Democrats and marginalize and penalize them on their return.

Flood Response Legislation

Only after redistricting passed did lawmakers turn to flood relief in the aftermath of the July 4 disaster along the Guadalupe River that took the lives of more than 130 people, including 27 children and staff at Camp Mystic.

The flash flood that overwhelmed camp facilities and homes along the river resulted in a weeks-long search for bodies of victims. When Democrats argued that flood response bills should have been prioritized above redistricting, Republicans countered that Democrats caused the delay of flood bills by their quorum break.

Lawmakers addressed the devastating floods with these legislative goals:

- **Early warning systems:** mandating siren systems, gauges, sensors, and local maintenance.
- **Disaster relief funding** for matching federal aid, plus preparedness and forecasting.
- **Emergency management:** licensing, drills, volunteer registry, and mass-fatality teams.
- **Youth camp safety:** alert systems, drills, evacuation planning, and banning of camps in floodplains.

Legislators tapped the Rainy Day Fund for $294 million in flood response money. It included $200 million in FEMA/state disaster recovery matching dollars, $50 million for local flood warning systems and sirens, $24 million for weather forecasting improvements, and $20 million for a swift-water rescue training facility for first responders. They mandated outdoor flood-warning sirens, reversing prior years of local resistance.

Among the legislation approved was a bill known as Heaven's 27 Camp Safety Act, so named for lives lost at Camp Mystic. It requires youth camps to have evacuation plans, weather-alert systems, and regular drills, while banning new camps in 100-year floodplains. Many of the girls' parents, watching in the galleries, wept and clutched each other as both chambers voted on bills meeting their demands to make the camps safer.

The bills reflected a broader shift in policy after the Texas Hill Country disaster — one that moved beyond immediate recovery to emphasize prevention, coordination, and training, indicating that Texas was committed to a more aggressive approach to flood preparedness.

A Texas Tradition

Though dramatic, the 2025 walkout was not unprecedented. Previous quorum breaks include the 1979 "Killer Bees," who hid out to block a primary bill; the 2003 Democratic flight to Oklahoma over mid-decade redistricting; and a 2021 walkout to Washington, D.C., against GOP voting restrictions.

In an effort to stop future standoffs, lawmakers considered a bill added to the second special session to create new fines for lawmakers breaking quorum.

Other Special Session Business

Lawmakers also:

- Approved a plan to replace the once-a-year STAAR test with three shorter exams for public school students.
- Barred local governments and schools from allowing transgender people to use bathrooms matching their preferred gender identity.
- Advanced bills restricting out-of-state abortion pill distribution by allowing private citizens to sue distributors.
- Considered bills to ban or regulate the retail sale of hemp-based THC consumables.

—Carolyn Barta

THE 89TH TEXAS LEGISLATURE

The Texas Legislature has 181 members: 31 in the Senate and 150 in the House of Representatives. Regular sessions convene on the second Tuesday of January in odd-numbered years, but the governor may call special sessions. Article III of the Texas Constitution details the structure and power of the Legislature.

The following lists are of members of the 89th Legislature, which convened for its Regular Session on January 4, 2025, and adjourned on June 2, 2025. The 90th Legislature is scheduled to convene on January 12, 2027, and adjourn May 31, 2027.

Salary: The salary of all members of the Legislature, both Senators and Representatives, is $7,200 per year and $221 per diem during legislative sessions; mileage allowance at same rate provided by law for state employees. The per diem payment applies during each regular and special session of the Legislature.

State Senate

All 31 members of the State Senate are elected to four-year, overlapping terms. Senatorial Districts include one or more whole counties; some counties have more than one Senator.

President of the Senate: Lt. Gov. Dan Patrick
President Pro Tempore: Brandon Creighton
Secretary of the Senate: Patsy Spaw
Sergeant-at-Arms: Austin Osborn

TEXAS STATE SENATORS

District, Member, Party-Hometown, Occupation

1. Bryan Hughes, R-Mineola; attorney
2. Bob Hall, R-Edgewood; retired military
3. Robert Nichols, R-Jacksonville; engineer
4. Brandon Creighton, R-Conroe; attorney
5. Charles Schwertner, R-Georgetown; surgeon
6. Carol Alvarado, D-Houston; small business owner
7. Paul Bettencourt, R-Houston; tax advisor
8. Angela Paxton, R-McKinney; consultant, former educator
9. Kelly Hancock, R-North Richland Hills; business owner
10. Phil King, R-Weatherford; attorney and small business owner
11. Mayes Middleton, R-Galveston; oil and gas
12. Tan Parker, R-Flower Mound; businessman
13. Borris L. Miles, D-Houston; insurance and real estate developer
14. Sarah Eckhardt, D-Austin; attorney
15. Molly Cook, D-Houston; emergency room nurse
16. Nathan Johnson, D-Dallas; attorney
17. Joan Huffman, R-Houston; attorney
18. Lois W. Kolkhorst, R-Brenham; business owner
19. Roland Gutierrez, D-San Antonio; attorney
20. Juan "Chuy" Hinojosa, D-McAllen; attorney
21. Judith Zaffirini, D-Laredo; communications specialist, former educator
22. Brian Birdwell, R-Granbury; retired military
23. Royce West, D-Dallas; attorney
24. Pete Flores, R-Pleasanton; retired game warden
25. Donna Campbell, R-New Braunfels; physician
26. José Menéndez, D-San Antonio; businessman
27. Adam Hinojosa, R-Corpus Christi; small business owner

WIKIPEDIA

28. Charles Perry, R-Lubbock; certified public accountant
29. César Blanco, D-El Paso; consultant
30. Brent Hagenbuch, R-Denton; business owner
31. Kevin Sparks, R-Midland; oil and gas operator

House of Representatives

This is a list of the 150 current members of the House of Representatives. They were elected for two-year terms from the districts shown below. Representatives and Senators receive the same salary.

Speaker: Dustin Burrows
Chief Clerk: Stephen Brown
Sergeant-at-Arms: Kara Coffee

TEXAS STATE REPRESENTATIVES

District, Member, Party-Hometown, Occupation

1. Gary VanDeaver, R-New Boston; retired educator
2. Brent Money, R-Greenville; attorney
3. Cecil Bell Jr., R-Magnolia; contractor
4. Keith Bell, R-Forney; electrical contractor
5. Cole Hefner, R-Mount Pleasant; insurance agent
6. Daniel Alders, R-Tyler; business owner
7. Jay Dean, R-Longview; business owner
8. Cody Harris, R-Palestine; ranch broker
9. Trent Ashby, R-Lufkin; title insurance executive
10. Brian Harrison, R-Midlothian; consultant
11. Joanne Shofner, R-Nacogdoches; consultant
12. Trey Wharton, R-Huntsville; business owner
13. Angelia Orr, R-Hillsboro; asset manager
14. Paul Dyson, R-Bryan; lawyer
15. Steve Toth, R-Conroe; business owner
16. Will Metcalf, R-Conroe; banker
17. Stan Gerdes, R-Smithville; consultant
18. Janis Holt, R-Silsbee; retired
19. Ellen Troxclair, R-Lakeway; self-employed
20. Terry M. Wilson, R-Georgetown; retired military
21. Dade Phelan, R-Beaumont; real estate developer
22. Christian Manuel, D-Port Arthur; state employee
23. Terri Leo-Wilson, R-Galveston; retired teacher
24. Greg Bonnen, R-Friendswood; neurosurgeon
25. Cody Vasut, R-Angleton; attorney
26. Matt Morgan, R-Richmond; business owner
27. Ron Reynolds, D-Missouri City; attorney
28. Gary Gates, R-Richmond; real estate, property management
29. Jeffrey Barry, R-Pearland; insurance agent
30. A.J. Louderback, R-Victoria; law enforcement
31. Ryan Guillen, R-Rio Grande City; investor, rancher
32. Todd Hunter, R-Corpus Christi; attorney
33. Katrina Pierson, R-Rockwall; communications executive
34. Denise Villalobos, R-Corpus Christi; engineer
35. Oscar Longoria, D-Mission; attorney
36. Sergio Muñoz Jr., D-Mission; attorney
37. Janie Lopez, R-San Benito; mental health professional
38. Erin Gámez, D-Brownsville; attorney
39. Armando "Mando" Martinez, D-Weslaco; contractor
40. Terry Canales, D-Edinburg; attorney
41. RD "Bobby" Guerra, D-Mission; attorney
42. Richard Peña Raymond, D-Laredo; mediator
43. J.M. Lozano, R-Kingsville; businessman
44. Alan Schoolcraft, R-McQueeney; CEO
45. Erin Zwiener, D-Driftwood; writer
46. Sheryl Cole, D-Austin; attorney, CPA
47. Vikki Goodwin, D-Austin; real estate broker
48. Donna Howard, D-Austin; community advocate
49. Gina Hinojosa, D-Austin; attorney
50. James Talarico, D-Austin; nonprofit director
51. Maria Luisa Flores, D-Austin; attorney
52. Caroline Harris Davila, R-Round Rock; policy advisor
53. Wes Virdell, R-Brady; self-employed
54. Brad Buckley, R-Salado; veterinarian
55. Hillary Hickland, R-Belton; homemaker
56. Pat Curry, R-Waco; self-employed
57. Richard Hayes, R-Hickory Creek; attorney
58. Helen Kerwin, R-Glen Rose; retired
59. Shelby Slawson, R-Stephenville; attorney
60. Mike Olcott, R-Fort Worth; retired biochemist
61. Keresa Richardson, R-McKinney; entrepreneur
62. Shelley Luther, R-Tom Bean; business owner
63. Benjamin Bumgarner, R-Flower Mound; self-employed
64. Andy Hopper, R-Decatur; software engineer
65. Mitch Little, R-Lewisville; attorney
66. Matt Shaheen, R-Plano; technology executive
67. Jeff Leach, R-Allen; attorney
68. David Spiller, R-Jacksboro; attorney
69. James Frank, R-Wichita Falls; business owner
70. Mihaela Plesa, D-Dallas; fashion merchandising and design
71. Stan Lambert, R-Abilene; retired banker
72. Drew Darby, R-San Angelo; attorney, businessman
73. Carrie Isaac, R-Dripping Springs; consultant
74. Eddie Morales Jr., D-Eagle Pass; attorney
75. Mary González, D-Clint; consultant, professor
76. Suleman Lalani, D-Sugar Land; physician
77. Vincent Perez, D-El Paso; consultant
78. Joe Moody, D-El Paso; attorney
79. Claudia Ordaz, D-El Paso, self-employed
80. Don McLaughlin Jr., R-Uvalde; sales
81. Brooks Landgraf, R-Odessa; attorney, rancher
82. Tom Craddick, R-Midland; business development manager
83. Dustin Burrows, R-Lubbock; attorney
84. Carl Tepper, R-Lubbock; commercial real estate
85. Stan Kitzman, R-Pattison; small business owner
86. John Smithee, R-Amarillo; attorney
87. Caroline Fairly, R-Amarillo; contractor
88. Ken King, R-Canadian; oil and gas service executive
89. Candy Noble, R-Lucas; educator
90. Ramón Romero Jr., D-Fort Worth; CEO
91. David Lowe, R-North Richland Hills; retired military
92. Salman Bhojani, D-Euless; attorney, real estate investor

93. Nate Schatzline, R-Fort Worth; operations director, pastor
94. Tony Tinderholt, R-Arlington; retired military
95. Nicole Collier, D-Fort Worth; attorney
96. David Cook, R-Mansfield; attorney
97. John McQueeney, R-Fort Worth; small business owner
98. Giovanni Capriglione, R-Southlake; small-business owner
99. Charlie Geren, R-Fort Worth; restaurant owner, rancher
100. Venton Jones, D-Dallas; nonprofit CEO
101. Chris Turner, D-Grand Prairie; communications consultant
102. Ana-María Rodríguez Ramos, D-Richardson; attorney, professor
103. Rafael Anchía, D-Dallas; attorney
104. Jessica González, D-Dallas; attorney
105. Terry Meza, D-Irving; attorney
106. Jared Patterson, R-Frisco; energy services
107. Linda Garcia, D-Mesquite; author
108. Morgan Meyer, R-University Park; attorney
109. Aicha Davis, D-Dallas; education
110. Toni Rose, D-Dallas; independent contractor
111. Yvonne Davis, D-Dallas; small business owner
112. Angie Chen Button, R-Garland; marketing
113. Rhetta Andrews Bowers, D-Rowlett; educator
114. John Bryant, D-Dallas; attorney
115. Cassandra Garcia Hernandez, D-Farmers Branch; lawyer
116. Trey Martinez Fischer, D-San Antonio; contractor
117. Philip Cortez, D-San Antonio; public relations
118. John Lujan, R-San Antonio; small business owner
119. Elizabeth "Liz" Campos, D-San Antonio; self-employed
120. Barbara Gervin-Hawkins, D-San Antonio; education
121. Marc LaHood, R-San Antonio; lawyer
122. Mark Dorazio, R-San Antonio; self-employed
123. Diego Bernal, D-San Antonio; attorney
124. Josey Garcia, D-San Antonio; retired military
125. Ray Lopez, D-San Antonio
126. E. Sam Harless, R-Spring; automobile dealer
127. Charles Cunningham, R-Humble; retired businessman
128. Briscoe Cain, R-Deer Park; attorney
129. Dennis Paul, R-Houston; engineer
130. Tom Oliverson, R-Cypress; anesthesiologist
131. Alma A. Allen, D-Houston; educational consultant
132. Mike Schofield, R-Katy; attorney
133. Mano DeAyala, R-Houston; attorney
134. Ann Johnson, D-Houston; attorney
135. Jon E. Rosenthal, D-Houston; engineer
136. John H. Bucy III, D-Austin; small business owner
137. Gene Wu, D-Houston; attorney
138. Lacey Hull, R-Houston; consultant
139. Charlene Ward Johnson, D-Houston; claims manager
140. Armando Lucio Walle, D-Houston; legal assistant
141. Senfronia Thompson, D-Houston; attorney
142. Harold V. Dutton Jr., D-Houston; attorney
143. Ana Hernandez, D-Houston; attorney
144. Mary Ann Perez, D-Houston; insurance agent
145. Christina Morales, D-Houston; funeral director
146. Lauren Ashley Simmons, D-Houston; union organizer
147. Jolanda "Jo" Jones, D-Houston; attorney
148. Penny Morales Shaw, D-Houston; attorney
149. Hubert Vo, D-Houston; businessman
150. Valoree Swanson, R-Spring; businesswoman

TEXAS STATE HOUSE OF REPRESENTATIVES, 89TH LEGISLATURE

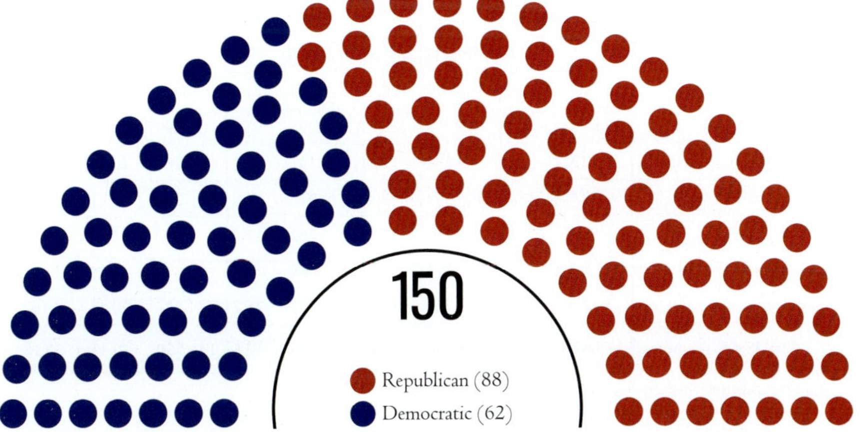

GOVERNMENT FINANCIALS

Taxes are the state government's primary source of income. These are summaries of state revenues and expenditures, tax collections, tax revenue by type of tax, a summary of the state budgets for the 2024-2025 and 2026-2027 bienniums, Texas Lottery income and expenditures, and the amount of federal payments to state agencies. Totals may not sum due to rounding.

State Revenues by Source and Expenditures by Function, Total of All Funds
Amounts (in Millions) and Percent Change from Previous Year

Revenues by Source	2024	%	2023	%	2022	%	2021	%	2020	%
Tax Collections	$81,874	-0.3	82,146	6.4	77,211	25.6	61,473	7.1	57,380	–3.4
Federal Income	$58,866	-14.3	68,707	-5.5	72,739	-11.2	81,940	41.0	58,117	38.7
Licenses, Fees, Permits, Fines, and Penalties	$6,937	4.1	6,663	2.0	6,532	2.9	6,347	1.7	6,241	–4.6
State Health Service Fees and Rebates	$14,148	29.6	10,920	6.2	10,285	51.4	6,794	-9.4	7,497	5.8
Net Lottery Proceeds	$3,090	-7.8	3,350	9.5	3,058	3.5	2,955	23.5	2,392	–4.7
Land Income	$3,540	-6.8	3,797	-11.9	4,312	100.8	2,148	18.7	1,809	–19.6
Interest and Investment Income	$5,755	37.0	4,201	72.3	2,438	23.4	1,975	-21.9	2,529	1.0
Settlements of Claims	$848	34.4	631	-4.7	662	-13.0	761	21.9	624	–3.4
Escheated Estates	$1,281	17.4	1,091	7.8	1,012	2.7	793	10.8	715	3.2
Sales of Goods and Services	$259	-15.9	308	-2.0	314	-2.2	321	26.1	255	–8.6
Other Revenues	$4,519	-24.4	5,975	24.9	4,783	-4.1	4,989	24.2	4,016	–3.0
Total Net Revenues	**181,118**	**-3.6**	**187,789**	**2.4**	**183,345**	**7.5**	**170,496**	**20.4**	**141,576**	**10.7**
Expenditures by Function	**2024**	**%**	**2023**	**%**	**2022**	**%**	**2021**	**%**	**2020**	**%**
General Government	$5,805	3.4	5,614	-5.7	5,955	25.6	4,741	27.7	3,714	5.4
Education	$61,062	21.3	50,352	1.8	49,468	10.4	44,821	4.6	42,869	13.9
Employee Benefits	$7,024	6.0	6,628	17.9	5,622	10.7	5,077	2.1	4,972	0.2
Health and Human Services	$67,715	-7.8	73,433	-1.5	74,571	11.5	66,857	16.9	57,197	10.3
Public Safety and Corrections	$7,019	5.7	6,639	10.7	5,998	25.4	4,782	-1.9	4,877	–6.1
Transportation	$18,133	31.7	13,766	12.0	12,293	-3.2	12,699	0.4	12,647	20.5
Natural Resources/Recreational Services	$4,222	-7.9	4,584	11.0	4,131	9.7	3,764	20.8	3,116	10.8
Regulatory Agencies	$418	18.3	353	2.4	345	4.5	330	-0.2	331	–1.5
Lottery Winnings Paid*	$831	-12.7	953	26.7	752	-1.9	767	41.6	541	–20.9
Debt Service – Interest	$1,203	3.6	1,161	6.0	1,096	-21.3	1,392	-16.2	1,661	1.0
Capital Outlay	$2,379	38.0	1,724	12.8	1,528	15.7	1,321	10.8	1,192	40.2
Total Net Expenditures	**175,812**	**6.4**	**165,206**	**2.1**	**161,758**	**10.4**	**146,550**	**10.1**	**133,118**	**10.9**

* Does not include payments made by retailers.

All amounts rounded. Revenue and expenditures exclude trust funds. Fiscal years end August 31.

Source: 2024 State of Texas Annual Cash Report, Comptroller of Public Accounts.

STATE GOVERNMENT BUDGET SUMMARY (2026–2027 BIENNIUM)

The Legislative Budget Board's (LBB) baseline appropriations for state government operations for the 2026-2027 biennium total $338 billion from All Funds functions of state government. The funding is a $4.0 billion, or 1.2%, increase from the 2024–2025 biennial level of $334 billion.

General Revenue Funds, including funds dedicated within the General Revenue Fund, total $149.2 billion for the 2026–2027 biennium, an increase of $7.2 billion, or 5.1%, from the estimated 2024–2025 biennial spending level of $141.9 billion. The table below details the difference in spending by article.

General Revenue Funds by Article

Article (Governmental Division)	Estimated/ Budgeted 2024–2025	2026–2027 Budget	Biennial Change	Percentage Change
Art. I: General Government	$11,040.2	$6,321.5	-4,718.7	-42.7%
Art. II: Health and Human Services	43,252.8	45,196.0	1,943.3	4.5%
Art. III: Agencies of Education	68,921.3	73,613.2	4,691.9	6.8%
Public Education	47,445.7	49,697.3	2,251.6	4.7%
Higher Education	21,475.6	23,915.9	2,440.3	11.4%
Art. IV: The Judiciary	850.9	829.0	-22.0	-2.6%
Art. V: Public Safety & Criminal Justice	13,401.1	19,244.8	5,843.7	43.6%
Art. VI: Natural Resources	2,639.9	1,598.8	-1,041.2	-39.4%
Art. VII: Business & Economic Dev.	881.1	958.6	77.5	8.8%
Art. VIII: Regulatory	428.3	562.9	134.6	31.4%
Art. IX: General Provisions	0.0	308.2	308.2	N/A
Art. X: The Legislature	520.8	540.1	19.3	3.7%
Total, All Articles	$141,936.3	$149,173.1	$7,236.7	**5.1%**

Totals may not sum due to rounding. All dollar figures in millions.
Source: Summary of Conference Committee Report on House Bill 1: Highlights of the Appropriations for the 2026–27 Biennium, May 2025.

State Tax Collections (2004–2024)

FY	State Tax Collections (in millions)	Resident Population	Per Capita Tax Collections	Taxes as % of Personal Income
2024	$81,874.20	30,515,222	$2,683	4.00%
2023	82,145.60	30,476,193	2,695	4.20%
2022	77,210.70	29,963,286	2,577	4.20%
2021	61,473.50	29,511,094	2,083	3.50%
2020	57,379.80	29,183,745	1,966	3.60%
2019	59,380.70	28,950,175	2,051	4.10%
2018	55,584.80	28,668,600	1,939	4.00%
2017	49,643.40	28,255,300	1,757	3.80%
2016	48,476.20	27,845,500	1,741	3.80%
2015	51,683.10	27,389,200	1,887	4.00%
2014	50,992.60	26,788,600	1,896	4.30%
2013	47,781.00	26,399,510	1,810	4.20%
2012	44,079.10	26,005,770	1,695	4.00%
2011	38,856.20	25,592,790	1,518	3.80%
2010	35,368.90	25,191,450	1,404	3.70%
2009	37,822.50	24,737,000	1,529	4.10%
2008	41,357.90	24,250,000	1,705	4.30%
2007	36,955.60	23,778,000	1,554	4.30%
2006	33,544.50	23,339,000	1,437	4.10%
2005	29,838.30	22,808,000	1,308	4.00%
2004	26,279.10	21,673,000	1,213	4.20%

Sources: 2024 State of Texas Annual Cash Report; historic data collected from older reports.

Tax Revenues (2023–2024)

Type of Tax	FY 2023	Change	FY 2024	Change
Sales	46,581.1	8.4%	$47,159.9	1.2%
Motor Vehicle Sales/ Rentals*	6,821.7	5.8%	6,835.1	0.2%
Motor Fuels	3,832.1	1.3%	3,846.5	0.4%
Franchise	6,820.2	20.2%	6,861.3	0.6%
Oil Production	5,931.0	-6.8%	6,304.2	6.3%
Insurance	4,064.6	30.2%	4,157.6	2.3%
Cigarettes & Tobacco	1,218.3	0.6%	1,069.8	–12.2%
Natural Gas Production	3,350.4	-25.0%	2,133.6	-36.3%
Alcoholic Beverages	1,771.6	7.8%	1,773.2	0.1%
Hotel	778.9	11.1%	755.8	-2.8%
Utility	625.2	12.3%	664.6	6.3%
Other Taxes	351.4	31.1%	312.6	-11.1%
Total	**$82,145.60**	6.4 %	**$81,874.20**	**-0.3%**

Totals may not sum due to rounding.
All dollar figures in millions.
*Includes tax on manufactured housing sales.
Source: 2024 State of Texas Annual Cash Report.

Source: Legislative Budget Board.

FEDERAL REVENUE BY AGENCY

Texas received $58.9 billion in federal funds during fiscal 2024, a decrease of $9.8 billion, or 14.3%, from fiscal 2023. Federal funds accounted for 32.5% of total net revenue, the second-largest source of revenue in fiscal 2024.

Agency	FY 2024	FY 2023	FY 2022	FY 2021
Health and Human Services	$33,922.9	$40,049.2	$42,026.00	$34,764.00
Texas Education Agency	11,668.9	12,843.0	12,104.80	6,317.40
Texas Department of Transportation	5,279.6	4,389.4	4,523.30	5,504.60
Texas Division of Emergency Management	568,503.0	1,150.0	3,487.30	7,481.40
Texas Workforce Commission	2,568.7	4,303.4	3,485.70	4,715.60
General Land Office	1,286.2	1,324.3	1,462.90	1,110.50
Department of State Health Services	676.6	803.7	967.7	616.3
Department of Agriculture	935,477.2	879,398.3	813.1	1,251.30
All Other Agencies	1,458.0	2,451.2	3,361.2	19,636.7
Total	**$58,866.3**	**$68,707.0**	**$72,738.70**	**$81,940.10**

Totals may not sum due to rounding. All figures in millions. *Source: 2024 State of Texas Annual Cash Report.*

TEXAS LOTTERY

The State Lottery Act was passed by the Texas Legislature in July 1991. Texas voters approved a constitutional amendment authorizing a state lottery in an election on November 5, 1991, by a vote of 1,326,154 to 728,994. Since the first ticket was sold on May 29, 1992, the Texas Lottery has generated $37.8 billion in revenue for the state.

Since 1997, the Texas Lottery has contributed $31.8 billion to the Foundation School Fund, which supports public education. Before September 1997, revenues were only deposited in the General Revenue Fund.

As authorized by the Legislature, certain Texas Lottery revenues have been earmarked to benefit state programs, including the Fund for Veterans Assistance, which is administered by the Texas Veterans Commission. Sales and unclaimed prizes from the veterans' designated scratch-off games have totaled more than $221 million since 2010.

Other Texas Lottery funds, such as unclaimed prizes, contribute to other causes and programs as authorized by the Texas Legislature.

Distribution of Texas Lottery proceeds for fiscal year 2023:

- 66.9% to prizes paid
- 24.5% to the Foundation School Fund
- 5.3% to retailer commissions
- 3.0% for lottery administration
- 0.3% to the Texas Veterans Commission.

Source: Texas Lottery Commission.

Texas Lottery Financial Data

Period	Sales	Value of Prizes Won	Retailer Commissions	Revenue to State of Texas*
FY 2023	$8,725.7	$5,907.0	$436.8	$2,161.5
FY 2022	$8,296.9	$5,599.7	$415.4	$1,998.4
FY 2021	$8,107.2	$5,418.3	$405.8	$1,998.3
FY 2020	$6,704.0	$4,442.4	$335.6	$1,683.7
FY 2019	$6,251.5	$4,056.5	$313.1	$1,636.6
FY 2018	$5,626.8	$3,666.1	$281.5	$1,450.5
FY 2017	$5,077.5	$3,257.4	$253.9	$1,334.0
FY 2016	$5,067.5	$3,186.4	$253.5	$1,392.3
FY 2015	$4,529.7	$2,858.3	$226.7	$1,242.7
FY 2014	$4,384.6	$2,741.2	$219.5	$1,220.7
FY 2013	$4,376.3	$2,767.4	$218.9	$1,214.1
FY 2012	$4,190.8	$2,632.6	$209.8	$1,155.5
FY 2011	$3,811.3	$2,387.2	$190.8	$1,023.8
FY 2010	$3,738.4	$2,300.2	$187.3	$1,063.1
FY 2009	$3,720.1	$2,299.8	$186.1	$1,062.2
FY 2008	$3,671.5	$2,281.1	$183.8	$1,034.9
FY 2007	$3,774.2	$2,315.3	$188.8	$1,093.0
FY 2006	$3,774.7	$2,310.6	$188.8	$1,090.3
FY 2005	$3,662.5	$2,228.0	$183.2	$1,070.3
FY 2004	$3,487.9	$2,068.6	$174.4	$1,051.0
FY 2003	$3,130.7	$1,845.2	$156.6	$949.1
FY 2002	$2,966.3	$1,715.4	$148.4	$928.9
FY 2001	$2,825.3	$1,643.2	$141.3	$864.0
FY 2000	$2,657.3	$1,508.8	$133.0	$862.8
FY 1999	$2,571.6	$1,329.0	$128.8	$953.4
FY 1998	$3,090.0	$1,648.1	$154.6	$1,097.8
FY 1997	$3,745.5	$2,151.7	$187.4	$1,182.8
FY 1996	$3,432.3	$1,951.1	$171.7	$1,098.3
FY 1995	$3,036.5	$1,689.3	$151.8	$1,015.0
FY 1994	$2,760.2	$1,528.7	$138.0	$927.7
FY 1993	$1,856.1	$981.7	$92.8	$656.8
Start up to FY 1992	$591.6	$268.9	$29.6	$250.0

All figures in millions.
*Revenue to the state presented on an accrual basis.
Source: Texas Lottery Commission Summary Financial Report.

UNSPLASH/ANDY BODEMER

DECLARATION OF INDEPENDENCE OF THE REPUBLIC OF TEXAS

The Declaration of Independence of the Republic of Texas was adopted in general convention at Washington-on-the-Brazos on March 2, 1836.

Richard Ellis, president of the convention, appointed a committee of five to write the declaration for submission to the convention. However, there is much evidence that George C. Childress, one of the members, wrote the document with little or no help from the other members. Childress is therefore generally accepted as the author.

The text of the declaration is followed by the names of the signers of the document. The names are presented here as the signers actually signed the document.

UNANIMOUS

DECLARATION OF INDEPENDENCE,

BY THE

DELEGATES OF THE PEOPLE OF TEXAS,

IN GENERAL CONVENTION,

AT THE TOWN OF WASHINGTON,

ON THE SECOND DAY OF MARCH, 1836.

WHEN A GOVERNMENT has ceased to protect the lives, liberty and property of the people from whom its legitimate powers are derived, and for the advancement of whose happiness it was instituted; and so far from being a guarantee for the enjoyment of those inestimable and inalienable rights, becomes an instrument in the hands of evil rulers for their oppression. When the Federal Republican Constitution of their country, which they have sworn to support, no longer has a substantial existence, and the whole nature of their government has been forcibly changed without their consent, from a restricted federative republic, composed of sovereign states, to a consolidated central military despotism, in which every interest is disregarded but that of the army and the priesthood — both the eternal enemies of civil liberty, and the ever-ready minions of power, and the usual instruments of tyrants; When long after the spirit of the Constitution has departed, moderation is at length, so far lost, by those in power that even the semblance of freedom is removed, and the forms, themselves, of the constitution discontinued; and so far from their petitions and remonstrances being regarded, the agents who bear them are thrown into dungeons; and mercenary armies sent forth to force a new government upon them at the point of the bayonet.

When, in consequence of such acts of malfeasance and abdication, on the part of the government, anarchy prevails, and civil society is dissolved into its original elements: In such a crisis, the first law of nature, the right of self-preservation — the inherent and inalienable right of the people to appeal to first principles and take their political affairs into their own hands in extreme cases — enjoins it as a right towards themselves and a sacred obligation to their posterity, to abolish such government and create another in its stead, calculated to rescue them from impending dangers, and to secure their future welfare and happiness.

Nations, as well as individuals, are amenable for their acts to the public opinion of mankind. A statement of a part of our grievances is, therefore, submitted to an impartial world, in justification of the hazardous but unavoidable step now taken of severing our political connection with the Mexican people, and assuming an independent attitude among the nations of the earth.

The Mexican Government, by its colonization laws, invited and induced the Anglo-American population of Texas to colonize its wilderness under the pledged faith of a written constitution, that they should continue to enjoy that constitutional liberty and republican government to which they had been habituated in the land of their birth, the United States of America. In this expectation they have been cruelly disappointed, inasmuch as the Mexican nation has acquiesced in the late changes made in the government by General Antonio Lopez de Santa Anna, who, having overturned the constitution of his country, now offers us the cruel alternative either to abandon our homes, acquired by so many privations, or submit to the most intolerable of all tyranny, the combined despotism of the sword and the priesthood.

It has sacrificed our welfare to the state of Coahuila, by which our interests have been continually depressed, through a jealous and partial course of legislation carried on at a far distant seat of government, by a hostile majority, in an unknown tongue; and this too, notwithstanding we have petitioned in the humblest terms, for the establishment of a separate state government, and have, in accordance with the provisions of the national constitution, presented the general Congress, a republican constitution which was without just cause contemptuously rejected.

It incarcerated in a dungeon, for a long time, one of our citizens, for no other cause but a zealous endeavor to procure the acceptance of our constitution and the establishment of a state government.

It has failed and refused to secure on a firm basis, the right of trial by jury; that palladium of civil liberty, and only safe guarantee for the life, liberty, and property of the citizen.

It has failed to establish any public system of education, although possessed of almost boundless resources (the public domain) and, although, it is an axiom, in political science, that unless a people are educated and enlightened it is idle to expect the continuance of civil liberty, or the capacity for self-government.

It has suffered the military commandants stationed among us to exercise arbitrary acts of oppression and tyranny; thus trampling upon the most sacred rights of the citizen and rendering the military superior to the civil power.

It has dissolved by force of arms, the state Congress of Coahuila and Texas, and obliged our representatives to fly for their lives from the seat of government; thus depriving us of the fundamental political right of representation.

It has demanded the surrender of a number of our citizens, and ordered military detachments to seize and carry them into the Interior for trial; in contempt of the civil authorities, and in defiance of the laws and constitution.

It has made piratical attacks upon our commerce; by commissioning foreign desperadoes, and authorizing them to seize our vessels, and convey the property of our citizens to far distant ports of confiscation.

It denies us the right of worshipping the Almighty according to the dictates of our own consciences, by the support of a national religion calculated to promote the temporal interests of its human functionaries rather than the glory of the true and living God.

It has demanded us to deliver up our arms; which are essential to our defense, the rightful property of freemen, and formidable only to tyrannical governments.

It has invaded our country, both by sea and by land, with intent to lay waste our territory and drive us from our homes; and has now a large mercenary army advancing to carry on against us a war of extermination.

It has, through its emissaries, incited the merciless savage, with the tomahawk and scalping knife, to massacre the inhabitants of our defenseless frontiers.

It hath been, during the whole time of our connection with it, the contemptible sport and victim of successive military revolutions and hath continually exhibited every characteristic of a weak, corrupt and tyrannical government.

These, and other grievances, were patiently borne by the people of Texas until they reached that point at which forbearance ceases to be a virtue. We then took up arms in defense of the national constitution. We appealed to our Mexican brethren for assistance. Our appeal has been made in vain. Though months have elapsed, no sympathetic response has yet been heard from the Interior. We are, therefore, forced to the melancholy conclusion that the Mexican people have acquiesced in the destruction of their liberty, and the substitution therefor of a military government — that they are unfit to be free and incapable of self-government.

The necessity of self-preservation, therefore, now decrees our eternal political separation.

We, therefore, the delegates, with plenary powers, of the people of Texas, in solemn convention assembled, appealing to a candid world for the necessities of our condition, do hereby resolve and DECLARE *that our political connection with the Mexican nation has forever ended; and that the people of Texas do now constitute a* FREE, SOVEREIGN *and* INDEPENDENT REPUBLIC, *and are fully invested with all the rights and attributes which properly belong to the independent nations; and, conscious of the rectitude of our intentions, we fearlessly and confidently commit the issue to the decision of the Supreme Arbiter of the destinies of nations.*

RICHARD ELLIS,
president of the convention and Delegate from Red River.
Charles B. Stewart
Thomas Barnett
John S.D. Byrom
Francis Ruis
J. Antonio Navarro
Jesse B. Badgett
Wm D. Lacy
William Menifee
Jn. Fisher
Matthew Caldwell
William Motley
Lorenzo de Zavala
Stephen H. Everitt
George W. Smyth
Elijah Stapp
Claiborne West
Wm B. Scates
M.B. Menard
A.B. Hardin
J.W. Bunton
Thos. J. Gazley
R. M. Coleman
Sterling C. Robertson
Benj. Briggs Goodrich
G.W. Barnett
James G. Swisher
Jesse Grimes
S. Rhoads Fisher
John W. Moore
John W. Bower
Saml. A. Maverick (from Bejar)
Sam P. Carson
A. Briscoe
J.B. Woods
James Collinsworth
Edwin Waller
Asa Brigham
Geo. C. Childress
Bailey Hardeman
Rob. Potter
Thomas Jefferson Rusk
Chas. S. Taylor
John S. Roberts
Robert Hamilton
Collin McKinney
Albert H. Latimer
James Power
Sam Houston
David Thomas
Edwd. Conrad
Martin Parmer
Edwin O. LeGrand
Stephen W. Blount
Jms. Gaines
Wm. Clark Jr.
Sydney O. Penington
Wm. Carrol Crawford
Jno. Turner
H.S. Kimble, Secretary

JOINT RESOLUTION FOR ANNEXING TEXAS TO THE UNITED STATES

Resolved

by the Senate and House of Representatives of the United States of America in Congress assembled,

That Congress doth consent that the territory properly included within and rightfully belonging to the Republic of Texas, may be erected into a new State to be called the State of Texas, with a republican form of government adopted by the people of said Republic, by deputies in convention assembled, with the consent of the existing Government in order that the same may by admitted as one of the States of this Union.

2. *And be it further resolved,* That the foregoing consent of Congress is given upon the following conditions, to wit:

First, said state to be formed, subject to the adjustment by this government of all questions of boundary that may arise with other governments; and the Constitution thereof, with the proper evidence of its adoption by the people of said Republic of Texas, shall be transmitted to the President of the United States, to be laid before Congress for its final action on, or before the first day of January, one thousand eight hundred and forty-six.

Second, said state when admitted into the Union, after ceding to the United States all public edifices, fortifications, barracks, ports and harbors, navy and navy yards, docks, magazines and armaments, and all other means pertaining to the public defense, belonging to the said Republic of Texas, shall retain funds, debts, taxes and dues of every kind which may belong to, or be due and owing to the said Republic; and shall also retain all the vacant and unappropriated lands lying within its limits, to be applied to the payment of the debts and liabilities of said Republic of Texas, and the residue of said lands, after discharging said debts and liabilities, to be disposed of as said State may direct; but in no event are said debts and liabilities to become a charge upon the Government of the United States.

Third — New States of convenient size not exceeding four in number, in addition to said State of Texas and having sufficient population, may, hereafter by the consent of said State, be formed out of the territory thereof, which shall be entitled to admission under the provisions of the Federal Constitution; and such states as may be formed out of the territory lying south of thirty-six degrees thirty minutes north latitude, commonly known as the Missouri Compromise Line, shall be admitted into the Union, with or without slavery, as the people of each State, asking admission shall desire; and in such State or States as shall be formed out of said territory, north of said Missouri Compromise Line, slavery, or involuntary servitude (except for crime) shall be prohibited.

3. *And be it further resolved,* That if the President of the United States shall in his judgment and discretion deem it most advisable, instead of proceeding to submit the foregoing resolution of the Republic of Texas, as an overture on the part of the United States for admission, to negotiate with the Republic; then,

Be it resolved, That a State, to be formed out of the present Republic of Texas, with suitable extent and boundaries, and with two representatives in Congress, until the next appointment of representation, shall be admitted into the Union, by virtue of this act, on an equal footing with the existing States, as soon as the terms and conditions of such admission, and the cession of the remaining Texian territory to the United States shall be agreed upon by the governments of Texas and the United States:

And that the sum of one hundred thousand dollars be, and the same is hereby, appropriated to defray the expenses of missions and negotiations, to agree upon the terms of said admission and cession, either by treaty to be submitted to the Senate, or by articles to be submitted to the two houses of Congress, as the President may direct.

Approved, March 1, 1845.

Source: Peters, Richard, ed., The Public Statutes at Large of the United States of America, v.5, pp. 797–798, Boston, Chas. C. Little and Jas. Brown, 1850.

UNSPLASH/LUCAS BECK

TWENTY-NINTH CONGRESS: SESSION 1 — RESOLUTIONS [NO. 1.] JOINT RESOLUTION FOR THE ADMISSION OF THE STATE OF TEXAS INTO THE UNION

Whereas

the Congress of the United States, by a joint resolution approved March the first, eighteen hundred and forty-five, did consent that the territory properly included within, and rightfully belonging to, the Republic of Texas, might be erected into a new State, to be called _The State of Texas,_ with a republican form of government, to be adopted by the people of said republic, by deputies in convention assembled, with the consent of the existing government, in order that the same might be admitted as one of the States of the Union;

which consent of Congress was given upon certain conditions specified in the first and second sections of said joint resolution;

and whereas the people of the said Republic of Texas, by deputies in convention assembled, with the consent of the existing government, did adopt a constitution, and erect a new State with a republican form of government, and, in the name of the people of Texas, and by their authority, did ordain and declare that they assented to and accepted the proposals, conditions, and guaranties contained in said first and second sections of said resolution:

and whereas the said constitution, with the proper evidence of its adoption by the people of the Republic of Texas, has been transmitted to the President of the United States and laid before Congress, in conformity to the provisions of said joint resolution:

Therefore—

Resolved by the Senate and House of Representatives of the United States of America in Congress assembled, That the State of Texas shall be one, and is hereby declared to be one, of the United States of America, and admitted into the Union on an equal footing with the original States in all respects whatever.

Sec. 2. And be it further resolved, That until the representatives in Congress shall be apportioned according to an actual enumeration of the inhabitants of the United States, the State of Texas shall be entitled to choose two representatives.

Approved, December 29, 1845.

Source: Minot, Geo., ed., Statutes at Large and Treaties of the United States of America from Dec. 1, 1845, to March 3, 1851, V. IX, p. 108.

CONSTITUTION OF TEXAS

The Constitution of Texas was adopted on February 15, 1876. According to the Legislative Reference Library of Texas, "The Texas Constitution is one of the longest in the nation and is still growing. As of 2024 (the 88th Legislature), the Texas Legislature has proposed a total of 714 amendments. Of these, 530 have been adopted and 181 have been defeated by Texas voters."

Amending the Texas Constitution requires a two-thirds favorable vote by both the Texas House of Representatives and the Texas Senate, followed by a majority vote of approval by voters in a statewide election.

Prior to 1973, amendments to the constitution could not be submitted by a special session of the Legislature. But the constitution was amended in 1972 to allow submission of amendments if the special session was opened to the subject by the governor.

Constitutional amendments are not subject to a gubernatorial veto. Once submitted, voters have the final decision on whether to change the constitution as proposed.

TEXAS' CHIEF GOVERNMENTAL OFFICIALS

The following are lists of the principal administrative officials who have served the Republic and State of Texas with dates of their tenures in office. In a few instances, there are disputes as to the exact dates of tenures. Dates listed here are those that appear the most authentic.

GOVERNORS AND PRESIDENTS

Spanish Royal Governors

(Some authorities would include Texas under administrations of several earlier Spanish governors. The late Dr. C.E. Castañeda, Latin-American librarian of The University of Texas and authority on the history of Texas and the Southwest, would include the following four: Francisco de Garay, 1523–1526; Pánfilo de Narváez, 1526–28; Nuño de Guzmán, 1528–1530; and Hernando de Soto, 1538–1543.)

Domingo Terán de los Rios 1691–1692
Gregorio de Salinas Varona. 1692–1697
Francisco Cuervo y Valdés. 1698–1702
Mathías de Aguirre 1703–1705
Martín de Alarcón 1705–1708
Simón Padilla y Córdova 1708–1712
Pedro Fermin de Echevers y Subisa 1712–1714
Juan Valdéz 1714–1716
Martín de Alarcón 1716–1719
José de Azlor y Virto de Vera, Marqués de San Miguel de Aguayo 1719–1722
Fernando Pérez de Almazán 1722–1727
Melchor de Mediavilla y Azcona 1727–1731
Juan Antonio Bustillo y Ceballos 1731–1734
Manuel de Sandoval. 1734–1736
Carlos Benites Franquis de Lugo 1736–1737
Joseph Fernández de Jáuregui y Urrutia. 1737–1737
Prudencio de Orobio y Basterra 1737–1741
Tomás Felipe Winthuisen (or Winthuysen) . . 1741–1743
Justo Boneo y Morales 1743–1744
Francisco García Larios. 1744–1748
Pedro del Barrio Junco y Espriella 1748–1750
Jacinto de Barrios y Jáuregui 1751–1759
Angel de Martos y Navarrete 1759–1767
Hugo Oconór 1767–1770
Juan María Vicencio, Barón de Ripperdá 1770–1778
Domingo Cabello y Robles 1778–1786
Rafael Martínez Pacheco. 1787–1790
Manuel Muñoz. 1790–1799
Juan Bautista de Elguezábal. 1799–1805
Antonio Cordero y Bustamante 1805–1808
Manuel María de Salcedo 1808–1813
(Mexico's War of Independence 1810–1812 created governmental instability.)
Juan Bautista de las Casas 1811–1811
(Revolutionary governor.)
Cristóbal Domínguez, Benito de Armiñan, ... Mariano Varela, Juan Ignacio Pérez, ... Manuel Pardo *(ad interim)* 1813–1817
Antonio María Martínez. 1817–1821

Governors Under Mexican Rule

The first two governors under Mexican rule, Trespalacios and García, were of Texas only as Texas was then constituted. Beginning with Gonzáles, 1824, the governors were for the joint State of Coahuila y Texas.

José Felix Trespalacios 1822–1823
Luciano García 1823–1824
Rafael Gonzáles 1824–1826
Victor Blanco 1826–1827

EARLY LEADERS OF TEXAS

The presidents of the Republic of Texas and the state's first Governor: **David G. Burnet**, provisional president; **Sam Houston**, second and fourth president; **Mirabeau B. Lamar**, third president; **Anson Jones**, the Republic's last president; and **J. Pinckney Henderson**, the Lone Star State's first governor.

José María Viesca 1827–1830
Ramón Eca y Múzquiz 1830–1831
José María Letona 1831–1832
Ramón Eca y Múzquiz 1832–1832
Juan Martín de Veramendi 1832–1833
José Vidáurri y Villaseñor 1833–1834
Juan José Elguezábal 1834–1835
José María Cantú 1835–1835
Agustín M. Viesca 1835–1835
Marciel Borrego 1835–1835
Ramón Eca y Múzquiz 1835–1835

Provisional Colonial Governor, Before Independence

Henry Smith (Impeached) 1835–Jan. 1836
(James W. Robinson served as acting governor after Smith was impeached.)

Presidents of the Republic of Texas

David G. Burnet .... Mar. 16, 1836–Oct. 22, 1836
(Provisional.)
Sam Houston .... Oct. 22, 1836–Dec. 10, 1838
Mirabeau B. Lamar .... Dec. 10, 1838–Dec. 13, 1841
Sam Houston .... Dec. 13, 1841–Dec. 9, 1844
Anson Jones .... Dec. 9, 1844–Feb. 19, 1846

Governors Since Annexation

Abbreviations: (D) Democrat, (R) Republican, (I) Independent. Many of the early Governors ran with no party affiliation.

J. Pinckney Henderson . . . . . Feb. 19, 1846–Dec. 21, 1847
(Albert C. Horton served as acting governor while Henderson was away in the Mexican War.)
George T. Wood . . . . Dec. 21, 1847–Dec. 21, 1849
Peter Hansbrough Bell . . . . Dec. 21, 1849–Nov. 23, 1853
(Resigned to enter the U.S. House of Representatives.)
J. W. Henderson . . . . Nov. 23, 1853–Dec. 21, 1853
Elisha M. Pease . . . . Dec. 21, 1853–Dec. 21, 1857
Hardin R. Runnels (D) . . . . Dec. 21, 1857–Dec. 21, 1859
Sam Houston . . . . Dec. 21, 1859–Mar. 16, 1861
(Resigned because of the state's secession from the Union.)
Edward Clark . . . . Mar. 16, 1861–Nov. 7, 1861
Francis R. Lubbock . . . . Nov. 7, 1861–Nov. 5, 1863
(Resigned to enter the Confederate Army.)
Pendleton Murrah . . . . Nov. 5, 1863–June 17, 1865
(Fled to Mexico upon the fall of Confederacy. Lt. Gov. Fletcher S. Stockdale briefly acted as governor after Murrah's departure.)
Andrew J. Hamilton . . . . June 17, 1865–Aug. 9, 1866
(Hamilton received a commission as "military governor of Texas" from President Abraham Lincoln on Nov. 14, 1862. He appears to have served in that capacity continuously until his "reappointment" as "provisional governor" by President Andrew Johnson on June 17, 1865. Apparently Johnson used the term "reappointment" because Hamilton was already serving as military governor.)
James W. Throckmorton . . . . . Aug. 9, 1866–Aug. 8, 1867
Elisha M. Pease (R) . . . . Aug. 8, 1867–Sept. 30, 1869
(Appointed under martial law after Throckmorton was removed on July 30, 1867, by Gen. Philip Sheridan. Pease formally took possession of the office on Aug. 8. He resigned and vacated the office Sept. 30, 1869, but no successor was named until Jan. 8, 1870. Some historians extend Pease's term to that date, but in reality Texas was without a head of government for that period.)
Edmund J. Davis (R) . . . . Jan. 8, 1870–Jan. 15, 1874
(Appointed provisional governor after being elected.)
Richard Coke (D) . . . . Jan. 15, 1874–Dec. 1, 1876
(Resigned to enter the U.S. Senate.)
Richard B. Hubbard (D) . . . . Dec. 1, 1876–Jan. 21, 1879
Oran M. Roberts (D) . . . . Jan. 21, 1879–Jan. 16, 1883
John Ireland (D) . . . . Jan. 16, 1883–Jan. 18, 1887
Lawrence Sullivan Ross (D) . Jan. 18, 1887–Jan. 20, 1891
James Stephen Hogg (D) . . . . Jan. 20, 1891–Jan. 15, 1895
Charles A. Culberson (D) . . . Jan. 15, 1895–Jan. 17, 1899
Joseph D. Sayers (D) . . . . Jan. 17, 1899–Jan. 20, 1903
S. W. T. Lanham (D) . . . . Jan. 20, 1903–Jan. 15, 1907
Thos. Mitchell Campbell (D) Jan. 15, 1907–Jan. 17, 1911
Oscar Branch Colquitt (D) . . . Jan. 17, 1911–Jan. 19, 1915
James E. Ferguson (D) . . . . . Jan. 19, 1915–Sept. 25, 1917
(Impeached in August 1917. Lt. Gov. Hobby served as acting governor during the impeachment proceedings. Ferguson was removed from office Sept. 25.)
William Pettus Hobby (D) . . Aug. 25, 1917–Jan. 18, 1921
Pat Morris Neff (D) . . . . Jan. 18, 1921–Jan. 20, 1925
Miriam A. Ferguson (D) . . . . Jan. 20, 1925–Jan. 17, 1927
Dan Moody (D) . . . . Jan. 17, 1927–Jan. 20, 1931
Ross S. Sterling (D) . . . . Jan. 20, 1931–Jan. 17, 1933
Miriam A. Ferguson (D) . . . . Jan. 17, 1933–Jan. 15, 1935
James V. Allred (D) . . . . Jan. 15, 1935–Jan. 17, 1939
W. Lee O'Daniel (D) . . . . Jan. 17, 1939–Aug. 4, 1941
(Resigned to the enter U.S. Senate.)
Coke R. Stevenson (D) . . . . Aug. 4, 1941–Jan. 21, 1947
Beauford H. Jester (D) . . . . . . Jan. 21, 1947–July 11, 1949
(Died in office. Succeeded by Lt. Gov. Shivers.)
Allan Shivers (D) . . . . July 11, 1949–Jan. 15, 1957
Price Daniel (D) . . . . Jan. 15, 1957–Jan. 15, 1963
John Connally (D) . . . . Jan. 15, 1963–Jan. 21, 1969
Preston Smith (D) . . . . Jan. 21, 1969–Jan. 16, 1973
Dolph Briscoe (D) . . . . Jan. 16, 1973–Jan. 16, 1979
(Effective in 1975, the term of office was increased from 2 to 4 years.)
William P. Clements (R) . . . . Jan. 16, 1979–Jan. 18, 1983
Mark White (D) . . . . Jan. 18, 1983–Jan. 20, 1987
William P. Clements (R) . . . . Jan. 20, 1987–Jan. 15, 1991
Ann W. Richards (D) . . . . . . Jan. 15, 1991–Jan. 17, 1995
George W. Bush (R) . . . . Jan. 17, 1995–Dec. 21, 2000
(Resigned to become U.S. President.)
Rick Perry (R) . . . . Dec. 21, 2000–Jan. 20, 2015
Greg Abbott (R) . . . . Jan. 20, 2015–Present

VICE PRESIDENTS AND LIEUTENANT GOVERNORS

Vice Presidents of the Republic

Lorenzo de Zavala . . . . Mar. 16, 1836–Oct, 17, 1836
(Provisional.)
Mirabeau B. Lamar . . . . Oct. 22, 1836–Dec.10, 1838
David G. Burnet . . . . Dec. 10, 1838–Dec.13, 1841
Edward Burleson . . . . Dec. 13, 1841–Dec. 9, 1844
Kenneth L. Anderson . . . . Dec. 9, 1844–July 3, 1845
(Died in office.)

Lieutenant Governors

Albert C. Horton (D) ..... May 2, 1846–Dec. 21, 1847
John A. Greer (D).........Dec. 21, 1847–Dec. 22, 1851
J. W. Henderson (D) ..... Dec. 22, 1851–Nov. 23, 1853
(Briefly succeeded to governorship when Gov. Bell resigned to enter the U.S. House of Representatives.)
D. C. Dickson (D) ....Dec. 21, 1853–Dec. 21, 1855
H. R. Runnels (D) ....Dec. 21, 1855–Dec. 21, 1857
F. R. Lubbock (D) ....Dec. 21, 1857–Dec. 21, 1859
Edward Clark (I) ....Dec. 21, 1859–Mar. 16, 1861
(Succeeded Gov. Sam Houston when Houston refused to take oath to the Confederacy.)
John M. Crockett (D) ....Nov. 7, 1861–Nov. 5, 1863
Fletcher S. Stockdale (D)....Nov. 7, 1863–June 17, 1865
(Fall of Confederacy.)
George W. Jones (D) .... Aug. 9, 1866–July 30, 1867
(Jones was removed by Gen. Philip Sheridan.)
J. W. Flanagan (R) 1869
(Elected in 1869, Flanagan was appointed U.S. Senator and was never inaugurated as Lt. Governor.)
R. B. Hubbard (D)......... Jan. 15, 1873–Dec. 1, 1876
(Succeeded Gov. Richard Coke when he resigned to become U.S. Senator.)
J. D. Sayers (D)............ Jan. 21, 1879–Jan. 18, 1881
L. J. Storey (D)............ Jan. 18, 1881–Jan. 16, 1883
Marion Martin (D) ....Jan. 16, 1883–Jan. 20, 1885
Barnett Gibbs (D)..........Jan. 20, 1885–Jan. 19, 1887
T. B. Wheeler (D)..........Jan. 19, 1887– Jan. 21, 1891
George C. Pendleton (D).....Jan. 21, 1891–Jan. 17, 1893
M. M. Crane (D) .... Jan. 17, 1893–Jan. 15, 1895
George T. Jester (D)........ Jan. 15, 1895–Jan. 17, 1899
J. N. Browning (D)........ Jan. 17, 1899– Jan. 20, 1903
George D. Neal (D) ....Jan. 20, 1903–Jan. 15, 1907
A. B. Davidson (D)......... Jan. 15, 1907–Jan. 21, 1913
Will H. Mayes (D).........Jan. 21, 1913–Aug. 14, 1914
(Resigned.)
William P. Hobby (D)......Jan. 19, 1915–Aug. 25, 1917
(Served as acting governor during the impeachment of Gov. Jim Ferguson. Took oath as governor after Ferguson was removed from office Sept. 25.)
W. A. Johnson (D)........ Sept. 29, 1917–Jan. 18, 1921
(Selected as president of the state Senate and acting lt. governor, serving Hobby's unexpired term. He was then elected statewide to the office in 1918.)
Lynch Davidson (D)........ Jan. 18, 1921–Jan. 16, 1923
T. W. Davidson (D) ....Jan. 16, 1923–Jan. 20, 1925
Barry Miller (D)...........Jan. 20, 1925–Jan. 20, 1931
Edgar E. Witt (D) .... Jan. 20, 1931–Jan. 15, 1935
Walter Woodul (D)........ Jan. 15, 1935–Jan. 17, 1939
Coke R. Stevenson (D).......Jan. 17, 1939–Aug. 4, 1941
(Became governor upon resignation of Gov. W. Lee O'Daniel to become U.S. Senator.)
John Lee Smith (D) .... Jan. 19, 1943–Jan. 21, 1947
Allan Shivers (D) .... Jan. 21, 1947–July 11, 1949
(Shivers succeeded to the governorship after the death of Gov. Beauford H. Jester.)
Ben Ramsey (D) .... Jan. 16, 1951–Sept. 18, 1961
(Ramsey resigned to become a member of the Texas Railroad Commission.)
Preston Smith (D) ....Jan. 15, 1963–Jan. 21, 1969
Ben Barnes (D)............ Jan. 21, 1969–Jan. 16, 1973
William P. Hobby Jr. (D) ...Jan. 16, 1973–Jan. 15, 1991
Robert D. Bullock (D)...... Jan. 15, 1991–Jan. 19, 1999
Rick Perry (R) .... Jan. 19, 1999–Dec. 21, 2000
Bill Ratliff (R) .... Dec. 28, 2000–Jan. 14, 2003
(Elected by State Senate when Perry succeeded to governorship.)
David Dewhurst (R)........Jan. 21, 2003–Jan. 20, 2015
Dan Patrick (R) ....Jan. 20, 2015–Present

SECRETARIES OF STATE OF THE REPUBLIC

The Year Book for Texas, 1901, gives the following record of Secretaries of State during the era of the Republic of Texas:

Under David G. Burnet: Samuel P. Carson, James Collingsworth, and W. H. Jack.

Under Sam Houston (first term): Stephen F. Austin, 1836. J. Pinckney Henderson and Dr. Robert A. Irion, 1837–1838.

Under Mirabeau B. Lamar: Bernard Bee appointed Dec. 16, 1838; James Webb appointed Feb. 6, 1839; D. G. Burnet appointed Acting Secretary of State, May 31, 1839; N. Amory appointed Acting Secretary of State, July 23, 1839; D. G. Burnet appointed Acting Secretary of State, Aug. 5, 1839; Abner S. Lipscomb appointed Secretary of State, Jan. 31, 1840, and resigned Jan. 22, 1841; Joseph Waples appointed Acting Secretary of State, Jan. 23, 1841, and served until Feb. 8, 1841; James S. Mayfield appointed Feb. 8, 1841; Joseph Waples appointed April 30, 1841, and served until May 25, 1841; Samuel A. Roberts appointed May 25, 1841; reappointed Sept. 7, 1841.

Under Sam Houston (second term): E. Lawrence Stickney, Acting Secretary of State until Anson Jones was appointed Dec. 13, 1841. Jones served as Secretary of State throughout this term except during the summer and part of this term of 1842, when Joseph Waples filled the position as Acting Secretary of State.

Under Anson Jones: Ebenezer Allen served from Dec. 10, 1844, until Feb. 5, 1845, when Ashbel Smith became Secretary of State. Allen was again named Acting Secretary of State, March 31, 1845, and later named Secretary of State.

In addition to the above, documents in the Texas State Archives indicate that **Joseph C. Eldredge**, Chief Clerk of the State Department during much of the Republic's existence, signed a number of documents in the absence of the office-holder in the capacity of "Acting Secretary of State."

State Secretaries of State

Charles Mariner ....Feb. 20, 1846–May 4, 1846
David G. Burnet .... May 4, 1846–Jan. 1, 1848
Washington D. Miller ....Jan. 1, 1848–Jan. 2, 1850
James Webb................Jan. 2, 1850–Nov. 14, 1851
Thomas H. Duval........ Nov. 14, 1851–Dec. 22, 1853
Edward Clark ....Dec. 22, 1853–Dec. 1857
T. S. Anderson .... Dec. 1857–Dec. 27, 1859
E. W. Cave...............Dec. 27, 1859–Mar. 16, 1861

Name	Term
Bird Holland	Mar. 16, 1861–Nov. 1861
Charles West	Nov. 1861–Sept. 1862
Robert J. Townes	Sept. 1862–May 2, 1865
Charles R. Pryor	May 2, 1865–Aug, 1865
James H. Bell	Aug. 1865–Aug. 1866
John A. Green	Aug. 1866–Aug. 1867
D. W. C. Phillips	Aug. 1867–Jan. 1870
J. P. Newcomb	Jan. 1, 1870–Jan. 17, 1874
George Clark	Jan. 17, 1874–Jan. 27, 1874
A. W. DeBerry	Jan. 27, 1874–Dec. 1, 1876
Isham G. Searcy	Dec. 1, 1876–Jan. 23, 1879
J. D. Templeton	Jan. 23, 1879–Jan. 22, 1881
T. H. Bowman	Jan. 22, 1881–Jan. 18, 1883
J. W. Baines	Jan. 18, 1883–Jan. 21, 1887
John M. Moore	Jan. 21, 1887–Jan. 22, 1891
George W. Smith	Jan. 22, 1891–Jan. 17, 1895
Allison Mayfield	Jan. 17, 1895–Jan. 5, 1897
J. W. Madden	Jan. 5, 1897–Jan. 18, 1899
D. H. Hardy	Jan. 18, 1899–Jan. 19, 1901
John G. Tod	Jan. 19, 1901–Jan., 1903
J. R. Curl	Jan. 1903–April 1905
O. K. Shannon	April 1905–Jan. 1907
L. T. Dashiel	Jan. 1907–Feb. 1908
W. R. Davie	Feb. 1908–Jan. 1909
W. B. Townsend	Jan. 1909–Jan. 1911
C. C. McDonald	Jan. 1911–Dec. 1912
J. T. Bowman	Dec. 1912–Jan. 1913
John L. Wortham	Jan. 1913–June 1913
F. C. Weinert	June 1913–Nov. 1914
D. A. Gregg	Nov. 1914–Jan. 1915
John G. McKay	Jan. 1915–Dec. 1916
C. J. Bartlett	Dec. 1916–Nov. 1917
George F. Howard	Nov. 1917–Nov. 1920
C. D. Mims	Nov. 1920–Jan. 1921
S. L. Staples	Jan. 1921–Aug. 1924
J. D. Strickland	Sept. 1924–Jan. 1, 1925
Henry Hutchings	Jan. 1, 1925–Jan. 20, 1925
Mrs. Emma G. Meharg	Jan. 20, 1925–Jan. 1927
Mrs. Jane Y. McCallum	Jan. 1927–Jan. 1933
W. W. Heath	Jan. 1933–Jan. 1935
Gerald C. Mann	Jan. 1935–Aug. 31, 1935
R. B. Stanford	Aug. 31, 1935–Aug. 25, 1936
B. P. Matocha	Aug. 25, 1936–Jan. 18, 1937
Edward Clark	Jan. 18, 1937–Jan. 1939
Tom L. Beauchamp	Jan. 1939–Oct. 1939
M. O. Flowers	Oct. 26, 1939–Feb. 25, 1941
William J. Lawson	Feb. 25, 1941–Jan. 1943
Sidney Latham	Jan. 1943–Feb. 1945
Claude Isbell	Feb. 1945–Jan. 1947
Paul H. Brown	Jan. 1947–Jan. 19, 1949
Ben Ramsey	Jan. 19, 1949–Feb. 9, 1950
John Ben Shepperd	Feb. 9, 1950–April 30, 1952
Jack Ross	April 30, 1952–Jan. 9, 1953
Howard A. Carney	Jan. 9, 1953–Apr. 30, 1954
C. E. Fulgham	May 1, 1954–Feb. 15, 1955
Al Muldrow	Feb. 16, 1955–Nov. 1, 1955
Tom Reavley	Nov. 1, 1955–Jan. 16, 1957
Zollie Steakley	Jan. 16, 1957–Jan. 2, 1962
P. Frank Lake	Jan. 2, 1962–Jan. 15, 1963
Crawford C. Martin	Jan. 15, 1963–Mar. 12, 1966
John L. Hill	Mar. 12, 1966–Jan. 22, 1968
Roy Barrera	Mar. 7, 1968–Jan. 23, 1969
Martin Dies Jr.	Jan. 23, 1969–Sept. 1, 1971
Robert D. (Bob) Bullock	Sept. 1, 1971–Jan. 2, 1973
V. Larry Teaver Jr.	Jan. 2, 1973–Jan. 19, 1973
Mark W. White Jr.	Jan. 19, 1973–Oct. 27,1977
Steven C. Oaks	Oct. 27, 1977–Jan. 16, 1979
George W. Strake Jr.	Jan. 16, 1979–Oct. 6, 1981
David A. Dean	Oct. 22, 1981–Jan. 18, 1983
John Fainter	Jan. 18, 1983–July 31, 1984
Myra A. McDaniel	Sept. 6, 1984–Jan. 26, 1987
Jack Rains	Jan. 26, 1987–June 15, 1989
George Bayoud Jr.	June 19, 1989–Jan. 15, 1991
John Hannah Jr.	Jan. 17, 1991–Mar. 11, 1994
Ronald Kirk	April 4, 1994–Jan. 10, 1995
Antonio O. "Tony" Garza Jr.	Jan. 18, 1995–Dec. 2, 1997
Alberto R. Gonzales	Dec. 2, 1997–Jan. 10, 1999
Elton Bomer	Jan. 11, 1999–Dec. 31, 2000
Henry Cuellar	Jan. 2, 2001–Oct. 5, 2001
Gwyn Shea	Jan. 2, 2002–Aug. 4, 2003
Geoff Connor	Sept. 26, 2003–Jan. 1, 2005
J. Roger Williams	Jan. 1, 2005–July 1, 2007
Phil Wilson	July 1, 2007–July 6, 2008
Esperanza (Hope) Andrade	July 23, 2008–Nov. 23,2012
John T. Steen Jr.	Nov. 27, 2012–Jan. 7, 2014
Nandita Berry	Jan. 7, 2014–Jan. 21, 2015
Carlos H. Cascos	Jan. 21, 2015–Jan. 5, 2017
Rolando B. Pablos	Jan. 5, 2017–Dec. 17, 2018
David Whitley *(Senate refused to confirm.)*	Dec. 17, 2018–May 27, 2019
Ruth Ruggero Hughs *(Resigned.)*	Aug. 19, 2019–May 31, 2021
John B. Scott	Oct. 21,2021–Dec. 31, 2022
Jane Nelson	Jan. 5, 2023–Present

ATTORNEYS GENERAL OF THE REPUBLIC

Name	Term
David Thomas and Peter W. Grayson	Mar. 2–Oct. 22, 1836
J. Pinckney Henderson, Peter W. Grayson, John Birdsall, and A.S. Thurston	1836–1838
J.C. Watrous	Dec. 1838–June 1, 1840
Joseph Webb and F.A. Morris	1840–1841
George W. Terrell, Ebenezer Allen	1841–1844
Ebenezer Allen	1844–1846

State Attorneys General

Name	Term
Volney E. Howard (D)	Feb. 21, 1846–May 7, 1846
John W. Harris (D)	May 7, 1846–Oct. 31, 1849
Henry P. Brewster	Oct. 31, 1849–Jan. 15, 1850
A. J. Hamilton	Jan. 15, 1850–Aug. 5, 1850

(The first few attorneys general held office by appointment of the governor. The office was made elective in 1850 by constitutional amendment. Ebenezer Allen was the first elected attorney general.)

Name	Term
Ebenezer Allen	Aug. 5, 1850–Aug. 2, 1852
Thomas J. Jennings	Aug. 2, 1852–Aug. 4, 1856
James Willie	Aug. 4, 1856–Aug. 2, 1858

Malcolm D. Graham (D)....Aug. 2, 1858–Aug. 6, 1860
George M. Flournoy (D).... Aug. 6, 1860–Jan. 15, 1862
N. G. Shelley (D)........... Feb. 3, 1862–Aug. 1, 1864
B. E. Tarver (D) .... Aug. 1, 1864–Dec. 11, 1865
Wm. Alexander (Unionist) .Dec. 11, 1865–June 25, 1866
W. M. Walton (D)........June 25, 1866–Aug. 27, 1867
Wm. Alexander (R) ....Aug. 27, 1867–Nov. 5, 1867
Ezekiel B. Turner (I) .... Nov. 5, 1867–July 11, 1870
Wm. Alexander (R) .... July 11, 1870–Jan. 27, 1874
George Clark (D)..........Jan. 27, 1874–Apr. 25, 1876
H. H. Boone (D)...........Apr. 25, 1876–Nov. 5, 1878
George McCormick........ Nov. 5, 1878–Nov. 2, 1880
J. H. McLeary (D) .... Nov. 2, 1880–Nov. 7, 1882
John D. Templeton (D) ..... Nov. 7, 1882–Nov. 2, 1886
James S. Hogg (D) .... Nov. 2, 1886–Nov. 4, 1890
C. A. Culberson (D)........ Nov. 4, 1890–Nov. 6, 1894
M. M. Crane (D) .... Nov. 6, 1894–Nov. 8, 1898
Thomas S. Smith (D).......Nov. 8, 1898–Mar. 15,1901
C. K. Bell (D) .... Mar. 20, 1901–Jan. 1904
R. V. Davidson (D) .... Jan. 1904–Dec. 31, 1909
Jewel P. Lightfoot (D) ....Jan. 1, 1910–Aug. 31, 1912
James D. Walthall (D)....... Sept. 1, 1912–Jan. 1, 1913
B. F. Looney (D)............... Jan. 1, 1913–Jan., 1919
C. M. Cureton (D)...............Jan. 1919–Dec. 1921
W. A. Keeling (D)................Dec. 1921–Jan. 1925
Dan Moody (D) .... Jan. 1925–Jan. 1927
Claude Pollard (D).............. Jan. 1927–Sept. 1929
R. L. Bobbitt (D) .... Sept. 1929–Jan. 1931 *(Appointed)*
James V. Allred (D) ....Jan. 1931–Jan. 1935
William McCraw (D) .... Jan. 1935–Jan. 1939
Gerald C. Mann (D) ......Jan. 1939–Jan. 1944 *(Resigned)*
Grover Sellers (D)................ Jan. 1944–Jan. 1947
Price Daniel (D)................. Jan. 1947–Jan. 1953
John Ben Shepperd (D) .... Jan. 1953–Jan. 1, 1957
Will Wilson (D)............ Jan. 1, 1957–Jan. 15, 1963
Waggoner Carr (D) .... Jan. 15, 1963–Jan. 1, 1967
Crawford C. Martin (D) .....Jan. 1, 1967–Dec. 29, 1972
John Hill (D) .... Jan. 1, 1973–Jan. 16, 1979
Mark White (D)...........Jan. 16, 1979–Jan. 18, 1983
Jim Mattox (D)............Jan. 18, 1983–Jan. 15, 1991
Dan Morales (D) ....Jan. 15, 1991–Jan. 13, 1999
John Cornyn (R).......... Jan. 13, 1999–Dec. 2, 2002
Greg Abbott (R)...........Dec. 2, 2002–Jan. 20, 2015
Ken Paxton (R).................Jan. 20, 2015–Present

TREASURERS OF THE REPUBLIC

Asa Brigham 1838–1840
James W. Simmons.......................1840–1841
Asa Brigham 1841–1844
Moses Johnson 1844–1846

State Treasurers

James H. Raymond.........Feb. 24, 1846–Aug. 2, 1858
C.H. Randolph...............Aug. 2, 1858–June 1865

(Randolph fled to Mexico upon the collapse of Confederacy. No exact date is available for his departure from office or for Harris' succession to the post. It is believed Harris took office Oct. 2, 1865.)

Samuel Harris.............Oct. 2, 1865–June 25, 1866
W.M. Royston .... June 25, 1866–Sept. 1, 1867
John T. Allan .... Sept. 1, 1867–Jan. 1869
George W. Honey................ Jan. 1869–Jan. 1874

(Honey was removed from office for a short period in 1872 and B. Graham served in his place.)

B. Graham *(short term)* ....Beginning May 27, 1872
A. J. Dorn .... Jan. 1874–Jan. 1879
F. R. Lubbock.................... Jan. 1879–Jan. 1891
W. B. Wortham .... Jan. 1891–Jan. 1899
John W. Robbins .... Jan. 1899–Jan. 1907
Sam Sparks .... Jan. 1907–Jan. 1912
J. M. Edwards................... Jan. 1912–Jan. 1919
John W. Baker....................Jan. 1919–Jan. 1921
G. N. Holton .... July 1921–Nov. 21, 1921
C. V. Terrell ....Nov. 21, 1921–Aug. 15, 1924
S. L. Staples.............. Aug. 16, 1924–Jan. 15, 1925
W. Gregory Hatcher......... Jan. 16, 1925–Jan. 1, 1931
Charley Lockhart...........Jan. 1, 1931–Oct. 25, 1941
Jesse James.............. Oct. 25, 1941–Sept. 29, 1977
Warren G. Harding ....Oct. 7, 1977–Jan. 3, 1983
Ann Richards ....Jan. 3, 1983–Jan. 2, 1991
Kay Bailey Hutchison...........Jan. 2, 1991–June 1993
Martha Whitehead..............June 1993–Aug. 1996

The office of treasurer was eliminated by constitutional amendment in an election Nov. 7, 1995, effective the last day of August 1996.

RAILROAD COMMISSIONERS

After the first three names in the following list, each commissioner's name is followed by a surname in parentheses. The name in parentheses is the name of the commissioner whom that commissioner succeeded.

John H. Reagan........... June 10, 1891–Jan. 20, 1903
L. L. Foster .... June 10, 1891–April 30, 1895
W. P. McLean............June 10, 1891–Nov. 20, 1894
L. J. Storey (McLean)..... Nov. 21, 1894–Mar. 28,1909
N. A. Stedman (Foster)...... May 1, 1895–Jan. 4, 1897
Allison Mayfield (Stedman) . . Jan. 5, 1897–Jan. 23, 1923
O. B. Colquitt (Reagan)..... Jan. 21, 1903–Jan. 17, 1911
William D. Williams (Storey)April 28, 1909–Oct. 1, 1916
John L. Wortham (Colquitt)...Jan. 21, 1911–Jan. 1, 1913
Earle B. Mayfield (Wortham). Jan. 2, 1913–Mar. 1, 1923
Charles Hurdleston (Williams)Oct. 10, 1916–Dec. 31,1918
Clarence Gilmore (Hurdleston) Jan. 1, 1919–Jan. 1, 1929
N. A. Nabors (A. Mayfield) . Mar. 1, 1923–Jan. 18, 1925
William Splawn (E. Mayfield)Mar. 1, 1923–Aug. 1, 1924
C. V. Terrell (Splawn) ...... Aug. 15, 1924–Jan. 1, 1939
Lon A. Smith (Nabors)...... Jan. 29, 1925–Jan. 1, 1941
Pat M. Neff (Gilmore)........ Jan. 1, 1929–Jan. 1, 1933
Ernest O. Thompson (Neff)... Jan. 1, 1933–Jan. 8, 1965
G. A. (Jerry) Sadler (Terrell)... Jan. 1, 1939–Jan. 1, 1943
Olin Culberson (Smith)......Jan. 1, 1941–June 22, 1961
Beauford Jester (Sadler) ...... Jan. 1, 1943–Jan. 21, 1947
William J. Murray Jr. (Jester)Jan. 21, 1947–Apr. 10, 1963
Ben Ramsey (Culberson) . . .Sept. 18, 1961–Dec. 31, 1976

Jim C. Langdon (Murray) . May 28, 1963–Dec. 31, 1977
Byron Tunnell (Thompson) Jan. 11, 1965–Sept. 15, 1973
Mack Wallace (Tunnell) . Sept. 18, 1973–Sept. 22, 1987
Jon Newton (Ramsey) . . . . Jan. 10, 1977–Jan. 4, 1979
John H. Poerner (Langdon). . . . Jan. 2, 1978–Jan. 1, 1981
James E. Nugent (Newton) . . . . .Jan. 4, 1979–Jan. 3,1995
Buddy Temple (Poerner) . . . . . Jan. 2, 1981–Mar. 2, 1986
Clark Jobe (Temple). . . . . Mar. 3, 1986–Jan. 5, 1987
John Sharp (Jobe). . . . . Jan. 6, 1987–Jan. 2, 1991
Kent Hance (Wallace) . . . . . . Sept. 23, 1987–Jan. 2, 1991
Robert Krueger (Hance) . . . . . Jan. 3, 1991–Jan. 22, 1993

(Krueger resigned when Gov. Ann Richards appointed him interim U.S. Senator on the resignation of Sen. Lloyd Bentsen.)

Lena Guerrero (Sharp). . . . .Jan. 23, 1991–Sept. 25, 1992
James Wallace (Guerrero) . . . . Oct. 2, 1992–Jan. 4, 1993
Barry Williamson (Wallace). . . Jan. 5, 1993–Jan. 4, 1999
Mary Scott Nabers (Krueger) . Feb. 9, 1993–Dec. 9, 1994
Carole K. Rylander (Nabers). Dec. 10, 1994–Jan. 4, 1999
Charles Matthews (Nugent) . . Jan. 3, 1995–Jan. 31, 2005
Antonio Garza (Williamson) Jan. 4, 1999–Nov. 18, 2002
Michael Williams (Rylander) Jan. 4, 1999–Mar. 31, 2011
Victor G. Carrillo (Garza). . . .Feb. 19, 2003–Jan. 3, 2011
Elizabeth A. Jones (Matthews)Feb. 2, 2005–Feb. 28, 2012
David Porter (Carrillo). . . . . Jan. 5, 2011–Jan. 2, 2017
Barry T. Smitherman (Williams)July 8, 2011–Jan. 2, 2015
Buddy Garcia (Jones) . . . . . . April 16, 2012–Dec. 7, 2012

(Appointed by Gov. Perry.)

Ryan Sitton (Smitherman). . . . .Jan. 5, 2015–Jan. 4, 2021
Christi Craddick (Garcia) . . . . Dec. 17, 2012–Present
Wayne Christian (Porter) . . . . Jan. 9, 2017–Present
Jim Wright (Sitton) . . . . Jan. 4, 2021–Present

COMPTROLLERS OF PUBLIC ACCOUNTS FOR THE REPUBLIC

John H. Money . . . . Dec. 30, 1835–Jan. 17, 1836
H. C. Hudson . . . . Jan. 17, 1836–Oct. 22, 1836
Elisha M. Pease. . . . . June 1837–Dec. 1837
F. R. Lubbock . . . . .Dec. 1837–Jan. 1839
Jas. W. Simmons. . . . . Jan. 15, 1839–Sept. 30, 1840
Jas. B. Shaw . . . . .Sept. 30, 1840–Dec. 24, 1841
F. R. Lubbock . . . . Dec. 24, 1841–Jan. 1, 1842
Jas. B. Shaw . . . . .Jan. 1, 1842–Jan. 1, 1846

State Comptrollers of Public Accounts

Jas. B. Shaw . . . . .Feb. 24, 1846–Aug. 2, 1858
Clement R. Johns . . . . .Aug. 2, 1858–Aug. 1, 1864
Willis L. Robards. . . . . Aug. 1, 1864–Oct. 12, 1865
Albert H. Latimer . . . . Oct. 12, 1865–Mar. 27, 1866
Robert H. Taylor . . . . Mar. 27, 1866–June 25, 1866
Willis L. Robards. . . . . .June 25, 1866–Aug. 27, 1867
Morgan C. Hamilton. . . . . . . .Aug. 27, 1867–Jan. 8, 1870
A. Bledsoe . . . . .Jan. 8, 1870–Jan. 20, 1874
Stephen H. Darden. . . . . .Jan. 20, 1874–Nov. 2, 1880
W. M. Brown . . . . .Nov. 2, 1880–Jan. 16, 1883
W. J. Swain . . . . .Jan. 16, 1883–Jan. 18, 1887
John D. McCall . . . . Jan. 18, 1887–Jan. 15, 1895
R. W. Finley . . . . .Jan. 15, 1895–Jan. 15, 1901
R. M. Love . . . . Jan. 15, 1901–Jan. 1903
J. W. Stephen. . . . . Jan. 1903–Jan. 1911
W. P. Lane. . . . . .Jan. 1911–Jan. 1915
H. B. Terrell . . . . Jan. 1915–Jan. 1920
M. L. Wiginton . . . . Jan. 1920–Jan. 1921
Lon A. Smith . . . . Jan. 1921–Jan. 1925
S. H. Terrell . . . . Jan. 1925–Jan. 1931
Geo. H. Sheppard. . . . . Jan., 1931–Jan. 17, 1949
Robert S. Calvert . . . . .Jan. 17, 1949–Jan., 1975
Robert D. (Bob) Bullock . . . . Jan. 1975–Jan. 3, 1991
John Sharp . . . . Jan. 3, 1991–Jan. 2, 1999
Carole Keeton Strayhorn . . . . . .Jan. 2, 1999–Jan. 1, 2007
Susan Combs. . . . . .Jan. 1, 2007–Jan. 1, 2015
Glenn Hegar . . . . Jan. 2, 2015–June 2025
Kelly Hancock . . . . .June 2025-Present

U.S. SENATORS FROM TEXAS

U.S. Senators were selected by the legislatures of the states until the U.S. Constitution was amended in 1913 to require popular elections. In Texas, the first Senator chosen by the voters in a general election was Charles A. Culberson in 1916. Because of political pressures, however, the rules of the Democratic Party of Texas were changed in 1904 to require that all candidates for office stand before voters in the primary. Consequently, Texas' Senators faced voters in 1906, 1910, and 1912 before the U.S. Constitution was changed.

Following is the succession of Texas representatives in the United States Senate since the annexation of Texas to the Union in 1845:

Houston Succession

Sam Houston (I) . . . . .Feb. 21, 1846–Mar. 4, 1859
John Hemphill (D). . . . . Mar. 4, 1859–July 11, 1861

(Louis T. Wigfall and W. S. Oldham took their seats in the Confederate Senate, Nov. 16, 1861, and served until the Confederacy collapsed. After that event, the State Legislature on Aug. 21, 1866, elected David G. Burnet and Oran M. Roberts to the U.S. Senate, anticipating immediate readmission to the Union, but they were not allowed to take their seats.)

Morgan C. Hamilton (R) . . .Feb. 22, 1870–Mar. 3, 1877
Richard Coke (D). . . . . Mar. 4, 1877–Mar. 3, 1895
Horace Chilton (D) . . . . Mar. 3, 1895–Mar. 3, 1901
Joseph W. Bailey (D) . . . . Mar. 3, 1901–Jan. 8, 1913

(Resigned.)

Rienzi Melville Johnston (D) . . Jan. 8, 1913–Feb. 3, 1913

(Appointed to fill vacancy.)

Morris Sheppard (D) . . . . Feb. 13, 1913–Apr. 9, 1941

(Died in office.)

Andrew J. Houston (D) . . . . June 2–26, 1941

(Appointed to fill vacancy; died in office.)

W. Lee O'Daniel (D) . . . . .Aug. 4, 1941–Jan. 3, 1949
Lyndon B. Johnson (D) . . . . . .Jan. 3, 1949–Jan. 20, 1961

(Resigned to become U.S. Vice President.)

William A. Blakley (D) . . . . .Jan. 20, 1961–June 15, 1961

(Appointed to fill vacancy.)

John G. Tower (R) . . . . .June 15, 1961–Jan. 21, 1985
Phil Gramm (R) . . . . Jan. 21, 1985–Dec. 2, 2002
John Cornyn (R). . . . . Dec. 2, 2002–Present

Rusk Succession

Thomas J. Rusk (D)........Feb 21, 1846–July 29, 1857
(Died in office.)
J. Pinckney Henderson (D)...Nov. 9, 1857–June 4, 1858
(Died in office.)
Matthias Ward (D) .... Sept. 29, 1858–Dec. 5, 1859
(Appointed to fill vacancy.)
Louis T. Wigfall (D) ...... Dec. 5, 1859–Mar. 23, 1861
(Succession was broken by secession. See note above under Houston Succession.)
James W. Flanagan (R) .....Feb. 22, 1870–Mar. 3, 1875
Samuel B. Maxey (D)....... Mar. 3, 1875–Mar. 3, 1887
John H. Reagan (D)........Mar. 3, 1887–June 10, 1891
(Resigned to head the Texas Railroad Commission.)
Horace Chilton (D) .... Dec. 7, 1891–Mar. 30,1892
(Appointed to fill vacancy.)
Roger Q. Mills (D)........Mar. 30, 1892–Mar. 3, 1899
Charles A. Culberson (D) ... Mar. 3, 1899–Mar. 4, 1923
Earle B. Mayfield (D)....... Mar. 4, 1923–Mar. 4, 1929
Tom Connally (D) .... Mar. 4, 1929–Jan. 3, 1953
Price Daniel (D)............Jan. 3, 1953–Jan. 15, 1957
(Resigned to become governor.)
William A. Blakley (D) .....Jan. 15, 1957–Apr. 27, 1957
(Appointed to fill vacancy.)
Ralph W. Yarborough (D)...Apr. 27, 1957–Jan. 12, 1971
Lloyd Bentsen (D) ....Jan. 12, 1971–Jan. 20, 1993
(Resigned to become U.S. Secretary of Treasury.)
Robert Krueger (D) .... Jan. 20, 1993–June 14, 1993
(Appointed to fill vacancy.)
Kay Bailey Hutchison (R).. June 14, 1993–Jan. 20, 2013
Ted Cruz (R) ....Jan. 20, 2013–Present

GENERAL LAND OFFICE COMMISSIONERS FOR THE REPUBLIC

John P. Borden .... Aug. 23, 1837–Dec. 12, 1840
H. W. Raglin .... Dec. 12, 1840–Jan. 4, 1841
Thomas William Ward ... Jan. 4, 1841–Mar. 20, 1848
(Part of the term after annexation.)

State Land Commissioners

George W. Smyth......... Mar. 20, 1848–Aug. 4, 1851
Stephen Crosby............Aug. 4, 1851–Mar. 1, 1858
Francis M. White.......... Mar. 1, 1858–Mar. 1, 1862
Stephen Crosby...........Mar. 1, 1862–Sept. 1, 1865
Francis M. White.......... Sept. 1, 1865–Aug. 7, 1866
Stephen Crosby............ Aug. 7, 1866–Aug. 27, 1867
Joseph Spence ....Aug. 27, 1867–Jan. 19, 1870
Jacob Kuechler ....Jan. 19, 1870–Jan. 20, 1874
J. J. Groos .... Jan. 20, 1874–June 15, 1878
W. C. Walsh ....July 30, 1878–Jan. 10, 1887
R. M. Hall................ Jan. 10, 1887–Jan. 16, 1891
W. L. McGaughey .... Jan. 16, 1891–Jan. 26, 1895
A. J. Baker ....Jan. 26, 1895–Jan. 16, 1899
George W. Finger.......... Jan. 16, 1899–May 4, 1899
Charles Rogan............ May 11, 1899–Jan. 10, 1903
John J. Terrell ....Jan. 10, 1903–Jan. 11, 1909
J. T. Robison............... Jan. 1909–Sept. 11, 1929
J. H. Walker .... Sept. 11, 1929–Jan. 1937
William H. McDonald ....Jan. 1937–Jan. 1939
Bascom Giles.................. Jan. 1939–Jan. 5, 1955
J. Earl Rudder...............Jan. 5, 1955–Feb. 1, 1958
Bill Allcorn ....Feb. 1, 1958–Jan. 1, 1961
Jerry Sadler .... Jan. 1, 1961–Jan. 1, 1971
Bob Armstrong............. Jan. 1, 1971–Jan. 1, 1983
Garry Mauro................ Jan. 1, 1983–Jan. 7, 1999
David Dewhurst ....Jan. 7, 1999–Jan. 3, 2003
Jerry Patterson ....Jan. 3, 2003–Jan. 2, 2015
George P. Bush ....Jan. 2, 2015–Jan. 10, 2023
Dawn Buckingham M.D..........Jan. 10, 2023–Present

SPEAKERS OF THE HOUSE FOR THE REPUBLIC

Speaker	Term	Congress
Ira Ingram	1836–37	1st
Branch Tanner Archer	1837	2nd
Joseph Rowe	1838	2nd
John M. Hansford	1838–39	3rd
David Spangler Kaufman	1840–41	4th, 5th
Kenneth L. Anderson	1841–42	6th
Nicholas H. Darnell	1842–43	7th
Richardson A. Scurry	1843–44	8th
John M. Lewis	1844–45	9th

State Speakers of the House

Speaker, Residence	Term	Leg.
William E. Crump (D), Bellville	1846	1st
John Brown (D), Brownsboro	1846	1st
Edward T. Branch (D), Liberty	1846	1st
William H. Bourland (D), Paris	1846	1st
Stephen W. Perkins (D), Columbia	1846	1st
James W. Henderson (D), Houston	1847–48	2nd
Charles G. Keenan (D), Huntsville	1849–51	3rd
David C. Dickson (D), Anderson	1851–53	4th
Hardin R. Runnels (D), Boston	1853–55	5th
Hamilton P. Bee (D), Laredo	1855–57	6th
William S. Taylor (D), Larissa	1857–58	7th
Matt F. Locke (D), Lafayette	1858–59	7th
Marion DeKalb Taylor (D), Jefferson	1859–61	8th
Constantine W. Buckley (D), Richmond	1861	9th
Nicholas H. Darnell (D), Dallas	1861–62	9th
Constantine W. Buckley (D), Richmond	1863	9th
Marion DeKalb Taylor (D), Jefferson	1863–65	10th
Nathaniel M. Burford (Unionist), Dallas	1866	11th
(Vacant under Congressional Reconstruction and military administration, 1867-1870.)		
Ira H. Evans (R), Corpus Christi	1870–71	12th
William H. Sinclair (R), Galveston	1871–73	12th
Marion DeKalb Taylor (D), Jefferson	1873–74	13th
Guy M. Bryan (D), Galveston	1874–76	14th
Thomas R. Bonner (D), Tyler	1876–79	15th
John H. Cochran (D), Dallas	1879–81	16th
George R. Reeves (D), Pottsboro	1881–83	17th

Speaker, Residence	Term	Leg.
Charles R. Gibson (D), Waxahachie	1883–85	18th
Lafayette L. Foster (D), Groesbeck	1885–87	19th
George C. Pendleton (D), Belton	1887–89	20th
Frank P. Alexander (D), Greenville	1889–91	21st
Robert T. Milner (D), Henderson	1891–93	22nd
John H. Cochran (D), Dallas	1893–95	23rd
Thomas Slater Smith (D), Hillsboro	1895–97	24th
L. Travis Dashiell (D), Jewett	1897–99	25th
J. S. Sherrill (D), Greenville	1899–1901	26th
Robert E. Prince (D), Corsicana	1901–03	27th
Pat M. Neff (D), Waco	1903–05	28th
Francis W. Seabury (D), Rio Grande City	1905–07	29th
Thomas B. Love (D), Lancaster	1907–09	30th
Austin M. Kennedy (D), Waco	1909	31st
(Resigned during 31st session.)		
John W. Marshall (D), Whitesboro	1909–11	31st
Sam Rayburn (D), Bonham	1911–13	32nd
Chester H. Terrell (D), San Antonio	1913–15	33rd
John W. Woods (D), Rotan	1915–17	34th
Franklin O. Fuller (D), Coldspring	1917–19	35th
R. Ewing Thomason (D), El Paso	1919–21	36th
Charles G. Thomas (D), Lewisville	1921–23	37th
Richard E. Seagler (D), Palestine	1923–25	38th
R. Lee Satterwhite (D), Amarillo	1925–27	39th
Robert L. Bobbitt (D), Laredo	1927–29	40th
W. S. Barron (D), Bryan	1929–31	41st
Fred H. Minor (D), Denton	1931–33	42nd
Coke R. Stevenson (D), Junction	1933–37	43rd–44th
Robert W. Calvert (D), Hillsboro	1937–39	45th
R. Emmett Morse (D), Houston	1939–41	46th
Homer L. Leonard (D), McAllen	1941–43	47th
Price Daniel (D), Liberty	1943–45	48th
Claud H. Gilmer (D), Rocksprings	1945–47	49th
William O. Reed (D), Dallas	1947–49	50th
Durwood Manford (D), Smiley	1949–51	51st
Reuben Senterfitt (D), San Saba	1951–55	52nd–53rd
Jim T. Lindsey (D), Texarkana	1955–57	54th
Waggoner Carr (D), Lubbock	1957–61	55th–56th
James A. Turman (D), Gober	1961–63	57th
Byron M. Tunnell (D), Tyler	1963–65	58th
Ben Barnes (D), De Leon	1965–69	59th–60th
Gus F. Mutscher (D), Brenham	1969–72	61st–62nd
(Resigned during 62nd session.)		
Rayford Price (D), Palestine	1972–73	62nd
Price Daniel Jr. (D), Liberty	1973–75	63rd
Bill Clayton (D), Springlake	1975–83	64th–67th
Gib Lewis (D), Fort Worth	1983–93	68th–72nd
Pete Laney (D), Hale Center	1993–2003	73rd–77th
Tom Craddick (R), Midland	2003–09	78th–80th
Joe Straus (R), San Antonio	2009–19	81st–85th
Dennis Bonnen (R), Angleton	2019–21	86th
Dade Phelan (R), Beaumont	2021–25	87th–88th
Dustin Burrows (R), Lubbock	2025–Present	89th

CHIEF JUSTICE OF THE SUPREME COURT REPUBLIC OF TEXAS

James Collinsworth . . . . Dec. 16, 1836–July 23, 1838
John Birdsall . . . . Nov. 19–Dec. 12, 1838
(Senate refused to confirm.)
Thomas J. Rusk . . . . Dec. 12, 1838–Dec. 5, 1840
John Hemphill . . . . Dec. 5, 1840–Dec. 29, 1845

Under Constitutions of 1845 and 1861

John Hemphill . . . . Mar. 2, 1846–Oct. 10, 1858
Royall T. Wheeler . . . . Oct. 11, 1858–April 1864
Oran M. Roberts . . . . Nov. 1, 1864–June 30, 1866

Under Constitution of 1866 (Presidential Reconstruction)

George F. Moore. . . . . Aug. 16, 1866–Sept. 10, 1867
(Removed under Congressional Reconstruction by military authorities who appointed members of the next court.)

Under Constitution of 1866 (Congressional Reconstruction)

Amos Morrill . . . . Sept. 10, 1867–July 5, 1870

Under Constitution of 1869

Lemuel D. Evans. . . . . July 5, 1870–Aug. 31, 1873
Wesley Ogden. . . . . Aug. 31, 1873–Jan. 29, 1874
Oran M. Roberts . . . . Jan. 29, 1874–Apr. 18, 1876

Under Constitution of 1876

Oran M. Roberts . . . . Apr. 18, 1876–Oct. 1, 1878
George F. Moore. . . . . Nov. 5, 1878–Nov. 1, 1881
Robert S. Gould . . . . Nov. 1, 1881–Dec. 23, 1882
Asa H. Willie . . . . Dec. 23, 1882–Mar. 3, 1888
John W. Stayton . . . . Mar. 3, 1888–July 5, 1894
Reuben R. Gaines. . . . . July 10, 1894–Jan. 5, 1911
Thomas J. Brown . . . . Jan. 7, 1911–May 26, 1915
Nelson Phillips. . . . . June 1, 1915–Nov. 16, 1921
C. M. Cureton. . . . . Dec. 2, 1921–Apr. 8, 1940
Hortense Sparks Ward. . . . . . Jan. 8, 1925–May 23, 1925
(Mrs. Ward headed a special Supreme Court to hear one case in 1925.)
W. F. Moore . . . . Apr. 17, 1940–Jan. 1, 1941
James P. Alexander . . . . Jan. 1, 1941–Jan. 1, 1948
J. E. Hickman . . . . Jan. 5, 1948–Jan. 3, 1961
Robert W. Calvert . . . . Jan. 3, 1961–Oct. 4, 1972
Joe R. Greenhill . . . . Oct. 4, 1972–Oct. 25, 1982
Jack Pope. . . . . Nov. 29, 1982–Jan. 5, 1985
John L. Hill Jr. . . . . Jan. 5, 1985–Jan. 4, 1988
Thomas R. Phillips . . . . Jan. 4, 1988–Sept. 3 2004
Wallace B. Jefferson . . . . Sept. 14, 2004–Oct. 1, 2013
Nathan L. Hecht . . . . Oct. 1, 2013–Dec. 31, 2024
Jimmy Blacklock. . . . . Jan. 6, 2025–Present

PRESIDING JUDGES, COURT OF APPEALS (1876–1891), AND COURT OF CRIMINAL APPEALS (1891–PRESENT)

Mat D. Ector. . . . . May 6, 1876–Oct. 29, 1879
John P. White . . . . Nov. 9, 1879–Apr. 26, 1892

James M. Hurt . . . . May 4, 1892–Dec. 31, 1898
W. L. Davidson. . . . . Jan. 2, 1899–June 27, 1913
A. C. Prendergast . . . . June 27, 1913–Dec. 31, 1916
W. L. Davidson. . . . . Jan. 1, 1917–Jan. 25, 1921
Wright C. Morrow . . . . Feb. 8, 1921–Oct. 16, 1939
Frank Lee Hawkins . . . . Oct. 16, 1939–Jan. 2, 1951
Harry N. Graves . . . . Jan. 2, 1951–Dec. 31, 1954
W. A. Morrison . . . . Jan. 1, 1955–Jan. 2, 1961
Kenneth K. Woodley . . . . Jan. 3, 1961–Jan. 4, 1965
W. T. McDonald . . . . Jan. 4, 1965–June 25, 1966
W. A. Morrison . . . . June 25, 1966–Jan. 1, 1967
Kenneth K. Woodley . . . . Jan. 1, 1967–Jan. 1, 1971
John F. Onion Jr.. . . . . Jan. 1, 1971–Jan. 1, 1989
Michael J. McCormick . . . . Jan. 1, 1989–Jan. 1, 2001
Sharon Keller . . . . Jan. 1, 2001–Dec. 31, 2024
David Schenck . . . . Jan. 31, 2025–Present

ADMINISTRATORS OF PUBLIC EDUCATION, SUPERINTENDENTS OF PUBLIC INSTRUCTION

Pryor Lea. . . . . Nov. 10, 1866–Sept. 12, 1867
Edwin M. Wheelock . . . . . . Sept. 12, 1867–May 6, 1871
Jacob C. DeGress . . . . May 6, 1871–Jan. 20, 1874
O. H. Hollingsworth . . . . Jan. 20, 1874–May 6, 1884
B. M. Baker . . . . May 6, 1884–Jan. 18, 1887
O. H. Cooper . . . . Jan. 18, 1887–Sept. 1, 1890
H. C. Pritchett . . . . Sept. 1, 1890–Sept. 15, 1891
J. M. Carlisle . . . . Sept. 15, 1891–Jan. 10, 1899
J. S. Kendall. . . . . Jan. 10, 1899–July 2, 1901
Arthur Lefevre . . . . July 2, 1901–Jan. 12, 1905
R. B. Cousins . . . . Jan. 12, 1905–Jan. 1, 1910
F. M. Bralley . . . . Jan. 1, 1910–Sept. 1, 1913
W. F. Doughty . . . . Sept. 1, 1913–Jan. 1, 1919
Annie Webb Blanton . . . . Jan. 1, 1919–Jan. 16, 1923
S. M. N. Marrs . . . . Jan. 16, 1923–April 28, 1932
C. N. Shaver . . . . April 28, 1932–Oct. 1, 1932
L. W. Rogers. . . . . Oct. 1, 1932–Jan. 16, 1933
L. A. Woods . . . . Jan. 16, 1933–1951

The office of State Superintendent of Public Instruction was abolished by the **Gilmer-Aikin Laws of 1949** and the office of Commissioner of Education was created. The Commissioner is appointed by the State Board of Education.

State Commissioners of Education

J. W. Edgar . . . . May 31, 1951–June 30, 1974
Marlin L. Brockette . . . . July 1, 1974–Sept. 1, 1979
Alton O. Bowen . . . . Sept. 1, 1979–June 1, 1981
Raymon Bynum . . . . June 1, 1981–Oct. 31, 1984
W. N. Kirby . . . . April 13, 1985–July 1, 1991
Lionel R. Meno. . . . . July 1, 1991–Mar. 1, 1995
Michael A. Moses. . . . . Mar. 9, 1995–Aug. 18, 1999
Jim Nelson . . . . Aug. 18, 1999–Mar. 25, 2002
Felipe Alanis. . . . . Mar. 25, 2002–July 31, 2003
Shirley J. Neeley . . . . Jan. 12, 2004–July 1, 2007
Robert Scott . . . . July 1, 2007–July 2, 2012
Michael Williams. . . . . Sept. 1, 2012–Dec. 31, 2015
Michael H. Morath . . . . Jan. 4, 2016–Present

STATE COMMISSIONERS OF AGRICULTURE

Robert Teague Milner 1907–1908
Edward Reeves Kone 1908–1914
Fred Davis 1915–1920
George B. Terrell 1921–1930
James E. McDonald 1931–1950
John C. White. 1951–1977
Reagan V. Brown 1977–1982
Jim Hightower 1983–1990
Rick Perry. 1991–1998
Susan Combs. 1999–2006
Todd Staples 2007–2015
Sidney C. Miller 2015–Present

FIRST LADIES OF TEXAS

Martha Evans Gindratt Wood 1847–1849
Bell Administration 1849–1853
(Gov. Peter Hansbrough Bell was not married while in office.)
Lucadia Christiana Niles Pease 1853–57; 1867–69
Runnels Administration 1857–1859
(Gov. Hardin R. Runnels never married.)
Margaret Moffette Lea Houston 1859–1861
Martha Evans Clark 1861
Adele Barron Lubbock 1861–1863
Susie Ellen Taylor Murrah 1863–1865
Mary Jane Bowen Hamilton 1865–1866
Annie Rattan Throckmorton 1866–1867
Ann Elizabeth Britton Davis 1870–1874
Mary Home Coke 1874–1876
Janie Roberts Hubbard 1876–1879
Frances Wickliff Edwards Roberts 1879–1883
Anne Maria Penn Ireland 1883–1887
Elizabeth Dorothy Tinsley Ross 1887–1891
Sarah Stinson Hogg 1891–1895
Sally Harrison Culberson 1895–1899
Orlene Walton Sayers 1899–1903
Sarah Beona Meng Lanham 1903–1907
Fannie Brunner Campbell 1907–1911
Alice Fuller Murrell Colquitt 1911–1915
Miriam A. Wallace Ferguson 1915–1917
(Miriam A. Wallace Ferguson was Mistress of the Mansion while her husband, James E. Ferguson, was governor, 1915–1917. She served as both Governor and Mistress of the Mansion, 1925–1927 and 1933–1935.)
Willie Cooper Hobby 1917–1921
Myrtle Mainer Neff 1921–1925
Mildred Paxton Moody 1927–1931
Maud Gage Sterling 1931–1933
Jo Betsy Miller Allred 1935–1939
Merle Estella Butcher O'Daniel 1939–1941
Fay Wright Stevenson 1941–1942
(Died in the Governor's Mansion on Jan. 3, 1942.)
Edith Will Scott Stevenson 1942–1946
(Mother of Gov. Coke R. Stevenson and Mistress of the Mansion upon the death of the governor's wife.)
Mabel Buchanan Jester 1946–1949
Marialice Shary Shivers 1949–1957
Jean Houston Baldwin Daniel 1957–1963
Idanell Brill Connally 1963–1969
Ima Mae Smith 1969–1973
Betty Jane Slaughter Briscoe 1973–1979
Rita Crocker Bass Clements 1979–1983
Linda Gale Thompson White 1983–1987
Rita Crocker Bass Clements 1987–1991
Richards Administration 1991–1995
(Gov. Ann Richards was not married while in office.)
Laura Welch Bush 1995–2000
Anita Thigpen Perry 2000–2015
Cecilia Abbott 2015–Present

TEXAS STATE JUDICIARY

The judiciary of the state consists of nine justices of the Supreme Court of Texas; nine judges of the Court of Criminal Appeals; 80 justices of the 14 Courts of Appeals; 459 judges of the State District Courts; 13 judges of the Criminal District Courts; 527 County Court judges; 805 Justice Court judges; and more than 1,200 Municipal Court judges in 944 cities.

Since 1876, judges at all levels have been elected by voters in partisan elections. The Judicial Campaign Fairness Act was added to the Texas Election Code in 1995 by the 74th Legislature and limits individual campaign contributions to $5,000 for a statewide judicial office and $1,000 to $5,000 for other judicial offices, depending on judicial district population. The exception is law firms, for which a $50 limit is set.

In addition to its system of formal courts, the State of Texas has established 18 Alternative Dispute Resolution Centers. The centers are headed by a director and help ease the caseload of Texas courts by using mediation, arbitration, negotiation, and moderated settlement conferences to handle disputes.

Centers are located in Amarillo, Austin, Beaumont, Bryan–College Station, Conroe, Corpus Christi, Dallas, Denton, El Paso, Fort Worth, Houston, Kerrville, Lubbock, Paris, Richmond, San Antonio, San Marcos, and Waco.

State Higher Courts

The state's higher courts include the Supreme Court, the Court of Criminal Appeals, the Courts of Appeals, and District Courts. Justices of the Supreme Court, Court of Criminal Appeals, and Courts of Appeals are elected to six-year, overlapping terms. District Court judges are elected to four-year terms.

The justices listed below are current as of June 2025. Notations in parentheses are terms of office expiration dates. Elsewhere in this section are lists of District Court judges by district number, district court numbers in each county, and county court judges.

Supreme Court

Chief Justice, Jimmy Blacklock (12/31/26). **Justices:** Jane Bland (12/31/31); Jeff Boyd (12/31/26); Brett Busby (12/31/26); John Phillip Devine (12/31/31); Rebeca Huddle (12/31/28); Debra Lehrmann (12/31/28); and Evan A. Young (12/31/28).
Clerk of Court, Blake A. Hawthorne.

Court of Criminal Appeals

Presiding Judge, David J. Schenck (12/31/30). **Judges:** Lee Finley (12/31/31); Mary Lou Keel (12/31/28); Jesse F. McClure III (12/31/28); David Newell (12/31/26); Gina G. Parker (12/31/31); Bert Richardson (12/31/26); Scott Walker (12/31/28); and Kevin Patrick Yeary (12/31/26).
State Prosecuting Attorney, Stacey M. Soule.
Clerk of Court, Deana Williamson.

COURT OF APPEALS

Texas has 15 courts of appeals with intermediate appellate jurisdiction. The first 14 courts have jurisdiction in specific regions of Texas, while the fifteenth has statewide jurisdiction. The fifteenth court was established during the 88th Legislature to focus on certain civil appeals, including those from the Texas Business Court, cases brought by or against the state, and challenges to state law.

Judges are elected from the district for six-year terms. Terms end on December 31 of the year in parentheses.

First District, Houston§: Chief Justice Terry Adams (2028). **Justices:** Jennifer Caughey (2030); Susanna Dokupil (2030); Amparo M. Guerra (2026); Kristin Guiney (2030); David M. Gunn (2026); Andrew Johnson (2030); Clint Morgan (2030); and Veronica Rivas-Malloy (2026). **Clerk of Court,** Deborah M. Young. **Counties in the First District:** Austin, Brazoria, Chambers, Colorado, Fort Bend, Galveston, Grimes, Harris, Waller, Washington.

Second District, Fort Worth: Chief Justice Bonnie Sudderth (2030). **Justices:** Dabney Bassel (2030); J. Wade Birdwell (2030); Elizabeth Kerr (2028); Brian Walker (2026); Mike Wallach (2030); Dana Womack (2026). **Clerk of Court,** Clarissa Hodges. **Counties in the Second District:** Archer, Clay, Cooke, Denton, Hood, Jack, Montague, Parker, Tarrant, Wichita, Wise, Young.

Third District, Austin: Chief Justice Darlene Byrne (2026). **Justices:** Karin Crump (2030); Maggie Ellis (2030); Chari L. Kelly (2030); Rosa Lopez Theofanis (2029); and Gisela D. Triana (2030). **Clerk of Court,** Jeffrey D. Kyle. **Counties in the Third District:** Bastrop, Bell, Blanco, Burnet, Caldwell, Coke, Comal, Concho, Fayette, Hays, Irion, Lampasas, Lee, Llano, McCulloch, Milam, Mills, Runnels, San Saba, Schleicher, Sterling, Tom Green, Travis, Williamson.

Fourth District, San Antonio: Chief Justice Rebeca C. Martinez (2026). **Justices:** Lori Massey Brissette (2030); Todd McCray (2030); Velia J. Meza (2030); Irene Rios (2028); Adrian A. Spears II (2030); and Lori I. Valenzuela (2030). **Clerk of Court,** Caitlin A. McCamish. **Counties in the Fourth District:** Atascosa, Bandera, Bexar, Brooks, Dimmit, Duval, Edwards, Frio, Gillespie, Guadalupe, Jim Hogg, Jim Wells, Karnes, Kendall, Kerr, Kimble, Kinney, La Salle, Mason, Maverick, McMullen, Medina, Menard, Real, Starr, Sutton, Uvalde, Val Verde, Webb, Wilson, Zapata, Zavala.

Fifth District, Dallas: Chief Justice J.J. Koch (2030). **Justices:** Cynthia M. Barbare (2030); Maricela Moore Breedlove (2029); Tina Clinton (2030); Dennise Garcia (2026); Bonnie Lee Goldstein (2026); Earl Jackson (2030); Nancy Kennedy (2028); Mike Lee (2030); Jessica Lewis (2030); Emily Miskel (2030); Gino J. Rossini (2030); and Craig Smith (2026). **Clerk of Court,** Ruben Morin. **Counties in the Fifth District:** Collin, Dallas, Grayson, Hunt, Kaufman, Rockwall.

Sixth District, Texarkana: Chief Justice Scott E. Stevens (2028). **Justices:** Jeff Rambin (2030) and Charles van Cleef (2028). **Clerk of Court,** Debbie Autrey. **Counties in the Sixth District:** Bowie, Camp, Cass, Delta, Fannin, Franklin, Gregg, Harrison, Hopkins, Hunt, Lamar, Marion, Morris, Panola, Red River, Rusk, Titus, Upshur, Wood.

Seventh District, Amarillo: Chief Justice Brian Quinn (2026). **Justices:** Lawrence M. Doss (2028); Judy C. Parker (2030); and Alex L. Yarbrough (2030). **Clerk of Court,** Bobby Ramirez. **Counties in the Seventh District:** Armstrong, Bailey, Briscoe, Carson, Castro, Childress, Cochran, Collingsworth, Cottle, Crosby, Dallam, Deaf Smith, Dickens, Donley, Floyd, Foard, Garza, Gray, Hale, Hall, Hansford, Hardeman, Hartley, Hemphill, Hockley, Hutchinson, Kent, King, Lamb, Lipscomb, Lubbock, Lynn, Moore, Motley, Ochiltree, Oldham, Parmer, Potter, Randall, Roberts, Sherman, Swisher, Terry, Wheeler, Wilbarger, Yoakum.

Eighth District, El Paso: Chief Justice Maria Salas-Mendoza (2026). **Justices:** Gina M. Palafox (2030) and Lisa Soto (2030). **Clerk of Court,** Elizabeth G. Flores. **Counties in the Eighth District:** Andrews, Brewster, Crane, Crockett, Culberson, El Paso, Hudspeth, Jeff Davis, Loving, Pecos, Presidio, Reagan, Reeves, Terrell, Upton, Ward, Winkler.

Ninth District, Beaumont: Chief Justice Scott Golemon (2026). **Justices:** Kent Chambers (2030); Leanne Johnson (2030); and Jay Wright (2028). **Clerk of Court,** Carly Latiolais. **Counties in the Ninth District:** Hardin, Jasper, Jefferson, Liberty, Montgomery, Newton, Orange, Polk, San Jacinto, Tyler.

Tenth District, Waco: Chief Justice Matt Johnson (2030). **Justices:** Lee Harris (2026) and Steven Lee Smith (2028). **Clerk of Court,** Sherry Williamson. **Counties in the Tenth District:** Bosque, Brazos, Burleson, Coryell, Ellis, Falls, Freestone, Hamilton, Hill, Johnson, Leon, Limestone, Madison, McLennan, Navarro, Robertson, Somervell, Walker.

Eleventh District, Eastland: Chief Justice John M. Bailey (2030). **Justices:** W. Stacy Trotter (2028) and Bruce Williams (2026). **Clerk of Court,** Marla Hanks. **Counties in the Eleventh District:** Baylor, Borden, Brown, Callahan, Coleman, Comanche, Dawson, Eastland, Ector, Erath, Fisher, Gaines, Glasscock, Haskell, Howard, Jones, Knox, Martin, Midland, Mitchell, Nolan, Palo Pinto, Scurry, Shackelford, Stephens, Stonewall, Taylor, Throckmorton.

Twelfth District, Tyler: Chief Justice James T. Worthen (2026). **Justices:** Brian Hoyle (2028) and Greg Neeley (2030). **Clerk of Court,** Katrina McClenny. **Counties in the Twelfth District:** Anderson, Angelina, Cherokee, Gregg, Henderson, Houston, Nacogdoches, Rains, Rusk, Sabine, San Augustine, Shelby, Smith, Trinity, Upshur, Van Zandt, Wood.

Thirteenth District, Corpus Christi: Chief Justice Jaime E. Tijerina (2030). **Justices:** Jenny Cron (2030); Ysmael D. Fonseca (2030); Lionel Aron Peña Jr. (2028); Clarissa Silva (2026); and Jon West (2030). **Clerk of Court,** Kathy S. Mills. **Counties in the Thirteenth District:** Aransas, Bee, Calhoun, Cameron, DeWitt, Goliad, Gonzales, Hidalgo, Jackson, Kenedy, Kleberg, Lavaca, Live Oak, Matagorda, Nueces, Refugio, San Patricio, Victoria, Wharton, Willacy.

Fourteenth District, Houston: Chief Justice Tracy Christopher (2026). **Justices:** Maritza M. Antu (2030); Katy Boatman (2030); Chad Bridges (2030); Brad Hart (2030); Kevin Jewell (2028); Tonya McLaughlin (2030); Randy Wilson (2028); and Ken Wise (2026). **Clerk of Court,** Deborah M. Young. **Counties in the Fourteenth District:** Austin, Brazoria, Chambers, Colorado, Fort Bend, Galveston, Grimes, Harris, Waller, Washington.

Fifthteenth District, Austin: Chief Justice Scott Brister (2026). **Justices:** April Farris (2026); and Scott Field (2026). **Clerk of Court,** Christopher A. Prine.

§The location of the First Court of Appeals was changed from Galveston to Houston by the 55th Legislature, with the provision that all cases originated in Galveston County be tried in that city and with the further provision that any case may, at the discretion of the court, be tried in either city.

DISTRICT JUDGES IN TEXAS

Below are the names of all district judges in Texas, as of July 2025, listed in district court order.

Dist.	Judge
1	Craig M. Mixson (R)
1-A	Delinda Gibbs-Walker (R)
2	R. Chris Day (R)
3	Mark A. Calhoun (R)
4	David H. Hill (R)
5	Bill Miller Jr. (R)
6	Wesley Tidwell (R)
7	Kerry L. Russell (R)
8	Eddie Northcutt (R)
9	Phil A. Grant (R)
10	Rebecca Millo (R)
11	Kristen B. Hawkins (D)
12	David W. Moorman (R)
13	James E. Lagomarsino (R)
14	Eric V. Moyé (D)
15	Jim Fallon (R)
16	Sherry Shipman (R)
17	Melody Wilkinson (R)
18	Sydney B. Hewlett (R)
19	Thomas West (R)
20	John W. Youngblood (R)
21	Carson Campbell (R)
22	Bruce Boyer (R)
23	John C. Maher (R)
24	Lisa Harvey-Moore (R)
25	William D. Old III (R)
25-A	Jessica R. Crawford (R)
26	Donna King (R)
27	Debbie Garrett (R)
28	Michael McCauley (R)
29	Michael Moore (R)
30	Jeff McKnight (R)
31	Steven R. Emmert (R)
32	Glen N. Harrison (R)
33	Allan Garrett (R)
34	William E. Moody (D)
35	Michael L. Smith (R)
36	Starr Bauer (R)
37	Nicole Garza (D)
38	Kelley T. Kimble (R)
39	Shane Hadaway (R)
40	Bob Carroll (R)
41	Annabell Perez (D)
42	Arimy Beasley (R)
43	Craig Towson (R)
44	Veretta Frazier (D)
45	Mary Lou Alvarez (D)
46	Cory Curtis (R)
47	Dee Johnson (R)
48	Christopher Taylor (R)
49	Joe Lopez (D)
50	Jennifer A. Habert (R)
51	Carmen Symes Dusek (R)
52	Trent D. Farrell (R)
53	Maria Cantu Hexel (D)
54	Susan Kelly (R)
55	Latosha L. Payne (D)
56	Lonnie Cox (R)
57	Toni Arteaga (D)
58	Kent Walston (D)
59	Larry Phillips (R)
60	Justin Sanderson (D)
61	Lee Kathryn Schuchart (R)
62	Gary D. Young (R)
63	Roland Andrade (R)
64	Danah Zirpoli (R)

Dist.	Judge
65	Selina Saenz (D)
66	Justin W. Lewis (R)
67	Donald J. Cosby (R)
68	Martin Hoffman (D)
69	Kimberly Allen (R)
70	Denn Whalen (R)
71	Brad Morin (R)
72	John Grace (R)
73	Elizabeth Martinez (D)
74	Position Vacant
75	Position Vacant
76	Angela Saucier (R)
77	Roy Defriend (R)
78	Meredith Kennedy (R)
79	Michael Ventura Garcia (D)
80	Sonya Lillie Aston (R)
81	Jennifer Margaret Dillingham (R)
82	Bryan F. Russ Jr. (R)
83	Robert E. Cadena (R)
84	Curtis W. Brancheau (R)
85	Kyle Hawthorne (R)
86	Casey Blair (R)
87	Amy Thomas Ward (R)
88	Earl Stover III (R)
89	Dobie Kosub (R)
90	Phillip C. Gregory (R)
91	Steven R. Herod (R)
92	Luis M. Singleterry (D)
93	Fernando Mancias (D)
94	Bobby Galvan (D)
95	Monica Purdy (D)
96	Pat Gallagher (R)
97	Trish Coleman Byars (R)
98	Sandra Avila Ramirez (D)
99	Phillip Hays (R)
100	Dale A. Rabe Jr. (R)
101	Staci Williams (D)
102	Jeff M. Addison (R)
103	Janet Leal (D)
104	Jeff Propst (R)
105	Jack W. Pulcher (R)
106	Reed Filley (R)
107	Benjamin Euresti, Jr. (D)
108	Timothy Gene Pirtle (R)
109	John L. Pool (R)
110	Bill Smith (R)
111	Monica Zapata Notzon (D)
112	Pete Gomez Jr. (D)
113	Rabeea Collier (D)
114	Austin Reeve Jackson (R)
115	Dean Fowler (R)
116	Tonya Parker (D)
117	Susan Barclay (R)
118	R. Shane Seaton (R)
119	Gonzalo Rios Jr. (R)
120	Ben L. Ivey III (R)
121	Trey Didway (R)
122	Jeth Jones II (R)
123	LeAnn Kay Rafferty (R)
124	F. Alfonso Charles (R)
125	Kyle Carter (D)
126	Aurora Martinez Jones (D)
127	Denise Renee Adkison Brown (D)
128	Courtney Arkeen (R)
129	Michael Gomez (D)
130	Denise M. Fortenberry (R)
131	Norma Gonzales (D)
132	Dana Cooley (R)
133	Nicole Vyrosteh Perdue (D)
134	Dale B. Tillery (D)
135	Stephen Williams (R)
136	Baylor Wortham (D)
137	Trey McClendon (R)
138	Gabriela Garcia (D)
139	Bobby Flores (D)
140	Douglas H. Freitag (R)
141	John P. Chupp (R)
142	David G. Rogers (R)
143	Alan J. Nicholas (R)
144	Michael Mery (D)
145	Jeff Davis (R)
146	Joe Michael Russell (R)
147	Clifford A. Brown (D)
148	David Klein (R)
149	Jessica Pulcher (R)
150	Monique Diaz (D)
151	Erica R. Hughes (D)
152	Takasha Francis (D)
153	Susan McCoy (R)
154	Scott Say (R)
155	Jeff Steinhauser (R)
156	Patrick L. Flanigan (R)
157	Tanya Garrison (D)
158	Steve Burgess (R)
159	Todd Kassaw (R)
160	Aiesha Redmond (D)
161	Justin Low (R)
162	Kim Bailey (D)
163	Rex Wayne Peveto (R)
164	Cheryl E. Thornton (D)
165	Bruce Ward Bain (R)
166	Laura Salinas (D)
167	Dayna Blazey (D)
168	Marcos Lizarraga (D)
169	Cari L. Starritt-Burnett (R)
170	Jim Meyer (R)
171	Bonnie Rangel (D)
172	Mitch Templeton (R)
173	Dan Moore (R)
174	Hazel B. Jones (D)
175	Catherine Torres-Stahl (D)
176	Nikita Harmon (D)
177	Emily Munoz Detoto (R)
178	Kelli Johnson (D)
179	Ana Martinez (D)
180	DaSean A. Jones (D)
181	Titiana D. Frausto (R)
182	Danny Lacayo (D)
183	Lance Long (R)
184	Kat Thomas (D)
185	Andrea Beall (D)
186	Kristina Escalona (D)
187	Stephanie R. Boyd (D)
188	Scott Novy (R)
189	Tami Craft (D)
190	Beau Miller (D)
191	Gena Slaughter (D)
192	Maria Aceves (D)
193	Bridgett Whitmore (D)
194	Ernest B. White III (D)
195	Hector Garza (D)
196	Andrew Bench (R)
197	Adolfo Cordova Jr. (D)
198	Pat Maguire (R)
199	Angela Tucker (R)
200	Jessica Mangrum (D)
201	Amy Clark Meachum (D)
202	John Tidwell (R)
203	Rocky Jones (D)
204	Tammy Kemp (D)
205	Francisco X. Dominguez (D)
206	Rose Guerra Reyna (D)
207	Tracie Wright-Reneau (R)
208	Beverly Armstrong (D)
209	Brian E. Warren (D)
210	Alyssa G. Perez (D)
211	Brody Shanklin (R)
212	Patricia V. Grady (R)
213	Christopher R. Wolfe (R)
214	Inna Klein (R)
215	Nathan Joseph Milliron (R)
216	Albert D. Patillo III (R)
217	Robert K. Inselmann Jr. (R)
218	Russell Wilson (R)
219	Jennifer Edgeworth (R)
220	Shaun Carpenter (R)
221	Lisa Ann Michalk (R)
222	Roland Saul (R)
223	Phil Vanderpool (R)
224	Marisa Flores (D)
225	Christine Vasquez Hortick (D)
226	Benjamin Garrett Robertson (NP)
227	Christine Del Prado (D)
228	Caroline Stephanie Dozier (D)
229	Balde Garza (D)
230	Chris Morton (D)
231	Jesse Nevarez Jr. (R)
232	Josh Hill (D)
233	Kenneth E. Newell (R)
234	Lauren Reeder (D)
235	Janelle M. Haverkamp (R)
236	Tom Lowe (R)
237	Les Hatch (R)
238	Elizabeth Leonard (R)
239	Greg Hill (R)
240	Surendran K. Pattel (D)
241	Debby Gunter (R)
242	Kregg Hukill (R)
243	Selena N. Solis (D)
244	Lori Ruiz-Crutcher (R)
245	Angela Lancelin (D)
246	Angela Graves-Harrington (D)
247	Janice Berg (D)
248	Hilary Unger (D)
249	Tiffany Strother (R)
250	Cory Ren Liu (D)
251	Ana Estevez (R)
252	Raquel West (D)
253	Chap B. Cain III (R)
254	Kim Brown (D)
255	Vonda Bailey (D)
256	Sandre Streete (D)
257	Sandra Peake (D)
258	Travis Kitchens Jr. (R)
259	Brooks H. Hagler (D)
260	Steve Parkhurst (R)
261	Daniela Deseta Lyttle (D)
262	Lori C. Gray (D)
263	Melissa Marie Morris (D)
264	Paul LePak (R)
265	Jennifer Bennett (D)
266	Jason Cashon (R)
267	Julie Bauknight (R)
268	Steve Rogers (R)
269	Cory Sepolio (D)
270	Dedra Davis (D)
271	Brock Smith (R)
272	John Brick (R)
273	James A. Payne Jr. (R)
274	Gary L. Steel (R)
275	Marla Cuellar (D)
276	Michael P. Kopech (R)
277	Stacey Mathews (R)

Dist.	Judge
278	Hal R. Ridley (R)
279	Randy Shelton (D)
280	Dianne Curvey (D)
281	Christine Weems (D)
282	Amber Givens-Davis (D)
283	Lela D. Mays (D)
284	Kristin Bays (R)
285	Nadine Melissa Nieto (D)
286	Pat Phelan (R)
287	Kathryn Gurley (R)
288	Cynthia Marie Chapa (D)
289	Rose Sosa (D)
290	Jennifer Peña (D)
291	Stephanie Mitchell (D)
292	Brandon Birmingham (D)
293	Maribel Flores (D)
294	Chris Martin (R)
295	Donna Roth (D)
296	John Roach Jr. (R)
297	Amy Allin (R)
298	Emily G. Tobolowsky (D)
299	Karen Sage (D)
300	Chad Bradshaw (R)
301	Mary Brown (D)
302	Sandra Jackson (D)
303	LaDeitra Adkins (D)
304	Andrea Martin (D)
305	Cheryl Lee Shannon (D)
306	Emily Fisher (R)
307	Tim Womack (R)
308	Gloria Lopez (D)
309	Linda Marie Dunson (D)
310	Sonya Leah Heath (D)
311	Germaine Tanner (D)
312	Teresa J. Waldrop (D)
313	Natalia Oakes (D)
314	Michelle Moore (D)
315	Leah Shapiro (D)
316	James Mosley (R)
317	Gordon Friesz (R)
318	David W. Lindemood (R)
319	David Stith (R)
320	Steven Denny (R)
321	Robert Wilson (R)
322	James B. Munford (R)
323	Alex Kim (R)
324	Beth A. Poulos (R)
325	Cynthia Terry (R)
326	Paul Rotenberry (R)
327	Monique Velarde Reyes (D)
328	Monica Rawlins (D)
329	Randy M. Clapp (R)
330	Andrea Plumlee (D)
331	Chantal Melissa Eldridge (D)
332	Juan R. Alvarez (D)
333	Tracy D. Good (D)
334	Dawn Rogers (D)
335	John Winkelmann (R)
336	Christina Tillett (R)
337	Colleen Gaido (D)
338	Michele Satterelli Oncken (R)
339	Te'iva Bell (D)
340	Jay Weatherby (R)
341	Beckie Palomo (D)
342	Kimberly Fitzpatrick (R)
343	Janna Whatley (R)
344	Randy McDonald (R)
345	Jan Soifer (D)
346	Patricia Baca (D)
347	Missy Medary (R)
348	Megan Fahey (R)
349	Pam Foster Fletcher (R)
350	Thomas Wheeler (R)
351	Nata Cornelio (D)
352	Josh Burgess (R)
353	Sherine E. Thomas (D)
354	Keli Aiken (R)
355	Bryan Bufkin (R)
356	Steven Thomas (R)
357	Juan A. Magallanes (D)
358	John F. Shrode (R)
359	Kathleen A. Hamilton (R)
360	Patricia Baca Bennett (R)
361	David Hilburn (R)
362	Bruce McFarling (R)
363	Tracy Holmes (D)
364	Billy Eichman (R)
365	Amado Abascal III (D)
366	Tom Nowak (R)
367	Brent Hill (R)
368	Sarah Bruchmiller (R)
369	C. Michael Davis (R)
370	Noe Gonzalez (D)
371	Ryan Hill (R)
372	Julie Lugo (R)
377	Eli Garza (R)
378	Doug Wallace (R)
379	Ron Rangel (D)
380	Ben N. Smith (R)
381	Jose L. Garza (D)
382	Brett Hall (R)
383	Lyda Ness Garcia (D)
384	Patrick M. Garcia (D)
385	Leah G. Robertson (R)
386	Jackie Valdez (D)
387	Oscar Telfair III (D)
388	Marlene Gonzalez (D)
389	Letty Lopez (D)
390	Julie H. Kocurek (D)
391	Brad Goodwin (R)
392	Scott McKee (R)
393	Karen Ann Alexander (R)
394	Monty Wayne Kimball (R)
395	Ryan D. Larson (R)
396	Vince Giardino (R)
397	Brian Keith Gary (R)
398	Keno Vasquez (D)
399	Frank J. Castro (D)
400	Edward Michael Krenek (R)
401	Kimberly M. Laseter (R)
402	J. Brad McCampbell (R)
403	Brandy Mueller (D)
404	Ricardo M. Adobbati (D)
405	Jared Robinson (R)
406	David E. Garcia (D)
407	Tina Torres (D)
408	Angelica Jimenez (D)
409	Sam Medrano Jr. (D)
410	Jennifer Robin (R)
411	John Wells III (R)
412	Justin R. Gilbert (R)
413	William C. Bosworth Jr. (R)
414	Ryan Alexander Luna (R)
415	Graham Quisenberry (R)
416	Andrea Thompson (R)
417	Cyndi Wheless (R)
418	Tracy A. Gilbert (R)
419	Catherine A. Mauzy (D)
420	John "Malcolm" Bales (R)
421	Amanda Montgomery (R)
422	Shelton Gibbs IV (R)
423	Chris Duggan (D)
424	Evan Stubbs (R)
425	Betsy F. Lambeth (R)
426	Steven Duskie (R)
427	Tamara Needles (D)
428	Joe Pool (D)
429	Jill R. Willis (R)
430	Orlando Javier Esquivel (D)
431	Jim Johnson (R)
432	Ruben Gonzalez Jr. (R)
433	Dib Waldrip (R)
434	Christian Becerra (D)
435	Patty Maginnis (R)
436	Cruz Shaw III (D)
437	Joel Perez (D)
438	Rosemarie Alvarado (D)
439	David Rakow (R)
440	Grant Kinsey (R)
441	Jeff Robnett (R)
442	Tiffany Haertling (R)
443	Grace Ruth Patricia Pandithurai (R)
444	David A. Sanchez (D)
445	Gloria M. Rincones (D)
446	Sara Kate Billingsley (R)
448	Sergio H. Enriquez (D)
449	Renee Rodriguez-Betancourt (D)
450	Brad Urrutia (D)
451	Kirsten Cohoon (R)
452	Robert Hofmann (R)
453	Sherri Tibbe (D)
454	Danny Kindred (R)
455	Laurie Eiserloh (D)
456	Heather Hines Wright (R)
457	Vince Santini (R)
458	Maggie P. Jaramillo (R)
459	Maya Guerra Gamble (D)
460	Selena Alvarenga (D)
461	Patrick Bulanek Jr. (R)
462	Lee Ann Breading (R)
464	Joe Ramirez (D)
465	Elizabeth Beyer (R)
466	Stephanie Bascon (R)
467	Derbha Jones (R)
468	Lindsey Wynne (R)
469	Piper McCraw (R)
470	Brook Fulks (R)
471	Bryan Gantt (R)
472	Jerrell J. Wise (R)
474	Edward (Alan) A. Bennett (NP)
475	Taylor Heaton (R)
476	Nereida Lopez-Singleterry (D)
477	Michael G. Dickens (R)
478	Wade Faulkner (R)
480	Terence Davis (R)
481	Crystal Edmonson Levonius (R)
482	Veronica M. Nelson (D)
483	Alicia Key (D)
484	Adela Kowalski-Garza (D)
485	Steven Jumes (R)
486	Aaron Edward Burdette (R)
487	Stacy Monique Allen Barrow (D)
488	Matthew R. Peneguy (R)
489	Tracy Booker Gray (R)
493	Christine A. Nowak (R)
494	Kathryn Lanigan Pruitt (R)
495	Lori Ann DeAngelo (R)
496	Dan Wayne Simons (R)
497	Peyton Peebles
505	Kali Morgan (D)
506	Gary W. Chaney (R)
507	Lillian Henny Alexander (D)

ADMINISTRATIVE JUDICIAL REGIONS OF TEXAS

There are 11 administrative judicial regions in the state for administrative purposes. Presiding Judges are appointed by the Governor to four-year terms. They must be active or retired region judges or active or retired appellate judges with judicial experience in a region court. They receive extra compensation of $5,000, paid by counties in the administrative region.

The Presiding Judge convenes an annual conference of judges in the administrative region to consult on business in the courts and to adopt rules for administering cases in the region.

The Presiding Judge may assign active or retired region judges residing within the administrative region to any of its regional courts. The Presiding Judge of one administrative region may request the Presiding Judge of another administrative region to assign a judge from that region to sit in a regional court in the requesting Judge's administrative region.

The Chief Justice of the Supreme Court of Texas convenes an annual conference of the 11 Presiding Judges to determine the need for assignment of judges and to promote the uniform administration of the assignments. The Chief Justice can assign judges of one administrative region for service in another region. Terms end in the year in parentheses.

First Region: Ray Wheless, McKinney (2026): Collin, Dallas, Ellis, Fannin, Grayson, Kaufman, Rockwall.

Second Region: Robert H. Trapp, Conroe (2026): Angelina, Bastrop, Brazos, Burleson, Chambers, Grimes, Hardin, Jasper, Jefferson, Lee, Liberty, Madison, Montgomery, Newton, Orange, Polk, San Jacinto, Trinity, Tyler, Walker, Waller, Washington.

Third Region: Dibrell "Dib" Waldrip, New Braunfels (2026): Austin, Bell, Blanco, Bosque, Burnet, Caldwell, Colorado, Comal, Comanche, Coryell, Falls, Fayette, Gonzales, Guadalupe, Hamilton, Hays, Hill, Lampasas, Lavaca, Llano, McLennan, Milam, Navarro, Robertson, San Saba, Travis, Williamson.

Fourth Region: Sid Harle, San Antonio (2025): Aransas, Atascosa, Bee, Bexar, Calhoun, DeWitt, Dimmit, Frio, Goliad, Jackson, Karnes, La Salle, Live Oak, Maverick, McMullen, Refugio, San Patricio, Victoria, Webb, Wilson, Zapata, Zavala.

Fifth Region: Missy Medary, Corpus Christi (2028): Brooks, Cameron, Duval, Hidalgo, Jim Hogg, Jim Wells, Kenedy, Kleberg, Nueces, Starr, Willacy.

Sixth Region: Kirsten B. Cohoon, Boerne (2029): Bandera, Brewster, Crockett, Culberson, Edwards, El Paso, Gillespie, Hudspeth, Jeff Davis, Kendall, Kerr, Kimble, Kinney, Mason, McCulloch, Medina, Menard, Pecos, Presidio, Reagan, Real, Sutton, Terrell, Upton, Uvalde, Val Verde.

Seventh Region: Ben Woodward, San Angelo (2027): Andrews, Borden, Brown, Callahan, Coke, Coleman, Concho, Crane, Dawson, Ector, Fisher, Gaines, Garza, Glasscock, Haskell, Howard, Irion, Jones, Kent, Loving, Lynn, Martin, Midland, Mills, Mitchell, Nolan, Reeves, Runnels, Schleicher, Scurry, Shackelford, Sterling, Stonewall, Taylor, Throckmorton, Tom Green, Ward, Winkler.

Eighth Region: David Evans, Fort Worth (2026): Archer, Clay, Cooke, Denton, Eastland, Erath, Hood, Jack, Johnson, Montague, Palo Pinto, Parker, Somervell, Stephens, Tarrant, Wichita, Wise, Young.

Ninth Region: Ana Estevez, Amarillo (2028): Armstrong, Bailey, Baylor, Briscoe, Carson, Castro, Childress, Cochran, Collingsworth, Cottle, Crosby, Dallam, Deaf Smith, Dickens, Donley, Floyd, Foard, Gray, Hale, Hall, Hansford, Hardeman, Hartley, Hemphill, Hockley, Hutchinson, King, Knox, Lamb, Lipscomb, Lubbock, Moore, Motley, Ochiltree, Oldham, Parmer, Potter, Randall, Roberts, Sherman, Swisher, Terry, Wheeler, Wilbarger, Yoakum.

Tenth Region: Alfonso Charles, Longview (2026): Anderson, Bowie, Camp, Cass, Cherokee, Delta, Franklin, Freestone, Gregg, Harrison, Henderson, Hopkins, Houston, Hunt, Lamar, Leon, Limestone, Marion, Morris, Nacogdoches, Panola, Rains, Red River, Rusk, Sabine, San Augustine, Shelby, Smith, Titus, Upshur, Van Zandt, Wood.

Eleventh Region: Susan Brown, Houston (2026): Brazoria, Fort Bend, Galveston, Harris, Matagorda, Wharton.

Texas Courts by County

Below are listed the state district court or courts, court of appeals district, administrative judicial district, and U.S. judicial district for each county in Texas as of July 2025.

County	State Dist. Court(s)	Ct. of Appeals Dist.	Adm. Jud. Reg.	U.S. Jud. Dist.
Anderson	3, 87, 349, 369	12	10	E-Tyler
Andrews	109	8	7	W-Midland
Angelina	159, 217	12	2	E-Lufkin
Aransas	36, 156, 343	13	4	S-C.Christi
Archer	97	2	8	N-W. Falls
Armstrong	47	7	9	N-Amarillo

County	State Dist. Court(s)	Ct. of Appeals Dist.	Adm. Jud. Reg.	U.S. Jud. Dist.
Atascosa	81, 218	4	4	W-San Ant.
Austin	155	1, 14	3	S-Houston
Bailey	287	7	9	N-Lubbock
Bandera	198	4	6	W-San Ant.
Bastrop	21,335,423,465	3	2	W-Austin
Baylor	50	11	9	N-W. Falls

County	State Dist. Court(s)	Ct. of Appeals Dist.	Adm. Jud. Reg.	U.S. Jud. Dist.
Bee	36, 156, 343	13	4	S-C. Christi
Bell	27, 146, 169, 264, 426, 478	3	3	W-Waco
Bexar	37, 45, 57, 73, 131, 144, 150, 166, 175, 186, 187, 224, 225, 226, 227, 285, 288, 289, 290, 379, 386, 399, 407, 408, 436, 437, 438	4	4	W-San Ant.
Blanco	33, 424	3	3	W-Austin
Borden	132	11	7	N-Lubbock
Bosque	220	10	3	W-Waco
Bowie	5, 102, 202	6	10	E-Texark
Brazoria	149, 239, 300, 412, 461	1, 14	11	S-Galves
Brazos	85, 272, 361	10	2	S-Houston
Brewster	394	8	6	W-Pecos
Briscoe	110	7	9	N-Amarillo
Brooks	79	4	5	S-C. Christi
Brown	35	11	7	N-S. Angelo
Burleson	21, 335	10	2	W-Austin
Burnet	33, 424	3	3	W-Austin
Caldwell	22, 207, 421	3	3	W-Austin
Calhoun	24, 135, 267	13	4	S-Victoria
Callahan	42	11	7	N-Abilene
Cameron	103, 107, 138, 197, 357, 404, 444, 445, 484	13	5	S-Brownsville
Camp	76, 276	6	10	E-Marshall
Carson	100	7	9	N-Amarillo
Cass	5	6	10	E-Marshall
Castro	64, 242	7	9	N-Amarillo
Chambers	253, 344	1, 14	2	S-Galves
Cherokee	2, 369	12	10	E-Tyler
Childress	100	7	9	N-Amarillo
Clay	97	2	8	N-W. Falls
Cochran	286	7	9	N-Lubbock
Coke	51	3	7	N-S. Angelo
Coleman	42	11	7	N-S. Angelo
Collin	199, 219, 296, 366, 380, 401, 416, 417, 428, 429, 468, 469, 470, 471	5	1	E-Sherman
Collingsworth	100	7	9	N-Amarillo
Colorado	25, 25-A	1, 14	3	S-Houston
Comal	22, 207, 274, 433, 463, 466	3	3	W-San Ant.
Comanche	220	11	3	N-Ft. Worth
Concho	119	3	7	N-S. Angelo
Cooke	235	2	8	E-Sherman
Coryell	52, 440	10	3	W-Waco
Cottle	50	7	9	N-W. Falls
Crane	109	8	7	W-Midland
Crockett	112	8	6	N-S. Angelo
Crosby	72	7	9	N-Lubbock
Culberson	205, 394	8	6	W-Pecos
Dallam	69	7	9	N-Amarillo
Dallas	14, 44, 68, 95, 101, 116, 134, 160, 162, 191, 192, 193, 194, 195, 203, 204, 254, 255, 256, 265, 282, 283, 291, 292, 298, 301, 302, 303, 304, 305, 330, 363, Cr. 1, Cr. 2, Cr. 3, Cr. 4, Cr. 5, Cr. 6, Cr. 7,	5	1	N-Dallas
Dawson	106	11	7	N-Lubbock
Deaf Smith	222	7	9	N-Amarillo
Delta	8, 62	6	10	E-Sherman
Denton	16, 158, 211, 362, 367, 393, 431, 442, 462, 467, 481	2	8	E-Sherman
DeWitt	24, 135, 267	13	4	S-Victoria
Dickens	110	7	9	N-Lubbock
Dimmit	293, 365	4	4	W-San Ant.
Donley	100	7	9	N-Amarillo
Duval	229	4	5	S-C. Christi
Eastland	91	11	8	N-Abilene
Ector	70, 161, 244, 358, 446	11	7	W-Midland
Edwards	452	4	6	W-Del Rio
Ellis	40, 378, 443	10	1	N-Dallas
El Paso	34, 41, 65, 120, 168, 171, 205, 210, 243, 327, 346, 383, 384, 388, 409, 448, Cr. 1	8	6	W-El Paso
Erath	266	11	8	N-Ft. Worth
Falls	82	10	3	W-Waco
Fannin	336	6	1	E-Sherman
Fayette	155	3	3	S-Houston
Fisher	32	11	7	N-Abilene
Floyd	110	7	9	N-Lubbock
Foard	46	7	9	N-W. Falls
Fort Bend	240, 268, 328, 387, 400, 434, 458, 505	1, 14	11	S-Houston
Franklin	8, 62	6	10	E-Texark
Freestone	77, 87	10	10	W-Waco
Frio	81, 218	4	4	W-San Ant.
Gaines	106	11	7	N-Lubbock
Galveston	10, 56, 122, 212, 306, 405	1, 14	11	S-Galves
Garza	106	7	7	N-Lubbock
Gillespie	216	4	6	W-Austin
Glasscock	118	11	7	N-S. Angelo
Goliad	24, 135, 267	13	4	S-Victoria
Gonzales	25, 25-A	13	3	W-San Ant.
Gray	31, 223	7	9	N-Amarillo
Grayson	15, 59, 397	5	1	E-Sherman
Gregg	124, 188, 307	6, 12	10	E-Tyler
Grimes	12, 506	1, 14	2	S-Houston
Guadalupe	25, 25-A, 274, 456	4	3	W-San Ant.
Hale	64, 242	7	9	N-Lubbock
Hall	100	7	9	N-Amarillo
Hamilton	220	10	3	W-Waco
Hansford	84	7	9	N-Amarillo
Hardeman	46	7	9	N-W. Falls
Hardin	88, 356	9	2	E-B'mont
Harris	11, 55, 61, 80, 113, 125,127, 129, 133, 151, 152, 157, 164, 165, 174, 176, 177, 178, 179, 180, 182, 183, 184, 185, 189, 190, 208, 209, 215, 228, 230, 232, 234, 245, 246, 247, 248, 257, 262, 263, 269, 270, 280, 281, 295, 308, 309, 310, 311, 312, 313, 314, 315, 333, 334, 337, 338, 339, 351, 507, 482	1, 14	11	S-Houston
Harrison	71	6	10	E-Marshall
Hartley	69	7	9	N-Amarillo
Haskell	39	11	7	N-Abilene
Hays	22, 207, 274, 428, 453, 483	3	3	W-Austin
Hemphill	31	7	9	N-Amarillo
Henderson	3, 173, 392	12	10	E-Tyler
Hidalgo	92, 93, 139, 206, 275, 332, 370, 389, 398, 430, 449, 464, 476	13	5	S-McAllen
Hill	66	10	3	W-Waco
Hockley	286	7	9	N-Lubbock
Hood	355	2	8	N-Ft. Worth
Hopkins	8, 62	6	10	E-Sherman
Houston	3, 349	12	10	E-Lufkin
Howard	118	11	7	N-Abilene
Hudspeth	205, 394	8	6	W-Pecos
Hunt	196, 354	5, 6	10	N-Dallas
Hutchinson	84, 316	7	9	N-Amarillo
Irion	51	3	7	N-S. Angelo
Jack	271	2	8	N-Ft. Worth
Jackson	24, 135, 267	13	4	S-Victoria
Jasper	1, 1-A	9	2	E-B'mont
Jeff Davis	394	8	6	W-Pecos
Jefferson	58, 60, 136, 172, 252, 279, 317, Cr. 1	9	2	E-B'mont
Jim Hogg	229	4	5	S-Laredo
Jim Wells	79	4	5	S-C. Christi
Johnson	18, 249, 413	10	8	N-Dallas
Jones	259	11	7	N-Abilene
Karnes	81, 218	4	4	W-San Ant.
Kaufman	86, 422	5	1	N-Dallas
Kendall	451	4	6	W-San Ant.
Kenedy	105	13	5	S-C. Christi
Kent	39	7	7	N-Lubbock
Kerr	198, 216	4	6	W-San Ant.
Kimble	452	4	6	W-Austin
King	50	7	9	N-W. Falls
Kinney	63	4	6	W-Del Rio
Kleberg	105	13	5	S-C. Christi
Knox	50	11	9	N-W. Falls
Lamar	6, 62	6	10	E-Sherman
Lamb	154	7	9	N-Lubbock
Lampasas	27	3	3	W-Austin
La Salle	81, 218	4	4	S-Laredo

County	State Dist. Court(s)	Ct. of Appeals Dist.	Adm. Jud. Reg.	U.S. Jud. Dist.
Lavaca	25, 25-A	13	3	S-Victoria
Lee	21, 335	3	2	W-Austin
Leon	87, 278, 369	10	10	W-Waco
Liberty	75, 253	9	2	E-B'mont
Limestone	77, 87	10	10	W-Waco
Lipscomb	31	7	9	N-Amarillo
Live Oak	36, 156, 343	13	4	S-C. Christi
Llano	33, 424	3	3	W-Austin
Loving	143	8	7	W-Pecos
Lubbock	72, 99, 137, 140, 237, 364	7	9	N-Lubbock
Lynn	106	7	7	N-Lubbock
Madison	12, 278	10	2	S-Houston
Marion	115, 276	6	10	E-Marshall
Martin	118	11	7	W-Midland
Mason	452	4	6	W-Austin
Matagorda	23, 130	13	11	S-Galves
Maverick	293, 365	4	4	W-Del Rio
McCulloch	452	3	6	W-Austin
McLennan	19, 54, 74, 170, 414, 474	10	3	W-Waco
McMullen	36, 156, 343	4	4	S-Laredo
Medina	454	4	6	W-San Ant.
Menard	452	4	6	N-S. Angelo
Midland	142, 238, 318, 385, 441	11	7	W-Midland
Milam	20	3	3	W-Waco
Mills	35	3	7	N-S. Angelo
Mitchell	32	11	7	N-Abilene
Montague	97	2	8	N-W. Falls
Montgomery	9, 221, 284, 359, 410, 418, 435, 457	9	2	S-Houston
Moore	69	7	9	N-Amarillo
Morris	76, 276	6	10	E-Marshall
Motley	110	7	9	N-Lubbock
Nacogdoches	145, 420	12	10	E-Lufkin
Navarro	13	10	3	N-Dallas
Newton	1, 1-A	9	2	E-B'mont
Nolan	32	11	7	N-Abilene
Nueces	28, 94, 105, 117, 148, 214, 319, 347	13	5	S-C. Christi
Ochiltree	84	7	9	N-Amarillo
Oldham	222	7	9	N-Amarillo
Orange	128, 163, 260	9	2	E-B'mont
Palo Pinto	29	11	8	N-Ft. Worth
Panola	123	6	10	E-Tyler
Parker	43, 415	2	8	N-Ft. Worth
Parmer	287	7	9	N-Amarillo
Pecos	83, 112	8	6	W-Pecos
Polk	258, 411	9	2	E-Lufkin
Potter	47, 108, 181, 251, 320	7	9	N-Amarillo
Presidio	394	8	6	W-Pecos
Rains	8, 354	12	10	E-Tyler
Randall	47, 181, 251	7	9	N-Amarillo
Reagan	112	8	6	N-S. Angelo
Real	38	4	6	W-San Ant.
Red River	6, 102	6	10	E-Texark
Reeves	143	8	7	W-Pecos
Refugio	24, 135, 267	13	4	S-Victoria
Roberts	31	7	9	N-Amarillo
Robertson	82	10	3	W-Waco
Rockwall	382, 439	5	1	N-Dallas
Runnels	119	3	7	N-S. Angelo
Rusk	4	6, 12	10	E-Tyler
Sabine	1, 273	12	10	E-Lufkin
San Augustine	1, 273	12	10	E-Lufkin

County	State Dist. Court(s)	Ct. of Appeals Dist.	Adm. Jud. Reg.	U.S. Jud. Dist.
San Jacinto	258, 411	9	2	S-Houston
San Patricio	36, 156, 343	13	4	S-C. Christi
San Saba	33, 424	3	3	W-Austin
Schleicher	51	3	7	N-S. Angelo
Scurry	132	11	7	N-Lubbock
Shackelford	259	11	7	N-Abilene
Shelby	123, 273	12	10	E-Lufkin
Sherman	69	7	9	N-Amarillo
Smith	7, 114, 241, 321, 475	12	10	E-Tyler
Somervell	18, 249	10	8	W-Waco
Starr	229, 381	4	5	S-McAllen
Stephens	90	11	8	N-Abilene
Sterling	51	3	7	N-S. Angelo
Stonewall	39	11	7	N-Abilene
Sutton	112	4	6	N-S. Angelo
Swisher	64, 242	7	9	N-Amarillo
Tarrant	17, 48, 67, 96, 141, 153, 213, 231, 233, 236, 297, 322, 323, 324, 325, 342, 348, 352, 360, 371, 372, 396, 432, 485, Cr. 1, Cr. 2, Cr. 3, Cr. 4	2	8	N-Ft. Worth
Taylor	42, 104, 326, 350	11	7	N-Abilene
Terrell	63, 83	8	6	W-Del Rio
Terry	121	7	9	N-Lubbock
Throckmorton	39	11	7	N-Abilene
Titus	76, 276	6	10	E-Texark
Tom Green	51, 119, 340, 391	3	7	N-S. Angelo
Travis	53, 98, 126, 147, 167, 200, 201, 250, 261, 299, 331, 345, 353, 390, 403, 419, 427, 450, 455, 459, 460	3	3	W-Austin
Trinity	258, 411	12	2	E-Lufkin
Tyler	1-A, 88	9	2	E-Lufkin
Upshur	115	6, 12	10	E-Marshall
Upton	112	8	6	W-Midland
Uvalde	38	4	6	W-Del Rio
Val Verde	63, 83	4	6	W-Del Rio
Van Zandt	294	12	10	E-Tyler
Victoria	24, 135, 267, 377	13	4	S-Victoria
Walker	12, 278	10	2	S-Houston
Waller	506	1, 14	2	S-Houston
Ward	143	8	7	W-Pecos
Washington	21, 335	1, 14	2	W-Austin
Webb	49, 111, 341, 406	4	4	S-Laredo
Wharton	23, 329	13	11	S-Houston
Wheeler	31	7	9	N-Amarillo
Wichita	30, 78, 89	2	8	N-W. Falls
Wilbarger	46	7	9	N-W. Falls
Willacy	197	13	5	S-Brownsville
Williamson	26, 277, 368, 395, 425, 480	3	3	W-Austin
Wilson	81, 218	4	4	W-San Ant.
Winkler	109	8	7	W-Pecos
Wise	271	2	8	N-Ft. Worth
Wood	402	6, 12	10	E-Tyler
Yoakum	121	7	9	N-Lubbock
Young	90	2	8	N-W. Falls
Zapata	49	4	4	S-Laredo
Zavala	293, 365	4	4	W-Del Rio

TEXAS STATE AGENCIES

Texas Commission on Environmental Quality

The Texas Commission on Environmental Quality (TCEQ) is the state's leading environmental agency. The TCEQ works to protect Texas' human and natural resources in a manner consistent with sustainable economic development. The agency has about 2,800 employees working in 17 offices.

One of the TCEQ's major functions is issuing permits and other authorizations for the control of air pollution, the safe operation of water and wastewater utilities, and the management of hazardous and nonhazardous waste.

The agency promotes voluntary compliance with environmental laws through pollution prevention programs, regulatory workshops, and assistance to businesses and local governments. When environmental laws are violated, the TCEQ has the authority to levy penalties as much as $25,000 a day per violation for administrative cases.

Source: Texas Commission on Environmental Quality.

Office of Air

Texas is home to some of the largest U.S. cities, with several metropolitan populations of greater than one million people. With these concentrated populations, vehicular traffic and other emissions can create air quality issues among the most challenging in the country.

The state has a fast-growing population, a large industrial base concentrated along the Gulf Coast, and an oil and gas industry expanding throughout much of the state. The TCEQ conducts survey activities along with targeted and/or specialized monitoring activities to evaluate changing air quality conditions across the state.

The TCEQ measures air quality across the state for compliance with federal standards, as well as for localized compounds of concern. Texas' air toxic monitoring network is one of the most comprehensive in the country with more than 200 monitoring sites located across the state.

The TCEQ is responsible for developing a state implementation plan to bring metropolitan areas into compliance with federal air quality standards, such as the ozone standard. The leading areas of concern for ozone issues are the Houston-Galveston-Brazoria and Dallas–Fort Worth areas.

Office of Water

The TCEQ preserves and improves the quality of the state's surface waters by establishing surface water quality standards; monitoring, assessing, and reporting conditions; and implementing plans to reduce pollution and improve water quality. It protects surface water users through the water rights permitting process and the watermaster programs.

The TCEQ is also responsible for most state and federal regulatory programs that protect groundwater, administers permits for the discharge of wastewater and stormwater, and conducts Section 401 certifications of federal permits.

The agency enforces the federal Safe Drinking Water Act, oversees the protection of the state's approximately 7,000 public water systems providing drinking water to roughly 29 million customers, and has general supervision of water districts.

Office of Land

Waste management projects at the TCEQ include Superfund projects, pesticide collections, and permits and authorizations for municipal and industrial waste management. Another major cleanup program focuses on leaking petroleum storage tanks.

The TCEQ issues permits and other authorizations for municipal and industrial waste management, including landfills and storage, processing, and recycling operations. In addition, the safe recycling of both municipal and industrial waste streams is encouraged.

The TCEQ also regulates the disposal of radioactive material, with the exception of naturally occurring radioactive material (NORM) generated as a result of oil and gas exploration. This includes the regulation of the receipt, processing, storage, and disposal of by-product and low-level radioactive waste, the licensing of uranium and thorium recovery facilities, decommissioning of inactive uranium-recovery facilities, permitting for underground injection control, and legacy radioactive material disposal sites.

HEALTH AND HUMAN SERVICES

Texas Health and Human Services (HHS) is the oversight agency for the state's health and human services system. HHS also administers state and federal programs that provide financial, health, and social services to Texans. Executive Commissioner Cecile Erwin Young was appointed on August 14, 2020.

In 2003, the 78th Texas Legislature mandated an unprecedented transformation of the state's health and human services system, blending 12 agencies into five. The system transformed again in 2017, with the goal of removing bureaucratic silos, creating clear lines of accountability, and making it easier for people to find out about services or benefits they might qualify for.

Today's HHS consists of two main agencies: Texas Health and Human Services Commission (HHSC) and the Texas Department of State Health Services (DSHS). The executive commissioner is appointed by the governor and confirmed by the Senate. The Department of Family and Protective Services is an independent agency under the HHSC umbrella.

Health and Human Services Commission

The HHSC oversees the licensing and credentialing of facilities for long-term care, including nursing homes and assisted living; licenses child care providers; and manages daily operations at state-supported hospitals and living centers.

It also delivers benefits and services such as Medicaid, SNAP food benefits, and TANF cash assistance; services for women and people with special health needs; long-term care for the aging and those with disabilities; and behavioral health services.

Department of State Health Services

DSHS serves as the public health authority for Texas, providing vital statistics and health data to the public, leading the public-health response in times of disaster or outbreaks, and administering chronic and infectious disease prevention and testing. The department also licenses and regulates facilities on topics including youth camps and mobile food establishments. It is led by Commissioner of Public Health Dr. Jennifer Shuford.

The client services DSHS previously provided were transferred to HHSC in 2016.

Source: Texas Health and Human Services.

Department of Family and Protective Services

The Department of Family and Protective Services (DFPS) works to protect children and vulnerable adults through prevention programs, investigations, and services and referrals. DFPS has four major programs:

- Adult Protective Services
- Child Protective Services
- Investigations
- Statewide Intake

Other HHSC Programs

The Family Violence program offers emergency shelter and services to victims and their children.

The Disaster Assistance program processes grant applications for victims of presidentially declared disasters, such as tornadoes, floods, and hurricanes.

Major HHS Programs

The Medicaid program provides healthcare coverage for approximately half of all children in Texas and pays for half of all births. In 2025, over four million Texans received healthcare coverage through Medicaid.

The **Children's Health Insurance Program (CHIP)** is designed for families who earn too much money to qualify for Medicaid yet cannot afford private insurance.

The **Temporary Assistance for Needy Families (TANF)** program provides basic financial assistance for needy children and the parents or caretakers with whom they live. As a condition of eligibility, caretakers must sign and abide by a personal-responsibility agreement. Time limits for benefits have been set by both state and federal welfare-reform legislation.

SNAP food benefits, formerly known as food stamps, is a federally funded program that helps low-income families, the elderly, and single adults obtain a nutritionally adequate diet.

THE GENERAL LAND OFFICE

The Texas General Land Office (GLO) is one of the oldest governmental entities in the state, dating back to the Republic of Texas. The first General Land Office was established in 1836 by the Republic of Texas Congress, and the first Texas Congress enacted the provision into law in 1837. The GLO was established to oversee distribution of public lands, register titles, issue patents on land, and maintain records of land granted.

In the early years of statehood, beginning in 1845, Texas established the precedent of using its vast public domain for public benefit. The first use was to sell or trade land to eliminate the huge debt remaining from Texas' War for Independence and the early years of the Republic.

Texas also gave away land to settlers as homesteads; to veterans as compensation for service; for internal improvements, including building railroads, shipbuilding, and improving rivers for navigation; and to build the state Capitol.

The public domain was closed in 1898 when the Texas Supreme Court declared there was no more vacant and unappropriated land in Texas. In 1900, all remaining unappropriated land was set aside by the Legislature to benefit public schools.

Today, 13 million acres of land and minerals, owned by the Permanent School Fund, the Permanent University Fund, various other state agencies, and the Veterans Land Board, are managed by the GLO and the Commissioner of the Texas General Land Office. This includes over 3,400 miles of coastline and tidelands extending over 10 miles into the Gulf of Mexico.

The GLO is the steward of the Texas Gulf Coast, serving as the premier state agency for protecting and renourishing the coast and fighting coastal erosion. In 1999, the Legislature created the Coastal Erosion Planning and Response Act and put the GLO in charge of facilitating restoration and preservation of eroding beaches, dunes, wetlands, and other bay shorelines along the Texas coast.

Texas Veterans Land Board Programs

The Veterans Land Board (VLB) was formally established by the Legislature to administer benefits for Texas Veterans in 1946, with the first loan made in 1949.

Since then, the programs have evolved to include low-interest land, housing, and home improvement loans. In a joint effort with the Texas Veterans Commission, the VLB operates the Texas Veterans Call Service Center to connect veterans, military members, and their families with the benefits and services they need.

Texas State Veterans

In 1997, the 75th Legislature approved legislation authorizing the Veterans Land Board to construct and operate Texas State Veterans Homes under a cost-sharing program with the U.S. Department of Veterans Affairs (USDVA).

Source: General Land Office of Texas.

The homes provide affordable, quality, long-term care for Texas' veterans.

The VLB owns and operates several cemeteries under USDVA guidelines. The USDVA funds the design and construction of the cemeteries, but the land must be donated.

The Alamo

In 2011, the 82nd Legislature granted authority over the Alamo to the GLO. The Alamo hosts millions of visitors from around the world each year. UNESCO designated the Alamo and four other Spanish missions in San Antonio as U.S. World Heritage sites in 2015.

Texas Historical Commission

The Texas Historical Commission protects and preserves the state's historic and prehistoric resources. The Texas State Legislature established the Texas State Historical Survey Committee in 1953 to identify important historic sites across the state.

The Texas Legislature changed the agency's name to the Texas Historical Commission in 1973 and increased its mission and its protective powers. Today, the agency's concerns include archaeology, architecture, community heritage development, historic sites, history programs, and education.

The commission:

- Works with communities and individuals to help identify important historic resources and develop a plan to preserve them.
- Provides leadership and training to county historical commissions, heritage organizations, and museums in Texas' 254 counties.
- Helps protect Texas' diverse architectural heritage, including historic county courthouses.
- Partners with communities to stimulate tourism and economic development.
- Assists Texas cities in the revitalization of their historic downtowns through the Texas Main Street Program.
- Administers the state's historical marker program, which has around 15,000 markers across the state.
- Consults with citizens and groups to nominate properties as Recorded Texas Historic Landmarks, State Archeological Landmarks, and to the National Register of Historic Places.
- Operates 41 state historic sites, including house museums, military forts, and archeological sites.
- Works with property owners to save archeological sites on private land and ensures archeological sites are protected as land is developed for highways and other public construction projects.

Railroad Commission of Texas

The Railroad Commission of Texas has primary regulatory jurisdiction over the oil and natural gas industry, pipeline transporters, the natural gas and hazardous liquid pipeline industry, natural gas utilities, the liquefied petroleum gas (LP-gas) industry, rail industry, and coal and uranium surface mining operations. It also promotes the use of LP-gas as an alternative fuel in Texas through research and education.

The commission exercises its statutory responsibilities under provisions of the Texas Constitution, the Texas Natural Resources Code, the Texas Water Code, the Texas Utilities Code, the Coal and Uranium Surface Mining and Reclamation Acts, the Pipeline Safety Acts, and the Railroad Safety Act.

The commission has regulatory and enforcement responsibilities under federal law, including the Federal Railroad Safety Act, the Local Rail Freight Assistance Act, the Surface Coal Mining Control and Reclamation Act, the Pipeline Safety Acts, the Resource Conservation Recovery Act, and the Clean Water Act.

The Railroad Commission was established by the Texas Legislature in 1891 and given jurisdiction over rates and operations of railroads, terminals, wharves, and express companies. In 1917, the Legislature declared pipelines to be common carriers and gave the commission regulatory authority over them. It was also given the responsibility to administer conservation laws relating to oil and natural gas production.

The Railroad Commission exists to protect the environment, public safety, and the rights of mineral interest owners; to prevent waste of natural resources; and to assure fair and equitable utility rates in those industries over which it has authority.

Texas Department of Juvenile Justice

The Texas Department of Juvenile Justice was created on December 1, 2011, by Senate Bill 653 in the 82nd Legislature. Its creation abolished both the Texas Youth Commission and the Texas Juvenile Probation Commission.

The agency's executive director is Shandra Carter, and it has a 13-member commission who are appointed to six-year terms. It is chaired by Manny Ramirez of Fort Worth.

The Texas Department of Juvenile Justice is a unified state juvenile justice agency that works in partnership with local county governments, courts, and communities to promote public safety by providing services to youth from initial contact through end of supervision. Its expressed goals are to:

- Support development of county-based programs and services for youth and families that reduce the need for out-of-home placement;

- Seek alternatives to placing youthful offenders in secure state facilities, while also addressing treatment of youth and protecting the public;
- Locate facilities as geographically close as possible to workforce and other services, and support youths' connection to their families;
- Encourage regional and county collaboration;
- Enhance the continuity of care throughout the juvenile justice system; and
- Use secure facilities of a size that supports effective youth rehabilitation and public safety.

Texas Workforce Commission

The Texas Workforce Commission (TWC) is the state government agency charged with overseeing and providing workforce development services to employers and job seekers of Texas. It is led by three appointed commissioners representing the public (Chairman Bryan Daniel), labor (Alberto Treviño III), and employers (Joe Esparza).

For employers, TWC offers recruiting, retention, training and retraining, outplacement services, and information on labor law and labor market statistics.

For job seekers, TWC offers career development information, job search resources, training programs, and unemployment benefits. While targeted populations receive intensive assistance to overcome barriers to employment, all Texans can benefit from the services offered by TWC and its network of workforce partners.

The Texas Workforce Commission is part of a local and state network dedicated to developing the workforce of Texas. The network is composed of the statewide efforts of the commission coupled with planning and service provision on a regional level by 28 local workforce boards. This network gives customers access to local workforce solutions and statewide services in a single location.

Primary services of the Texas Workforce Commission and its network partners are funded by federal tax revenue and are generally free to all Texans.

TEXAS STATE BOARDS AND COMMISSIONS

Economic Development

- Aerospace and Aviation Advisory Committee
- Aerospace Research and Space Economy Consortium Executive Committee, Texas
- Broadband Development Council, Governor's
- Broadband Development Office Board of Advisors
- Cancer Prevention and Research Institute of Texas Oversight Committee
- Economic Development Corporation Board of Directors, Texas
- Economic Incentive Oversight Board
- Emergency Management, Business Advisory Council to the Texas Division of
- Industry-Based Certification Advisory Council
- Jobs and Education for Texans (JET) Grant Program Advisory Board
- Real Estate Research Advisory Committee
- Semiconductor Innovation Consortium Executive Committee, Texas
- Small Business Assistance Advisory Task Force, Office of
- Space Commission Board of Directors, Texas
- University Research Initiative Advisory Board, Governor's
- Workforce Investment Council, Texas
- Workforce of the Future Fund Advisory Board, Lone Star

Financial

- Affordable Housing Corporation Board of Directors, Texas State
- County and District Retirement System Board of Trustees, Texas
- Emergency Services Retirement System Board of Trustees, Texas
- Employees Retirement System of Texas Board of Trustees
- Housing and Community Affairs, Texas Department of
- Lease of Texas Department of Criminal Justice Lands, Board for
- Lease of Texas Parks and Wildlife Lands, Board for
- Municipal Retirement System, Texas
- Opioid Abatement Fund Council, Texas
- Pension Review Board, State
- Permanent School Fund Corporation Board of Directors, Texas
- Public Finance Authority, Texas
- School Land Board
- Teacher Retirement System of Texas Board of Trustees

Healthcare

- Alzheimer's Disease and Related Disorders, Texas Council on
- Behavioral Health Executive Council, Texas
- Cardiovascular Disease and Stroke, Council on
- Chronic Kidney Disease Task Force
- Correctional Managed Health Care Committee
- Diabetes Council, Texas
- Emergency Medical Services, Advisory Council on
- Health Coordinating Council, Statewide
- Health Services Authority Board of Directors, Texas
- Infectious Disease Preparedness and Response, Task Force on
- Medical or Mental Impairments, Adv. Comm. to the Texas Board of Criminal Justice on Offenders with
- Pediatric Acute-Onset Neuropsychiatric Syndrome Advisory Council
- Pharmaceutical Initiative Governing Board, Texas

Higher Education

- A&M University System Board of Regents, Texas
- Family Practice Residency Advisory Committee
- Higher Education Coordinating Board, Texas
- Postsecondary Education for Persons with Intellectual and Developmental Disabilities, Advisory Council on
- Prepaid Higher Education Tuition Board
- Texas Southern University Board of Regents
- Texas State Technical College System Board of Regents
- Texas State University System Board of Regents
- Texas Tech University System Board of Regents
- Texas Woman's University Board of Regents
- University of Houston System Board of Regents
- University of North Texas System Board of Regents
- University of Texas System Board of Regents

Human Services

- Aging, Legislative Committee on
- Aging Services Coordinating Council, Statewide Interagency
- Community-Based Care Transition, Director of the Office of
- Developmental Disabilities, Texas Council for
- Disabilities, Governor's Committee on People with
- Disaster Issues Affecting Persons who are Elderly and Persons with Disabilities, Task Force on
- Early Childhood Intervention Advisory Committee
- Family and Protective Services Council
- Family and Protective Services, Commissioner of the Department
- Family and Protective Services, Commissioner of the Department
- Health and Human Services, Executive Commissioner of
- Health and Human Services, Inspector General for
- Homeless, Texas Interagency Council for the
- Housing and Health Services Coordination Council
- Independent Living Council, State
- OneStar Foundation
- OneStar National Service Commission
- Rehabilitation Council of Texas
- State Employee Charitable Campaign Advisory Committee
- State Supported Living Centers, Independent Ombudsman for
- Workforce and Social Services, Task Force on Consolidation of

Humanities

- Arts, Texas Commission on the
- Bicentennial Commission, Committee to Study the Formation of a Texas
- Cultural Affairs, Advisory Council on
- Emergency Medical First Responders' Star of Texas Award Advisory Committee
- Firefighters' Star of Texas Award Advisory Committee
- Historian, Texas State
- Historical Commission, Texas
- Historical Records Advisory Board, Texas
- Holocaust, Genocide, and Antisemitism Advisory Commission, Texas
- Humanities Texas
- Peace Officers' Star of Texas Award Advisory Committee
- Poet Laureate, State Musician and State Artists Committee, Texas
- Women, Governor's Commission for

Legal

- Administrative Law Judge, Chief
- Indigent Defense Commission, Governing Board of the Texas
- Judge, Business Courts, Various Regions
- Judicial Compensation Commission
- Judicial Council, Texas
- Judicial Districts Board
- Presiding Judge, Various Judicial Regions
- Real Estate Broker Lawyer Committee, Texas
- Specialty Courts Advisory Council
- Uniform State Laws, Commission on

Natural Resources

- Angelina and Neches River Authority Board of Directors
- Brazos River Authority Board of Directors
- Canadian River Compact Commissioner
- Coastal Water Authority Board of Directors
- Colorado River Authority, Lower
- Colorado River Authority, Upper
- Evergreen Underground Water Conservation District
- Farm and Ranch Lands Conservation Council, Texas
- Guadalupe River Authority, Upper
- Guadalupe-Blanco River Authority Board of Directors
- Gulf Coast Authority Board of Directors
- Gulf Coast Protection District Board of Directors
- Gulf States Marine Fisheries Commission
- Lavaca-Navidad River Authority
- Low-Level Radioactive Waste Disposal Compact Commission
- Oyster Mariculture Advisory Board, Commercial
- Neches River Municipal Water Authority Board of Directors, Upper
- Neches Valley Authority Board of Directors, Lower
- Nueces River Authority Board of Directors
- Pecos River Compact Commission
- Red River Authority of Texas Board of Directors
- Red River Boundary Commission
- Red River Compact Commission
- Rio Grande Compact Commission
- Rio Grande Regional Water Authority
- Sabine River Authority Board of Directors
- Sabine River Compact Administration
- San Jacinto River Authority Board of Directors
- Soil and Water Conservation Board, State
- Sulphur River Basin Authority Board of Directors
- TexNet Technical Advisory Committee
- Trinity River Authority Board of Directors

Public Education
- 1836 Project Advisory Committee, Texas
- Adult High School Charter School Program Advisory Committee
- Blind and Visually Impaired, Governing Board of the Texas School for the
- Deaf, Governing Board of the Texas School for the
- Early Learning Council, Texas
- Education Commission of the States
- Educator Certification, State Board for
- Mathematics and Science Advisory Board, Texas Academy of
- P-TECH Advisory Council
- Special Education, Continuing Advisory Committee for

Public Safety
- Crime Stoppers Council, Texas
- Crime Victims' Institute Advisory Council
- Emergency Communications, Commission on State
- Emergency Management Chief, Texas Division of
- Motor Vehicle Crime Prevention Authority
- One-Call Board of Texas
- Pardons and Paroles, Board of
- School Safety Center Board, Texas
- Violent Gang Task Force, Texas

Regulatory-Industry
- Alcoholic Beverage Commission, Texas
- Animal Health Commission, Texas
- Credit Union Commission
- Finance Commission of Texas
- Fire Protection, Texas Commission on
- Forensic Science Commission, Texas
- Funeral Service Commission, Texas
- Galveston County Ports, Board of Pilot Commissioners for
- Harris County Ports, Board of Pilot Commissioners for
- Industrialized Building Code Council, Texas
- Jefferson and Orange County Board of Pilot Commissioners
- Law Enforcement, Texas Commission on
- Lottery Commission, Texas
- Manufactured Housing Board
- Public Utility Commission of Texas
- Racing Commission, Texas
- Radiation Advisory Board
- Securities Board, State
- Sex Offender Treatment, Council on
- Small Business Compliance Assistance Advisory Panel
- Workers' Compensation, Commissioner of

Regulatory-Professional
- Accountancy, Texas State Board of Public
- Acupuncture Examiners, Texas State Board of
- Appraisal Management Companies Advisory Committee
- Appraiser Licensing and Certification Board, Texas
- Architectural Examiners, Texas Board of
- Chiropractic Examiners, Texas Board of
- Counselors, Texas State Board of Examiners of Professional
- Dental Examiners, State Board of
- Dental Review Committee
- Engineers and Land Surveyors, Texas Board of Professional
- Geoscientists, Texas Board of Professional
- Judicial Conduct, State Commission on
- Marriage and Family Therapists, Texas State Board of Examiners of
- Medical Board District Four Review Committee, Texas
- Medical Board District One Review Committee, Texas
- Medical Board District Three Review Committee, Texas
- Medical Board District Two Review Committee, Texas
- Medical Board, Texas
- Medical Radiologic Technology, Texas Board of
- Nursing Facility Administrators Advisory Committee
- Nursing, Texas Board of
- Occupational Therapy Examiners, Texas Board of
- Optometry Board, Texas
- Pharmacy, Texas State Board of
- Physical Therapy and Occupational Therapy Examiners, Executive Council of
- Physical Therapy Examiners, Texas Board of
- Physician Assistant Board, Texas
- Plumbing Examiners, Texas State Board of
- Podiatric Medical Examiners Advisory Board
- Psychologists, Texas State Board of Examiners of
- Real Estate Commission, Texas
- Respiratory Care, Texas Board of
- Social Worker Examiners, Texas State Board of
- Veterinary Medical Examiners, State Board of

State Oversight
- Artificial Intelligence Advisory Council
- Cemetery Committee, State
- Civil Commitment Office, Governing Board of the Texas
- Committee to Support the Military, Governor's
- Criminal Justice, Texas Board of
- Education, State Commissioner of
- Energy Plan Advisory Committee, State
- Energy Reliability Council, Texas
- Environmental Quality, Texas Commission on
- ERCOT Board Selection Committee
- Ethics Commission, Texas
- Facilities Commission, Texas
- Information Resources, Department of
- Injured Employee Public Counsel
- Inspector General for Health and Human Services
- Insurance Counsel, Office of Public
- Insurance, Commissioner of
- Jail Standards, Commission on
- Juvenile Justice Advisory Board
- Juvenile Justice Board, Texas
- Juvenile Justice Department, Office of Independent Ombudsman for the Texas
- Library and Archives Commission, Texas State
- Licensing and Regulation, Texas Commission of

- Military Preparedness Commission, Texas
- Motor Vehicles Board, Texas Department of
- Mutual Insurance Company Board of Directors, Texas
- Parks and Wildlife Commission
- Preservation Board, State
- Public Safety Commission
- Public Utility Counsel, Office of
- Regulatory Compliance Division, Director of the
- Risk Management Board
- Secretary of State
- State-Federal Relations, Director of the Office of
- Transportation Commission, Texas
- Veterans Commission, Texas
- Veterans' Land Board
- Water Development Board, Texas
- Workforce Commission, Texas

Transportation

- North Texas Tollway Authority Board of Directors
- Regional Mobility Authority, Alamo
- Regional Mobility Authority, Brazos County
- Regional Mobility Authority, Cameron County
- Regional Mobility Authority, Camino Real
- Regional Mobility Authority, Central Texas
- Regional Mobility Authority, Grayson County
- Regional Mobility Authority, Hidalgo County
- Regional Mobility Authority, North East Texas
- Regional Mobility Authority, Sulphur River
- Regional Mobility Authority, Webb County - City of Laredo
- Transportation Advisory Committee, Public

UNSPLASH/JEREMY DODDRIDGE

Texas

LOCAL GOVERNMENT

UNSPLASH/KATERYNA HLIZNITSOVA

TEXAS MAYORS & CITY MANAGERS

This list was compiled from online sources. It includes the name of each city's mayor **(M)**, as well as the name of the city manager **(CM)**, city administrator **(CA)**, or town administrator **(TA)**. Home-rule cities are marked in this list by a single-dagger symbol (†) after the name.

A

Abbott . . . . Anthony R. Pustejovsky (M)
Abernathy . . . . . Ron Johnson (M), Don Provost (CM)
Abilene † . Weldon W. Hurt (M), Mindy Patterson (CM)
Ackerly . . . . Scott Ragle (M)
Addison † . . . . Bruce Arfsten (M), David Gaines (CM)
Adrian . . . . Maggie Gruhlkey (M)
Agua Dulce . . . . John Howard (M)
Alamo † . . . . . J.R. Garza (M), Robert L. Salinas (CM)
Alamo Heights † Al Honigblum (M), Buddy Kuhn (CM)
Alba . . . . Paul Kelbe (M)
Albany . . . Susan Montgomery (M), Billy Holson (CM)
Aledo † . . . . . Nick Stanley (M), Noah A. Simon (CM)
Alice † Cynthia A. Carrasco (M), Michael Esparza (CM)
Allen † . . . . Baine L. Brooks (M), Eric Ellwanger (CM)
Alma . . . . Renee Jones (M), Linda Blazek (CA)
Alpine † . . . Catherine Eaves (M), Megan Antrim (CM)
Alto . . . . Jimmy Allen (M)
Alton † . . . . . Salvador Vela (M), Jeff Underwood (CM)
Alvarado † . . . . . Jacob Wheat (M), Paul DeBuff (CM)
Alvin † . . . . . . Gabe Adame (M), Junru Roland (CM)
Alvord . . . . Caleb Caviness (M), Troy Gregg (CA)
Amarillo † . . . . . Cole Stanley (M), Grayson Path (CM)
Ames . . . . Barbara L. Domain (M)
Amherst . . . . Clinton Sawyer (M)
Anahuac . . Charles Hightower (M), Kenneth Kathan (CA)
Anderson . . . . Marc Benton (M)
Andrews † . . . Jason Harper (M), Steve Eggleston (CM)
Angleton † . . . John Wright (M), Chris Whittaker (CM)
Angus . . . . Julie Humphries (M)
Anna † . . . . . . Pete Cain (M), Ryan Henderson (CM)
Annetta . . . . . . Sandy Roberts (M), Jamee Long (CA)
Annetta North . . . . Robert Schmidt (M)
Annetta South . . . . Charles Marsh (M)
Annona . . . . Marcella Dean (M)
Anson † . . . Richard Abila (M), Sonny Campbell (CM)
Anthony † . . . . Martin Lerma (M)
Anton . . . . Blake Cate (M), Mike Sea (CM)
Appleby . . . . Robbie Box (M), Kevin Pierce (CM)
Aquilla . . . . James Hamner Sr. (M)
Aransas Pass † . . . . Ram Gomez (M)
. . . . Mary Juarez (Interim CM)
Archer City . Steven Schroeder (M), Ronnie Meyer (CM)
Arcola . . Veeda Williams (M), Dr. Annette Guajardo (CA)
Argyle . . . . . Ronald Schmidt (M), Mike Sims (CM)
Arlington † . . . Jim R. Ross (M), Trey Yelverton (CM)
Arp . . . . Terry Lowry (M)
Asherton . . . . Mario DJ Ruiz (M)
Aspermont . . . Steven Ellis (M), Lorenzo Calamaco (CA)
Athens † . . . . Aaron (Bubba) Smith (M)
. . . . Elizabeth Borstad (CM)
Atlanta † . . Marshall James Brooks (M), Danica Porter (CM)
Aubrey † . . . . . Chris Rich (M), Charles Kreidler (TA)
Aurora . . . . Bryan Dolan (M), Kristi Gilbert (CA)
Austin † . . . . . Kirk Watson (M), T.C. Broadnax (CM)
Austwell . . . . Andrew Biery (M)
Avery . . . . Alex Ackley (M)
Avinger . . . . Jeff Patterson (M)
Azle † . . . . Randa Goode (M), Tom Muir (CM)

B

Bailey . . . . Kenneth Burks (M)
Bailey's Prairie . . . . Tammy Mutina (M)
Baird . . . . Scottt Davis (M), Lori Higgins (CA)
Balch Springs † . . Rodney Taylor (M), Charles Fenner (CM)
Balcones Heights . . . . . . Johnny A. Rodriguez Jr. (M)
Ballinger † . . Dawni Seymore (M), Lindsey Gayoso (CM)
Balmorhea . . . . John L. Davis (M)
Bandera . . . . Denise Griffin (M)
Bangs . . . . . . Steve Whittenberg (M), Erica Berry (CA)
Bardwell . . . . Joseph R. Odlozil (M)
Barry . . . . Charles Worsham (M)
Barstow . . . . Manuel Lujan Jr. (M)
Bartlett . . . . Chad Mees (M), Adrian Flores (CA)
Bartonville . . . Jaclyn Carrington (M), Kirk Riggs (TA)
Bastrop † . . . . Ishamel Harris (M), Sylvia Carrillo (CM)
Bay City † . . . . Robert Nelson (M), Scotty Jones (CM)
Bayou Vista . . . . Paula J. Eshelman (M)
Bayside . . . . Sharon Scott (M)
Baytown † . Charles Johnson (M), Jason Reynolds (CM)
Bayview . . . . Gary E. Paris (M)
Beach City . . . . Ken Pantin (M)
Bear Creek . . . . Mark Bohm (M)
Beasley . . . . Kenneth Reid (M)
Beaumont † . Roy West (M), Kenneth R. Williams (CM)
Beckville . . . . Andrew Nixon (M)
Bedford † . . . . . . Dan Cogan (M), Andrea Roy (CM)
Bedias . . . . Gwen Boullion (M)
Bee Cave † . . . . . . Kara King (M), Julie Oakley (CM)
Beeville † . . Michael R. Willow (M), John Benson (CM)

Bellaire † . . . . Gus E. Pappas (M), Sharon Citino (CM)
Bellevue . . . . Robert Ratliff (M)
Bellmead † . . . James Cleveland (M), Yousry Zakhary (CM)
Bells . . . . Joe Paul Smith (M), Cody Dale Nelson (CA)
Bellville . . . James Harrison (M), Shawn Jackson (CA)
Belton † . . . . . David K. Leigh (M), Sam A. Listi (CM)
Benavides . . . . Ramiro Saenz (M)
Benbrook † . . . . Jason Ward (M), Jim Hinderaker (CM)
Benjamin . . . . Shelby Russell (M)
Berryville . . . . Dennis Selby (M)
Bertram . . . . Mike Dickinson (M)
. . . . Georgina Hernandez (CA)
Beverly Hills . . . . David Gonzales (M)
Bevil Oaks . . . . Cheri Mitchell (M)
Big Lake . . . . David Melms (M), Sheri K. Benson (CA)
Big Sandy . . . . . . Linda Baggett (M), Laura Rex (CA)
Big Spring † . . . Robert Moore (M), Todd Darden (CM)
Big Wells . . . . Robert D. Juarez Jr. (M)
Bishop . . . . Noel Barrera Lopez (M)
Bishop Hills . . . . Betty Benham (M)
Blackwell . . . . Laura Rozzlle (M)
Blanco . . . . . Candy Cargill (M), Warren Escovy (CA)
Blanket . . . . Judy Eoff (M)
Bloomburg . . . . Delores Simmons (M)
Blooming Grove . . . . Ashley Mahone (M)
Blossom . . . . Phillip Bolton (M)
Blue Mound . . . . Darlene Copeland (M)
Blue Ridge . . . . Rhonda Williams (M)
Blum . . . . Chryle Hackler (M)
Boerne † . . . . Frank Ritchie (M)
. . . . Ben Thatcher (CM)
Bogata . . . . Larry Hinsley (M)
Bonham † . . . . . H.L. Compton (M), Sean Pate (CM)
Bonney . . . . Raymond Cantu (M)
Booker . . . . Stephen Skipper (M)
Borger † . . . Karen Felker (M), Garrett Spradling (CM)
Bovina . . Frank Gonzalez Jr. (M), Cesar Marquez (CM)
Bowie † . . Gaylynn Burris (M), Bert Cunningham (CM)
Boyd . . . . . Rodney Holmes (M), Dwayne Taylor (CA)
Brackettville . . Miguel Aguirre (M), Nora Y. Rivas (CA)
Brady † . . . . Anthony Groves (M), James Stewart (CM)
Brazoria . . . . . . Philip Ray (M), David Kocurek (CM)
Brazos Country . . . . Bob Ray (M)
Breckenridge † . . Bob Sims (M), Cynthia Northrop (CM)
Bremond . . . . Andy Burnett (M)
Brenham † . . . . Atwood C. Kenjura (M)
. . . . Carolyn D. Miller (CM)
Briarcliff . . . . . Al Hostetler (M), Aaron Johnson (VA)
Briaroaks . . . . Howard Bogart (M)
Bridge City † . . . . David Rutledge (M)
. . . . Brett Bartkowiak (CM)
Bridgeport † . Randy Singleton (M), Mike Murray (CM)
Broaddus . . . . Shirley Parker (M)
Brock . . . . Jay Hamilton (M)
Bronte . . . . Paul Gohman (M)
Brookshire . . . . Darrell Branch (M)
. . . . Jennifer Jones Ward (CA)
Brookside Village . . . . Apollo Gonzales (M)
Browndell . . . . Donna Brooks (M)
Brownfield † . . . . . . Eric Horton (M), Jeff Davis (CM)
Brownsboro . . . . Adam McLean (M)
Brownsville † . . John Cowen Jr. (M), Helen Ramirez (CM)
Brownwood † . . . . Stephen E. Haynes (M)
. . . . Emily Crawford (CM)
Bruceville-Eddy . . Linda Owens (M), Kent Manton (CA)
Bryan † . . . . Bobby Gutierrez (M), Kean Register (CM)
Bryson . . . . Lutitia Ford (M)
Buckholts . . . . Ricky McCall (M)
Buda † . . . . . Lee Urbanovsky (M), Micah Grau (CM)
Buffalo . . . . Jerrod Jones (M)
Buffalo Gap . . . . Bryan Cunningham (M)
Buffalo Springs . . . . Dennis Wardroup (M)
Bullard . . . . . . Shirley Coe (M), Pam Frederick (CM)
Bulverde † . . . . . . Helen Hays (M), Danny Batts (CM)
Bunker Hill Village . . . . Keith Brown (M)
. . . . Gerardo Barrera (CA)
Burkburnett † . . . . Lori Kemp (M)
. . . . Lindsey McNabb-Fox (CM)
Burke . . . . John Thomas Jones (M)
Burleson † . . Chris Fletcher (M), Tommy Ludwig (CM)
Burnet † . . . Gary Wideman (M), David Vaughn (CM)
Burton . . . . Karen Buck (M)
Byers . . . . Norrieca Dalton (M)
Bynum . . . . Lori Youngblood (M)

C

Cactus . . . Socorro Marquez (M), Aldo Gallegos (CM)
Caddo Mills † . . . . Chris Davies (M), John Adel (CM)
Caldwell . . . . Janice Easter (M), Camden White (CM)
Callisburg . . . . Nathan Caldwell (M)
Calvert . . . . . . James M. Evans (M), Sergio Loya (CA)
Cameron † . . . . Nathan Fuchs (M), Ricky Tow Jr. (CM)
Campbell . . . . Terry Trapp (M)
Camp Wood . . . . Juan Gomez (M)
Canadian . . . . . . Terrill Bartlett (M), Joe Jarosek (CM)
Caney City . . . . Steve Pine (M)
Canton . . . . . Lou Ann Everett (M), Lonny Cluck (CM)
Canyon † . . . . Gary Hinders (M), Joe Price (CM)
Carbon . . . . Corey Hull (M)
Carl's Corner . . . . Susan Ezell (M)
Carmine . . . . Wade Eilers (M)
Carrizo Springs † . . Mario Ruiz (M), Azalia Garcia (CM)
Carrollton † . . . Steve Babick (M), Erin Rinehart (CM)
Carthage † . . . . Olin Joffrion Jr. (M)
. . . . Stephen K. Williams (CM)
Cashion . . . . Debra Carr (M)
Castle Hills . . . . JR Treviño (M)
. . . . Gilbert T. Perales (Interim CM)
Castroville . . . Darrin Schroeder (M), Scott Dixon (CA)
Cedar Hill † . . . . Stephen Mason (M)
. . . . Melissa A. Valadez (CM)
Cedar Park † . . . . Jim Penniman-Morin (M)
. . . . Brenda Eivens (CM)
Celeste . . . . Shaunna Cole (M)
Celina † . . . . . . Ryan Tubbs (M), Robert Ranc (CM)

Center † . . . David Chadwick (M), Chad Nehring (CM)
Centerville . . . . N.R. Goolsby (M)
Chandler . . Cy Ditzler (M), Robert Turner (Interim CA)
Channing . . . . Troy Williams (M)
Charlotte . . . . Stephen Porter (M)
Chester . . . . Robert Poynter (M)
Chico . . . . Richard Todd Blair (M)
Childress † . . . . Cary Preston (M), Kevin Hodges (CM)
Chillicothe . . . . Cathy Young (M)
China . . . . Matthew Lopez (M)
China Grove . . . . Mary A. Hajek (M)
Chireno . . Susan Higginbotham (M), Steven Spencer (CA)
Christine . . . . Jerry Flores (M)
Cibolo † . . . . Mark Allen (M), Wayne Reed (CM)
Cisco † . . . . Stephen Forester (M), Sarah Adams (CM)
Clarendon . . . Jacob Fangman (M), Brian Barboza (CA)
Clarksville . . . . Ann Rushing (M)
Clarksville City . . Joe B. Spears (M), Matt Maines (CA)
Claude . . . . Twila Baldwin (M)
Clear Lake Shores . . . . Randy Chronister (M)
Cleburne † . . Scott Cain (M), Michael R. Marerro (CM)
Cleveland † . . . . . . Danny Lee (M), Lee Tipton (CM)
Clifton . . . Damaris Neelley (M), David McDowell (CA)
Clint . . . . Ramon Cano Jr. (M)
Clute † . . . . Calvin Shiflet (M), CJ Snipes (CM)
Clyde . . Paul McGuire (M), Rodger Brown (Interim CA)
Coahoma . . . . Jay Holt (M)
Cockrell Hill . . Luis D. Carrera (M), Bret Haney (CA)
Coffee City . . . . Jeff Blackstone (M)
Coldspring . . . . John Benestante (M)
Coleman † . . . . Tommy Sloan (M), Diana Lopez (CM)
College Station † . . John Nichols (M), Bryan Woods (CM)
Colleyville † . . Bobby Lindamood (M), Jerry Ducay (CM)
Collinsville . . Derek M. Kays (M), Dannielle Talley (CA)
Colmesneil . . . . Duane Crews (M)
Colorado City † . Ruben Hurt (M), Donna Madrid (CM)
Columbus . . Lori An Gobert (M), Donald Warschak (CM)
Comanche . . Mary A. Boyd (M), Jim Winklemann (CA)
Combes . . . Silvestre Garcia (M), Aida Gutierrez (TA)
Combine . . . . . . Tim Ratcliff (M), Jack Gilbert (CM)
Commerce † . . Teddy Reel (M), Howdy Lisenbee (CM)
Como . . . . Jerry Radney (M)
Conroe † . . . . Duke W. Coon (M), Gary A. Scott (CM)
Converse † . . . . Alfred Suarez (M)
. . . . Lennie S. Lambert (Interim CM)
Cool . . . . Dorothy Hall (M)
Coolidge . . . . Tonia Bruckner (M)
Cooper . . . . Darren Braddy (M)
Coppell † . . . . Wes Mays (M), Mike Land (CM)
Copperas Cove † . . Dan Yancey (M), Ryan Haverlah (CM)
Copper Canyon . . Ron Robertson (M), Troy Meyer (CA)
Corinth † . . Bill Heidemann (M), Scott Campbell (CM)
Corpus Christi † . . . . Paulette M. Guajardo (M)
. . . . Peter Zanoni (CM)
Corral City . . . . Jamie Sue Harris (M)
Corrigan . . Johnna Gibson (M), Paloma E. Carbajal (CM)
Corsicana † . . . . . Joe Hill (M), James Holgersson (CM)
Cottonwood . . . . Karen Deloney (M)
Cottonwood Shores . . Jared Dodd (M), J.C. Hughes (CA)
Cotulla . . . . . . Sandra Luna (M), Juanita Fonesca (CA)
Coupland . . . . Russell Schmidt (M)
Cove . . . . Leroy Stevens (M)
Covington . . . . Shirley Erickson (M)
Coyote Flats . . . . Doug Peterson (M)
Crandall . . . . David Lindsey (M)
. . . . David Sanchez (Interim CM)
Crane . . . . Manuel Cadena Jr. (M), Jason R. Little (CA)
Cranfills Gap . . . . David D. Witte (M)
Crawford . . . . . . Bobby Bain (M), Brian Bolfing (CM)
Creedmoor . . . . . Jeff Jakobeit (M), Anna L. Ortiz (CA)
Cresson . . . . Ronald G. Becker (M)
Crockett † . . . Ianthia Fisher (M), John Angerstein (CA)
Crosbyton . . . Dusty Cornelius (M), Amy Wallace (CA)
Cross Plains . . . Gary Moses (M), Debbie Gosnell (CA)
Cross Roads . . . . T. Lynn Tompkins Jr. (M)
. . . . Jason Laumer (TA)
Cross Timber . . . . Patti Meier (M)
Crowell . . . . Ronnie Allen (M)
Crowley † . . . . Billy P. Davis (M), Lori Watson (CM)
Crystal City † . . . . Frank Moreno Jr. (M)
. . . . Felix Benavides (CM)
Cuero † . . . . . . Emil Garza (M), Wayne Berger (CM)
Cumby . . . . Amber L. Hardy (M)
Cuney . . . . Tammy Lewis (Pro Term M)
Cushing . . . . Robert Sides (M)
Cut and Shoot . . . . Nyla Akin Dalhaus (M)

D

Daingerfield † . . . Wade Kerley (M), Teresa Jones (CM)
Daisetta . . . . Chancie Bailey (M)
Dalhart † . . . . James Stroud (M), John Oznick Jr. (CM)
Dallas † . . . Eric Johnson (M), Kimberly Tolbert (CM)
Dalworthington Gardens . . . . Laurie Bianco (M)
. . . . Greg Petty (CA)
Danbury . . . . Suzanne Powell (M)
Darrouzett . . . . . Alan Meier (M), Wynona Lusk (CA)
Dawson . . . . Stephen Sanders (M)
Dayton † . . . . Martin Mudd (M)
. . . . Derek Woods (Interim CM)
Dayton Lakes . . . . Justin McCormick (M)
Dean . . . . Steve L. Sicking (M)
Decatur † . Mike McQuiston (M), Nate R. Mara (CM)
DeCordova . . . . Dave Hanson (M)
Deer Park † . . Jerry Mouton Jr. (M) James J. Stokes (CM)
De Kalb . . . . Lowell Walker (M)
De Leon † . . . . Jan Grisham (M), David Denman (CA)
Dell City . . . . Rudy Bustamante (M)
Del Rio † . . . . Alvaro Arreola (M)
. . . . Shawna D. Burkhart (CM)
Denison † . . . . Robert Crawley (M)
. . . . Bobby Atteberry (Interim CM)
Dennis . . . . James Synowsky (M)
Denton † . . . Gerard Hudspeth (M), Sara Hensley (CM)
Denver City † . . . Ronald Weir (M), Stan David (CM)
Deport . . . . Patrick Watson (M)

DeSoto † . . Rachel L. Proctor (M), Majed Al-Ghafry (CM)
Detroit . . . . . Kenneth Snodgrass (M)
Devers . . . . . Steven Horelica (M)
Devine . . . . . Butch Cook (M), David Lee Jordan (CA)
Diboll † . . Trey Wilkerson (M), Jason A. Arnold (CM)
Dickens . . . . . David Warren (M)
Dickinson † . . . . . Travis Magliolo (M)
. . . . . Chaise Cary (Interim CM)
Dilley . . Mary Ann Obregon (M), Henry Arredondo (CA)
Dimmitt † . . . . Scott Sheffy (M), Daniel Jackson (CM)
Dish . . . . . William Sciscoe (M)
Dodd City . . . . . Timothy Davis (M)
Dodson . . . . . Steve Kane (M)
Domino . . . . . Moria White (M)
Donna † . . . . . David Moreno (M), Jorge Pena (CM)
Dorchester . . . . . David Smith (M)
Double Horn . . . . . Cathy Sereno (M)
Double Oak . . . . . Patrick Johnson (M)
. . . . . Chris W. Laugenour (TA)
Douglassville . . . . . Douglass Heath (M)
Dripping Springs . . . . . Bill Foulds Jr. (M)
. . . . . Michelle Fischer (CA)
Driscoll . . . . . Mark Gonzalez (M)
. . . . . Paula R. Wakefield (Interim CA)
Dublin . . . . . David Leatherwood (M)
. . . . . Cameron Ray (Interim CM)
Dumas † . . . . . Pat L. Sims (M), Mark Hall (CM)
Duncanville † . . Greg Contreras (M), Douglas Finch (CM)

E

Eagle Lake . . . . . Timothy L. Kelley (M)
. . . . . Charles Jackson (CM)
Eagle Pass † . . . . . Rolando Salinas Jr. (M)
. . . . . Homero Balderas (CM)
Early . . . . . Robert Mangrum (M), Tony Aaron (CA)
Earth . . . . . John Kelley (M)
East Bernard . . . . . Lance Rejsek (M)
Eastland † . . Larry Vernon (M), Savannah Fortenberry (CM)
East Mountain . . . . . Marc Covington (M)
Easton . . . . . Walter Ward (M), Leah Robertson (CA)
East Tawakoni . . . . . Harold D. Chandler (M)
Ector . . . . . Jerry M. Newell (M)
Edcouch . . . . . Virginio Gonzalez Jr. (M)
. . . . . Marisela Aguilar (Interim CM)
Eden . . . . . Renae Rodgers (M), Priscilla Aguirre (CA)
Edgecliff Village . . . . . Sammye Bartley (M)
. . . . . Veronica Gamboa (CA)
Edgewood . . . Stevan Steadham (M), Petra Marley (CA)
Edinburg † . . Ramiro Garza Jr. (M), Myra L. Ayala (CM)
Edmonson . . . . . Todd Crawford (M)
Edna † . . . . . Lance Smiga (M), Gary Broz (CM)
Edom . . . . . Barbara Crow (M)
El Campo † . . . . . Eugene Bustamante (M)
. . . . . Courtney Sladek (CM)
El Cenizo . . Carina Hernandez (M), Jaime Montes (CA)
Eldorado . . . . . Oscar Martinez (M)
Electra † . . . . . Christina Neumann (M)
Elgin † . . . . . Theresa McShan (M)
. . . . . Isaac D. Turner (Interim CM)
Elkhart . . . . . Jennifer McCoy (M)
El Lago . . . . . Shawn Findley (M)
Ellinger . . . . . Matt Mikulenka (M)
Elmendorf . Michael J. Gonzales (M), Cody D. Dailey (CM)
El Paso † . . . Renard Johnson (M), Dionne Mack (CM)
Elsa † . . . . . Alonzo R. Perez (M), Juan Ybarra (CM)
Emhouse . . . . . Jimmy Barkley (M)
Emory . . . . . Earl Hill III (M), Angie Allen (CA)
Enchanted Oaks . Natalie Oñate (M), Regina Kiser (CA)
Encinal . . . . . Debra Weikel (M), Velma Davila (CM)
Ennis † . . . . . Kameron Raburn (M)
. . . . . Andrea Weckmueller-Behringer (CM)
Escobares . . . . . Ivan Escobar (M)
Estelline . . . . . Jeff Jones (M)
Euless † . . . Linda Martin (M), Chris D. Barker (CM)
Eureka . . . . . Tammy Cantrell (M)
Eustace . . . . . Dustin Shelton (M)
Evant . . . . . Charles Weeks (M)
Everman † . . Ray Richardson (M), Craig Spencer (CM)

F

Fairchilds . . . . . Lance Bertolino (M)
Fairfield . . . . . Robert Nichols (M)
Fair Oaks Ranch † . . . . . Greg Maxton (M)
. . . . . Scott Huizenga (CM)
Fairview † . . . . . John Hubbard (M), Julie Couch (CM)
Falfurrias . . . . . David G. Longoria (Pro Term M)
. . . . . Martin Saenz (CA)
Falls City . . . . Corey Albert (M), Jeremy Mandel (CA)
Farmers Branch † . . Terry Lynne (M), Ben Williamson (CM)
Farmersville . . Bryon Wiebold (M), Ben L. White (CM)
Farwell . . . . . Stephen Schilling (M)
Fate † . . . David Billings (M), Michael W. Kovacs (CM)
Fayetteville . . . . . Mike Stroup (M)
Ferris . . . . . Fred Pontley (M), Brooks Williams (CM)
Flatonia . . Travis Seale (M), Raymond Miller Jr. (CM)
Florence . . . . Ben Daniel (M), Tamela N. Louvier (CA)
Floresville † . . . . . Gloria Morales Cantu (M)
. . . . . Monica Veliz (Interim CM)
Flower Mound † . . . . . Cheryl Moore (M)
. . . . . James W. Childers (TM)
Floydada . . . Bobby Gilliland (M), Darrell Gooch (CM)
Follett . . . . . Lynn Blau (M)
Forest Hill † . . . . . Stephanie Boardingham (M)
. . . . . Venus Wehle (CM)
Forney † . . Jason Roberson (M), Charles Daniels (CM)
Forsan . . . . . Steve Park (M)
Fort Stockton † . . . . . Paul Casias (M)
. . . . . Frank Rodriguez III (CM)
Fort Worth † . . . . . Mia Hall (M), Jesus Chapa (CM)
Franklin . . . . . Molly Hedrick (M)
Frankston . . . . . Tommy Carr (M)
Fredericksburg † . . Jeryl Hoover (M), Clinton Bailey (CM)
Freeport † . . . . . Jerry Cain (M), Lance Petty (CM)
Freer . . . . . Martin Martinez Jr. (M)

Friendswood † . . Mike Foreman (M), Morad Kabiri (CM)
Friona . . . . Greg Lewellen (M), Leander Davila (CM)
Frisco † . . . . Jeff Cheney (M), Wesley S. Pierson (CM)
Fritch . . Shelby Deatherage (M), Christina Arhey (CM)
Frost . . . . Anthony Harris (M)
Fruitvale . . . . Susan Murre (M)
Fulshear † . . Don McCoy (M), Zach J. Goodlander (CM)
Fulton . . . . Kelli Cole (M)

G

Gainesville † . . Tommy Moore (M), Barry L. Sullivan (CM)
Galena Park † . . . . Esmeralda Moya (M)
Gallatin . . . . Kathy Dethlefs (M)
Galveston † . . . Craig Brown (M), Brian Maxwell (CM)
Ganado . . . . Clinton W. Tegeler (M)
Garden Ridge † . . . Lisa Swint (M), Ryan Rapelye (CM)
Garland † . . . . Dylan Hedrick (M), Judson Rex (CM)
Garrett . . . . Matt Newsom (M)
Garrison . . . . Keith Yarbrough (M)
Gary . . . . Jason Woodfin (M)
Gatesville † . . . . Gary Chumley (M)
. . . . Bradford William Hunt (CM)
Georgetown † . Josh Schroeder (M), David Morgan (CM)
George West † . . Andrew Garza (M), Darrell Pullin (CM)
Gholson . . . . Eddie Oliver (M)
Giddings † . . . Joel Lopez (M), Spencer Schneider (CM)
Gilmer † . . . Tim A. Marshall (M), Greg Hutson (CM)
Gladewater † . . Brandy Flanagan (M), Charlie Smith (CM)
Glenn Heights † . . . . Sonja A. Brown (M)
. . . . Clifford Blackwell (CM)
Glen Rose . . . . Joe Boles (M), Troy Hill (CA)
Godley . . Christopher J. Lenker (M), Angela Winkle (CA)
Goldsmith . . . . Richard Bradley (M)
Goldthwaite . . J. Wilson (M), Robert E. Lindsey III (CM)
Goliad . . . . Brenda Moses (M), Julia Post (CA)
Golinda . . . . Joyce Farar (M)
Gonzales † . . . . . . Steve Sucher (M), Tim Crow (CM)
Goodlow . . . . Johnny Moss Sr. (M)
Goodrich . . . . Kelly Nelson (M)
Gordon . . . . . Sherrye Mills (M), Teresa Johnson (CA)
Goree . . . . Randy Hibdon (M)
Gorman † . . . . David Perry (M)
Graford . . . . Janet Francies (M)
Graham † . . Alex Heartfield (M), Eric Garretty (CM)
Granbury † . . James Jarratt (M), Chris Coffman (CM)
Grandfalls . . . . Position Vacant (M)
Grand Prairie † . . . . Ron Jensen (M), Bill Hills (CM)
Grand Saline . . . . Ridge Tardy (M), Dana Clair (CM)
Grandview . . William Houston (M), Katherine Reading (M)
Granger . . . . Monica Stojanik (M)
. . . . Christy Cavness Bradshaw (CM)
Granite Shoals † . . Ron Munos (M), Sarah Novo (CM)
Granjeno . . . . Yvette Cabrera (M)
Grapeland . . . . Velda Green (M)
Grapevine † . . . . William D. Tate (M)
. . . . Bruno R. Rumbelow (CM)
Grays Prairie . . . . Brandon Coogler (M)
Greenville † . . Jerry Ransom (M), Summer Spurlock (CM)
Gregory . . . Estella Boyes (M), Blyth Swartsfager (CA)
Grey Forest . . . . Paul Garro (M)
Groesbeck . . Matthew Dawley (M), Chris Henson (CA)
Groom . . . . Tim Case (M)
Groves † . . . . . Chris Borne (M), Kevin Carruth (CM)
Groveton . . . . Hayden Lee (M)
Gruver . . . . Steven Davis (M), Johnnie Williams (CM)
Gun Barrel City † . . . Brian Crull (M), Angela Smith (CM)
Gunter . . . . Karen Souther (M)
Gustine . . . . Ken Huey (M)

H

Hackberry . . Ronald Austin (M), Brenda Lewallen (CA)
Hale Center . . . . W.H. Johnson (M)
. . . . Michael Neighbors (CM)
Hallettsville . . Alice Jo Summers (M), Grace Ward (CA)
Hallsburg . . . . Mike Glockzin (M)
Hallsville . . . . . Jesse Casey (M), Marty D. Byers (CA)
Haltom City † . . . An Truong (M), Rex L. Phelps (CM)
Hamilton . . Richard Buchanan (M), Stacey Norris (CA)
Hamlin . . . . . . Tucker Teague (M), Brian Weaver (CA)
Happy . . . . Sara Tirey (M)
Hardin . . . . Harry Johnson (M)
Harker Heights † . . . . Michael Blomquist (M)
. . . . David R. Mitchell (CM)
Harlingen † . . . . Norma Sepulveda (M)
. . . . Gabriel Gonzalez (CM)
Hart . . . . . . Eliazar Castillo (M), Luis Martinez (CA)
Haskell . . . Christina Isbell (M), Winston Stephens (CA)
Haslet . . . . Gary Hulsey (M)
Hawk Cove . . Dotty Spence (M), Rhonda McKeehan (CA)
Hawkins . . . . Debbie Rushing (M)
Hawley . . . . Billy Richardson (M)
Hays . . . . Harvey Davis (M)
Hearne † . . . . Ruben Gomez (M)
. . . . Alonzo Echavarria-Garza (CM)
Heath † . . Jeremiah McClure (M), Steven J. Alexander (CM)
Hebron . . . . Kelly Clem (M)
Hedley . . . . Trisha Chambless (M)
Hedwig Village . . Tom Jinks (M), Wendy Baimbridge (CA)
Helotes . . . . . Rich Whitehead (M), Henry Hayes (CA)
Hemphill . . . . Stephen Crowell (M), Thad Smith (CA)
Hempstead † . . . . Katherine Ragston Ward (M)
Henderson † . . Henry Pace (M), Jay M. Abercrombie (CM)
Henrietta . . . . Billy Carlton (M)
Hereford † . . . . . Cathy Bunch (M), Ryan Polster (CM)
Hewitt † . . . . Steve Fortenberry (M)
. . . . Everett Thomas (CM)
Hickory Creek . . Lynn Clark (M), John M. Smith Jr. (TA)
Hico . . . . . . Eddie Needham (M), Jason Dominy (CA)
Hidalgo † . . Sergio I. Coronado (M), Julian J. Gonzalez (CM)
Hideaway . . . . Chet Thomas (M)
Higgins . . . . Mark McKnight (M)
Highland Haven . . Olan Kelley (M), Andy Adams (CA)
Highland Park † . . . . Will C. Beecherl (M)
. . . . Tobin E. Maples (TA)

Highland Village † . . . . Charlotte Wilcox (M)
. . . . Paul Stevens (CM)
Hill Country Village . . . . Gabriel Durand-Hollis (M)
. . . . Frank Morales Jr. (CA)
Hillcrest Village . . . Kendall McGilvray (Pro Term M)
Hillsboro † . . . . Scott Johnson (M)
. . . . Megan S. Henderson (CM)
Hilshire Village . . . . Robert (Bob) Buesinger (M)
. . . . Cassie Stephens (CA)
Hitchcock † . . Chris Armacost (M), Marie Gelles (CA)
Holiday Lakes . . . . Norman C. Schroeder (M)
Holland . . Johnny C. Kallus (M), Sandy L. Starks (CA)
Holliday . . . . Brad Litteken (M)
Hollywood Park . . . . Chester Drash (M)
Hondo † . . . John McAnelly Jr. (M), John Naron (CM)
Honey Grove . . . . Claude Caffee (M)
Hooks . . . . Marc Reiter (M)
Horizon City † . . . . Andres Renteria (M)
Horseshoe Bay † . . Elsie Thurman (M), Jeff Koska (CM)
Houston † . . . . John Whitmire (M)
Howardwick . . . . Johnny F. Floyd (M)
Howe . . . . . Karla McDonald (M), Monte Walker (CA)
Hubbard . . . . Mary Alderman (M), Jason Patrick (CM)
Hudson . . . Robert Smith (M), Rodney McCarty (CA)
Hudson Oaks Tom Fitzpatrick (M), Sterling Naron (CA)
Hughes Springs . . . . Lee A. Newsom (M)
. . . . Tim L. Lambert (CM)
Humble † . . . . Norman Funderburk (M)
. . . . Jason Stuebe (CM)
Hunters Creek Village . . . Jim Pappas (M), Tom Fullen (CA)
Huntington . . . . . . Todd Ricks (M), Bill Stewart (CA)
Huntsville † . . . . Russell Humphrey (M)
. . . . Scott E. Swigert (CM)
Hurst † . . . . Henry Wilson (M), Clay Caruthers (CM)
Hutchins . . . Mario Vasquez (M), James W. Quin (CA)
Hutto † . . . . . . Mike Snyder (M), James R. Earp (CM)
Huxley . . . . Larry Vaughn (M)

I

Idalou . . . . William Russ Perkins (M)
. . . . Suzette Williams (CA)
Impact . . . . Trevor Dickson (M)
Indian Lake . . . . James Chambers (M)
Industry . . . . Mable Meyers (M)
Ingleside † . . . . Pedro Oscar Adame (M)
. . . . Brenton B. Lewis (CM)
Ingleside on the Bay . . . . Jo Ann Ehmann (M)
Ingram . . . . Claud Jordan Jr. (M)
Iola . . . . Christina Stover (M)
Iowa Colony † . . . . Wil Kennedy (M)
Iowa Park † . . Jeffrey Pogatshnik (M), Jerry Flemming (CM)
Iraan . . . . Karina Browning (M)
Iredell . . . . Ricardo Vergara (M)
Irving † . . . . . Rick Stopfer (M), Chris Hillman (CM)
Italy . . Clinton Sulka-Tovar (M), Keith Whitfield (CM)
Itasca . . James Bouldin (M), Steve Daniels (Interim CA)
Ivanhoe . . . . Skip Blackstone (M)

J

Jacinto City † . . . Ana Diaz (M), Lon D. Squyres (CM)
Jacksboro . . . . Alton Morris Jr. (M)
. . . . Michael R. Smith (CM)
Jacksonville † Randy Gorham (M), James Hubbard (CM)
Jamaica Beach . . . . Mary Morse (M)
. . . . Gilbert Salas (Interim CA)
Jarrell . . . . Patrick Sherek (M)
. . . . Jorge L. Hernandez (Interim CM)
Jasper † . . . . . Clark McClane (M), Greg Kelley (CM)
Jayton . . . . George Chisum (M)
Jefferson . . Patricia A. Finstrom (M), Melissa Boyd (CA)
Jersey Village † . . Bobby Warren (M), Austin Bleess (CM)
Jewett . . . . John Sitton (M)
Joaquin . . . . Jessie Griffith (M)
Johnson City . . . . Stephanie Fisher (M)
Jolly . . . . D. LeAnn Skinner (M)
Jones Creek . . . . Corey Thomas (M)
Jonestown . . . Paul Johnson (M), Tracie Hlavinka (CA)
Josephine . . . . . Jason Turney (M), Lisa Palomba (CA)
Joshua † . . . . . Scott Kimble (M), Mike Peacock (CM)
Jourdanton . . . . Robert A. Williams (M)
. . . . Debbie G. Molina (CM)
Junction . . . . Russell Hammonds (CM)
Justin † . . . James Clark (M), Jarrod Greenwoods (CM)

K

Karnes City . . Leroy T. Skloss (M), Veronica Butler (CM)
Katy † . . . William H. Thiele (M), Byron J. Hebert (CM)
Kaufman † . . . . . Jeff Jordan (M), Mike Holder (CM)
Keene † . . . . . . Lisa Parrish (M), Jonathan Seitz (CM)
Keller † . . . . Armin Mizani (M), Aaron Rector (CM)
Kemah . . . . . . Robin Collins (M), Cesar Garcia (CA)
Kemp . . . . Christi Neal (M), Dean Winters (CA)
Kempner . . John Wilkerson (M), Rebecca D. Ramos (CM)
Kendleton . . . . Position Vacant (M)
Kenedy . . Brandon Briones (M), Melissa Gonzalez (CM)
Kenefick . . . . Rory Handley (M)
Kennard . . . . . Position Vacant (M), April Wright (CA)
Kennedale † . . . . Brad Horton (M), Darrell Hull (CM)
Kerens . . . . Jeffrey Saunders (M)
Kermit † . . . . David Holbrook (M)
. . . . Mike Arismendez Jr. (CM)
Kerrville † . . . . Joe Herring Jr. (M), Dalton Rice (CM)
Kilgore † . . . Ronnie E. Spradlin III (M), Rachel Rowe (CM)
Killeen † . . . Debbie Nash-King (M), Kent Cagle (CM)
Kingsbury . . . . Shirley Nolen (M)
Kingsville † . . . . Sam R. Fugate (M)
. . . . Charles Sosa (Interim CM)
Kirby † . . . Janeshia Grider (M), Brian Rowland (Interim CM)
Kirbyville . . . . Frank George (M)
Kirvin . . . . J.W. Walthall (M)
Knollwood . . . . Rosalie Dunn (M)
Knox City . . . . Henry Moya (M), Dustin Bradley (CA)
Kosse . . . . Brooks Valls (M)
Kountze . . . . . Fred Williams (M), George Drake (CA)

Kress . . . . Johnny Taylor (M)
Krugerville . . . . Jeff Parrent (M)
Krum † . . Rhonda Harrison (M), Nicholas Vincent (CA)
Kurten . . . . Chris Court (M)
Kyle † . . . . Travis Mitchell (M), Bryan Langley (CM)

L

La Coste . . . . Andy Keller (M), Darrell Rawlings (CA)
Lacy Lakeview † . . Charles Wilson (M), Calvin Hodde (CA)
Ladonia . . . . Patricia Harrod (M)
La Feria † . . Olga H. Maldonado (M), Frank Rios Jr. (CM)
Lago Vista † . . . Kevin Sullivan (M), Charles West (CM)
La Grange † . . Jan Dockery (M), Jack Thompson (CM)
La Grulla . . . . Macario Villarreal III (M)
. . . . Roberto A. Salinas (CM)
Laguna Vista † . . . Michael Carter (M), Victor Treviño (TM)
La Joya † . . Isidro Casanova (M), Jaime S. Sandoval (CA)
Lake Bridgeport . . . Nick Bilby (M), Wanda Vick (CA)
Lake City . . . . Shannan Smith (M)
Lake Dallas † . . . . Andi Nolan (M), Luke Olson (CM)
Lake Jackson † . . . . Gerald Roznovsky (M)
. . . . Modesto Mundo (CM)
Lakeport . . . . Johnny Sammons (M)
Lakeside (San Patricio Co.) . . . . Jeff Mason (M)
Lakeside (Tarrant Co.) . . . . Patrick Jacob (M)
. . . . Norman Craven (TA)
Lakeside City . Cory Glassburn (M), Cory C. Aspinwall (CA)
Lake Tanglewood . . . . Tiffany Rogers (M)
Lakeview . . . . Kelly Clark (M)
Lakeway † . . Thomas Kilgore (M), Joseph Molis (CM)
Lakewood Village . . . Mark E. Vargus (M), Linda Ruth (TA)
Lake Worth † . . . . Walter E. Bowen (M)
. . . . Stacey Almond (CM)
La Marque † . . . . Keith Bell (M), Joshua Pritchett (CM)
Lamesa † . . . . Hayden Davis (M), Joe Hines (CM)
Lampasas † . . . . Herb Pearce (M), Erin Corbell (CM)
Lancaster † . . . . Clyde C. Hairston (M)
. . . . Opal D. Mauldin-Jones (CM)
La Porte † . . Rick Helton (M), Corby D. Alexander (CM)
Laredo † . . . Victor D. Treviño (M), Joseph Neeb (CM)
Latexo . . . . Robert Hernandez M)
La Vernia . . Martin Poore (M), Lindsey Boyd-Wheeler (CA)
La Villa . . . . . . Rosa Perez (M), Antonio Barco (CA)
Lavon † . . . . Vicki Sanson (M), Kim Dobbs (CA)
La Ward . . . . William R. Koch (M)
Lawn . . . . Veronica Burleson (M)
League City † . . Nick Long (M), John Baumgartner (CM)
Leakey . . . . Hazel Pendley (M)
Leander † . . Christine DeLisle (M), Todd Parton (CM)
Leary . . . . . . B.J. Martin (M), Randy Mansfield (CA)
Lefors . . . . Michael Ray (M)
Leona . . . . Ernest Oden (M)
Leonard . . . . . Michael Pye (M), George Evanko (CA)
Leon Valley † . . Chris Riley (M), Crystal Caldera (CM)
Leroy . . . . Ernest Moravec (M)
Levelland † . . Breann Buxkemper (M), James Fisher (CM)
Lewisville † . . TJ Gilmore (CM), Claire E. Powell (CM)
Lexington . . . . Allen Retzlaff (M)
Liberty † . . . John Hebert Jr. (M), Bryan Kendrick (CM)
Liberty Hill . . Crystal Mancilla (M), Paul Brandenburg (CM)
Lindale † . . . Gavin Rasco (M), Carolyn Caldwell (CM)
Linden . . . . . Lynn Reynolds (M), Stephen Barnes (CA)
Lindsay . . . . Scott Neu (M)
Lipan . . . . Mike Stowe (M)
Little Elm † . . Curtis J. Cornelious (M), Matt Mueller (CA)
Littlefield † . . . . Eric Turpen (M), Ray Resendez (CM)
Little River-Academy . . . . . Domingo Montalbo (CM)
Live Oak † . Mary M. Dennis (M), Anas Garfaoui (CM)
Liverpool . . . . Ric Bogue (M)
Livingston . . . Judy B. Cochran (M), Bill Wiggins (CM)
Llano . . . . Laura Almond (M), Martin Mangum (CM)
Lockhart † . . . . . Lew White (M), Steven Lewis (CM)
Lockney . . . Aaron Wilson (M), Buster Poling Jr. (CM)
Log Cabin . . . . Paul Eckeberger (M)
Lometa . . . . Derek Talley (M)
Lone Oak . . . . Steve Forgy (M)
Lone Star . . . . Brianna McClain (M)
Longview † . . Kristen Ishihara (M), Rolin C. McPhee (CM)
Loraine . . . . Susanna Epperson (M)
Lorena . . . . . . Russell Walizer (M), Kevin Neal (CM)
Lorenzo . Lori A. Landin (M), Michael Chambers (CA)
Los Fresnos † . . . . Alejandro Flores (M)
. . . . Mark W. Milum (CM)
Los Indios . . Jaime Gonzalez (M), Jared Hockema (CA)
Los Ybanez . . Mary A. Ybanez (M), John Castillo (CM)
Lott . . . . David Stimmel (M)
Lovelady . . . . William B. Shoemaker (M)
Lowry Crossing . . . . . Bob Petitt (M), Janis Cable (CA)
Lubbock † . . Mark McBrayer (M), Jarrett Atkinson (CM)
Lucas † . . . Dusty Kuykendall (M), John Whitsell (CM)
Lueders . . . . Benny Jarvis (M)
Lufkin † . . . . Mark Hicks (M), Kevin Gee (CM)
Luling † . . . . . CJ Watts (M), Mark McLaughlin (CM)
Lumberton † . . . . . Don Surratt (M), Steve Clark (CM)
Lyford . . . . Jose G. Solis (M)
Lytle . . Ruben Gonzalez (M), Zachary Meadows (CM)

M

Mabank . . . . . Randy Teague (M), Bryant Morris (CA)
Madisonville . . . . William L. Parten (M)
. . . . Fabrice Kabona (CM)
Magnolia . . . . Matthew Dantzer (M)
Malakoff . . Nicole Mason-Driver (M), Tim Whitley (CA)
Malone . . . . John Stewart (M)
Manor † . . Christopher Harvey (M), Scott Moore (CM)
Mansfield † . . Michael Evans Sr. (M), Joe Smolinski (CM)
Manvel † . . . . . Dan Davis (M), Daniel Johnson (CM)
Marble Falls † . . John Packer (M), Mickiel Hodge (CM)
Marfa . . . Manuel V. Baeza (M), Kelly Perez (Interim CM)
Marietta . . . Position Vacant (M), Charles Elliott (CM)
Marion . . . . Daniel H. Loyola (M)
Marlin † . . . Susan R. Byrd (M), Justin Parker (Interim CM)
Marquez . . . . Stynette Clary (M), Lauren Powers (CM)
Marshall † . . . Amy Ware (M), Melissa Byrne Vossmer (CM)

Mart . . . . Robert Kaiser (M)
Martindale . . . Katherine Glaze (M), Jared Anable (CA)
Mason . . . . . Robert Rayburn (M), Amanda Hill (CA)
Matador . . . . Gerald Conner (M)
Mathis † . . Ciri Villarreal (M), Cedric W. Davis Sr. (CM)
Maud . . . . Jimmy Clary (M)
Maypearl . . . . Chance Lynch (M)
McAllen † . . Javier Villalobos (M), Isaac J. Tawil (CM)
McCamey . . . . Pedro L. Rosales (M)
McGregor † . . . . . Jim Lilley (M), Kevin P. Evans (CM)
McKinney † . . . . . . Bill Cox (M), Paul Grimes (CM)
McLean . . . . Tanner Hess (M)
McLendon-Chisholm † . . . . Bryan McNeal (M)
. . . . Beverly Stibbens (Interim CA)
Meadow . . Natalie Howard (M), Terri McClanahan (CA)
Meadowlakes . . . Mark Bentley (M), William De Roos (CM)
Meadows Place . . . Audrey St. Germain (M), Nick Haby (CA)
Megargel . . . . Randall Williams (M)
Melissa † . . . . . . Jay Northcut (M), Jason Little (CM)
Melvin . . . . Marelina Brown (M)
Memphis . . . . Joe Davis (M), Jack Owens (CA)
Menard . . Barbara Hooten (M), Donald R. Kerns (CA)
Mercedes † . . . . Oscar D. Montoya Sr. (M)
. . . . Alberto Perez (CM)
Meridian . . . . Ryan Nieuwenhuis (M), Kris Garza (CA)
Merkel . . . Ray Cobb (M), Evelyn Morse (Interim CM)
Mertens . . . . Barbara S. Crass (M)
Mertzon . . Aubrey Stewart (M), Michele Rabenaldt (CA)
Mesquite † . . . . Daniel Alemán Jr. (M)
. . . . Clifford V. Keheley Jr. (CM)
Mexia † . . . . . . Geary Smith (M), Joshua Barron (CM)
Miami . . . . Chad Breeding (M)
Midland † . . . Lori Blong (M), Tomas Gonzalez (CM)
Midlothian † . . . Justin Coffman (M), Chris Dick (CM)
Midway . . . . Randal Dorman (M)
Milano . . . . Karl Westbrook (M)
Mildred . . . . Bryan Roach (M)
Miles . . . . Tammy Pitt (M)
Milford . . . . Bruce Perryman (M)
Miller's Cove . . . . Willie B. Garrett (M)
Millsap . . . . . . Jamie French (M), Ashley Davis (CM)
Mineola . . Jayne L. Lankford (M), Cynthia Karch (CM)
Mineral Wells † . . . . Regan Johnson (M)
. . . . Jason B. Weeks (CM)
Mingus . . . . Vincent Huckaba (M)
Mission † . . . . Norie Gonzalez Garza (M)
. . . . Mike R. Perez (CM)
Missouri City † . . . . Robin J. Elackatt (M)
. . . . Angel L. Jones (CM)
Mobeetie . . . . John Charles Helton Jr. (M)
Mobile City . . . . Kenny Phillips (M)
Monahans † . . . . Adam Steen (M), Rex M. Thee (CM)
Mont Belvieu † . . . . Joey McWilliams (M)
. . . . Brian Winningham (CM)
Montgomery . . . . Sara Countryman (M)
. . . . Anthony Solomon (Interim CA)
Moody . . . . . . Charleen Dowell (M), Keith Fisher (CA)
Moore Station . . . . Greg Davis (Pro Term M)

Moran . . . . Tyler George (M)
Morgan . . . . Jonathan W. Croom II (M)
Morgan's Point . . Tim Harris (M), Brian Schneider (CA)
Morgan's Point Resort . . . . James Snyder (M)
. . . . Dennis M. Baldwin (CM)
Morton . . . Richard Levitt (M), Veronica Olguin (CM)
Moulton . . Mark Zimmerman (M), LuAnn D. Rogers (CA)
Mountain City . . . . Ralph McClendon Jr. (M)
. . . . Tiffany Curnutt (CA)
Mount Calm . . . . Jimmy Tucker (M)
Mount Enterprise . . . . Jim Reese (M)
Mount Pleasant † . . . . Wesley R. Lyon II (M)
. . . . Candias Webster (Interim CM)
Mount Vernon . Brad Hyman (M), Craig Lindholm (CA)
Muenster . . . Tim Felderhoff (M), Adam Deweber (CA)
Muleshoe † . . . . Colt Ellis (M), Ramon Sanchez (CM)
Mullin . . . . . M. Jean Smith (M), Dexter Morris (CM)
Munday . . . . Bob Bowen (M), Frank D. Treviño (CA)
Murchison . . . . Brad Gray (M)
Murphy † . . . Scott Bradley (M), Aretha Adams (CM)
Mustang Ridge David Bunn (M), Christina Gomez (CA)

N

Nacogdoches † . . . . Randy Johnson (M)
. . . . Richard B. Beverlin III (CM)
Naples . . . . Joyce Birdsong (M)
Nash . . . . Robert Bunch (M), Doug Bowers (CM)
Nassau Bay † . . . . Phil Johnson (M)
. . . . Paul Lopez (Interim CM)
Natalia . . . . Tommy F. Ortiz (M), Nichole Bermea (CA)
Navarro . . . . Vickie Lynn Farmer (M)
Navasota † . . . . William A. (Bert) Miller III (M)
. . . . Robert Hemminger (CM)
Nazareth . . . . . Marlin Durbin (M), Lacey Farris (CM)
Nederland † . . . . Jeffrey P. Darby (M)
. . . . Cheryl Dowden (Interim CM)
Needville . . . . Chad Nesvadba (M)
Nevada . . . . Donald Deering (M)
Newark . . . . Crystal Cardwell (M)
New Berlin . . . . Walter C. Williams (M)
New Boston . . Ronald Humphrey (M), Wayne Dial (CA)
New Braunfels † . . . . Neal Linnartz (M)
. . . . Robert Camareno (CM)
Newcastle . . . . Dickey Baynes (M)
New Chapel Hill . . . . Riley Harris (M)
New Deal . . . . John Salter (M)
New Fairview . . John R. Taylor (M), John Cabrales Jr. (CA)
New Home . . . . Brad Emert (M)
New Hope . . . . Andy Reitinger (M)
New London . . . . Dale McNeel (M)
New Summerfield . . . . Jane Barrow (M)
Newton . . . . John Pollock (M), Donald H. Meek (CA)
New Waverly . . . . Nathaniel James (M)
Neylandville . . . . Kathy Wilson (M)
Niederwald . . Connie Wood (M), Reynell Smith (CA)
Nixon . . . . Ellie Dominguez (M), Darryl Becker (CM)
Nocona . . Robert H. Fenoglio (M), Lynn Henley (CM)
Nolanville † . . Andy Williams (M), Teresa Chandler (CM)
Nome . . . . Kerry Abney (M)
Noonday . . . . Mike Turman (M)
Nordheim . . . . Dennis Pfeifer (Pro Term M)
Normangee . . . . Troy Noey (M)
North Cleveland . . . . Bob Bartlett (M)
Northlake † . . . Brian Montini (M), Drew Corn (CM)
North Richland Hills † . . . . Jack McCarty (M)
. . . . Paulette A. Hartman (CM)
Novice . . . . . Frankie Berry (M), Melissa Mullins (CA)

O

Oak Grove . . . . Jeffrey Davis (M)
Oak Leaf . . . . Tom Leverentz (M)
Oak Point † . . . . Dena Meek (M), Joni Vaughn (CM)
Oak Ridge (Cooke Co.) . . . . Chad Ramsey (M)
Oak Ridge (Kaufman Co.) . . . . Al Rudin (M)
Oak Ridge North . . Paul Bond (M), Heather Neeley (CM)
Oak Valley . . . . Jarrett Greer (M)
Oakwood . . . . Jacquelyn Morrow (M)
O'Brien . . . . Chris Casillas (M)
Odem . . . . Cal Hendrick (M)
Odessa † . . . . . . Javier Joven (M), David A. Vela (CM)
O'Donnell . . . . Max Mendieta (M)
Oglesby . . . . Bruce Pomerenke (M)
Old River-Winfree . . . . Joe Landry (M)
Olmos Park . . . . Erin Harrison (M)
. . . . Ashley Wayman Maus (CM)
Olney † . . . . Rue Rogers (M), Simon Dwye (CA)
Olton . . . . . Mark McFadden (M), Keeley Adams (CA)
Omaha . . . . Robert A. Holland (M)
Onalaska . . . . . . James Arnett (M), Angela Stutts (CA)
Opdyke West . . . . Wayne Riggins (M)
Orange † . . . . . Larry Spears Jr. (M), Mike Kunst (CM)
Orange Grove . . . . Carl D. Srp (M), Todd Wright (CA)
Orchard . . . . Matt Perreault (M)
Ore City . . . . Angie Edwards (M)
Overton . . . . . . Curtis Gilbert (M), Shane West (CM)
Ovilla . . Richard Dormier (M), David D. Henley (CM)
Oyster Creek . . . . Justin Mills (M)

P

Paducah . . . . Rodger Brannen (M)
Paint Rock . . . . Frances Maupin (M)
Palacios † . . . . Rick Cink (M), Cynthia Raleigh (CM)
Palestine † . . Mitchell Jordan (M), Teresa Herrera (CM)
Palisades . . . . Jerry Lane (M)
Palmer . . . . . Kenneth Bateman (M), Alicia Baran (CA)
Palmhurst . . . Fred del Barrio (M), Lori A. Lopez (CM)
Palm Valley . . . . Michael R. Galvan (M)
. . . . Rendie Gonzales (CA)
Palmview † . . Ricardo Villareal (M), Michael R. Leo (CM)
Pampa † . . . . . . Mike Borger (M), Shane Stokes (CM)
Panhandle . . . Doyle Robinson (M), Terry Coffee (CM)
Panorama Village . . . . Lynn Scott (M)
Pantego . . . . . . Russ Brewster (M), Joe Ashton (CM)

Paradise . . . Amanda Black (M)
Paris † . . Mihir "Mark" Pankaj (M), Rose Beverly (CM)
Parker . . . Lee Pettle (M)
Pasadena † . . . Jeff A. Wagner (M)
Pattison . . . Daphney Kirby (M)
Patton Village . . . Scott Anderson (M)
Payne Springs . . . Andrea Miller (M)
Pearland † . . . Kevin Cole (M), Trent Epperson (CM)
Pearsall † . . Ben T. Briscoe (M), Federico Reyes Jr. (CM)
Peaster . . . Gerald Hobson (M)
Pecan Gap . . . Eddy Frey (M)
Pecan Hill . . Don Schmerse (M), Shelley Martinez (CA)
Pecos † . . . . Teresa Winkles (M), Charles E. Lino (CM)
Pelican Bay . . . Tamra Olague (M)
Penelope . . . Phillip Esparza (M)
Peñitas † . . Ramiro Loya (M), Humberto Garza III (CM)
Perryton . . Kerry Symons (M), Patrick C. Comiskey (CM)
Petersburg . . Susie Martinez (M), Mario Martinez (CM)
Petrolia . . . Troy Inman (M)
Petronila . . . Todd Wright (M)
Pflugerville † . . . Victor Gonzales (M)
. . . Sereniah Breland (CM)
Pharr † . . . Ambrosio Hernandez (M)
. . . Jonathan B. Flores (CM)
Pilot Point † . . . . Chad Major (M), Britt M. Lusk (CM)
Pine Forest . . . Cathy Nagel (M)
Pinehurst . . . . Sarah McClendon (M), Jerry Hood (CA)
Pine Island . . . Steve Nagy (M)
Pineland . . . Joe Lane (M)
Piney Point Village . . . Aliza Dutt (M)
. . . Bobby Pennington (CA)
Pittsburg † David Abernathy (M), Clint Hardeman (CM)
Plains . . . Elsa Moya (M), Steve Vasquez (CA)
Plainview † . . . Charles Starnes (M)
. . . Theodore E. Chancellor (CM)
Plano † . . . John B. Muns (M), Mark D. Israelson (CM)
Plantersville . . . Kimberly Allphin (M)
Pleak . . . Michael A. John (M)
Pleasanton † . . . JR Gallegos (M), Johnny Huizar (CM)
Pleasant Valley . . . Jerry G. Gholson (M)
Plum Grove . . . Mary Arrendell (M)
Poetry . . . Michael Ross Jaffe (M)
Point . . . Dustin Briggs (M)
Point Blank . . . Mark T. Wood (M), Kelly Hoot (CM)
Point Comfort . . Stephen Lambden (M), Don Doering (CA)
Point Venture . . . Justin Hamilton (M)
Ponder . . . Nick McGregor (M)
Port Aransas † . . . Wendy Moore (M), David Parsons (CM)
Port Arthur † . . . Thurman Bill Bartie (M)
. . . Ron Burton (CM)
Port Isabel † . . Martin Cantu Jr. (M), Jared Hockema (CM)
Portland † . Cathy Skurow (M), Randy L. Wright (CM)
Port Lavaca † Jack Whitlow (M), JoAnna P. Weaver (CM)
Port Neches † . . . R. Glenn Johnson (M)
. . . André S. Wimer (CM)
Post . . . Marvin Self (M), J. Rhett Parker (CM)
Post Oak Bend . . . Mike Parker (M), Jana Shelton (CA)
Poteet . . Denise Leal Sanchez (M), Melissa Popham (CA)
Poth . . . Chrystal Eckel (M)
Pottsboro . . Tom Ceci (M), Kandace Tappen Lesley (CM)
Powell . . . Clay Jackson (M)
Poynor . . . Dannie Smith (M)
Prairie View † . . . Ron Leverett (M)
. . . Wendy Parker (Interim CM)
Premont . . . Idolina Perez (M)
Presidio . John Ferguson (M), Pablo E. Rodriguez (CA)
Primera . . . Robert D. Kusch Jr. (M), Celina Gonzales (CM)
Princeton † . Eugene Escobar Jr. (M), Michael Mashburn (CM)
Progreso . . . . Hugo Gamboa (M), Pedro Treviño (CM)
Progreso Lakes . . . David Martin (M)
Prosper † . . David F. Bristol (M), Mario Canizares (TM)
Providence Village † . . . Linda Inman (M)
. . . Brian D. Roberson (TM)
Putnam . . . Hubert Donaway (M)
Pyote . . . Abigail Pritchard (M)

Q

Quanah † . . . . . Kathy Butler (M), Paula Wilson (CA)
Queen City . . . Harold Martin (M)
Quinlan . . . . . . Jacky Goleman (M), John Adel (CM)
Quintana . . . Mike Cassata (M), Tammi Cimiotta (CA)
Quitaque . . . Phil Barefield (M)
Quitman . . . Randy C. Dunn (M), James Attaway (CM)

R

Ralls . . . Terry Hitt (M), Kim Perez (CA)
Rancho Viejo . . Todd Day (M), Isabel Perales (Interim TA)
Ranger † . . . . Robert Butler (M), Charlie Archer (CM)
Rangerville . . . Wayne M. Halbert (M)
Rankin . . . . Brandon Brown (M), Renee Lee (CA)
Ransom Canyon . . . Val Meixner (M)
. . . Maria Elena Quintanilla (CA)
Ravenna . . . Erik Premont (M)
Raymondville † . . . Gilbert Gonzales (M)
. . . Andres Chavez (CM)
Red Lick . . . Michael D. Peek (M)
Red Oak † . . . Mark L. Stanfill (M), Todd Fuller (CM)
Redwater . . . . Clay Parker (M), Dessie Whelchel (CA)
Refugio . . . Wanda Dukes (M)
Reklaw . . . Bob Parrott (M)
Reno (Lamar Co.) . . . Stacey Nichols (M)
Reno (Parker Co.) . . Hector Bas (M), Scott Passmore (CA)
Retreat . . . Janice Barfknecht (M)
Rhome . . . Kenny Crenshaw (M), Amanda DeGan (CA)
Rice . . . Christi Campbell (M)
Richardson † . . . Amir Omar (M), Don Magner (CM)
Richland . . . Jerry Morris (M)
Richland Hills † . . . Curtis A. Bergthold (M)
. . . Candice Edmondson (CM)
Richland Springs . . . J. Frank Pearce (M)
Richmond † . . . . Rebecca Haas (M), Terri Vela (CM)
Richwood † . . . Michael W. Durham (M)
. . . Eric Foerster (CM)
Riesel . . . Marshall Shaw (M)

Rio Bravo † . . . . Amanda Perez Aguero (M)
. . . . Jesus M. Olivares (CA)
Rio Grande City † . . . . Gilberto Falcon (M)
. . . . Gilbert Millan Jr. (CM)
Rio Hondo . . Gustavo Olivares (M), Ben Medina Jr. (CA)
Rio Vista . . . . Jeff Faraizi (M)
Rising Star . . . . Betsy Herron (M), Jan Clark (CA)
River Oaks † . . . Darren Houk (M), Marvin Gregory (CA)
Riverside . . . . Heidi Tutor (M)
Road Runner . . . . David Ortega Jr. (M)
Roanoke † . . . Carl E. Gierisch (M), Cody Petree (CM)
Roaring Springs . . . . Jeff Thacker (M)
Robert Lee . . . Steven Arens (M), Amanda Mendoza (CA)
Robinson † . . . . . . Greg May (M), Craig Lemin (CM)
Robstown † . . . . David Martinez (M)
Roby . . . . Eli Sepeda (M), Jack W. Brown (CM)
Rochester . Marvin Stegemoeller (M), Gail Nunn (CM)
Rockdale † . . Ward Roddam (M), Timothy Kelty (CM)
Rockport † . . . . Lowell Timothy Jayroe (M)
. . . . Vanessa Shrauner (CM)
Rocksprings . . . . Homer Jimenez (M)
Rockwall † . . . Trace Johannesen (M), Mary Smith (CM)
Rocky Mound . . . . Noble T. Smith (M)
. . . . Norris E. Smith (CM)
Rogers . . . . . Jeff Watson (M), Tammy Cockrum (CA)
Rollingwood . . Gavin Massingill (M), Alun Thomas (CA)
Roma † . . Jaime Escobar Jr. (M), Alejandro Barrera (CM)
Roman Forest . . Chris Parr (M), Scott Castleberry (CA)
Ropesville . Brenda Rabel (M), Susan D. Thompson (CA)
Roscoe . . . David Ralph (M), Jack Brown (Interim CM)
Rosebud . Marlene Zipperlen (M), Kenny Ray Murray (CA)
Rose City . . . . Tony Wilcoxson (M)
Rose Hill Acres . . . . David Lang (M)
Rosenberg † . . William Benton (M), Joyce Vasut (CM)
Ross . . . . Jim Jaska (M)
Rosser . . . . Shannon R. Corder (M)
Rotan . . . Zachary Johnson (M), Carla Thornton (CM)
Round Mountain . . . . Julian Gutierrez (M)
Round Rock † . Craig Morgan (M), Brooks Bennett (CM)
Round Top . . . . Judith Vincent (M)
Rowlett † . . . . Jeff Winget (M), David Hall (CM)
Roxton . . . . Paul Helms (M), Janet Wheeler (CM)
Royse City † . . . Janet Nichol (M), Carl Alsabrook (CM)
Rule . . . . Delle Watkins (M)
Runaway Bay . . . . Herman White (M)
Runge . . . . Christopher Parker (M)
Rusk † . . . . Ben Middlebrooks (M)
. . . . Ben Goldsberry (Interim CM)

S

Sabinal . . . . Erik Jason Gomez (M)
Sachse † . . . . . . Jeff Bickerstaff (M), Gina Nash (CM)
Sadler . . . . Jackie Moss (M), Jaime Vannoy (CA)
Saginaw † . . . Todd Flippo (M), Gabriel Reaume (CM)
Saint Hedwig Dee Grimm (M), Maria Hernandez (CM)
Saint Jo . . . . Kelly Williamson (M)
Salado . . . . Bert Henry (M), Manuel De La Rosa (CA)
San Angelo † . . Brenda Gunter (M), Daniel Valenzuela (CM)
San Antonio † . . Gina Ortiz Jones (M), Erik Walsh (CM)
San Augustine . Leroy Hughes (M), Jeaneyse Mosby (CM)
San Benito † . . . . Ricardo (Rick) Guerra (M)
. . . . Federico R. Sandoval (CM)
Sanctuary . . . . Megg Galloway (M)
San Diego . . . . Araseli Sally Lichtenberger (M)
. . . . Aleida L. Luera (CM)
Sandy Oaks . . . . Michael Martinez Jr. (M)
Sandy Point . . . . Charles J. Waller Jr. (M)
San Elizario . Miguel A. Chacon (M), Adriana Gaucin (CA)
San Felipe . . . . Bobby Byars (M)
Sanford . . . . Dallis Shelton (M)
Sanger † . . . . . . Thomas Muir (M), John Noblitt (M)
San Juan † . . . . . Mario Garza (M), Tirso Garza (CM)
San Leanna . . . Molly Quirk (M), Rebecca Howe (CA)
San Marcos † Jane Hughson (M), Stephanie Reyes (CM)
San Patricio . . . . Jackie Hale (M)
San Perlita . . . . George M. Guadiana (M)
San Saba . . . . . Ken Jordan (M), Scott Edmonson (CM)
Sansom Park . . . . Jim Barnett Jr. (M)
Santa Anna . . . . Kevin Morris (M)
Santa Clara . . . . Jeff Hunt (M)
Santa Fe † . . . Brandon Noto (M), Ramon Covan (CM)
Santa Rosa . . . . Jaime Quiroga (M)
Savoy . . . . Joe Petree (M)
Schertz † . . Ralph Gutierrez (M), Steve Williams (CM)
Schulenburg . . Connie Koopmann (M), Tami Walker (CA)
Scotland . . . . Ron Hoff (M)
Scottsville . . . . Kerry L. Cade (M)
Scurry . . . . Johnny Blazek (M)
Seabrook † . . . . . Jim Sweeney (M), Gayle Cook (CM)
Seadrift . . . . Tracey L. Johnson (M)
Seagoville † . . . . Lackey Stepper Sebastian (M)
. . . . Cindy Brown (CM)
Seagraves . . . . Mike Terrell (M)
Sealy † . . . . . . Carolyn Bilski (M), Kimbra Hill (CM)
Seguin † . . . . . Donna Dodgen (M), Steve Parker (CM)
Selma . . . . Tom Daly (M), Johnny Casias (CA)
Seminole † . . . . . . Chet Clark (M), Mary Furlow (CA)
Seven Oaks . . . . Centa Evans (M)
Seven Points . . . . Keith Betts (M)
Seymour . . . . . . Mark McCord (M), Jeff Brasher (CA)
Shady Shores . . . . Cindy Aughinbaugh (M)
. . . . Wendy Withers (TA)
Shallowater . . Royking Potter (M), Russel Moses (CM)
Shamrock . . . . . Lynn Ramsey (M), Troy Potts (CM)
Shavano Park . . . . . . Bob Werner (M), Bill Hill (CM)
Shenandoah . . . . . John Escoto (M), Kathie Reyer (CA)
Shepherd . . . . Charles Minton (M)
Sherman † . Shawn C. Teamann (M), Zachary Flores (CM)
Shiner . . . . Fred Hilscher (M)
Shoreacres . . David Jennings (M), Troy Harrison (CM)
Silsbee † . . Danny Reneau (M), DeeAnn Zimmerman (CM)
Silverton . . . . Lane B. Garvin (M), John Hall (CA)
Simonton . . . . Laurie Boudreaux (M)
Sinton † . Mary M. Speidel (M), John D. Hobson (CM)
Skellytown . . . . Amanda Dickerson (M)

Slaton † . . . . . . Clifton Shaw (M), Wade Wilson (CA)
Smiley . . . . Lisa Benavides (M)
Smithville . . Sharon Foerster (M), Robert Tamble (CM)
Smyer . . . . Gena Pittman (M)
Snook . . . . Frank Fields (M), David Junek (CA)
Snyder † . . . . Stephanie Ducheneaux (M)
. . . . Eli Torres (Interim CM)
Socorro † . . Rudy Cruz Jr. (M), Adriana Rodarte (CM)
Somerset . Lydia P. Hernandez (M), James R. Cano (CA)
Somerville . . . . Tommy Thompson (M)
Sonora . . . . Juanita Gomez (M), Arturo Fuentes (CM)
Sour Lake . . . Bruce Robinson (M), Jack Provost (CM)
South Frydek . . . . Joe Mike Young (M)
South Houston . . . . Joe Soto (M)
Southlake † . . Shawn McCaskill (M), Alison Ortowski (CM)
Southmayd . . . . Debra Thompson (M)
South Mountain . . . . Position Vacant (M)
South Padre Island † . . . . Patrick McNulty (M)
. . . . William R. Smith (CM)
Southside Place . . . Andy Chan (M), David Moss (CM)
Spearman . . . . . Tobe Shields (M), Justin Parker (CM)
Splendora . . . Dorothy Welch (M), Danna Welter (CA)
Spofford . . . . Nyshe Smith (M)
Spring Branch . . . . James Mayer (M)
Springlake . . . . Chuck Conner (M)
Springtown . . . . . Greg Hood (M), David Miller (CA)
Spring Valley . . Marcus Vajdos (M), John McDonald (CA)
Spur . . . . John Schmidt (M)
Stafford † . . . . Ken Mathew (M)
Stagecoach . . . . James Osteen (M)
Stamford † . . . . James M. Decker (M)
. . . . Steven Paul Norwood (CM)
Stanton . . . . Sally Poteet (M), Jessie Montez (CA)
Staples . . . . Ronnie Clark (M)
Star Harbor . Steve Watson (M), Adabeth Shumate (CA)
Stephenville † . . . . . Doug Svien (M), Jason King (CM)
Sterling City . . . . George Rodriguez (M)
Stinnett . . . . . . Jeff Irvin (M), Marisa Webster (CA)
Stockdale . . . Ray Wolff (M), Stephen Mayfield (CM)
Stockton Bend . . . . Edward Reiter (M)
St. Paul . . . . Kent Swaner (M)
Stratford . . . . . Greg Wright (M), Tommy Bogart (CA)
Strawn . . . . . . Aron Johnson (M), Danny Miller (CA)
Streetman . . . . Johnny A. Robinson (M)
Sudan . . . . Michael Williamson (M)
Sugar Land † . . . . Thomas Schoenbein (M)
. . . . Mike Goodrum (CM)
Sullivan City † Alma D. Salinas (M), Richard Ozuna (CM)
Sulphur Springs † . . . . Harold Nash Sr. (M)
. . . . Marc Maxwell (CM)
Sundown . Jonathan Strickland (M), Billy Hernandez (CA)
Sunnyvale † . . . . . . Saji George (M), Jeff Jones (TM)
Sunray . . . . Bruce Broxson (M), K.J. Perry (CM)
Sunrise Beach Village . . . . . . Rob Hardy, MHA (M)
Sunset Valley . . Marc Bruner (M), Matt Lingafelter (CA)
Sun Valley . . . . Tom Wagnon (M)
Surfside Beach . . . . Zack Parsch (M)
Sweeny † . . . . Dusty Hopkins (M), David Jordan (CM)
Sweetwater † . . . Jerod Peek (M), Bryan Sheridan (CM)

T

Taft . . . . . . Leonard Vasquez (M), Ryan Smith (CM)
Tahoka . . . . . . Ronny Jolly (M), Derek Stephens (CA)
Talco . . . . Mike Sloan (M)
Talty . . . . . Frank Garrison (M), James Stroman (CM)
Tatum . . . . Michael Henry (M)
Taylor † . . . . Dwayne Ariola (M), Brian LaBorde (CM)
Taylor Lake Village . . Jon Keeney (M), Stacey Fields (CA)
Taylor Landing . . . . John Phillip Owens (M)
Teague . . . . James Monks (M)
Tehuacana . . . . James Trantham (M)
Temple † . . . . Tim Davis (M), Brynn Myers (CM)
Tenaha . . O'Neal Jones Jr. (M), Amanda Treat-Brock (CA)
Terrell † . . . . Rick Carmona (M), Mark C. Mills (CM)
Terrell Hills † . . . . . . John Low (M), Bill Foley (CM)
Texarkana † . . . . Bob Bruggeman (M), David Orr (CM)
Texas City † . . . . Dedrick D. Johnson Sr. (M)
Texhoma . . . . Lazaro Salamanca (M)
Texline . . . . . Trever Greene (M), Marcia French (CM)
The Colony † . . Richard Boyer (M), Troy Powell (CM)
The Hills (Village of) . . . . Kevin Proud (M)
. . . . Angie Massey (CA)
Thompsons . . . . Freddie Newsome (M)
Thorndale . . . . George Galbreath Jr. (M)
. . . . Myron F. Trethewey (CA)
Thornton . . . Paul Miller (M), Victoria Winstead (CA)
Thorntonville . . . . Bryan Mann (M)
Thrall . . . . Troy Marx (M)
Three Rivers . . . . Felipe Q. Martinez (M)
. . . . Thomas Salazar (CA)
Throckmorton . . . . Will Carroll (M)
Tiki Island . . . . Vernon Teltschick (M)
Timbercreek Canyon . . . . Brian Giffin (M)
. . . . Amber Gerber (CM)
Timpson . . . . Debra Smith (M)
Tioga . . . . Craig Jezek (M)
Tira . . . . Allen Joslin (M)
Toco . . . . Christopher Gray (M)
Todd Mission . Stephen Mensing (M), Neal Wendele (CM)
Tolar . . . . . Matt Hutsell (M), Michelle Burdette (CA)
Tom Bean . . . . Ricky Thomas (M)
Tomball † Lori Klein Quinn (M), David Esquivel (CM)
Tool . . . . Mike Dumont (M), Julius Kizzee (CA)
Toyah . . . . Gordon Hoyt (M)
Trent . . . . Leanna West (M)
Trenton . . . . Rodney Alexander (M)
Trinidad . . . Leslie Parker (M), Terri R. Newhouse (CA)
Trinity . . . . Billy Goodin (M), Tracy Hutto (CA)
Trophy Club † . . . . Jeannette Tiffany (M)
. . . . Brandon Wright (TM)
Troup . . . . Jeff Hale (M), Gene Cottle (M)
Troy . . . . . Michael Morgan (M), Gary O. Smith (CA)
Tulia † . . . . Dusty George (M), B.J. Potts (CM)
Turkey . . . . . Christy Yates (M), Larry Plumlee (CM)
Tuscola . . . . Joe Quick (M)

Tye . . . . Nancy Moore (M), Eileen Hayman (CA)
Tyler † . . Don Warren (M), Edward A. Broussard (CM)

U

Uhland . . Lacee Duke (M), Kimberly Weatherford (CA)
Uncertain . . . . Judye Patterson (M)
Union Grove . . . . Mallory Dippold Shelton (M)
Union Valley . . . . Craig Waskow (M)
Universal City † . Tom Maxwell (M), Kim Turner (CM)
University Park † . . . . Thomas H. Stewart (M)
. . . . Robbie Corder (CM)
Uvalde † . Hector R. Luevano (M), Vince DiPiazza (CM)

V

Valentine . . . . Summer Webb (M)
Valley Mills . . . . Craig Godby (M)
Valley View . . . . Milton Boyle (M)
Van . . . . Ernie Burns (M), Jeff Hudgens (CM)
Van Alstyne † . . . Jim Atchison (M), Lane Jones (CM)
Van Horn . . Michael Garibay (M), Mark A. Cabezuela (CA)
Vega . . . . Roudy Blasingame (M)
Venus . . . . . Alejandro Galaviz (M), Joshua Jones (CA)
Vernon † . . . . . Pam Gosline (M), Darell Kennon (CM)
Victoria † . . . Duane Crocker (M), Jesús A. Garza (CM)
Vidor † . . Misty Songe (M), Gerard "Rod" Carroll (CM)
Vinton . . . Rachel Quintana (M), Andrea Carrillo (VA)
Volente . . . . Tom Blauvelt (M), Lacie Hale (CA)
Von Ormy . . Casey Homer (M), Valerie Michelle Naff (CA)

W

Waco † . . . . James C. Holmes (M), Bradley Ford (CM)
Waelder . . . . . Michael Harris (M), Paul Zepeda (CM)
Wake Village † . . Sheryl Collum (M), Jim Roberts (CA)
Waller . . . . Danny Marburger (M)
Wallis . . . . Belinda Halfin (M)
Walnut Springs . . . . Sammy Ortega (M)
Warren City . . . . Ricky Wallace (M)
Waskom . . . . Keith Slone (M)
Watauga † . Arthur L. Miner (M), Sandra Gibson (CM)
Waxahachie † . . Billie Wallace (M), Michael Scott (CM)
Weatherford † . Paul Paschall (M), James Hotopp (CM)
Webberville . . . . Hector Gonzales (M)
Webster † Donna Rogers (M), Michael K. Ahrens (CM)
Weimar . . Milton Koller (M), Donald D. Dixon (CM)
Weinert . . . . Doug Carrol (M)
Weir . . . . John Fox (M), Joy Hart (CA)
Wellington . . . . Larry Adams (M), Jon Sessions (CM)
Wellman . . . . Eddie Garza (M)
Wells . . . . Tony A. McKnight (M)
Weslaco † . . Adrian Gonzales (M), Martin Garza (CM)
West . . . . David Pratka (M), Shannon Cox (CA)
Westbrook . . . . Ramiro Fuentes (M)
West Columbia . . . . Laurie B. Kincannon (M
. . . . Debbie Sutherland (CM)
Westlake . . . . Kim D. Greaves (M), Wade Carroll (TM)
West Lake Hills . . James Vaughan (M), Trey Fletcher (CA)
Weston . . . . Jerry Randall (M)
Weston Lakes . . . . Bob Wall (M)
West Orange † . . . . Randy Branch (M)
Westover Hills . . . . Kelly Thompson (M)
West Tawakoni . Kevin Featherston (M), Tyler Collins (CA)
West University Place † . . . . Susan Sample (M)
. . . . Dave Beach (CM)
Westworth Village . .L. Kelly Jones (M), Brandy Barrett (CA)
Wharton † . . . . Tim Barker (M), Joseph R. Pace (CM)
Wheeler . . . . Dale Kidd (M), Dan Sams (CA)
White Deer . . . . Nick Ball (M)
Whiteface . . . . James Solis (M)
Whitehouse † . . James Wansley (M), Leslie Black (CM)
White Oak † . . . Kyle Kutch (M), Jimmy Purcell (CM)
Whitesboro . .David Blaylock (M), Phil Craig Harris (CA)
White Settlement † . Faron Young (M), Jeffrey James (CM)
Whitewright . . . . Sarah Beth Owen (M)
Whitney . . . . Janice Sanders (M)
Wichita Falls † . . Tim Short (M), Jeffery Jenkins (CM)
Wickett . . . . Xavier Estrada (M)
Willis † . William Deon Brown (M), Sheyi I. Ipaye (CM)
Willow Park . . . Teresa Palmer (M), Bryan Grimes (CA)
Wills Point . . Mike D. Jones (M), Charlie Brown-Conway (CA)
Wilmer . . . . Sheila Petta (M), Rona Stringfellow (CA)
Wilson . . . . Randy Dunn (M)
Wimberley . . . . . Jim Chiles (M), Timothy Patek (CA)
Windcrest † . . Dan Reese (M), Rafael Castillo Jr. (CM)
Windom . . . . Liena Fox (M)
Windthorst . . . . Justin Keener (M)
Winfield . . . . Debbie Cruitt (M)
Wink . . . . Eric Hawkins (M)
Winnsboro . Richard Parris (M), Makenzie Lyons (CA)
Winona . . . . Rachel Moreno (M)
Winters . . . . Chris Bahlman (M)
Wixon Valley . . . . James Soefje (M)
Wolfe City . . . . Sharion Scott (M)
Wolfforth † . . . . Charles Addington II (M)
. . . . Randy Criswell (CM)
Woodbranch Village . . . . Mike Tyson (M)
Woodcreek . . . . Jeff Rasco (M), Jim Burton (CA)
Woodloch . . . . Donald J. Nichols (M)
Woodsboro . . . . Brenda Roach (M)
Woodson . . . . Bobby Mathiews (M)
Woodville . . Amy Bythewood (M), Mandy K. Risinger (CA)
Woodway † . . . . Amine Quorzal (M)
Wortham . . . . Pellie Goolsby (M)
Wylie † . . . . . Matthew Porter (M), Brent Parker (CM)

Y

Yantis . . . . John D. (Trey) Norris III (M)
Yoakum † . . . . Carl O'Neill (M)
Yorktown . . . . . Bill Baker (M), Michele Warwas (CA)

Z

Zavalla . . . . Pam Hooks (M)

TEXAS COUNTY AND DISTRICT OFFICIALS — TABLE NO. 1

County	County Seat	County Judge	County Clerk	County Attorney	County Treasurer	Assessor–Collector	Sheriff
Anderson	Palestine	Carey McKinney	Mark Staples	Allyson Mitchell	Tara Holliday	Tommy G. Cross	W.R. (Rudy) Flores
Andrews	Andrews	Sam Jones	Vicki Scott	Sean Galloway	*Office abolished 11-5-1985.*	Robin Harper	Rusty Stewart
Angelina	Lufkin	Keith Wright	Amy Fincher	Layne Thompson	Jill Brewer	Terri Collier	Tom Selman
Aransas	Rockport	Ray A. Garza	Misty R.F. Kimbrough	Amanda Oster	Alma Cartwright	Anna Marshall	William (Bill) Mills
Archer	Archer City	Randall C. Jackson	Karren Winter	Jordyn Berend	Patricia A. Vieth	Dawn Vieth	Jack Curd
Armstrong	Claude	Adam Ensey	Tawnee Blodgett	Jason Herring	Susan Overcast McGrath	Jamie Craig	Melissa Anderson
Atascosa	Jourdanton	Weldon Cude	Theresa Carrasco	Molly Groesbeck Solis	Laura Pawelek	Loretta Holley	Joe Guerra
Austin	Bellville	Tim Lapham	Diane Day	Brandy Robinson	Bryan Haevischer	Kim Rinn	Jack Brandes
Bailey	Muleshoe	Basil Nash	Dyana Limon-Mercado	Michaela Kee	Tracy Torres	Maria Gonzalez	Richard Wills
Bandera	Bandera	Richard Evans	Tandie Mansfield	Janna Lindig	Beverly Schmidt	Andrea K. Jankoski	Joshua Teitge
Bastrop	Bastrop	Gregory Klaus	Krista Bartsch		Brittney Ross	Ellen Owens	Maurice Cook
Baylor	Seymour	Rusty A. Stafford	Chris Jakubicek	Susan Elliot	Kevin Hostas	Jeanette Holub	Darcy White
Bee	Beeville	George (Trace) Morill III	Michele Bridge	Mike Knight	*Office abolished 11-2-1982.*	Michelle Matus	Randy Aguirre
Bell	Belton	David Blackburn	Shelley Coston	James E. Nichols	Gaylon Evans	Shay Luedeke	Bill Cooke
Bexar	San Antonio	Peter Sakai	Lucy Adame-Clark	*Office abolished.*	*Office abolished 11-5-1985.*	Albert Uresti	Javier Salazar
Blanco	Johnson City	Brett Bray	Laura Walla	Deborah Earley	Camille Swift	Kristen Spies	Don Jackson
Borden	Gail	Shane Walker	Jana Underwood	Marlo Holbrooks	Shawna Gass	Benny Allison	Benny Allison
Bosque	Meridian	Cindy Vanlandingham	Tabatha Ferguson	Natalie Koehler	Pam Browning	Arlene Swiney	Trace Hendricks
Bowie	New Boston	Bobby Howell	Tina Petty		Donna Burns	Josh Davis	Jeff Neal
Brazoria	Angleton	L.M. (Matt) Sebesta Jr.	Joyce Hudman		Angela Dees	Kristin R. Bulanek	Bo Stallman
Brazos	Bryan	Duane Peters	Karen McQueen	Earl Gray	Laura Taylor Davis	Melissa Leonard	Wayne Dicky
Brewster	Alpine	Greg P. Henington	Sarah Vasquez	Marisol Skelton	Julie K. Morton	Sylvia Vega	Ronny Dodson
Briscoe	Silverton	Rank Cogdell	Amy Fuston	Taryn Minter (Pro Term)	Mary Jo Brannon	Jon Etta Ziegler	Garrett Davis
Brooks	Falfurrias	Eric Ramos	Elvaray B. Silvas	David T. Garcia	Alan Hernandez	Urbino (Benny) Martinez	Urbino (Benny) Martinez
Brown	Brownwood	Shane Britton	Sharon Ferguson	Jennifer Broughton	Ann Krpoun	Christine Pentecost	Vance W. Hill
Burleson	Caldwell	Keith Schroeder	Anna L. Schielack	Susan Deski	Stephanie Smith	Jessica Lucero	Gene Hermes
Burnet	Burnet	Bryan Wilson	Vicinta Stafford	Eddie Arredondo	Karrie Crownover	DeAnne Fisher	Calvin Boyd
Caldwell	Lockhart	Hoppy Haden	Teresa Rodriguez		Gloria Garcia	Debbie Sanders	Mike Lane
Calhoun	Port Lavaca	Vern Lyssy	Anna Goodman		Rhonda Kokena	Kerri Boyd	Bobbie Vickery
Callahan	Baird	Nicki Harle	Nicole Crocker	Shane Deel	Melissa Preijers	Debbie Hatchett	Eric Pechacek
Cameron	Brownsville	Eddie Treviño Jr.	Sylvia Garza-Perez	Luis V. Saenz	David A. Betancourt	Edelmiro Garcia	Manuel Treviño
Camp	Pittsburg	A.J. Mason	Sandra Knight	James (Jas) W. Wallace III	Kim Pittman	Missy Huffman	John Cortelyou
Carson	Panhandle	Dan Looten	Gayla Cates	Scott Sherwood	Eileen Pulliam	Ashley Montgomery	Tam Terry
Cass	Linden	Travis Ransom	Arturo Guajardo Jr.		Janice Ayers	Angela Young	Larry Rowe
Castro	Dimmitt	Mandy Gfeller	Amanda Fisher	Shalyn Hamlin	Elaine D. Flynt	Connie Gilbreath	Salvador Rivera
Chambers	Anahuac	Jimmy Sylvia	Heather Hawthorne	Ashley Cain Land	Nicole M. Whittington	Laurie G. Payton	Brian C. Hawthorne
Cherokee	Rusk	Chris Davis	Laverne Lusk	Dana Young	Erin Curtis	Shonda McCutcheon Potter	Brent Dickson
Childress	Childress	Kim Jones	Tiffany Howard	Greg Buckley	Brenda Overstreet	Kathy Dobbs	Matthew Bradley

County	County Seat	County Judge	County Clerk	County Attorney	County Treasurer	Assessor–Collector	Sheriff
Clay	Henrietta	Mike Campbell	Sasha Kelton	Seth C. Slagle	Danja Bloodworth	Patti Jackson	Sidney (Kirk) Horton
Cochran	Morton	Pat Sabala Henry	Lisa Smith	Amanda Martin	Tommy Smith	Dixie Mendoza	Scott Prothro, Acting Sheriff
Coke	Robert Lee	Hal Spain	Jennifer Burdett	Cody McCabe	Therese Emert	Gina Williams	Bill Williams
Coleman	Coleman	Billy D. Bledsoe	Stacey Mendoza	Hayden J. Wise	Jeana Farrow	Jamie Dodgen	Les Cogdill
Collin	McKinney	Chris Hill	Stacey Kemp			Scott Grigg	Jim Skinner
Collingsworth	Wellington	Scot Martindale	Jackie Johnson	Gaylon Davis	Gina Harris	Sharon Sherwood	Kent Riley
Colorado	Columbus	Ty Prause	Kimberly Menke	Jay E. Johannes	Joyce Guthmann	Meilnda A. Zajicek	Justin K. Lindemann
Comal	New Braunfels	Sherman Krause	Bobbie Koepp		Renee Couch	Kristen H. Hoyt	Mark Reynolds
Comanche	Comanche	Stephanie L. Davis	Ruby Lesley	Craig Willingham	Patsy Phifer	Grace Everhart	Chris Pounds
Concho	Paint Rock	David Dillard	Amber Hall	Ginger Paul	Jenifer Gierisch	Brent Frazier	Brent Frazier
Cooke	Gainesville	John O. Roane	Pam Harrison	Edmund J. Zielinski	Susan Wells	Brandy Ann Carr	Ray Sappington
Coryell	Gatesville	Roger A. Miller	Jennifer Newton	Brandon Belt	Randi McFarlin	Justin K. Carothers	Scott Williams
Cottle	Paducah	Karl Holloway	Vickey Wederski	Greg Buckley	Crystal Tucker	Kayla Box	Mark Box
Crane	Crane	Roy Hodges	Andrea Flores	Austin Rawls	Syndi Cadena	Judy Crumrine	Andrew Aguilar
Crockett	Ozona	Frank Tambunga	Ninfa Preddy	Jody K. Upham	Laura Conner	Michelle M. Medley	Antonio Alejandro III
Crosby	Crosbyton	Rusty Forbes	Tammy Marshall	Michael Sales	Debra Riley	Michele Cook	Corey Nunley
Culberson	Van Horn	Carlos G. Urias	Tina Urias		Adrian Hinojos	Aida O. Balcazar	Oscar Carrillo
Dallam	Dalhart	Wes Ritchey	Terri Banks	Whitney Hill	Kenda McKay	Jami Parr	Shane Stevenson
Dallas	Dallas	Clay Jenkins	John F. Warren		Pauline Medrano	John R. Ames	Marian Brown
Dawson	Lamesa	Foy O'Brien	Clare Christy	Steven B. Payson	Terri Stahl	Cheryl Miller	Matt Hogg
Deaf Smith	Hereford	D.J. Wagner	Rachel Garman		Christina Treviño	Gina Nunez	J. Dale Butler
Delta	Cooper	Tanner Crutcher	Janice Roberts	Jay Garrett	Debbie Huie	Dawn Moody	Marshall Lynch
Denton	Denton	Andy Eads	Juli Luke		Cindy Yeatts Brown	Dawn Waye	Tracy Murphree
DeWitt	Cuero	Daryl L. Fowler	Natalie Carson	A. Jay Condie	Desirae Poth-Garibay	Ashley D. Mraz	Carl Bowen
Dickens	Dickens	Kevin Brendle	Danay Carnes	Aaron Clements	Brandi Abbott	Rhonda Brendie	Jay Allen
Dimmit	Carrizo Springs	Martha Alicia Gomez Ponce	Mario Z. Garcia	Daniel M. Gonzalez	Oscar Ortiz	Mary E. Sandoval	Chris Casteneda
Donley	Clarendon	John C. Howard	Vicky Tunnell	Landon Lambert	Wanda Smith	Kristy Christopher	Charles (Butch) Blackburn
Duval	San Diego	Arnoldo Cantu	Sally Lichtenberger	Baldemar Gutierrez	Sylvia Lazo	Roberto Elizondo	Romeo R. Ramirez
Eastland	Eastland	David Hullum	Cathy Jentho		Christina Dodrill	Andrea May	Jason Weger
Ector	Odessa	Dustin Fawcett	Jennifer Martin	Julie Prentice	Cleopatra Anderson-Callaway	Lindy Wright	Mike Griffis
Edwards	Rocksprings	Souli Asa Shanklin	Olga Lydia Reyes	Amanda Poole	Lupe S. Enriquez	Mistee D. Splawn	James W. Guthrie
Ellis	Waxahachie	Todd Little	Krystal Valdez	Lindy Beatty	Cheryl Chambers	Richard Rozier	Brad Norman
El Paso	El Paso	Ricardo A. Samaniego	Delia Briones	Christina Sanchez	*Office abolished 1989.*	Ruben P. Gonzalez	Oscar Ugarte
Erath	Stephenville	Brandon J. Huckabee	Gwinda Jones	Bethany Espinoza	Angie Shawver	Valerie Stephen	Matt Coates
Falls	Marlin	Jay Elliott	Elizabeth Perez	Kathryn (Jody) Gilliam	Sheryl Pringle	Kayci Nehring	Jason Campbell
Fannin	Bonham	Newt Cunningham	Jenny Garner		David E. Woodson	Amber Sutherland	Cody Shook
Fayette	La Grange	Dan Mueller	Brenda Fietsam	Peggy Supak	*Office abolished 11-3-87.*	Sylvia Mendoza	Keith Korenek
Fisher	Roby	Ken Holt	Pat Thomson	Michael Hall	Jeanna Parks	Jonnye Lu Gibson	John Patrick Dickinson
Floyd	Floydada	Marty Lucke	KeeLee Rawls	Lex Herrington	Lori Morales	Priscilla DeHoyos	Paul Raissez
Foard	Crowell	Mark Christopher	Debra Hopkins	Marshall Capps	Darcy Moore	Mike Brown	Mike Brown
Fort Bend	Richmond	KP George	Laura Richard	Bridgette Smith-Lawson	Bill Rickert	Carmen P. Turner	Eric Fagan
Franklin	Mount Vernon	Scott Lee	Brook Bussell	Landon Ramsay	Paris Tillery	Melissa McSwain Clawson	Ricky Jones
Freestone	Fairfield	Linda K. Grant	Brook Emerson Bussell	Brian Evans	Mandy Chavers	Daniel M. Ralstin	Jeremy Shipley
Frio	Pearsall	Rochelle Lozano Camacho	Renee Gregory Reynolds	Joseph Sindon	Pete Jasso Martinez	Anna L. Alaniz	Peter Salinas
Gaines	Seminole	Cindy Therwhanger	Terri Berry	Joe H. Nagy Jr.	Michael Lord Jr.	Tarran DeLeon	J.A Vest

County	County Seat	County Judge	County Clerk	County Attorney	County Treasurer	Assessor–Collector	Sheriff
Galveston	Galveston	Mark Henry	Dwight D. Sullivan		Hank Dugie	Cheryl E. Johnson	Jimmy Fullen
Garza	Post	Lee Norman	Terri Laurence	Annhya Valez	LuAnne Terry	Nancy Wallace	Michael Isbell
Gillespie	Fredericksburg	Daniel Jones	Lindsey Brown	Sarah Neel	Vicki J. Schmidt	Carol Rode Durst	Chris Ayala
Glasscock	Garden City	Billy Ray Reynolds	Rebecca Batla	Joshua Hamby	Vikki Calloway	Tina Flores	Keith Burnett
Goliad	Goliad	Mike Bennett	Vickie Quinn	Terry Breen	Christina Hernandez	Michelle Garcia	Roy Boyd
Gonzales	Gonzales	Patrick C. Davis	Lona Ackman	Eduardo Xavier Escobar	Sheryl Barborak	Crystal Cedillo	Keith Schmidt
Gray	Pampa	Chris Porter	Dee Dee Laramore	Josh Seabourn	Terri Kitchens	Christie Johnson	Michael Ryan
Grayson	Sherman	Bruce Dawsey	Deana Patterson		Gayla Hawkins	Bruce Stidham	Tony Bennie
Gregg	Longview	Bill Stoudt	Michelle Gilley		*Office abolished 1-1-88.*	Michelle Terry	Maxey Cerliano
Grimes	Anderson	Joe Fauth III	Vanessa Burzynski	Megan Moody Barcak	Tom Maynard	Mary Ann Waters	Donald G. Sowell
Guadalupe	Seguin	Kyle Kutscher	Teresa Kiel	Dave Willborn	Linda Douglass	Daryl John	Joshua Ray
Hale	Plainview	David Mull	Christine Reyna	Jim Tirey	Ida A. Tyler	Israel Flores	David Cochran
Hall	Memphis	Ray Powell	Patricia Snyder	Harley Caudle	Janet Bridges	Teresa Altman	Tom Heck
Hamilton	Hamilton	James Yates	Cynthia K. Puff	Mark Henkes	Tonya Cox	Terry Payne Short	Justin Caraway
Hansford	Spearman	Tim Glass	Janet Torres	Cheryl Nelson	Cindy Lopez	Linda Cummings	Robert Mahaffee
Hardeman	Quanah	Ronald Ingram	Stella Doyal	Stanley Watson	Traysha Newsom	Jan Evans	Pat Laughery
Hardin	Kountze	Wayne McDaniel	Connie Becton	Matthew Minick	Deborah McWilliams	Shirley Cook	Mark Davis
Harris	Houston	Lina Hidalgo	Teneshia Hudspeth	Christian D. Menefee	Carla L. Wyatt	Ann Harris Bennett	Ed Gonzalez
Harrison	Marshall	Chad Sims	Liz James		Sherry Rushing	Veronica King	Brandon (BJ) Fletcher
Hartley	Channing	Ronnie Gordon	Melissa Mead	Robert Elliott	Dinkie Parman	Chanze Fowler	Chanze Fowler
Haskell	Haskell	Kenny Thompson	Belia Abila	Kris Fouts	Stacia Leach	Connie Benton	David Halliburton
Hays	San Marcos	Ruben Becerra	Elaine Cárdenas		Daphne Tenorio	Jenifer O'Kane	Gary Cutler
Hemphill	Canadian	Lisa Johnson	Sylvia Guerrero	Kyle Miller	Kay Smallwood	Chris Jackson	Brent Clapp
Henderson	Athens	Wade McKinney	Mary Margaret Wright	Clint Davis	Michael Bynum	Peggy Goodall	Botie Hillhouse
Hidalgo	Edinburg	Richard F. Cortez	Arturo Guajardo Jr.		Lita Leo	Pablo (Paul) Villarreal Jr.	J.E. (Eddie) Guerra
Hill	Hillsboro	Justin Lewis	Nicole Tanner	David Holmes	Rachel Parker	Krissi Hightower	Rodney B. Watson
Hockley	Levelland	Sharla Baldridge	Jennifer Nicole Palermo	Anna Hord	Kelli Martin	Debra C. Bramlett	Ray Scifres
Hood	Granbury	Ron Massingill	Katie Lang	Matthew A. Mills	Leigh Ann McCoy	Andrea Ferguson	Roger Deeds
Hopkins	Sulphur Springs	Robert Newsom	Tracy Smith	Dusty Rabe	Danny Davis	Debbie Pogue Mitchell	Lewis Tatum
Houston	Crockett	Jim L. Lovell	Terri Meadows	Daphne Lynette Session	Janis Omelina	Laronica Wooten Smith	Randy Hargrove
Howard	Big Spring	Randy Johnson	Brent Zitterkopf	Joshua Hamby	Sharon Adams	Tiffany Sayles	Stan Parker
Hudspeth	Sierra Blanca	Joanna (Jojo) Mackenzie	Brenda Sanchez		Blanca Rosa Santana	Patricia Rose	Arvin West
Hunt	Greenville	Bobby W. Stovall	Becky Landrum	G. Calvin Grogan	Brittni Turner	Randy L. Wineinger	Terry Jones
Hutchinson	Stinnett	Cindy Irwin	Kelly Ratliff	Craig Jones	Amy Back	Carrie Kimmell	Blaik Kemp
Irion	Mertzon	Molly Criner	Shirley Graham	James Ridge	Carolyn Huelster	Joyce Gray	W.A. Estes
Jack	Jacksboro	Brian Keith Umphress	Vanessa James	Michael Brad Dixon	Brad Campsey	Sharon Robinson	Thomas Spurlock
Jackson	Edna	Jill S. Sklar	Katherine R. Brooks		Mary Horton	Monica Foster	Kelly Janicka
Jasper	Jasper	Mark Allen	Holly Thomas		Rene Kelley-Ellis	Bobby Biscamp	Mitchel Newman
Jeff Davis	Fort Davis	Curtis Evans	Jennifer Wright	Teresa L. Todd	Dawn Kitts	William (Bill) Kitts	William (Bill) Kitts
Jefferson	Beaumont	Jeff Branick	Roxanne Acosta-Hellberg		Tim Funchess	Allison Nathan Getz	Zena Stephens
Jim Hogg	Hebbronville	Juan Carlos Guerra	Zonia G. Morales	Rodolfo Gutierrez	Gloria (Gigi) Benavides	Norma Liza S. Hinojosa	Erasmo Alarcon Jr.
Jim Wells	Alice	Pedro (Pete) Treviño Jr.	J.C. Perez III	Michael Guerra	Mark Dominguez	Mary Lozano	Danny Bueno
Johnson	Cleburne	Christopher Boedeker	April Long	Bill Moore	Kathy Blackwell	Scott Porter	Adam King
Jones	Anson	Dale Spurgin	LeeAnn Jennings	Chad Cowan	Kristian Smith	Gloria Little	Danny Jimenez
Karnes	Karnes City	Wade J. Hedtke	Carol Swize	David Chapman	Vi Swierc	Tammy Braudaway	Dwayne Villanueva

County	County Seat	County Judge	County Clerk	County Attorney	County Treasurer	Assessor–Collector	Sheriff
Kaufman	Kaufman	Jakie Allen	Laura Hughes		Chuck Mohnkern	Teressa Floyd	Bryan W. Beavers
Kendall	Boerne	Shane Stolarczyk	Denise Maxwell		Sheryl D'Spain	James Hudson	Al Auxier
Kenedy	Sarita	Charles Burns	Veronica Vela	Allison Strauss	Cynthia M. Salinas	Irma G. Longoria	Ramon Salinas III
Kent	Jayton	Layne Coulter	Craig Harrison	Katie Lackey	Christy Long	William Scogin	William Scogin
Kerr	Kerrville	Rob Kelly	Jackie (JD) Dowdy	Heather Stebbins	Tracy Soldan	Bob Reeves	Larry L. Leitha
Kimble	Junction	Harold (Hal) Rose	Karen E. Page	Andrew James Heap	Billie Stewart	Allen Castleberry	Allen Castleberry
King	Guthrie	Duane Lee Daniel	Jammye D. Timmons	George (Trey) Poage	Maggie Oliver	Amy McCauley	Michael R. McWhirter
Kinney	Brackettville	John Paul Schuster	Rick Alvarado	Brent Smith	Diana Gutierrez	Martha Peña-Padron	Brad Coe
Kleberg	Kingsville	Rudy Madrid	Salvador (Sonny) Barrera III	Kira Talip Sanchez	Priscilla Alaniz Cantu	Maria Victoria Valadez	Richard Kirkpatrick
Knox	Benjamin	Stan Wojcik	Lisa Cypert	Lina Reyes Treviño	Julie Bradley	Penny Eaton	Bridger Bush
Lamar	Paris	Brandon Bell	Ruth Sisson	Gary Young	Camey Boyer	Haskell Maroney	Scott Cass
Lamb	Littlefield	James M. DeLoach	Tonya Ritchie	Rickie Redman	Jerry Yarbrough	Tammy Kirkland	Gary Maddox
Lampasas	Lampasas	Randall J. Hoyer	Dianne Miller	John K. Greenwood	Melissa Karcher	Betty Salinas	Jesus (Jess) G. Ramos
La Salle	Cotulla	Leodoro Martinez III	Sonia Maldonado	Elizabeth Martinez	Maria Perez	Dora A. Gonzales	Anthony Zertuche
Lavaca	Hallettsville	Keith Mudd	Barbara K. Steffek	Kyle A. Denney	Karen Bludau	Deborah A. Sevcik	Micah Harmon
Lee	Giddings	Frank J. Malinak	Sharon Blasig	Martin Placke	Melinda (Lyndy) Krause	David Matthijetz	Casey Goetz
Leon	Centerville	Byron Ryder	Christie Wakefield	Keith Cook	Brandi S. Hill	Robin Shafer	Kevin Ellis
Liberty	Liberty	Jay H. Knight	Lee Haidusek Chambers	Matthew Poston	Kim Harris	Richard Brown	Robert (Bobby) Rader
Limestone	Groesbeck	Richard Duncan	Kerrie Cobb	William Roy DeFriend	Carol Pickett	Stacy L. Hall	Murray Agnew
Lipscomb	Lipscomb	Dori Artis	Kim Blau	Matthew D. Bartosiewicz	Kimberly L. Long	Gailan Winegarner	Ty Lane
Live Oak	George West	James Liska	Donna VanWay	Dwayne McWilliams	Kitley Moffatt-Wasicek	Deanna Atkinson	Larry Busby
Llano	Llano	Ron Cunningham	Marci Hadeler	Dwain K. Rogers	Cheryl Regmund	Kris Fogelberg	Bill Blackburn
Loving	Mentone	Skeet Lee Jones	Mozelle Carr	Steve Simonsen	Regina Wilkinson	Chris H. Busse	Chris H. Busse
Lubbock	Lubbock	Curtis Parrish	Kelly Pinion		Chris Winn	Ronnie Keister	Kelly S. Rowe
Lynn	Tahoka	Mike Braddock	Karen Strickland	Rebekah Filley	Amy Schuknecht	Donna Willis	Wanda Mason
Madison	Madisonville	Clark Osborne	Adrian Lawson		Judi Delesandri	Karen M. Lane	Bobby Adams
Marion	Jefferson	Leward J. LaFleur	Kim Wise	Angela Smoak	B.J. Westbrook	Karen Jones	David Capps
Martin	Stanton	Bryan Cox	Linda Gonzales	James Napper	Cynthia O'Donnell	Kathy Hull	Brad Ingram
Mason	Mason	Sheree Hardin	Pam Beam	Rebekah Whitworth	Ally Yonker	Joe Lancaster	Joe Lancaster
Matagorda	Bay City	Bobby Seiferman	Stephanie Wurtz	Jennifer Kim Chau	Loretta K. Griffin	Becky Cook	Frank D. Osborne
Maverick	Eagle Pass	Ramsey English Cantú	Sara Montemayor	Jaime (AJ) Iracheta	Rito Valdez	Asalia Casares	Tom Schmerber
McCulloch	Brady	Frank Trull	Christine Jones	Greg Torres	Mikkie Williams	Silvia Campos	Matt Andrews
McLennan	Waco	Scott Felton	Andy Harwell		Bill Helton	Randy H. Riggs	Parnell McNamara
McMullen	Tilden	James E. Teal	Mattie S. Sadovsky	Kimberly Kreider-Dusek	Jill Atkinson	Bessilia (Bessie) Guerrero	Emmett Shelton
Medina	Hondo	Keith Lutz	Gina Champion		Debbie Southwell	Melissa Lutz	Randy Brown
Menard	Menard	Brandon Corbin	Christy Eggleston	Luke Davis	Tami Russell	Tim Powell	Buck Miller
Midland	Midland	Terry Johnson	Alison Haley	Russell Malm	Sara Gray	Karen Hood	David Criner
Milam	Cameron	Bill Whitmire	Jodi Morgan	Bill Torrey	Linda Acosta	Sherry Mueck	Mike Clore
Mills	Goldthwaite	Jett J. Johnson	Sonya Scott	Gerald Hale	Summer Campbell	Lori King	Clint Hammonds
Mitchell	Colorado City	Mike Redwine	Carla Kern	Sterling T. Burleson II	Jennifer Rivera	Teresa Hughes	Patrick Toombs
Montague	Montague	Kevin Benton	Kim Jones	Clay V. Riddle	Jennifer Fenoglio	Kathryn Phillips	Marshall Thomas
Montgomery	Conroe	Mark J. Keough	L. Brandon Steinmann	B.D. Griffin	Melanie Bush	Tammy J. McRae	Rand Henderson
Moore	Dumas	Rowdy Rhoades	Brenda McKanna	Scott Higginbotham	Kara Milligan	Chris A. Rivera	Morgan W. Hightower
Morris	Daingerfield	Doug Reeder	Brittany Andrews	Ricky Shelton	Molly Cummings	Kim Thomasson	Jack Martin
Motley	Matador	James B. (Jim) Meador	D'anna Russell	Tom Edwards	Misty Jones	Ronda Miller	Robert Fisk

County	County Seat	County Judge	County Clerk	County Attorney	County Treasurer	Assessor–Collector	Sheriff
Nacogdoches	Nacogdoches	Greg Sowell	Sandra (Sandy) Yates	John Fleming	Denise Baublet	Kim Morton	Jason Bridges
Navarro	Corsicana	H.M. Davenport Jr.	Sherry Dowd		Ryan Douglas	Mike Dowd	Elmer Tanner
Newton	Newton	Ronald J. Cochran	Sandra K. Duckworth		Ginger Sims	Melissa J. Burks	Robert Burby
Nolan	Sweetwater	Whitley May	Sharla Keith	Samantha Morrow	Jeanne Wells	Kathy Bowen	David Warren
Nueces	Corpus Christi	Connie Scott	Kara Sands	Jenny P. Dorsey	*Office abolished 11-3-87.*	Kevin Kieschnick	J.C. Hooper
Ochiltree	Perryton	Charles E. Kelly	Sandra Limas	Jose N. Meraz	Tambra J. Kile	Linda Womble	Terry Bouchard
Oldham	Vega	Shawn Ballew	Darla Lookingbill	Kent Birdsong	Rebecca Hatfield	Linda Brown	Brent Warden
Orange	Orange	John Gothia	Brandy Robertson	John Kimbrough	Christy Khoury	Karen Fisher	Jimmy Lane Mooney
Palo Pinto	Palo Pinto	Shane Long	Janette K. Green	Maegan Kostiha	Deanna Copeland	Stacy L. Choate	Brett E. McGuire
Panola	Carthage	Rodger McLane	Bobbie Davis		Joni Reed	Holly Gibbs	Cutter Clinton
Parker	Weatherford	Pat Deen	Lila Deakle	John Forrest	Becky McCullough	Jenny Gentry	Russ Authier
Parmer	Farwell	Isabel (Izzy) Carrasco	Susie Spring	Jeff W. Actkinson	Sharon May	Awyna Sanchez	Eric Geske
Pecos	Fort Stockton	Joe Shuster	Liz Chapman	Frank Lacy	Sonia Murphy	Santa Acosta	Thomas J. (TJ) Perkins
Polk	Livingston	Sydney Murphy	Schelana Hock		Terri Williams	Leslie Jones Burks	Byron A. Lyons
Potter	Amarillo	Nancy Tanner	Julie Smith	Scott Brumley	Brooke Graves	Sherri Aylor	Brian Thomas
Presidio	Marfa	Jose Portillo Jr.	Florcita Zubia	Rod Ponton	Frances Garcia	Natalia Williams	Danny Dominguez
Rains	Emory	Linda Wallace	Mandy Sawyer	Robert Vititow	Teresa Northcutt	Sheila Floyd	Michael Hopkins
Randall	Canyon	Christy Dyer	Susan Allen		Angie Parker	Christina McMurray	Christopher Forbis
Reagan	Big Lake	Jim O'Bryan	Tammy Hodge	Michele Dodd	Leticia Quiñonez	Cynthia Aguilar	Jeff N. Garner
Real	Leakey	Bella A. Rubio	D'Ann Green	Bobby Jack Rushing	Jennifer Manchester	Terrie Pendley	Nathan T. Johnson
Red River	Clarksville	Robert Bridges	Shawn Weemes	Val Varley	Lorena De la Torre	Tonya R. Martin	Jimmy Caldwell
Reeves	Pecos	Leo Hung	Evangelina (Yvonne) Abila	Alva Alvarez	Zulema E. Rodriguez	Rosemary Chabarria	Arturo (Art) Granado
Refugio	Refugio	Jhiela (Gigi) Poynter	Ida Ramirez	Deborah A. Bauer	Rita Trojcak	Ida Turner	Raul (Pinky) Gonzales
Roberts	Miami	Mitchell D. Locke	Toni Rankin	William P. Weiman	Amy Tennant	Hether Williams	Bruce Skidmore
Robertson	Franklin	Joe David Scarpinato	Stephanie M. Sanders	W. Coty Siegert	Melinda Turner	Michael (Duba) Brewer	Gerald Yezak
Rockwall	Rockwall	Frank New	Jennifer Fogg		David Peek	Kim Sweet	Terry Garrett
Runnels	Ballinger	Julia Miller	Jennifer Hoffpauir	Ben Clayton	Laura Pospichal	Robin Burgess	Carl L. Squyres
Rusk	Henderson	Joel Hale	Trudy McGill	Micheal E. Jimerson	Andy Vinson	Nesha Partin	Johnwayne Valdez
Sabine	Hemphill	Daryl Melton	Jamie Clark	Robert G. Neal Jr.	Tricia Jacks	Martha M. Stone	Thomas N. Maddox
San Augustine	San Augustine	Jeff Boyd	Margo Noble	Jon Bates	Pam Smith	Regina Barthol	Robert Cartwright
San Jacinto	Coldspring	Fritz Faulkner	Dawn Wright		Dianna (Dee Dee) Adams	Betty Davis	Greg Capers
San Patricio	Sinton	David Krebs	Gracie Alaniz-Gonzales	Tamara Cochran-May	Denise Janak	Marcela Thormaehlen	Oscar Rivera
San Saba	San Saba	Jody Fauley	Kim Wells	Randall Robinson	Lois VanBeck	David Jenkins	David Jenkins
Schleicher	Eldorado	Charlie Bradley	Mary Ann Gonzalez	Clint T. Griffin	Jennifer L. Henderson	Vanessa Covarrubiaz	Jason Chatham
Scurry	Snyder	Dan Hicks	Melody Appleton	Michael Hartman	Kirsta Koennecke	Jana Young	Trey Wilson
Shackelford	Albany	John Viertel	Cheri Hawkins	Rollin Rauschl	Tammy Brown	Edward A. Miller	Edward A. Miller
Shelby	Center	Allison Harbison	Jennifer Fountain	John Price	Ann Blackwell	Debora Riley	Kevin Windham
Sherman	Stratford	Terri Beth Carter	Laura Rogers	Erin Lands Anchondo	Alicia Law	Kalee Flippin	Ted Allen
Smith	Tyler	Neal Franklin	Karen Phillips		Kelli R. White	Gary Barber	Larry Smith
Somervell	Glen Rose	Danny L. Chambers	Michelle Reynolds	Trey Brown	Valerie Williams	April Campos	Alan West
Starr	Rio Grande City	Eloy Vera	Humberto Gonzalez	Rene Montalvo	Romeo Gonzalez	Ameida Salinas	Rene (Orta) Fuentes
Stephens	Breckenridge	Michael Roach	Jackie Ensey	Gary Trammel	Sharon Trigg	Christie Latham	Kevin Roach
Sterling	Sterling City	Deborah Horwood	Jerri McCutchen	Lilli Hensley	Rhea McGinnis	Ellen Clark	Russell Irby
Stonewall	Aspermont	Ronnie Moorhead	Holly McLaury	Riley Branch	Anya Mullen	Lacy English	William (Bill) Mullen
Sutton	Sonora	Joseph Harris	Pam Thorp	Dawn Cahill	Janell Martin	Kathy Sanchez Marshall	DuWayne Castro

County	County Seat	County Judge	County Clerk	County Attorney	County Treasurer	Assessor–Collector	Sheriff
Swisher	Tulia	Harold Keeter	C.J. Chasco	J. Michael Criswell	Jolina Flowers	Deborah Lemons	Jim McCaslin
Tarrant	Fort Worth	Tim O'Hare	Mary Louise Nicholson		*Office abolished 4-2-83.*	Wendy Burgess	Bill E. Waybourn
Taylor	Abilene	Phil Crowley	Brandi DeRemer		Lesa Hart Crosswhite	Kay Middleton	Ricky Bishop
Terrell	Sanderson	Dale Lynn Carruthers	Raeline Thompson	Kenneth D. Bellah	Rebecca Luevano	Thaddeus C. (Thad) Cleveland	Thaddeus C. (Thad) Cleveland
Terry	Brownfield	Tony Serbantez	Kim Carter	Jo'Shae Ferguson-Worley	Andrea Perry	Rexann W. Furlow	Timothy Click
Throckmorton	Throckmorton	Caleb Hodges	Dianna Moore	Kris Fouts	Michelle Clark	Doc Wigington	Doc Wigington
Titus	Mount Pleasant	Kent Cooper	Leslie Brosnan	John Mark Cobern	Dana Wallace-Applewhite	Melissa Stevens	Tim C. Ingram
Tom Green	San Angelo	Lane Carter	Christina Ubando	Chris Taylor	Dianna Spieker	Becky Robles	J. Nick Hanna
Travis	Austin	Andy Brown	Dyana Limon-Mercado	Delia Garza	Dolores Ortega Carter	Bruce Elfant	Sally Hernandez
Trinity	Groveton	Danny Martin	Shasta Bergman	Colton Hay	Orrin Hargrave	Nancy Shanafelt	Woody Wallace
Tyler	Woodville	Milton Powers	Donece Gregory		Leann Monk	Lynnette Cruse	Bryan Weatherford
Upshur	Gilmer	Todd Tefteller	Terri Ross		Brandy Vick	Luana Howell	Larry Webb
Upton	Rankin	Dusty W. Kilgore	LaWanda McMurray	Paige Skehan	Vivian Venegas	Monica Zarate	William Mitch Upchurch
Uvalde	Uvalde	William R. Mitchell	Donna M. Williams	John Dodson	Joni Deorsam	Rita C. Verstuyft	Ruben Nolasco
Val Verde	Del Rio	Lewis Owens	Teresa Esther Chapoy	David E. Martinez	Aaron D. Rodriguez	Elodia Garcia	Joe Frank Martinez
Van Zandt	Canton	Andy Reese	Susan Strickland		Kenny Edwards	Misty Stanberry	Joe Carter
Victoria	Victoria	Ben Zeller	Heidi Easley		Paige Foster	Ashley Hernandez	Justin Marr
Walker	Huntsville	Colt Christian	Kari French		Amy Klawinsky	Diana L. McRae	Clint McRae
Waller	Hempstead	Carbett (Trey) J. Duhon III	Debbie Hollan	Elton Mathis	Joan Sargent	Ellen C. Shelburne	Troy Guidry
Ward	Monahans	Greg M. Holly	Denise Valles	Alan Nicholas	Carleigh Ennis	Vicki Heflin	Frarin Valle
Washington	Brenham	John Durrenberger	Beth A. Rothermel	Renee Ann Mueller	Peggy Kramer	Cheryl Gaskamp	Otto H. Hanak
Webb	Laredo	Tano E. Tijerina	Margie Ramirez Ibarra	Marco A. Montemayor	Raul Reyes	Patricia Barrera	Martin Cuellar
Wharton	Wharton	Phillip Spenrath	Barbara Svatek	G.A. (Trey) Maffett	Audrey Scearce	Cindy Hernandez	Shannon Srubar
Wheeler	Wheeler	Pat McDowell	Margaret Dorman	Leslie Timmons	Renee Warren	Cindy Brown	Johnny Carter
Wichita	Wichita Falls	Jim Johnson	Annette Stanley		Stephen Jones	Tommy Smyth	David Duke
Wilbarger	Vernon	Greg Tyra	Jana Kennon	Cornell Curtis	Joann Carter	Tissha Taylor	Brian Fritze
Willacy	Raymondville	Aurelio (Keter) Guerra	Susana R. Garza	Annette C. Hinojosa	Ruben Cavazos	Elizabeth Barnhart	Jose Salazar
Williamson	Georgetown	Bill Gravell Jr.	Nancy E. Rister	Doyle (Dee) Hobbs Jr.	D. Scott Heselmeyer	Larry Gaddes	Mike Gleason
Wilson	Floresville	Henry L. (Hank) Whitman Jr.	Genevieve Martinez	Tom Caldwell	Christina Mutz	Dawn Polasek Barnett	Jim Stewart
Winkler	Kermit	Charles M. Wolf	Pam Greene	Thomas Duckworth Jr.	Susan Willhelm	Minerva Soltero	Darin Mitchell
Wise	Decatur	J.D. Clark	Blanca Tuma	Che Rotramble	Katherine Hudson	Monte Shaw	Lane Akin
Wood	Quitman	Kevin White	Kelley Price		Daphne Carter	Carol Taylor	Kelly Cole
Yoakum	Plains	Michael C. Ybarra	Summer Lovelace		Darla Welch	Ann Saxon	David Bryant
Young	Graham	Edwin S. (Win) Graham, IV	Ann Ford	Chris Baran	Kathy Mishler	Christy Centers	Travis Babcock
Zapata	Zapata	Joe Rathmell	Mary Jayne Villarreal-Bonoan	Said Alfonso Figueroa	Romeo Salinas	Delia Mendoza	Raymundo Del Bosque
Zavala	Crystal City	Cindy Martínez-Rivera	Michelle B. Urrabazo	Eduardo Serna	Elizabeth Tovar	Rosario (Chari) Benavidez	Eusevio Salinas

TEXAS COUNTY AND DISTRICT OFFICIALS — TABLE NO. 2

County	District Clerk	District Attorney	Comm. Precinct 1	Comm. Precinct 2	Comm. Precinct 3	Comm. Precinct 4
Anderson	Teresia Coker	Allyson Mitchell	Greg Chapin	Rashad Mims	Kenneth Dickson	Joey Hill
Andrews	Sherry Dushane	Sean Galloway	Kerry Pack	Mark Savell	Jeneane Anderegg	Jim Waldrop
Angelina	Reba Squyres	Janet Cassels	Kent Walker	Kermit Kennedy	Terry Pitts	Kenneth Jeffrey
Aransas	Pam Heard		Jack Chaney	Leslie (Bubba) Casterline	Pat Rousseau	Bob Dupnik
Archer	Lori Rutledge	Casey Hall	Wade Scarbrough	Darin Wolf	Pat Martin III	Todd Herring
Armstrong	Tawnee Blodgett	Randall C. Sims	Shawn Smith	Clint Cornell	Robert Harris	Joe Neely
Atascosa	Margaret E. Littleton	Audrey Gossett Louis	Mark Gillespie	Mark Bowen	Eliseo Perez	Kennard (Bubba) Riley
Austin	Sue Murphy	Travis J. Koehn	Mark Lamp	Robert (Bobby) Rinn	Leroy Cerny	Chip Reed
Bailey	Becky Espinoza	Jackie R. Claborn II	Gary Don Gartin	Mike Slayden	Cody Black	Jim Daniel
Bandera	Tammy Kneuper	Stephen Harpold	Bruce Eliker	Greg P. Grothues	Jack Moseley	Jordan (Jody) Rutherford
Bastrop	Sarah Loucks	Bryan Goertz	Mel Hamner	Clara Beckett	Mark Meuth	David Glass
Baylor	Chris Jakubicek	Hunter Brooks	Rick Gillispie	Larry Elliott	Reed Slaggle	Jim Stout
Bee	Zenaida Silva	Jose Aliseda	Kristofer Linney	Dennis DeWitt	Sammy G. Farias	Tino Olivares
Bell	Joanna Staton	Henry Garza	Russell Schneider	Bobby Whitson	Bill Schumann	Louie Minor
Bexar	Gloria A. Martinez	Joe Gonzales	Rebeca Clay-Flores	Justin Rodriguez	Grant Moody	Tommy Calvert
Blanco	Celia Doyle	Wiley B. (Sonny) McAfee	Tommy Weir	Emil Ray Uecker	Chris Liesmann	Charles Riley
Borden	Jana Underwood	Ben R. Smith	Norman (Jibber) Herridge	Randy Adcock	Ernest Reyes	Greg Stansell
Bosque	Juanita Miller	Adam Sibley	Billy Hall	Terry Townley	Larry (Shotgun) Philipp	Ronny Liardon
Bowie	Lori Caraway	Jerry Rochelle	Sammy Stone	Tom Whitten	James Strain	Mike Carter
Brazoria	Cassandra Tigner	Tom Selleck	Donald (Dude) Payne	Ryan Cade	Stacy Adams	David Linder
Brazos	Gabriel Garcia	Jarvis Parsons	Steve Aldrich	Russ Ford	Nancy Berry	Irma Cauley
Brewster	Sarah Fellows Martinez	Ori T. White	Jim Westermann	Sara Allen Colando	Ruben Ortega	Mo Morrow
Briscoe	Amy Fuston	Emily Teegardin	Ken Wood	Jack Wellman	Danny Francis	John Burson
Brooks	Elvaray B. Silvas	Carlos Omar Garcia	Eduardo (Eddy) Garza	Rolando Gutierrez	Horacio Villareal III	Ernesto (Pepe) Williams
Brown	Cheryl Jones	Micheal Murray	Gary Worley	Joel Kelton	Wayne Shaw	Larry Traweek
Burleson	Dana Fritsche	Susan Deski	Dwayne Faust	Vincent Svec Jr.	David Hildebrand	Robert (Bobby) Urbanovsky
Burnet	Casie Walker	Wiley B. (Sonny) McAfee	Jim Luther Jr.	Damon Beierle	Billy Wall	Joe Don Dockery
Caldwell	Juanita Allen	Fred Weber	B.J. Westmoreland	Rusty Horne	Edward (Ed) Theriot	Dyral Thomas
Calhoun	Anna Kabela	Dan Heard	David Hall	Vern Lyssy	Joel Behrens	Gary Reese
Callahan	Sharon Owens	Shane Deel	Ashley McGowen	Bryan Farmer	Tom Windham	Erwin Clark
Cameron	Laura Perez-Reyes	Luis V. Saenz	Sofia C. Benavides	Joey Lopez	David A. Garza	Gus Ruiz
Camp	Kelly Gunn	David Colley	George French	Tommy Rozell	Perry Weeks	Steve Lindley
Carson	Gayla Cates	Luke M. Inman	Mike Britten	James Martin	Mike Jennings	Kevin Howell
Cass	Jamie Albertson	Courtney Shelton	Brett Fitts	Kevin Young	Paul Cothren	Darrell Godwin
Castro	JoAnna Blanco	Shalyn Hamlin	Paul Ramirez	Tim Elliott	Michael Goolsby	Ralph Brockman
Chambers	Patti L. Henry	Cheryl Swope Lieck	Jimmy Gore	Kenneth Mark Tice	Tommy Hammond	Ryan J. Dagley
Cherokee	Alison Dotson	Elmer Beckworth	Kelly Traylor	Steven Norton	Patrick Reagan	Billy McCutcheon
Childress	Barbara Spitzer	Luke Inman	Jeremy Hill	Mark Ross	Kevin Hackler	Rick Elliot

County	District Clerk	District Attorney	Comm. Precinct 1	Comm. Precinct 2	Comm. Precinct 3	Comm. Precinct 4
Clay	Marianne Bowles	Casey Hall	Richard Lowery	Jack Pickett	Retta Collins	Chase Broussard
Cochran	Lisa Smith	Angela Overman	Timothy Roberts	Matt Evans	Eric Silhan	Reynaldo Morin
Coke	Jennifer Burdett	Allison Palmer	Donald Robertson	Paul Williams	Marshall Millican	Joe Sefcik
Coleman	Darlene Huddle-Boyd	Heath Hemphill	Matt Henderson	Jim Rice	Scotty Lawrence	Alan Davis
Collin	Michael Gould	Greg Willis	Susan Fletcher	Cheryl Williams	Darrell Hale	Duncan Webb
Collingsworth	Jackie Johnson	Luke M. Inman	Farris Nation	James Ellis	Joel Sherwood	Richard Johnson
Colorado	Valerie Harmon	Jay E. Johannes	Doug Wessels	Ryan Brandt	Keith Neuendorff	Darrell Gertson
Comal	Heather Kellar	Jennifer Tharp	Donna Eccleston	Scott Haag	Kevin Webb	Jen Crownover
Comanche	Brandy Jones	Adam Sibley	Gary (Corky) Underwood	Russell Gillette	Sherman Sides	Jimmy Dale Johnson
Concho	Amber Hall	John Best	Trey Bradshaw	Eric Gully	Gary Gierisch	Keith Dillard
Cooke	Marci A. Gilbert	John Warren	Gary Hollowell	Jason Snuggs	Adam Arendt	Matt Sicking
Coryell	Becky Moore	Dusty Boyd	Kyle Matthews	Scott Weddle	Ryan Basham	Keith Taylor
Cottle	Vickey Wederski	Hunter Brooks	Arty Tucker	Steven Beck Jr.	Harvey Truelock	John B. Brothers
Crane	Janie Macias Hodges	Amanda Navarette	Manuella Kirkpatrick	Dennis Young	Domingo Escobedo	Danny Castro
Crockett	Ninfa Preddy	Laurie English	Elsa Fierro	G.L. Bunger V	Wesley Bean	Mike Medina Jr.
Crosby	Shari Smith	Michael Sales	Larry McCauley	Frank Mullins	Donald Kirksey	Kevin Langdon
Culberson	Linda McDonald	Bill D. Hicks	Frank Franco	Raul Rodriguez	Gilda Morales	Adrian Norman
Dallam	Terri Banks	Erin Lands Archondo	Carl McCarty	Corey Crabtree	Levi James	Floyd French
Dallas	Felicia Pitre	John Creuzot	Theresa Daniel	Andy Sommerman	John Wiley Price	Elba Garcia
Dawson	Adreana Gonzalez	Philip Mack Furlow	Mark Shofner	Ryan Webb	Nicky Goode	Russell Cox
Deaf Smith	Elaine Gerber	Chris Strowd	Chris Kahlich	Jerry O'Connor	Mike Brumley	Dale Artho
Delta	Janice Roberts	Will Ramsay	Morgan Baker	Jimmy Sweat	Anthony Roberts	Mark Brantley
Denton	David Trantham	Paul Johnson	Ryan Williams	Kevin Falconer	Bobbie J. Mitchell	Dianne Edmondson
DeWitt	Esther Ruiz	Robert C. Lassmann	Curtis G. Afflerbach	James B. Pilchiek Sr.	James Kaiser	Brian Carson
Dickens	Danay Carnes	Emily Teegardin	Dennis Wyatt	Mike Smith	Charles Morris	Greg Arnold
Dimmit	Maricela G. Gonzalez	Roberto Serna	Jose A. Urenda	Alonso G. Carmona	Juan Carmona	Valerie Rubalcaba
Donley	Fay Vargas	Luke M. Inman	Mark White	Daniel Ford	Neil Koetting	Dan Sawyer
Duval	Rachel S. Vela	G. Allen Ramirez	Pete Guerra	Adalberto (Chaico) Vera	Marla Garza	Marty Perez
Eastland	Chelsea Henry	Brad Stephenson	Andy Maxwell	James Crenshaw	Ronnie Wilson	Robert Rains
Ector	Clarissa Webster	Dusty Gallivan	Mike Gardner	Greg Simmons	Don Stringer	Billy Hall
Edwards	Olga Lydia Reyes	Tonya Ahlschwede	Marty H. Graham	Steve Smith	Matt Fry	Mike Grooms
Ellis	Melanie Reed	Ann Montgomery	Randy Stinson	Lane Grayson	Paul Perry	Kyle Butler
El Paso	Norma Favela Barceleau	Bill D. Hicks	Carlos Leon	David Stout	Iliana Holguin	Sergio Coronado
Erath	Wanda Greer	Alan Nash	Dee Stephens	Albert Ray	Joe Brown	Jim Buck
Falls	Laurie Smith	Kathryn (Jody) Gilliam	Milton Albright	F.A. Green	Jason Willberg	Nita Wuebker
Fannin	April Gibbs	Richard E. Glaser	Edwina Lane	A.J. Self	Jerry Magness	Doug Kopf
Fayette	Linda Svrcek	Peggy Supak	Jason McBroom	Luke Sternadel	Harvey Berckenhoff	Drew Brossmann
Fisher	Gina Pasley	Richard Thompson	Gordon Pippin	Dexter Elrod	Preston Martin	Micah Evans
Floyd	Patty Davenport	Emily Teegardin	Tanner R. Smith	Clint Bigham	Nathan Johnson	David Martinez
Foard	Debra Hopkins	John Staley Heatly	Ricky Hammonds	Rockne Wisdom	Larry Wright	Anthony Hinsley
Fort Bend	Beverley McGrew Walker	Brian Middleton	Vincent Morales Jr.	Grady Prestage	Andy Meyers	Dexter L. McCoy
Franklin	Ellen Jaggers	Will W Ramsay	Jerry Cooper	Toby Godfrey	Charlie Emerson	Scott Smith
Freestone	Teresa Black	Brian Evans	Andy Bonner	Will McSwane	Lloyd Lane	Clyde Ridge Jr.
Frio	Ofilia M. Treviño	Audrey Gossett Louis	Joe Vela	Mario Martinez	Raul Carrizales	Danny Cano

County	District Clerk	District Attorney	Comm. Precinct 1	Comm. Precinct 2	Comm. Precinct 3	Comm. Precinct 4
Gaines	Susan Murphree	Philip Mack Furlow	Brian Rosson	Josh Elder	David Murphree	Biz Houston
Galveston	John D. Kinard	Jack Roady	Darrell Apffel	Joe Giusti	Stephen D. Holmes	Robin Armstrong
Garza	Terri Laurence	Philip Mack Furlow	Jeff Williams	Kim Wilks	Ted Brannon	Giles W. Dalby Jr.
Gillespie	Jan Davis	Lucy Wilke	Charles Olfers	Keith Kramer	Dennis Neffendorf	Don Weinheimer
Glasscock	Rebecca Batla	Joshua Hamby	Charles Gully	Mark Halfmann	Brian Frerich	John Seidenberger
Goliad	Vickie Quinn	Rob Lassmann	Kenneth Edwards	David Young	Kirby Brumby	Kevin Fagg
Gonzales	Janice Sutton		K.O. (Dell) Whiddon	Donnie R. Brzozowski	Kevin T. La Fleur	Collie Boatright
Gray	Phyllis Carroll	Franklin McDonough	Logan Hudson	Lake Arrington	John Mark Baggerman	Jeff Haley
Grayson	Kelly Ashmore	J. Brett Smith	Jeff Whitmire	Art Arthur	Phyllis James	Matt Hardenburg
Gregg	Trey Hattaway	John Moore	Ronnie L. McKinney	Ray Bostick. Jr.	Floyd Wingo	Danny Craig Sr.
Grimes	Diane Leflore	Andria Bender	Chad Mallett	David Tullos	Barbara Walker	Phillip Cox
Guadalupe	Linda Balk		Greg Seidenberger	Drew Engelke	Michael Carpenter	Stephen Germann
Hale	Carla Cannon	Wally Hatch	Harold King	Jerry Bright	Vickie Milner	Benny Cantwell
Hall	Kaci Mills	Luke M. Inman	Ronny Wilson	Terry Lindsey	Gary Proffitt	Troy Glover
Hamilton	Sandy Layhew	Adam Sibley	Johnny Wagner	Keith Allen Curry	Lloyd Huggins	Dickie Clary
Hansford	Janet Torres	Mark Snider	Ira G. (Butch) Reed	Robert Whitaker	Tim Stedje	Wylee Maupin
Hardeman	Stella Doyal	Staley Heatly	Chris Call	Haden Braziel	Barry Haynes	Rodney Foster
Hardin	Dana Hogg	Rebecca Walton	L.W. Cooper Jr.	Chris Kirkendall	Amanda Young	Ernie Koch
Harris	Marilyn Burgess	Kim Ogg	Rodney Ellis	Adrian Garcia	Tom S. Ramsey	Lesley Briones
Harrison	Sherry Griffis	Reid McCain	William D. Hatfield	Zephaniah Timmins	Phillip Mauldin	Jay Ebarb
Hartley	Melissa Mead	Erin Lands Anchondo	David Vincent	David Spinhirne	Chad Hicks	Robert (Eutch) Owens
Haskell	Cynthia Jones	Mike Fouts	Jerry Don Garcia	Bill Steele	Matt Sanders	Russell Beakley
Hays	Avrey Anderson	Kelly Higgins	Debbie Ingalsbe	Michelle Cohen	Lon Shell	Walt Smith
Hemphill	Sylvia Guerrero	Franklin McDonough	Dawn E. Webb	Tim Alexander	Curt McPherson	Nicholas Thomas
Henderson	Betty Herriage	Jenny Palmer	Wendy Spivey	Scott Tuley	Charles (Chuck) McHam	Mark Richardson
Hidalgo	Laura Hinojosa	Ricardo Rodriguez Jr.	David L. Fuentes	Eduardo (Eddie) Cantu	Everardo (Ever) Villareal	Ellie Torres
Hill	Marchel Eubank	Mark Pratt	Jim Holcomb	Larry Crumpton	Scotty Hawkins	Martin Lake
Hockley	Oralie Gutierrez	Angela L. Overman	Alan Wisdom	Larry Carter	Seth Graf	Tommy Clevenger
Hood	Tonna Trumble Hitt	Ryan Sinclair	Kevin Andrews	Nannette Samuelson	Jack Wilson	Dave Eagle
Hopkins	Cheryl Fulcher	Will Ramsay	Mickey Barker	Greg Anglin	Wade Bartley	Joe Price
Houston	Laura Goolsby	Donna Gordon Kaspar	Gary Lovell	Willie Kitchen	Gene Stokes	Jimmy Henderson
Howard	Joanna Gonzales	Joshua Hamby	Eddilisa Ray	Cash Berry	Jimmie Long	Doug Wagner
Hudspeth	Brenda Sanchez	Bill D. Hicks	Andrew Virdell	Sergio Quijas	Johny Sheets	Canuto Mariscal
Hunt	Susan Spradling	Noble D. Walker	Mark Hutchins	David Monroe	Phillip Martin	Steven Harrison
Hutchinson	Tammy McBrayer	Mark Snider	Gary Alexander	Dwight Kirksey	Ben Bentley	Chris Prock
Irion	Shirley Graham	Allison Palmer	Tia Paxton	Jeff Davidson	John Nanny	Bill (Beaver) McManus III
Jack	Tracie Pippin	James Stainton	Gary Oliver	Kenny Salazar	Henry Birdwell Jr.	Terry Ward
Jackson	Sharon Mathis	Pam Guenther	Wayne Hunt	Wayne Bubela	Glenn Martin	Dennis Karl
Jasper	Rosa Norsworthy	Anne Pickle	Seth Martindale	Kevin Holloway	Willie Stark	Dennis Marks
Jeff Davis	Jennifer Wright	Ori T. White	Jody Adams	Roy Hurley	John Davis	Royce Laskoske
Jefferson	Jamie Smith	Keith Giblin	Vernon Pierce	Cary Erickson	Michael Sinegal	Everette (Bo) Alfred
Jim Hogg	Zonia G. Morales	Gocha A. Ramirez	Antonio (Tony) Flores III	Abelardo Alaniz	Sandalio Ruiz	Cynthia Guerra Betancourt
Jim Wells	R. David Guerrero	Carlos Omar Garcia	Margie H. Gonzalez	Ventura Garcia	Renee Kirchoff Chapa	Wicho Gonzalez
Johnson	David Lloyd	Dale Hanna	Rick Bailey	Kenny Howell	Mike White	Larry Woolley

County	District Clerk	District Attorney	Comm. Precinct 1	Comm. Precinct 2	Comm. Precinct 3	Comm. Precinct 4
Jones	Lacey Hansen	Joe Edd Boaz	Roy Spalding	Lonnie Vivian	Ross Davis	Joel Spraberry
Karnes	Denise Rodriguez	Audrey Gossett Louis	Shelby Dupnik	Benny Lyssy	James Rosales	Wesley Gisler
Kaufman	Rhonda Hughey	Erleigh Norville Wiley	Mike Hunt	Skeet Phillips	Terry Barber	Tommy Moore
Kendall	Susan Jackson	Nicole S. Bishop	Christina Bergmann	Andra M. Wisian	Richard Chapman	Chad Carpenter
Kenedy	Veronica Vela	John T. Hubert	Joe Recio	Israel Vela Jr.	Sarita Armstrong Hixon	Jose Salazar
Kent	Craig Harrison	Mike Fouts	Roy W. Chisum	Don Long	Daryl Ham	Robert Graham
Kerr	Dawn Lantz	Stephen Harpold (198th); Lucy Wilke (216th)	Harley David Belew	Rich Paces	Jonathan Letz	Don Harris
Kimble	Karen E. Page	Tonya Ahlschwede	Brayden Schulze	Kelly Simon	Dennis Dunagan	Kenneth Hoffman
King	Jammye D. Timmons	Hunter Brooks	Reggie Hatfield	Chris McCauley	Dwayne Green	Jay Hurt
Kinney	Rick Alvarado	Suzanne West	Mark Frerich	Joe Montalvo	Dennis Dodson	Tim Ward
Kleberg	Jennifer Whittington	John T. Hubert	David Rosse	Chuck Schultz	Jerry Martinez	Marcus Salinas
Knox	Lisa Cypert	Hunter Brooks	Johnny McCown	Kim Sealy	Ray Herring	Nathan Urbanczyk
Lamar	Shawntel Golden	Gary Young	Alan Skidmore	Lonnie Layton	Ronnie Bass	Kevin Anderson
Lamb	Debbie Long	Rickie Redman	Cory DeBerry	Kent Lewis	Danny Short	Lee Logan
Lampasas	Edith Wagner Harrison	John K. Greenwood	Bobby Carroll	Jamie Smart	Lewis Bridges	Mark Rainwater
La Salle	Sonia Maldonado	Audrey Gossett Louis	Noel Niavez	Joaquin Alba	Erasmo Ramirez Jr.	Raul Ayala
Lavaca	Lori A. Wenske	Kyle A. Denney	Edward Pustka	Wayne Faircloth	Kenny Siegel	Dennis W. Kocian
Lee	Lisa Teinert	Martin Placke	Mark Matthijetz	Richard Wagner	Alan Turner	Steven Knobloch
Leon	Cassandra Noey	James (Caleb) Henson	Joey Sullivan	Newman Paul Bing	Kyle Workman	Thomas J. Foley
Liberty	Delia Sellers	Jennifer L. Bergman	Bruce Karbowski	Greg Arthur	David S. Whitmire	Leon Wilson
Limestone	Carol Jenkins	William Roy DeFriend	Bill David Sadler	Micah Anderson	Stephen Friday	Bobby Forrest
Lipscomb	Kim Blau	Franklin McDonough	Juan Cantu	Merle Miller	Scotty Schilling	Dan Cockrell
Live Oak	Melanie Matkin	Jose Aliseda	Richard Lee	Randy Kopplin	Mitchell Williams	Lucio Morin
Llano	Ashley Inge	Wiley B. (Sonny) McAfee	Peter R. Jones	Linda Raschke	Mike Sandoval	Jerry Don Moss
Loving	Mozelle Carr	Randall (Randy) Reynolds	Harlan Hopper	Ysidro (Joe) Renteria	Raymond W. King	Brad Cook
Lubbock	Sara L. Smith	K. Sunshine Stanek	Terence Kovar	Jason Corley	Gilbert A. Flores	Jordan Rackler
Lynn	Courtney Odom	Philip Mack Furlow	Mark Woodley	John Hawthorne	Don Blair	Larry Durham
Madison	Rhonda Savage	Courtney Cain	Ken Starr	Carl Wiseman	Carl L. Cannon	David Pohorelsky
Marion	Susan Anderson	Angela Smoak	J.R. Ashley	Jacob Pattison	Ralph Meisenheimer	Gered Lee
Martin	Linda Gonzales	Joshua hamby	Kenny Stewart	Auggie Ramos	Bobby Holland	Koy Blocker
Mason	Pam Beam	Tonya Ahlschwede	Reggie Loeffler	Fred Estes	Buddy Schuessler	Dave Underwood
Matagorda	Janice L. Hawthorne	Steven Reis	Edward (Bubba) Cook	Mike Estlinbaum	Troy Shimek	Charles (Bubba) Frick
Maverick	Leopoldo Vielma	Roberto Serna	Gerardo (Jerry) Morales	Rosanna (Roxi) Rios	Olga Ramos	Roberto Ruiz
McCulloch	Michelle Pitcox	Tonya Ahlschwede	Carol Anderson	Randy Deans	Jason Behrens	Don Bratton
McLennan	Jon Gimble	Josh Tetens	Jim Smith	Patricia Miller	Will Jones	Ben Perry
McMullen	Mattie S. Sadovsky	Jose Aliseda	Larry Garcia	Murray Swaim	Scotty McClaugherty	Max Quintanilla Jr.
Medina	Cindy Fowler	Mark P. Haby	Tim Neuman	Larry Sittre	David Lynch	Daniel Lawler
Menard	Christy Eggleston	Tonya Ahlschwede	Frank Davis	Jay Cunningham	Ed Keith	Tyler Wright
Midland	Alex (Lex) Archuleta	Laura A. Noldolf	Scott Ramsey	Jeff Somers	Luis Sánchez	Dianne Anderson
Milam	Karen Berry	Bill Torrey	Henry (Hub) Hubnik	James Denman	Art Neal	Wesley Payne
Mills	Sonya Scott	Micheal Murray	Mike Wright	Robert Head	Dale Partin	Jason Williams
Mitchell	Belinda Blassingame	Ricky Thompson	Dennis Jones	Jeremy Strain	Jesse Munoz	Ricky Bailey
Montague	Robin Woods	Casey Hall	Roy Darden	Mike Mayfield	Mark Murphey	Bob Langford

County	District Clerk	District Attorney	Comm. Precinct 1	Comm. Precinct 2	Comm. Precinct 3	Comm. Precinct 4
Montgomery	Melisa Miller	Brett Ligon	Robert C. Walker	Charlie Riley	James Noack	Matt Gray
Moore	Mayra Rivero	Erin Lands Anchondo	Daniel Garcia	Miles Mixon	Dee Vaughan	Colt Farni
Morris	Gwen Ashworth	Ricky Shelton	Greg Frazier	Kerry McCoy	Michael Clair	Todd Freeman
Motley	D'anna Russell	Emily Teegardin	Douglas Campbell	Roegan Cruse	Franklin Jameson	Timmy Brooks
Nacogdoches	Loretta Cammack	Andrew Jones	Jerry Don Williamson	Sandy McCorvey	Robin Dawley	Mark Harkness
Navarro	Joshua B. Tackett	William Thompson	Jason Grant	Eddie Perry	Eddie Moore	David Brewer
Newton	Nikki Windham	Courtney Tracy Ponthier	Danny Bentsen	Phillip A. White	Gary Fomby	Leanord (Bubba) Powell
Nolan	Jamie Clem	Richard Thompson	Terry Willman	Seth Mahaffey	Tommy White	Henry Ortega Jr.
Nueces	Anne Lorentzen	Mark A. Gonzalez	Robert Hernandez	Joe A. (JAG) Gonzalez	John Marez	Brent Chesney
Ochiltree	Shawn Bogard	Jose N. Meraz	Duane Pshigoda	Joe Johnson	JW DeWitt	Kevin Walker
Oldham	Darla Lookingbill		Quincy Taylor	Jim Watkins	Roger Morris	Daniel Gruhlkey
Orange	Anne Reed	John Kimbrough	Johnny Trahan	Chris Sowell	Kirk Roccaforte	Robert Viator
Palo Pinto	Jonna Banks	Kriste Burnett	Gary Glover	Mike Reed	Mike Pierce	Jeff Fryer
Panola	Lindsey Smith	Danny Buck Davidson	Billy Alexander	David A. Cole	Craig M. Lawless	Dale LaGrone
Parker	Sharena Gilliland	Jeff Swain	George Conley	Jacob Holt	Larry Walden	Mike Hale
Parmer	Sandra Warren	Jackie R. Claborn II	Kirk Frye	Charles Wilkins	Kenny White	Casey Russell
Pecos	Darla Cude	Ori T. White (83rd); Laurie English (112th)	Tom Chapman	Robert Gonzales	Mickey Jack Perry	Nathan Reeves
Polk	Bobbye Richards	Shelly Bush-Sitton	Guylene Robertson	Mark DuBose	Milt Purvis	Jerry Cassity
Potter	Stephnie Menke	Randall Sims	H.R. Kelly	Blair Schaffer	John Coffee	Warren Coble Sr.
Presidio	Florcita Zubia	Ori T. White	Brenda Silva Bentley	Margarito Hernandez	Jose Cabezuela	David Beebe
Rains	Laura Pate	Robert Vititow	Jeremy Cook	Mike Willis	Korey Young	Lori Northcutt
Randall	Joel Forbis	Robert Love	Rusty Carnes	Eric Barry	Bob Robinson	Tam Boatler
Reagan	Tammy Hodge	Laurie English	Mike Vargas	Tim Sellman	Tommy Holt	Mary Loftin
Real	D'Ann Green	Christina Mitchell Busbee	Brad Hart	Shawn D. Gray	Ramon Ybarra	Charles E. Hunger
Red River	Brenna Williams	Val Varley	Donnie Gentry	David Hutson	Jeff Moore	Bruce Emery
Reeves	Julia Perez	Randall W. Reynolds	Rojelio Alvarado	Israel Campos	Paul Hinojos	Tony Trujillo
Refugio	Sylvia M. Lopez	Robert C. Lassmann	Roy Payne	Stanley Tuttle	Gary Lee Wright	Blaine Wolfshohl
Roberts	Toni Rankin	Franklin McDonough	Cleve Wheeler	William Gill	Kelly Flowers	James F. Duvall
Robertson	Barbara W. Axtell	W. Coty Siegert	Ty Rampy	Donald Threadgill	Chuck Hairston	James Taylor
Rockwall	Lea Carlson	Kenda Culpepper	Cliff Sevier	Dana Macalik	Dennis Bailey	John Stacy
Runnels	Tammy Burleson	John Best	Carl King	Chris Ocker	Brandon Poehls	Juan Ornelas
Rusk	Terri Pirtle Willard	Micheal E. Jimerson	Randy Gaut	Robert Kuykendall	Greg Gibson	Bennie Whitworth
Sabine	Lisa Pitre	Paul A. Robbins	Brent Cox	Keith Nabours	Stanley Jacks	James Lowe
San Augustine	Jeanette Bryan	Paul A. Robbins	Tommy Pickard	Daniel Holman	Joey Holloway	Steve Bryan
San Jacinto	Tammy Currie	Todd Dillon	Laddie McAnally	Donny Marrs	David Brandon	Mark Nettuno
San Patricio	Heather B. Marks	Samuel B. Smith	Sonia Lopez	Tom Yardley	Lilly Wilkinson	Howard Gillespie
San Saba	Kim Wells	Wiley B. (Sonny) McAfee	James Lebow	Mike Poe	Kenley Kroll	Greg McGregor
Schleicher	Mary Ann Gonzalez	Allison Palmer	Gary Gibson	Steve Nelson	Kirk Griffin	Chris Meador
Scurry	Candace Jones	Ben Smith	Terry D. Williams	Doug Scott	Shawn McCowen	Jeff Mitchell
Shackelford	Cheri Hawkins	Joe Edd Boaz	Steve Riley	Ace Reames	Lanham Martin	Cody Jordan
Shelby	Lori Oliver	Karren Price	Roscoe McSwain	Jimmy Lout	Stevie Smith	Tom Bellmyer
Sherman	Laura Rogers	Erin Lands Anchondo	Dan Law	Terry Mathews	Jeff Crippen	David Davis
Smith	Penny Clarkston	Jacob Putman	Pam Frederick	John Moore	Terry Lee Phillips	Ralph Caraway Sr.

County	District Clerk	District Attorney	Comm. Precinct 1	Comm. Precinct 2	Comm. Precinct 3	Comm. Precinct 4
Somervell	Virginia Dickson	Dale Hanna	Jeff Harris	Richard Talavera	Tammy Ray	Wade Busch
Starr	Orlando Velasquez	Gocha A. Ramirez	Jose Francisco (Kiki) Perez	Raul (Roy) Peña III	Eloy Garza	Ruben D. Saenz
Stephens	Christie Coapland	Dee Hudson Peavy	David Fambro	Mark McCullough	William H. Warren	Eric O'Dell
Sterling	Jerri McCutchen	Allison Palmer	Ross Copeland	Edward Michulka Jr.	Tommy Wright Jr.	Reed Stewart
Stonewall	Holly McLaury	Mike Fouts	Charles (Shorty) Martin	Gerry Messick	Billy Kirk Meador	Gary Myers
Sutton	Pam Thorp	Laurie K. English	Lee C. Bloodworth	Bob Brockman	Carl Teaff	Harold Martinez
Swisher	C.J. Chasco	J. Michael Criswell	Lloyd Rahlfs	Danny Morgan	Joe Murrell	Larry Buske
Tarrant	Thomas A. Wilder	Phil Sorrells	Roy Charles Brooks	Alisa Simmons	Gary Fickes	Manny Ramirez
Taylor	Tammy Robinson	James Hicks	Randall D. Williams	Kyle Kendrick	Brad Birchum	Chuck Statler
Terrell	Raeline Thompson	Suzanne West	Adam Johnson	Lupe Garza	Arnulfo Serna	Gene Chavez
Terry	Tiffany O'Briant	Jo'Shae Ferguson-Worley	Mike Swain	Richard Cavazos	Martin Lefevere	Ernesto Elizardo
Throckmorton	Dianna Moore	Mike Fouts	Casey Wells	Kasey Hibbitts	Greg Brockman	Klay Mitchell
Titus	Marcus Carlock	David Colley	Jeff Parchman	Joe D. Mitchell	Dana Applewhite	Jimmy Parker
Tom Green	Anthony Joseph Monico	Allison Palmer (51st); John H. Best (119th)	Ralph Hoelscher	Sammy Farmer	Rick Bacon	Shawn Nanny
Travis	Velva L. Price	José Garza	Jeff Travillion	Brigid Shea	Ann Howard	Margaret Gómez
Trinity	Jillian Steptoe	Bennie L. Schiro	Tommy Park	Mike Loftin	Neal Smith	Steven Truss
Tyler	Pamela Reneé Crews	Lucas Babin	Joe Blacksher	Doug Hughes	Mike Marshall	Charles (Buck) Hudson
Upshur	Nicole Hernandez	Billy Byrd	Gene Dolle	Dustin Nicholson	Michael Ashley	Jay Miller
Upton	LaWanda McMurray	Laurie English	Pete Jackson	Cody Owens	Mike Smart	Cody Zamora
Uvalde	Christina J. Ovalle	Christina Mitchell Busbee	John Yeackle	Mariano Pargas Jr.	Jerry W. Bates	Ronald (Ronnie) Garza
Val Verde	Jo Ann Cervantes	Suzanne West	Martin Wardlaw	Juan Carlos Vazquez	Robert Beau Nettleton	Gustavo (Gus) Flores
Van Zandt	Karen L. Wilson	Tonda Curry	Chad LaPrade	Virgil Melton Jr.	Keith Pearson	Brandon Barton
Victoria	Kim Plummer	Constance Filley Johnson	Danny Garcia	Jason Ohrt	Gary Burns	Kenneth Saxton
Walker	Leslie Woolley	Will Durham	Danny Kuykendall	Ronnie White	Bill Daugette	Brandon Decker
Waller	Liz Pirkle	Elton Mathis	John A. Amsler	Walter E. Smith	Kendric D. Jones	Justin Beckendorff
Ward	Valerie Romo	Randall W. Reynolds	Tino Sanchez	Larry Hanna	Dexter Nichols	Eddie Nelms
Washington	Tammy Brauner	Julie Renken	Don Koester	Candice Bullock	Kirk Hanath	Dustin Majewski
Webb	Esther Degollado	Isidro R. (Chilo) Alaniz	Jesse Gonzalez	Rosaura (Wawi) Tijerina	John Galo	Ricardo A. Jaime
Wharton	Kendra Charbula	Dawn Elizabeth Allison	Richard Zahn	Bud Graves	Steven Goetsch	Doug Mathews
Wheeler	Sherri Jones	Franklin McDonough	Jackie Don May Jr.	Phillip Gaines	David Simpson	John Walker
Wichita	Leslee Mannon	John Gillespie	Mark Beauchamp	Mickey Fincannon	Barry Mahler	Jeff Watts
Wilbarger	Brenda Peterson	Staley Heatly	Billy Taylor	Phillip Graf	Scott Inglish	Josh Patterson
Willacy	Isabel Adame	Annette C. Hinojosa	Eliberto (Beto) Guerra	Mario Tijerina	Henry De La Paz	Ernie Garcia
Williamson	Lisa David	Shawn Dick	Terry Cook	Cynthia Long	Valerie Covey	Russ Boles
Wilson	Deborah Bryan	Audrey Gossett Louis	Gary Martin	Russell A. King	Jeffery Pierdolla	John (Scott) Akin
Winkler	Geneva Baker	Amanda Navarette	Billy J. Stevens	Robbie Wolf	Victor Berzoza	Billy Ray Thompson
Wise	Loucrecia Biggerstaff	James Stainton	Biff Hayes	Kevin D. Burns	Danny Lambert	Colby Shawn
Wood	Suzy Wright	Angela Albers	Virgil Holland	Jerry Gaskill	Mike Simmons	Russell Acker
Yoakum	Sandra Roblez	Bill Helwig	Woodson W. Lindsey	Ray Marion	Tommy Box	Tim Addison
Young	Jamie Freeze Land	Dee Peavy	Stacy Creswell	Scott Shook	Stacey Rogers	Jimmy Wiley
Zapata	Dora Martinez Castañon	Isidro R. (Chilo) Alaniz	Paco Mendoza	Olga M. Elizondo	Jose A. Solis	Norberto Garza
Zavala	Rachel Ramirez	Robert Serna	Joe Cruz	Raul Gomez	Jesse Gonzalez	Florencio (Flo) Melendrez

★

REGIONAL COUNCILS

The concept of regional planning and cooperation, fostered by enabling legislation in 1965, has spread across Texas since the organization of the North Central Texas Council of Governments in 1966.

Regional councils are voluntary associations of local governments that deal with problems and planning needs that cross the boundaries of individual local governments or that require regional attention.

These concerns include: criminal justice, emergency communications, job-training programs, solid-waste management, transportation, and water-quality management. The councils make recommendations to member governments and may assist in implementing the plans. Financing is provided by local, state, and federal governments.

The Texas Association of Regional Councils is located in Austin. Following is a list of the 24 regional councils and its member counties.

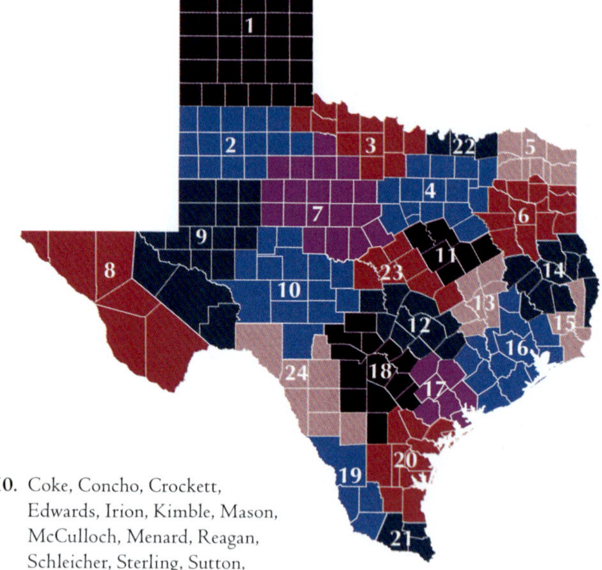

1. Armstrong, Briscoe, Carson, Castro, Childress, Collingsworth, Dallam, Deaf Smith, Donley, Gray, Hall, Hansford, Hartley, Hemphill, Hutchinson, Lipscomb, Moore, Ochiltree, Oldham, Parmer, Potter, Randall, Roberts, Sherman, Swisher, and Wheeler
2. Bailey, Cochran, Crosby, Dickens, Floyd, Garza, Hale, Hockley, King, Lamb, Lubbock, Lynn, Motley, Terry, and Yoakum
3. Archer, Baylor, Clay, Cottle, Foard, Hardeman, Jack, Montague, Wichita, Wilbarger, and Young
4. Collin, Dallas, Denton, Ellis, Erath, Hood, Hunt, Johnson, Kaufman, Navarro, Palo Pinto, Parker, Rockwall, Somervell, Tarrant, and Wise
5. Bowie, Cass, Delta, Franklin, Hopkins, Lamar, Morris, Red River, and Titus
6. Anderson, Camp, Cherokee, Gregg, Harrison, Henderson, Marion, Panola, Rains, Rusk, Smith, Upshur, Van Zandt, and Wood
7. Brown, Callahan, Coleman, Comanche, Eastland, Fisher, Haskell, Jones, Kent, Knox, Mitchell, Nolan, Runnels, Scurry, Shackelford, Stephens, Stonewall, Taylor, and Throckmorton
8. Brewster, Culberson, El Paso, Hudspeth, Jeff Davis, Presidio, and Doña Ana County, N.M.
9. Andrews, Borden, Crane, Dawson, Ector, Gaines, Glasscock, Howard, Loving, Martin, Midland, Pecos, Reeves, Terrell, Upton, Ward, and Winkler
10. Coke, Concho, Crockett, Edwards, Irion, Kimble, Mason, McCulloch, Menard, Reagan, Schleicher, Sterling, Sutton, and Tom Green
11. Bosque, Falls, Freestone, Hill, Limestone, and McLennan
12. Bastrop, Blanco, Burnet, Caldwell, Fayette, Hays, Lee, Llano, Travis, and Williamson
13. Brazos, Burleson, Grimes, Leon, Madison, Robertson, and Washington
14. Angelina, Houston, Nacogdoches, Newton, Polk, Sabine, San Augustine, San Jacinto, Shelby, Trinity, and Tyler
15. Hardin, Jasper, Jefferson, and Orange
16. Austin, Brazoria, Chambers, Colorado, Fort Bend, Galveston, Harris, Liberty, Matagorda, Montgomery, Walker, Waller, and Wharton
17. Calhoun, DeWitt, Goliad, Gonzales, Jackson, Lavaca, and Victoria
18. Atascosa, Bandera, Bexar, Comal, Frio, Gillespie, Guadalupe, Karnes, Kendall, Kerr, McMullen, Medina, and Wilson
19. Jim Hogg, Starr, Webb, and Zapata
20. Aransas, Bee, Brooks, Duval, Jim Wells, Kenedy, Kleberg, Live Oak, Nueces, Refugio, and San Patricio
21. Cameron, Hidalgo, and Willacy
22. Cooke, Fannin, and Grayson
23. Bell, Coryell, Hamilton, Lampasas, Milam, Mills, and San Saba
24. Dimmit, Kinney, La Salle, Maverick, Real, Uvalde, Val Verde, and Zavala

Source: Texas Association of Regional Councils.

WET-DRY COUNTIES

Although the laws regulating the alcoholic beverage industry are consistent statewide, the Alcoholic Beverage Code allows for local-option elections to determine the types of alcoholic beverages that may be sold and how they can be sold.

Elections can be held by counties, cities, or individual justice of the peace precincts. In the time since our last edition went to press, one county moved from Part Wet to Wet: Dallam.

As of March 2025, there were 60 completely wet counties in Texas and three completely dry counties.

Texas has become "wetter" over time. In 2003, there were 35 completely wet counties and 51 completely dry. In 1995, there were 53 dry counties, and in 1986, there were 62 dry counties. The following list reflects the wet, part wet, and dry coding on the map.

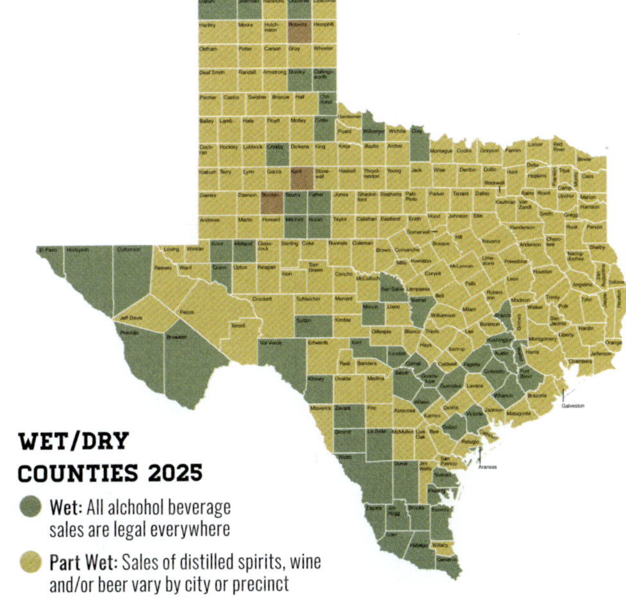

COUNTIES THAT ARE PARTIALLY WET (191):
Anderson, Andrews, Angelina, Archer, Armstrong, Atascosa, Bailey, Bandera, Bastrop, Baylor, Bee, Bell, Blanco, Bosque, Bowie, Brazoria, Briscoe, Brown, Burleson, Caldwell, Calhoun, Callahan, Camp, Carson, Cass, Castro, Chambers, Cherokee, Cochran, Coke, Coleman, Collin, Comanche, Concho, Cooke, Coryell, Crockett, Dallas, Dawson, Deaf Smith, Delta, Denton, DeWitt, Dickens, Eastland, Edwards, Ellis, Erath, Falls, Fannin, Floyd, Foard, Franklin, Freestone, Frio, Gaines, Galveston, Garza, Gillespie, Glasscock, Gray, Grayson, Gregg, Grimes, Hale, Hall, Hamilton, Hansford, Hardeman, Hardin, Harris, Harrison, Hartley, Haskell, Hays, Hemphill, Henderson, Hill, Hockley, Hood, Hopkins, Houston, Howard, Hunt, Hutchinson, Irion, Jack, Jackson, Jasper, Jeff Davis, Jefferson, Jim Wells, Johnson, Jones, Karnes, Kaufman, Kimble, King, Knox, Lamar, Lamb, Lampasas, Lavaca, Lee, Leon, Liberty, Limestone, Lipscomb, Live Oak, Llano, Loving, Lubbock, Lynn, Madison, Marion, Martin, Matagorda, Maverick, McCulloch, McLennan, McMullen, Medina, Menard, Milam, Mills, Montague, Montgomery, Moore, Morris, Motley, Nacogdoches, Navarro, Newton, Oldham, Orange, Palo Pinto, Panola, Parker, Parmer, Pecos, Polk, Potter, Rains, Randall, Reagan, Real, Red River, Reeves, Refugio, Robertson, Rockwall, Runnels, Rusk, Sabine, San Augustine, San Jacinto, San Patricio, Schleicher, Shackelford, Shelby, Smith, Somervell, Stephens, Sterling, Stonewall, Swisher, Tarrant, Taylor, Terrell, Terry, Throckmorton, Titus, Tom Green, Travis, Trinity, Tyler, Upshur, Upton, Uvalde, Van Zandt, Walker, Ward, Wheeler, Wichita, Willacy, Williamson, Winkler, Wise, Wood, Yoakum, Young.

COUNTIES WHERE ALL ALCOHOLIC BEVERAGE SALES ARE LEGAL EVERYWHERE (60):
Aransas, Austin, Bexar, Brazos, Brewster, Brooks, Burnet, Cameron, Childress, Clay, Collingsworth, Colorado, Comal, Cottle, Crane, Crosby, Culberson, Dallam, Dimmit, Donley, Duval, Ector, El Paso, Fayette, Fisher, Fort Bend, Goliad, Gonzales, Guadalupe, Hidalgo, Hudspeth, Jim Hogg, Kendall, Kenedy, Kerr, Kinney, Kleberg, La Salle, Mason, Midland, Mitchell, Nolan, Nueces, Ochiltree, Presidio, San Saba, Scurry, Sherman, Starr, Sutton, Val Verde, Victoria, Waller, Washington, Webb, Wharton, Wilbarger, Wilson, Zapata, Zavala.

COUNTIES WHERE NO SALES OF ALCOHOLIC BEVERAGES ARE LEGAL ANYWHERE (3):
Borden, Kent, Roberts.

Source: Texas Alcoholic Beverage Commission.

UNSPLASH/CALEB FISHER

Texas

FEDERAL GOVERNMENT

UNSPLASH / TIM MOSSHOLDER

TEXANS IN CONGRESS

Texas has two members in the U.S. Senate and was allocated 38 members in the U.S. House of Representatives for the 119th Congress. Senators serve six-year terms. The term of office for members of the House is two years.

U.S. SENATORS

JOHN CORNYN
Republican-Austin
Committees: Foreign Relations, Finance, Judiciary, Intelligence, Budget

TED CRUZ
Republican-Houston
Committees: Foreign Relations, Judiciary, Rules & Administration, Commerce, Science, & Transportation

U.S. HOUSE OF REPRESENTATIVES

DISTRICT 1: Nathaniel Moran, R-Tyler
Ethics, Ways & Means, Strategic Competition Between the U.S. and Chinese Communist Party

DISTRICT 2: Dan Crenshaw, R-Kingwood
Energy & Commerce, Intelligence

DISTRICT 3: Keith Self, R-McKinney
Foreign Affairs, Veterans' Affairs, Science, Space, & Technology

DISTRICT 4: Pat Fallon, R-Sherman
Armed Services, Oversight & Government Reform, Intelligence

DISTRICT 5: Lance Gooden, R-Terrell
Armed Services, Judiciary

DISTRICT 6: Jake Ellzey, R-Midlothian
Appropriations, Small Business

DISTRICT 7: Lizzie Fletcher, D-Houston
Energy & Commerce

DISTRICT 8: Morgan Luttrell, R-Magnolia
Armed Services, Homeland Security, Veterans' Affairs

DISTRICT 9: Al Green, D-Houston
Financial Services, Homeland Security

DISTRICT 10: Michael McCaul, R-West Lake Hills
Foreign Affairs, Homeland Security

DISTRICT 11: August Pfluger, R-San Angelo
Energy & Commerce, Homeland Security

DISTRICT 12: Craig Goldman, R-Fort Worth
Energy & Commerce

DISTRICT 13: Ronny Jackson, R-Amarillo
Agriculture, Armed Services, Foreign Affairs, Intelligence

DISTRICT 14: Randy Weber, R-Friendswood
Energy & Commerce, Science, Space, & Technology

DISTRICT 15: Monica De La Cruz, R-Edinburg
Agriculture, Financial Services

DISTRICT 16: Veronica Escobar, D-El Paso
Appropriations, Budget

DISTRICT 17: Pete Sessions, R-Waco
Financial Services, Oversight & Government Reform

DISTRICT 18: VACANT

DISTRICT 19: Jodey Arrington, R-Lubbock
Budget, Ways & Means, Joint Economic Committee

DISTRICT 20: Joaquin Castro, D-San Antonio
Foreign Affairs, Intelligence

DISTRICT 21: Chip S. Roy, R-Dripping Springs
Rules, Budget, Judiciary

DISTRICT 22: Troy E. Nehls, R-Richmond
Judiciary, Transportation & Infrastructure

DISTRICT 23: Tony Gonzales, R-San Antonio
Appropriations, Homeland Security

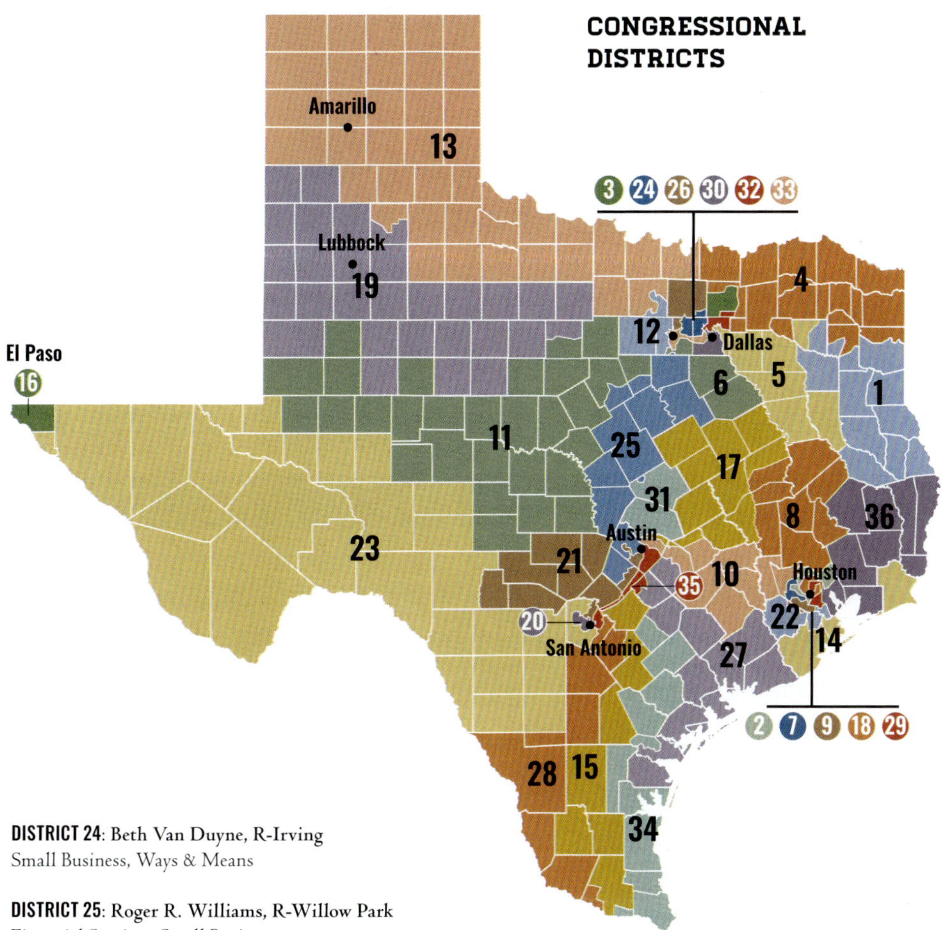

DISTRICT 24: Beth Van Duyne, R-Irving
Small Business, Ways & Means

DISTRICT 25: Roger R. Williams, R-Willow Park
Financial Services, Small Business

DISTRICT 26: Brandon Gill, R-Flower Mound
Oversight & Government Reform, Budget, Judiciary

DISTRICT 27: Michael Cloud, R-Victoria
Appropriations, Oversight & Government Reform

DISTRICT 28: Henry Cuellar, D-Laredo
Appropriations

DISTRICT 29: Sylvia Garcia, D-Houston
Ethics, Financial Services

DISTRICT 30: Jasmine Crockett, D-Dallas
Oversight & Government Reform, Judiciary

DISTRICT 31: John Carter, R-Round Rock
Appropriations

DISTRICT 32: Julie Johnson, D-Farmers Branch
Foreign Affairs, Homeland Security, House Administration, Library

DISTRICT 33: Marc Veasey, D-Fort Worth
Energy & Commerce

DISTRICT 34: Vicente Gonzalez, D-McAllen
Financial Services

DISTRICT 35: Greg Casar, D-Austin
Education & Workforce, Oversight & Government Reform

DISTRICT 36: Brian Babin, R-Woodville
Science, Space, & Technology, Transportation & Infrastructure

DISTRICT 37: Lloyd Doggett, D-Austin
Budget, Ways & Means, Joint Committee on Taxation

DISTRICT 38: Wesley Hunt, R-Houston
Natural Resources, Judiciary

U.S. Tax Collections in Texas

(in thousands) *Information for fiscal years furnished by the Internal Revenue Service.*

Fiscal Year	Individual Income and Employment Taxes	Corporation Income Taxes	Estate Taxes	Gift Taxes	Excise Taxes	TOTAL U.S. Taxes Collected in Texas
2023	$346,764,665	$33,595,913	$9,026,040	$151,027	$23,473,316	$413,010,962
2022	340,961,422	36,394,970	2,108,978	349,218	21,053,057	400,867,645
2021	265,528,807	27,143,965	1,996,227	259,352	17,143,535	312,071,886
2020	242,548,320	14,508,511	1,023,884	113,036	17,291,862	275,485,613
2019	245,361,121	18,470,193	1,620,965	148,057	22,661,021	292,330,171
2018	240,169,156	15,756,288	1,395,067	135,733	22,592,120	280,048,364
2017	225,236,761	22,939,596	1,314,828	123,822	21,340,788	270,955,237
2016	218,950,277	19,021,716	1,318,116	140,191	21,698,393	261,138,693
2015	226,945,577	32,083,819	1,167,572	115,516	19,591,942	279,904,425
2014	211,993,178	32,585,544	1,557,068	89,865	19,110,528	265,336,183
2013	195,542,035	33,933,242	890,069	596,861	18,950,003	249,912,209
2012	171,880,127	27,984,282	796,227	180,060	18,619,137	219,459,878
2011	160,086,749	21,880,905	117,936	359,987	15,850,240	198,295,817
2010	147,748,859	24,991,374	1,210,600	287,181	14,904,099	189,142,112

Federal Funds Distribution in Texas

	2023		2024
TOTAL	$293.6 billion		$270.9 billion
Direct Payments	$138.9 billion	Direct Payments	$145.7 billion
Contracts	82.1 billion	Grants	65.6 billion
Grants	70.1 billion	Contracts	58.8 billion
Other Financial Assistance	3.0 billion	Other Financial Assistance	1.0 billion
Loans	-496.5 million	Loans	-183.9 million
TOP 5 BY PROGRAM			
Social Security Retirement	$72.7 billion	Social Security Retirement	$64.0 billion
Medical Assistance	37.0 billion	Medical Assistance	38.0 billion
Veterans Compensation	15.6 billion	Veterans Compensation	13.9 billion
SNAP	9.6 billion	SNAP	11.5 billion
Social Security Disability	9.5 billion	Social Security Disability	9.1 billion
TOP 5 BY AGENCY			
Social Security Administration	$95.5 billion	Social Security Administration	$102.8 billion
Department of Defense	61.8 billion	Department of Health and Human Services	49.4 billion
Department of Health and Human Services	57.3 billion	Department of Defense	39.3 billion
Department of Veterans Affairs	32.5 billion	Department of Veterans Affairs	31.7 billion
Department of Agriculture	16.8 billion	Department of Agriculture	13.0 billion

Information for fiscal years from USAspending.gov.

Federal Funds Distribution to States (Trailing 12 Months)

Rank	State	Total	Rank	State	Total
1	California	$325.1 billion	11	South Carolina	90.5 billion
2	Florida	213.8 billion	12	Illinois	88.6 billion
3	**Texas**	**185.0 billion**	13	Ohio	86.4 billion
4	Pennsylvania	184.8 billion	14	Michigan	85.8 billion
5	New York	175.8 billion	15	North Carolina	83.5 billion
6	Minnesota	171.0 billion	16	Tennessee	80.3 billion
7	Indiana	142.8 billion	17	Wisconsin	75.6 billion
8	Kentucky	121.5 billion	18	Arizona	70.0 billion
9	Virginia	119.8 billion	19	Georgia	69.5 billion
10	Connecticut	98.5 billion	20	Maryland	66.0 billion

Source: USAspending.gov.

MAJOR MILITARY INSTALLATIONS

U.S. NAVY

NAVAL AIR STATION CORPUS CHRISTI

CORPUS CHRISTI (EST. 1941)
Personnel: 2,836 (active duty)
Major Units: Naval Air Training Command Headquarters; Training Air Wing 4; Marine Aviation Training Support Group; Coast Guard Air Group; Corpus Christi Army Depot (est. 1961)

NAVAL AIR STATION JOINT RESERVE BASE FORT WORTH

FORT WORTH (EST. 1994)
Personnel: 4,500 (active duty)
Major Units: Navy Fleet Logistics Support Squadron 59; 8th Marine Corps District; Marine Air Group 41; 14th Marine Regiment; Marine Aviation Logistics Squadron 41; Marine Fighter Attack Squadron 112; 136th Airlift Wing, Texas Air National Guard; U.S. Army 90th Aviation Support Battalion; 10th Air Force, 301st Fighter Wing, Air Force Reserve

NAVAL AIR STATION KINGSVILLE

KINGSVILLE (EST. 1942)
Personnel: 494 (active duty)
Major Units: Training Air Wing Two; Training Squadrons 21 and 22; Naval Auxiliary Landing Field Orange Grove; McMullen Target Range, Escondido Ranch

U.S. ARMY

FORT BLISS

EL PASO (EST. 1849)
Personnel: 25,546 (active duty)
Major Units: 1st Armored Division; 32nd Air and Missile Defense Command; 15th Sustainment Brigade; 5th Armored Brigade; Air Defense Artillery School; 11th Air Defense Artillery Brigades; Joint Task Force North; 204th Military Intelligence Battalion; 212th Fires Brigade; 402nd Field Artillery Brigade; Biggs Army Airfield (est. 1916)

FORT CAVAZOS

KILLEEN (EST. 1942)
Personnel: 28,784 (active duty)
Major Units: III Corps, Headquarters Command; First Army Division West; 1st Cavalry Division; 13th Sustainment Command; 89th Military Police Brigade; 3rd Cavalry Regiment; 41st Fires Brigade; 504th Battlefield Surveillance Brigade; Army Operational Test Command; Darnell Army Medical Center

RED RIVER ARMY DEPOT

TEXARKANA (EST. 1941)
Personnel: 2 (active duty)
Major Unit: Defense Distribution Center; U.S. Army Tank-Automotive and Armaments Command

U.S. AIR FORCE

JOINT BASE SAN ANTONIO (FORT SAM HOUSTON, LACKLAND AFB, AND RANDOLPH AFB)

SAN ANTONIO (EST. 2010)
Personnel: 80,000 (active duty)
Major Units: 502nd Air Base Wing; 59th Medical Wing; 37th and 12th Training Wing; 616th Operations Center; 67th and 688th Cyberspace Wing; 350th Spectrum Warfare Wing; 22nd, 10th, and 4th Air Force Reserves; Texas Air Guard 149th Fighter Wing; US Army Medical Command; US Army Veterinary Corps; 7th Signal Command; 470th Military Intelligence Brigade

DYESS AIR FORCE BASE

ABILENE (EST. 1942 AS TYE ARMY AIRFIELD, CLOSED AT END OF WORLD WAR II, RE-ESTABLISHED IN 1956)
Personnel: 4,151 (active duty)
Major Units: 7th Bomb Wing (Air Combat Command); 317th Airlift Group

GOODFELLOW AIR FORCE BASE

SAN ANGELO (EST. 1940)
Personnel: 5,074 (active duty)
Major Units: 17th Training Wing; 517th Training Squadron; 17th Medical Group; 17th Mission Support Group

LAUGHLIN AIR FORCE BASE

DEL RIO (EST. 1942)
Personnel: 1,309 (active duty)
Major Unit: 47th Flying Training Wing

SHEPPARD AIR FORCE BASE

WICHITA FALLS (EST. 1941)
Personnel: 1,967 (active duty)
Major Units: 82nd Training Wing; 80th Flying Training Wing; NCO Academy

WIKIMEDIA COMMONS/LEONARDO COGNOSCENTI

TEXAS MILITARY FORCES

Tracing their history to early frontier days, the Texas Military Forces are organized into the Texas Army National Guard, Texas Air National Guard, and the Texas State Guard.

The governor is commander-in-chief of the Texas Military Forces. This command function is exercised through the adjutant general appointed by the governor and approved by federal and state legislative authority. Major General Thomas Suelzer has served as the current adjutant general since 2022.

When not in active federal service, Camp Mabry serves as the administrative and storage headquarters. Camp Mabry was established in the early 1890s as a summer encampment of the Texas Volunteer Guard, a forerunner of the Texas National Guard. The name honors Woodford Haywood Mabry, adjutant general from 1891–1898.

The State Guard, an all-volunteer backup force, was created by the Legislature in 1941. It became an active element of the state military forces in 1965 with a mission of reinforcing the National Guard in emergencies and replacing National Guard units called into federal service.

The Army National Guard is available for state and national emergencies and has been used extensively during natural disasters.

When the military forces were reorganized following World War II, the Texas Air National Guard was added. Its units augment major Air Force commands.

When called into active federal service, National Guard units come within the chain of command of the Army and Air Force units.

CAMP MABRY

AUSTIN

Major Units: Joint Force Headquarters; Standing Joint Interagency Task Force; 36th Infantry Division; 147th Reconnaissance Wing; 149th Fighter Wing; 136th Airlift Wing; Texas Air National Guard

FEDERAL COURTS IN TEXAS

Texas is divided into four federal judicial districts, each of which is comprised of several divisions. Appeal from all Texas federal courts is to the U.S. Fifth Circuit Court of Appeals in New Orleans, Louisiana.

U.S. COURT OF APPEALS, FIFTH CIRCUIT

The Fifth Circuit is composed of Louisiana, Mississippi, and Texas. Sessions are held in each of the states at least once per year and may be scheduled at any location having adequate facilities. U.S. circuit judges are appointed for life and received a salary of $262,300 in 2025.

Circuit Judges:
- Jennifer Walker Eldrod (Houston, Chief)
- Andrew S. Oldham (Austin)
- Priscilla Richman (Austin)
- Stuart Kyle Duncan (Baton Rouge, LA)
- Catharina Haynes (Dallas)
- James C. Ho (Dallas)
- Irma Ramirez (Dallas)
- Don R. Willett (Dallas)
- Edith H. Jones (Houston)
- Jerry E. Smith (Houston)
- James E. Graves Jr. (Jackson, Miss.)
- Leslie H. Southwick (Jackson, Miss.)
- Cory T. Wilson (Jackson, Miss.)
- Dana M. Douglas (New Orleans, LA)
- Kurt D. Engelhardt (New Orleans, LA)
- Stephen A. Higginson (New Orleans, LA)
- Carl E. Stewart (Shreveport, LA)

Senior Judges:
- James L. Dennis (Baton Rouge, LA)
- Patrick E. Higginbotham (Dallas)
- Carolyn Dineen King (Houston)
- Rhesa H. Barksdale (Jackson, Miss.)
- E. Grady Jolly (Jackson, Miss.)
- W. Eugene Davis (New Iberia, LA)
- John M. Duhé Jr. (New Iberia, LA)
- Edith Brown Clement (New Orleans, LA)
- Jacques L. Wiener Jr. (Shreveport, LA)

Clerk of Court: Lyle W. Cayce (New Orleans, LA)

U.S. DISTRICT COURTS

U.S. district judges are appointed for life and received a salary of $247,400 in 2025.

NORTHERN TEXAS DISTRICT

District Judges: David C. Godbey (Dallas, Chief), Matthew J. Kacsmaryk (Amarillo), Jane J. Boyle (Dallas), Ada Brown (Dallas), Ed Kinkeade (Dallas), Sam A. Lindsay (Dallas), Karen Gren Scholer (Dallas), Brantley Starr (Dallas), Reed O'Connor (Fort Worth), Mark T. Pittman (Fort Worth), James Wesley Hendrix (Lubbock)
Senior Judges: A. Joe Fish (Dallas), Sidney A. Fitzwater (Dallas), Barbara M.G. Lynn (Dallas), Terry R. Means (Fort Worth), Sam R. Cummings (Lubbock)
Clerk of Court: Karen Mitchell (Dallas)
U.S. Attorney: Chad Meacham
Federal Public Defender: Jason Hawkins
U.S. Marshal: Vacant
Bankruptcy Judges: Stacey G.C. Jernigan (Dallas, Chief), Scott W. Everett (Dallas), Michelle V. Larson (Dallas), Edward L. Morris (Fort Worth) Mark X. Mullin (Fort Worth), Brad Odell (Lubbock)

Following are the divisions of the Northern District and the counties in each division:

ABILENE DIVISION

Coverage Areas: Callahan, Eastland, Fisher, Haskell, Howard, Jones, Mitchell, Nolan, Shackelford, Stephens, Stonewall, Taylor, Throckmorton
Magistrate Judge: John R. Parker
Courtroom Deputy: Jennifer Chittum

AMARILLO DIVISION

Coverage Areas: Armstrong, Briscoe, Carson, Castro, Childress, Collingsworth, Dallam, Deaf Smith, Donley, Gray, Hall, Hansford, Hartley, Hemphill, Hutchinson, Lipscomb, Moore, Ochiltree, Oldham, Parmer, Potter, Randall, Roberts, Sherman, Swisher, Wheeler
Magistrate Judge: Lee Ann Reno
Courtroom Deputy: Christopher Kordes

DALLAS DIVISION

Coverage Areas: Dallas, Ellis, Hunt, Johnson, Kaufman, Navarro, Rockwall
Magistrate Judges: David L. Horan, Rebecca Rutherford, Renee H. Toliver
Courtroom Deputies: Marie Gonzales, Lavenia Price, Shakira Todd, Mervin Wright

FORT WORTH DIVISION

Coverage Areas: Comanche, Erath, Hood, Jack, Palo Pinto, Parker, Tarrant, Wise
Magistrate Judges: Jeffrey L. Cureton, Hal R. Ray Jr.
Courtroom Deputies: Julie Harwell, Elsherie Mooree

LUBBOCK DIVISION

Coverage Areas: Bailey, Borden, Cochran, Crosby, Dawson, Dickens, Floyd, Gaines, Garza, Hale, Hockley, Kent, Lamb, Lubbock, Lynn, Motley, Scurry, Terry, Yoakum
Magistrate Judge: Amanda R. Burch
Courtroom Deputy: Zelma Zertuche

SAN ANGELO DIVISION

Coverage Areas: Brown, Coke, Coleman, Concho, Crockett, Glasscock, Irion, Menard, Mills, Reagan, Runnels, Schleicher, Sterling, Sutton, Tom Green
Magistrate Judge: John R. Parker
Division Manager: Erik Paltrow

WICHITA FALLS DIVISION

Coverage Areas: Archer, Baylor, Clay, Cottle, Foard, Hardeman, King, Knox, Montague, Wichita, Wilbarger, Young
Magistrate Judge: Hal R. Ray Jr.

WESTERN TEXAS DISTRICT

District Judges: Alia Moses (Del Rio, Chief), Ernest Gonzalez (Del Rio), Robert Pitman (Austin), Kathleen Cardone (El Paso), Leon Schydlower (El Paso), David Counts (Midland), Fred Biery (San Antonio), Orlando L. Garcia (San Antonio), Jason Pulliam (San Antonio), Xavier Rodriguez (San Antonio), Alan Albright (Waco)
Senior Judges: James R. Nowlin (Austin), Sam Sparks (Austin), David Briones (El Paso), David C. Guaderrama (El Paso), Frank Montalvo (El Paso), Robert A. Junell (Pecos), David A. Ezra (San Antonio)
Clerk of District Court: Philip J. Devlin (San Antonio)
U.S. Attorney: Margaret Leachman
Federal Public Defender: Maureen Scott Franco
U.S. Marshal: Susan L. Pamerleau
Bankruptcy Judges: Craig A. Gargotta (San Antonio, Chief), Christopher G. Bradley (Austin), Shad M. Robinson (Austin), Ronald B. King (San Antonio), Michael M. Parker (San Antonio)

Following are the divisions of the Western District and the counties in each division.

AUSTIN DIVISION

Coverage Areas: Bastrop, Blanco, Burleson, Burnet, Caldwell, Gillespie, Hays, Kimble, Lampasas, Lee, Llano, Mason, McCulloch, San Saba, Travis, Washington, Williamson
Magistrate Judges: Susan Hightower, Dustin M. Howell, Mark Lane
Courtroom Deputies: Stephanie Cruz, Kyra Fink, Victoria Rivera

DEL RIO DIVISION

Coverage Areas: Edwards, Kinney, Maverick, Terrell, Uvalde, Val Verde, Zavala
Magistrate Judges: Matthew H. Watters, Joseph Cordova
Courtroom Deputies: Mary Cienega, Carmen Levrie

EL PASO DIVISION

Coverage Areas: El Paso, Hudspeth
Magistrate Judges: Anne T. Berton, Robert F. Castañeda, Miguel A. Torres
Courtroom Deputies: Myrna Gallegos, Veronica Montoya, Fidel Morales

FORT CAVAZOS DIVISION

Coverage Areas: Fort Cavazos Military Reservation
Magistrate Judge: Jeffery C. Manske
Courtroom Deputy: Michelle Ortiz

MIDLAND–ODESSA DIVISION

Coverage Areas: Andrews, Crane, Ector, Martin, Midland, Upton
Magistrate Judge: Ronald C. Griffin
Courtroom Deputy: Monica Ramirez

PECOS DIVISION

Coverage Areas: Brewster, Culberson, Jeff Davis, Loving, Pecos, Presidio, Reeves, Ward, Winkler
Magistrate Judge: David B. Fannin
Courtroom Deputy: Yvette Lujan

SAN ANTONIO DIVISION

Coverage Areas: Atascosa, Bandera, Bexar, Comal, Dimmit, Frio, Gonzales, Guadalupe, Karnes, Kendall, Kerr, Medina, Real, Wilson
Magistrate Judges: Henry J. Bemporad, Elizabeth S. "Betsy" Chestney, Richard B. Farrer
Courtroom Deputies: Amber Baillio, Abigail Chaparro, Cindy Miranda

WACO DIVISION

Coverage Areas: Bell, Bosque, Coryell, Falls, Freestone, Hamilton, Hill, Leon, Limestone, McLennan, Milam, Robertson, Somervell
Magistrate Judges: Derek T. Gilliland, Jeffrey C. Manske
Courtroom Deputies: Melissa Copp, Abigail Ernstes

FEDERAL JUDICIAL DISTRICTS

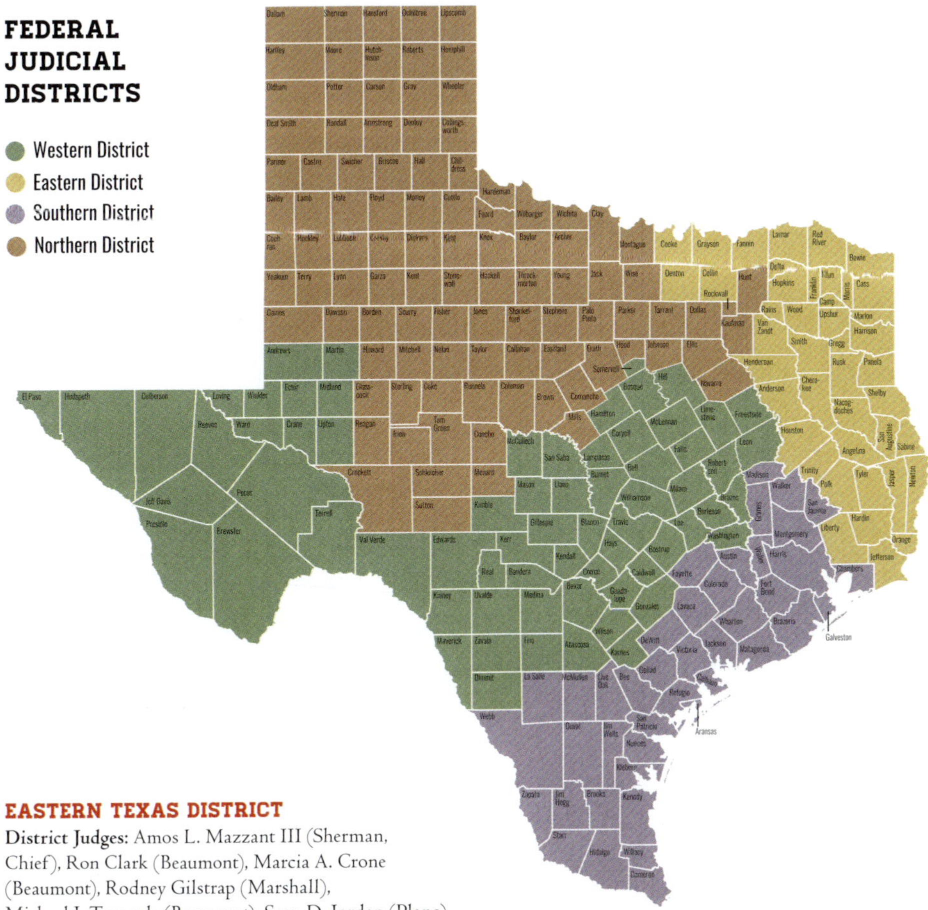

EASTERN TEXAS DISTRICT

District Judges: Amos L. Mazzant III (Sherman, Chief), Ron Clark (Beaumont), Marcia A. Crone (Beaumont), Rodney Gilstrap (Marshall), Michael J. Truncale (Beaumont), Sean D. Jordan (Plano), Richard Schell (Plano), Robert W. Schroeder III (Texarkana), J. Campbell Barker (Tyler), Jeremy D. Kernodle (Tyler)
Clerk of District Court: David A. O'Toole (Tyler)
U.S. Attorney: Abe McGlothin Jr.
Federal Public Defender: John D. McElroy
U.S. Marshal: Vacant
Bankruptcy Judges: Brenda T. Rhoades (Plano, Chief), Joshua P. Searcy (Tyler)

Following are the divisions of the Eastern District and the counties in each division:

BEAUMONT DIVISION

Coverage Areas: Hardin, Jasper, Jefferson, Liberty, Newton, Orange
Magistrates: Zack Hawthorn, Christine L. Stetson
Courtroom Deputies: Tonya Piper, Sherre White

LUFKIN DIVISION

Coverage Areas: Angelina, Houston, Nacogdoches, Polk, Sabine, San Augustine, Shelby, Trinity, Tyler
Deputy-in-Charge: Brandy Fairley

MARSHALL DIVISION

Coverage Areas: Camp, Cass, Harrison, Marion, Morris, Upshur
Magistrate: Roy Payne
Courtroom Deputy: Wendy Asbel

SHERMAN DIVISION

Coverage Areas: Collin, Cooke, Delta, Denton, Fannin, Grayson, Hopkins, Lamar
Magistrates: Aileen Goldman Durrett
Courtroom Deputies: Karen Lee

TEXARKANA DIVISION

Coverage Areas: Bowie, Franklin, Red River, Titus
Magistrate: Boone Baxter
Courtroom Deputy: Nicole Peavy

TYLER DIVISION

Coverage Areas: Anderson, Cherokee, Gregg, Henderson, Panola, Rains, Rusk, Smith, Van Zandt, Wood
Magistrates: John D. Love and K. Nicole Mitchell
Courtroom Deputies: Sharon Baum and Lisa Hardwick

SOUTHERN TEXAS DISTRICT

District Judges: Randy Crane (McAllen, Chief), Rolando Olvera (Brownsville), Fernando Rodriguez Jr. (Brownsville), David S. Morales (Corpus Christi), Nelva Gonzales Ramos (Corpus Christi), Drew B. Tipton (Corpus Christi), Jeffrey V. Brown (Galveston), Alfred H. Bennett (Houston), Keith P. Ellison (Houston), Charles Eskridge (Houston), George C. Hanks Jr. (Houston), Lynn N. Hughes (Houston), John A. Kazen (Laredo), Marina Garcia Marmolejo (Laredo), Diana Saldaña (Laredo), Ricardo H. Hinojosa (McAllen)

Senior Judges: Janis Graham Jack (Corpus Christi), Andrew S. Hanen (Houston), David Hittner (Houston), Kenneth M. Hoyt (Houston), Sim Lake (Houston), Gray H. Miller (Houston), Lee H. Rosenthal (Houston), Ewing Werlein Jr. (Houston), Micaela Alvarez (McAllen), John D. Rainey (Victoria)

Clerk of Court: Nathan Ochsner (Houston)

U.S. Attorney: Alamdar Hamdani

Federal Public Defender: Marjorie A. Meyers

U.S. Marshal: T. Michael O'Connor

Bankruptcy Judges: Eduardo V. Rodriguez (McAllen, Chief), Marvin Isgur (Houston), David R. Jones (Houston), Christopher M. Lopez (Houston), Jeffrey P. Norman (Houston)

Following are the divisions of the Southern District and the counties in each division:

BROWNSVILLE DIVISION

Coverage Areas: Cameron, Willacy

Magistrate Judges: Ignacio Torteya III

Deputy-in-Charge: Rosy D'Venturi

CORPUS CHRISTI DIVISION

Coverage Areas: Aransas, Bee, Brooks, Duval, Jim Wells, Kenedy, Kleberg, Live Oak, Nueces, San Patricio

Magistrate Judges: Julie K. Hampton, Jason B. Libby, Mitchel Neurock

Deputy-in-Charge: Anna Salazar

GALVESTON DIVISION

Coverage Areas: Brazoria, Chambers, Galveston, Matagorda

Magistrate Judge: Andrew M. Edison

Deputy-in-Charge: Lucia Smith

HOUSTON DIVISION

Coverage Areas: Austin, Brazos, Colorado, Fayette, Fort Bend, Grimes, Harris, Madison, Montgomery, San Jacinto, Walker, Waller, Wharton

Magistrate Judges: Richard Bennett, Peter Bray, Christina A. Bryan, Yvonne Y. Ho, Dena Hanovice Palermo

Deputy-in-Charge: Darlene Hansen

LAREDO DIVISION

Coverage Areas: Jim Hogg, La Salle, McMullen, Webb, Zapata

Magistrate Judges: Christopher A. dos Santos, Diana Song Quiroga

Deputy-in-Charge: Aimee Veliz

MCALLEN DIVISION

Coverage Areas: Hidalgo, Starr

Magistrate Judges: Juan F. Alanis, J. Scott Hacker, Nadia S. Medrano

Deputy-in-Charge: Velma T. Barrera

VICTORIA DIVISION

Coverage Areas: Calhoun, DeWitt, Goliad, Jackson, Lavaca, Refugio, Victoria

Magistrate Judges: Julie K. Hampton, Jason B. Libby, Mitchel Neurock

Deputy-in-Charge: Lana Reimann

UNSPLASH/JENNIFER BURK

Texas

ELECTIONS

UNSPLASH/SJ OBJIO

2024 PRESIDENTIAL ELECTION RESULTS

Below are the official results by county. The leading candidates for President of the United States were: Donald J. Trump for the Republican Party, Kamala Harris for the Democratic Party, Chase Oliver for the Libertarian Party, and Jill Stein for the Green Party.

Incumbent President Joe Biden withdrew his bid for reelection in July 2024.

The total number of votes counted in the presidential race — 11,388,674 — equaled 61.15 percent of the registered voters. The voting-age population in November 2024 was estimated at 22,938,482. The statewide turnout in the previous presidential election in 2020 was 66.73 percent of the registered voters.

President Trump won the 2024 election with 312 electoral college votes, including 40 from Texas.

Source: Texas Secretary of State.

County	Registered Voters	Turnout %	Presidential Race							
			TRUMP	%	HARRIS	%	OLIVER	%	STEIN	%
Statewide	**18,623,931**	**61.15%**	**6,393,597**	**56.14%**	**4,835,250**	**42.46%**	**68,557**	**0.60%**	**82,701**	**0.73%**
Anderson	30,613	63.23%	15,597	80.57%	3,635	18.78%	76	0.39%	45	0.23%
Andrews	10,739	56.43%	5,205	85.89%	806	13.30%	35	0.58%	13	0.21%
Angelina	55,965	61.51%	26,049	75.68%	8,146	23.67%	143	0.42%	81	0.24%
Aransas	19,849	65.65%	10,090	77.43%	2,831	21.73%	67	0.51%	40	0.31%
Archer	7,008	73.23%	4,592	89.48%	520	10.13%	12	0.23%	8	0.16%
Armstrong	1,429	77.61%	1,029	92.79%	77	6.94%	3	0.27%	0	0.00%
Atascosa	32,142	57.38%	13,142	71.25%	5,153	27.94%	72	0.39%	75	0.41%
Austin	22,116	69.56%	12,457	80.98%	2,816	18.31%	60	0.39%	46	0.30%
Bailey	3,172	54.89%	1,395	80.13%	332	19.07%	9	0.52%	4	0.23%
Bandera	19,026	71.48%	10,939	80.43%	2,532	18.62%	76	0.56%	45	0.33%
Bastrop	61,403	64.83%	23,301	58.54%	15,989	40.17%	299	0.75%	199	0.50%
Baylor	2,430	68.93%	1,471	87.82%	184	10.99%	7	0.42%	8	0.48%
Bee	15,979	55.01%	6,111	69.52%	2,606	29.65%	40	0.46%	32	0.36%
Bell	240,207	54.40%	75,161	57.52%	53,973	41.31%	844	0.65%	579	0.44%
Bexar	1,295,580	58.53%	337,545	44.51%	411,389	54.25%	4,310	0.57%	4,303	0.57%
Blanco	11,014	77.38%	6,447	75.64%	1,973	23.15%	67	0.79%	31	0.36%
Borden	487	79.47%	370	95.61%	16	4.13%	1	0.26%	0	0.00%
Bosque	13,638	70.22%	7,969	83.22%	1,524	15.91%	51	0.53%	27	0.28%
Bowie	62,656	58.48%	27,122	74.01%	9,282	25.33%	138	0.38%	87	0.24%
Brazoria	249,840	64.86%	95,867	59.16%	63,976	39.48%	932	0.58%	1,175	0.73%
Brazos	133,384	68.94%	56,671	61.63%	33,844	36.80%	796	0.87%	536	0.58%
Brewster	7,408	61.80%	2,545	55.59%	1,969	43.01%	40	0.87%	22	0.48%
Briscoe	1,037	71.84%	666	89.40%	72	9.66%	4	0.54%	2	0.27%
Brooks	4,945	48.57%	1,077	44.84%	1,308	54.45%	8	0.33%	9	0.37%
Brown	25,500	66.09%	14,593	86.59%	2,132	12.65%	80	0.47%	48	0.28%
Burleson	13,840	67.70%	7,590	81.01%	1,705	18.20%	52	0.56%	18	0.19%
Burnet	39,186	71.84%	21,795	77.42%	6,114	21.72%	172	0.61%	66	0.23%
Caldwell	27,097	57.91%	8,880	56.59%	6,618	42.17%	93	0.59%	95	0.61%
Calhoun	13,223	59.23%	5,939	75.83%	1,853	23.66%	24	0.31%	16	0.20%
Callahan	10,439	66.94%	6,180	88.44%	761	10.89%	33	0.47%	11	0.16%
Cameron	238,215	48.76%	60,991	52.51%	54,258	46.71%	442	0.38%	431	0.37%
Camp	8,424	62.23%	4,011	76.52%	1,201	22.91%	22	0.42%	8	0.15%
Carson	4,297	73.94%	2,866	90.21%	290	9.13%	8	0.25%	8	0.25%
Cass	21,812	64.84%	11,693	82.68%	2,406	17.01%	32	0.23%	9	0.06%
Castro	3,694	54.76%	1,594	78.79%	418	20.66%	4	0.20%	5	0.25%
Chambers	37,026	67.45%	20,567	82.36%	4,192	16.79%	144	0.58%	68	0.27%
Cherokee	32,121	63.84%	16,593	80.91%	3,744	18.26%	91	0.44%	74	0.36%
Childress	3,804	59.73%	1,991	87.63%	263	11.58%	11	0.48%	7	0.31%
Clay	8,291	71.26%	5,288	89.51%	584	9.88%	21	0.36%	13	0.22%
Cochran	1,676	53.28%	735	82.31%	148	16.57%	9	1.01%	1	0.11%
Coke	2,460	73.74%	1,623	89.47%	179	9.87%	9	0.50%	3	0.17%
Coleman	6,139	67.70%	3,712	89.32%	428	10.30%	11	0.26%	4	0.10%

PRESIDENTIAL VOTE 2024

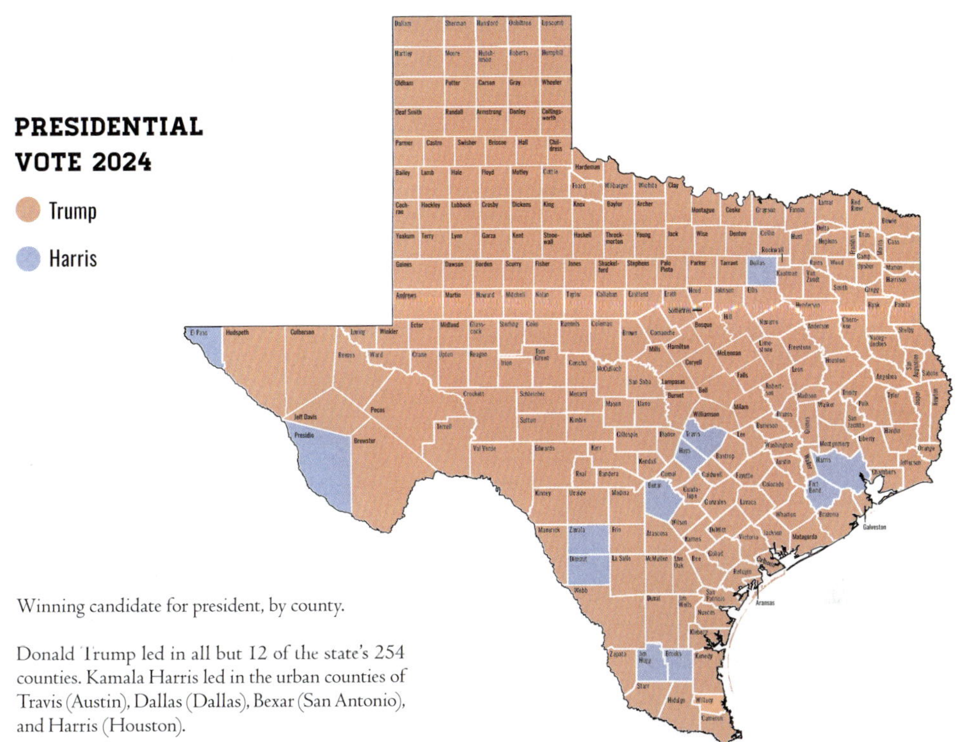

Winning candidate for president, by county.

Donald Trump led in all but 12 of the state's 254 counties. Kamala Harris led in the urban counties of Travis (Austin), Dallas (Dallas), Bexar (San Antonio), and Harris (Houston).

County	Registered Voters	Turnout %	Presidential Race							
			TRUMP	%	HARRIS	%	OLIVER	%	STEIN	%
Collin	748,752	68.86%	279,534	54.22%	222,115	43.08%	3,508	0.68%	10,010	1.94%
Collingsworth	1,887	63.65%	1,066	88.76%	135	11.24%	0	0.00%	0	0.00%
Colorado	14,775	67.64%	7,824	78.29%	2,108	21.09%	45	0.45%	17	0.17%
Comal	143,696	72.02%	74,756	72.23%	27,680	26.75%	699	0.68%	330	0.32%
Comanche	10,022	65.30%	5,679	86.78%	834	12.74%	25	0.38%	6	0.09%
Concho	1,795	66.74%	1,038	86.64%	153	12.77%	3	0.25%	4	0.33%
Cooke	30,193	67.72%	16,975	83.02%	3,310	16.19%	107	0.52%	40	0.20%
Coryell	46,995	50.91%	16,688	69.75%	6,959	29.09%	161	0.67%	103	0.43%
Cottle	994	66.10%	565	86.00%	89	13.55%	2	0.30%	1	0.15%
Crane	2,674	51.94%	1,195	86.03%	186	13.39%	3	0.22%	3	0.22%
Crockett	2,289	61.90%	1,087	76.71%	323	22.79%	3	0.21%	4	0.28%
Crosby	3,638	51.68%	1,416	75.32%	451	23.99%	10	0.53%	3	0.16%
Culberson	1,707	45.75%	451	57.75%	319	40.85%	10	1.28%	1	0.13%
Dallam	2,873	50.37%	1,285	88.80%	152	10.50%	5	0.35%	5	0.35%
Dallas	1,467,410	57.92%	322,569	37.96%	511,118	60.14%	6,273	0.74%	8,988	1.06%
Dawson	6,776	51.84%	2,810	79.99%	667	18.99%	24	0.68%	10	0.28%
Deaf Smith	8,756	48.95%	3,233	75.43%	1,019	23.78%	19	0.44%	15	0.35%
Delta	4,112	64.64%	2,250	84.65%	397	14.94%	8	0.30%	3	0.11%
Denton	661,565	67.90%	250,521	55.77%	191,503	42.63%	3,100	0.69%	3,605	0.80%
DeWitt	11,357	68.90%	6,515	83.26%	1,270	16.23%	24	0.31%	15	0.19%
Dickens	1,433	69.30%	844	84.99%	146	14.70%	2	0.20%	1	0.10%
Dimmit	6,706	51.10%	1,653	48.23%	1,765	51.50%	5	0.15%	4	0.12%
Donley	2,414	70.92%	1,512	88.32%	174	10.16%	8	0.47%	18	1.05%
Duval	8,031	55.55%	2,439	54.67%	2,003	44.90%	13	0.29%	6	0.13%
Eastland	12,520	66.81%	7,397	88.44%	918	10.98%	27	0.32%	21	0.25%
Ector	86,640	49.19%	32,429	76.10%	9,881	23.19%	190	0.45%	115	0.27%
Edwards	1,496	67.18%	869	86.47%	133	13.23%	1	0.10%	2	0.20%
Ellis	147,399	67.54%	64,763	65.05%	33,850	34.00%	521	0.52%	351	0.35%
El Paso	521,945	48.20%	105,124	41.79%	143,156	56.91%	1,461	0.58%	1,630	0.65%

County	Registered Voters	Turnout %	Presidential Race							
			TRUMP	%	HARRIS	%	OLIVER	%	STEIN	%
Erath	25,961	70.69%	15,349	83.64%	2,871	15.64%	95	0.52%	35	0.19%
Falls	10,562	59.43%	4,520	72.01%	1,713	27.29%	18	0.29%	25	0.40%
Fannin	24,942	65.73%	13,648	83.24%	2,607	15.90%	82	0.50%	48	0.29%
Fayette	18,353	72.64%	10,699	80.26%	2,515	18.87%	76	0.57%	37	0.28%
Fisher	2,705	67.65%	1,487	81.26%	330	18.03%	10	0.55%	2	0.11%
Floyd	3,660	57.10%	1,715	82.06%	358	17.13%	11	0.53%	5	0.24%
Foard	806	67.62%	448	82.20%	92	16.88%	3	0.55%	2	0.37%
Fort Bend	555,569	65.25%	173,592	47.88%	179,310	49.46%	1,929	0.53%	7,428	2.05%
Franklin	7,599	69.89%	4,473	84.22%	813	15.31%	17	0.32%	7	0.13%
Freestone	13,406	67.47%	7,500	82.92%	1,499	16.57%	37	0.41%	9	0.10%
Frio	9,526	51.91%	3,060	61.88%	1,848	37.37%	15	0.30%	10	0.20%
Gaines	10,467	61.30%	5,840	91.02%	538	8.39%	22	0.34%	16	0.25%
Galveston	245,695	64.71%	100,295	63.08%	56,732	35.68%	997	0.63%	909	0.57%
Garza	2,651	60.32%	1,374	85.93%	213	13.32%	9	0.56%	3	0.19%
Gillespie	21,884	75.36%	13,202	80.05%	3,160	19.16%	91	0.55%	29	0.18%
Glasscock	840	78.93%	623	93.97%	38	5.73%	2	0.30%	0	0.00%
Goliad	5,833	68.35%	3,178	79.71%	778	19.51%	16	0.40%	12	0.30%
Gonzales	13,174	58.87%	5,981	77.12%	1,729	22.30%	28	0.36%	17	0.22%
Gray	12,317	61.54%	6,691	88.27%	845	11.15%	31	0.41%	13	0.17%
Grayson	100,124	65.83%	50,556	76.70%	14,800	22.45%	343	0.52%	189	0.29%
Gregg	76,263	61.29%	33,026	70.66%	13,294	28.44%	248	0.53%	131	0.28%
Grimes	21,080	66.66%	11,197	79.69%	2,734	19.46%	72	0.51%	40	0.28%
Guadalupe	130,489	65.24%	54,691	64.24%	29,573	34.74%	527	0.62%	306	0.36%
Hale	18,272	50.82%	7,283	78.44%	1,903	20.50%	57	0.61%	35	0.38%
Hall	1,886	60.92%	992	86.34%	149	12.97%	5	0.44%	3	0.26%
Hamilton	6,260	71.33%	3,809	85.31%	625	14.00%	23	0.52%	7	0.16%
Hansford	3,002	66.59%	1,842	92.15%	146	7.30%	9	0.45%	2	0.10%
Hardeman	2,388	58.84%	1,210	86.12%	188	13.38%	3	0.21%	4	0.28%
Hardin	43,116	65.31%	24,691	87.69%	3,347	11.89%	89	0.32%	30	0.11%
Harris	2,693,055	57.83%	722,695	46.40%	808,771	51.93%	9,727	0.62%	15,117	0.97%
Harrison	47,283	63.96%	22,658	74.92%	7,369	24.37%	135	0.45%	64	0.21%
Hartley	2,846	70.84%	1,843	91.42%	163	8.09%	8	0.40%	2	0.10%
Haskell	3,442	65.28%	1,918	85.36%	313	13.93%	12	0.53%	3	0.13%
Hays	186,198	67.58%	58,438	46.44%	65,528	52.08%	979	0.78%	743	0.59%
Hemphill	2,347	68.68%	1,412	87.59%	190	11.79%	7	0.43%	3	0.19%
Henderson	59,479	64.80%	31,379	81.42%	6,919	17.95%	152	0.39%	78	0.20%
Hidalgo	446,417	48.67%	110,760	50.98%	104,517	48.11%	805	0.37%	1,112	0.51%
Hill	26,962	61.96%	13,669	81.82%	2,919	17.47%	78	0.47%	37	0.22%
Hockley	13,984	57.12%	6,616	82.82%	1,323	16.56%	34	0.43%	14	0.18%
Hood	51,704	70.70%	30,174	82.55%	6,070	16.61%	194	0.53%	100	0.27%
Hopkins	25,383	66.10%	13,754	81.98%	2,917	17.39%	65	0.39%	37	0.22%
Houston	13,901	67.37%	7,247	77.38%	2,065	22.05%	33	0.35%	17	0.18%
Howard	17,198	56.06%	7,817	81.08%	1,759	18.24%	44	0.46%	20	0.21%
Hudspeth	2,212	46.93%	759	73.12%	275	26.49%	4	0.39%	0	0.00%
Hunt	72,860	64.14%	36,137	77.33%	10,212	21.85%	237	0.51%	117	0.25%
Hutchinson	13,442	61.33%	7,273	88.22%	913	11.07%	40	0.49%	15	0.18%
Irion	1,230	70.57%	761	87.67%	105	12.10%	2	0.23%	0	0.00%
Jack	5,857	71.73%	3,819	90.91%	363	8.64%	12	0.29%	7	0.17%
Jackson	9,894	63.97%	5,386	85.10%	907	14.33%	23	0.36%	13	0.21%
Jasper	24,496	64.67%	13,162	83.09%	2,615	16.51%	48	0.30%	14	0.09%
Jeff Davis	1,574	74.27%	699	59.79%	450	38.49%	14	1.20%	6	0.51%
Jefferson	147,938	58.34%	46,596	53.98%	38,936	45.11%	410	0.48%	330	0.38%
Jim Hogg	3,548	44.67%	725	45.74%	856	54.01%	3	0.19%	1	0.06%
Jim Wells	26,414	50.23%	7,636	57.55%	5,577	42.03%	32	0.24%	23	0.17%
Johnson	129,287	62.44%	60,752	75.26%	19,247	23.84%	454	0.56%	238	0.29%
Jones	10,883	63.83%	5,988	86.20%	907	13.06%	33	0.48%	18	0.26%
Karnes	8,449	60.07%	4,001	78.84%	1,051	20.71%	16	0.32%	7	0.14%
Kaufman	108,165	64.17%	44,063	63.49%	24,726	35.63%	320	0.46%	257	0.37%
Kendall	38,959	75.25%	22,668	77.33%	6,355	21.68%	195	0.67%	77	0.26%
Kenedy	270	58.52%	115	72.78%	41	25.95%	2	1.27%	0	0.00%
Kent	599	74.29%	390	87.64%	50	11.24%	5	1.12%	0	0.00%

County	Registered Voters	Turnout %	Presidential Race							
			TRUMP	%	HARRIS	%	OLIVER	%	STEIN	%
Kerr	40,065	70.31%	21,615	76.73%	6,315	22.42%	161	0.57%	65	0.23%
Kimble	3,318	72.45%	2,126	88.44%	261	10.86%	10	0.42%	5	0.21%
King	165	81.82%	129	95.56%	6	4.44%	0	0.00%	0	0.00%
Kinney	2,175	65.24%	1,063	74.91%	346	24.38%	7	0.49%	3	0.21%
Kleberg	18,689	53.58%	5,612	56.04%	4,338	43.32%	36	0.36%	24	0.24%
Knox	2,230	61.70%	1,156	84.01%	214	15.55%	1	0.07%	5	0.36%
Lamar	33,110	64.29%	17,044	80.08%	4,079	19.16%	71	0.33%	42	0.20%
Lamb	7,883	52.66%	3,398	81.86%	729	17.56%	13	0.31%	11	0.26%
Lampasas	16,913	66.82%	8,961	79.29%	2,232	19.75%	63	0.56%	40	0.35%
La Salle	4,210	56.06%	1,417	60.04%	933	39.53%	4	0.17%	6	0.25%
Lavaca	14,389	72.91%	9,215	87.84%	1,235	11.77%	19	0.18%	17	0.16%
Lee	12,168	69.16%	6,724	79.90%	1,640	19.49%	35	0.42%	14	0.17%
Leon	12,654	71.63%	7,982	88.06%	1,033	11.40%	34	0.38%	11	0.12%
Liberty	54,530	57.44%	25,241	80.58%	5,952	19.00%	88	0.28%	35	0.11%
Limestone	14,443	62.83%	7,081	78.03%	1,921	21.17%	44	0.48%	23	0.25%
Lipscomb	1,818	69.25%	1,125	89.36%	123	9.77%	11	0.87%	0	0.00%
Live Oak	7,774	65.51%	4,307	84.57%	761	14.94%	13	0.26%	11	0.22%
Llano	18,455	73.85%	10,902	79.99%	2,613	19.17%	75	0.55%	32	0.23%
Loving	128	75.78%	86	88.66%	10	10.31%	0	0.00%	1	1.03%
Lubbock	197,198	63.41%	86,547	69.22%	37,148	29.71%	793	0.63%	484	0.39%
Lynn	4,385	58.54%	2,175	84.73%	371	14.45%	14	0.55%	7	0.27%
Madison	5,424	64.77%	3,033	86.34%	455	12.95%	17	0.48%	8	0.23%
Marion	159,331	62.56%	64,606	64.82%	33,863	33.97%	696	0.70%	325	0.33%
Martin	644	75.62%	448	91.99%	37	7.60%	2	0.41%	0	0.00%
Mason	8,471	64.80%	4,498	81.95%	964	17.56%	17	0.31%	10	0.18%
Matagorda	7,822	60.27%	3,577	75.88%	1,101	23.36%	18	0.38%	18	0.38%
Maverick	3,497	59.57%	1,825	87.61%	247	11.86%	7	0.34%	4	0.19%
McCulloch	3,278	77.09%	2,076	82.15%	434	17.17%	12	0.47%	4	0.16%
McLennan	22,394	59.44%	9,957	74.80%	3,231	24.27%	67	0.50%	53	0.40%
McMullen	35,947	43.80%	9,285	58.97%	6,373	40.48%	46	0.29%	39	0.25%
Medina	38,525	63.90%	17,464	70.94%	6,950	28.23%	103	0.42%	81	0.33%
Menard	1,516	68.60%	861	82.79%	170	16.35%	5	0.48%	3	0.29%
Midland	99,004	59.40%	46,944	79.83%	11,351	19.30%	363	0.62%	142	0.24%
Milam	17,208	64.49%	8,691	78.31%	2,331	21.00%	42	0.38%	29	0.26%
Mills	3,626	75.62%	2,418	88.18%	310	11.31%	9	0.33%	4	0.15%
Mitchell	4,526	55.52%	2,144	85.32%	352	14.01%	11	0.44%	6	0.24%
Montague	15,649	70.94%	9,825	88.51%	1,208	10.88%	36	0.32%	28	0.25%
Montgomery	453,832	67.70%	221,964	72.24%	82,277	26.78%	1,672	0.54%	1,221	0.40%
Moore	10,130	52.93%	4,458	83.14%	860	16.04%	25	0.47%	16	0.30%
Morris	8,948	60.73%	4,092	75.30%	1,312	24.14%	22	0.40%	7	0.13%
Motley	849	76.56%	612	94.15%	35	5.38%	2	0.31%	1	0.15%
Nacogdoches	40,051	63.63%	17,575	68.96%	7,690	30.17%	127	0.50%	78	0.31%
Navarro	32,955	60.18%	14,983	75.55%	1,708	23.74%	76	0.38%	62	0.31%
Newton	9,486	60.61%	4,781	83.16%	952	16.56%	7	0.12%	9	0.16%
Nolan	8,494	60.22%	4,048	79.14%	1,020	19.94%	26	0.51%	20	0.39%
Nueces	218,753	55.62%	67,201	55.23%	53,248	43.76%	663	0.54%	502	0.41%
Ochiltree	5,201	57.87%	2,723	90.47%	269	8.94%	12	0.40%	4	0.13%
Oldham	1,340	72.69%	895	91.89%	74	7.60%	4	0.41%	1	0.10%
Orange	56,232	64.62%	30,191	83.08%	5,945	16.36%	128	0.35%	64	0.18%
Palo Pinto	20,351	65.53%	11,093	83.18%	2,143	16.07%	54	0.40%	43	0.32%
Panola	17,836	64.13%	9,500	83.05%	1,905	16.65%	23	0.20%	9	0.08%
Parker	127,635	71.17%	75,168	82.75%	14,872	16.37%	534	0.59%	228	0.25%
Parmer	4,549	55.05%	2,123	84.78%	368	14.70%	9	0.36%	4	0.16%
Pecos	8,328	50.83%	3,042	71.86%	1,144	27.03%	24	0.57%	23	0.54%
Polk	44,308	54.83%	19,216	79.10%	4,910	20.21%	100	0.41%	59	0.24%
Potter	59,681	53.82%	23,007	71.63%	8,748	27.23%	210	0.65%	126	0.39%
Presidio	4,429	45.02%	686	34.40%	1,289	64.64%	9	0.45%	10	0.50%
Rains	9,404	69.72%	5,649	86.17%	869	13.26%	23	0.35%	13	0.20%
Randall	100,105	66.83%	53,314	79.69%	12,935	19.33%	403	0.60%	202	0.30%
Reagan	1,803	52.63%	800	84.30%	141	14.86%	2	0.21%	6	0.63%
Real	2,698	72.57%	1,625	82.99%	315	16.09%	12	0.61%	6	0.31%

County	Registered Voters	Turnout %	Presidential Race							
			TRUMP	%	HARRIS	%	OLIVER	%	STEIN	%
Red River	8,746	66.27%	4,682	80.78%	1,103	19.03%	7	0.12%	4	0.07%
Reeves	7,838	43.88%	2,340	68.04%	1,070	31.11%	22	0.64%	7	0.20%
Refugio	4,938	62.27%	2,134	69.40%	919	29.89%	12	0.39%	7	0.23%
Roberts	722	79.22%	547	95.63%	20	3.50%	3	0.52%	0	0.00%
Robertson	12,600	64.75%	6,177	75.72%	1,926	23.61%	38	0.47%	13	0.16%
Rockwall	87,932	70.81%	43,542	69.93%	18,092	29.05%	374	0.60%	243	0.39%
Runnels	6,807	59.59%	3,580	88.26%	452	11.14%	15	0.37%	9	0.22%
Rusk	34,277	63.33%	17,234	79.40%	4,337	19.98%	81	0.37%	50	0.23%
Sabine	8,446	66.08%	4,972	89.09%	590	10.57%	12	0.22%	7	0.13%
San Augustine	6,038	62.06%	2,917	77.85%	809	21.59%	17	0.45%	4	0.11%
San Jacinto	20,406	62.67%	10,524	82.29%	2,175	17.01%	49	0.38%	41	0.32%
San Patricio	45,265	56.51%	17,337	67.78%	8,025	31.37%	131	0.51%	79	0.31%
San Saba	3,795	71.38%	2,412	89.04%	276	10.19%	12	0.44%	3	0.11%
Schleicher	1,732	63.97%	906	81.77%	192	17.33%	7	0.63%	3	0.27%
Scurry	9,366	61.08%	4,945	86.44%	734	12.83%	27	0.47%	14	0.24%
Shackelford	2,439	70.85%	1,565	90.57%	146	8.45%	12	0.69%	4	0.23%
Shelby	16,355	60.83%	8,164	82.07%	1,741	17.50%	27	0.27%	16	0.16%
Sherman	1,448	60.29%	817	93.59%	48	5.50%	5	0.57%	2	0.23%
Smith	162,009	64.12%	74,862	72.07%	28,041	26.99%	559	0.54%	353	0.34%
Somervell	7,420	71.35%	4,493	84.87%	751	14.19%	28	0.53%	13	0.25%
Starr	36,420	45.09%	9,487	57.77%	6,862	41.79%	36	0.22%	34	0.21%
Stephens	5,881	63.95%	3,385	90.00%	384	10.21%	5	0.13%	4	0.11%
Sterling	892	70.52%	583	92.69%	43	6.84%	1	0.16%	2	0.32%
Stonewall	955	74.97%	604	84.36%	110	15.36%	1	0.14%	1	0.14%
Sutton	2,348	59.63%	1,167	83.36%	228	16.29%	3	0.21%	2	0.14%
Swisher	3,900	58.08%	1,840	81.24%	403	17.79%	13	0.57%	9	0.40%
Tarrant	1,309,456	62.87%	426,626	51.82%	384,501	46.70%	5,534	0.67%	6,019	0.73%
Taylor	89,791	61.72%	41,198	74.34%	13,624	24.58%	371	0.67%	193	0.35%
Terrell	626	64.70%	314	77.53%	91	22.47%	0	0.00%	0	0.00%
Terry	6,412	53.34%	2,815	82.31%	587	17.16%	13	0.38%	4	0.12%
Throckmorton	1,217	73.95%	823	91.44%	73	8.11%	2	0.22%	2	0.22%
Titus	18,026	56.66%	7,861	76.96%	2,275	22.27%	48	0.47%	24	0.23%
Tom Green	72,586	62.63%	33,399	73.47%	11,585	25.48%	308	0.68%	146	0.32%
Travis	926,313	62.75%	170,787	29.38%	398,981	68.64%	4,631	0.80%	5,886	1.01%
Trinity	12,283	60.03%	6,136	83.21%	1,195	16.21%	26	0.35%	17	0.23%
Tyler	14,888	64.33%	8,286	86.51%	1,249	13.04%	28	0.29%	14	0.15%
Upshur	30,374	65.47%	16,939	85.18%	2,820	14.18%	78	0.39%	45	0.23%
Upton	2,114	61.64%	1,149	88.18%	146	11.20%	3	0.23%	5	0.38%
Uvalde	17,929	54.50%	6,482	66.33%	3,218	32.93%	37	0.38%	32	0.33%
Val Verde	30,117	48.44%	9,162	62.81%	5,282	36.21%	73	0.50%	61	0.42%
Van Zandt	27,950	66.95%	24,351	58.33%	3,450	8.26%	98	0.23%	36	0.09%
Victoria	58,087	60.80%	25,010	70.82%	9,998	28.31%	136	0.39%	95	0.27%
Walker	38,958	64.62%	17,515	69.57%	7,461	29.64%	117	0.46%	77	0.31%
Waller	44,330	62.17%	17,077	61.96%	10,183	36.95%	133	0.48%	152	0.55%
Ward	7,047	53.43%	3,115	82.74%	627	16.65%	16	0.42%	6	0.16%
Washington	25,794	70.62%	14,020	76.96%	4,058	22.28%	99	0.54%	31	0.17%
Webb	148,536	44.34%	33,384	50.69%	31,952	48.51%	226	0.34%	283	0.43%
Wharton	26,422	62.27%	12,439	75.60%	3,910	23.76%	63	0.38%	40	0.24%
Wheeler	3,408	66.73%	2,093	92.04%	169	7.43%	8	0.35%	2	0.09%
Wichita	79,805	55.80%	31,818	71.45%	12,237	27.48%	295	0.66%	147	0.33%
Wilbarger	8,126	54.97%	3,566	79.83%	860	19.25%	28	0.63%	9	0.20%
Willacy	11,703	47.53%	2,856	51.34%	2,673	48.05%	18	0.32%	16	0.29%
Williamson	445,326	69.27%	155,310	50.35%	147,766	47.90%	2,546	0.83%	2,541	0.82%
Wilson	39,092	69.77%	20,894	76.60%	6,247	22.90%	80	0.29%	49	0.18%
Winkler	4,086	47.31%	1,646	85.15%	283	14.64%	3	0.16%	0	0.00%
Wise	55,864	68.46%	32,385	84.68%	5,605	14.66%	167	0.44%	73	0.19%
Wood	35,589	68.52%	20,621	84.56%	3,618	14.84%	100	0.41%	42	0.17%
Yoakum	4,289	55.79%	2,039	85.21%	342	14.29%	7	0.29%	5	0.21%
Young	12,394	67.08%	7,298	87.78%	962	11.57%	30	0.36%	19	0.23%
Zapata	8,182	59.53%	2,970	60.97%	1,877	38.53%	15	0.31%	9	0.18%
Zavala	7,810	44.71%	1,482	42.44%	1,984	56.82%	20	0.57%	6	0.17%

2024 GENERAL ELECTION RESULTS

Abbreviations used are **(D)** Democrat, **(R)** Republican, **(L)** Libertarian, **(Ind.)** Independent, and **(W-I)** Write-in.

Below are the official voting results for the general election held November 5, 2024, as canvassed by the State Canvassing Board. Federal races include presidential, Senate, and House of Representatives elections. Statewide races include railroad commissioner, courts of criminal appeals, and Texas Supreme Court. District races include the Texas State Senate and State Board of Education.

FEDERAL RACES

PRESIDENT

Candidate	Votes	Percent
Donald J. Trump (R)	6,393,597	56.14%
Kamala Harris (D)	4,835,250	42.46%
Jill Stein (Green)	82,701	0.73%
Chase Oliver (L)	68,557	0.60%
Peter Sonski (W-I)	3,780	0.03%
Claudia De la Cruz (W-I)	2,374	0.02%
Cornel West (W-I)	1,858	0.02%
Shiva Ayyadurai (W-I)	433	0.00%
Jessie Cuellar (W-I)	98	0.00%
Cherunda Fox (W-I)	26	0.00%
Total Vote		**11,388,674**

U.S. SENATE

Candidate	Votes	Percent
Ted Cruz (R)	5,990,741	53.05%
Colin Allred (D)	5,031,249	44.56%
Ted Brown (L)	267,039	2.36%
Analisa Roche (W-I)	1,906	0.02%
Tracy Andrus (W-I)	919	0.01%
Total Vote		**11,291,854**

U.S. HOUSE OF REPRESENTATIVES

District 2

Candidate	Votes	Percent
Dan Crenshaw (R)	214,631	65.66%
Peter Filler (D)	112,252	34.34%
Total Vote		**326,883**

District 3

Candidate	Votes	Percent
Keith Self (R)	237,794	62.45%
Sandeep Srivastava (D)	142,953	37.55%
Total Vote		**380,747**

District 4

Candidate	Votes	Percent
Pat Fallon (R)	241,603	68.38%
Simon Cardell (D)	111,696	31.62%
Total Vote		**353,299**

District 5

Candidate	Votes	Percent
Lance Gooden (R)	192,185	64.08%
Ruth "Truth" Torres (D)	107,712	35.92%
Total Vote		**299,897**

District 6

Candidate	Votes	Percent
Jake Ellzey (R)	188,119	65.68%
John Love III (D)	98,319	34.32%
Total Vote		**286,438**

District 7

Candidate	Votes	Percent
Lizzie Fletcher (D)	149,820	61.28%
Caroline Kane (R)	94,651	38.72%
Total Vote		**244,471**

District 8

Candidate	Votes	Percent
Morgan Luttrell (R)	233,423	68.22%
Laura Jones (D)	108,754	31.78%
Total Vote		**342,177**

District 10

Candidate	Votes	Percent
Michael T. McCaul (R)	221,229	63.6%
Theresa Boisseau (D)	118,280	34.01%
Jeff Miller (L)	8,309	2.39%
Total Vote		**347,818**

District 12

Candidate	Votes	Percent
Craig Goldman (R)	215,564	63.45%
Trey J. Hunt (D)	124,154	36.55%
Total Vote		**339,718**

District 14

Candidate	Votes	Percent
Randy Weber (R)	210,320	68.69%
Rhonda Hart (D)	95,875	31.31%
Total Vote		**306,195**

District 15

Candidate	Votes	Percent
Monica De La Cruz (R)	127,804	57.11%
Michelle Vallejo (D)	95,965	42.89%
Total Vote		**223,769**

District 16

Veronica Escobar (D)	131,391	59.50%
Irene Armendariz-Jackson (R)	89,281	40.43%
D. "DMB" Montanez (W-I)	156	0.07%
Total Vote		**220,828**

District 17

Pete Sessions (R)	193,101	66.35%
Mark Lorenzen (D)	97,941	33.65%
Total Vote		**291,042**

District 18

Sylvester Turner (D)	151,834	69.42%
Lana Centonze (R)	66,810	30.55%
Total Vote		**218,720**

District 19

Jodey C. Arrington (R)	214,950	80.69%
Nathan Lewis (Ind.)	27,461	10.31%
Bernard Johnson (L)	23,964	9.00%
Total Vote		**266,375**

District 21

Chip Roy (R)	263,744	61.85%
Kristin Hook (D)	153,765	36.06%
Bob King (L)	8,914	2.09%
Total Vote		**426,423**

District 22

Troy E. Nehls (R)	209,285	62.12%
Marquette Greene-Scott (D)	127,604	37.88%
Total Vote		**336,889**

District 23

Tony Gonzales (R)	180,720	62.3%
S. Limon (D)	109,373	37.7%
Total Vote		**290,093**

District 24

Beth Van Duyne (R)	227,108	60.30%
Sam Eppler (D)	149,518	39.70%
Total Vote		**376,626**

District 25

Roger Williams (R)	263,042	99.37%
Chad Hagg (W-I)	1,661	0.63%
Total Vote		**264,703**

District 26

Brandon Gill (R)	241,096	62.07%
Ernest R. Lineberger III (D)	138,558	35.67%
Phil Gray (L)	8,773	2.26%
Total Vote		**388,427**

District 27

Michael Cloud (R)	183,980	66.04%
Tanya Lloyd (D)	94,596	33.96%
Total Vote		**278,576**

District 28

Henry Cuellar (D)	125,280	52.79%
Jay Furman (R)	112,018	47.21%
Total Vote		**237,298**

District 29

Sylvia Garcia (D)	99,379	65.29%
Alan Garza (R)	52,830	34.71%
Total Vote		**152,209**

District 30

Jasmine Crockett (D)	197,650	84.89%
Jrmar "JJ" Jefferson (L)	35,175	15.11%
Total Vote		**232,825**

District 31
John Carter (R) . . . . 229,087 . . . . 64.43%
Stuart Whitlow (D) . . . . . 126,470 . . . . 35.57%
Total Vote 355,557

District 32
Julie Johnson (D) . . . . . . 140,536 . . . . 60.45%
Darrell Day (R) . . . . .85,941 . . . . 36.97%
Kevin A. Hale (L) . . . . 5,987 . . . . .2.58%
Total Vote 232,464

District 33
Marc Veasey (D). . . . . . . 114,289 . . . . 68.79%
Patrick David Gillespie (R) . .51,864 . . . . 31.21%
Total Vote 166,153

District 34
Vicente Gonzalez (D) . . . . 102,780 . . . . 51.29%
Mayra Flores (R). . . . . . . .97,603 . . . . 48.71%
Total Vote 200,383

District 35
Greg Casar (D). . . . . 170,509 . . . . 67.36%
Steven Wright (R) . . . . . . .82,610 . . . . 32.64%
Total Vote 253,119

District 36
Brian Babin (R) . . . . . . .206,009 . . . . 69.36%
Dayna Steele (D). . . . . . . .91,009 . . . . 30.64%
Total Vote 297,018

District 37
Lloyd Doggett (D). . . . . . 252,980 . . . . 74.22%
Jenny Garcia Sharon (R) . . .80,366 . . . . 23.58%
Girish Altekar (L) . . . . .7,511 . . . . .2.20%
Total Vote 340,857

District 38
Wesley P. Hunt (R) . . . . . 215,030 . . . . 62.73%
Melissa McDonough (D). . . 127,640 . . . . 37.24%
Total Vote 342,764

STATE RACES

RAILROAD COMMISSIONER

Christi Craddick (R) . . . 6,100,218 . . . . 55.63%
Katherine Culbert (D) . . . 4,275,904 . . . . 39.00%
Eddie Espinoza (Green) . . . 301,793 . . . . 2.75%
Hawk Dunlap (L) . . . . . .285,544 . . . . 2.60%
Total Vote 10,965,115

SUPREME COURT

Justice, Place 2
Jimmy Blacklock (R) . . . 6,372,584 . . . . 58.23%
Dasean Jones (D). . . . . . 4,571,171 . . . . 41.77%
Total Vote 10,943,755

Justice, Place 4
John Devine (R) . . . . . . 6,256,496 . . . . 57.33%
Christine Vinh Weems (D) 4,656,560 . . . . 42.67%
Total Vote 10,913,056

Justice, Place 6
Jane Bland (R) . . . . 6,145,167 . . . . 56.24%
Bonnie Lee Goldstein (D). 4,425,189 . . . . 40.50%
J. David Roberson (L) . . . . 355,485 . . . . 3.25%
Total Vote 10,925,841

COURT OF CRIMINAL APPEALS

Presiding Judge
David J. Schenck (R). . . . 6,330,389 . . . . 58.13%
Holly Taylor (D). . . . . . 4,558,856 . . . . 41.87%
Total Vote 10,889,245

Judge, Place 7
Gina Parker (R) . . . . . . 6,340,949 . . . . 58.35%
Nancy Mulder (D). . . . . 4,526,924 . . . . 41.65%
Total Vote 10,867,873

Judge, Place 8
Lee Finley (R) . . . . 6,385,238 . . . . 58.87%
Chika Anyiam (D). . . . . 4,461,229 . . . . 41.13%
Total Vote 10,846,467

DISTRICT RACES

STATE BOARD OF EDUCATION

District 1
Gustavo Reveles (D). . . . . 314,162 . . . . 50.94%
Michael (Travis) Stevens (R) . 302,544 . . . . 49.06%
Total Vote 616,706

District 10
Tom Maynard (R). . . . . . 594,496 . . . . 67.56%
Raquel Saenz Ortiz (L) . . . 285,508 . . . . 32.44%
Total Vote 880,004

District 11
Brandon Hall (R) . . . . . . 519,163 . . . . 61.51%
Rayna Glasser (D) . . . . . . 303,180 . . . . 35.92%
Hunter Crow (Green) . . . . .21,679 . . . . 2.57%
Total Vote 844,022

District 12
Pam Little (R) . . . . 565,011 . . . . 63.30%
George King (D). . . . . . . 327,645 . . . . 36.70%
Total Vote 892,656

District 15
Aaron Kinsey (R) . . . . . . 512,043 . . . . 76.26%
Morgan Kirkpatrick (D). . . 137,759 . . . . 20.52%
Jack B. Westbrook (L). . . . .21,639 . . . . 3.22%
Total Vote 671,441

STATE SENATOR

District 6

Candidate	Votes	Percent
Carol Alvarado (D)	119,280	63.01%
Martha Fierro (R)	70,013	36.99%
Total Vote		**189,293**

District 7

Candidate	Votes	Percent
Paul Bettencourt (R)	251,489	63.41%
Michelle Gwinn (D)	145,100	36.59%
Total Vote		**396,589**

District 8

Candidate	Votes	Percent
Angela Paxton (R)	269,743	59.36%
Rachel Mello (D)	184,642	40.64%
Total Vote		**454,385**

District 10

Candidate	Votes	Percent
Phil King (R)	227,475	61.71%
Andy Morris (D)	141,163	38.29%
Total Vote		**368,638**

District 12

Candidate	Votes	Percent
Tan Parker (R)	277,734	61.36%
Stephanie Draper (D)	174,875	38.64%
Total Vote		**452,609**

District 15

Candidate	Votes	Percent
Molly Cook (D)	200,680	61.90%
Joseph L. Trahan (R)	123,515	38.10%
Total Vote		**324,195**

District 17

Candidate	Votes	Percent
Joan Huffman (R)	238,328	64.16%
Kathy Cheng (D)	133,127	35.84%
Total Vote		**371,455**

District 25

Candidate	Votes	Percent
Donna Campbell (R)	321,653	63.57%
Merrie Fox (D)	184,312	36.43%
Total Vote		**505,965**

District 27

Candidate	Votes	Percent
Adam Hinojosa (R)	126,073	49.38%
Morgan Lamantia (D)	123,305	48.29%
Robin Lee Vargas (Green)	5,956	2.33%
Total Vote		**255,334**

District 30

Candidate	Votes	Percent
Brent Hagenbuch (R)	289,981	65.03%
Dale Frey (D)	155,949	34.97%
Total Vote		**445,930**

STATE REPRESENTATIVE

District 2

Candidate	Votes	Percent
Brent A. Money (R)	71,222	80.56%
Kristen Washington (D)	17,182	19.44%
Total Vote		**88,404**

District 4

Candidate	Votes	Percent
Keith Bell (R)	60,287	69.67%
Alex Bar-Sela (D)	26,240	30.33%
Total Vote		**86,527**

District 5

Candidate	Votes	Percent
Cole Hefner (R)	74,381	98.79%
Nancy A. Nichols (W-I)	910	1.21%
Total Vote		**75,291**

District 6

Candidate	Votes	Percent
Daniel Alders (R)	56,497	71.83%
Cody J. Grace (D)	22,158	28.17%
Total Vote		**78,655**

District 7

Candidate	Votes	Percent
Jay Dean (R)	59,056	74.21%
Marlena R. Cooper (D)	20,520	25.79%
Total Vote		**79,576**

District 8

Candidate	Votes	Percent
Cody Harris (R)	60,938	81.36%
Carolyn F. Salter (D)	13,961	18.64%
Total Vote		**74,899**

District 10

Candidate	Votes	Percent
Brian Harrison (R)	68,706	98.67%
Jennifer Brummell (W-I)	888	1.28%
Jeremy Schroppel (W-I)	40	0.06%
Total Vote		**69,634**

District 12

Candidate	Votes	Percent
Trey Wharton (R)	64,105	76.84%
Dee Howard Mullins (D)	19,325	23.16%
Total Vote		**83,430**

District 13

Candidate	Votes	Percent
Angelia Orr (R)	55,317	76.18%
Albert Hunter (D)	17,301	23.82%
Total Vote		**72,618**

District 14

Candidate	Votes	Percent
Paul Dyson (R)	40,262	60.46%
Fred Medina (D)	26,332	39.54%
Total Vote		**66,594**

District 16

Candidate	Votes	Percent
Will Metcalf (R)	73,385	80.36%
Mike Midler (D)	17,930	19.64%
Total Vote		**91,315**

District 17

Candidate	Votes	Percent
Stan Gerdes (R)	53,531	66.15%
Desiree Venable (D)	27,389	33.85%

Total Vote 80,920

District 18
Janis Holt (R) . . . . .69,326 . . . . 86.58%
Seth Steele (L) . . . . 10,749 . . . . 13.42%
Total Vote 80,075

District 19
Ellen Troxclair (R). . . . . . . 87,416 . . . . 70.85%
Dwain Handley (D) . . . . . .31,486 . . . . 25.52%
Kodi Sawin (Ind.) . . . . 4,478 . . . . 3.63%
Total Vote 123,380

District 20
Terry M. Wilson (R) . . . . .64,086 . . . . 59.76%
Stephen M. Wyman (D) . . .43,148 . . . . 40.24%
Total Vote 107,234

District 23
Terri Leo Wilson (R) . . . . .53,841 . . . . 66.87%
Dev Merugumala (D) . . . . .26,680 . . . . 33.13%
Total Vote 80,521

District 25
Cody Thane Vasut (R) . . . .47,002 . . . . 61.04%
J. Daggett (D) . . . . .29,999 . . . . 38.96%
Total Vote 77,001

District 26
Matt Morgan (R) . . . . . . .48,561 . . . . 59.17%
Daniel Lee (D). . . . . .33,505 . . . . 40.83%
Total Vote 82,066

District 27
Ronald Reynolds (D) . . . . .57,594 . . . . 69.81%
Ibifrisolam Max-Alalibo (R) 24,908 . . . . 30.19%
Total Vote 82,502

District 28
Gary Gates (R). . . . . .56,890 . . . . 60.55%
Marty Rocha (D) . . . . . . .37,058 . . . . 39.45%
Total Vote 93,948

District 29
Jeffrey Barry (R). . . . . . . .49,655 . . . . 61.52%
Adrienne Bell (D) . . . . . . .31,060 . . . . 38.48%
Total Vote 80,715

District 30
AJ Louderback (R). . . . . . . 57,180 . . . . 76.96%
Stephanie R. Bassham (D). . . 17,120 . . . . 23.04%
Total Vote 74,300

District 32
Todd Hunter (R) . . . . . . .54,091 . . . . 68.69%
Cathy Mcauliffe (D). . . . . .24,656 . . . . 31.31%
Total Vote 78,747

District 34
Denise Villalobos (R). . . . .28,553 . . . . 55.37%
Solomon P. Ortiz Jr. (D) . . .23,013 . . . . 44.63%
Total Vote 51,566

District 37
Janie Lopez (R) . . . . .30,590 . . . . 55.01%
Jonathan Gracia (D). . . . . .25,014 . . . . 44.99%
Total Vote 55,604

District 39
Armando Martinez (D) . . . .26,962 . . . . 60.90%
Jimmie Garcia (R) . . . . . . .17,308 . . . . 39.10%
Total Vote 44,270

District 41
Bobby Guerra (D) . . . . . . .30,589 . . . . 53.47%
John Robert Guerra (R). . . .26,618 . . . . 46.53%
Total Vote 57,207

District 43
J.M. Lozano (R). . . . . . . .43,812 . . . . 66.73%
Mariana Casarez (D) . . . . .21,842 . . . . 33.27%
Total Vote 65,654

District 44
Alan Schoolcraft (R) . . . . .57,466 . . . . 65.12%
Eric Norman (D) . . . . . . .30,780 . . . . 34.88%
Total Vote 88,246

District 45
Erin Zwiener (D) . . . . . . .52,912 . . . . 56.76%
Tennyson G. Moreno (R) . . .40,312 . . . . 43.24%
Total Vote 93,224

District 46
Sheryl Cole (D) . . . . .60,832 . . . . 73.24%
Nikki Kosich (R) . . . . . . .22,223 . . . . 26.76%
Total Vote 83,055

District 47
Vikki Goodwin (D) . . . . . . 59,016 . . . . 60.17%
Scott Firsing (R). . . . . . . .39,066 . . . . 39.83%
Total Vote 98,082

District 48
Donna Howard (D) . . . . . .72,631 . . . . 83.00%
Daniel Jerome McCarthy (L). . 14,871 . . . . 17.00%
Total Vote 87,502

District 52
Caroline Harris Davila (R) . .62,830 . . . . 56.24%
Jennie Birkholz (D) . . . . . .48,884 . . . . 43.76%
Total Vote 111,714

District 53
Wes Virdell (R) . . . . 76,176 . . . . 76.59%

Joe P. Herrera (D) . . . . . . .21,058 . . . . 21.17%
B. W. Holk (L). . . . . 2,230 . . . . .2.24%
Total Vote . . . . **.99,464**

District 54
Brad Buckley (R). . . . . . . .34,526 . . . . 61.09%
Dawn Richardson (D). . . . .21,993 . . . . 38.91%
Total Vote . . . . **.56,519**

District 55
Hillary Hickland (R) . . . . .39,455 . . . . 57.41%
Jennifer Alicia Lee (D) . . . .29,269 . . . . 42.59%
Total Vote . . . . **.68,724**

District 56
Pat Curry (R) . . . . .56,195 . . . . 68.59%
Erin Shank (D) . . . . .25,733 . . . . 31.41%
Total Vote . . . . **.81,928**

District 57
Richard Hayes (R). . . . . . .51,865 . . . . 58.27%
Collin Johnson (D) . . . . . .34,279 . . . . 38.51%
Darren Hamilton (L) . . . . . 2,870 . . . . .3.22%
Total Vote **89,014**

District 58
Helen Kerwin (R) . . . . . . .63,760 . . . . 82.06%
Richard Windmann (L). . . . 13,935 . . . . 17.94%
Total Vote . . . . **.77,695**

District 59
Shelby Slawson (R) . . . . . .64,147 . . . . 80.67%
Hannah Bohm (D). . . . . . .15,367 . . . . 19.33%
Total Vote . . . . **.79,514**

District 61
Keresa Richardson (R) . . . .58,513 . . . . 59.62%
Tony Adams (D). . . . . . . .39,632 . . . . 40.38%
Total Vote **98,145**

District 62
Shelley Luther (R). . . . . . .67,062 . . . . 77.71%
Tiffany Drake (D). . . . . . .19,240 . . . . 22.29%
Total Vote . . . . **.86,302**

District 63
Ben Bumgarner (R) . . . . . .46,861 . . . . 55.66%
Michelle Beckley (D) . . . . .37,326 . . . . 44.34%
Total Vote **84,187**

District 64
Andy Hopper (R) . . . . . . .59,542 . . . . 63.12%
Angela Brewer (D). . . . . . .34,786 . . . . 36.88%
Total Vote . . . . **.94,328**

District 65
Mitch Little (R) . . . . 60,284 . . . . 60.30%
Detrick Deburr (D) . . . . . .39,686 . . . . 39.70%
Total Vote . . . . **.99,970**

District 66
Matt Shaheen (R) . . . . . . .58,294 . . . . 61.11%
David W. Carstens (D) . . . .37,098 . . . . 38.89%
Total Vote . . . . **.95,392**

District 67
Jeff Leach (R) . . . . .56,107 . . . . 60.23%
Makala L. Washington (D). . 37,051 . . . . 39.77%
Total Vote . . . . **.93,158**

District 68
David Spiller (R). . . . . . . .79,554 . . . . 87.17%
Stacey Swann (D) . . . . 11,705 . . . . 12.83%
Total Vote **91,259**

District 69
James B. Frank (R). . . . . . .53,583 . . . . 78.68%
Walter Coppage (D). . . . . . 14,518 . . . . 21.32%
Total Vote . . . . **.68,101**

District 70
Steve Kinard (R). . . . . . . .34,933 . . . . 47.78%
Mihaela Elizabeth Plesa (D) .38,183 . . . . 52.22%
Total Vote . . . . **.73,116**

District 71
Stan Lambert (R) . . . . . . .58,413 . . . . 81.03%
Linda Goolsbee (D) . . . . . . 13,678 . . . . 18.97%
Total Vote . . . . **.72,091**

District 73
Carrie Isaac (R) . . . . .91,924 . . . . 71.47%
Sally Duval (D) . . . . .36,686 . . . . 28.52%
Total Vote **128,610**

District 74
Eddie Morales Jr. (D) . . . . .28,203 . . . . 51.67%
Robert Garza (R) . . . . . . .26,378 . . . . 48.33%
Total Vote . . . . **.54,581**

District 76
Suleman Lalani (D) . . . . . .39,770 . . . . 56.50%
Lea C.S. Simmons (R). . . . .30,615 . . . . 43.50%
Total Vote . . . . **.70,385**

District 80
Don McLaughlin Jr. (R). . . . 31,182 . . . . 59.49%
Cecilia Castellano (D). . . . .21,231 . . . . 40.51%
Total Vote . . . . **.52,413**

District 82
Tom Craddick (R). . . . . . .50,546 . . . . 82.73%
Steven Schafersman (D) . . .10,555 . . . . 17.27%
Total Vote . . . . **.61,101**

District 84

Carl H. Tepper (R) . . . . . . 37,021 . . . . 64.1%
Noah Lopez (D). . . . . 20,733 . . . . 35.9%
Total Vote 57,754

District 89
Candy Noble (R) . . . . 55,900 . . . . 60.63%
Darrel Evans (D). . . . . 36,292 . . . . 39.37%
Total Vote 92,192

District 93
Nate Schatzline (R) . . . . . . 53,532 . . . . 60.55%
Perla Bojorquez (D) . . . . . . 34,871 . . . . 39.45%
Total Vote 88,403

District 94
Tony Tinderholt (R). . . . . . 43,785 . . . . 55.62%
Denise Wilkerson (D). . . . . 34,937 . . . . 44.38%
Total Vote 78,722

District 96
David Cook (R) . . . . 48,814 . . . . 57.37%
Ebony M. Turner (D) . . . . . 36,276 . . . . 42.63%
Total Vote 85,090

District 97
John McQueeney (R) . . . . . 51,432 . . . . 58.07%
Carlos Walker (D). . . . . . . 37,132 . . . . 41.93%
Total Vote 88,564

District 98
Giovanni Capriglione (R) . . . 64,833 . . . . 65.70%
Scott Bryan White (D) . . . . 33,845 . . . . 34.30%
Total Vote 98,678

District 99
Charlie Geren (R) . . . . 47,708 . . . . 62.82%
Mimi Coffey (D). . . . . 28,233 . . . . 37.18%
Total Vote 75,941

District 101
Chris Turner (D). . . . . 40,337 . . . . 64.94%
Clint Burgess (R) . . . . 21,781 . . . . 35.06%
Total Vote 62,118

District 105
Terry Meza (D) . . . . 22,850 . . . . 54.69%
Rose Cannaday (R) . . . . . . 18,928 . . . . 45.31%
Total Vote 41,778

District 106
Jared Patterson (R) . . . . . . 61,381 . . . . 60.58%
Hava Johnston (D). . . . . . . 39,941 . . . . 39.42%
Total Vote 101,322

District 108
Morgan Meyer (R). . . . . . . 60,227 . . . . 57.61%
Elizabeth Ginsberg (D) . . . . 44,307 . . . . 42.39%
Total Vote 104,534

District 112
Angie Chen Button (R) . . . . 47,456 . . . . 53.87%
Averie Bishop (D) . . . . 40,645 . . . . 46.13%
Total Vote 88,101

District 113
Rhetta Andrews Bowers (D) . 33,547 . . . . 56.59%
Stephen Stanley (R) . . . . . . 25,732 . . . . 43.41%
Total Vote 59,279

District 114
John Bryant (D) . . . . 43,554 . . . . 62.76%
Aimee Ramsey (R). . . . . . . 25,839 . . . . 37.24%
Total Vote 69,393

District 115
Cassandra Hernandez (D). . . 37,692 . . . . 54.31%
John Jun (R) . . . . 31,709 . . . . 45.69%
Total Vote 69,401

District 116
Trey Martinez Fischer (D) . . 38,044 . . . . 66.00%
Darryl W. Crain (R). . . . . . 19,596 . . . . 34.00%
Total Vote 57,640

District 117
Philip Cortez (D) . . . . 40,066 . . . . 57.99%
Ben Mostyn (R) . . . . 29,021 . . . . 42.01%
Total Vote 69,087

District 118
John Lujan Iii (R) . . . . 39,246 . . . . 51.73%
Kristian Carranza (D). . . . . 36,624 . . . . 48.27%
Total Vote 75,870

District 119
Elizabeth "Liz" Campos (D) 38,160 . . . . 63.68%
Brandon J. Grable (R) . . . . . 21,763 . . . . 36.32%
Total Vote 59,923

District 121
Marc Lahood (R) . . . . 51,013 . . . . 52.53%
Laurel Jordan Swift (D). . . . 46,104 . . . . 47.47%
Total Vote 97,117

District 122
Mark Dorazio (R). . . . . . . 64,018 . . . . 58.09%
Kevin Geary (D) . . . . 46,180 . . . . 41.91%
Total Vote 110,198

District 124
Josey Garcia (D) . . . . 30,345 . . . . 61.52%
Sylvia Soto (R). . . . . 18,981 . . . . 38.48%
Total Vote 49,326

District 126
E. Sam Harless (R) . . . . . . 59,749 . . . . 98.98%
Sarah Smith (W-I). . . . . 616 . . . . 1.02%

Total Vote 60,365

District 127
Charles Cunningham (R) . . .55,048 . . . . . . 60.51%
John Lehr (D) . . . . . .35,932 . . . . . . 39.49%
Total Vote 90,980

District 128
Briscoe Cain (R) . . . . . .45,372 . . . . . . 68.24%
Chuck Crews (D) . . . . . . 19,181 . . . . . . 28.85%
Kevin J. Hagan (L) . . . . . .1,932 . . . . . . 2.91%
Total Vote 66,485

District 129
Dennis Paul (R) . . . . . .52,419 . . . . . . 60.83%
Doug Peterson (D) . . . . . .33,758 . . . . . . 39.17%
Total Vote 86,177

District 130
Tom Oliverson (R) . . . . . .63,270 . . . . . . 68.82%
Brett Robinson (D) . . . . . .28,671 . . . . . . 31.18%
Total Vote 91,941

District 132
Mike Schofield (R) . . . . . .53,928 . . . . . . 58.76%
Chase West (D) . . . . . .37,846 . . . . . . 41.24%
Total Vote 91,774

District 134
Ann Johnson (D) . . . . . .61,037 . . . . . . 61.33%
Audrey Douglas (R) . . . . . .38,480 . . . . . . 38.67%
Total Vote 99,517

District 136
John H. Bucy III (D) . . . . . .45,185 . . . . . . 62.02%
Amin Salahuddin (R) . . . . . .27,665 . . . . . . 37.98%
Total Vote 72,850

District 137
Gene Wu (D) . . . . . .19,286 . . . . . . 76.31%
Lee Sharp (L) . . . . . . 5,988 . . . . . . 23.69%
Total Vote 25,274

District 138
Lacey Hull (R) . . . . . .42,022 . . . . . . 57.02%
Stephanie Morales (D) . . . .31,671 . . . . . . 42.98%
Total Vote 73,693

District 146
Lauren Ashley Simmons (D) 42,840 . . . . . . 77.72%
Lance York (R) . . . . . .12,282 . . . . . . 22.28%
Total Vote 55,122

District 147
Jolanda Jones (D) . . . . . .47,828 . . . . . . 74.54%
Claudio Gutierrez (R) . . . . .16,332 . . . . . . 25.46%
Total Vote 64,160

District 148
Penny Morales Shaw (D) . . .28,341 . . . . . . 54.94%
Kay Smith (R) . . . . . .23,246 . . . . . . 45.06%
Total Vote 51,587

District 149
Hubert Vo (D) . . . . . .26,921 . . . . . . 57.02%
Lily Truong (R) . . . . . .20,291 . . . . . . 42.98%
Total Vote 47,212

District 150
Valoree Swanson (R) . . . . 48,000 . . . . . . 59.86%
Marisela "MJ" Jimenez (D). . 32,181 . . . . . . 40.14%
Total Vote 80,181

UNSPLASH/HAL GATEWOOD

TEXAS ELECTION TURNOUT BY VOTING AGE POPULATION

Year	2024	2020	2016	2012	2008	2004	2000	1996	1992	1988	1984	1980
Major Candidates	Trump/Harris	Biden/Trump	Trump/Clinton	Obama/Romney	Obama/McCain	Bush/Kerry	Bush/Gore	Clinton/Dolet	Clinton/ Bush/Perot	Bush/Dukakis	Reagan/Mondale	Reagan/Carter
Percent of VAP that voted	49.7	52.4	46.5	43.7	45.6	46.1	44.3	41.0	47.6	44.3	47.6	45.6
Percent of registered voters that voted	61.2	66.7	58.6	59.5	56.6	51.8	53.2	72.9	66.2	68.3	68.4	64.8

The **voting age population** (VAP) refers to the total number of persons of voting age regardless of citizenship, military status, felony conviction, or mental state. The Bureau of the Census is the source for the VAP estimates.

Since the National Voter Registration Act of 1993, non-voters cannot be removed from registration rolls of a county until two federal elections have been held.

So, for instance, if a person moved in December 2020 from one county to another, that person could be counted as a non-voter in the previous county of residence through the general election of November 2024. These are called "suspense voters" on county rolls and have affected the statistical reports of the percentage of registered voters participating in elections.

The presidential elections have a larger voter turnout than off-year and state elections.

Sources: Federal Election Commission and Texas Secretary of State.

UNSPLASH/JOSH JOHNSON

2024 PRESIDENTIAL PRIMARY RESULTS

Below are the official canvass results by county in the party primaries for president held March 5, 2024.

This table lists the top candidates in the Democratic and Republican primaries. Joe Biden received 84.64 percent of votes cast in the Democratic primary. Donald J. Trump received 77.84 percent of votes cast in the Republican primary.

Alongside the number of votes received by each candidate is listed the percent of the total vote received.

Source: Texas Secretary of State.

Republican Primary		County	Democratic Primary	
Trump	%		Biden	%
1,808,269	77.84%	Statewide	831,247	84.64%
7,087	85.56%	Anderson	593	86.32%
1,671	85.43%	Andrews	74	70.48%
9,205	84.60%	Angelina	1,008	86.97%
3,697	79.71%	Aransas	430	88.30%
1,928	85.80%	Archer	65	83.33%
488	83.42%	Armstrong	5	71.43%
4,723	83.70%	Atascosa	943	84.27%
4,653	85.03%	Austin	433	89.83%
610	85.20%	Bailey	34	85.00%
4,827	83.12%	Bandera	413	86.40%
8,724	78.78%	Bastrop	3,167	87.95%
550	88.85%	Baylor	24	80.00%
2,929	77.10%	Bee	426	80.38%
22,866	75.68%	Bell	7,550	88.07%
77,852	74.26%	Bexar	65,881	86.70%
2,548	80.03%	Blanco	464	91.16%
204	90.27%	Borden	2	100.00%
3,121	84.12%	Bosque	245	89.42%
10,330	83.72%	Bowie	1,417	86.72%
27,757	81.45%	Brazoria	9,684	89.28%
14,598	69.17%	Brazos	3,097	80.59%
973	76.92%	Brewster	509	83.31%
396	85.90%	Briscoe	14	70.00%
117	90.70%	Brooks	566	58.90%
4,872	85.44%	Brown	224	85.82%
3,042	87.04%	Burleson	326	88.59%
7,680	79.27%	Burnet	1,114	91.09%
3,071	79.50%	Caldwell	1,340	88.62%
2,742	80.22%	Calhoun	184	83.64%
2,270	83.92%	Callahan	70	83.33%
12,633	85.96%	Cameron	11,213	66.42%
1,779	84.88%	Camp	204	85.36%
1,179	84.27%	Carson	36	97.30%
4,920	87.56%	Cass	414	83.81%
539	83.05%	Castro	48	82.76%
6,910	87.09%	Chambers	430	83.66%
5,690	86.91%	Cherokee	642	93.31%
727	85.73%	Childress	25	83.33%
2,092	85.32%	Clay	62	86.11%
332	81.57%	Cochran	14	73.68%
770	85.65%	Coke	14	70.00%
1,845	87.82%	Coleman	46	79.31%
70,148	69.74%	Collin	29,938	86.18%
507	82.71%	Collingsworth	9	90.00%
3,941	83.96%	Colorado	291	89.81%
21,335	78.90%	Comal	4,104	91.67%
2,202	86.29%	Comanche	126	85.71%
517	81.55%	Concho	30	83.33%
6,517	83.03%	Cooke	384	82.40%

Republican Primary		County	Democratic Primary	
Trump	%		Biden	%
5,172	81.64%	Coryell	887	87.13%
380	85.01%	Cottle	16	69.57%
502	89.48%	Crane	18	72.00%
493	83.84%	Crockett	51	76.12%
672	76.19%	Crosby	42	84.00%
94	89.52%	Culberson	169	49.71%
556	86.74%	Dallam	13	72.22%
69,540	66.25%	Dallas	106,211	86.85%
1,415	79.63%	Dawson	41	75.93%
1,490	77.40%	Deaf Smith	115	71.43%
1,309	83.16%	Delta	53	84.13%
68,203	73.04%	Denton	25,376	89.79%
2,659	84.33%	DeWitt	190	89.62%
528	83.28%	Dickens	12	80.00%
189	89.57%	Dimmit	1,025	59.63%
599	86.81%	Donley	25	86.21%
214	86.99%	Duval	805	65.02%
2,472	86.77%	Eastland	83	79.81%
7,866	85.95%	Ector	802	78.86%
564	81.86%	Edwards	12	60.00%
18,385	79.89%	Ellis	5,112	92.16%
16,814	81.70%	El Paso	29,044	84.00%
5,173	83.69%	Erath	346	87.37%
1,691	85.36%	Falls	301	82.47%
5,660	83.84%	Fannin	375	88.24%
4,702	81.96%	Fayette	455	91.18%
577	87.29%	Fisher	63	87.50%
702	82.30%	Floyd	42	75.00%
305	81.33%	Foard	6	85.71%
42,611	75.35%	Fort Bend	31,363	79.86%
1,898	83.98%	Franklin	115	85.19%
2,589	87.08%	Freestone	252	79.00%
650	91.94%	Frio	830	64.19%
1,906	88.53%	Gaines	38	61.29%
26,961	79.78%	Galveston	8,969	91.94%
722	84.25%	Garza	29	78.38%
6,370	77.79%	Gillespie	693	93.78%
333	90.24%	Glasscock	3	100.00%
1,515	84.83%	Goliad	121	84.03%
2,674	83.02%	Gonzales	213	84.19%
2,540	86.48%	Gray	64	73.56%
17,945	79.60%	Grayson	2,080	84.97%
9,951	81.45%	Gregg	2,119	87.89%
4,926	85.83%	Grimes	433	80.78%
16,610	80.55%	Guadalupe	1,387	92.69%
2,620	81.14%	Hale	191	78.28%
476	90.84%	Hall	15	71.43%
1,994	82.02%	Hamilton	65	91.55%
1,062	86.76%	Hansford	10	58.82%
444	88.80%	Hardeman	25	89.29%
8,593	88.80%	Hardin	424	86.18%
153,193	75.63%	Harris	151,875	88.78%
7,628	85.06%	Harrison	1,097	84.97%
886	84.30%	Hartley	20	52.63%
828	84.23%	Haskell	43	75.44%
12,864	71.07%	Hays	12,377	85.94%
596	82.66%	Hemphill	22	95.65%
10,538	84.94%	Henderson	1,183	89.35%
15,665	87.50%	Hidalgo	19,301	65.42%
4,841	83.75%	Hill	433	91.93%
2,725	83.03%	Hockley	111	88.80%
11,156	79.94%	Hood	911	90.65%
5,197	84.79%	Hopkins	371	86.89%
3,701	88.37%	Houston	462	89.19%
2,638	86.61%	Howard	186	83.04%
517	78.45%	Hudspeth	41	80.39%

2024 DEMOCRATIC PARTY PRESIDENTIAL PRIMARY

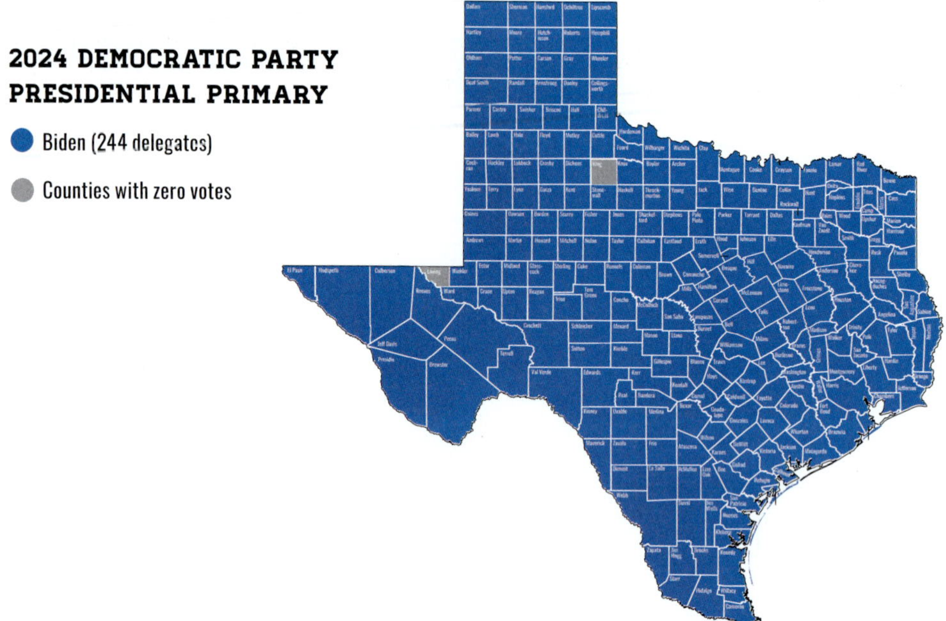

Republican Primary		County	Democratic Primary	
Trump	%		Biden	%
11,633	82.08%	Hunt	1,266	87.25%
2,697	86.47%	Hutchinson	103	78.03%
353	87.81%	Irion	23	88.46%
1,878	88.50%	Jack	57	86.36%
2,390	88.95%	Jackson	121	80.67%
7,134	87.75%	Jasper	409	86.84%
420	66.77%	Jeff Davis	82	93.18%
15,378	81.81%	Jefferson	10,441	92.29%
49	85.96%	Jim Hogg	519	56.29%
1,827	88.05%	Jim Wells	2,010	69.53%
18,561	82.04%	Johnson	2,326	90.58%
2,499	84.74%	Jones	116	77.33%
2,294	82.82%	Karnes	158	79.40%
13,605	82.30%	Kaufman	3,034	87.41%
8,244	77.26%	Kendall	990	93.57%
24	85.71%	Kenedy	10	55.56%
70	30.30%	Kent	13	86.67%
9,288	80.07%	Kerr	1,099	90.45%
1,155	84.06%	Kimble	26	78.79%
88	92.63%	King	0	0.00%
536	79.64%	Kinney	78	82.98%
2,066	77.70%	Kleberg	893	83.22%
504	84.71%	Knox	31	93.94%
7,453	83.51%	Lamar	569	88.63%
1,240	86.65%	Lamb	72	82.76%
3,609	82.06%	Lampasas	389	87.81%
155	91.72%	La Salle	369	43.21%
4,636	87.69%	Lavaca	198	82.85%
2,690	86.36%	Lee	259	85.76%
3,163	88.75%	Leon	161	88.46%
9,424	89.17%	Liberty	802	83.89%
2,851	87.51%	Limestone	291	83.38%
601	85.73%	Lipscomb	14	66.67%
1,996	87.05%	Live Oak	132	83.02%
4,982	77.10%	Llano	494	91.31%
68	76.40%	Loving	0	0.00%

Republican Primary		County	Democratic Primary	
Trump	%		Biden	%
23,551	78.36%	Lubbock	4,103	81.04%
781	84.80%	Lynn	21	61.76%
1,504	85.94%	Madison	49	92.45%
22,324	74.84%	Marion	4,714	88.86%
210	87.14%	Martin	7	87.50%
1,778	89.48%	Mason	88	80.73%
1,433	86.59%	Matagorda	240	88.24%
983	85.18%	Maverick	9	69.23%
1,011	78.98%	McCulloch	71	88.75%
4,388	85.12%	McLennan	618	86.19%
1,141	93.60%	McMullen	2,194	56.80%
6,420	83.92%	Medina	847	80.90%
482	76.63%	Menard	17	89.47%
12,233	80.02%	Midland	1,023	84.27%
3,579	84.37%	Milam	383	86.46%
1,380	86.03%	Mills	36	83.72%
860	86.87%	Mitchell	37	84.09%
3,591	85.64%	Montague	127	83.01%
66,458	80.82%	Montgomery	9,015	89.92%
1,941	83.59%	Moore	42	65.63%
1,623	85.60%	Morris	224	82.96%
301	91.49%	Motley	7	100.00%
7,262	74.88%	Nacogdoches	878	83.07%
5,531	83.80%	Navarro	691	85.84%
2,609	86.68%	Newton	82	88.17%
1,673	78.29%	Nolan	107	80.45%
16,978	79.61%	Nueces	10,583	90.21%
1,238	87.06%	Ochiltree	19	70.37%
414	86.07%	Oldham	9	75.00%
13,363	87.29%	Orange	881	84.71%
5,154	80.39%	Palo Pinto	275	84.62%
4,576	89.24%	Panola	358	86.06%
26,813	81.79%	Parker	1,919	86.99%
815	84.72%	Parmer	20	68.97%
1,345	82.06%	Pecos	273	74.79%
6,654	84.46%	Polk	650	91.16%
7,357	78.67%	Potter	1,031	81.63%
102	85.00%	Presidio	602	57.22%
1,993	86.95%	Rains	143	88.82%
16,610	78.97%	Randall	1,371	86.83%
389	83.12%	Reagan	12	70.59%
755	86.58%	Real	83	88.30%
2,256	88.78%	Red River	185	84.86%
279	93.00%	Reeves	499	44.00%
1,254	79.32%	Refugio	176	82.63%
359	88.86%	Roberts	1	100.00%
3,003	82.89%	Robertson	243	84.97%
14,828	75.35%	Rockwall	2,554	90.15%
1,589	84.57%	Runnels	56	88.89%
6,340	85.85%	Rusk	590	87.80%
2,217	91.12%	Sabine	101	90.18%
1,349	91.09%	San Augustine	193	88.13%
5,214	87.09%	San Jacinto	393	86.18%
4,800	83.23%	San Patricio	1,575	80.52%
1,455	86.04%	San Saba	26	81.25%
407	87.90%	Schleicher	40	78.43%
1,550	84.15%	Scurry	68	82.93%
563	84.16%	Shackelford	14	77.78%
3,975	88.35%	Shelby	181	87.86%
402	87.20%	Sherman	4	50.00%
24,759	81.11%	Smith	4,693	89.41%
1,960	81.77%	Somervell	106	80.30%
398	89.84%	Starr	856	45.15%
1,475	86.26%	Stephens	43	91.49%
326	82.74%	Sterling	1	100.00%
273	90.40%	Stonewall	22	78.57%

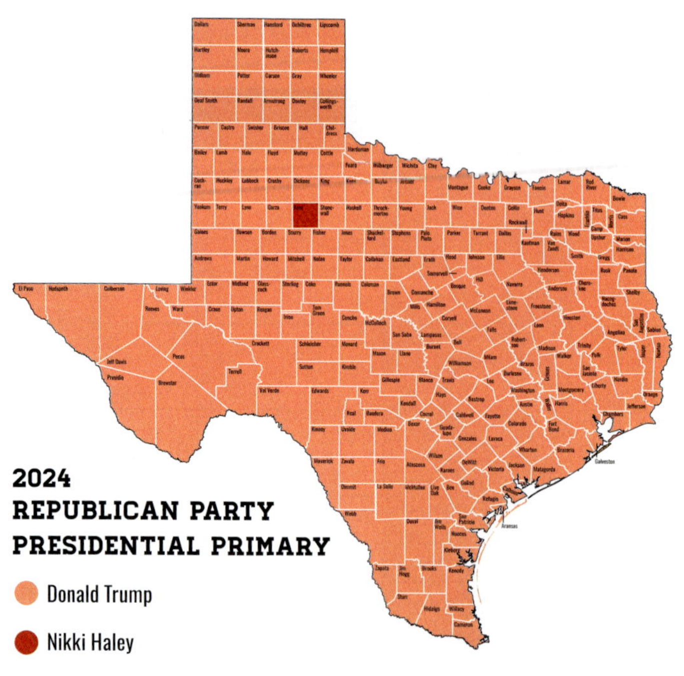

POLITICAL PARTY ORGANIZATIONS

Democratic State Executive Committee
Chairman: Gilberto Hinojosa

Republican State Executive Committee
Chairman: Abraham George

Libertarian State Executive Committee
Chairman: Andrew Amelang

Green State Executive Committee
Co-Chairs: Aly Schmidt, Matt Bauman

Republican Primary		County	Democratic Primary	
Trump	%		Biden	%
625	83.67%	Sutton	30	78.95%
748	81.13%	Swisher	61	81.33%
106,043	72.96%	Tarrant	57,202	86.29%
14,112	72.66%	Taylor	1,428	85.82%
171	88.14%	Terrell	18	78.26%
1,107	85.42%	Terry	69	75.82%
321	88.43%	Throckmorton	7	87.50%
3,029	86.12%	Titus	320	84.21%
11,716	77.76%	Tom Green	1,089	69.85%
30,872	58.68%	Travis	78,771	83.94%
2,665	88.19%	Trinity	253	93.36%
3,391	87.87%	Tyler	194	88.58%
5,960	87.61%	Upshur	444	85.71%
504	88.27%	Upton	21	77.78%
3,147	80.38%	Uvalde	619	79.16%
2,652	85.19%	Val Verde	1,062	69.05%
9,511	87.64%	Van Zandt	565	88.01%
8,626	81.09%	Victoria	1,174	86.51%
6,723	81.18%	Walker	885	87.02%
4,928	84.07%	Waller	1,095	84.30%
1,620	84.20%	Ward	94	68.12%
6,252	80.10%	Washington	699	90.78%
3,976	87.93%	Webb	11,551	65.84%
5,093	85.94%	Wharton	594	90.69%
1,361	88.20%	Wheeler	17	77.27%
7,253	81.03%	Wichita	1,408	86.75%
1,660	83.50%	Wilbarger	115	85.82%
413	93.65%	Willacy	995	54.52%
39,585	71.30%	Williamson	21,402	89.15%
6,560	83.80%	Wilson	881	87.92%
509	87.46%	Winkler	13	68.42%
11,345	86.35%	Wise	663	86.22%
7,612	85.91%	Wood	599	88.74%
1,065	83.92%	Yoakum	18	56.25%
3,148	83.95%	Young	121	79.61%
221	88.76%	Zapata	800	40.14%
144	95.36%	Zavala	1,040	63.53%

2024 TEXAS PRIMARY ELECTIONS

Following are the official results for the contested races in the Democratic and Republican primaries held March 5, 2024. Included are selected federal, statewide, and selected district races. Runoffs were held on May 28.

Some data was omitted for space, including the Texas House of Representatives, judges in the Court of Appeals, judges in the Criminal Court of Appeals, judges in the state Supreme Court, district level races, races in which only a single candidate was running, select races in the U.S. House of Representatives, and some party propositions.

Source: Texas Secretary of State.

DEMOCRATIC PRIMARY

FEDERAL RACES: PRESIDENT

Candidate	Votes	Percent
Joseph Biden	831,247	84.64%
Marianne Williamson	43,667	4.45%
Armando "Mando" Perez-Serrato	27,473	2.80%
Dean Phillips	26,473	2.70%
Gabriel A. Cornejo	17,196	1.75%
Cenk Uygur	16,100	1.64%
Frankie Lozada	11,311	1.15%
Star Locke	8,602	0.88%
Total Vote		**982,069**

U.S. SENATE

Candidate	Votes	Percent
Colin Allred	569,585	58.87%
Roland Gutierrez	160,978	16.64%
Mark Gonzalez	85,228	8.81%
Meri Gomez	44,166	4.56%
Carl Oscar Sherman	31,694	3.28%
A. "Robert" Hassan	21,855	2.26%
Steven J. Keough	21,801	2.25%
Heli Rodriguez Prilliman	18,801	1.94%
Thierry Tchenko	13,395	1.38%
Total Vote		**967,503**

U.S. HOUSE OF REPRESENTATIVES

District 7

Candidate	Votes	Percent
Lizzie Fletcher	27,902	74.24%
Pervez Agwan	9,679	25.76%
Total Vote		**37,581**

District 10

Candidate	Votes	Percent
Theresa Boisseau	14,702	72.20%
Keith McPhail	5,661	27.80%
Total Vote		**20,363**

District 12

Candidate	Votes	Percent
Trey J. Hunt	11,935	58.01%
Sebastian K. Gehrig	8,638	41.99%
Total Vote		**20,573**

District 15

Candidate	Votes	Percent
Michelle Vallejo	21,456	74.70%
John Villarreal Rigney	7,268	25.30%
Total Vote		**28,724**

District 16

Candidate	Votes	Percent
Veronica Escobar	28,129	86.29%
Leeland White	4,470	13.71%
Total Vote		**32,599**

District 18

Candidate	Votes	Percent
Sheila Jackson Lee	23,629	60.04%
Amanda Edwards	14,668	37.27%
Robert Slater	1,059	2.69%
Total Vote		**39,356**

District 22

Candidate	Votes	Percent
Marquette Greene-Scott	17,290	81.68%
Wayne Raasch	3,877	18.32%
Total Vote		**21,167**

District 23

Candidate	Votes	Percent
S. Limon	16,316	58.49%
Lee Bausinger	11,577	41.51%
Total Vote		**27,893**

District 24

Candidate	Votes	Percent
Sam Eppler	17,451	58.63%
Francine Ly	12,314	41.37%
Total Vote		**29,765**

District 27

Candidate	Votes	Percent
Tanya Lloyd	10,305	53.34%
Anthony (A.J.) Tristan	9,013	46.66%
Total Vote		**19,318**

District 30

Candidate	Votes	Percent
Jasmine Crockett	43,059	91.54%
Jared D. Davis	3,982	8.46%
Total Vote		**47,041**

District 31

Stuart Whitlow . . . . 10,023 . . . . 48.42%
Brian Walbridge . . . . 5,346 . . . . 25.82%
Rick Von Pfeil . . . . 5,332 . . . . 25.76%
Total Vote 20,701

District 32

Julie Johnson . . . . 17,633 . . . . 50.44%
Brian Williams. . . . . 6,704 . . . . 19.18%
Justin A. Moore . . . . 2,483 . . . . 7.10%
Jan McDowell . . . . 1,722 . . . . 4.93%
Zachariah Manning . . . . . . 1,617 . . . . 4.63%
Raja Chaudhry. . . . . 1,258 . . . . 3.60%
Callie Butcher . . . . 1,169 . . . . 3.34%
Kevin Felder . . . . 1,101 . . . . 3.15%
Alex Cornwallis . . . . 909 . . . . 2.60%
Christopher Panayiotou . . . . . 361 . . . . 1.03%
Total Vote 34,957

District 33

Marc Veasey . . . . 15,313 . . . . 68.32%
Carlos Quintanilla. . . . . . . 7,102 . . . . 31.68%
Total Vote 22,415

District 37

Lloyd Doggett . . . . 57,762 . . . . 86.1%
Christopher "Chris" McNerney . 5,279 . . . . 7.87%
Eduardo "Lalito" Romero. . . 4,048 . . . . 6.03%
Total Vote 67,089

District 38

Melissa McDonough . . . . . 18,486 . . . . 82.54%
Gion Christopher Thomas . . . 3,910 . . . . 17.46%
Total Vote 22,396

STATEWIDE RACES: RAILROAD COMMISSIONER

Katherine Culbert . . . . . . 615,965 . . . . 67.64%
Bill Burch. . . . . 294,628 . . . . 32.36%
Total Vote 910,593

SUPREME COURT

Place 2

Dasean Jones . . . . 529,623 . . . . 59.57%
Randy Sarosdy . . . . 359,402 . . . . 40.43%
Total Vote 889,025

Place 6

Bonnie Lee Goldstein . . . . 646,690 . . . . 73.14%
Joe Pool. . . . . 237,465 . . . . 26.86%
Total Vote 884,155

DISTRICT RACES: STATE BOARD OF EDUCATION

District 10

Raquel Saenz Ortiz . . . . . 35,622 . . . . 78.59%
DC Caldwell . . . . 9,703 . . . . 21.41%
Total Vote 45,325

STATE SENATE

District 7

Michelle Gwinn . . . . 12,707 . . . . 55.66%
Nasir H. Malik . . . . 10,122 . . . . 44.34%
Total Vote 22,829

District 15

Jarvis D. Johnson. . . . . 17,953 . . . . 36.19%
Molly Cook . . . . 10,213 . . . . 20.59%
Todd Litton . . . . 7,859 . . . . 15.84%
Michelle Anderson Bonton . . 5,291 . . . . 10.67%
Alberto "Beto" Cardenas . . . 5,196 . . . . 10.48%
Karthik Soora . . . . 3,091 . . . . 6.23%
Total Vote 49,603

District 16

Nathan Johnson . . . . 19,734 . . . . 59.19%
Victoria Neave Criado. . . . 13,604 . . . . 40.81%
Total Vote 33,338

District 30

Michael Braxton . . . . 7,833 . . . . 37.72%
Dale Frey . . . . 6,856 . . . . 33.02%
Matthew McGhee . . . . 6,077 . . . . 29.26%
Total Vote 20,766

DEMOCRATIC RUNOFF

FEDERAL RACES: U.S. HOUSE OF REPRESENTATIVES

District 31

Stuart Whitlow . . . . 3,512 . . . . 68.51%
Brian Walbridge . . . . 1,614 . . . . 31.49%
Total Vote 5,126

DISTRICT RACES: STATE SENATE

District 15

Molly Cook . . . . 9,506 . . . . 50.16%
Jarvis D. Johnson. . . . . 9,444 . . . . 49.84%
Total Vote 18,950

District 30

Dale Frey . . . . 1,737 . . . . 56.99%
Michael Braxton . . . . 1,311 . . . . 43.01%
Total Vote 3,048

REPUBLICAN PRIMARY

FEDERAL RACES: PRESIDENT

Donald J. Trump. . . . . . 1,808,269 . . . . 77.84%
Nikki Haley . . . . 405,472 . . . . 17.45%
Uncommitted . . . . 45,568 . . . . 1.96%
Ron DeSantis . . . . 36,302 . . . . 1.56%
Vivek Ramaswamy. . . . . . . 10,582 . . . . 0.46%

Chris Christie	8,938	0.38%
Asa Hutchinson	2,964	0.13%
Ryan L. Binkley	2,585	0.11%
David Stuckenberg	2,339	0.10%
Total Vote		**2,323,019**

U.S. SENATE

Ted Cruz	1,977,961	88.30%
Holland "Redd" Gibson	134,011	5.98%
R. E. (Rufus) Lopez	127,986	5.71%
Total Vote		**2,239,958**

U.S. HOUSE OF REPRESENTATIVES

District 2

Dan Crenshaw	40,379	59.50%
Jameson Ellis	27,482	40.50%
Total Vote		**67,861**

District 3

Keith Self	55,888	72.81%
Suzanne Harp	14,215	18.52%
Tre Pennie	2,797	3.64%
John Porro	2,634	3.43%
Jeremy D. Ivanovskis	1,224	1.59%
Total Vote		**76,758**

District 4

Pat Fallon	70,801	80.28%
Don Horn	17,396	19.72%
Total Vote		**88,197**

District 6

Jake Ellzey	38,143	60.77%
James Buford	12,782	20.36%
Cliff Wiley	11,843	18.87%
Total Vote		**62,768**

District 7

Kenneth Omoruyi	9,834	41.90%
Caroline Kane	5,764	24.56%
Carolyn B. Bryant	4,382	18.67%
Tina Blum Cohen	3,489	14.87%
Total Vote		**23,469**

District 10

Michael T. McCaul	59,998	72.14%
Jared B. Lovelace	23,175	27.86%
Total Vote		**83,173**

District 15

Monica De La Cruz	30,972	88.21%
Vangela Churchill	4,140	11.79%
Total Vote		**35,112**

District 17

Pete Sessions	67,798	84.91%
Joseph T. Langone	12,052	15.09%
Total Vote		**79,850**

District 18

Lana Centonze	6,202	53.28%
Aaron Ray Hermes	5,438	46.72%
Total Vote		**11,640**

District 19

Jodey C. Arrington	70,705	83.45%
Chance Ferguson	6,316	7.45%
Vance W. Boyd	5,116	6.04%
Ryan Zink	2,586	3.05%
Total Vote		**84,723**

District 23

Tony Gonzales	25,988	45.09%
Brandon Herrera	14,201	24.64%
Julie Clark	7,994	13.87%
Frank Lopez Jr.	6,266	10.87%
Victor Avila	3,181	5.52%
Total Vote		**57,630**

District 25

Roger Williams	66,345	78.04%
Matthew Lucci	11,929	14.03%
Vince Crabb	6,738	7.93%
Total Vote		**85,012**

District 26

Brandon Gill	49,876	58.37%
Scott Armey	12,400	14.51%
John Huffman	8,559	10.02%
Luisa Del Rosal	3,949	4.62%
Doug Robison	2,999	3.51%
Mark "Big Rut" Rutledge	2,130	2.49%
Joel A. Krause	1,959	2.29%
Neena Biswas	1,665	1.95%
Burt Thakur	975	1.14%
Vlad De Franceschi	572	0.67%
Total Vote		**85,450**

District 27

Michael Cloud	53,304	74.57%
Scott Mandel	10,791	15.1%
Luis A. Espindola	3,838	5.37%
Chris Mapp	3,553	4.97%
Total Vote		**71,486**

District 28

Jay Furman	12,036	44.84%
Lazaro Garza Jr.	7,283	27.13%
Jose Sanz	5,502	20.5%
Jimmy León	2,021	7.53%
Total Vote		**26,842**

District 29

Christian V. Garcia	3,716	44.74%

Alan Garza	2,418	29.11%
Angel Fierro	1,346	16.21%
Jose Angel Casares	825	9.93%
Total Vote		**8,305**

District 31

John Carter	55,092	65.28%
Mike Williams	9,355	11.09%
Mack Latimer	6,593	7.81%
Abhiram Garapati	6,256	7.41%
William Abel	4,362	5.17%
John Carnan Anderson	2,732	3.24%
Total Vote		**84,390**

District 32

David Blewett	10,706	44.42%
Darrell Day	9,211	38.22%
Juan Feria	2,397	9.95%
Gulrez "Gus" Khan	1,787	7.41%
Total Vote		**24,101**

District 33

Patrick David Gillespie	6,144	61.58%
Kurt Schwab	3,833	38.42%
Total Vote		**9,977**

District 34

Mayra Flores	18,307	81.19%
Laura Cisneros	1,991	8.83%
Mauro Garza	1,388	6.16%
Gregory Scott Kunkle Jr.	863	3.83%
Total Vote		**22,549**

District 35

Michael Rodriguez	4,085	27.07%
Steven Wright	3,715	24.61%
Dave Cuddy	3,079	20.40%
Brandon Craig Dunn	2,700	17.89%
Rod Lingsch	1,514	10.03%
Total Vote		**15,093**

District 36

Brian Babin	58,635	81.34%
Jonathan "Pipeliner" Mitchell	13,448	18.66%
Total Vote		**72,083**

STATEWIDE RACE: RAILROAD COMMISSIONER

Christi Craddick	982,457	50.42%
James "Jim" Matlock	517,624	26.56%
Christie Clark	228,395	11.72%
Corey Howell	122,802	6.30%
Petra Reyes	97,280	4.99%
Total Vote		**1,948,558**

SUPREME COURT

Place 4

John Devine	921,556	50.44%
Brian Walker	905,418	49.56%
Total Vote		**1,826,974**

COURT OF CRIMINAL APPEALS

Presiding Judge

David J. Schenck	1,174,795	62.58%
Sharon Keller	702,464	37.42%
Total Vote		**1,877,259**

Place 7

Gina Parker	1,210,956	66.08%
Barbara Parker Hervey	621,660	33.92%
Total Vote		**1,832,616**

Place 8

Lee Finley	988,824	53.88%
Michelle Slaughter	846,549	46.12%
Total Vote		**1,835,373**

DISTRICT RACES: STATE BOARD OF EDUCATION

District 10

Tom Maynard	101,741	49.29%
Mary Bone	83,497	40.45%
DC Caldwell	21,162	10.25%
Total Vote		**206,400**

District 11

Brandon Hall	89,139	53.23%
Pat (Patricia) Hardy	78,326	46.77%
Total Vote		**167,465**

District 12

Pam Little	63,633	36.38%
Jamie Kohlmann	47,288	27.04%
Chad Green	35,446	20.27%
Matt Rostami	28,542	16.32%
Total Vote		**174,909**

STATE SENATE

District 30

Brent Hagenbuch	35,262	36.38%
Jace Yarbrough	32,899	33.94%
Carrie De Moor	17,069	17.61%
Cody Clark	11,704	12.07%
Total Vote		**96,9349**

PROPOSITIONS

1 – Eliminate property taxes without increasing Texas' overall tax burden.

In Favor	1,741,825	77.97%
Against	492,231	22.03%
Total Vote		**2,234,056**

2 – Create a border protection unit and deploy additional state law enforcement and military forces, to seal the border, to use physical force to prevent illegal entry and trafficking, and to deport undocumented people to Mexico or to their nations of origin.

In Favor	2,088,151	91.53%
Against	193,190	8.47%
Total Vote		**2,281,341**

3 – Require the use of e-verify by all employers in Texas to protect jobs for legal workers by preventing the hiring of undocumented people.

In Favor	2,029,971	89.90%
Against	228,102	10.10%
Total Vote		**2,258,073**

4 – End all subsidies and public services, including in-state college tuition and enrollment in public schools, for undocumented people.

In Favor	1,978,723	87.63%
Against	279,347	12.37%
Total Vote		**2,258,070**

REPUBLICAN RUNOFF

FEDERAL RACES: U.S. HOUSE OF REPRESENTATIVES

District 7

Caroline Kane	2,539	50.44%
Kenneth Omoruyi	2,495	49.56%
Total Vote		**5,034**

District 12

Craig Goldman	16,787	62.90%
John C. O'Shea	9,903	37.10%
Total Vote		**26,690**

District 23

Tony Gonzales	15,023	50.60%
Brandon Herrera	14,669	49.40%
Total Vote		**29,692**

District 28

Jay Furman	8,297	65.29%
Lazaro Garza Jr.	4,410	34.71%
Total Vote		**12,707**

District 29

Alan Garza	421	53.77%
Christian V. Garcia	362	46.23%
Total Vote		**783**

District 32

Darrell Day	3,394	64.82%
David Blewett	1,842	35.18%
Total Vote		**5,236**

District 35

Steven Wright	1,082	50.12%
Michael Rodriguez	1,077	49.88%
Total Vote		**2,159**

DISTRICT RACES: STATE BOARD OF EDUCATION

District 10

Tom Maynard	24,658	51.82%
Mary Bone	22,924	48.18%
Total Vote		**47,582**

District 12

Pam Little	31,968	50.81%
Jamie Kohlmann	30,948	49.19%
Total Vote		**62,916**

District 30

Brent Hagenbuch	18,779	56.65%
Jace Yarbrough	14,368	43.35%
Total Vote		**33,147**

UNSPLASH/ELEMENT5 DIGITAL

UNSPLASH/HISTORY IN HD

10 FUN FACTS ABOUT SPACE IN TEXAS

1
The country's third-largest meteor impact crater was formed just south of Odessa more than 60,000 years ago. The Odessa Meteor Crater measures roughly 550 feet in diameter and was designated a National Natural Landmark in 1965.

2
Between 1894 and 1895, Austin erected 31 165-foot towers to cast "artificial moonlight" onto the city streets. The 17 remaining moon towers are the only ones left in the country.

3
American astrophysicist and author Neil DeGrasse Tyson earned a Master of Arts in astronomy from the University of Texas at Austin in 1983.

4
The National Center for Electron Beam Research at Texas A&M University in College Station partners with NASA to produce about 30 percent of the food items that astronauts consume in space.

5
The Perot Museum of Nature and Science in Dallas features a permanent "Expanding Universe" exhibit offering stargazing and other interactive children's activities about the solar system and beyond.

6
Challenger Elementary School opened in Pearland in 1993 to honor the crew of Space Shuttle Challenger, who died shortly after liftoff on January 28, 1986.

7
August 25, 1951 was the first of several days when witnesses saw V-shaped formations of blue-green lights in the sky over Lubbock. The case of the "Lubbock Lights" remains a mystery.

8
In 2005, Hemphill unveiled a memorial to the crew of Space Shuttle Columbia, who were lost upon re-entry on February 1, 2003. The 20-foot-diameter circular monument sits at the intersection of State Highway 87 and Farm-to-Market Road 83.

9
The Planetarium on the campus of Sam Houston State University in Huntsville hosts free shows for the public about astronomy and other space topics every Thursday evening.

10
The Neutral Buoyancy Laboratory at the Johnson Space Center includes one of the world's largest indoor pools for astronaut training. It's 202 feet long, 102 feet wide, 40 feet deep, and holds more than six million gallons of water.

UNSPLASH/RYUNOSUKE KIKUNO

UNSPLASH/CALEB FISHER

UNSPLASH/CALEB FISHER

A

ANDERSON
COUNTY

Named for Republic of Texas Vice President K.L. Anderson.

Cities/Towns: Palestine, Cayuga, Elkhart, Frankston, Neches, Tenessee Colony

Land Area (Square Miles): 1,062.62
Elevation (Approx. Feet): 51

Population: 59,512
Population Change: 2.70%

Race:
White: 56.9%
Black: 21.4%
Hispanic: 19.6%
Asian: 1.1%
Other: 1.1%

Vital Statistics:
Births: 517
Deaths: 712
Marriages: 294
Divorces: 39

2024 Rainfall: 62.46 in.
January Avg. Temp.: 43.2°F
July Avg. Temp.: 81.3°F

Unemployment Rate: 4.4
Per Capita Income: $46,478
Tourism Earnings: $18.1 million
Avg. Home Value: $173,400

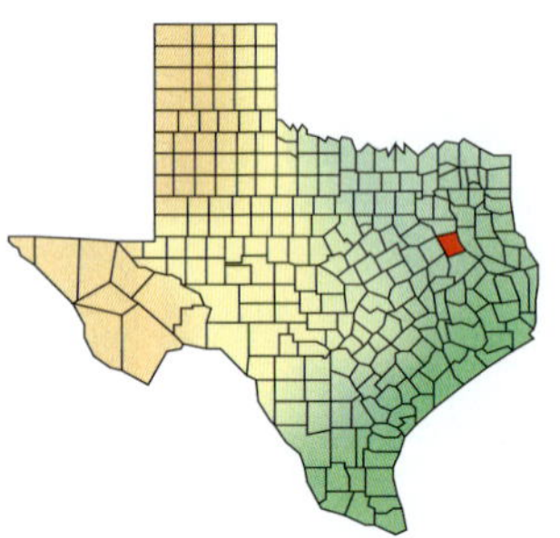

ANDREWS
COUNTY

Named for Texas Revolutionary soldier Richard Andrews.

Cities/Towns: Andrews, McKinney Acres

Land Area (Square Miles): 1,500.72
Elevation (Approx. Feet): 3,156

Population: 18,923
Population Change: 1.70%

Race:
White: 38.3%
Black: 2.2%
Hispanic: 58.2%
Asian: 0.8%
Other: 1.7%

Vital Statistics:
Births: 316
Deaths: 144
Marriages: 93
Divorces: 87

2024 Rainfall: 9.29 in.
January Avg. Temp.: 41.6°F
July Avg. Temp.: 81.9°F

Unemployment Rate: 3
Per Capita Income: $57,526
Tourism Earnings: $8.4 million
Avg. Home Value: $188,200

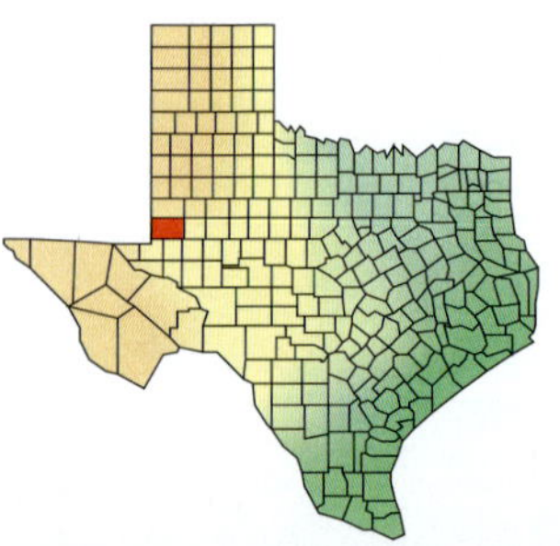

ANGELINA
COUNTY

Named for legendary Indigenous maiden Angelina.

Cities/Towns: Lufkin, Burke, Diboll, Hudson, Huntington, Redland, Zavalla

Land Area (Square Miles): 797.87
Elevation (Approx. Feet): 236

Population: 88,094
Population Change: 1.80%

Race:
White: 58.7%
Black: 15.6%
Hispanic: 23.8%
Asian: 1.1%
Other: 0.9%

Vital Statistics:
Births: 1,082
Deaths: 1,031
Marriages: 549
Divorces: 250

2024 Rainfall: 76.44 in.
January Avg. Temp.: 45.7°F
July Avg. Temp.: 81.7°F

Unemployment Rate: 4.3
Per Capita Income: $51,080
Tourism Earnings: $36.3 million
Avg. Home Value: $149,800

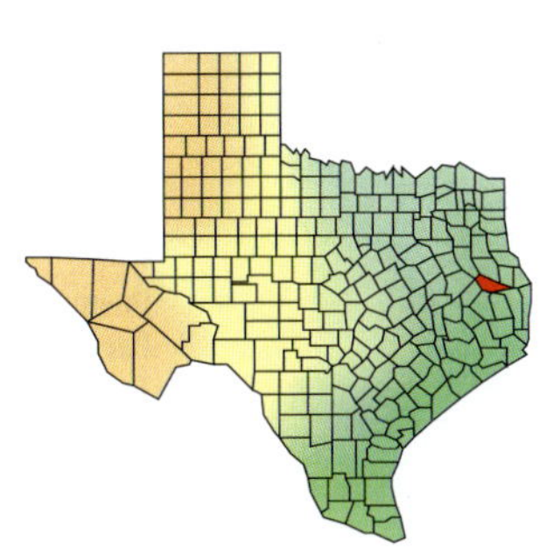

ARANSAS
COUNTY

Named for the Aransas Bay.

Cities/Towns: Rockport, Fulton, Holiday Beach, Lamar

Land Area (Square Miles): 252.07
Elevation (Approx. Feet): N/A

Population: 25,595
Population Change: 7.40%

Race:
White: 67.1%
Black: 2.1%
Hispanic: 27.3%
Asian: 1.9%
Other: 1.6%

Vital Statistics:
Births: 197
Deaths: 404
Marriages: 136
Divorces: 95

2024 Rainfall: 28.15 in.
January Avg. Temp.: 54.5°F
July Avg. Temp.: 84.6°F

Unemployment Rate: 4.8
Per Capita Income: $68,361
Tourism Earnings: $39.1 million
Avg. Home Value: $236,800

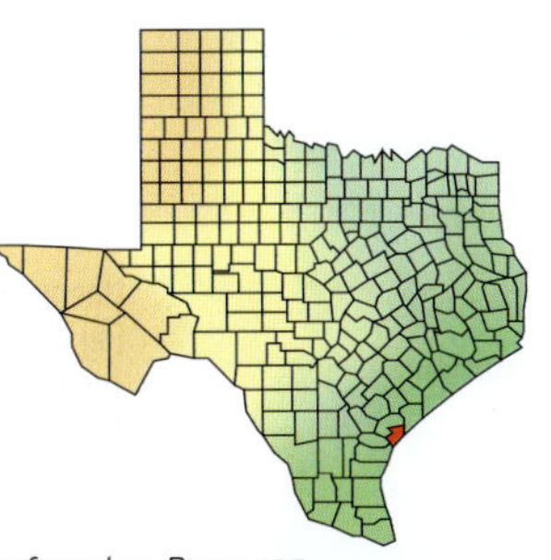

Source information for this chapter can be found on Page 407.

A

ARCHER
COUNTY

Named for Republic Commissioner Dr. B.T. Archer.

Cities/Towns: Archer City, Holliday, Lakeside City, Megargel, Scotland, Windhorst

Land Area (Square Miles): 903.29
Elevation (Approx. Feet): 991

Population: 9,155
Population Change: 7%

Race:
White: 85.5%
Black: 1.6%
Hispanic: 9.6%
Asian: 0.7%
Other: 1.8%

Vital Statistics:
Births: 92
Deaths: 89
Marriages: 15
Divorces: 28

2024 Rainfall: 34.99 in.
January Avg. Temp.: 39.6°F
July Avg. Temp.: 84.2°F

Unemployment Rate: 3.7
Per Capita Income: $67,573
Tourism Earnings: $200,000
Avg. Home Value: $175,300

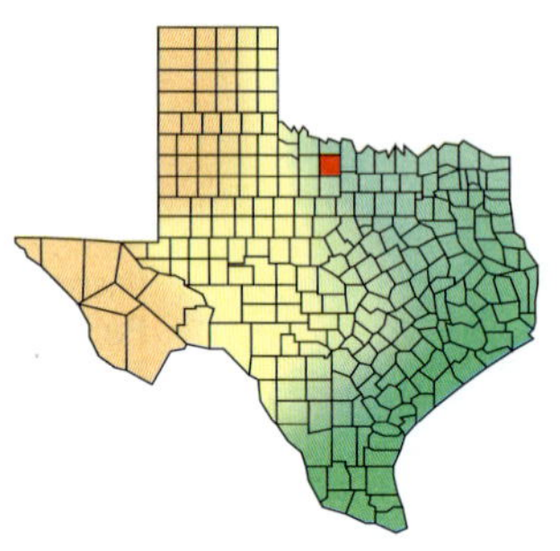

ARMSTRONG
COUNTY

Named for one of several Texas pioneer families.

Cities/Towns: Claude, Washburn

Land Area (Square Miles): 909.12
Elevation (Approx. Feet): 3,347

Population: 1,809
Population Change: -2.10%

Race:
White: 84.7%
Black: 2.0%
Hispanic: 11.0%
Asian: 0.2%
Other: 1.9%

Vital Statistics:
Births: 20
Deaths: 31
Marriages: 9
Divorces: 11

2024 Rainfall: 20.24 in.
January Avg. Temp.: 35.4°F
July Avg. Temp.: 81.8°F

Unemployment Rate: 3.1
Per Capita Income: $71,357
Tourism Earnings: $130,000
Avg. Home Value: $185,700

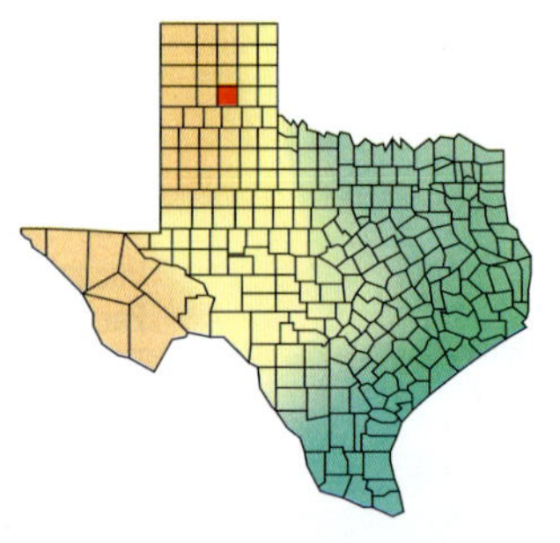

A

ATASCOSA
COUNTY

Named for the Atascosa River.

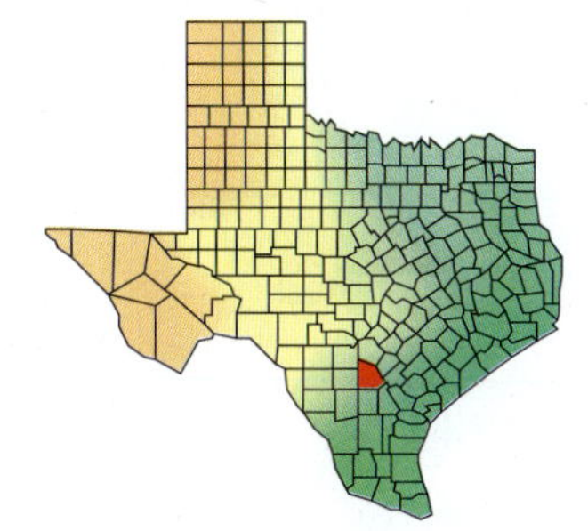

Cities/Towns: Jourdanton, Pleasanton, Campbellton, Charlotte, Christine, Leming, Lytle, Peggy, Poteet

Land Area (Square Miles): 1,219.54
Elevation (Approx. Feet): 427

Population: 52,783
Population Change: 7.40%

Race:
White: 31.0%
Black: 1.8%
Hispanic: 66.0%
Asian: 0.8%
Other: 1.8%

Vital Statistics:
Births: 666
Deaths: 541
Marriages: 188
Divorces: 107

2024 Rainfall: 23.67 in.
January Avg. Temp.: 50.1°F
July Avg. Temp.: 84.4°F

Unemployment Rate: 4.1
Per Capita Income: $48,387
Tourism Earnings: $27.7 million
Avg. Home Value: $157,400

MELISSA SUTHERLAND HUNT/COURTESY OF ATASCOSA COUNTY

A

AUSTIN
COUNTY

Named for Stephen F. Austin, commonly known as the "Father of Texas."

Cities/Towns: Bellville, Sealy, Bleiberville, Brazos Country, Cat Spring, Industry, Kenney, New Ulm, San Felipe, South Frydek, Wallis

Land Area (Square Miles): 646.5
Elevation (Approx. Feet): 223

Population: 32,546
Population Change: 7.90%

Race:
White: 60.7%
Black: 9.4%
Hispanic: 28.2%
Asian: 0.9%
Other: 1.2%

Vital Statistics:
Births: 349
Deaths: 378
Marriages: 113
Divorces: 99

2024 Rainfall: 49.45 in.
January Avg. Temp.: 50.3°F
July Avg. Temp.: 83.9°F

Unemployment Rate: 3.7
Per Capita Income: $65,441
Tourism Earnings: $18 million
Avg. Home Value: $270,900

UNSPLASH/LEON CONTRERAS

B

BAILEY
COUNTY

Named for Alamo hero Peter J. Bailey.

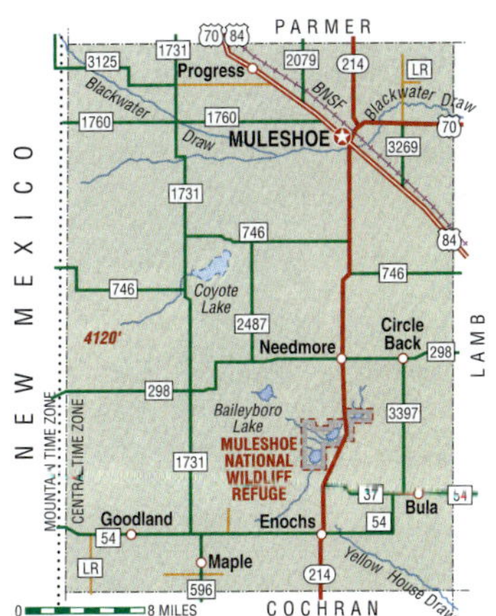

Cities/Towns: Muleshoe, Enochs, Maple

Land Area (Square Miles): 826.97
Elevation (Approx. Feet): 3,901

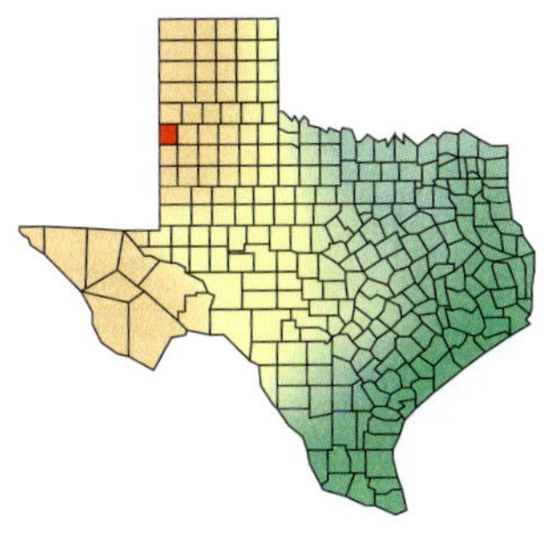

Population: 7,031
Population Change: 1.9

Race:
White: 29.8%
Black: 4.0%
Hispanic: 66.3%
Asian: 1.0%
Other: 3.9%

Vital Statistics:
Births: 130
Deaths: 60
Marriages: 20
Divorces: 14

2024 Rainfall: 18.94 in.
January Avg. Temp.: 36.2°F
July Avg. Temp.: 78.3°F

Unemployment Rate: 4.2
Per Capita Income: $57,209
Tourism Earnings: $1.4 million
Avg. Home Value: $104,400

BANDERA
COUNTY

Named for the Bandera Mounains.

Cities/Towns: Bandera, Medina, Pipe Creek, Tarpley, Vanderpool, Lakehills, Lake Modina Shores

Land Area (Square Miles): 790.99
Elevation (Approx. Feet): 1,906

Population: 22,830
Population Change: 9.50%

Race:
White: 74.2%
Black: 1.7%
Hispanic: 21.6%
Asian: 0.7%
Other: 1.7%

Vital Statistics:
Births: 182
Deaths: 318
Marriages: 115
Divorces: 68

2024 Rainfall: 21.41 in.
January Avg. Temp.: 45.9°F
July Avg. Temp.: 82.1°F

Unemployment Rate: 4
Per Capita Income: $62,073
Tourism Earnings: $26.2 million
Avg. Home Value: $249,800

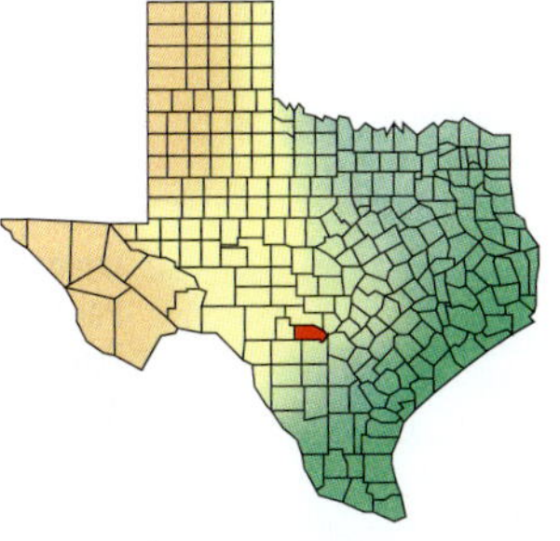

B

BASTROP
COUNTY

Named for Baron de Bastrop, who aided Moses and Stephen F. Austin in establishing the colony in the 1820s.

Cities/Towns: Bastrop, Elgin, Smithville, Cedar Creek, Circle D-KC Estates, McDade, Paige, Red Rock, Resanky

Land Area (Square Miles): 888.23
Elevation (Approx. Feet): 361

Population: 114,931
Population Change: 18.20%

Race:
White: 45.2%
Black: 6.9%
Hispanic: 45.9%
Asian: 1.1%
Other: 2.4%

Vital Statistics:
Births: 1,429
Deaths: 917
Marriages: 370
Divorces: 182

2024 Rainfall: 37.09 in.
January Avg. Temp.: 47.8°F
July Avg. Temp.: 84°F

Unemployment Rate: 3.6
Per Capita Income: $47,331
Tourism Earnings: $106.4 million
Avg. Home Value: $269,500

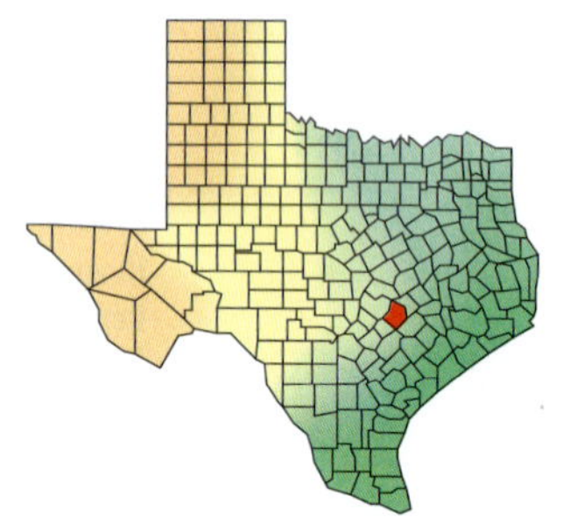

BAYLOR
COUNTY

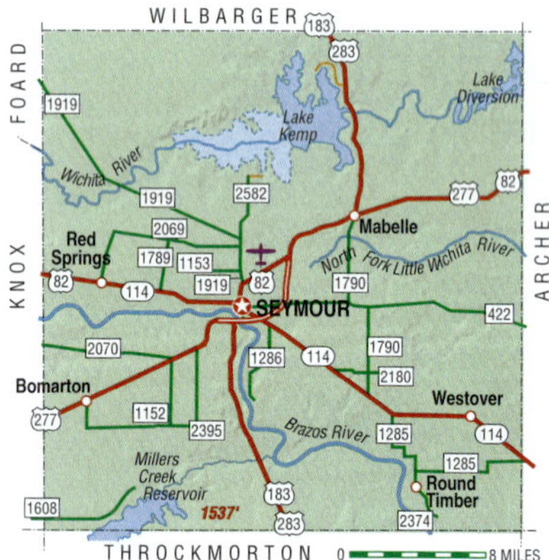

Named for Texas Ranger surgeon H.W. Baylor.

Cities/Towns: Seymour

Land Area (Square Miles): 867.48
Elevation (Approx. Feet): 1,339

Population: 3,533
Population Change: 2.00%

Race:
White: 79.0%
Black: 3.8%
Hispanic: 14.1%
Asian: 0.4%
Other: 1.7%

Vital Statistics:
Births: 48
Deaths: 64
Marriages: 13
Divorces: 3

2024 Rainfall: 30.67 in.
January Avg. Temp.: 39.8°F
July Avg. Temp.: 84.5°F

Unemployment Rate: 3
Per Capita Income: $62,964
Tourism Earnings: $1 million
Avg. Home Value: $93,300

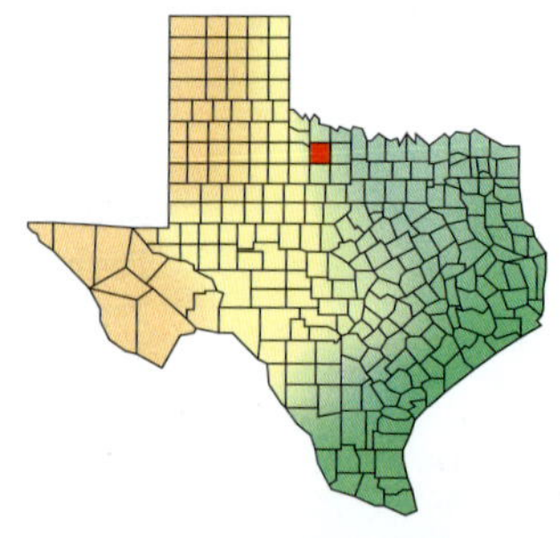

B

BEE
COUNTY

Named for Republic Secretary of State and diplomat Barnard Bee Sr.

Cities/Towns: Beeville, Blueberry Hill, Mineral, Normanna, Pawnee, Pettus, Skidmore, Tuleta, Tynan

Land Area (Square Miles): 880.24
Elevation (Approx. Feet): 233

Population: 31,226
Population Change: 0.60%

Race:
White: 28.2%
Black: 9.0%
Hispanic: 61.7%
Asian: 0.8%
Other: 1.2%

Vital Statistics:
Births: 309
Deaths: 305
Marriages: 110
Divorces: 58

2024 Rainfall: 24.74 in.
January Avg. Temp.: 52.6°F
July Avg. Temp.: 84.1°F

Unemployment Rate: 4.6
Per Capita Income: $37,156
Tourism Earnings: $11.2 million
Avg. Home Value: $102,800

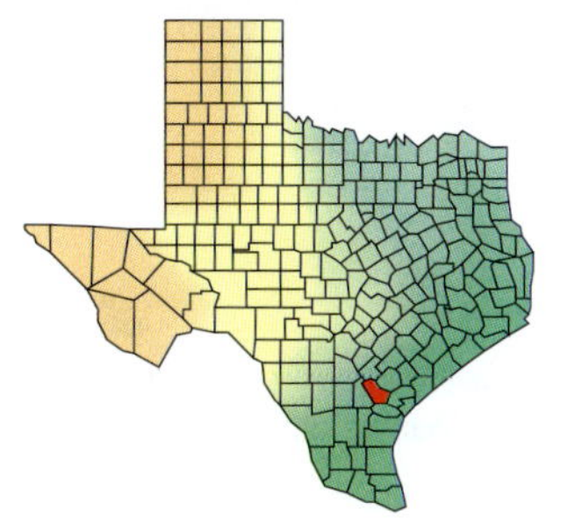

BELL
COUNTY

Named for Governor P.H. Bell.

Cities/Towns: Belton, Killeen, Temple, Harker Heights, Heidenheimer, Holland, Little River-Academy, Morgan's Point Resort, Nolanville, Pendleton, Rogers, Salado, Troy, Bartlett, Fort Cavazos

Land Area (Square Miles): 1,053.83
Elevation (Approx. Feet): 637

Population: 399,578
Population Change: 7.80%

Race:
White: 42.9%
Black: 24.9%
Hispanic: 26.6%
Asian: 3.3%
Other: 2.0%

Vital Statistics:
Births: 6,092
Deaths: 3,013
Marriages: 3,541
Divorces: 2,035

2024 Rainfall: 34.22 in.
January Avg. Temp.: 45°F
July Avg. Temp.: 82.9°F

Unemployment Rate: 4.4
Per Capita Income: $51,898
Tourism Earnings: $210.2 million
Avg. Home Value: $221,100

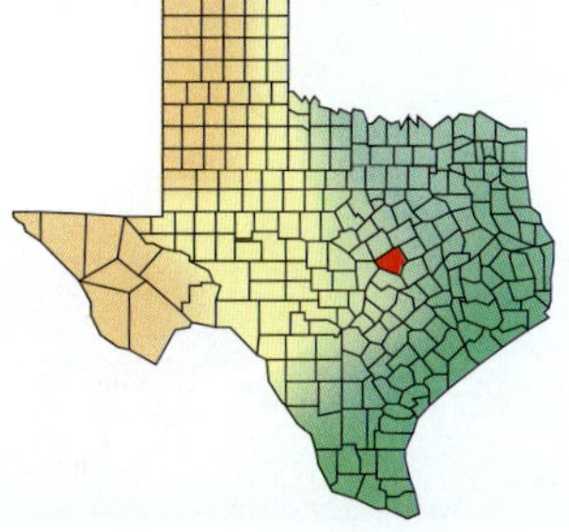

B

BEXAR
COUNTY

Named for San Antonio de Béxar, a Spanish municipality in Texas.

Cities/Towns: San Antonio, Alamo Heights, Balcones Heights, Castle Hills, China Grove, Converse, Elmendorf, Fair Oaks Ranch, Grey Forest, Helotes, Hill Country Village, Heywood Park, Kirby, Leon Valley, Live Oak, Macdona, Olmos Park, St. Hedwig, Selma, Shavano Park, Somerset, Terrel Hills, Universal City, Von Ormy, Windcrest, Schertz, Lackland Air Force Base, Randolph Air Force Base

Land Area (Square Miles): 1,240.32
Elevation (Approx. Feet): 679

Population: 2,127,737
Population Change: 5.90%

Race:
White: 26.6%
Black: 9.4%
Hispanic: 59.8%
Asian: 3.7%
Other: 1.6%

Vital Statistics:
Births: 26,609
Deaths: 16,496
Marriages: 9,120
Divorces: 2,693

2024 Rainfall: 24.07 in.
January Avg. Temp.: 48.4°F
July Avg. Temp.: 84.2°F

Unemployment Rate: 3.8
Per Capita Income: $57,096
Tourism Earnings: $3.2 billion
Avg. Home Value: $244,100

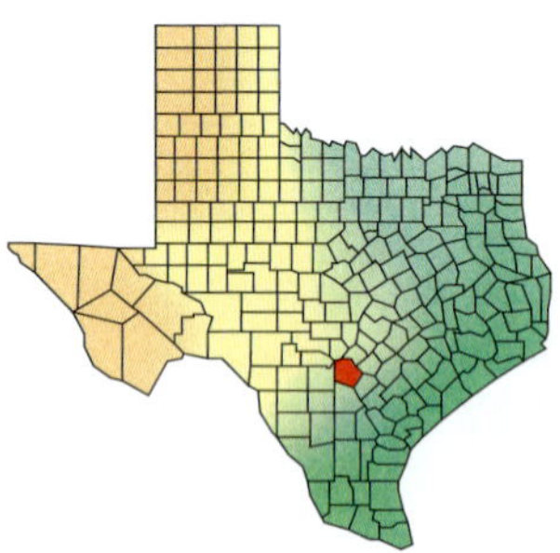

BLANCO COUNTY

Named for the Blanco River.

Cities/Towns: Johnson City, Blanco, Hye, Round Mountain

Land Area (Square Miles): 709.25
Elevation (Approx. Feet): 1,230

Population: 13,358
Population Change: 17.40%

Race:
White: 77.1%
Black: 1.6%
Hispanic: 18.5%
Asian: 1.0%
Other: 1.5%

Vital Statistics:
Births: 99
Deaths: 149
Marriages: 31
Divorces: 51

2024 Rainfall: 28.26 in.
January Avg. Temp.: 45.9°F
July Avg. Temp.: 82.4°F

Unemployment Rate: 3.5
Per Capita Income: $78,045
Tourism Earnings: $9 million
Avg. Home Value: $396,200

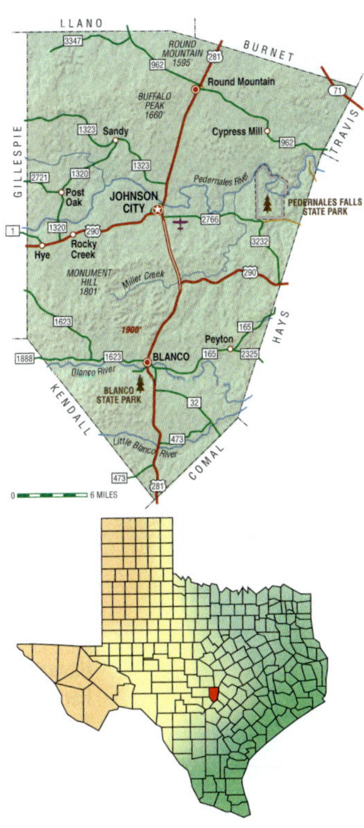

BORDEN COUNTY

Named for patriot, inventor, and editor Gail Borden.

Cities/Towns: Gail

Land Area (Square Miles): 897.44
Elevation (Approx. Feet): 2,533

Population: 557
Population Change: -11.40%

Race:
White: 80.9%
Black: 1.7%
Hispanic: 14.9%
Asian: 0.2%
Other: 0.9%

Vital Statistics:
Births: N/A
Deaths: N/A
Marriages: 4
Divorces: N/A

2024 Rainfall: 18.85 in.
January Avg. Temp.: 39.7°F
July Avg. Temp.: 83.1°F

Unemployment Rate: 3
Per Capita Income: $155,670
Tourism Earnings: $10,000
Avg. Home Value: $105,400

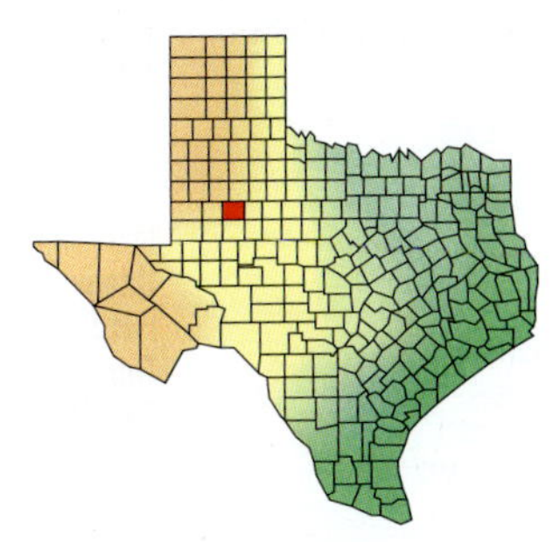

B

BOSQUE
COUNTY

Named for the Bosque River.

Cities/Towns: Meridian, Clifton, Cranfills Gap, Iredell, Kopperl, Laguna Park, Morgan, Valley Mills, Walnut Springs

Land Area (Square Miles): 982.98
Elevation (Approx. Feet): 742

Population: 19,013
Population Change: 4.30%

Race:
White: 75.8%
Black: 2.5%
Hispanic: 19.6%
Asian: 0.8%
Other: 1.2%

Vital Statistics:
Births: 179
Deaths: 298
Marriages: 81
Divorces: 38

2024 Rainfall: 40.77 in.
January Avg. Temp.: 42.8°F
July Avg. Temp.: 82.9°F

Unemployment Rate: 3.9
Per Capita Income: $57,123
Tourism Earnings: $5.2 million
Avg. Home Value: $184,500

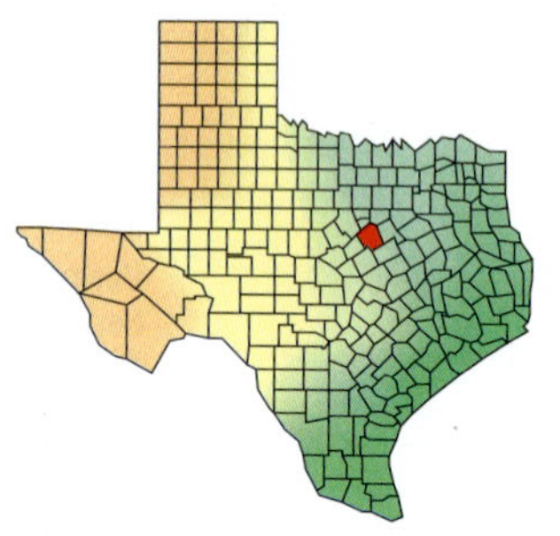

BOWIE
COUNTY

Named for Alamo hero James Bowie.

Cities/Towns: New Boston, Texarkana, De Kalb, Hooks, Leary, Maud, Nash, Red Lick, Redwater, Simms, Wake Village

Land Area (Square Miles): 884.93
Elevation (Approx. Feet): 354

Population: 91,992
Population Change: -1.00%

Race:
White: 61.4%
Black: 26.0%
Hispanic: 8.7%
Asian: 1.3%
Other: 1.3%

Vital Statistics:
Births: 995
Deaths: 1,281
Marriages: 357
Divorces: 435

2024 Rainfall: 60.43 in.
January Avg. Temp.: 40.8°F
July Avg. Temp.: 81.9°F

Unemployment Rate: 4.1
Per Capita Income: $51,132
Tourism Earnings: $37.5 million
Avg. Home Value: $161,300

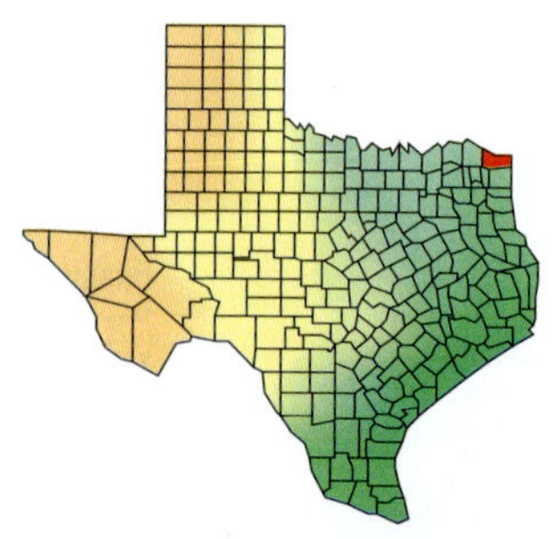

BRAZORIA
COUNTY

Named for the Brazos River.

Cities/Towns: Angleton, Brazosport, Clute, Freeport, Jones Creek, Lake Jackson, Oyster Creek, Quintana, Richwood, Surfside Beach, Pearland, Alvin, Bailey's Prairie, Bonney, Brazoria, Brookside Village, Damon, Danbury, Danciger, Hillcrest Village, Holiday Lakes, Iowa Colony, Liverpool, Manvel, Old Ocean, Rosharon, Sandy Point, Sweeny, West Columbia

Land Area (Square Miles): 1,363.33
Elevation (Approx. Feet): 30

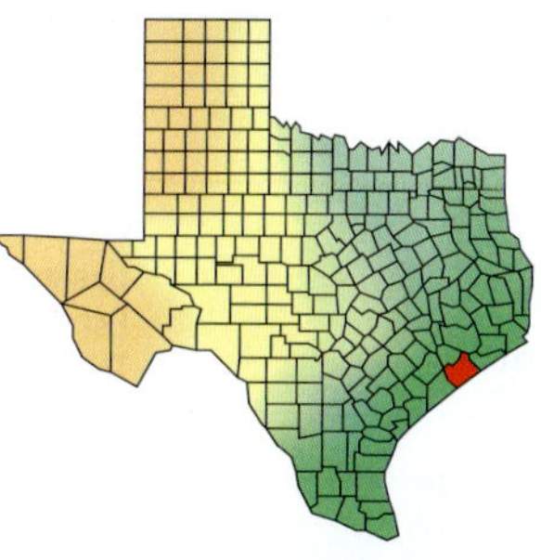

Population: 413,224
Population Change: 11.10%

Race:
White: 41.5%
Black: 17.8%
Hispanic: 31.8%
Asian: 7.9%
Other: 1.0%

Vital Statistics:
Births: 4,827
Deaths: 2,873
Marriages: 1,786
Divorces: 1,211

2024 Rainfall: 60.86 in.
January Avg. Temp.: 52.1°F
July Avg. Temp.: 83.1°F

Unemployment Rate: 4.4
Per Capita Income: $60,088
Tourism Earnings: $166.2 million
Avg. Home Value: $276,800

UNSPLASH/JAKE BALLARD

B

BRAZOS
COUNTY

Named for the Brazos River.

Cities/Towns: Bryan, College Station, Kurten, Lake Bryan, Millican, Wellborn, Wixon Valley

Land Area (Square Miles): 586.14
Elevation (Approx. Feet): 289

Population: 249,624
Population Change: 6.70%

Race:
White: 54.2%
Black: 11.4%
Hispanic: 27.5%
Asian: 5.7%
Other: 0.8%

Vital Statistics:
Births: 2,752
Deaths: 1,306
Marriages: 1,159
Divorces: 161

2024 Rainfall: 50.02 in.
January Avg. Temp.: 47°F
July Avg. Temp.: 82.8°F

Unemployment Rate: 3.4
Per Capita Income: $50,236
Tourism Earnings: $262.5 million
Avg. Home Value: $279,700

BREWSTER
COUNTY

Named for Republic Secretary of War Henry P. Brewster.

Cities/Towns: Alpine, Marathon, Basin, Study Butte, Terlingua

Land Area (Square Miles): 6,183.76
Elevation (Approx. Feet): 3,055

Population: 9,508
Population Change: -0.40%

Race:
White: 50.6%
Black: 3.0%
Hispanic: 42.0%
Asian: 2.6%
Other:2.1%

Vital Statistics:
Births: 72
Deaths: 83
Marriages: 49
Divorces: N/A

2024 Rainfall: 6.31 in.
January Avg. Temp.: 47.6°F
July Avg. Temp.: 81.7°F

Unemployment Rate: 2.9
Per Capita Income: $58,475
Tourism Earnings: $56.4 million
Avg. Home Value: $216,000

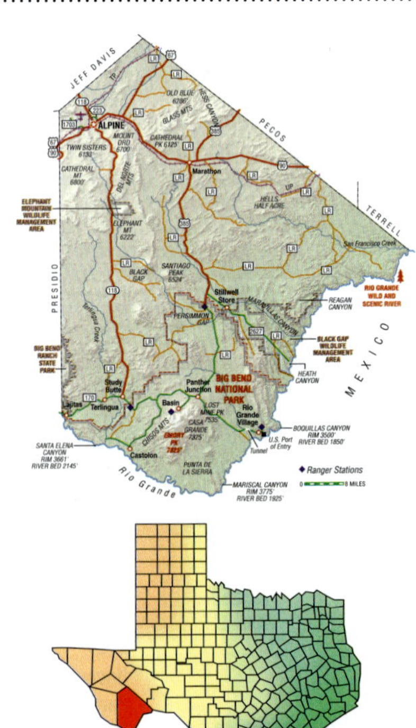

BRISCOE COUNTY

Named for Republic of Texas soldier Andrew Briscoe.

Cities/Towns: Silverton, Quitaque

Land Area (Square Miles): 900
Elevation (Approx. Feet): 3,202

Population: 1,494
Population Change: 4.00%

Race:
White: 63.9%
Black: 4.4%
Hispanic: 28.5%
Asian: 0.1%
Other: 1.4%

Vital Statistics:
Births: 13
Deaths: 14
Marriages: 9
Divorces: 1

2024 Rainfall: 22.53 in.
January Avg. Temp.: 36.2°F
July Avg. Temp.: 82.3°F

Unemployment Rate: 3.3
Per Capita Income: $62,907
Tourism Earnings: $200,000
Avg. Home Value: $82,900

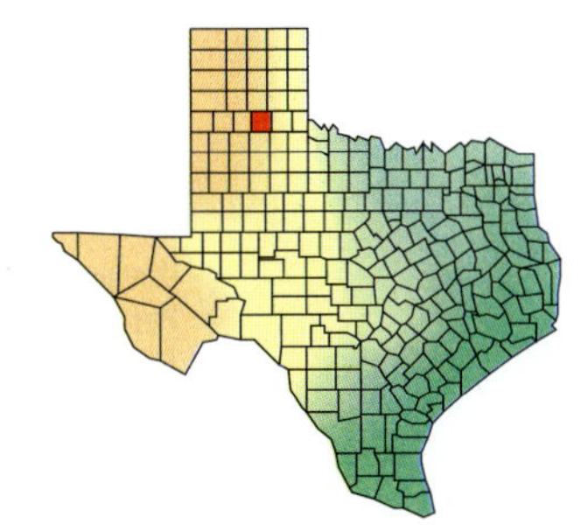

BROOKS COUNTY

Named for Texas Ranger and legislator J.A. Brooks.

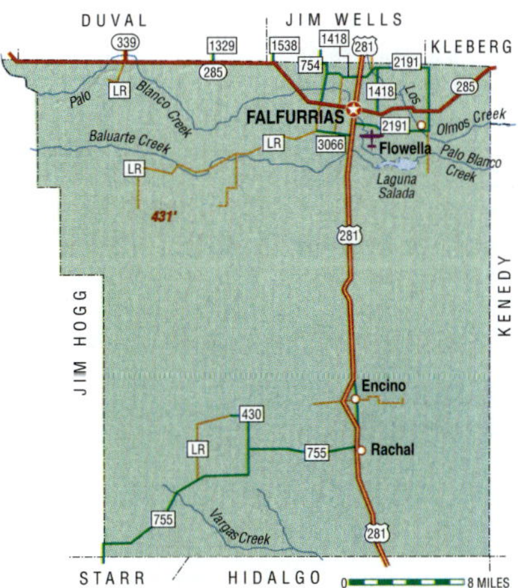

Cities/Towns: Falfurrias, Encino

Land Area (Square Miles): 943.36
Elevation (Approx. Feet): 171

Population: 6,740
Population Change: -5.40%

Race:
White: 8.3%
Black: 3.3%
Hispanic: 86.9%
Asian: 1.3%
Other: 1.0%

Vital Statistics:
Births: 102
Deaths: 110
Marriages: 30
Divorces: 4

2024 Rainfall: 22.09 in.
January Avg. Temp.: 57°F
July Avg. Temp.: 85.5°F

Unemployment Rate: 4.2
Per Capita Income: $45,257
Tourism Earnings: $1.8 million
Avg. Home Value: $82,700

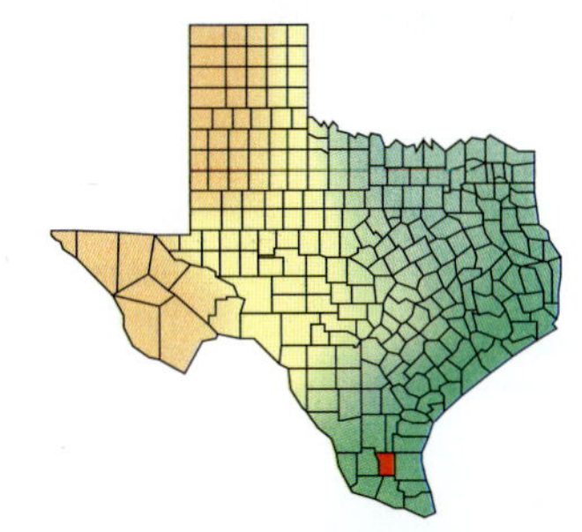

B

BROWN
COUNTY

Named for frontiersman Henry S. Brown.

Cities/Towns: Brownwood, Early, Bangs, Blanket, Brookesmith, May, Zephyr, Lake Brownwood

Land Area (Square Miles): 944.45
Elevation (Approx. Feet): 1,368

Population: 38,631
Population Change: 1.40%

Race:
White: 70.7%
Black: 4.2%
Hispanic: 22.9%
Asian: 0.8%
Other: 1.9%

Vital Statistics:
Births: 374
Deaths: 621
Marriages: 227
Divorces: 55

2024 Rainfall: 33.13 in.
January Avg. Temp.: 43°F
July Avg. Temp.: 83.2°F

Unemployment Rate: 3.7
Per Capita Income: $49,825
Tourism Earnings: $21.6 million
Avg. Home Value: $149,900

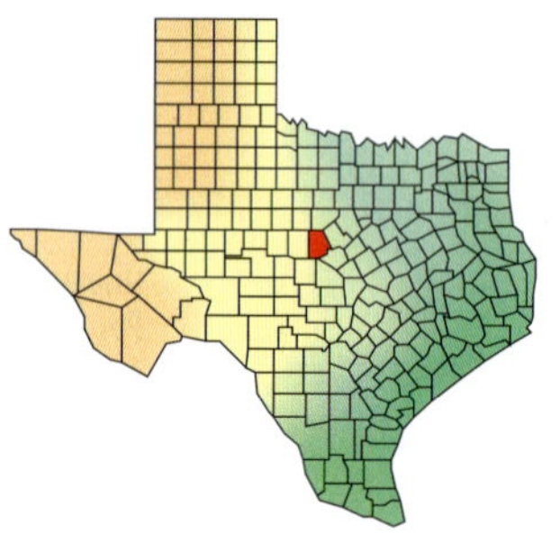

BURLESON
COUNTY

Named for Texas Revolution hero Edward Burleson.

Cities/Towns: Caldwell, Somerville, Chriesman, Lyons, Snook

Land Area (Square Miles): 659.08
Elevation (Approx. Feet): 354

Population: 20,179
Population Change: 14.40%

Race:
White: 63.6%
Black: 11.1%
Hispanic: 23.2%
Asian: 0.8%
Other: 0.4%

Vital Statistics:
Births: 210
Deaths: 256
Marriages: 49
Divorces: 21

2024 Rainfall: 45.05 in.
January Avg. Temp.: 47.7°F
July Avg. Temp.: 83.2°F

Unemployment Rate: 3.7
Per Capita Income: $61,181
Tourism Earnings: $6.7 million
Avg. Home Value: $174,000

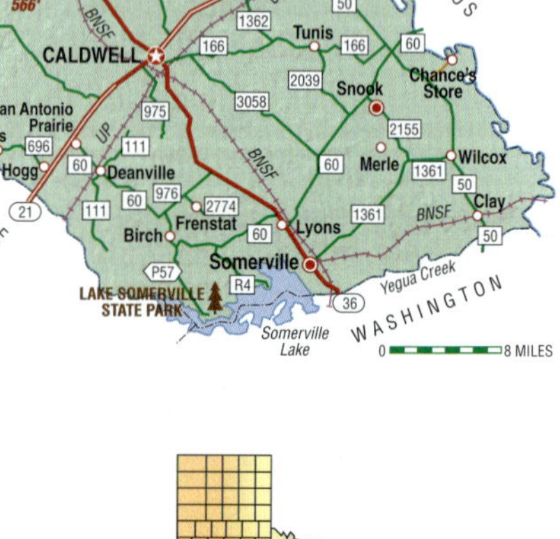

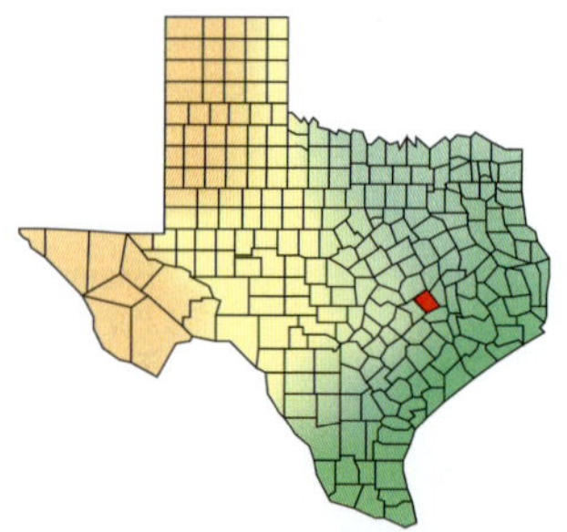

BURNET
COUNTY

Named for provisional president of the Republic, David G. Burnet.

Cities/Towns: Burnet, Marble Falls, Bertram, Cottonwood Shores, Granite Shoals, Highland Haven, Meadowlakes, Horseshoe Bay

Land Area (Square Miles): 994.8
Elevation (Approx. Feet): 1,385

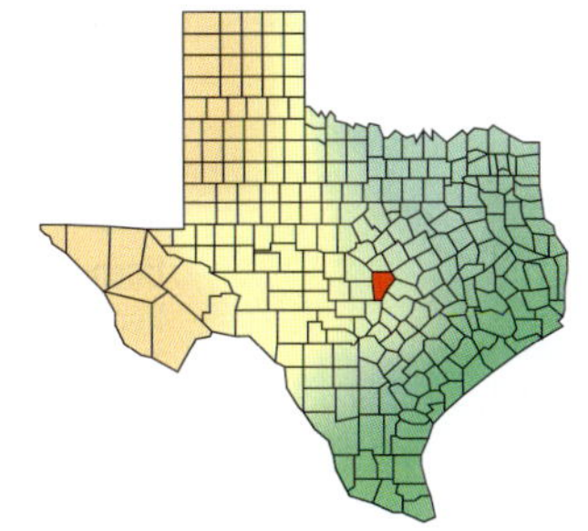

Population: 55,722
Population Change: 13.40%

Race:
White: 71.8%
Black: 2.1%
Hispanic: 23.5%
Asian: 1.2%
Other: 1.4%

Vital Statistics:
Births: 594
Deaths: 639
Marriages: 254
Divorces: 172

2024 Rainfall: 28.11 in.
January Avg. Temp.: 45°F
July Avg. Temp.: 82.9°F

Unemployment Rate: 3.5
Per Capita Income: $67,112
Tourism Earnings: $54.3 million
Avg. Home Value: $310,500

UNSPLASH/SHEEYAM

C

CALDWELL
COUNTY

Named for frontiersman Mathew Caldwell.

Cities/Towns: Lockhart, Luling, Dale, Fentress, Martindale, Maxwell, Prairie Lea

Land Area (Square Miles): 544.54
Elevation (Approx. Feet): 482

Population: 52,430
Population Change: 14.30%

Race:
White: 35.1%
Black: 6.1%
Hispanic: 57.6%
Asian: 0.9%
Other: 1.9%

Vital Statistics:
Births: 659
Deaths: 431
Marriages: 165
Divorces: 104

2024 Rainfall: 31.73 in.
January Avg. Temp.: 48.3°F
July Avg. Temp.: 84.8°F

Unemployment Rate: 3.6
Per Capita Income: $44,202
Tourism Earnings: $24.5 million
Avg. Home Value: $215,600

CALHOUN
COUNTY

Named for American statesman John C. Calhoun.

Cities/Towns: Port Lavaca, Point Comfort, Port O' Connor, Seadrift

Land Area (Square Miles): 506.94
Elevation (Approx. Feet): 10

Population: 19,942
Population Change: -0.80%

Race:
White: 41.7%
Black: 3.1%
Hispanic: 49.7%
Asian: 5.1%
Other: 1.2%

Vital Statistics:
Births: 228
Deaths: 228
Marriages: 110
Divorces: 12

2024 Rainfall: 39.76 in.
January Avg. Temp.: 53.1°F
July Avg. Temp.: 83.4°F

Unemployment Rate: 3.3
Per Capita Income: $59,827
Tourism Earnings: $19.1 million
Avg. Home Value: $150,000

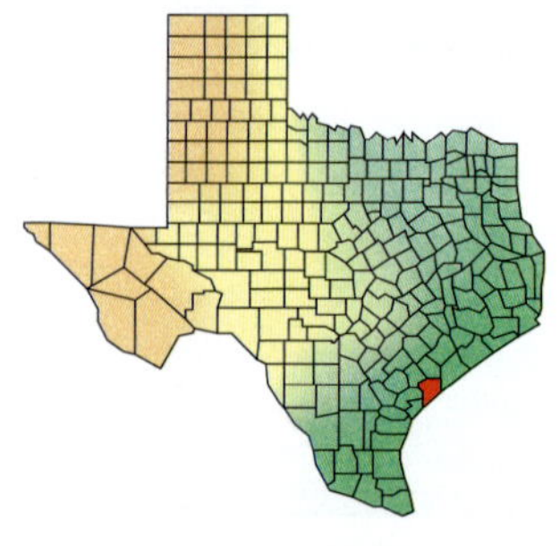

C

CALLAHAN
COUNTY

Named for Texas Ranger J.H. Callahan.

Cities/Towns: Baird, Clyde, Cross Plains, Putnam

Land Area (Square Miles): 899.37
Elevation (Approx. Feet): 1,818

Population: 14,615
Population Change: 6.60%

Race:
White: 83.1%
Black: 2.2%
Hispanic: 11.8%
Asian: 0.8%
Other: 1.2%

Vital Statistics:
Births: 155
Deaths: 176
Marriages: 45
Divorces: 14

2024 Rainfall: 34.56 in.
January Avg. Temp.: 41.4°F
July Avg. Temp.: 82.8°F

Unemployment Rate: 3.4
Per Capita Income: $54,394
Tourism Earnings: $1.2 million
Avg. Home Value: $144,800

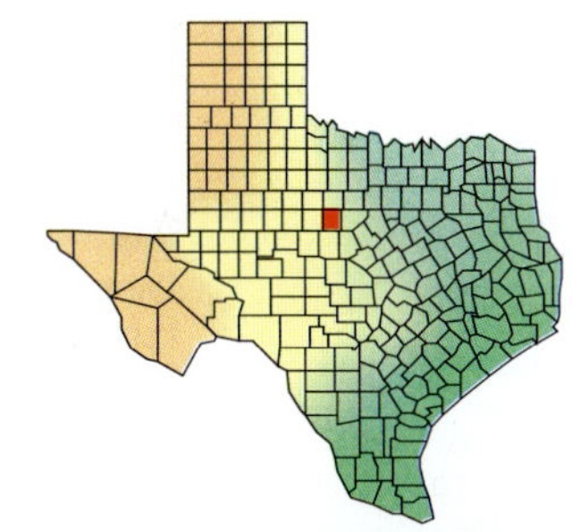

UNSPLASH/K. MITCH HODGE

CAMERON
COUNTY

Named for Mier Expedition Captain Ewen Cameron.

Cities/Towns: Brownsville, Harlingen, San Benito, South Padre Island, Bayview, Bluetown, Cameron Park, Combes, Encantada-Ranchito El Calaboz, Indian Lake, La Feria, Laguna Heights, Laguna Vista, Laureles, Los Fresnos, Los Indios, Olmito, Palm Valley, Port Isabel, Primera, Rancho Viejo, Rangerville, Rio Hondo, Santa Maria, Santa Rosa

Land Area (Square Miles): 891.71
Elevation (Approx. Feet): 13

Population: 431,874
Population Change: 2.60%

Race:
White: 9.0%
Black: 1.1%
Hispanic: 89.2%
Asian: 0.9%
Other: 0.8%

Vital Statistics:
Births: 6,112
Deaths: 3,506
Marriages: 1,701
Divorces: 403

2024 Rainfall: 31.89 in.
January Avg. Temp.: 59.9°F
July Avg. Temp.: 84.8°F

Unemployment Rate: 5.2
Per Capita Income: $38,523
Tourism Earnings: $304.6 million
Avg. Home Value: $120,000

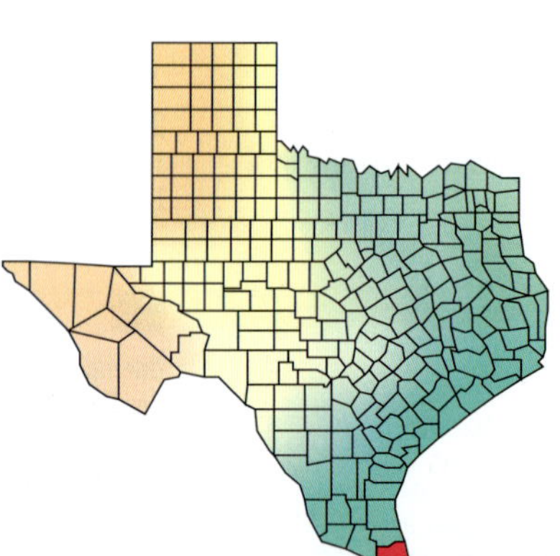

UNSPLASH/JESWIN THOMAS

C

CAMP COUNTY

Named for jurist J.L. Camp.

Cities/Towns: Pittsburg, Leesburg, Rocky Mound

Land Area (Square Miles): 195.85
Elevation (Approx. Feet): 387

Population: 13,164
Population Change: 5.60%

Race:
White: 53.3%
Black: 15.9%
Hispanic: 27.9%
Asian: 1.5%
Other: 1.6%

Vital Statistics:
Births: 163
Deaths: 171
Marriages: 67
Divorces: 3

2024 Rainfall: 57.62 in.
January Avg. Temp.: 42.3°F
July Avg. Temp.: 82°F

Unemployment Rate: 4.5
Per Capita Income: $50,426
Tourism Earnings: $2.1 million
Avg. Home Value: $159,900

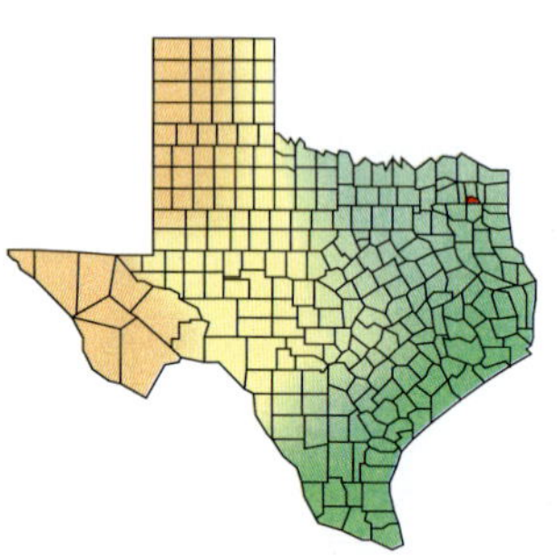

CARSON COUNTY

Named for Republic Secretary of State S.P. Carson.

Cities/Towns: Panhandle, Groom, Skellytown, White Deer

Land Area (Square Miles): 920.24
Elevation (Approx. Feet): 3,452

Population: 5,822
Population Change: 0.40%

Race:
White: 83.1%
Black: 1.7%
Hispanic: 11.3%
Asian: 0.7%
Other: 1.7%

Vital Statistics:
Births: 60
Deaths: 82
Marriages: 24
Divorces: 8

2024 Rainfall: 20.81 in.
January Avg. Temp.: 34.5°F
July Avg. Temp.: 80.9°F

Unemployment Rate: 2.9
Per Capita Income: $61,595
Tourism Earnings: $500,000
Avg. Home Value: $140,600

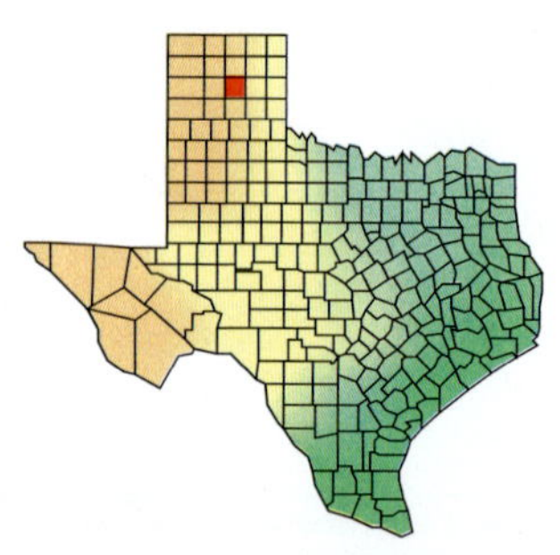

C

CASS
COUNTY

Named for U.S. Senator Lewis Cass.

Cities/Towns: Linden, Atlanta, Avinger, Bivins, Bloomburg, Domino, Douglassville, Hughes Springs, Kildare, Marietta, McLeod, Queen City

Land Area (Square Miles): 936.95
Elevation (Approx. Feet): 361

Population: 28,622
Population Change: 0.60%

Race:
White: 83.1%
Black: 1.7%
Hispanic: 11.3%
Asian: 0.7%
Other: 1.7%

Vital Statistics:
Births: 293
Deaths: 499
Marriages: 129
Divorces: 117

2024 Rainfall: 60.7 in.
January Avg. Temp.: 42°F
July Avg. Temp.: 81.6°F

Unemployment Rate: 5.2
Per Capita Income: $49,130
Tourism Earnings: $6.8 million
Avg. Home Value: $133,500

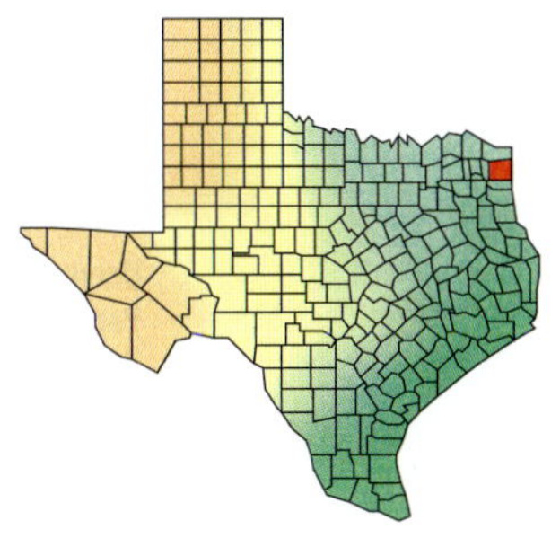

CASTRO
COUNTY

Named for Texas colonizer Henri Castro.

Cities/Towns: Dimmitt, Hart, Nazareth

Land Area (Square Miles): 894.44
Elevation (Approx. Feet): 3,822

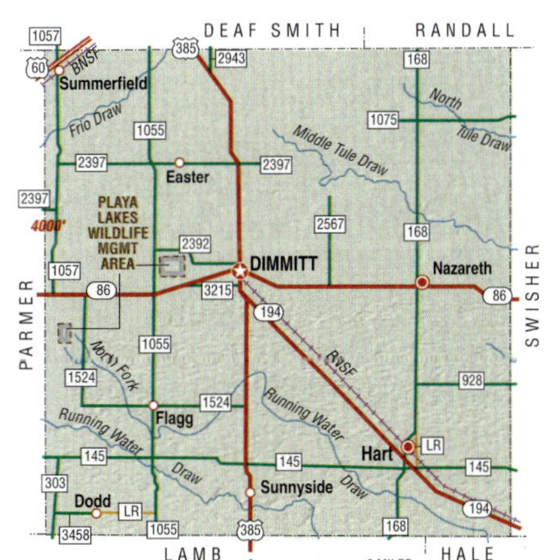

Population: 7,380
Population Change: 0.10%

Race:
White: 30.5%
Black: 2.9%
Hispanic: 65.6%
Asian: 1.0%
Other: 2.4%

Vital Statistics:
Births: 110
Deaths: 65
Marriages: 36
Divorces: 8

2024 Rainfall: 17.14 in.
January Avg. Temp.: 35.5°F
July Avg. Temp.: 78.9°F

Unemployment Rate: 2.8
Per Capita Income: $108,479
Tourism Earnings: $570,000
Avg. Home Value: $94,900

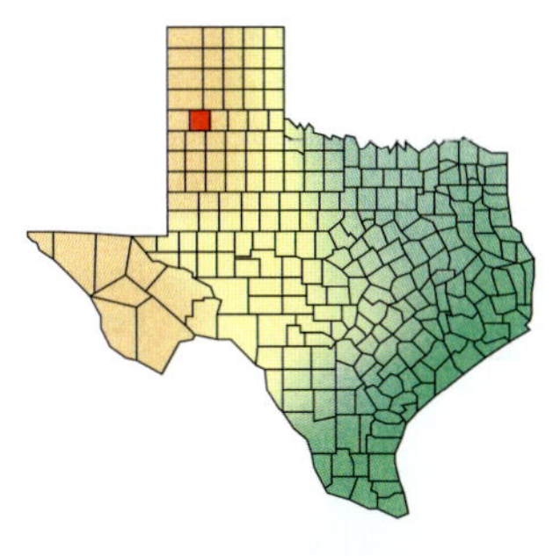

C

CHAMBERS
COUNTY

Named for General T.J. Chambers.

Cities/Towns: Anahuac, Winnie, Beach City, Cove, Hankamer, Mont Belvieu, Old River-Winfree, Stowell, Wallisville, Bayton

Land Area (Square Miles): 597.08
Elevation (Approx. Feet): 13

Population: 56,179
Population Change: 20.70%

Race:
White: 60.8%
Black: 9.4%
Hispanic: 27.3%
Asian: 1.6%
Other: 1.4%

Vital Statistics:
Births: 675
Deaths: 346
Marriages: 220
Divorces: 135

2024 Rainfall: 66.15 in.
January Avg. Temp.: 50.8°F
July Avg. Temp.: 82.6°F

Unemployment Rate: 4.6
Per Capita Income: $65,907
Tourism Earnings: $17.9 million
Avg. Home Value: $289,900

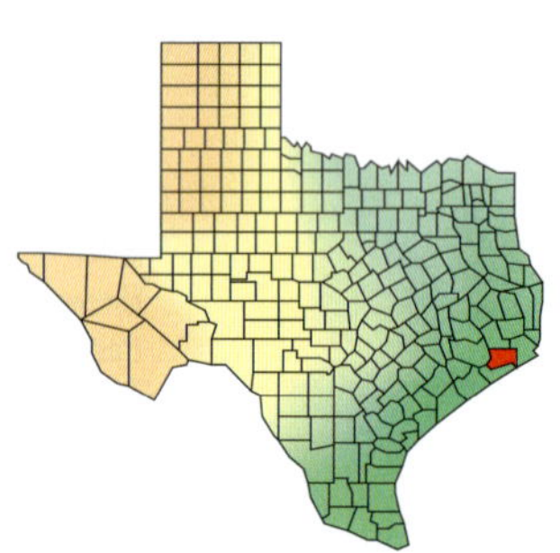

CHEROKEE
COUNTY

Named for the Indigenous community.

Cities/Towns: Rusk, Jacksonville, Alto, Cuney, Gallatin, Maydelle, New Summerfeld, Reklaw, Shadybrook, Wells, Bullard, Troup

Land Area (Square Miles): 1,052.96
Elevation (Approx. Feet): 614

Population: 53,223
Population Change: 5.30%

Race:
White: 59.8%
Black: 13.9%
Hispanic: 24.2%
Asian: 0.7%
Other: 1.7%

Vital Statistics:
Births: 679
Deaths: 576
Marriages: 247
Divorces: 92

2024 Rainfall: 68.97 in.
January Avg. Temp.: 43.7°F
July Avg. Temp.: 80.8°F

Unemployment Rate: 4.4
Per Capita Income: $46,221
Tourism Earnings: $10.3 million
Avg. Home Value: $160,300

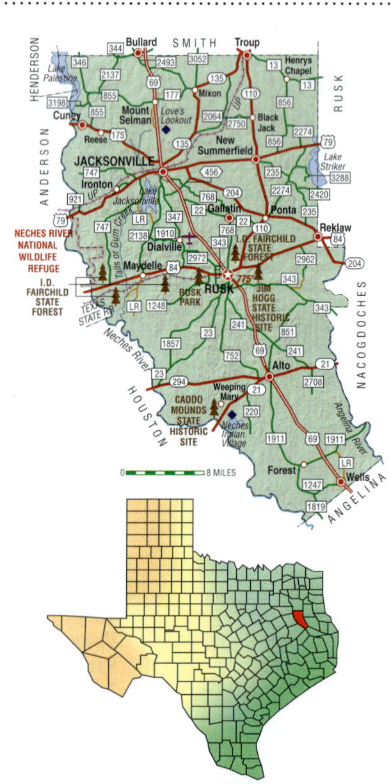

UNSPLASH/INVADINGKINGDOM

C

CHILDRESS COUNTY

Named for George C. Childress, the primary writer of the Texas Declaration of Independence.

Cities/Towns: Childress, Tell

Land Area (Square Miles): 696.51
Elevation (Approx. Feet): 1,696

Population: 6,679
Population Change: 0.20%

Race:
White: 55.5%
Black: 10.2%
Hispanic: 31.3%
Asian: 1.1%
Other: 1.3%

Vital Statistics:
Births: 72
Deaths: 92
Marriages: 34
Divorces: 10

2024 Rainfall: 20.08 in.
January Avg. Temp.: 36.7°F
July Avg. Temp.: 84.3°F

Unemployment Rate: 2.8
Per Capita Income: $44,285
Tourism Earnings: $4.3 million
Avg. Home Value: $115,100

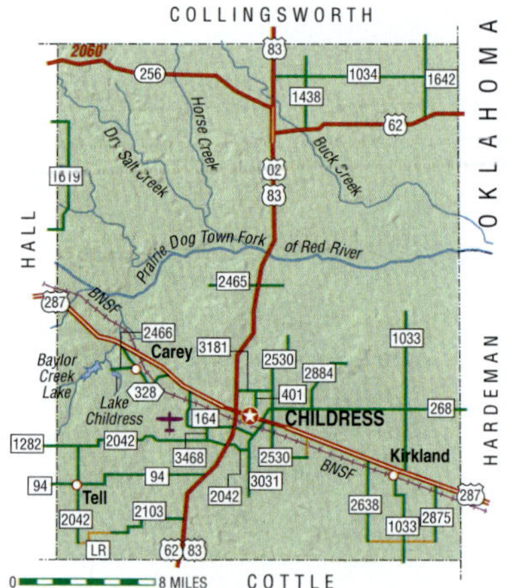

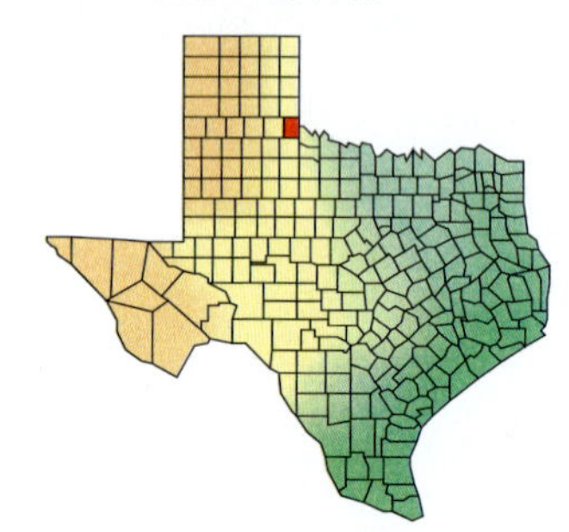

CLAY COUNTY

Named for American statesman Henry Clay.

Cities/Towns: Henrietta, Bellevue, Bluegrove, Byers, Dean, Jolly, Petrolia

Land Area (Square Miles): 1,088.76
Elevation (Approx. Feet): 886

Population: 10,730
Population Change: 5.00%

Race:
White: 86.7%
Black: 1.6%
Hispanic: 7.3%
Asian: 1.0%
Other: 1.8%

Vital Statistics:
Births: 91
Deaths: 151
Marriages: 25
Divorces: 16

2024 Rainfall: 38.71 in.
January Avg. Temp.: 38.8°F
July Avg. Temp.: 83.8°F

Unemployment Rate: 3.7
Per Capita Income: $57,095
Tourism Earnings: $880,000
Avg. Home Value: $161,300

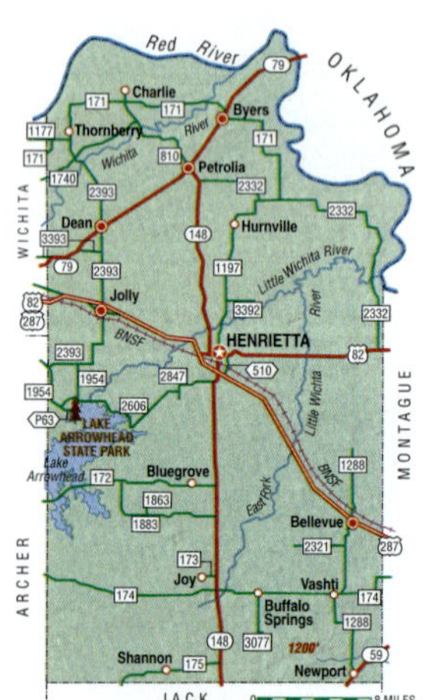

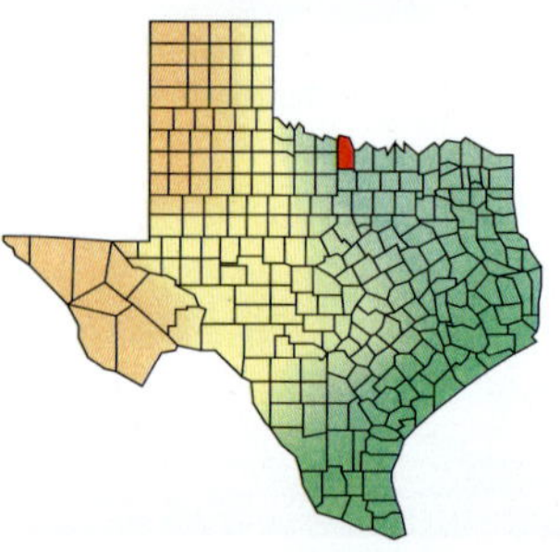

COCHRAN COUNTY

Named for soldier Robert Cochran, who died at the Alamo.

Cities/Towns: Morton, Bledsoe, Whiteface

Land Area (Square Miles): 775.08
Elevation (Approx. Feet): 3,809

Population: 2,583
Population Change: 1.30%

Race:
White: 33.5%
Black: 5.0%
Hispanic: 60.2%
Asian: 0.7%
Other: 4.1%

Vital Statistics:
Births: 52
Deaths: 28
Marriages: 17
Divorces: 5

2024 Rainfall: 15.29 in.
January Avg. Temp.: 37.1°F
July Avg. Temp.: 78.8°F

Unemployment Rate: 4.1
Per Capita Income: $49,855
Tourism Earnings: $260,000
Avg. Home Value: $57,700

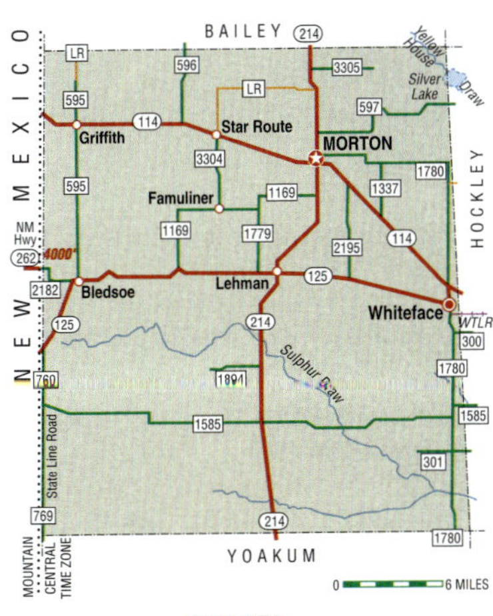

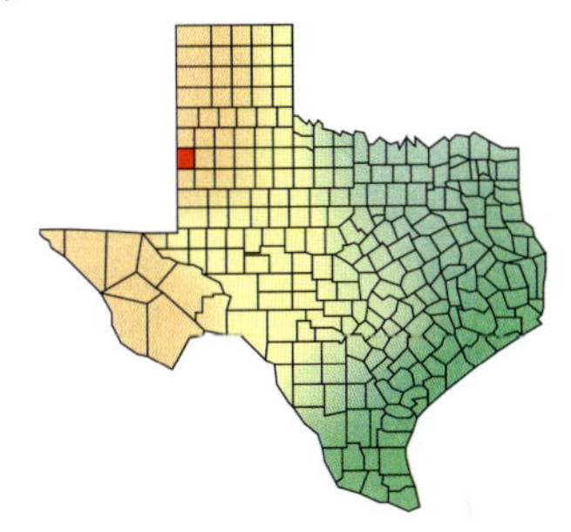

COKE COUNTY

Named for Governor Richard Coke.

Cities/Towns: Robert Lee, Bronte, Silver, Tennyson, Blackwell

Land Area (Square Miles): 911.65
Elevation (Approx. Feet): 1,860

Population: 3,396
Population Change: 2.80%

Race:
White: 74.3%
Black: 1.0%
Hispanic: 21.8%
Asian: 0.1%
Other: 2.9%

Vital Statistics:
Births: 35
Deaths: 62
Marriages: 11
Divorces: 9

2024 Rainfall: 23 in.
January Avg. Temp.: 42.6°F
July Avg. Temp.: 84°F

Unemployment Rate: 2.9
Per Capita Income: $56,377
Tourism Earnings: $960,000
Avg. Home Value: $112,900

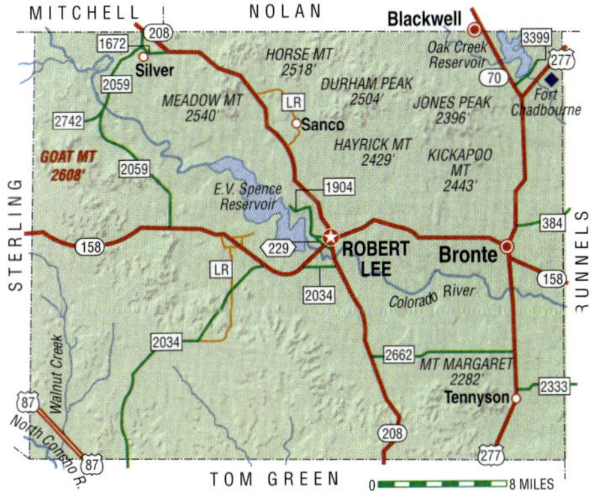

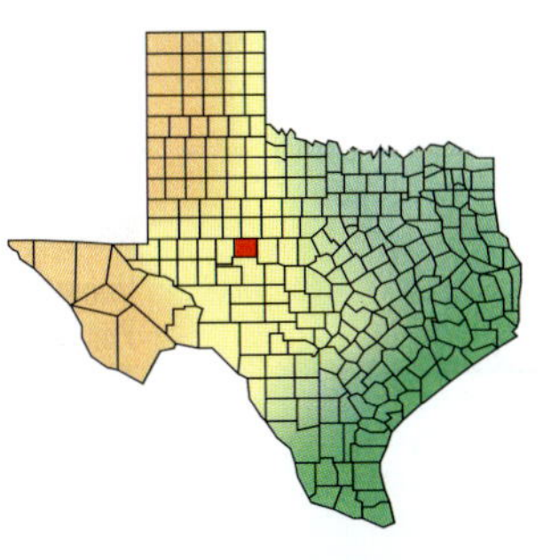

C

COLEMAN
COUNTY

Named for Houston's aide-de-camp R.M. Coleman.

Cities/Towns: Coleman, Santa Anna, Burkett, Gouldbusk, Novice, Talpa, Valera

Land Area (Square Miles): 1,262.91
Elevation (Approx. Feet): 1,663

Population: 7,990
Population Change: 4.00%

Race:
White: 76.6%
Black: 3.8%
Hispanic: 16.9%
Asian: 1.2%
Other: 1.5%

Vital Statistics:
Births: 85
Deaths: 162
Marriages: 54
Divorces: 25

2024 Rainfall: 33.17 in.
January Avg. Temp.: 43.2°F
July Avg. Temp.: 83.2°F

Unemployment Rate: 3.7
Per Capita Income: $62,085
Tourism Earnings: $1.8 million
Avg. Home Value: $91,200

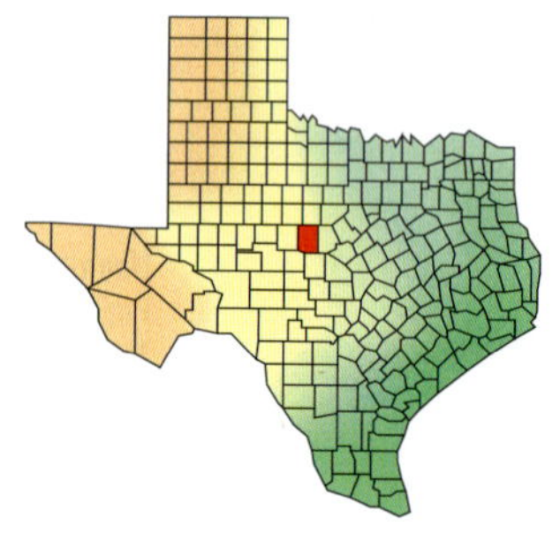

COLLIN
COUNTY

Named for pioneer settler Collin McKinney.

Cities/Towns: McKinney, Plano, Frisco, Allen, Anna, Blue Ridge, Celina, Copeville, Fairview, Farmersville, Josephine, Lavon, Lowry Crossing, Lucas, Melissa, Murphy, Nevada, New Hope, Parker, Princeton, Prosper, St. Paul, Westminster, Weston, Wylie, Dallas, Richardson, Sachse

Land Area (Square Miles): 841.26
Elevation (Approx. Feet): 512

Population: 1,254,658
Population Change: 17.70%

Race:
White: 49.9%
Black: 12.0%
Hispanic: 16.1%
Asian: 19.7%
Other: 0.8%

Vital Statistics:
Births: 12,808
Deaths: 6,023
Marriages: 4,456
Divorces: 1,886

2024 Rainfall: 43.48 in.
January Avg. Temp.: 41°F
July Avg. Temp.: 84.1°F

Unemployment Rate: 3.8
Per Capita Income: $86,860
Tourism Earnings: $1 billion
Avg. Home Value: $447,600

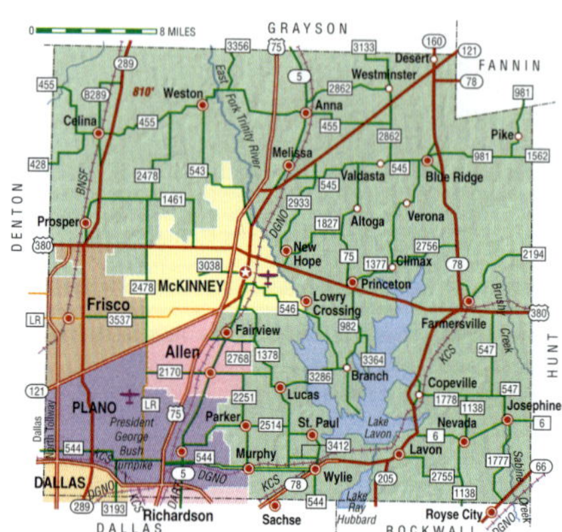

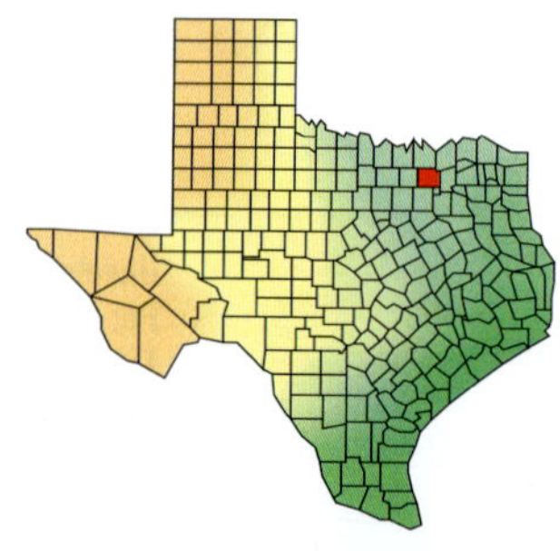

COLLINGSWORTH
COUNTY

Named for Republic of Texas' first Chief Justice James Collinsworth.

Cities/Towns: Wellington, Dodson, Quail, Samnorwood

Land Area (Square Miles): 918.44
Elevation (Approx. Feet): 2,067

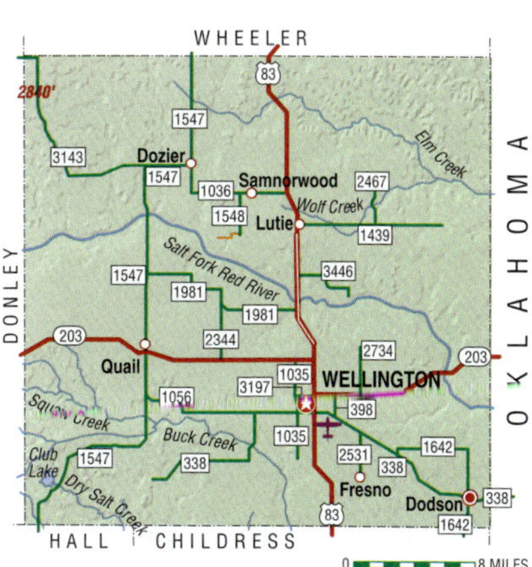

Population: 2,611
Population Change: -1.60%

Race:
White: 58.8%
Black: 6.8%
Hispanic: 31.3%
Asian: 0.7%
Other: 3.6%

Vital Statistics:
Births: 27
Deaths: 30
Marriages: 8
Divorces: 1

2024 Rainfall: 21.49 in.
January Avg. Temp.: 35.3°F
July Avg. Temp.: 82.7°F

Unemployment Rate: 3.1
Per Capita Income: $58,742
Tourism Earnings: $310,000
Avg. Home Value: $108,400

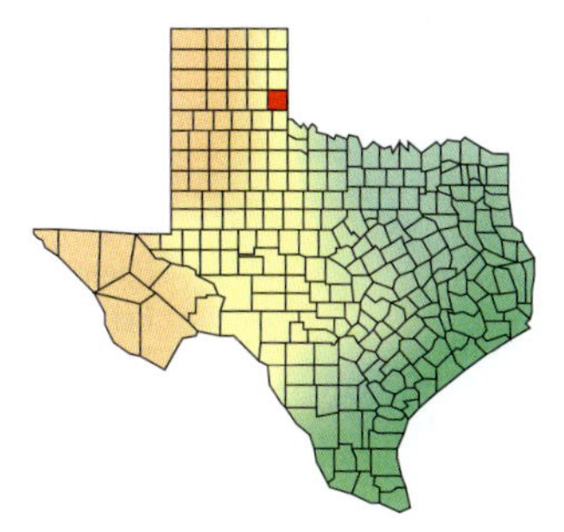

COLORADO
COUNTY

Named for the Colorado River.

Cities/Towns: Columbus, Eagle Lake, Weimar, Altair, Garwood, Gildden, Lone Oak, Nada, Oakland, Rock Island, Sheridan

Land Area (Square Miles): 960.29
Elevation (Approx. Feet): 236

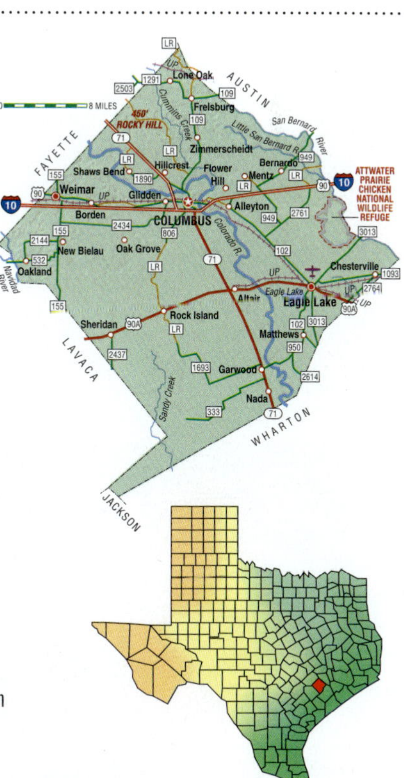

Population: 21,475
Population Change: 4.00%

Race:
White: 55.2%
Black: 12.4%
Hispanic: 31.0%
Asian: 0.8%
Other: 1.3%

Vital Statistics:
Births: 258
Deaths: 287
Marriages: 86
Divorces: 53

2024 Rainfall: 43.51 in.
January Avg. Temp.: 50.6°F
July Avg. Temp.: 84.3°F

Unemployment Rate: 3.8
Per Capita Income: $64,084
Tourism Earnings: $20.8 million
Avg. Home Value: $194,000

C

COMAL
COUNTY

Named for the Comal River.

Cities/Towns: New Braunfels, Canyon Lake, Bulverde, Garden Ridge, Fair Oaks Ranch, Schertz, Selma

Land Area (Square Miles): 559.53
Elevation (Approx. Feet): 1,296

Population: 201,628
Population Change: 24.90%

Race:
White: 64.4%
Black: 3.5%
Hispanic: 28.8%
Asian: 1.8%
Other:1.1%

Vital Statistics:
Births: 1,912
Deaths: 1,654
Marriages: 982
Divorces: 192

2024 Rainfall: 27.92 in.
January Avg. Temp.: 47.2°F
July Avg. Temp.: 83.4°F

Unemployment Rate: 3.6
Per Capita Income: $77,224
Tourism Earnings: $236.6 million
Avg. Home Value: $398,800

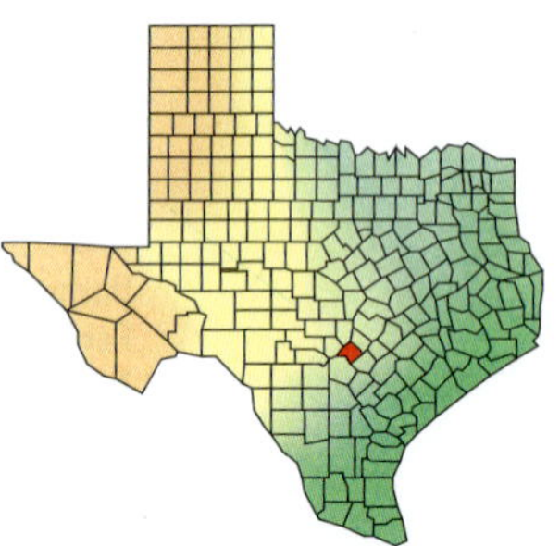

UNSPLASH/DOCUMERICA

COMANCHE
COUNTY

Named for the Indigenous community.

Cities/Towns: Comanche, De Leon, Energy, Gustine, Proctor, Sidney

Land Area (Square Miles): 937.75
Elevation (Approx. Feet): 1,260

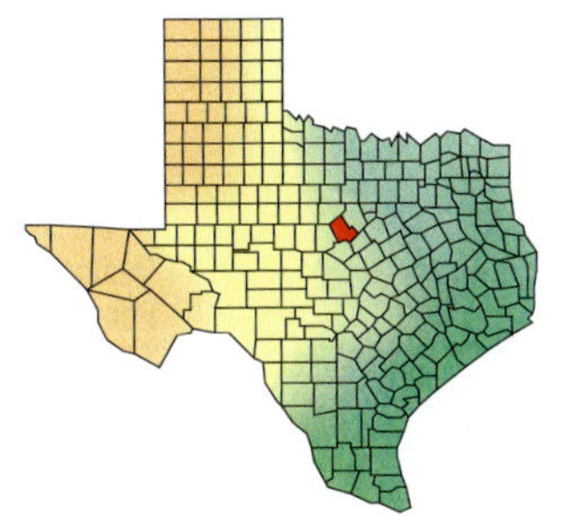

Population: 14,359
Population Change: 5.70%

Race:
White: 66.8%
Black: 1.6%
Hispanic: 29.8%
Asian: 0.9%
Other: 1.5%

Vital Statistics:
Births: 176
Deaths: 202
Marriages: 56
Divorces: 50

2024 Rainfall: 35.4 in.
January Avg. Temp.: 42.4°F
July Avg. Temp.: 83.3°F

Unemployment Rate: 3
Per Capita Income: $55,417
Tourism Earnings: $3.4 million
Avg. Home Value: $137,800

CONCHO
COUNTY

Named for the Concho River.

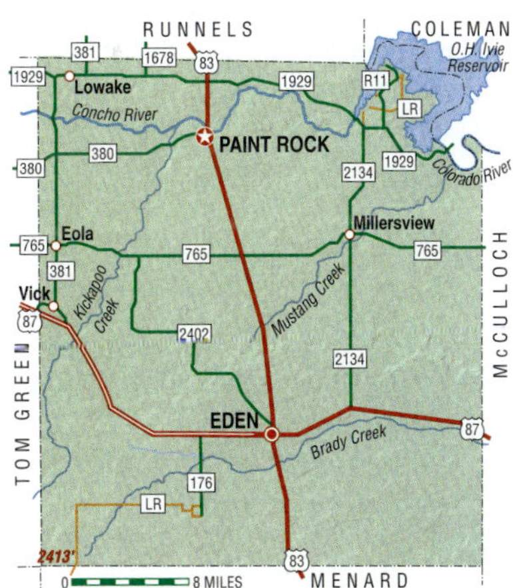

Cities/Towns: Paint Rock, Eden, Eola, Lowake, Millersview

Land Area (Square Miles): 983.76
Elevation (Approx. Feet): 1,946

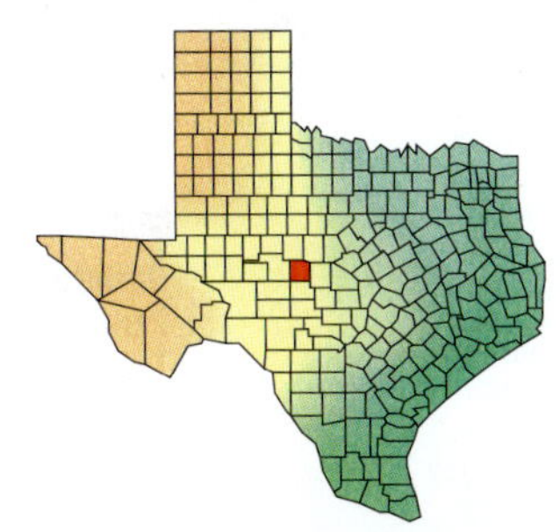

Population: 3,326
Population Change: 0.80%

Race:
White: 53.9%
Black: 12.6%
Hispanic: 31.5%
Asian: 1.6%
Other: 1.1%

Vital Statistics:
Births: 13
Deaths: 33
Marriages: 3
Divorces: 2

2024 Rainfall: 22.99 in.
January Avg. Temp.: 44.4°F
July Avg. Temp.: 83.4°F

Unemployment Rate: 3.3
Per Capita Income: $41,175
Tourism Earnings: $490,000
Avg. Home Value: $105,800

C

COOKE
COUNTY

Named for Texas Revolution Captain W.G. Cooke.

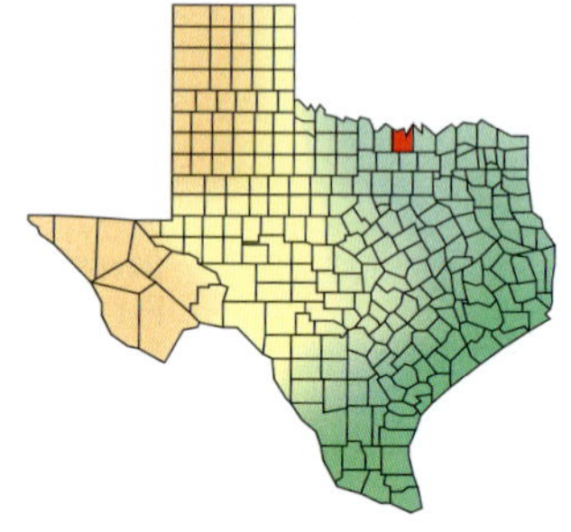

Cities/Towns: Gainesville, Meunster, Callisburg, Era, Lindsay, Myra, Oak Ridge, Rosston, Valley View, Lake Kiowa

Land Area (Square Miles): 874.83
Elevation (Approx. Feet): 774

Population: 44,258
Population Change: 6.20%

Race:
White: 72.1%
Black: 3.6%
Hispanic: 21.1%
Asian: 1.1%
Other: 1.6%

Vital Statistics:
Births: 491
Deaths: 465
Marriages: 306
Divorces: 107

2024 Rainfall: 38.49 in.
January Avg. Temp.: 38.9°F
July Avg. Temp.: 83.2°F

Unemployment Rate: 3.6
Per Capita Income: $62,126
Tourism Earnings: $960,000
Avg. Home Value: $224,600

CORYELL
COUNTY

Named for local pioneer James Coryell.

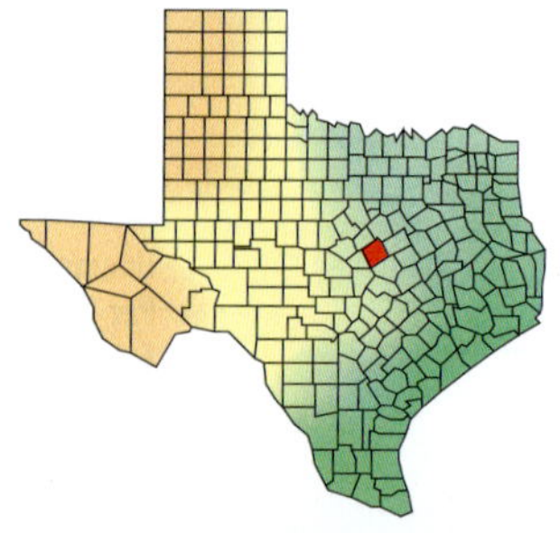

Cities/Towns: Gatesville, Copperas Cove, Evant, Flat, Jonesboro, Mound, Oglesvy, Purmela, South Mountain, Fort Cavazos

Land Area (Square Miles): 1,052.25
Elevation (Approx. Feet): 922

Population: 86,370
Population Change: 4.00%

Race:
White: 55.3%
Black: 17.8%
Hispanic: 21.1%
Asian: 2.5%
Other: 2.5%

Vital Statistics:
Births: 974
Deaths: 653
Marriages: 323
Divorces: 271

2024 Rainfall: 33.3 in.
January Avg. Temp.: 43.9°F
July Avg. Temp.: 82.8°F

Unemployment Rate: 4.5
Per Capita Income: $39,462
Tourism Earnings: $13.6 million
Avg. Home Value: $177,400

COTTLE
COUNTY

Named for Alamo hero George W. Cottle.

Cities/Towns: Paducah, Hackberry

Land Area (Square Miles): 900.56
Elevation (Approx. Feet): 1,952

Population: 1,263
Population Change: -8.50%

Race:
White: 60.4%
Black: 10.5%
Hispanic: 27.2%
Asian: 0.2%
Other: 0.9%

Vital Statistics:
Births: N/A
Deaths: 20
Marriages: 3
Divorces: N/A

2024 Rainfall: 24.26 in.
January Avg. Temp.: 37.8°F
July Avg. Temp.: 84.1°F

Unemployment Rate: 2.2
Per Capita Income: $106,885
Tourism Earnings: $210,000
Avg. Home Value: $54,100

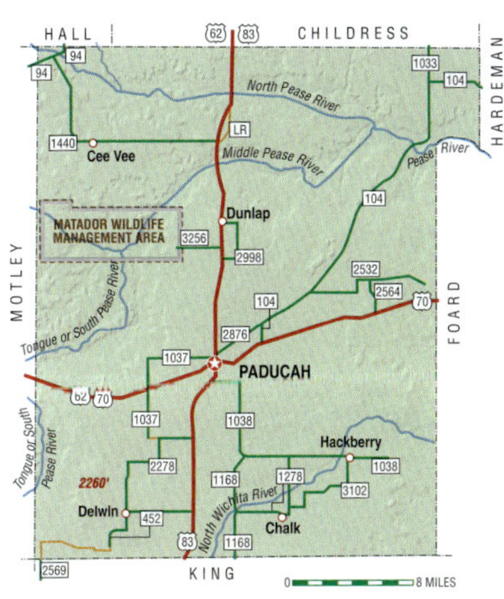

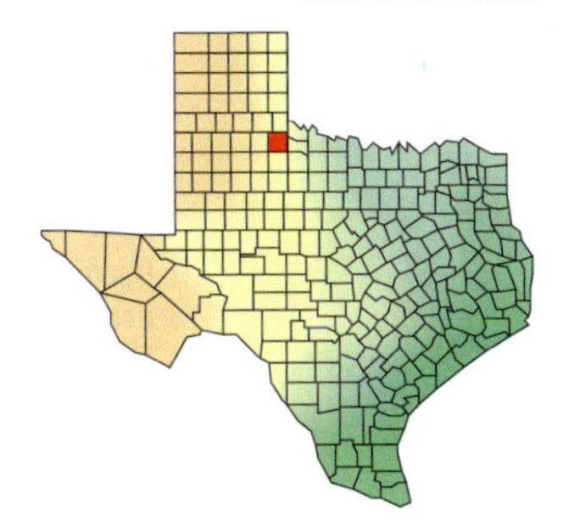

CRANE
COUNTY

Named for Baylor University President W. C. Crane.

Cities/Towns: Crane

Land Area (Square Miles): 785.07
Elevation (Approx. Feet): 2,510

Population: 4,594
Population Change: -1.80%

Race:
White: 24.3%
Black: 4.1%
Hispanic: 70.2%
Asian: 1.1%
Other: 2.3%

Vital Statistics:
Births: 71
Deaths: 49
Marriages: 18
Divorces: 6

2024 Rainfall: 8.12 in.
January Avg. Temp.: 46.2°F
July Avg. Temp.: 85°F

Unemployment Rate: 2.6
Per Capita Income: $57,616
Tourism Earnings: $730,000
Avg. Home Value: $119,900

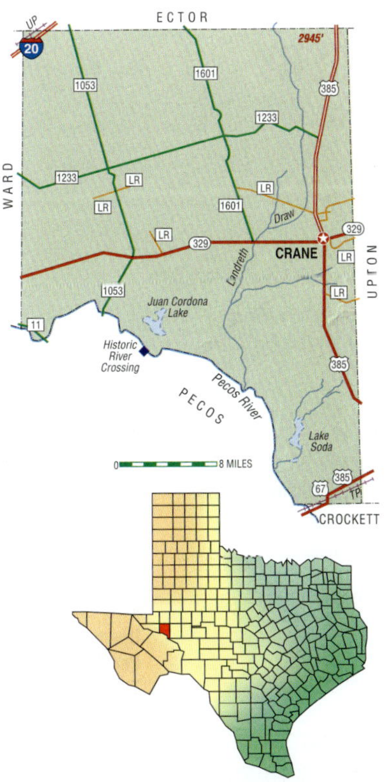

C

CROCKETT COUNTY

Named for Alamo hero Davy Crockett.

Cities/Towns: Ozona

Land Area (Square Miles): 2,807.32
Elevation (Approx. Feet): 2,356

Population: 2,799
Population Change: -9.60%

Race:
White: 32.9%
Black: 3.0%
Hispanic: 63.1%
Asian: 1.4%
Other: 3.4%

Vital Statistics:
Births: 32
Deaths: 38
Marriages: 23
Divorces: 5

2024 Rainfall: 11.73 in.
January Avg. Temp.: 44.8°F
July Avg. Temp.: 83.8°F

Unemployment Rate: 3.3
Per Capita Income: $68,799
Tourism Earnings: $3.2 million
Avg. Home Value: $140,000

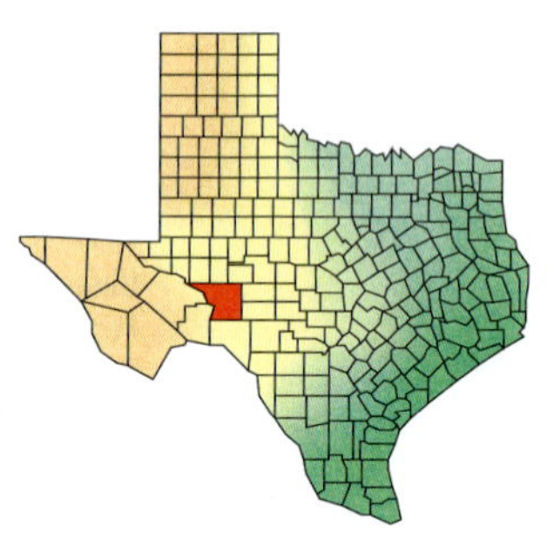

CROSBY COUNTY

Named for Texas Land Commissioner Stephen Crosby.

Cities/Towns: Crosbyton, Lorenzo, Ralls

Land Area (Square Miles): 900.2
Elevation (Approx. Feet): 3,035

Population: 5,030
Population Change: -1.90%

Race:
White: 37.9%
Black: 4.6%
Hispanic: 56.6%
Asian: 0.4%
Other: 1.8%

Vital Statistics:
Births: 71
Deaths: 62
Marriages: 17
Divorces: 8

2024 Rainfall: 19.32 in.
January Avg. Temp.: 38°F
July Avg. Temp.: 81.6°F

Unemployment Rate: 4
Per Capita Income: $55,085
Tourism Earnings: $540,000
Avg. Home Value: $75,500

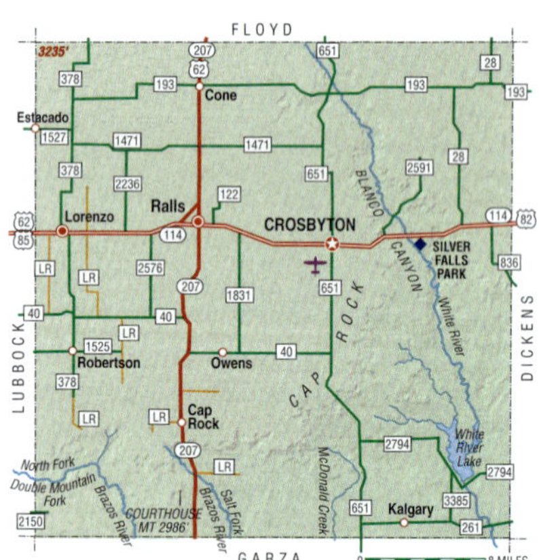

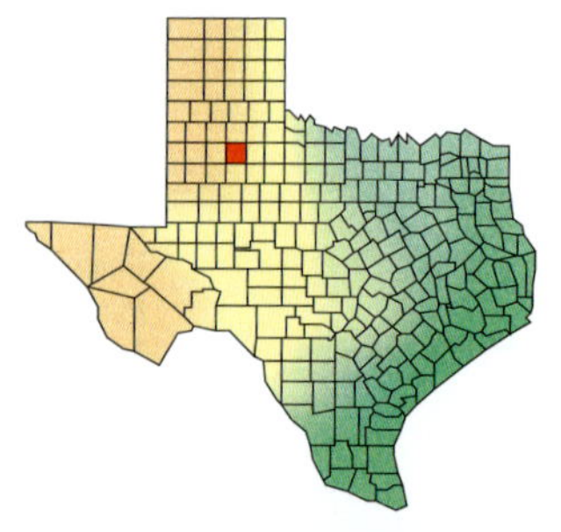

CULBERSON
COUNTY

Named for Texas Congressman D.B. Culberson.

Cities/Towns: Van Horn, Kent

Land Area (Square Miles): 3,812.16
Elevation (Approx. Feet): 4,679

Population: 2,254
Population Change: 3.10%

Race:
White: 24.3%
Black: 3.1%
Hispanic: 68.3%
Asian: 2.4%
Other: 2.5%

Vital Statistics:
Births: 32
Deaths: 29
Marriages: 0
Divorces: N/A

2024 Rainfall: 15.98 in.
January Avg. Temp.: 43.7°F
July Avg. Temp.: 80.5°F

Unemployment Rate: 3.3
Per Capita Income: $96,410
Tourism Earnings: $7.4 million
Avg. Home Value: $84,500

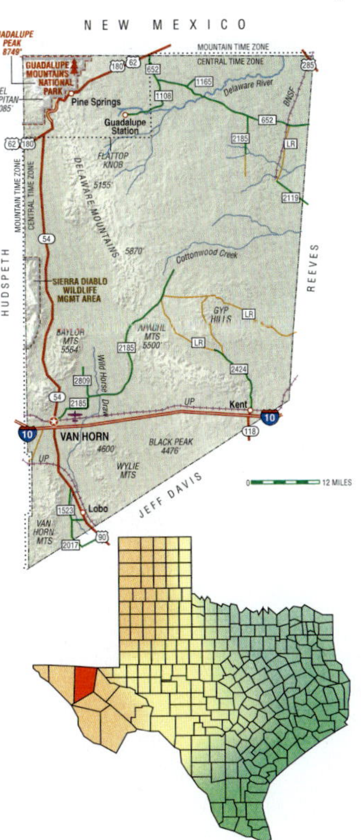

DALLAM
COUNTY

Named for lawyer and editor James W. Dallam.

Cities/Towns: Dalhart, Kerrick, Texline

Land Area (Square Miles): 1,503.13
Elevation (Approx. Feet): 4,190

Population: 7,526
Population Change: 5.50%

Race:
White: 40.4%
Black: 2.8%
Hispanic: 54.9%
Asian: 1.4%
Other: 4.0%

Vital Statistics:
Births: 142
Deaths: 69
Marriages: 39
Divorces: 28

2024 Rainfall: 15.98 in.
January Avg. Temp.: 31.2°F
July Avg. Temp.: 77.6°F

Unemployment Rate: 2.8
Per Capita Income: $82,618
Tourism Earnings: $9.3 million
Avg. Home Value: $140,500

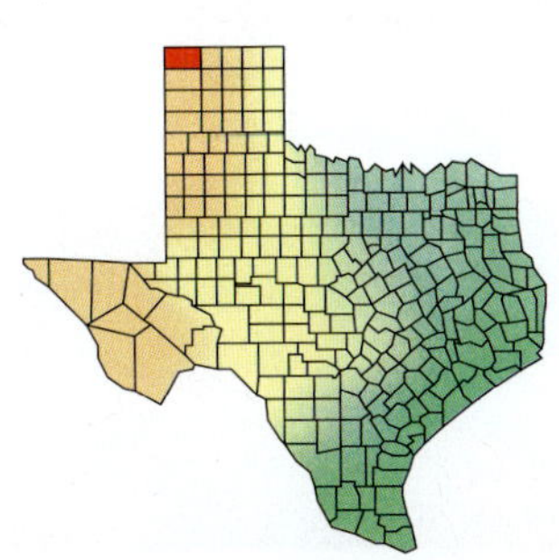

UNSPLASH/ZABDIEL GONZALEZ

D

DALLAS
COUNTY

Named for U.S. Vice President George Mifflin Dallas.

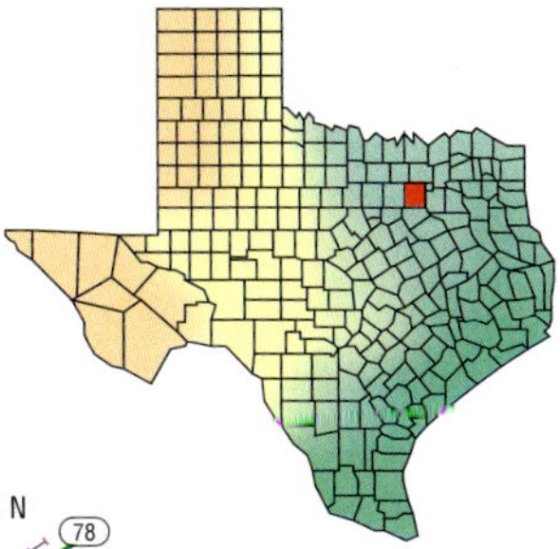

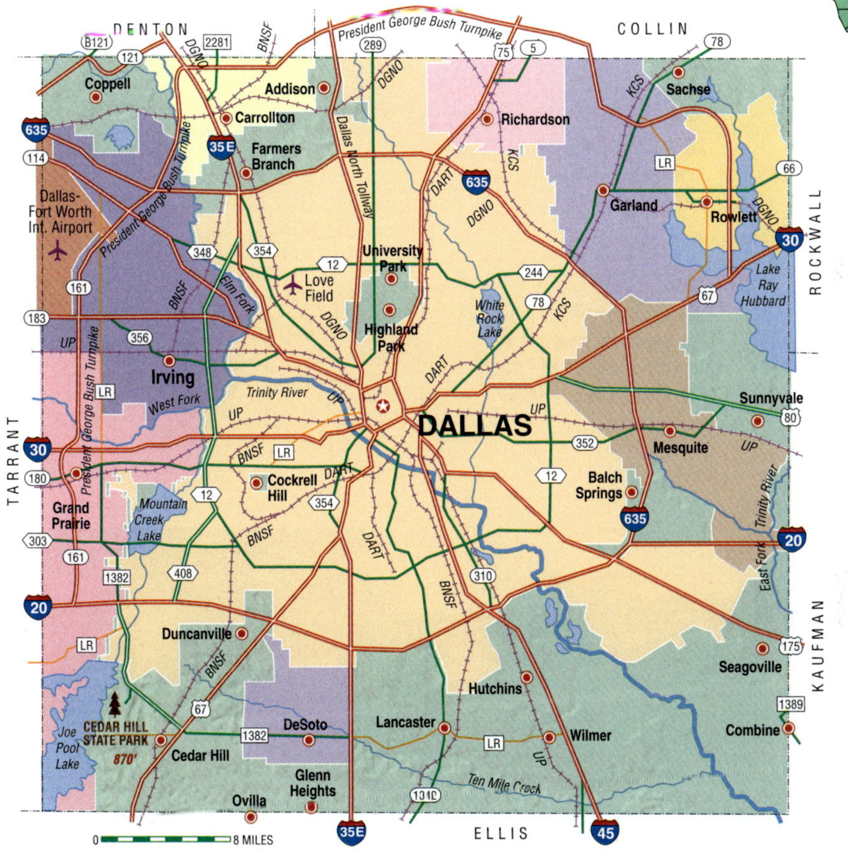

Cities/Towns: Dallas, Garland, Irving, Addison, Balch Springs, Cedar Hill, Cockrell Hill, Coppell, Duncanville, Farmers Branch, Glenn Heights, Grand Prairie, Highland Park, Hutchins, Lancaster, Mesquite, Richardson, Rowlett, Sachse, Seagoville, Sunnyvale, University Park, Wilmer, Combine, Ovilla, Wylie

Land Area (Square Miles): 873.06
Elevation (Approx. Feet): 443

Population: 2,656,028
Population Change: 1.70%

Race:
White: 26.6%
Black: 24.1%
Hispanic: 41.4%
Asian: 7.4%
Other: 1.2%

Vital Statistics:
Births: 37,228
Deaths: 18,708
Marriages: 8,723
Divorces: 7,966

2024 Rainfall: 46.3 in.
January Avg. Temp.: 42°F
July Avg. Temp.: 84.1°F

Unemployment Rate: 4.1
Per Capita Income: $79,626
Tourism Earnings: $5.8 billion
Avg. Home Value: $277,900

D

DAWSON
COUNTY

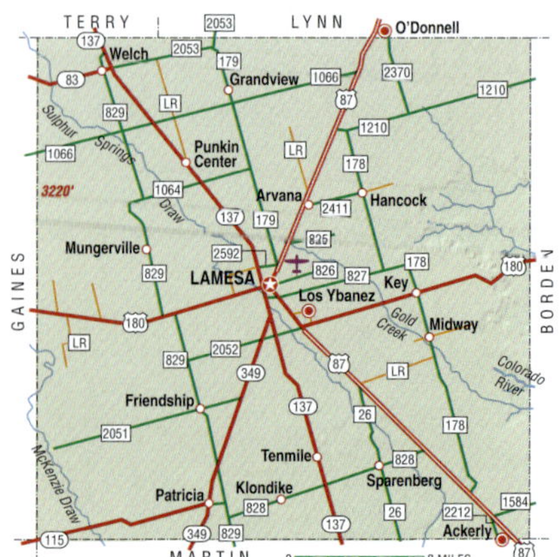

Named for San Jacinto veteran Nicholas M. Dawson.

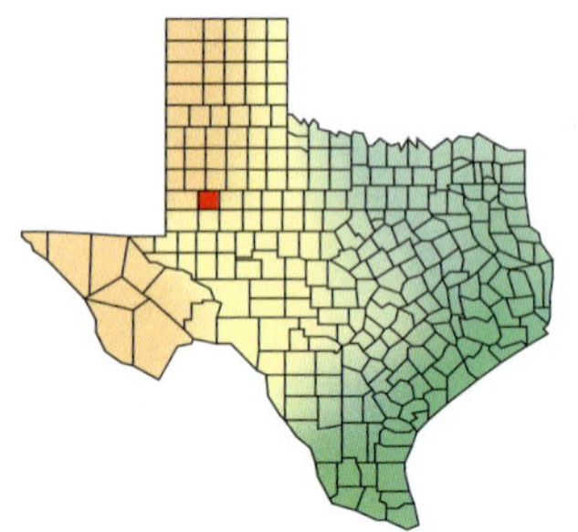

Cities/Towns: Lamesa, Ackerly, Los Ybanez, Welch, O'Donnell

Land Area (Square Miles): 900.31
Elevation (Approx. Feet): 2,992

Population: 11,758
Population Change: -5.60%

Race:
White: 34.9%
Black: 7.6%
Hispanic: 56.4%
Asian: 1.2%
Other: 1.5%

Vital Statistics:
Births: 154
Deaths: 180
Marriages: 46
Divorces: 36

2024 Rainfall: 15.41 in.
January Avg. Temp.: 39.1°F
July Avg. Temp.: 81.8°F

Unemployment Rate: 4.3
Per Capita Income: $54,953
Tourism Earnings: $4.7 million
Avg. Home Value: $90,800

UNSPLASH/DAVID HOLIFIELD

DEAF SMITH
COUNTY

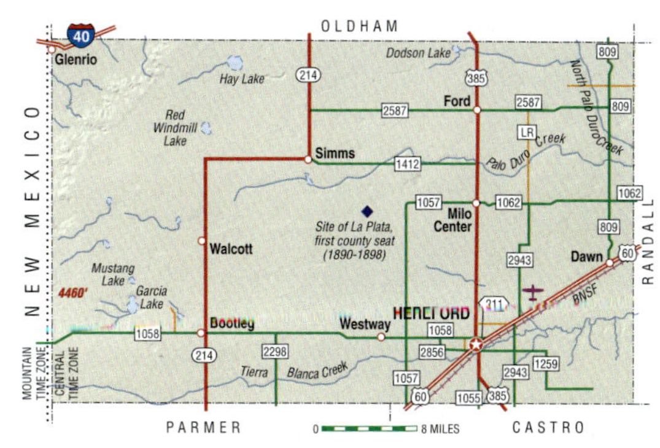

Named for Texas Revolution scout Erastus "Deaf" Smith.

Cities/Towns: Hereford, Dawn

Land Area (Square Miles): 1,496.82
Elevation (Approx. Feet): 4,131

Population: 18,495
Population Change: -0.50%

Race:
White: 20.3%
Black: 2.3%
Hispanic: 77.1%
Asian: 0.6%
Other: 2.3%

Vital Statistics:
Births: 313
Deaths: 152
Marriages: 92
Divorces: 13

2024 Rainfall: 17.14 in.
January Avg. Temp.: 34.5°F
July Avg. Temp.: 78.9°F

Unemployment Rate: 3.3
Per Capita Income: $75,549
Tourism Earnings: $4.2 million
Avg. Home Value: $116,000

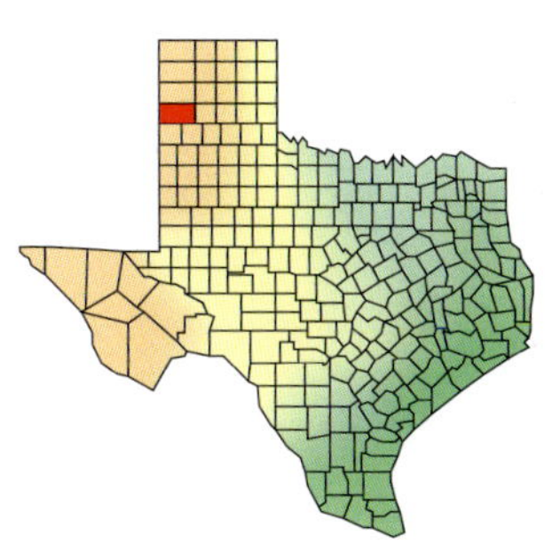

DELTA
COUNTY

Named for the Greek letter delta due to the county's triangular shape.

Cities/Towns: Cooper, Ben Franklin, Enloe, Klondike, Lake Creek, Pecan Gap

Land Area (Square Miles): 256.83
Elevation (Approx. Feet): 453

Population: 5,647
Population Change: 8.10%

Race:
White: 78.6%
Black: 6.3%
Hispanic: 10.0%
Asian: 0.7%
Other: 2.8%

Vital Statistics:
Births: 81
Deaths: 72
Marriages: 14
Divorces: 22

2024 Rainfall: 51.28 in.
January Avg. Temp.: 39.7°F
July Avg. Temp.: 81.9°F

Unemployment Rate: 4.4
Per Capita Income: $49,467
Tourism Earnings: $420,000
Avg. Home Value: $149,400

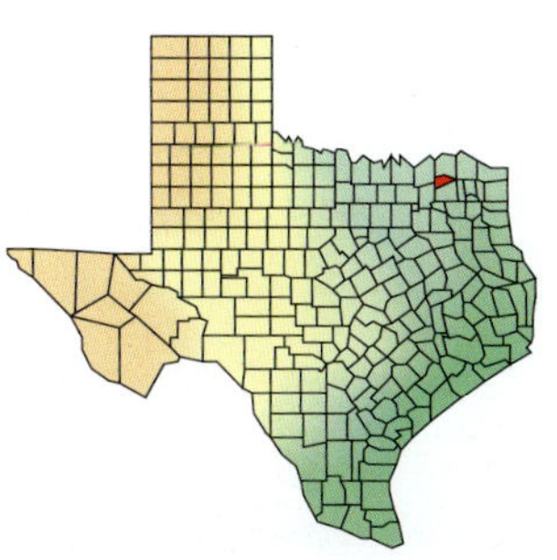

UNSPLASH/BAILEY ALEXANDER

DENTON
COUNTY

Named for pioneer Methodist minister John B. Denton.

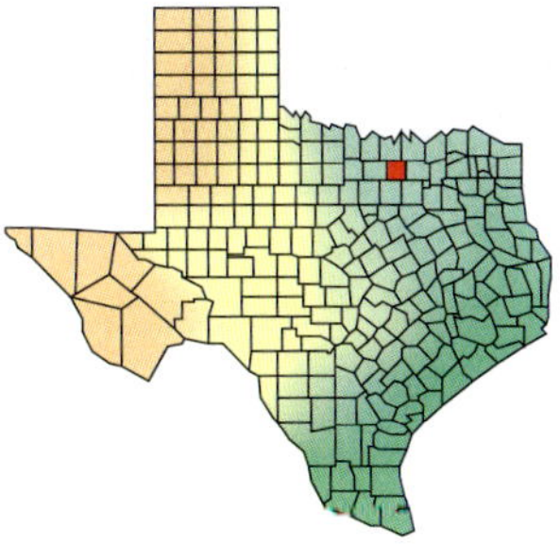

Cities/Towns: Denton, Lewisville, Flower Mound, Carrollton, Argyle, Aubrey, Bartonville, Cooper Canyon, Corinth, Corral City, Cross Roads, Dish, Double Oak, Hackberry, Hebron, Hickory Creek, Highland Village, Justin, Krugerville, Krum, Lake Dallas, Lakewood Village, Lantana, Little Elm, Northlake, Oak Point, Pilot Point, Providence Village, Roanoke, Sanger, Shady Shores, The Colony, Trophy Club, Dallas, Forth Worth, Frisco, Plano, Coppell, Celina, Prosper, Southlake

Land Area (Square Miles): 878.51
Elevation (Approx. Feet): 617

Population: 1,045,120
Population Change: 15.30%

Race:
White: 52.9%
Black: 12.5%
Hispanic: 20.5%
Asian: 12.1%
Other: 0.9%

Vital Statistics:
Births: 11,506
Deaths: 5,118
Marriages: 4,295
Divorces: 2,779

2024 Rainfall: 39.64 in.
January Avg. Temp.: 40.8°F
July Avg. Temp.: 84.5°F

Unemployment Rate: 3.7
Per Capita Income: $77,733
Tourism Earnings: $387.3 million
Avg. Home Value: $403,400

D

DEWITT
COUNTY

Named for colonizer Green DeWitt.

Cities/Towns: Cuero, Yorktown, Hochheim, Mayersville, Nordheim, Thomaston, Westhoff, Yoakum

Land Area (Square Miles): 397.56
Elevation (Approx. Feet): 230

Population: 20,252
Population Change: 2.10%

Race:
White: 54.5%
Black: 9.0%
Hispanic: 36.1%
Asian: 0.6%
Other: 1.2%

Vital Statistics:
Births: 213
Deaths: 260
Marriages: 71
Divorces: N/A

2024 Rainfall: 32.84 in.
January Avg. Temp.: 51.2°F
July Avg. Temp.: 84.5°F

Unemployment Rate: 4.5
Per Capita Income: $77,489
Tourism Earnings: $11.3 million
Avg. Home Value: $167,200

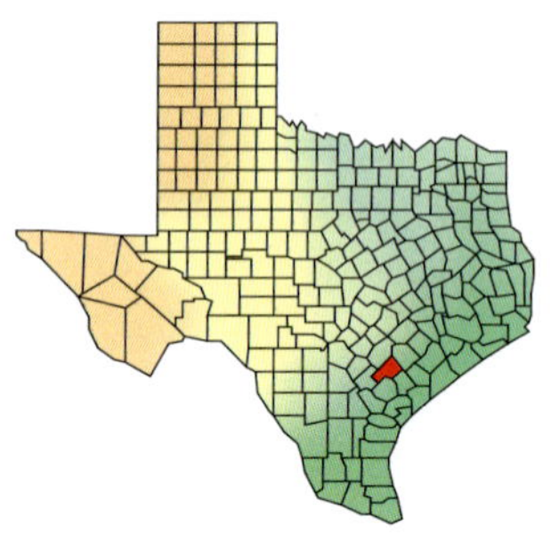

DICKENS
COUNTY

Named for Alamo hero who is variously listed as James R. Demkins, Dimpkins, and J. Dickens.

Cities/Towns: Dickens, Spur, Afton, McAdoo

Land Area (Square Miles): 901.72
Elevation (Approx. Feet): 2,323

Population: 1,725
Population Change: -2.60%

Race:
White: 65.8%
Black: 3.8%
Hispanic: 27.6%
Asian: 1.5%
Other: 3.2%

Vital Statistics:
Births: 18
Deaths: 24
Marriages: 5
Divorces: 7

2024 Rainfall: 23.35 in.
January Avg. Temp.: 38.3°F
July Avg. Temp.: 83.3°F

Unemployment Rate: 4.3
Per Capita Income: $56,301
Tourism Earnings: $140,000
Avg. Home Value: $65,000

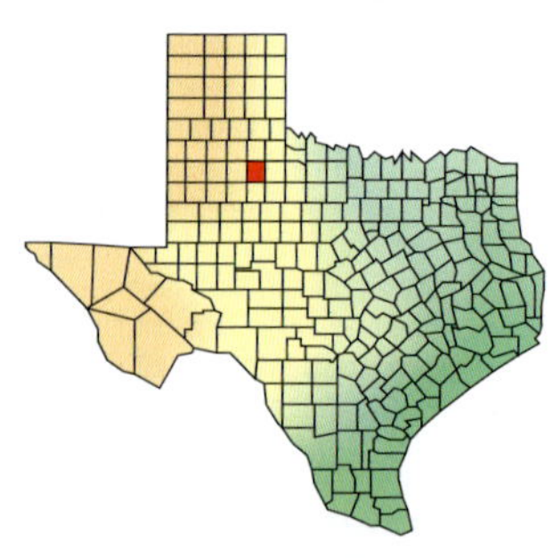

DIMMIT
COUNTY

Named for Texas Revolution officer Philip Dimmitt.

Cities/Towns: Carrizo Springs, Asherton, Big Wells, Carrizo Hill, Catrina

Land Area (Square Miles): 1,328.89
Elevation (Approx. Feet): 577

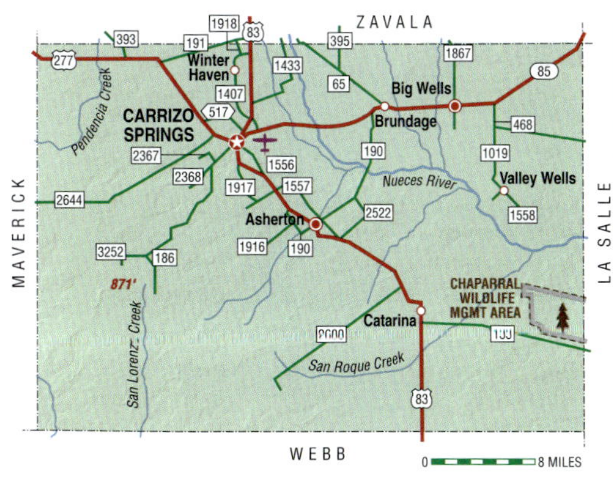

Population: 8,181
Population Change: -5.00%

Race:
White: 9.7%
Black: 2.3%
Hispanic: 87.4%
Asian: 1.0%
Other: 1.3%

Vital Statistics:
Births: 116
Deaths: 120
Marriages: 27
Divorces: N/A

2024 Rainfall: 14.88 in.
January Avg. Temp.: 51.8°F
July Avg. Temp.: 87.1°F

Unemployment Rate: 6.8
Per Capita Income: $55,714
Tourism Earnings: $8.6 million
Avg. Home Value: $80,300

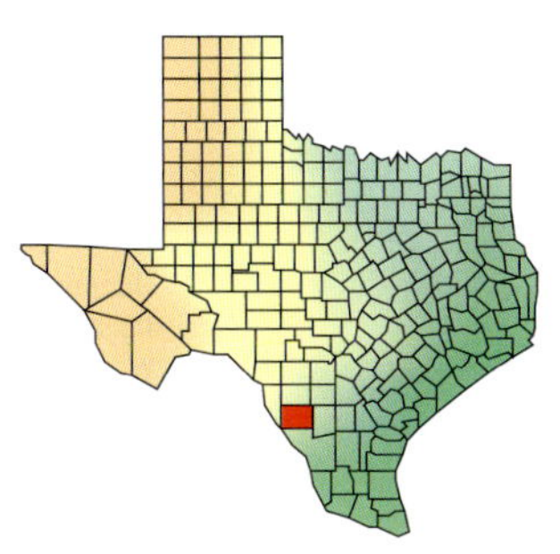

DONLEY
COUNTY

Named for Texas Supreme Court Justice S.P. Donley.

Cities/Towns: Clarendon, Hedley, Howardwick, Leila Lake

Land Area (Square Miles): 926.91
Elevation (Approx. Feet): 2,677

Population: 3,193
Population Change: -2.10%

Race:
White: 77.6%
Black: 5.7%
Hispanic: 13.3%
Asian: 0.9%
Other: 1.3%

Vital Statistics:
Births: 18
Deaths: 66
Marriages: 20
Divorces: 5

2024 Rainfall: 20.07 in.
January Avg. Temp.: 35.2°F
July Avg. Temp.: 81.9°F

Unemployment Rate: 4.5
Per Capita Income: $52,905
Tourism Earnings: $2.4 million
Avg. Home Value: $90,500

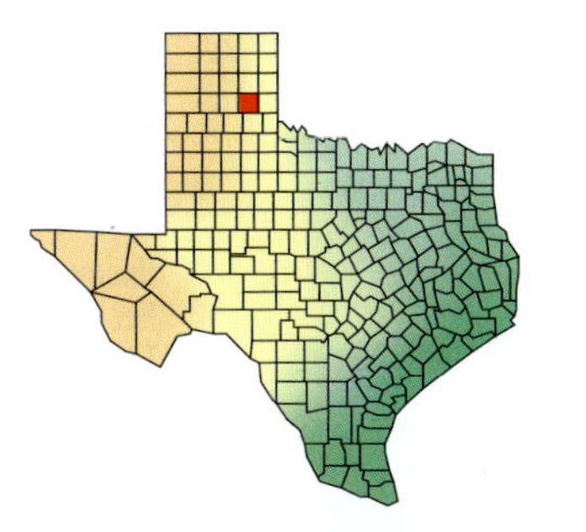

DUVAL
COUNTY

Named for Burr H. Duval, a victim of the Goliad massacre.

Cities/Towns: San Diego, Freer, Benavides, Concepcion, Realitos

Land Area (Square Miles): 1,793.48
Elevation (Approx. Feet): 525

Population: 9,585
Population Change: -2.50%

Race:
White: 14.5%
Black: 2.7%
Hispanic: 82.0%
Asian: 0.6%
Other: 1.5%

Vital Statistics:
Births: 144
Deaths: 148
Marriages: 33
Divorces: 16

2024 Rainfall: 22.75 in.
January Avg. Temp.: 54.8°F
July Avg. Temp.: 84.8°F

Unemployment Rate: 5.3
Per Capita Income: $52,669
Tourism Earnings: $1.2 million
Avg. Home Value: $86,400

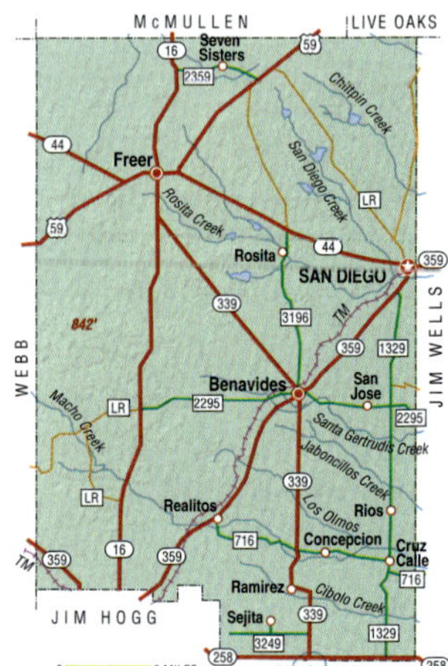

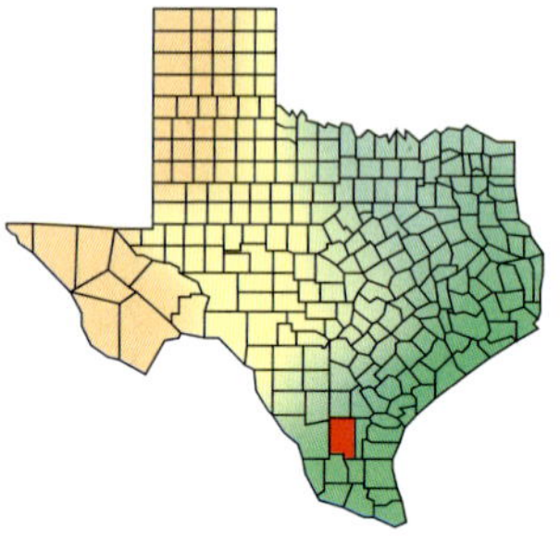

EASTLAND
COUNTY

Named for Mier Expedition Captain W.M. Eastland.

Cities/Towns: Eastland, Cisco, Ranger, Carbon, Desdamona, Gorman, Olden, Rising Star

Land Area (Square Miles): 926.51
Elevation (Approx. Feet): 1,558

Population: 18,290
Population Change: 3.00%

Race:
White: 77.5%
Black: 2.5%
Hispanic: 17.2%
Asian: 0.9%
Other: 1.5%

Vital Statistics:
Births: 204
Deaths: 335
Marriages: 104
Divorces: 22

2024 Rainfall: 36.05 in.
January Avg. Temp.: 40.9°F
July Avg. Temp.: 82.9°F

Unemployment Rate: 5.3
Per Capita Income: $56,246
Tourism Earnings: $6.5 million
Avg. Home Value: $121,700

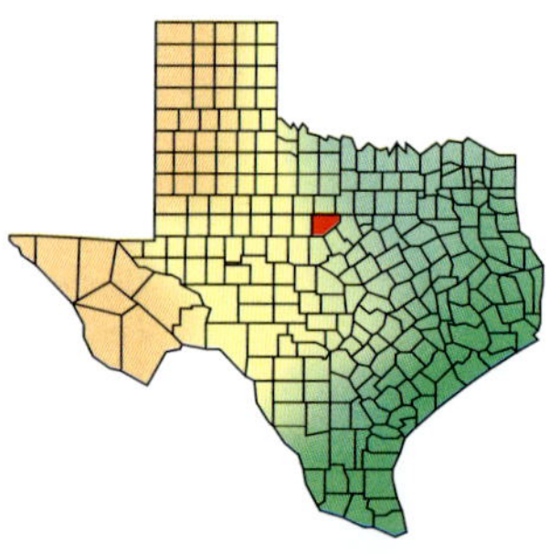

ECTOR
COUNTY

Named for jurist M.D. Ector.

Cities/Towns: Odessa, Gardendale, Goldsmith, Notrees, Penwell, West Odessa

Land Area (Square Miles): 897.96
Elevation (Approx. Feet): 3,019

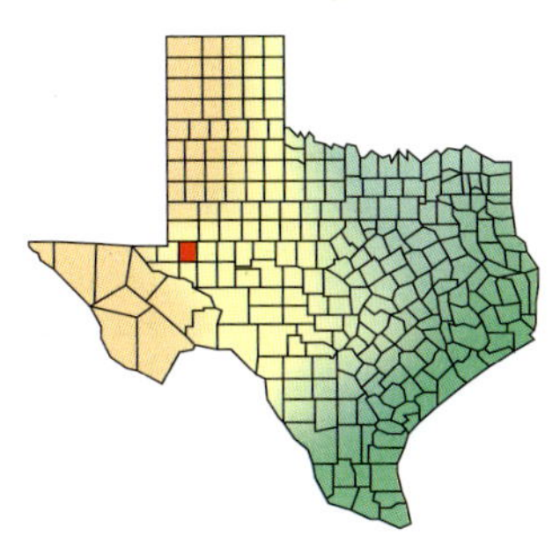

Population: 170,022
Population Change: 2.90%

Race:
White: 28.1%
Black: 5.5%
Hispanic: 64.5%
Asian: 1.5%
Other: 1.8%

Vital Statistics:
Births: 3,015
Deaths: 1,516
Marriages: 1,048
Divorces: 747

2024 Rainfall: 8.38 in.
January Avg. Temp.: 43.4°F
July Avg. Temp.: 82.8°F

Unemployment Rate: 3.5
Per Capita Income: $58,961
Tourism Earnings: $120.2 million
Avg. Home Value: $190,500

EDWARDS
COUNTY

Named for Nacogdoches empresario Hayden Edwards.

Cities/Towns: Rocksprings, Barksdale

Land Area (Square Miles): 2,117.87
Elevation (Approx. Feet): 2,293

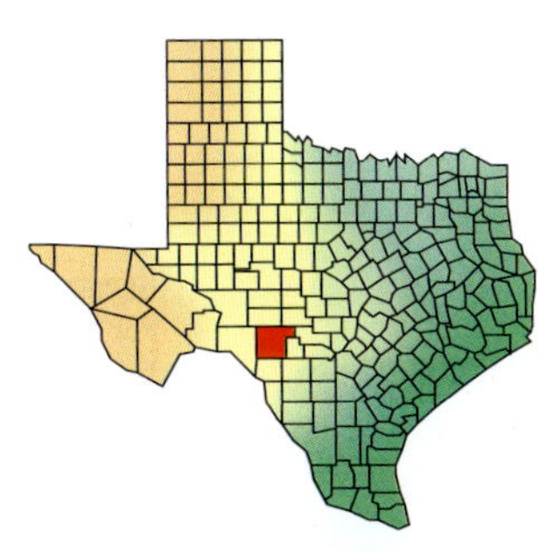

Population: 1,383
Population Change: -2.80%

Race:
White: 45.8%
Black: 2.8%
Hispanic: 49.7%
Asian: 1.2%
Other: 3.3%

Vital Statistics:
Births: 20
Deaths: 28
Marriages: 6
Divorces: N/A

2024 Rainfall: 15.16 in.
January Avg. Temp.: 45.9°F
July Avg. Temp.: 81.9°F

Unemployment Rate: 3.1
Per Capita Income: $82,497
Tourism Earnings: $160,000
Avg. Home Value: $78,300

ELLIS
COUNTY

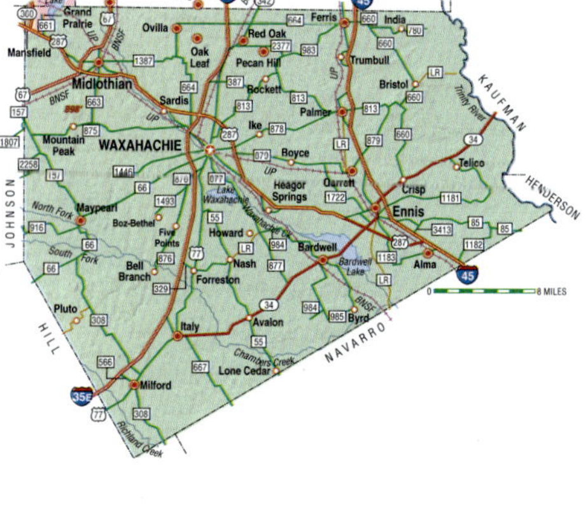

Named for Richard Ellis, president of convention that declared Texas' independence.

Cities/Towns: Waxahachie, Ennis, Midlothian, Alma, Avalon, Bardwell, Bristol, Ferris, Forreston, Garrett, Howard, Italy, Maypearl, Milford, Oak Leaf, Ovilla, Palmer, Pecan Hill, Red Oak, Glenn Heights, Grand Prairie, Mansfield

Land Area (Square Miles): 935.75
Elevation (Approx. Feet): 492

Population: 232,387
Population Change: 20.80%

Race:
White: 51.9%
Black: 17.3%
Hispanic: 28.4%
Asian: 1.2%
Other: 1.1%

Vital Statistics:
Births: 2,820
Deaths: 1,655
Marriages: 910
Divorces: 330

2024 Rainfall: 47.04 in.
January Avg. Temp.: 42.4°F
July Avg. Temp.: 83.5°F

Unemployment Rate: 3.7
Per Capita Income: $57,977
Tourism Earnings: $78.5 million
Avg. Home Value: $306,400

EL PASO
COUNTY

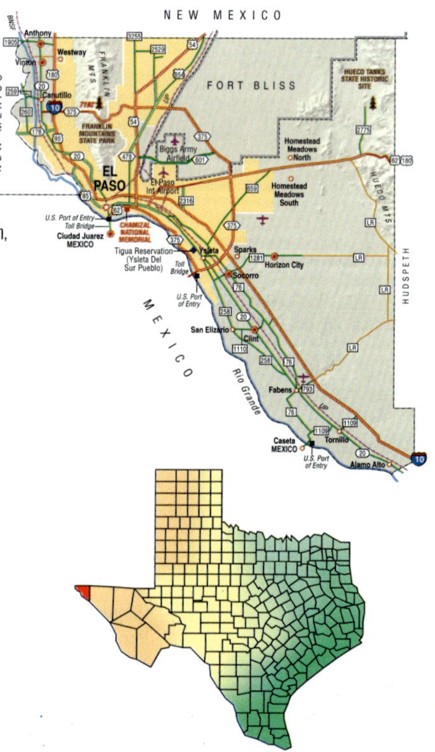

Named for historic pass Paso del Norte..

Cities/Towns: El Paso, Anthony, Canutillo, Clint, Fabens, Homestead Meadows North, Homestead Meadows South, Horizon City, Prado Verde, San Elizario, Socorro, Sparks, Tornillo, Vinton, Westway, Ysleta, Fort Bliss

Land Area (Square Miles): 1,013.23
Elevation (Approx. Feet): 4,016

Population: 875,784
Population Change: 1.20%

Race:
White: 11.1%
Black: 4.5 %
Hispanic: 82.8%
Asian: 1.5%
Other: 1.3%

Vital Statistics:
Births: 11,597
Deaths: 6,946
Marriages: 6,128
Divorces: 21

2024 Rainfall: 5.1 in.
January Avg. Temp.: 47.1°F
July Avg. Temp.: 84.9°F

Unemployment Rate: 4.2
Per Capita Income: $46,753
Tourism Earnings: $647.4 million
Avg. Home Value: $167,300

ERATH
COUNTY

Named for Texas Revolution figure George B. Erath.

Cities/Towns: Stephenville, Dublin, Bluff Dale, Lingleville, Morgan Mill, Thurber

Land Area (Square Miles): 1,083.18
Elevation (Approx. Feet): 1,270

Population: 44,496
Population Change: 4.60%

Race:
White: 72.6%
Black: 2.2%
Hispanic: 22.4%
Asian: 1.2%
Other: 1.6%

Vital Statistics:
Births: 520
Deaths: 398
Marriages: 249
Divorces: 136

2024 Rainfall: 36.01 in.
January Avg. Temp.: 42.1°F
July Avg. Temp.: 83.6°F

Unemployment Rate: 3.5
Per Capita Income: $53,610
Tourism Earnings: $21.4 million
Avg. Home Value: $251,900

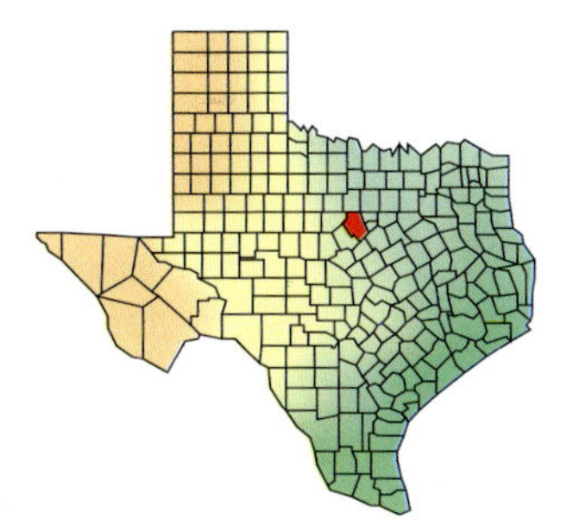

FALLS
COUNTY

Named for Brazos River falls.

Cities/Towns: Marlin, Chilton, Golinda, Lott, Reagan, Rosebud, Satin

Land Area (Square Miles): 765.5
Elevation (Approx. Feet): 338

Population: 17,752
Population Change: 4.60%

Race:
White: 50.3%
Black: 22.9%
Hispanic: 25.9%
Asian: 0.7%
Other: 1.5%

Vital Statistics:
Births: 185
Deaths: 208
Marriages: 47
Divorces: 7

2024 Rainfall: 41.8 in.
January Avg. Temp.: 44.5°F
July Avg. Temp.: 82.6°F

Unemployment Rate: 4.3
Per Capita Income: $47,110
Tourism Earnings: $3 million
Avg. Home Value: $97,300

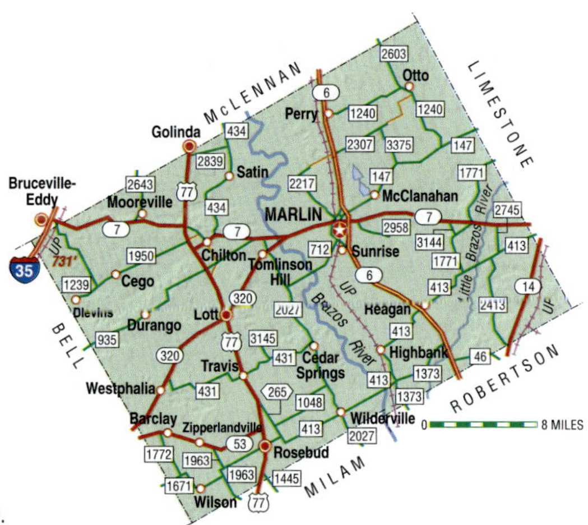

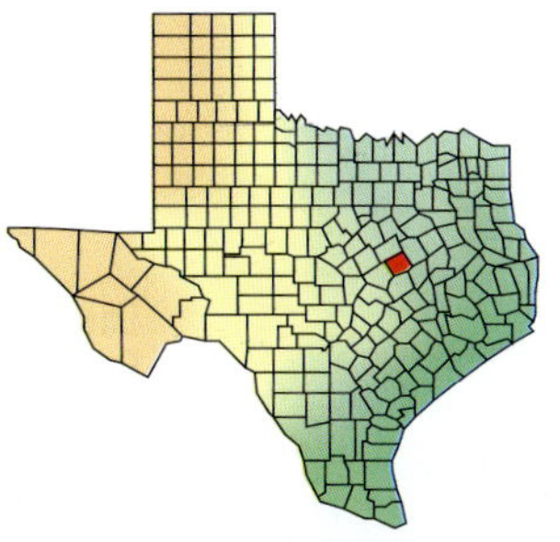

F

FANNIN
COUNTY

Named for military figure James W. Fannin, who was a victim of the Goliad massacre.

Cities/Towns: Bonham, Bailey, Dodd City, Ector, Gober, Honey Grove, Ladonia, Leonard, Randolph, Ravenna, Savoy, Telephone, Trenton, Windom

Land Area (Square Miles): 890.84
Elevation (Approx. Feet): 607

Population: 38,650
Population Change: 7.80%

Race:
White: 75.9%
Black: 6.8%
Hispanic: 13.7%
Asian: 0.8%
Other: 1.5%

Vital Statistics:
Births: 371
Deaths: 535
Marriages: 151
Divorces: 83

2024 Rainfall: 49.26 in.
January Avg. Temp.: 39.1°F
July Avg. Temp.: 82.9°F

Unemployment Rate: 3.7
Per Capita Income: $49,380
Tourism Earnings: $4 million
Avg. Home Value: $213,500

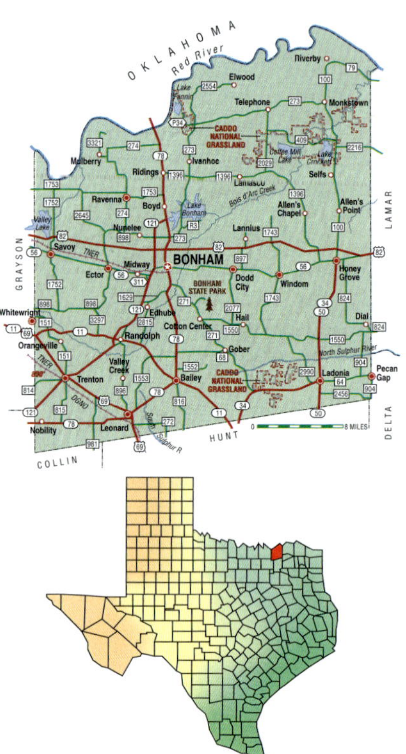

FAYETTE
COUNTY

Named for American Revolution hero Marquis de Lafayette.

Cities/Towns: La Grange, Schulenburg, Round Top, Carmine, Ellinger, Fayetteville, Flatonia, Plum, Warda, Warrenton

Land Area (Square Miles): 949.93
Elevation (Approx. Feet): 253

Population: 25,488
Population Change: 4.10%

Race:
White: 69.9%
Black: 6.3%
Hispanic: 22.2%
Asian: 0.6%
Other: 1.6%

Vital Statistics:
Births: 242
Deaths: 393
Marriages: 83
Divorces: 62

2024 Rainfall: 42.2 in.
January Avg. Temp.: 49.5°F
July Avg. Temp.: 84.5°F

Unemployment Rate: 3.8
Per Capita Income: $72,230
Tourism Earnings: $13.8 million
Avg. Home Value: $271,100

FISHER
COUNTY

Named for Republic of Texas Secretary of Navy S.R. Fisher.

Cities/Towns: Roby, Rotan, McCaulley, Sylvester

Land Area (Square Miles): 898.95
Elevation (Approx. Feet): 1,955

Population: 3,665
Population Change: -0.20%

Race:
White: 65.8%
Black: 4.7%
Hispanic: 27.3%
Asian: 0.5%
Other: 1.4%

Vital Statistics:
Births: 31
Deaths: 69
Marriages: 8
Divorces: 6

2024 Rainfall: 24.76 in.
January Avg. Temp.: 40.6°F
July Avg. Temp.: 84.2°F

Unemployment Rate: 3.1
Per Capita Income: $62,676
Tourism Earnings: $200,000
Avg. Home Value: $77,600

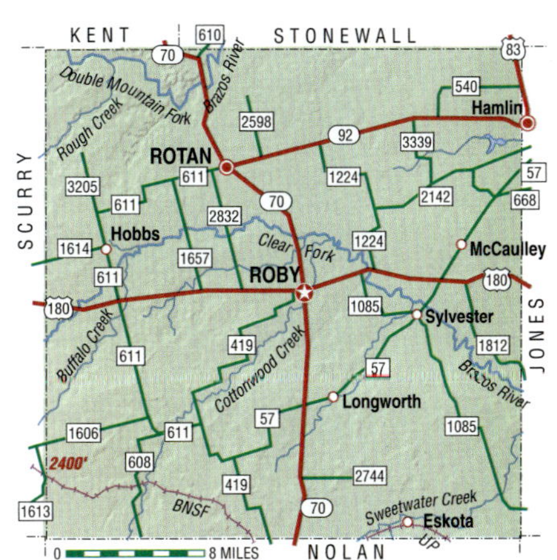

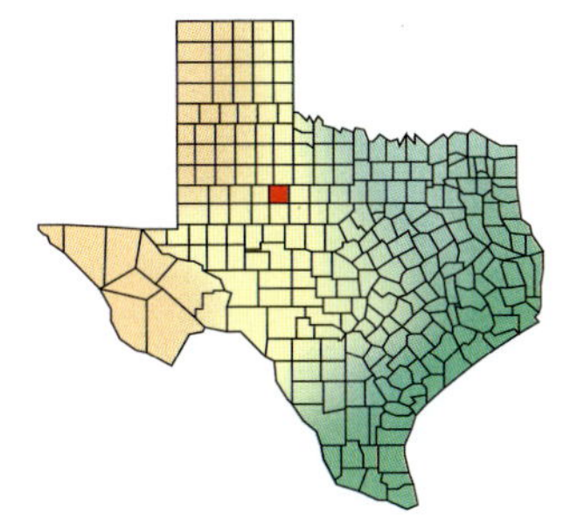

FLOYD
COUNTY

Named for soldier Dolphin Ward Floyd, who died at the Alamo.

Cities/Towns: Floydada, Lockney, Aiken, Dougherty, South Plains

Land Area (Square Miles): 992.14
Elevation (Approx. Feet): 3,156

Population: 5,042
Population Change: -6.60%

Race:
White: 35.9%
Black: 4.8%
Hispanic: 58.7%
Asian: 0.5%
Other: 1.7%

Vital Statistics:
Births: 63
Deaths: 71
Marriages: 26
Divorces: 11

2024 Rainfall: 21.92 in.
January Avg. Temp.: 36.4°F
July Avg. Temp.: 80.3°F

Unemployment Rate: 4.2
Per Capita Income: $51,829
Tourism Earnings: $650,000
Avg. Home Value: $101,000

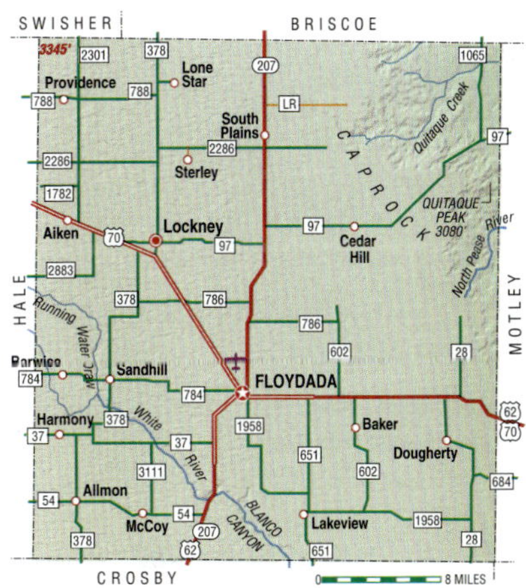

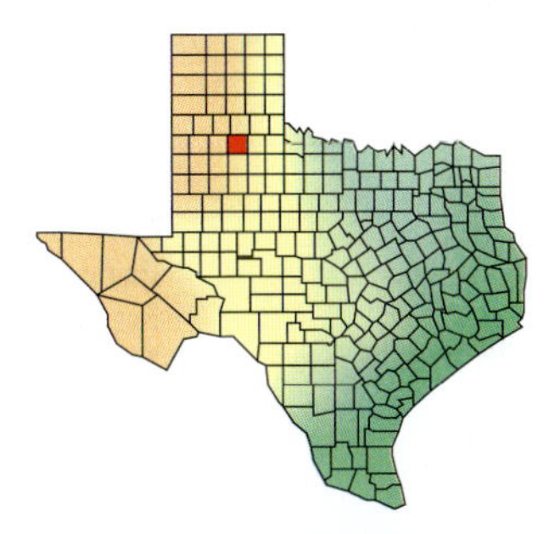

F

UNSPLASH/PETER SCHULZ

FOARD
COUNTY

Named for Confederate Army Major Robert L. Foard.

Cities/Towns: Crowell

Land Area (Square Miles): 704.4
Elevation (Approx. Feet): 1,575

Population: 1,053
Population Change: -4.00%

Race:
White: 71.5%
Black: 5.9%
Hispanic:19.3%
Asian: 1.0%
Other: 1.2%

Vital Statistics:
Births: N/A
Deaths: 22
Marriages: 6
Divorces: 4

2024 Rainfall: 27.03 in.
January Avg. Temp.: 38.4°F
July Avg. Temp.: 84°F

Unemployment Rate: 3.4
Per Capita Income: $65,386
Tourism Earnings: $120,000
Avg. Home Value: $71,400

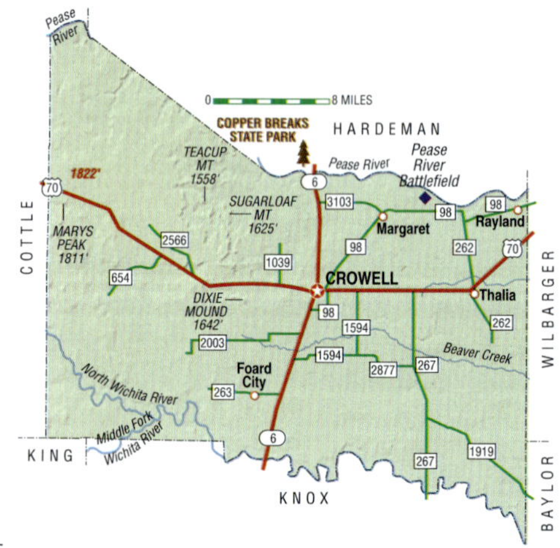

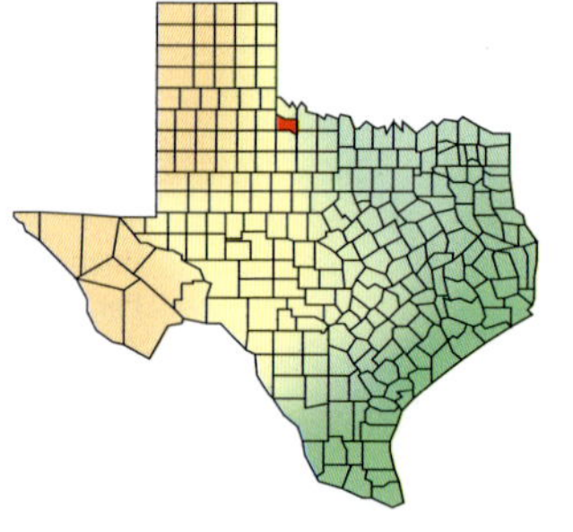

FORT BEND
COUNTY

Named for the blockhouse built at the bend in the Brazos River that served as a point of defense from Native groups.

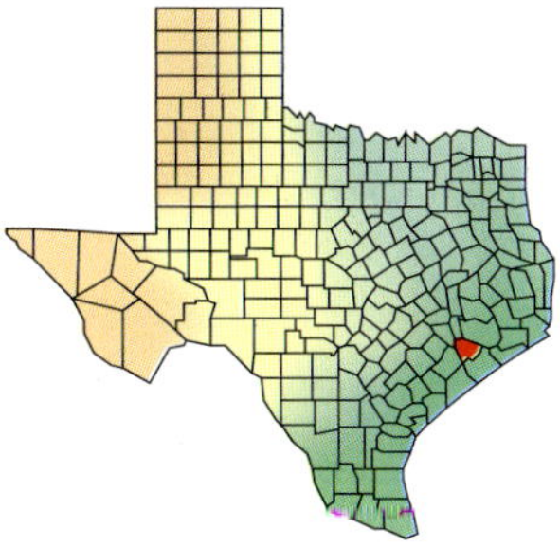

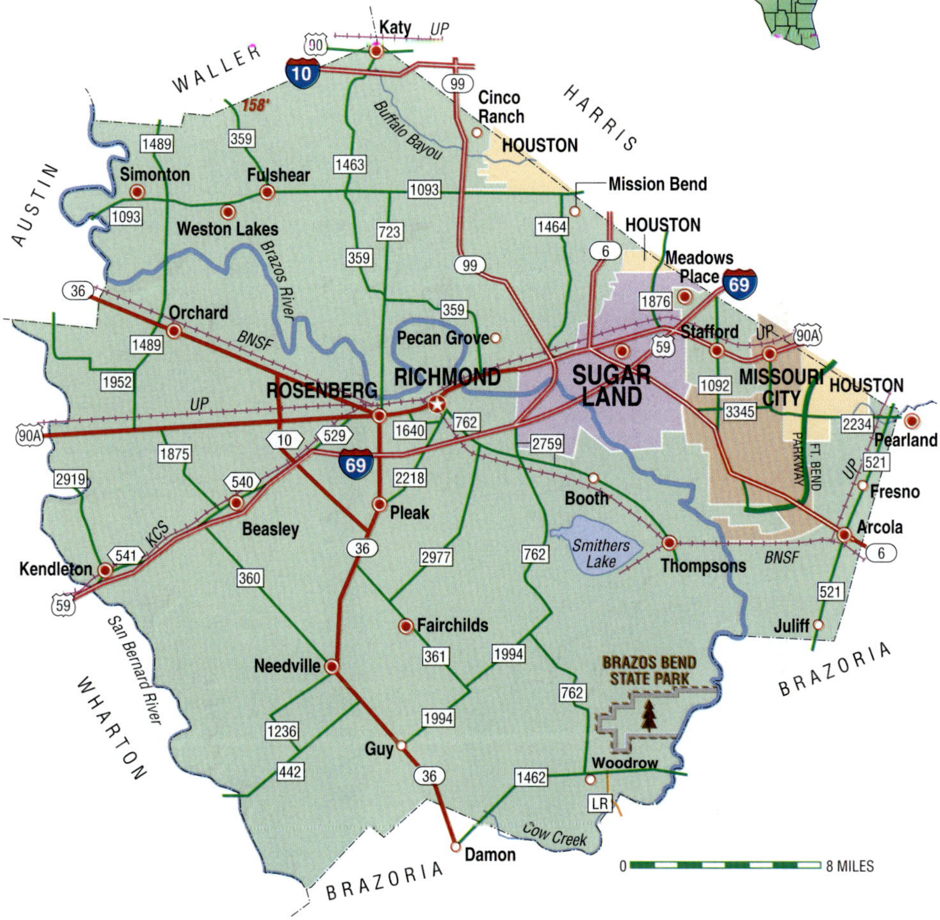

Cities/Towns: Richmond, Sugar Land, Missouri City, Rosenberg, Arcola, Beasley, Cinco Ranch, Fairchilds, Fresno, Fulshear, Guy, Kendleton, Meadows Place, Mission Bend, Needville, Orchard, Pecan Grove, Pleak, Simonton, Stafford, Thompsons, Weston Lakes, Houston, Katy, Pearland

Land Area (Square Miles): 861.72
Elevation (Approx. Feet): 92

Population: 958,434
Population Change: 16.50%

Race:
White: 28.9%
Black: 22.7%
Hispanic: 24.7%
Asian: 22.7%
Other: 0.7%

Vital Statistics:
Births: 9,587
Deaths: 4,561
Marriages: 2,880
Divorces: 1,883

2024 Rainfall: 54.05 in.
January Avg. Temp.: 51.5°F
July Avg. Temp.: 83.5°F

Unemployment Rate: 4.1
Per Capita Income: $73,855
Tourism Earnings: $267.2 million
Avg. Home Value: $350,300

F

FRANKLIN COUNTY

Named for jurist B.C. Franklin.

Cities/Towns: Mount Vernon, Scroggins, Winnsboro

Land Area (Square Miles): 284.39
Elevation (Approx. Feet): 499

Population: 10,912
Population Change: 5.40%

Race:
White: 77.4%
Black: 5.0%
Hispanic: 14.4%
Asian: 1.2%
Other: 1.4%

Vital Statistics:
Births: 103
Deaths: 143
Marriages: 27
Divorces: 33

2024 Rainfall: 58.86 in.
January Avg. Temp.: 41.2°F
July Avg. Temp.: 81.6°F

Unemployment Rate: 3.8
Per Capita Income: $56,987
Tourism Earnings: $2.7 million
Avg. Home Value: $213,200

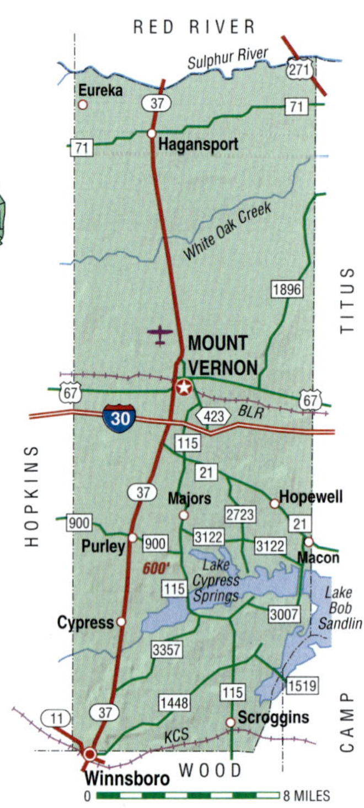

FREESTONE COUNTY

Named for the indigenous stone.

Cities/Towns: Fairfield, Teague, Donie, Streetman, Wortham

Land Area (Square Miles): 877.73
Elevation (Approx. Feet): 404

Population: 20,645
Population Change: 6.20%

Race:
White: 65.6%
Black: 14.9%
Hispanic: 17.4%
Asian: 1.0%
Other: 1.6%

Vital Statistics:
Births: 212
Deaths: 289
Marriages: 90
Divorces: 31

2024 Rainfall: 52.09 in.
January Avg. Temp.: 43.8°F
July Avg. Temp.: 82.6°F

Unemployment Rate: 4.7
Per Capita Income: $47,097
Tourism Earnings: $7.1 million
Avg. Home Value: $164,400

FRIO
COUNTY

Named for the Frio River.

Cities/Towns: Pearsall, Dilley, Bigfoot, Hilltop, Moore, North Pearsall

Land Area (Square Miles): 1,133.50
Elevation (Approx. Feet): 587

Population: 19,520
Population Change: 6.10%

Race:
White: 15.4%
Black: 5.1%
Hispanic: 77.7%
Asian: 2.8%
Other: 1.3%

Vital Statistics:
Births: 209
Deaths: 186
Marriages: 69
Divorces: 26

2024 Rainfall: 18.45 in.
January Avg. Temp.: 50.7°F
July Avg. Temp.: 85.9°F

Unemployment Rate: 5.9
Per Capita Income: $41,270
Tourism Earnings: $9.6 million
Avg. Home Value: $110,100

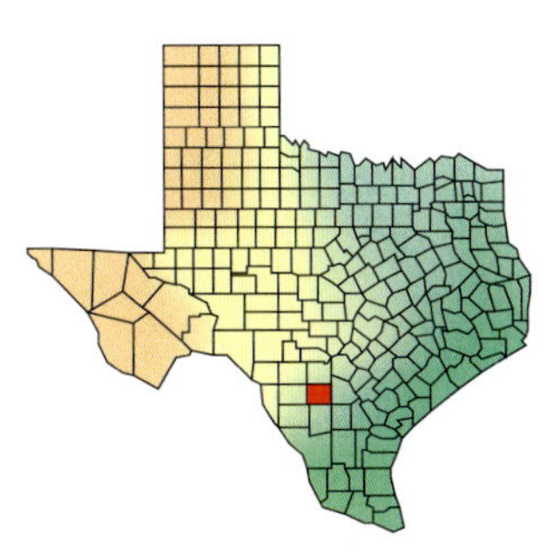

GAINES
COUNTY

Named for James Gaines, a signer of the Texas Declaration of Independence.

Cities/Towns: Seminole, Seagraves, Loop, Denver City

Land Area (Square Miles): 1,502.36
Elevation (Approx. Feet): 3,307

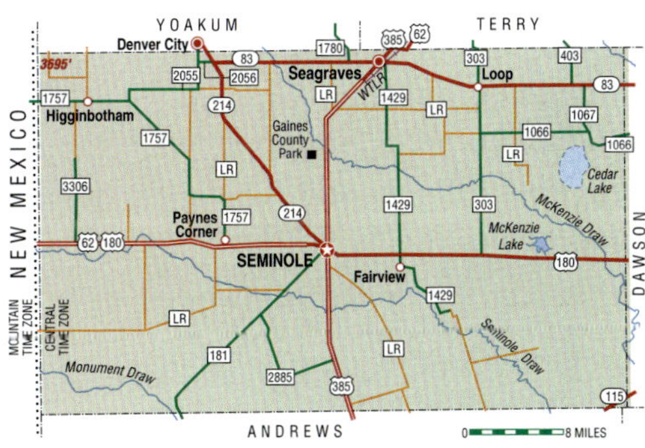

Population: 22,892
Population Change: 6.00%

Race:
White: 56.0%
Black: 2.2%
Hispanic: 40.7%
Asian: 0.7%
Other: 1.1%

Vital Statistics:
Births: 467
Deaths: 155
Marriages: 165
Divorces: 32

2024 Rainfall: 10.33 in.
January Avg. Temp.: 39.4°F
July Avg. Temp.: 81.5°F

Unemployment Rate: 3.2
Per Capita Income: $56,478
Tourism Earnings: $4.1 million
Avg. Home Value: $185,300

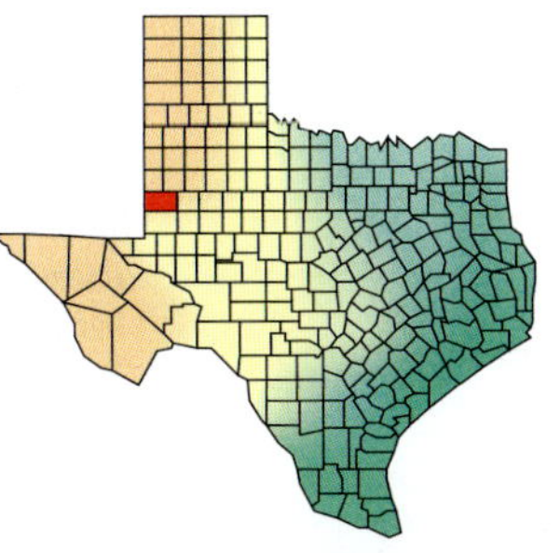

G

GALVESTON
COUNTY

Named for the Governor of Spanish Louisiana Bernardo de Gálvez.

Cities/Towns: Galveston, League City, Texas City, Bolivar Peninsula, Port Bolivar, Crystal Beach, Gilchrist, High Island, Bacliff, Bayou Vista, Clear Lake Shores, Friendswood, Jamaica Beach, Kemah, La Marque, San Leon, Santa Fe, Tiki Island

Land Area (Square Miles): 379.29
Elevation (Approx. Feet): 0 or N/A

Population: 367,407
Population Change: 4.80%

Race:
White: 54.8%
Black: 13.5%
Hispanic: 26.7%
Asian: 3.7%
Other: 0.9%

Vital Statistics:
Births: 3,881
Deaths: 3,300
Marriages: 1,128
Divorces: 1,180

2024 Rainfall: 64.02 in.
January Avg. Temp.: 52°F
July Avg. Temp.: 83.3°F

Unemployment Rate: 4.3
Per Capita Income: $64,574
Tourism Earnings: $483.1 million
Avg. Home Value: $284,900

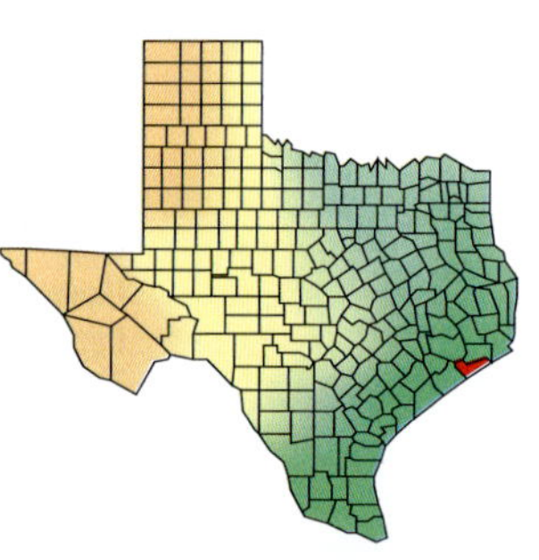

UNSPLASH/LESLI WHITECOTTON

GARZA COUNTY

Named for a pioneer Bexar County family.

Cities/Towns: Post

Land Area (Square Miles): 893.42
Elevation (Approx. Feet): 2,425

Population: 4,645
Population Change: -20.20%

Race:
White: 37.8%
Black: 7.5%
Hispanic: 53.4%
Asian: 1.1%
Other: 1.9%

Vital Statistics:
Births: 55
Deaths: 66
Marriages: 28
Divorces: 11

2024 Rainfall: 19.61 in.
January Avg. Temp.: 39.3°F
July Avg. Temp.: 83.8°F

Unemployment Rate: 3.8
Per Capita Income: $49,585
Tourism Earnings: $2.8 million
Avg. Home Value: $79,300

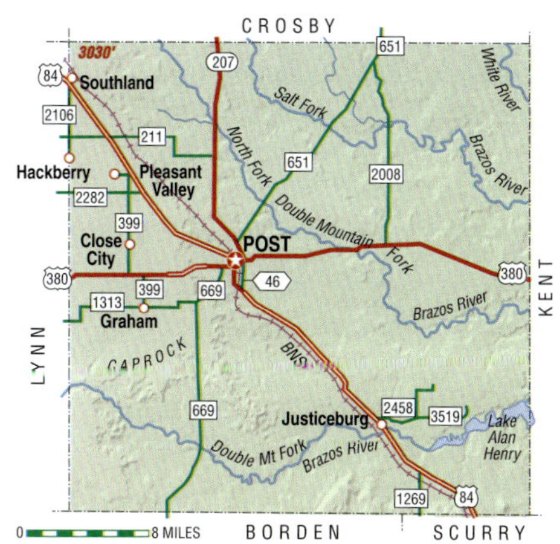

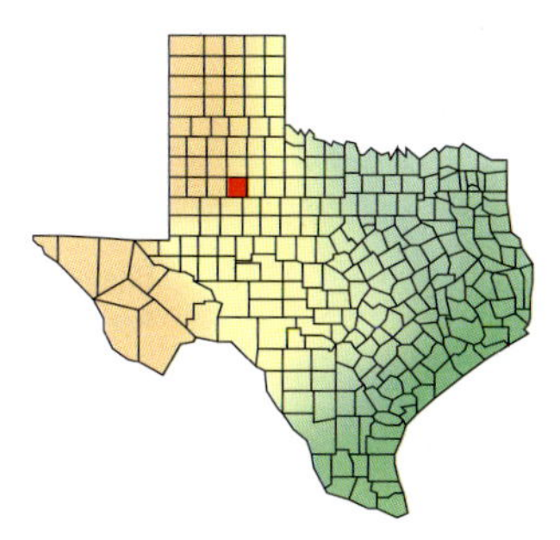

GILLESPIE COUNTY

Named for Texas Ranger Captain R.A. Gillespie.

Cities/Towns: Fredericksburg, Doss, Harper, Luckenbach, Stonewall, Willow City

Land Area (Square Miles): 1,058.20
Elevation (Approx. Feet): 1,962

Population: 28,159
Population Change: 5.30%

Race:
White: 74.1%
Black: 0.9%
Hispanic: 23.3%
Asian: 0.7%
Other: 1.4%

Vital Statistics:
Births: 248
Deaths: 393
Marriages: 157
Divorces: 73

2024 Rainfall: 25.99 in.
January Avg. Temp.: 44.3°F
July Avg. Temp.: 81.4°F

Unemployment Rate: 3
Per Capita Income: $93,310
Tourism Earnings: $52.2 million
Avg. Home Value: $432,300

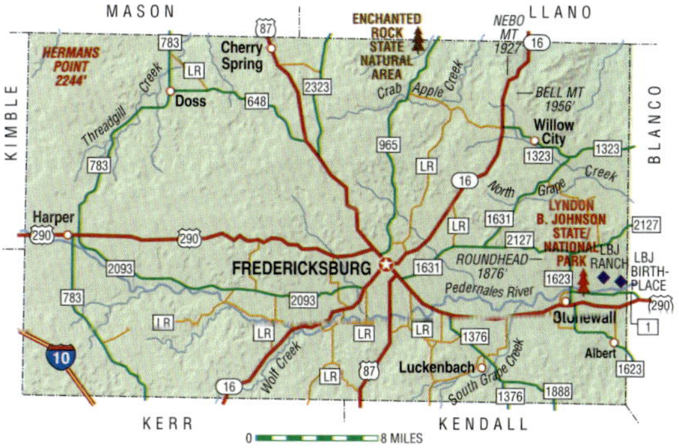

G

GLASSCOCK
COUNTY

Named for Texas pioneer George W. Glasscock.

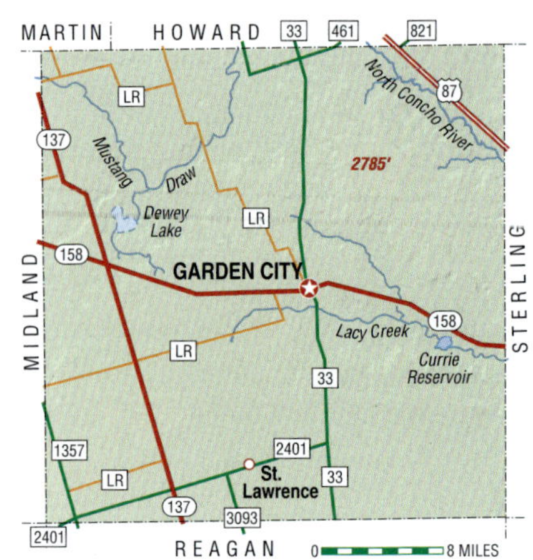

Cities/Towns: Garden City, St. Lawrence

Land Area (Square Miles): 900.22
Elevation (Approx. Feet): 2,684

Population: 1,153
Population Change: 3.40%

Race:
White: 61.6%
Black: 2.8%
Hispanic: 34.4%
Asian: 0.3%
Other: 1.4%

Vital Statistics:
Births: 17
Deaths: N/A
Marriages: 1
Divorces: N/A

2024 Rainfall: 14.27 in.
January Avg. Temp.: 42.2°F
July Avg. Temp.: 82.7°F

Unemployment Rate: 3.1
Per Capita Income: $132,049
Tourism Earnings: $50,000
Avg. Home Value: $248,600

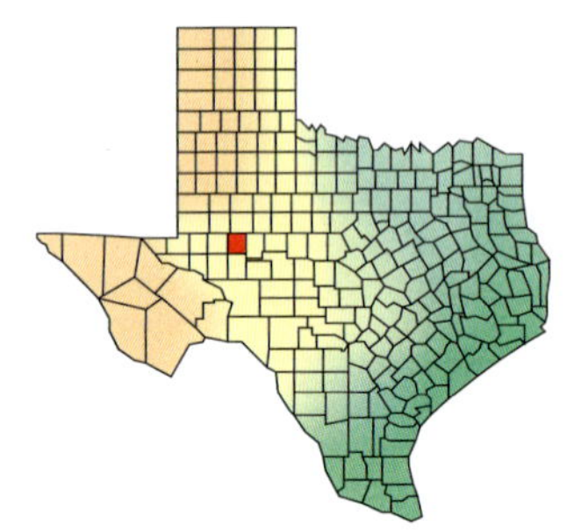

GOLIAD
COUNTY

Named for the Mexican Municipality of Goliad.

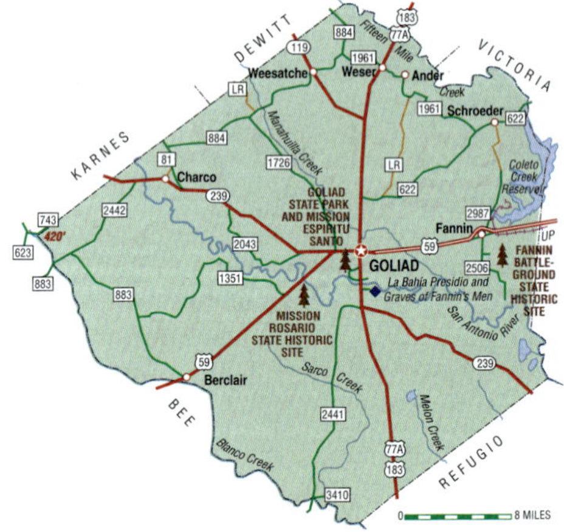

Cities/Towns: Goliad, Berclair, Fannin, Weesatche

Land Area (Square Miles): 852.01
Elevation (Approx. Feet): 141

Population: 7,221
Population Change: 2.90%

Race:
White: 61.9%
Black: 5.2%
Hispanic: 31.5%
Asian: 0.7%
Other: 1.3%

Vital Statistics:
Births: 75
Deaths: 92
Marriages: 19
Divorces: 5

2024 Rainfall: 28.34 in.
January Avg. Temp.: 52.3°F
July Avg. Temp.: 84.1°F

Unemployment Rate: 4.2
Per Capita Income: $62,484
Tourism Earnings: $2 million
Avg. Home Value: $182,800

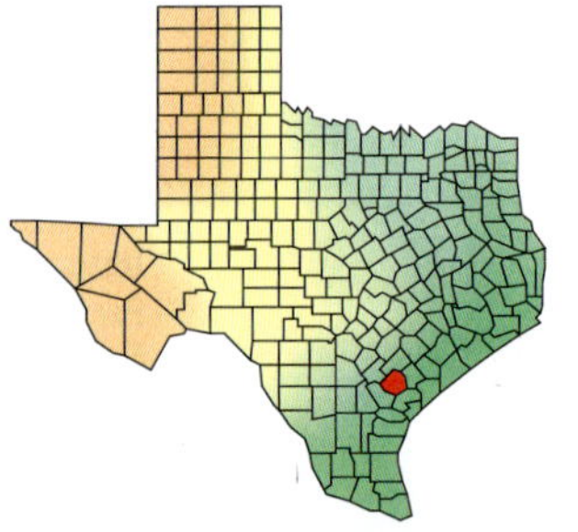

G

GONZALES
COUNTY

Named for Coahuila y Texas Governor Rafael Gonzales.

Cities/Towns: Gonzales, Belmont, Cost, Harwood, Leesville, Nixon, Ottine, Smiley, Waelder

Land Area (Square Miles): 1,066.69
Elevation (Approx. Feet): 292

Population: 20,040
Population Change: 1.90%

Race:
White: 41.1%
Black: 7.2%
Hispanic: 51.2%
Asian: 0.7%
Other: 2.0%

Vital Statistics:
Births: 298
Deaths: 240
Marriages: 75
Divorces: 58

2024 Rainfall: 30.02 in.
January Avg. Temp.: 49.9°F
July Avg. Temp.: 85°F

Unemployment Rate: 3.8
Per Capita Income: $64,553
Tourism Earnings: $6.9 million
Avg. Home Value: $158,900

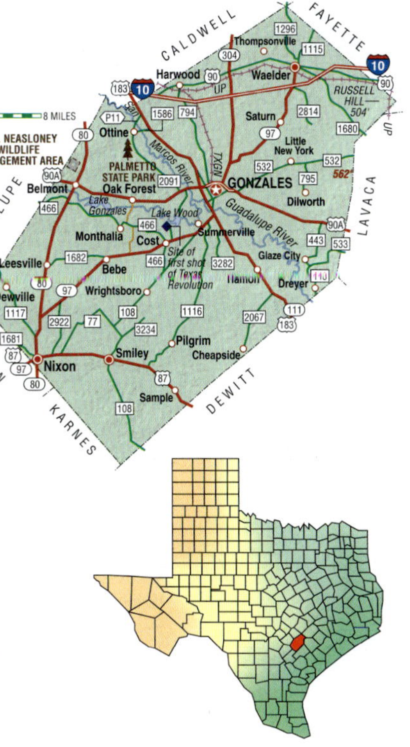

GRAY
COUNTY

Named for Peter W. Gray, who represented Texas in the Confederate House of Representatives.

Cities/Towns: Pampa, Alanreed, Lefors, McLean

Land Area (Square Miles): 925.97
Elevation (Approx. Feet): 2,864

Population: 20,888
Population Change: -1.60%

Race:
White: 59.6%
Black: 5.3%
Hispanic: 32.3%
Asian: 0.8%
Other: 1.8%

Vital Statistics:
Births: 240
Deaths: 296
Marriages: 111
Divorces: 97

2024 Rainfall: 24.81 in.
January Avg. Temp.: 34.8°F
July Avg. Temp.: 80.9°F

Unemployment Rate: 3.9
Per Capita Income: $53,508
Tourism Earnings: $13.3 million
Avg. Home Value: $100,400

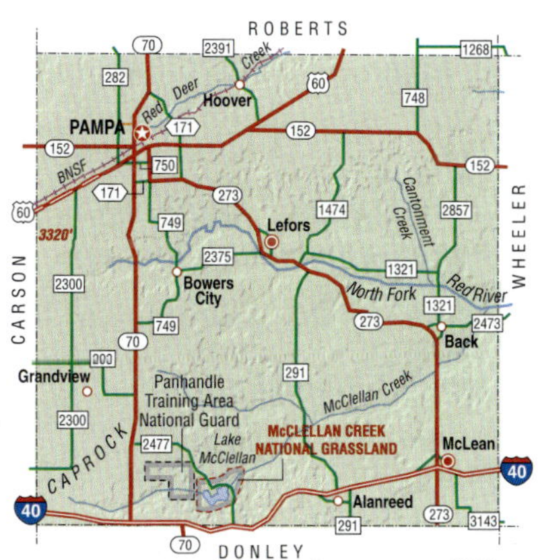

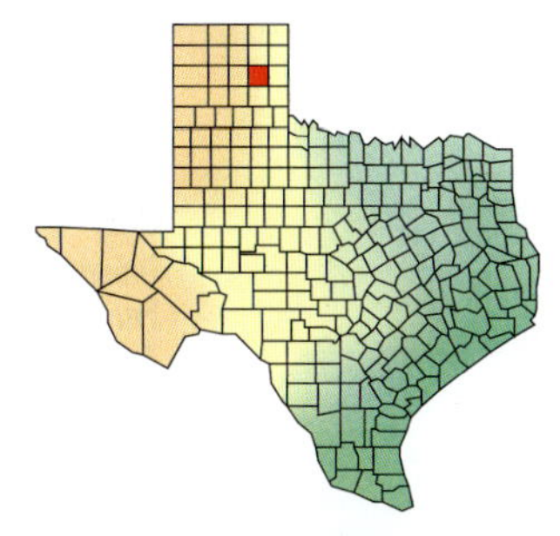

G

GRAYSON
COUNTY

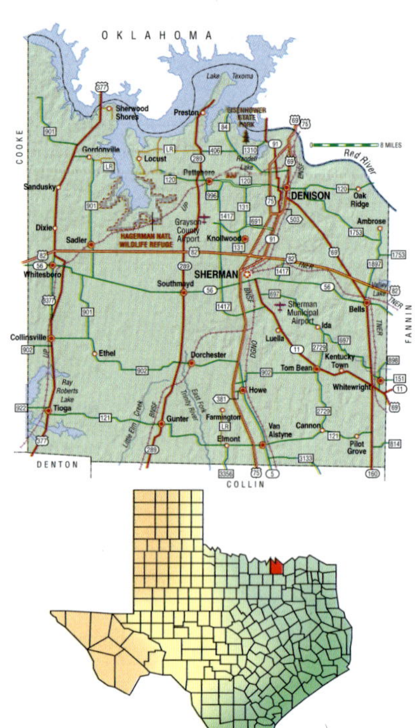

Named for Republic Attorney General Peter W. Grayson.

Cities/Towns: Sherman, Denison, Bells, Collinsville, Dorchester, Gordonville, Gunter, Howe, Knollwood, Pottsboro, Preston, Sadler, Southmayd, Tioga, Tom Bean, Van Alstyne, Whitesboro, Whitewright

Land Area (Square Miles): 932.84
Elevation (Approx. Feet): 814

Population: 150,532
Population Change: 11.00%

Race:
White: 71.9%
Black: 6.3%
Hispanic: 16.7%
Asian: 1.6%
Other: 2.0%

Vital Statistics:
Births: 1,687
Deaths: 1,716
Marriages: 767
Divorces: 176

2024 Rainfall: 42.42 in.
January Avg. Temp.: 39.1°F
July Avg. Temp.: 83.2°F

Unemployment Rate: 3.9
Per Capita Income: $55,946
Tourism Earnings: $54.1 million
Avg. Home Value: $228,300

GREGG
COUNTY

Named for Confederate General John Gregg.

Cities/Towns: Longview, Kilgore, Gladewater, Clarksville City, Easton, Judson, Lakeport, Liberty City, Warren City, White Oak

Land Area (Square Miles): 273.38
Elevation (Approx. Feet): 269

Population: 126,679
Population Change: 1.90%

Race:
White: 55.3%
Black: 21.1%
Hispanic: 20.5%
Asian: 1.5%
Other: 1.1%

Vital Statistics:
Births: 1,735
Deaths: 1,570
Marriages: 922
Divorces: 528

2024 Rainfall: 65.98 in.
January Avg. Temp.: 43.2°F
July Avg. Temp.: 81.2°F

Unemployment Rate: 4.8
Per Capita Income: $59,997
Tourism Earnings: $89.4 million
Avg. Home Value: $185,800

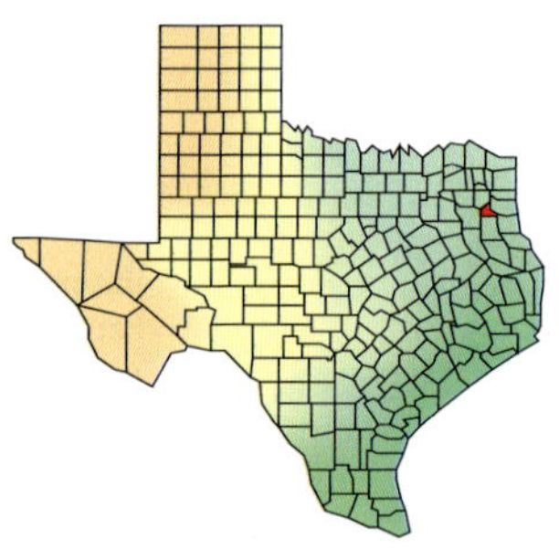

GRIMES
COUNTY

Named for Jesse Grimes, a signer of the Texas Declaration of Independence.

Cities/Towns: Anderson, Navasota, Bedias, Iola, Plantersville, Richards, Roans Prairie, Shiro, Todd Mission

Land Area (Square Miles): 787.47
Elevation (Approx. Feet): 335

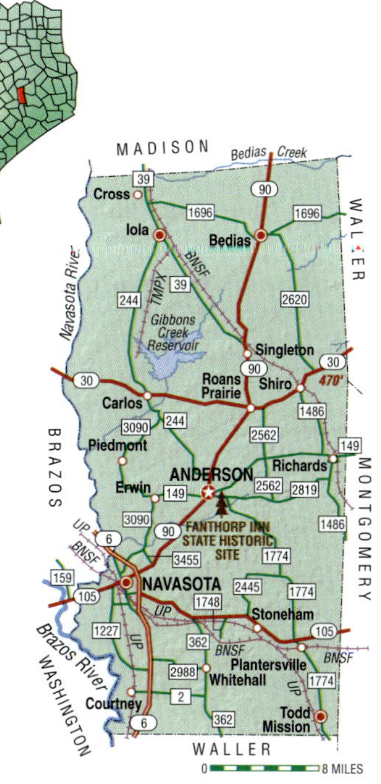

Population: 33,448
Population Change: 14.20%

Race:
White: 58.6%
Black: 13.8%
Hispanic: 25.7%
Asian: 0.6%
Other: 1.1%

Vital Statistics:
Births: 359
Deaths: 361
Marriages: 105
Divorces: 73

2024 Rainfall: 58.91 in.
January Avg. Temp.: 47.5°F
July Avg. Temp.: 82.5°F

Unemployment Rate: 4.4
Per Capita Income: $44,487
Tourism Earnings: $11.4 million
Avg. Home Value: $226,600

GUADALUPE
COUNTY

Named for the Guadalupe River.

Cities/Towns: Seguin, Schertz, Cibolo, Geronimo, Kingsbury, Lake Dunlap, Marion, McQueeney, New Berlin, Redwood, Santa Clara, Staples, New Braunfels, Delma, San Marcos

Land Area (Square Miles): 711.25
Elevation (Approx. Feet): 538

Population: 195,166
Population Change: 13.00%

Race:
White: 47.7%
Black: 9.2%
Hispanic: 39.5%
Asian: 2.3%
Other: 1.4%

Vital Statistics:
Births: 2,099
Deaths: 1,439
Marriages: 536
Divorces: 525

2024 Rainfall: 27.47 in.
January Avg. Temp.: 48.6°F
July Avg. Temp.: 84.6°F

Unemployment Rate: 3.6
Per Capita Income: $58,644
Tourism Earnings: $105.3 million
Avg. Home Value: $285,900

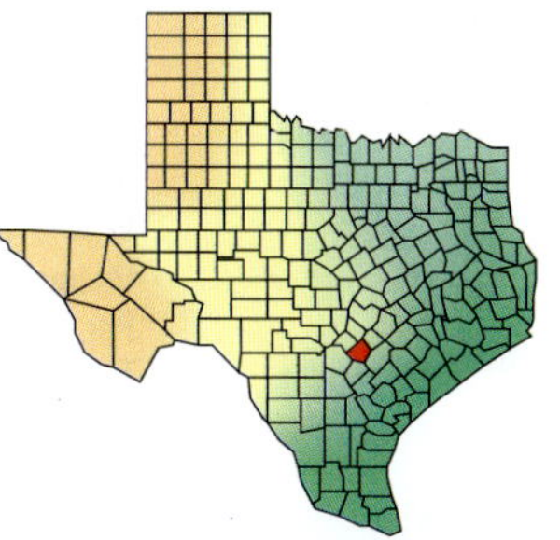

H

HALE COUNTY

Named for Lieutenant J.C. Hale, who died at San Jacinto.

Cities/Towns: Plainview, Hale Center, Abernathy, Cotton Center, Edmonson, Petersburg, Seth Ward

Land Area (Square Miles): 1,004.68
Elevation (Approx. Feet): 3,409

Population: 31,953
Population Change: -1.80%

Race:
White: 31.5%
Black: 5.7%
Hispanic: 62.0%
Asian: 0.6%
Other: 2.1%

Vital Statistics:
Births: 442
Deaths: 338
Marriages: 153
Divorces: 33

2024 Rainfall: 19.42 in.
January Avg. Temp.: 36.3°F
July Avg. Temp.: 79.8°F

Unemployment Rate: 4.1
Per Capita Income: $45,103
Tourism Earnings: $13.4 million
Avg. Home Value: $106,100

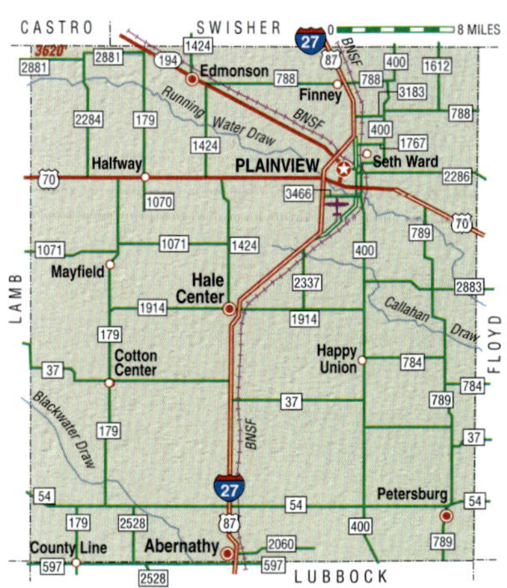

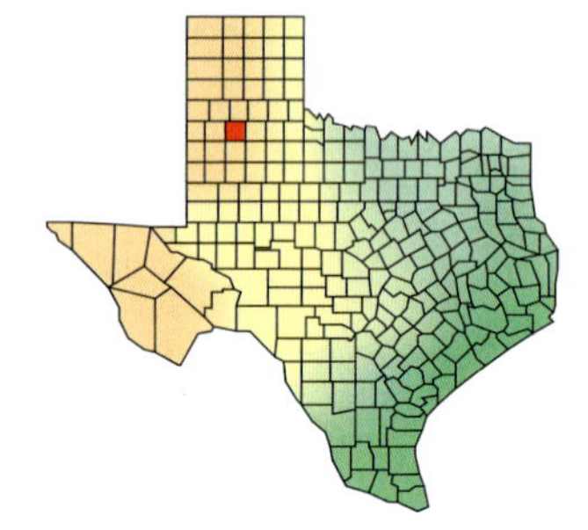

HALL COUNTY

Named for Republic of Texas Secretary of War Warren D.C. Hall.

Cities/Towns: Memphis, Esteline, Lakeview, Turkey

Land Area (Square Miles): 883.49
Elevation (Approx. Feet): 1,887

Population: 2,828
Population Change: 0.30%

Race:
White: 52.7%
Black: 9.5%
Hispanic: 35.9%
Asian: 0.6%
Other: 1.9%

Vital Statistics:
Births: 21
Deaths: 47
Marriages: 5
Divorces: N/A

2024 Rainfall: 21.26 in.
January Avg. Temp.: 36.8°F
July Avg. Temp.: 83.8°F

Unemployment Rate: 4.6
Per Capita Income: $49,814
Tourism Earnings: $490,000
Avg. Home Value: $80,200

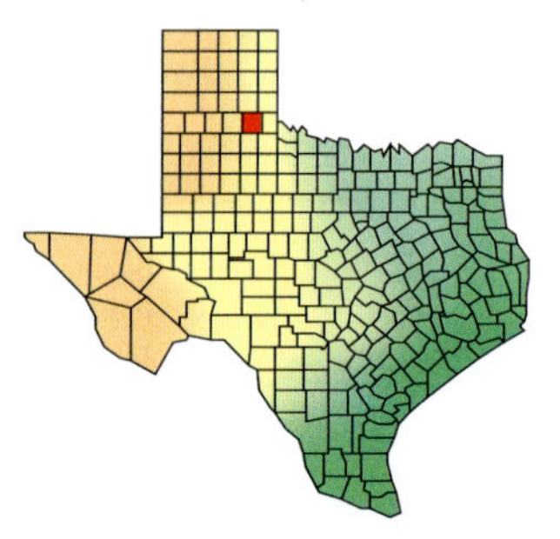

H

HAMILTON
COUNTY

Named for South Carolina Governor James Hamilton, who aided the Texas Revolution and Republic.

Cities/Towns: Hamilton, Hico, Carlton, Evant, Jonesboro, Pottsville

Land Area (Square Miles): 835.92
Elevation (Approx. Feet): 1,227

Population: 8,644
Population Change: 5.20%

Race:
White: 81.8%
Black: 1.4%
Hispanic: 14.5%
Asian: 1.0%
Other: 2.2%

Vital Statistics:
Births: 74
Deaths: 148
Marriages: 42
Divorces: 35

2024 Rainfall: 32.91 in.
January Avg. Temp.: 42.6°F
July Avg. Temp.: 83.3°F

Unemployment Rate: 4.1
Per Capita Income: $70,580
Tourism Earnings: $2.3 million
Avg. Home Value: $124,800

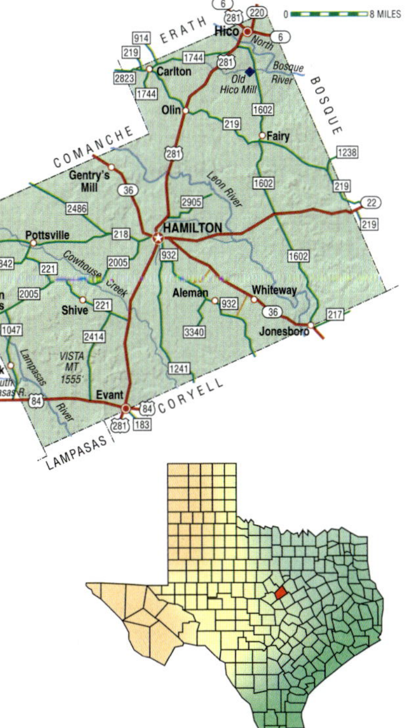

HANSFORD
COUNTY

Named for jurist J.M. Hansford.

Cities/Towns: Spearman, Gruver, Morse

Land Area (Square Miles): 919.81
Elevation (Approx. Feet): 3,101

Population: 5,006
Population Change: -5.10%

Race:
White: 47.0%
Black: 1.6%
Hispanic: 50.0%
Asian: 0.5%
Other: 1.9%

Vital Statistics:
Births: 71
Deaths: 67
Marriages: 24
Divorces: 11

2024 Rainfall: 21.61 in.
January Avg. Temp.: 33.6°F
July Avg. Temp.: 80.2°F

Unemployment Rate: 3.3
Per Capita Income: $103,818
Tourism Earnings: $360,000
Avg. Home Value: $132,100

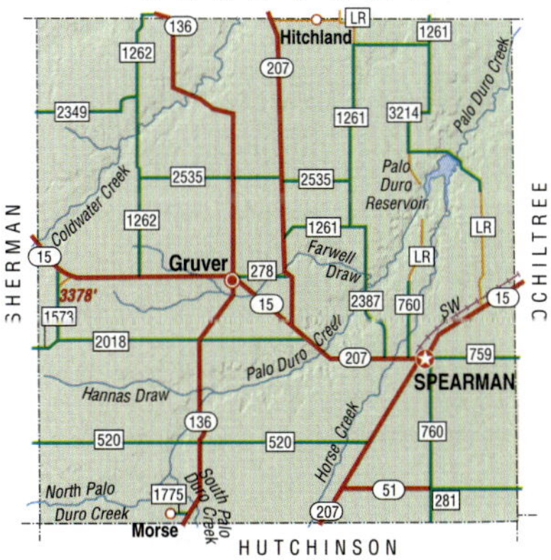

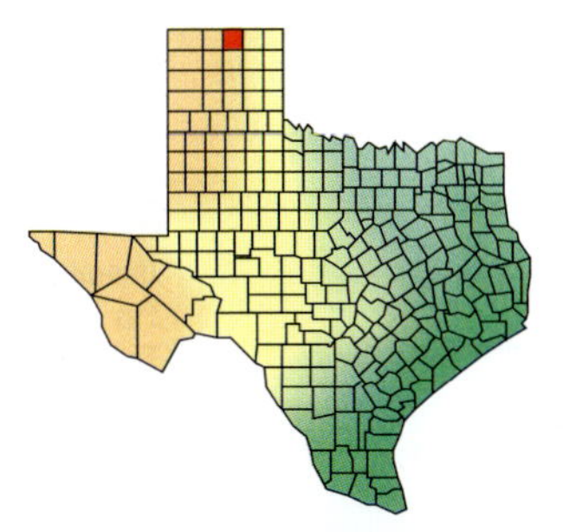

H

HARDEMAN
COUNTY

Named for pioneer brothers Bailey and T.J. Hardeman.

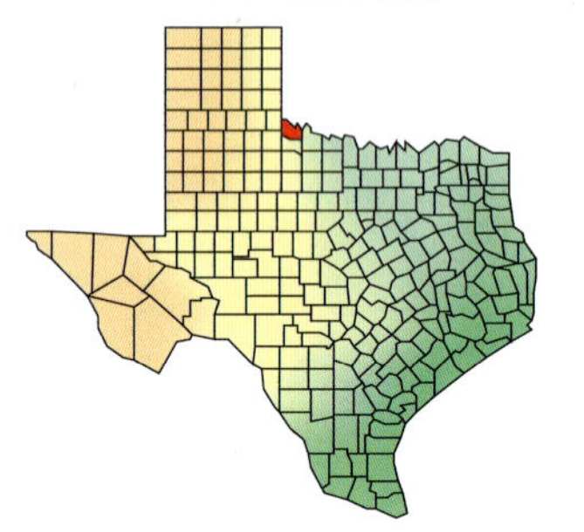

Cities/Towns: Quanah, Chillicothe

Land Area (Square Miles): 695.11
Elevation (Approx. Feet): 1,581

Population: 3,417
Population Change: -3.70%

Race:
White: 65.7%
Black: 7.0%
Hispanic: 24.3%
Asian: 0.9%
Other: 1.5%

Vital Statistics:
Births: 38
Deaths: 55
Marriages: 15
Divorces: 14

2024 Rainfall: 23.19 in.
January Avg. Temp.: 37.4°F
July Avg. Temp.: 84.2°F

Unemployment Rate: 3.7
Per Capita Income: $60,392
Tourism Earnings: $620,000
Avg. Home Value: $76,500

HARDIN
COUNTY

Named for Texas Revolutionary leader William Hardin.

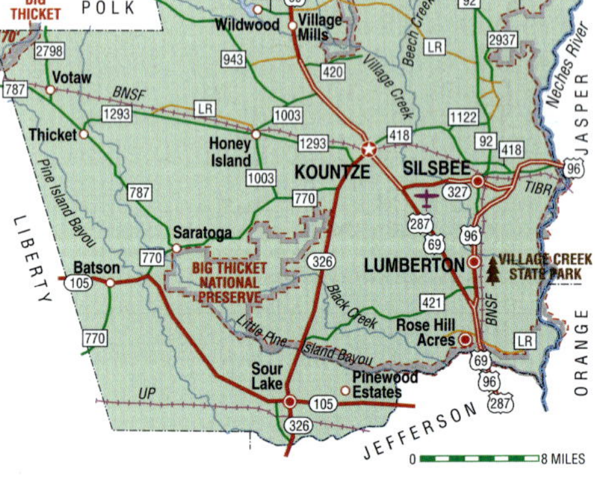

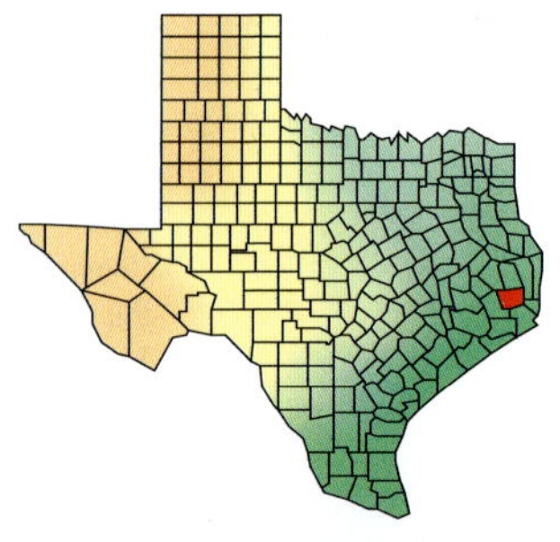

Cities/Towns: Kountze, Silsbee, Lumberton, Batson, Pinewood Estates, Rose Hill Acres, Saratoga, Sour Lake, Thicket, Village Mills, Votaw, Wildwood

Land Area (Square Miles): 890.59
Elevation (Approx. Feet): 69

Population: 58,670
Population Change: 4.30%

Race:
White: 84.1%
Black: 6.1%
Hispanic: 7.2%
Asian: 0.9%
Other: 0.7%

Vital Statistics:
Births: 647
Deaths: 689
Marriages: 282
Divorces: 279

2024 Rainfall: 77.65 in.
January Avg. Temp.: 48.1°F
July Avg. Temp.: 81.9°F

Unemployment Rate: 4.5
Per Capita Income: $56,424
Tourism Earnings: $13.4 million
Avg. Home Value: $188,200

HARRIS
COUNTY

Named for John R. Harris, founder of Harrisburg (now part of Houston).

COURTESY OF HOUSTON FIRST CORPORATION/LANCE CHILDERS

Cities/Towns: Houston, Pasadena, Baytown, El Lago, Nassau Bay, Seabrook, Taylor Lake Village, Webster, Aldine, Atascocita, Barrett, Bellaire, Bunker Hill Village, Channelview, Crosby, Cypress, Deer Park, Galena Park, Hedwig Village, Highlands, Hilshire Village, Hockley, Huffman, Humble, Hunters Creek Village, Jacinto City, Jersey Village, Katy, La Porte, Mission Bend, Morgan's Point, Piney Point Village, Sheldon, Shoreacres, South Houston, Southside Place, Spring, Spring Valley, Tomball, West University Place, Cinco Ranch, Missouri City, Stafford, Friendswood, League City, Pearland, Waller, Addicks, Alief, Kingwood

Land Area (Square Miles): 1,706.96
Elevation (Approx. Feet): 72

Population: 5,009,302
Population Change: 5.90%

Race:
White: 27.0%
Black: 21.1%
Hispanic: 44.1%
Asian: 7.7%
Other: 1.3%

Vital Statistics:
Births: 66,112
Deaths: 31,359
Marriages: 19,587
Divorces: 10,247

2024 Rainfall: 59.27 in.
January Avg. Temp.: 50.9°F
July Avg. Temp.: 83.3°F

Unemployment Rate: 4.4
Per Capita Income: $73,862
Tourism Earnings: $6.8 billion
Avg. Home Value: $255,000

H

HARRISON COUNTY

Named for Texas Revolution advocate Jonas Harrison.

Cities/Towns: Marshall, Elysian Fields, Hallsville, Jonesville, Karnack, Nesbitt, Scottsville, Uncertain, Waskom, Woodlawn, Longview

Land Area (Square Miles): 900.06
Elevation (Approx. Feet): 407

Population: 71,370
Population Change: 3.70%

Race:
White: 61.4%
Black: 21.2%
Hispanic: 15.1%
Asian: 0.9%
Other: 1.5%

Vital Statistics:
Births: 795
Deaths: 726
Marriages: 350
Divorces: 99

2024 Rainfall: 72.46 in.
January Avg. Temp.: 43.2°F
July Avg. Temp.: 81.2°F

Unemployment Rate: 4.9
Per Capita Income: $50,269
Tourism Earnings: $17.7 million
Avg. Home Value: $178,200

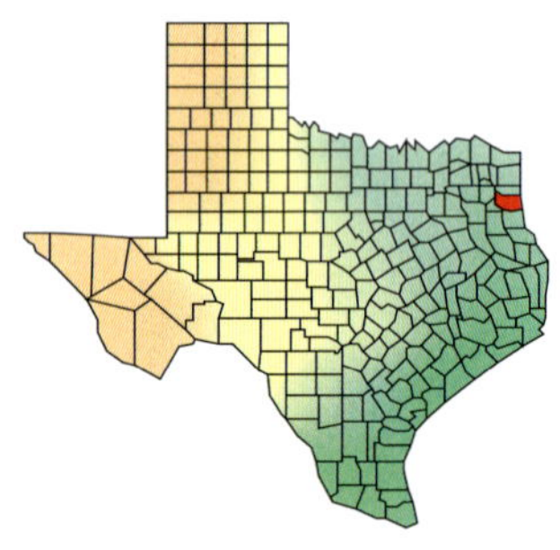

HARTLEY COUNTY

Named for Texas pioneers O.C. and R.K. Hartley.

Cities/Towns: Channing, Dalhart, Hartley

Land Area (Square Miles): 1,461.95
Elevation (Approx. Feet): 3,881

Population: 4,996
Population Change: -6.90%

Race:
White: 60.7%
Black: 6.1%
Hispanic: 31.5%
Asian: 0.9%
Other: 0.9%

Vital Statistics:
Births: 75
Deaths: 58
Marriages: 1
Divorces: 14

2024 Rainfall: 15.86 in.
January Avg. Temp.: 32.5°F
July Avg. Temp.: 78.7°F

Unemployment Rate: 3.1
Per Capita Income: $107,013
Tourism Earnings: $180,000
Avg. Home Value: $213,200

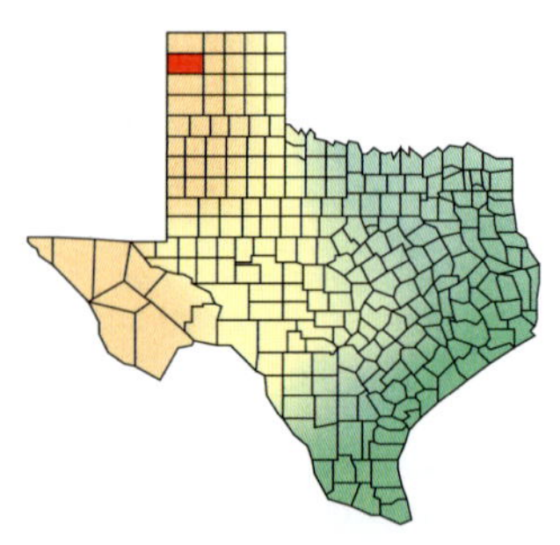

H

HASKELL
COUNTY

Named for Goliad victim C.R. Haskell.

Cities/Towns: Haskell, O'Brien, Rochester, Rule, Weinert

Land Area (Square Miles): 903.13
Elevation (Approx. Feet): 1,601

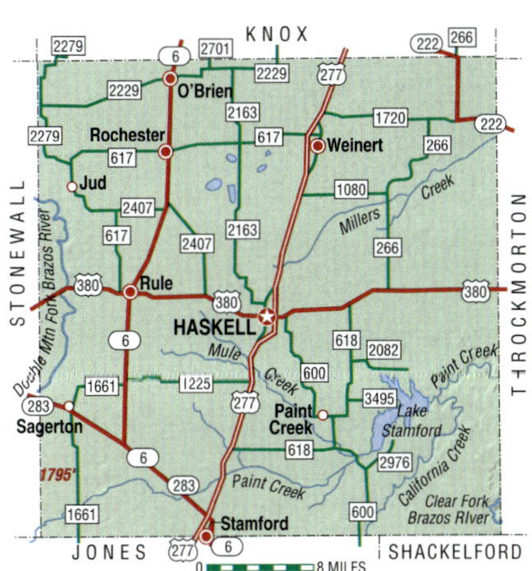

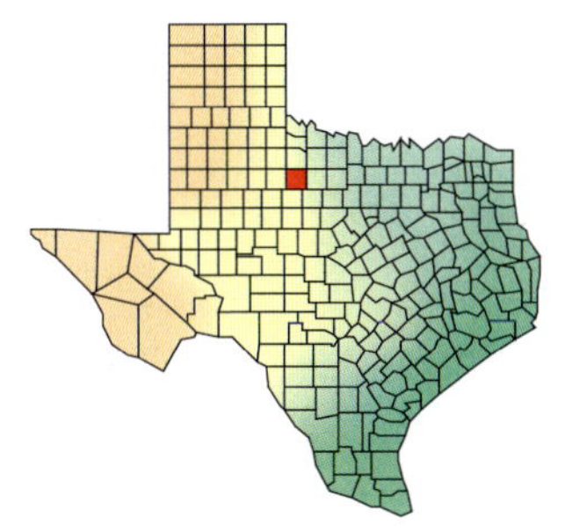

Population: 5,435
Population Change: 0.40%

Race:
White: 65.4%
Black: 5.5%
Hispanic: 26.8%
Asian: 1.0%
Other: 1.5%

Vital Statistics:
Births: 33
Deaths: 83
Marriages: 16
Divorces: 13

2024 Rainfall: 28.85 in.
January Avg. Temp.: 40.5°F
July Avg. Temp.: 84.6°F

Unemployment Rate: 3.9
Per Capita Income: $53,538
Tourism Earnings: $1.4 million
Avg. Home Value: $92,000

HAYS
COUNTY

Named for famous Texas Ranger Captain Jack Hays.

Cities/Towns: San Marcos, Kyle, Bear Creek, Buda, Driftwood, Dripping Springs, Hays, Mountain City, Neiderwald, Uhland, Wimberly, Woodcreek

Land Area (Square Miles): 676.85
Elevation (Approx. Feet): 1,109

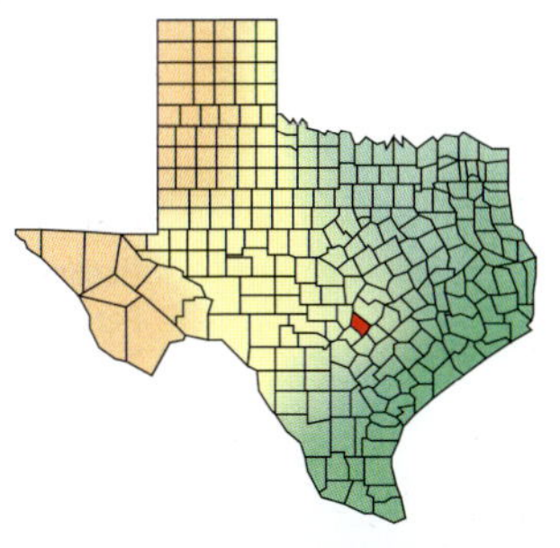

Population: 292,029
Population Change: 21.10%

Race:
White: 51.7%
Black: 5.0%
Hispanic: 39.6%
Asian: 2.5%
Other: 1.4%

Vital Statistics:
Births: 3,250
Deaths: 1,586
Marriages: 861
Divorces: 601

2024 Rainfall: 30.36 in.
January Avg. Temp.: 46.7°F
July Avg. Temp.: 83°F

Unemployment Rate: 3.4
Per Capita Income: $64,671
Tourism Earnings: $319.4 million
Avg. Home Value: $371,400

H

HEMPHILL
COUNTY

Named for Republic of Texas Justice John Hemphill.

Cities/Towns: Canadian

Land Area (Square Miles): 906.29
Elevation (Approx. Feet): 2,418

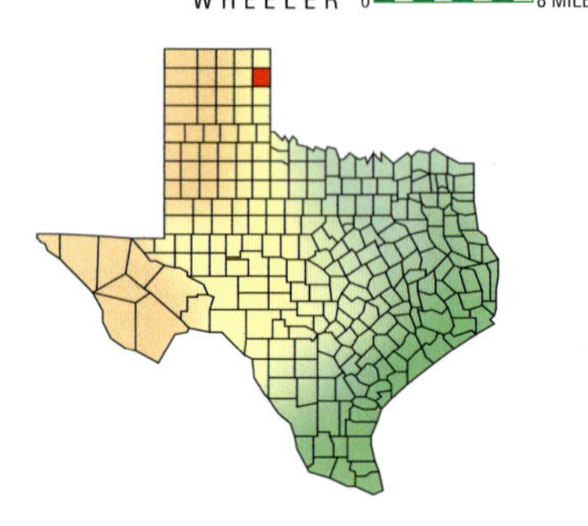

Population: 3,134
Population Change: -7.40%

Race:
White: 62.6%
Black: 1.5%
Hispanic: 32.9%
Asian: 1.5%
Other: 2.1%

Vital Statistics:
Births: 30
Deaths: 41
Marriages: 18
Divorces: 8

2024 Rainfall: 22.57 in.
January Avg. Temp.: 34.1°F
July Avg. Temp.: 81.4°F

Unemployment Rate: 4.6
Per Capita Income: $90,724
Tourism Earnings: $1.3 million
Avg. Home Value: $214,900

HENDERSON
COUNTY

Named for Govenor J. Pinckney Henderson.

Cities/Towns: Athens, Gun Barrel City, Malakoff, Berryville, Brownsboro, Caney City, Chandler, Coffee City, Enchanted Oaks, Eustace, Larue, Log Cabin, Moore Station, Murchison, Payne Springs, Poyner, Seven Points, Star Harbor, Tool, Trinidad, Mabank

Land Area (Square Miles): 873.78
Elevation (Approx. Feet): 479

Population: 87,467
Population Change: 6.50%

Race:
White: 75.2%
Black: 6.4%
Hispanic: 15.4%
Asian: 0.8%
Other: 1.2%

Vital Statistics:
Births: 967
Deaths: 1,310
Marriages: 470
Divorces: 53

2024 Rainfall: 53.9 in.
January Avg. Temp.: 42.1°F
July Avg. Temp.: 81.6°F

Unemployment Rate: 4.5
Per Capita Income: $52,297
Tourism Earnings: $30.3 million
Avg. Home Value: $189,600

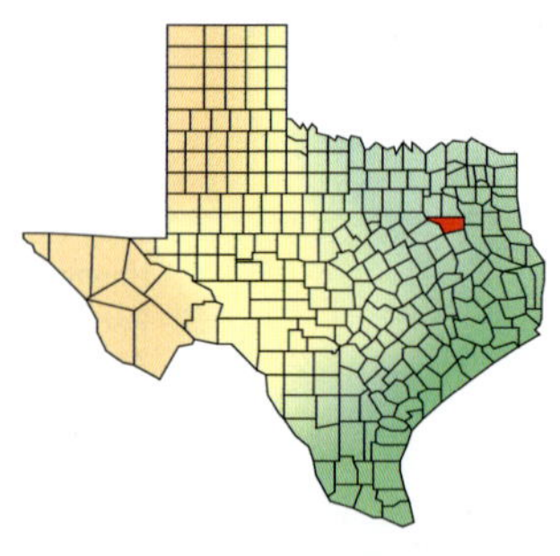

H

UNSPLASH/DAIGA ELLABY

H

HIDALGO COUNTY

Named for Father Miguel Hidalgo y Costilla, a leader of Mexico's independence movement of 1810.

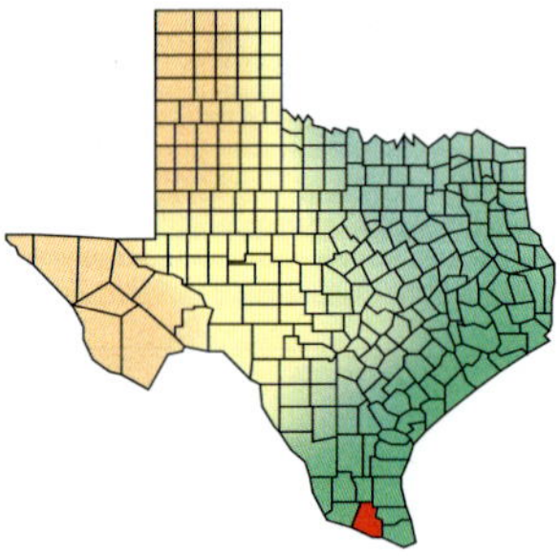

Cities/Towns: Edinburg, McAllen, Mission, Pharr, Abram, Alamo, Alton, Doffing, Donna, Edcouch, Elsa, Granjeno, Hargill, Hidalgo, La Blanca, La Homa, La Joya, La Villa, Linn, Los Ebanos, Mercedes, Mila Doce, Monte Alto, Murillo, North Alamo, Palmhurst, Palmview, Palmview South, Peñitas, Perezville, Progeso, Progreso Lakes, San Carlos, San Juan, South Alamo, Sullivan City, Weslaco

Land Area (Square Miles): 1,570.96
Elevation (Approx. Feet): 85

Population: 914,820
Population Change: 5.10%

Race:
White: 0.7%
Black: 0.0%
Hispanic: 99.0%
Asian: 0.0%
Other: 0.0%

Vital Statistics:
Births: 14,400
Deaths: 5,624
Marriages: 3,992
Divorces: 3

2024 Rainfall: 24.4 in.
January Avg. Temp.: 58.8°F
July Avg. Temp.: 86°F

Unemployment Rate: 6
Per Capita Income: $34,373
Tourism Earnings: $542.3 million
Avg. Home Value: $124,000

HILL
COUNTY

Named for Republic of Texas official G.W. Hill.

Cities/Towns: Hillsboro, Whitney, Abbott, Aquilla, Blum, Brandon, Bynum, Carl's Corner, Covington, Hubbard, Irene, Itasca, Malone, Mertens, Mount Calm, Penelope

Land Area (Square Miles): 958.86
Elevation (Approx. Feet): 568

Population: 38,771
Population Change: 8.10%

Race:
White: 68.0%
Black: 6.3%
Hispanic: 23.5%
Asian: 0.8%
Other: 1.3%

Vital Statistics:
Births: 431
Deaths: 558
Marriages: 166
Divorces: 136

2024 Rainfall: 46.49 in.
January Avg. Temp.: 42.9°F
July Avg. Temp.: 83.1°F

Unemployment Rate: 3.9
Per Capita Income: $52,054
Tourism Earnings: $15.7 million
Avg. Home Value: $163,100

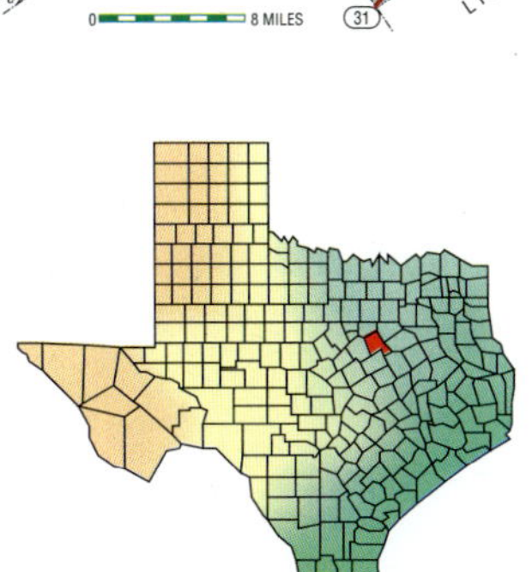

HOCKLEY
COUNTY

Named for the Republic of Texas Secretary of War General G.W. Hockley.

Cities/Towns: Levelland, Anton, Opdyke West, Pep, Ropesville, Smyer, Sundown, Whitharral

Land Area (Square Miles): 908.39
Elevation (Approx. Feet): 3,521

Population: 21,505
Population Change: -0.10%

Race:
White: 44.7%
Black: 4.2%
Hispanic: 49.9%
Asian: 0.5%
Other: 1.7%

Vital Statistics:
Births: 285
Deaths: 294
Marriages: 98
Divorces: 45

2024 Rainfall: 16.71 in.
January Avg. Temp.: 37.4°F
July Avg. Temp.: 79.6°F

Unemployment Rate: 3.7
Per Capita Income: $53,348
Tourism Earnings: $7.7 million
Avg. Home Value: $112,700

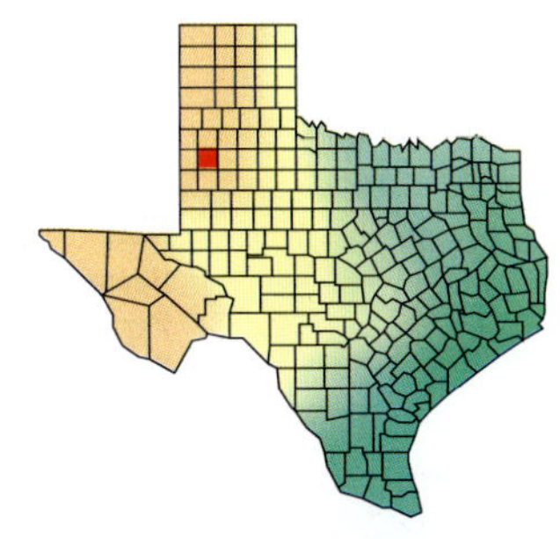

COURTESY OF VISIT GRANBURY

HOOD
COUNTY

Named for Confederate General John B. Hood.

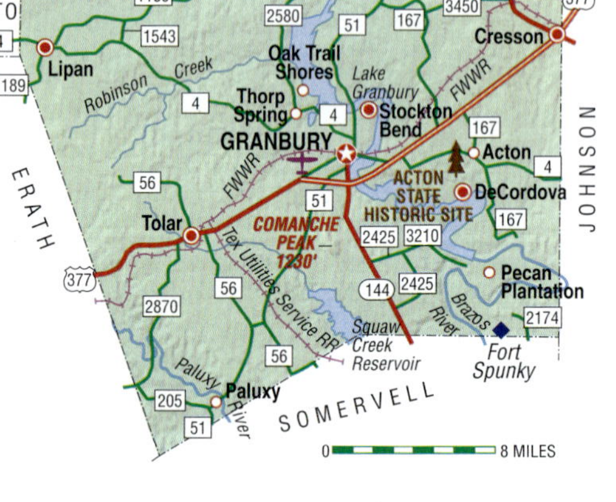

Cities/Towns: Granbury, Acton, Lipan, Cresson, DeCordova, Lipan, Oak Trail Shores, Pecan Plantation, Stockton Bend, Tolar

Land Area (Square Miles): 420.69
Elevation (Approx. Feet): 869

Population: 69,126
Population Change: 12.20%

Race:
White: 81.5%
Black: 1.5%
Hispanic: 14.2%
Asian: 1.0%
Other: 1.1%

Vital Statistics:
Births: 666
Deaths: 920
Marriages: 301
Divorces: 190

2024 Rainfall: 38.72 in.
January Avg. Temp.: 42.3°F
July Avg. Temp.: 83.8°F

Unemployment Rate: 4.2
Per Capita Income: $66,521
Tourism Earnings: $23.1 million
Avg. Home Value: $281,300

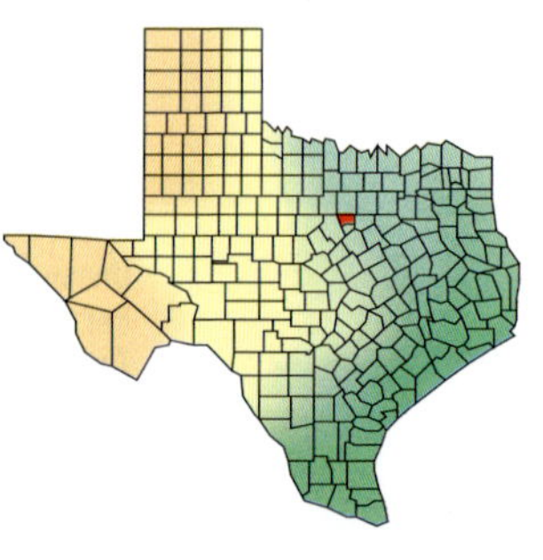

H

HOPKINS
COUNTY

Named for the David Hopkins family of pioneers.

Cities/Towns: Sulphur Springs, Brashear, Como, Cumby, Dike, Pickton, Saltillo, Suphur Bluff, Tira

Land Area (Square Miles): 767.43
Elevation (Approx. Feet): 446

Population: 38,784
Population Change: 5.40%

Race:
White: 70.9%
Black: 7.1%
Hispanic: 19.2%
Asian: 0.9%
Other: 1.2%

Vital Statistics:
Births: 459
Deaths: 488
Marriages: 255
Divorces: 121

2024 Rainfall: 54.55 in.
January Avg. Temp.: 40.6°F
July Avg. Temp.: 81.4°F

Unemployment Rate: 3.3
Per Capita Income: $55,098
Tourism Earnings: $19.7 million
Avg. Home Value: $193,200

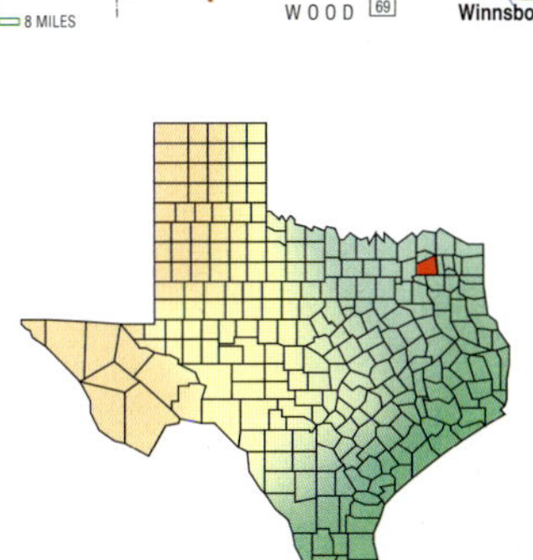

HOUSTON
COUNTY

Named for General Sam Houston.

Cities/Towns: Crockett, Grapeland, Kennard, Latexo, Lovelady, Ratcliff

Land Area (Square Miles): 1,231.00
Elevation (Approx. Feet): 335

Population: 22,197
Population Change: 0.50%

Race:
White: 70.9%
Black: 7.1%
Hispanic: 19.2%
Asian: 0.9%
Other: 1.2%

Vital Statistics:
Births: 257
Deaths: 365
Marriages: 96
Divorces: 21

2024 Rainfall: 70.04 in.
January Avg. Temp.: 44.8°F
July Avg. Temp.: 81.3°F

Unemployment Rate: 4.4
Per Capita Income: $53,657
Tourism Earnings: $7.3 million
Avg. Home Value: $155,100

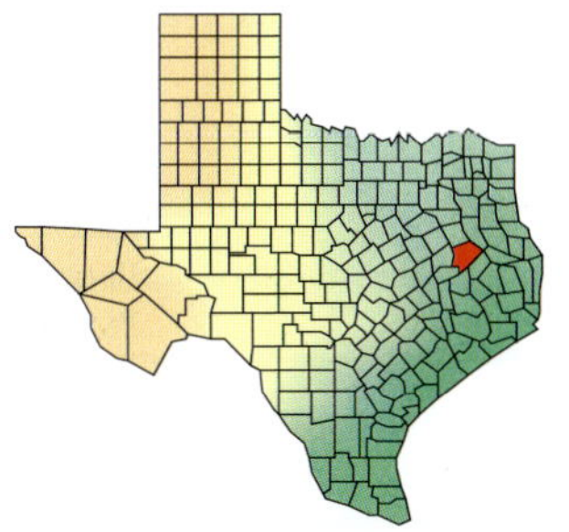

H

HOWARD COUNTY

Named for legislator V.E. Howard.

Cities/Towns: Big Spring, Coahoma, Forsan, Knott, Sand Springs

Land Area (Square Miles): 900.79
Elevation (Approx. Feet): 2,559

Population: 30,833
Population Change: -11.60%

Race:
White: 44.1%
Black: 6.0%
Hispanic: 47.9%
Asian: 1.3%
Other: 1.9%

Vital Statistics:
Births: 379
Deaths: 434
Marriages: 177
Divorces: 87

2024 Rainfall: 16.57 in.
January Avg. Temp.: 41°F
July Avg. Temp.: 83.4°F

Unemployment Rate: 3.4
Per Capita Income: $66,751
Tourism Earnings: $26.7 million
Avg. Home Value: $150,300

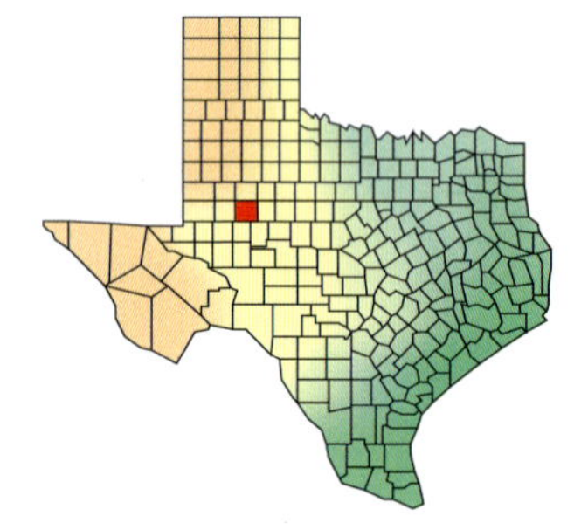

HUDSPETH COUNTY

Named for Texas political leader Claude B. Hudspeth.

Cities/Towns: Sierra Blanca, Acala, Dell City, Fort Hancock

Land Area (Square Miles): 4,570.53
Elevation (Approx. Feet): 4,475

Population: 3,608
Population Change: 12.70%

Race:
White: 19.6%
Black: 7.5%
Hispanic: 68.2%
Asian: 2.9%
Other: 1.5%

Vital Statistics:
Births: 25
Deaths: 45
Marriages: 0
Divorces: N/A

2024 Rainfall: 5.23 in.
January Avg. Temp.: 44.2°F
July Avg. Temp.: 80.8°F

Unemployment Rate: 4.1
Per Capita Income: $41,438
Tourism Earnings: $350,000
Avg. Home Value: $57,400

HUNT
COUNTY

Named for Republic Secretary of Navy Memucan Hunt.

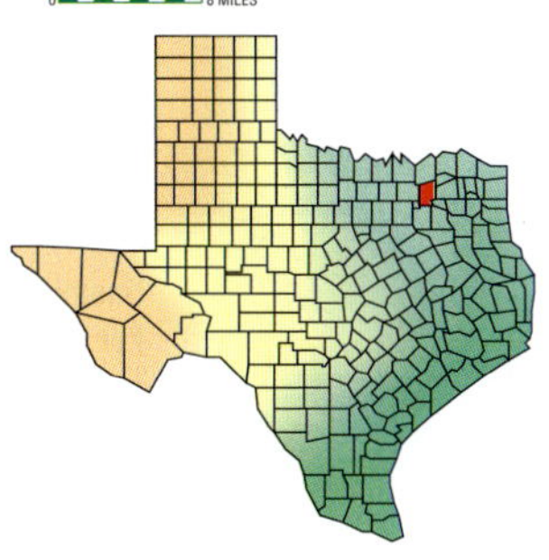

Cities/Towns: Greenville, Caddo Mills, Campbell, Celeste, Hawk Cove, Lone Oak, Merit, Neylandville, Quinlan, Union Valley, West Tawakoni, Wolfe City

Land Area (Square Miles): 840.42
Elevation (Approx. Feet): 505

Population: 118,729
Population Change: 18.80%

Race:
White: 65.2%
Black: 8.9%
Hispanic: 22.2%
Asian: 1.7%
Other: 1.8%

Vital Statistics:
Births: 1,475
Deaths: 1,175
Marriages: 473
Divorces: 201

2024 Rainfall: 53.04 in.
January Avg. Temp.: 40.7°F
July Avg. Temp.: 82.4°F

Unemployment Rate: 4.1
Per Capita Income: $50,287
Tourism Earnings: $47.7 million
Avg. Home Value: $210,900

HUTCHINSON
COUNTY

Named for pioneer jurist Anderson Hutchinson.

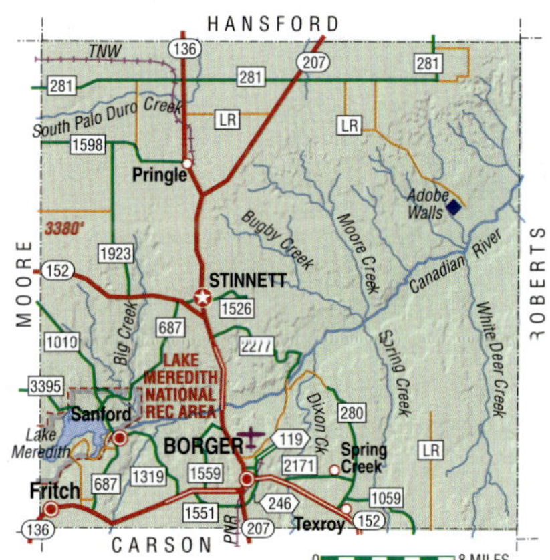

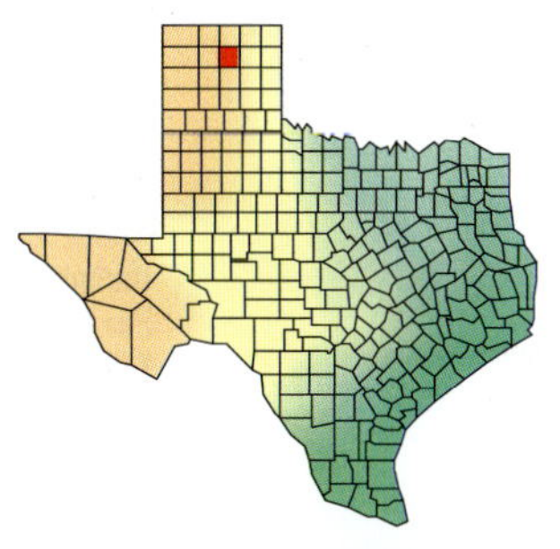

Cities/Towns: Stinnett, Borger, Fritch, Sanford

Land Area (Square Miles): 887.42
Elevation (Approx. Feet): 3,045

Population: 19,721
Population Change: -4.40%

Race:
White: 68.4%
Black: 3.0%
Hispanic: 25.3%
Asian: 0.7%
Other: 2.3%

Vital Statistics:
Births: 215
Deaths: 292
Marriages: 90
Divorces: 70

2024 Rainfall: 18.93 in.
January Avg. Temp.: 34.9°F
July Avg. Temp.: 82°F

Unemployment Rate: 4.5
Per Capita Income: $52,596
Tourism Earnings: $11.8 million
Avg. Home Value: $102,200

IRION COUNTY

Named for Republic leader R.A. Irion.

Cities/Towns: Mertzon, Barnhart

Land Area (Square Miles): 1,051.54
Elevation (Approx. Feet): 2,379

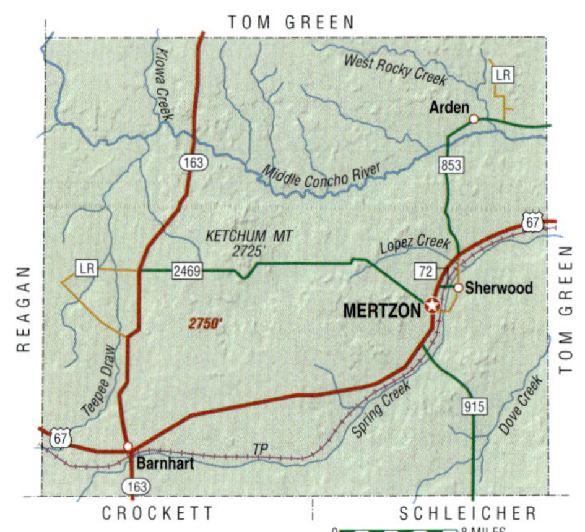

Population: 1,526
Population Change: 0.80%

Race:
White: 69.7%
Black: 1.7%
Hispanic: 25.6%
Asian: 0.5%
Other: 1.5%

Vital Statistics:
Births: 18
Deaths: 15
Marriages: 8
Divorces: 3

2024 Rainfall: 17.12 in.
January Avg. Temp.: 42.7°F
July Avg. Temp.: 83.4°F

Unemployment Rate: 3
Per Capita Income: $85,857
Tourism Earnings: $530,000
Avg. Home Value: $152,600

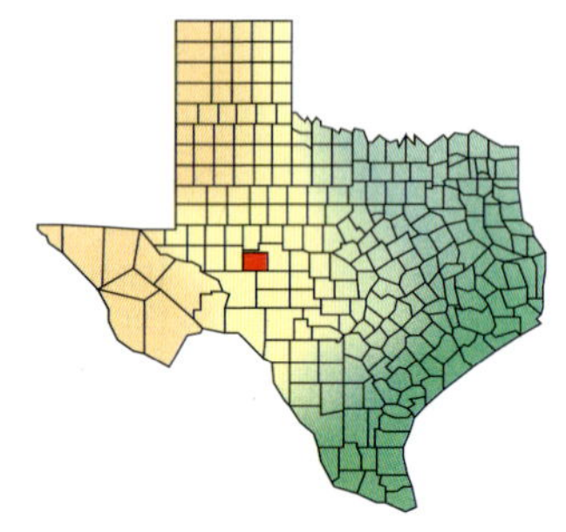

JACK COUNTY

Named for brothers P.C. and W.H. Jack, who were leaders in Texas' independence effort.

Cities/Towns: Jacksboro, Bryson, Jermyn, Perrin

Land Area (Square Miles): 910.97
Elevation (Approx. Feet): 1,060

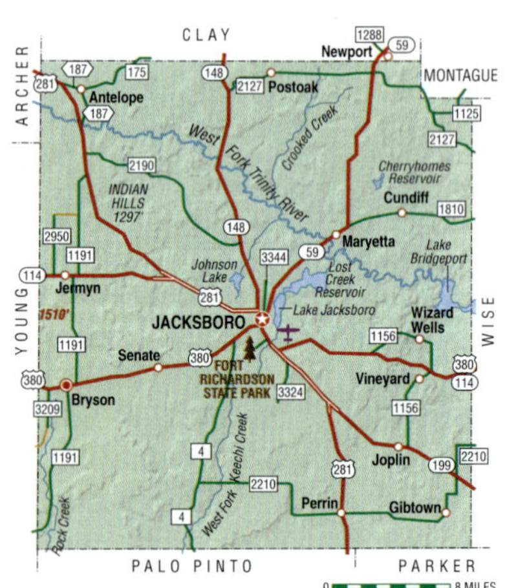

Population: 9,398
Population Change: 10.90%

Race:
White: 75.3%
Black: 3.8%
Hispanic: 18.8%
Asian: 0.9%
Other: 1.4%

Vital Statistics:
Births: 96
Deaths: 118
Marriages: 46
Divorces: 31

2024 Rainfall: 36.18 in.
January Avg. Temp.: 39.5°F
July Avg. Temp.: 83.3°F

Unemployment Rate: 5.1
Per Capita Income: $52,599
Tourism Earnings: $970,000
Avg. Home Value: $174,800

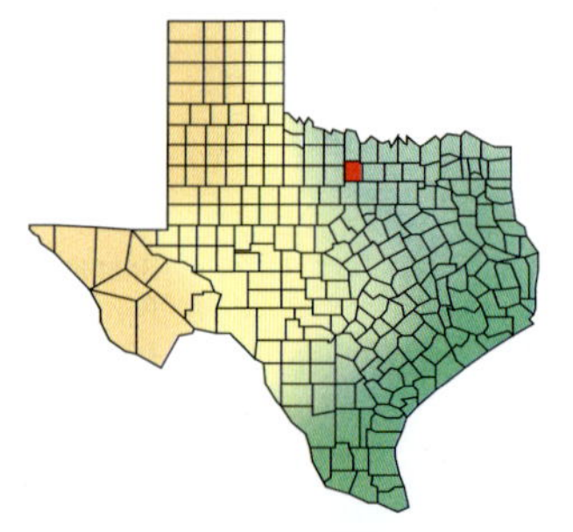

JACKSON COUNTY

Named for U.S. President Andrew Jackson.

Cities/Towns: Edna, Francitas, Ganado, La Salle, La Ward, Lolita, Vanderbilt

Land Area (Square Miles): 829.44
Elevation (Approx. Feet): 52

Population: 15,284
Population Change: 2.00%

Race:
White: 57.7%
Black: 6.8%
Hispanic: 33.4%
Asian: 1.2%
Other: 0.9%

Vital Statistics:
Births: 209
Deaths: 181
Marriages: 52
Divorces: 42

2024 Rainfall: 42.18 in.
January Avg. Temp.: 51.7°F
July Avg. Temp.: 83.4°F

Unemployment Rate: 4.1
Per Capita Income: $54,702
Tourism Earnings: $2.6 million
Avg. Home Value: $175,500

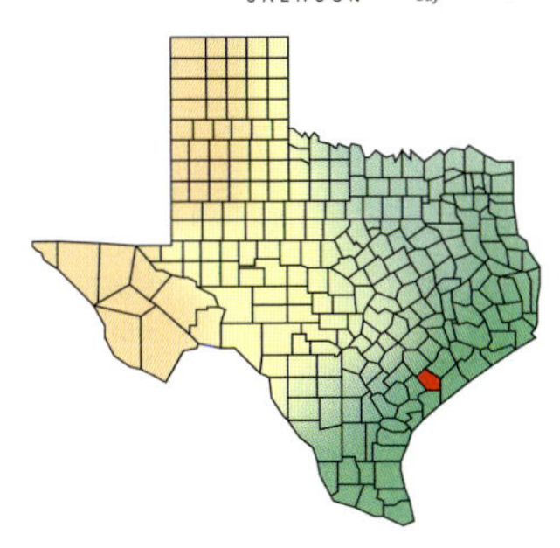

JASPER COUNTY

Named for American Revolution Sergeant William Jasper.

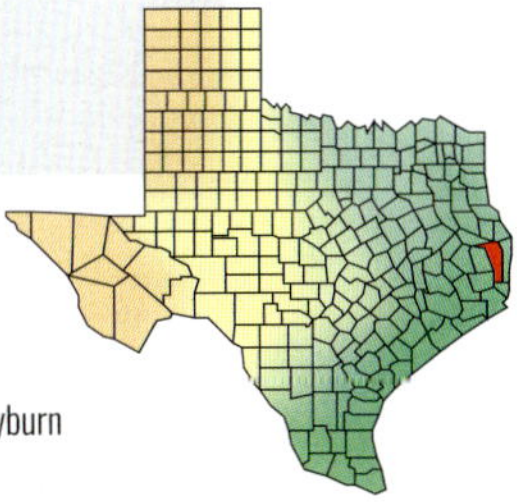

Cities/Towns: Jasper, Browndell, Buna, Evadale, Kirbyville, Sam Rayburn

Land Area (Square Miles): 938.66
Elevation (Approx. Feet): 184

Population: 32,907
Population Change: -0.20%

Race:
White: 74.2%
Black: 15.9%
Hispanic: 7.3%
Asian: 0.7%
Other: 1.0%

Vital Statistics:
Births: 401
Deaths: 516
Marriages: 195
Divorces: 77

2024 Rainfall: 77.48 in.
January Avg. Temp.: 46.2°F
July Avg. Temp.: 81.3°F

Unemployment Rate: 5.9
Per Capita Income: $53,205
Tourism Earnings: $13.5 million
Avg. Home Value: $125,900

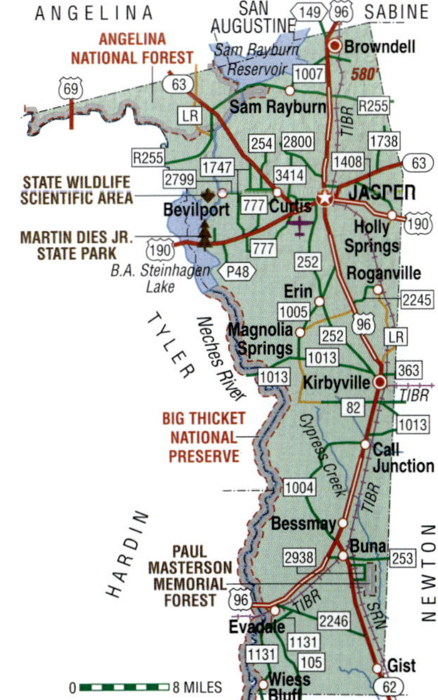

J

JEFF DAVIS COUNTY

Named for U.S. Secretary of War and Confederate President Jefferson Davis.

Cities/Towns: Fort Davis, Valentine

Land Area (Square Miles): 2,264.56
Elevation (Approx. Feet): 6,057

Population: 1,778
Population Change: -11.00%

Race:
White: 64.1%
Black: 1.6%
Hispanic: 29.6%
Asian: 1.9%
Other: 2.3%

Vital Statistics:
Births: 14
Deaths: 35
Marriages: 12
Divorces: N/A

2024 Rainfall: 7.12 in.
January Avg. Temp.: 44.4°F
July Avg. Temp.: 77.9°F

Unemployment Rate: 4.9
Per Capita Income: $67,092
Tourism Earnings: $4.9 million
Avg. Home Value: $234,400

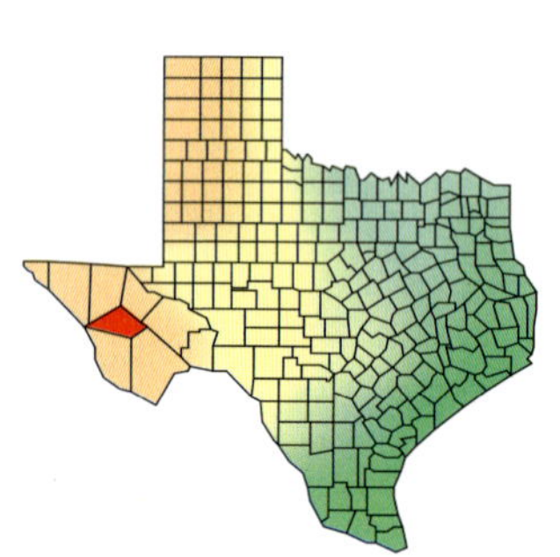

JEFFERSON COUNTY

Named for U.S. President Thomas Jefferson.

Cities/Towns: Beaumont, Port Arthur, Beauxart Gardens, Bevil Oaks, Central Gardens, China, Fannett, Groves, Hamshire, Nederland, Nome, Port Neches, Taylor Landing

Land Area (Square Miles): 876.76
Elevation (Approx. Feet): 10

Population: 253,948
Population Change: -1.00%

Race:
White: 36.5%
Black: 34.4%
Hispanic: 24.6%
Asian: 4.0%
Other: 1.3%

Vital Statistics:
Births: 3,263
Deaths: 2,702
Marriages: 1,450
Divorces: 410

2024 Rainfall: 67.48 in.
January Avg. Temp.: 50.3°F
July Avg. Temp.: 82.4°F

Unemployment Rate: 5.9
Per Capita Income: $50,131
Tourism Earnings: $146.8 million
Avg. Home Value: $159,600

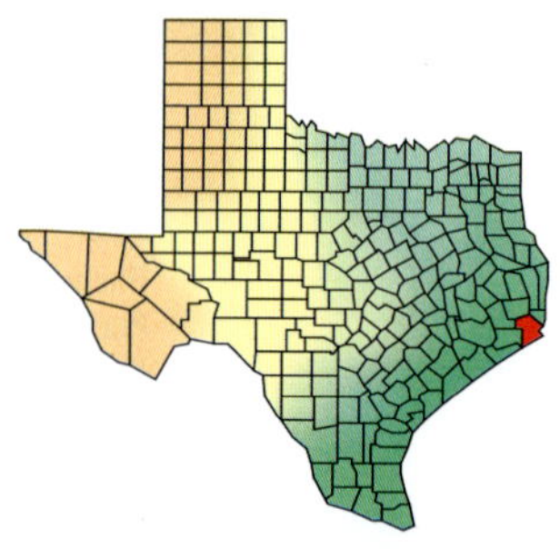

JIM HOGG
COUNTY

Named for Govenor James Stephen Hogg.

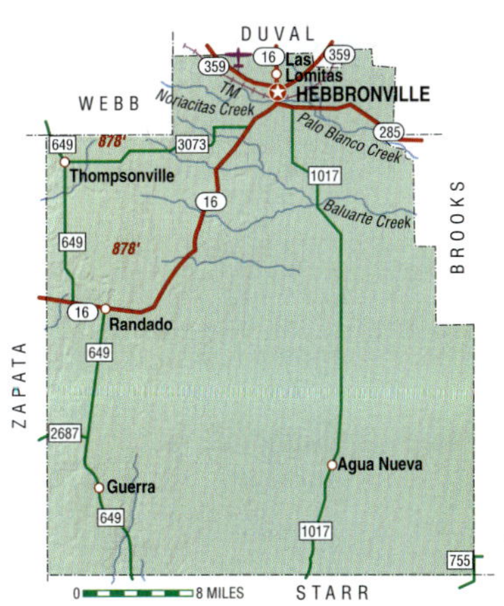

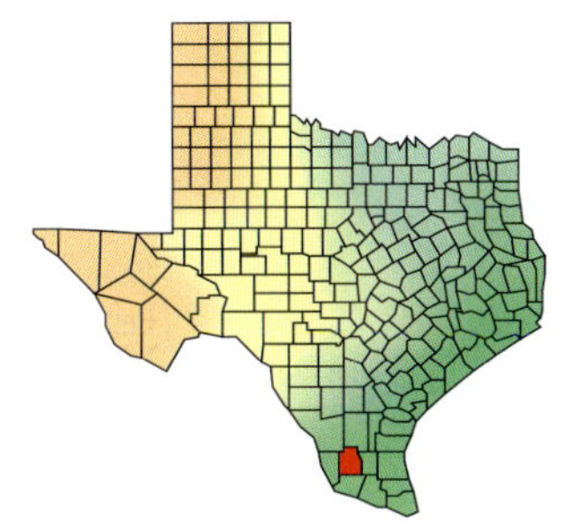

Cities/Towns: Hebbronville, Las Lomitas, South Fork Estates, Thompsonville

Land Area (Square Miles): 1,136.17
Elevation (Approx. Feet): 525

Population: 4,583
Population Change: -5.20%

Race:
White: 8.6%
Black: 1.5 %
Hispanic: 88.6%
Asian: 0.7%
Other: 0.6%

Vital Statistics:
Births: 52
Deaths: 65
Marriages: 19
Divorces: 1

2024 Rainfall: 19.61 in.
January Avg. Temp.: 56.5°F
July Avg. Temp.: 85.6°F

Unemployment Rate: 4.7
Per Capita Income: $44,294
Tourism Earnings: $1.5 million
Avg. Home Value: $125,600

JIM WELLS
COUNTY

Named for developer J.B. Wells Jr.

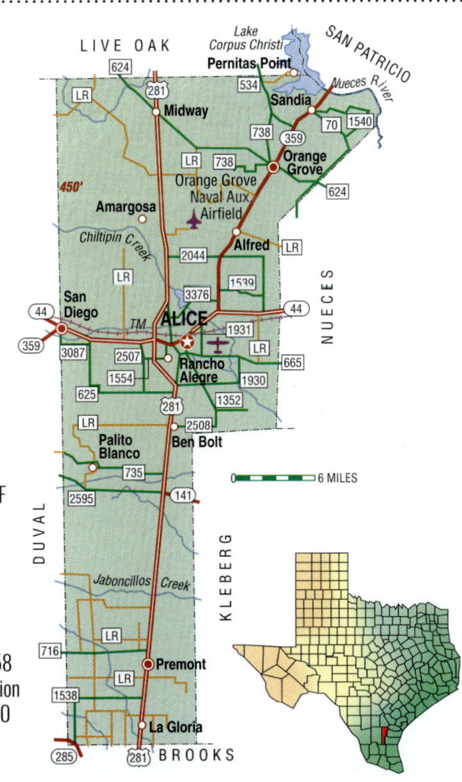

Cities/Towns: Alice, Alfred, Amargosa, Ben Bolt, Orange Grove, Premont, Rancho Alegre, Sandia, San Diego

Land Area (Square Miles): 865.18
Elevation (Approx. Feet): 217

Population: 38,886
Population Change: 0.00%

Race:
White: 18.2%
Black: 1.3%
Hispanic: 79.6%
Asian: 0.7%
Other: 1.3%

Vital Statistics:
Births: 546
Deaths: 491
Marriages: 140
Divorces: 132

2024 Rainfall: 23.51 in.
January Avg. Temp.: 54.9°F
July Avg. Temp.: 84.8°F

Unemployment Rate: 5.2
Per Capita Income: $51,458
Tourism Earnings: $18 million
Avg. Home Value: $104,800

JOHNSON
COUNTY

Named for Colonel M.T. Johnson of the Mexican War and Confederacy.

Cities/Towns: Cleburne, Burleson, Alvarado, Briaroaks, Coyota Flats, Cross Timber, Godley, Grandview, Joshua, Keene, Lillian, Rio Vista, Venus, Cresson, Mansfield

Land Area (Square Miles): 724.78
Elevation (Approx. Feet): 774

Population: 210,547
Population Change: 17.00%

Race:
White: 64.4%
Black: 6.3%
Hispanic: 25.9%
Asian: 1.4%
Other: 1.5%

Vital Statistics:
Births: 2,401
Deaths: 1,885
Marriages: 926
Divorces: 460

2024 Rainfall: 39.81 in.
January Avg. Temp.: 42.6°F
July Avg. Temp.: 83°F

Unemployment Rate: 3.6
Per Capita Income: $55,487
Tourism Earnings: $53.9 million
Avg. Home Value: $254,600

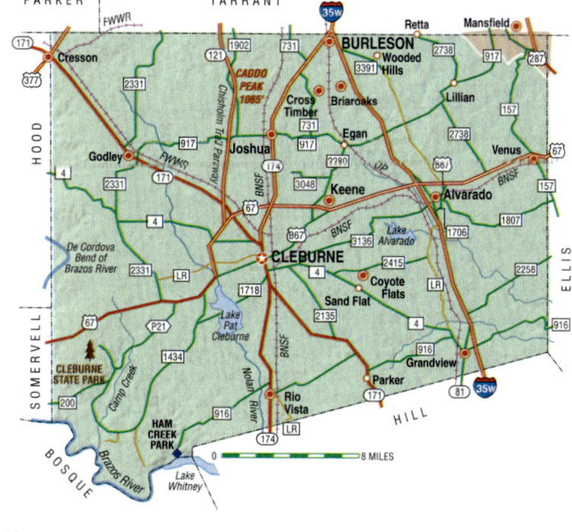

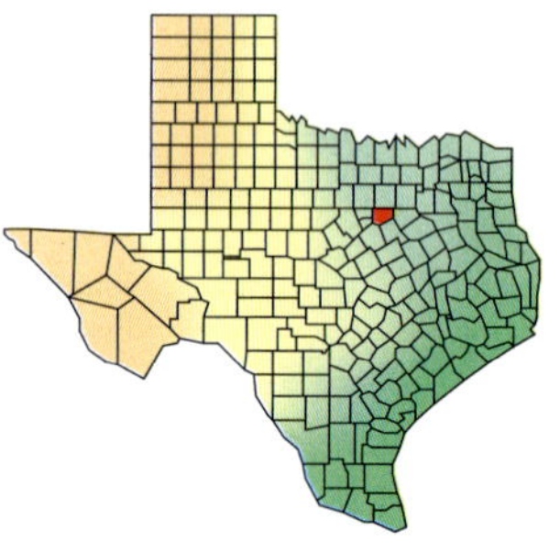

COURTESY OF CITY OF BURLESON

JONES
COUNTY

Named for Anson Jones, the last president of the Republic.

Cities/Towns: Anson, Stamford, Hamlin, Hawley, Lueders, Abilene

Land Area (Square Miles): 928.61
Elevation (Approx. Feet): 1,732

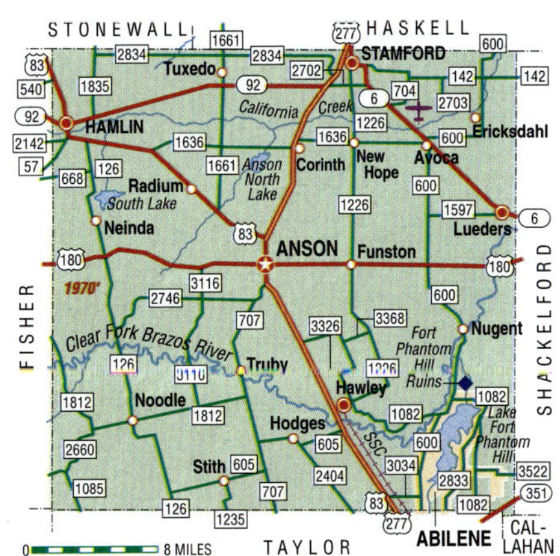

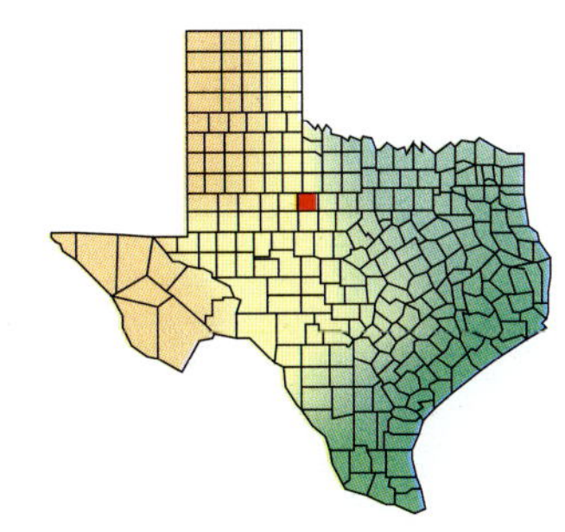

Population: 20,850
Population Change: 6.00%

Race:
White: 56.9%
Black: 13.6%
Hispanic: 28.8%
Asian: 0.7%
Other: 1.7%

Vital Statistics:
Births: 168
Deaths: 215
Marriages: 54
Divorces: 41

2024 Rainfall: 28.87 in.
January Avg. Temp.: 41°F
July Avg. Temp.: 84.1°F

Unemployment Rate: 3.7
Per Capita Income: $41,722
Tourism Earnings: $2.9 million
Avg. Home Value: $92,700

KARNES
COUNTY

Named for Texas Revolutionary figure Henry W. Karnes.

Cities/Towns: Karnes City, Kenedy, Falls City, Runge

Land Area (Square Miles): 747.75
Elevation (Approx. Feet): 338

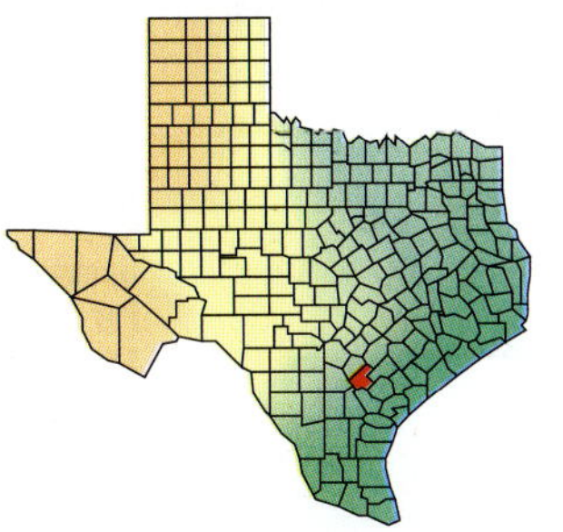

Population: 15,137
Population Change: 2.50%

Race:
White: 34.9%
Black: 11.2%
Hispanic: 53.6%
Asian: 0.7%
Other: 1.2%

Vital Statistics:
Births: 140
Deaths: 175
Marriages: 18
Divorces: 33

2024 Rainfall: 28.25 in.
January Avg. Temp.: 50.6°F
July Avg. Temp.: 84°F

Unemployment Rate: 4.1
Per Capita Income: $83,442
Tourism Earnings: $14.4 million
Avg. Home Value: $136,900

CHRISTINA MCDANIEL PHOTOGRAPHY/COURTESY OF TERRELL CVB

KAUFMAN
COUNTY

Named for Texas and U.S. Congressman D.S. Kaufman.

Cities/Towns: Kaufman, Terrell, Forney, Combine, Cottonwood, Crandall, Elmo, Grays Prairie, Kemp, Mabank, Oak Grove, Oak Ridge, Post Oak Bend, Rosser, Scurry, Talty

Land Area (Square Miles): 780.79
Elevation (Approx. Feet): 417

Population: 197,829
Population Change: 36.10%

Race:
White: 46.6%
Black: 21.6%
Hispanic: 28.1%
Asian: 2.4%
Other: 1.2%

Vital Statistics:
Births: 2,768
Deaths: 1,318
Marriages: 628
Divorces: 433

2024 Rainfall: 52.31 in.
January Avg. Temp.: 41.4°F
July Avg. Temp.: 82.2°F

Unemployment Rate: 4
Per Capita Income: $53,843
Tourism Earnings: $50.7 million
Avg. Home Value: $290,800

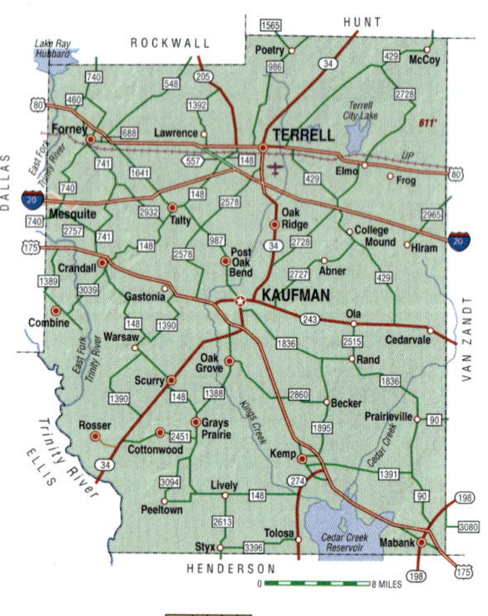

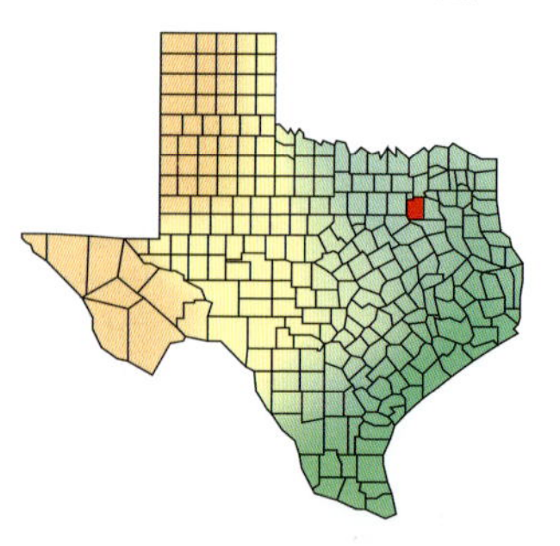

KENDALL
COUNTY

Named for journalist, pioneer sheepman, and early contributor to *Texas Almanac*, George W. Kendall.

Cities/Towns: Boerne, Comfort, Kendalia, Sisterdale, Waring, Fair Oaks Ranch

Land Area (Square Miles): 662.45
Elevation (Approx. Feet): 1,276

Population: 51,828
Population Change: 17.00%

Race:
White: 69.8%
Black: 1.8%
Hispanic: 24.8%
Asian: 1.9%
Other: 0.9%

Vital Statistics:
Births: 443
Deaths: 514
Marriages: 355
Divorces: 65

2024 Rainfall: 26.45 in.
January Avg. Temp.: 45.8°F
July Avg. Temp.: 82.1°F

Unemployment Rate: 3.3
Per Capita Income: $110,116
Tourism Earnings: $54 million
Avg. Home Value: $489,800

KENEDY
COUNTY

Named for pioneer steamboat operator and cattleman, Captain Mifflin Kenedy.

Cities/Towns: Sarita, Armstrong

Land Area (Square Miles): 1,458.56
Elevation (Approx. Feet): 13

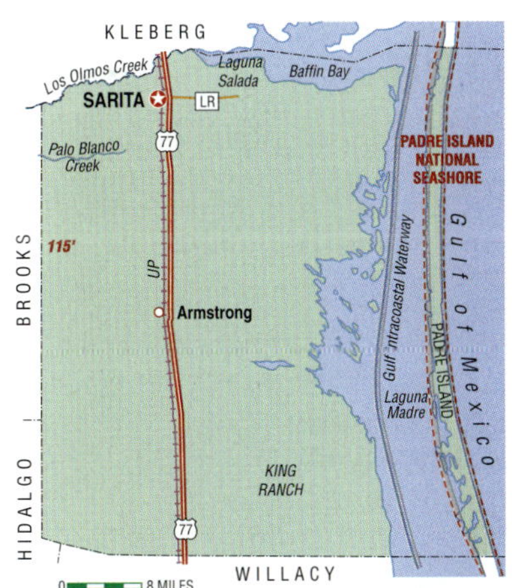

Population: 330
Population Change: -6.00%

Race:
White: 20.4%
Black: 5.2%
Hispanic: 73.2%
Asian: 1.5%
Other: 0.9%

Vital Statistics:
Births: N/A
Deaths: N/A
Marriages: 0
Divorces: N/A

2024 Rainfall: 28.08 in.
January Avg. Temp.: 57.8°F
July Avg. Temp.: 84.9°F

Unemployment Rate: 8
Per Capita Income: $45,802
Tourism Earnings: $370,000
Avg. Home Value: N/A

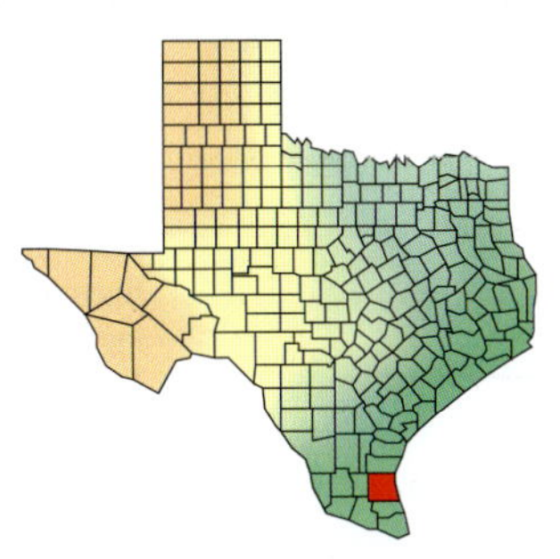

K

KENT COUNTY

Named for Andrew Kent, one of 32 volunteers from Gonzales who died at the Alamo.

Cities/Towns: Jayton, Girard

Land Area (Square Miles): 902.51
Elevation (Approx. Feet): 2,106

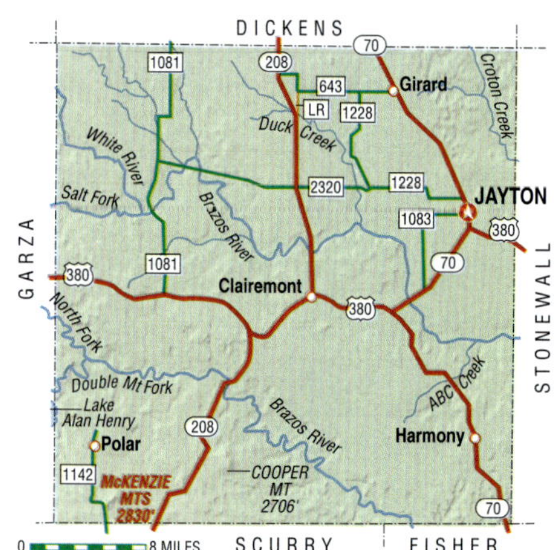

Population: 703
Population Change: -6.40%

Race:
White: 78.9%
Black: 1.2%
Hispanic: 17.2%
Asian: 0.3%
Other: 1.7%

Vital Statistics:
Births: N/A
Deaths: 18
Marriages: 0
Divorces: 1

2024 Rainfall: 24.63 in.
January Avg. Temp.: 39.5°F
July Avg. Temp.: 84.7°F

Unemployment Rate: 4.5
Per Capita Income: $71,715
Tourism Earnings: $190,000
Avg. Home Value: $108,900

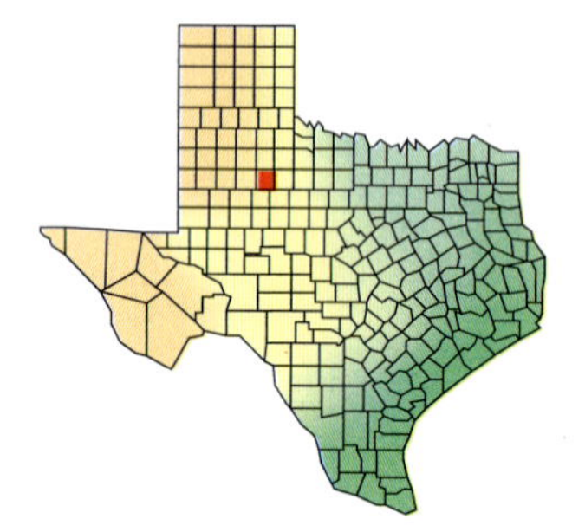

KERR COUNTY

Named for James Kerr, a member of Austin's Colony.

Cities/Towns: Kerrville, Camp Verde, Center Point, Hunt, Mountain Home

Land Area (Square Miles): 1,103.33
Elevation (Approx. Feet): 1,982

Population: 53,900
Population Change: 2.50%

Race:
White: 68.2%
Black: 2.1%
Hispanic: 27.1%
Asian: 1.3%
Other: 1.3%

Vital Statistics:
Births: 501
Deaths: 819
Marriages: 274
Divorces: 157

2024 Rainfall: 23.07 in.
January Avg. Temp.: 44°F
July Avg. Temp.: 80.6°F

Unemployment Rate: 3.3
Per Capita Income: $69,038
Tourism Earnings: $51 million
Avg. Home Value: $285,100

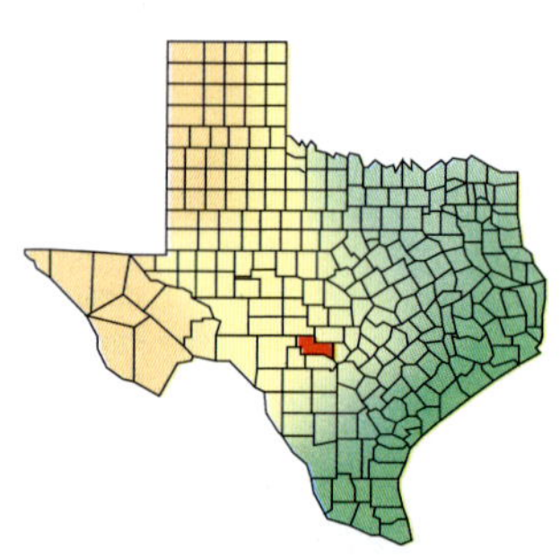

COURTESY OF KERRVILLE CVB

KIMBLE COUNTY

Named for George C. Kimble, a Gonzales volunteer who died at the Alamo.

Cities/Towns: Junction, London, Roosevelt

Land Area (Square Miles): 1,250.98
Elevation (Approx. Feet): 1,778

Population: 4,401
Population Change: 2.80%

Race:
White: 73.4%
Black: 1.4%
Hispanic: 23.0%
Asian: 0.9%
Other: 1.7%

Vital Statistics:
Births: 45
Deaths: 55
Marriages: 13
Divorces: 10

2024 Rainfall: 22.66 in.
January Avg. Temp.: 43.3°F
July Avg. Temp.: 81.1°F

Unemployment Rate: 3.4
Per Capita Income: $59,148
Tourism Earnings: $2.9 million
Avg. Home Value: $173,100

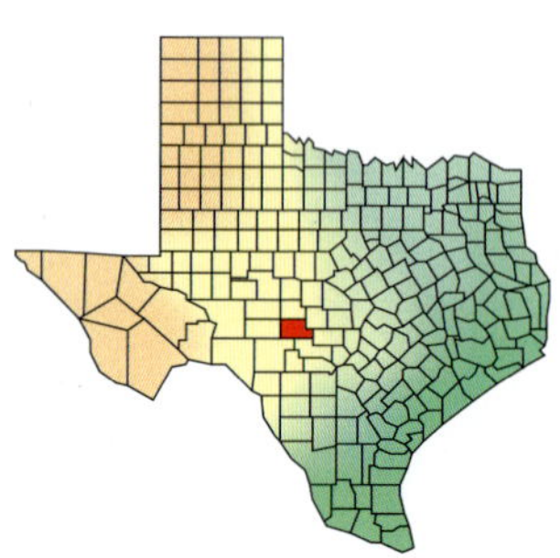

KING COUNTY

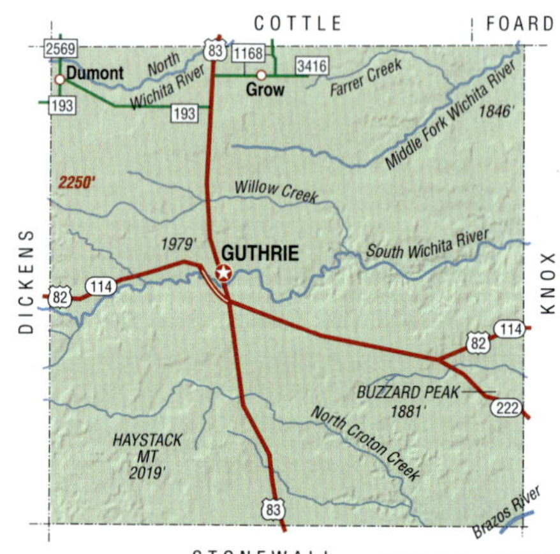

Named for William P. King, a volunteer from Gonzales who died at the Alamo.

Cities/Towns: Guthrie

Land Area (Square Miles): 910.87
Elevation (Approx. Feet): 1,759

Population: 215
Population Change: -18.30%

Race:
White: 79.3%
Black: 2.3%
Hispanic: 14.3%
Asian: 0.0%
Other: 1.9%

Vital Statistics:
Births: N/A
Deaths: N/A
Marriages: 0
Divorces: N/A

2024 Rainfall: 26.96 in.
January Avg. Temp.: 39.2°F
July Avg. Temp.: 84.5°F

Unemployment Rate: 2.5
Per Capita Income: $139,825
Tourism Earnings: $10,000
Avg. Home Value: N/A

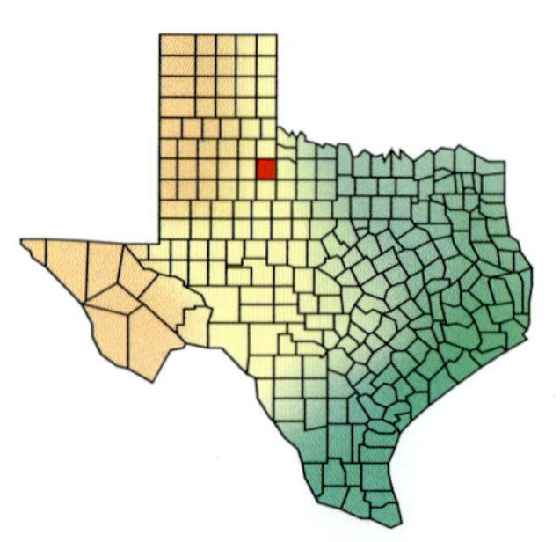

KINNEY
COUNTY

Named for founder of Corpus Christi H.L. Kinney.

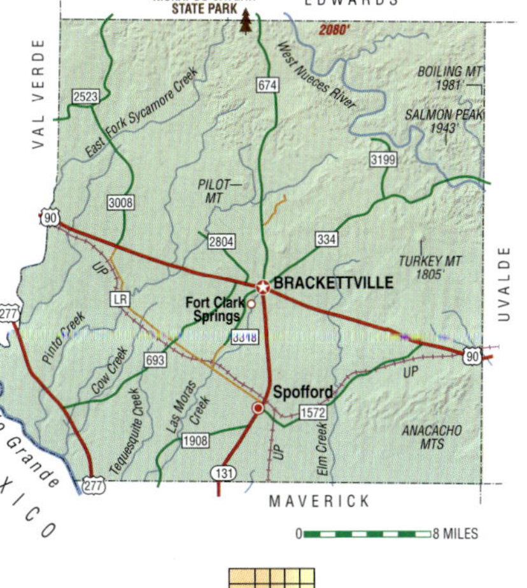

Cities/Towns: Brackettville, Fort Clark Springs, Spofford

Land Area (Square Miles): 1,360.53
Elevation (Approx. Feet): 1,201

Population: 3,191
Population Change: 1.90%

Race:
White: 41.0%
Black: 3.6%
Hispanic: 53.1%
Asian: 1.0%
Other: 2.5%

Vital Statistics:
Births: 35
Deaths: 38
Marriages: 15
Divorces: 4

2024 Rainfall: 14.4 in.
January Avg. Temp.: 49.6°F
July Avg. Temp.: 86.2°F

Unemployment Rate: 4.1
Per Capita Income: $44,642
Tourism Earnings: $2.9 million
Avg. Home Value: $88,500

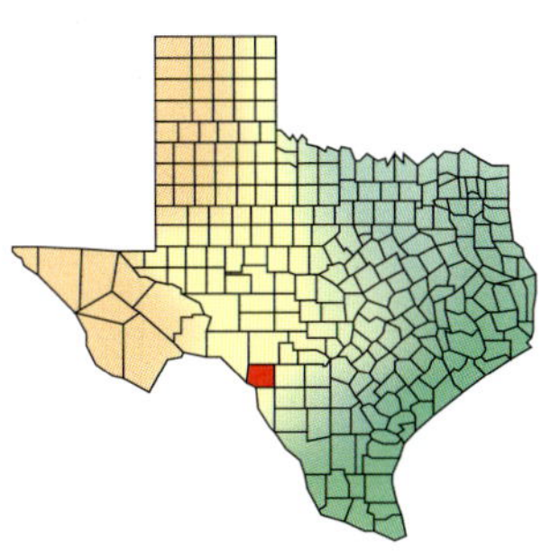

KLEBERG
COUNTY

Named for San Jacinto veteran and rancher Robert Kleberg.

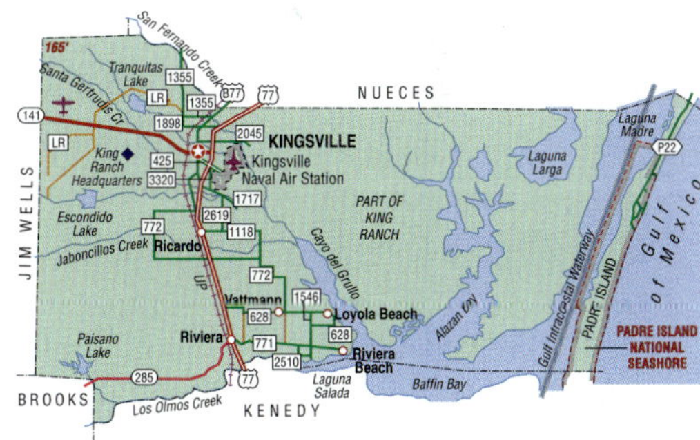

Cities/Towns: Kingsville, Ricardo, Riviera

Land Area (Square Miles): 881.31
Elevation (Approx. Feet): 23

Population: 30,442
Population Change: -1.90%

Race:
White: 21.0%
Black: 4.4%
Hispanic: 71.9%
Asian: 2.3%
Other: 1.3%

Vital Statistics:
Births: 373
Deaths: 284
Marriages: 166
Divorces: 79

2024 Rainfall: 23.54 in.
January Avg. Temp.: 56.1°F
July Avg. Temp.: 85.5°F

Unemployment Rate: 4.4
Per Capita Income: $49,333
Tourism Earnings: $18.6 million
Avg. Home Value: $152,200

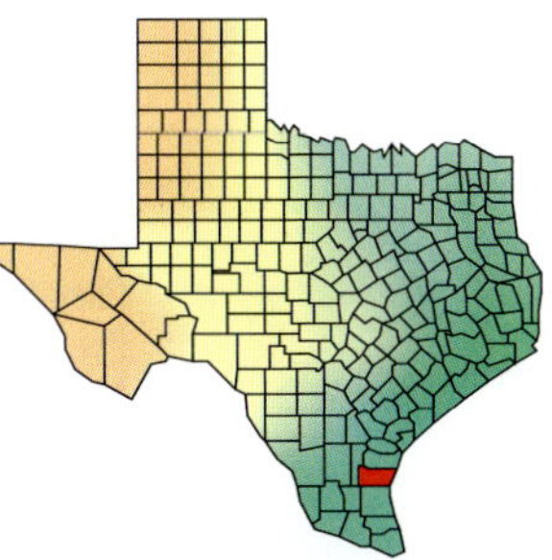

Source information for this chapter can be found on Page 407.

KNOX
COUNTY

Named for U.S. Secretary of War Henry Knox.

Cities/Towns: Benjamin, Munday, Knox City, Goree, Rhineland

Land Area (Square Miles): 850.62
Elevation (Approx. Feet): 1,496

Population: 3,255
Population Change: -3.00%

Race:
White: 57.1%
Black: 5.9%
Hispanic: 33.6%
Asian: 0.8%
Other: 1.4%

Vital Statistics:
Births: 39
Deaths: 54
Marriages: 8
Divorces: 17

2024 Rainfall: 29.96 in.
January Avg. Temp.: 39.7°F
July Avg. Temp.: 84.2°F

Unemployment Rate: 3.5
Per Capita Income: $52,798
Tourism Earnings: $450,000
Avg. Home Value: $66,800

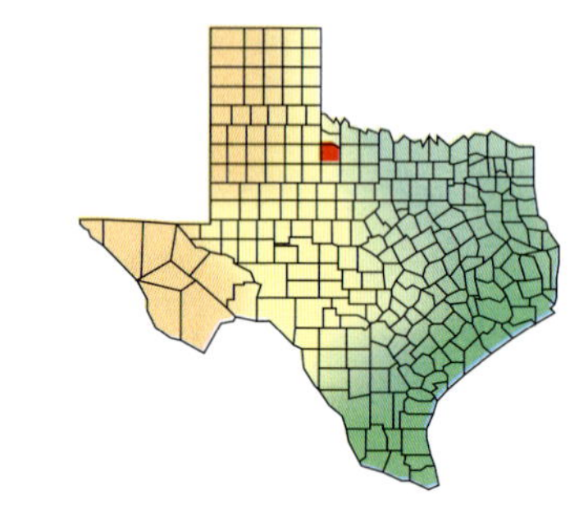

LAMAR
COUNTY

Named for the second president of Republic, Mirabeau B. Lamar.

Cities/Towns: Paris, Arthur City, Blossom, Brookston, Deport, Pattonville Petty, Powderly, Reno, Roxton, Sun Valley, Toco

Land Area (Square Miles): 907.33
Elevation (Approx. Feet): 568

Population: 51,249
Population Change: 2.30%

Race:
White: 71.6%
Black: 13.6%
Hispanic: 10.0%
Asian: 0.8%
Other: 2.1%

Vital Statistics:
Births: 615
Deaths: 695
Marriages: 317
Divorces: 237

2024 Rainfall: 50.26 in.
January Avg. Temp.: 38.7°F
July Avg. Temp.: 82.2°F

Unemployment Rate: 4
Per Capita Income: $51,936
Tourism Earnings: $26.2 million
Avg. Home Value: $175,500

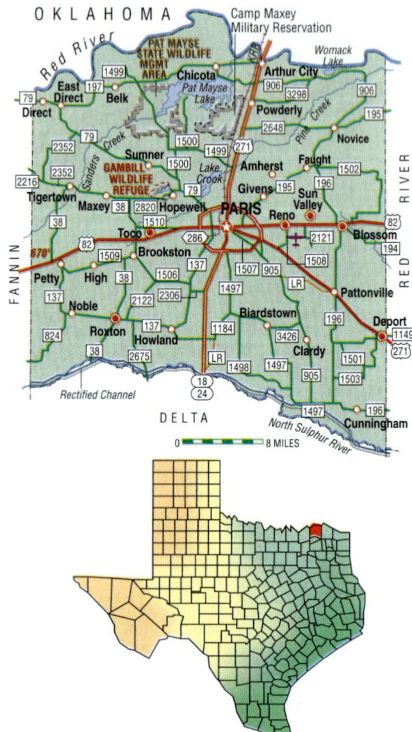

LAMB
COUNTY

Named for Lieutenant G.A. Lamb, who died in the Battle of San Jacinto.

Cities/Towns: Littlefield, Olton, Amherst, Earth, Fieldton, Spade, Springlake, Sudan

Land Area (Square Miles): 1,016.18
Elevation (Approx. Feet): 3,642

Population: 12,687
Population Change: -2.70%

Race:
White: 36.0%
Black: 4.9%
Hispanic: 58.4%
Asian: 0.7%
Other: 2.3%

Vital Statistics:
Births: 167
Deaths: 179
Marriages: 48
Divorces: 15

2024 Rainfall: 17.2 in.
January Avg. Temp.: 36°F
July Avg. Temp.: 78.8°F

Unemployment Rate: 3.8
Per Capita Income: $63,169
Tourism Earnings: $2.1 million
Avg. Home Value: $76,600

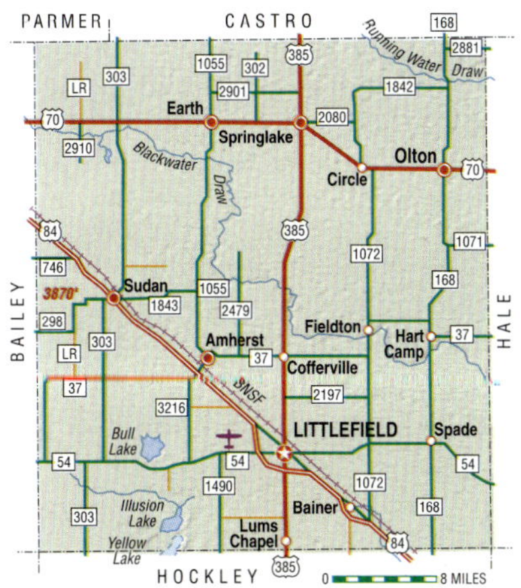

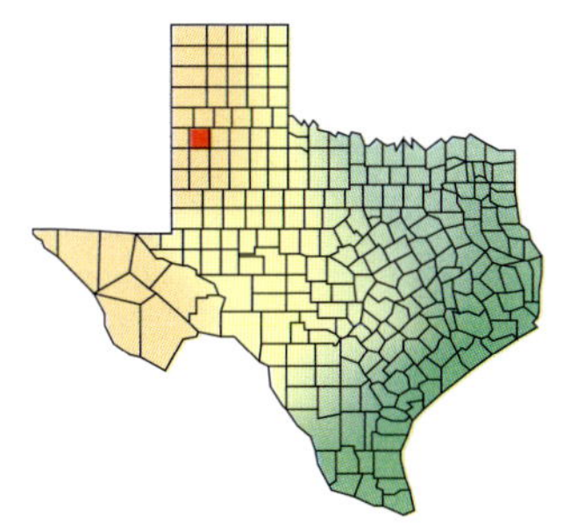

LAMPASAS
COUNTY

Named for the Lampasas River.

Cities/Towns: Lampasas, Izoro, Kempner, Lometa

Land Area (Square Miles): 712.53
Elevation (Approx. Feet): 1,247

Population: 23,539
Population Change: 8.90%

Race:
White: 69.9%
Black: 5.0%
Hispanic: 21.0%
Asian: 1.5%
Other: 2.0%

Vital Statistics:
Births: 213
Deaths: 292
Marriages: 103
Divorces: 64

2024 Rainfall: 29.63 in.
January Avg. Temp.: 43.7°F
July Avg. Temp.: 83°F

Unemployment Rate: 4
Per Capita Income: $62,665
Tourism Earnings: $4.2 million
Avg. Home Value: $236,000

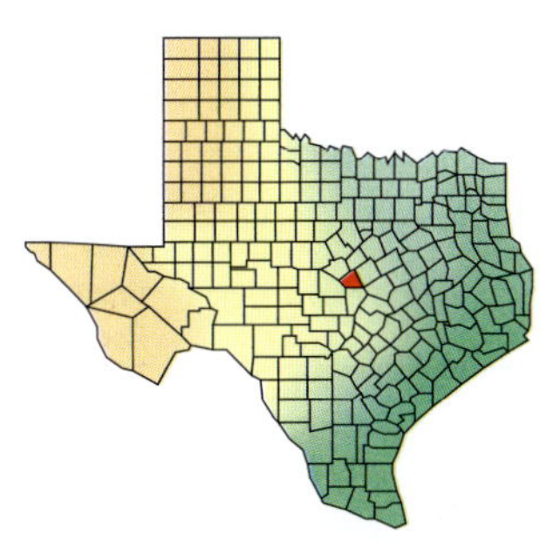

L

LA SALLE
COUNTY

Named for Robert Cavelier Sieur de La Salle, a French explorer who died in Texas.

Cities/Towns: Cotulla, Encinal, Fowlerton

Land Area (Square Miles): 1,486.70
Elevation (Approx. Feet): 407

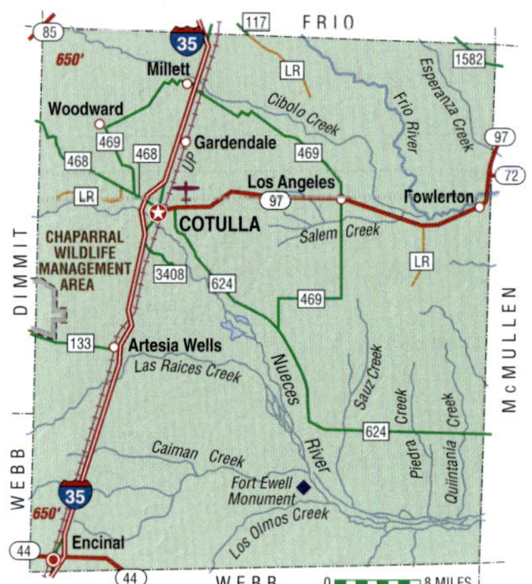

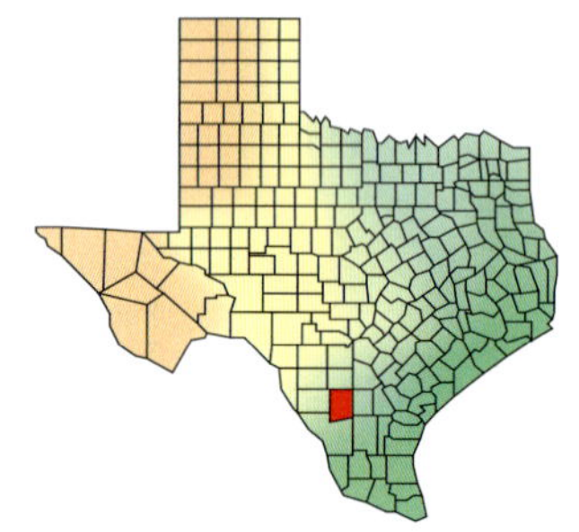

Population: 6,679
Population Change: 0.30%

Race:
White: 18.5%
Black: 2.7%
Hispanic: 77.5%
Asian: 0.7%
Other: 1.6%

Vital Statistics:
Births: 65
Deaths: 77
Marriages: 34
Divorces: N/A

2024 Rainfall: 19.05 in.
January Avg. Temp.: 53.1°F
July Avg. Temp.: 86.8°F

Unemployment Rate: 4.6
Per Capita Income: $50,247
Tourism Earnings: $12.7 million
Avg. Home Value: $101,000

LAVACA
COUNTY

Named for the Lavaca River.

Cities/Towns: Halletsville, Yoakum, Shiner, Moulton, Sublime, Sweet Home

Land Area (Square Miles): 969.71
Elevation (Approx. Feet): 259

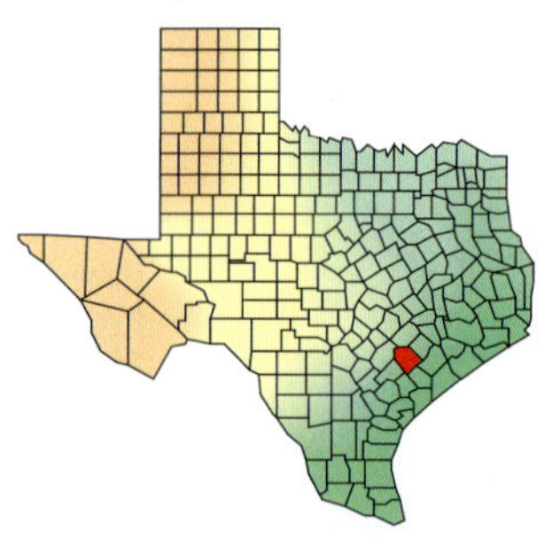

Population: 20,605
Population Change: 1.30%

Race:
White: 72.4%
Black: 6.4%
Hispanic: 20.1%
Asian: 0.7%
Other: 0.8%

Vital Statistics:
Births: 244
Deaths: 253
Marriages: 77
Divorces: 48

2024 Rainfall: 37.13 in.
January Avg. Temp.: 50.7°F
July Avg. Temp.: 84.6°F

Unemployment Rate: 3.1
Per Capita Income: $71,664
Tourism Earnings: $4.7 million
Avg. Home Value: $220,900

LEE
COUNTY

Named for General Robert E. Lee.

Cities/Towns: Giddings, Dime Box, Lexington, Lincoln, Serbin

Land Area (Square Miles): 629.04
Elevation (Approx. Feet): 456

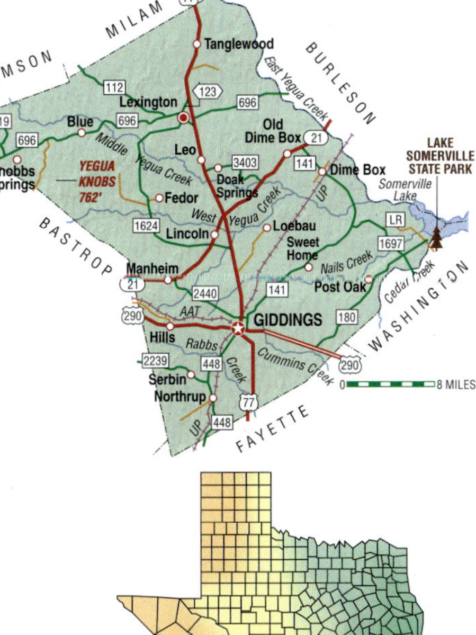

Population: 18,451
Population Change: 5.50%

Race:
White: 61.7%
Black:9.6%
Hispanic: 27.0%
Asian: 0.6%
Other: 1.4%

Vital Statistics:
Births: 220
Deaths: 198
Marriages: 73
Divorces: 65

2024 Rainfall: 43.07 in.
January Avg. Temp.: 47.9°F
July Avg. Temp.: 83.4°F

Unemployment Rate: 3.5
Per Capita Income: $59,542
Tourism Earnings: $8.8 million
Avg. Home Value: $247,500

LEON
COUNTY

Named for the founder of the city of Victoria, Martín de León.

Cities/Towns: Centerville, Buffalo, Hilltop Lakes, Jewett, Leona, Marquez, Normangee, Oakwood

Land Area (Square Miles): 1,073.16
Elevation (Approx. Feet): 367

Population: 16,698
Population Change: 5.90%

Race:
White: 74.0%
Black: 6.6%
Hispanic: 17.0%
Asian: 1.0%
Other: 1.0%

Vital Statistics:
Births: 181
Deaths: 269
Marriages: 62
Divorces: 52

2024 Rainfall: 61.73 in.
January Avg. Temp.: 44.4°F
July Avg. Temp.: 82°F

Unemployment Rate: 4
Per Capita Income: $62,631
Tourism Earnings: $5.8 million
Avg. Home Value: $177,400

UNSPLASH/SOMBRERO CRAFT

L

LIBERTY
COUNTY

Named for the Spanish municipality Villa de la Santísima Trinidad de la Libertad.

Cities/Towns: Liberty, Dayton, Cleveland, Ames, Daisetta, Dalton Lakes, Devers, Hardin, Hull, Kenefick, North Cleveland, Plum Grove, Raywood, Romayer, Rye

Land Area (Square Miles): 1,158.35
Elevation (Approx. Feet): 30

Population: 115,042
Population Change: 25.50%

Race:
White: 48.0%
Black: 8.9%
Hispanic: 41.8%
Asian: 0.9%
Other: 1.7%

Vital Statistics:
Births: 1,517
Deaths: 959
Marriages: 437
Divorces: 300

2024 Rainfall: 69.2 in.
January Avg. Temp.: 49.5°F
July Avg. Temp.: 82.2°F

Unemployment Rate: 5.3
Per Capita Income: $44,184
Tourism Earnings: $24.5 million
Avg. Home Value: $167,100

LIMESTONE
COUNTY

Named for the limestone deposits found in the region.

Cities/Towns: Groesbeck, Mexia, Coolidge, Kosse, Prairie Hill, Tehuacana

Land Area (Square Miles): 905.43
Elevation (Approx. Feet): 492

Population: 22,569
Population Change: 1.90%

Race:
White: 56.8%
Black: 17.1%
Hispanic: 23.9%
Asian: 1.1%
Other: 1.5%

Vital Statistics:
Births: 273
Deaths: 331
Marriages: 106
Divorces: 72

2024 Rainfall: 44.83 in.
January Avg. Temp.: 44°F
July Avg. Temp.: 82.6°F

Unemployment Rate: 4.3
Per Capita Income: $52,196
Tourism Earnings: $3.7 million
Avg. Home Value: $154,400

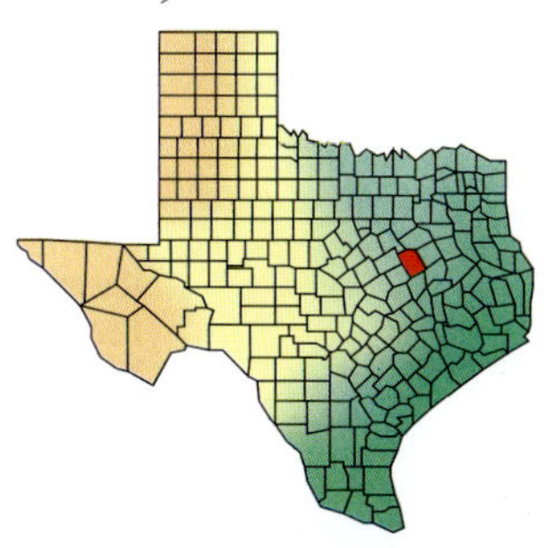

L

LIPSCOMB
COUNTY

Named for Republic of Texas leader A.S. Lipscomb.

Cities/Towns: Lipscomb, Booker, Darrouzett, Follett, Higgins

Land Area (Square Miles): 932.21
Elevation (Approx. Feet): 2,494

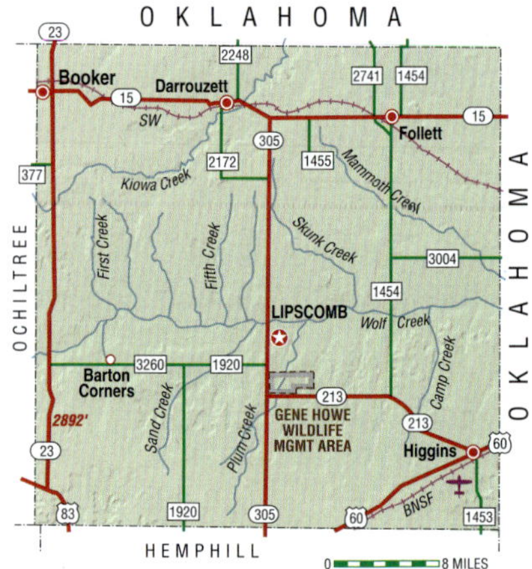

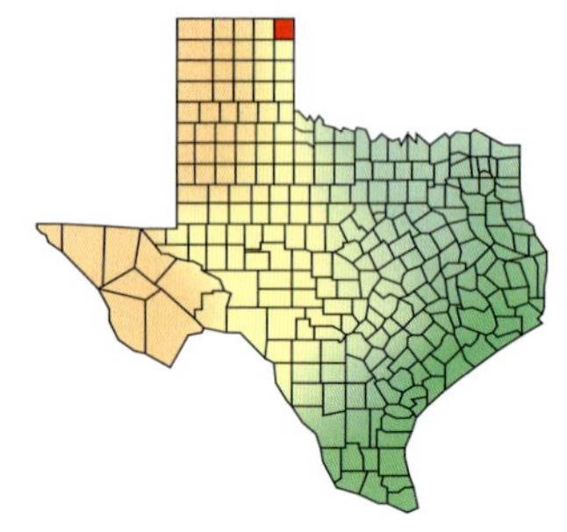

Population: 2,880
Population Change: -5.90%

Race:
White: 55.7%
Black: 2.7%
Hispanic: 38.3%
Asian: 1.0%
Other: 2.6%

Vital Statistics:
Births: 35
Deaths: 33
Marriages: 8
Divorces: 14

2024 Rainfall: 21.85 in.
January Avg. Temp.: 32.7°F
July Avg. Temp.: 80.4°F

Unemployment Rate: 3.2
Per Capita Income: $141,712
Tourism Earnings: $240,000
Avg. Home Value: $128,400

LIVE OAK
COUNTY

Named for live oak trees prominent in the area.

Cities/Towns: George West, Three Rivers, Dinero, Lagarto, Pernitas Point, Whitsett

Land Area (Square Miles): 1,039.70
Elevation (Approx. Feet): 148

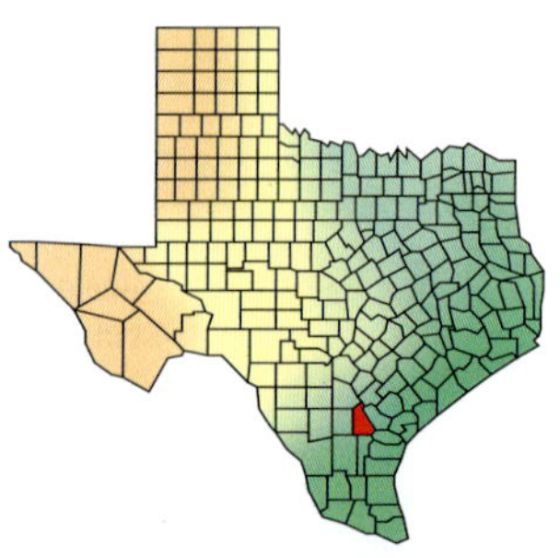

Population: 11,967
Population Change: 5.60%

Race:
White: 48.4%
Black: 7.3%
Hispanic: 42.2%
Asian: 1.3%
Other: 1.9%

Vital Statistics:
Births: 96
Deaths: 134
Marriages: 50
Divorces: 39

2024 Rainfall: 24.6 in.
January Avg. Temp.: 52.4°F
July Avg. Temp.: 84.3°F

Unemployment Rate: 4.8
Per Capita Income: $50,483
Tourism Earnings: $5 million
Avg. Home Value: $142,300

LLANO
COUNTY

Named for the Llano River.

Cities/Towns: Llano, Kingsland, Bluffton, Buchannon Lake Village, Horseshoe Bay, Sunrise Beach Village, Tow

Land Area (Square Miles): 934.06
Elevation (Approx. Feet): 1,089

Population: 23,163
Population Change: 8.90%

Race:
White: 82.1%
Black: 1.5%
Hispanic: 14.1%
Asian: 0.8%
Other: 1.1%

Vital Statistics:
Births: 195
Deaths: 379
Marriages: 77
Divorces: 62

2024 Rainfall: 29.35 in.
January Avg. Temp.: 45.3°F
July Avg. Temp.: 83.6°F

Unemployment Rate: 4.1
Per Capita Income: $72,121
Tourism Earnings: $51.8 million
Avg. Home Value: $322,300

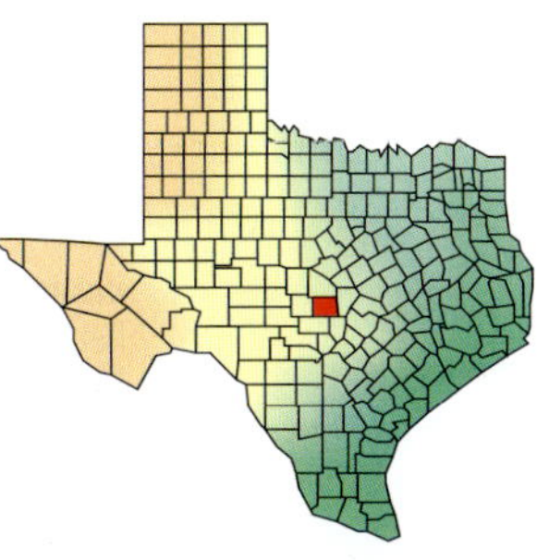

UNSPLASH/J. AMILL SANTIAGO

L

LOVING
COUNTY

Named for cattle rancher Oliver Loving, who developed the Goodnight-Loving Trail alongside Charles Goodnight.

Cities/Towns: Mentone

Land Area (Square Miles): 668.82
Elevation (Approx. Feet): 2,943

Population: 48
Population Change: -26.20%

Race:
White: 81.4%
Black: 7.0%
Hispanic: 11.6%
Asian: 0.0%
Other: 0.0%

Vital Statistics:
Births: *
Deaths: *
Marriages: 0
Divorces: N/A

2024 Rainfall: 4.93 in.
January Avg. Temp.: 44.6°F
July Avg. Temp.: 85.1°F

Unemployment Rate: 1.3
Per Capita Income: $223,419
Tourism Earnings: 0
Avg. Home Value: N/A

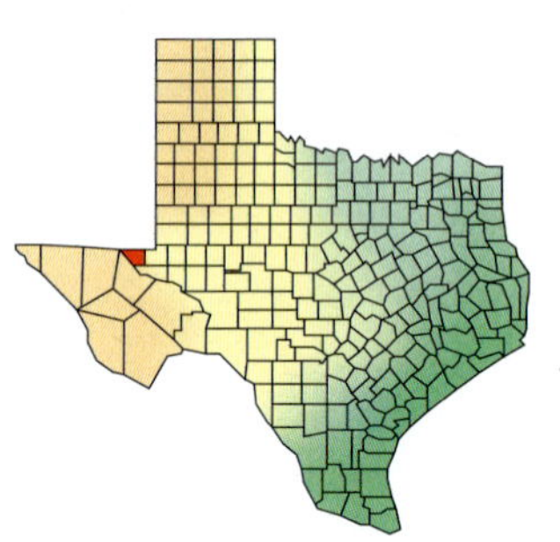

LUBBOCK
COUNTY

Named for Colonel Tom S. Lubbock, an organizer of the Confederate Terry's Rangers.

Cities/Towns: Lubbock, Buffalo Springs, Idalou, New Deal, Ransom Canyon, Shallowater, Slaton, Wolfforth, Abernathy

Land Area (Square Miles): 895.6
Elevation (Approx. Feet): 3,225

Population: 327,394
Population Change: 5.40%

Race:
White: 52.0%
Black: 8.1%
Hispanic: 36.6%
Asian: 2.5%
Other: 1.4%

Vital Statistics:
Births: 4,146
Deaths: 3,116
Marriages: 1,734
Divorces: 747

2024 Rainfall: 19.63 in.
January Avg. Temp.: 37.9°F
July Avg. Temp.: 80.8°F

Unemployment Rate: 3.5
Per Capita Income: $54,313
Tourism Earnings: $413.1 million
Avg. Home Value: $199,600

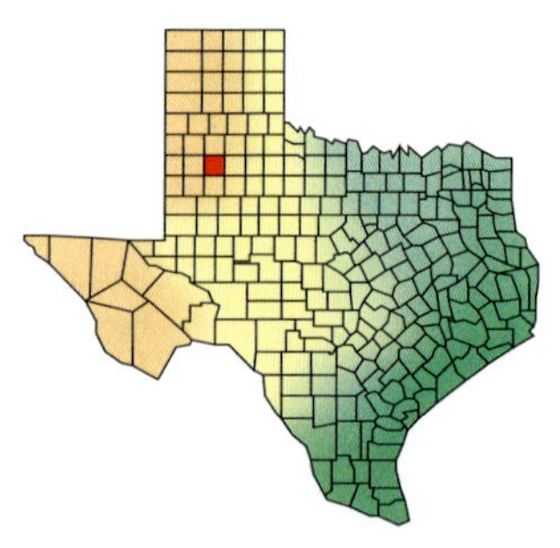

LYNN
COUNTY

Named for Alamo victim W. Lynn.

Cities/Towns: Tahoka, O'Donnell, New Home, Wilson

Land Area (Square Miles): 891.87
Elevation (Approx. Feet): 3,110

Population: 5,952
Population Change: 6.50%

Race:
White: 55.4%
Black: 3.2%
Hispanic: 40.3%
Asian: 0.5%
Other: 2.3%

Vital Statistics:
Births: 93
Deaths: 65
Marriages: 14
Divorces: 9

2024 Rainfall: 17.12 in.
January Avg. Temp.: 38.5°F
July Avg. Temp.: 81.4°F

Unemployment Rate: 3.4
Per Capita Income: $65,814
Tourism Earnings: $520,000
Avg. Home Value: $130,800

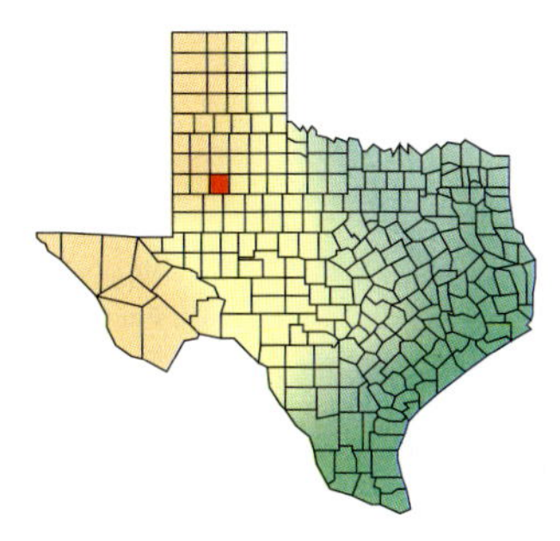

MADISON
COUNTY

Named for U.S. President James Madison.

Cities/Towns: Madisonville, Midway, Normangee

Land Area (Square Miles): 466.07
Elevation (Approx. Feet): 266

Population: 13,877
Population Change: 3.10%

Race:
White: 52.7%
Black: 18.6%
Hispanic: 26.6%
Asian: 1.1%
Other: 1.4%

Vital Statistics:
Births: 172
Deaths: 165
Marriages: 77
Divorces: 13

2024 Rainfall: 63.36 in.
January Avg. Temp.: 45.5°F
July Avg. Temp.: 82.1°F

Unemployment Rate: 4.6
Per Capita Income: $45,527
Tourism Earnings: $2.8 million
Avg. Home Value: $149,100

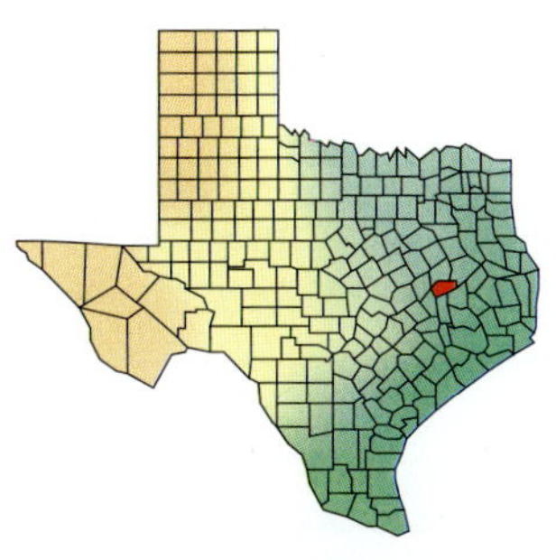

M

MARION
COUNTY

Named for American Revolution General Francis Marion.

Cities/Towns: Jefferson, Lodi, Pine Harbor

Land Area (Square Miles): 380.9
Elevation (Approx. Feet): 220

Population: 9,704
Population Change: -1.40%

Race:
White: 70.6%
Black: 19.7%
Hispanic: 5.4%
Asian: 1.0%
Other:1.4%

Vital Statistics:
Births: 76
Deaths: 187
Marriages: 50
Divorces: 40

2024 Rainfall: 67.2 in.
January Avg. Temp.: 42.6°F
July Avg. Temp.: 81.2°F

Unemployment Rate: 5.7
Per Capita Income: $52,570
Tourism Earnings: $2.6 million
Avg. Home Value: $110,500

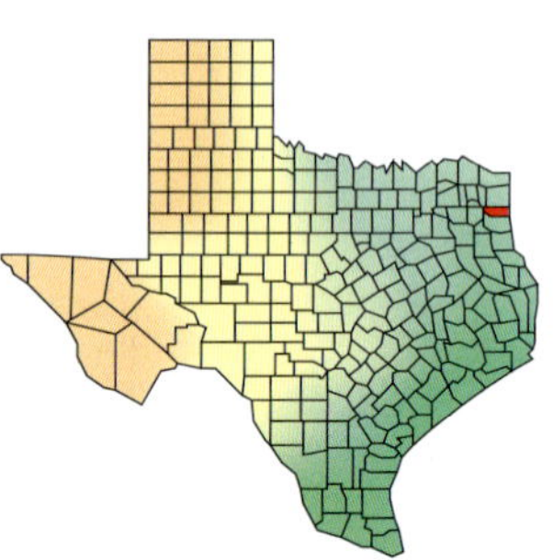

UNSPLASH/JOSHUA J. COTTEN

MARTIN COUNTY

Named for Senator of Republic of Texas Wylie Martin.

Cities/Towns: Stanton, Ackerly, Lenorah, Tarzan

Land Area (Square Miles): 914.90
Elevation (Approx. Feet): 2,832

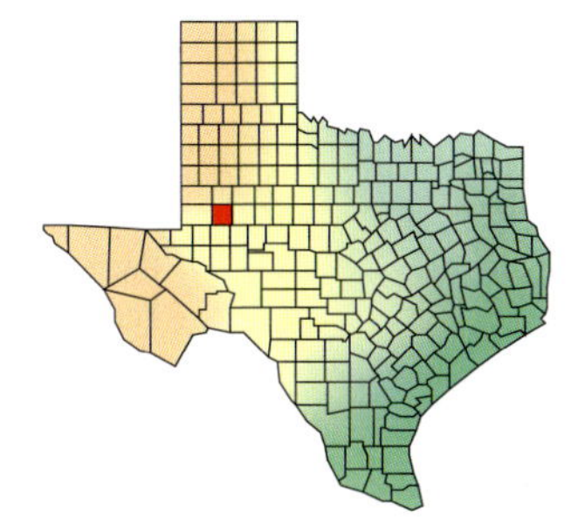

Population: 5,179
Population Change: -1.30%

Race:
White: 49.5%
Black: 3.7%
Hispanic: 45.6%
Asian: 0.7%
Other: 1.8%

Vital Statistics:
Births: 66
Deaths: 43
Marriages: 20
Divorces: 11

2024 Rainfall: 13.9 in.
January Avg. Temp.: 41.3°F
July Avg. Temp.: 82.4°F

Unemployment Rate: 3
Per Capita Income: $107,395
Tourism Earnings: $3.3 million
Avg. Home Value: $162,200

MASON COUNTY

Named for Mexican War victim U.S. Army Lieutenant G.T. Mason.

Cities/Towns: Mason, Art, Fredonia, Pontotoc

Land Area (Square Miles): 928.84
Elevation (Approx. Feet): 1,575

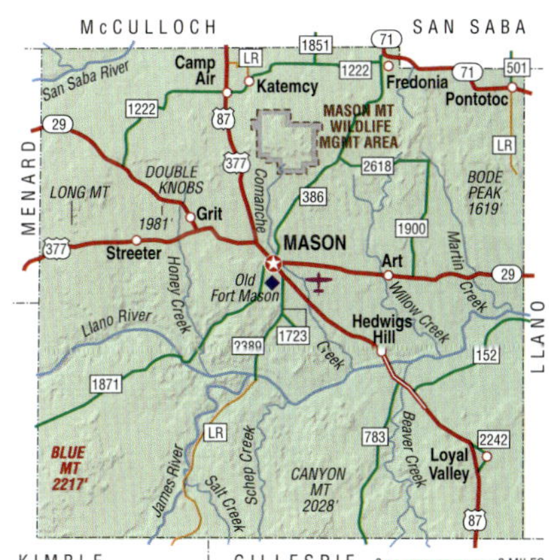

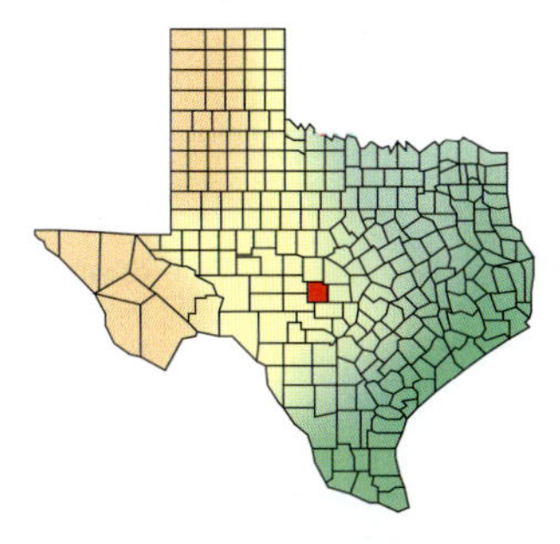

Population: 3,987
Population Change: 0.90%

Race:
White: 74.4%
Black: 1.1%
Hispanic: 23.5%
Asian: 0.3%
Other: 1.2%

Vital Statistics:
Births: 38
Deaths: 81
Marriages: 14
Divorces: 5

2024 Rainfall: 25.03 in.
January Avg. Temp.: 44.3°F
July Avg. Temp.: 83.2°F

Unemployment Rate: 3.8
Per Capita Income: $63,450
Tourism Earnings: $1 million
Avg. Home Value: $274,600

M

MATAGORDA COUNTY

Named for canebrakes that once grew along the coast.

Cities/Towns: Bay City, Palacios, Blessing, Cedar Lane, Collegeport, Elmaton, Markham, Matagorda, Midfield, Pledger, Sargent, Van Vleck, Wadsworth

Land Area (Square Miles): 1,092.92
Elevation (Approx. Feet): 16

Population: 36,391
Population Change: 0.40%

Race:
White: 42.5%
Black: 11.0%
Hispanic: 44.1%
Asian: 2.0%
Other: 1.7%

Vital Statistics:
Births: 475
Deaths: 443
Marriages: 178
Divorces: 66

2024 Rainfall: 52.51 in.
January Avg. Temp.: 51.7°F
July Avg. Temp.: 83.3°F

Unemployment Rate: 5.7
Per Capita Income: $53,090
Tourism Earnings: $27.5 million
Avg. Home Value: $162,200

MAVERICK COUNTY

Named for lawyer, politician, and signer of the Texas Declaration of Independence Samuel A. Maverick.

Cities/Towns: Eagle Pass, Chula Vista, Eldson Road, Las Quintas Fronterizas, Rosita, Elm Creek, Fabrica, Seco Mines, Siesta Acres, Quemado

Land Area (Square Miles): 1,279.47
Elevation (Approx. Feet): 814

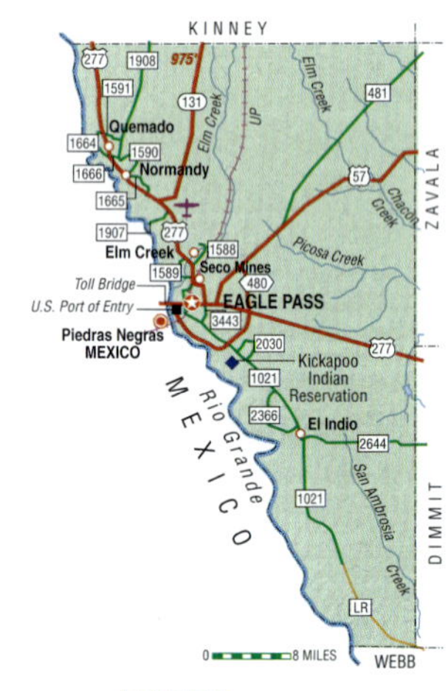

Population: 58,829
Population Change: 1.60%

Race:
White: 2.9%
Black: 1.0%
Hispanic: 94.7%
Asian: 0.6%
Other: 2.0%

Vital Statistics:
Births: 991
Deaths: 546
Marriages: 385
Divorces: N/A

2024 Rainfall: 13.47 in.
January Avg. Temp.: 51.1°F
July Avg. Temp.: 87.6°F

Unemployment Rate: 7.9
Per Capita Income: $41,009
Tourism Earnings: $19.1 million
Avg. Home Value: $151,500

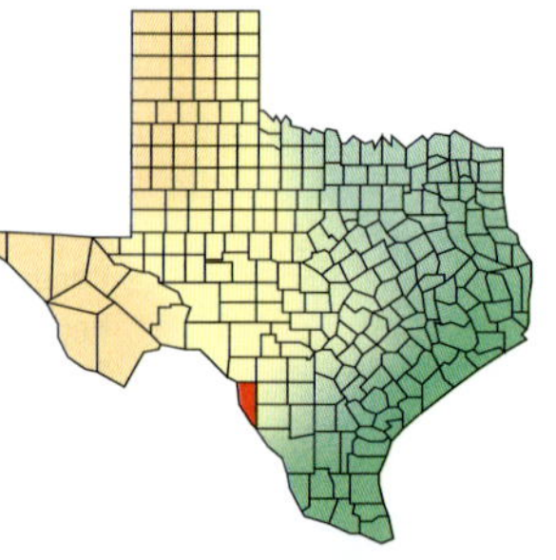

MCCULLOCH
COUNTY

Named for San Jacinto Veteran General Ben McCulloch.

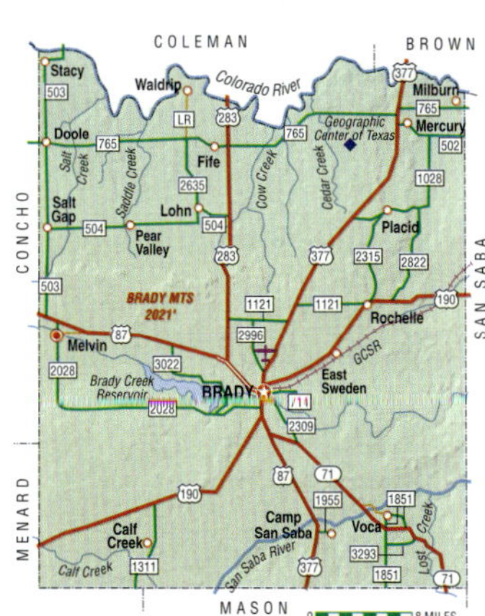

Cities/Towns: Brady, Doole, Lohn, Melvin, Mercury, Rochelle, Voca

Land Area (Square Miles): 1,065.60
Elevation (Approx. Feet): 1,782

Population: 7,448
Population Change: -2.40%

Race:
White: 64.8%
Black: 3.3%
Hispanic: 30.2%
Asian: 0.8%
Other: 1.6%

Vital Statistics:
Births: 99
Deaths: 144
Marriages: 61
Divorces: 28

2024 Rainfall: 24.01 in.
January Avg. Temp.: 44°F
July Avg. Temp.: 83.2°F

Unemployment Rate: 4.4
Per Capita Income: $53,630
Tourism Earnings: $2.8 million
Avg. Home Value: $104,400

MCLENNAN
COUNTY

Named for settler Neil McLennan Sr.

Cities/Towns: Waco, Hewitt, West, Axtell, Bellmead, Beverly Hills, Bruceville-Eddy, Gholson, Hallsburg, Lacy-Lakeview, Leroy, Lorena, Mart, McGregor, Moody, Riesel, Robinson, Ross, Woodway, Golinda, Valley Mills

Land Area (Square Miles): 1,036.66
Elevation (Approx. Feet): 522

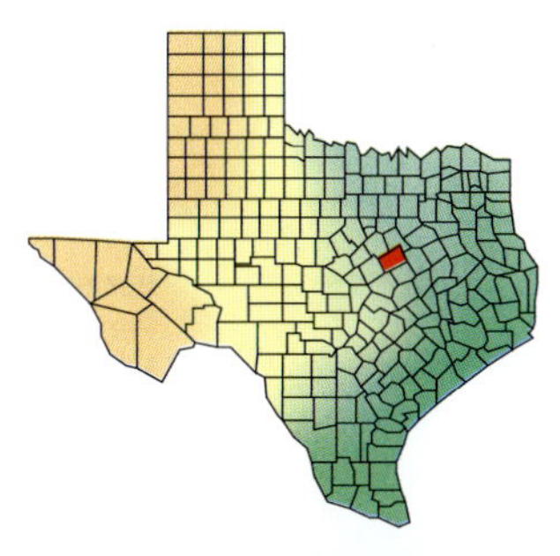

Population: 270,358
Population Change: 3.80%

Race:
White: 54.8%
Black: 15.0%
Hispanic: 27.2%
Asian: 2.0%
Other: 1.3%

Vital Statistics:
Births: 3,328
Deaths: 2,652
Marriages: 1,376
Divorces: 778

2024 Rainfall: 41.77 in.
January Avg. Temp.: 43.8°F
July Avg. Temp.: 82.8°F

Unemployment Rate: 3.8
Per Capita Income: $53,941
Tourism Earnings: $183.5 million
Avg. Home Value: $219,200

M

MCMULLEN
COUNTY

Named for Nueces River pioneer-empresario John McMullen.

Cities/Towns: Tilden, Calliham

Land Area (Square Miles): 1,139.80
Elevation (Approx. Feet): 295

Population: 565
Population Change: -5.70%

Race:
White: 54.8%
Black: 2.8%
Hispanic: 39.4%
Asian: 1.4%
Other: 0.2%

Vital Statistics:
Births: 11
Deaths: 12
Marriages: 3
Divorces: N/A

2024 Rainfall: 21.64 in.
January Avg. Temp.: 52.7°F
July Avg. Temp.: 85.3°F

Unemployment Rate: 6.1
Per Capita Income: $117,599
Tourism Earnings: $530,000
Avg. Home Value: $108,800

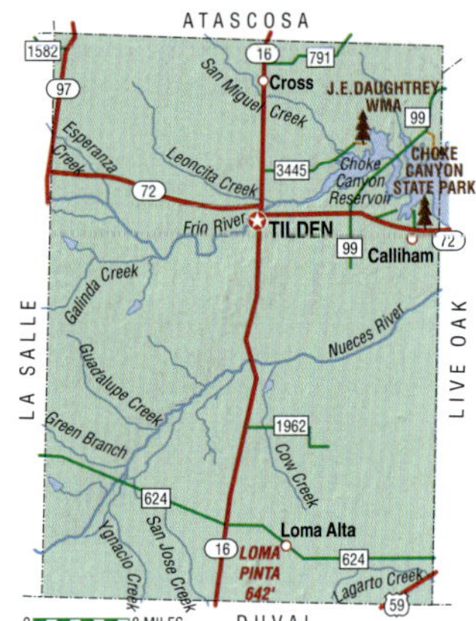

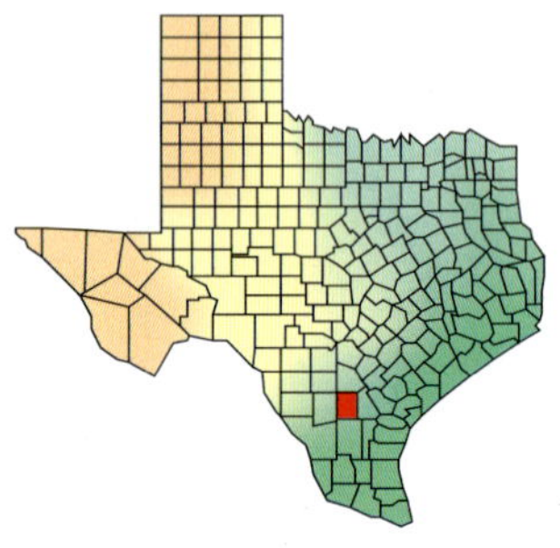

MEDINA
COUNTY

Named for the Medina River.

Cities/Towns: Hondo, Castroville, Devine, D'Hanis, La Coste, Natalia, Riomedina, Yancey, Lytle

Land Area (Square Miles): 1,325.36
Elevation (Approx. Feet): 863

Population: 55,619
Population Change: 9.40%

Race:
White: 42.2%
Black: 4.2%
Hispanic: 52.1%
Asian: 0.9%
Other: 1.4%

Vital Statistics:
Births: 544
Deaths: 526
Marriages: 209
Divorces: 142

2024 Rainfall: 16.98 in.
January Avg. Temp.: 48.6°F
July Avg. Temp.: 84.7°F

Unemployment Rate: 4.1
Per Capita Income: $52,854
Tourism Earnings: $11.1 million
Avg. Home Value: $220,000

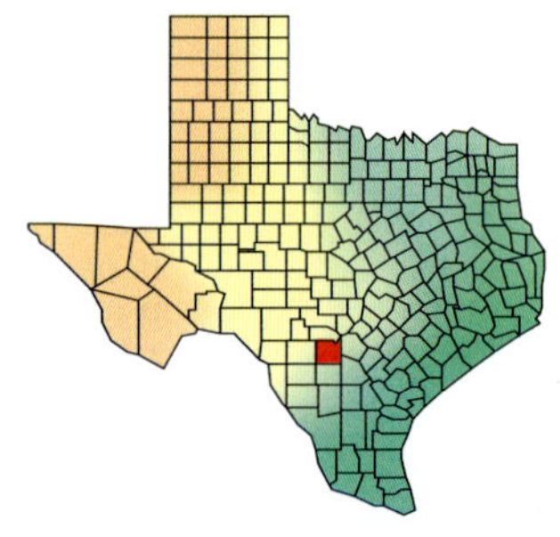

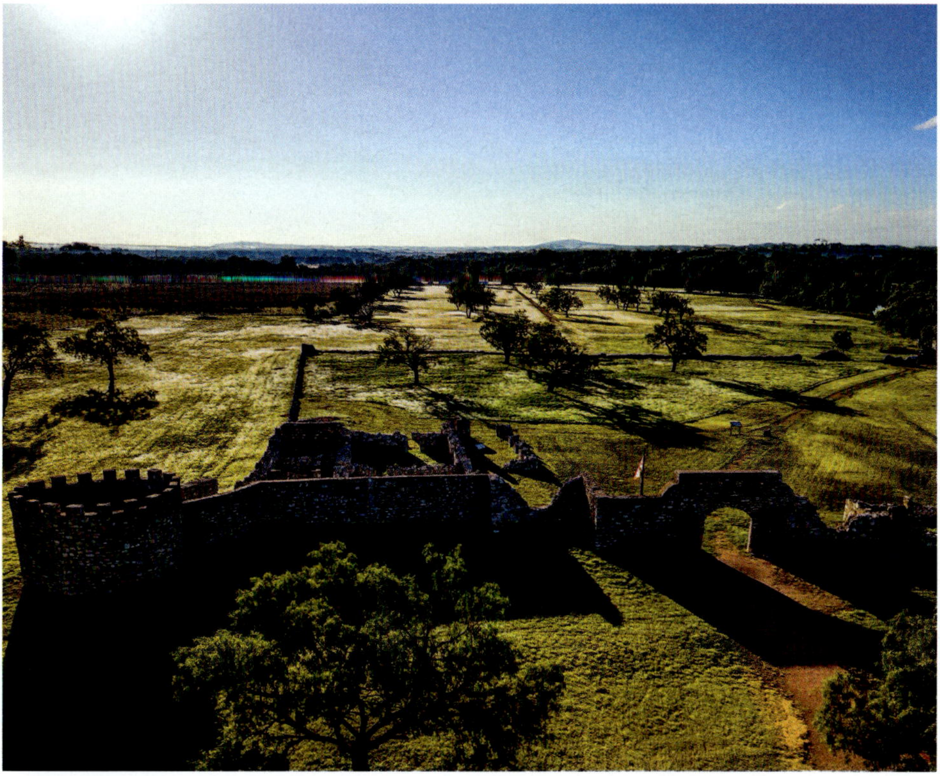

MENARD
COUNTY

Named for Galveston's co-founder, Michel B. Menard.

Cities/Towns: Menard, Fort McKavett, Hext

Land Area (Square Miles): 902.03
Elevation (Approx. Feet): 1,972

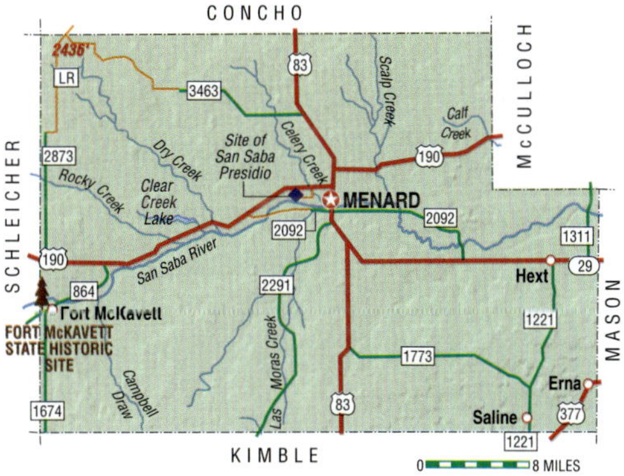

Population: 1,911
Population Change: -2.70%

Race:
White: 62.1%
Black: 2.7%
Hispanic: 33.7%
Asian: 0.4%
Other: 1.9%

Vital Statistics:
Births: 12
Deaths: 35
Marriages: 1
Divorces: 4

2024 Rainfall: 21.32 in.
January Avg. Temp.: 43.2°F
July Avg. Temp.: 81.8°F

Unemployment Rate: 3.3
Per Capita Income: $52,791
Tourism Earnings: $380,000
Avg. Home Value: $105,300

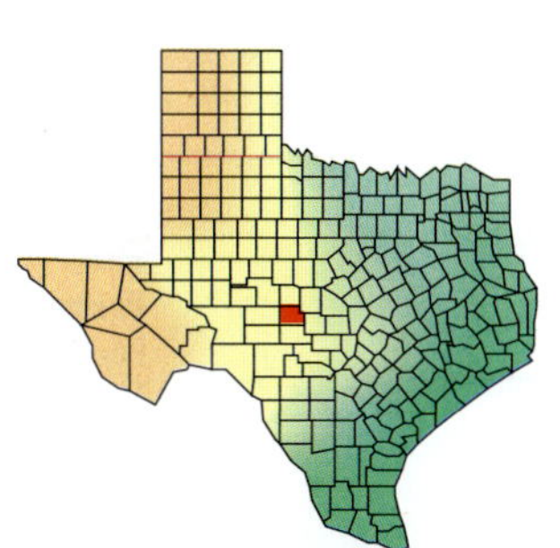

MIDLAND COUNTY

Named for the halfway location on the Texas and Pacific Railway between El Paso and Fort Worth.

Cities/Towns: Midland, Odessa

Land Area (Square Miles): 900.36
Elevation (Approx. Feet): 2,782

Population: 183,587
Population Change: 7.80%

Race:
White: 42.2%
Black: 7.5%
Hispanic: 47.1%
Asian: 2.3%
Other: 1.3%

Vital Statistics:
Births: 2,980
Deaths: 1,337
Marriages: 1,228
Divorces: 719

2024 Rainfall: 11.73 in.
January Avg. Temp.: 43°F
July Avg. Temp.: 82.9°F

Unemployment Rate: 2.9
Per Capita Income: $114,532
Tourism Earnings: $150.4 million
Avg. Home Value: $293,000

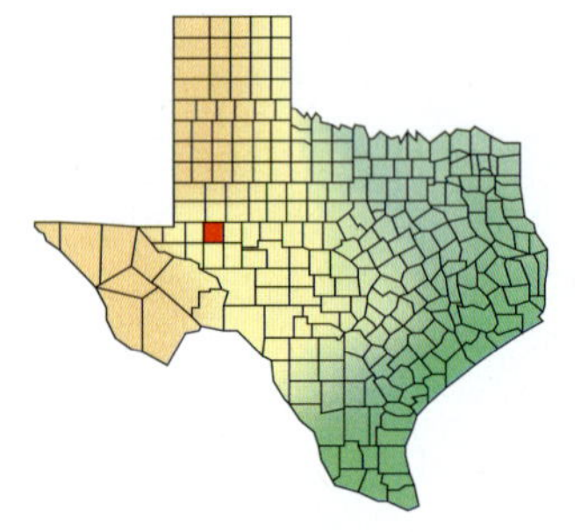

MILAM COUNTY

Named for Texas Revolution soldier Ben Milam.

Cities/Towns: Cameron, Rockdale, Buckholts, Davilla, Gause, Milano, Thorndale

Land Area (Square Miles): 1,016.36
Elevation (Approx. Feet): 384

Population: 26,159
Population Change: 5.70%

Race:
White: 62.8%
Black: 9.3%
Hispanic: 26.0%
Asian: 0.9%
Other: 1.5%

Vital Statistics:
Births: 311
Deaths: 359
Marriages: 90
Divorces: 52

2024 Rainfall: 39.12 in.
January Avg. Temp.: 45.9°F
July Avg. Temp.: 82.8°F

Unemployment Rate: 4.3
Per Capita Income: $51,236
Tourism Earnings: $10.2 million
Avg. Home Value: $168,900

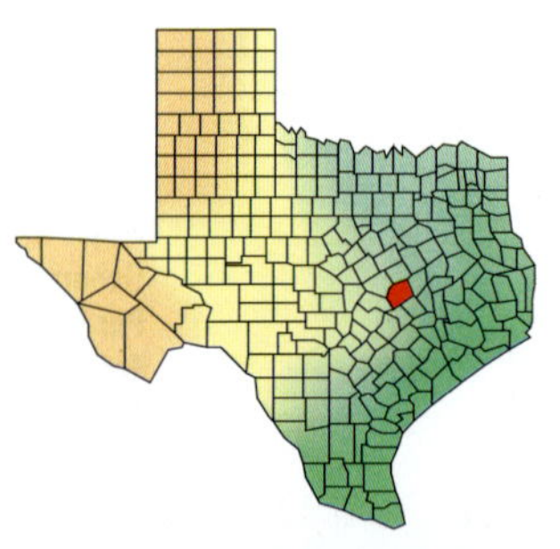

COURTESY OF DISCOVER ODESSA

M

MILLS COUNTY

Named for pioneer jurist John T. Mills.

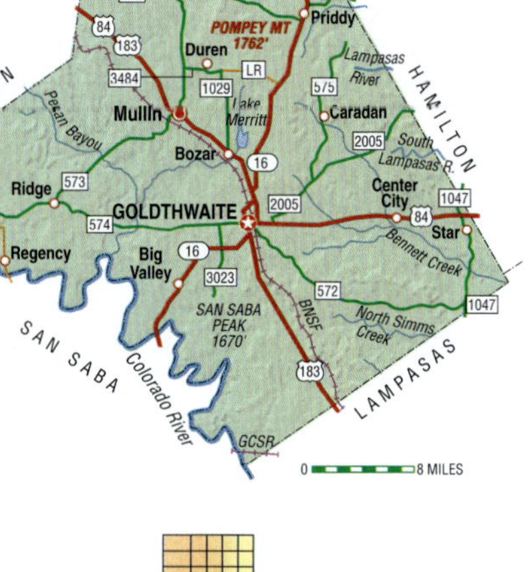

Cities/Towns: Goldthwaite, Mullin, Priddy, Star

Land Area (Square Miles): 748.23
Elevation (Approx. Feet): 1,549

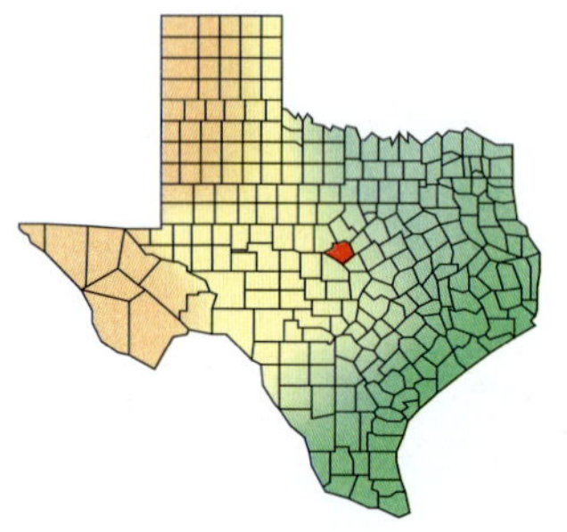

Population: 4,563
Population Change: 2.40%

Race:
White: 78.6%
Black: 1.8%
Hispanic: 17.4%
Asian: 0.9%
Other: 1.3%

Vital Statistics:
Births: 34
Deaths: 82
Marriages: 18
Divorces: 17

2024 Rainfall: 29.16 in.
January Avg. Temp.: 42.9°F
July Avg. Temp.: 83.1°F

Unemployment Rate: 3.3
Per Capita Income: $58,522
Tourism Earnings: $600,000
Avg. Home Value: $200,200

MITCHELL COUNTY

Named for pioneer brothers Asa and Eli Mitchell.

Cities/Towns: Colorado City, Loraine, Westbrook, Lake Colorado City

Land Area (Square Miles): 911.09
Elevation (Approx. Feet): 2,077

Population: 8,968
Population Change: -0.30%

Race:
White: 47.3%
Black: 12.6%
Hispanic: 38.9%
Asian: 1.0%
Other: 2.0%

Vital Statistics:
Births: 77
Deaths: 93
Marriages: 33
Divorces: 28

2024 Rainfall: 18.92 in.
January Avg. Temp.: 41.2°F
July Avg. Temp.: 84.4°F

Unemployment Rate: 3.3
Per Capita Income: $40,541
Tourism Earnings: $2.5 million
Avg. Home Value: $85,700

MONTAGUE
COUNTY

Named for pioneer Daniel Montague.

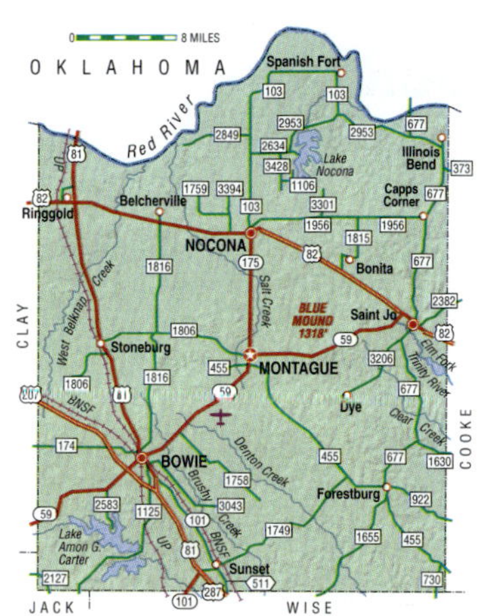

Cities/Towns: Montague, Bowie, Nocona, Ringgold, Saint Jo, Sunset

Land Area (Square Miles): 930.91
Elevation (Approx. Feet): 1,030

Population: 21,890
Population Change: 9.40%

Race:
White: 83.5%
Black: 1.1%
Hispanic: 12.4%
Asian: 0.6%
Other: 1.6%

Vital Statistics:
Births: 218
Deaths: 334
Marriages: 88
Divorces: 42

2024 Rainfall: 42.27 in.
January Avg. Temp.: 38.7°F
July Avg. Temp.: 83.4°F

Unemployment Rate: 4.3
Per Capita Income: $50,251
Tourism Earnings: $9.3 million
Avg. Home Value: $189,400

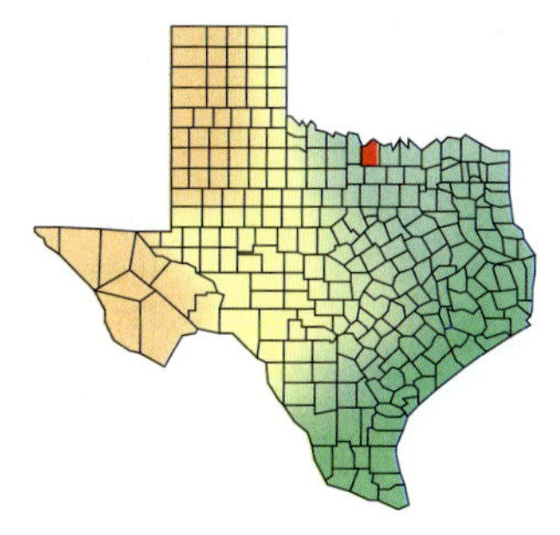

MONTGOMERY
COUNTY

Named for American Revolution General Richard Montgomery.

Cities/Towns: Conroe, The Woodlands, Cut and Shoot, Dobbin, Grangerland, Magnolia, Montgomory, Oak Ridge North, Panorama Village, Patton Village, Pinehurst, Porter Heights, Roman Forest, Shenandoah, Splendora, Stagecoach, Willis, Woodbranch, Woodloch, Houston

Land Area (Square Miles): 1,042.18
Elevation (Approx. Feet): 141

Population: 749,613
Population Change: 20.80%

Race:
White: 58.8%
Black: 7.8%
Hispanic: 28.3%
Asian: 3.8%
Other: 1.2%

Vital Statistics:
Births: 8,474
Deaths: 4,875
Marriages: 2,825
Divorces: 2,041

2024 Rainfall: 65.56 in.
January Avg. Temp.: 49.2°F
July Avg. Temp.: 82.4°F

Unemployment Rate: 4
Per Capita Income: $78,644
Tourism Earnings: $465.3 million
Avg. Home Value: $317,500

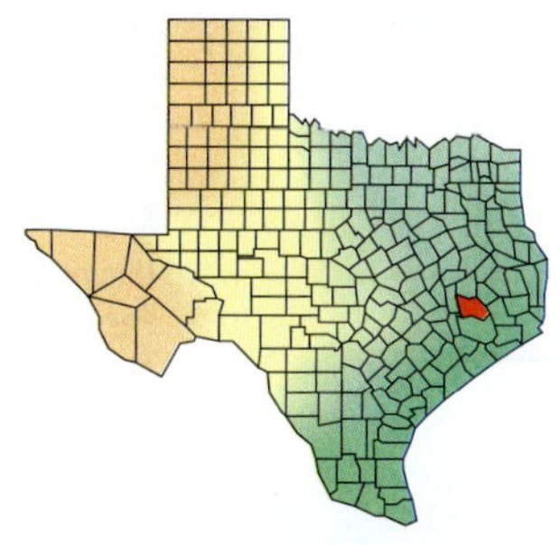

M

MOORE COUNTY

Named for commander-in-chief of the Navy of Republic of Texas E.W. Moore.

Cities/Towns: Dumas, Cactus, Sunray

Land Area (Square Miles): 899.7
Elevation (Approx. Feet): 3,550

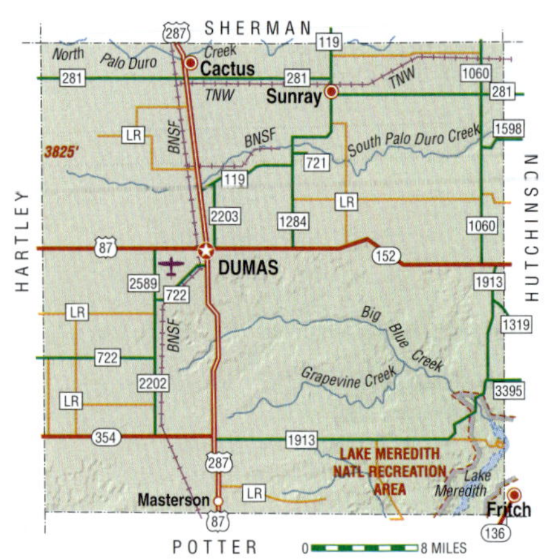

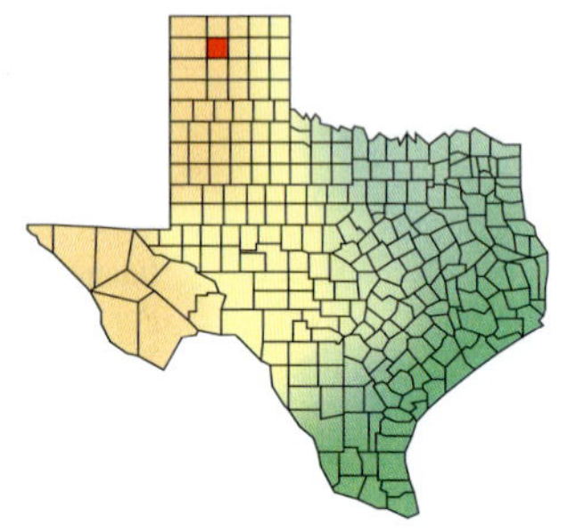

Population: 21,872
Population Change: 2.40%

Race:
White: 28.0%
Black: 5.5%
Hispanic: 61.5%
Asian: 4.3%
Other: 2.3%

Vital Statistics:
Births: 402
Deaths: 164
Marriages: 113
Divorces: 87

2024 Rainfall: 15.8 in.
January Avg. Temp.: 33.7°F
July Avg. Temp.: 80.4°F

Unemployment Rate: 3
Per Capita Income: $61,988
Tourism Earnings: $7.4 million
Avg. Home Value: $135,400

MORRIS COUNTY

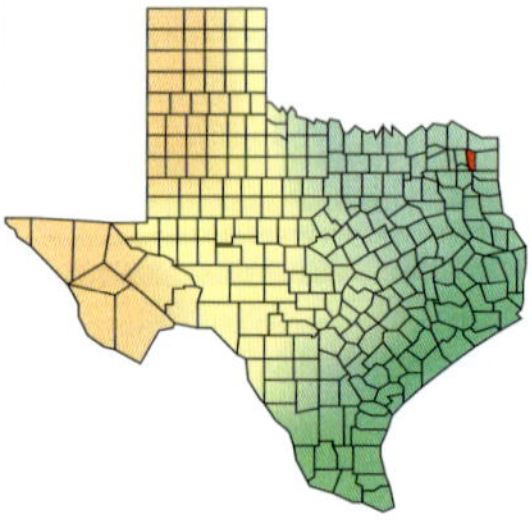

Named for legislator and jurist W.W. Morris.

Cities/Towns: Dangerfield, Cason, Lone Star, Naples, Omaha

Land Area (Square Miles): 251.99
Elevation (Approx. Feet): 367

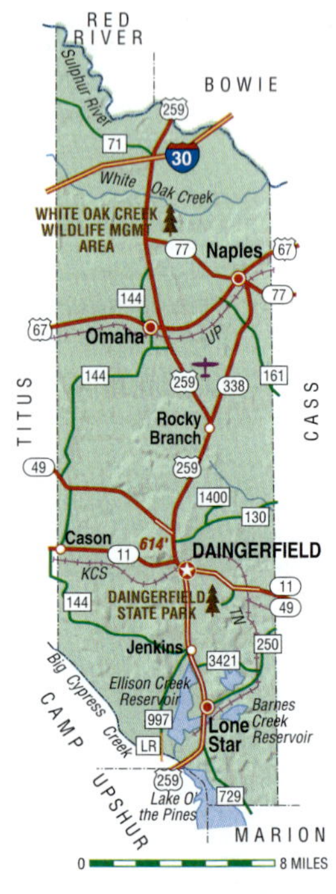

Population: 12,184
Population Change: 1.80%

Race:
White: 62.6%
Black: 22.1%
Hispanic: 11.6%
Asian: 0.9%
Other: 1.7%

Vital Statistics:
Births: 140
Deaths: 219
Marriages: 53
Divorces: 7

2024 Rainfall: 57.37 in.
January Avg. Temp.: 42.3°F
July Avg. Temp.: 82°F

Unemployment Rate: 5.5
Per Capita Income: $50,538
Tourism Earnings: $1.4 million
Avg. Home Value: $110,200

MOTLEY
COUNTY

Named for Dr. J.W. Mottley, a signer of the Texas Declaration of Independence.

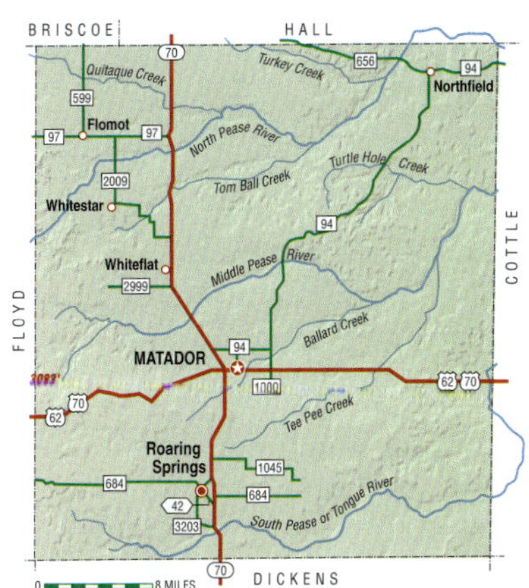

Cities/Towns: Matador, Flomot, Roaring Springs

Land Area (Square Miles): 989.57
Elevation (Approx. Feet): 2,346

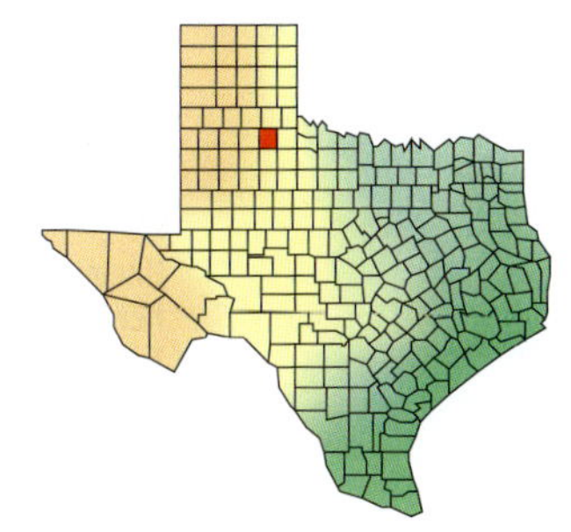

Population: 1,015
Population Change: -4.60%

Race:
White: 77.5%
Black: 3.0%
Hispanic: 16.1%
Asian: 0.2%
Other: 2.1%

Vital Statistics:
Births: 11
Deaths: 22
Marriages: 5
Divorces: 2

2024 Rainfall: 23.01 in.
January Avg. Temp.: 37.3°F
July Avg. Temp.: 83.3°F

Unemployment Rate: 3.9
Per Capita Income: $55,185
Tourism Earnings: $120,000
Avg. Home Value: $81,100

NACOGDOCHES
COUNTY

Named for the Nacogdoches tribe of the Caddo community.

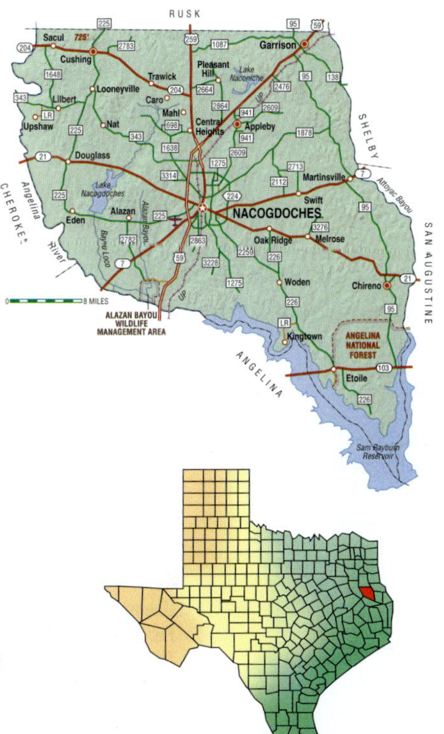

Cities/Towns: Nacogdoches, Appleby, Cireno, Cushing, Douglass, Etoile, Garrison, Martinsville, Redfield, Woden

Land Area (Square Miles): 946.32
Elevation (Approx. Feet): 404

Population: 65,728
Population Change: 1.60%

Race:
White: 58.1%
Black: 17.3%
Hispanic: 21.8%
Asian: 1.4%
Other: 1.0%

Vital Statistics:
Births: 797
Deaths: 703
Marriages: 323
Divorces: 155

2024 Rainfall: 75.47 in.
January Avg. Temp.: 44.3°F
July Avg. Temp.: 81.3°F

Unemployment Rate: 4.3
Per Capita Income: $50,541
Tourism Earnings: $27 million
Avg. Home Value: $158,200

NAVARRO
COUNTY

Named for Republic of Texas leader José Antonio Navarro.

Cities/Towns: Corsicana, Angus, Barry, Blooming Grove, Dawson, Emhouse, Eureka, Frost, Goodlow, Kerens, Mildred, Navarro, Oak Valley, Powell, Purdon, Retreat, Rice, Richland

Land Area (Square Miles): 1,009.70
Elevation (Approx. Feet): 436

Population: 56,533
Population Change: 7.40%

Race:
White: 51.1%
Black: 12.6%
Hispanic: 32.8%
Asian: 1.0%
Other: 1.7%

Vital Statistics:
Births: 731
Deaths: 612
Marriages: 220
Divorces: 77

2024 Rainfall: 44.37 in.
January Avg. Temp.: 43.3°F
July Avg. Temp.: 83.4°F

Unemployment Rate: 4.5
Per Capita Income: $46,891
Tourism Earnings: $16.5 million
Avg. Home Value: $159,900

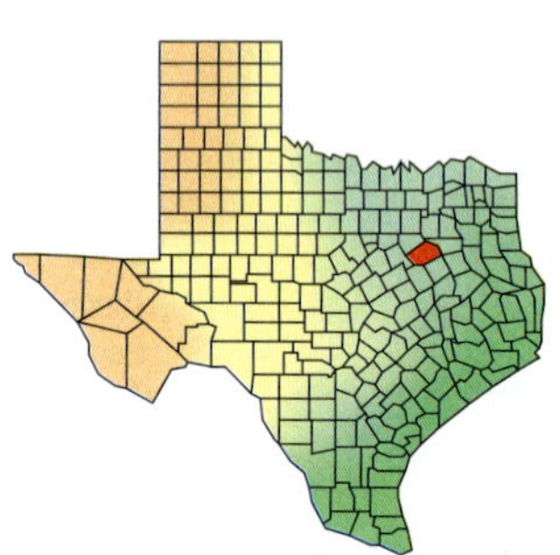

NEWTON
COUNTY

Named for American Revolutionary soldier John Newton.

Cities/Towns: Newton, Deweyville, Bon Wier, Burkeville, Call, South Toledo Bend, Wiergate

Land Area (Square Miles): 933.68
Elevation (Approx. Feet): 135

Population: 11,908
Population Change: -2.50%

Race:
White: 75.8%
Black: 16.8%
Hispanic: 3.9%
Asian: 0.6%
Other: 1.1%

Vital Statistics:
Births: 113
Deaths: 187
Marriages: 38
Divorces: 32

2024 Rainfall: 76.89 in.
January Avg. Temp.: 46.7°F
July Avg. Temp.: 81.4°F

Unemployment Rate: 6.5
Per Capita Income: $44,866
Tourism Earnings: $890,000
Avg. Home Value: $83,100

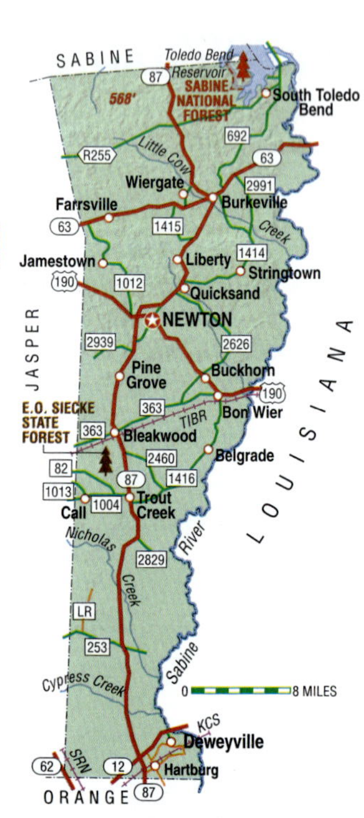

NOLAN
COUNTY

Named for adventurer Philip Nolan, who was killed near Waco.

Cities/Towns: Sweetwater, Blackwell, Maryneal, Nolan, Roscoe

Land Area (Square Miles): 912
Elevation (Approx. Feet): 2,599

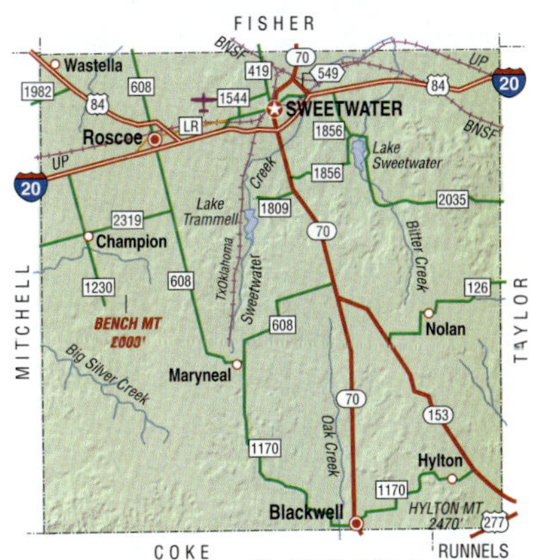

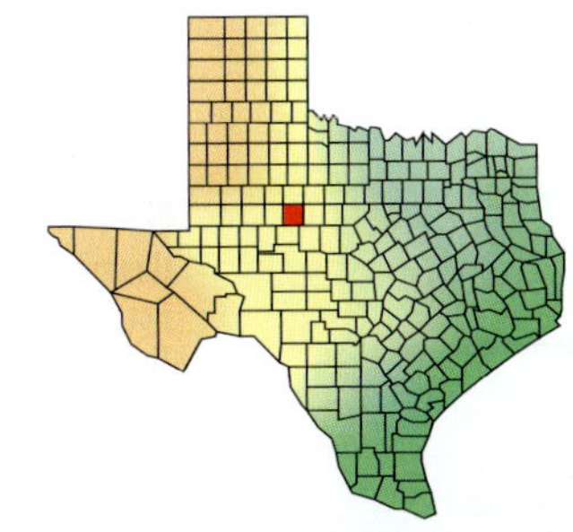

Population: 14,182
Population Change: -3.80%

Race:
White: 54.9%
Black: 5.5%
Hispanic: 37.9%
Asian: 0.9%
Other: 1.4%

Vital Statistics:
Births: 176
Deaths: 201
Marriages: 80
Divorces: 9

2024 Rainfall: 23.37 in.
January Avg. Temp.: 41.5°F
July Avg. Temp.: 83.2°F

Unemployment Rate: 3.8
Per Capita Income: $56,320
Tourism Earnings: $10.5 million
Avg. Home Value: $98,300

UNSPLASH/DUNCAN SANCHEZ

O

NUECES
COUNTY

Named for the Nueces River.

Cities/Towns: Corpus Christi, Port Aransas, Robstown, Agua Dulce, Banquete, Bishop, Chapman Ranch, Driscoll, La Paloma-Lost Creek, North San Pedro, Petronila, Rancho Banquete, Sandy Hollow-Escondidas, Spring Gardens, Tierra Grande, Tierra Verde

Land Area (Square Miles): 839.07
Elevation (Approx. Feet): 43

Population: 353,125
Population Change: -0.10%

Race:
White: 29.6%
Black: 4.6%
Hispanic: 62.9%
Asian: 2.5%
Other: 1.1%

Vital Statistics:
Births: 4,170
Deaths: 3,616
Marriages: 1,670
Divorces: 382

2024 Rainfall: 26.25 in.
January Avg. Temp.: 55.6°F
July Avg. Temp.: 85.2°F

Unemployment Rate: 4.2
Per Capita Income: $56,833
Tourism Earnings: $506.3 million
Avg. Home Value: $194,700

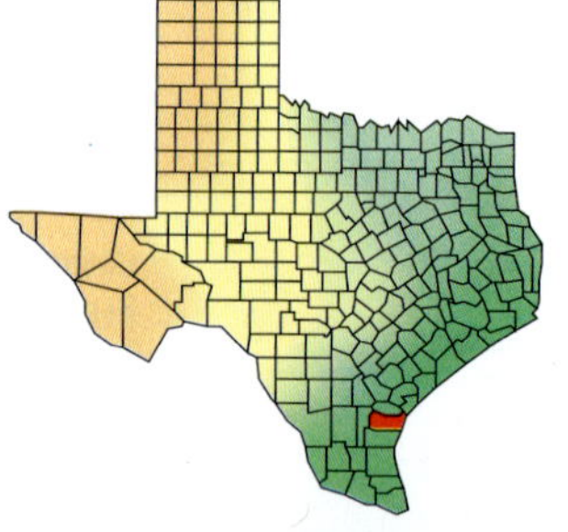

UNSPLASH/OBED ESQUIVEL PICKETT

O

OCHILTREE
COUNTY

Named for Republic of Texas leader W.B. Ochiltree.

Cities/Towns: Perryton, Farnsworth, Waka

Land Area (Square Miles): 917.69
Elevation (Approx. Feet): 2,927

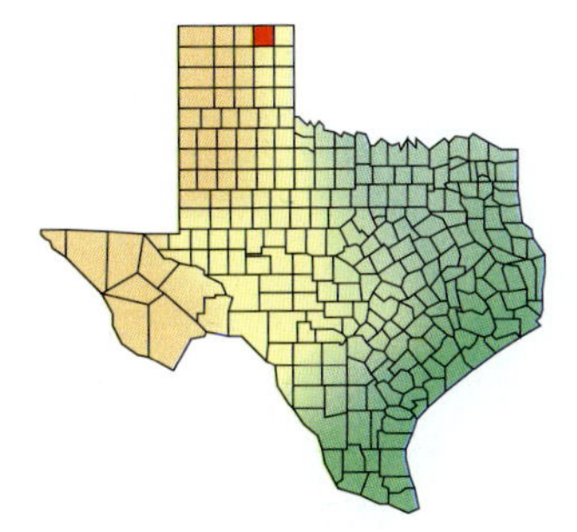

Population: 9,717
Population Change: -3.00%

Race:
White: 39.4%
Black: 1.5%
Hispanic: 57.8%
Asian: 0.7%
Other: 2.5%

Vital Statistics:
Births: 104
Deaths: 73
Marriages: 49
Divorces: 32

2024 Rainfall: 23.36 in.
January Avg. Temp.: 33.3°F
July Avg. Temp.: 80.4°F

Unemployment Rate: 3.2
Per Capita Income: $72,100
Tourism Earnings: $3.3 million
Avg. Home Value: $137,200

OLDHAM
COUNTY

Named for editor and Confederate senator W.S. Oldham.

Cities/Towns: Vega, Adrian, Wildorado, Cal Farley's Boys Ranch

Land Area (Square Miles): 1,500.52
Elevation (Approx. Feet): 3,767

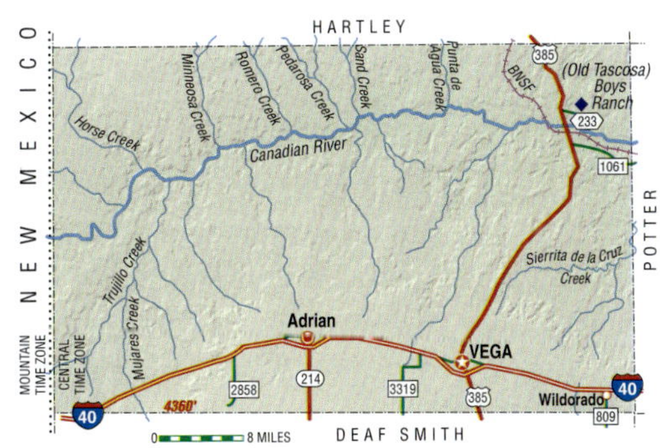

Population: 1,823
Population Change: 3.70%

Race:
White: 71.2%
Black: 3.8%
Hispanic: 20.6%
Asian: 2.3%
Other: 2.0%

Vital Statistics:
Births: 27
Deaths: 21
Marriages: 3
Divorces: 2

2024 Rainfall: 15.91 in.
January Avg. Temp.: 33.9°F
July Avg. Temp.: 79.6°F

Unemployment Rate: 3.4
Per Capita Income: $89,268
Tourism Earnings: $980,000
Avg. Home Value: $144,800

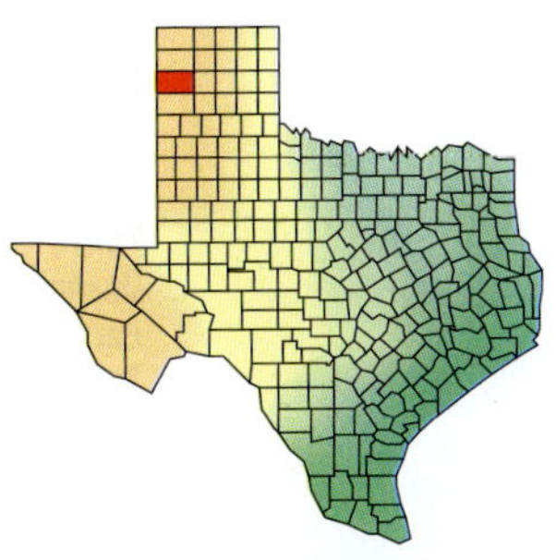

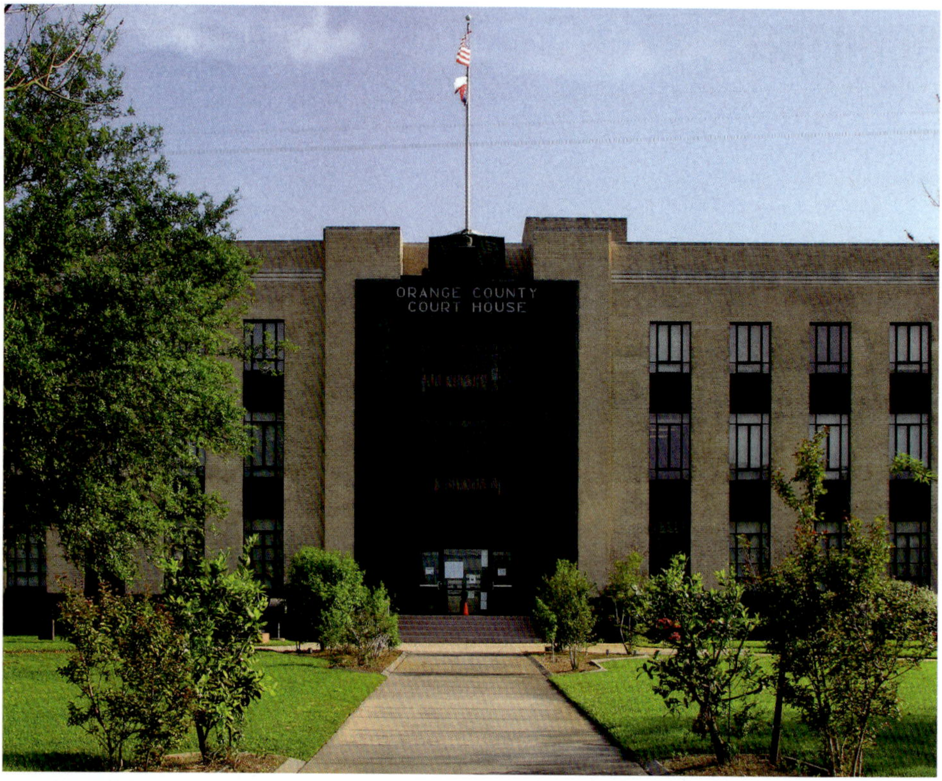

P

ORANGE
COUNTY

Named for an orange grove planted by settlers.

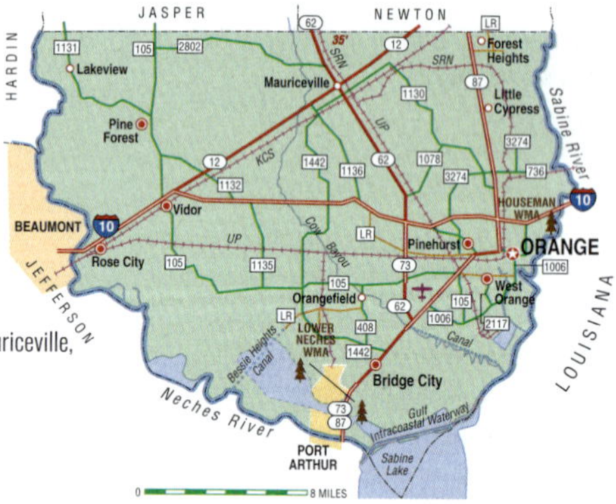

Cities/Towns: Orange, Bridge City, Vidor, Forest Heights, Little Cypress, Mauriceville, Orangefield, Pine Forest, Pinehurst, Rose City, West Orange

Land Area (Square Miles): 333.79
Elevation (Approx. Feet): 16

Population: 86,115
Population Change: 1.50%

Race:
White: 77.7%
Black: 9.4%
Hispanic: 10.0%
Asian: 1.2%
Other: 0.9%

Vital Statistics:
Births: 1,038
Deaths: 1,039
Marriages: 382
Divorces: 259

2024 Rainfall: 68.5 in.
January Avg. Temp.: 49.4°F
July Avg. Temp.: 82.1°F

Unemployment Rate: 4.7
Per Capita Income: $51,982
Tourism Earnings: $40.4 million
Avg. Home Value: $163,400

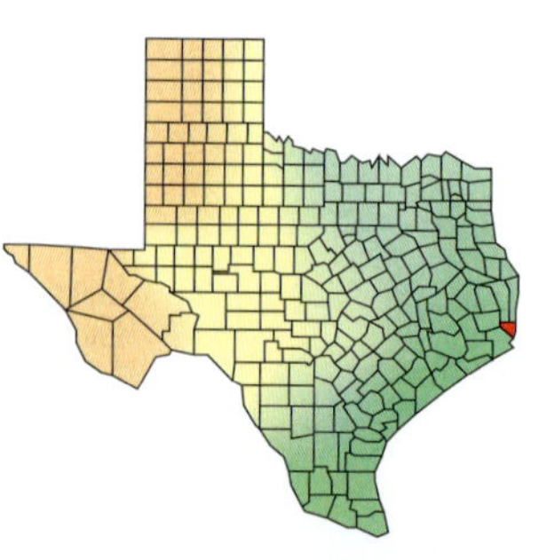

PALO PINTO
COUNTY

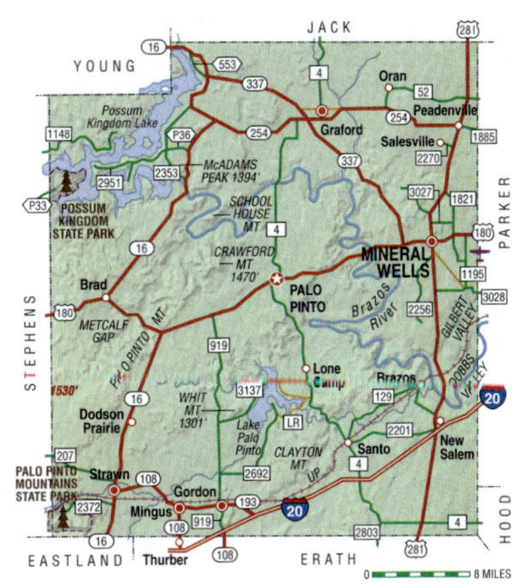

Named for the Palo Pinto Creek.

Cities/Towns: Palo Pinto, Mineral Wells, Gordon, Graford, Mingus, Santo, Strawn

Land Area (Square Miles): 952.55
Elevation (Approx. Feet): 1,175

Population: 30,231
Population Change: 6.40%

Race:
White: 74.0%
Black: 2.7%
Hispanic: 20.8%
Asian:0.9%
Other:1.3%

Vital Statistics:
Births: 351
Deaths: 405
Marriages: 131
Divorces: 142

2024 Rainfall: 34.85 in.
January Avg. Temp.: 41°F
July Avg. Temp.: 84.1°F

Unemployment Rate: 4
Per Capita Income: $54,995
Tourism Earnings: $18.6 million
Avg. Home Value: $167,300

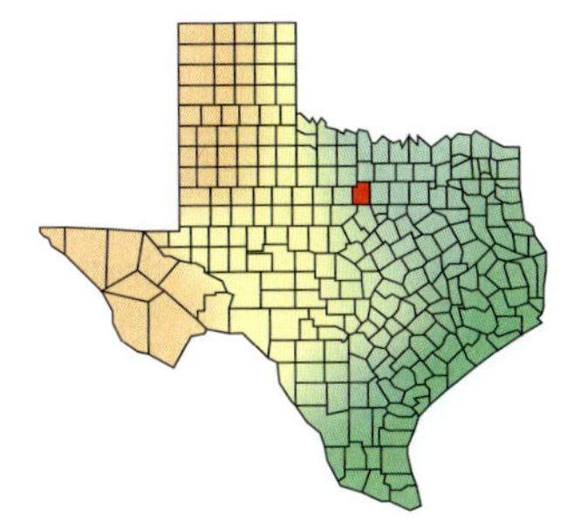

PANOLA
COUNTY

Named for the Cherokee word for cotton.

Cities/Towns: Carthage, Beckville, Clayton, DeBerry, Garu, Long Branch, Panola

Land Area (Square Miles): 811.36
Elevation (Approx. Feet): 233

Population: 23,022
Population Change: 2.30%

Race:
White: 71.5%
Black: 15.4%
Hispanic: 10.6%
Asian: 0.6%
Other: 1.0%

Vital Statistics:
Births: 262
Deaths: 347
Marriages: 114
Divorces: 82

2024 Rainfall: 73.55 in.
January Avg. Temp.: 43.9°F
July Avg. Temp.: 81.3°F

Unemployment Rate: 5.2
Per Capita Income: $60,434
Tourism Earnings: $4.2 million
Avg. Home Value: $146,000

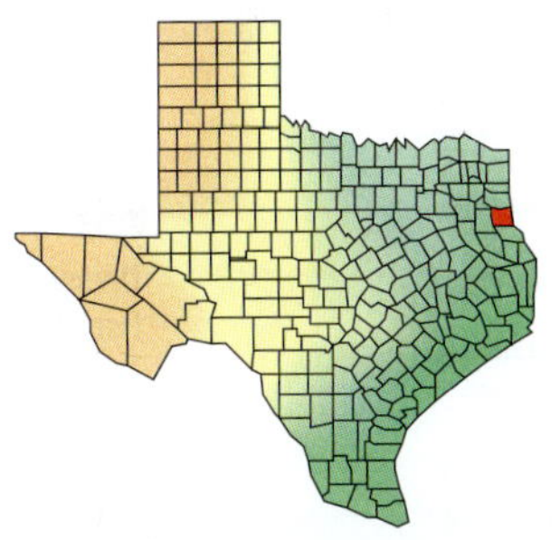

P

PARKER
COUNTY

Named for pioneer legislator Isaac Parker.

Cities/Towns: Weatherford, Aledo, Annetta, Annetta North, Annetta South, Briar, Dennis, Hudson Oaks, Peaster, Reno, Springtown, Willow Park

Land Area (Square Miles): 903.72
Elevation (Approx. Feet): 1,050

Population: 179,707
Population Change: 21.20%

Race:
White: 79.6%
Black: 2.1%
Hispanic: 15.1%
Asian: 1.0%
Other: 1.1%

Vital Statistics:
Births: 1,931
Deaths: 1,620
Marriages: 686
Divorces: 437

2024 Rainfall: 35.06 in.
January Avg. Temp.: 41.4°F
July Avg. Temp.: 83.6°F

Unemployment Rate: 3.4
Per Capita Income: $74,009
Tourism Earnings: $46 million
Avg. Home Value: $343,600

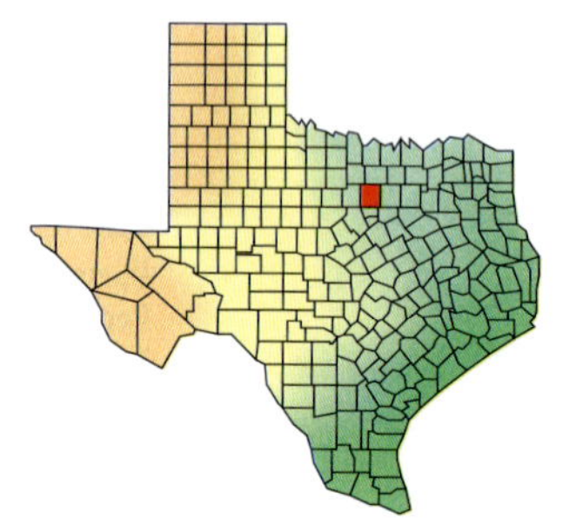

PARMER
COUNTY

Named for Republic figure Martin Parmer.

Cities/Towns: Farwell, Friona, Bovina, Lazbuddie

Land Area (Square Miles): 880.82
Elevation (Approx. Feet): 4,055

Population: 9,669
Population Change: -2.00%

Race:
White: 30.4%
Black: 1.9%
Hispanic: 66.8%
Asian: 1.0%
Other: 2.2%

Vital Statistics:
Births: 148
Deaths: 92
Marriages: 7
Divorces: 24

2024 Rainfall: 17.4 in.
January Avg. Temp.: 35.4°F
July Avg. Temp.: 78.8°F

Unemployment Rate: 2.8
Per Capita Income: $77,006
Tourism Earnings: $1 million
Avg. Home Value: $127,300

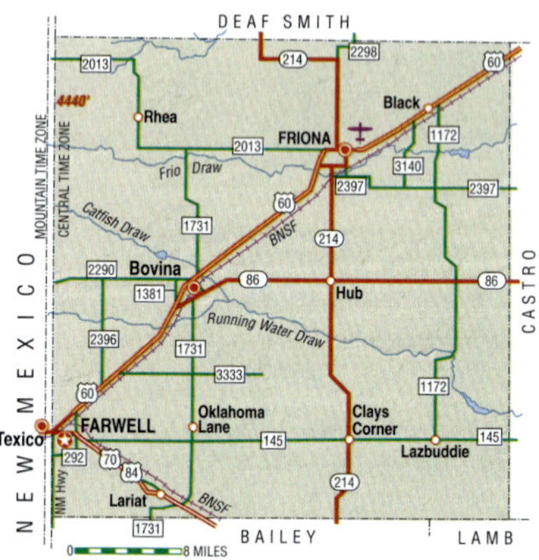

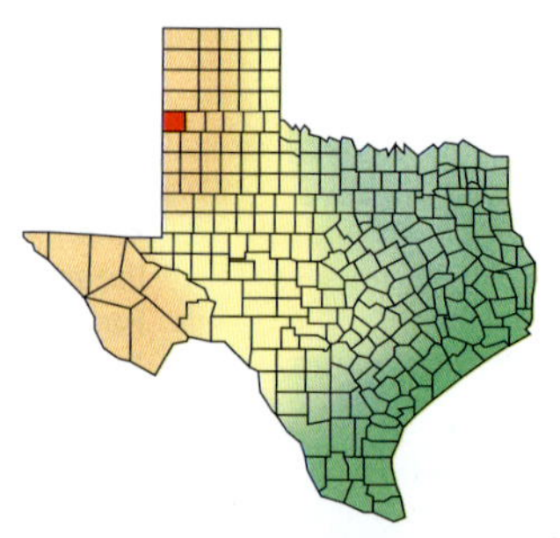

PECOS
COUNTY

Named for the Pecos River.

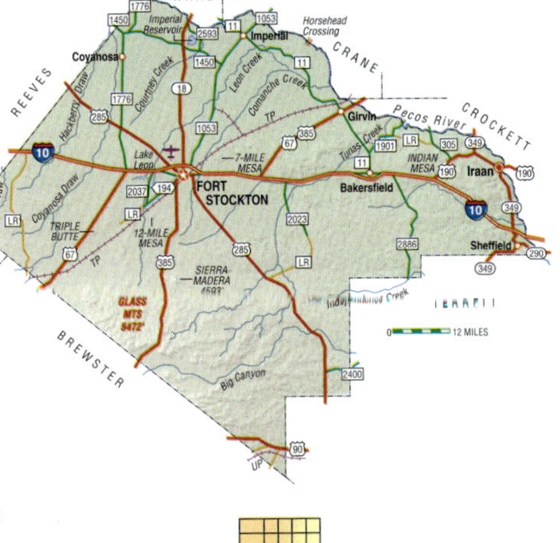

Cities/Towns: Fort Stockton, Iraan, Coyanosa, Imperial, Sheffield

Land Area (Square Miles): 4,763.84
Elevation (Approx. Feet): 3,025

Population: 14,712
Population Change: -3.20%

Race:
White: 22.1%
Black: 4.7%
Hispanic: 71.4%
Asian: 1.6%
Other: 1.8%

Vital Statistics:
Births: 186
Deaths: 145
Marriages: 70
Divorces: 13

2024 Rainfall: 7.76 in.
January Avg. Temp.: 47.4°F
July Avg. Temp.: 82.8°F

Unemployment Rate: 4
Per Capita Income: $49,691
Tourism Earnings: $7.1 million
Avg. Home Value: $142,900

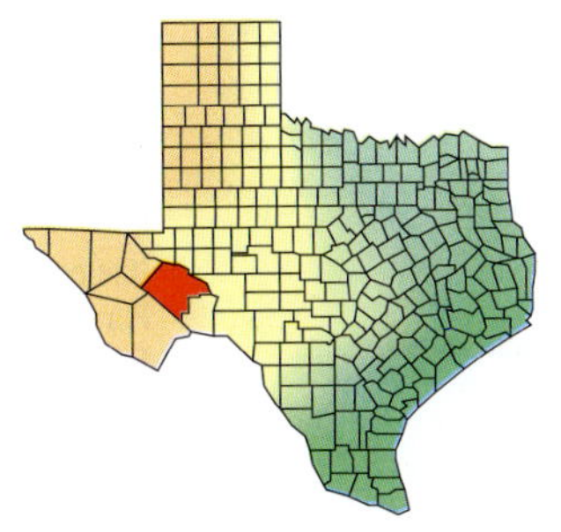

POLK
COUNTY

Named for U.S. President James K. Polk.

Cities/Towns: Livingston, West Livingston, Camden, Corrigan, Dallardsville, Goodrich, Onalaska, Pleasant Hill, Seven Oaks

Land Area (Square Miles): 1,057.05
Elevation (Approx. Feet): 272

Population: 54,258
Population Change: 8.30%

Race:
White: 71.4%
Black: 9.3%
Hispanic: 15.6%
Asian: 1.0%
Other: 2.2%

Vital Statistics:
Births: 496
Deaths: 782
Marriages: 273
Divorces: N/A

2024 Rainfall: 77.61 in.
January Avg. Temp.: 47°F
July Avg. Temp.: 81.7°F

Unemployment Rate: 5.1
Per Capita Income: $49,945
Tourism Earnings: $24.2 million
Avg. Home Value: $154,000

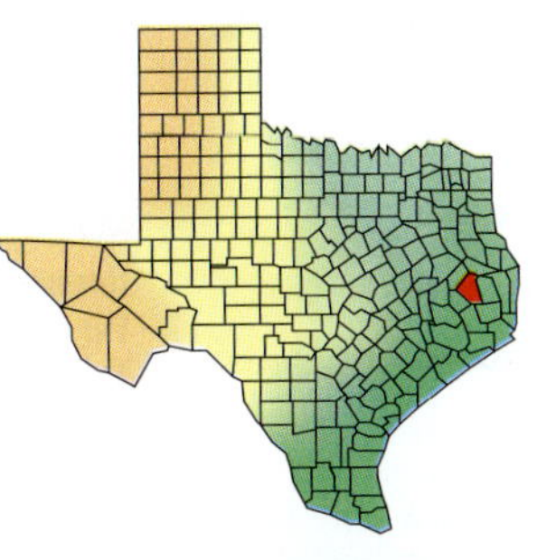

POTTER
COUNTY

Named for Republic leader Robert Potter.

Cities/Towns: Amarillo, Bishop Hills, Bushland

Land Area (Square Miles): 908.39
Elevation (Approx. Feet): 3,304

Population: 114,649
Population Change: -3.30%

Race:
White: 42.8%
Black: 11.4%
Hispanic: 39.9%
Asian: 4.9%
Other:1.4%

Vital Statistics:
Births: 1,579
Deaths: 1,415
Marriages: 955
Divorces: 235

2024 Rainfall: 17.03 in.
January Avg. Temp.: 34.5°F
July Avg. Temp.: 81.2°F

Unemployment Rate: 3.4
Per Capita Income: $58,933
Tourism Earnings: $231.4 million
Avg. Home Value: $134,900

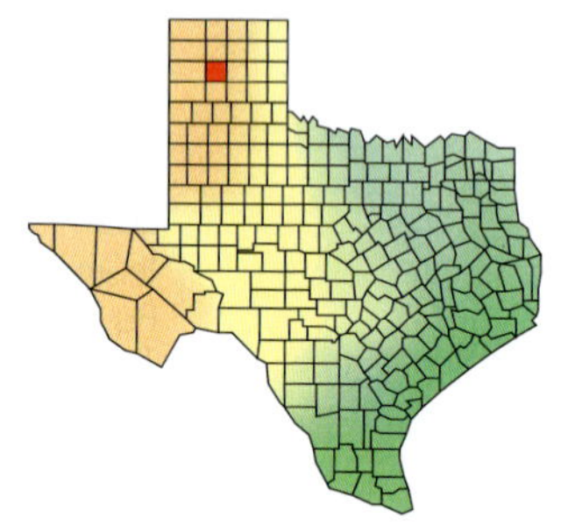

PRESIDIO
COUNTY

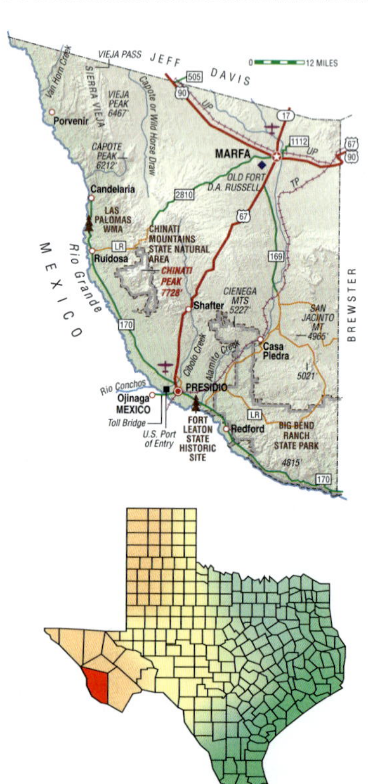

Named for Spanish Presidio del Norte.

Cities/Towns: Marfa, Presidio, Redford, Shafter

Land Area (Square Miles): 3,855.25
Elevation (Approx. Feet): 5,171

Population: 5,686
Population Change: -7.30%

Race:
White: 13.3%
Black: 2.7%
Hispanic: 82.4%
Asian: 1.8%
Other: 2.2%

Vital Statistics:
Births: 87
Deaths: 68
Marriages: 22
Divorces: N/A

2024 Rainfall: 5.87 in.
January Avg. Temp.: 47.2°F
July Avg. Temp.: 81.1°F

Unemployment Rate: 6.5
Per Capita Income: $65,420
Tourism Earnings: $5.8 million
Avg. Home Value: $123,100

R

RAINS
COUNTY

Named for Republic leader Emory Rains.

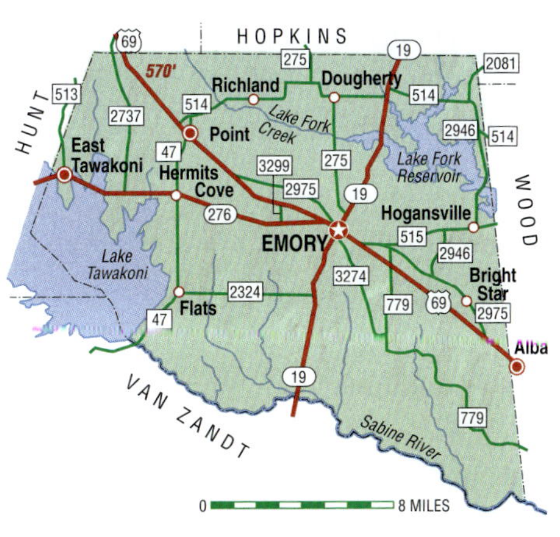

Cities/Towns: Emory, East Tawakoni, Point

Land Area (Square Miles): 229.45
Elevation (Approx. Feet): 502

Population: 13,306
Population Change: 9.50%

Race:
White: 82.1%
Black: 3.1%
Hispanic: 10.7%
Asian: 1.2%
Other: 1.6%

Vital Statistics:
Births: 125
Deaths: 173
Marriages: 81
Divorces: 48

2024 Rainfall: 58.31 in.
January Avg. Temp.: 41.2°F
July Avg. Temp.: 81.1°F

Unemployment Rate: 4
Per Capita Income: $44,559
Tourism Earnings: $4.2 million
Avg. Home Value: $214,900

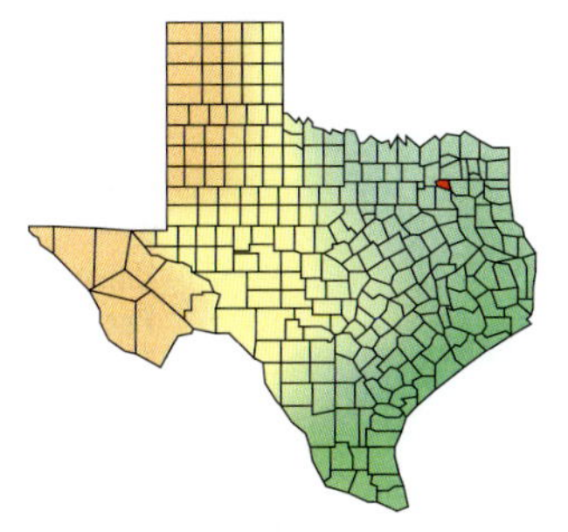

RANDALL
COUNTY

Named for Confederate General Horace Randal.

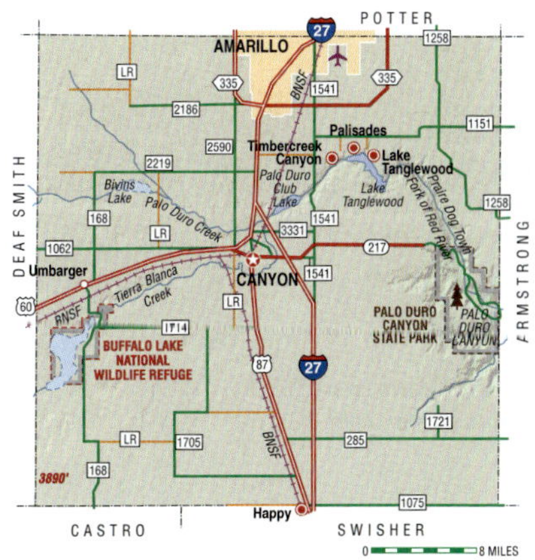

Cities/Towns: Canyon, Amarillo, Lake Tanglewood, Palisades, Rockwell Place, Timber Creek Canyon, Umbarger

Land Area (Square Miles): 912.71
Elevation (Approx. Feet): 3,494

Population: 150,547
Population Change: 7.00%

Race:
White: 66.7%
Black: 4.4%
Hispanic: 25.3%
Asian: 2.2%
Other: 1.1%

Vital Statistics:
Births: 1,731
Deaths: 1,416
Marriages: 521
Divorces: 410

2024 Rainfall: 19.11 in.
January Avg. Temp.: 34.9°F
July Avg. Temp.: 80°F

Unemployment Rate: 3
Per Capita Income: $60,604
Tourism Earnings: $36.3 million
Avg. Home Value: $227,500

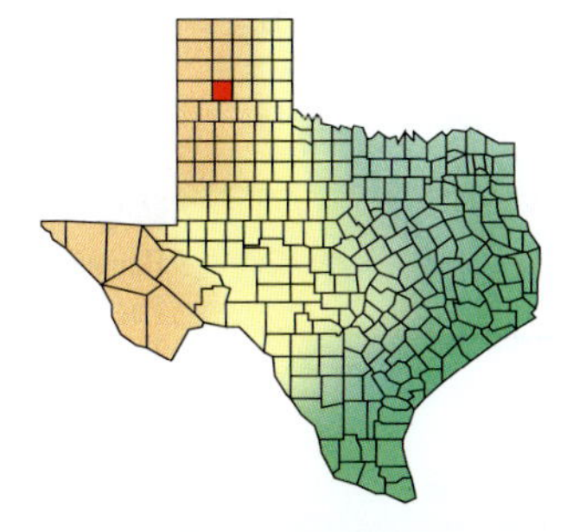

REAGAN COUNTY

Named for Texas' U.S. Senator John H. Reagan, the first chairman of the Texas Railroad Commission.

Cities/Towns: Big Lake

Land Area (Square Miles): 1,175.31
Elevation (Approx. Feet): 2,589

Population: 3,139
Population Change: -8.40%

Race:
White: 25.7%
Black: 4.3%
Hispanic: 68.5%
Asian: 1.3%
Other: 1.7%

Vital Statistics:
Births: 43
Deaths: 45
Marriages: 14
Divorces: 15

2024 Rainfall: 13.43 in.
January Avg. Temp.: 43.5°F
July Avg. Temp.: 83.1°F

Unemployment Rate: 4
Per Capita Income: $71,887
Tourism Earnings: $4.5 million
Avg. Home Value: $163,700

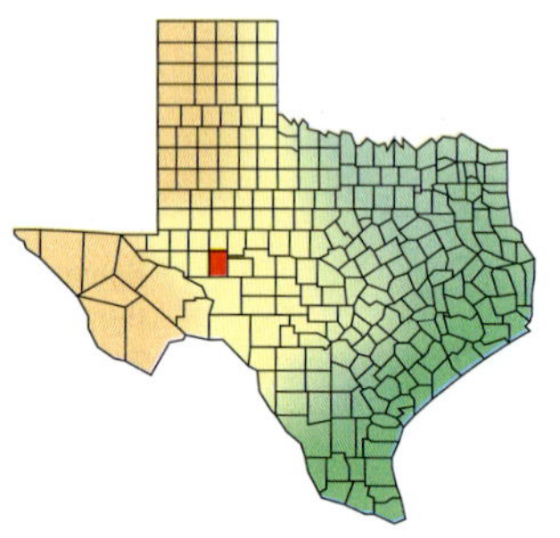

REAL COUNTY

Named for legislator and ranchman Julius Real.

Cities/Towns: Leakey, Camp Wood, Rio Frio

Land Area (Square Miles): 669.16
Elevation (Approx. Feet): 2,316

Population: 2,772
Population Change: 0.50%

Race:
White: 66.8%
Black: 2.1%
Hispanic: 27.7%
Asian: 0.6%
Other: 3.1%

Vital Statistics:
Births: 24
Deaths: 66
Marriages: 1
Divorces: N/A

2024 Rainfall: 16.91 in.
January Avg. Temp.: 45.9°F
July Avg. Temp.: 81.2°F

Unemployment Rate: 4.7
Per Capita Income: $61,576
Tourism Earnings: $2.1 million
Avg. Home Value: N/A

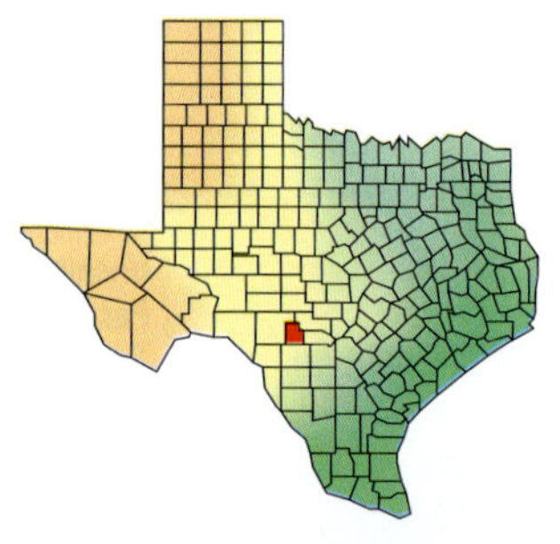

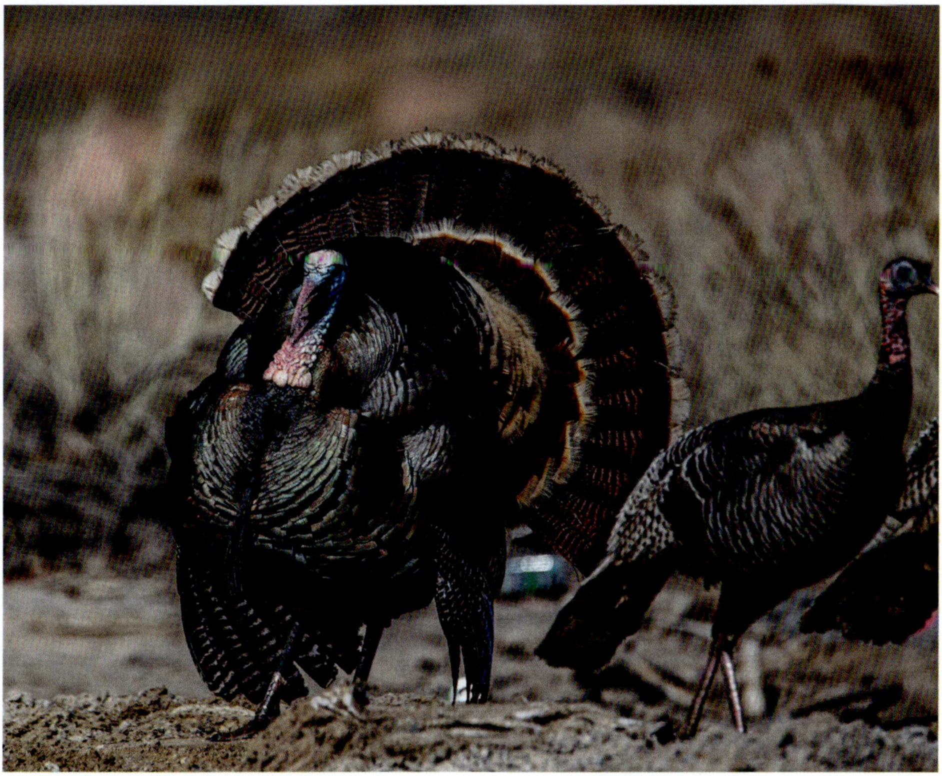

RED RIVER
COUNTY

Named for the Red River.

Cities/Towns: Clarksville, Annona, Avery, Bagwell, Bogota, Detroit

Land Area (Square Miles): 1,043.90
Elevation (Approx. Feet): 443

Population: 11,696
Population Change: 1.00%

Race:
White: 73.1%
Black: 15.7%
Hispanic: 8.0%
Asian: 0.5%
Other: 1.9%

Vital Statistics:
Births: 115
Deaths: 215
Marriages: 32
Divorces: 42

2024 Rainfall: 58.26 in.
January Avg. Temp.: 39.6°F
July Avg. Temp.: 81.8°F

Unemployment Rate: 4.7
Per Capita Income: $55,403
Tourism Earnings: $1.2 million
Avg. Home Value: $133,800

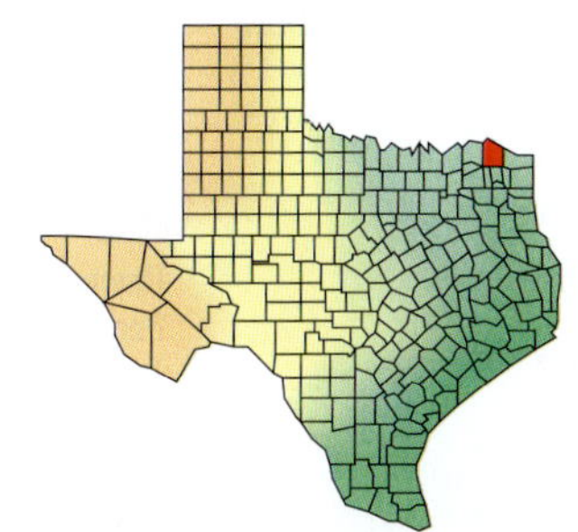

R

REEVES
COUNTY

Named for Confederate Colonel George R. Reeves.

Cities/Towns: Pecos, Balmorhea, Lindsay, Saragosa, Toyah, Toyahvale

Land Area (Square Miles): 2,635.35
Elevation (Approx. Feet): 2,782

Population: 11,956
Population Change: -18.90%

Race:
White: 10.2%
Black: 3.3%
Hispanic: 85.7%
Asian: 1.4%
Other: 1.4%

Vital Statistics:
Births: 184
Deaths: 121
Marriages: 70
Divorces: 16

2024 Rainfall: 5.49 in.
January Avg. Temp.: 45.9°F
July Avg. Temp.: 84.3°F

Unemployment Rate: 3.2
Per Capita Income: $76,555
Tourism Earnings: $46.1 million
Avg. Home Value: $113,700

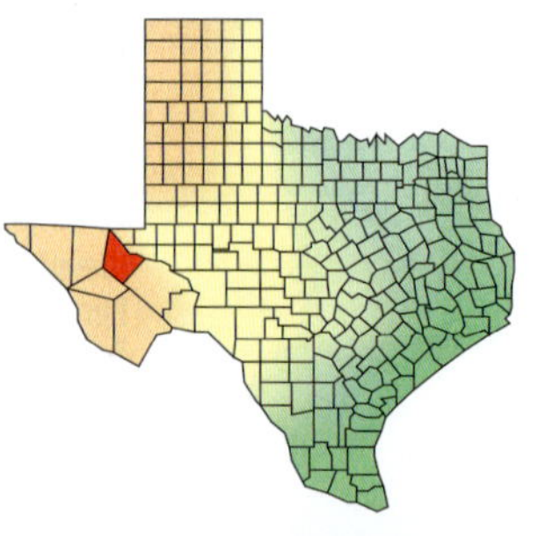

AUALLISO/WIKIMEDIA COMMONS

REFUGIO
COUNTY

Named for the Spanish mission Nuestra Señora del Refugio, which means "Our Lady of Refuge."

Cities/Towns: Refugio, Austwell, Bayside, Tivoli, Woodsboro

Land Area (Square Miles): 770.48
Elevation (Approx. Feet): 43

Population: 6,739
Population Change: 0.0%

Race:
White: 40.7%
Black: 7.1%
Hispanic: 51.0%
Asian: 0.9%
Other: 1.2%

Vital Statistics:
Births: 82
Deaths: 104
Marriages: 19
Divorces: 17

2024 Rainfall: 27.7 in.
January Avg. Temp.: 53.7°F
July Avg. Temp.: 84°F

Unemployment Rate: 4.6
Per Capita Income: $57,772
Tourism Earnings: $3.6 million
Avg. Home Value: $94,400

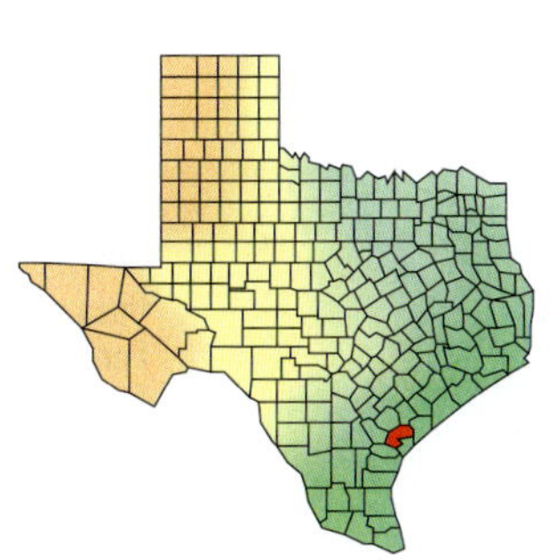

ROBERTS
COUNTY

Named for Texas leaders John S. Roberts and Governor O.M. Roberts.

Cities/Towns: Miami

Land Area (Square Miles): 924.06
Elevation (Approx. Feet): 2,697

Population: 837
Population Change: 1.00%

Race:
White: 82.7%
Black: 1.0%
Hispanic: 12.7%
Asian: 0.2%
Other: 3.5%

Vital Statistics:
Births: N/A
Deaths: N/A
Marriages: 5
Divorces: 5

2024 Rainfall: 23.56 in.
January Avg. Temp.: 34.7°F
July Avg. Temp.: 81.7°F

Unemployment Rate: 4.3
Per Capita Income: $64,762
Tourism Earnings: $50,000
Avg. Home Value: $176,800

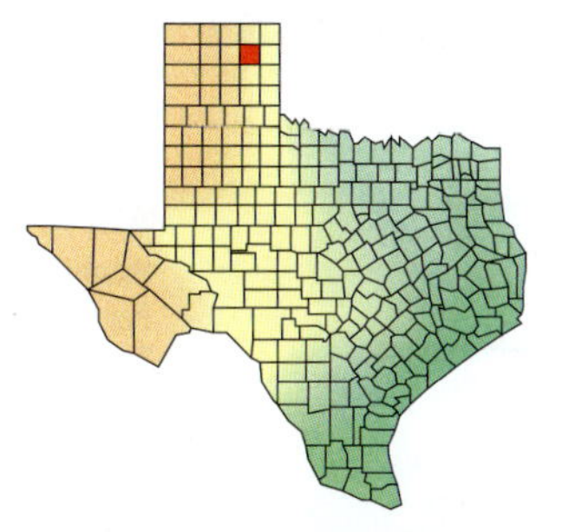

R

ROBERTSON
COUNTY

Named for pioneer Sterling Clack Robertson.

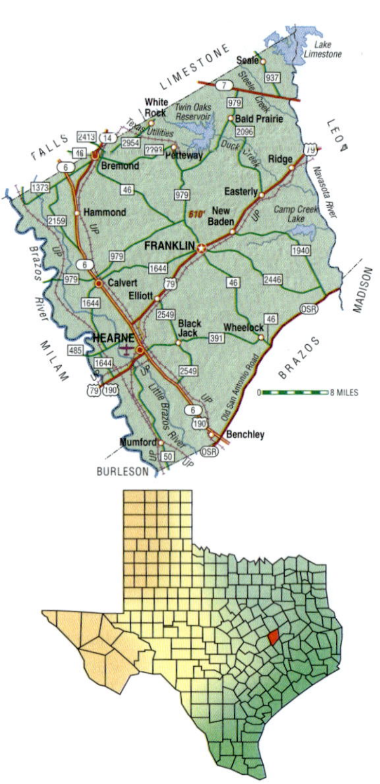

Cities/Towns: Franklin, Hearne, Bremond, Calvert, Mumford, New Baden, Wheelock

Land Area (Square Miles): 855.16
Elevation (Approx. Feet): 427

Population: 17,659
Population Change: 5.40%

Race:
White: 56.4%
Black: 19.2%
Hispanic: 22.7%
Asian: 0.9%
Other: 1.4%

Vital Statistics:
Births: 216
Deaths: 240
Marriages: 51
Divorces: 35

2024 Rainfall: 45.45 in.
January Avg. Temp.: 45.2°F
July Avg. Temp.: 82.4°F

Unemployment Rate: 4.3
Per Capita Income: $58,609
Tourism Earnings: $5.3 million
Avg. Home Value: $172,200

ROCKWALL
COUNTY

Named for the wall-like rock formation discovered by early settlers.

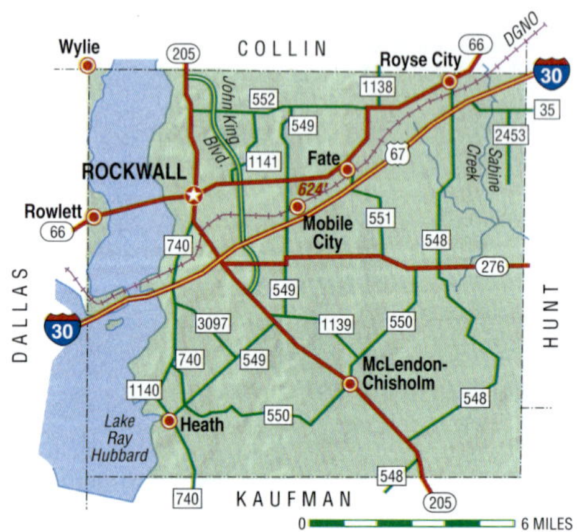

Cities/Towns: Rockwall, Fate, Heath, McLendon-Chisholm, Mobile City, Royse City, Rowlett, Wylie

Land Area (Square Miles): 127.21
Elevation (Approx. Feet): 587

Population: 137,044
Population Change: 27.00%

Race:
White: 62.1%
Black: 10.5%
Hispanic: 21.5%
Asian: 4.0%
Other: 1.0%

Vital Statistics:
Births: 1,390
Deaths: 810
Marriages: 1,152
Divorces: 321

2024 Rainfall: 47.63 in.
January Avg. Temp.: 41.4°F
July Avg. Temp.: 83.2°F

Unemployment Rate: 3.5
Per Capita Income: $77,307
Tourism Earnings: $51.2 million
Avg. Home Value: $386,000

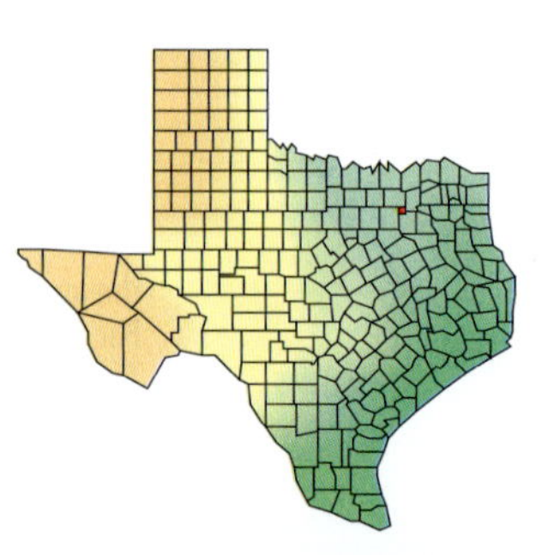

RUNNELS
COUNTY

Named for planter and legislator H.G. Runnels.

Cities/Towns: Ballinger, Miles, Rowena, Wingate, Winters

Land Area (Square Miles): 1,051.07
Elevation (Approx. Feet): 1,719

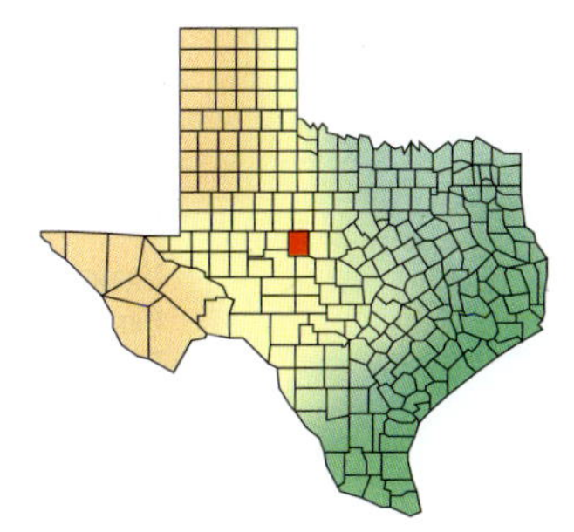

Population: 9,751
Population Change: -1.50%

Race:
White: 59.8%
Black: 2.9%
Hispanic: 35.4%
Asian: 1.3%
Other: 2.0%

Vital Statistics:
Births: 115
Deaths: 155
Marriages: 53
Divorces: 24

2024 Rainfall: 29.45 in.
January Avg. Temp.: 43°F
July Avg. Temp.: 83.8°F

Unemployment Rate: 3.4
Per Capita Income: $55,707
Tourism Earnings: $2.1 million
Avg. Home Value: $103,700

RUSK
COUNTY

Named for Republic state leader Thomas J. Rusk.

Cities/Towns: Henderson, Laird Hill, Lake Cherokee, Laneville, Minden, Mount Enterprise, New London, Overton, Price, Tatum, Turnertown-Selman City, Reklaw, Kilgore

Land Area (Square Miles): 924.2
Elevation (Approx. Feet): 417

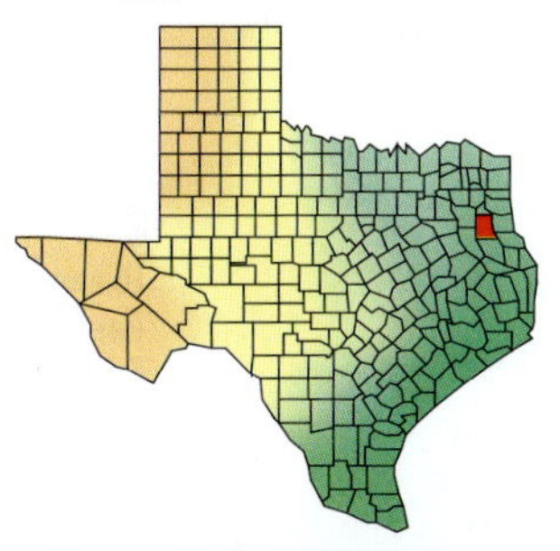

Population: 53,391
Population Change: 2.30%

Race:
White: 45.4%
Black: 29.7%
Hispanic: 19.5%
Asian: 1.5%
Other: 1.1%

Vital Statistics:
Births: 568
Deaths: 642
Marriages: 235
Divorces: 178

2024 Rainfall: 69.97 in.
January Avg. Temp.: 43.7°F
July Avg. Temp.: 81°F

Unemployment Rate: 4.5
Per Capita Income: $47,312
Tourism Earnings: $10.2 million
Avg. Home Value: $166,900

S

SABINE
COUNTY

Named for the Sabine River.

Cities/Towns: Hemphill, Bronson, Brookeland, Geneva, Milam, Pineland

Land Area (Square Miles): 491.71
Elevation (Approx. Feet): 259

Population: 10,058
Population Change: 1.70%

Race:
White: 84.7%
Black: 7.0%
Hispanic: 4.7%
Asian: 0.7%
Other: 1.1%

Vital Statistics:
Births: 107
Deaths: 215
Marriages: 56
Divorces: 10

2024 Rainfall: 80.35 in.
January Avg. Temp.: 45.2°F
July Avg. Temp.: 81.5°F

Unemployment Rate: 6
Per Capita Income: $47,303
Tourism Earnings: $2.3 million
Avg. Home Value: $131,900

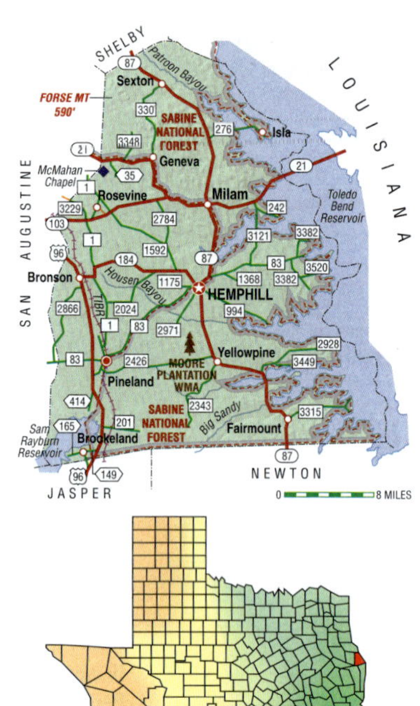

SAN AUGUSTINE
COUNTY

Named for the town of San Augustine.

Cities/Towns: San Augustine, Broaddus

Land Area (Square Miles): 530.66
Elevation (Approx. Feet): 279

Population: 7,767
Population Change: -2.00%

Race:
White: 68.1%
Black: 21.4%
Hispanic: 8.4%
Asian: 0.5%
Other: 1.0%

Vital Statistics:
Births: 72
Deaths: 146
Marriages: 37
Divorces: 1

2024 Rainfall: 78.42 in.
January Avg. Temp.: 44.5°F
July Avg. Temp.: 81.3°F

Unemployment Rate: 5.2
Per Capita Income: $58,852
Tourism Earnings: $2.8 million
Avg. Home Value: $83,500

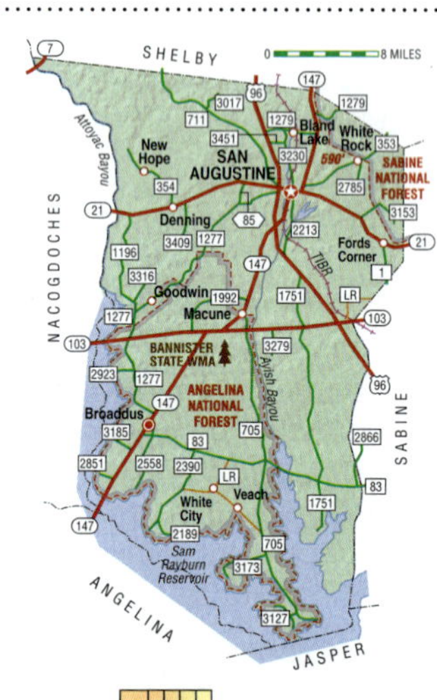

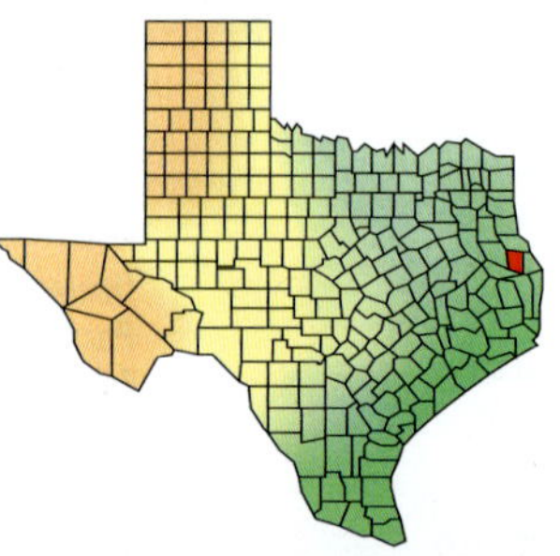

SAN JACINTO
COUNTY

Named for the Battle of San Jacinto.

Cities/Towns: Coldspring, Shepherd, Oakhurst, Point Blank

Land Area (Square Miles): 569.24
Elevation (Approx. Feet): 272

Population: 29,326
Population Change: 7.00%

Race:
White: 68.6%
Black: 9.0%
Hispanic: 19.9%
Asian: 0.7%
Other: 1.4%

Vital Statistics:
Births: 350
Deaths: 388
Marriages: 106
Divorces: 108

2024 Rainfall: 72.22 in.
January Avg. Temp.: 47.8°F
July Avg. Temp.: 81.6°F

Unemployment Rate: 5.3
Per Capita Income: $47,030
Tourism Earnings: $2.9 million
Avg. Home Value: $183,100

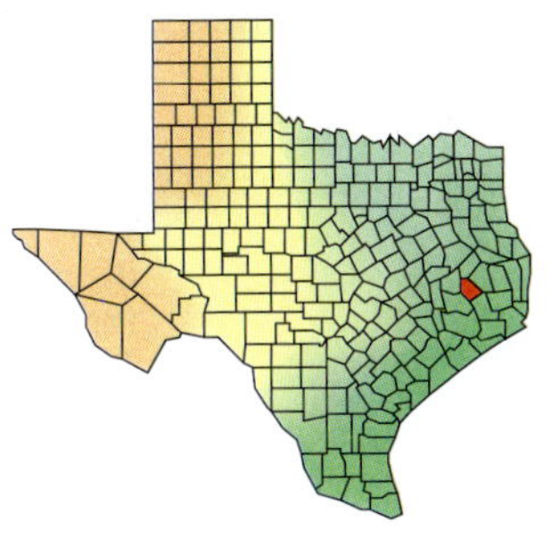

SAN PATRICIO
COUNTY

Named for San Patricio de Hibernia, an Irish colony named for Saint Patrick.

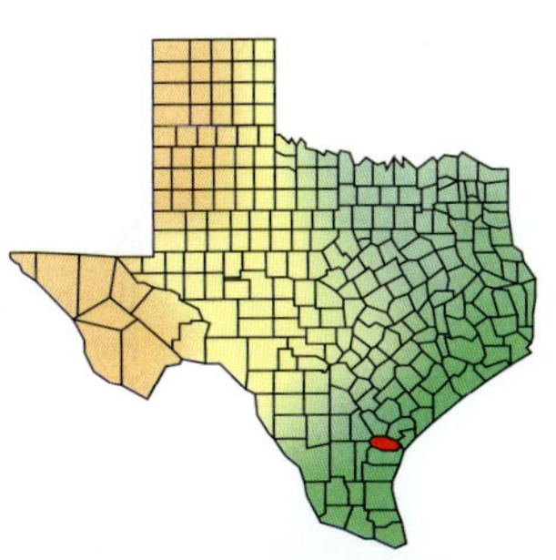

Cities/Towns: Sinton, Aransas Pass, Portland, Edroy, Gregory, Ingleside, Ingleside-on-the-Bay, Lake City, Lakeside, Mathis, Odem, St. Paul, San Patricio, Taft, Taft Southwest

Land Area (Square Miles): 693.44
Elevation (Approx. Feet): 52

Population: 71,467
Population Change: 3.90%

Race:
White: 39.1%
Black: 2.3%
Hispanic: 56.6%
Asian: 1.4%
Other: 1.3%

Vital Statistics:
Births: 851
Deaths: 777
Marriages: 248
Divorces: 191

2024 Rainfall: 26.24 in.
January Avg. Temp.: 54.4°F
July Avg. Temp.: 84.4°F

Unemployment Rate: 4.9
Per Capita Income: $53,429
Tourism Earnings: $50.5 million
Avg. Home Value: $180,400

S

SAN SABA
COUNTY

Named for the San Saba River.

Cities/Towns: San Saba, Bend, Cherokee, Richland Springs

Land Area (Square Miles): 1,135.31
Elevation (Approx. Feet): 1,309

Population: 5,508
Population Change: -3.80%

Race:
White: 62.1%
Black: 4.6%
Hispanic: 30.7%
Asian: 0.7%
Other: 1.7%

Vital Statistics:
Births: 50
Deaths: 86
Marriages: 17
Divorces: 2

2024 Rainfall: 28.18 in.
January Avg. Temp.: 44°F
July Avg. Temp.: 83.4°F

Unemployment Rate: 3.8
Per Capita Income: $48,235
Tourism Earnings: $1.4 million
Avg. Home Value: $161,800

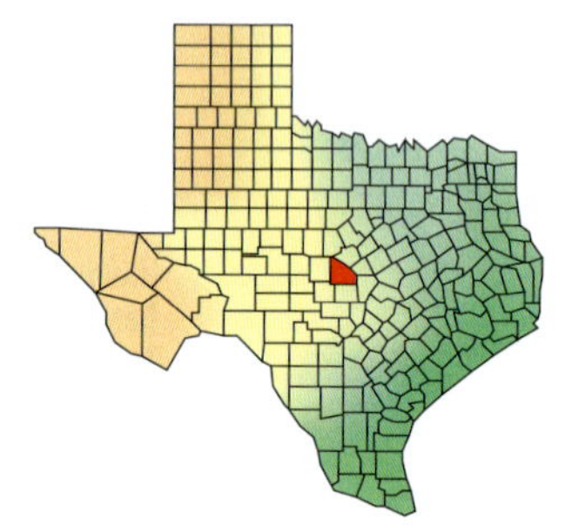

SCHLEICHER
COUNTY

Named for engineer and U.S. Congressman Gustav Schleicher.

Cities/Towns: Eldorado

Land Area (Square Miles): 1,310.64
Elevation (Approx. Feet): 2,415

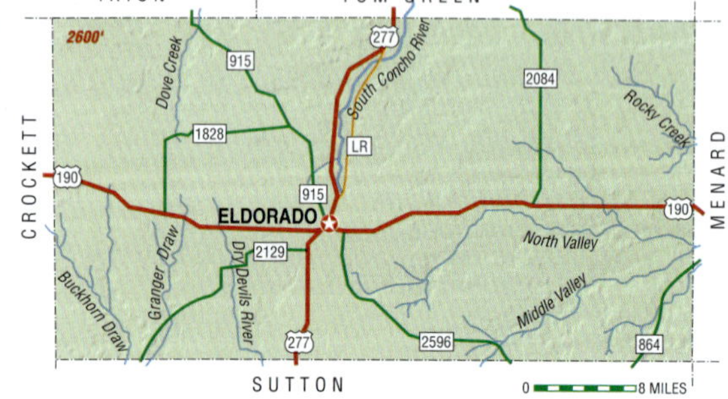

Population: 2,302
Population Change: -6.10%

Race:
White: 42.6%
Black: 2.4%
Hispanic: 53.7%
Asian: 0.6%
Other: 1.4%

Vital Statistics:
Births: 20
Deaths: 25
Marriages: 6
Divorces: 7

2024 Rainfall: 17.77 in.
January Avg. Temp.: 42.9°F
July Avg. Temp.: 82.2°F

Unemployment Rate: 4.6
Per Capita Income: $61,904
Tourism Earnings: $150,000
Avg. Home Value: $113,400

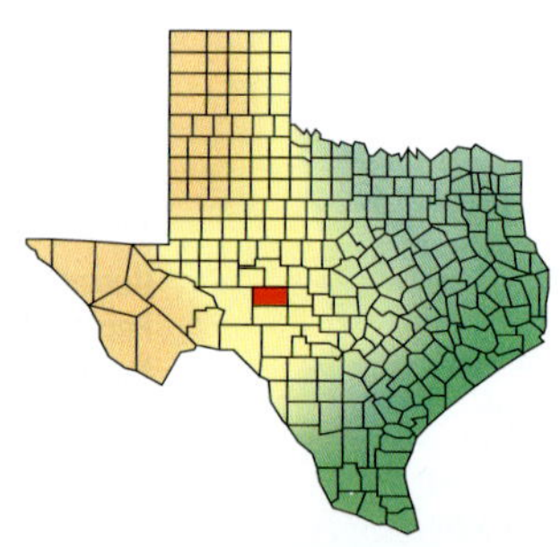

SCURRY
COUNTY

Named for Confederate General W.R. Scurry.

Cities/Towns: Snyder, Dunn, Fluvanna, Hermleigh, Ira

Land Area (Square Miles): 905.45
Elevation (Approx. Feet): 2,392

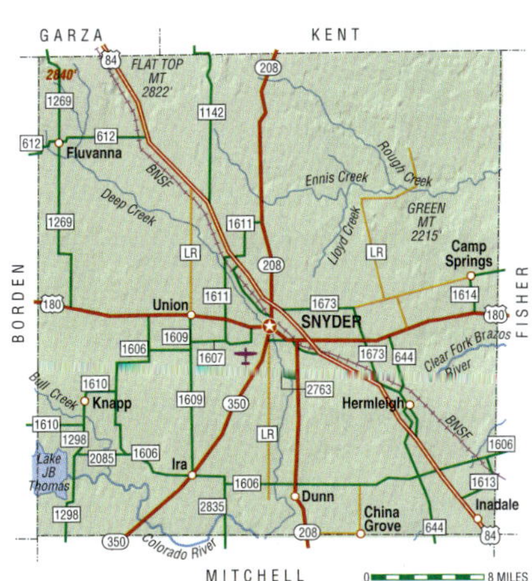

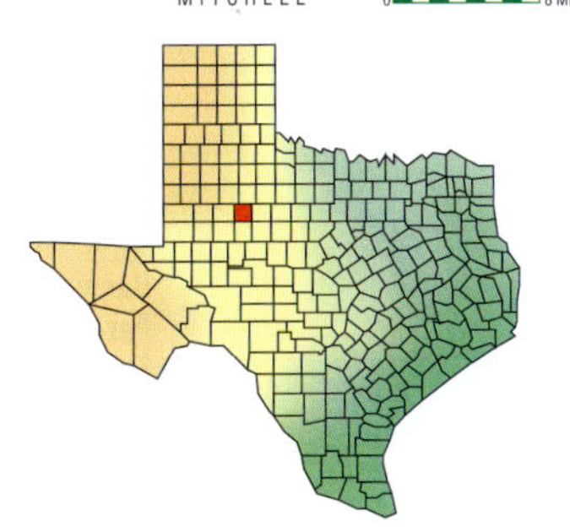

Population: 16,211
Population Change: -4.10%

Race:
White: 49.8%
Black: 4.4%
Hispanic: 43.9%
Asian: 1.1%
Other: 1.5%

Vital Statistics:
Births: 199
Deaths: 194
Marriages: 68
Divorces: 60

2024 Rainfall: 21.82 in.
January Avg. Temp.: 39.7°F
July Avg. Temp.: 83.9°F

Unemployment Rate: 3.8
Per Capita Income: $54,065
Tourism Earnings: $16.3 million
Avg. Home Value: $110,800

SHACKELFORD
COUNTY

Named for Texas Revolution hero Dr. Jack "John" Shackelford.

Cities/Towns: Albany, Moran

Land Area (Square Miles): 914.29
Elevation (Approx. Feet): 1,539

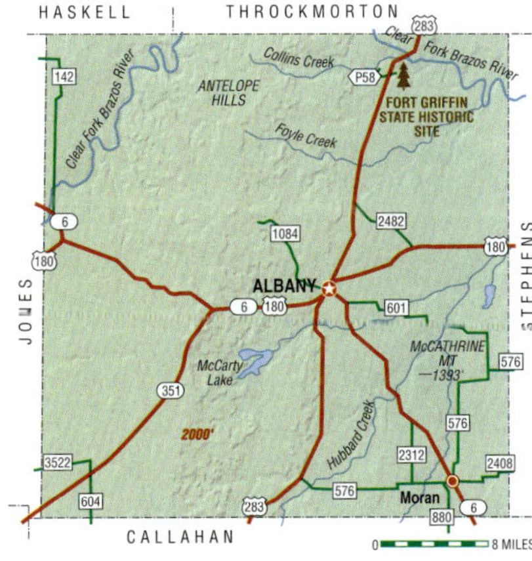

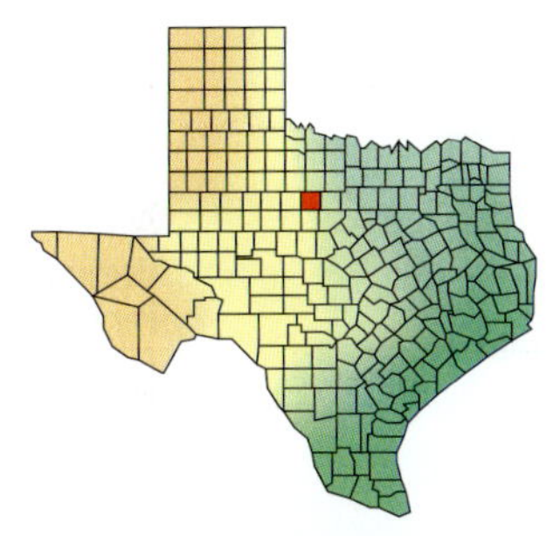

Population: 3,169
Population Change: 2.00%

Race:
White: 82.6%
Black: 2.3%
Hispanic: 13.1%
Asian: 0.5%
Other: 1.3%

Vital Statistics:
Births: 26
Deaths: 44
Marriages: 11
Divorces: 8

2024 Rainfall: 31.69 in.
January Avg. Temp.: 40.9°F
July Avg. Temp.: 84.1°F

Unemployment Rate: 3.4
Per Capita Income: $91,109
Tourism Earnings: $1.1 million
Avg. Home Value: $176,900

S

SHELBY
COUNTY

Named for American Revolution officer Isaac Shelby.

Cities/Towns: Center, Huxley, Joaquin, Shelbyville, Tenaha, Timpson

Land Area (Square Miles): 795.59
Elevation (Approx. Feet): 345

Population: 24,192
Population Change: 0.20%

Race:
White: 59.9%
Black: 17.1%
Hispanic: 20.1%
Asian: 1.7%
Other: 1.3%

Vital Statistics:
Births: 334
Deaths: 322
Marriages: 128
Divorces: 72

2024 Rainfall: 78.77 in.
January Avg. Temp.: 44°F
July Avg. Temp.: 81.2°F

Unemployment Rate: 4.9
Per Capita Income: $64,203
Tourism Earnings: $11.2 million
Avg. Home Value: $110,700

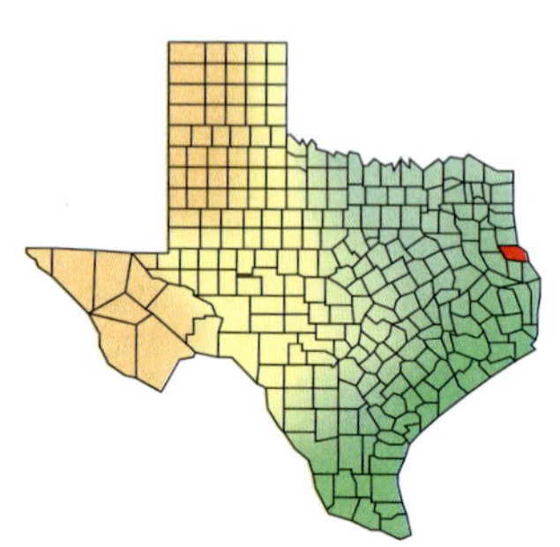

SHERMAN
COUNTY

Named for Republic of Texas General Sidney Sherman.

Cities/Towns: Stratford, Texhoma

Land Area (Square Miles): 922.86
Elevation (Approx. Feet): 3,521

Population: 2,771
Population Change: -0.50%

Race:
White: 48.5%
Black: 2.1%
Hispanic: 48.0%
Asian: 1.1%
Other: 1.9%

Vital Statistics:
Births: 47
Deaths: 29
Marriages: 10
Divorces: 1

2024 Rainfall: 18.17 in.
January Avg. Temp.: 32.7°F
July Avg. Temp.: 79.2°F

Unemployment Rate: 2.8
Per Capita Income: $173,932
Tourism Earnings: $680,000
Avg. Home Value: $125,500

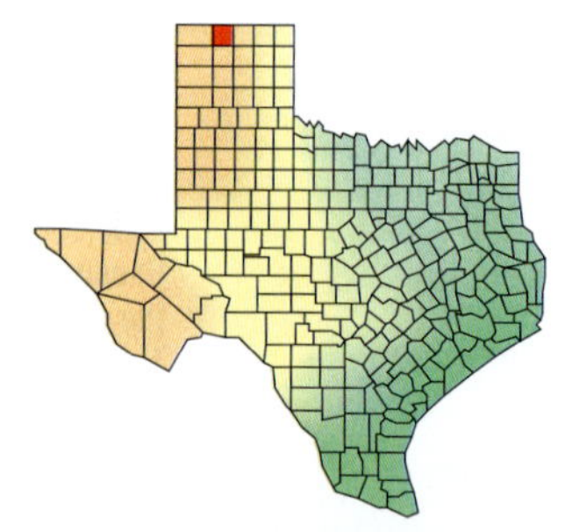

S

SMITH
COUNTY

Named for Texas Revolution General James Smith.

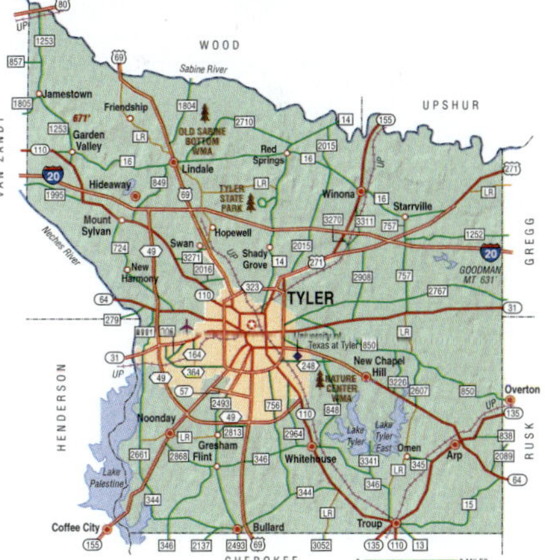

Cities/Towns: Tyler, Whitehouse, Arp, Bullard, Emerald Bay, Hideaway, Lindale, New Chapel Hill, Noonday, Troup, Winona, Overton

Land Area (Square Miles): 921.47
Elevation (Approx. Feet): 495

Population: 249,091
Population Change: 6.70%

Race:
White: 58.0%
Black: 17.7%
Hispanic: 21.2%
Asian: 1.8%
Other: 1.0%

Vital Statistics:
Births: 3,115
Deaths: 2,572
Marriages: 1,395
Divorces: 782

2024 Rainfall: 59.48 in.
January Avg. Temp.: 42.2°F
July Avg. Temp.: 80.7°F

Unemployment Rate: 3.8
Per Capita Income: $66,887
Tourism Earnings: $147.2 million
Avg. Home Value: $220,800

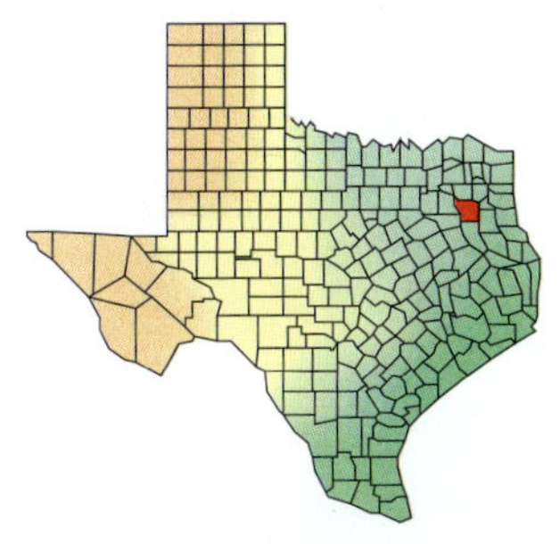

UNSPLASH/DANICA STRADECKE

S SOMERVELL COUNTY

Named for Republic of Texas General Alexander Somervell.

Cities/Towns: Glen Rose, Nemo, Rainbow

Land Area (Square Miles): 186.38
Elevation (Approx. Feet): 669

Population: 10,098
Population Change: 9.70%

Race:
White: 77.4%
Black: 1.3%
Hispanic: 18.0%
Asian: 1.1%
Other: 1.8%

Vital Statistics:
Births: 82
Deaths: 116
Marriages: 48
Divorces: 21

2024 Rainfall: 42.24 in.
January Avg. Temp.: 42.5°F
July Avg. Temp.: 83.5°F

Unemployment Rate: 4
Per Capita Income: $62,988
Tourism Earnings: $8.1 million
Avg. Home Value: $253,600

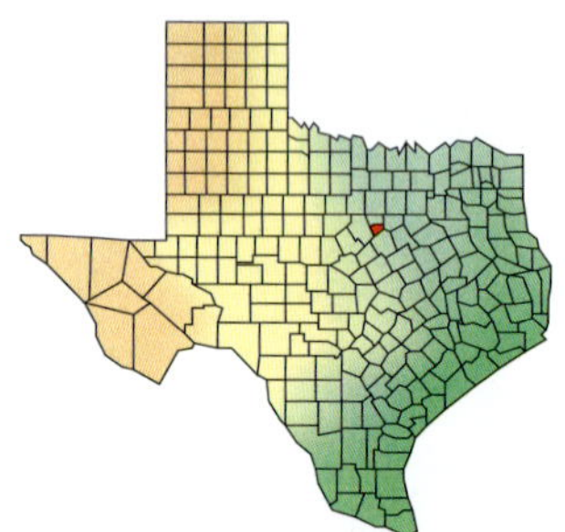

UNSPLASH/LORI STEVENS

STARR
COUNTY

Named for Republic Secretary of Treasury Dr. J.H. Starr.

Cities/Towns: Rio Grande City, Roma-Los Saenz, Delmita, El Cenizo, Escobares, Fronton, Garceño, Garciasville, La Grulla, La Puerta, La Rosita, Las Lomas, La Victoria, Los Alvarez, North Escobares, Salineño, San Isidro, Valle Vista

Land Area (Square Miles): 1,223.18
Elevation (Approx. Feet): 410

Population: 66,587
Population Change: 1.00%

Race:
White: 2.5%
Black: 0.6%
Hispanic: 97.0%
Asian: 0.3%
Other: 0.5%

Vital Statistics:
Births: 1,097
Deaths: 525
Marriages: 306
Divorces: N/A

2024 Rainfall: 19.89 in.
January Avg. Temp.: 57.6°F
July Avg. Temp.: 86.3°F

Unemployment Rate: 9.5
Per Capita Income: $32,785
Tourism Earnings: $7 million
Avg. Home Value: $93,300

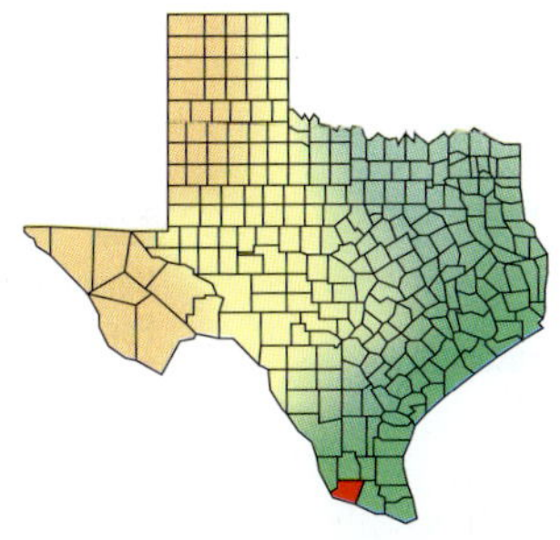

LIBRARY OF CONGRESS

S

STEPHENS COUNTY

Named for Confederate Vice President Alexander H. Stephens.

Cities/Towns: Breckenridge, Caddo

Land Area (Square Miles): 896.72
Elevation (Approx. Feet): 1,348

Population: 9,475
Population Change: 4.10%

Race:
White: 67.9%
Black: 3.7%
Hispanic: 25.7%
Asian: 1.1%
Other: 1.7%

Vital Statistics:
Births: 96
Deaths: 109
Marriages: 35
Divorces: 31

2024 Rainfall: 34.6 in.
January Avg. Temp.: 40.1°F
July Avg. Temp.: 84°F

Unemployment Rate: 4.4
Per Capita Income: $49,206
Tourism Earnings: $2.2 million
Avg. Home Value: $105,700

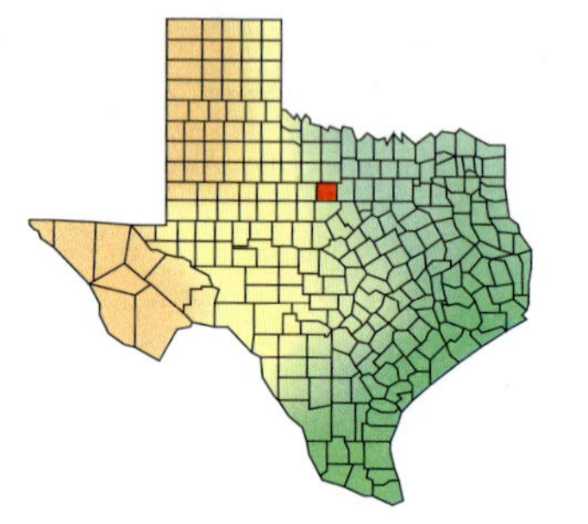

STERLING COUNTY

Named for buffalo hunter W.S. Sterling.

Cities/Towns: Sterling City

Land Area (Square Miles): 923.45
Elevation (Approx. Feet): 2,330

Population: 1,387
Population Change: 1.10%

Race:
White: 59.8%
Black: 1.6%
Hispanic: 35.2%
Asian: 0.3%
Other: 2.4%

Vital Statistics:
Births: 18
Deaths: 15
Marriages: 0
Divorces: N/A

2024 Rainfall: 17.01 in.
January Avg. Temp.: 42.1°F
July Avg. Temp.: 83.5°F

Unemployment Rate: 3.2
Per Capita Income: $71,876
Tourism Earnings: $330,000
Avg. Home Value: $143,200

STONEWALL
COUNTY

Named for Confederate General T.J. "Stonewall" Jackson.

Cities/Towns: Aspermont, Old Glory

Land Area (Square Miles): 916.31
Elevation (Approx. Feet): 1,719

Population: 1,235
Population Change: 0.80%

Race:
White: 73.0%
Black: 3.7%
Hispanic: 20.3%
Asian: 1.7%
Other: 1.6%

Vital Statistics:
Births: 13
Deaths: 22
Marriages: 4
Divorces: 2

2024 Rainfall: 28.41 in.
January Avg. Temp.: 40.1°F
July Avg. Temp.: 84.8°F

Unemployment Rate: 2.2
Per Capita Income: $95,644
Tourism Earnings: $300,000
Avg. Home Value: $54,700

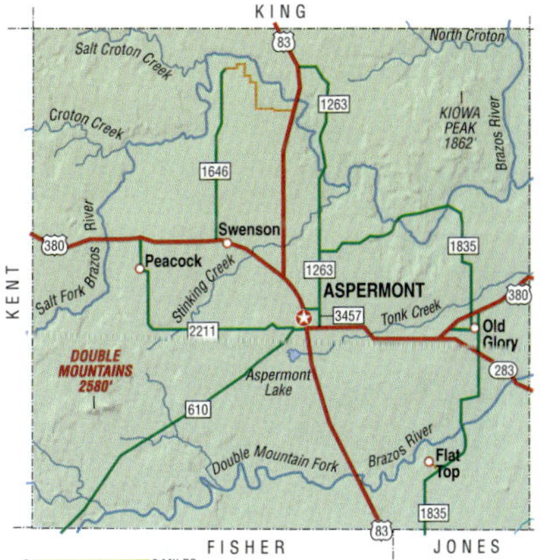

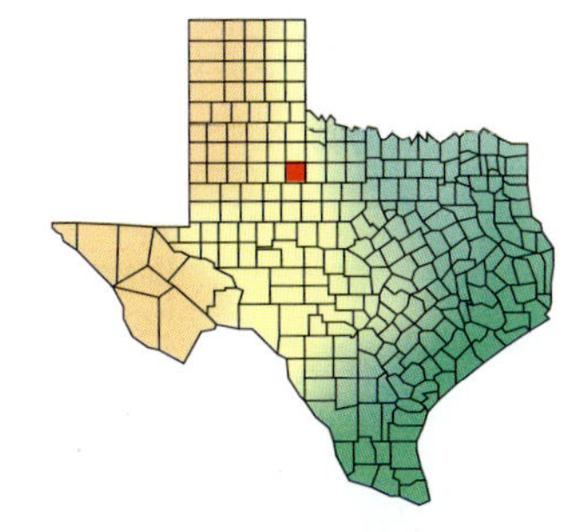

UNSPLASH/RAYCHEL SANNER

S

SUTTON
COUNTY

Named for Confederate Colonel John S. Sutton.

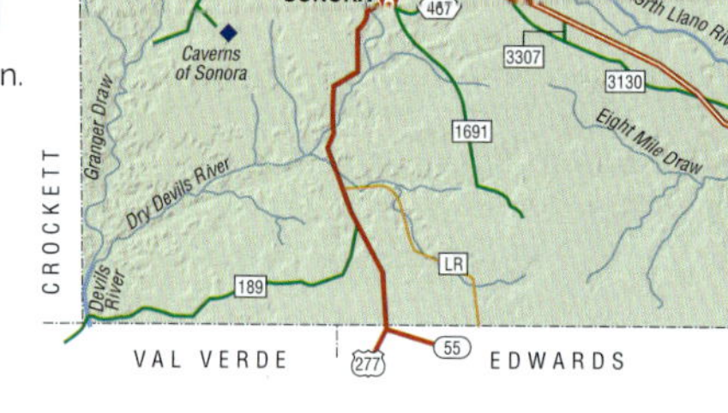

Cities/Towns: Sonora

Land Area (Square Miles): 1,453.94
Elevation (Approx. Feet): 2,231

Population: 3,269
Population Change: -3.10%

Race:
White: 34.7%
Black: 1.6%
Hispanic: 63.6%
Asian: 0.8%
Other: 1.6%

Vital Statistics:
Births: 27
Deaths: 45
Marriages: 14
Divorces: 6

2024 Rainfall: 16.76 in.
January Avg. Temp.: 43.8°F
July Avg. Temp.: 81.9°F

Unemployment Rate: 5.5
Per Capita Income: $75,645
Tourism Earnings: $3.6 million
Avg. Home Value: $140,600

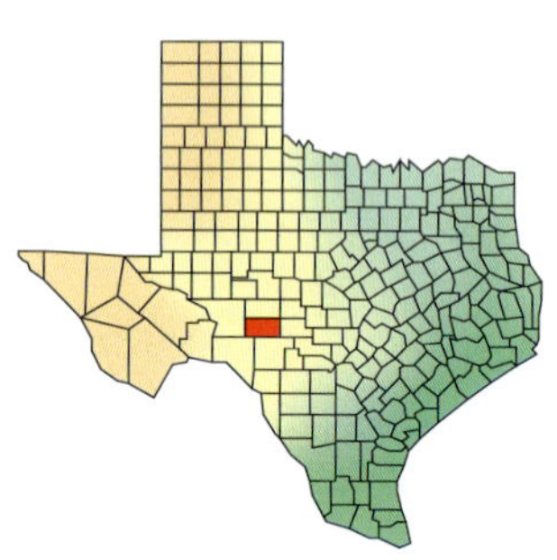

SWISHER
COUNTY

Named for J.G. Swisher of the Texas Revolution.

Cities/Towns: Tulia, Happy, Kress, Vigo Park

Land Area (Square Miles): 890.16
Elevation (Approx. Feet): 3,448

Population: 6,877
Population Change: -1.40%

Race:
White: 42.3%
Black: 9.3%
Hispanic: 46.7%
Asian: 0.8%
Other: 2.1%

Vital Statistics:
Births: 72
Deaths: 101
Marriages: 15
Divorces: N/A

2024 Rainfall: 20.15 in.
January Avg. Temp.: 35.4°F
July Avg. Temp.: 80°F

Unemployment Rate: 4.5
Per Capita Income: $85,037
Tourism Earnings: $900,000
Avg. Home Value: $89,200

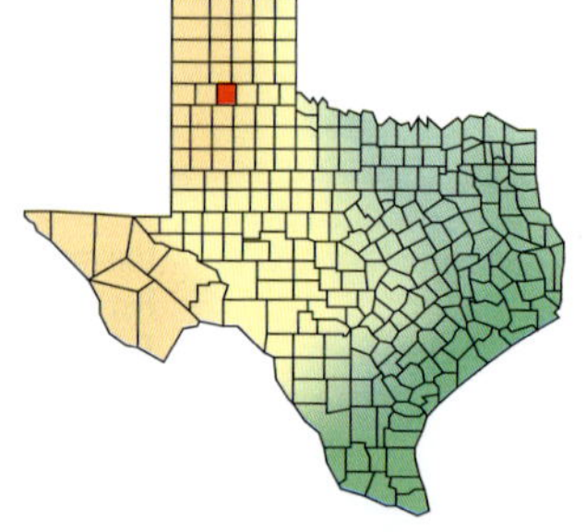

T

TARRANT
COUNTY

Named for Republic of Texas General Edward H. Tarrant.

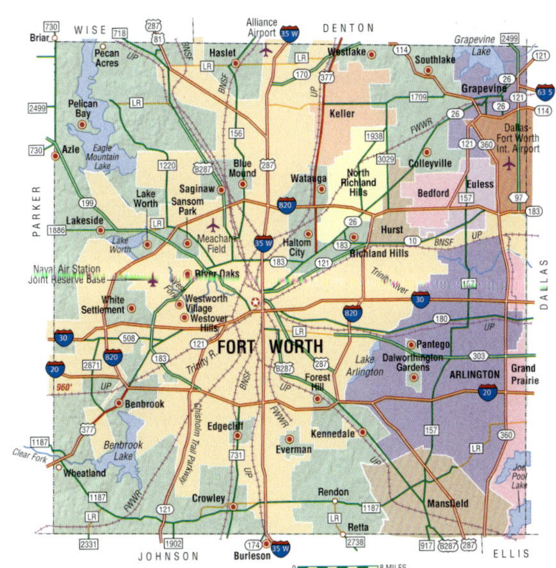

Cities/Towns: Fort Worth, Arlington, Hurst, Euless, Bedford, Azle, Benbrook, Blue Mound, Briar, Colleyville, Crowley, Dalworthington Gardens, Edgecliff Village, Everman, Forest Hill, Grapevine, Haltom City, Haslet, Keller, Kennedale, Lakeside, Lake Worth, Mansfield, North Richland Hills, River Oaks, Saginaw, Sansom Park, Southlake, Watauga, Westlake, Westover Hills, Westworth Village, White Settlement, Burleson, Grand Prairie

Land Area (Square Miles): 865.29
Elevation (Approx. Feet): 554

COURTESY OF VISIT FORT WORTH

Population: 2,230,708
Population Change: 5.70%

Race:
White: 42.2%
Black: 19.3%
Hispanic: 30.5%
Asian: 6.4%
Other: 1.2%

Vital Statistics:
Births: 28,137
Deaths: 15,785
Marriages: 10,991
Divorces: 7,553

2024 Rainfall: 36.83 in.
January Avg. Temp.: 42.3°F
July Avg. Temp.: 84.4°F

Unemployment Rate: 3.9
Per Capita Income: $65,765
Tourism Earnings: $6.6 billion
Avg. Home Value: $294,100

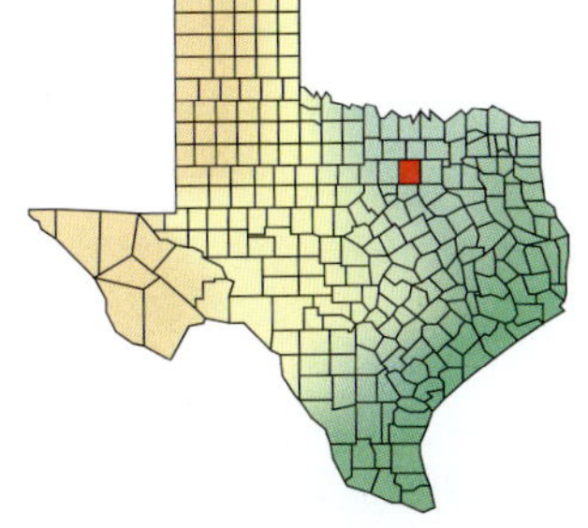

S

UNSPLASH/MATTHEW JUNGLING

TAYLOR
COUNTY

Named for three brothers who died defending the Alamo: Edward, James, and George Taylor.

Cities/Towns: Abilene, Buffalo Gap, Impact, Lawn, Merkel, Ovalo, Potosi, Trent, Tuscola, Tye

Land Area (Square Miles): 915.54
Elevation (Approx. Feet): 2,320

Population: 148,813
Population Change: 3.90%

Race:
White: 61.6%
Black: 9.0%
Hispanic: 25.4%
Asian: 2.2%
Other: 1.3%

Vital Statistics:
Births: 1,963
Deaths: 1,580
Marriages: 1,010
Divorces: 163

2024 Rainfall: 30.8 in.
January Avg. Temp.: 41.7°F
July Avg. Temp.: 83.3°F

Unemployment Rate: 3.4
Per Capita Income: $58,181
Tourism Earnings: $142.8 million
Avg. Home Value: $190,300

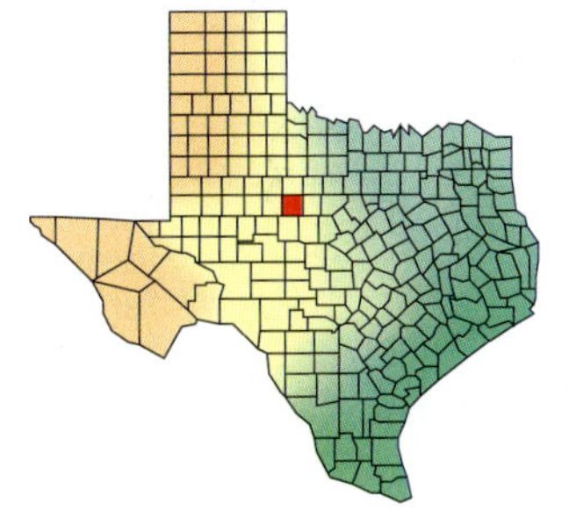

TERRELL
COUNTY

Named for Confederate General A.W. Terrell.

Cities/Towns: Sanderson, Dryden

Land Area (Square Miles): 2,357.96
Elevation (Approx. Feet): 2,392

Population: 718
Population Change: -5.50%

Race:
White: 44.0%
Black: 2.9%
Hispanic: 49.9%
Asian: 0.7%
Other: 4.5%

Vital Statistics:
Births: N/A
Deaths: N/A
Marriages: 2
Divorces: N/A

2024 Rainfall: 9.77 in.
January Avg. Temp.: 47.4°F
July Avg. Temp.: 84.5°F

Unemployment Rate: 3.7
Per Capita Income: $66,721
Tourism Earnings: $320,000
Avg. Home Value: $152,200

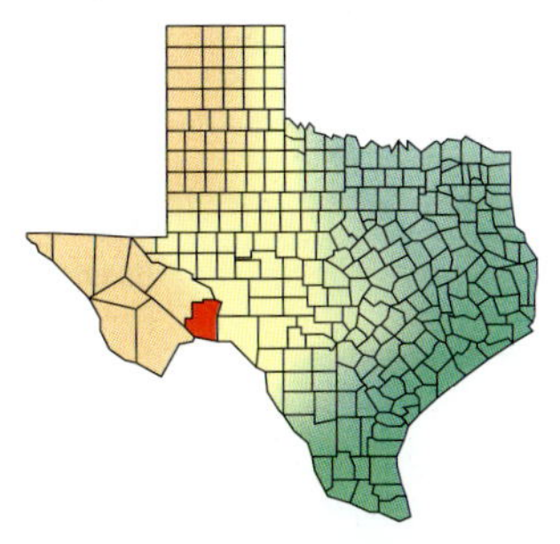

T

TERRY
COUNTY

Named for Confederate Colonel B.F. Terry, the head of the Eighth Texas Cavalry (Terry's Texas Rangers).

Cities/Towns: Brownfield, Meadow, Wellman

Land Area (Square Miles): 888.84
Elevation (Approx. Feet): 3,347

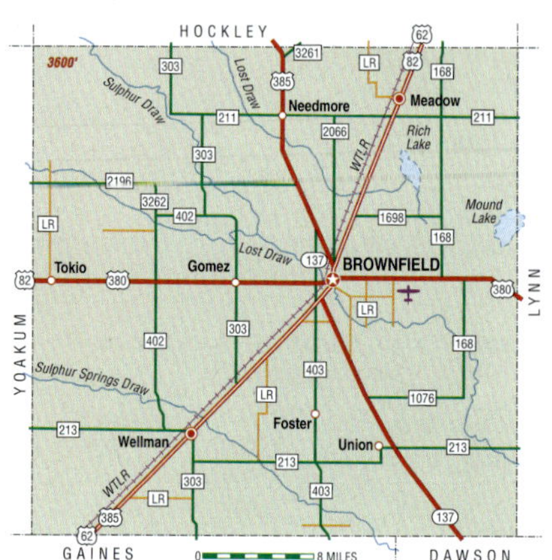

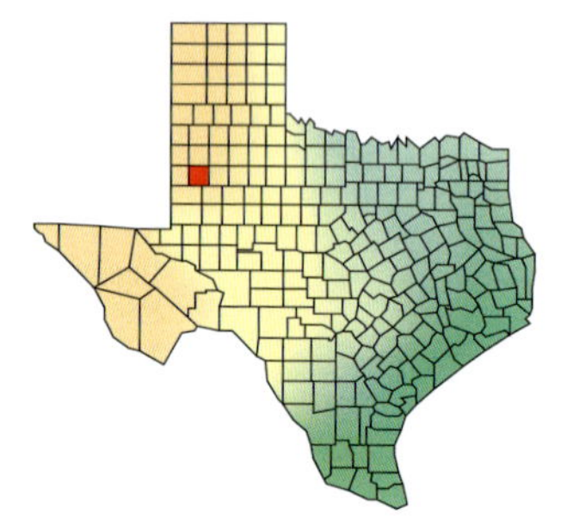

Population: 11,602
Population Change: -1.90%

Race:
White: 37.3%
Black: 4.8%
Hispanic: 57.2%
Asian: 0.7%
Other: 1.5%

Vital Statistics:
Births: 198
Deaths: 164
Marriages: 63
Divorces: 24

2024 Rainfall: 14.05 in.
January Avg. Temp.: 38.1°F
July Avg. Temp.: 80.9°F

Unemployment Rate: 3.7
Per Capita Income: $49,822
Tourism Earnings: $3.4 million
Avg. Home Value: $111,200

THROCKMORTON
COUNTY

Named for Dr. W.E. Throckmorton, the father of Governor J.W. Throckmorton.

Cities/Towns: Throckmorton, Elbert, Woodson

Land Area (Square Miles): 912.55
Elevation (Approx. Feet): 1,401

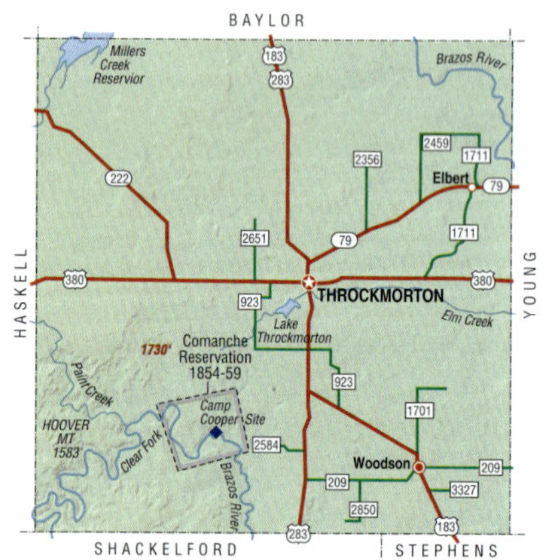

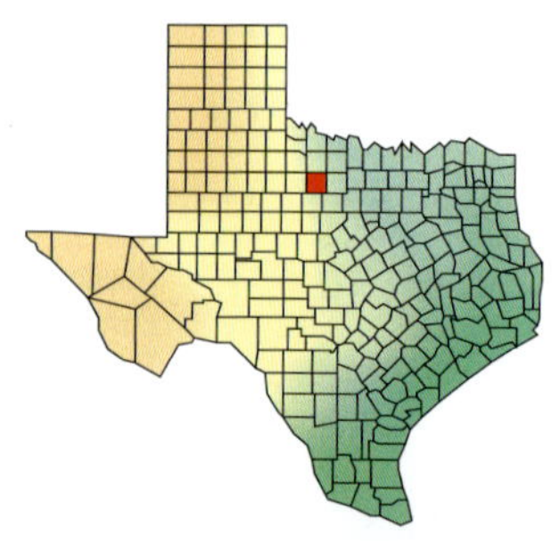

Population: 1,532
Population Change: 6.30%

Race:
White: 84.1%
Black: 1.2%
Hispanic: 12.1%
Asian: 0.7%
Other: 1.2%

Vital Statistics:
Births: 23
Deaths: 36
Marriages: 5
Divorces: 1

2024 Rainfall: 31.22 in.
January Avg. Temp.: 41°F
July Avg. Temp.: 84.6°F

Unemployment Rate: 4
Per Capita Income: $53,588
Tourism Earnings: $260,000
Avg. Home Value: $84,200

T

TITUS
COUNTY

Named for pioneer settler A.J. Titus.

Cities/Towns: Mount Pleasant, Cookville, Millers Cove, Talco, Winfield

Land Area (Square Miles): 406.06
Elevation (Approx. Feet): 423

Population: 31,547
Population Change: 1.00%

Race:
White: 42.5%
Black: 10.2%
Hispanic: 45.4%
Asian: 1.3%
Other: 2.4%

Vital Statistics:
Births: 436
Deaths: 338
Marriages: 178
Divorces: 50

2024 Rainfall: 58.09 in.
January Avg. Temp.: 41.9°F
July Avg. Temp.: 82.4°F

Unemployment Rate: 3.9
Per Capita Income: $52,359
Tourism Earnings: $14.2 million
Avg. Home Value: $157,900

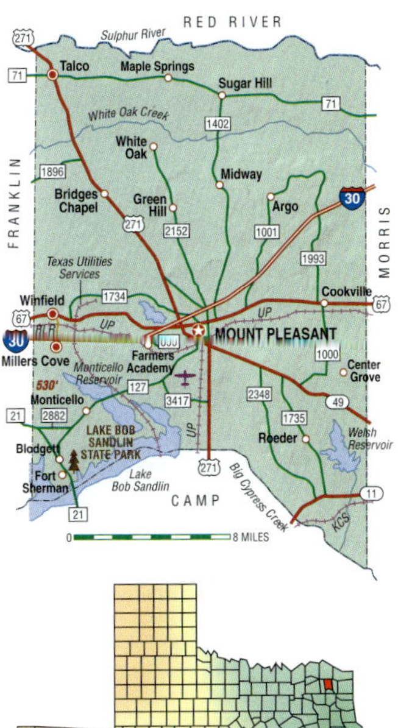

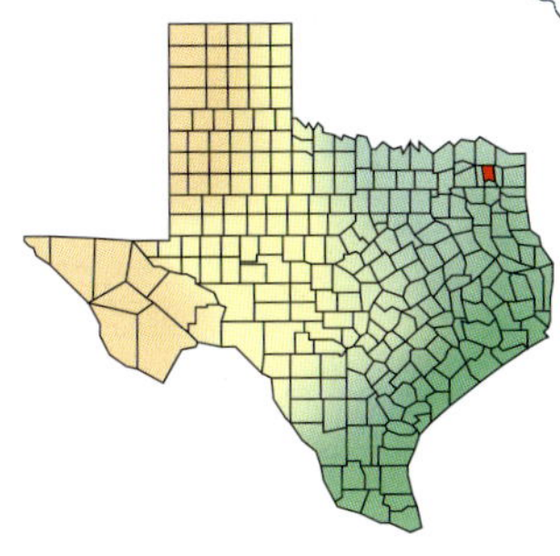

TOM GREEN
COUNTY

Named for Texas Revolution General Tom Green.

Cities/Towns: San Angelo, Carlsbad, Christoval, Grape Creek, Knickerbocker, Mereta, Vancourt, Veribest, Wall, Water Valley

Land Area (Square Miles): 1,522.00
Elevation (Approx. Feet): 1,864

Population: 120,103
Population Change: 0.10%

Race:
White: 51.9%
Black: 4.4%
Hispanic: 41.2%
Asian: 1.5%
Other: 1.4%

Vital Statistics:
Births: 1,444
Deaths: 1,252
Marriages: 827
Divorces: 345

2024 Rainfall: 20.35 in.
January Avg. Temp.: 43.3°F
July Avg. Temp.: 83.8°F

Unemployment Rate: 3.2
Per Capita Income: $65,314
Tourism Earnings: $104.5 million
Avg. Home Value: $186,700

TRAVIS
COUNTY

Named for Alamo commander Colonel William B. Travis.

Cities/Towns: Austin, Bee Cave, Briar Cliff, Creedmoor, Garfield, Hornsby Bend, Hudson Bend, Jonestown, Lago Vista, Lakeway, Manchaca, Manor, Mustang Ridge, Pflugerville, Point Venture, Rollingwood, San Leanna, Steiner Ranch, Sunset Valley, Wells Branch, West Lake Hills, Cedar Park, Round Rock, Elgin

Land Area (Square Miles): 994.05
Elevation (Approx. Feet): 492

Population: 1,363,767
Population Change: 5.70%

Race:
White: 47.9%
Black: 9.5%
Hispanic: 32.4%
Asian: 8.8%
Other: 1.3%

Vital Statistics:
Births: 16,433
Deaths: 6,829
Marriages: 7,382
Divorces: 3,494

2024 Rainfall: 29.96 in.
January Avg. Temp.: 46.5°F
July Avg. Temp.: 83.4°F

Unemployment Rate: 3.5
Per Capita Income: $91,887
Tourism Earnings: $3.4 billion
Avg. Home Value: $487,600

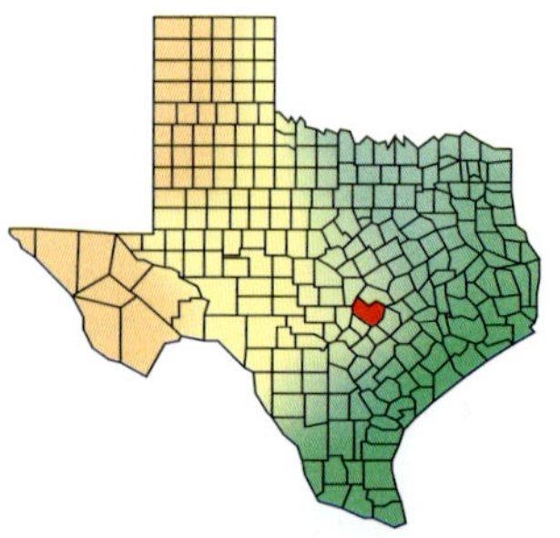

TRINITY
COUNTY

Named for the Trinity River.

Cities/Towns: Groveton, Trinity, Apple Springs, Centralia, Pennington, Sebastopol, Westwood Shores

Land Area (Square Miles): 693.8
Elevation (Approx. Feet): 312

Population: 14,489
Population Change: 6.50%

Race:
White: 76.5%
Black: 8.8%
Hispanic: 12.0%
Asian: 0.7%
Other: 1.2%

Vital Statistics:
Births: 110
Deaths: 239
Marriages: 45
Divorces: 26

2024 Rainfall: 74.67 in.
January Avg. Temp.: 46°F
July Avg. Temp.: 81.5°F

Unemployment Rate: 5.1
Per Capita Income: $49,195
Tourism Earnings: $8 million
Avg. Home Value: $110,100

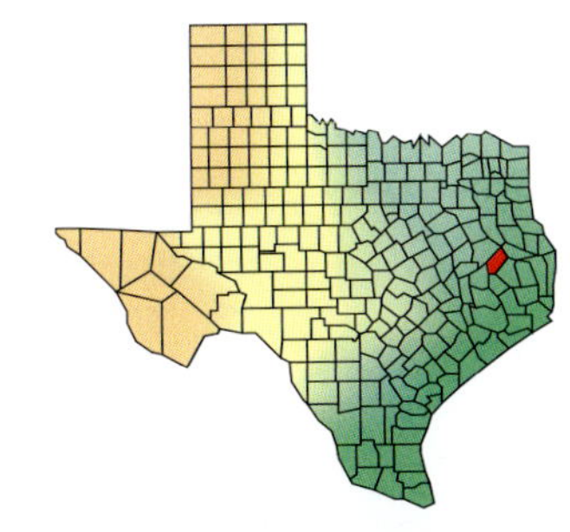

UNSPLASH/JESS ZOERB

T

TYLER
COUNTY

Named for U.S. President John Tyler.

Cities/Towns: Woodville, Chester, Colmesneil, Doucette, Fred, Hillister, Ivanhoe, Spurger, Warren

Land Area (Square Miles): 924.39
Elevation (Approx. Feet): 269

Population: 20,560
Population Change: 3.70%

Race:
White: 76.9%
Black: 11.9%
Hispanic: 8.9%
Asian: 0.7%
Other: 1.2%

Vital Statistics:
Births: 198
Deaths: 303
Marriages: 85
Divorces: 96

2024 Rainfall: 79.78 in.
January Avg. Temp.: 46.3°F
July Avg. Temp.: 81.5°F

Unemployment Rate: 6.1
Per Capita Income: $44,662
Tourism Earnings: $2.4 million
Avg. Home Value: $138,400

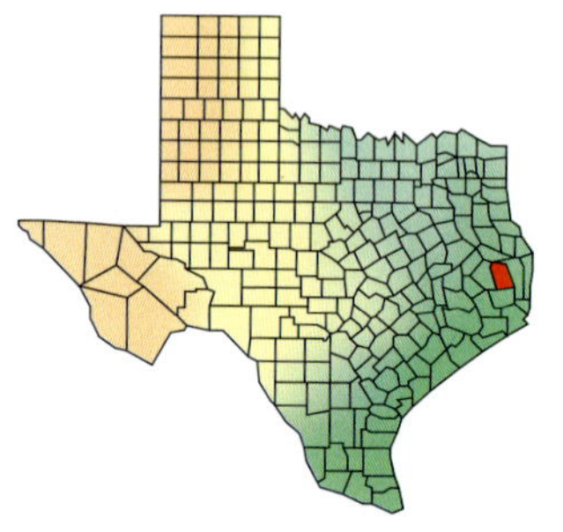

UPSHUR
COUNTY

Named for U.S. Secretary of State A.P. Upshur.

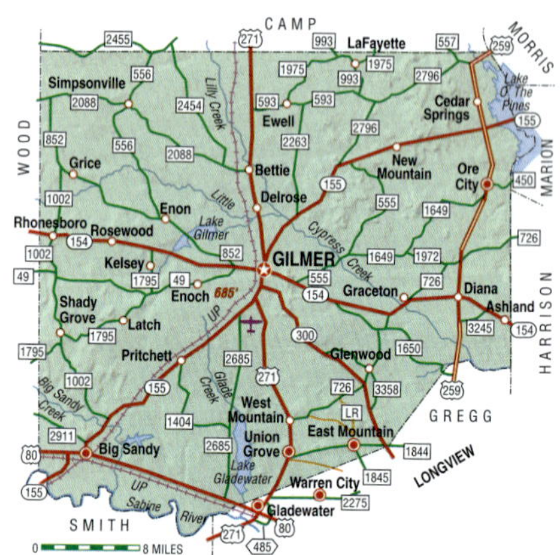

Cities/Towns: Gilmer, Big Sandy, Diana, East Mountain, Ore City, Union City, Gladewater

Land Area (Square Miles): 582.98
Elevation (Approx. Feet): 345

Population: 44,050
Population Change: 7.70%

Race:
White: 77.9%
Black: 8.0%
Hispanic: 10.7%
Asian: 0.8%
Other: 1.3%

Vital Statistics:
Births: 518
Deaths: 568
Marriages: 162
Divorces: 150

2024 Rainfall: 62.41 in.
January Avg. Temp.: 42.6°F
July Avg. Temp.: 81.2°F

Unemployment Rate: 4.5
Per Capita Income: $46,654
Tourism Earnings: $5 million
Avg. Home Value: $171,200

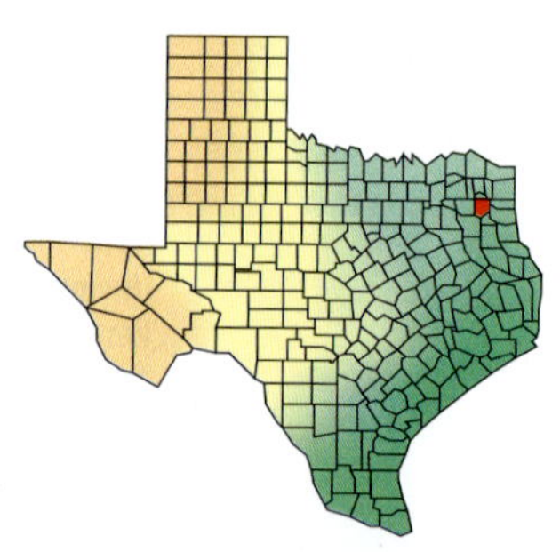

UPTON
COUNTY

Named for brothers John and William Upton, who served as Confederate colonels.

Cities/Towns: Rankin, McCamey, Midkiff

Land Area (Square Miles): 1,241.32
Elevation (Approx. Feet): 2,740

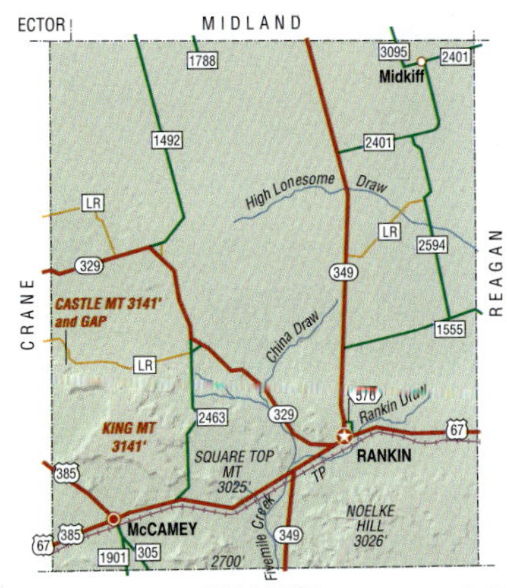

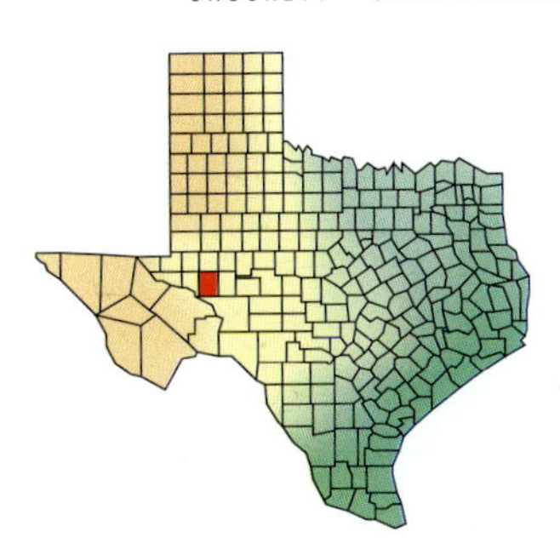

Population: 3,138
Population Change: -5.50%

Race:
White: 77.9%
Black: 8.0%
Hispanic: 10.7%
Asian: 0.8%
Other: 1.1%

Vital Statistics:
Births: 40
Deaths: 34
Marriages: 18
Divorces: 20

2024 Rainfall: 10.01 in.
January Avg. Temp.: 45.6°F
July Avg. Temp.: 83.8°F

Unemployment Rate: 1.7
Per Capita Income: $88,874
Tourism Earnings: $970,000
Avg. Home Value: $106,300

UVALDE
COUNTY

Named for Spanish governor of Coahuila, Juan de Ugalde.

Cities/Towns: Uvalde, Sabinal, Concan, Knippa, Utopia, Uvalde Estates

Land Area (Square Miles): 1,151.92
Elevation (Approx. Feet): 1,119

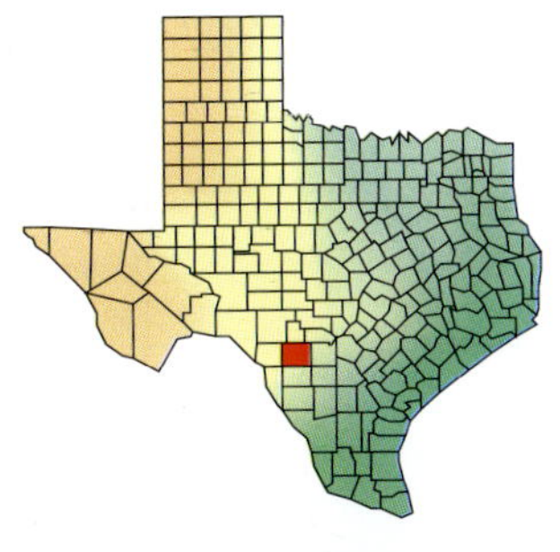

Population: 25,138
Population Change: 2.30%

Race:
White: 77.9%
Black: 8.0%
Hispanic: 10.7%
Asian: 0.8%
Other: 1.3%

Vital Statistics:
Births: 400
Deaths: 333
Marriages: 152
Divorces: 5

2024 Rainfall: 13.85 in.
January Avg. Temp.: 48.6°F
July Avg. Temp.: 85°F

Unemployment Rate: 4.2
Per Capita Income: $55,211
Tourism Earnings: $31.2 million
Avg. Home Value: $144,400

V

COURTESY OF LAUGHLIN AIRFORCE BASE/AIRMAN 1ST CLASS CODY MOTT

VAL VERDE
COUNTY

Named for a Civil War battle.

Cities/Towns: Del Rio, Laughlin Air Force Base, Cienegas Terrace, Comstock, Langtry, Val Verde Park

Land Area (Square Miles): 3,144.75
Elevation (Approx. Feet): 1,588

Population: 47,999
Population Change: 0.90%

Race:
White: 15.6%
Black: 2.5%
Hispanic: 81.2%
Asian: 0.9%
Other: 1.2%

Vital Statistics:
Births: 773
Deaths: 448
Marriages: 344
Divorces: 113

2024 Rainfall: 11.1 in.
January Avg. Temp.: 47°F
July Avg. Temp.: 85.3°F

Unemployment Rate: 5.2
Per Capita Income: $50,112
Tourism Earnings: $18.8 million
Avg. Home Value: $151,500

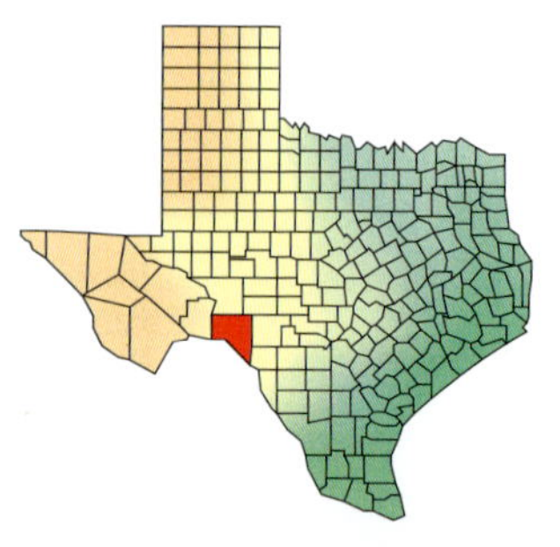

V

VAN ZANDT

COUNTY

Named for Republic leader Isaac Van Zandt.

Cities/Towns: Canton, Wills Point, Ben Wheeler, Edgewood, Edom, Fruitvale, Grand Saline, Van

Land Area (Square Miles): 842.57
Elevation (Approx. Feet): 512

Population: 65,304
Population Change: 9.70%

Race:
White: 80.2%
Black: 3.2%
Hispanic: 14.0%
Asian: 0.6%
Other: 1.1%

Vital Statistics:
Births: 674
Deaths: 828
Marriages: 309
Divorces: 200

2024 Rainfall: 59.2 in.
January Avg. Temp.: 41.4°F
July Avg. Temp.: 80.9°F

Unemployment Rate: 4.1
Per Capita Income: $48,399
Tourism Earnings: $14.8 million
Avg. Home Value: $199,500

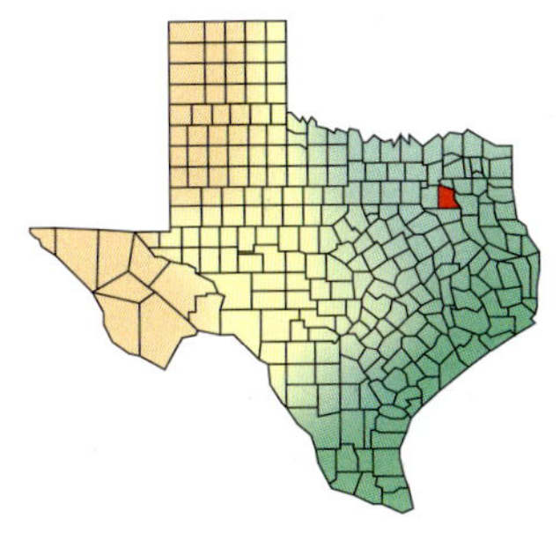

VICTORIA

COUNTY

Named for Mexican President Guadalupe Victoria.

Cities/Towns: Victoria, Bloomington, Inez, Nursery, Placedo, Telferner, Quail Creek

Land Area (Square Miles): 882.11
Elevation (Approx. Feet): 82

Population: 91,949
Population Change: 0.70%

Race:
White: 43.1%
Black: 6.5%
Hispanic: 48.4%
Asian: 1.4%
Other: 1.0%

Vital Statistics:
Births: 1,249
Deaths: 1,061
Marriages: 283
Divorces: 344

2024 Rainfall: 36.86 in.
January Avg. Temp.: 52.3°F
July Avg. Temp.: 82.8°F

Unemployment Rate: 4.1
Per Capita Income: $58,912
Tourism Earnings: $47.6 million
Avg. Home Value: $197,600

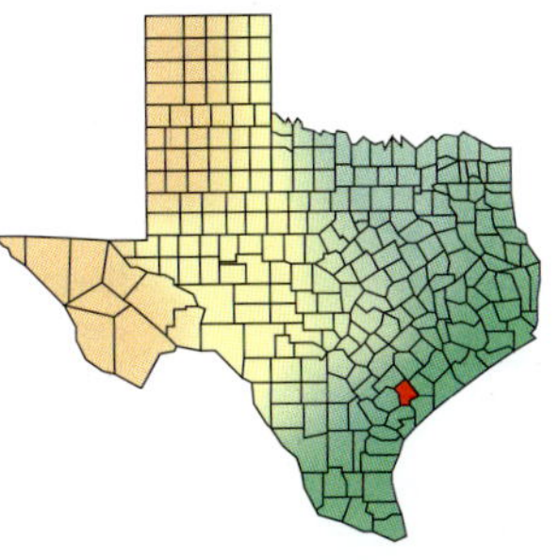

W

WALKER
COUNTY

Named for U.S. Secretary of the Treasury R.J. Walker. The county was renamed in 1863 for Texas Ranger Captain S.H. Walker.

Cities/Towns: Huntsville, Dodge, New Waverly, Riverside

Land Area (Square Miles): 784.22
Elevation (Approx. Feet): 390

Population: 83,722
Population Change: 9.60%

Race:
White: 53.8%
Black: 22.3%
Hispanic: 21.7%
Asian: 1.2%
Other: 1.0%

Vital Statistics:
Births: 694
Deaths: 682
Marriages: 385
Divorces: 210

2024 Rainfall: 71.57 in.
January Avg. Temp.: 46.8°F
July Avg. Temp.: 81.6°F

Unemployment Rate: 4.1
Per Capita Income: $35,913
Tourism Earnings: $30.2 million
Avg. Home Value: $207,900

WALLER
COUNTY

Named for Republic leader Edwin Waller.

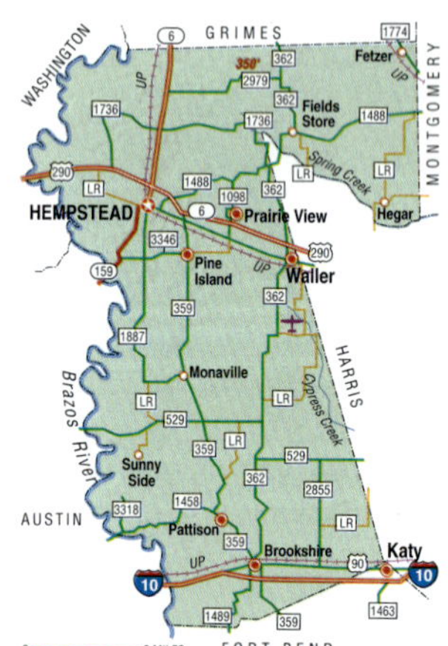

Cities/Towns: Hempstead, Prairie View, Brookshire, Pattison, Pine Island, Waller

Land Area (Square Miles): 513.3
Elevation (Approx. Feet): 233

Population: 65,109
Population Change: 14.70%

Race:
White: 38.2%
Black: 24.8%
Hispanic: 34.0%
Asian: 2.4%
Other: 1.7%

Vital Statistics:
Births: 770
Deaths: 466
Marriages: 288
Divorces: 68

2024 Rainfall: 52.75 in.
January Avg. Temp.: 50°F
July Avg. Temp.: 83.4°F

Unemployment Rate: 4.7
Per Capita Income: $55,463
Tourism Earnings: $14 million
Avg. Home Value: $292,000

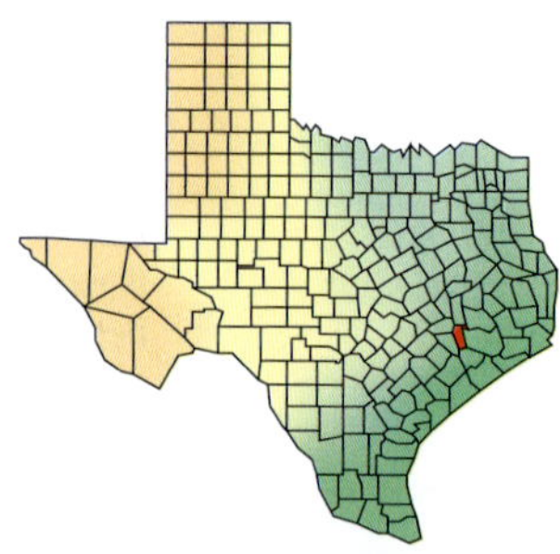

W

WARD
COUNTY

Named for Republic leader Thomas W. Ward.

Cities/Towns: Monahans, Barstow, Grandfalls, Pyote, Southwest Sandhill, Thorntonville, Wickett

Land Area (Square Miles): 835.6
Elevation (Approx. Feet): 2,612

Population: 11,038
Population Change: -5.20%

Race:
White: 36.1%
Black: 5.4%
Hispanic: 57.1%
Asian: 1.0%
Other: 1.8%

Vital Statistics:
Births: 184
Deaths: 136
Marriages: 73
Divorces: 38

2024 Rainfall: 5.62 in.
January Avg. Temp.: 45.8°F
July Avg. Temp.: 85.6°F

Unemployment Rate: 3.3
Per Capita Income: $67,647
Tourism Earnings: $14.6 million
Avg. Home Value: $138,800

WASHINGTON
COUNTY

Named for George Washington.

Cities/Towns: Brenham, Burton, Chappell Hill, Washington

Land Area (Square Miles): 604.19
Elevation (Approx. Feet): 236

Population: 37,810
Population Change: 5.60%

Race:
White: 62.6%
Black: 16.4%
Hispanic: 18.7%
Asian: 1.6%
Other: 0.7%

Vital Statistics:
Births: 342
Deaths: 439
Marriages: 164
Divorces: 92

2024 Rainfall: 49.78 in.
January Avg. Temp.: 49.2°F
July Avg. Temp.: 83.6°F

Unemployment Rate: 3.8
Per Capita Income: $73,880
Tourism Earnings: $27.7 million
Avg. Home Value: $270,100

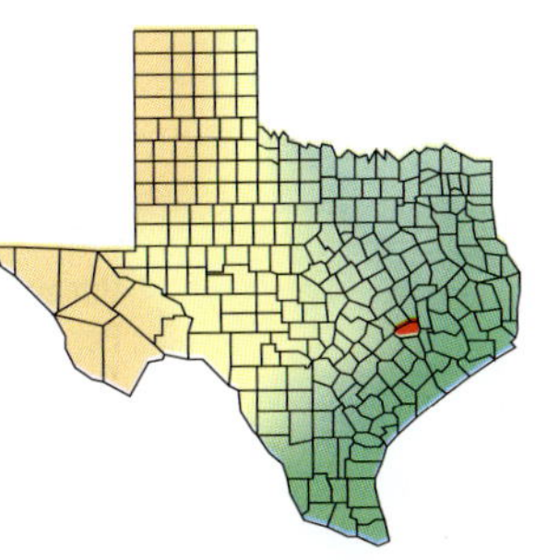

W

WEBB
COUNTY

Named for Republic leader James Webb.

Cities/Towns: Laredo, Bruni, El Cenizo, Mirando City, Oilton, Rio Bravo

Land Area (Square Miles): 3,361.48
Elevation (Approx. Feet): 558

Population: 272,823
Population Change: 2.10%

Race:
White: 3.9%
Black: 0.9%
Hispanic: 94.9%
Asian: 0.6%
Other: 0.7%

Vital Statistics:
Births: 4,534
Deaths: 1,809
Marriages: 1,456
Divorces: 16

2024 Rainfall: 15.68 in.
January Avg. Temp.: 54.3°F
July Avg. Temp.: 86.4°F

Unemployment Rate: 4.2
Per Capita Income: $42,757
Tourism Earnings: $191.6 million
Avg. Home Value: $178,900

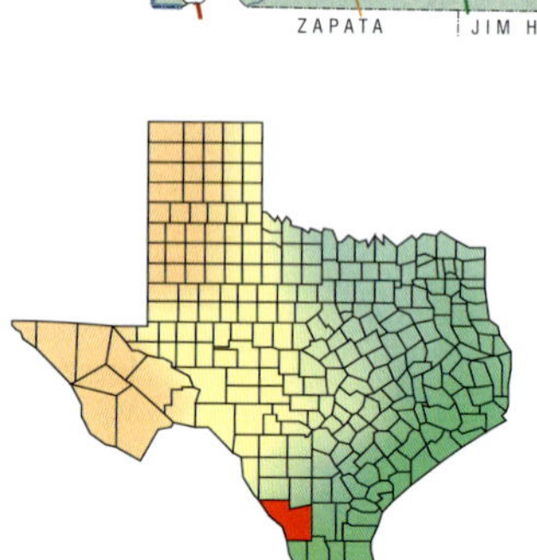

WHARTON
COUNTY

Named for brothers John A. and William H. Wharton, who were active in the Texas Revolution.

Cities/Towns: Wharton, El Campo, Boling, Danevang, East Bernard, Glen Flora, Hungerford, Lane City, Louise, Pierce

Land Area (Square Miles): 1,086.14
Elevation (Approx. Feet): 112

Population: 42,035
Population Change: 1.10%

Race:
White: 43.6%
Black: 13.8%
Hispanic: 42.3%
Asian: 0.8%
Other: 0.9%

Vital Statistics:
Births: 545
Deaths: 513
Marriages: 198
Divorces: 86

2024 Rainfall: 48.33 in.
January Avg. Temp.: 51.2°F
July Avg. Temp.: 83.9°F

Unemployment Rate: 4.3
Per Capita Income: $55,902
Tourism Earnings: $12.6 million
Avg. Home Value: $182,700

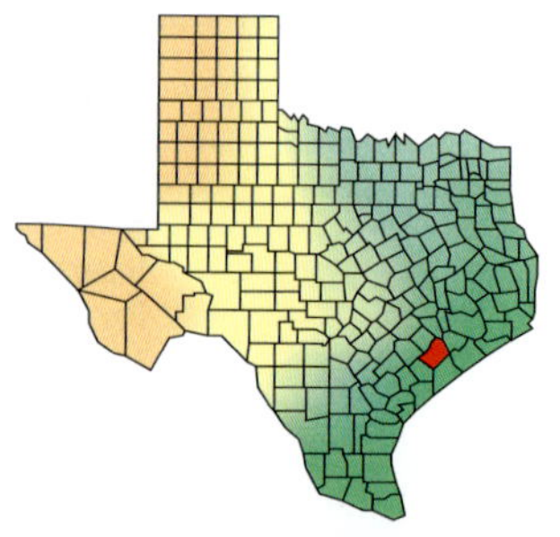

WHEELER
COUNTY

Named for pioneer jurist R.T. Wheeler.

Cities/Towns: Wheeler, Shamrock, Allison, Briscoe, Mobeetie

Land Area (Square Miles): 914.53
Elevation (Approx. Feet): 2,556

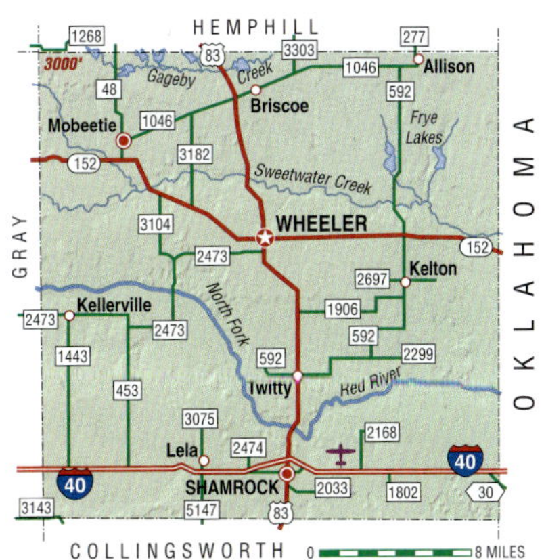

Population: 4,824
Population Change: -3.30%

Race:
White: 68.6%
Black: 3.2%
Hispanic: 25.0%
Asian: 0.9%
Other: 2.2%

Vital Statistics:
Births: 46
Deaths: 80
Marriages: 41
Divorces: 2

2024 Rainfall: 24.33 in.
January Avg. Temp.: 35°F
July Avg. Temp.: 81.8°F

Unemployment Rate: 3.3
Per Capita Income: $54,067
Tourism Earnings: $2.7 million
Avg. Home Value: $97,600

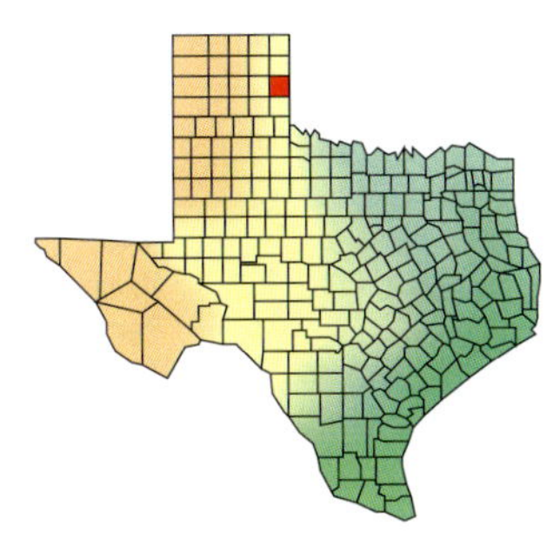

WICHITA
COUNTY

Named for the Wichita Native Americans.

Cities/Towns: Wichita Falls, Burkburnett, Cashion, Electra, Iowa Park, Kamay, Pleasant Valley

Land Area (Square Miles): 627.59
Elevation (Approx. Feet): 1,034

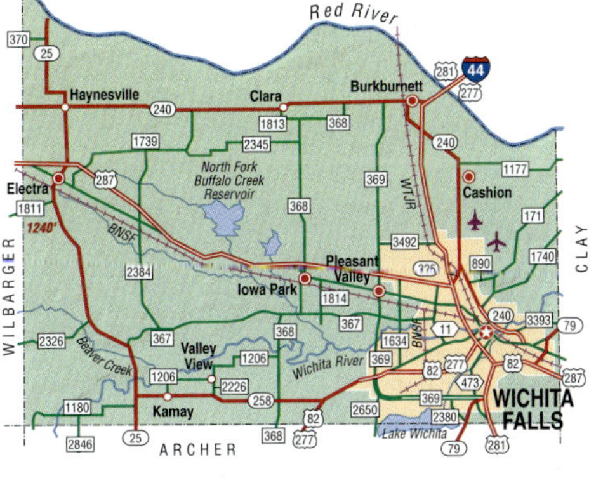

Population: 129,984
Population Change: 0.50%

Race:
White: 62.9%
Black: 11.3%
Hispanic: 20.9%
Asian: 2.3%
Other: 1.7%

Vital Statistics:
Births: 1,526
Deaths: 1,616
Marriages: 772
Divorces: 328

2024 Rainfall: 34.43 in.
January Avg. Temp.: 38.4°F
July Avg. Temp.: 84.2°F

Unemployment Rate: 3.8
Per Capita Income: $55,278
Tourism Earnings: $67.1 million
Avg. Home Value: $141,600

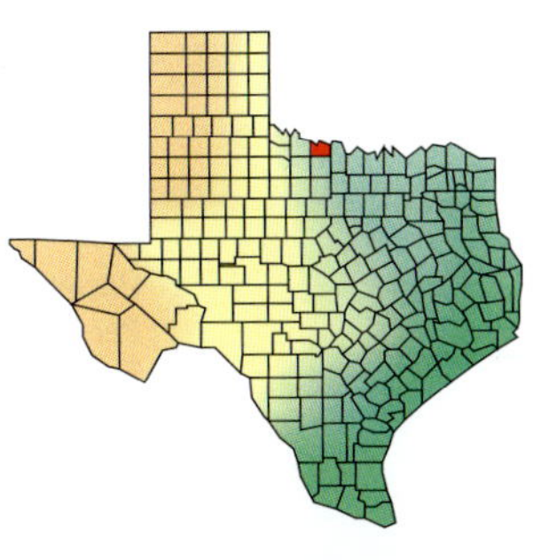

W

WILBARGER
COUNTY

Named for pioneers Josiah and Mathias Wilbarger.

Cities/Towns: Vernon, Harrold, Lockett, Odell, Oklaunion

Land Area (Square Miles): 970.95
Elevation (Approx. Feet): 1,260

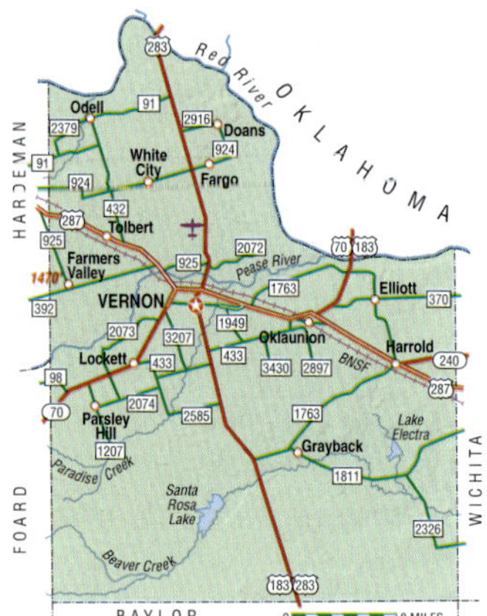

Population: 12,455
Population Change: -3.40%

Race:
White: 55.2%
Black: 8.7%
Hispanic: 30.8%
Asian: 3.4%
Other: 1.7%

Vital Statistics:
Births: 158
Deaths: 189
Marriages: 90
Divorces: 33

2024 Rainfall: 26.83 in.
January Avg. Temp.: 38.1°F
July Avg. Temp.: 84.4°F

Unemployment Rate: 3.7
Per Capita Income: $67,115
Tourism Earnings: $7.3 million
Avg. Home Value: $98,800

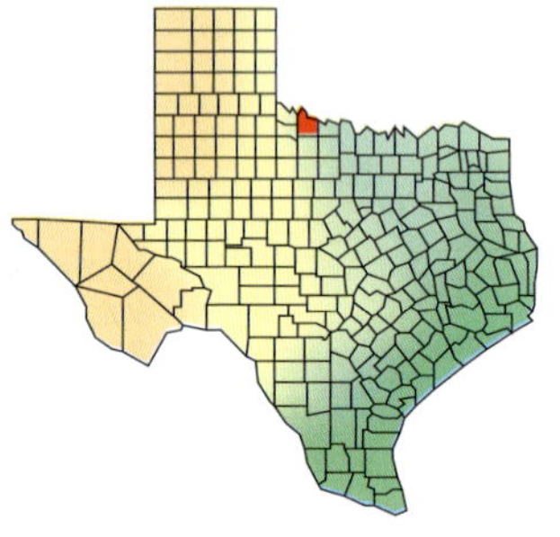

WILLACY
COUNTY

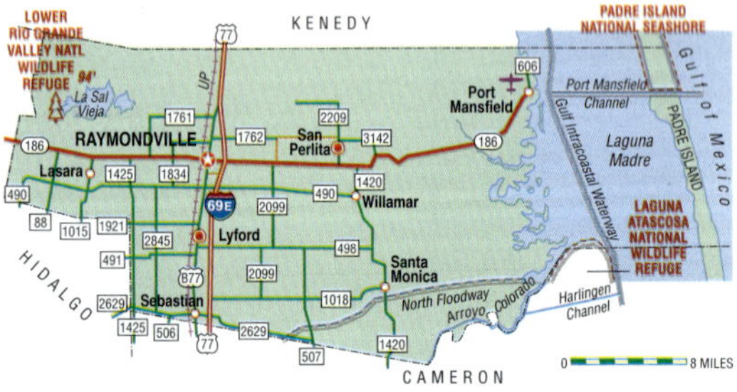

Named for legislator John G. Willacy.

Cities/Towns: Raymondville, Lasara, Lyford, Port Mansfield, San Perlita, Sebastian

Land Area (Square Miles): 590.6
Elevation (Approx. Feet): 20

Population: 20,027
Population Change: -0.70%

Race:
White: 9.5%
Black: 3.1%
Hispanic: 87.2%
Asian: 0.9%
Other: 0.8%

Vital Statistics:
Births: 234
Deaths: 228
Marriages: 59
Divorces: 39

2024 Rainfall: 30.92 in.
January Avg. Temp.: 59.1°F
July Avg. Temp.: 84.8°F

Unemployment Rate: 5.5
Per Capita Income: $35,832
Tourism Earnings: $6.2 million
Avg. Home Value: $60,800

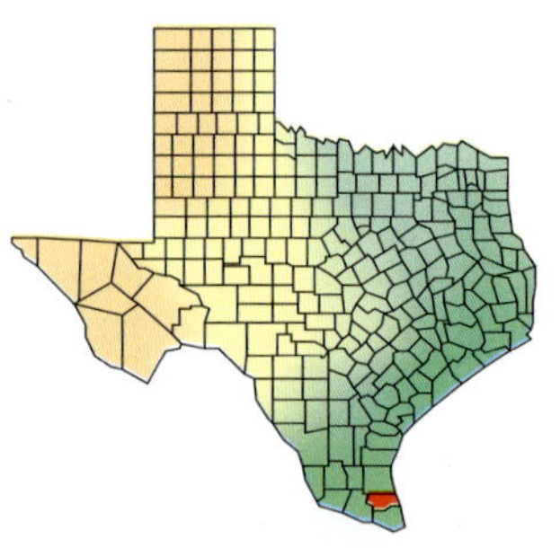

W

WILLIAMSON
COUNTY

Named for pioneer leader Robert M. Williamson.

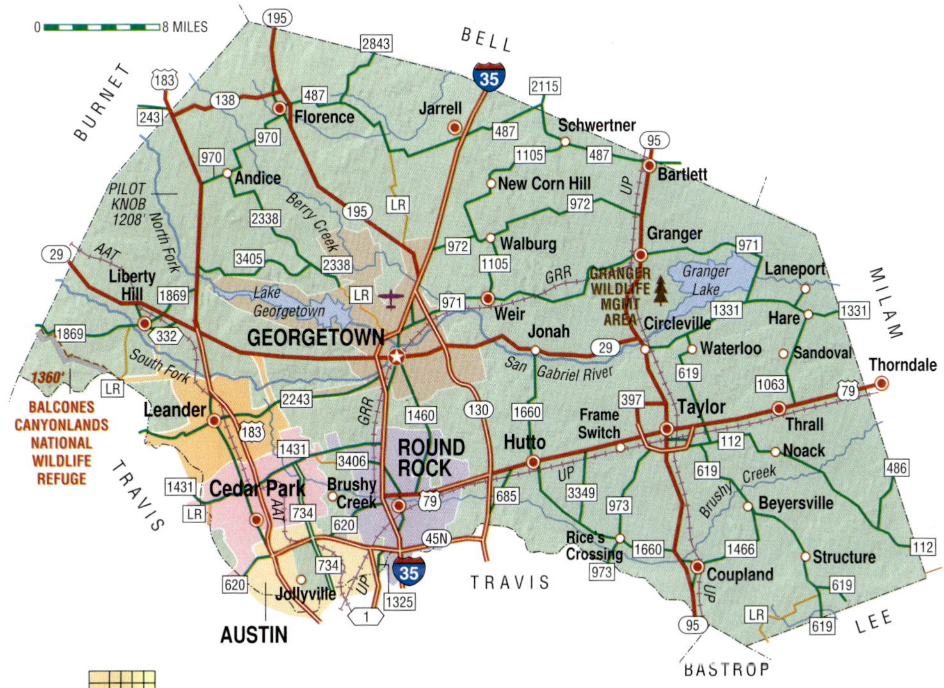

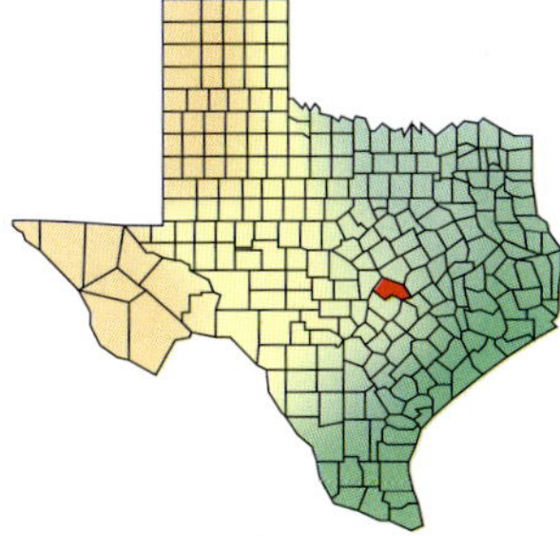

Cities/Towns: Georgetown, Round Rock, Cedar Park, Leander, Taylor, Bartlett, Brushy Creek, Coupland, Florence, Granger, Hutto, Jarrell, Jollyville, Liberty Hill, Schwertner, Thrall, Walburg, Weir

Land Area (Square Miles): 1,115.83
Elevation (Approx. Feet): 669

Population: 727,480
Population Change: 19.40%

Race:
White: 53.4%
Black: 8.1%
Hispanic: 24.9%
Asian: 11.7%
Other: 1.1%

Vital Statistics:
Births: 8,077
Deaths: 3,913
Marriages: 2,551
Divorces: 798

2024 Rainfall: 32.15 in.
January Avg. Temp.: 45.8°F
July Avg. Temp.: 83°F

Unemployment Rate: 3.6
Per Capita Income: $72,828
Tourism Earnings: $357.2 million
Avg. Home Value: $414,600

WILSON COUNTY

Named for Mier Expedition member James C. Wilson.

Cities/Towns: Floresville, La Vernia, Pandora, Poth, Stockdale, Sutherland Springs

Land Area (Square Miles): 803.73
Elevation (Approx. Feet): 486

Population: 55,415
Population Change: 11.40%

Race:
White: 55.0%
Black: 2.4%
Hispanic: 40.7%
Asian: 0.9%
Other: 1.2%

Vital Statistics:
Births: 546
Deaths: 480
Marriages: 183
Divorces: 117

2024 Rainfall: 26.79 in.
January Avg. Temp.: 49.3°F
July Avg. Temp.: 84.1°F

Unemployment Rate: 3.4
Per Capita Income: $59,578
Tourism Earnings: $15.5 million
Avg. Home Value: $286,300

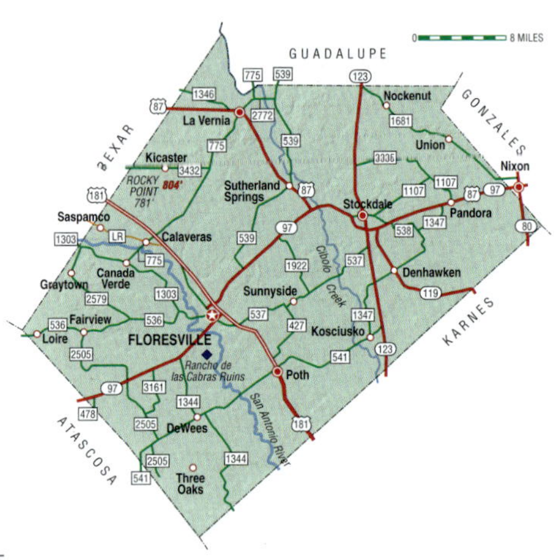

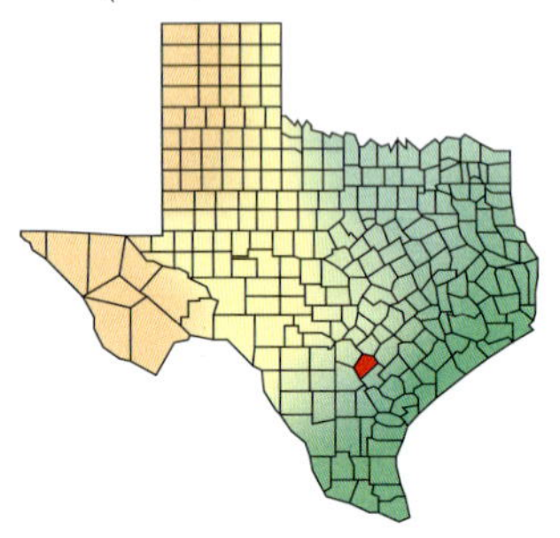

WINKLER COUNTY

Named for Confederate Colonel C.M. Winkler.

Cities/Towns: Kermit, Wink

Land Area (Square Miles): 841.27
Elevation (Approx. Feet): 2,877

Population: 7,381
Population Change: -5.30%

Race:
White: 31.3%
Black: 3.8%
Hispanic: 63.8%
Asian: 1.1%
Other: 2.4%

Vital Statistics:
Births: 108
Deaths: 65
Marriages: 46
Divorces: 15

2024 Rainfall: 5.78 in.
January Avg. Temp.: 44.4°F
July Avg. Temp.: 84.5°F

Unemployment Rate: 3.1
Per Capita Income: $75,821
Tourism Earnings: $3.7 million
Avg. Home Value: $121,200

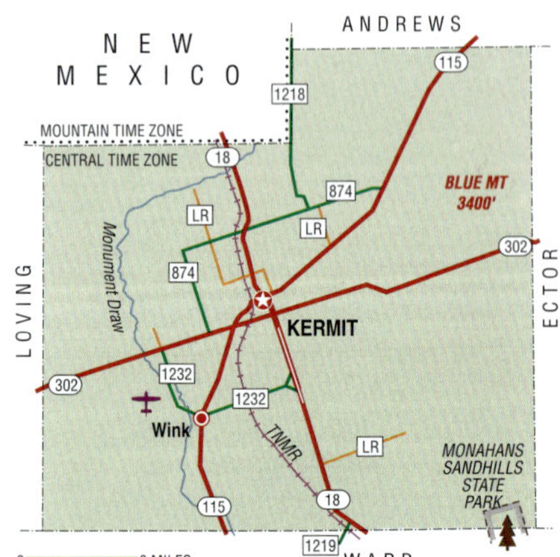

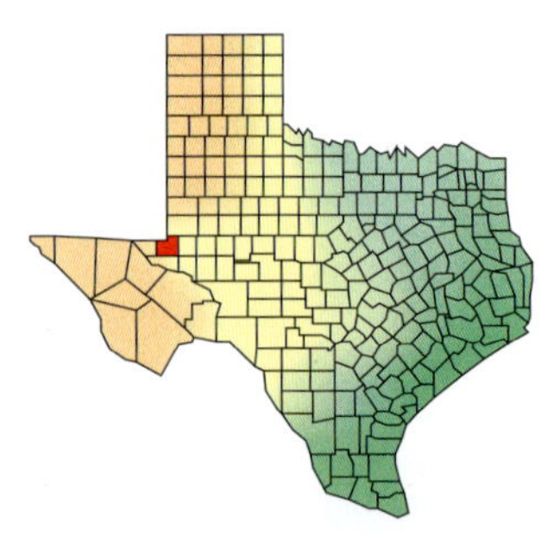

WISE
COUNTY

Named for Virginian U.S. Representative Henry A. Wise, who favored the annexation of Texas.

Cities/Towns: Decatur, Bridgeport, Alvord, Aurora, Boyd, Chico, Greenwood, Lake Bridgeport, Newark, New Fairview, Paradise, Pecan Acres, Rhome, Runaway Bay, Slidell

Land Area (Square Miles): 904.39
Elevation (Approx. Feet): 837

Population: 81,275
Population Change: 18.40%

Race:
White: 73.5%
Black: 2.1%
Hispanic: 21.5%
Asian: 0.8%
Other: 1.3%

Vital Statistics:
Births: 866
Deaths: 805
Marriages: 345
Divorces: 297

2024 Rainfall: 38.25 in.
January Avg. Temp.: 40.1°F
July Avg. Temp.: 83.8°F

Unemployment Rate: 3.7
Per Capita Income: $59,092
Tourism Earnings: $24 million
Avg. Home Value: $277,200

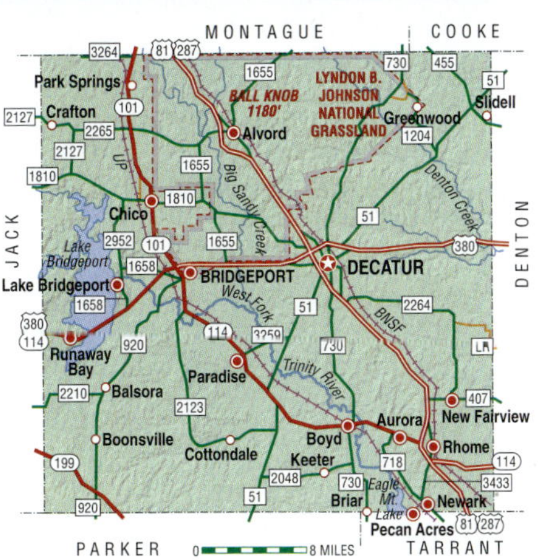

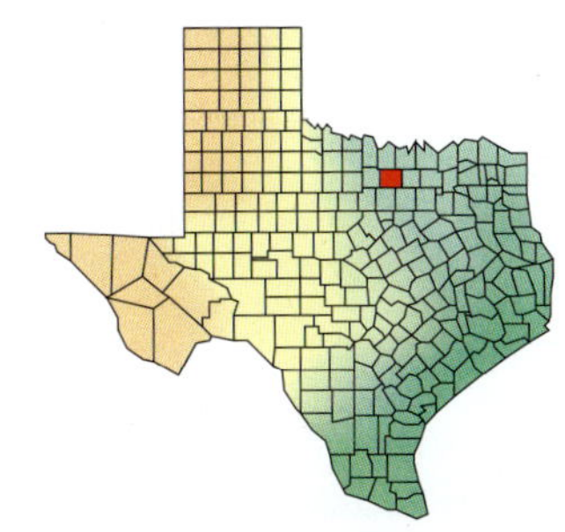

UNSPLASH/LESLIE KOENIG

UNSPLASH/YS

WOOD
COUNTY

Named for Governor George T. Wood.

Cities/Towns: Quitman, Mineola, Winnsboro, Alba, Golden, Hawkins, Holly Lake Ranch, Yantis

Land Area (Square Miles): 645.24
Elevation (Approx. Feet): 410

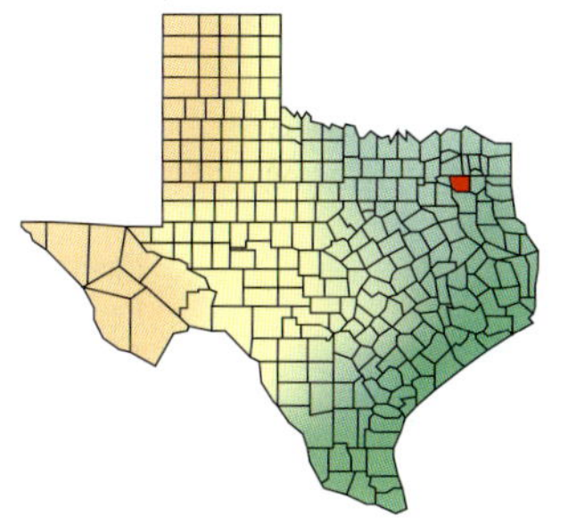

Population: 48,742
Population Change: 8.70%

Race:
White: 81.5%
Black: 4.4%
Hispanic: 11.7%
Asian: 0.8%
Other: 1.2%

Vital Statistics:
Births: 444
Deaths: 799
Marriages: 191
Divorces: 151

2024 Rainfall: 60.08 in.
January Avg. Temp.: 41.8°F
July Avg. Temp.: 81°F

Unemployment Rate: 4.8
Per Capita Income: $50,674
Tourism Earnings: $10.3 million
Avg. Home Value: $195,100

YOAKUM
COUNTY

Named for pioneer historian Henderson Yoakum.

Cities/Towns: Plains, Denver City

Land Area (Square Miles): 799.72
Elevation (Approx. Feet): 3,655

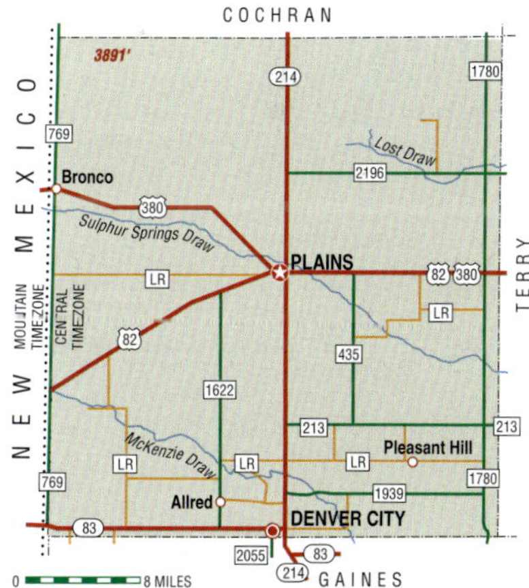

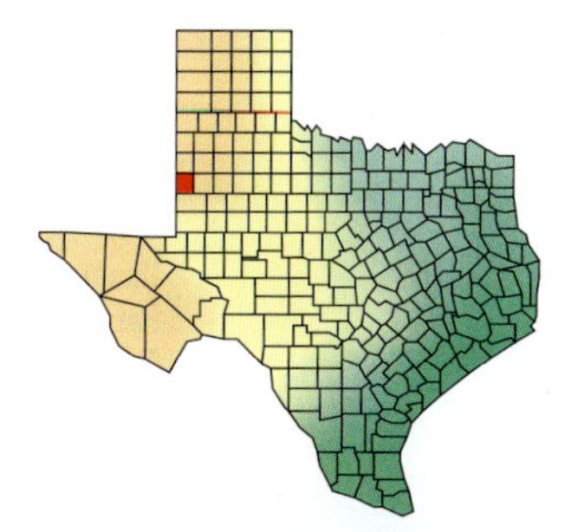

Population: 7,581
Population Change: -1.40%

Race:
White: 30.9%
Black: 1.8%
Hispanic: 65.8%
Asian: 0.7%
Other: 2.2%

Vital Statistics:
Births: 136
Deaths: 82
Marriages: 45
Divorces: 30

2024 Rainfall: 10.01 in.
January Avg. Temp.: 38.2°F
July Avg. Temp.: 80.2°F

Unemployment Rate: 3.5
Per Capita Income: $61,028
Tourism Earnings: $1.4 million
Avg. Home Value: $183,000

Y

YOUNG
COUNTY

Named for Colonel William Cooke Young.

Cities/Towns: Graham, Loving, Newcastle, Olney, South Bend

Land Area (Square Miles): 914.5
Elevation (Approx. Feet): 1,211

Population: 18,236
Population Change: 2.10%

Race:
White: 75.0%
Black: 1.8%
Hispanic: 21.0%
Asian: 0.8%
Other: 1.5%

Vital Statistics:
Births: 217
Deaths: 288
Marriages: 79
Divorces: 54

2024 Rainfall: 34.08 in.
January Avg. Temp.: 40.2°F
July Avg. Temp.: 84°F

Unemployment Rate: 3.5
Per Capita Income: $69,691
Tourism Earnings: $9.1 million
Avg. Home Value: $165,300

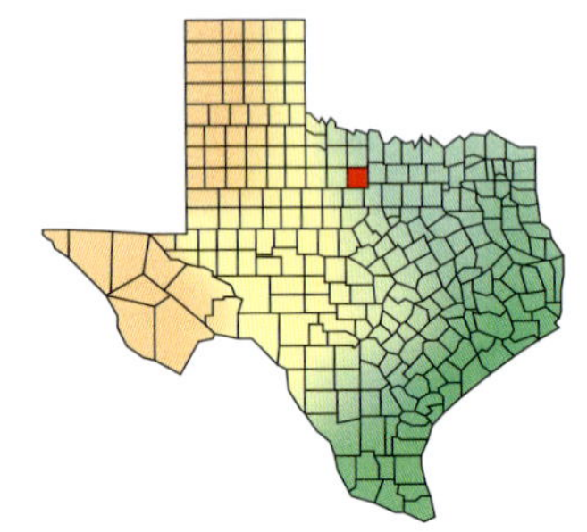

ZAPATA
COUNTY

Named for pioneer rancher Colonel Antonio Zapata.

Cities/Towns: Zapata, Falcon Lake Estates, Lopeño, Medina, San Ygnacio

Land Area (Square Miles): 998.41
Elevation (Approx. Feet): 381

Population: 13,819
Population Change: -0.50%

Race:
White: 4.8%
Black: 0.9%
Hispanic: 94.2%
Asian: 0.3%
Other: 0.6%

Vital Statistics:
Births: 175
Deaths: 123
Marriages: 37
Divorces: N/A

2024 Rainfall: 14.54 in.
January Avg. Temp.: 56.4°F
July Avg. Temp.: 86.8°F

Unemployment Rate: 6.9
Per Capita Income: $34,154
Tourism Earnings: $3.7 million
Avg. Home Value: $88,800

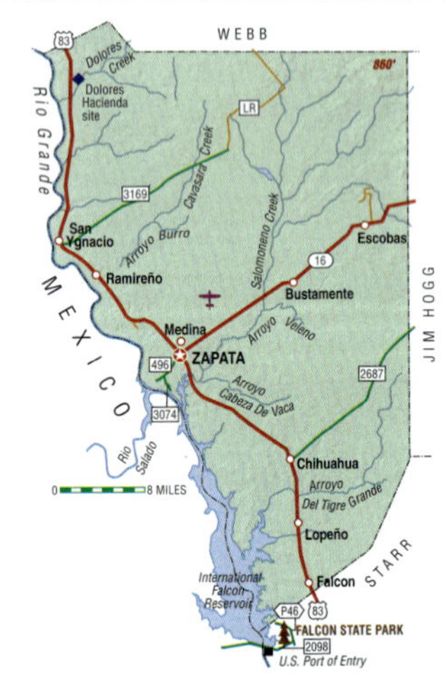

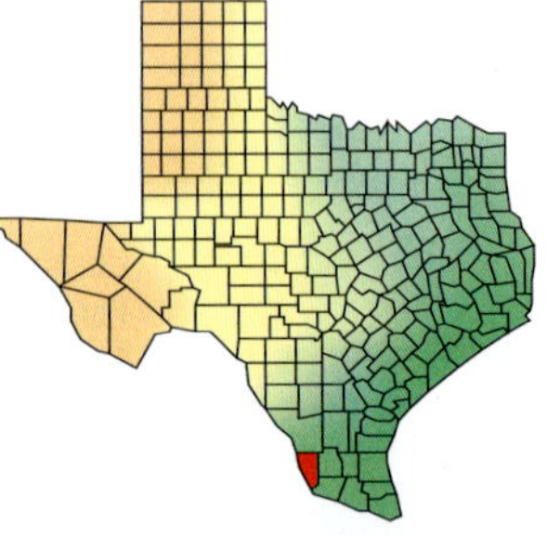

ZAVALA
COUNTY

Named for Texas Revolutionary leader Lorenzo de Zavala.

Cities/Towns: Crystal City, Batesville, Chula Vista, La Pryor

Land Area (Square Miles): 1,297.41
Elevation (Approx. Feet): 663

Population: 9,209
Population Change: -4.70%

Race:
White: 5.7%
Black: 1.9%
Hispanic: 92.7%
Asian: 0.4%
Other: 1.7%

Vital Statistics:
Births: 158
Deaths: 114
Marriages: 30
Divorces: N/A

2024 Rainfall: 14.51 in.
January Avg. Temp.: 50.6°F
July Avg. Temp.: 86.8°F

Unemployment Rate: 6.1
Per Capita Income: $47,333
Tourism Earnings: $1.1 million
Avg. Home Value: $88,100

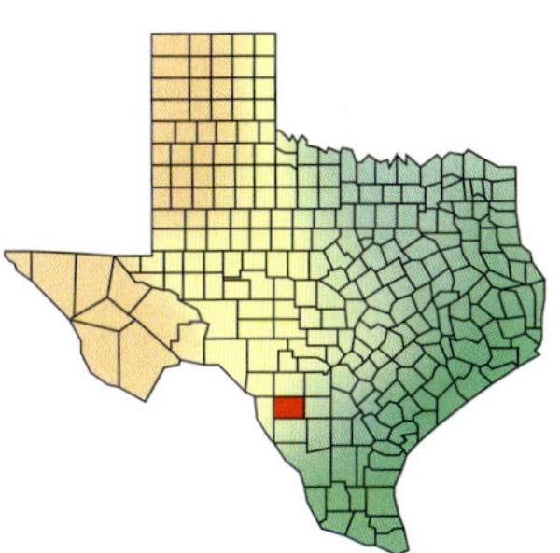

UNSPLASH/CHARLIE FAIR

The information in this chapter came from the following sources. Years in parentheses indicate the most recent data available at the time of this publication.

All "Named for" blurbs and maps are from previous editions of the *Texas Almanac*.

Land Area: *U.S. Census Bureau.*
Elevation: *U.S. Geological Survey.*
Population: *U.S. Census Bureau* (2024 estimates).
Population Change: *U.S. Census Bureau, change from 2020 Census data.*
Race: *U.S. Census Bureau* (2024).
Births and Deaths: *Texas Department of State Health Services, Center for Health Statistics* (2022).
Marriage and Divorces*: Texas Department of State Health Services, Marriage/Divorce Indexes* (2019, 2017).
Climate: *National Centers for Environmental Information* (2024).
Unemployment Rate: *Texas Workforce Commission* (2024).
Per Capita Income: *Bureau of Economic Analysis* (2023).
Tourism Earnings: *Texas Travel Research Dashboard* (2024).
Average Home Value: *U.S. Census Bureau* (2024).

fort worth zoo

Texas

ENVIRONMENT

UNSPLASH/AARON OWENS

PHYSICAL REGIONS

GULF COASTAL PLAINS

Texas' Gulf Coastal Plains are the western extension of the coastal plain extending from the Atlantic Ocean to beyond the Rio Grande. Its characteristic rolling to hilly surface covered with a heavy growth of pine and hardwoods extends into East Texas. In the increasingly arid west, however, its forests become secondary in nature, consisting largely of post oaks and, farther west, prairies and brushlands.

The interior limit of the Gulf Coastal Plains in Texas is the line of the Balcones Fault and Escarpment. This geologic fault or shearing of underground strata extends eastward from a point on the Rio Grande near Del Rio. It extends to the northwestern part of Bexar County, where it turns northeastward and extends through Comal, Hays, and Travis counties, intersecting the Colorado River immediately north of Austin. The fault line is a single, definite geologic feature, accompanied by a line of southward- and eastward-facing hills.

The resemblance of the hills to balconies when viewed from the plain below accounts for the Spanish name for this area: balcones.

North of Waco, features of the fault zone are sufficiently inconspicuous that the interior boundary of the Coastal Plain follows the traditional geologic contact between upper and lower Cretaceous rocks. This contact is along the eastern edge of the Eastern Cross Timbers.

This fault line is usually accepted as the boundary between lowland and upland Texas. Below the fault line, the surface is characteristically coastal plains. Above the Balcones Fault, the surface is characteristically interior rolling plains.

This section was reviewed by Dr. David R. Butler, Texas State University System Regents' Professor of Geography.

Pine Belt or "Piney Woods"

The Pine Belt, called the "Piney Woods," extends 75 to 125 miles into Texas from the east. From north to south, it extends from the Red River to within about 25 miles of the Gulf Coast. Interspersed among the pines are hardwood timbers, usually in valleys of rivers and creeks. This area is the source of practically all of Texas' commercial timber production. It was settled early in Texas' history and is one of the oldest farming areas in the state.

This area's soils and climate are adaptable to the production of a variety of fruit and vegetable crops. Cattle raising is widespread, along with the development of pastures planted to improved grasses. There is a large iron-and-steel industry near Daingerfield in Morris County based on nearby iron deposits.

A great oil field discovered in Gregg, Rusk, and Smith counties in 1931 has contributed greatly to the region's economic growth. This area has a variety of clays, lignite, and other minerals as potentials for development.

Post Oak Belt

The main Post Oak Belt of Texas is wedged between the Pine Belt on the east, Blacklands on the west, and the Coastal Prairies on the south, covering a considerable area in East-Central Texas. The principal industry is diversified farming and livestock raising.

It is spotty in character, with some insular areas of blackland soil and some that closely resemble those of the Pine Belt. There is a small, isolated area of loblolly pines in Bastrop, Caldwell, Fayette, and Lee counties known as the "Lost Pines" — the westernmost southern pines in the United States. The Post Oak Belt has lignite, commercial clays, and some other minerals.

Blackland Belt

The Blackland Belt stretches from the Rio Grande to the Red River, lying just below the line of the Balcones Fault. It is narrowest below the segment of the Balcones Fault from the Rio Grande to Bexar County and gradually widens as it runs northeast to the Red River.

Its rolling prairie, easily turned by the plow, developed rapidly as a farming area until the 1930s and was the principal cotton-producing area of Texas. Now, other Texas areas that are irrigated and mechanized lead in farming.

Because of the early growth, the Blackland Belt is still the most thickly populated area in the state and contains within it and along its border more of the state's large and middle-sized cities than any other area.

Coastal Prairies

The Coastal Prairies extend along the Gulf of Mexico from the Sabine River to the Lower Rio Grande Valley. The eastern half is covered with a heavy growth of grass; the western half, which is more arid, is covered with short grass and, in some places, with small timber and brush. Grass supports the densest cattle population in Texas, and cattle ranching is the principal agricultural industry. Rice is a major crop, grown under irrigation from wells and rivers.

Coastal Prairie areas have seen the greatest industrial development in Texas history since World War II. Chief concentration has been from Orange and Beaumont to Houston, and much of the development has been in petrochemicals and the aerospace industry.

Corpus Christi, in the Coastal Bend, and Brownsville, in the Lower Rio Grande Valley, have seaports and agricultural and industrial sections. Cotton, grain, vegetables, and citrus fruits are the principal crops. Cattle production is significant, with the famed King Ranch and other large ranches located here.

Lower Rio Grande Valley

The deep alluvial soils and distinctive economy cause the Lower Rio Grande Valley to be classified as a subregion of the Gulf Coastal Plains. "The Valley" — as it is called locally — is Texas' greatest citrus and winter vegetable growing region because of the normal absence of freezing weather and the rich delta soils of the Rio Grande. The Lower Valley ranks high among the nation's fruit and truck-farming regions. Much of the acreage is irrigated, although dry-land farming is also practiced.

Rio Grande Plain

This area may be roughly defined as lying south of San Antonio between the Rio Grande and the Gulf Coast. The Rio Grande Plain shows characteristics of both the Gulf Coastal Plains and the North Mexico Plains because of similar topography, climate, and plant life all the way from the Balcones Escarpment in Texas to the Sierra Madre Oriental in Mexico, which runs past Monterrey approximately 160 miles south of Laredo.

The Rio Grande Plain is partly prairie, but much of it is covered with a dense growth of prickly pear, mesquite, dwarf oak, catclaw, guajillo, huisache, blackbrush, cenizo, and other cactus and wild shrubs. It is devoted primarily to raising cattle, sheep, and goats. The Texas Angora goat and mohair industry centers in this area. San Antonio and Laredo are its chief commercial centers, with San Antonio dominating trade.

Over a large area in the central and western parts of the Rio Grande Plain, the growth of small oaks, mesquite, prickly pear (Opuntia) cactus, and a variety of wild shrubs is very dense, and it is often called the Brush Country. It is also referred to as the chaparral and the monte, from a Spanish word that can mean dense brush.

INTERIOR LOWLANDS

North Central Plains

The North Central Plains of Texas are a southwestern extension into Texas of the interior lowlands that extend northward to the Canadian border, paralleling the Great Plains to the West. The North Central Plains of Texas extend from the Blackland Belt on the east to the Caprock Escarpment on the west. From north to south, they extend from the Red River to the Colorado River.

UNSPLASH/JOSH REDD

West Texas Rolling Plains

The West Texas Rolling Plains rise from east to west in altitude from about 750 feet to 2,000 feet at the base of the Caprock Escarpment. In general, as one progresses westward in Texas, the precipitation not only declines but also becomes more variable from year to year. This area still has a large cattle-raising industry with many of the state's largest ranches.

Grand Prairie

Near the eastern edge of the North Central Plains is the Grand Prairie, extending south from the Red River in an irregular band through Cooke, Montague, Wise, Denton, Tarrant, Parker, Hood, Johnson, Bosque, Coryell, and some adjacent counties.

It is a limestone-based area, usually treeless except along the numerous streams, and adapted primarily to raising livestock and growing staple crops. Sometimes called the Fort Worth Prairie, it has an agricultural economy and largely rural population, with no large cities, except Fort Worth on its eastern boundary.

Eastern and Western Cross Timbers

Hanging over the top of the Grand Prairie and dropping down on each side are the Eastern and Western Cross Timbers. The two southward-extending bands are connected by a narrow strip along the Red River.

The Eastern Cross Timbers extend southward from the Red River through eastern Denton County and along the boundary between Dallas and Tarrant counties. It then stretches through Johnson County to the Brazos River and into Hill County.

The much larger Western Cross Timbers extend from the Red River south through Clay, Montague, Jack, Wise, Parker, Palo Pinto, Hood, Erath, Eastland, Comanche, Brown, and Mills counties to the Colorado River, where they meet the Llano Basin.

Their soils are adapted to fruit and vegetable crops, which reach considerable commercial production in some areas in Parker, Erath, Eastland, and Comanche counties.

GREAT PLAINS

High Plains

The Great Plains, which lie to the east of the Rocky Mountains base, extend into northwestern Texas. This area, commonly known as the High Plains, is a vast, flat, high plain covered with thick layers of alluvial material. It is also known as the Staked Plains or Llano Estacado.

Historians differ as to the origin of this name. Some say it came from the fact that the explorer Coronado's expedition used stakes to mark its route across the trackless sea of grass so that it would be guided on its return trip. Others think that the estacado refers to the palisaded appearance of the Caprock in many places, especially the west-facing escarpment in New Mexico.

The Caprock Escarpment is the dividing line between the High Plains and the lower West Texas Rolling Plains. Like the Balcones Escarpment, the Caprock Escarpment is a striking physical feature, rising abruptly 200 feet, 500 feet, and in some places almost 1,000 feet above the plains. Unlike the Balcones Escarpment, the Caprock was caused by surface erosion.

Where rivers issue from the eastern face of the Caprock, there frequently are notable canyons, such as Palo Duro Canyon on the Prairie Dog Town Fork of the Red River, Blanco Canyon on the White River, as well as the breaks along the Canadian River as it crosses the Panhandle north of Amarillo.

Along the eastern edge of the Panhandle, there is a gradual descent of the land's surface from high to low plains. At the Red River, the Caprock Escarpment becomes a striking surface feature.

It continues as an east-facing wall south through Briscoe, Floyd, Motley, Dickens, Crosby, Garza, and Borden counties, gradually decreasing in elevation. South of Borden County, the escarpment is less obvious, and the boundary between the High Plains and the Edwards Plateau occurs where the alluvial cover of the High Plains disappears.

Stretching over the largest level plain of its kind in the United States, the High Plains rise gradually from about 2,700 feet on the east to more than 4,000 in spots along the New Mexico border.

Chiefly because of climate and the resultant agriculture, subdivisions are called the North Plains and South Plains. The North Plains, from Hale County north, has primarily wheat and grain sorghum farming, but with significant ranching and petroleum developments. Amarillo is the largest city, with Plainview on the south and Borger on the north as important commercial centers.

The South Plains, also a leading grain sorghum region, leads Texas in cotton production. Lubbock County is one of the state's largest cotton producers. Irrigation from underground reservoirs, centered around Lubbock and Plainview, waters much of the crop acreage.

Edwards Plateau

Geographers usually consider that the Great Plains at the foot of the Rocky Mountains actually continue southward from the High Plains of Texas to the Rio Grande and the Balcones Escarpment. This southern and lower extension of the Great Plains in Texas is known as the Edwards Plateau.

It lies between the Rio Grande and the Colorado River. Its southeastern border is the Balcones Escarpment from the Rio Grande at Del Rio eastward to San Antonio and thence to Austin on the Colorado River. Its upper boundary is the Pecos River, though the Stockton Plateau is geologically and topographically classed with the Edwards Plateau.

The Edwards Plateau varies from about 750 feet high at its southern and eastern borders to about 2,700 feet in places. Almost the entire surface is a thin, limestone-based soil covered with a medium to thick growth of cedar, small oak, and mesquite and a varying growth of prickly pear. Grass for cattle, weeds for sheep, and tree foliage for the browsing goats support three industries — cattle, goat, and sheep raising — upon which the area's economy depends. It is the nation's leading Angora goat and mohair producing region and one of the nation's leading sheep and wool areas.

Hill Country

The Hill Country is a popular name for the eastern portion of the Edwards Plateau south of the Llano Basin. Its notable large springs include Barton Springs at Austin, San Marcos Springs at San Marcos, Comal Springs at New Braunfels, and several springs at San Antonio.

The Hill Country is characterized by rugged hills with relatively steep slopes and thin soils overlying limestone bedrock. High gradient streams combine with these steep hillslopes and occasionally heavy precipitation to produce an area with a significant flash-flood hazard.

Toyah Basin

To the northwest of the Edwards and Stockton plateaus is the Toyah Basin, a broad, flat remnant of an old sea floor that occupied the region as recently as Quaternary time.

Located in the Pecos River Valley, this region has become important for many agricultural products as a result of irrigation. Additional economic activity is afforded by local oil fields.

Llano Basin

The Llano Basin lies at the junction of the Colorado and Llano rivers in Burnet and Llano counties. Earlier, this was known as the "Central Mineral Region" because of evidence of a large number of minerals.

On the Colorado River in this area, a succession of dams impounds a number of reservoirs. Uppermost is Lake Buchanan between Burnet and Llano counties. Below it in the western part of Travis County is Lake Travis.

Between these two large reservoirs are three smaller ones — Inks, Lyndon B. Johnson, and Marble Falls reservoirs — used primarily to produce electric power from the overflow from Lake Buchanan. Lake Austin is along the western part of the city of Austin. Another small lake, Lady Bird Lake, is formed by a low-water dam in Austin.

The recreational area around these lakes has been called the Highland Lakes Country. This is an interesting area with Precambrian and Paleozoic rocks found on the surface. Granitic domes, exemplified by Enchanted Rock north of Fredericksburg, form the core of this area of ancient rocks.

UNSPLASH/SAM GOODGAME

BASIN AND RANGE PROVINCE

The Basin and Range Province, with its center in Nevada, surrounds the Colorado Plateau on the west and south and enters far West Texas from southern New Mexico on the east. It consists of broad interior drainage basins interspersed with scattered fault-block mountain ranges.

The region of Texas west of the Edwards Plateau, bordered by New Mexico to the north and the Rio Grande to the south, is distinctive in both its physical and economic conditions. Traversed from north to south by fault-block mountains, the area contains all of Texas' true mountains.

Guadalupe Mountains

Highest of the Trans-Pecos Mountains is the Guadalupe Range, which enters Texas from New Mexico. It abruptly ends about 20 miles south of the boundary line, where Guadalupe Peak, (8,751 feet — the highest in Texas) and El Capitan (8,085 feet) are situated. El Capitan, because of perspective, appears to the observer on the plain below to be higher than Guadalupe.

The Diablo Plateau lies west of the Guadalupe Range and extends to the Hueco Mountains a short distance east of El Paso. The runoff from the scant rain that falls on its surface drains into a series of salt lakes that lie just west of the Guadalupe Mountains. These lakes are dry during periods of low rainfall, exposing bottoms of solid salt. For years, they were a source of commercial salt. West of the Hueco Mountains are the Franklin Mountains in El Paso, with the Hueco Bolson separating the two fault-block ranges.

Davis Mountains

The Davis Mountains are principally in Jeff Davis County. The highest peak, Mount Livermore (8,378 feet), is one of the highest in Texas. These mountains intercept the moisture-bearing winds and receive more precipitation than elsewhere in the Trans-Pecos, so they have more vegetation than the other Trans-Pecos mountains.

Big Bend

South of the Davis Mountains lies the Big Bend country, so called because it is encompassed on three sides by a great southward swing of the Rio Grande. It is a mountainous country of scant rainfall and sparse population. Its principal mountains, the Chisos, rise to 7,825 feet in the tallest peak, Mount Emory.

Along the Rio Grande are the Santa Elena, Mariscal, and Boquillas canyons with rim elevations of 3,500 to 3,775 feet. They are among the noteworthy canyons of North America.

Because of its remarkable topography and plant and animal life, the southern part of this region along the Rio Grande is home to Big Bend National Park, with headquarters in the Chisos Basin, a deep valley in the Chisos Mountains.

Upper Rio Grande Valley

The Upper Rio Grande Valley, or El Paso Valley, is a narrow strip of irrigated land running down the river from El Paso for approximately 75 miles, or more.

In this area are the historic towns and missions of Ysleta, Socorro, and San Elizario — some of the oldest in Texas. Cotton is the chief product of this valley, much of it the long-staple variety. This limited area has a dense urban and rural population, in marked contrast to the territory surrounding it.

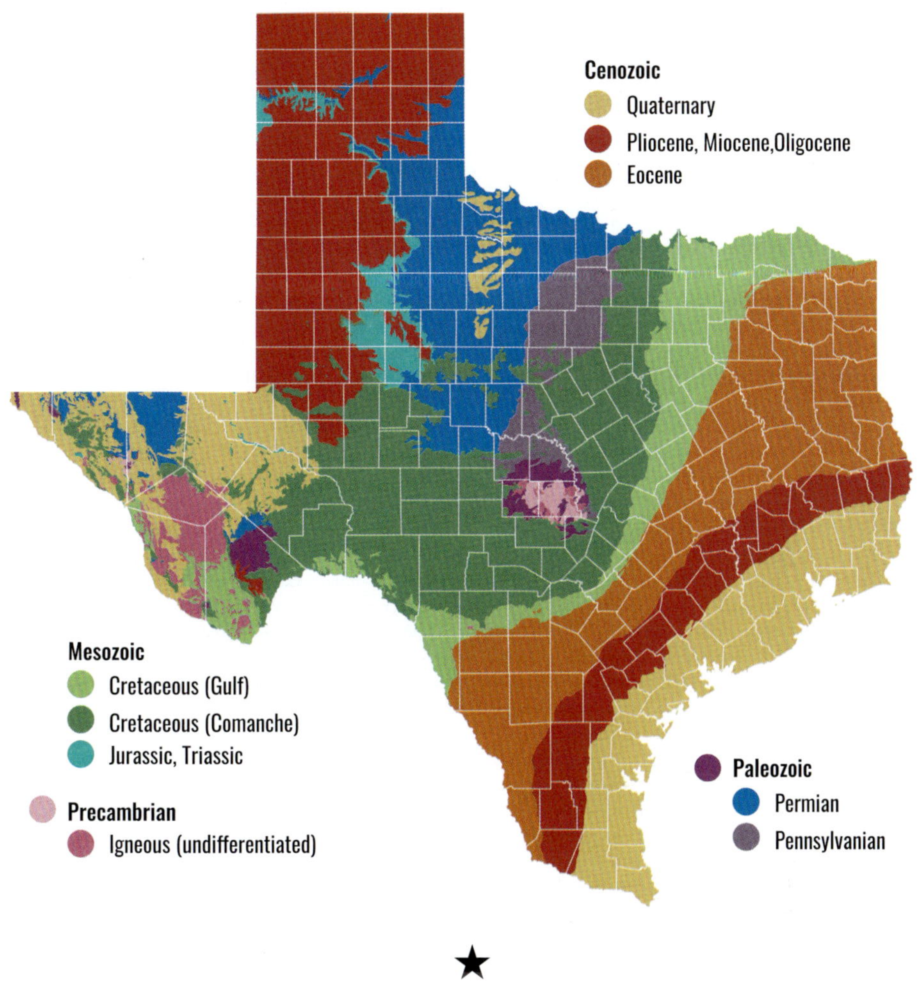

★

GEOLOGY OF TEXAS

Stratigraphy is the study of the composition, sequence, and origin of rocks: what rocks are made of, how they were formed, and the order in which the layers were formed.

Structural geology reveals the architecture of rocks: the locations of the mountains, volcanoes, sedimentary basins, and earthquake belts.

The map shows where rocks of various geologic ages are visible on the surface of Texas today.

PRECAMBRIAN ERA

Precambrian rocks, more than 600 million years old, are exposed at the surface in the Llano Uplift of Central Texas and in scattered outcrops in West Texas, around and north of Van Horn and near El Paso.

These rocks, some more than a billion years old, include complexly deformed rocks that were originally formed by cooling from a liquid state, as well as rocks that were altered from pre-existing rocks.

Precambrian rocks, often called the "basement complex," are thought to form the foundation of continental masses. They underlie all of Texas. The outcrop in Central Texas is only the exposed part of the Texas Craton, which is primarily buried by younger rocks. A craton is a stable, almost immovable portion of the earth's crust that forms the nuclear mass of a continent.

PALEOZOIC ERA

During the early part of the Paleozoic Era (approximately 600 million to 350 million years ago), broad, relatively shallow seas repeatedly inundated the Texas Craton and much of North and West Texas. The evidence for these events is found exposed around the Llano Uplift and in

Sources: Bureau of Economic Geology and The University of Texas at Austin.

far West Texas near Van Horn and El Paso, and also in the subsurface throughout most of West and North Texas.

The evidence includes early Paleozoic rocks, sandstones, shales, and limestones, similar to sediments that form in seas today, and the fossils of animals, similar to modern crustaceans: the brachiopods, clams, snails, and related organisms that live in modern marine environments.

By late Paleozoic (approximately 350 million to 240 million years ago), the Texas Craton was bordered on the east and south by a long, deep marine basin called the Ouachita Trough. Sediments slowly accumulated in this trough until late in the Paleozoic Era.

Plate-tectonic theory postulates that the collision of the North American Plate (upon which the Texas Craton is located) with the European and African–South American plates uplifted the thick sediments that had accumulated in the trough to form the Ouachita Mountains.

At that time, the Ouachitas extended across Texas. Today, the Texas portion of the old mountain range is mostly buried by younger rocks. Ancient remnants can be seen in the Marathon Basin of West Texas due to uplift and erosion of younger sediments.

The public can see the remains of this once-majestic Ouachita Mountain range at Post Park, just south of Marathon in Brewster County. Other remnants at the surface are exposed in southeastern Oklahoma and southwestern Arkansas.

During the Pennsylvanian Period the Ouachita Mountains bordered the eastern margin of shallow inland seas that covered most of West Texas. Rivers flowed westward from the mountains to the seas bringing sediment to form deltas along an ever-changing coastline.

The sediments were then reworked by the waves and currents of the inland sea. Today, these fluvial, delta, and shallow marine deposits compose the late Paleozoic rocks that crop out and underlie the surface of North-Central Texas.

Broad marine shelves divided the West Texas seas into several sub-basins, or deeper areas, that received more sediments than accumulated on the limestone shelves. Limestone reefs rimmed the deeper basins. Today, these limestone reefs are important oil reservoirs in West Texas.

These seas gradually withdrew from Texas, and by the late Permian Period, all that was left in West Texas were shallow basins and wide tidal flats in which salt, gypsum, and red muds accumulated in a hot, arid land. Strata deposited during the Permian Period are exposed today along the edge of the Panhandle, as far east as Wichita Falls and south to Concho County, and in the Trans-Pecos.

MESOZOIC ERA

Approximately 240 million years ago, the major geologic events in Texas shifted from West Texas to East and Southeast Texas. The European and African-South American plates, which had collided with the North American plate to form the Ouachita Mountains, began to separate from North America.

A series of faulted basins, or rifts, extending from Mexico to Nova Scotia were formed. These rifted basins received sediments from adjacent uplifts. As Europe and the southern continents continued to drift away from North America, the Texas basins were eventually buried beneath thick deposits of marine salt within the newly formed East Texas and Gulf Coast basins.

Jurassic and Cretaceous rocks in East and Southeast Texas document a sequence of broad limestone shelves at the edge of the developing Gulf of Mexico. From time to time, the shelves were buried beneath deltaic sandstones and shales, which built the northwestern margin of the widening Gulf of Mexico to the south and southeast.

As the underlying salt was buried more deeply by dense sediments, the salt became unstable and moved toward areas of least pressure. As the salt moved, it arched or pierced overlying sediments forming, in some cases, columns known as "salt domes." In some cases, these salt domes moved to the surface; others remain beneath a sedimentary overburden. This mobile salt formed numerous structures that would later serve to trap oil and natural gas.

By the early Cretaceous (approximately 140 million years ago), the shallow Mesozoic seas covered a large part of Texas, eventually extending west to the Trans-Pecos area and north almost to present-day state boundaries.

Today, the limestone deposited in those seas is exposed in the walls of the magnificent canyons of the Rio Grande in the Big Bend National Park area, the canyons and headwaters of streams that drain the Edwards Plateau, and in Central Texas.

Animals of many types lived in the shallow Mesozoic seas, tidal pools, and coastal swamps. Today, these lower Cretaceous rocks are some of the most fossiliferous in the state. Tracks of dinosaurs occur in several places, and remains of terrestrial, aquatic, and flying reptiles have been collected from Cretaceous rocks.

During most of the late Cretaceous, much of Texas lay beneath marine waters that were deeper than those of the early Cretaceous seas, except where rivers, deltas, and shallow marine shelves existed.

River delta and strandline sandstones are the reservoir rocks for the most prolific oil field in Texas. When discovered in 1930, this East Texas oil field contained recoverable reserves estimated at 5.6 billion barrels.

The chalky rock that we now call the "Austin Chalk" was deposited when the Texas seas became deeper. Today, the chalk and other Upper Cretaceous rocks crop out in a wide band that extends from near Eagle Pass on the Rio Grande, east to San Antonio, north to Dallas, and east to the Texarkana area. The Austin Chalk and other upper Cretaceous rocks dip southeastward beneath the East Texas and Gulf Coast basins.

The late Cretaceous was the time of the last major seaway across Texas because mountains were forming in the western United States that influenced areas as far away as Texas.

A chain of volcanoes formed beneath the late Cretaceous seas in an area roughly parallel to and south and east of the old, buried Ouachita Mountains. The eruptions of these volcanoes were primarily on the sea floor and great clouds of steam and ash likely accompanied them.

Between eruptions, invertebrate marine animals built reefs on the shallow volcanic cones. Pilot Knob, located southeast of Austin, is one of these old volcanoes that is now exposed at the surface.

CENOZOIC ERA

At the dawn of the Cenozoic Era, approximately 65 million years ago, deltas fed by rivers were in the northern and northwestern margins of the East Texas Basin. These streams flowed eastward, draining areas to the north and west. Although there were minor incursions of the seas, the Cenozoic rocks principally document extensive seaward building by broad deltas, marshy lagoons, sandy barrier islands, and embayments.

Thick vegetation covered the levees and areas between the streams. Coastal plains were taking shape under the same processes still at work today.

The Mesozoic marine salt became buried by thick sediments in the coastal plain area. The salt began to form ridges and domes in the Houston and Rio Grande areas. The heavy load of sand, silt, and mud deposited by the deltas eventually caused some areas of the coast to subside and form large fault systems, essentially parallel to the coast.

Many of these coastal faults moved slowly and probably generated little earthquake activity. Movement along the Balcones and Luling-Mexia-Talco zones, a complex system of faults along the western and northern edge of the basins, likely generated large earthquakes millions of years ago.

Predecessors of modern animals roamed the Texas Cenozoic coastal plains and woodlands. Bones and teeth of horses, camels, sloths, giant armadillos, mammoths, mastodons, bats, rats, large cats, and other modern or extinct mammals have been excavated from coastal plain deposits.

Vegetation in the area included varieties of plants and trees both similar and dissimilar to modern ones. Fossil palmwood, the Texas "state stone," is found in sediments of early Cenozoic age.

The Cenozoic Era in Trans-Pecos Texas was entirely different. There, extensive volcanic eruptions formed great calderas and produced copious lava flows. These eruptions ejected great clouds of volcanic ash and rock particles into the air.

Ash from the eruptions drifted eastward and is found in many of the sand-and-siltstones of the Gulf Coastal Plains. Lava flowed over older Paleozoic and Mesozoic rocks, and igneous intrusions melted their way upward into crustal rocks. These volcanic and intrusive igneous rocks are well exposed in arid areas of the Trans-Pecos today.

In the Texas Panhandle, streams originating in the recently elevated southern Rocky Mountains brought floods of gravel and sand into Texas. As the braided streams crisscrossed the area, they formed great alluvial fans.

These fans, which were deposited on the older Paleozoic and Mesozoic rocks, occur from northwestern Texas into Nebraska. Between one million and two million years ago, the streams of the Panhandle were isolated from their Rocky Mountain source, and the eastern edge of this sheet of alluvial material began to retreat westward, forming the Caprock of the modern High Plains.

Late in the Cenozoic Era, a great Ice Age descended on northern North America. For more than two million years, there were successive advances and retreats of the thick sheets of glacial ice. Four periods of extensive glaciation were separated by warmer interglacial periods. Although the glaciers never reached as far south as Texas, the state's climate and sea level underwent major changes with each period of glacial advance and retreat.

Sea level during times of glacial advance was 300 to 450 feet lower than during the warmer interglacial periods because so much sea water was captured in the ice sheets. The climate was both more humid and cooler than today, and the major Texas rivers carried more water and more sand and gravel to the sea. These deposits underlie the outer 50 miles or more of the Gulf Coastal Plain.

Approximately 3,000 years ago, sea level reached its modern position. The rivers, deltas, lagoons, beaches, and barrier islands that we know as coastal Texas today have formed since that time.

UNSPLASH/K. MITCH HODGE

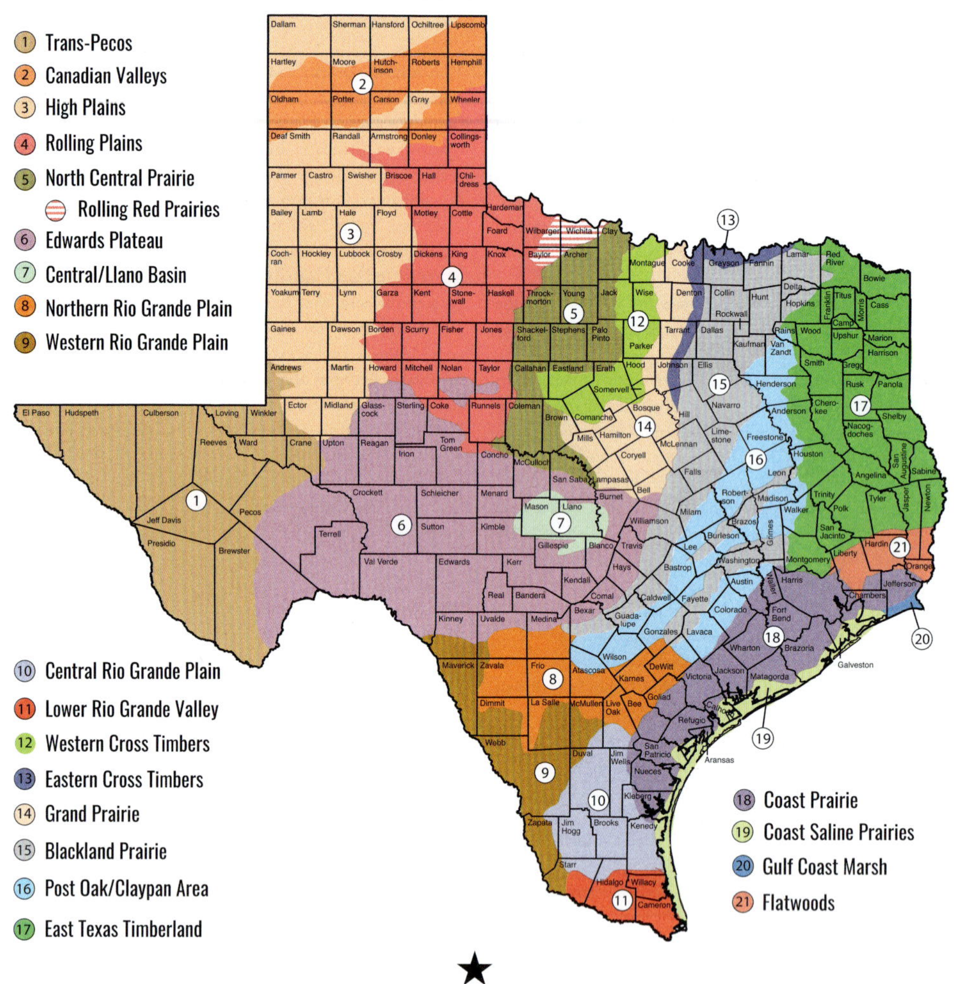

SOILS OF TEXAS

Texas can be divided into 21 Major Land Resource Areas that have similar or related soils, vegetation, topography, climate, and land uses.

Trans-Pecos Soils

The 19 million acres of the Trans-Pecos, mostly west of the Pecos River, are diverse plains and valleys intermixed with mountains. This arid region is used mainly as rangeland. A small amount of irrigated cropland lies on the more fertile soils along the Rio Grande and the Pecos River. Vineyards are a more recent use of these soils, as is the disposal of large volumes of municipal wastes.

Upland soils are mostly well-drained, light reddish-brown to brown clay loams, clays, and sands. Some have a large amount of gypsum or other salts. Many areas have shallow soils and rock outcrops, and sizable areas have deep sands.

Bottomland soils are deep, well-drained, dark grayish-brown to reddish-brown silt loams, loams, clay loams, and clays. The lack of soil moisture and wind erosion are the major soil-management problems. Only irrigated crops can be grown on these soils, and most areas lack an adequate source of good water.

Upper Pecos, Canadian Valleys, and Plains Soils

The Upper Pecos, Canadian Valleys, and Plains area occupies a little over a half-million acres and is in the northwest part of Texas near the Texas-New Mexico border. It is characterized by broad rolling plains and tablelands broken by drainageways and tributaries of the Canadian River. It includes the Canadian Breaks, which are rough, steep lands

Source: Natural Resources Conservation Service and U.S. Department of Agriculture.

below the adjacent High Plains. The soils are well drained and alkaline. The mostly reddish-brown clay loams and sandy loams were formed mostly in material weathered from sandstone and shale.

The area is used mainly as rangeland and wildlife habitat. Native vegetation is mid- to short-grass prairie species, such as hairy grama, sideoats grama, little bluestem, alkali sacaton, vine-mesquite, and galleta in the plains and tablelands. Juniper and mesquite grow on the relatively higher breaks. Soil management problems include low soil moisture and brush control.

High Plains Soils

The High Plains area comprises a vast high plateau of more than 19 million acres in northwestern Texas. It lies in the southern part of the Great Plains province that includes large, similar areas in Oklahoma and New Mexico. The flat, nearly level treeless plain has few streams to cause local relief. Several major rivers originate in the High Plains or cross the area. The largest is the Canadian River, which has cut a deep valley across the Panhandle section.

More than 19,000 playas — shallow wetlands — are scattered through the area, and they lie up to 20 feet below the surrounding plains. These lakes serve as an important source for the Ogallala Aquifer, recharging up to 95 percent of the water in the aquifer's southern portion.

Upland soils are mostly well-drained, deep, neutral to alkaline clay loams and sandy loams in shades of brown or red. Sandy soils are in the southern part. Many soils have large amounts of lime at various depths and some are shallow over caliche. Soils of bottomlands are minor in extent.

The area is used mostly for cropland, but significant areas of rangeland are in the southwestern and extreme northern parts. Millions of cattle populate the many large feedlots in the area. The soils are moderately productive, and the flat surface encourages irrigation and mechanization. Limited soil moisture, constant danger of wind erosion, and irrigation water management are the major soil-management problems. The region is Texas' leading producer of three important crops: cotton, grain sorghums, and wheat.

Rolling Plains Soils

The Rolling Plains include 21.7 million acres east of the High Plains in northwestern Texas. The area lies west of the North Central Prairies and extends from the edge of the Edwards Plateau in Tom Green County northward into Oklahoma. The landscape is nearly level to strongly rolling, and surface drainage is moderate to rapid. Outcrops of red beds, geologic materials, and associated reddish soils have led some scientists to use the name "Red Plains." Limestone underlies the soils in the southeastern part. The eastern part contains large areas of badlands (dry terrain with extensive erosion).

Upland soils are mostly deep, pale-brown through reddish-brown to dark grayish-brown, neutral to alkaline sandy loams, clay loams, and clays. Some are deep sands. Many soils have a large amount of lime in the lower part, and a few others are saline. Some are shallow and stony. Bottomland soils are mostly reddish-brown and sandy to clayey. Some are saline.

This area is used mostly for rangeland, but cotton, grain sorghums, and wheat are important crops. The major soil-management problems are brush control, wind erosion, low fertility, and lack of soil moisture.

North Central Prairie Soils

The North Central Prairie occupies approximately seven million acres in North Central Texas. Adjacent to this area on the north is the rather small area (less than one million acres) called Rolling Red Prairies, which extends into Oklahoma and is included here because the soils and land use are similar.

This area is predominantly grassland intermixed with small wooded areas. Upland soils are mostly deep, well-drained, brown or reddish-brown, slightly acidic loams over neutral to alkaline, clayey subsoils. Some soils are shallow or moderately deep to shale. Bottomland soils are mostly well-drained, dark-brown or gray loams and clays.

This area is used mostly as rangeland, but wheat, grain sorghums, and other crops are grown on the better soils. Brush control, wind and water erosion, and limited soil moisture are the major management concerns.

Edwards Plateau Soils

The 22.7 million acres of the Edwards Plateau are in South Central Texas east of the Trans-Pecos and west of the Blackland Prairie. Uplands are nearly level to undulating except near large stream valleys, where the landscape is hilly with deep canyons and steep slopes.

Upland soils are mostly shallow, stony, or gravelly, dark alkaline clays and clay loams underlain by limestone. Lighter-colored soils are on steep side slopes and deep, less-stony soils are in the valleys. Bottomland soils are mostly deep, dark-gray or brown, alkaline loams and clays.

Raising beef cattle is the main enterprise in this region, but it is also the center of the nation's mohair and wool production. Cropland is mostly in the valleys on the deeper soils and is used mainly for growing forage crops and hay. The major soil-management concerns are brush control, large stones, low fertility, excess lime, and limited soil moisture.

Central or Llano Basin Soils

The Central Basin, also known as the Llano Basin, occupies a relatively small area in Central Texas. It includes parts or all of Llano, Mason, Gillespie, and adjoining counties. The total area is approximately 1.6 million acres of undulating to hilly landscape.

Upland soils are mostly shallow, reddish-brown to brown, mostly gravelly and stony, neutral to slightly acidic sandy loams over granite, limestone, gneiss, and schist bedrock. Large boulders are on the soil surface in some areas. Deeper, less stony sandy-loam soils are in the valleys. Bottomland soils are minor areas of deep, dark-gray or brown loams and clays.

Ranching is the main enterprise, with some farms producing peaches, grain sorghum, and wheat. Brush control, large stones, and limited soil moisture are soil-management concerns.

Northern Rio Grande Plain Soils

The Northern Rio Grande Plain comprises more than six million acres in South Texas extending from Uvalde to Beeville. The landscape is nearly level to rolling, mostly brush-covered plains with slow to rapid surface drainage.

The major upland soils are deep, reddish-brown or dark grayish-brown, neutral to alkaline loams and clays. Bottomland soils are mostly dark-colored loams.

The area is mostly rangeland with significant areas of cropland. Grain sorghums, cotton, corn, and small grains are the major crops. Crops are irrigated in the western part, especially in the Winter Garden area, where vegetables such as spinach, carrots, and cabbage are grown. Brush control, soil fertility, and irrigation-water management are the major soil-management concerns.

Western Rio Grande Plain Soils

The Western Rio Grande Plain comprises more than five million acres in an area of southwestern Texas from Del Rio to Rio Grande City. The landscape is nearly level to undulating except near the Rio Grande where it is hilly. The major soils are mostly deep, brown or gray alkaline clays and loams. Some soils are saline.

Most of the soils are used for rangeland. Irrigated grain sorghums and vegetables are grown along the Rio Grande. Brush control and limited soil moisture are the major soil-management problems.

Central Rio Grande Plain Soils

The Central Rio Grande Plain comprises nearly six million acres in an area of South Texas from Live Oak County to Hidalgo County. It includes the South Texas Sand Sheet, an area of deep, sandy soils and active sand dunes. The landscape is nearly level to gently undulating. Upland soils are mostly deep, light-colored, neutral to alkaline sands and loams. Many soils are saline or sodic.

Most of the area is used for raising beef cattle. A few areas, mostly in the northeast part, are used for growing grain sorghums, cotton, and small grains. Brush control is the major soil-management problem on rangeland; wind erosion and limited soil moisture are major concerns on cropland.

Lower Rio Grande Valley Soils

The Lower Rio Grande Valley comprises about two million acres in extreme southern Texas. The landscape is level to gently sloping with slow surface drainage.

Upland soils are mostly deep, grayish-brown, neutral to alkaline loams; coastal areas are mostly gray, silty clay loam and silty clay. Some are saline.

Most of the soils are used for growing irrigated vegetables and citrus, along with cotton, grain sorghums, and sugar cane. Some areas are used for growing beef cattle. Irrigation water management and wind erosion are the major soil-management problems on cropland. Brush control is the major problem on rangeland.

Western Cross Timbers Soils

The Western Cross Timbers area comprises approximately 2.6 million acres. It includes the wooded section west of the Grand Prairie and extends from the Red River southward to the north edge of Brown County. The landscape is undulating and is dissected by many drainageways including the Brazos and Red rivers.

Upland soils are mostly deep, grayish-brown, slightly acidic loams with loamy and clayey subsoils. Bottomland soils along the major rivers are deep, reddish-brown, neutral to alkaline silt loams and clays.

The area is used mostly for grazing beef and dairy cattle on native range and improved pastures. Crops are peanuts, grain sorghums, small grains, peaches, pecans, and vegetables. The major soil-management problem on grazing lands is brush control. Waste management on dairy farms is a more recent concern. Wind and water erosion are the major problems on cropland.

Eastern Cross Timbers Soils

The Eastern Cross Timbers area comprises about one million acres in a long, narrow strip of wooded land that separates the northern parts of the Blackland Prairie and Grand Prairie and extends from the Red River southward to Hill County. The landscape is gently undulating to rolling and is dissected by many streams, including the Red and Trinity rivers.

The upland soils are mostly deep, light-colored, slightly acidic sandy loams and loamy sands with reddish loamy or clayey subsoils. Bottomland soils are reddish-brown to dark gray, slightly acidic to alkaline loams or gray clays.

Grassland consisting of native range and improved pastures is the major land use. Peanuts, grain sorghums, small grains, peaches, pecans, and vegetables are grown in some areas. Brush control, water erosion, and low fertility are the major soil concerns in management.

Grand Prairie Soils

The Grand Prairie comprises more than six million acres in North Central Texas. It extends from the Red River to about the Colorado River. It lies between the Eastern and Western Cross Timbers in the northern part and just west of the Blackland Prairie in the southern part. The landscape is undulating to hilly and is dissected by many streams including the Red, Trinity, and Brazos rivers.

Upland soils are mostly dark-gray, alkaline clays; some are shallow over limestone and some are stony. Some areas have light-colored loamy soils over chalky limestone. Bottomland soils along the Red and Brazos rivers are reddish silt loams and clays. Other bottomlands have dark-gray loams and clays.

Land use is a mixture of rangeland, pastureland, and cropland. The area is mainly used for growing beef cattle. Some small grain, grain sorghums, corn, and hay are grown. Brush control and water erosion are the major management concerns.

Blackland Prairie Soils

The Blackland Prairies consist of more than 12 million acres of East-Central Texas extending southwesterly from the Red River to Bexar County. The landscape is undulating with few scattered wooded areas that are mostly in the bottomlands.

Both upland and bottomland soils are deep, dark-gray to black alkaline clays. Some soils in the western part are shallow to moderately deep over chalk. Some soils on the eastern edge are neutral to slightly acidic, grayish clays and loams over mottled clay subsoils.

Blackland soils are known as "cracking clays" because of the large, deep cracks that form in dry weather. This high shrink-swell property can cause serious damage to foundations, highways, and other structures and is a safety hazard in pits and trenches.

Land use is divided about equally between cropland and grassland. Cotton, grain sorghums, corn, wheat, oats, and hay are grown. Grassland is mostly improved pastures, with native range on the shallower and steeper soils. Water erosion, cotton root rot, soil tilth, and brush control are the major management problems.

Claypan Area Soils

The Claypan Area consists of approximately six million acres in East-Central Texas just east of the Blackland Prairie. The landscape is a gently undulating to rolling, moderately dissected woodland also known as the Post Oak Belt or Post Oak Savannah.

Upland soils commonly have a thin, light-colored, acid sandy loam surface layer over dense, mottled red, yellow, and gray claypan subsoils. Some deep, sandy soils with less clayey subsoils exist. Bottomlands are deep, highly fertile, reddish-brown to dark-gray loamy to clayey soils.

Land use is mainly rangeland. Most cropland is in bottomlands that are protected from flooding. Major crops are cotton, grain sorghums, corn, hay, and forage crops, most of which are irrigated. Brush control on rangeland and irrigation water management on cropland are the major soil-management problems. Water erosion is a serious problem on the highly erosive claypan soils, especially where they are overgrazed.

East Texas Timberland Soils

The East Texas Timberlands area comprises about 16 million acres of the forested eastern part of the state. The land is gently undulating to hilly and well dissected by many streams.

This area has many kinds of upland soils but most are deep, light-colored, acidic sands and loams over loamy and clayey subsoils. Deep sands are in scattered areas, and red clays are in areas of "redlands." Bottomland soils are mostly brown to dark-gray, acidic loams and some clays.

The land is used mostly for growing commercial pine timber and for woodland grazing. Improved pastures are scattered throughout and are used for grazing beef and dairy cattle and for hay production. Some commercial hardwoods are in the bottomlands.

Woodland management problems include seedling survival, invasion of hardwoods in pine stands, effects of logging on water quality, and control of the southern pine beetle. Lime and fertilizers are necessary for productive cropland and pastures.

Coast Prairie Soils

The Coast Prairie includes about 8.7 million acres near the Gulf Coast. It ranges from 30 miles to 80 miles in width and parallels the coast from the Sabine River in Orange County in Southeast Texas to Baffin Bay in Kleberg County in South Texas. The landscape is level to gently undulating with slow surface drainage.

Upland soils are mostly deep, dark-gray, neutral to slightly acidic clay loams and clays. Lighter-colored and more-sandy soils are in a strip on the northwestern edge. Some soils in the southern part are alkaline. Some are saline and sodic. Bottomland soils are mostly deep, dark-colored clays and loams along small streams but are greatly varied along the rivers.

Land use is mainly for grazing lands and cropland. Many areas are also managed for wetland wildlife habitat. The nearly level topography and productive soils encourage farming. Rice, grain sorghums, cotton, corn, and hay are the main crops. Brush management on grasslands and removal of excess water on cropland are the major management concerns.

Coast Saline Prairies Soils

The Coast Saline Prairies area includes more than three million acres along a narrow strip of wet lowlands adjacent to the coast. It includes the barrier islands that extend from Mexico to Louisiana. The surface is at or only a few feet above sea level with many areas of salt-water marsh.

The soils are mostly deep, dark-colored clays and loams. Many soils are saline and sodic. Light-colored sandy soils are on the barrier islands. The water table is at or near the surface of most soils.

Cattle grazing is the chief economic use of the various salt-tolerant cordgrasses and sedges. Major management concerns include providing fresh water and access to grazing areas.

Gulf Coast Marsh Soils

This 150,000-acre area lies in the extreme southeastern corner of Texas. The area can be subdivided into four parts: freshwater, intermediate, brackish, and saline (saltwater) marsh. The degree of salinity of this system grades landward from saltwater marshes along the coast to freshwater marshes inland.

This area contains many lakes, bayous, tidal channels, and man-made canals. About one-half of the marsh is fresh, while the other half is salty. Most of it is susceptible to flooding by fresh water drained from lands adjacent to the marsh or by saltwater from the Gulf of Mexico.

Most of the soils are poorly drained, continuously saturated, soft, and can carry little weight. In general, the organic soils have a thick layer of dark gray, relatively

UNSPLASH/MATTHEW WILLIAMS

undecomposed organic material over a gray, clayey subsoil. The mineral soils have a surface of dark gray, highly decomposed organic material over a gray, clayey subsoil.

Most of the almost treeless and uninhabited area is in marsh vegetation, such as grasses, sedges, and rushes. It is used mainly for wildlife habitat. Part of the fertile and productive estuarine complex supports marine life of the Gulf of Mexico. It also provides wintering ground for waterfowl and habitat for many fur-bearing animals and alligators. A significant acreage is firm enough to support livestock and is used for winter grazing of cattle. The major management problems are providing fresh water and access to grazing areas.

Flatwoods Soils

The Flatwoods area includes approximately 2.5 million acres of woodland in humid Southeast Texas just north of the Coast Prairie and extending into Louisiana. The landscape is level to gently undulating.

Upland soils are mostly deep, light-colored, acidic loams with gray, loamy, or clayey subsoils. Bottomland soils are deep, dark-colored, acid clays and loams.

The land is mainly used for forest, although cattle are grazed in some areas. Woodland management problems include seedling survival, invasion of hardwoods in pine stands, effects of logging on water quality, and control of the southern pine beetle.

MAJOR AQUIFERS OF TEXAS

Aquifers are water-bearing rock formations beneath the earth's surface. Texas has a wealth of fresh to slightly saline groundwater in nine major and 22 minor aquifers.

Ogallala

The Ogallala Aquifer underlies most of the Texas Panhandle. It is the southernmost extension of the largest aquifer (High Plains Aquifer) in North America. The Ogallala Formation of late Miocene to early Pliocene age consists of heterogeneous sequences of coarse-grained sand and gravel in the lower part, grading upward into clay, silt, and fine sand.

The formation reaches a maximum thickness of 800 feet, and its freshwater saturated thickness averages 95 feet. In Texas, the Panhandle is the most extensive region irrigated with groundwater. About 95 percent of the water pumped from the Ogallala Aquifer is used for irrigation.

Extensive pumping that exceeds the amount of recharge has resulted in consistently declining water levels throughout much of the aquifer. Water conservation measures promoted by agricultural and municipal users have slowed the rate of decline, and water levels have risen in a few areas.

Gulf Coast

The Gulf Coast Aquifer system forms a broad belt parallel to the Texas coastline, extending through 56 counties from the Rio Grande northeastward to the Louisiana border. The aquifer system is composed of Quaternary- and Tertiary-age layers, including the Catahoula, Oakville, Fleming, Goliad, Willis, Lissie, Bentley, Montgomery, and Beaumont formations.

The Gulf Coast Aquifer system includes the Chicot, Evangeline, and Jasper aquifers. These aquifers are composed of discontinuous layers of sand, silt, clay, and gravel beds.

The maximum total sand thickness of the Gulf Coast Aquifer system ranges from 700 feet in the south to 1,300 feet in the north. Freshwater saturated thickness averages 1,000 feet. The Gulf Coast Aquifer system is used primarily for municipal, industrial, and agricultural purposes.

Water quality is generally good in the central and northeastern parts of the aquifer but deteriorates to the southwest. Years of heavy pumping have caused significant water-level declines in portions of the aquifer. Some of these declines have resulted in land subsidence, particularly in the Houston-Galveston area.

Edwards Balcones Fault Zone

The Edwards Aquifer (Balcones Fault Zone) forms a narrow belt extending through the south-central part of the state from a groundwater divide in Kinney County through the San Antonio area to the northeast of the Leon River in Bell County. A groundwater divide in Hays County hydrologically separates the aquifer into the San Antonio and Austin regions.

The aquifer is highly permeable, with water occurring in fractures, honeycomb-like zones (or intergranular pores), and solution channels that characterize the Edwards and associated limestone formations of Cretaceous age. Because the aquifer is highly permeable, water levels and spring flows respond quickly to rainfall, drought, and pumping. Aquifer thickness ranges from 200 to 600 feet, and freshwater saturated thickness averages 560 feet in the southern part of the aquifer.

Water from the Edwards BFZ is used primarily for municipal, irrigation, and recreational purposes. The City of San Antonio meets the majority of its water needs with Edwards BFZ water. The aquifer also feeds several well-known recreational springs and underlies some of Texas' most environmentally sensitive areas.

In 1993, the Texas Legislature created the Edwards Aquifer Authority (EAA) to regulate pumping from the aquifer to benefit all users within EAA's jurisdiction. The Barton Springs/Edwards Aquifer Conservation District and the Kinney County Groundwater Conservation District also provide aquifer management in the areas of the aquifer that are not within the EAA boundaries.

WIKIPEDIA

Source: Texas Water Development Board.

Carrizo-Wilcox

The Carrizo-Wilcox Aquifer extends from south of the Rio Grande in Mexico through Texas northeastward into Arkansas and Louisiana in a wide band parallel to and northwest of the Gulf Coast Aquifer.

The aquifer consists of the Tertiary-age Wilcox Group and overlying Carrizo Sand Formation of the Claiborne Group. The aquifer is composed of a hydrologically connected system of sand locally interbedded with clay, silt, lignite, and gravel. Although the Carrizo-Wilcox Aquifer reaches 3,000 feet in thickness, the freshwater saturated thickness of the sands averages 670 feet.

Throughout most of its extent in Texas, the aquifer yields fresh to slightly saline water. A little more than half of the water pumped from the aquifer is used for irrigation. The remaining amount pumped is used for municipal, industrial, domestic, and livestock purposes.

Trinity

The Trinity Aquifer consists of Cretaceous-age Trinity Group formations that extend from the Red River in North Texas southward to the Hill Country of Central Texas. It is composed of several smaller aquifers contained within the Trinity Group. Depending on where they occur in the state, they are referred to as the Antlers, Glen Rose, Paluxy, Twin Mountains, Travis Peak, Hensell, and Hosston aquifers.

These aquifers consist of limestones, sands, clays, gravels, and conglomerates. Their combined freshwater saturated thickness averages about 600 feet in North Texas, and about 1,900 feet in Central Texas.

The Trinity Aquifer is primarily used to meet municipal water demands, but also provides water for irrigation, livestock, and other domestic purposes. Extensive development of the Trinity Aquifer in the Dallas–Fort Worth and Waco areas has resulted in water-level declines of 350 feet to more than 1,000 feet, though these declines have slowed with more reliance on surface water and reductions in groundwater pumping.

Edwards-Trinity Plateau

The Edwards-Trinity Plateau Aquifer extends from the Hill Country of Central Texas westward and southwestward to the Trans-Pecos region, covering much of the southwestern part of the state. The aquifer consists of early Cretaceous limestone and dolomites of the Edwards Group and sands. Although the maximum saturated thickness of the aquifer is greater than 800 feet, freshwater saturated thickness averages 433 feet.

The aquifer lies beneath the Edwards Plateau. Near the plateau's edge — along the northern, eastern, and southern margins of the aquifer — groundwater flows toward streams, where water discharges from springs. Irrigation, mainly in the northwestern portion of the region, accounts for more than two-thirds of aquifer use.

Seymour

The Seymour Aquifer extends across North-Central Texas. It consists of Quaternary-age, alluvial sediments unconformably overlying Permian-age rocks. Water is contained within isolated patches of discontinuous beds of poorly sorted gravel, conglomerate, sand, and silty clay. These deposits may reach 360 feet in thickness, but most of the Seymour is less than 100 feet thick.

Approximately 90 percent of the water pumped from the Seymour is used for irrigation. Water quality generally ranges from fresh to slightly saline. However, some areas have moderate to very high water salinity. Nitrate concentrations occur above primary drinking water standards throughout much of the aquifer.

Hueco-Mesilla Bolsons

The Hueco-Mesilla Bolsons Aquifer is located in El Paso and Hudspeth counties in far West Texas. The aquifer consists of Tertiary and Quaternary basin-fill deposits of silt, sand, gravel, and clay that extend northward into New Mexico and westward into Mexico in two basins. The Hueco Bolson, located on the eastern side of the Franklin Mountains, has a maximum thickness of 9,000 feet and is an important source of drinking water for both El Paso and Juárez, Mexico. The Mesilla Bolson, located on the western side of the Franklin Mountains, has a maximum thickness of 2,000 feet.

Historical large-scale groundwater withdrawals, especially for the municipal uses of El Paso and Juárez, have caused major water-level declines. This pumping has also caused a deterioration of the chemical quality of the groundwater in the aquifer, according to El Paso Water Utilities and the United States Geological Survey.

Nearly 90 percent of the water pumped from the aquifer in the Texas extent of the bolsons is used for public supply. The City of El Paso has reduced its use of groundwater from the Hueco Bolson since 1989, and observation wells indicate that water levels have stabilized from a previously declining trend. El Paso and Fort Bliss also have built the world's largest inland desalination plant (Kay Bailey Hutchison) in El Paso County, which uses brackish groundwater from the Hueco Bolson.

Statewide Water Usage (2022)

Source	Volume	Percentage
Groundwater	8.2 million acre-feet	54%
Surface Water	6.4 million acre-feet	42%
Reuse	0.6 million acre-feet	4%

* One acre-foot equals 325,851 gallons of water. *Source: Texas Water Use Summary.*

Pecos Valley

The Pecos Valley Aquifer is located in the upper Pecos River Valley of West Texas. This aquifer, formerly called the Cenozoic Pecos Alluvium, consists of up to 1,500 feet of Tertiary and Quaternary alluvial fill and windblown deposits.

The aquifer occupies two hydrologically separate basins: the Pecos Trough in the west and the Monument Draw Trough in the east. The alluvial fill reaches 1,500 feet thick, and freshwater saturated thickness averages about 250 feet. Naturally occurring arsenic and radionuclides occur in excess of primary drinking water standards.

More than 80 percent of groundwater pumped from the aquifer is used for irrigation, and the remainder is withdrawn for industrial, power supply, and municipal uses. Water-level declines have occurred in Reeves and Pecos counties but have slowed since the mid-1970s as irrigation pumping has decreased. Declines continue in Ward County due to increased municipal and industrial pumping.

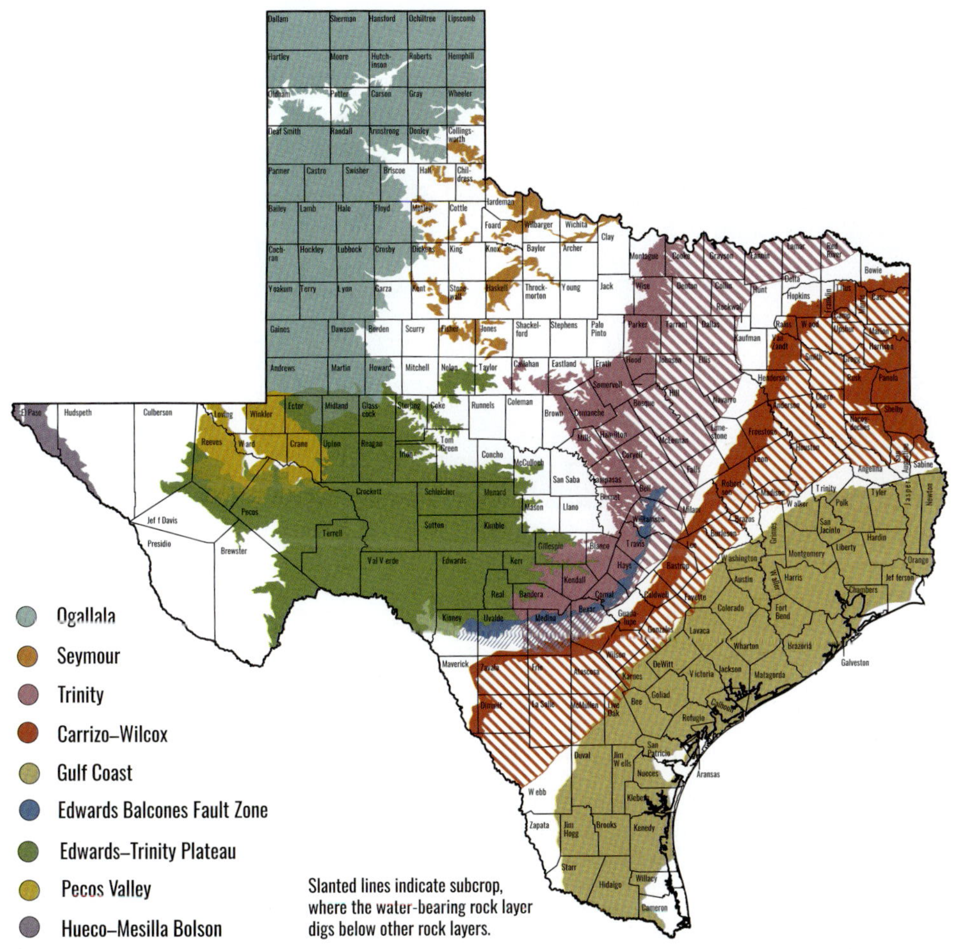

MAJOR AQUIFERS OF TEXAS

UNSPLASH/MEGAN BUCKNALL

MAJOR RIVERS OF TEXAS

Texas contains approximately 191,000 miles of streams. Amongst all these creeks, brooks, and branches, the 14 major rivers listed here are essential to everyday life.

Rio Grande

The Pueblo community called this river P'osoge, which means the "river of great water." In 1582, Antonio de Espejo of Nueva Vizcaya, Mexico, followed the course of the Río Conchos to its confluence with a great river, which he named Río del Norte (River of the North). The name Rio Grande was apparently first used by the explorer Juan de Oñate, who arrived on its banks near present-day El Paso in 1598.

Thereafter the names were often consolidated as Río Grande del Norte. It was shown also on early Spanish maps as Río San Buenaventura and Río Ganapetuán. In its lower course, it acquired the name Río Bravo, which is its name on most Mexican maps. At times it has also been known as Río Turbio, probably because of its muddy appearance during its frequent rises. Some people erroneously call this watercourse the "Rio Grande River."

This river forms the boundary of Texas and the international U.S.-Mexican border for 889 or 1,254 river miles, depending upon method of measurement.

The snow-fed flow of the Rio Grande is used for irrigation in Colorado below the San Juan Mountains, where the river rises at the Continental Divide. Turning south, it flows through a canyon in northern New Mexico and again irrigates a broad valley of central New Mexico. Southern New Mexico impounds Rio Grande waters in Elephant Butte Reservoir for irrigation of the valley above and below El Paso.

Sources: Texas Water Development Board and U.S. Geological Survey.

The valley near El Paso is thought to be the oldest irrigated area in Texas because Native Americans were irrigating crops here when Spanish explorers arrived in the early 1500s.

From source to mouth, the Rio Grande drops 12,000 feet to sea level as a mountain torrent, desert stream, and meandering coastal river. Along its banks and in its valley, Europeans established some of their first North American settlements. Here are situated three of the oldest towns in Texas: Ysleta, Socorro, and San Elizario.

Because of the extensive irrigation, the Rio Grande virtually ends at the lower end of the El Paso valley, except in seasons of above-normal flow.

The river starts again as a perennially flowing stream where the Río Conchos of Mexico flows into it at Presidio-Ojinaga. Through the Big Bend, the Rio Grande flows through three successive canyons, the Santa Elena, the Mariscal, and the Boquillas. The Santa Elena has a river bed elevation of 2,145 feet and a canyon-rim elevation of 3,661. Corresponding figures for Mariscal are 1,925 and 3,625, and for Boquillas, 1,850 and 3,490. The river here flows for approximately 100 miles around the base of the Chisos Mountains as the southern boundary of Big Bend National Park.

Below the Big Bend, the Rio Grande gradually emerges from mountains onto the Coastal Plains. A 191.2-mile strip on the U.S. side from Big Bend National Park downstream to the Terrell–Val Verde county line has federal designation as the Rio Grande Wild and Scenic River.

The Rio Grande, where it joins the Gulf of Mexico, has created a fertile delta called the Lower Rio Grande Valley, a major vegetable- and fruit-growing area. On the Mexican side are Río Conchos, Río Salado, and Río San Juan. About three-fourths of the water running into the Rio Grande below El Paso comes from the Mexican side.

Pecos River

The Pecos, one of the major tributaries of the Rio Grande, rises on the western slope of the Santa Fe Mountains in the Sangre de Cristo Range of northern New Mexico. It enters Texas as the boundary between Loving and Reeves counties and flows 350 miles southeast as the boundary for several other counties, entering Val Verde County at its northwestern corner and angles across that county to its mouth on the Rio Grande, northwest of Del Rio.

According to the *Handbook of Texas*, the origins of the river's several names began with Antonio de Espejo, who called the river the Río de las Vacas ("river of the cows") because of the number of buffalo in the vicinity. Gaspar Castaño de Sosa, who followed the Pecos northward, called it the Río Salado because of its salty taste, which caused it to be shunned by men and animals alike.

It is believed that the name "Pecos" first appears in Juan de Oñate's reports concerning the Native American pueblo of Cicuye, now known as the Pecos Pueblo in New Mexico, and is of unknown origin.

Through most of its 926-mile-long course from its headwaters, the Pecos River parallels the Rio Grande. Most of its tributaries flow from the west. These include the Delaware River and Toyah Creek.

The topography of the river valley in Texas ranges from semi-arid irrigated farmlands, desert with sparse vegetation, and, in the lowermost reaches of the river, deep canyons.

Nueces River

The Nueces River rises in two forks in Edwards and Real counties and flows 315 miles to Nueces Bay on the Gulf near Corpus Christi. The spring-fed stream flows through canyons until it issues from the Balcones Escarpment onto the Coastal Plains in northern Uvalde County.

Alonso de León, in 1689, gave it its name. Nueces, plural of nuez, means nuts in Spanish. (More than a century earlier, Cabeza de Vaca had referred to a Río de las Nueces in this region, but that is now thought to have been the Guadalupe.)

The original Native American name for this river seems to have been Chotilapacquen. Crossing Texas in 1691, Terán de los Ríos named the river San Diego.

The Nueces was the boundary line between the Spanish provinces of Texas and Nuevo Santander. After the Texas Revolution of 1836, both Texas and Mexico claimed the territory between the Nueces and the Rio Grande, a dispute that was settled in 1848 by the Treaty of Guadalupe Hidalgo, which fixed the international boundary at the Rio Grande.

Principal water supply projects are Lake Corpus Christi and Choke Canyon Reservoir. Principal tributaries of the Nueces are the Frio and the Atascosa rivers. The river terminates in Nueces and Corpus Christi bays along the Coastal Bend.

San Antonio River

The San Antonio River has at its source large springs within and near the city limits of San Antonio. It flows 180 miles across the Coastal Plains to a junction with the Guadalupe River to enter San Antonio Bay along the Gulf Coast. Its channel through San Antonio has been developed into a parkway known as the River Walk.

Its principal tributaries are the Medina River and Cibolo Creek, both spring-fed streams, and this, with its own spring origin, gives it remarkably clear water and makes it one of the steadiest of Texas rivers.

The river was first named the León by Alonso de León in 1689; the name was not for himself, but he called it "lion" because its channel was filled with a rampaging flood.

Guadalupe River

The Guadalupe rises in its North and South forks in western Kerr County. A spring-fed stream, it flows eastward through the Hill Country until it issues from the Balcones Escarpment near New Braunfels. It then crosses the Coastal Plains to San Antonio Bay. Its principal tributaries are the Comal, which joins it at New Braunfels; the San Marcos, another spring-fed stream, which joins it in Gonzales County; and the San Antonio, which joins it just above its mouth on San Antonio Bay.

The name Guadalupe is derived from Nuestra Señora de Guadalupe, the name given the stream by Alonso de León.

MAJOR RIVERS OF TEXAS

Lavaca River

The Lavaca rises in extreme southwestern Fayette County and flows 117 miles to terminate in Lavaca Bay. Without a spring-fed water source and with only a small watershed, including that of its principal tributary, the Navidad, its flow is intermittent. The Spanish called it the Lavaca (the cow) because of the numerous bison found near it. It is the principal stream flowing to the Texas Coast between the Guadalupe and the Colorado. The principal lake on the Navidad is Lake Texana.

Colorado River

The Colorado River rises in east-central Dawson County and flows 600 miles to Matagorda Bay. Its name is a Spanish word meaning "reddish." There is evidence that Spanish explorers originally named the muddy Brazos "Colorado," but Spanish mapmakers later transposed the two names.

The river flows through a rolling, mostly prairie terrain to the vicinity of San Saba County, where it enters the rugged Hill Country and Llano Basin. It passes through a picturesque series of canyons until it issues from the Balcones Escarpment at Austin and flows across the Coastal Plains.

In the Hill Country, a remarkable series of reservoirs has been built to provide hydroelectric power, flood control, and water supply. The largest of these are Lake Buchanan in Burnet and Llano counties and Lake Travis in Travis County. Between the two in Burnet County are three smaller reservoirs: Inks, Lyndon B. Johnson (formerly Granite Shoals), and Marble Falls. Below Lake Travis is the older Lake Austin, largely filled with silt, whose dam is used to produce power from waters flowing down from the lakes above. Lady Bird Lake (formerly Town Lake) is in the city of Austin. This entire area is known as the Highland Lakes Country.

As early as the 1820s, Anglo-Americans settled on the banks of the lower Colorado, and in 1839, the Capital Commission of the Republic of Texas chose the picturesque area where the river flows from the Balcones Escarpment as the site of a new capital of the Republic — now Austin, the capital of the state.

The early colonists encouraged navigation along the lower channel with some success. However, a natural log raft that formed 10 miles from the Gulf blocked river traffic after 1839, although shallow-draught vessels occasionally ventured as far upstream as Austin.

Conservation and utilization of the waters of the Colorado are under the jurisdiction of two agencies created by the Texas Legislature — the Lower and Upper Colorado River authorities.

The principal tributaries of the Colorado River are the several prongs of the Concho River on its upper course, Pecan Bayou (farthest west "bayou" in the United States), and the Llano, San Saba, and Pedernales rivers. All except Pecan Bayou flow into the Colorado River from the Edwards Plateau and are spring-fed, perennially flowing rivers. In the numerous mussels found along these streams, pearls occasionally have been found. On early Spanish maps, the Middle Concho was called Río de las Perlas.

Brazos River

The Brazos River proper is considered to begin where the Double Mountain and Salt Forks flow together in northeastern Stonewall County. It then flows 840 miles across Texas. It is the second-largest river basin in Texas, after the Rio Grande. It flows directly into the Gulf southwest of Freeport in Brazoria County.

The Brazos' third upper fork is the Clear Fork, which joins the main stream in Young County, just above Possum Kingdom Lake. The Brazos crosses most of the main physiographic regions of Texas: High Plains, West Texas Rolling Plains, Western Cross Timbers, Grand Prairie, and Gulf Coastal Plains.

The original name of this river was Brazos de Dios, meaning "Arms of God." There are several legends as to why. One story is that the Coronado expedition, wandering on the trackless Llano Estacado, exhausted its water and was threatened with death from thirst. Arriving at the bank of the river, they gave it the name "Brazos de Dios" in thankfulness.

Another legend is that a ship exhausted its water supply, and its crew was saved when they found the mouth of the Brazos. Still another story is that miners on the San Saba were forced by drought to seek water near present-day Waco and in gratitude called it Brazos de Dios.

Much early Anglo-American colonization of Texas took place in the Brazos Valley. Along its channel were San Felipe de Austin, capital of Austin's colony; Washington-on-the-Brazos, where Texans declared independence from Mexico; and other historic settlements. There was some navigation of the lower channel of the Brazos in this period. Near its mouth, it intersects the Gulf Intracoastal Waterway, which provides connection with commerce throughout Texas and the Gulf Coast.

Most of the Brazos Valley lies within the boundaries of the Brazos River Authority, which conducts a multipurpose program for development. A large reservoir on the main channel of the Brazos is Lake Whitney, where it is the boundary line between Hill and Bosque counties. Lake Waco on the Bosque and Belton Lake on the Leon are among the principal reservoirs on its tributaries. In addition to its three upper forks, other chief tributaries are the Paluxy, Little, and Navasota rivers.

San Jacinto River

The San Jacinto is a short river formed by the junction of its East and West forks in northeastern Harris County and runs to the Gulf through Galveston Bay. Its total length, including the East Fork, is about 85 miles.

Lake Conroe is on the West Fork, and Lake Houston is at the junction of the West Fork and the East Fork. The Houston Ship Channel runs through the lower course of the San Jacinto and its tributary, Buffalo Bayou, connecting the Port of Houston to the Gulf.

There are two stories concerning the origin of its name. One is that when early explorers discovered it, its channel was choked with hyacinth ("jacinto" is the Spanish word for hyacinth). The other is that it was discovered on August 17 — St. Hyacinth's Day.

The Battle of San Jacinto was fought on the bank of this river on April 21, 1836, when Texas won its independence from Mexico. San Jacinto Battleground State Historic Site and monument commemorate the battle.

Trinity River

The Trinity rises in its East Fork, Elm Fork, West Fork, and Clear Fork in Grayson, Montague, Archer, and Parker counties, respectively. The main stream begins with the junction of the Elm and West forks at Dallas.

The Trinity derives its name from the Spanish "Trinidad." Alonso de León named it La Santísima Trinidad (the Most Holy Trinity).

Navigation was developed along its lower course with several riverport towns, such as Sebastopol in Trinity County. For many years, there has been a basin-wide movement for navigation, conservation, and utilization of its water. The Trinity River Authority is a state agency and the Trinity Improvement Association is a publicly supported nonprofit organization that has advocated its development.

The Trinity has in its valley more large cities, greater population, and more industrial development than any other river basin in Texas. On the Coastal Plains, there is large use of its waters for rice irrigation. Large reservoirs on the Elm Fork are Lewisville Lake and Ray Roberts Lake. There are four reservoirs above Fort Worth: Lake Worth, Eagle Mountain Lake, and Lake Bridgeport on the West Fork, and Benbrook Lake on the Clear Fork.

Lake Lavon in southeast Collin County and Lake Ray Hubbard in Collin, Dallas, Kaufman, and Rockwall counties are on the East Fork. Lake Livingston is in Polk, San Jacinto, Trinity, and Walker counties. Two other reservoirs in the Trinity basin below the Dallas–Fort Worth area are Cedar Creek Reservoir and Richland-Chambers Reservoir.

Neches River

The Neches rises in Van Zandt County in East Texas and flows 416 miles to Sabine Lake near Port Arthur. The river takes its name from the Neches community, who the early Spanish explorers found living along its banks. Principal tributary of the Neches, and comparable with the Neches in length and flow above their confluence, is the Angelina River, so named for Angelina (Little Angel), a Hainai Native American girl who converted to Christianity and played an important role in the early development of this region.

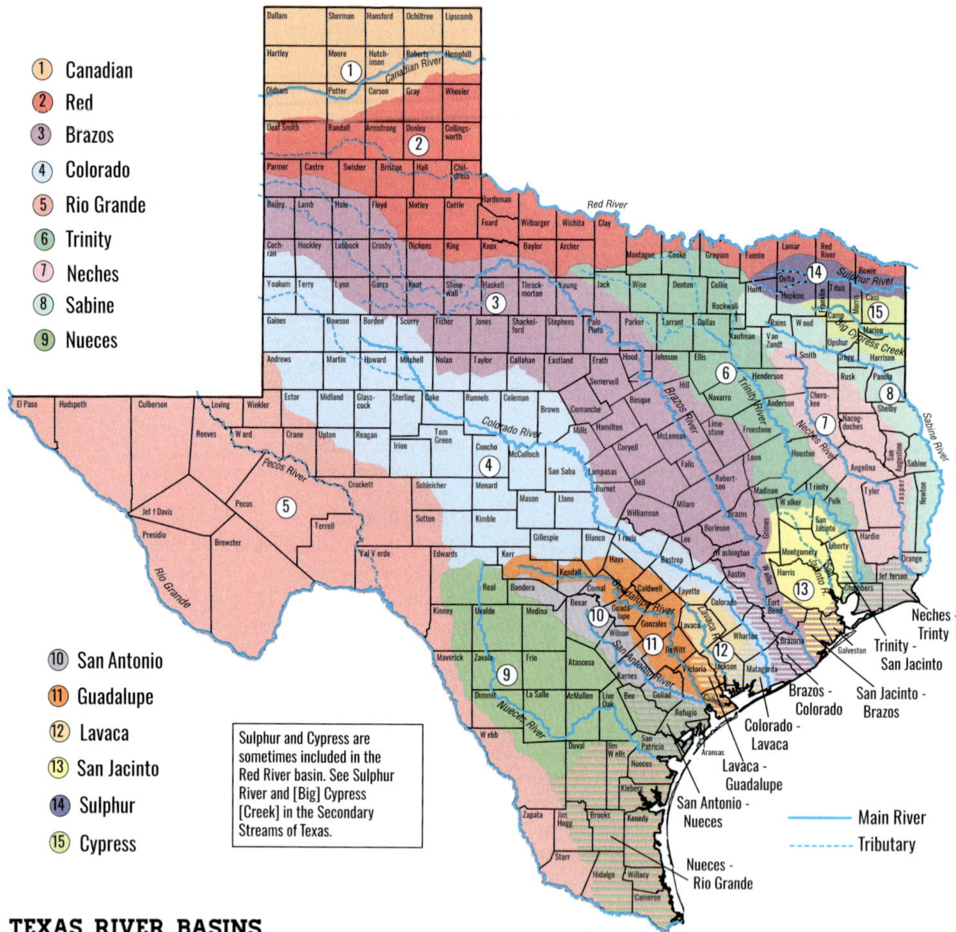

TEXAS RIVER BASINS

Both the Neches and the Angelina run most of their courses in the Piney Woods, and there was much settlement along them as early as the 1820s.

Sam Rayburn Reservoir, near Jasper on the Angelina River, was completed and dedicated in 1965. It is the fourth-largest reservoir in or shared with Texas by total storage capacity. Reservoirs located on the Neches River include Lake Palestine in the upper basin and B. A. Steinhagen Lake located at the junction of the Neches and the Angelina rivers.

Sabine River

The Sabine River is formed by three forks rising in Collin and Hunt counties. From its sources to its mouth on Sabine Lake, it flows approximately 360 miles. Sabine comes from the Spanish word for cypress, as does the name of the Sabinal River, which flows into the Frio River in Southwest Texas.

Throughout most of Texas history, the lower Sabine has been the eastern Texas boundary line, although for a while there was doubt as to whether the Sabine or the Arroyo Hondo, east of the Sabine in Louisiana, was the boundary. For a number of years, the outlaw-infested neutral ground lay between them. There was also a boundary dispute in which it was alleged that the Neches River was really the Sabine and, therefore, the boundary.

Travelers over the part of the Camino Real known as the Old San Antonio Road crossed the Sabine at the Gaines Ferry in Sabine County, and there were crossings for the Atascosito Road and other travel and trade routes of that day.

Red River

The Red River, with a length of 1,360 miles from its headwaters, is exceeded in length only by the Rio Grande among rivers associated with Texas. Its original source is water in Curry County, New Mexico, near the Texas boundary, forming a definite channel as it crosses Deaf Smith County, Texas, in tributaries that flow into the Prairie Dog Town Fork of the Red River. These waters carve the spectacular

Surface Water Usage, 2022

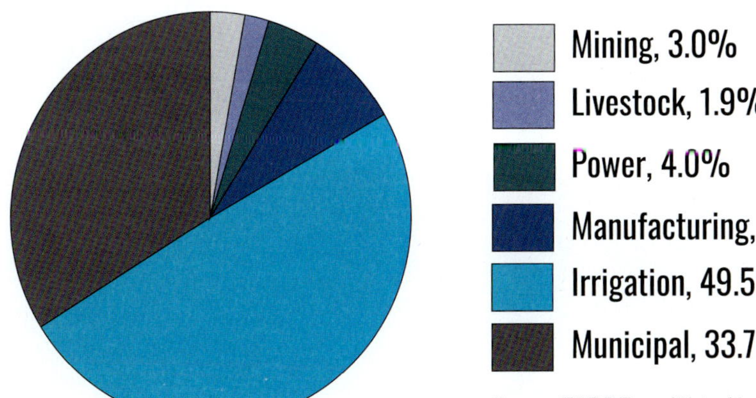

Source: TWDB Texas Water Use Summary.

Palo Duro Canyon of the High Plains before the Red River leaves the Caprock Escarpment, flowing eastward.

Where the Red River crosses the 100th meridian at the bottom of the Panhandle, the river becomes the Texas-Oklahoma boundary and is soon joined by Buck Creek to form the main channel, according to the U.S. Geological Survey.

The Red River is a part of the Mississippi drainage basin, and at one time it emptied all of its water into the Mississippi. In recent years, however, part of its water, especially at flood stage, has flowed to the Gulf via the Atchafalaya River in Louisiana.

The Red River takes its name from the red color of the water. This caused every explorer who came to its banks to call it "red" regardless of the language he spoke — Río Rojo or Río Roxo in Spanish, Rivière Rouge in French. At an early date, the river became the axis for French advance from Louisiana northwestward as far as present-day Montague County. There was consistent early navigation of the river from its mouth on the Mississippi to Shreveport, above which navigation was blocked by a natural log raft.

A number of important gateways into Texas from the north were established along the stream, such as Pecan Point and Jonesborough in Red River County, Colbert's Ferry and Preston in Grayson County, and later, Doan's Store Crossing in Wilbarger County. The river was a menace to the early traveler because of both its variable current and its quicksands, which brought disaster to many trail-herd cows, as well as ox teams and covered wagons.

The Red River's high content of salt and other minerals limits the usefulness of its water along its upper reaches. Ten salt springs and tributaries in Texas and Oklahoma contribute most of these minerals.

The uppermost tributaries of the Red River in Texas are Tierra Blanca Creek, which rises in Curry County, N.M., and flows easterly across Deaf Smith and Randall counties to meet Palo Duro Creek and form the Prairie Dog Town Fork a few miles east of Canyon.

Other principal tributaries in Texas are the Pease and the Wichita in North Central Texas and the Sulphur in Northeast Texas, which flows through Wright Patman Lake, then into the Red River after it has crossed the boundary line into Arkansas.

The last major tributary in Northeast Texas is the Cypress Creek system, which flows into Louisiana before joining with the Red River. Major reservoirs in this basin are Lake O' The Pines and Caddo Lake.

From Oklahoma, the principal tributary is the Washita, which has its headwaters in Roberts County, Texas. The Ouachita, a river with the same pronunciation though spelled differently, is the principal tributary to the Red River's lower course in Arkansas.

The Red River boundary dispute, a long-standing feud between Oklahoma and Texas, was finally settled in 2000 when the boundary was set at the vegetation line on the south bank, except for Lake Texoma, where the boundary was set within the channel of the lake.

Canadian River

The Canadian River heads near Raton Pass in northern New Mexico near the Colorado boundary line and flows into Texas on the west line of Oldham County. It crosses the Texas Panhandle into Oklahoma and there flows into the Arkansas River — a total distance of 906 miles. A tributary, the North Canadian River, dips briefly into the Texas Panhandle in Sherman County before it joins the main channel in Oklahoma.

One of several theories as to how the Canadian got its name is that some early explorers thought it flowed into Canada. Lake Meredith, formed by Sanford Dam, provides water for several Panhandle cities.

Because of the deep gorge and the quicksand that occurs in many places, the Canadian River has been a particularly difficult stream to bridge. It is known, especially in its lower course in Oklahoma, as outstanding among the streams of the country for the great amount of quicksand in its channel.

SECONDARY STREAMS OF TEXAS

In addition to the principal rivers, Texas has many other streams of various sizes. The following list gives a few of these streams and counties they go through as designated by the U.S. Geological Survey.

- **Alamito Creek** (Presidio)
- **Angelina River** (Rusk, Cherokee, Nacogdoches, Angelina, San Augustine, Jasper)
- **Aransas River** (Bee, San Patricio, Refugio, Aransas)
- **Atascosa River** (Atascosa, Live Oak)
- **Attoyac Bayou** (Rusk County, Shelby, San Augustine, Nacogdoches)
- **Barton Creek** (Hays, Travis)
- **Beals Creek** (Howard, Mitchell)
- **Big Cypress Creek** (Hopkins, Marion)
- **Blackwater Draw** (Bailey, Lamb, Hale, Lubbock)
- **Blanco Creek** (Bee, Goliad, Karnes, Refugio)
- **Blanco Creek** (Uvalde)
- **Blanco River** (Kendall, Blanco, Hays)
- **Bosque River** (McLennan)
- **Bosque River, North** (Erath, Hamilton, Bosque, McLennan)
- **Bosque River, South** (Coryell, McLennan)
- **Brady Creek** (Concho, McCulloch, San Saba)
- **Brazos River, Clear Fork** (Scurry, Fisher, Jones, Haskell, Throckmorton, Shackelford, Stephens, Young)
- **Brazos River, Double Mountain Fork** (Lynn, Garza, Kent, Fisher, Haskell)
- **Brazos River, North Fork** (Crosby, Garza, Kent)
- **Brazos River, Salt Fork** (Garza, Kent, Stonewall)
- **Buck Creek** (Donley, Collingsworth, Childress, Hardeman)
- **Buffalo Bayou** (Fort Bend, Houston, Harris)
- **California Creek** (Fisher, Jones, Haskell)
- **Caney Creek** (Wharton, Matagorda)
- **Capote/Wildhorse Draw** (Culberson, Jeff Davis, Presidio)
- **Cedar Bayou** (Liberty, Harris, Chambers)
- **Chambers Creek** (Ellis, Navarro)

UNSPLASH/JOHN BRAY

Sources: Texas Water Development Board and U.S. Geological Survey.

- **Cibolo Creek** (Kendall, Bexar, Comal, Guadalupe, Wilson, Karnes)
- **Coleto Creek** (Victoria, Goliad)
- **Comal River** (Comal)
- **Concho River** (Tom Green, Concho)
- **Concho River, Middle** (Sterling, Irion, Reagan, Tom Green)
- **Concho River, North** (Howard, Glasscock, Sterling, Coke, Tom Green)
- **Concho River, South** (Schleicher, Tom Green)
- **Cowleech Fork Sabine River** (Hunt)
- **Deep Creek** (Callahan, Shackelford)
- **Deep Creek** (Scurry)
- **Delaware River** (Culberson)
- **Devils River** (Sutton, Val Verde)
- **Elm Creek** (Nolan, Taylor, Jones)
- **Frio River** (Real, Uvalde, Medina, Frio, La Salle, McMullen, Live Oak)
- **Greens Bayou** (Harris)
- **Hondo Creek** (Bandera, Medina, Frio)
- **Howard Draw** (Crockett, Reagan, Val Verde)
- **Hubbard Creek** (Callahan, Shackelford, Stephens)
- **James River** (Kimble, Mason)
- **Jim Ned Creek** (Taylor, Callahan, Coleman, Brown)
- **Johnson Draw** (Crockett, Val Verde)
- **Lampasas River** (Mills, Hamilton, Lampasas, Burnet, Bell)
- **Leon River** (Eastland, Comanche, Hamilton, Coryell, Bell)
- **Leona River** (Uvalde, Zavala, Frio)
- **Limpia Creek** (Jeff Davis, Pecos)
- **Little Brazos River** (Thornton, Limestone, Falls, Robertson, Brazos)
- **Little River** (Bell, Milam)
- **Llano River** (Kimble, Mason, Llano)
- **Llano River, North** (Sutton, Kimble)
- **Llano River, South** (Edwards, Kimble)
- **Los Olmos Creek** (Duval, Jim Wells, Brooks, Kenedy, Kleberg)
- **Madera Canyon** (Jeff Davis, Reeves)
- **Medina River** (Bandera, Medina, Bexar)
- **Medio Creek** (Karnes, Bee, Refugio)
- **Mission River** (Refugio)
- **Mulberry Creek** (Armstrong, Donley, Briscoe, Hall)
- **Navasota River** (Hill, Limestone, Leon, Madison, Robertson, Brazos, Grimes)
- **Navidad River** (Lavaca, Jackson)
- **Nolan River** (Johnson, Hill)
- **Onion Creek** (Hays, Blanco, Travis)
- **Paint Creek** (Jones, Stonewall, Haskell, Throckmorton)
- **Palo Blanco Creek** (Hogg, Duval, Brooks, Kenedy)
- **Palo Duro Creek** (Deaf Smith, Randall)
- **Paluxy River** (Erath, Hood, Somervell)
- **Pease River** (Cottle, Hardeman, Foard, Wilbarger)
- **Pease River, Middle** (Motley, Cottle)
- **Pease River, North** (Floyd, Motley, Hall, Cottle)
- **Pease River, South** (Motley, Cottle)
- **Pecan Bayou** (Callahan, Coleman, Brown, Mills)
- **Pedernales River** (Kerr, Kimble, Gillespie, Blanco, Hays, Travis)
- **Pine Island Bayou** (Liberty, Hardin, Jefferson)
- **Red River, Prairie Dog Town Fork** (Randall, Armstrong, Briscoe, Hall, Childress, Hardeman)
- **Red River, North Fork** (Gray, Wheeler, Wilbarger)
- **Red River, Salt Fork** (Armstrong, Donley, Collingsworth)
- **Richland Creek** (Hill, Ellis, Navarro, Freestone)
- **Running Water Draw** (Parmer, Castro, Lamb, Hale, Floyd)
- **Sabana River** (Callahan, Eastland, Comanche)
- **Sabinal River** (Bandera, Uvalde)
- **San Bernard River** (Austin, Colorado, Wharton, Fort Bend, Brazoria)
- **San Gabriel River** (Williamson, Milam)
- **San Jacinto River, East** (Walker, San Jacinto, Liberty, Montgomery, Harris)
- **San Jacinto River, West** (Grimes, Walker, Montgomery, Harris)
- **San Marcos River** (Hays, Guadalupe, Caldwell, Gonzales)
- **Sandy Creek** (Colorado, Lavaca, Wharton, Jackson)
- **San Saba River** (Schleicher, Menard, Mason, McCulloch, San Saba)
- **Spring Creek** (Waller, Harris, Montgomery)
- **Sulphur River** (Delta, Franklin, Red River, Titus, Morris, Bowie, Cass, Miller)
- **Sulphur River, North** (Fannin, Delta, Lamar)
- **Sulphur River, South** (Fannin, Hunt, Hopkins, Delta)
- **Sulphur Springs Draw** (Yoakum, Terry, Gaines, Dawson, Martin, Howard)
- **Sweetwater Creek** (Nolan, Fisher, Jones)
- **Terlingua Creek** (Brewster)
- **Tierra Blanca Creek** (Deaf Smith, Parmer, Randall)
- **Toyah Creek** (Jeff Davis, Reeves)
- **Trinity River, Clear Fork** (Parker, Tarrant)
- **Trinity River, East Fork** (Grayson, Collin, Rockwall, Dallas, Kaufman)
- **Trinity River, Elm Fork** (Montague, Cooke, Denton, Dallas)
- **Trinity River, West Fork** (Archer, Jack, Wise, Tarrant, Dallas)
- **Tule Creek** (Swisher, Briscoe)
- **Turkey Creek** (Kinney, Uvalde, Zavala, Dimmit)
- **Washita River** (Roberts, Hemphill)
- **West Caney Creek** (Leon, Madison, Brazos)
- **White River** (Floyd, Crosby, Garza, Kent)
- **Wichita River** (Knox, Baylor, Archer, Wichita, Clay)
- **Wichita River, Little** (Archer, Clay)
- **Wichita River, North** (Dickens, King, Cottle, Foard, Knox, Baylor)
- **Wichita River, South** (Dickens, King, Knox)
- **Yellow House Draw** (Bailey, Cochran, Hockley, Lubbock)

LAKES AND RESERVOIRS

The table that begins below lists the lakes and reservoirs in Texas that have more than 5,000 acre-feet of storage capacity. Some industrial cooling reservoirs are not included in this table.

The surface area listed in the table is the area at conservation elevation as calculated by the Texas Water Development Board (TWDB). Because sediment deposition constantly changes reservoir volumes over time, storage capacity figures are from the most recent surveys available.

Various methods of computing capacity area are used, and detailed information may be obtained from the TWDB, from the U.S. Army Corps of Engineers, or from local sources. Boundary reservoir capacities include water designated for Texas and non-Texas water. Texas' share will be included in the description.

Lakes and Reservoirs	Date of Origin	County	Surface Area (acres)	Storage Capacity (acre-ft.)
Abilene, Lake	1921	Taylor	595	7,900
Addicks Reservoir	Dec. 1948	Harris	16,780	204,500
Alan Henry Lake	Oct. 1993	Garza/Kent	2,800	96,207
Alcoa Lake	Oct. 1952	Milam	914	15,650
Amistad Reservoir	1964-1969	Val Verde	62,765	1,813,408
Amon G. Carter, Lake	Aug. 1956	Montague	1,848	27,500
Anahuac Lake	July 1954	Chambers	5,035	33,348
Aquilla Lake	May 1983	Hill	7,000	43,243
Arlington, Lake	March 1957	Tarrant	1,926	40,157
Arrowhead, Lake	Dec. 1956	Clay	14,506	230,359
Athens, Lake	May 1963	Henderson	1,799	29,503
Austin, Lake	1839	Travis	1,589	23,972
Ballinger Lake	1947	Runnels	500	8,215
Balmorhea Lake	1917	Reeves	573	6,350
Bardwell Lake	March 1966	Ellis	6,040	43,856
Barker Reservoir	Feb. 1945	Harris/Fort Bend	17,225	207,000
B.A Steinhagen Lake	June 1953	Tyler/Jasper	10,235	69,259
Bastrop Lake	1964	Bastrop	906	16,590
Baylor Lake	Feb. 1950	Childress	610	9,220
Belton Lake	1954	Bell	12,135	432,631
Benbrook Lake	Dec. 1950	Tarrant	3,635	85,648
Bivins Lake	1927	Randall	379	5,120
Bob Sandlin, Lake	1978	Titus/Camp	8,888	192,412
Bonham, Lake	Nov. 1969	Fannin	1,012	11,027
Brady Creek Reservoir	May 1963	McCulloch	2,020	28,808
Brady Branch Reservoir	—	—	—	—
Brazoria Reservoir	May 1954	Brazoria	1,865	21,970
Bridgeport, Lake	Dec. 1931	Wise	11,712	372,183
Brownwood, Lake	1933	Brown	6,814	130,868
Bryan Utilities	—	—	—	—
Buchanan, Lake	1938	Burnet/Llano	22,137	886,626
Buffalo Lake	June 1938	Randall	1,900	18,150
Caddo Lake	June 1971	Harrison/Marion	26,800	29,898
Calveras Lake	—	—	—	—
Camp Creek	Jan. 1949	Robertson	750	8,550
Canyon Lake	1964	Comal	12,890	378,781
Casa Blanca Lake	1951	Webb	1,680	20,000

Lakes and Reservoirs	Date of Origin	County	Surface Area (acres)	Storage Capacity (acre-ft.)
Cedar Creek Reservoir	1965	Henderson/Kaufman	32,873	644,686
Champion Creek Reservoir	April 1959	Mitchell	1,560	41,580
Cherokee, Lake	Nov. 1948	Gregg/Rusk	3,749	40,094
Choke Canyon Reservoir	May 1982	Live Oak	25,438	662,820
Cisco Lake	Sept. 1923	Eastland	1,193	29,003
Clyde, Lake	1970	Callahan	449	5,748
Coffee Mill Lake	1938	Fannin	650	8,000
Coleman Lake	May 1966	Coleman	1,811	38,075
Coleto Creek Reservoir	1980	Victoria	3,100	30,758
Colorado City, Lake	Sept. 1949	Mitchell	1,612	31,040
Conroe Lake	Jan. 1973	Walker/Monroe	19,640	417,577
Corpus Christi, Lake	1929	Live Oak/San Patricio/Jim Wells	18,700	256,062
Cox Creek Reservoir	—	—	—	—
Crook, Lake	1923	Lamar	1,063	9,196
Cypress Springs, Lake	Feb. 1971	Franklin	3,252	66,756
Daniel Lake	Sept. 1948	Stephen	924	9,515
Davis, Lake	1959	Kmox	585	5,454
Delta Lake Reservoir	1939	Hidalgo	2,371	14,000
Diversion, Lake	1924	Archer/Baylor	3,397	35,325
Dunlap, Lake	1928	Guadalupe	410	5,900
Eagle Lake	1900	Colorado	1,200	9,600
Eagle Mountain Lake	Oct. 1932	Tarrant	9,246	185,087
Eagle Nest Lake	1949	Brazoria	—	18,000
Eastman Lakes	—	—	—	—
Electra Lake	1950	Witchita	—	8,730
Ellison Creek Reservoir	1943	Morris	—	—
E.V Spence Reservoir	Nov. 1969	Coke	14,640	517,272
Fairfield Lake	Dec. 1969	Freestone	2,159	44,169
Falcon International Reservoir	April 1954	Zapata	88,621	2,646,817
Fayette County Reservoir	1978	Fayette	2,400	71,400
Forest Grove Reservoir	Sept. 1976	Henderson	1,502	20,038
Fort Phantom Hill, Lake	Oct. 1938	Jones	4,213	70,030
Georgetown Lake	Oct. 1980	Williamson	1,287	38,005
Gibbons Creek Reservoir	1981	Grimes	2,576	25,721
Gonzales, Lake	June 1929	Gonzales	696	6,500
Graham Lake	1929	Young	2,444	45,288
Granbury Lake	Sept. 1969	Hood	8,282	132,949
Granger Lake	Feb. 1980	Williamson	4,159	51,822
Grapevine Lake	June 1952	Denton/Tarrant	12,710	163,064
Greenbelt Lake	Mar. 1966	Donley	1,990	59,968
Greenville City Lakes	—	—	—	—
Halbert, Lake	1921	Navarro	603	6,033
Hawkins, Lake	Sept. 1962	Wood	776	11,890
Holbrook, Lake	Nov. 1962	Wood	653	7,990
Hords Creek	June 1948	Coleman	510	8,109
Houston, Lake	Dec. 1953	Harris	11,282	132,298
Houston County Lake	Dec. 1966	Houston	1,330	17,113
Hubbard Creek Reservoir	Nov. 1962	Stephens	15,687	313,298
Hubert H. Moss Lake	Sept. 1966	Cooke	1,140	24,670
Imperial Reervoir	1910	Pecos	1,530	6,000

Lakes and Reservoirs	Date of Origin	County	Surface Area (acres)	Storage Capacity (acre-ft.)
Inks Lake	1938	Burnet/Llano	788	13,729
Jacksonville, Lake	Aug. 1957	Cherokee	1,164	25,670
J.B Thomas, Lake	Sept. 1952	Scurry	7,282	199,931
J.D Murphree Wildlife Management Area Impoundments	1960	Jefferson	—	32,000
Jim Chapman Lake	1991	Delta/Hopkins	17,998	258,723
Joe Pool Lake	Dec. 1985	Tarrant/Dallas/Ellis	6,680	149,629
Johnson Creek Reservoir	Aug. 1961	Marion	650	10,100
Kemp, Lake	Aug. 1923	Baylor	15,357	245,307
Kickapoo, Lake	Dec. 1954	Archer	5,864	86,345
Kiowa Lake	Jan. 1970	Cooke	563	7,000
Kirby Lake	1928	Taylor	740	7,620
Kurth Lake	July 1961	Angelina	726	14,769
Lady Bird Lake	1960	Travis	465	7,151
Lake Creek Lake	May 1952	McLennan	550	8,400
Lake Fork Reservoir	Dec. 1985	Wood	26,889	636,504
Lake O' the PInes	1959	Marion	17,638	241,638
Lavon Lake	Sept. 1953	Collin	20,622	409,757
Leon Lake	June 1954	Eastland	1,756	27,762
Lewis Creek Reservoir	Aug. 1969	Montgomery	1,010	16,400
Lewisville Lake	1927	Denton	27,175	563,228
Limestone, Lake	1978	Leon/Robertson	12,486	203,780
Livingston, Lake	Aug. 1969	Polk/San Jacinto	91,730	1,603,504
Loma Alta Lake	Mar. 1963	Cameron	2,490	26,500
Lost Creek Reservoir	1990	Jack	413	11,950
Lyndon B. Johnson Lake	Nov. 1951	Burnet/Llano	6,273	112,778
Mackenzie Reservoir	April 1974	Briscoe	910	46,450
Marble Falls Lake	Oct. 1951	Burnet	608	7,597
Martin Creek Lake	Sept. 1974	Rusk	4,954	75,726
McQueeney, Lake	1928	Guadalupe	396	5,000
Medina Lake	May 1913	Medina	6,066	254,823
Meredith, Lake	Aug. 1965	Hutchinson/Moore/Potter	21,639	500,000
Millers Creek Reservoir	1974	Baylor/Throckmorton	2,212	26,767
Mineral Wells, Lake	Sept. 1920	Parker	477	5,273
Mitchell County Reservoir	1991	Mitchell	1,463	27,266
Monticello Reservoir	1973	Titus	2,001	34,740
Mountain Creek Lake	Dec. 1936	Dallas	2,710	22,850
Murvaul Lake	June 1958	Panola	3,507	38,285
Nacogdoches, Lake	May 1976	Nacogdoches	2,212	39,522
Naconiche Lake	—	—	—	—
Nasworthy Lake	June 1930	Tom Green	1,380	9,615
Natural Dam Lake	—	—	—	—
Navarro Mills Lake	May 1963	Navarro	4,736	49,827
Nocona Lake	Oct. 1960	Montague	1,362	21,444
North Fork Buffalo Creek Reservoir	Nov. 1964	Witchita	1,730	15,400
North Lake	Aug. 1957	Dallas	800	17,000
Oak Creek Reservoir	May 1952	Coke	2,375	39,210
O.C. Fisher Lake	Feb. 1952	Tom Green	12,697	115,742
O.H. Ivie Reservoir	March 1990	Concho/Coleman/Runnels	19,149	554,340
Palestine, Lake	March 1971	Henderson/Anderson/Smith/Cherokee	23,112	367,303

Lakes and Reservoirs	Date of Origin	County	Surface Area (acres)	Storage Capacity (acre-ft.)
Palo Duro Reservoir	March 1991	Hansford	2,407	61,066
Palo Pinto, Lake	April 1964	Palo Pinto	2,176	26,766
Pat Cleburne, Lake	1964	Johnson	1,568	26,008
Pat Mayse Lake	Oct. 1964	Lamar	7,680	113,683
Pinkston Reservoir	1977	Shelby	523	7,380
Possum Kingdom Lake	March 1941	Palo Pinto	17,914	538,139
Proctor Lake	1963	Comanche	4,615	54,762
Quitman, Lake	June 1962	Wood	814	7,440
Randell Lake	1909	Grayson	311	6,290
Ray Hubbard ,Lake	1964	Dallas/Kaufman/Collin/Rockwall	20,947	439,559
Ray Roberts Lake	June 1987	Denton	28,646	788,167
Red Bluff Reservoir	Sept. 1936	Reeves	7,495	151,110
Red Draw Reservoir	1985	Howard	374	5,538
Richland-Chambers Reservoir	Nov. 1987	Freestone/Navarro	45,500	1,099,417
Rita Blanca Lake	1941	Hartley	524	12,050
River Crest Lake	1954	Red River	555	7,000
Sam Rayburn Reservoir	1966	Jasper/Angelina/Sabine	142,700	2,857,077
San Esteban Lake	1911	Presidio	762	18,770
Santa Rosa Lake	1929	Wilbarger	1,500	11,570
Smithers Lake	July 1957	Fort Bend	2,480	18,000
Somerville Lake	Oct. 1967	Burleson	11,395	150,293
South Texas Project Reservoir	July 1983	Matagorda	7,000	202,600
Squaw Creek Reservoir	1979	Somerville	3,169	151,250
Stamford Lake	March 1953	Haskell	5,124	51,570
Stillhouse Hollow Lake	July 1968	Bell	11,830	229,796
Striker Creek Reservoir	—	—	—	17,747
Sulphur Springs Lake	Jan. 1974	Hopkins	1,340	17,747
Sweetwater, Lake	1930	Nolan	630	12,267
Tawakoni Lake	Oct. 1960	Rains/Van Zandt	37,325	871,685
Terrell City Lake	Nov. 1955	Kaufman	849	8,594
Texana, Lake	1979	Jackson	9,676	159,845
Texoma, Lake	Feb. 1944	Grayson	74,686	1,243,801
Toledo Bend Reservoir	1969	Newton/Sabine/Panola/Shelby	181,600	2,236,450
Tradinghouse Creek Reservoir	Sept. 1968	McClennan	2,010	37,814
Travis, Lake	July 1939	Travis/Burnet	29,160	1,098,044
Trinidad Lake	1925	Henderson	690	6,200
Truscott Brine Lake	1983	Knox	3,146	111,147
Twin Buttes Reservoir	Feb. 1963	Tom Green	9,082	182,454
Twin Oaks Reservoir	July 1974	Robertson	2,330	30,319
Tyler, Lake/Lake Tyler East	May 1949	Smith	4,714	72,073
Upper Nueces Lake	March 1948	Zavala	316	5,200
Valley Lake	Sept. 1961	Fannin	1,080	16,400
Victor Braunig Lake	Dec. 1962	Bexar	1,350	26,500
Waco, Lake	1929	McClennan	8,434	189,418
Walter E. Long Lake	Oct. 1967	Travis	1,269	33,940
Waxahachie, Lake	Aug. 1957	Ellis	656	11,060
Weatherford Lake	1957	Parker	1,112	17,812
Welsh Reservoir	1975	Titus	1,269	20,242
White River Lake	Nov. 1963	Crosby	1,642	29,880
White Rock Lake	Sept. 1911	Dallas	995	10,230
Whitney Lake	April 1951	Hill/Bosque	23,220	564,808

Lakes and Reservoirs	Date of Origin	County	Surface Area (acres)	Storage Capacity (acre-ft.)
Wichita Lake	1901	Wichita	2,220	14,000
William Harris Reservoir	—	—	—	—
Winnsboro, Lake	Sept. 1962	Wood	806	8,100
Winters, Lake	1983	Runnels	638	7,779
Worth, Lake	Oct. 1914	Tarrant	3,458	24,419
Wright Patman Lake	1953	Bowie/Cass	18,247	122,593
Winters, Lake	1983	Runnels	638	7,779
Worth, Lake	1914	Tarrant	3,377	33,495
Wright Patman Lake	1957	Bowie/Cass/Morris/Titus/Red River	18,247	97,927

ESTUARIES AND BAYS

Texas has 367 miles of coastline along which 11 major river basins and eight coastal basins terminate, bringing fresh water from rivers, streams, and surface runoff to the coast to mix with the Gulf of Mexico seawater. These unique zones, known as estuaries, are a significant feature of the Texas coast.

Texas has seven major estuaries, which are formed by a complex of individual bays separated from the Gulf by barrier islands, and five minor, riverine estuaries, which occur near the mouths of major rivers that flow directly into the Gulf.

Texas estuaries range from the nearly freshwater Sabine-Neches, which borders Louisiana, to the frequently hypersaline Laguna Madre along the southern coast.

Although each estuary differs in size and hydrological and ecological characteristics, together they support a diverse array of species that serve as the raw materials for a variety of economic activities associated with commercial and recreational fishing, hunting, and birding.

In addition, estuaries provide many other ecological services, such as:

- Water filtration and nutrient regulation through nutrient cycling
- Storm surge protection
- Shoreline stabilization through trapping sediments that support the growth of wetlands

The major estuaries, in order from east to west, include:

Sabine-Neches Estuary (Sabine Lake)

The Sabine-Neches Estuary — commonly known as Sabine Lake — is located along the Texas-Louisiana border and is the smallest of Texas' seven major estuaries with an area of 45,320 acres.

This estuary receives approximately 14 million acre-feet of freshwater inflow per year from the Sabine and Neches rivers and surrounding coastal watersheds, making it the freshest estuary along the Texas coast. The Sabine-Neches Waterway and Gulf Intracoastal Waterway are important shipping channels in this system.

The estuary is connected to the Gulf by Sabine Pass and lies within Orange and Jefferson counties on the Texas side.

Trinity-San Jacinto Estuary (Galveston Bay)

The Trinity-San Jacinto Estuary, also known as Galveston Bay, is located on the upper Texas coast. It is the largest estuary in Texas, with an area of 345,280 acres, and is the seventh largest in the United States.

Key features include: Trinity Bay, Galveston Bay, East Bay, West Bay, and connections with the Gulf at Bolivar Roads, San Luis Pass, and Rollover Pass.

The Houston Ship Channel and the Gulf Intracoastal Waterway are notable man-made features of the system.

This estuary receives on average 11 million acre-feet of freshwater inflow annually from the Trinity and San Jacinto rivers and surrounding coastal watersheds. It is bounded by Bolivar Peninsula and Galveston Island and lies within Chambers, Harris, Galveston, and Brazoria counties.

Source: Texas Water Development Board.

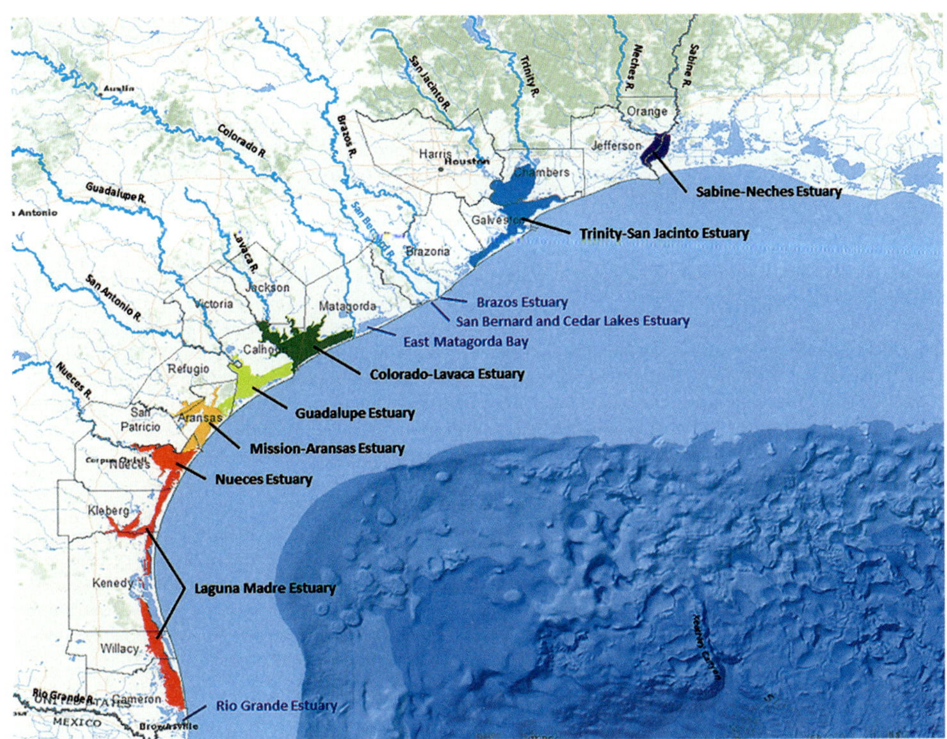

Colorado-Lavaca Estuary (Matagorda Bay System)

The Colorado-Lavaca Estuary — or Matagorda Bay system — is located along the mid-Texas coast and covers an area of 244,490 acres. The estuary is bounded by Matagorda Island and consists of Matagorda Bay, Lavaca Bay, and several smaller bays, including Carancahua Bay, Tres Palacios Bay, Keller Bay, Cox Bay, and Turtle Bay.

Other key features include: Pass Cavallo, the Matagorda Ship Channel, and the Gulf Intracoastal Waterway.

The estuary averages 3.5 million acre-feet of freshwater inflow annually from the Colorado, Lavaca, and Tres Palacios rivers and surrounding coastal watersheds. It is bordered by Matagorda, Jackson, Victoria, and Calhoun counties.

Guadalupe Estuary

The Guadalupe Estuary is located on the mid-Texas coast. The estuary includes San Antonio Bay, Mission Lake, Hynes Bay, Espiritu Santo Bay, and Mesquite Bay.

This estuary is largely protected from the Gulf by Matagorda Island and typically does not have a direct connection to the Gulf except through Cedar Bayou.

The other closest connection with the Gulf is through Pass Cavallo to the northeast in the Colorado-Lavaca Estuary.

The Guadalupe Estuary typically receives an average of 2.5 million acre-feet of freshwater inflow per year from the Guadalupe and San Antonio rivers and from surrounding coastal watersheds. The estuary lies adjacent to Calhoun, Aransas, and Refugio counties.

Mission-Aransas Estuary

The Mission-Aransas Estuary, located in the Coastal Bend, covers 111,780 acres and consists of Aransas Bay, Copano Bay, and several smaller bays, including Saint Charles Bay, Mission Bay, and Redfish Bay.

The estuary has a direct connection to the Gulf through Aransas Pass but is largely protected by a barrier island: San Jose Island.

Typically, the estuary receives 490,000 acre-feet of freshwater inflow per year from the Aransas and Mission rivers and surrounding coastal basins. The estuary is bordered by Aransas, Refugio, and San Patricio counties.

Nueces Estuary

The Nueces Estuary, located in the Coastal Bend, consists of Nueces Bay, Corpus Christi Bay, and Oso Bay. It spans 106,990 acres and is separated from the Gulf by Mustang Island, except for a direct connection through Aransas Pass.

The Corpus Christi Ship Channel and the Gulf Intracoastal Waterway are notable man-made features of the system.

This estuary typically receives 587,000 acre-feet of freshwater inflow per year from the Nueces River, Oso Creek, and surrounding coastal watersheds. The estuary is bordered by San Patricio and Nueces counties.

Laguna Madre Estuary

The Laguna Madre Estuary is the southernmost major estuary in Texas and extends almost to the Texas-Mexico border.

The Laguna Madre is the only hypersaline estuary in the nation and one of only a handful that exists worldwide.

The estuary spans 280,910 acres but is divided by a coastal landmass known as Saltillo Flats, though more commonly referred to as the Landcut, and separated from the Gulf by Padre Island.

The Upper Laguna Madre has one major bay, Baffin Bay, and is hydrologically connected to the Nueces Estuary on its northern end and to the Gulf via the Packery Channel.

San Fernando Creek is the principal source of freshwater inflow to this arid estuary. The Lower Laguna Madre has one major bay, South Bay, and is connected to the Gulf via the Port Mansfield Channel and Brazos-Santiago Pass.

The Arroyo Colorado and surrounding coastal watersheds are principal sources of freshwater inflow to the Lower Laguna Madre.

The estuary is bordered by Nueces, Kleberg, Kenedy, Willacy, and Cameron counties.

MINOR ESTUARIES AND BAYS

Christmas Bay

Southwest of Galveston Bay, this system includes both Bastrop Bay and Drum Bay, and it is protected from the Gulf of Mexico by Follet's Island. It has two connections to the Gulf, through Cold Pass and San Luis Pass. It receives fresh water from runoff and through Bastrop Bayou.

Brazos River Estuary

The Brazos River Estuary, located on the upper Texas coast, is a riverine estuary that flows directly into the Gulf rather than into a system of bays. The estuarine portion of the river occurs near the mouth where tidal water from the Gulf mixes with river water. Typically, this estuary receives 6.3 million acre-feet of freshwater inflow per year. It is located in Brazoria county.

San Bernard Estuary

The San Bernard Estuary is a minor estuary located along the mid-Texas coast, covering an area of 3,760 acres. While the San Bernard River flows directly into the Gulf, creating a riverine estuary, neighboring Cowtrap Lake and Cedar Lake are small bays that connect with the Gulf through small tidal inlets. On average, this estuary receives 683,753 acre-feet of freshwater inflow per year from the San Bernard River and surrounding coastal watersheds. It is located in Brazoria and Matagorda counties.

East Matagorda Bay

East Matagorda Bay is a small bay covering an area of 37,810 acres and is separated from the larger estuary by the Colorado River delta. There are no direct sources of river inflow into this bay, which receives an average of 536,165 acre-feet of fresh water per year from runoff of surrounding coastal watersheds.

Rio Grande Estuary

The Rio Grande Estuary forms a natural border between the United States and Mexico and is a riverine estuary, which flows directly into the Gulf with no associated bay system. The estuarine portion of the river occurs where tides from the Gulf mix with fresh water from the river. Annual average inflow from the Rio Grande is 370,722 acre-feet per year. The estuary is bordered by Cameron County on the north, and Mexico on the south.

UNSPLASH/DAN DENNIS

TEXAS PLANT LIFE

The types of plants found in Texas vary widely from one region to the next. This is due to the amount and frequency of rainfall, diversity of soils, and the number of frost-free days. From the forests of East Texas to the deserts of West Texas, from the grassy plains of North Texas to the semi-arid brushlands of South Texas, plant species continuously change.

More than 100 million acres of Texas are devoted to grazing, both for domestic and wild animals. This is the largest single use of land in the state. More than 80 percent of the acreage is devoted to range in the Edwards Plateau, Cross Timbers and Prairies, South Texas Plains, and Trans-Pecos Mountains and Basins.

Sideoats grama, which occurs on more different soils in Texas than any other native grass, was officially designated as the state grass by the Texas Legislature in 1971.

The 10 principal plant life areas of Texas, starting in the east, are:

Piney Woods

Most of this area of some 16 million acres ranges from about 200 to 500 feet above sea level. Many rivers, creeks, and bayous drain the region. Nearly all of Texas' commercial timber comes from this area. There are three native species of pine, the principal timber: longleaf, shortleaf, and loblolly. An introduced species, the slash pine, also is widely grown. Hardwoods include oaks, elm, hickory, magnolia, sweet and black gum, tupelo, and others.

The area is interspersed with native and improved grasslands. Cattle are the primary grazing animals. Deer and quail are abundant in properly managed habitats. Primary forage plants, under proper grazing management, include species of bluestems, rosettegrass, panicums, paspalums, blackseed needlegrass, Canada and Virginia wildryes, purpletop, broadleaf and spike woodoats, switchcane, lovegrasses, Indiangrass, and numerous legume species.

Highly disturbed areas have understory and overstory of undesirable woody plants that suppress growth of pine and desirable grasses. The primary forage grasses have been reduced, and the grasslands have been invaded by threeawns, annual grasses, weeds, broomsedge bluestem, red lovegrass, and shrubby woody species.

Gulf Prairies and Marshes

The Gulf Prairies and Marshes cover approximately 10 million acres. There are two subunits: (a) the marsh and salt grasses immediately at tidewater, and (b) a little farther inland, a strip of bluestems and tall grasses, with some gramas in the western part. Many of these grasses make excellent grazing.

Oaks, elm, and other hardwoods grow to some extent, especially along streams, and the area has some post oak and brushy extensions along its borders. Much of the Gulf Prairies is fertile farmland, and the area is well suited for cattle.

Principal grasses of the Gulf Prairies are tall bunchgrasses, including big bluestem, little bluestem, seacoast bluestem, Indiangrass, eastern gamagrass, Texas wintergrass, switchgrass, and gulf cordgrass. Saltgrass occurs on moist saline sites.

Heavy grazing has changed the native vegetation in many cases so the predominant grasses are the less desirable broomsedge bluestem, smutgrass, threeawns, tumblegrass, and many other less desirable grasses. Other plants that have invaded the productive grasslands include oak underbrush, Macartney rose, huisache, mesquite, prickly pear, ragweed, bitter sneezeweed, broomweed, and others.

Vegetation of the Gulf Marshes consists primarily of sedges, bullrush, flat-sedges, beakrush and other rushes, smooth cordgrass, marshhay cordgrass, marshmillet, and maidencane. The marshes are grazed best during winter.

Post Oak Savannah

This secondary forest area, also called the Post Oak Belt, covers some eight million acres. It is immediately west of the primary forest region, with less annual rainfall and a little higher elevation. Principal trees are post oak, blackjack oak, and elm. Pecans, walnuts, and other kinds of

Source: This article was previously updated by Stephan L. Hatch, Director, S.M. Tracy Herbarium and professor, Department of Ecosystem Science and Management, Texas A&M University.

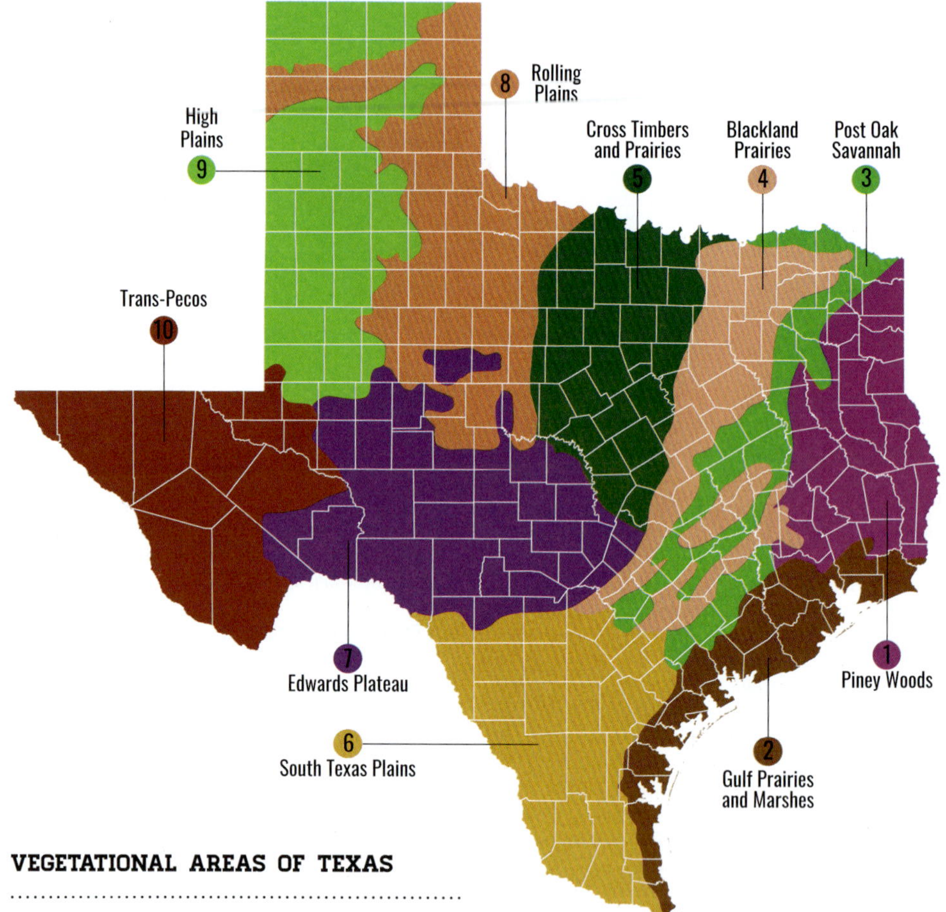

VEGETATIONAL AREAS OF TEXAS

water-demanding trees grow along streams. The southwestern extension of this belt is often poorly defined, with large areas of prairie.

The upland soils are sandy and sandy loam, while the bottomlands are sandy loams and clays.

The original vegetation consisted mainly of little bluestem, big bluestem, Indiangrass, switchgrass, purpletop, silver bluestem, Texas wintergrass, woodoats, narrowleaf, post oak, and blackjack oak. The area is still largely native or improved grasslands, with small farms located throughout. Intensive grazing has contributed to dense stands of a woody understory of yaupon, greenbriar, and oak brush.

Mesquite has become a serious problem. Good forage plants have been replaced by such plants as split-beard bluestem, red lovegrass, broomsedge bluestem, broomweed, bullnettle, and western ragweed.

Blackland Prairies

This area of approximately 12 million acres, while called a "prairie," has much timber along the streams, including a variety of oaks, pecan, elm, bois d'arc, and mesquite. In its native state, it was largely a grassy plain — the first native grassland in the westward extension of the Southern Forest Region.

Most of this fertile area has been cultivated, and only small acreages of grassland remain in original vegetation. In heavily grazed pastures, the tall bunchgrass has been replaced by buffalograss, Texas grama, and other less productive grasses. Mesquite, lotebush, and other woody plants have invaded the grasslands.

The original grass vegetation includes big and little bluestem, Indiangrass, switchgrass, sideoats grama, hairy grama, tall dropseed, Texas wintergrass, and buffalograss. Non-grass vegetation is largely legumes and composites.

Cross Timbers and Prairies

Approximately 17 million acres of alternating woodlands and prairies, often called the Western Cross Timbers, constitute this region. Sharp changes in the vegetational cover are associated with different soils and topography, but the grass composition is rather uniform.

The prairie grasses are big bluestem, little bluestem, Indiangrass, switchgrass, Canada wildrye, sideoats grama, hairy grama, tall grama, tall dropseed, Texas wintergrass, blue grama, and buffalograss.

On Cross Timbers soils, the vegetation is composed of big bluestem, little bluestem, hooded windmillgrass, sand lovegrass, Indiangrass, switchgrass, and many species of legumes. The woody vegetation includes shinnery, blackjack, post, and live oaks.

The entire area has been invaded heavily by woody brush plants of oaks, mesquite, juniper, and other unpalatable plants that furnish little forage for livestock.

South Texas Plains

South of San Antonio, between the coast and the Rio Grande, are some 18 million acres of subtropical dryland vegetation, consisting of small trees, shrubs, cactus, weeds, and grasses. The area is noteworthy for extensive brushlands and is known as the Brush Country, or the Spanish equivalents of chaparral or monte. Principal plants are mesquite, small live oak, post oak, prickly pear (*Opuntia*) cactus, catclaw, blackbrush, whitebrush, guajillo, huisache, cenizo, and others that often grow very densely.

The original vegetation was mainly perennial warm-season bunchgrasses in savannahs of post oak, live oak, and mesquite. Other brush species form dense thickets on the ridges and along streams. Long-continued grazing has contributed to the dense cover of brush. Most of the desirable grasses have only persisted under the protection of brush and cacti.

There are distinct differences in the original plant communities on various soils. Dominant grasses on the sandy loam soils are seacoast bluestem, bristlegrass, paspalum, windmillgrass, silver bluestem, big sandbur, and tanglehead. Dominant grasses on the clay and clay loams are silver bluestem, Arizona cottontop, buffalograss, common curlymesquite, bristlegrass, pappusgrass, gramas, plains lovegrass, Texas cupgrass, vinemesquite, other panicums, and Texas wintergrass.

Low saline areas are characterized by gulf cordgrass, saltgrass, alkali sacaton, and switchgrass. In the post oak and live oak savannahs, the grasses are mainly seacoast bluestem, Indiangrass, switchgrass, crinkleawn, paspalums, and panicums. Today much of the area has been reseeded to buffelgrass.

Edwards Plateau

These 24 million acres are rolling to mountainous, with woodlands in the eastern part and grassy prairies in the west. There is a good deal of brushy growth in the central and eastern areas. The combination of grasses, weeds, and small trees is ideal for cattle, sheep, goats, deer, and wild turkey.

This limestone-based area is characterized by the large number of springfed, perennially flowing streams that originate in its interior and flow across the Balcones Escarpment, which bounds it on the south and east. The soils are shallow, ranging from sands to clays, and are calcareous in reaction. This area is predominantly rangeland, with cultivation confined to the deeper soils.

In the east-central portion is the well-marked Central or Llano Basin, centering in Mason, Llano, and Burnet counties, with a mixture of granitic and sandy soils. The western portion of the area comprises the semi-arid Stockton Plateau.

Noteworthy is the growth of cypress along the perennially flowing streams. Separated by many miles from the cypress growth of the moist Southern Forest Belt, they constitute one of Texas' several "islands" of vegetation. These trees, which grow to stately proportions, were commercialized in the past.

The principal grasses of the clay soils are cane bluestem, silver bluestem, little bluestem, sideoats grama, hairy grama, Indiangrass, curly-mesquite, buffalograss, fall witchgrass, plains lovegrass, wildryes, and Texas wintergrass.

The rocky areas support tall or mid-grasses with an overstory of live oak, shinnery oak, juniper, and mesquite. The heavy clay soils have a mixture of tobosagrass, buffalograss, sideoats grama, and mesquite.

Throughout the Edwards Plateau, live oak, shinnery oak, mesquite, and juniper dominate the woody vegetation. Woody plants have invaded to the degree that they must be controlled before range forage plants can re-establish.

Rolling Plains

This is a region of approximately 24 million acres of alternating woodlands and prairies. The area is half mesquite woodland and half prairie. Mesquite trees have steadily invaded and increased in the grasslands for many years, despite constant control efforts.

Soils range from coarse sands along outwash terraces adjacent to streams to tight or compact clays on redbed clays and shales. Rough broken lands on steep slopes are found in the western portion. About two-thirds of the area is rangeland, but cultivation is important in certain localities.

The original vegetation includes big, little, sand and silver bluestems, Texas wintergrass, Indiangrass, switchgrass, sideoats and blue gramas, wildryes, tobosagrass, and buffalograss on the clay soils.

The sandy soils support tall bunchgrasses, mainly sand bluestem. Sand shinnery oak, sand sagebrush, and mesquite are the dominant woody plants.

Continued heavy grazing contributes to the increase in woody plants, low-value grasses such as red grama, red lovegrass, tumblegrass, gummy lovegrass, Texas grama, sand dropseed, and sandbur, with western ragweed, croton, and many other weedy forbs. Yucca is a problem plant on certain rangelands.

High Plains

The High Plains, some 20 million treeless acres, are an extension of the Great Plains to the north. Its level nature and porous soils prevent drainage over wide areas.

The relatively light rainfall flows into the numerous shallow "playa" lakes or sinks into the ground to feed the great underground aquifer that is the source of water for the countless wells that irrigate the surface of the plains. A large part of this area is under irrigated farming, but native grassland remains in about one-half of the High Plains.

Blue grama and buffalograss comprise the principal vegetation on the clay and clay loam "hardland" soils. Important grasses on the sandy loam "sandy land" soils are little bluestem, western wheatgrass, Indiangrass, switchgrass, and sand reedgrass. Sand shinnery oak, sand sagebrush, mesquite, and yucca are conspicuous invading brushy plants.

UNSPLASH/JAKE FAGAN

Trans-Pecos Mountains and Basins

With little annual rainfall, long hot summers, and usually cloudless skies to encourage evaporation, this 19-million-acre area produces only drought-resistant vegetation without irrigation. Grass is usually short and sparse.

The principal vegetation consists of lechuguilla, ocotillo, yucca, cenizo, prickly pear, and other arid land plants. In the more arid areas, gyp and chino grama, and tobosagrass prevail. There is some mesquite. The vegetation includes creosote-tarbush, desert shrub, grama grassland, yucca and juniper savannahs, pine oak forest, and saline flats.

The mountains are 3,000 to 8,749 feet in elevation and support piñon pine, juniper, and some ponderosa pine and other forest vegetation on a few of the higher slopes. The grass vegetation, especially on the higher mountain slopes, includes many southwestern and Rocky Mountain species not present elsewhere in Texas. On the desert flats, black grama, burrograss, and fluffgrass are frequent.

More productive sites have numerous species of grama, muhly, Arizona cottontop, dropseed, and perennial three-awn grasses. At the higher elevations, plains bristlegrass, little bluestem, Texas bluestem, sideoats grama, chino grama, blue grama, piñon ricegrass, wolftail, and several species of needlegrass are frequent.

The common invaders on all depleted ranges are woody plants, burrograss, fluffgrass, hairy erioneuron, ear muhly, sand muhly, red grama, broom snakeweed, croton, cacti, and several poisonous plants.

FORESTS AND GRASSLANDS IN TEXAS

There are four national forests and five national grasslands in Texas. These federally owned lands are administered by the U.S. Department of Agriculture Forest Service and by district rangers. The five state forests in Texas are managed by the Texas A&M Forest Service.

NATIONAL FORESTS

National forests in Texas were established by invitation of the Texas Legislature by an Act of 1934, authorizing the purchase of lands in Texas for the establishment of national forests. President Franklin D. Roosevelt proclaimed these purchases on October 15, 1936.

The national forests cover approximately 640,000 acres in parts of 12 Texas counties.

The four East Texas forests and two North Texas grasslands are under the supervision of the National Forests and Grasslands in Lufkin. The three West Texas grasslands (Black Kettle, McClellan Creek, and Rita Blanca) are administered by the Forest Supervisor in Albuquerque, N.M., as units of the Cibola National Forest.

Each of Texas' National Forests contain wilderness areas, made possible by the Texas Wilderness Act of 1984, introduced by Representative John W. Bryant of Texas' 5th Congressional district, and signed into law by President Ronald Regan.

Angelina National Forest is spread across five East Texas counties: San Augustine, Angelina, Jasper, Nacogdoches, and Tyler. The southern portion of the forest is predominantly covered by the longleaf pine. Loblolly and shortleaf pine cover much of the rest of the forest. Angelina National Forest is home to two wilderness areas: Upland Island, found south of the Sam Rayburn Reservoir, and Turkey Hill, north of the reservoir.

Davy Crockett National Forest is found in Houston and Trinity counties. This is a diverse forest, with both hardwoods (including white oak, red oak, hickory, chestnut oak, cherry-bark oak, sweetgum, nuttall oak, and willow) and pines (loblolly and shortleaf). In the northern part of Davy Crockett National Forest, you'll find the Big Slough Wilderness Area. The forest also contains the Alabama Creek Wildlife Management Area.

Sabine National Forest is another wide ranging forest that touches five different counties: Sabine, Shelby, San Augustine, Newton, and Jasper, and even forms part of the border between Texas and Louisiana. The forest contains both hardwoods (American beech and southern red oak) and pines (loblolly, shortleaf, and longleaf). The Toledo Bend Reservoir runs along the eastern edge of much of the forest, including the Indian Mounds Wilderness Area near the middle.

Sam Houston National Forest is approximately 50 miles north of Houston, with parts found in San Jacinto, Walker, and Montgomery counties. It contains a variety of pines and hardwoods, and features redbuds and dogwoods, which are said to create a spectacular show of flowers in mid-February (redbud) and March (dogwood). Part of the forest stretches around the northern end of Lake Conroe, including the Little Lake Creek Wilderness. Big Creek Scenic Area is near the eastern-most part of the forest.

NATIONAL GRASSLANDS

The national grasslands were originally submarginal Dust Bowl project lands, purchased by the federal government primarily under the Bankhead-Jones Farm Tenant Act (1937). Today, they are well covered with grasses and native shrubs.

The national grasslands cover nearly 120,000 acres in six Texas counties. Two of these grasslands extend into Oklahoma.

Lyndon B. Johnson National Grassland and Caddo National Grassland are located northeast and northwest of DFW, with a district ranger office at Decatur. These grasslands provide grazing land for cattle, but also habitat for native wildlife, including white-tailed deer, bobcats, red foxes, and several game birds. Lyndon B. Johnson National Grassland is found mostly in Wise County. Caddo National Grassland is only in Fannin County. The Bois d'Arc unit of Caddo contains Lake Fannin, Coffee Mill Lake, and Lake Crockett, which are popular for fishing.

Black Kettle National Grassland and McClellan Creek National Grassland are both administered by the Cibola National Forest & National Grasslands in Albuquerque, New Mexico. Black Kettle National Grassland lies mostly in Oklahoma, with a mere 576 acres in Texas' Hemphill County near the town of Canadian. This portion of the grassland is also part of the Lake Marvin Recreation Area. McClellan Creek National Grassland is found near Pampa in Gray County and includes the Lake McClellan Recreation Area. Both grasslands allow livestock grazing, have active oil and gas wells installed, and lie within the Anadarko Basin.

Rita Blanca National Grassland is also managed by Cibola National Forest & National Grasslands, in Albuquerque. These grasslands also stretch across the Texas border, from Dallam County into Oklahoma. These grasslands are home to local wildlife and provide food for grazing livestock.

Sources: U.S. Forest Service and the Texas A&M Forest Service.

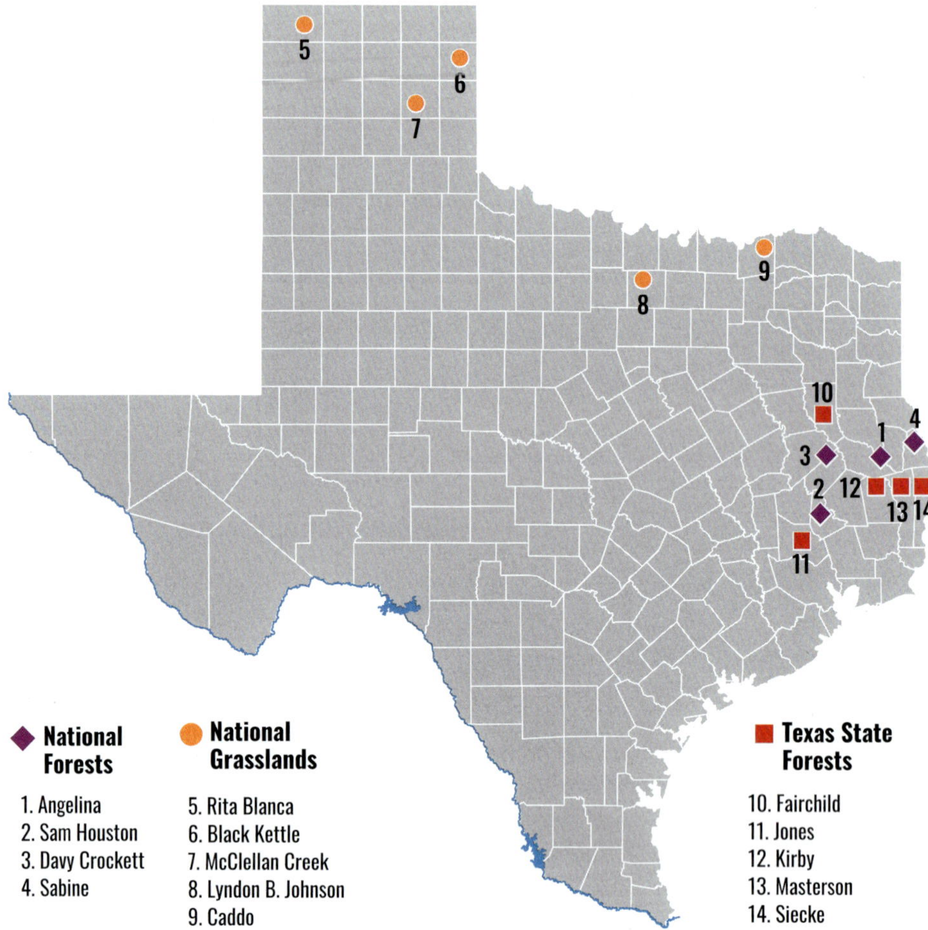

FORESTS AND GRASSLANDS IN TEXAS

STATE FORESTS

Texas has five state forests, all of which are used primarily for demonstration and research.

I.D. Fairchild State Forest: Texas' largest forest is located west of Rusk in Cherokee County. This forest was transferred from the state prison system in 1925. Additional land was obtained in 1963 from the Texas State Hospitals and Special Schools for a total acreage of 2,788.

W. Goodrich Jones State Forest: Located south of Conroe in Montgomery County, it comprises 1,722 acres and is one of the largest working urban forests in the country. It was purchased in 1926 and named for the founder of the Texas Forestry Association.

John Henry Kirby Memorial State Forest: This approximately 600-acre forest in Tyler County was donated by lumberman John Henry Kirby in 1929, as well as later donors. Revenue from this forest is given to the Association of Former Students of Texas A&M University for student-loan purposes.

Paul N. Masterson Memorial Forest: Mrs. Leonora O'Neal Masterson of Beaumont donated these 519 acres in Jasper County in 1984 in honor of her husband, who was a tree farmer and an active member of the Texas Forestry Association.

E.O. Siecke State Forest: The first Texas state forest, it was purchased by the state in 1924. It contains 1,722 acres of pine land in Newton County. An additional 100 acres was obtained by a 99-year lease in 1946.

TEXAS WILDLIFE

The wide variation in soils, climate, and vegetation in Texas has resulted in a rich diversity of animal life. There are hundreds of species of vertebrates (animals with backbones) found in Texas, categorized into five groups or classes: fishes, amphibians, reptiles, birds, and mammals.

A summary of each class is listed, followed by a condensed list of examples of species in each of the five groups. Those marked by an asterisk (*) are non-native species.

FISHES

Fishes are a large group of gilled aquatic vertebrates, which include jawless fish, cartilaginous fish, and bony fish. Jawless fish include both hagfish and lampreys, the latter of which only two species are known from Texas. Cartilaginous fish are a class of fish that have skeletons primarily composed of cartilage (rather than bone) and include sharks, skates, and rays.

The final group, the bony fish, is the most diverse and abundant class of fish and is named due to their skeletons being primarily composed of bone (rather than cartilage). More than 34,000 species of bony fish are recognized and include species that range widely in size, shape, and behaviors, making them the most diverse group of vertebrates.

There are more than 560 species of fish from 117 different families in freshwater and marine environments in Texas. In addition to native species, many non-native species of fish have become established in Texas.

Fish are all aquatic, gilled animals that lack limbs with digits. Like amphibians and reptiles, most fish are cold-blooded (or ectothermic), meaning that their body temperatures vary as environmental temperatures change, and they cannot self-regulate their temperature. Most

UNSPLASH/LAURA ESPAÑA

Source: This section was written for the Texas Almanac by Drew R. Davis, Associate Research Scientist, UT Rio Grande Valley, and Travis J. LaDuc, curator of herpetology, Biodiversity Center at UT Austin.

fish are covered in scales, which help protect them from predators and pathogens and can help serve as camouflage, but some species like catfish and eels lack scales altogether.

Barracuda: Three species of barracuda are known from Texas, including the Great Barracuda (*Sphyraena barracuda*), Northern Sennet (*Sphyraena borealis*), and the Guaguanche (*Sphyraena guachancho*). Barracudas are large, predatory fishes that occur in marine waters along the Texas coast, and have large jaws with fang-like teeth, and two dorsal fins that are widely separated.

Catfish: Two families of native catfish are known in Texas. North American catfish consist of at least 11 freshwater species, including the Yellow Bullhead (*Ameiurus natalis*), Channel Catfish (*Ictalurus punctatus*), and Tadpole Madtom (*Noturus gyrinus*). Most species have relatively widespread distributions across the state and vary in their body size and shape, but all species have four pairs of barbels (*whiskers*). Additionally, three species of blind, aquifer-dwelling species are part of this group: the Toothless Blindcat (*Trogloglanis pattersoni*), Widemouth Blindcat (*Satan eurystomus*), and Mexican Blindcat (*Prietella phreatophila*), which was only discovered in 2016. The second group, sea catfish, is marine, and only two species are known: Hardhead Catfish (*Ariopsis felis*) and Gafftopsail Catfish (*Bagre marinus*). Sea catfish are large fish that lack scales, typically are gray in coloration, and have two or three pairs of barbels. A third, non-native family of catfish called suckermouth armored catfish have been introduced in Texas from Central and South America, and are covered in tough, bony plates, and have a sucker-like mouth.

Eel: At least six different families of eels are known to occur in marine habitats along the Texas coast. There are seven species of cusk-eel, including the Crested Cusk-eel (*Ophidion josephi*). Cusk-eels have long dorsal and anal fins and their pelvic fins are modified into barbel-like structures occurring below the mouth. There are seven species of snake eels, including the Speckled Worm Eel (*Myrophis punctatus*) and Shrimp Eel (*Ophichthus gomesii*). Snake eels have long, snake-like bodies and often bury among sand or mud substrates. Additional eels, like the Conger Eel (*Conger oceanicus*), Ridged Eel (*Neoconger mucronatus*), Blackedge Moray (*Gymnothorax nigromarginatus*), and Environment 77 Freckled Pikeconger (*Hoplunnis macrura*) also occur along the Texas coast, but are less abundant. In addition to marine species, one native species of freshwater eel occurs in Texas, the American Eel (*Anguilla rostrata*). This eel has small scales embedded in the skin giving it a smooth appearance, a long snake-like body, and a single continuous dorsal, caudal, and anal fin.

Herring: Ten species of herrings are found in both marine and freshwater habitats in Texas. Four of the more common species include the Gizzard Shad (*Dorosoma cepedianum*), Threadfin Shad (*Dorosoma petenense*), Gulf Menhaden (*Brevoortia patronus*), and Skipjack Herring (*Alosa chrysochloris*). These silvery fish are important as food for many other fishes and can reach lengths up to two feet. Herrings are variable in their body shape and typically have forked caudal fins.

Puffer: Two families of puffers are known from marine habitats along the Texas coastline: puffers and porcupinefish. Puffers, including the Least Putter (*Sphoeroides parvus*), have elongated, globular-shaped bodies covered in small spines (*sometimes unnoticeable*), loose skin on the underside, a beaklike mouth with two teeth in the upper and lower jaw. Porcupinefish, such as the Striped Burrfish (*Chilomycterus schoepfii*), have globular bodies covered in short spines and a beaklike mouth with one upper and lower tooth. Both families can swallow water to expand their bodies when threatened.

Sea Bass: This group of fish are popular saltwater sport fishes and include hind and grouper. At least 25 species occur along the Texas coast, including the Rock Sea Bass (*Centropristis philadelphica*) and Warsaw Grouper (*Epinephelus nigritus*). Species in this diverse group range in size and shape, but many species are brightly colored, have robust bodies, and large teeth.

Shark: Sharks include both the requiem and hammerhead sharks, with 13 species found in marine habitats along the Texas coast. Species include the Atlantic Sharpnose Shark (*Rhizoprionodon terraenovae*), which is relatively small, only reaching lengths up to four feet, has a pointed snout, and is typically gray in coloration with lighter undersides. The Scalloped Hammerhead (*Sphyrna lewini*) and the Bonnethead (*Sphyrna tiburo*) are easily differentiated from other sharks by their flattened heads that resemble a hammer or shovel and eyes on the outer edges.

Stingray: Four species of whiptail stingrays occur in Texas, and the most common is the Atlantic Stingray (*Dasyatis sabina*). The Atlantic Stingray has a pointed snout and a long, whip-like tail with a serrated spine.

Tarpon: The Tarpon (*Megalops atlanticus*) is a large marine fish that is present along the Gulf Coast of Texas. It can reach lengths of up to eight feet in length and weigh more than 350 pounds. The mouth is turned upwards, the last ray of the dorsal fin is elongated, the caudal fin is deeply forked, and it is covered in shiny silver scales.

Tetra: The Mexican Tetra (*Astyanax mexicanus*) is a small (*less than four inches long*) freshwater fish found throughout flowing river systems in South, Central and West Texas, and has an oblong, laterally compressed body shape. It is silver in body coloration but has a small black band at the base of the caudal fin. Adult males will have red coloration on the anal fins.

UNSPLASH/PATTI BLACK

AMPHIBIANS

Amphibians include frogs, toads, salamanders, newts, and caecilians. More than 6,000 amphibian species are found worldwide, and new species are described each year. Texas is home to 71 native species of amphibians, comprising 13 different families and two orders. These species include frogs, toads, salamanders, and newts, but no caecilians. Texas is also home to one introduced species: the Greenhouse Frog.

Amphibians lack claws, although arboreal frogs often have toe pads that assist in climbing, and burrowing toads may have spades on the hind feet for digging. Amphibians typically have moist, smooth skin, although species like toads have dry, warty skin. The skin of aquatic frogs is highly permeable to allow gas exchange in aquatic environments. Toads have parotid glands just behind the head. These glands release a toxin to deter predators by irritating their mouths.

All amphibians play important roles in ecosystems. Frogs and toads are primarily herbivorous as larvae and carnivorous as adults, eating insects and other invertebrate pests. Larval salamanders are known to consume mosquito larvae. Further, amphibians are an essential food source for many animals and help to move nutrients from aquatic habitats into upland, terrestrial food webs.

Several of our native amphibians have been accidentally spread and introduced to areas of Texas where they do not naturally occur. For example, the Rio Grande Chirping Frog was widely introduced across the state due to the horticultural trade, and the Green Treefrog became established at Big Bend National Park due to individuals likely hitchhiking on RVs or other camping equipment from areas where this species is native.

Blind Salamander: Five species of blind salamanders occur in Texas, all occurring along the Edwards Plateau and Balcones Faultline in central Texas. These five species include the Texas Blind Salamander (*Eurycea rathbuni*), Blanco Blind Salamander (*Eurycea robusta*), Comal Blind Salamander (*Eurycea tridentifera*), Valdina Farms Salamander (*Eurycea troglodytes*), and Austin Blind Salamander (*Eurycea waterlooensis*). Like the closely related spring salamanders, these species are fully aquatic but have reduced or absent vision, as these species occur in aquifers, spring outflows, or within karst habitats where there is little visible light. Several species, such as the Texas Blind Salamander, have lost skin pigmentation and appear white, with elongated limbs.

Bullfrog: The American Bullfrog (*Rana catesbeiana*) occurs statewide and is the largest species of frog in North America, having a body length up to seven inches, and is capable of jumping three to six feet. This large frog lives in large, permanent lakes and wetlands and breeds throughout the summer on warm, humid nights. This species has been widely introduced around the world where it is often farmed for human consumption.

Burrowing Toad: The Mexican Burrowing Toad (*Rhinophrynus dorsalis*) is an odd-looking, secretive frog that only occurs in extreme South Texas. These frogs are dark gray with small white spots with a red or orange line running down their back. Mexican Burrowing Toads spend the majority of their lives underground and only emerge after heavy rains, often associated with hurricanes or tropical storms. The larval development of Mexican Burrowing Toads is extremely rapid, as the ponds they frequently use dry quickly after filling up after rains.

Chirping Frog: Texas is home to three species of native chirping frog and one introduced species. The Spotted Chirping Frog (*Eleutherodactylus guttilatus*) can be found in montane regions of West Texas such as Big Bend and the Cliff Chirping Frog (*Eleutherodactylus marnockii*) can be found in the Edwards Plateau. The third native species is the Rio Grande Chirping Frog (*Eleutherodactylus cystignathoides*), which is native to the Rio Grande Valley in South Texas but has spread throughout much of central and East Texas through the horticultural trade. The non-native Greenhouse Frog* (*Eleutherodactylus planirostris*) — originally from the Caribbean Islands — has established populations in Houston, Corpus Christi, and South Padre Island. All chirping frogs are small, mostly leaf-litter-dwelling frogs that get their name from the sound of their call. Additionally, all chirping frogs have direct development, meaning that there is no aquatic swimming tadpole stage and small juvenile frogs hatch from eggs.

Chorus Frog: Four species of chorus frog occur in Texas. Chorus frogs are closely related to treefrogs and have expanded toe pads on the ends of their digits that allow them to climb up vegetation. The Spotted Chorus Frog (*Pseudacris clarkii*) has a gray background color with irregular green markings and ranges from the Panhandle south through Central and North Texas into South Texas. Both the Spring Peeper (*Pseudacris crucifer*) and the Cajun Chorus Frog (*Pseudacris fouquettei*) occur in wooded habitats in East Texas. The Strecker's Chorus Frog (*Pseudacris streckeri*) occurs throughout Central, East, and North Texas. Most chorus frogs are considerably smaller than treefrogs, except the Strecker's Chorus Frog. Chorus frogs primarily use temporary wetlands that fill up after heavy rains for reproduction. Despite their small size, their calls can be surprisingly loud.

Newt: Two species of newts occur in Texas: the Eastern Newt (*Notophthalmus viridescens*) and the Black-spotted Newt (*Notophthalmus meridionalis*). The Eastern Newt occurs throughout East Texas and parts of coastal Texas while the Black-spotted Newt is restricted to South Texas, where it experienced widespread population declines in recent decades. As a result, the Black-spotted Newt is listed as state-threatened and is a proposed species for federal protection. The Eastern Newt is known to have a terrestrial immature stage called an eft, which is typically bright orange with orange spots outlined in black. As efts mature into adults, they often return to aquatic habitats.

Spring Salamander: Eight species of spring salamanders occur in central Texas, all occurring in spring outflows and associated stream runs. Most of these species occur in a limited number of localities and have very small ranges. These species include the Salado Salamander (*Eurycea chisholmensis*), Cascade Caverns Salamander (*Eurycea latitans*), San Marcos Salamander (*Eurycea nana*), Georgetown Salamander (*Eurycea naufragia*), Texas Salamander (*Eurycea neotenes*), Fern Bank Salamander (*Eurycea pterophila*), Barton Springs Salamander (*Eurycea sosorum*), and Jollyville Plateau Salamander (*Eurycea tonkawae*). Most species are federally and state-protected due to their limited occurrence in Texas and the threats these species face.

True Frog: True frogs are a group of large frogs which also include leopard frogs and bullfrogs. Species of true frogs that occur in Texas include the Pickerel Frog (*Rana palustris*) and Green Frog (*Rana clamitans*), which both have relatively large distributions throughout East Texas. The Pickerel Frog looks similar to leopard frogs but has squarish blotches instead of round blotches and yellow or orange coloration on the inside of its hind legs. Despite their name, Green Frogs can also be tan or bronze in coloration and can look similar to American Bullfrogs. These two species can be differentiated by looking at the dorsolateral fold (*a fold of skin occurring from behind the eye*). In Green Frogs, the dorsolateral fold extends to the hind limb, but in American Bullfrogs, the dorsolateral fold curves around the tympanum (*eardrum*) and never reaches the hind limb. Both the Pig Frog (*Rana grylio*) and Crawfish Frog (*Rana areolata*) also occur in East Texas but have a much more limited distribution in the state.

True Toad: Ten species of toads occur throughout Texas, all varying in size, distribution, and preferred habitats. The largest toad that occurs in Texas is the Mesoamerican Cane Toad (*Rhinella horribilis*) that occurs in extreme South Texas, which can exceed seven inches in length. The smallest toad in Texas is the Green Toad (*Anaxyrus debilis*), rarely exceeding two inches in length, which is found across much of the state except East Texas. All other species of toads are similar in size. Likely the rarest toad in Texas is the Houston Toad (*Anaxyrus houstonensis*). The Houston Toad only occurs in a handful of counties in the east-central portion of the state, has suffered widespread population declines, and is both federally- and state-protected. Two of the most widespread and abundant toads in Texas are the Texas Toad (*Anaxyrus speciosus*), which occurs throughout much of Texas except the eastern portion of the state and is also the state amphibian, and the Gulf Coast Toad (*Incilius nebulifer*), which occurs throughout South, Central, and East Texas. The American Toad (*Anaxyrus americanus*) occurs in the extreme northeast corner of the state and is similar in appearance to the Fowler's Toad (*Anaxyrus fowleri*), which occupies a larger distribution throughout East Texas. The Great Plains Toad (*Anaxyrus cognatus*) primarily occurs in the Texas Panhandle and the Trans-Pecos region. Widespread across West, North, and Central Texas, the Red-spotted Toad (*Anaxyrus punctatus*) can be found in rocky, limestone habitats. The Woodhouse's Toad (*Anaxyrus woodhousii*) historically ranged from the Texas Panhandle down the Gulf Coast but has experienced declines across much of its range in Central Texas. Despite these declines, there remain areas where populations are still robust. Toads typically have dry, warty skin, bony ridges on the top of their head, and large poison glands called parotoid glands behind their eyes. These parotoid glands can secrete noxious compounds which are distasteful and irritating to potential predators.

Waterdog: These salamanders are also occasionally called mudpuppies and one species occurs in Texas: the Gulf Coast Waterdog (*Necturus beyeri*). The Gulf Coast Waterdog occurs in small creek systems in the Big Thicket of East Texas. This species is fully aquatic, has four limbs, and bushy external gills on the sides of its head.

UNSPLASH/DAVID CADENAS

REPTILES

The order Reptilia consists of more than 1,200 genera and 11,000 species and includes lizards, snakes, turtles, and crocodilians. Texas is home to 153 native species of reptiles and 10 introduced species: Florida Red-bellied Cooter, Bent-toed Gecko, Common House Gecko, Indo-Pacific House Gecko, Tropical House Gecko, Sri Lankan Spotted House Gecko, Mediterranean Gecko, Mexican Spiny-tailed Iguana, Brown Anole, and the Brahminy Blindsnake.

Unlike amphibians, all reptiles have skin that is covered in scales. These scales serve as protection, but also help to prevent water loss, allowing reptiles to tolerate more arid habitats than amphibians.

Most species of reptiles lay eggs, but some species will give birth to live young, such as rattlesnakes. For egg-laying species, young develop in hard or leathery-shelled eggs, which are often laid in a nest and abandoned by the female.

Most reptiles have a well-developed sense of smell and use their tongue to collect chemical compounds from the air and move the compounds to the Jacobson's organ. This chemosensory organ is located on the roof of the mouth and provides sensory feedback for detecting airborne chemicals.

Reptiles also have relatively good vision. Snakes often detect movement with their eyes, and visual cues help them locate prey or attract mates.

Like amphibians, reptiles play an important role in nature as part of the food chain. Within Texas, the highest reptile diversity is located in South and West Texas. The Chihuahuan Desert of West Texas is home to most of the diversity of venomous snakes found in the state, including six species of rattlesnakes. Species such as the Pond Slider, Texas Spiny Lizard, and Coachwhip are found across almost the entire state, while species like the Rough-footed Mud Turtle, Reticulate Banded Gecko, and Speckled Racer have extremely limited occurrences in the state.

Alligator: The American Alligator (*Alligator mississippiensis*) is the largest reptile in North America and is found across the eastern third of Texas.

Copperhead: VENOMOUS. The Copperhead (*Agkistrodon contortrix*) is found in most of the state, except South Texas and the Panhandle. Its copper-colored body with rusty orange or grayish bands help camouflage the snake in leaf litter. They feed on small mammals and insects, particularly, freshly-molted cicadas in the summer.

Coral Snake: VENOMOUS. The Texas Coral Snake (*Micrurus tener*) is a common species across South, Central, and East Texas. It is infrequently seen because it spends the majority of its life underground, and it feeds almost exclusively on other snakes. Because of variability in color intensity and pattern in Texas Coral Snakes, the commonly used rhyme "red next to yellow, kill a fellow; red next to black, venom lack" is not a reliable method to distinguish venomous coralsnakes from look-a-likes, such as the non-venomous Milksnake (*Lampropeltis triangulum*).

Gecko: The Texas Banded Gecko (*Coleonyx brevis*) is the smaller of the two native geckos in the state and is found in West and South Texas. The Reticulate Banded Gecko (*Coleonyx reticulatus*) is native to the Big Bend. Six species of geckos have been introduced to Texas. The Mediterranean Gecko* (*Hemidactylus turcicus*) first arrived in Brownsville in the 1950s and is now found as far north as Lubbock and the Red River. Other species like the Tropical House Gecko* (*Hemidactylus mabouia*) and the Sri Lankan Spotted Gecko* (*Hemidactylus parvimaculatus*) are recent arrivals to the state.

Horned Lizard: The Texas Horned Lizard (*Phrynosoma cornutum*), or Horny Toad, is the state reptile. Originally found across the majority of the state, it is now restricted to pockets in West, South, and North Texas due to habitat loss and the introduction of invasive grasses and insects. The Greater Short-horned Lizard (*Phrynosoma hernandesi*) is found at higher elevations in the Davis, Guadalupe, and Hueco mountains. The Round-tailed Horned Lizard (*Phrynosoma modestum*) is found mostly in West Texas and the Panhandle and blends into its arid habitats as a rock mimic.

Iguana: The Mexican Spiny-tailed Iguana* (*Ctenosaura pectinata*) is the only species of iguana found in the state. It was introduced in Brownsville in the 1960s but has not expanded its range outside of Cameron County.

Rattlesnake: VENOMOUS. Rattlesnakes are seen in every habitat in Texas, with 11 species represented in the state. The largest, the Western Diamond-backed Rattlesnake (*Crotalus atrox*), can reach lengths over seven feet and is found everywhere except far East Texas. The Timber Rattlesnake (*Crotalus horridus*) is a heavy-bodied snake found in the hardwood bottomlands of East and North Texas. The Rock Rattlesnake (*Crotalus lepidus*) can reach more than two feet in length and is restricted to the Trans-Pecos. The smallest rattlesnake species in Texas, the Pygmy Rattlesnake (*Sistrurus miliarius*) is found in East Texas, rarely growing longer than 20 inches.

Sea Turtle: Five species of sea turtles can be found in saltwater habitats along the Texas coastline. The largest of all sea turtles, the Leatherback Sea Turtle (*Dermochelys coriacea*), has a shell length that exceeds seven feet in length and can weigh almost a ton. The Kemp's Ridley Sea Turtle (*Lepidochelys kempii*) is among the rarest and smallest of the sea turtles, which primarily nest along South Padre Island and into coastal Mexico and is designated as the State Sea Turtle. Other sea turtles include the Green Sea Turtle (*Chelonia mydas*), Hawksbill Sea Turtle (*Eretmochelys imbricata*), and Loggerhead Sea Turtle (*Caretta caretta*). All species of sea turtle are federally- and state-protected and any observed nesting or stranded along the coastline should be reported to appropriate individuals, such as TPWD.

Snapping Turtle: Snapping turtles are among the largest freshwater turtles in North America and have a generalist diet, consuming almost anything in the water it encounters, including carrion. Two species of snapping turtles are found in Texas. The Snapping Turtle (*Chelydra serpentina*) is found throughout the central and eastern regions while the Alligator Snapping Turtle (*Macrochelys temminckii*) is restricted to East Texas.

Tortoise: One species of tortoise occurs in Texas: the Berlandier's Tortoise (*Gopherus berlandieri*). This tortoise occurs throughout South Texas and into Mexico and has a domed shell and elephant-like feet. Unlike most other turtles, tortoises spend the majority of their time on land foraging on vegetation.

BIRDS

The order Aves consists of more than 2,000 genera and over 10,000 species. Texas is home to 639 species of birds, including purposefully introduced species (e.g., House Sparrow, European Starling) and accidental releases (e.g., Monk Parakeet), as well as recent introductions or range expansions (e.g., Cattle Egret, Red-crowned Parrot).

Because many species migrate long distances, flying between spring breeding grounds and overwintering sites, some individuals find themselves off-course and are recorded as accidental visitors in the state each year.

Birds are well-known for their vocalizations, which are unique to each species. Calls include courtship songs, alarm calls, and threat displays. Both males and females will vocalize, but the males typically have elaborate songs used to attract mates. Song attractiveness may be enhanced by behavioral displays in some species that include bright colorations and elaborate dances or flight patterns. Some bird species will form single pair bonds (some for life), while other species may breed with more than one partner.

All birds lay eggs; some species may construct elaborate nests from vegetation or build nests in cavities, while some species like Killdeer and nighthawks lay camouflaged eggs directly on the ground. A few species are nest parasites, laying eggs in the nests of other species.

When chicks hatch, they may be altricial (naked, helpless, blind; e.g., songbirds), semi-precocial (downy, dependent, eyes open; e.g., gulls), or precocial (downy, independent, eyes open; e.g., ducklings).

Bird diets vary from scavenging and eating carrion to hunting small and medium-sized vertebrates. Other diet items can include invertebrates from grasshoppers to spiders, snails to worms, and many other bird species eat a variety of seeds, fruit, and even nectar. Birds also serve as important diet items for many species.

Dove: Many species occur in Texas. Several species are game species, including Mourning Dove (*Zenaida macroura*), White-winged Dove (*Zenaida asiatica*), and White-tipped Dove (*Leptotila verreauxi*). The Rock Dove (*Columba livia*), or Pigeon, can be found in large numbers in urban areas. The Eurasian Collared-dove* (*Steptopelia decaocto*) first arrived in the state in 1995 and can now be found in every county.

Eagle: The Bald Eagle (*Haliaeetus leucocephalus*) is the largest raptor in Texas, feeding on fish and ducks primarily in the eastern third of the state. It can be seen in most of Texas during migration. The Golden Eagle (*Aquila chrysaetos*), with its seven-foot wingspan, is often associated with mountainous regions where it feeds on mammals, birds, and reptiles.

Hawk: Hawks are birds of prey in the same family as eagles, kites, and harriers. The Cooper's Hawk (*Accipiter cooperii*) feeds on birds and is often seen in wooded urban backyards. The Northern Harrier (*Circus cyaneus*) can be found gliding low across prairies searching for small vertebrates. The Harris's Hawk (*Parabuteo unicinctus*) is known for cooperatively hunting in social groups. The Red-tailed Hawk (*Buteo jamaicensis*) is found statewide, often seen soaring or perched on telephone poles and fence posts.

UNSPLASH/ZDENEK MACHACEK

Hummingbird: Texas is home to at least 18 species, some species being residents, others only brief migratory visitors. The Ruby throated Hummingbird (*Archilochus colubris*) is a summer resident in the eastern third of the state; the Black-chinned Hummingbird (*Archilochus alexandri*) is commonly seen in the western two-thirds of the state. The Lucifer Hummingbird (*Calothorax lucifer*) can be found in the Christmas and Chisos mountains in the Big Bend during the summer; the Green-breasted Mango (*Anthracothorax prevostii*) has been seen sporadically in the Lower Rio Grande Valley, primarily in the fall.

Mockingbird: The Northern Mockingbird (*Mimus polyglottos*) is the State Bird of Texas. Known for mimicking songs of other birds to attract mates and intimidate other males, unmated males will sing at night in the spring. Both males and females may vigorously attack would-be predators to defend their eggs and young.

Owl: Seventeen species are observed in the state. With large eyes, incredible hearing, and wings adapted to maintain silence in flight, owls are amazing nocturnal predators. More frequently seen owls include the Barn Owl (*Tyto alba*), Great Horned Owl (*Bufo virginianus*), Eastern Screech Owl (*Megascops asio*), Burrowing Owl (*Athene cunicularia*), and Barred Owl (*Strix varia*). In the summer, the small Elf Owl (*Micrathene whitneyi*) can be seen in West Texas.

Parrot: A single species, the Red-crowned Parrot (*Amazona viridigenalis*) is found in Texas, common in the metropolitan areas of Cameron, Hidalgo, and Starr counties along the lower Rio Grande border.

Roadrunner: The Greater Roadrunner (*Geococcyx californicus*) is found across the state, though uncommon in East Texas. They feed on a variety of prey, including insects, spiders, small mammals, small birds, lizards, and snakes, including rattlesnakes, but will also eat fruit and seeds. Other names include Paisano and Chaparral Cock.

Shorebird: Shorebirds' long bills are used to probe moist sand and sediment for invertebrates and featherless legs adapted for wading. The Willet (*Tringa semipalmata*) breeds along the Gulf Coast, identified by its black-and-white wing pattern visible during flight. The Spotted Sandpiper (*Actitis macularius*) can be identified by the exaggerated bobbing of its longish tail when walking. The Mountain Plover (*Charadrius montanus*) is a summer resident in open grasslands of the northern Panhandle with some populations wintering in central and South Texas. The secretive and solitary Wilson's Snipe (*Callinago delicata*), the focus of many invented hunts, is an actual game bird found along grassy marshes and meadows.

Vulture: Both species of vultures are experts at soaring, generally only flapping their wings when they take off from feeding or roosting. Featherless heads and curved bills are adaptations to feeding on carrion. The Black Vulture (*Coragyps atratus*) has a black head and white wing-tips when viewed from below; the Turkey Vulture (*Cathartes aura*) has a red head and two-toned (*black and white*) wings from below: black on the leading edge, gray or white on the trailing edge. Turkey Vultures use both sight and smell to find food; Black Vultures rely more on sight.

MAMMALS

Mammals, with a few notable exceptions (the egg-laying monotremes: four species of echidna and the Platypus), are a large group of vertebrates with hair that give birth to live young. There are more than 6,400 species worldwide (approximately 1,200 genera), including species-rich groups like rodents, bats, and shrews.

A total of 145 species of native terrestrial mammals occur in Texas, a number exceeded in the United States only by California and New Mexico. Also, 28 species of marine mammals have been reported from the Texas coast or are expected to occur there. A single species of marsupial, the Virginia Opossum, is found in the state.

Mammals are found in every ecoregion across the state, with species diversity highest in the Trans-Pecos. Mammals occupy many different habitats, such as species that live almost entirely underground (moles and gophers), are primarily aquatic (American Beaver, Nutria, River Otter), or can fly (bats) or glide (Flying Squirrel).

Recreational hunting is an important economic activity for the state, with the breeding and hunting of deer impacting the Texas economy by over $1 billion each year. Game animals include White-tailed Deer, Mule Deer, Pronghorn, Javelina, and squirrels. There are also 18 exotics or non-native species that have been introduced by man either accidentally (e.g., Japanese Macaque, House Mouse, Black Rat, Norway Rat) or intentionally (e.g., Nutria, Red Fox, Feral Pig, Axis Deer, Fallow Deer, Sika Deer, Nilgai, Greater Kudu, Eastern Thomson's Gazelle, Sable Antelope, Scimitar-horned Oryx, Common Eland, Aoudad, Blackbuck) and have become established.

Armadillo: The Nine-banded Armadillo (*Dasypus novemcinctus*) is one of Texas' most iconic mammals and is the state's small mammal. It is found in most of the state except the western Trans-Pecos. It is now common as far north and east as Kansas and Mississippi.

Bat: Thirty-two species of these winged mammals have been found in Texas, more than in any other state in the United States. Of these, 27 species are known residents, though they are seldom seen by the casual observer. The Mexican Free-tailed Bat (*Tadarida brasiliensis*) and the Cave Myotis (*Myotis velifer*) constitute most of the cave-dwelling bats of central and West Texas. They have some economic value for their deposits of nitrogen-rich guano. Some commercial guano has been produced from Beaver Creek Cavern (Burnet County) and James River Bat Cave (Mason County), and from large deposits in other caves, including Bandera Bat Cave (Bandera County), Blowout Cave (Blanco County), and Devil's Sinkhole (Edwards County). The largest concentration of bats in the world is found at Bracken Cave in Comal County, which is thought to hold between 20 and 40 million bats. The Big Brown Bat (*Eptesicus fuscus*), the Eastern Red Bat (*Lasiurus borealis*), and the Evening Bat (*Nycticeius humeralis*) are found in East and Southeast Texas. The Evening Bat and Big Brown Bat are forest and woodland dwelling mammals. The rarer species of Texas bats have been found along the Rio Grande and in the Trans-Pecos. Bats can be observed at dusk near a water source, and many species may also be found foraging on insects attracted to streetlights. The State Flying Mammal of Texas is the Mexican Free-tailed Bat.

UNSPLASH/GOUTHAM GANESH SIVANANDAM

Bison: The largest of native terrestrial wild mammals of North America, the American Bison (*Bos bison*), commonly called buffalo, was formerly found in the western two-thirds of the state. Today, it is extirpated or confined on ranches. Deliberate slaughter of this majestic animal for hides and to eliminate the Plains Natives' main food source reached a peak about 1877 to 1878, and the American Bison was almost eradicated by 1885. Estimates of the number of buffalo killed vary, but as many as 200,000 hides were sold in Fort Worth at a single two-day sale. Except for the interest of the late Colonel Charles Goodnight and a few other foresighted men, the American Bison might be extinct.

Javelina: The Javelina or Collared Peccary (*Pecari tajacu*) is found in brushy semidesert areas where Prickly Pear, a favorite food, is found. The Javelina was hunted commercially for its hide until 1939. They are harmless to livestock and to people, though they can defend themselves ferociously when attacked by hunting dogs.

Opossum: A marsupial, the Virginia Opossum (*Didelphis virginiana*) is found in nearly all parts of the state. The opossum has economic value for its pelt, and its meat is considered a delicacy by some.

Otter: Northern River Otters (*Lontra canadensis*) are found in the eastern third of the state. This species has probably been extirpated from the Panhandle and some north-central locations but over the past 20 years, it has been expanding its range back into remaining suitable habitat in East and South Texas.

Rabbit: The Black-tailed Jackrabbit (*Lepus californicus*) is found throughout Texas except the Big Thicket area of East Texas. It breeds rapidly, and its long hind legs make it one of the world's faster-running animals. The Eastern Cottontail (*Sylvilagus floridanus*) is found mostly in the eastern three-quarters of the state. The Desert Cottontail (*Sylvilagus audubonii*) is found in the western half of the state, usually in the open range. The Swamp Rabbit (*Sylvilagus aquaticus*) is found in East Texas and the coastal area. The Davis Mountains Cottontail (*Sylvilagus robustus*) is restricted to Jeff Davis County.

Rats, Mice, and Voles: There are 40 to 50 species of rats, mice, and voles in Texas of varying characteristics, habitats, and economic destructiveness. The Norway Rat* (*Rattus norvegicus*) and the Roof Rat* (*Rattus rattus*), both non-native species, are probably the most common and most destructive. They also are instrumental in the transmission of several dread diseases, including bubonic plague and typhus. Populations of the Common House Mouse* (*Mus musculus*) are estimated in the hundreds of millions annually. The Mogollon Vole (*Microtus mogolollonensis*) is found only in the higher elevations of Guadalupe Mountains National Park. With its long tail tipped with a white tuft of fur, the state-threatened Texas Kangaroo Rat (*Dipodomys elator*) is restricted to less than a dozen Texas counties near the Red River.

Skunk: There are five species of skunk in Texas. The Eastern Spotted Skunk (*Spilogale putorius*) is found in the eastern half of the state, the Gulf Coast, and across north-central Texas to the Panhandle. A small skunk, it is often erroneously called a civet cat. The Western Spotted Skunk (*Spilogale gracilis*) is found in the southwestern part of the state north to Garza and Howard counties and east to Bexar and Duval counties. The Striped Skunk (*Mephitis mephitis*) is found statewide, mostly in brush or wooded areas. The Hooded Skunk (*Mephitis macroura*) was found in limited numbers in the Big Bend and adjacent parts of the Trans-Pecos but may be extirpated from the state. The Hog-nosed Skunk (*Conepatus leuconotus*) is found across the western, central, and southern portion of the state, as well as the upper Gulf Coast.

TEXAS' THREATENED AND ENDANGERED SPECIES

Endangered species are those the Texas Parks and Wildlife Department has named as being at risk of statewide extinction. Threatened species are likely to become endangered in the future. The following lists include species that are listed by the TPWD as either threatened or endangered as of January 2025 (the most recent list available at the time of this publication).

The species on these lists vary from those on the federal list of threatened and endangered species managed by the United States Fish and Wildlife Service.

THREATS AND SUCCESSES

The distribution and abundance of Texas wildlife have changed dramatically over the last 100 years. While a few native species have increased their numbers and expanded their ranges during this period (e.g., White-tailed Deer, Coyote, White-winged Dove), these species are the exceptions. Many species have declined and face continued threats across their shrinking distributions in Texas.

In general, these threats are not focused on individual species, but are widespread risks to ecoregions as a whole, impacting both plant and animal communities. Habitat loss is the primary threat and can include land lost to urbanization and agriculture. The development of land for resource extraction activities contributes to habitat loss and fragmentation. Some technologies, such as wind turbines, have led to the direct mortality of some groups of animals (e.g., birds and bats).

The loss of riparian habitats is often linked to the reallocation or reprioritization of water resources. The suppression of wildfire across many habitats has removed the natural cycle of vegetative change important for maintaining species diversity. Modifications to rainfall patterns and temperatures due to climate change affect the distribution of plant and animal communities as well as the timing of processes and behaviors (e.g., dates for plants to flower and birds to begin migration).

The introduction of invasive grasses (e.g., King Ranch Bluestem, Buffelgrass), aquatic plants (e.g., Hydrilla, Giant Reed), trees (e.g., Chinaberry, Tamarisk), and animals (e.g., Red Imported Fire Ant, Zebra Mussel) has allowed non-native species to outcompete and replace populations of native species across the state. Historical instances of overhunting led to the demise of native Bighorn Sheep, Bison, and Elk. Predator control efforts removed the Jaguar and Gray Wolf from the state as well.

Focused conservation efforts have removed species such as the Black-capped Vireo, Concho Water Snake, and American Alligator from the Federal Threatened and Endangered Species List. However, many species still require thoughtful and intensive management plans at local, state, and federal levels to help them remain a part of the state's natural heritage.

THREATENED SPECIES

Plants: Cacti: Bunched Cory Cactus, Chisos Mountains Hedgehog Cactus, Lloyd's Mariposa Cactus; **Grasses:** Dune Umbrella-sedge, Small-headed Pipewort; **Trees, Shrubs, Sub-shrubs:** Gypsum Scalebroom, Hinckley's Oak; **Quillworts:** Rock Quillwort; **Wildflowers:** Brushpea, Earth Fruit, Houston Daisy, Leoncita False Foxglove, Livermore Sweet-cicely, Neches River Rose-mallow, Pecos Sunflower

Invertebrates: Bivalves: Brazos Heelsplitter, Guadalupe Fatmucket, Louisiana Pigtoe, Mexican Fawnsfoot, Salina Mucket, Sandbank Pocketbook, Southern Hickorynut, Texas Fatmucket, Texas Fawnsfoot, Texas Heelsplitter, Texas Pigtoe, Trinity Pigtoe; **Crustaceans:** Clear Creek Amphipod, Texas Troglobitic Water Slater; **Snails:** Carolinae Tryonia, Caroline's Springs Pyrg, Crowned Cave Snail, Limpia Creek Springsnail, Metcalf's Tryonia, Presidio County Springsnail

Fishes: Catfish: Headwater Catfish, Toothless Blindcat, Widemouth Blindcat; **Coastal Fishes:** Mexican Goby, River Goby; **Large River Fish:** Paddlefish, Shovelnose Sturgeon; **Livebearers:** Spotfin Gambusia; **Minnows:** Arkansas River Shiner, Bluehead Shiner, Chihuahua Shiner, Chub Shiner, Devils River Minnow, Frio Roundnose Minnow, Medina Roundnose Minnow, Mexican Stoneroller, Plateau Shiner, Prairie Chub, Proserpine Shiner, Rio Grande Chub, Rio Grande Shiner, Roundnose Minnow, Speckled Chub, Tamaulipas Shiner; **Perches:** Blackside Darter, Guadalupe Darter, Rio Grande Darter; **Pupfish:** Conchos Pupfish, Pecos Pupfish, Red River Pupfish; **Sharks:** Great Hammerhead, Oceanic Whitetip, Shortfin Mako; **Suckers:** Blue Sucker, Western Creek Chubsucker

Amphibians: Black-Spotted Newt, Blanco Blind Salamander, Cascade Caverns Salamander, Georgetown Salamander, Jollyville Plateau Salamander, Mexican Burrowing Toad, Mexican Treefrog, Salado Springs Salamander, San Marcos Salamander, Sheep Frog, South Texas Siren (*Large Form*), Texas Salamander, White-Lipped Frog

Reptiles: Lizards: Mountain Short-Horned Lizard, Texas Horned Lizard; **Snakes:** Black-Striped Snake, Brazos Water

Snake, Louisiana Pine Snake, Northern Cat-Eyed Snake, Northern Scarlet Snake, Speckled Racer, Texas Scarlet Snake, Trans-Pecos Black-Headed Snake; **Turtles:** Alligator Snapping Turtle, Cagle's Map Turtle, Chihuahuan Mud Turtle, Green Sea Turtle, Loggerhead Sea Turtle, Texas Tortoise

Birds: Parrots: Red-Crowned Parrot; **Raptors:** American Peregrine Falcon, Cactus Ferruginous Pygmy-Owl, Common Black Hawk, Gray Hawk, Mexican Spotted Owl, Peregrine Falcon, Swallow-Tailed Kite, White-Tailed Hawk, Zone-Tailed Hawk; **Shorebirds:** Black Rail, Piping Plover, Rufa Red Knot, Sooty Tern; Bachman's Sparrow, Northern Beardless-Tyrannulet, Rose-Throated Becard, Texas Botteri's Sparrow, Tropical Parula; **Waterbirds:** Reddish Egret, White-Faced Ibis, Wood Stork

Mammals: Bats: Rafinesque's Big-Eared Bat, Spotted Bat; **Carnivores:** American Black Bear, Louisiana Black Bear, White-Nosed Coati; **Marine Mammals:** Atlantic Spotted Dolphin, Cuvier's Beaked Whale, Dwarf Sperm Whale, False Killer Whale, Gervais' Beaked Whale, Killer Whale, Pygmy Killer Whale, Pygmy Sperm Whale, Rough-toothed Dolphin, Short-finned Pilot Whale, West Indian Manatee; **Rodents:** Coues' Rice Rat, Palo Duro Mouse, Tawny-bellied Cotton Rat, Texas Kangaroo Rat

ENDANGERED SPECIES

Plants: Cacti: Black Lace Cactus, Davis' Green Pitaya, Star Cactus, Tobusch Fishhook Cactus; **Grasses:** Guadalupe Fescue, Little Aguja Pondweed, Texas Wild Rice; **Orchids:** Navasota Ladies'-tresses; **Trees, Shrubs, Sub-shrubs:** Texas Ayenia, Texas Snowbells, Walker's Manioc; **Wildflowers:** Ashy Dogweed, Large-fruited Sand-verbena, Slender Rushpea, South Texas Ambrosia, Terlingua Creek Cat's-eye, Texas Golden Gladecress, Texas Poppy-mallow, Texas Prairie Dawn, Texas Trailing Phlox, White Bladderpod, Zapata Bladderpod

Invertebrates: Beetles: Comal Springs Dryopid Beetle, Comal Springs Riffle Beetle; **Bivalves:** Balcones Spike, False Spike, Guadalupe Orb, Texas Hornshell, Texas Pimpleback; **Crustaceans:** Diminutive Amphipod, Peck's Cave Amphipod, Pecos Amphipod; **Snails:** Diamond Y Springsnail, Gonzales Tryonia, Pecos Assiminea Snail, Phantom Springsnail, Phantom Tryonia

Fishes: Catfish: Mexican Blindcat; **Coastal Fishes:** Smalltooth Sawfish; **Livebearers:** Big Bend Gambusia, Clear Creek Gambusia, Pecos Gambusia; **Minnows:** Peppered Chub, Sharpnose Shiner, Smalleye Shiner; **Perches:** Fountain Darter; **Pupfish:** Comanche Springs Pupfish, Leon Springs Pupfish

Amphibians: Austin Blind Salamander, Barton Springs Salamander, Houston Toad, Texas Blind Salamander

Reptiles: Lizards: Dunes Sagebrush Lizard; **Turtles:** Hawksbill Sea Turtle, Kemp's Ridley Sea Turtle, Leatherback Sea Turtle

Birds: Raptors: Northern Aplomado Falcon; **Shorebirds:** Eskimo Curlew, Interior Least Tern; **Songbirds:** Golden-Cheeked Warbler, Southwestern Willow Flycatcher; **Upland Birds:** Attwater's Greater Prairie Chicken, Lesser Prairie Chicken; **Waterbirds:** Whooping Crane; **Woodpeckers:** Red-Cockaded Woodpecker

Mammals: Bats: Mexican Long-nosed Bat; **Carnivores:** Ocelot; **Marine Mammals:** Blue Whale, Bryde's Whale, Finback Whale, North Atlantic Right Whale, Rice's Whale, Sei Whale, Sperm Whale

TEXAS WILDLIFE MANAGEMENT AREAS

The Texas Parks and Wildlife Department is responsible for managing more than 50 wildlife management areas (WMAs) in the state totaling more than 748,000 acres. Every ecological region in the state has at least one WMA.

Wildlife management areas are used principally for hunting, but many are also used for research, fishing, wildlife viewing, hiking, camping, bicycling, and horseback riding, when those activities are compatible with the primary goals for which the WMA was established.

Name (Acreage)	Hunting	Fishing	Camping	Wildlife Viewing	Hiking	Driving	Bicycling	Equestrian	County
Alabama Creek (14,561)	★	★	★	★	★	★	★	★	Trinity
Alazan Bayou (2,063)	★	★	★	★				★	Nacogdoches
Angelina-Neches/Dam B (12,636)	★	★	★	★	★		★		Jasper/Tyler
Atkinson Island (150)		★		★					Harris
Bannister (25,695)	★	★	★	★	★		★	★	San Augustine
Big Lake Bottom (3,894)	★	★		★					Anderson
Black Gap (103,000)	★	★	★	★	★	★	★	★	Brewster
Caddo Lake (8,124)	★	★	★	★				★	Marion/Harrison
Caddo Nat. Grasslands (16,140)	★	★	★	★	★		★	★	Fannin
Candy Cain Abshier (207)				★					Chambers
Cedar Creek Islands (160)		★		★					Henderson
Chaparral (15,200)	★		★	★	★	★	★		La Salle/Dimmit
Cooper (14,480)	★	★		★	★		★		Delta/Hopkins
D.R. Wintermann (246)				★					Wharton
Elephant Mountain (23,147)	★		★	★	★	★			Brewster
Gene Howe (5,394)	★	★	★	★	★		★	★	Hemphill
Gene Howe: W.A. "Pat" Murphy (889)	★	★		★	★				Hemphill
Guadalupe Delta (7,411)	★	★		★	★		★		Calhoun/Refugio
Gus Engeling (10,958)	★	★	★	★	★	★	★	★	Anderson
J.D. Murphree (25,852)	★	★		★					Jefferson
James E. Daughtrey (34,000)	★			★					Live Oak/McMullen
Justin Hurst (15,612)	★	★		★	★		★		Brazoria
Keechi Creek (1,500)	★								Leon
Kerr (6,493)	★	★		★		★	★		Kerr
Las Palomas: Anacua (222)	★			★					Cameron
Las Palomas: Lower Rio Grande Valley (3,311)	★			★	★				Cameron/Hidalgo/Presidio
Lower Neches (7,998)	★	★		★	★				Orange
M.O. Neasloney (100)				★	★				Gonzales
Mad Island (7,200)	★			★					Matagorda
Mason Mountain (5,300)	★								Mason
Matador (28,183)	★	★	★	★	★	★		★	Cottle
Matagorda Island (56,688)	★	★	★	★	★		★		Calhoun
McGillivray & Leona McKie Muse (1,973)	★								Brown
Moore Plantation (26,772)	★	★	★	★	★		★	★	Sabine/Jasper
Nannie M. Stringfellow (3,666)	★			★					Brazoria
Nature Center (82)				★	★				Smith
North Toledo Bend (3,650)	★	★	★	★	★			★	Shelby
Old Sabine Bottom (5,158)	★	★	★	★	★		★	★	Smith
Pat Mayse (8,925)	★	★	★	★	★			★	Lamar

Source: Texas Parks and Wildlife Department.

NATIONAL WILDLIFE REFUGES IN TEXAS

Texas is home to 20 national wildlife refuges. Each refuge works to conserve native species and also provides recreational opportunities for the public such as bird watching, wildlife viewing, hunting, and fishing.

Aransas (1937): This refuge complex comprises more than 115,000 acres including Blackjack Peninsula, Matagorda Island, and three satellite units in Aransas and Refugio counties. Besides providing wintering grounds for the largest wild flock of endangered whooping cranes, the refuge includes hundreds of species of waterfowl and other migratory birds.

Attwater Prairie Chicken (1972): Established in Colorado County to preserve habitat for the endangered Attwater's prairie chicken *(a ground-dwelling grouse)*, the refuge comprises more than 10,000 acres of native tallgrass prairie, sandy knolls, and wooded areas.

Balcones Canyonlands (1992): This approximately 25,000-acre refuge is located in Burnet, Travis, and Williamson counties northwest of Austin. It was established to protect the nesting habitat of two endangered birds: black-capped vireo and golden-cheeked warbler.

Big Boggy (1983): This refuge, designated an Internationally Significant Shorebird Site, occupies almost 5,000 acres of coastal prairie and salt marsh along East Matagorda Bay for the benefit of wintering waterfowl. The marsh protects the threatened eastern black rail.

Brazoria (1966): More than 45,000 acres make up this refuge, located along the Gulf Coast in Brazoria County. The area serves as a haven for wintering waterfowl and a wide variety of other migratory birds. The refuge also supports many marsh and water birds, from roseate spoonbills and great blue herons to white-faced ibis and sandhill cranes.

Buffalo Lake (1958): Comprising 7,664 acres in the Central Flyway in Randall County in the Panhandle, this refuge contains some of the best remaining shortgrass prairie in the United States. Buffalo Lake is now typically dry; a marsh area is artificially maintained for the numerous birds, reptiles, and mammals.

Caddo Lake (2000): Established on portions of the approximately 8,500-acre Longhorn Army Ammunition Plant in Harrison County, this refuge contains a mature flooded bald cypress forest, with some trees nearly 400 years old. The bottomland hardwood forest ecosystem provides essential habitat for migratory and resident wildlife. The wetlands of Caddo Lake are important to migratory birds within the Central Flyway. The area supports one of the highest breeding populations of wood ducks and prothonotary warblers.

Hagerman (1946): Hagerman National Wildlife Refuge lies on the Big Mineral arm of Lake Texoma in Grayson County. The 3,000 acres of marsh and water and 8,000 acres of upland and farmland provide a feeding and resting place for migrating waterfowl.

Jocelyn Nungaray (1963): *(renamed from Anahuac)* The 39,000 acres of this refuge are located along the upper Gulf Coast in Chambers County. Fresh and saltwater marshes and miles of sweeping coastal prairie provide wintering habitat for large flocks of waterfowl, including geese, ducks, and rails. Roseate spoonbills, great and snowy egrets, and white-faced ibis are among the other birds frequenting the refuge. Other species include alligator, muskrat, and bobcat.

Laguna Atascosa (1946): This refuge is the southernmost waterfowl refuge in the Central Flyway and contains more than 110,000 acres fronting on the Laguna Madre in the Lower Rio Grande Valley in Cameron and Willacy counties. Open lagoons, coastal prairies, salt flats, and brushlands support a wide diversity of wildlife. The United States' largest concentration of redhead ducks winters here, along with many other species of waterfowl and shorebirds. White-tailed deer, javelina, and armadillo can be found, along with endangered ocelot.

Lower Rio Grande Valley (1979): Part of the South Texas Refuge Complex, this nearly 40,000-acre refuge lies within Cameron, Hidalgo, Starr, and Willacy counties. The refuge includes a variety of habitats, including sabal palm forest, tidal flats, coastal brushland, mid-delta thorn forest, woodland potholes and basins, upland thorn scrub, flood forest, barretal, riparian woodland, and Chihuahuan thorn forest.

McFaddin (1980): This refuge's more than 58,000 acres in Jefferson and Chambers counties are of great importance to wintering populations of migratory waterfowl. One of the densest populations of alligators in Texas is found here. From October through March, 24 duck species can number up to 100,000.

Moody (1961): Authorized under the Migratory Bird Treaty Act of 1918, a law establishing treaties for conserving migratory birds, this refuge is protected by a conservation easement and is closed to the public.

Source: U.S. Fish and Wildlife Service, U.S. Department of the Interior.

UNSPLASH/CHANDLER CRUTTENDEN

Muleshoe (1935): Oldest of the national refuges in Texas, Muleshoe provides winter habitat for waterfowl and the continent's largest wintering population of sandhill cranes. Comprising 6,440 acres in the High Plains of Bailey County, the refuge contains playa lakes, marsh areas, caliche outcroppings, and native grasslands.

Neches River (2013): Located in the Anderson and Cherokee counties, the 7,000-acre refuge was established to protect wintering and nesting habitat for migratory birds of the Central Flyway and the bottomland hardwoods for their diverse biological value.

San Bernard (1968): Located in Brazoria and Matagorda counties on the Gulf Coast near Freeport, this refuge's more than 64,000 acres attract migrating waterfowl, including thousands of white-fronted and Canada geese and several duck species, which spend the winter on the refuge. Habitats, consisting of coastal prairies, salt-mud flats, and saltwater and freshwater ponds and potholes, also attract yellow rails, roseate spoonbills, reddish egrets, and American bitterns.

Santa Ana (1943): Santa Ana is located on the north bank of the Rio Grande in Hidalgo County. Santa Ana's 2,088 acres of subtropical forest and native brushland are at an ecological crossroads of subtropical, Gulf Coast, Great Plains, and Chihuahuan desert habitats. Santa Ana attracts birders from across the United States who can view many species of Mexican birds as they reach the northern edge of their ranges in South Texas.

Texas Point (1980): Texas Point's approximately 8,900 acres are located in Jefferson County on the upper Gulf Coast, where they serve a large wintering population of waterfowl and migratory birds. The endangered southern bald eagle and peregrine falcon may occasionally be seen during peak fall and spring migrations.

Trinity River (1994): Established to protect remnant bottomland hardwood forests and associated wetlands, this refuge, located in northern Liberty County, provides habitat for wintering, migrating, and breeding waterfowl, and a variety of other wetland-dependent wildlife.

Texas Wildlife Management Areas Continued

Name (Acreage)	Hunting	Fishing	Camping	Wildlife Viewing	Hiking	Driving	Bicycling	Equestrian	County
Playa Lakes: Armstrong (160)				★					Castro
Playa Lakes: Dimmitt (422)	★								Cottle
Playa Lakes: Taylor Lakes (530)	★			★	★				Donley
Powderhorn (15,069)	★			★					Calhoun
Redhead Pond (37)				★					Nueces
Richland Creek (13,783)	★	★	★	★	★		★	★	Freestone/Navarro
Roger R. Fawcett (5,459)	★	★							Palo Pinto
Sam Houston National Forest (161,508)	★	★	★	★	★	★	★	★	San Jacinto/Walker
Sierra Diablo (11,624)	★								Hudspeth/Culberson
Tawakoni (2,335)	★	★	★	★	★			★	Hunt/Van Zandt
Tony Houseman/Blue Elbow Swamp (3,985)	★	★	★	★	★				Orange
Welder Flats (1,480)		★		★					Calhoun
White Oak Creek (25,777)	★	★		★	★			★	Bowie/Cass/Morris/Titus
Yoakum Dunes (14,037)	*In development, not yet open to the public. Commissioned and authorized in 2014, this site will preserve the breeding and nesting habitats of the lesser prairie-chicken, as well as many other native wildlife, including quail, mule deer, and Texas horned lizards. (Cochran/Terry/Yoakum)*								

UNSPLASH/MATTHEW LANCASTER

DISCOVER TEXAS HISTORY
THROUGH
THE TEXAS HERITAGE TRAILS PROGRAM
BY SOFIA TREVIÑO
Lady Bird Johnson Wildflower Center
COURTESY OF HILL COUNTRY TRAIL REGION

Encompassing all 254 counties,

the 10 regions of the Texas Heritage Trails Program (THTP) each embody a unique identity. Through these trail regions, travelers can engage with the state's broad spectrum of culture, history, geography, and stories.

The program originated with the 1968 HemisFair convention, a world's fair that marked the 250th anniversary of the founding of San Antonio. To promote tourism across the state, Governor John Connally and the Texas Highway Department (now the Texas Department of Transportation) established the Texas Travel Trails. Blue roadside signs marked the paths of 10 scenic driving routes, and regionally themed maps helped visitors explore Texas one region at a time.

"The trails were seen as a way for travelers to break Texas down into bite-sized pieces," Margaret Hoogstra, publisher at *Authentic Texas,* said. "If travelers had the time, they could explore a different piece of the state or come back another time."

Nearly 30 years later, in 1997, the Texas Legislature directed the Texas Historical Commission (THC) to create a statewide heritage tourism program. The original driving trails were reimagined and expanded into the Texas Heritage Trails, using the driving routes and blue signs as a foundation for the 10 regions.

The Texas Heritage Trails Program is centered on local, regional, and state partnerships. Each trail region is a nonprofit organization with a regionally-based volunteer board of directors and a paid executive director. Working with economic development, tourism, and preservation partners — as well as with city and county officials and community organizations — each region crafts and implements its own unique blend of programs and promotions.

The THTP received national recognition in 2005 with the Preserve America Presidential Award. The Governor's Award for Historic Preservation was presented to each of the 10 regional boards in 2018.

Heritage tourism supports both historical preservation and economic growth. A 2025 THC-commissioned study found that 3.4 million people visit THC sites annually. In 2024, travel and tourism across Texas contributed $199.5 billion to the state's economy, with heritage travelers accounting for $11.7 billion — or 12% — of all direct travel spending.

"Our state is so diverse that when a non-Texan visits, they begin to comprehend how large our state is," Hoogstra said. "Even many lifelong Texans haven't seen all of the state. It's a lifelong endeavor to see all the different parts and pieces of Texas and personally experience what makes this state so great."

Whether you're a lifelong resident or just passing through, the THTP opens the door to learning about the state's history and connecting to its communities.

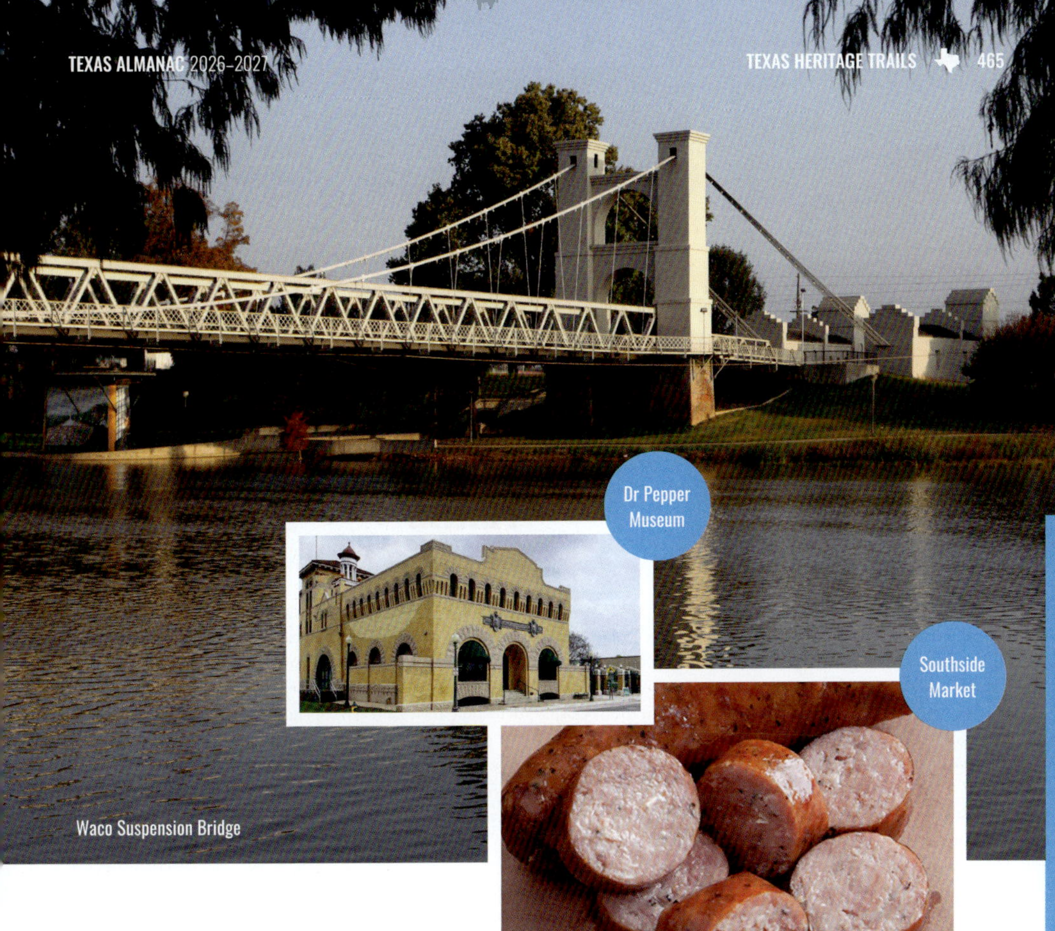

Waco Suspension Bridge

COURTESY OF WACO CVB; COURTESY OF BRAZOS TRAIL REGION; COURTESY OF SOUTHSIDE MARKET

TEXAS BRAZOS TRAIL REGION

The fertile soil along the Brazos River made Central Texas an ideal spot for cotton to grow, attracting immigrants that settled there and made it a productive region. Transporting cotton from the region proved difficult until the development of railroads in the late 19th and early 20th centuries. Towns such as Waco and Bryan became major commercial centers for shipping cotton along the tracks.

The 18 counties of the region are distinguished by the strong agricultural industry and diverse communities. Spots to visit include various museums such as the **Camp Hearne WWII Historic Site and Exhibit** (Hearne), **Museum of the American G.I.** (College Station), and the **Brazos Valley African American Museum** (Bryan).

Attend a Heritage Festival

Many communities within the region pay homage to their European roots with festivals. Known as the "Norwegian Capital of Texas," Clifton hosts a **Norwegian Country Christmas Tour** every December. The Bosque Museum highlights the stories of the Norwegian settlers who arrived in 1854.

In Salado — recognized as the "Scottish Capital of Texas" — the Salado Museum and College Park throws the **Scottish Gathering and Highland Games** every November with bagpipe bands, traditional Highland sports, and dancing. Bremond, the "Polish Capital of Texas," celebrates with an annual "**Polski Dzien.**" **Festa Italiana** in Bryan commemorates when Sicilian immigrants arrived in the late 19th century. Caldwell's annual **Kolache Festival** in September honors the community's Czech heritage.

Savor Texas BBQ

A variety of barbecue establishments are featured throughout this region. The 1995 Texas Legislature designated Elgin as the "Sausage Capital of Texas," and **Southside Market** helps that claim with its "Elgin Hot Sausage." Self-proclaimed the oldest barbecue joint in the state, the company dates back to 1882. **Louie Mueller Barbecue** opened in Taylor in 1949 and remains a family-run establishment in its third generation of Muellers.

Sightsee in Waco

Walk through the **Waco Suspension Bridge**, which was completed in 1870 and was once the longest single-span suspension bridge west of the Mississippi. Major attractions in Waco include the **Dr Pepper Museum**, the **Texas Ranger Hall of Fame and Museum**, and the **Texas Sports Hall of Fame.**

Fort Concho

TEXAS FOREST TRAIL REGION

Located in East Texas, the "Gateway to Texas" encompasses 35 counties characterized by dense forests and a history of timber production. Native American groups, including the Caddo, once lived and traded in these forests. In the 1800s, waves of westward expansion and European immigration led to the displacement of Native American communities.

The arrival of railroads and opening of sawmills in the late 19th and early 20th centuries led to a prospering timber industry that bolstered the economy. Another major industry emerged in 1901, when the Lucas Gusher erupted at the Spindletop oil field, marking the first Texas oil boom.

Journey Through Regional Forests

Home to the only national preserve in the state, the **Big Thicket National Preserve**, the Forest Trail is an ideal spot for those wanting to get outdoors. This region includes the only national forests in Texas: **Angelina N.F.**, **Davy Crockett N.F.**, **Sabine N.F.**, and **Sam Houston N.F.** State forests also include the **E.O. Siecke S.F.**, **Fairchild S.F.**, **J.H. Kirby Memorial S.F.**, **Masterson S.F.**, and **W.G. Jones S.F.**

Travel Along El Camino Real de los Tejas

This National Historic Trail dates back to the 1690s and extended from Mexico City to Louisiana. Connecting Indigenous trails and trade routes across the state, the trail later functioned as the primary overland route for Spanish colonization. Travelers can stop at East Texas towns of **Alto, Crockett, Milam, Nacogdoches,** and **San Augustine** to discover stories of the trail. In Alto, stop at the **Caddo Mounds State Historic Site** to learn more about the Caddo community, whose established trade routes were the foundation for the trail.

Uncover the History of the Timber Industry

While the timber industry remains important to Texas' economy, East Texas has shifted from rapid logging to more sustainable practices. Remnants of historic sawmill towns still remain, however. The **Aldridge Sawmill Historic Site** located in the Angelina N.F. shows the rise and fall of the timber industry in East Texas.

TEXAS FORTS TRAIL REGION

Debuting in 1998, this region served as the pilot for the Texas Heritage Trail Program. Twenty-nine counties in Central West Texas showcase the history of Indigenous communities defending their land. The Spanish established missionaries in the mid-18th century as they aimed to Christianize Native Americans in the southern plains.

After the Spanish withdrew from Texas, nomadic groups were mostly undisputed under Mexican rule (1821-36) and the Texas Republic (1836-45). An initial line of frontier forts was created by the U.S. Army once Texas became a state in 1845, but a second line was added when settlements moved west in the 1850s. The Army built more outposts after the Civil War.

Stop by Abilene

Kickstart a trip around the Forts Trail Region with a visit to Abilene. **Frontier Texas!** boasts a state-of-the-art interactive museum and serves as the official visitors center for the city and region. Other landmarks include the **National Center for Children's Illustrated Literature**, **The Grace Museum**, and the **Paramount Theatre**.

Tour the Presidio de San Sabá

The Colonial Spanish Army founded the **Presidio de San Sabá** — previously known as the Presidio San Luis de las Amarillas — in 1757, but the fortress burned down a year later during a raid by neighboring tribes. Located near Menard, visitors can participate in a self-guided tour to observe the ruins.

Visit Frontier Forts

The historic U.S. Army forts in this region exist in different states of construction today. While some stand as restored grounds, others feature crumbling structures. Make a stop at the forts to experience a time as a frontier soldier. Those established in the 1850s included **Fort Phantom Hill** (near Abilene), **Fort Mason** (Mason), **Fort Belknap** (Graham), **Fort McKavett S.H.S.** (near Menard), and **Fort Chadbourne** (Bronte). The forts constructed after the Civil War were **Fort Concho N.H.L.** (San Angelo), **Fort Griffin S.H.S.** (Albany), and **Fort Richardson** (Jacksboro).

WIKIMEDIA COMMONS

Enchanted Rock

Gruene Hall

UNSPLASH/JAKE FAGAN; COURTESY OF HILL COUNTRY TRAIL REGION

TEXAS HILL COUNTRY TRAIL REGION

Marked by its rolling hills, streaming rivers, and scenic views, the 19 counties of this region offer plenty of activities for travelers. It features major cities such as Austin and San Antonio and numerous small towns such as Comfort, Fredericksburg, and Stonewall. While offering many outdoor ventures, the region also holds significant history from large military installations to the shaping of powerful politicians such as Lyndon B. Johnson and John Nance "Cactus Jack" Garner.

Enjoy Nature

This Central Texas region provides abundant opportunities for getting outside. From natural areas to state parks to lakes, some recommended areas include **Balcones Canyonlands National Wildlife Refuge** (Marble Falls), **Inner Space Caverns** (Georgetown), **Enchanted Rock State Natural Area** (Fredericksburg), **Lady Bird Johnson Wildflower Center** (Austin), and **Garner State Park** (Concan).

Have a Ball in Dance Halls

Years ago, German Texans built dance halls where live music, drinks, and two-stepping still exist today under one roof. Constructed in 1878, **Gruene Hall** in New Braunfels remains the oldest-running dance hall in Texas. Other locations to enjoy a night of fun include **Anhalt Hall** (Spring Branch), **Kendalia Halle** (Kendalia), **Luckenbach Dance Hall** (Fredericksburg), and **Twin Sisters Dance Hall** (Blanco).

Step into Cowboy Boots in Bandera

Called the "Cowboy Capital of the World," this small town founded in the 1800s contains cowboy charm. The **Frontier Times Museum** holds more than 30,000 items, including a rare Native American buffalo hide, Edison phonographs, and rare Russian sleigh bells. At the **Silver Dollar Saloon**, country music reverberates around the honky-tonk, with artists like Willie Nelson performing there.

VISIT GALVESTON; NATALIE LACY LANGECOURTESY OF VISIT BRENHAM

TEXAS INDEPENDENCE TRAIL REGION

This region features 28 counties where many major events of the Texas Revolution occurred. From the Texans' first shot fired at the Battle of Gonzales in 1835 to Sam Houston's forces defeating the Mexican army at the Battle of San Jacinto in 1836, visitors can retrace the steps of Texas independence.

Revisit Key Moments of the Texas Revolution

Although Texans lost at the battle at **The Alamo**, a strong sense of unity inspired their forces after the defeat, leading to the victory at the Battle of San Jacinto. This fortress, along with the rest of the **San Antonio missions**, is the only UNESCO World Heritage Site in Texas. Other locations pivotal to the Revolution include **San Jacinto Battleground State Historic Site** (La Porte), **Fannin Battleground S.H.S.** (Fannin), **Goliad State Park** (Goliad), and **Presidio La Bahía S.H.S.** (Goliad).

Gain Insight From Museums

In Galveston, the **Bryan Museum** carries more than 70,000 objects that spotlight the American West. The **Buffalo Soldiers National Museum** in Houston details African American troops' stories from the American Revolution to the Persian Gulf War. Other museums include the **Matagorda County Museum** (Bay City), **Oil Patch Museum** (Luling), and **Bayou Bend Collection and Gardens** (Houston).

Drop by Brenham

As the world headquarters of Blue Bell ice cream since 1911, this small town founded in 1844 has charming locations for family fun. Stop at the oldest wooden carousel in Texas at **Fireman's Park** or get a scoop of ice cream at the **Blue Bell Creamery**. Every May, the town celebrates **Maifest**, a traditional German festival.

Washington-on-the-Brazos S.H.S., where the signing of the Texas Declaration of Independence occurred, is just 20 minutes away.

TEXAS LAKES TRAIL REGION

Thirty-one counties in North Central Texas make up this region, which is anchored by the Dallas-Fort-Worth Metroplex and known for renowned museums, storied downtowns, cowboy culture, and major rivers and lakes. Once enveloped in sea, the area later became inhabited by Indigenous communities such as the Wichita and Caddo tribes. In the 19th century, cowboys drove herds of longhorn cattle north to Kansas via the Chisholm Trail.

Increasing populations in Dallas and Fort Worth transformed the area into commercial and metropolitan hubs. Later, the building of major lakes and reservoirs created new opportunities for recreation.

Swim

Cool off at any of the numerous lakes in the region. Popular sites include **Lake Tawakoni** (Wills Point), **Cooper Lake State Park** (Sulphur Springs), **Lake Texoma** (Denison), and **Meridian State Park** (Meridian). For something unique, visit **Athens Scuba Park**, an all-inclusive diving facility where pros and beginners can snorkel or scuba dive in a 28-foot-deep lake.

Shop at the World's Largest Flea Market

For more than 150 years, Canton has hosted **First Monday Trade Day,** the largest and oldest continually operating flea market in the U.S. What started in the 1850s as a place for locals to trade goods during court sessions has grown into a monthly tradition drawing over thousands of vendors and shoppers from across the country.

Take Part in Cowboy Culture

Symbolized by the 52-foot-tall cowboy figure of Big Tex in Dallas, the Lakes Trail Region takes pride in its cowboy roots. Fort Worth became "Cowtown" after it became a major stop on the Chisolm Trail in the 19th century. Today, the **Stockyards Collection & Museum** in Fort Worth preserves heritage sites with attractions like the **Fort Worth Herd Cattle Drive**, where Texas Longhorns are driven through the streets twice daily. Other highlights include the **National Cowgirl Museum and Hall of Fame, the Texas Cowboy Hall of Fame,** and the **Amon Carter Museum of American Art.**

TEXAS MOUNTAIN TRAIL REGION

This region's location in Far West Texas presents a rugged and scenic landscape where six counties offer outdoor adventures, breathtaking views, and small towns rich in art and culture.

In the 1500s, Spanish explorers set up a provincial capital in San Juan Pueblo, New Mexico. This site connected to

COURTESY OF HOTEL PASO DEL NORTE

Mexico City by El Camino Real de Tierra Adentro, a historic trade route that passed through El Paso. In 1680, Pueblo tribes in New Mexico revolted against Spanish rule, prompting Spanish settlers to flee south and establish Texas' oldest communities: Ysleta and Socorro.

Later, in the 1800s, the territory faced frequent raids by Apache and Comanche groups, and the U.S. Army built forts to help with westward travel. After four railroads arrived in the 1880s, El Paso transformed into a commercial hub, spurring ranching and mining. Now, the region attracts visitors with its remote location and recreational opportunities.

Hike

With six national parks and historic sites, the Mountain Trail Region offers great terrain for hiking. The region includes: **Big Bend National Park, Chamizal National Memorial** (El Paso), **Fort Davis National Historic Site** (Fort Davis), and **Rio Grande Wild and Scenic River.** East of El Paso, hike to the tallest point in the state at the **Guadalupe Mountains National Park.**

Also, be sure to visit the **Blackwell School National Historic Site** in Marfa.

Rest in Historic Hotels

While exploring Far West Texas, take time to relax in the region's historic hotels. Cattlemen, ranchers, and miners lodged in many of these hotels after railroads reached the area in the 1880s.

Originally built in 1927 as a headquarters for Alfred Gage's ranch, the **Gage Hotel** in Marathon became a hotel in 1978. Decor inspired by West Texas and Mexican influences create an appealing atmosphere, along with the Desert Moon spa and 27 acres of gardens.

Other historic hotels include **Hotel Paso del Norte** (El Paso), **Plaza Hotel** (El Paso), **Cibolo Creek Ranch** (between Marfa and Presidio), **Holland Hotel** (Alpine), **Indian Lodge** (Fort Davis), **Hotel Limpia** (Fort Davis), and **The Hotel Paisano** (Marfa).

Stargaze

The wide open skies and remoteness of West Texas transforms the night sky into a mesmerizing blanket of stars. Aside from Big Bend, including the Greater Big Bend International Dark Sky Reserve, the University of Texas' **McDonald Observatory** in the Davis Mountains hosts guided tours of the world's third-largest optical telescope: the Hobby-Eberly.

Caprock Canyon State Park

TEXAS PECOS TRAIL REGION

This West Texas region covers 35,000 square miles throughout 22 counties and tells the stories of Indigenous peoples, cowboys and pioneers, oil executives and crews, and more. Native American populations hunted game in the region for centuries. Nomadic Comanche groups displaced these existing Native Americans in the mid-1700s and often raided Mexico along the Comanche Trail.

After the U.S.-Mexico War of 1846 through 1848, Americans pushed into West Texas, which led to the establishment of frontier forts in the 1850s. **Fort Clark, Fort Lancaster S.H.S.**, and **Fort Stockton** still stand today, and tourists can visit these sites.

Years later in the 1920s, the discovery of oil in this region transformed Midland and Odessa into bustling cities and turned ranchers into millionaires.

See Old Rock Art

Dating back more than 4,000 years, the Indigenous communities left rock art that expresses their stories. These paintings remain in the **Seminole Canyon State Park and Historic Site,** as well as the **White Shaman Preserve.** Though the meaning behind these paintings still remains under debate, they offer educational opportunities centered around the people living in the region thousands of years ago.

Go Outdoors

The world's largest spring-fed swimming pool is in **Balmorhea State Park**. Located in Toyahvale, the pool receives more than 200,000 visitors annually. Another popular park, **Monahans Sandhills State Park**, offers a unique outdoor experience with around 4,000 acres of sand dunes. Other recommended places to visit include **South Llano River State Park** (Junction), **Amistad National Recreation Area** (Del Rio), and the **Eaton Hill Nature Center & Preserve** (Sonora).

Find Out More: Permian Basin Oil Boom

In the town of Big Lake in 1923, the Permian Basin's first oil gusher blew in. The Santa Rita No. 1 oil well opened up oil exploration in West Texas and resulted in an economic boom to the region. The **Hickman Museum** in Big Lake features a working scale model of Santa Rita No. 1 and exhibits on the oil industry.

The **Permian Basin Petroleum Museum** in Midland offers interactive exhibitions about the oil and gas industry, and has dozens of oil drilling rigs and machinery outdoors.

TEXAS PLAINS TRAIL REGION

With 52 counties across 50,000 square miles, this region covers the northern part of the state. Apaches lived here during the 16th century but after 1700, the Comanches took over, dominating the region for two centuries. Though these Native groups traded with Anglo and Spanish settlers for a while, tensions grew between them by 1870. Anglo-Americans encroached on their territory and hunted their buffalo, later relocating Natives to Oklahoma.

The next era brought millions of cattle to northern markets, along with advancements in the windmill, railroad, agricultural, and all-weather highways like Route 66. Remnants of history can be found across the region in historic buildings, sites, and more than 80 museums.

Explore the Quanah Parker Trail

Outside of Amarillo, the **Quanah Parker Trail** is marked by giant arrow sculptures created by artist Charles A. Smith. More than 80 steel arrows 20-feet-tall showcase where the Comanches lived and roamed. The trail is named after Quanah Parker, who served as the last war leader of the Comanches.

Catch Live Music at a Festival

Buddy Holly, born in Lubbock, is the region's most famous musician, and fans can stop by the **Buddy Holly Center** (Lubbock) to learn more about his life and career. Festivals throughout the year present live music in genres from Western swing to rock.

Some notable festivals include:

- **Bob Wills Day,** *Turkey*, April
- **TEXAS Outdoor Musical,** *Canyon*, June–August
- **West Texas Western Swing Music Festival**, *Snyder*, June

Venture Outside

Each of the five state parks of the Plains Trails Region offer fun outdoor activities. Outside of Amarillo, **Palo Duro Canyon S.P.** is the second-largest canyon in the nation. **Lake Colorado City S.P.** provides space for fishing, boating, and birdwatching. For stargazing, visit **Copper Breaks S.P.**, between Quanah and Crowell, or **Caprock Canyons S.P.** (outside of Turkey). Lastly, **Big Spring S.P.** allows you to look out from a 200-foot bluff to the area below.

COURTESY OF PLAINS TRAIL REGION

World Birding Center

Port Isabel Lighthouse

COURTESY OF TROPICAL TRAIL REGION; COURTESY OF PORT ISABEL LIGHTHOUSE STATE HISTORIC SITE

TEXAS TROPICAL TRAIL REGION

At the southernmost end of Texas — with palm trees and sandy beaches attracting visitors — 20 counties extend hundreds of miles along the U.S. border with Mexico.

The early 20th century attracted tourists because of the region's coastlines. Today, residents honor their diverse heritage and roots through language, food, and music.

Celebrate Hispanic Heritage

The region's close proximity to the Mexican border instills a sense of biculturalism in many residents. Conjunto and orquestras merged to create the unique sounds of Tejano music in the region. The Queen of Tejano Music, Selena Quintanilla, launched her career from Corpus Christi, and fans flock to the **Selena Museum** there to see her awards and costumes. In San Benito, the **Texas Conjunto Music Hall of Fame and Museum** shows the evolution of Tejano music.

Bird Watch

Because of the region's ecologically diverse nature, avid bird watchers enjoy their time here. The region includes more than three-quarters of America's bird species. Places to visit include the **World Birding Center** (across the Rio Grande Valley), **Laguna Atascosa National Wildlife Refuge** (Los Fresnos), and **Sabal Palm Sanctuary** (Brownsville).

Stop Along the Coast

More than 300 miles of coastline span the eastern edge of the region, making a trip to a beach a necessity. South Padre Island is located at the southern tip of Texas, and its beaches attract more than seven million visitors each year. The gateway to SPI, Port Isabel maintains one of the most popular historic sites in the region, the **Port Isabel Lighthouse S.H.S.** Other places to visit include **Port Aransas, Rockport,** and **Corpus Christi.** ★

Texas

RECREATION

UNSPLASH/SHREYAS SANE

TEXAS STATE PARKS AND NATURAL AREAS

Texas' diverse system of state parks and natural areas offers contrasting attractions: mountains and canyons, arid deserts and lush forests, spring-fed streams, sandy dunes, and saltwater surf.

The Texas Parks and Wildlife Department (TPWD) operates the state parks, state natural areas, and state historic sites listed in this section unless otherwise noted. TPWD is dedicated to managing and conserving the state's natural resources and providing recreation opportunities for all to enjoy the outdoors. The department celebrated its 100th anniversary in 2023.

Abilene State Park, southwest of Abilene in Taylor County, consists of 529 acres that were deeded by the City of Abilene in 1933. Large groves of pecan trees that once shaded bands of Comanches now shade visitors at picnic tables. Nearby is Buffalo Gap, the original Taylor County seat (1878) and one of the early frontier settlements.

Atlanta State Park is 1,475 acres and located northwest of Atlanta in Cass County, adjacent to Wright Patman Dam and Reservoir. The land was acquired from the U.S. Army in 1954 by license to 2004 with option to renew to 2054. Nearby is the historic town of Jefferson, Caddo Lake State Park, and Daingerfield State Park.

Balmorhea State Park is 751 acres located southwest of Balmorhea between Balmorhea and Toyahvale in Reeves County. The land was deeded between 1934 and 1935 by private owners and Reeves County Water Improvement District No. 1. Nearby are the city of Pecos, Fort Davis National Historic Site, Davis Mountains State Park, and McDonald Observatory.

Bastrop State Park is 6,600 acres. The park was acquired by deeds from the City of Bastrop and private owners between 1933 and 1935. The site is famous for the "Lost Pines" — an isolated region of loblolly pines and hardwoods. A 13-mile drive through forest leads to Buescher State Park.

Bentsen–Rio Grande Valley State Park, is a scenic park along the Rio Grande in Hidalgo County. Originally acquired from private owners in 1944, the park's subtropical resaca woodlands and brushlands has grown to 797 acres. The park is one of last natural refuges in Texas for ocelots. Nearby are Santa Ana National Wildlife Refuge, Falcon State Park, and Sabal Palm Sanctuary.

Big Bend Ranch State Park, encompasses more than 300,000 acres of Chihuahuan Desert wilderness in Brewster and Presidio counties along the Rio Grande, and was purchased from private owners in 1988. The purchase more than doubled the size of the state park system (220,000). Nearby is Big Bend National Park.

Big Spring State Park is 382 acres located within the city limits of Big Spring in Howard County. Both the city and park were named for a natural spring that was replaced by an artificial one. The park was deeded by the City of Big Spring in 1934 and 1935. The top of Scenic Mountain offers a panoramic view of the surrounding country. It was used extensively as campsites for early Natives, explorers, and settlers.

Blanco State Park is 105 acres along the Blanco River in Blanco County. The land was used as a campsite by early explorers and settlers and deeded by private owners in 1933. Lyndon B. Johnson State Park and Historic Site and Lyndon B. Johnson National Historic Park are nearby.

Bonham State Park is a 261-acre park in Fannin County. It includes a 65-acre lake, rolling prairies, and woodlands. The land was acquired in 1933 from the City of Bonham. Sam Rayburn House State Historic Site and Eisenhower Birthplace State Historic Site are nearby.

Brazos Bend State Park is in Fort Bend County. The 5,000-acre park was purchased from private owners in 1976 to 1977. George Observatory, part of the Houston Museum of Natural Science, is there. Nearby attractions: Varner-Hogg Plantation State Historic Site and Sea Center Texas.

Buescher State Park is a scenic 1,017 acres in Bastrop County. Acquired between 1933 and 1936, El Camino Real once ran near the park, connecting San Antonio de Béxar with Spanish missions in East Texas. The park land was part of Stephen F. Austin's colonial grant. A scenic park road connects with Bastrop State Park through the Lost Pines area.

Caddo Lake State Park, in Harrison County, consists of 484 acres along Cypress Bayou, which runs into Caddo Lake. A scenic area, it was acquired from private owners in 1933. Caddo legend attributes the formation of Caddo Lake to a huge flood. Nearby: Starr Family Home State Historic Site, Marshall, and Karnack (the birthplace of Lady Bird Johnson).

Source: Texas Parks and Wildlife.

BRAZOS BEND STATE PARK

Caprock Canyons State Park and Trailway, in the Briscoe, Floyd, and Hall counties, covers 15,313 acres. Purchased in 1975, these canyons provided camping areas for Natives of Folsom culture more than 10,000 years ago. A 64-mile trailway extends from South Plains to Estelline.

Cedar Hill State Park, an urban park on 1,826 acres around Joe Pool Lake, was acquired by long-term lease from the U.S. Army Corps of Engineers in 1982. Penn Farm Agricultural History Center includes reconstructed buildings of the 19th-century Penn Farm and exhibits.

Choke Canyon State Park consists of two units — South Shore and Calliham — located on the 26,000-acre Choke Canyon Reservoir. The park was acquired in 1981 in a 50-year agreement among Bureau of Reclamation, City of Corpus Christi, and Nueces River Authority. Nearby is the James E. Daughtrey Wildlife Management Area.

Cleburne State Park is a 528-acre park in Johnson County with an 116-acre spring-fed lake. It was acquired from the City of Cleburne and private owners in 1935 and 1936. Nearby are Fossil Rim Wildlife Center and dinosaur tracks in the Paluxy River at Dinosaur Valley State Park.

Colorado Bend State Park, encompassing 5,328 acres, is in Lampasas and San Saba counties. The park site was purchased partly in 1984, with the balance acquired in 1987. Gorman Falls is a top attraction.

Cooper Lake State Park comprises 3,026 acres in Delta and Hopkins counties. The park was acquired in 1991 from the U.S. Army Corps of Engineers. Two units — Doctors Creek and South Sulphur — adjoin Cooper Lake. Cooper Wildlife Management Area is nearby.

Copper Breaks State Park, in Hardeman County, was acquired by purchase from a private owner in 1970. The park features rugged scenic beauty on 1,899 acres, two lakes, grass-covered mesas, and juniper breaks. Nearby medicine mounds were important ceremonial sites of Comanches. Nearby, the Pease River was the site of the 1860 battle in which Cynthia Ann Parker was recovered from Comanches. Part of the state longhorn herd lives at the park.

Daingerfield State Park, in Morris County, is a 507-acre recreational area that includes an 80-acre lake. Deeded in 1935 by private owners, this area is the center of the iron industry in Texas. Nearby is Lone Star Steel Company.

Davis Mountains State Park is 2,709 acres in Jeff Davis County. The scenic area was deeded between 1933 and 1937 by private owners. A four-mile hiking trail leads to Fort Davis National Historic Site. Other nearby attractions include the McDonald Observatory and a 74-mile scenic loop through the Davis Mountains.

Devils River State Natural Area comprises 37,000 acres in Val Verde County. Ecologically, it is in a transitional

UNSPLASH/RYUTA F.

area between the Edwards Plateau, the Trans-Pecos desert, and the South Texas brush country. Archaeological studies suggest occupation and use by cultures from both the east and west.

Devil's Sinkhole State Natural Area, covering 1,860 acres in Edwards County, is a vertical cavern. The sinkhole, discovered by Anglo settlers in 1867, was purchased in 1985 from private owners. The cavern opening is about 40 feet by 60 feet, with a vertical drop of approximately 140 feet. Kickapoo Cavern State Park is nearby.

Dinosaur Valley State Park, in Somervell County, is a 1,587-acre scenic park. The land was acquired from private owners in 1968. Dinosaur tracks in the bed of Paluxy River and two full-scale dinosaur models — originally created for New York World's Fair in 1964 to 1965 — are on display. The riverbed featuring the dinosaur tracks was designated a national landmark in 1968. Cleburne State Park is nearby.

Eisenhower State Park, 463 acres in Grayson County, was acquired by an Army lease in 1954. The park was named after Dwight D. Eisenhower, the 34th U.S. President, who was born nearby at the Eisenhower Birthplace State Historic Site.

Enchanted Rock State Natural Area is 1,644 acres on Big Sandy Creek. Acquired in 1978 by the Nature Conservancy of Texas and by the state in 1984, Enchanted Rock is a huge, pink granite boulder rising 425 feet above ground and covering 640 acres. It is the second-largest batholith (underground rock formation uncovered by erosion) in the United States. The TPWD purchased more than 3,000 acres for $43 million in 2025.

Estero Llano Grande State Park, part of the World Birding Center network, is a 230-acre wetlands refuge 3.2 miles southeast of Weslaco. Birds seen here include waders, shorebirds and migrating waterfowl, as well as coastal species such as roseate spoonbill and ibis. Rare sightings include red-crowned parrots and green parakeets.

Falcon State Park is 576 acres in Starr and Zapata counties. The park has been leased from the International Boundary and Water Commission since 1949. Nearby are Mexico, Fort Ringgold in Rio Grande City, and the historic city of Roma.

Fort Boggy State Park is 1,847 acres of wooded, rolling hills in Leon County near Boggy Creek. The land was donated to the TPWD in 1985 by Eileen Crain Sullivan. The area was once home to Keechi and Kickapoo communities. Nearby attractions include Fort Parker State Park and the Texas State Railroad.

Fort Parker State Park, composed of 759 acres of land and a 750-acre lake, is in Limestone County. Named for the former private fort built near the present park in 1836, the site was acquired from private owners and the City of Mexia from 1935 to 1937. Nearby is the Old Fort Parker Historic Site, which is operated by the City of Groesbeck.

Fort Richardson State Park, Historic Site, and Lost Creek Reservoir State Trailway contains 454 acres in Jack County. It was acquired in 1968 from the City of Jacksboro. The fort — originally named Fort Jacksboro — was founded in 1867 and was the northernmost of a line of federal forts established after the Civil War for protection from Native Americans. The fort was abandoned in May 1878 and now contains seven restored buildings and two replicas.

Franklin Mountains State Park, created by an act of the Legislature in 1979 to protect the mountain range as a wilderness preserve and acquired by the TPWD in 1981, comprises 24,248 acres, all within El Paso city limits. One of the largest urban parks in the nation, it includes virtually an entire Chihuahuan Desert mountain range, with an elevation of 7,192 feet at the summit. Other area attractions include Hueco Tanks State Park and Magoffin Home State Historic Site.

Galveston Island State Park, on the west end of Galveston Island, is a 2,013-acre site acquired in 1969 from private owners. Study nature amid sand dunes and grassland, or enjoy the beach.

Garner State Park is 1,774 acres in Uvalde County. Named for John Nance Garner, the U.S. Vice President from 1933 to 1941, the park was deeded between 1934 and 1936 by private owners. Nearby is John Nance "Cactus Jack" Garner Museum in Uvalde. Ruins of historic Mission Nuestra Señora de la Candelaria del Cañón, Camp Sabinal (a U.S. Cavalry post and later Texas Ranger camp), and Fort Inge are all close by.

Goliad State Park and Mission Espíritu Santo Historic Site are on 188 acres along the San Antonio River in Goliad County. The land was deeded to the state in 1931 by the City and County of Goliad and transferred to the TPWD in 1949. On site is the restored Mission Nuestra Señora del Espíritu Santo de Zúñiga and the El Camino Real de los Tejas Visitors Center. Presidio La Bahía State Historic Site and Fannin Battleground State Historic Site are both close by.

Goose Island State Park, 321 acres in Aransas County, was deeded by private owners between 1931 and 1935. The park is home to "Big Tree" — an estimated 1,000-year-old live oak. Nearby is Aransas National Wildlife Refuge.

Government Canyon State Natural Area is a 12,244-acre area in Bexar County. The trail to Zizelmann House (built in the 1880s) passes dinosaur tracks. San Antonio and Landmark Inn State Historic Site are nearby.

GALVESTON ISLAND STATE PARK

COURTESY OF VISIT GALVESTON

Guadalupe River State Park and Honey Creek State Natural Area are comprised of nearly 5,000 acres on cypress-shaded Guadalupe River in Kendall and Comal counties. The 1,939 acres of parkland were acquired by deed from private owners in 1974 and has four miles of river frontage with several white-water rapids located in a stretch of Guadalupe River noted for canoeing, tubing, and nature study.

Hill Country State Natural Area is in Bandera and Medina counties. The 5,370-acre site was acquired by gift and purchase in 1976. The park is located in the Texas Hill Country on West Verde Creek and contains several spring-fed streams.

Hueco Tanks State Park and Historic Site, in El Paso County, was obtained from the county in 1969, with an additional 121 acres purchased in 1970. The 860-acre park is known for the large natural rock basins that provided water for Native hunter-gatherers, Butterfield Overland Mail coach horses and passengers, and other travelers in this arid region. The park features pictographs, an old ranch house, and the relocated ruins of a stage station.

Huntsville State Park, a 2,083-acre recreational area in Walker County, was acquired by deeds from private owners in 1937. Heavily wooded park adjoins Sam Houston National Forest and encloses Lake Raven.

Inks Lake State Park is 1,201 acres of recreational facilities along Inks Lake in Burnet County. It was acquired by deeds from the Lower Colorado River Authority and private owners in 1940. Nearby are Buchanan Dam, Longhorn Cavern State Park, and Enchanted Rock.

Kickapoo Cavern State Park is 6,368 acres and contains 20 known caves. Kickapoo Cavern, approximately 1,400 feet in length, has impressive formations, and Stuart Bat Cave, slightly shorter, supports a large colony of Mexican freetail bats in the summer.

Lake Arrowhead State Park consists of 524 acres in Clay County. Acquired in 1970 from the City of Wichita Falls, Lake Arrowhead is a reservoir on the Little Wichita River with 106 miles of shoreline. The park features boat ramps, a disc golf course, and hosts annual events, including fishing contests.

Lake Bob Sandlin State Park, on the wooded shoreline of 9,400-acre Lake Bob Sandlin, is located in Titus County. Trees in the 640-acre park include oak, hickory, dogwood, redbud, maple, and pine. The park also features a historical cemetery.

Lake Brownwood State Park in Brown County is 538 acres. During WWII, the park was a popular rest site for soldiers stationed at nearby Camp Bowie.

Lake Casa Blanca International State Park was formerly operated by the City of Laredo and Webb County and was acquired by the TPWD in 1990. The park features an amphitheater, and fossils found on site by Lamar University students are exhibited at park headquarters.

Lake Colorado City State Park, in Mitchell County, is 500 acres and leased from a utility company. The region features drought-tolerant mesquite trees and abundant wildflowers in the spring and summer.

Lake Corpus Christi State Park is a 356-acre park in San Patricio, Jim Wells, and Live Oak counties. It was leased from the City of Corpus Christi in 1934 and features a 400-foot-long fishing pier. Nearby are Mustang Island State Park, Choke Canyon State Park, and Fulton Mansion State Historic Site.

Lake Livingston State Park, in Polk County, contains 635 acres along Lake Livingston. Acquired by deed from private landowners in 1971, the park is near the ghost town of Swartwout as well as Big Thicket National Preserve and Sam Houston National Forest.

Lake Mineral Wells State Park and Trailway, in Parker County, consists of 3,283 acres encompassing Lake Mineral Wells. In 1975, the City of Mineral Wells donated 1,095 land acres and the lake to the TPWD. The federal government transferred additional land from Fort Wolters.

Lake Somerville State Park and Trailway, in Lee and Burleson counties, was leased from the federal government in 1969. Birch Creek Unit (2,365 acres) and Nails Creek Unit (3,155 acres) are connected by a 13-mile trailway. Somerville Wildlife Management Area and San Felipe State Historic Site are nearby.

Lake Tawakoni State Park is a 376-acre park in Hunt County along the shore of its namesake reservoir. It was acquired in 1984 through a lease agreement with the Sabine River Authority and opened in 2001. Lake Tawakoni is known for its blue-fin catfish and is host to several fishing tournaments.

Lake Whitney State Park is 1,281 acres in Hill County. Acquired in 1954 by a Department of the Army lease, the park is located near ruins of Towash, an early Texas settlement inundated by the lake. Towash Village is named for the leader of the Hainai.

Lockhart State Park is 264 acres in Caldwell County. The land was deeded by private owners between 1934 and 1937. After the Comanche raid at Linnville, the Battle of Plum Creek (1840) was fought in the area.

Longhorn Cavern State Park, in Burnet County, is 646 acres and was dedicated as a natural landmark in 1971. It was acquired between 1932 and 1937 from private owners. Visitors can camp at nearby Inks Lake State Park.

Lost Maples State Natural Area consists of 2,174 scenic acres on the Sabinal River in Bandera and Real counties. It was acquired by purchase from private owners between 1973 and 1974.

Lyndon B. Johnson State Park and Historic Site contains 718 acres in Gillespie County. Acquired in 1965 with private donations, the home of Lyndon B. Johnson is located on the north bank of the Pedernales River. In Johnson City is the Lyndon B. Johnson National Historic Park, the boyhood home of President Johnson.

Martin Creek Lake State Park, 287 acres, is located in Rusk County. It was deeded to the TPWD by Texas Utilities in 1976. The roadbed of Trammel's Trace, an old Native trail that became a major route for settlers moving to Texas from Arkansas, can be seen.

Martin Dies Jr. State Park is 705 acres in Jasper and Tyler counties on the B. A. Steinhagen Reservoir. The land has been leased from the Corps of Engineers since 1964. Named after the decorated WWII veteran, who later served as a State Senator and Secretary of State, the park is located at the edge of Big Thicket National Preserve and near Angelina National Forest.

McKinney Falls State Park is 641 acres in Austin. Acquired in 1970 as a gift from private owners, it is named for Thomas F. McKinney, one of Stephen F. Austin's first 300 colonists. Ruins of his homestead can be viewed.

Meridian State Park in Bosque County is a 505-acre park. The heavily wooded land was acquired from private owners between 1933 and 1935. The Texas-Santa Fe expedition of 1841 passed through Bosque County near the present site of the park on Bee Creek.

Mission Tejas State Park is a 364-acre park in Houston County at the north end of Davy Crockett National Forest. The park was acquired from the Texas Forest Service in 1957. In the park is a representation of Mission San Francisco de los Tejas, the first mission in East Texas (1690). The restored Rice Family Log Home, which was built around 1828, is also in the park.

Monahans Sandhills State Park consists of 3,840 acres of sand dunes, some up to 70 feet high, in Ward and Winkler counties. The land is leased by the state from a private foundation until 2056. The Odessa meteor crater and Balmorhea State Park are nearby.

Mother Neff State Park was the first official state park in Texas. It originated with six acres donated by Mrs. I. E. Neff, the mother of Pat M. Neff, who was the Governor of Texas from 1921 to 1925. Gov. Neff and Frank Smith donated the remainder of the land in 1934. The park now contains 259 acres along the Leon River in Coryell County.

PEDERNALES FALLS STATE PARK

UNSPLASH/KYLE VENA

Mustang Island State Park, 3,954 acres on the Gulf of Mexico in Nueces County, was acquired from private owners in 1972. Mustang Island is a barrier island with a complicated ecosystem, dependent upon sand dunes. Padre Island National Seashore, Texas State Aquarium, and the USS Lexington Museum are nearby.

Old Tunnel State Park sits on 16 acres of land, making it the smallest state park in Texas. The abandoned railroad tunnel provides a home to more than three million Mexican free-tailed bats and 3,000 cave myotises (mouse-eared bats) from May to October.

Palmetto State Park, a scenic park of 270 acres, is located in Gonzales County. The land was deeded between 1934 and 1936 by private owners and the City of Gonzales. Nearby Gonzales and Ottine are important in early Texas history.

Palo Duro Canyon State Park consists of 27,123 acres found in Armstrong and Randall counties. The land was deeded by private owners in 1933. A spectacular one-million-year-old scenic canyon exposes rocks spanning about 200 million years of geological time. Part of the state longhorn herd is kept here.

Palo Pinto Mountains State Park is currently under development. Comprising 4,871 acres of former ranchland, the new park will have trails for hikers, bikers, and horses, and overnight spaces for RVs and tents. Tucker Lake will also be available.

Pedernales Falls State Park, 5,212 acres in Blanco County, was acquired from private owners in 1970. The falls, where the river elevation drops by 50 feet across 3,000 feet of rocky limestone riverbed, are the main scenic attraction. Lyndon B. Johnson State Park is nearby.

Possum Kingdom State Park, in Palo Pinto County, is 1,529 acres adjacent to Possum Kingdom Lake (20,000 acres) in the Palo Pinto Mountains and Brazos River Valley. It was acquired from the Brazos River Authority in 1940.

Purtis Creek State Park is 1,582 acres in Henderson and Van Zandt counties. It was acquired in 1977 from private owners. The 355-acre Purtis Creek State Park Lake was designed specifically for fishing. The Texas Freshwater Fisheries Center and Cedar Creek Reservoir are nearby.

Ray Roberts Lake State Park is comprised of nine units. The Isle du Bois Unit consists of 1,397 acres on the south side of Ray Roberts Lake in Denton County. Johnson Branch Unit contains 1,514 acres on the north side of the lake in Denton and Cooke counties. The Jordan Unit (477 acres on the east side of the lake) features the Lone Star Lodge & Marina. The Greenbelt Unit is a 20-mile multi-use trail between Ray Roberts Dam and Lake Lewisville.

Resaca de la Palma State Park is 1,700 semi-tropical acres in Cameron County. It is part of the World Birding Center network.

San Angelo State Park, on O.C. Fisher Reservoir adjacent to the city of San Angelo in Tom Green County, contains 7,677 acres of land, most of which will remain undeveloped. It was leased from the U.S. Corps of Engineers in 1995. Part of the state longhorn herd is in the park. Nearby is Lake Nasworthy and Fort Concho National Historic Landmark.

Sea Rim State Park in Jefferson County contains 4,141 acres of marshland and more than five miles of Gulf beach shoreline. Acquired from private owners in 1972, it is near the McFaddin National Wildlife Refuge.

Seminole Canyon State Park and Historic Site in Val Verde County contains 2,173 acres. It was purchased from private owners between 1973 and 1977. Fate Bell Shelter in the canyon contains several important prehistoric Native pictographs. Nearby are Amistad National Recreation Area and the Judge Roy Bean Visitor Center (in Landry).

Sheldon Lake State Park and Environmental Learning Center sit on 2,800 acres in Harris County. Acquired by purchase in 1952 from the City of Houston, the John Jacob Observation Tower is a top attraction.

South Llano River State Park is a 2,600-acre site donated to the TPWD by a private owner in 1977. The wooded bottomland along the winding South Llano River is the largest and oldest winter roosting site for the Rio Grande turkey in Central Texas.

Stephen F. Austin State Park is 473 acres along the Brazos River in San Felipe in Austin County. The area was deeded by the San Felipe de Austin Corporation and the San Felipe Park Association in 1940. San Felipe was the home of Stephen F. Austin and other famous early Texans.

Tyler State Park is 986 acres in Smith County and includes a 64-acre lake. The land was deeded by private owners between 1934 and 1935. Nearby Tyler is called the "Rose Capital of America."

Village Creek State Park, comprising 2,466 heavily forested acres, is located in Hardin County. Purchased in 1979 from a private owner, the Big Thicket National Preserve is nearby.

Walter Umphrey State Park is operated by Jefferson County on the south end of Pleasure Island. McFadden National Wildlife Refuge is nearby.

Texas State Parks & State Natural Areas

Park	NEAREST TOWN	Day Use Only	Historic Site	Exhibit/Interpretive/Museum	Restrooms	Showers	Trailer Dump Station	Camping	Screened Shelters	Cabins	Group Facilities	Nature Trail	Hiking Trail	Picnicking	Boat Ramp	Fishing	Swimming	Canoe Rentals	Activities/Amenities
Abilene SP	BUFFALO GAP				★	★	★	★	★	★	BG	★	★	★	★	★	★	★	B1, B2, E, H,
Atlanta SP	ATLANTA				★	★	★	★			DG	★	★	★	★	★	★	★	
Balmorhea SP	BALMORHEA				★	★	★	★			BG	★		★			★		H, L
Bastrop SP	BASTROP				★	★	★	★		★	BG		★	★		★	★		B2, H
Bentsen–Rio Grande Valley SP	MISSION			★	★	★		★			DG	★	★	★		★			B1, B2, H
Big Bend Ranch SP	LAJITAS			★	★	★	★	★			NG	★	★	★	★	★			B1, E, H, L
Big Spring SP	BIG SPRING	★		★	★						DG	★	★	★					B1, B2
Blanco SP	BLANCO				★	★	★	★	★		DG		★	★		★	★		H
Bonham SP	BONHAM				★	★	★	★			BG		★	★	★	★	★	★	B1, H
Brazos Bend SP	RICHMOND			★	★	★	★	★	★	★	BG	★	★	★		★			B1, B2, E, H
Buescher SP	SMITHVILLE				★	★	★	★	★	★	DG		★	★		★		★	B1, B2, H
Caddo Lake SP	KARNACK			★	★	★	★	★	★	★	DG	★	★	★	★	★		★	H
Caprock Canyons SP & TW	QUITAQUE			★	★	★	★	★			DG	★	★	★	★	★	★		B1, B2, E, H
Cedar Hill SP	CEDAR HILL		★		★	★	★	★			DG	★	★	★	★	★	★		B1, B2, H
Choke Canyon SP, Calliham Unit	THREE RIVERS				★	★	★	★		★	BG	★	★	★	★	★	★		H
South Shore Unit	THREE RIVERS	★			★						DG			★	★	★	★		B2, H
Cleburne SP	CLEBURNE				★	★	★	★	★	★	BG		★	★	★	★	★		B1, B2, H
Colorado Bend SP	BEND				★			★			NG		★	★	★	★	★		B1, H
Cooper Lake SP, Doctors Creek Unit	COOPER				★	★	★	★	★	★	BG	★	★	★	★	★	★		B1, H
South Sulphur Unit	SULPHUR SPRINGS				★	★	★	★	★	★	DG	★	★	★	★	★	★		B1, E, H
Copper Breaks SP	QUANAH			★	★	★	★	★			BG	★	★	★	★	★	★		B1, B2, E, H
Daingerfield SP	DAINGERFIELD			★	★	★		★		★	BG		★	★	★	★	★	★	H
Davis Mountains SP	FORT DAVIS			★	★	★	★	★			DG	★	★	★					B1, B2, E, H, L
Devils River SNA	DEL RIO				★	★		★			NG		★	★		★	★		L
Devil's Sinkhole SNA	ROCKSPRINGS	No access to cavern. Tours of SNA by special request only.																	
Dinosaur Valley SP	GLEN ROSE			★	★	★	★	★			BG	★	★	★		★	★		B1, B2, E, H
Eisenhower SP	DENISON				★	★	★	★	★	★	BG	★	★	★	★	★	★	★	B1, H, R
Enchanted Rock SNA	FREDERICKSBURG			★	★	★		★			NG	★	★	★		★			R
Estero Llano Grande SP	WESLACO	★			★						BG	★	★	★					B1, B2, H
Falcon SP	ZAPATA				★	★	★	★	★	★	DG	★	★	★	★	★	★		B1
Fort Boggy SP	CENTERVILLE				★	★		★		★	DG		★	★	★	★	★		B1, H

Texas State Parks & State Natural Areas

Park	NEAREST TOWN	Day Use Only	Historic Site	Exhibit/Interpretive/Museum	Restrooms	Showers	Trailer Dump Station	Camping	Screened Shelters	Cabins	Group Facilities	Nature Trail	Hiking Trail	Picnicking	Boat Ramp	Fishing	Swimming	Canoe Rentals	Activities/Amenities
Fort Parker SP	MEXIA		★	★	★	★	★	★	★	★	BG	★	★	★	★	★	★	★	BI, H
Fort Richardson SP, HS & Lost Creek Res. TW	JACKSBORO		★	★	★	★	★	★		★	BG	★	★	★		★	★		BI, B2, E, H
Franklin Mountains SP	EL PASO	★		★	★			★			NG	★	★	★					BI, H, R
Galveston Island SP	GALVESTON			★	★	★	★	★		★	DG	★	★	★		★	★		BI, B2, H
Garner SP	CONCAN				★	★	★	★	★	★	BG		★	★		★	★		B2, H
Goliad SP & Mission Espíritu Santo HS	GOLIAD		★	★	★	★	★	★	★		DG	★	★	★		★			BI, B2, H
Goose Island SP	ROCKPORT				★	★	★	★			DG	★		★	★	★			H
Government Canyon SNA	SAN ANTONIO				★	★		★			BG	★	★	★					BI, H
Guadalupe River SP & Honey Creek SNA	BOERNE			★	★	★	★	★				★	★	★		★	★		BI, E, H
Hill Country SNA	BANDERA				★			★			NG	★	★	★					BI, E, H
Hueco Tanks SP & HS	EL PASO		★	★	★	★	★	★			NG	★	★	★					H, R
Huntsville SP	HUNTSVILLE			★	★	★	★	★	★	★	DG	★	★	★	★	★	★	★	BI, H
Inks Lake SP	BURNET				★	★	★	★		★	BG	★	★	★	★	★	★	★	H
Kickapoo Cavern SP	BRACKETTVILLE				★	★	★	★			DG		★	★					BI, H
Lake Arrowhead SP	WICHITA FALLS				★	★	★	★			DG	★	★	★	★	★	★		BI, B2, E, H
Lake Bob Sandlin SP	MOUNT PLEASANT				★	★	★	★	★	★	DG	★	★	★	★	★	★		BI, H
Lake Brownwood SP	BROWNWOOD				★	★	★	★	★	★	DG	★	★	★	★	★	★		BI, B2, H
Lake Casa Blanca International SP	LAREDO			★	★	★	★	★			DG	★	★	★	★	★	★		BI, H
Lake Colorado City SP	COLORADO CITY				★	★	★	★		★	DG	★	★	★	★	★	★		
Lake Corpus Christi SP	MATHIS				★	★	★	★	★	★	DG	★	★	★	★	★	★		BI, B2, H
Lake Livingston SP	LIVINGSTON			★	★	★	★	★	★		DG	★	★	★	★	★	★	★	BI, B2, H
Lake Mineral Wells SP & TW	MINERAL WELLS				★	★	★	★	★		DG		★	★	★	★	★	★	BI, E, H, R
Lake Somerville SP & TW , Birch Creek Unit	SOMERVILLE				★	★	★	★			BG	★	★	★	★	★	★	★	B2, E, H
Nails Creek Unit	LEDBETTER				★	★	★	★			DG	★	★	★	★	★	★	★	E, H
Lake Tawakoni SP	WILLS POINT				★	★	★	★			BG	★	★	★	★	★	★		BI, H
Lake Whitney SP	WHITNEY				★	★	★	★	★	★	BG	★	★	★	★	★	★		BI, H
Lockhart SP	LOCKHART				★	★	★	★			BG	★	★	★		★	★		BI, H
Longhorn Cavern SP	BURNET	★		★	★							★	★	★					
Lost Maples SNA	VANDERPOOL			★	★	★	★	★				★	★	★		★			
Lyndon B. Johnson SP & HS	STONEWALL	★	★	★	★						DG	★		★		★	★		BI, B2, H
Martin Creek Lake SP	TATUM				★	★	★	★	★	★	DG	★	★	★	★	★	★	★	BI, H
Martin Dies Jr. SP	JASPER			★	★	★	★	★	★	★	DG	★	★	★	★	★	★	★	B2, H
McKinney Falls SP	AUSTIN		★	★	★	★	★	★		★	BG	★	★	★		★	★		BI, B2, H, R
Meridian SP	MERIDIAN				★	★	★	★	★	★	BG	★	★	★	★	★	★		H
Mission Tejas SP	WECHES		★	★	★	★	★	★			BG	★	★	★		★			BI, B2, H
Monahans Sandhills SP	MONAHANS			★	★	★	★	★			DG	★	★	★					E, H
Mother Neff SP	MOODY			★	★	★		★		★		★	★	★					H
Mustang Island SP	PORT ARANSAS				★	★	★	★					★	★		★	★		BI,B2, H
Old Tunnel SP	FREDERICKSBURG	★			★							★		★					H
Palmetto SP	LULING				★	★	★	★		★	BG	★	★	★		★	★	★	BI, B2, H
Palo Duro Canyon SP	CANYON			★	★	★	★	★		★	BG		★	★					BI, E, H
Pedernales Falls SP	JOHNSON CITY				★	★	★	★			NG	★	★	★		★	★		BI, E, H
Possum Kingdom SP	CADDO				★	★	★	★		★			★	★	★	★	★	★	H
Purtis Creek SP	EUSTACE				★	★	★	★			DG	★	★	★	★	★	★		BI, B2, H
Ray Roberts Lake SP, Isle du Bois Unit	PILOT POINT			★	★	★	★	★			BG	★	★	★	★	★	★		BI, B2, E, H
Johnson Branch Unit	VALLEY VIEW			★	★	★	★	★			NG	★	★	★	★		★		H
Resaca de la Palma SP	BROWNSVILLE	★			★						DG	★	★	★					B2, H
San Angelo SP	SAN ANGELO				★	★	★	★		★	BG	★	★	★	★	★	★		E
Sea Rim SP	PORT ARTHUR				★		★	★		★		★		★	★	★	★	★	E, H
Seminole Canyon SP & HS	COMSTOCK		★	★	★	★	★	★				★	★	★					BI, H
Sheldon Lake SP	HOUSTON	★		★	★							★	★	★	★	★			H
South Llano River SP	JUNCTION				★	★	★	★				★	★	★		★	★		BI, H
Stephen F. Austin SP	SAN FELIPE			★	★	★	★	★	★	★	NG	★	★	★					BI, B2, H
Tyler SP	TYLER			★	★	★	★	★	★	★	BG	★	★	★	★	★	★	★	BI, H
Village Creek SP	LUMBERTON			★	★	★	★	★		★	BG	★	★	★		★	★	★	BI, H
Walter Umphrey SP	PORT ARTHUR				★	★	★	★			BG		★	★	★	★	★		

ACTIVITIES/AMENITIES CODES

BI	Mountain biking	E	Equestrian facilities and/or trails	DG	Day-use group facilities
B2	Surfaced bike trail	L	Hotel-type facilities	NG	Overnight group facilities
H	Some handicap accessible facilities	R	Rock climbing	BG	Both day and night group facilities

FACILITIES CODES	★	Activities Permitted

STATE HISTORIC SITES

Acton State Historic Site is a small cemetery plot in Hood County where Davy Crockett's second wife, Elizabeth, was buried in 1860. Nearby attractions include Dinosaur Valley State Park and Lake Whitney State Park.

Barrington Plantation State Historic Site, in Washington County, marks the final home of Dr. Anson Jones, the fifth and final president of the Republic of Texas. Visitors can take a self-guided tour of the plantation and Independence Hall.

Battleship Texas State Historic Site usually sits within the San Jacinto Battleground State Historic Site in Harris County. Battleship Texas once took part in naval battles during both world wars and was acquired by the state of Texas in 1948. Today the ship serves as a memorial to the servicemen who fought both world wars and as an engineering landmark.

Bush Family Home State Historic Site in Midland County became the 36th designated historic site in Texas in 2022. The 1,400-square-foot house was built in 1940 and acquired by the Bush family in 1951. First opened to the public as a museum in 2006, the home has been restored to its appearance in the 1950s and features exhibits about the town and the Bush family.

Caddo Mounds State Historic Site in Cherokee County was acquired in 1975 and sits on more than 90 acres. The park offers exhibits and interpretive trails through reconstructed Caddo dwellings and ceremonial areas. Nearby are Jim Hogg Park, Mission Tejas State Park, and the Texas State Railroad.

Casa Navarro State Historic Site in downtown San Antonio was donated by the San Antonio Conservation Society Foundation in 1975. The furnished Navarro House, built around 1848, was the home of statesman, rancher, and Texas patriot José Antonio Navarro.

Confederate Reunion Grounds State Historic Site, located in Limestone County on the Navasota River, comprises 77 acres. It was acquired in 1983 by deed from Joseph E. Johnston Camp No. 94 CSA. Nearby are Fort Parker State Park and Fort Boggy State Park.

Eisenhower Birthplace State Historic Site was acquired in 1958 from the Eisenhower Birthplace Foundation. Restoration of the home of President Dwight D. Eisenhower includes furnishings and some personal effects. Hagerman National Wildlife Refuge and Eisenhower State Park are nearby.

Fannin Battleground State Historic Site is located in Goliad County. The 14-acre site was acquired by the state in 1914 and transferred to the TPWD by legislative enactment in 1965. At this site on March 20, 1836, Colonel James Fannin surrendered to Mexican General José Urrea after the Battle of Coleto. The Fannin Memorial Monument and burial site is south of Goliad, near Presidio la Bahía State Historic Site and Goliad State Park.

Fanthorp Inn State Historic Site includes a historic double-pen cedar-log dogtrot house. It was purchased in 1977 from a Fanthorp descendant and opened to the public in 1987. Inn records report visits from many prominent civic and military leaders, including Sam Houston, Anson Jones, and generals Ulysses S. Grant, Robert E. Lee, and Stonewall Jackson. Originally built in 1834, it has been restored to its 1850 use as a family home and travelers' hotel.

Fort Griffin State Historic Site is 506 acres in Shackelford County. The state was deeded the land by the county in 1935. The site was selected as the permanent home for Texas longhorns in 1948, followed by the 61st Legislature officially recognizing the State of Texas Longhorn Herd in 1969. Nearby are Albany, Abilene, and Possum Kingdom State Park.

Fort Lancaster State Historic Site sits on 82 acres in Crockett County. Acquired in 1968 by deed from Crockett County, Henry Meadows donated 41 acres in 1975. Fort Lancaster was originally established in 1855 to guard San Antonio–El Paso Road and protect movement of supplies and immigrants from Native groups.

Fort Leaton State Historic Site, in Presidio County, was acquired in 1967 from private owners. In 1848, Ben Leaton built the fortified adobe trading post known as Fort Leaton near present Presidio. It is operated by the TPWD and serves as the western entrance to Big Bend Ranch State Park.

Fort Martin Scott State Historic Site, located near Fredericksburg, is a restored U.S. Army outpost, which served as protection for settlers through westward expansion between 1848 and 1853. The City of Fredericksburg took ownership of the property in 1949 to preserve the fort. Enchanted Rock State Park is nearby.

Fort McKavett State Historic Site is 80 acres and was acquired from Fort McKavett Restoration, Inc., Menard County, and private individuals. Originally called Camp San Saba, the fort was built by the War Department in 1852 to protect frontier settlers and travelers on Upper El Paso

Sources: Texas Historical Commission and Texas Parks and Wildlife.

LANDMARK INN STATE HISTORIC SITE

WIKIPEDIA/MICHAEL BARERA

Road from Natives. The camp was later renamed for Captain Henry McKavett, who was killed at the Battle of Monterrey.

French Legation State Historic Site, located near downtown Austin, was built in 1841 as a private home for Alphones Dubois, French chargé d'affaires to the Republic of Texas. In 1848, it was purchased by Dr. Joseph W. Robertson, who lived there with his large family and nine enslaved workers. Daughter Lillie Robertson lived in the house her entire life. The state acquired the house after her death and appointed the Daughters of the Republic as custodian. In 2017, HB 3810 transferred the French Legation to the Texas Historical Commission (THC).

Fulton Mansion State Historic Site is in Aransas County. The 2.3-acre property was acquired by purchase from a private owner in 1976. A three-story wooden structure built between 1874 and 1877, it was the home of George W. Fulton, who was prominent in South Texas for economic and commercial influence.

Goodnight Ranch State Historic Site, in Armstrong County, is the home of Charles and Mary Ann Goodnight. The J. Evetts Haley Visitor and Education Center is a top attraction. Caprock Canyons State Park is nearby.

Iwo Jima Museum and Monument State Historic Site is located on the Marine Military Academy campus in Cameron County. On February 23, 1945, six Marines placed an American flag on Iwo Jima terrain, marking the end of the World War II American campaign in the Pacific. Visitors can see the monument sculpted by Dr. Felix W. de Weldon and tour the adjacent museum.

Landmark Inn State Historic Site was donated by Miss Ruth Lawler in 1974. Castroville, settled in the 1840s by Alsatian farmers, is called Little Alsace of Texas. The Landmark Inn was built around 1844 as a residence and store for Cesar Monod, the mayor of Castroville from between 1851 and 1864.

Levi Jordan Plantation State Historic Site, in Brazoria County, was a sugar and cotton plantation established in the 1850s. Owned by descendants until 2001, it was acquired by the Houston Endowment and donated to the TPWD in 2022. Today, the 90-acre plantation is both an attraction and an active archeological site.

Lipantitlán State Historic Site is five acres in Nueces County. The property was deeded by private owners in 1937. A fort constructed here in 1833 by the Mexican government fell to Texas forces in 1835. Lake Corpus Christi State Park is nearby.

Magoffin Home State Historic Site, in El Paso, is a 19-room territorial-style adobe on a 1.5-acre site. Purchased by the state and City of El Paso in 1976, the home was built in 1875 by El Pasoan Joseph Magoffin and furnished with original family artifacts.

Mission Dolores State Historic Site in San Augustine memorializes the location of a Spanish mission built in 1721 near the Texas–Louisiana border. There are no longer any above-ground remains of the mission.

Monument Hill State Historic Site and Kreische Brewery State Historic Site are operated as one park unit. Monument Hill consists of 40 acres in Fayette County. The monument and tomb area were acquired by the state in 1907. Additional acreage was acquired from the Archdiocese of San Antonio in 1956. The Kreische Complex, on 36 acres, is linked to Monument Hill by an interpretive trail.

National Museum of the Pacific War and Admiral Nimitz State Historic Site is on seven acres in Gillespie County. First established as a state agency in 1969 by the Texas Legislature, it is overseen by the THC and operated by the Admiral Nimitz Foundation. It is named for Admiral Chester W. Nimitz.

Old Socorro Mission State Historic Site was established in 1682 by Franciscans to help Spanish and Native American people displaced from New Mexico during the Pueblo Revolt. Located in El Paso County, it is the oldest known mission site in the state and protected as a State Antiquities Landmark.

Palmito Ranch Battlefield State Historic Site consists of 9,391 acres in Cameron County. The area covers where the last land battle of the Civil War took place, which occurred May 12-13, 1865 and resulted in a Confederate victory.

Port Isabel Lighthouse State Historic Site is in Cameron County. Acquired from private owners in 1950, the lighthouse was constructed in 1852. It is operated by the City of Port Isabel.

Presidio la Bahía State Historic Site comprises 45 acres. Established at this site in 1749, the fort took part in six revolutions, making it the most fought-over fort in Texas. Today, the site is operated by the Catholic Diocese of Victoria. "Our Lady of Loreto" chapel is the oldest building on the site, and it housed Fannin's troops for a time after they were captured.

Sabine Pass Battleground State Historic Site in Jefferson County contains 58 acres acquired from Kountze and Couch Trust in 1972. Lieutenant Richard W. Dowling, with a small Confederate force, repelled an attempted 1863 invasion of Texas by Union gunboats.

Sam Bell Maxey House State Historic Site, in Lamar County, was donated by the City of Paris in 1976. It features an 1868 Victorian Italianate-style frame house, plus outbuildings.

Sam Rayburn House State Historic Site in Fannin County preserves personal belongings, original furniture, and photos just as they were when Sam Rayburn lived there. Visitors can explore the home and grounds to the once powerful and influential Texas politician.

San Felipe de Austin State Historic Site, in Austin County, marks the headquarters for Stephen F. Austin's colony in Mexican Texas. Visitors are able to walk the grounds of the former political and economic center of American immigration to Texas before its fall in the war of Texas independence. Stephen F. Austin State Park is nearby.

San Jacinto Battleground State Historic Site is in east Harris County. The park is 1,200 acres with a 570-foot-tall monument erected between 1936 and 1939 in honor of Texans who defeated Mexican General Antonio López de Santa Anna on April 21, 1836, to win Texas' independence from Mexico. The park was purchased by the state in a series of acquisitions between 1899 and the 1930s. It was transferred to the TPWD in 1965.

Sebastopol House State Historic Site, in Guadalupe County, was purchased in 1976 from Seguin Conservation Society. It is owned and operated by the City of Seguin. Built around 1856 by Colonel Joshua W. Young, the Greek Revival-style house has been restored to its 1880 appearance.

Slaton Harvey House State Historic Site in Lubbock County was added as a Texas Historical Commission's historic site in 2024. Created by Scottish immigrant Fred Harvey in 1876 as a restaurant for those traveling on the Santa Fe railroad line, the site exemplifies services associated with railroad travel.

Star of the Republic Museum State Historic Site in Washington County was created by the 61st Texas Legislature to study Texas' Republic period (1836-1846). It is located on the same site as Washington-on-the-Brazos State Historic Site.

Starr Family Home State Historic Site is in Harrison County. Called Maplecroft mansion, the Greek Revival-style house was home to four generations of the Starr family, who were powerful and economically influential Texans. Two other family homes are also in the park. Acquired by gift in 1976, additional land was donated in 1982. Caddo Lake State Park is nearby.

Stephen F. Austin Memorial State Historic Site is a lawn and marker located in Brazoria County designating where Stephen F. Austin died in 1836. Referred to as the "Father of Texas," he began the colonization of the state by settling over 1,500 families in the Tejas region of Mexico. There are no facilities at this site.

Varner–Hogg Plantation State Historic Site is 66 acres in Brazoria County. The land was originally owned by Martin Varner, a member of Stephen F. Austin's "Old

Three Hundred" colony, and later became the home of Texas Governor James Stephen Hogg. The property was deeded to the state in 1957 by Miss Ima Hogg, Gov. Hogg's daughter.

Washington-on-the-Brazos State Historic Site consists of 293 acres in Washington County. The land was acquired by deed from private owners in 1916, 1976, and 1996. The park includes the site of the signing of the Texas Declaration of Independence from Mexico as well as the site of the later signing of the Constitution of the Republic of Texas. Star of the Republic Museum State Historic Site and Barrington Plantation State Historic Site are on the same property.

Texas State Historic Sites

Park	NEAREST TOWN	Day Use Only	Exhibit/Interpretive Cntr	Restrooms	Showers	Trailer Dump Station	Camping	Cabins	Group Facilities	Nature Trail	Hiking Trail	Picnicking	Boat Ramp	Fishing	Canoe Rentals	Activities/Amenities
Acton SHS	ACTON	★														
Barrington Plantation SHS	WASHINGTON	★	★	★					DG			★				
Battleship Texas SHS	GALVESTON	★	★													
Bush Family Home SHS	MIDLAND	★		★												H
Caddo Mounds SHS	ALTO	★	★	★						★		★				H
Casa Navarro SHS	SAN ANTONIO	★		★												
Confederate Reunion Grounds SHS	MEXIA	★	★	★			★		BG		★	★		☆		H
Eisenhower Birthplace SHS	DENISON	★	★	★					DG							H
Fannin Battleground SHS	GOLIAD	★	★	★					DG			★				H
Fanthorp Inn SHS	ANDERSON	★	★	★												
Fort Griffin SHS	ALBANY		★	★	★	★	★	★		★	★	★		☆	★	H
Fort Lancaster SHS	OZONA	★	★	★								☆				
Fort Leaton SHS	PRESIDIO	★	★	★						★		★				
Fort Martin Scott SHS	FREDERICKSBURG	★		★						★		★				H
Fort McKavett SHS	FORT McKAVETT	★	★	★						★		★				
French Legation SHS	AUSTIN	★		★					DG							H
Fulton Mansion SHS	FULTON	★	★	★								★				H
Goodnight Ranch SHS	GOODNIGHT	★	★	★												
Iwo Jima Museum and Monument SHS	HARLINGEN	★		★												H
Landmark Inn SHS	CASTROVILLE		★	★					DG	★		★				L
Levi Jordan Plantation SHS	BRAZORIA	★	★	★						★						
Lipantitlán SHS	SAN PATRICIO	★														
Magoffin Home SHS	EL PASO	★	★	★								★				H
Mission Dolores SHS	SAN AUGUSTINE		★	★	★		★				★	★				H
Monument Hill & Kreische Brewery SHS	LA GRANGE	★	★	★					DG	★		★				H
National Museum of Pacific War & Adm. Nimitz SHS	FREDERICKSBURG	★	★	★					BG	★						H
Old Socorro Mission SHS	SOCORRO	No facilities and closed to the public.														
Palmito Ranch Battlefield SHS	BROWNSVILLE	No facilities.														
Port Isabel Lighthouse SHS	PORT ISABEL	★		★					DG			★				
Presidio la Bahía SHS	GOLIAD		★	★				★	DG	★						
Sabine Pass Battleground SHS	SABINE PASS	★	★	★								★	★	☆		H
Sam Bell Maxey House SHS	PARIS	★	★	★												H
Sam Rayburn House SHS	BONHAM	★	★	★								★				H
San Felipe de Austin SHS	SAN FELIPE	★		★												H
San Jacinto Battleground SHS	HOUSTON	★	★	★					DG	★	★	★		☆		H
Sebastopol House SHS	SEGUIN	★	★									★				
Slaton Harvey House SHS	LUBBOCK		★	★	★				BG							H
Star of the Republic Museum SHS	WASHINGTON	★	★	★					DG			★				
Starr Family Home SHS	MARSHALL	★	★	★					DG							H
Stephen F. Austin Memorial SHS	WEST COLUMBIA	No facilities.														
Varner-Hogg Plantation SHS	WEST COLUMBIA	★	★	★				★	DG	★		★		☆		H
Washington-on-the-Brazos SHS	WASHINGTON	★	★	★					DG			★				H

ACTIVITIES/AMENITIES CODES

B1	Mountain biking	E	Equestrian facilities and/or trails	DG	Day-use group facilities
B2	Surfaced bike trail	L	Hotel-type facilities	NG	Overnight group facilities
H	Some handicap accessible facilities	R	Rock climbing	BG	Both day and night group facilities

FACILITIES CODES	★	Facilities or services available for activity	☆	Permitted, but facilities not provided

★

RECREATION IN STATE FORESTS AND ARBORETUMS

Owned and operated by the Texas A&M Forest Service, these state forests are all working demonstration forests. All Texas State Forests are game sanctuaries with no firearms or hunting allowed, except for those organized by the Texas Parks and Wildlife Department.

W. GOODRICH JONES STATE FOREST

Texas State Forests and Arboretums

Forests	NEAREST TOWN	Reservations Required	Hiking	Biking	Horseback Riding	Wildlife Viewing	Bird Watching	Picnicking	Special Attractions
E.O. Siecke State Forest	Kirbyville		★	★	★	★	★	★	Historical fire tower, the oldest slash pine stand in Texas, Trout Creek
I.D. Fairchild State Forest	Rusk		★	★	★	★	★	★	Red-cockaded woodpecker management area, pond with picnic area
John Henry Kirby Memorial State Forest	Woodville	★	★			★	★		Pitcher plant bog, historical fire tower, John Henry Kirby Historical Marker
Masterson State Forest	Kirbyville	★	★		★		★		Educational loop, pond and picnic area, longleaf seed orchard
W. Goodrich Jones State Forest	Conroe		★	★	★	★	★	★	Red-cockaded woodpecker management area, orienteering course, Sweetleaf nature and fitness trail, two small lakes with limited knicking and fishing, environmental educator trainings
Arboretums									
Olive Scott Petty Arboretum	Jacksonville		★			★	★		Hazel Tilton outdoor classroom, demonstration gardens, historic trees
Ruth Bowling Nichols Arboretum	Kountze						★	★	Jimmy Hull memorial, ponds, tree identification

Source: Texas A&M Forest Service.

UNSPLASH/OBED ESQUIVEL PICKETT

NATIONAL PARKS, HISTORIC SITES, RECREATION AREAS

Below is a list of Texas' two national parks, a national seashore, a biological preserve, a marine sanctuary, and several historic sites, memorials, and recreation areas in the Lone Star State. Most are under supervision of the U.S. Department of Interior. Recreational opportunities in the state and national forests and national grasslands in Texas are under the jurisdiction of the U.S. Department of Agriculture.

- **Alibates Flint Quarries National Monument**
- **Amistad National Recreation Area**
- **Big Bend National Park**
- **Big Thicket National Preserve**
- **Blackwell School National Historic Site**
- **Butterfield Overland National Historic Trail**
- **Chamizal National Memorial**
- **El Camino Real de los Tejas National Historic Trail**
- **El Camino Real de Tierra Adentro National Historic Trail**
- **Flower Garden Banks National Marine Sanctuary**
- **Fort Davis National Historic Site**
- **Guadalupe Mountains National Park**
- **Lake Meredith National Recreation Area**
- **Lyndon B. Johnson National Historical Park**
- **Padre Island National Seashore**
- **Palo Alto Battlefield National Historical Park**
- **Rio Grande Wild & Scenic River**
- **Waco Mammoth National Monument**

Source: U.S. Department of Interior.

NATIONAL NATURAL LANDMARKS IN TEXAS

These Texas natural areas have been listed on the National Registry of Natural Landmarks.

The registry was established by the Secretary of the Interior in 1962 to identify and encourage the preservation of geological and ecological features that represent nationally significant examples of the nation's natural heritage. Below is the list of those landmarks found in Texas, as of July 2025, and their locations.

- **Attwater Prairie Chicken Preserve:** Colorado County (1968)
- **Bayside Resaca Area:** Cameron County (1980)
- **Catfish Creek:** Anderson County (1983)
- **Caverns of Sonora:** Sutton County (1965)
- **Cave Without a Name:** Kendall County (2009)
  Devil's Sinkhole State Natural Area: Edwards County (1972)
- **Dinosaur Valley:** Somervell County (1968)
- **Enchanted Rock:** Gillespie and Llano counties (1971)
- **Ezell's Cave:** Hays County (1971)
- **Fort Worth Nature Center and Refuge:** Tarrant County (1980)
- **Greenwood Canyon:** Montague County (1975)
- **High Plains Natural Area:** Randall County (1980)
- **Independence Creek Preserve:** Terrell County (2024)
- **Little Blanco River Bluff:** Blanco County (1982)
- **Longhorn Cavern:** Burnet County (1971)
- **Lost Maples State Natural Area:** Bandera and Real counties (1980)
- **Muleshoe National Wildlife Refuge:** Bailey County (1980)
- **Natural Bridge Caverns:** Comal County (1971)
- **Odessa Meteor Crater:** Ector County (1965)
- **Palo Duro Canyon State Park:** Armstrong and Randall counties (1976)
- **Santa Ana National Wildlife Refuge:** Hidalgo County (1966)

Source: National Natural Landmarks Directory.

UNSPLASH/JOSHUA J. COTTEN

BIRDING IN TEXAS

WORLD BIRDING CENTER

The World Birding Center features nine birding education centers and observation sites in the Lower Rio Grande Valley designed to protect wildlife habitat and offer visitors a view of more than 500 species of birds. The center has partnered with the Texas Parks and Wildlife Department, the U.S. Fish and Wildlife Service, and other communities to turn 10,000 acres back into natural areas for birds, butterflies, and other wildlife.

- **Bentsen–Rio Grande Valley State Park** (Mission, WBC Headquarters)
- **Edinburg Scenic Wetlands** (Edinburg)
- **Estero Llano Grande State Park** (Weslaco)
- **Harlingen Arroyo Colorado** (Harlingen)
- **Old Hidalgo Pumphouse** (Hidalgo)
- **Quinta Mazatlan** (McAllen)
- **Resaca de la Palma State Park** (Brownsville)
- **Roma Bluffs** (Roma)
- **South Padre Island Birding and Nature Center** (South Padre Island)

GREAT TEXAS COASTAL BIRDING TRAIL

This trail winds its way through 43 Texas counties along the entire Texas coastal region. The trail was completed in April 2000 and is divided into upper, central, and lower coastal regions. It includes more than 300 wildlife-viewing sites and amenities such as boardwalks, parking pullouts, kiosks, observation platforms, and landscaping to attract native wildlife.

I-20 WILDLIFE PRESERVE AND JENNA WELCH NATURE STUDY CENTER

The I-20 Wildlife Preserve is an 87-acre urban playa lake in its natural state in southwest Midland that opened in 2013. It was maintained for many years by the Midland Naturalists and other volunteers, including Jenna Welch, a birding enthusiast and a member of the group. It includes hiking trails, bird observation blinds, four teaching platforms, the 24-foot-tall Hawk Observation Platform, and the Merritt Pavilion.

The Jenna Welch Nature Study Center operates an educational outreach program to local schools and area colleges and universities.

TEXAS STATE AQUARIUM

The Texas State Aquarium, on Corpus Christi Beach, is operated by the Texas State Aquarium Association — a nonprofit, self-supporting organization established in 1978. Efforts to fund a public aquarium in South Texas began in 1952, and several nonprofit organizations founded over the years eventually grew into the Texas State Aquarium Association.

In 1985, the 69th Texas Legislature declared the project the "Official Aquarium of the State of Texas."

The Jesse H. and Mary Gibbs Jones Gulf of Mexico Exhibit Building was completed in July 1990. In 2003, Dolphin Bay opened for Atlantic bottlenose dolphins and the Environmental Discovery Center opened, featuring a library, a Family Learning Center, and the Flint Hills Resources Distance Learning Studio.

The aquarium's exhibits and research focus on the plants and animals of the Gulf of Mexico and the Caribbean. It is the first U.S. facility to do so.

The Port of Corpus Christi Wildlife Rescue, opened in 2023, is the largest coastal wildlife rescue facility in the state.

Sources: Handbook of Texas Online and Texas State Aquarium.

SEA CENTER TEXAS

The Texas Parks and Wildlife Department operates Sea Center Texas — a marine aquarium, fish hatchery, and nature center that educates and entertains visitors. It is located at Lake Jackson.

The visitor center opened in 1996 and has interpretive displays, a "touch tank," and native Texas habitat exhibits depicting a salt marsh, bay, jetty, reef, and open Gulf waters. Sea Center is one of three marine hatcheries on the Texas coast that produce juvenile red drum, spotted seatrout, and southern flounder for enhancing natural populations in Texas bays. The hatchery can produce 25 million juvenile fish yearly and is a testing ground for production of other marine species.

A half-acre youth fishing pond introduces kids to saltwater fishing through scheduled activities.

The center's wetland area is part of the Great Texas Coastal Birding Trail, where more than 150 species of birds have been identified. They include one acre of salt marsh and three acres of freshwater marsh. Damselflies, dragonflies, butterflies, turtles, and frogs can be sighted off the boardwalk, and an outdoor pavilion is adjacent to butterfly and hummingbird gardens.

Sea Center Texas is operated in partnership with The Dow Chemical Company and the Coastal Conservation Association.

Source: Texas Parks and Wildlife Department.

UNSPLASH/DAVID CLODE

HUNTING AND FISHING

The popularity of hunting and fishing in Texas cannot be denied. According to the 2024 State of Texas Annual Cash Report, public hunting, fishing and other participation fees (including sales of hunting and fishing licenses) brought in revenues of $2.9 million in 2023 and $2.7 million in 2024.

HUNTING LICENSES

- A hunting license is required of Texas residents and non-residents who hunt any legal bird or animal. Hunting licenses and endorsements are valid during the period September 1 through the following August 31 of each year, except licenses issued for a specific number of days or time periods.
- A hunting license (except the non-resident special hunting license and non-resident, five-day special hunting license) is valid for taking all legal species of wildlife in Texas including deer, turkey, javelina, antelope, aoudad (sheep), alligator, and all small game and migratory game birds. Endorsement and tag requirements apply.
- A trapper's license is required for all persons to hunt, shoot, or take for sale those species classified as fur-bearing animals or their pelts.

In addition to a valid hunting license:

- An Archery Endorsement is required to hunt deer or turkey during Archery-Only open season.
- An Upland Game Bird Endorsement is required to hunt turkey, pheasant, quail, or chachalaca. Non-residents who purchase the non-resident spring turkey license are exempt from this endorsement requirement.
- A Migratory Game Bird Endorsement and HIP (Harvest Information Program) Certification is required to hunt any migratory game birds, including waterfowl, coot, rail, gallinule, snipe, dove, sandhill crane, and woodcock.
- A valid Federal Duck Stamp is required of waterfowl hunters age 16 or older.

GAME HARVEST ESTIMATES

The TPWD conducts random surveys of hunters each year to create estimates of hunter and harvest trends in two categories: small game (23 species total, birds and small mammals) and big game (white-tailed deer, mule deer, and javelina). They collect data not just on what animals were hunted, but also where and how.

FISHING LICENSES

All fishing licenses and endorsements are valid only from September 1 through the following August 31, except licenses issued for a specific number of days or time periods. If you own any valid freshwater fishing package, you will be able to purchase a saltwater stamp and also fish saltwater.

If you own any valid saltwater fishing package, you will be able to purchase a freshwater stamp and also fish freshwater. An all-water fishing package is available that enables anglers to fish both fresh- and saltwater.

FRESHWATER FISHING

Freshwater fishing in Texas is an activity enjoyed by an estimated 1.78 million recreational anglers ages 16 and over. In 2022, these anglers contributed an economic output of approximately $1.7 billion to the Texas economy.

Among the 268 species of freshwater fish in Texas, the most popular fish for recreational fishing are: largemouth bass, catfish, crappie, and striped, white, and hybrid striped bass.

Texas anglers can fish in approximately 1,100 public reservoirs and about 191,000 miles of rivers and streams, together totaling 1.7 million acres.

The Texas Parks and Wildlife Department operates field stations, fish hatcheries, and research facilities to support the conservation and management of fishery resources. The hatcheries operated by TPWD raise largemouth and smallmouth bass, as well as catfish, striped and hybrid striped bass, and sunfish.

TPWD has continued its programs of stocking fish in public waters to increase angling opportunities. Many conservation-minded anglers who desire continued quality fishing practice catch-and-release fishing.

TEXAS FRESHWATER FISHERIES CENTER

The Texas Freshwater Fisheries Center in Athens is an $18-million hatchery and educational center, where visitors can learn about underwater life.

The interactive Visitors Center includes aquarium displays of fish in their natural environment. Visitors get an "eye-to-eye" view of three authentically designed Texas freshwater habitats: a Hill Country stream, an East Texas pond, and a reservoir. A marsh exhibit features live American alligators.

A casting pond stocked with rainbow trout in the winter and catfish year-round provides a place for visitors to learn how to bait a hook, cast a line, and land a fish.

SALTWATER FISHING

The most popular saltwater sport fish in Texas bays are spotted seatrout, sand seatrout, Atlantic croaker, red drum, southern flounder, black drum, sheepshead, and gafftopsail catfish.

Offshore, some of the fish that anglers target are red snapper, king mackerel, Spanish mackerel, dolphinfish, cobia, tarpon, and yellowfin tuna.

Source: Texas Parks and Wildlife Department.

UNSPLASH/DEREK LALIBERTE

Hunting and Fishing Licenses Sold

2023	Volume
Hunting Licenses	420,139
Fishing Licenses	1,331,023
Combined Licenses	650,035
TOTALS	2,401,197
2024*	**Volume**
Hunting Licenses	435,974
Fishing Licenses	1,313,398
Combined Licenses	649,050
TOTALS	2,398,422

*Volumes for 2024 are estimated.

Source: 2026–27 Legislative Appropriation Request, TPWD

2023–2024 Wildlife Game Harvest

Game	Hunters	Harvest Estimates
Dove, combined*	289,648	7,212,239
Duck	77,020	1,317,570
Gallinule	329	0
Goose	22,382	249,822
Pheasant	2,633	5,595
Quail, combined**	33,573	407,482
Rabbit	23,698	126,721
Rail	987	1,317
Snipe	3,950	69,121
Squirrel	36,535	337,045
Teal	27,319	406,495
Turkey (fall and spring)	67,188	32,471
Woodcock	1,646	658
White-tailed Deer	757,047	739,864
Mule Deer	30,692	11,656
Javalina	42,726	28,204

*Dove, combined includes the following species: Eurasian, mourning, white-tipped, and white-winged.
**Quail, combined includes the following species: bobwhite and scaled.

Source: TPWD Game Harvest Surveys

COURTESY OF VISIT TYLER

FAIRS, FESTIVALS, AND SPECIAL EVENTS

Fairs, festivals, and other special events provide year–round recreation in Texas. Some are of national interest, while many attract visitors from across the state.

- **Abilene: West Texas Fair & Rodeo;** September. Founded 1897.
- **Albany: Fort Griffin Fandangle;** June. Founded 1938.
- **Alvarado: Johnson County Pioneers & Old Settlers Reunion;** September. Founded 1893.
- **Amarillo: Tri-State Fair & Rodeo;** September. Founded 1903.
- **Anderson: Grimes County Fair;** June. Founded 1952.
- **Angleton: Brazoria County Fair;** October. Founded 1910.
- **Aransas Pass: Shrimporee;** May. Founded 1949.
- **Athens: Athens Old Fiddlers Contest & Reunion;** May. Founded 1932.
- **Austin: Rodeo Austin;** March. Founded 1938.
- **Austin: South By Southwest;** March. Founded 1987.
- **Austin: Eeyore's Birthday Party;** April. Founded 1966.
- **Austin: Austin City Limits Music Festival;** October. Founded 2002.
- **Bay City: Matagorda County Fair & Livestock Show;** February-March. Founded 1944.
- **Bay City: Bay City Rice Festival;** October. Founded 1945.
- **Beaumont: South Texas State Fair;** March. Founded 1907.
- **Bellville: Austin County Fair & Rodeo;** October. Founded 1927.
- **Belton: Belton 4th of July Celebration & PRCA Rodeo;** July. Founded 1919.
- **Belton: Central Texas State Fair;** August-September.
- **Big Spring: Howard County Fair;** September. Founded 1973.
- **Boerne: Kendall County Fair;** September. Founded 1905.
- **Brenham: Washington County Fair;** September. Founded 1870.
- **Brownsville: Charro Days Fiesta;** February-March. Founded 1938.
- **Burnet: Bluebonnet Festival;** April. Founded 1986.
- **Burton: Burton Cotton Gin Festival;** April. Founded 1990.
- **Caldwell: Kolache Festival;** September. Founded 1986.
- **Caldwell: Burleson County Fair;** September. Founded 1936.
- **Canyon: TEXAS Outdoor Musical;** June-August. Founded 1967.
- **Chappell Hill: Chappell Hill Bluebonnet Festival;** April. Founded 1964.
- **Clifton: Norse Smorgasbord;** November. Founded 1955.
- **Clute: Great Texas Mosquito Festival;** July. Founded 1981.
- **Columbus: Colorado County Fair & Rodeo;** September. Founded 1978.
- **Conroe: Montgomery County Fair & Rodeo;** March. Founded 1957.
- **Corpus Christi: Birdiest Festival in America;** April. Founded 2017.
- **Corpus Christi: Buc Days;** May. Founded 1938.
- **Corpus Christi: Corpus Christi Beer Festival;** June.
- **Corpus Christi: Dia de los Muertos Festival;** October. Founded 2008.
- **Corsicana: Derrick Days;** April. Founded 1976.
- **Dalhart: XIT Rodeo & Reunion;** August. Founded 1937.
- **Dallas: State Fair of Texas;** September-October. Founded 1886.
- **Decatur: Wise County Old Settlers Reunion;** July. Founded 1881.
- **De Leon: De Leon Peach and Melon Festival;** August. Founded 1917.
- **Denton: North Texas Fair & Rodeo;** August. Founded 1929.
- **Edna: Jackson County Youth Fair;** October. Founded 1949.
- **Ennis: National Polka Festival;** May. Founded 1967.
- **Fairfield: Freestone County Fair;** June. Founded 1915.
- **Flatonia: Czhilispiel;** October. Founded 1973.
- **Fort Worth: Fort Worth Stock Show & Rodeo;** January-February. Founded 1896.
- **Fredericksburg: Night in Old Fredericksburg;** July. Founded 1963.
- **Fredericksburg: Fredericksburg Food & Wine Fest;** October. Founded 1991.
- **Fredericksburg: Oktoberfest;** October. Founded 1981.
- **Freer: Freer Rattlesnake Roundup;** April. Founded 1966.
- **Galveston: Galveston Historic**

Homes Tour; May. Founded 1974.

- **Galveston: Dickens on The Strand;** December. Founded 1974.
- **Gilmer: East Texas Yamboree;** October. Founded 1938.
- **Glen Flora: Wharton County Youth Fair;** April. Founded 1976.
- **Graham: Food Truck Championship of Texas;** June. Founded 2015.
- **Granbury: Hometown 4th of July Festival;** July. Founded 1975.
- **Granbury: Harvest Moon Festival of the Arts;** October. Founded 1979.
- **Grand Prairie: Main Street Festival;** October. Founded 2014.
- **Grapevine: GrapeFest;** September. Founded 1986.
- **Greenville: Hunt County Fair & Livestock Show;** April. Founded 1967.
- **Groesbeck: Limestone County Fair;** March.
- **Hallettsville: Kolache Fest;** September. Founded 1996.
- **Helotes: Helotes Cornyval;** May. Founded 1966.
- **Hempstead: Waller County Fair & Rodeo;** September-October. Founded 1946.
- **Henderson: Heritage Syrup Festival;** November. Founded 1989.
- **Hico: Hico Old Settler's Reunion;** July. Founded 1883.
- **Hidalgo: Borderfest;** March-April. Founded 1976.
- **Hitchcock: Galveston County Fair & Rodeo;** April. Founded 1938.
- **Hondo: Medina County Fair;** September. Founded 1980.
- **Houston: Houston Livestock Show and Rodeo;** February-March. Founded 1932.
- **Hughes Springs: Wildflower Trails of Texas;** April. Founded 1971.
- **Huntsville: Prison City Film Festival;** February. Founded 2018.
- **Huntsville: Walker County Fair & Rodeo;** March-April. Founded 1979.
- **Ingram: Texas Arts and Crafts Fair;** October. Founded 1973.
- **Jefferson: Jefferson Historical Pilgrimage;** May. Founded 1948.
- **Johnson City: Blanco County Fair & Rodeo;** August. Founded 1932.
- **Kenedy: Bluebonnet Days;** April. Founded 1980.
- **Kerrville: Kerrville Folk Festival;** May-June. Founded 1972.
- **La Grange: Fayette County Fair;** September. Founded 1927.
- **Laredo: Washington's Birthday Celebration;** January-February. Founded 1898.
- **Laredo: Laredo International Fair and Exposition;** February-March. Founded 1963.
- **Longview: Gregg County Fair;** September. Founded 1949.
- **Lubbock: Panhandle-South Plains Fair;** September. Founded 1914.
- **Lufkin: Texas State Forest Festival;** September. Founded 1938.
- **Luling: Luling Watermelon Thump;** June. Founded 1954.
- **Marshall: FireAnt Festival;** October. Founded 1983.
- **Marshall: Wonderland of Lights;** November-December. Founded 1984.
- **McKinney: Texas Scottish Festival & Highland Games;** May. Founded 1986.
- **Mercedes: Rio Grande Valley Livestock Show;** March. Founded 1940.
- **Mesquite: Mesquite Championship Rodeo;** June-August. Founded 1957.
- **Monahans: Butterfield Festival;** July. Founded 1994.
- **Mount Pleasant: Titus County Fair;** September. Founded 1975.
- **Nacogdoches: Piney Woods Fair;** October. Founded 1978.
- **Nederland: Nederland Heritage Festival;** March. Founded 1973.
- **New Braunfels: Comal County Fair & Rodeo;** September. Founded 1894.
- **New Braunfels: Wurstfest;** November. Founded 1961.
- **Odessa: Permian Basin Fair & Expo;** September. Founded 1975.
- **Palestine: Texas Dogwood Trails Celebration;** March-April. Founded 1938.
- **Paris: Red River Valley Fair;** September-October. Founded 1911.
- **Pasadena: Pasadena Livestock Show & Rodeo;** September. Founded 1949.
- **Port Aransas: Whooping Crane Festival;** February. Founded 1996.
- **Port Arthur: cavOILcade;** October. Founded 1952.
- **Port Lavaca: Calhoun County Fair;** October. Founded 1935.
- **Poteet: Poteet Strawberry Festival;** April. Founded 1948.
- **Refugio: Refugio County Fair;** March. Founded 1961.
- **Rio Grande City: Starr County Fair;** March. Founded 1965.
- **Rosenberg: Fort Bend County Fair & Rodeo;** September-October. Founded 1937.
- **Salado: Scottish Gathering and Highland Games;** November. Founded 1961.
- **San Angelo: San Angelo Stock Show & Rodeo;** February. Founded 1932.
- **San Antonio: CarFest;** April. Founded 2016.
- **San Antonio: Fiesta San Antonio;** April. Founded 1891.
- **San Antonio: Texas Folklife Festival;** June. Founded 1972.
- **Sanderson: Prickly Pear Pachanga;** April. Founded 2001.
- **Sanderson: Cinco de Mayo Celebration;** May.
- **Sanderson: 4th of July Celebration;** July. Founded 1908.
- **Schulenburg: Schulenburg Festival;** August. Founded 1976.
- **Shamrock: St. Patrick's Day Celebration;** March. Founded 1938.
- **Stamford: Texas Cowboy Reunion;** July. Founded 1930.
- **Sulphur Springs: Hopkins County Fall Festival;** October. Founded 1970.
- **Sweetwater: Rattlesnake Roundup;** March. Founded 1958.
- **Terlingua: Terlingua International Chili Championship;** November. Founded 1967.
- **Texarkana: Four States Fair & Rodeo;** September. Founded 1940.
- **Todd Mission: Texas Renaissance Festival;** October-November. Founded 1974.
- **Tyler: East Texas State Fair;** September. Founded 1914.
- **Tyler: Texas Rose Festival;** October. Founded 1933.
- **Waco: Heart O' Texas Fair & Rodeo;** October. Founded 1954.
- **Waxahachie: Scarborough Renaissance Festival;** April-May. Founded 1980.
- **Waxahachie: Gingerbread Trail Tour of Homes;** June. Founded 1969.
- **Weatherford: Parker County Peach Festival;** July. Founded 1985.
- **Weatherford: Christmas on the Square;** December. Founded 1988.
- **West: Westfest;** September. Founded 1976.
- **Winnsboro: Autumn Trails Festival;** October. Founded 1959.
- **Woodville: Tyler County Dogwood Festival;** March-April. Founded 1940.
- **Yorktown: Yorktown Western Days;** October. Founded 1959.

Texas

TRAVEL GUIDE

AS VOTED BY TSHA MEMBERSHIP AND FRIENDS

VISIT GALVESTON

Favorite Texas Destinations

Galveston

Situated on the Gulf Coast, Galveston provides beaches, outdoor activities, and historical sites for Texans to visit. The city is also the birthplace of Juneteenth. On June 19, 1865, Union troops arrived in the city, announcing the emancipation of enslaved people. Every year, the Ashton Villa reads the General Order No. 3.

Popular attractions include the Moody Gardens, Galveston Island Historic Pleasure Pier, Galveston Island State Park, Bryan Museum, and The Strand.

Fredericksburg

Settled in 1846 by Germans, this Central Texas town is best known for its wineries and German heritage. Fredericksburg runs more than 75 vineyards and wineries, attracting visitors who want to sample wine. Its German roots are on clear display, with their food along the Main Street and museums such as the Pioneer Museum and Vereins Kirche Museum. Every October, the town hosts Oktoberfest, bringing live polka music, beer, food, and games.

San Antonio

Outside of the main trip to the Alamo, San Antonio brims with cultural diversity, sports pride, and unique attractions. Take a stroll along the River Walk, where you can stop at restaurants or shops. Cheer on the Spurs at an NBA game. While visiting main tourist spots from the Texas Revolution, also make sure to stop at the Japanese Tea Garden, Briscoe Western Art Museum, Witte Museum, Pearl district, and Six Flags Fiesta Texas.

VISIT GALVESTON; UNSPLASH/MARKUS SPISKE; ICK HAUPT

Favorite Event

The Houston Livestock Show and Rodeo (Houston)

Founded in 1932, the Houston Livestock Show and Rodeo has grown into one of the largest events of its kind in the world. It combines a livestock show, rodeo competitions, and concerts, working to promote agriculture and community. Each year, the four-day event, which takes place in February and March, gathers more than 200,000 attendees.

The rodeo hosts a competition in events such as bull riding, steer wrestling, and bareback riding. Musicians who've graced the Star Stage include: George Strait, Taylor Swift, Elvis Presley, Beyoncé, Bob Dylan, and Ariana Grande.

The State Fair of Texas (Dallas)

Taste deep fried food, take a ride on a roller coaster, or snap a photo with Big Tex at the State Fair of Texas in Dallas. Since 1866, the fair has brought in visitors from across the state from late September to mid-October. Activities include watching a livestock show, rooting for competitors in the rodeo, and enjoying an auto show. The fair hosts the popular Texas-Oklahoma college football game, also known as the Red River Showdown.

Fiesta San Antonio (San Antonio)

To honor those that fought at the Alamo and the Battle of San Jacinto, a group of women in 1891 led the Battle of Flowers Parade. This procession evolved into Fiesta, an 11-day celebration in San Antonio that attracts more than 2.5 million people each year. Held in April, the festival includes over 100 events such as live music, sporting events, pageant competitions, and exhibitions.

UNSPLASH/PERRY MERRITY

Favorite Texas Shop

Buc-ee's

Clean bathrooms, a plethora of gas pumps, and food like Beaver Nuggets and barbecue combine to make Buc-ee's a one-of-a-kind gas station chain. Since opening the first store in 1982 in Lake Jackson, more than 50 Buc-ee's locations have opened across the nation. Though a Texas-based brand, the chain recently expanded to newer states including Mississippi, Virginia, and Georgia. The store in Luling, Texas, holds the record as the world's largest convenience store at 75,593 square feet.

H-E-B

In 1905, Florence Thornton Butt established Mrs. C.C. Butt's Staple and Fancy Grocery, located in her family home in Kerrville. Butt passed down the store to her son, Howard Edward Butt, who renamed it to H-E-B in San Antonio in 1942. Today, H-E-B operates more than 440 stores across all of their divisions, including those in Mexico. The supermarket chain is beloved by Texans due to its affordable prices, high-quality produce, and community engagement.

Cavender's

Cavender's sells a collection of Western wear and cowboy boots. James and Patricia Cavender opened the first store in 1965 in Pittsburg, Texas. Since then, the company has expanded to more than 100 stores across more than 15 states, while collaborating with brands such as Wrangler and Justin. In 2019, the Texas Cowboy Hall of Fame inducted the Cavender family for supporting the western lifestyle.

UNSPLASH/JEREMY BRADY

Best Texas Hotel or Lodge

Menger Hotel (San Antonio)
Grand Galvez (Galveston)
Gage Hotel (Marathon)
The Driskill (Austin)
Indian Lodge (Fort Davis)

Best Outdoor Spot

Big Bend (West Texas region)
Palo Duro Canyon (Canyon)
Caddo Lake (Karnack)
South Padre Island (near Brownsville)
Enchanted Rock (near Fredericksburg)

Best Family Vacation Spot

San Antonio
South Padre Island
Galveston
Port Aransas
Big Bend

Favorite Historic Site or Museum

The Alamo (San Antonio)
San Jacinto Museum and Battlefield (La Porte)
The Bullock Texas State History Museum (Austin)
San Antonio Missions National Historic State Park (San Antonio)
The Bryan Museum (Galveston)

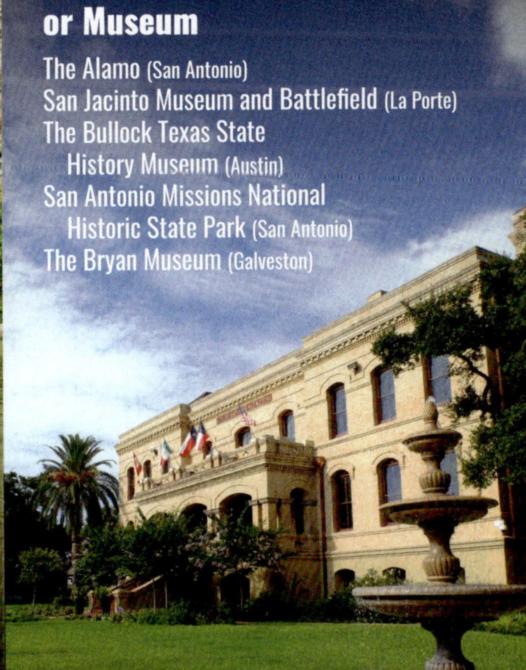

COURTESY OF GAGE HOTEL; UNSPLASH/BEN DUTTON; MICK HAUPT; VISIT GALVESTON

UNSPLASH/KATT GALVAN

Texas

TRANSPORTATION

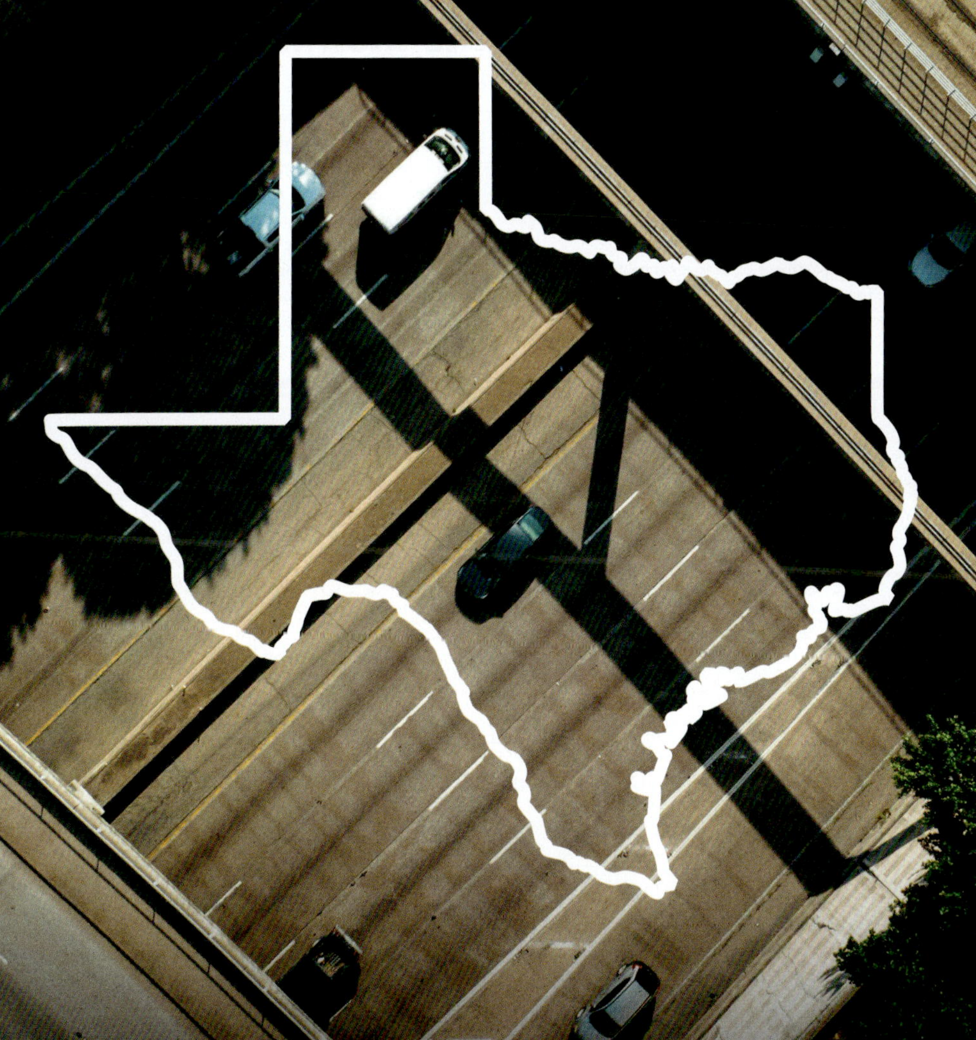

UNSPLASH/LANCE ASPER

UNSPLASH/DANIEL

TRAVELING TEXAS HIGHWAYS

Texans drove nearly 26 million motor vehicles in 2023 on 324,003 miles of roadways, including city- and county-maintained roads. That driving is calculated to have included more than 610 million miles driven daily on the 200,723 miles of state-maintained highways alone.

The Texas Department of Transportation (TxDOT) is responsible for state highway construction and maintenance, planning for future road expansion, administering Texas tollways and toll tags, and operating the state's 12 official Texas Travel Information Centers and 76 safety rest areas.

Mileage, maintenance, and construction figures (listed by county) refer only to roads that are maintained by the state: Interstates, U.S. highways, state highways, farm-to-market roads, and some loops around urban areas. Not included are city- or county-maintained streets and roads. A lane mile is one lane for one mile; i.e., one mile of four-lane highway equals four lane miles.

County	Vehicles Registered ('24)	Lane Miles of Highway ('23)	Vehicle Miles Driven Daily ('23)	State Construction Expenditures ('24)	Combined Construction Maintenance Expenditures ('24)	Total Vehicle Registration Fees ('24)	State Net Receipts ('24)	County Net Receipts ('24)
Anderson	48,081	1,013	1,305,165	$26,756,765	$35,980,799	$3,447,957	$2,498,448	$947,229
Andrews	23,901	556	907,430	$34,392,393	$67,506,310	$2,300,783	$1,800,900	$498,374
Angelina	81,449	985	2,137,672	$74,812,072	$100,840,270	$6,192,043	$4,850,828	$1,337,474
Aransas	28,638	231	552,235	$9,134,849	$11,702,687	$1,780,508	$1,199,604	$576,884
Archer	11,895	580	415,045	$5,844,853	$10,461,587	$1,185,638	$727,131	$457,543
Armstrong	2,641	379	409,206	$172,586	$2,642,680	$169,644	$9,248	$160,329
Atascosa	52,918	1,022	2,124,128	$17,692,194	$40,045,210	$3,478,132	$2,566,479	$909,345
Austin	44,486	660	1,671,769	$11,186,720	$17,939,074	$3,176,055	$2,355,254	$818,149
Bailey	6,221	491	247,211	$202,286	$2,066,678	$463,233	$90,121	$372,962
Bandera	30,945	414	417,819	$8,668,433	$17,876,136	$2,036,389	$1,375,781	$656,789
Bastrop	111,796	817	3,113,704	$10,934,785	$28,919,325	$8,159,297	$6,353,084	$1,795,414
Baylor	4,144	531	254,221	$18,773,477	$24,447,059	$245,087	$21,572	$223,317
Bee	22,150	679	659,021	$1,897,778	$6,526,053	$1,501,551	$912,525	$587,103
Bell	331,547	1,654	9,226,590	$67,274,609	$99,396,199	$22,915,707	$18,470,564	$4,421,535
Bexar	1,675,717	3,590	35,616,087	$881,648,315	$1,103,658,577	$167,590,369	$126,069,904	$41,410,448
Blanco	20,109	464	819,549	$7,570,926	$14,607,046	$1,361,758	$882,107	$477,201
Borden	924	344	63,366	$2,404,528	$6,841,404	$43,977	$2,966	$40,966
Bosque	24,606	697	578,693	$19,972,650	$46,184,563	$1,430,190	$831,251	$597,378
Bowie	83,330	1,199	3,108,079	$28,793,432	$57,308,583	$5,890,169	$4,570,693	$1,313,987
Brazoria	348,896	1,429	6,175,617	$266,333,335	$318,579,015	$24,766,599	$20,432,727	$4,303,724
Brazos	172,150	979	4,269,178	$51,921,671	$75,087,216	$13,296,237	$10,635,501	$2,627,715
Brewster	10,815	606	227,383	$685,202	$3,047,678	$638,114	$283,127	$351,756
Briscoe	1,927	325	52,454	$221,430	$2,392,476	$108,939	$5,913	$102,880
Brooks	6,072	354	690,299	$2,295,970	$12,076,323	$372,110	$112,266	$259,632

Sources: Texas Department of Transportation and Department of Motor Vehicles.

County	Vehicles Registered ('24)	Lane Miles of Highway ('23)	Vehicle Miles Driven Daily ('23)	State Construction Expenditures ('24)	Combined Construction Maintenance Expenditures ('24)	Total Vehicle Registration Fees ('24)	State Net Receipts ('24)	County Net Receipts ('24)
Brown	43,241	772	787,446	$11,365,840	$24,337,614	$2,774,475	$1,901,660	$870,794
Burleson	25,956	543	819,536	$17,496,598	$28,524,443	$1,779,477	$1,126,980	$650,585
Burnet	66,951	792	2,170,358	$16,131,645	$28,825,087	$4,684,522	$3,513,783	$1,162,113
Caldwell	50,267	711	1,604,257	$8,699,642	$19,445,651	$3,329,025	$2,401,626	$925,165
Calhoun	23,170	437	532,198	$4,710,219	$12,470,409	$1,731,940	$1,162,841	$567,933
Callahan	17,271	745	1,137,225	$6,969,382	$27,339,718	$1,314,791	$749,845	$564,002
Cameron	352,638	1,927	7,430,994	$43,313,654	$68,092,714	$30,424,819	$21,771,027	$8,639,359
Camp	18,280	263	287,360	$5,951,763	$8,459,324	$1,576,875	$1,093,485	$482,803
Carson	7,807	780	879,256	$11,501,009	$21,325,606	$529,246	$121,857	$407,025
Cass	33,238	980	854,744	$13,032,235	$25,681,274	$2,019,263	$1,298,518	$719,903
Castro	8,671	552	268,589	$7,495,856	$9,334,847	$1,100,095	$644,992	$454,987
Chambers	55,549	864	3,333,527	$19,234,675	$34,429,778	$3,863,322	$2,959,484	$900,328
Cherokee	52,267	1,145	1,329,333	$47,105,682	$60,874,773	$3,461,039	$2,533,721	$924,272
Childress	6,243	497	457,009	$8,009,480	$25,185,424	$396,970	$78,937	$317,795
Clay	13,457	756	821,223	$16,598,692	$28,099,773	$1,011,227	$488,887	$520,961
Cochran	2,792	469	104,469	$461,999	$2,366,902	$179,756	$8,419	$171,249
Coke	4,535	369	201,193	$12,551,396	$24,831,095	$253,753	$37,274	$216,323
Coleman	11,382	753	388,467	$4,434,747	$14,894,734	$649,939	$182,638	$466,779
Collin	926,336	1,609	11,223,015	$548,794,935	$598,988,150	$76,848,180	$63,652,109	$13,098,839
Collingsworth	3,217	454	76,051	$7,318,921	$25,395,858	$210,234	$23,192	$186,819
Colorado	30,202	765	2,145,270	$103,912,811	$111,279,431	$2,249,999	$1,549,020	$699,297
Comal	213,782	743	5,732,058	$122,962,251	$75,633,996	$17,112,696	$14,122,496	$2,961,984
Comanche	17,848	748	489,870	$14,769,520	$21,875,017	$1,347,606	$772,814	$574,339
Concho	3,520	478	281,823	$1,641,743	$4,883,356	$182,367	$15,682	$166,414
Cooke	57,614	847	2,009,527	$42,108,957	$56,301,000	$4,139,836	$3,099,656	$1,036,974
Coryell	63,757	782	1,310,031	$9,807,368	$23,369,878	$3,662,307	$2,679,043	$978,622
Cottle	1,508	390	65,414	$518,725	$2,037,691	$79,205	$4,492	$74,431
Crane	5,263	340	346,650	$1,875,115	$5,496,447	$394,071	$161,725	$232,181
Crockett	4,801	744	635,004	$3,278,886	$6,808,434	$494,655	$225,882	$268,681
Crosby	5,495	569	207,995	$5,459,174	$14,459,886	$318,963	$21,422	$297,090
Culberson	2,653	757	752,082	$41,352,878	$84,887,374	$170,020	$11,395	$158,395
Dallam	8,475	698	450,496	$1,942,183	$6,639,963	$716,609	$269,929	$446,534
Dallas	2,100,428	3,590	43,761,913	$618,069,827	$742,302,159	$174,022,164	$144,481,357	$29,414,323
Dawson	10,886	741	584,387	$2,305,705	$6,967,220	$1,881,325	$1,351,140	$528,815
Deaf Smith	20,432	603	483,901	$11,528,606	$19,546,604	$2,012,385	$1,400,459	$610,914
Delta	6,649	373	198,028	$9,199,905	$13,197,683	$374,460	$95,618	$278,710
Denton	797,549	1,846	12,841,791	$360,463,896	$430,815,158	$59,057,250	$48,829,460	$10,148,929
DeWitt	25,329	674	625,870	$22,130,511	$57,402,423	$1,656,771	$1,041,769	$613,721
Dickens	2,556	468	104,194	$361,022	$3,249,604	$132,593	$7,056	$125,515
Dimmit	10,543	506	588,564	$16,098,396	$21,269,066	$879,268	$512,496	$366,367
Donley	3,340	469	594,876	$2,805,635	$13,214,542	$204,209	$8,979	$195,145
Duval	10,842	642	361,852	$1,779,517	$6,413,880	$685,844	$252,374	$432,982
Eastland	27,122	1,033	1,454,551	$13,239,811	$40,758,484	$2,367,347	$1,699,041	$667,392
Ector	187,147	976	3,536,403	$41,844,845	$88,948,190	$18,942,242	$16,288,646	$2,645,937
Edwards	2,944	500	90,314	$1,619,244	$3,128,425	$175,204	$8,223	$166,813
Ellis	207,627	1,652	6,974,518	$98,100,244	$133,317,597	$14,118,196	$11,548,043	$2,554,504
El Paso	701,070	1,793	12,722,264	$268,062,775	$348,406,528	$58,240,019	$43,174,976	$15,041,462
Erath	46,350	851	1,295,444	$23,887,895	$32,085,799	$3,294,967	$2,448,652	$841,838
Falls	18,076	752	871,839	$3,780,578	$16,765,703	$1,281,425	$703,956	$577,025
Fannin	40,337	991	1,026,998	$8,079,483	$24,177,585	$2,617,345	$1,846,322	$768,473
Fayette	36,320	1,034	2,168,088	$39,710,092	$67,075,944	$2,586,709	$1,857,490	$725,765
Fisher	4,326	558	177,495	$3,166,882	$8,172,717	$227,387	$11,178	$216,064
Floyd	6,628	702	179,816	$504,681	$3,088,593	$427,930	$71,900	$355,490
Foard	1,607	298	59,677	$278,869	$2,599,847	$82,617	$4,430	$78,165
Fort Bend	692,374	1,453	9,511,999	$308,766,123	$322,786,679	$50,043,632	$41,248,054	$8,736,488
Franklin	12,939	344	543,441	$5,632,789	$11,566,547	$773,118	$349,789	$422,772
Freestone	23,408	824	1,769,186	$10,119,576	$32,557,743	$1,523,128	$927,198	$594,706
Frio	15,559	761	1,466,371	$9,707,950	$15,507,934	$1,015,604	$526,639	$488,230

County	Vehicles Registered ('24)	Lane Miles of Highway ('23)	Vehicle Miles Driven Daily ('23)	State Construction Expenditures ('24)	Combined Construction Maintenance Expenditures ('24)	Total Vehicle Registration Fees ('24)	State Net Receipts ('24)	County Net Receipts ('24)
Gaines	25,916	663	789,436	$11,176,869	$15,614,874	$2,169,885	$1,523,926	$644,721
Galveston	305,333	1,081	5,585,093	$189,008,010	$215,053,564	$21,102,210	$17,355,358	$3,715,592
Garza	4,871	457	494,946	$884,478	$5,117,198	$324,015	$72,021	$251,727
Gillespie	40,871	684	889,577	$8,100,653	$21,571,065	$2,598,226	$1,776,288	$816,241
Glasscock	2,925	357	347,608	$14,936,424	$17,168,719	$147,900	$1,715	$149,503
Goliad	9,629	535	338,856	$28,783,942	$39,540,489	$538,254	$149,104	$388,119
Gonzales	25,697	894	1,620,129	$14,623,947	$25,550,561	$2,019,795	$1,397,495	$620,965
Gray	21,835	762	675,312	$18,768,837	$27,152,455	$1,576,927	$972,866	$603,201
Grayson	149,776	1,283	4,284,436	$90,292,669	$150,673,636	$10,674,962	$8,582,931	$2,079,738
Gregg	134,069	824	3,087,269	$63,350,405	$103,981,538	$11,427,226	$9,590,860	$1,827,029
Grimes	37,591	652	1,429,238	$17,274,366	$39,914,218	$2,377,871	$1,641,366	$733,849
Guadalupe	175,734	1,016	4,364,263	$124,116,857	$159,554,727	$12,920,312	$10,327,723	$2,576,762
Hale	28,043	1,055	908,582	$2,231,427	$6,658,033	$2,045,011	$1,366,830	$676,721
Hall	2,912	459	277,251	$5,777,181	$20,687,987	$177,036	$7,913	$169,031
Hamilton	12,301	580	373,503	$8,692,796	$22,881,285	$743,391	$270,004	$472,572
Hansford	6,317	525	144,818	$4,168,605	$7,392,693	$456,318	$92,712	$363,378
Hardeman	3,810	465	393,590	$4,760,045	$21,372,852	$235,379	$11,488	$223,793
Hardin	60,579	586	1,414,865	$35,784,616	$44,972,412	$4,414,726	$3,333,031	$1,077,511
Harris	3,488,097	5,661	69,420,211	$959,013,026	$1,081,530,520	$296,777,490	$247,028,787	$49,513,267
Harrison	72,022	1,174	2,953,271	$16,618,164	$37,080,825	$5,040,903	$3,792,442	$1,244,410
Hartley	7,339	551	496,285	$7,327,339	$17,173,862	$1,008,637	$653,402	$354,552
Haskell	5,906	669	244,993	$4,697,983	$14,722,744	$422,053	$78,263	$343,510
Hays	229,229	756	6,135,064	$39,469,769	$93,428,654	$17,148,585	$14,191,774	$2,928,622
Hemphill	5,018	384	126,622	$6,940,243	$18,685,593	$342,149	$68,063	$273,786
Henderson	97,712	1,068	2,090,598	$16,103,835	$37,068,646	$6,301,990	$4,901,347	$1,395,233
Hidalgo	706,364	2,533	12,578,516	$184,522,687	$231,315,301	$63,195,642	$47,321,054	$15,848,875
Hill	49,262	1,162	3,105,934	$18,608,148	$41,973,192	$3,893,580	$3,019,883	$871,136
Hockley	25,273	752	619,491	$2,204,604	$5,958,741	$1,905,043	$1,274,131	$628,352
Hood	76,566	407	1,196,989	$27,911,415	$30,893,620	$6,889,650	$5,618,440	$1,262,717
Hopkins	44,915	1,009	1,832,882	$3,158,051	$19,184,627	$3,205,810	$2,316,487	$886,840
Houston	22,775	872	717,035	$9,949,085	$35,837,502	$1,341,898	$765,269	$575,208
Howard	29,852	910	1,477,917	$14,135,372	$39,213,564	$2,150,308	$1,467,871	$680,560
Hudspeth	3,672	829	1,524,499	$12,310,833	$33,793,212	$224,389	$12,025	$212,232
Hunt	113,278	1,371	3,577,149	$49,980,771	$107,561,872	$7,913,356	$6,185,883	$1,720,768
Hutchinson	23,662	493	331,976	$4,771,270	$22,978,618	$1,587,665	$1,028,478	$558,284
Irion	3,390	246	235,881	$3,386,314	$4,219,853	$530,779	$337,559	$193,022
Jack	11,516	583	348,370	$35,966,599	$40,048,684	$850,502	$406,812	$442,944
Jackson	18,009	637	979,646	$8,764,627	$20,825,158	$1,146,764	$608,155	$537,451
Jasper	40,329	778	1,216,463	$7,099,522	$28,009,255	$2,537,089	$1,753,796	$781,761
Jeff Davis	2,680	472	171,703	$1,726,129	$6,215,162	$155,343	$30,488	$124,147
Jefferson	206,510	1,123	5,572,371	$213,435,205	$280,808,370	$15,542,972	$12,756,733	$2,774,121
Jim Hogg	4,328	288	132,639	$3,266,978	$5,088,020	$296,144	$81,163	$214,531
Jim Wells	38,812	715	1,170,846	$40,190,649	$48,152,977	$2,822,597	$2,012,179	$808,610
Johnson	198,999	1,004	3,976,005	$57,435,436	$77,905,957	$15,735,926	$12,742,958	$2,979,399
Jones	18,789	1,005	525,272	$4,632,376	$21,673,139	$1,424,791	$855,428	$567,755
Karnes	19,981	709	706,491	$14,121,890	$30,536,540	$1,191,652	$665,766	$525,556
Kaufman	163,201	1,235	5,235,458	$138,929,141	$170,358,682	$10,956,154	$8,659,900	$2,285,610
Kendall	70,304	458	1,544,647	$13,536,546	$37,370,317	$7,462,778	$5,964,019	$1,483,508
Kenedy	921	192	517,237	$4,784,514	$6,619,053	$45,264	$2,683	$42,528
Kent	1,074	323	47,958	$2,020,231	$5,038,012	$44,138	$2,492	$41,602
Kerr	63,124	712	1,451,148	$6,221,242	$10,755,815	$4,415,943	$3,261,870	$1,138,671
Kimble	6,537	686	772,342	$6,301,078	$27,506,351	$376,279	$81,462	$294,425
King	444	229	84,174	$2,221,929	$6,652,992	$15,598	$4,135	$19,733
Kinney	3,609	407	211,545	$1,321,657	$4,667,220	$223,604	$55,916	$167,490
Kleberg	25,427	378	830,513	$51,751,171	$56,859,497	$1,745,724	$1,204,618	$539,301
Knox	4,195	470	149,203	$1,437,293	$10,523,982	$276,854	$24,034	$252,687
Lamar	52,434	1,014	1,363,532	$29,984,935	$49,648,172	$3,980,531	$3,010,997	$966,734
Lamb	12,807	802	488,343	$2,479,572	$5,938,171	$877,044	$373,876	$502,148

County	Vehicles Registered ('24)	Lane Miles of Highway ('23)	Vehicle Miles Driven Daily ('23)	State Construction Expenditures ('24)	Combined Construction Maintenance Expenditures ('24)	Total Vehicle Registration Fees ('24)	State Net Receipts ('24)	County Net Receipts ('24)
Lampasas	29,143	528	676,171	$13,868,821	$22,298,751	$1,961,736	$1,268,817	$691,046
La Salle	7,789	649	1,196,788	$59,373,316	$74,430,952	$677,912	$330,811	$346,799
Lavaca	30,659	667	597,899	$6,898,485	$13,064,688	$1,790,746	$1,149,763	$639,011
Lee	26,206	519	831,496	$5,831,581	$14,522,409	$1,807,584	$1,197,954	$608,702
Leon	23,697	836	1,792,310	$25,860,891	$36,717,374	$1,630,898	$1,057,131	$572,274
Liberty	100,442	933	2,527,260	$29,590,714	$80,956,645	$6,917,173	$5,483,871	$1,430,022
Limestone	24,786	770	671,840	$3,345,699	$10,821,894	$1,669,992	$1,038,111	$629,921
Lipscomb	3,960	414	89,722	$7,412,881	$18,683,115	$297,370	$31,485	$265,631
Live Oak	14,903	1,013	1,622,336	$6,311,027	$14,120,610	$960,629	$451,679	$508,147
Llano	31,610	514	637,506	$7,507,687	$15,430,701	$1,916,372	$1,205,544	$707,153
Loving	213	68	234,565	$8,179,481	$29,006,215	$10,157	$332	$9,824
Lubbock	264,046	1,737	4,188,153	$92,605,465	$143,802,333	$22,032,118	$18,328,690	$3,671,277
Lynn	6,770	709	448,088	$484,816	$3,878,008	$400,680	$61,332	$338,409
Madison	14,693	585	1,174,911	$25,147,127	$34,969,730	$2,193,138	$1,702,970	$489,381
Marion	10,371	330	285,046	$12,245,638	$16,857,873	$647,857	$232,764	$414,762
Martin	7,054	643	1,140,636	$7,343,842	$13,647,032	$622,831	$193,706	$428,603
Mason	6,880	417	177,319	$3,807,658	$8,047,514	$364,689	$81,089	$282,946
Matagorda	35,910	710	832,629	$4,074,750	$13,127,861	$2,230,706	$1,503,897	$724,959
Maverick	52,635	510	957,051	$6,869,241	$17,138,520	$3,992,413	$3,076,598	$913,864
McCulloch	9,567	616	328,112	$638,208	$6,117,617	$629,925	$194,317	$434,712
McLennan	232,550	1,766	7,578,775	$58,220,182	$102,578,651	$17,945,416	$14,500,053	$3,428,217
McMullen	1,782	325	213,705	$603,159	$2,083,320	$79,834	$1,323	$78,290
Medina	61,368	772	1,605,703	$9,693,886	$21,854,092	$4,555,890	$3,480,329	$1,071,521
Menard	2,911	348	174,935	$2,648,722	$4,098,769	$163,025	$17,727	$144,938
Midland	235,365	1,069	4,823,932	$74,998,742	$150,763,034	$22,417,447	$19,429,814	$2,974,483
Milam	30,959	712	945,008	$6,081,283	$18,779,879	$1,798,625	$1,140,406	$656,537
Mills	7,358	463	261,705	$7,500,192	$10,595,926	$461,897	$99,630	$361,617
Mitchell	7,014	662	738,865	$817,527	$7,749,693	$413,402	$81,768	$331,357
Montague	27,578	860	826,810	$23,026,758	$32,008,526	$2,019,587	$1,312,584	$704,420
Montgomery	631,384	1,630	12,945,657	$215,858,226	$241,866,584	$50,939,866	$43,274,358	$7,597,681
Moore	24,602	487	570,404	$3,835,594	$13,828,704	$1,836,432	$1,259,379	$576,542
Morris	13,288	360	472,222	$261,558	$3,924,498	$828,957	$419,089	$409,519
Motley	1,665	330	51,457	$143,822	$2,417,357	$88,104	$5,244	$82,794
Nacogdoches	58,607	980	1,821,034	$18,569,480	$39,010,890	$4,304,387	$3,221,965	$1,077,647
Navarro	56,125	1,276	2,383,592	$24,181,161	$39,341,316	$4,215,477	$3,207,052	$1,006,400
Newton	13,189	554	386,021	$2,766,760	$10,260,658	$810,675	$314,747	$495,170
Nolan	13,863	694	1,197,248	$63,867,182	$78,897,013	$1,029,460	$534,134	$494,213
Nueces	283,645	1,627	6,496,502	$73,560,028	$121,240,512	$21,743,643	$17,996,476	$3,727,676
Ochiltree	11,818	432	244,591	$109,238	$1,865,136	$971,369	$483,799	$486,898
Oldham	2,926	472	828,329	$8,629,697	$12,368,573	$215,479	$39,617	$175,774
Orange	79,338	657	2,814,890	$27,742,497	$56,383,591	$5,278,217	$4,059,172	$1,213,548
Palo Pinto	33,232	838	1,205,200	$13,666,298	$22,903,942	$2,171,915	$1,491,013	$678,106
Panola	26,603	775	1,086,354	$30,801,382	$38,584,638	$1,639,070	$1,187,300	$450,297
Parker	183,421	903	4,473,591	$40,527,667	$53,283,898	$13,673,906	$10,811,801	$2,841,420
Parmer	9,986	612	428,347	$2,919,558	$17,244,468	$729,216	$263,626	$465,359
Pecos	15,804	1,686	1,371,201	$26,286,818	$54,938,012	$1,182,683	$652,106	$529,604
Polk	57,870	867	1,926,396	$60,556,621	$69,224,337	$4,480,195	$3,412,877	$1,063,820
Potter	102,983	915	2,882,962	$118,064,263	$154,138,781	$8,724,560	$7,047,711	$1,668,320
Presidio	7,793	554	209,583	$8,936,912	$14,078,686	$526,422	$190,361	$335,693
Rains	16,715	269	378,199	$3,668,653	$6,612,186	$1,008,525	$551,547	$456,050
Randall	148,480	933	1,835,734	$16,609,376	$61,770,681	$11,820,443	$9,387,764	$2,417,219
Reagan	5,095	319	322,793	$23,902,705	$30,150,007	$370,327	$97,207	$272,988
Real	4,593	295	107,881	$2,002,399	$3,609,302	$282,490	$70,611	$211,373
Red River	14,032	760	441,871	$4,782,194	$17,543,223	$850,007	$352,282	$497,255
Reeves	16,855	1,177	1,765,531	$87,036,422	$138,143,135	$1,634,861	$1,079,621	$554,285
Refugio	8,002	491	773,425	$5,309,976	$9,847,733	$553,592	$220,518	$332,410
Roberts	1,252	244	78,516	$712,438	$1,848,198	$65,833	$3,498	$62,312
Robertson	21,533	661	958,076	$6,315,837	$22,588,687	$1,427,242	$832,455	$593,390

County	Vehicles Registered ('24)	Lane Miles of Highway ('23)	Vehicle Miles Driven Daily ('23)	State Construction Expenditures ('24)	Combined Construction Maintenance Expenditures ('24)	Total Vehicle Registration Fees ('24)	State Net Receipts ('24)	County Net Receipts ('24)
Rockwall	113,291	366	2,872,799	$150,946,367	$166,651,526	$9,233,188	$7,409,175	$1,809,787
Runnels	12,625	734	383,343	$3,057,241	$12,547,427	$815,630	$333,975	$480,985
Rusk	52,582	1,175	1,428,182	$17,301,783	$39,215,831	$3,601,193	$2,638,746	$959,276
Sabine	13,043	482	296,841	$1,985,324	$6,410,404	$810,927	$368,240	$441,950
San Augustine	9,387	536	305,224	$9,233,313	$17,366,204	$712,503	$288,643	$423,150
San Jacinto	30,242	534	930,574	$26,977,425	$42,468,159	$2,189,102	$1,480,103	$707,360
San Patricio	68,639	995	2,339,027	$36,297,906	$58,213,793	$4,663,932	$3,477,651	$1,181,277
San Saba	8,149	437	195,579	$5,992,862	$13,575,412	$462,707	$89,497	$372,880
Schleicher	4,172	361	111,024	$53,548	$1,143,550	$242,715	$43,932	$198,346
Scurry	24,053	687	656,803	$2,516,860	$12,534,974	$1,812,464	$1,226,392	$585,472
Shackelford	4,349	355	152,267	$295,916	$3,064,265	$431,831	$130,485	$300,912
Shelby	27,797	877	818,014	$12,740,590	$22,696,571	$2,023,705	$1,326,875	$695,484
Sherman	3,038	445	260,274	$4,077,199	$6,965,091	$260,431	$13,925	$246,483
Smith	236,945	1,616	6,014,951	$87,268,533	$132,904,372	$18,842,102	$15,161,491	$3,660,312
Somervell	11,739	199	280,531	$1,927,687	$4,091,062	$678,959	$313,855	$363,429
Starr	58,728	547	1,067,563	$22,488,445	$28,715,135	$4,014,784	$2,961,159	$1,051,714
Stephens	9,554	559	230,315	$3,723,188	$15,615,103	$657,510	$253,389	$403,568
Sterling	2,328	309	264,131	$1,086,626	$3,530,867	$117,816	$21,222	$96,436
Stonewall	1,844	327	75,760	$22,985,445	$29,440,342	$108,603	$13,613	$94,969
Sutton	5,363	591	701,446	$27,026,368	$33,951,665	$326,809	$83,660	$242,920
Swisher	6,671	819	414,305	$1,409,545	$8,001,682	$417,342	$69,500	$347,268
Tarrant	1,720,389	3,481	36,942,754	$624,896,698	$749,429,882	$146,710,045	$124,520,762	$22,004,585
Taylor	133,212	1,200	2,928,008	$43,602,890	$66,783,713	$10,403,592	$8,487,932	$1,904,102
Terrell	1,135	375	95,079	$671,633	$1,919,489	$45,011	$5,085	$50,070
Terry	11,410	628	561,354	$5,580,692	$20,810,925	$798,397	$307,492	$490,292
Throckmorton	2,213	343	65,562	$1,170,111	$7,426,790	$138,108	$5,350	$132,671
Titus	31,956	587	1,169,760	$18,590,963	$29,374,690	$2,437,564	$1,700,756	$735,710
Tom Green	121,021	1,055	1,935,676	$15,592,774	$40,768,402	$9,185,114	$7,199,590	$1,975,533
Travis	993,487	2,203	22,557,022	$767,948,878	$934,567,499	$94,471,884	$80,937,963	$13,409,178
Trinity	16,636	444	423,082	$749,478	$6,939,689	$1,001,087	$497,841	$502,385
Tyler	22,398	517	566,815	$45,120,215	$54,671,338	$1,405,149	$803,884	$600,573
Upshur	44,995	789	1,104,451	$11,500,992	$20,842,480	$2,745,662	$1,892,117	$851,728
Upton	4,990	392	339,318	$35,535,427	$41,856,640	$413,814	$153,197	$260,552
Uvalde	27,078	766	685,234	$2,075,961	$7,896,127	$1,936,222	$1,345,020	$590,032
Val Verde	47,838	748	566,174	$7,691,819	$13,429,621	$3,807,986	$2,851,460	$953,033
Van Zandt	65,789	1,174	2,697,886	$18,241,141	$54,140,790	$4,389,659	$3,251,151	$1,134,471
Victoria	88,713	935	2,262,000	$46,084,545	$70,421,875	$6,994,223	$5,451,890	$1,534,249
Walker	57,966	838	2,889,648	$40,823,482	$54,506,355	$3,959,996	$2,907,316	$1,047,409
Waller	62,093	607	2,382,737	$51,965,428	$71,223,856	$4,585,115	$3,554,961	$1,026,561
Ward	15,945	670	1,418,484	$12,554,440	$50,902,361	$1,280,985	$978,152	$302,329
Washington	45,174	660	1,539,269	$10,253,460	$25,423,778	$3,281,405	$2,431,875	$845,618
Webb	228,508	1,223	3,690,242	$161,651,324	$193,003,084	$24,321,647	$19,002,299	$5,312,279
Wharton	48,662	922	1,697,291	$73,273,704	$148,908,351	$3,689,632	$2,790,355	$896,931
Wheeler	6,249	674	561,400	$1,998,179	$13,028,366	$405,609	$65,796	$339,586
Wichita	109,333	1,132	2,390,126	$17,746,867	$33,081,848	$8,127,938	$6,407,571	$1,712,891
Wilbarger	12,164	729	683,968	$10,023,650	$20,697,769	$863,977	$360,981	$501,876
Willacy	15,855	525	564,475	$16,144,275	$21,236,692	$1,090,661	$574,138	$515,470
Williamson	552,110	1,733	11,215,394	$108,479,212	$121,923,575	$45,701,471	$37,795,640	$7,836,294
Wilson	65,757	741	1,185,692	$9,891,960	$25,243,459	$4,141,089	$3,132,089	$1,004,607
Winkler	10,454	292	594,068	$28,553,592	$55,641,505	$996,606	$674,092	$322,212
Wise	99,687	914	2,855,699	$26,392,285	$37,476,308	$7,324,905	$5,866,903	$1,452,201
Wood	56,743	910	1,022,171	$4,840,016	$17,451,090	$3,746,444	$2,696,921	$1,043,742
Yoakum	10,961	431	311,606	$1,442,177	$3,497,664	$889,001	$416,794	$471,713
Young	23,681	702	395,911	$2,145,191	$12,973,631	$1,708,590	$1,098,520	$608,577
Zapata	11,944	289	299,312	$12,906,347	$15,745,760	$773,877	$395,165	$378,515
Zavala	9,052	541	449,538	$980,001	$6,915,754	$614,669	$266,345	$348,214
Total	25,965,558	200,723	610,631,202	$11,342,538,372	$15,828,043,096	$2,110,958,756	$1,669,165,227	$439,752,946

Texas Major Toll Roads					
Facilities	Authority	2022	2020	2015	2010
Roads	(Tolls Collected in thousands of dollars)				
Camino Colombia Toll Road	TxDOT	—	$883,839	$1,073,604	$359,799
Central Texas Turnike System	Texas Turnpike Authority	$270,523	$253,015	$2,112,475	$109,850
Dallas North Tollway	Texas Turnpike Authority	$1,060,449	$1,077,391	$793,984	$1,383,578
U.S. 183A Toll Road	Central Texas Regional Mobility Authority	$179,185	$193,393	$172,811	$196,378
Fort Bend Toll Road	Fort Bend Toll Road Authority	$69,589	$8,313	$75,760	$16,328
Harris County Toll Facilities[1]	Harris County Toll Road Authority	$1,305,087	$15,662	$745,373	$1,858,583
TOTAL		$2,884,833	$2,431,613	$4,974,007	$3,924,516

[1]Including Harris County includes Harris County Toll Road and the Jesse Jones Memorial Toll Bridge.
Source: Highway Statistics annual, Federal Highway Administration; and local toll authorities.

Toll Bridges						
Facilities	Authority	2022	2021	2020	2015	2010
Bridge	(Tolls Collected in thousands of dollars)					
Cameron County International Toll Bridge	Cameron County	$34,447	$15,751	$20,789	$21,273	$22,102
Del Rio International	City of Del Rio	$8,302	$5,621	$8,313	$6,558	$4,144
Eagle Pass-Piedras Negras International	City of Eagle Pass	$20,646	$12,431	$15,662	$10,737	$8,106
Laredo-Nuevo Laredo International	City of Laredo	$79,841	$66,989	$71,036	$69,215	$41,449
McAllen International	City of McAllen	$13,716	$10,263	$18,734	$19,799	$11,036
Pharr-Reynosa International	City of Pharr	$41,990	$63,253	$14,539	$13,196	$10,639
Roma International	Starr County	$2,336	$1,789	$2,420	$2,988	$2,081
San Luis Pass–Vacek	Galveston County	$583	$597	$4,032	$3,128	$1,265
Zaragosa Bridge	City of El Paso	$27,284	$25,207	$23,875	$21,499	$16,094
Zaragosa	City of El Paso	$229,145	$201,901	$179,400	$168,393	$116,916
TOTAL		$179,400	$173,861	$177,197	$168,393	$132,404

Source: Highway Statistics annual, Federal Highway Administration.

TEXAS DRIVERS

The following list shows the number of licensed drivers by year for Texas and for all the states. Sources are the Texas Department of Public Safety (for state figures) and the Federal Highway Administration.

Year	Texas Licensed Drivers	Total U.S. Licensed Drivers
2023	19,159,360	237,655,885
2022	18,738,980	235,086,153
2021	18,297,900	232,781,797
2020	17,667,039	228,195,802
2010	16,808,359	210,114,939
2000	14,024,305	190,625,023
1990	11,136,694	167,015,250
1980	9,287,286	145,295,036
1970	6,380,057	111,542,787
1960	4,352,168	87,252,563
1950	2,687,349	59,322,278

MOTOR VEHICLE CRASHES AND DEATHS

Even though Texans traveled more miles in 2023, the number of motor vehicle traffic fatalities on Texas roadways decreased from 2022 to 2023 by 2.81%.

Based on data from the Texas Department of Transportation:

- 1 person died every 2 hours, 3 minutes.
- 1 person was injured every 2 minutes, 6 seconds.
- 1 reportable crash occurred every 56 seconds.
- Texas roadways did not experience any deathless days.

Year	Deaths	% Increase or Decrease (Deaths)	Vehicle Miles Traveled/VMT (in millions)	% Increase or Decrease (VMT)	Deaths per 100 mill miles	Economic loss (in millions)
2023	4,283	-2.81%	294,785	1.34%	1.45	$56,200
2022	4,407	-1.10%	290,891	2.06%	1.52	$57,800
2021	4,456	14.32%	285,028	9.38%	1.56	$55,600
2020	3,898	7.62%	260,580	-9.59%	1.5	$44,600
2019	3,622	-0.96%	288,227	2.19%	1.26	$40,400
2018	3,657	-1.85%	282,037	3.32%	1.3	$39,700
2017	3,726	-1.79%	272,981	0.63%	1.36	$39,400
2016	3,794	5.83%	271,263	5.09%	1.4	$38,800
2015	3,585	1.33%	258,122	6.23%	1.39	$36,700
2014	3,538	3.85%	242,989	-0.63%	1.46	$38,100
2013	3,407	-0.29%	244,536	2.82%	1.39	$27,800
2012	3,417	11.38%	237,821	0.16%	1.44	$26,000
2011	3,068	0.26%	237,443	1.36%	1.29	$23,400
2010	3,060	-1.99%	234,261	0.98%	1.31	$22,300
2009	3,122	-10.26%	231,976	-1.12%	1.35	$21,300
2008	3,479	0.49%	234,593	-2.96%	1.48	$22,900
2007	3,462	-1.68%	241,746	2.22%	1.43	$20,600
2006	3,521	-1.04%	236,486	0.96%	1.49	$20,400
2005	3,558	-3.84%	234,231	2.13%	1.52	$19,200
2004	3,700	-3.19%	229,345	5.10%	1.61	$19,400
2003	3,822	-0.03%	218,209	1.08%	1.75	$20,700

Source: Texas Department of Transportation (TxDOT).

FOREIGN CONSULATES IN TEXAS

In the list below, these abbreviations appear after the name of the city:
(CG) Consulate General; **(C)** Consulate; **(VC)** Vice Consulate; and **(HC)** Honorary Consulate.

ALBANIA: VACANT
ANGOLA: Houston (CG)
ARGENTINA: Houston (CG)
AUSTRALIA: Houston (CG)
AUSTRIA: Houston (C)
BAHAMAS: Houston (HC)
BARBADOS: Houston (HC)
BELGIUM: Austin (HC); Dallas (HC); Houston (HC)
BELIZE: Dallas (HC)
BOLIVIA: Houston (C)
BOTSWANA: Houston (HC)
BRAZIL: Houston (CG)
BURKINA FASO: Houston (HC)
CANADA: Dallas (CG); Houston (C); Austin (HC)
CHILE: Houston (CG); San Antonio (HC)
COLOMBIA: Houston (CG)
COSTA RICA: Houston (CG)
CROATIA: Houston (HC)
CYPRUS: Houston (HC)
CZECH REPUBLIC: Houston (HC)
DENMARK: Houston (CG); Dallas (HC)
DOMINICAN REPUBLIC: Houston (CG)
ECUADOR: Houston (CG)
EGYPT: Houston (CG)
EL SALVADOR: Dallas (CG); El Paso (CG); Houston (CG); San Antonio (CG); McAllen (CG)
EQUATORIAL GUINEA: Houston (CG)
ESTONIA: Dallas (HC); Houston (HC)
ETHIOPIA: Houston (HC)
FINLAND: Dallas (HC); Houston (HC)
FRANCE: Houston (CG); Dallas (HC); El Paso (HC); San Antonio (HC)
GEORGIA: Houston (HC)
GERMANY: Houston (CG); Austin (HC); Dallas (HC)
GREECE: Houston (C)
GUATEMALA: Houston (CG); Del Rio (C); McAllen (C)
GUYANA: Houston (HC)
HONDURAS: Dallas (CG); Houston (CG); McAllen (CG)
HUNGARY: Houston (CG)
ICELAND: Dallas (HC); Houston (HC)
INDIA: Houston (CG)
INDONESIA: Houston (CG)
IRELAND: Austin (CG)
ISRAEL: Houston (CG)
ITALY: Houston (CG); Dallas (HC)
JAMAICA: Houston (HC)
JAPAN: Houston (CG); Plano (HC)
KAZAKHSTAN: VACANT
KOREA: Houston (CG); Dallas (C)
LATVIA: Houston (HC)
LEBANON: VACANT
LITHUANIA: Houston (HC)
LUXEMBOURG: Austin (HC)
MALAWI: Wimberley (HC)
MALI: Austin (HC)
MALTA: Dallas (HC)
MEXICO: Austin (CG); Dallas (CG); Del Rio (C); Eagle Pass (C); El Paso (CG); Houston (CG); Laredo (CG); Presidio (CG); San Antonio (CG); Brownsville (C); McAllen (C)
MONACO: Dallas (HC)
NAMIBIA: Houston (HC); San Antonio (HC)
NEW ZEALAND: Houston (HC)
NICARAGUA: Houston (CG)
NORWAY: Dallas (HC); Katy (HC)
PAKISTAN: Houston (CG)
PANAMA: Houston (CG)
PARAGUAY: Bellaire (HC); Dallas (HC)
PERU: Dallas (CG); Houston (CG)
PHILIPPINES: Houston (CG)
POLAND: Houston (CG)
PORTUGAL: Houston (HC)
QATAR: Houston (CG)
ROMANIA: VACANT
RUSSIA: Houston (CG)
RWANDA: Houston (HC)
SAUDI ARABIA: Houston (CG)
SIERRA LEONE: Dallas (HC)
SLOVAKIA: Dallas (HC)
SLOVENIA: Houston (HC)
SOUTH AFRICA: Dallas (HC)
SPAIN: Houston (C); Austin (HC); Corpus Christi (HC); Dallas (HC); El Paso (HC); San Antonio (HC)
SRI LANKA: Houston (HC)
SWEDEN: Houston (HC); Dallas (HC)
SWITZERLAND: Dallas (HC); Houston (HC)
TAIWAN: Houston (DG);
THAILAND: Houston (HC)
TRINIDAD AND TOBAGO: Houston (HC)
TUNISIA: Houston (HC)
TURKEY: Houston (CG)
UKRAINE: Houston (CG)
UNITED ARAB EMIRATES: Houston (CG)
UNITED KINGDOM: Houston (CG); Dallas (HC); San Antonio (HC)
URUGUAY: Houston (HC)
VIETNAM: Houston (CG)

Source: Texas Secretary of State and individual consulates, as of March 2025.

FOREIGN-TRADE ZONES IN TEXAS

Foreign-trade-zone status endows a domestic site with certain customs privileges, causing it to be considered outside customs territory and therefore available for activities that might otherwise be carried on overseas.

Operated as public utilities for qualified corporations, the zones are established under grants of authority from the Foreign-Trade Zones board, which is chaired by the U.S. Secretary of Commerce. Zone facilities are available for operations involving storage, repacking, inspection, exhibition, assembly, manufacturing, and other processing.

A foreign-trade zone is especially suitable for export processing or manufacturing operations when foreign components or materials with a high U.S. duty are needed to make the end product competitive in markets abroad.

In 2024, 35 Foreign-Trade Zones existed in Texas.

Zone	Location	Port of Entry	Address	Phone
12	McAllen	Hidalgo	6401 S. 33rd Street, 78503	(956) 682-4306
36	Galveston	Galveston	123 Rosenberg Ave. 8th Floor, 77550	(409) 766-6203
39	Dallas/Fort Worth Airport	Dallas-Fort Worth	P.O. Box 619428, 2400 Aviation Drive, DFW Airport 75261	(972) 973-4649
62	Brownsville	Brownsville-Cameron	1000 Foust Road, 78521	(956) 592-3961
68	El Paso	El Paso	501 George Perry, Suite I, 79925	(915) 212-0480
80	San Antonio	San Antonio	100 W. Houston, Ste. 1800, 78205	(210) 207-3906
84	Houston	Houston	111 East Loop North, 77029-4327	(713) 670-2576
94	Laredo	Laredo	4719 Maher Av., 78041	(956) 795-2000 x2822
95	Starr County	Rio Grande City	P.O. Box 502, Rio Grande City 78582	(956) 487-2709
96	Eagle Pass	Eagle Pass	100 S. Monroe, 78852	(830) 773-1111 x2003
113	Ellis County	Dallas-Fort Worth	P.O. Box 788, Midlothian 75065	(972) 723-5522
115	Beaumont	Port Arthur	P.O. Drawer 2297, 77704	(409) 835-5367
116	Port Arthur	Port Arthur	P.O. Drawer 2297, Beaumont 77704	(409) 835-5367
117	Orange	Port Arthur	P.O. Drawer 2297, Beaumont 77704	(409) 835-5367
122	Corpus Christi	Corpus Christi	400 Charles Zahn, Jr. Drive, 78401	(361) 885-6187
149	Freeport	Freeport	1100 Cherry Street, 77541	(979) 233-2667 x4315
150	El Paso	El Paso	1865 Northwestern Dr., 79912	(915) 877-4300
155	Calhoun/Victoria counties	Port Lavaca	P.O. Drawer 397, Point Comfort 77978	(361) 987-2813
156	Hidalgo County	Progreso	100 E. Cano, Suite 201, Edinburg 78539	(956) 318-2600
165	Midland	Midland International Airport	9506 Laforce Blvd., P.O. Box 60305, Midland 79711	(432) 560-2200
168	Dallas	Dallas-Fort Worth	P.O. Box 613307, 75261	(972) 357-1044
171	Liberty County	Houston	117 Cook Street, Dayton 77535	(281) 659-7213
183	Austin	Austin	c/o Opportunity Austin 200 W. 6th Street, Suite 1750, 78701	(512) 595-0741
196	Fort Worth	Fort Worth Alliance Airport	9800 Hillwood Parkway, Suite 300, 76177	(817) 224-6356
199	Texas City	Houston	1801 9th Avenue N., 77590	(409) 643-5927
234	Gregg County	Shreveport-Bossier City, LA	269 Terminal Circle, Longview 75603	(903) 643-3031
246	Waco	Dallas-Fort Worth	P.O. Box 1220, 76703	(254) 752-6551
252	Amarillo	Amarillo	600 S. Tyler St., Suite 1600, 79101	(806) 379-6411
258	Bowie County	Shreveport-Bossier City, LA	107 Chapel Lane, New Boston 75570	(903) 223-9841
260	Lubbock	Lubbock	1500 Broadway, 6th Floor, 79401	(806) 723-8227
265	Conroe (Montgomery County)	Houston	300 W Davis, Suite 500, 77305	(936) 522-3530
269	Athens	Dallas-Fort Worth	201 W. Corsicana St., Suite 3, 75751	(903) 675-4617
297	Lufkin	Port Arthur	P.O. Box 190, 300 E. Shepherd, 75902	(936) 633-0221
299	Smith County	Shreveport-Bossier City, LA	315 N. Broadway, Suite 300, Tyler 75702	(903) 595-1064
302	Socorro	Tornillo	124 Horizon Boulevard, 79927	(915) 275-1039

Source: U.S. Department of Commerce.

UNSPLASH/VENTI VIEWS

ANNUAL TONNAGE HANDLED BY TEXAS PORTS

The table below gives consolidated tonnage (x1,000) handled by Texas ports. All figures are in short tons (2,000 lbs.). Note that "—" indicates no commerce was reported and "0" means tonnage reported was less than 500 tons.

Port	2022	2021	2020	2015	2010	2005	2000
Beaumont	74,343	74,555	70,567	87,170	76,959	78,887	76,894
Brownsville	9,105	8,860	6,782	7,779	4,616	5,105	3,268
Corpus Christi	174,327	164,448	150,755	85,647	73,663	77,637	81,164
Freeport	31,550	42,243	38,749	21,133	26,676	33,602	28,966
Galveston	13,530	12,012	11,945	10,381	13,949	8,008	10,402
Houston	293,834	266,524	275,940	240,933	227,133	211,666	186,567
Matagorda Channel (Port Lavaca)	4,424	4,008	4,760	11,821	8,879	11,607	10,552
Port Arthur	47,506	40,224	41,222	35,787	30,232	26,385	20,524
Sabine Pass	29,194	26,733	23,000	418	2,494	641	910
Texas City	32,855	27,951	33,347	42,924	56,591	57,839	58,109
Victoria Channel	1,995	1,855	2,033	6,733	2,792	3,224	5,104
Anahuac	—	—	—	—	—	—	—
Aransas Pass	29	48	38	917	173	128	6
Arroyo Colorado	1,768	2,454	1,658	260	411	791	837
Cedar Bayou	847	729	1,071	1,271	931	1,172	1,002
Chocolate Bayou	1,045	1,193	1,134	1,171	1,005	3,537	3,488
Clear Creek	—	—	—	—	—	—	—
Colorado River	1,063	799	781	848	671	501	445
Dickinson	422	429	365	491	93	688	904
Double Bayou	—	—	—	—	—	257	0
Greens Bayou	7,916	6,856	3,984	6,427	5,523	3,768	0
Harbor Island (Port Aransas)	32	55	77	28	1	10	151
Liberty Channel	—	—	808	16	5	—	—
Orange	4,068	2,315	4,095	838	684	627	681
Palacios	—	—	—	—	—	—	—
Port Isabel	8	108	31	0	0	—	5
Port Mansfield	—	—	—	—	—	—	—
Rockport	—	—	—	—	—	—	—
San Bernard River	40,071	33,885	41,203	317	371	773	633

Source: U.S. Army Corps of Engineers.

Foreign/Domestic Commerce: Breakdown for 2022

Data below represent inbound and outbound tonnage for major ports. Note that "—" means no tonnage was reported. All figures in short tons x1000.

Source: U.S. Army Corps of Engineers.

Port	Foreign		Domestic		
	Imports	Exports	Receipts	Shipments	Local
Beaumont	13,749	39,293	5,949	15,064	289
Brownsville	5,498	987	2,293	286	41
Corpus Christi	17,184	131,403	5,035	17,210	3,434
Freeport	5,263	20,037	2,955	3,294	—
Galveston	1,841	3,448	5,134	2,987	120
Houston	47,860	109,525	1,625	11,032	75,502
Matagorda Chl. (Port Lavaca)	697	1,677	21	386	1,643
Port Arthur	9,996	21,247	6,360	9,093	811
Sabine Pass	23	447	192	29	—
Texas City	4,518	15,213	3,352	9,598	176
Victoria	—	—	616	1,379	—

Gulf Intracoastal Waterway by Commodity (Texas portion)

All figures in short tons x1000.

Source: U.S. Army Corps of Engineers.

Commodity	2022	2021	2020	2015	2010	2005	2000
Coal	176	183	242	125	93	335	121
Petroleum products	57,963	50,264	50,103	57,224	49,219	39,538	34,816
Chemicals	17,378	17,784	16,791	17,475	17,553	20,668	21,382
Raw materials	2,250	2,902	5,540	3,910	3,123	4,898	5,822
Manufactured goods	2,163	1,443	1,705	1,631	1,646	2,449	2,301
Food, farm products	446	331	433	903	574	473	960
Total	**80,376**	**72,907**	**74,814**	**81,268**	**72,917**	**69,549**	**66,440**

U.S. Ports Ranked by Tonnage

(2022, short tons)

Houston Port Authority........... 293,833,530
Port of South Louisiana 226,188,142
Corpus Christi 174,327,410
New York, NY & NJ 141,290,423
Port of Long Beach, CA 92,958,926
New Orleans, LA 83,254,102
Beaumont 74,342,746
Port of Greater Baton Rouge, LA......73,371,577
Port of Virginia, VA.........................69,433,624
Lake Charles Harbor District, LA ...64,107,156

States Ranked by Tonnage

(2022, x1,000 short tons)

1. **Texas...651,711**
2. Louisiana..526,510
3. California 238,154
4. New Jersey 149,774
5. Washington 107,200
6. Florida 101,936
7. Kentucky 77,624
8. Illinois...72,403
9. Virginia..72,177
10. Alabama..64,969

BORDER CROSSINGS

Texas maintains 32 ports of entry into the United States, which is more than any other state in the country. The table below shows incoming border traffic through Texas ports of entry with data from the U.S. Bureau of Transportation Statistics.

Entering at Border	2024 U.S. total	2024 TX Total, % of U.S. Total	2024	2023	2022	2021
Buses	182,876	39.77%	72,731	64,322	59,303	51,990
Bus Passengers	3,288,966	48.15%	1,583,777	1,848,720	1,352,569	1,072,170
Personal Vehicles	99,448,048	35.09%	34,896,618	34,326,705	32,590,240	24,892,826
Personal Vehicle Passengers	183,133,011	36.12%	66,145,500	64,127,033	60,224,826	42,755,878
Pedestrians	41,036,476	42.20%	17,315,958	16,047,358	14,034,169	10,770,832
Trucks	13,167,757	40.75%	5,366,231	5,140,784	5,053,160	4,870,401
Truck Containers (Empty)	3,854,380	46.49%	1,791,971	1,598,889	1,433,034	1,581,440
Truck Containers (Loaded)	18,449,970	41.93%	7,736,223	3,991,728	3,489,418	3,269,601
Trains	32,307	30.84%	9,965	9,473	9,431	9,023
Train Passengers	319,327	8.20%	26,196	4,742	918	13,063
Rail Containers (Empty)	1,481,616	40.02%	592,899	540,733	541,963	586,375
Rail Containers (Loaded)	2,128,724	23.35%	497,148	506,617	480,630	448,006

TEXAS AIRPORTS

In 1945, the Texas Aeronautics Commission (TAC) was created and directed by the Legislature to encourage, foster, and assist in the development of aeronautics within the state, and to encourage the establishment of airports and air navigational facilities. The Commission's first annual report of December 31, 1946, stated that Texas had 592 designated airports and 7,756 civilian aircraft.

The TAC's commitment to providing air transportation was strengthened in 1989 when the TAC became the Texas Department of Aviation (TDA). On September 1, 1991, when the Texas Department of Transportation (TxDOT) was created, the TDA became the Aviation Division within the department.

The primary responsibilities of the Aviation Division include providing engineering and technical services for planning, constructing, and maintaining aeronautical facilities in the state. It is also responsible for long-range aviation facility development planning (statewide system of airports) and applying for, receiving, and disbursing federal funds.

In the Texas Airport System Plan, TxDOT has identified 289 airports and three heliports. Of the airports, 26 are commercial airports, 24 are reliever airports, and 239 are general aviation airports.

Additionally, TxDOT's Aviation Division has requested Federal Aviation Administration Reliever status for five airports. These include the privately owned Austin Executive and Houston Executive airports, as well as the publicly owned New Braunfels Municipal, Mid-Way Regional (at Midlothian), and Cleburne municipal airports.

Commercial-service airports provide scheduled passenger service. Reliever airports are a special class of general aviation airports designated by the Federal Aviation Administration (FAA). They provide alternative landing facilities in the metropolitan areas separate from the commercial-service airports and, together with the business/corporate airports, provide access for business and executive turbine-powered aircraft.

The community-service and basic-service airports provide access for single- and multi-engine, piston-powered aircraft to smaller communities throughout the state. Some community-service airports are also capable of accommodating light jets.

TxDOT is charged by the Legislature with planning, programming, and implementing improvement projects at the general aviation airports. In carrying out these responsibilities, TxDOT channels the Airport Improvement Program (AIP) funds provided by the FAA for all general aviation airports in Texas.

Since 1993, TxDOT has participated in the FAA's state block grant demonstration program. Under this program, TxDOT assumes most of the FAA's responsibility for the administration of the AIP funds for airports.

The Aviation Facilities Development Program (AFDP) oversees planning and research, assists with engineering and technical services, and provides financial assistance through state grants to public bodies operating airports for the purpose of establishing, constructing, reconstructing, enlarging, or repairing airports, airstrips, or navigational facilities.

UNSPLASH/ROYAL OXFORD

Source: Texas Transportation Institute.

PLANE PASSENGERS BY AIRPORT

Airport	2023	2022	2021	2020	2015
Abilene	79,831	70,419	75,402	44,202	88,959
Amarillo	397,983	358,360	303,904	173,469	347,304
Austin	10,833,443	10,382,573	6,666,215	3,141,505	5,643,251
Beaumont	32,150	24,882	21,914	15,792	35,557
Brownsville	176,056	127,239	167,957	93,145	147,831
College Station	60,072	54,542	67,033	41,790	91,243
Corpus Christi	352,224	319,687	285,195	162,161	339,105
DFW	39,246,212	35,345,138	30,005,266	18,593,421	31,356,173
Dallas/Love	8,559,052	7,819,129	6,487,563	3,669,930	6,495,869
Del Rio*	5,320	26,641	19,879	8,296	—
El Paso	2,018,137	1,931,067	1,438,321	760,165	1,370,243
Harlingen	536,510	508,867	355,190	172,878	263,423
Houston/Bush	22,228,844	19,814,052	16,242,821	8,682,558	20,346,164
Houston/Hobby	6,800,320	6,462,948	5,560,780	3,127,178	5,765,544
Killeen-Ft. Hood	113,701	126,160	142,253	102,324	153,698
Laredo	151,114	139,396	108,992	52,612	113,176
Longview	32,613	25,982	23,942	14,632	19,871
Lubbock	543,363	489,710	405,157	253,126	446,081
McAllen	513,770	452,925	477,636	191,497	390,358
Midland	684,419	633,964	504,264	319,570	533,049
San Angelo	51,865	54,347	60,115	35,595	64,901
San Antonio	5,336,684	4,751,610	3,677,643	1,919,958	4,057,345
Texarkana	41,951	35,590	26,888	17,340	35,469
Tyler	50,155	40,548	39,943	29,133	77,543
Victoria	11,293	7,505	6,610	2,837	3,129
Waco	51,867	54,899	47,541	27,704	63,256
Wichita Falls	25,075	27,720	32,038	21,272	45,426
TOTAL	**98,936,047**	**90,085,900**	**73,250,462**	**41,674,090**	**70,334,187**

*Del Rio lost commercial service in 2013 and regained service in 2018. Calendar year data.
Sources: FAA Terminal Area Forecasts and Passenger Enplanement for U.S. Airports 2023.

TEXAS AIR HISTORY

Passengers enplaned in Texas by scheduled carriers. A scheduled airline runs on specific routes at specific times. Texarkana is not included here.

Year	Passengers	Year	Passengers
2023	98,922,499	2000	65,090,784
2022	90,089,634	1995	57,166,515
2021	73,274,996	1990	49,317,029
2020	41,687,899	1985	40,659,223
2019	91,618,421	1980	26,216,873
2018	86,428,773	1975	13,182,957
2017	80,223,633	1970	10,256,691
2016	80,187,617	1965	5,757,689
2015	78,261,315	1960	3,113,582
2010	66,850,320	1950	1,169,051
2005	65,718,669		

Source: Federal Aviation Administration (by fiscal year).

Leading U.S. Airlines by Passengers (2023)		
Rank	Airline	Passengers
1	**Southwest Airlines**	**171,816,815**
2	**American Airlines**	**164,370,684**
3	Delta Air Lines	161,612,456
4	United Airlines	133,994,004
5	Spirit Airlines	44,019,368
6	JetBlue Airways	42,812,665
7	SkyWest Airlines	38,432,232
8	Alaska Airlines	35,169,842
9	Frontier Airlines	30,115,996
10	Republic Airways	17,573,620

Texas-based airlines in bold.
Source: U.S. Department of Transportation.

FREIGHT RAILROADS

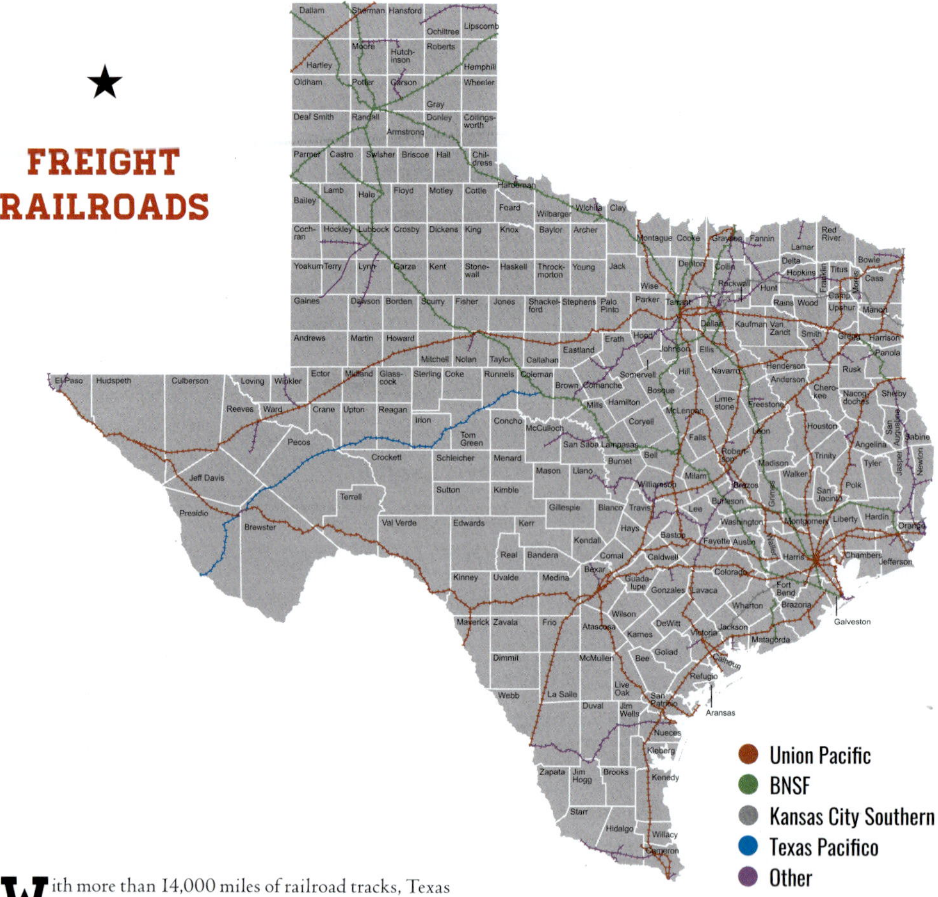

With more than 14,000 miles of railroad tracks, Texas boasts the most rail lines out of any state. Freight railroads transport essential goods such as coal, farm products, and chemicals across the nation and play a major role in Texas' economy. In 2023, railroads in the state carried some 129 million tons of freight. The leading commodities handled are listed in the table below.

In 2023, three Class I railroad companies operated through Texas. Their combined mileage made up nearly 87% of the state's total track mileage, in contrast to short line railroads, which made up about 13% of the state's total. Short line railroads connect local industries to larger rail networks.

Railroads in State	Miles Operated
Class I	12,825
Union Pacific Railroad Co.	6,498
BNSF Railway Co.	5,388
Canadian Pacific Kansas City	939
Total	**14,792**
Total excluding trackage rights*	**10,460**

*Trackage rights — track provided by another railroad.

Freight Traffic in Texas by Kind (2023)

Carloads Originated		Tons (Mil.)
Chemicals	451,500	42.5
Crushed Stone & Sand	302,900	33.0
Intermodal	899,300	12.4
Petroleum & Coal Products	124,200	10.3
Steel Products	81,800	7.5
All Other	342,800	23.4
Total	2,202.6K	129.1M

Carloads Terminated		Tons (Mil.)
Crushed Stone & Sand	442,400	48.7
Coal	352,300	42.4
Chemicals	345,500	32.8
Grain	160,700	17.3
Petroleum & Coal Products	184,300	16.3
All Other	1,587,400	58.9
Total	3,072.6K	216.4M

Source: Association of American Railroads.

U.S. FREIGHT GATEWAYS

Freight gateways serve as crucial locations for transporting goods across regions and countries. These gateways can take the form of airports, ports, or other transportation hubs. The table below highlights the top gateways in 2023 ranked by value of shipments, with Texas gateways highlighted. All figures are in billions of dollars.

Rank	Port	Mode	Exports	Imports	Total Trade	Exports as a percent of total
1	Laredo, TX	Land	$123.4	$189.5	$312.9	39.4%
2	Los Angeles, CA	Water	$32.8	$259.0	$291.8	11.2%
3	Chicago, IL	Air	$72.8	$197.3	$270.1	27.0%
4	Houston, TX	Water	$124.4	$102.0	$226.4	54.9%
5	Detroit, MI	Land	$84.9	$72.4	$157.2	54.0%
6	Los Angeles International Airport, CA	Air	$57.3	$72.9	$130.1	44.0%
7	Port Huron, MI	Land	$53.3	$57.0	$110.3	48.3%
8	Long Beach, CA	Water	$26.4	$81.4	$107.8	24.5%
9	Charleston, SC	Water	$26.8	$68.2	$94.9	28.2%
10	Buffalo-Niagara Falls, NY	Land	$45.7	$43.1	$88.8	51.5%
11	Corpus Christi, TX	Water	$80.4	$5.4	$85.8	93.7%
12	Cleveland, OH	Air	$47.8	$36.1	$83.9	57.0%
13	Baltimore, MD	Water	$21.8	$58.7	$80.5	27.1%
14	Ysleta Port of Entry, TX	Land	$25.8	$47.6	$73.4	35.1%
15	Dallas-Fort Worth, TX	Air	$27.3	$35.9	$63.2	43.2%
16	Otay Mesa, CA	Land	$22.2	$38.3	$60.6	36.6%
17	Anchorage, AK	Air	$18.5	$34.7	$53.1	34.8%
18	Hidalgo, TX	Land	$16.9	$27.6	$44.5	38.0%
19	Eagle Pass, TX	Land	$11.5	$25.5	$37.0	31.1%
20	Pembina, ND	Land	$17.7	$16.1	$33.9	52.2%
21	Nogales, AZ	Land	$10.3	$21.3	$31.6	32.6%
22	Santa Teresa, NM	Land	$9.9	$17.5	$27.4	36.1%
23	Champlain-Rouses Point, NY	Land	$10.2	$16.4	$26.6	38.3%
24	Blaine, WA	Land	$13.6	$12.5	$26.1	52.1%
25	Houston, TX	Land	$15.1	$6.9	$22.0	68.6%
26	Calexico-East, CA	Land	$8.5	$13.3	$21.8	39.0%
27	El Paso, TX	Land	$14.5	$7.0	$21.6	67.1%
28	Brownsville, TX	Land	$12.0	$9.1	$21.1	56.9%
29	Portal, ND	Land	$11.8	$8.5	$20.3	58.1%
30	Sweet Grass, MT	Land	$8.3	$11.5	$19.8	41.9%
31	Alexandria Bay, NY	Land	$8.7	$10.8	$19.5	44.6%
32	Cincinnati-Lawrenceburg, OH	Air	$7.3	$12.0	$19.3	37.8%
33	Houston Intercontinental Airport, TX	Air	$9.6	$7.1	$16.7	57.5%
34	Freeport, TX	Water	$11.7	$4.8	$16.6	70.5%
35	Port Hueneme, CA	Water	$0.8	$15.3	$16.1	5.0%

Source: U.S. Bureau of Transportation Statistics, National Transportation Statistics.

UNSPLASH/ADAM THOMAS

The Spanish General Bernardo de Gálvez
by Mariano Salvador Maella
c. 1783-1784

WIKIMEDIA COMMONS

WIKIMEDIA COMMONS

SPANISH TEXAS & THE AMERICAN *Revolution*

Robert T. C. Goodwin Ph.D
UNIVERSITY COLLEGE LONDON

N DECEMBER 21, 1779, a Spanish frigate sailed into the El Ferrol naval base in the far northwest of Spain. It had made the crossing from Cuba in 36 days thanks to a gale-force southwester. Captain Pedro del Barco offered a prayer of thanks for his safe homecoming, but the weather had been the least of his concerns: it was seven months to the day since Spain declared war on England. On the high seas, Barco's greatest fear was the British Royal Navy.

A militiaman from New Orleans named José Valliere disembarked with a rousing story. In the first Spanish military action of the American Revolution, Governor Bernardo de Gálvez of Louisiana had captured all the British strongholds along the lower Mississippi River in a daring campaign. It was a stunning triumph over the British that undermined their military presence on the American frontier and led to the return of Florida to Spanish control in the treaty that ended the Revolution.

In Madrid, the Universal Minister of the Indies, José de Gálvez, must have read the news with great pride. Gálvez, the hero of the moment, was his nephew. The official royal newspaper, the *Gazeta de Madrid*, published the story in its New Year edition. On January 4, 1780, Valliere reached Madrid with the Governor's dispatches and "a number of flags captured from the English."

"My lord," Gálvez wrote his uncle, "Valliere will place in Your Excellency's hands both this letter and at the same time a copy of the official report of the campaign."

Although Gálvez has been given posthumous honorary U.S. citizenship and his portrait was hung in the U.S. Capitol Building in Washington D.C., in 2014, the role played by Spain in the American Revolution has been overlooked by all but a handful of scholars. As the 250th anniversary of the Revolution approaches, a better understanding of that history is long

The Destruction of the Saint Sabá Mission in the Province of Texas and the Martyrdom of the Priests, Fray Alonso Giraldo de Terreros and Fray José de Santiesteban by José de Páez, c. 1758

overdue.[1] Spanish intervention changed the course of the war and arguably its outcome. The Spanish crown and individual Spaniards organized clandestine shipments of supplies to the rebels — most notably Diego Gardoqui, a Basque merchant who, intriguingly, is probably the same 'Mr. Gardoqui' appointed British vice-consul at Santander in 1776. Spain also provided vital strategic and financial support to the French navy that secured George Washington's victory at Yorktown. But most striking of all were Gálvez's victories on the Mississippi River in 1779, and later at Mobile (1780) and Pensacola (1781).

Bernardo's campaign on the Mississippi was a masterwork of courage, leadership, improvisation, and tactics. When a hurricane badly damaged his capital at New Orleans and sank his gunboats, delaying his march to confront professional British "redcoats," many other European military commanders would have sought an honorable capitulation. Instead, Bernardo rallied his rag-tag army of veterans, mi-

[1] The America&Spain250 initiative, launched by the Queen Sofía Spanish Institute (QSSI), highlights Spain's significant yet often overlooked role in the American Revolution and its broader contributions to U.S. history. Major projects include two history symposia led by academic directors Richard L. Kagan and Gonzalo Quintero Saravia in Madrid and D.C., events with local historical organizations across the U.S., and digital educational resources developed in partnership with the QSSI, Royal Academy of History of Spain, and the Gilder Lehrman Institute of American History.

Painting of Gálvez at the siege of Pensacola
by Augusto Ferrer-Dalmau

WIKIMEDIA COMMONS

litia, and volunteers (including free Blacks), persuaded a formidable force of Native Americans to join him, and took the fight to the enemy. He had attended the new state-of-the-art military academy at Ávila and, despite having been badly wounded in a failed attack on Algiers, conducted a careful campaign that included frontal assaults on British fortifications.

Gálvez reported to his uncle that on August 27, 1779, "our little army left the town, made up of 170 veterans, 330 raw recruits, 20 customs officers, 60 militiamen, 60 Blacks and mixed-race freemen, along with Oliver Pollock, an agent of the American Congress. . . , two American officers and seven [other American] volunteers' and 600 Arcadians and German-speakers from the Cote d'Allemandes."

In reports concerning his previous operations against the Apaches, Gálvez had recommended that Spanish commanders "take more Indian allies on campaign, for like the Apaches they are fleet of foot, skillful, and sure shots with a bow and arrow." In the following days, he persuaded 160 Opelousas and Atakapas to join him.

The *Gazeta de Madrid* reported that "the ardor with which these troops marched is inexplicable." But Gálvez had written that both Spaniards and Indian allies should be treated with "respect and friendship; indeed, if treated kindly they become so obedient that they will not complain even if you are leading them to their deaths."

They endured a grueling march through the insect-infested humidity of a Louisiana August and arrived at Fort Bute, a log post on the Mississippi northwest of New Orleans. The British left only a small defensive force, and Gálvez had the militia take it by storm, with his father-in-law leading the assault.

Gálvez then marched on Baton Rouge. Many of his men were sick, but they completed their journey "through ninety leagues of thick forest-swamp, along all but impassable roads, without tents and other equipment usually thought essential."

The British fort at Baton Rouge was formidable, with thick earthen walls, wooden palisades, a wide moat, 13 cannons, and 500 defenders (400 of whom were British soldiers). But Gálvez distracted the garrison by having his men noisily build an earthwork while he positioned his cannons on the other side of the fort. Hours of close-range bombardment convinced the British to capitulate, and their commander surrendered Fort Panmure at Natchez as well.

At Pensacola, Major General John Campbell reported to London that Gâlvez had moved so swiftly, while so effectively "stopping any communication of intelligence of his movements being sent to this place, that he had nearly effected the reduction of the western part of this province before we at Pensacola had the smallest communication of his having commenced hostilities." Spain had taken control of the lower Mississippi. The following year, Bernardo took Mobile, and the year after that, he occupied Pensacola.

It was a brilliant climax to many years of service for Gálvez, much of it in what would become the southwestern United States, including Texas. Born in July 1746 in the province of Malaga, he became a professional soldier at the age of sixteen. He arrived in New Spain in 1769 as a veteran of Spain's invasion of Portugal with the rank of lieutenant. His baptism of fire in the New World was fighting Mescalero Apaches in the Mimbres hills of southern New Mexico. The following year, he was appointed Commandant of the Nueva Vizcaya and Sonora frontier with orders to take the fight to Lipan Apache raiders in Texas. In November, he set out from Chihuahua and crossed the Rio Grande with 250 well-armed and well-provisioned troops. They pursued a large Apache force but were drenched by freezing rain that spoiled their provisions and dampened their spirits. Many deserted.

Gálvez reached the Pecos River with 130 remaining soldiers and Ópata allies at a place he named Matias's Ford after his father, now Horsehead Crossing. With so little food, his men were eating unripe dates, and there was plenty of talk in the ranks about the comfort and safety of Chihuahua. In his later report on warfare against the Apaches, Gálvez expressed his strong admiration for their resiliency and mobility, recalling that they easily outrode the more heavily encumbered Spanish soldiers. They were also skilled in surprise attacks, often striking at night.

At the Pecos, in 1770, Gálvez harangued his discordant men:

> *Soldiers, our time has come. This is our last chance to show our mettle to the world. You have confronted cold and snow with joy. We have seen Hunger thanks to rains sent from the Heavens that have spoiled our supplies. I know not how many days or months before we face the enemy. But should we go to Chihuahua now... we will blush for shame at the time and money we will have wasted.*
>
> *I will go on alone, even if none of you come with me. I will bring back a scalp to Chihuahua or I will die earning the king's bread that I have eaten. Over yonder is the road for home. Be gone, if your heart is base. But follow me if you yearn for glorious fight and no other reward than the Grace of God!*

With that, Gálvez spurred his horse into the swollen stream. His men allegedly shouted: "We will follow you to our deaths! We will eat our horses and then the very stones themselves!"

Years later, he rallied the faltering Spanish naval assault on Pensacola by shouting that he alone would sail into the bay. He subsequently chose *Yo Solo* as the motto on his coat-of-arms when Charles III elevated him as the first Count of Gálvez.

Gálvez's Indian scouts picked up the trail and his men spent the night in breathless, silent vigil, their horses saddled, all eager for the fray. As dawn approached, they surrounded the enemy camp. At first light, Gálvez yelled the ancient battle-shout of Castile: "Santiago!"

Taken unaware, some Apaches jumped into the river, where many drowned. Spaniards chased down the few who reached the other bank, taking 36 men and women captives along with 204 horses and mules. Gálvez did not lose a single soldier, while his troops killed 28 Apache men.

After two more years of military service on the northern frontier of New Spain, and having suffered several wounds, Gálvez returned to Spain with his uncle. Following military service in France and at Algiers, where he was badly wounded, he became an instructor at the Ávila academy with

Gálvez had written that both Spaniards and Indian allies should be treated with *"respect and friendship; indeed, if treated kindly they become so obedient that they will not complain even if you are leading them to their deaths"*

"No civilized person has ever seen a worse place!"

Domingo Terán de los Ríos
First Spanish Governor of Texas

the rank of colonel by the time he was 30. His uncle got him an appointment as governor of Louisiana in 1777, and during the next two years, Gálvez developed a network of friends and allies, and became a brigadier general, while pursuing an openly anti-British policy.

After all, the British had won the Seven Years' War, and as a result, Spain had lost Florida to them (although they gained Louisiana).

Gálvez's success on the lower Mississippi, and at Mobile and Pensacola, led to rapid promotions for him to lieutenant general and then field marshal. He became the governor and captain general of both Louisiana and Florida, as well as overall commander of the Spanish expeditionary army. Troops under his command occupied Nassau in the Bahamas, and only the end of the Revolution stopped him from invading Jamaica. Charles III not only made him a count, he also gave him his highest award by making him a knight. Gálvez later took charge of Cuba and finally succeeded his father as viceroy of New Spain before his death in 1786.

The victories on the lower Mississippi and at Mobile and Pensacola were not just important to Gálvez and the American Revolution, they were also high points in the history of Spain on the northern frontier of its New World empire. Spaniards had endured more than a century of military defeats and financial turmoil around the world by 1779, while provinces such as Texas had failed to yield much benefit. Throughout the history of imperial Spain, the geographic territory of modern Texas was always at the margin of the empire.

It may be useful to think of Texas as the "Beyond" — a land and people outside all but the thinnest of Spanish pretenses to colonial control. In 1691, after a year of struggle and setback, the first Spanish governor of Texas, Domingo Terán de los Ríos, sailed away from Matagorda Bay, concluding "no civilized person has ever seen a worse place." So it was a surprise to many when an officer with military experience in Texas, and with support from Texans, won such a great success against the British during the fight for American independence.

The first Spaniards to be reliably documented in Texas were the survivors of Pánfilo Narváez's failed expedition to Florida. In April 1528, 300 men disembarked somewhere near Tampa Bay and marched inland. Confused by geographical reality, struggling in an unfamiliar landscape, assailed by hostile Native Americans, and struck by disease, Narváez gave up. At Apalache Bay, he ordered his men to build five makeshift barges, hoping to follow the coast to what they believed to be the nearby Spanish outpost at Pánuco, in reality 1,500 miles away.

All five vessels wrecked on the Texas coast in November 1528, two on Galveston Island, which was ironically later named in honor of Gálvez. By 1530, only four survivors were known to have been alive: Álvar Núñez Cabeza de Vaca, Alonso del Castillo, Andrés Dorantes, and Dorantes's African slave, who had been baptized Esteban.

In 1536, Spanish slave-raiders in Sonora were amazed to meet these four men, dressed as shamans, and accompanied by 600 Native Americans. They had escaped from their Karankawa captors and had an extraordinary tale to tell about possible riches, which spread quickly and inspired several others to explore the northern frontier of New Spain.

When Cabeza de Vaca reached Spain, in 1537, Charles V appointed him governor of the River Plate because he had already granted the title of Adelantado of Florida to Hernando de Soto. De Soto had returned from conquering Peru "with more than a hundred thousand pesos in gold and silver." But he had to "leave behind many men of rank because of a lack of shipping."

They were the lucky ones: his next expedition foundered in the Deep South. De Soto himself died of fever on the banks of the Mississippi, on June 28, 1542. His lieutenant, Luis de Mocoso, led a party west but

Norteamérica, 1792, Jaillot-Elwe, Spanish Florida's borders after Bernardo Gálvez's military actions, which appear to include Spanish Louisiana and Spanish Texas, as well.

became lost in East Texas. They met a Native American woman who had escaped Francisco Vázquez de Coronado's expedition to the Great Plains, chasing the riches reported by De Vaca and his comrades. To their amazement, she named many of Coronado's captains. The two expeditions had come tantalizingly close to meeting, but neither found anything of value in Texas.

Texas continued to be a disappointment for Spain. In 1554, three ships bound for Spain were wrecked at Padre Island — only one of the roughly 300 passengers survived. In 1558, Guido de Lavazares recorded landing at Matagorda Bay and formally taking possession of the land for Spain, but gales blew him east to Florida. Spanish imperial ambitions in North America were by then focused on the Pueblos of the Upper Rio Grande. A handful of expeditions traveled through West Texas and north up the Pecos River. Juan de Oñate's massive expedition in 1598 settled the Upper Rio Grande.

In 1680, the Pueblos temporarily expelled the Spanish empire from New Mexico, leading to the establishment of Corpus Christi de la Ysleta, the first mission in Texas. Four years later, Spanish officials learned that a Frenchman, René-Robert Cavelier, Sieur de la Salle, was intending to establish a settlement somewhere between the Mississippi and the Rio Grande. Alonso de León led three expeditions into Texas but found no sign of La Salle.

Later, in 1688, an apparent survivor of the La Salle expedition was found living with Indians. He led De León to the site of La Salle's fort, but all they found was wreckage and some human remains. After speaking with two other French survivors living with local Indians, De León rode home and reported to the viceroy that only a strong military presence could control a territory such as Texas.

The viceroy ordered De León to help Father Damián Massanet, who had been with the last expedition searching for La Salle, found a mission in East Texas to counter more French intrusions. The first Spanish governor of Texas, Domingo Terán de los Ríos, crossed the Rio Grande in the spring of 1691 with 50 soldiers and a baker's dozen of Franciscans, and two missions were built in East Texas. But food was short, the priests and nearby Indians suffered from disease. When the latter became hostile, the surviving Franciscans burned the remaining mission and fled. In the dead of night, on October 25, Massanet set fire to his mission and fled. Texas remained a cemetery of colonial dreams.

WIKIMEDIA COMMONS

At Mission San Juan Bautista, on the Rio Grande near modern Laredo, a Franciscan brother who had been with Massanet, Francisco Hidalgo, refused to forget the Indians in East Texas. So, when the War of the Spanish Succession (1701-1714) led to an alliance between the crowns of France and Spain, Hidalgo begged the French governor of Louisiana to send priests to East Texas. Cadillac, keen to trade with New Spain, instead sent Louis Juchereau de Saint-Denis to investigate. When he reached San Juan Bautista in July 1714, Captain Diego Ramón arrested him, but imprisoned him in his own household. His 17-year-old granddaughter Manuela Sánchez caught the eye of his flamboyant guest, but before a wedding could be held, soldiers escorted Saint-Denis to Mexico City.

Saint-Denis told the viceroy that he was an emissary of the Téjas chiefs, who begged to be sent friars to preach the gospel. He was given a Spanish commission in an expedition to help Hidalgo reestablish the missions in East Texas. Back at San Juan Bautista, he married Manuela. Then, in 1716, he and Hidalgo initiated a multi-year effort that included building five missions with a presidio (or fort) to protect them in East Texas and another presidio and mission, later famed as the Alamo, at what is today known as San Antonio.

This campaign ended with Saint-Denis fleeing to Louisiana with Manuela after being arrested for smuggling, while the East Texas missions were abandoned when France and Spain went to war again.

At Christmas 1720, a new governor of Texas, the Marquis San Miguel de Aguayo, reached the Rio Grande with 500 men, 2,800 horses, 4,800 head of cattle, and 6,400 sheep and goats. While the livestock crossed the swollen river, he sent troops to occupy the site of La Salle's ruined fort. In East Texas, he met with local Indian leaders and exchanged gifts, then forced Saint-Denis, then in command at Natchitoches, to accept a truce on the condition that all Frenchmen vacate Texas. De Aguayo had two presidios constructed in East Texas to guard six missions, then resigned his governorship and retired into private life. Within 10 years, only one presidio and three missions remained in East Texas

Activity at San Antonio increased enough for it to become the center of politics, trade, and faith in Spanish Texas, but efforts to expand west failed miserably. In the 1700s, three short-lived missions were founded on the San Gabriel River. But the troops at the nearby presidio took up with Tonkawa women who came to the mission for spiritual enlightenment. The scandalized friars excommunicated the garrison. Later, when an Indian tailor complained that the captain had seduced his wife, the captain organized the first documented 'drive-by' shooting in Texan history.

One evening in May 1752, as two friars and the tailor were dining, a musket shot rang out. The tailor fell dead. One of the friars ran to the door. An arrow killed him outright. Soon, disaffected Tonkawa and horrified missionaries deserted the missions.

In the 1740s, Apaches began to ask for Spanish protection from Comanche raids. In Mexico City, the self-made mining magnate Pedro Romero de Terreros offered to fund his Franciscan cousin Alonso Giraldo de Terreros to found new missions intended to convert Lipan Apaches. In 1756, Terreros established a mission near the San Sabá River, with the usual presidio, and brought nine Tlaxcalan families as settlers. In June, 3,000 Apaches camped nearby, heading to the plains to hunt bison. A month later, the Apaches returned laden with meat and hides, rushing south "as if propelled by some unseen danger." As winter approached, more Apaches arrived, bringing rumors of a great Comanche army mustering to the north. The friars left the mission, reporting that "we find no reason to remain with this enterprise, which we think ill-conceived and illogical."

The end came on March 16, 1758. A volley of shots heralded an attack by Comanches and their Indian allies in which two remaining friars, seven soldiers, the mission administrator, his son, and a small child were killed, burned, or horribly mutilated. In Mexico City, Romero commissioned *The Destruction of San Sabá*, a painting attributed to José de Páez. Father Manuel Arroyo composed his *Account of the Sacrileges* in verse. Together, painting and poem offered a haunting representation of the tragedy. It was also a stark reminder of yet another military failure in Spanish Texas.

Remarkably, when a captain with 14 men arrived from the presidio, the attackers withdrew, allowing a lone Franciscan to escape. In August 1759, the Spanish launched a punitive expedition. The troops overran a Tonkawa village, killing 55 and taking 149 captives, but they failed to take a larger fortified village defended by Comanches, Wichitas, and others on the Red River. After suffering heavy casualties during a two-day battle, the Spanish retreated. Spanish Texas had met its match in the rising Comanche empire.

In 1767, the Marquis de Rubí visited Texas during an inspection tour of the northern frontier of New Spain that covered 7,600 miles in 23 months. He recommended the closing of three of the five remaining presidios in Texas, leaving only those at San Antonio and La Bahía (Goliad). The missions that depended on these garrisons for protection were also to be closed. Spanish officials accepted Rubí's declaration that the Texas operation was a "waste of money," and his recommendations were embodied in the New Regulations issued in 1772 that left the frontier province sparsely populated and thinly defended.

Such reforms made sense to leaders in Spain. The more profitable provinces south of Texas were safe since the French, whom they blamed for much of the Indian unrest, had lost Louisiana to Spain in the treaty signed in 1763, and the British had agreed to stay east of the Mississippi. Texas had never yielded much but disappointment for the Spanish empire. But then Britain's North American colonists rebelled, Spain joined the fray by declaring war on Britain in 1779, and Gálvez, a veteran of the Indian campaigns in Texas, won an unexpected, but entirely welcome, series of victories.

Moreover, Texans sent thousands of cattle and other supplies to support Gálvez's troops, expanding their contribution to American independence. Ironically, this marked the beginning of an age of revolution that would leave Spain shorn of most of its New World possessions, a portion of which went to the United States, but in 1781 no one was thinking of that. They were busy celebrating Gálvez's achievements, which led to a redrawing of the world map in favor of both the Spanish and the Americans. ★

COURTESY OF MD ANDERSON CANCER CENTER

Texas
HEALTH & SCIENCE
UNSPLASH/RYAN ZAZUETA

MEASLES OUTBREAK IN TEXAS

In 2025, Texas experienced one of the largest outbreaks of measles in recent years. As of July 1, 2025, the Texas Department of State Health Services confirmed 753 cases of measles, with 99 patients having been hospitalized. The airborne disease was declared eliminated in the United States in 2000, but declining vaccination rates, international travel, and the highly contagious nature of measles led to the outbreak.

Most cases of measles have been primarily concentrated in West Texas. With the highest number of cases, Gaines County made up 55 percent of cases in Texas in July 2025. Two school-aged children died from measles.

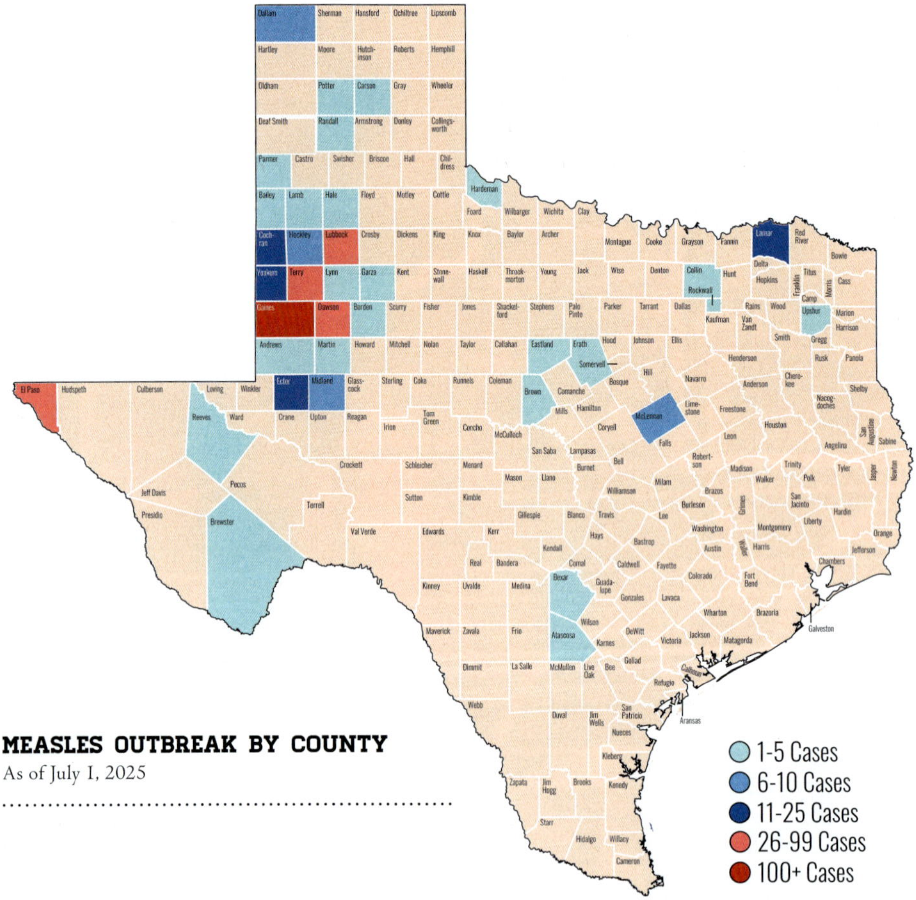

MEASLES OUTBREAK BY COUNTY

As of July 1, 2025

- 1-5 Cases
- 6-10 Cases
- 11-25 Cases
- 26-99 Cases
- 100+ Cases

Outbreak Cases by Vaccination Status

Vaccination Status	Cases
Unknown/Vaccinated	710
Vaccinated: 1 dose	22
Vaccinated: 2 doses	21

Note: The Texas Department of State Health Services updates its outbreak alert page every Tuesday. The data here is reflected as of July 1, 2025.

HEALTH IN TEXAS

The number of deaths in 2022 was 239,362, compared to 265,561 in 2021. Heart disease and cancer have been the leading causes of death in Texas and the nation since 1950 and remained the major causes of death in 2022. The leading causes of death are shown below for 2022, the latest year for which statistical breakdowns were available from the Center for Health Statistics, Texas Department of State Health Services.

LEADING CAUSES OF DEATH

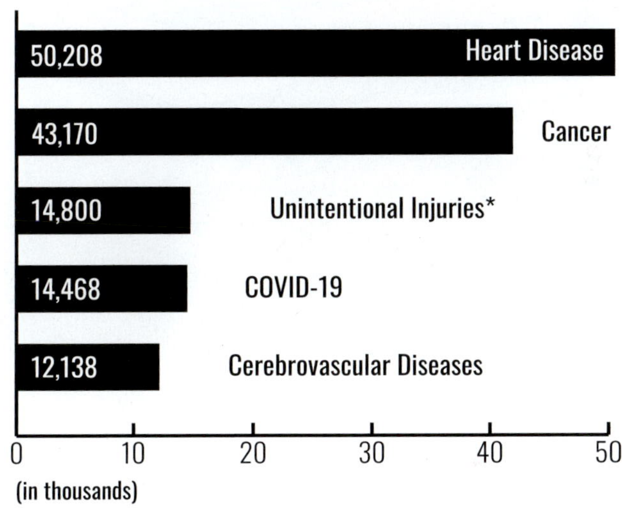

Motor vehicle accidents are included under "Unintentional Injuries"

MARRIAGE AND DIVORCE

Texas' marriage rate in 2023 was 5.8, while the divorce rate was 2.1. The rates are calculated per 1,000 total population. Meanwhile, the marriage rate for the entire United States in 2023 was 6.1, and the divorce rate was 2.4.

Texas

Year	Marriage Rate	Divorce Rate
2023	5.8	2.1
2022	5.8	1.9
2021	5.8	1.4
2020	5.3	1.5
2010	7.1	3.3
2000	9.4	4

United States

Year	Marriage Rate	Divorce Rate
2023	6.1	2.4
2022	6.2	2.4
2021	6.0	2.5
2020	5.1	2.3
2010	6.8	3.6
2000	8.2	4.0

Source: National Vital Statistics System, Texas Department of State Health Services: Vital Statistics and Center for Health Statistics.

COURTESY OF TEXAS HEALTH RESOURCES

HOSPITALS IN TEXAS

Texas hospitals reported more than 445,000 employees on their payroll in 2022. This number includes more than 358,000 full-time workers, but not the thousands of contracted staff and physicians at these hospitals.

In 2022, **64%** of Texas hospitals are operating with fewer beds and reduced services because of the decreased number of nurses.

In 2023, there were 4.9 million uninsured Texans.
Under federal law, Texas hospitals must treat anyone under an emergency setting even without insurance.

The registered nurse vacancy rate increased from

6% in 2019 to 17.6% in 2022.

The main reasons for Texas nurses leaving hospital employment included burnout/fatigue and a desire for greater pay and burnout/fatigue. In addition, 98% of Texas hospitals in 2022 reported that workplace violence against healthcare workers increased or stayed the same since the start of the pandemic.

Source: The Texas Hospital Association.

National Health Expenditures

GDP and Expenditures ($ billion)	2023	2022	2021	2020	2000
Total Health Expenditures	**$4,866.50**	**$4,525.80**	**$4,327.70**	**$4,153.90**	**$1,366.00**
Percent of GDP	17.60%	17.40%	18.30%	19.50%	13.30%
Per capita amount (in dollars)	$14,570.00	$13,617.00	$13,068.00	$12,563.00	$4,845.00
Personal health care expenditure	$4,107.40	$3,755.20	$3,581.30	$3,368.30	$1,156.50
Cost of private insurance	$1,464.70	$1,313.80	$1,230.30	$1,147.90	$441.00
Hospital care expenditures	$1,519.70	$1,376.70	$1,334.00	$1,267.60	$415.50
Gross Domestic Product (GDP)	**$27,720.70**	**$26,006.90**	**$23,681.20**	**$21,354.10**	**$10,251.00**

Source: U.S. Centers for Medicare and Medicaid Services.

Comparison of Vital Statistics

Data from 2021 with states that either border Texas or have large populations. ***Lowest and highest with number in bold.***

State/Country	Birthrate*	Death Rate*	Life Expectancy
Texas	12.7	9.1	76.5
Arkansas	11.9	13.2	73.8
California	10.7	8.5	**79.0**
Florida	9.9	12.0	77.5
Georgia	11.5	10.4	75.6
Louisiana	12.4	12.4	73.1
Michigan	10.4	11.7	76.0
New Hampshire	**8.7**	12.6	77.8
New Mexico	10.1	12.0	74.5
New York	10.6	9.1	77.7
Ohio	11.0	12.5	75.3
Oklahoma	12.1	12.8	74.1
Utah	**14.0**	**6.8**	78.6
West Virginia	9.6	**16.5**	**72.8**
United States	11.0	10.4	76.4
Afghanistan	34.8	12.1	**54.1**
Angola	**41.4**	7.8	62.5
Brazil	13.4	6.9	76.1
Canada	10.1	8.2	84.0
Germany	9.0	12.0	81.7
Italy	7.0	11.3	82.8
Japan	6.9	11.7	85.0
Monaco	**6.6**	10.9	**89.6**
Mexico	14.0	7.1	73.5
Qatar	9.3	**1.4**	80.0
Russia	9.2	**13.3**	72.7
South Sudan	37.1	9.2	59.7
United Kingdom	10.8	9.1	82.1
World	18.1	7.7	70.5

*Rates are number during one year per 1,000 persons. Sources: National Vital Statistics Report 2021; Centers for Disease Control and Prevention, National Center for Health Statistics, National Vital Statistics System 2018–2021; CIA World Factbook, 2023.

Life Expectancy at Birth for Texans by Sex (2021)

Sex	All
Total population	75.4
Males	72.7
Females	78.3

Source: Centers for Disease Control, National Vital Statistics Reports, Vol. 71, for 2021.

Texas Births by Race/Ethnicity and Sex

Race/Sex	2022	2020	2015	2000
All Races	389,806	368,317	403,439	363,325
All Male	199,172	288,551	205,972	185,591
All Female	190,634	179,766	197,467	177,734
White Total	120,463	118,242	136,663	142,553
White Male	61,844	60,995	69,935	72,972
White Female	58,619	57,247	66,728	69,581
Black Total	47,357	46,150	47,515	41,180
Black Male	24,127	23,421	24,140	21,128
Black Female	23,230	22,729	23,375	20,052
Hispanic Total	190,871	175,967	191,080	166,440
Hispanic Male	97,321	89,837	97,469	84,750
Hispanic Female	93,550	86,130	93,611	81,690
Other* Total	31,115	27,958	28,181	13,152
Other Male	15,880	14,298	14,428	6,741
Other Female	15,235	13,660	13,753	6,411

*Other includes births of unknown race/ethnicity.

Source: Texas Department of State Health Services.

Disposition of Bodies in Texas by Percent of Deaths*

Year	Burial	Cremation	Donation of Body	Removal from State/Other†
2022	40.1%	52.8%	1.6%	3.9%
2020	46.1%	45.7%	1.5%	6.7%
2019	44.4%	48.0%	1.7%	5.9%
2018	43.6%	50.0%	1.5%	4.9%
2017	46.8%	43.9%	1.4%	7.9%
2001	75.5%	17.3%	0.8%	6.3%
1995	81.7%	11.6%	0.8%	5.8%

*Resident Deaths: Deaths where decedent resided in Texas, regardless of where death occurred.
†Includes Removal from State, Entombment, Other, and Unknown.

Source: Texas Death Certificate Data; Texas Department of State Health Services, Center for Health Statistics.

MENTAL HEALTH AND SUBSTANCE ABUSE

Diagnosis of Adult Clients in Texas/United States (Fiscal Year 2023)

Diagnosis	Texas Clients	% of Clients with Diagnosis		Employed as % of Known Employment
		Texas	United States	Texas
Schizophrenia & Related Disorders	45,085	18.80%	12.90%	16.50%
Bipolar & Mood Disorders	145,696	60.70%	38.60%	35.30%
Other Psychoses	871	0.40%	2.10%	24.70%
All Other Diagnoses	6,268	2.60%	38.70%	37.50%
No Diagnosis/Deferred	41,999	17.50%	7.70%	35.20%
Total	**239,919**	**100%**	**100%**	**31.80%**

Source: U.S. Department of Health and Human Services, Center for Mental Health Services, Uniform Reporting System, 2023.

Readmission Within 180 Days of Mental Health Treatment (Fiscal Year 2023)

Age	Civil* Texas	Civil U.S.	States/Terr. Reporting	Forensic* Texas	Forensic U.S.
In percent of clients.					
0 to 5	0%	13.0%	2	—	—
6 to 12	20.0%	15.5%	9	0%	15.0%
13 to 17	16.5%	15.9%	19	2.0%	9.5%
18 to 20	13.2%	18.0%	29	0%	8.3%
21 to 24	17.3%	17.3%	34	5.4%	8.3%
25 to 44	20.1%	20.6%	44	7.0%	8.6%
45 to 64	20.9%	20.9%	42	7.0%	7.6%
65 to 74	14.3%	16.1%	34	3.1%	11.1%
75 and over	22.0%	12.8%	21	11.1%	11.6%
Total	**19.4%**	**19.6%**	**49**	**6.5%**	**8.5%**

*Forensic services are mental health services provided to persons directed into treatment by the criminal justice system; others are listed as "Civil."
Source: U.S. Department of Health and Human Services, Center for Mental Health Services, Uniform Reporting System, 2023.

Substance Abuse Treatment in Texas (2023)

Facility Operation	Number	%	Clients in Treatment on March 31, 2023		
			No.	%	Clients under 18
Private for-profit	244	49.1%	20,271	48.9%	746
Private non-profit	176	35.4%	14,982	36.2%	620
State	25	5.0%	2,294	5.5%	123
Local/county/community	37	7.4%	1,768	4.3%	144
Tribal	1	0.2%	18	—	—
Federal	14	2.8%	2,106	5.1%	—
Total	**497**	**100%**	**41,439**	**100%**	**1,633**
Problem Treated	**Number.**	**%**	**No.**	**%**	**...per 100,000 pop.**
Both alcohol & substances other than alcohol	267	73.2%	13,416	32.5%	44
Only alcohol	229	62.7%	5,370	13.0%	18
Only substances other than alcohol	293	80.3%	22,463	54.5%	74
Total	**365**	**—**	**41,249**	**100%**	**135**

Source: National Survey of Substance Abuse Treatment Services, 2023.

Estimated Drug Use in Texas and Bordering States (Annual Average Percentages, 2022 and 2023)

State	Any Illicit Drug	Marijuana	Other than Marijuana[1]	Cigarettes	Binge Alcohol[2]	Pain Reliever Misuse[4]
Current users[3] as ***percent of population, age 12+ years****. Selected states.*						
U.S. total	16.67%	15.20%	3.32%	14.10%	21.68%	3.01%
Texas	**11.66%**	**10.29%**	**2.77%**	**14.37%**	**20.93%**	**3.24%**
Arkansas	16.39%	14.63%	3.55%	19.59%	19.41%	3.55%
Louisiana	16.55%	14.48%	4.01%	20.37%	25.22%	4.41%
Oklahoma	21.13%	20.07%	2.99%	19.11%	18.97%	4.07%
New Mexico	25.90%	23.97%	4.09%	16.03%	21.10%	4.35%

[1]Marijuana users who have also used another drug are included. [2]Binge use is defined as drinking five or more drinks on the same occasion on at least one day in the past 30 days. [3]Used drugs at least once within month. [4]Within the last year.
Source: U.S. Substance Abuse and Mental Health Services Administration, National Survey on Drug Use and Health, 2023.

STATE INSTITUTIONS FOR MENTAL HEALTH SERVICES

Mental health services were provided to some 455,740 Texans in 2023 in various institutions, including community centers.

In 2004, the Texas Department of State Health Services was created (DSHS), bringing together:

- the Texas Department of Health,
- the Texas Department of Mental Health and Mental Retardation (MHMR),
- Commission on Alcohol and Drug Abuse,
- and the Texas Health Care Information Council.

In 2016, Texas Health and Human Services was created by the Legislature with two agencies: the Texas Health and Human Services Commission (HHSC) and DSHS, with many direct client services transferred from DSHS to HHSC, including mental health services.

In 2023, state mental health agency expenditure was $1,390,387,856, with $874,395,350 for community services, according to the federal Uniform Reporting System for the states.

Hospitals for Persons with Mental Illness

Following is a list of the 11 state hospitals, their location, and the year each was founded.

- **Austin State Hospital**: Austin; 1857.
- **Big Spring State Hospital**: Big Spring; 1937.
- **El Paso Psychiatric Center**: El Paso; 1974.
- **John S. Dunn Behavioral Sciences Center**: Houston; 2022.
- **Kerrville State Hospital**: Kerrville; 1950.
- **North Texas State Hospital**: Wichita Falls (1922) and Vernon (1969).
- **Rio Grande State Center**: Harlingen; 1962.
- **Rusk State Hospital**: Rusk; 1919.
- **San Antonio State Hospital**: San Antonio; 1892.
- **Terrell State Hospital**: Terrell; 1885.
- **Waco Center for Youth**: Waco; 1979.

Community Mental Health Centers

Following is a list of community mental health centers, the year each was founded, and the counties each serves.

- **Abilene**: *Betty Hardwick Center*; 1971; Callahan, Jones, Shackelford, Stephens, and Taylor.
- **Amarillo**: *Texas Panhandle Centers*; 1968; Armstrong, Carson, Collingsworth, Dallam, Deaf Smith, Donley, Gray, Hall, Hansford, Hartley, Hemphill, Hutchinson, Lipscomb, Moore, Ochiltree, Oldham, Potter, Randall, Roberts, Sherman, and Wheeler.
- **Austin**: *Integral Care*; 1967; Travis.
- **Beaumont**: *Spindletop Center*; 1967; Chambers, Hardin, Jefferson, and Orange.
- **Big Spring**: *West Texas Centers*; 1997; Andrews, Borden, Crane, Dawson, Fisher, Gaines, Garza, Glasscock, Howard, Kent, Loving, Martin, Mitchell, Nolan, Reeves, Runnels, Scurry, Terrell, Terry, Upton, Ward, Winkler, and Yoakum.
- **Brownwood**: *Center for Life Resources*; 1969; Brown, Coleman, Comanche, Eastland, McCulloch, Mills, and San Saba.
- **Bryan-College Station**: *MHMR Authority of Brazos Valley*; 1972; Brazos, Burleson, Grimes, Leon, Madison, Robertson, and Washington.
- **Conroe**: *Tri-County Behavioral Healthcare*; 1983; Liberty, Montgomery, and Walker.
- **Corpus Christi**: *Nueces Center for Mental Health & Intellectual Disabilities*; 1970; Nueces.
- **Dallas**: *North Texas Behavioral Health Authority (NTBHA)*; 1967; Dallas, Ellis, Hunt, Kaufman, Navarro, and Rockwall.
- **Denton**: *Denton County MHMR Center*; 1987; Denton.
- **Edinburg**: *Tropical Texas Behavioral Health*; 1967; Cameron, Hidalgo, and Willacy.
- **El Paso**: *Emergence Health Network*; 1968; El Paso.
- **Fort Worth**: *MHMR of Tarrant County*; 1969; Tarrant.
- **Granbury**: *Pecan Valley Centers for Behavioral & Developmental HealthCare*; 1977; Erath, Hood, Johnson, Palo Pinto, Parker, and Somervell.
- **Houston**: *The Harris Center for Mental Health and IDD*; 1965; Harris.
- **Jacksonville**: *Anderson-Cherokee Community Enrichment Services (ACCESS)*; 1995; Anderson and Cherokee.
- **Kerrville**: *Hill Country Mental Health & Developmental Disabilities Centers*; 1997; Bandera, Blanco, Comal, Edwards, Gillespie, Hays, Kendall, Kerr, Kimble, Kinney, Llano, Mason, Medina, Menard, Real, Schleicher, Sutton, Uvalde, and Val Verde.
- **Laredo**: *Border Region Behavioral Health Center*; 1969; Jim Hogg, Starr, Webb, and Zapata.
- **Longview**: *Community Healthcore*; 1970; Bowie, Cass, Gregg, Harrison, Marion, Panola, Red River, Rusk, and Upshur.
- **Lubbock**: *StarCare Specialty Health System*; 1969; Cochran, Crosby, Hockley, Lubbock, and Lynn.
- **Lufkin**: *Burke Center*; 1975; Angelina, Houston, Jasper, Nacogdoches, Newton, Polk, Sabine, San Augustine, San Jacinto, Shelby, Trinity, and Tyler.
- **Lytle**: *Camino Real Community Services*; 1996; Atascosa, Dimmit, Frio, La Salle, Karnes, Maverick, McMullen, Wilson, and Zavala.

Source: U.S. Department of Health and Human Services and the Texas Department of State Health Services.

- **McKinney**: *LifePath Systems*; 1986; Collin.
- **Midland**: *PermiaCare*; 1969; Brewster, Culberson, Ector, Hudspeth, Jeff Davis, Midland, Pecos, and Presidio.
- **Plainview**: *Central Plains Center*; 1969; Bailey, Briscoe, Castro, Floyd, Hale, Lamb, Motley, Parmer, and Swisher.
- **Portland**: *Coastal Plains Community Center*; 1996; Aransas, Bee, Brooks, Duval, Jim Wells, Kenedy, Kleberg, Live Oak, and San Patricio.
- **Rosenberg**: *Texana Center*; 1996; Austin, Colorado, Fort Bend, Matagorda, Waller and Wharton.
- **Round Rock**: *Bluebonnet Trails Community Services*; 1997; Bastrop, Burnet, Caldwell, Fayette, Gonzales, Guadalupe, Lee, and Williamson.
- **San Angelo**: *MHMR Services for the Concho Valley*; 1969; Coke, Concho, Crockett, Irion, Reagan, Sterling, and Tom Green.
- **San Antonio**: *The Center for Health Care Services*; 1966; Bexar.
- **Sherman**: *Texoma Community Center*; 1974; Cooke, Fannin, and Grayson.
- **Temple**: *Central Counties Services*; 1967; Bell, Coryell, Hamilton, Lampasas, and Milam.
- **Terrell**: *Lakes Regional MHMR Center*; 1996; Camp, Delta, Franklin, Hopkins, Lamar, Morris, and Titus.
- **Tyler**: *Andrews Center Behavioral Healthcare System*; 1970; Henderson, Rains, Smith, Van Zandt, and Wood.
- **Victoria**: *Gulf Bend Center*; 1970; Calhoun, DeWitt, Goliad, Jackson, Lavaca, Refugio, and Victoria.
- **Waco**: *Heart of Texas Behavioral Health Network*; 1969; Bosque, Falls, Freestone, Hill, Limestone, and McLennan.
- **Wichita Falls**: *Helen Farabee Centers*; 1969; Archer, Baylor, Childress, Clay, Cottle, Dickens, Foard, Hardeman, Haskell, Jack, King, Knox, Montague, Stonewall, Throckmorton, Wichita, Wilbarger, Wise, and Young.

TEXANS IN THE NATIONAL ACADEMY OF SCIENCES

The National Academy of Sciences is a private organization of researchers dedicated to the furtherance of science and its use for the general welfare. A total of 165 scientists who have had positions with Texas institutions have been named members or associates.

Established by congressional acts of incorporation, which were signed by President Abraham Lincoln in 1863, the academy acts as the official adviser to the federal government in matters of science and technology. Election to the academy is one of the highest honors that can be accorded a scientist. As of April 2025, the number of active members was 3,218.

Elected from Texas in 2024 were Sharon Y. Dent from The University of Texas MD Anderson Cancer Center and UT Health at Houston; Kristen M. Harris and Keiko Torii from The University of Texas at Austin; F.R. Harvey and Ramamoorthy Ramesh from Rice University; and William J. Murphy from Texas A&M University at College Station.

Margaret Goodell (Baylor College of Medicine), Lydia E. Kavraki (Rice), and James W. Pennebaker (UT-Austin) were elected in 2025.

In 1931, Robert Moore (UT-Austin 1920–69) and Hermann Muller (Rice 1915–18, UT-Austin 1920–32) became the first scientists from Texas institutions elected to the academy.

Academy Member	Affiliation	Elected
Perry L. Adkisson †	Texas A&M	1979
Richard W. Aldrich	UT-Austin	2008
James P. Allison	UT-MD Anderson Cancer	1997
Abram Amsel †	UT-Austin	1992
Neal R. Amundson †	University of Houston	1992
Leif Andersson	Texas A&M	2012
Dora E. Angelaki	Baylor Medical	2014
Charles J. Arntzen	Texas A&M	1983
David H. Auston	Rice	1991
Paul F. Barbara †	UT-Austin	2006
Allen J. Bard †	UT-Austin	1982
Bonnie Bartel	Rice	2016
D.H.R. Barton †	Texas A&M	1970
Frederic C. Bartter †	UT-Health Science at San Antonio	1979
John D. Baxter †	Houston Methodist Research Institute	2003
Arthur L. Beaudet	Baylor Medical	2011
Hugo Bellen	Baylor College of Medicine	2020
Brian J.L. Berry †	UT-Dallas	1975

Academy Member	Affiliation	Elected
Bruce Beutler †	UT-Southwestern Medical	2008
Lewis R. Binford †	Southern Methodist University	2001
R.H. Bing †	UT-Austin	1965
Harold C. Bold †	UT-Austin	1973
Norman E. Borlaug †	Texas A&M	1968
Maurice S. Brookhart	University of Houston	2001
Michael S. Brown	UT-Southwestern Medical	1980
James J. Bull	UT-Austin	2016
Karl W. Butzer †	UT-Austin	1996
Horace R. Byers †	Texas A&M	1952
Luis A. Caffarelli	UT-Austin	1991
C. Thomas Caskey †	Baylor Medical	1993
Joseph W. Chamberlain †	Rice	1965
Zhijian (James) Chen	UT-Southwestern Medical	2014
Wah Chiu	Baylor Medical	2012
C.W. Chu	University of Houston	1989

† – Deceased
UT – University of Texas

Source: National Academy of Sciences.

Academy Member	Affiliation	Elected
Melanie H. Cobb	UT-Southwestern Medical	2006
Jonathan C. Cohen	UT-Southwestern Medical	2022
Neal G. Copeland	Houston Methodist Research Institute	2009
F. Albert Cotton †	Texas A&M	1967
Robert F. Curl Jr. †	Rice	1997
Marcetta Darensbourg	Texas A&M	2017
Russell A. DeBose-Boyd	UT-Southwestern Medical	2023
Johann Deisenhofer	UT-Southwestern Medical	1997
Sharon Y. Dent	UT-MD Anderson Cancer, UT-Health Houston	2024
Ronald A. DePinho	UT-MD Anderson Cancer	2012
Gerard H. de Vaucouleurs †	UT-Austin	1986
Ronald DeVore	Texas A&M	2017
Bryce DeWitt †	UT-Austin	1990
Robert E. Dickinson	UT-Austin	1988
Anthony Di Fiore	UT-Austin	2021
Richard A. Dixon	University of North Texas	2007
Stephen J. Elledge	Baylor Medical	2003
Ronald W. Estabrook †	UT-Southwestern Medical	1979
Mary K. Estes	Baylor Medical	2007
Karl Folkers †	UT-Austin	1948
Marye Anne Fox †	UT-Austin	1994
Katherine Freese	UT-Austin	2020
Stephen A. Fuselier	Southwest Research Institute	2021
David L. Garbers †	UT-Southwestern Medical	1993
Wilson S. Geisler	UT-Austin	2008
Quentin H. Gibson †	Rice	1982
Alfred G. Gilman †	UT-Southwestern Medical	1985
Joseph L. Goldstein	UT-Southwestern Medical	1980
Margaret Goodell	Baylor College of Medicine	2025
John B. Goodenough †	UT-Austin	2012
Cameron M. Gordon	UT-Austin	2023
William E. Gordon †	Rice	1968
Verne E. Grant †	UT-Austin	1968
Jan-Åke Gustafsson	University of Houston	2002
Norman Hackerman †	Robert A. Welch Foundation	1971
Naomi J. Halas	Rice	2013
Kristen M. Harris	UT-Austin	2024
Carl G. Hartman †	UT-Austin	1937
F.R. Harvey	Rice	2024
Luis Herrera-Estrella	Texas Tech	2003
Dudley Herschbach	Texas A&M	1967
Donald W. Hilgemann	UT-Southwestern Medical	2021
David M. Hillis	UT-Austin	2008
Helen H. Hobbs	UT-Southwestern Medical	2007
Lora V. Hooper	UT-Southwestern Medical	2015
A. James Hudspeth	UT-Southwestern Medical	1991
Thomas J.R. Hughes	UT-Austin	2009
Nancy A. Jenkins	UT-MD Anderson Cancer	2008
V. Craig Jordan †	UT-MD Anderson Cancer	2009
Lydia E. Kavraki	Rice	2025
Robert C. Kennicutt, Jr.	Texas A&M	2006
James L. Kinsey †	Rice	1991
Mark Kirkpatrick	UT-Austin	2020
Steven A. Kliewer	UT-Southwestern Medical	2015
Ernst Knobil †	UT-Houston Health Science	1986
Jay K. Kochi †	University of Houston	1982
John Kormendy †	UT-Austin	2020
P. Kusch †	UT-Dallas	1956
Alan M. Lambowitz	UT-Austin	2004
Neal F. Lane	Rice	2009
David M. Lee	Texas A&M	1991
Beth Levine †	UT-Southwestern Medical	2013
Herbert Levine	Rice	2011
Gardner Lindzey †	UT-Austin	1989
Gigi Lozano	UT-MD Anderson Cancer	2017
Alan G. MacDiarmid †	UT-Dallas	2002
Allan H. MacDonald	UT-Austin	2010
David J. Mangelsdorf	UT-Austin	2008
John L. Margrave †	Rice	1974
Martin M. Matzuk	Baylor Medical	2014
S.M. McCann †	UT-Southwestern Medical	1983
Steven L. McKnight	UT-Southwestern Medical	1992
David J. Meltzer	Southern Methodist University	2009
Robert Moore †	UT-Austin	1931
Nancy A. Moran	UT-Austin	2004
Sean J. Morrison	UT-Southwestern Medical	2020
Hermann Muller †	Rice, UT-Austin	1931
Hans J. Muller-Eberhard †	UT-Houston Health Science	1974
Ferid Murad †	UT-Houston Health Science	1997
William J. Murphy	Texas A&M	2024
Jack Myers †	UT-Austin	1975
Kyriacos C. Nicolaou	Rice	1996
Robert N. Noyce †	SEMATECH/Austin	1980
David R. Nygren	UT-Arlington	2000
Eric N. Olson	UT-Southwestern Medical	2000
Bert W. O'Malley	Baylor Medical	1992
Jose N. Onuchic	Rice	2006
Kim Orth	UT-Southwestern Medical	2020
Theophilus S. Painter †	UT-Austin	1938
Duojia Pan	UT-Southwestern Medical	2023
Luis F. Parada	UT-Southwestern Medical	2011
John Patterson †	UT-Austin	1941
James W. Pennebaker	UT-Austin	2025
Margaret A. Phillips	UT-Southwestern Medical	2021
Kenneth L. Pike †	Summer Institute of Linguistics	1985
Helen Piwnica-Worms	UT-MD Anderson Cancer	2023
William H. Press	UT-Austin	1994
Darwin J. Prockop †	Texas A&M	1991
Lester J. Reed †	UT-Austin	1973
Peter M. Rentzepis	Texas A&M	1978
Rebecca Richards-Kortum	Rice	2015
Ignacio Rodriguez-Iturbe †	Texas A&M	2010
Michael K. Rosen	UT-Southwestern Medical	2020
A. Catharine Ross	Texas A&M	2003
Peter J. Rossky	UT-Austin	2011
David W. Russell	UT-Southwestern Medical	2006
Marlan O. Scully	Texas A&M	2001
Jonathan L. Sessler	UT-Austin	2021
Richard E. Smalley †	Rice	1990
Esmond E. Snell †	UT-Austin	1955
Richard C. Starr †	UT-Austin	1976
Patrick Stover	Texas A&M	2016
Thomas Südhof	UT-Southwestern Medical	2002
Max D. Summers	Texas A&M	1989
John Suppe	University of Houston	1995
Harry L. Swinney	UT-Austin	1992
Joseph S. Takahashi	UT-Southwestern Medical	2003
John T. Tate †	UT-Austin	1969
Keiko Torii	UT-Austin	2024
Karen K. Uhlenbeck	UT-Austin	1986
Jonathan W. Uhr	UT-Southwestern Medical	1984
Roger H. Unger †	UT-Southwestern Medical	1986
H.S. Vandiver †	UT-Austin	1934
Moshe Y. Vardi	Rice	2015
Ellen S. Vitetta	UT-Southwestern Medical	1994
Salih J. Wakil †	Baylor Medical	1990
Xiaodong Wang	UT-Southwestern Medical	2004
Steven Weinberg †	UT-Austin	1972
D. Fred Wendorf †	Southern Methodist University	1987
John Archibald Wheeler †	UT-Austin	1952
Roger J. Williams †	UT-Austin	1946
Jean D. Wilson †	UT-Southwestern Medical	1983
Peter G. Wolynes	Rice	1991
James E. Womack †	Texas A&M	1999
Richard D. Wood	UT-MD Anderson Cancer	2023
Karen L. Wooley	Texas A&M	2020
Masashi Yanagisawa	UT-Southwestern Medical	2003
Clarence Zener †	Texas A&M	1959
Huda Y. Zoghbi	Baylor Medical	2004

† – Deceased
UT – University of Texas

SCIENCE RESEARCH FUNDING AT UNIVERSITIES

The following chart shows funding for research and development by source at universities in Texas, in order of total R&D funding. Colleges and universities not listed received less. The figures are from the National Science Foundation's Higher Education Research and Development Survey (HERDS) and are for fiscal year 2023.

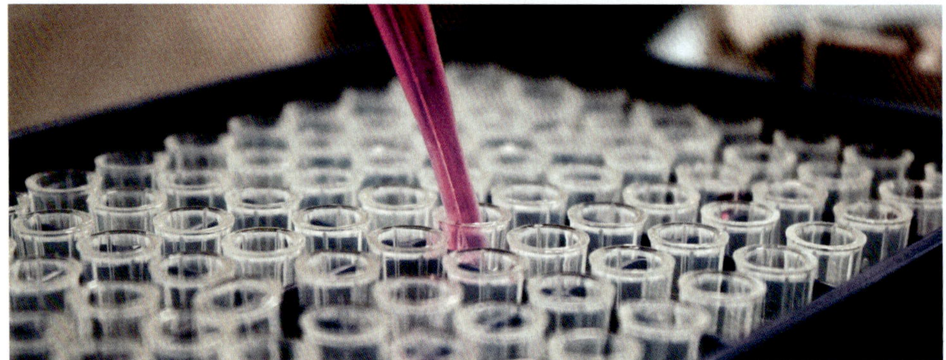

University	All R&D Expenditures	Federal Government	State/Local Government	Institutional Funds	Business	Nonprofit	All Other Sources
United States	$108,841,148	$59,678,935	$5,447,408	$27,702,412	$6,230,371	$6,684,772	$3,097,250
Texas (all colleges statewide)	**$8,330,578**	**$3,560,492**	**$1,055,701**	**$2,360,953**	**$560,247**	**$485,865**	**$307,320**
1. Texas A&M	$1,277,814	$546,481	$251,300	$353,916	$37,390	$53,710	$35,017
2. UT-M. D. Anderson Cancer Center	1,255,190	259,285	300,907	256,545	248,261	38,163	152,029
3. UT-Austin	1,035,838	621,223	37,601	235,987	79,753	52,764	8,510
4. Baylor College of Medicine	847,305	440,345	34,061	282,695	33,100	57,104	—
5. UT-Southwestern Medical Center	800,391	336,126	95,710	191,493	46,325	66,076	64,661
6. UT-HTC, Houston	374,105	197,759	48,815	66,008	17,466	34,341	9,716
7. UT-HSC, San Antonio	281,078	143,730	30,582	70,676	10,393	25,514	183
8. Rice University	255,115	119,853	9,801	78,447	7,506	33,684	5,824
9. Texas Tech University	240,107	58,922	28,095	122,202	15,461	14,994	433
10. UT-Medical Branch	233,192	150,272	7,479	58,807	6,138	10,496	—
11. University of Houston	231,942	99,450	28,641	84,315	8,565	6,492	4,479
12. UT-San Antonio	158,453	58,171	21,583	67,694	5,971	1,988	3,046
13. UT-Arlington	147,265	56,337	28,343	50,435	5,284	4,708	2,158
14. UT-Dallas	146,779	66,127	13,085	38,169	12,518	16,383	497
15. UT-El Paso	145,724	70,873	16,687	44,987	1,268	1,770	10,139
16. Texas State University	141,291	44,297	4,667	83,686	1,378	7,106	157
17. University of North Texas, Denton	106,665	30,017	5,695	63,577	1,907	2,170	3,299
18. University of North Texas, Health Science Center	94,652	77,660	3,180	11,773	847	1,003	189
19. UT-Rio Grande Valley	82,444	25,068	4,367	37,248	569	15,016	176
20. Baylor University	82,074	17,147	2,879	45,076	3,460	12,667	845
21. Southern Methodist University	59,749	19,986	1,393	33,204	33,204	3,399	166
22. Texas Tech University, HSC	48,638	14,732	18,670	9,432	608	3,205	1,991
23. Texas A&M University, Corpus Christi	39,305	17,742	10,790	5,118	230	2,783	2,642
24. UT-HSC, Tyler	32,077	12,555	10,087	3,795	172	5,468	—
25. Texas A&M University, Kingsville	26,401	9,584	7,058	3,311	487	5,932	29
26. Texas Christian University	24,050	7,627	658	12,066	2,491	1,069	139
27. Tarleton State University	23,345	5,478	4,392	12,689	286	500	—
28. Prairie View A&M University	21,791	12,354	4,391	3,550	490	1,006	—
29. Texas Southern University	16,287	10,969	1,227	4,042	—	49	—
30. Texas Tech University, HSC, El Paso	13,189	2,415	3,097	6,947	229	501	—

UT – University of Texas
HSC – Health Science Center

(Figures in Thousands of Dollars)

UNSPLASH/LOUIS REED

TEXAN NOBEL PRIZE WINNERS

On November 27, 1895, Alfred Nobel signed his last will and testament, giving the largest share of his fortune to a series of prizes in physics, chemistry, physiology or medicine, literature and peace — the Nobel Prizes.

In 1968, Sveriges Riksbank (Sweden's central bank) established The Sveriges Riksbank Prize in Economic Sciences in Memory of Alfred Nobel.

Between 1901 and 2024, the Nobel Prizes and the prize in economic sciences were awarded 627 times to 1,012 people and organizations. A small number of individuals and organizations have been honored more than once, which means that 976 unique individuals and 28 unique organizations have received the Nobel Prize in total.

There are some years when the Nobel Prizes have not been awarded. The total number of times are 49. Several occurred during World Wars I (1914–1918) and II (1939–1945). In the statutes of the Nobel Foundation it says: "If none of the works under consideration is found to be of the importance indicated in the first paragraph, the prize money shall be reserved until the following year. If, even then, the prize cannot be awarded, the amount shall be added to the Foundation's restricted funds."

NORMAN BORLAUG

ROBERT F. CURL JR.

JOHN GOODENOUGH

Texan Nobel Prize Winners

Year	Name	Nobel Prize in
2019	John Goodenough	Chemistry
2018	James Allison	Physiology or Medicine
2017	Michael W. Young	Physiology or Medicine
2015	Aziz Sancar	Chemistry
2011	Bruce Beutler	Physiology or Medicine
2003	John Maxwell Coetzee	Literature
2000	Alan MacDiarmid	Chemistry
2000	Jack Kilby	Physics
1996	Robert F. Curl Jr.	Chemistry
1994	Alfred Gilman	Physiology or Medicine
1993	Russell Alan Hulse	Physics
1990	E. Donnall Thomas	Physiology or Medicine
1988	Johann Deisenhofer	Chemistry
1985	Michael S. Brown and Joseph Goldstein	Physiology or Medicine
1979	Steven Weinberg	Physics
1977	Ilya Prigogine	Chemistry
1970	Norman Borlaug	Peace
1946	Hermann Joseph Muller	Physiology or Medicine

Source: The Nobel Foundation.

UNSPLASH/THOMAS WAVID JOHNS

Texas

EDUCATION

UNSPLASH / MOREN HSU

TEXAS PUBLIC SCHOOLS

During the 2023-2024 school year, 5,531,236 students were enrolled in Texas public schools. That's an increase of 0.23% over enrollment in the 2022-2023 school year, which saw the enrollment of 5,518,432 students, according to the Texas Education Agency.

In Texas, there are 1,207 independent and common school districts and 186 charter operators. Independent school districts are administered by an elected board of trustees and deal directly with the Texas Education Agency. Common districts are supervised by elected county school superintendents and county trustees.

As of the 2023-2024 school year, there were 16 school districts with more than 50,000 students enrolled in their various schools; 24.45% of all students in Texas attend school in these large districts. By contrast, only 1.83% of Texas students are enrolled at the 401 smallest districts in Texas, each of which has fewer than 500 students enrolled.

5 Largest School Districts, by Enrollment (May 2024)

School District	County	Enrollment
Houston ISD	Harris	184,109
Dallas ISD	Dallas	139,246
Cypress-Fairbanks ISD	Harris	118,470
Northside ISD	Bexar	101,095
Katy ISD	Harris, Fort Bend, Waller	94,785

5 Smallest School Districts, by Enrollment (May 2024)

School District	County	Enrollment
San Vicente ISD	Brewster	6
Doss Consolidated CSD	Gillespie	21
Ramirez CSD	Duval	22
Valentine ISD	Jeff Davis	24
Divide ISD	Kerr	35

BRIEF HISTORY OF PUBLIC EDUCATION IN TEXAS

Public education was one of the primary goals of the early settlers of Texas, who listed in the Texas Declaration of Independence the failure to provide education as one of their grievances against Mexico.

As early as 1838, President Mirabeau B. Lamar's message to the Republic of Texas Congress advocated setting aside public domain for public schools. His interest led to his nickname as the "Father of Education in Texas." In 1839, Congress designated three leagues of land to support public schools for each Texas county and 50 leagues for a state university. In 1840, each county was allocated one more league of land.

The Republic, however, did not establish a public school system or a university. After Texas was admitted into the Union, the 1845 Texas State Constitution advocated public education, instructing the Legislature to designate at least 10% of the tax revenue for schools. Further delay occurred until Gov. Elisha M. Pease, on January 31, 1854, signed the bill setting up the Texas public school system.

The public school system was made possible by setting aside $2 million out of $10 million Texas received for relinquishing its claim to land north and west of its present boundaries in the Compromise of 1850.

Sources: Texas Education Agency, Texas Tribune, and the Texas Permanent School Fund Annual Comprehensive Financial Report for 2023 and 2024.

UNSPLASH/LEOHOHO

UNSPLASH/DALLAS PENNER

Early Funding and Administration Changes

During 1854, legislation provided for state apportionment of funds based upon an annual census. Also, railroads receiving grants were required to survey alternate sections to be set aside for public school financing. The first school census that year showed 65,463 students. State fund apportionment was 62 cents per student.

When adopted in 1876, the present Texas Constitution provided: "All funds, lands, and other property heretofore set apart and appropriated for the support of public schools; all the alternate sections of land reserved by the state of grants heretofore made or that may hereafter be made to railroads, or other corporations, of any nature whatsoever; one half of the public domain of the state, and all sums of money that may come to the state from the sale of any portion of the same shall constitute a perpetual public school fund." More than 52 million acres of the Texas public domain were allotted for school purposes.

In 1949, the Gilmer-Aikin Laws reorganized the state system of public schools by making sweeping changes in administration and financing. The Texas Education Agency, headed by the governor-appointed Commissioner of Education, administers the public school system.

The policy-making body for public education is the 15-member State Board of Education, which is elected from separate districts for overlapping four-year terms.

Targeting Student Performance

The 68th Legislature passed one of the most historic education-reform bills of the past 50 years when lawmakers met in special session in 1984. House Bill 72 came in response to growing concern over deteriorating literacy among Texas' schoolchildren over two decades, reflected in students' scores on standardized tests.

Provisions of HB 72 raised teachers' salaries, but tied those raises to teacher performance. It also introduced more stringent teacher certification and initiated competency testing for teachers. Lawmakers also created the 22:1 class size ratio for kindergarten through fourth-grade classes and the no-pass, no-play rule.

Sweeping Reforms

In 1995, the 74th Legislature took on a monumental task and completely rewrote all the state's public education laws.

The Public Schools Reform Act of 1995 increased local control of public schools by limiting the Texas Education Agency to recommending and reporting on educational goals; overseeing charter schools; managing the permanent, foundation, and available school funds; administering an accountability system; creating and implementing the student testing program; recommending educator appraisal and counselor evaluation instruments; and developing plans for special, bilingual, compensatory, gifted and talented, vocational, and technology education.

It also reduced the authority of the State Board of Education. The goal was to return as much authority as possible to the local level. However, each subsequent Legislature has reinstated some state-level control.

Financial Reform

In 2019, the 86th Legislature focused on school finances and taking some of the financial burden for public education off of property owners. Maintenance and operations (M&O) property taxes fund much of public education in Texas.

The $11.6 billion finance bill included $6.5 billion in new public education spending and $5.1 billion for lowering property tax bills. Its measures included increased per-student base funding by 20%, provided raises for teachers, funded free full-day pre-K for eligible 4-year-olds, and reduced the amount of money that wealthier school districts spent subsidizing poorer districts, a recapture program informally known as "Robin Hood."

The bill also offered $3,000 to $12,000 to districts providing merit-pay bonuses to their best teachers, and school administrators are required to use part of their funding to offer raises and benefits for teachers with more than five years of experience.

Social and Safety Concerns

The 87th Legislature passed laws regulating how race, slavery, and history are taught in classes. Lawmakers took aim at "CRT" — or "critical-race theory" — which maintains that racism is baked into legal systems and is not limited to individual action alone. Although CRT is primarily taught at the university level, Senate Bill 3 restricts it at the public one, stating that a "teacher may not be compelled to discuss a widely debated and currently controversial issue of public policy or social affairs," with no definition of what a "controversial issue" might be.

Under House Bill 25, transgender athletes are required to play on teams that correspond to birth certificates issued on or near the time of their births. Under this law, modified birth certificates would only be accepted if they had been altered to fix clerical errors. According to Jamey Harrison, deputy director of the University Interscholastic League (UIL), schools that do not comply with these measures would face sanctions and forfeit competitions at minimum.

In 2023, the 88th Legislature approved House Bill 3, a school safety measure that requires an armed security officer at every Texas campus, offers mental health training for district employees who regularly interact with children, and creates regional safety teams that conduct intruder detection audits at least once a year. House Bill 3 also created a safety and security department within the Texas Education Agency. The Texas Education Agency was given the authority to compel school districts to formulate and follow active shooter protocols, with non-compliant districts put under state supervision. The Texas School Safety Center, a think tank located at Texas State University in San Marcos, was tasked with reviewing best practices for campus security every five years. House Bill 3 allocated $1.1 billion in funding to the Texas Education Agency for use in school safety grants, promising at least $15,000 per campus and $10 per student.

School Financing and Policy Changes

The 89th Legislature in 2025 passed Senate Bill 2, a private school voucher program that funds children's education for private schools through public taxpayer dollars. Under the program, families can receive up to $10,000 to send their children to private schools, and the money flows through Education Savings Accounts managed by the state. Public school funding received $8.5 billion for districts and teacher raises.

The session also brought changes in school policies, with lawmakers requiring teachers to post the Ten Commandments, adding more bans on diversity, equity, and inclusion programs, allowing parents to challenge books in school libraries, and restricting cell phone use for students.

PERMANENT SCHOOL FUND

The Texas public school system was established, and the Permanent School Fund (PSF or "the Fund") was set up by the Fifth Legislature on January 31, 1854. The 170-year-old PSF is managed by the State Board of Education and is the largest educational endowment in the United States. It is invested in global markets and broadly diversified.

In 2021, the 87th Legislature passed SB 1232, which separated the Fund from the Texas Education Agency in 2023. The PSF then became a standalone entity known as the Texas Permanent School Fund Corporation.

Every year, a distribution is made from PSF to pay a portion of educational costs in each public school district. The PSF balance, as of August 31, 2024, was $57.3 billion, an increase of $5 billion from the prior year.

Permanent School Fund

Year	Fund Value* (in millions)	Funds Distributed to Schools (in millions)
2024	$57,290.80	$2,156.40
2023	$52,316.80	$2,075.70
2022	$56,810.70	$2,142.30
2021	$55,624.10	$1,701.70
2020	$46,675.60	$1,701.70
2019	$46,500.40	$1,535.80
2018	$44,067.50	$1,235.80
2017	$41,418.00	$1,056.40
2016	$37,263.90	$1,056.40
2015	$33,833.50	$838.70
2014	$34,951.20	$838.00
2013	$27,277.00	$1,020.90
2012	$25,503.00	$1,020.90
2011	$24,091.60	$1,092.80
2010	$22,107.80	$60.70
2009	$20,545.30	$716.50
2008	$23,142.40	$716.50
2007	$25,311.80	$843.10
2006	$22,802.70	$841.90
2005	$21,354.30	$880.00
2004	$19,261.80	$825.10
2003	$18,037.30	—
2002	$17,047.20	—
2001	$19,021.80	—
2000	$22,275.60	—
1999	$19,615.70	$698.50
1998	$16,296.20	$661.90
1997	$15,496.60	$690.80
1996	$12,995.80	$692.70
1995	$12,273.20	$740.00
1994	$11,330.60	$737.00
1993	$11,822.50	$737.70
1992	$10,944.90	$739.50
1991	$10,227.80	$739.20
1990	$7,328.20	$700.30
1980	$2,464.60	$3.00
1970	$842.20	$287.20
1960	$425.80	$164.20
1950	$161.20	$94.00
1940	$68.30	$34.60
1930	$38.70	$27.30

*Prior to 1991, the PSF reported cash, bonds at par, and stock at book value. From 1991 to the present, the PSF has reported cash, bonds, and stocks at fair value.

Texas School Enrollment and Expenditures Per Student		
School Year	Enrollment	Spending Per Student
2023-2024	5,531,236	$18,125
2022-2023	5,518,432	$16,792
2021–2022	5,427,370	$15,705
2020–2021	5,371,586	$14,797
2019–2020	5,493,940	$14,058
2018–2019	5,431,910	$13,108
2017–2018	5,399,682	$12,861
2016–2017	5,343,893	$12,634
2015–2016	5,284,306	$12,264
2014–2015	5,232,065	$11,704
2013–2014	5,151,925	$10,971
2012–2013	5,058,939	$10,549
2011–2012	4,978,120	$10,556
2010–2011	4,912,385	$11,142
2009–2010	4,824,778	$11,543

Graduates and Dropouts		
School Year	Graduates	Dropouts*
2022-2023	377,367	41,597
2021-2022	368,686	43,909
2020–2021	358,842	46,299
2019–2020	360,220	30,921
2018–2019	355,615	34,477
2017–2018	347,893	33,697
2016–2017	334,424	33,050
2015–2016	324,311	33,466
2014–2015	313,397	33,437
2013–2014	303,109	35,358
2012–2013	301,418	34,696
2011–2012	292,636	36,276
2010–2011	290,581	34,363
2009–2010	280,520	33,235
2008–2009	264,275	40,923

*Grades 7–12.

Public School Personnel and Salaries

Personnel Category*	Personnel 2022-2023	Personnel 2023-2024	% Change from Previous	Average Base Salaries 2022-2023	Average Base Salaries 2023-2024	% Change from Previous
Teachers	371,778	374,922	0.85%	$60,705	$62,463	2.90%
Campus Administration	25,301	25,836	2.11%	$85,166	$86,738	1.85%
Central Administration	9,501	9,488	-0.14%	$112,702	$116,028	2.95%
Professional Support	83,120	86,316	3.85%	$71,996	$73,758	2.45%
Total Professionals	**489,700**	**496,562**	**1.40%**	**$64,894**	**$66,713**	**2.80%**
Paraprofessionals	86,235	88,258	2.35%	$24,135	$24,963	3.43%
Auxiliary Staff	188,375	191,701	1.77%	$31,817	$33,173	4.26%
Total Staff	**764,310**	**776,521**	**1.60%**	**$52,143**	**$53,688**	**2.96%**

*Personnel figures are full-time equivalent.
The Professional Support category includes supervisors, counselors, educational diagnosticians, librarians, nurses/physicians, therapists, and psychologists.

Source: TEA Staff Salary reports for 2022–2023 and 2023–2024.

UNIVERSITY INTERSCHOLASTIC LEAGUE WINNING SCHOOLS (2023–2024 AND 2024–2025)

The UIL Lone Star Cup is awarded annually to six high schools — one in each of the six UIL classifications — based on their team performance in district and state championships. The winning schools receive the UIL Lone Star Cup trophy and a $1,000 scholarship.

Lone Star Cup Champions						
YEAR	1A	2A	3A	4A	5A	6A
2024	Gail Borden County	Shiner	Holliday	Canyon Randall	Lucas Lovejoy	Southlake Carroll
2025	Jayton	Shelbyville	Holliday	Wimberley	Aledo	Austin Vandegrift

ACADEMICS

The schools of individuals who won state championships in the academic, music, and the arts categories are listed. An em-dash (—) in the box means there was no competition in that conference in that category for that year.

YEAR	1A	2A	3A	4A	5A	6A
Overall State Meet Academic Champions						
2024	Gail Borden County	Martins Mill	Gladewater Sabine	Lindale	Argyle	Katy Seven Lakes
2025	Gail Borden County	Shelbyville	Gladewater Sabine	Dallas Sci. & Eng.	Argyle	Katy Seven Lakes
Accounting						
2024	Happy	Douglass	Holliday	Caddo Mills	Sharyland Pioneer	Edinburg
2025	Jayton	Douglass	Tuscola Jim Ned	Dallas Sci. & Eng.	Argyle	Waller
Calculator Applications						
2024	Newcastle	Latexo	Canadian	Dallas Sci. & Eng.	Argyle	Allen
2025	Newcastle	Three Rivers	Gladewater Sabine	Dallas Sci. & Eng.	Canutillo	Conroe Grand Oaks
Computer Applications						
2024	Rocksprings	Sanford-Fritch	Mount Pleasant Chapel Hill	Needville	Melissa	Waller
2025	—	—	—	—	—	—
Computer Science						
2024	Aspermont	Ozona	FW Harmony Innovation	Dallas Sci. & Eng.	Joshua	Plano West
2025	Rankin	Olney	Wall	Dallas Sci. & Eng.	CC Flour Bluff	Round Rock Westwood
Current Issues						
2024	Vernon Northside	Era	Mansfield Frontier	Hereford	Nacogdoches	Mansfield
2025	Lasara	Hico	Leonard	Hereford	Leander Rouse	Fort Bend Clements

Source: University Interscholastic League.

YEAR	1A	2A	3A	4A	5A	6A
Editorial Writing						
2024	Nazareth	Lipan	Comanche	Sulphur Springs	Argyle	Austin Lake Travis
2025	San Isidro	Martins Mill	Grandview	Sulphur Springs	Frisco Independence	Cedar Park Vista Ridge
Feature Writing						
2024	Nazareth	Gladewater Union Grove	Canadian	Fredericksburg	Comal Smithson Valley	Austin Westlake
2025	Gail Borden County	Gladewater Union Grove	White Oak	Dallas Sci. & Eng.	Nacogdoches	Lewisville Hebron
Headline Writing						
2024	Gail Borden County	Stinnett West Texas	Comal Memorial EC	Lindale	Forney	Alvin Shadow Creek
2025	Nazareth	Lindsay	Buna	Dallas Sci. & Eng.	Gregory-Portland	Schertz Clemens
Informative Speaking						
2024	Gail Borden County	Era	Callisburg	Wimberley	College Station A&M Consolidated	Northside O'Connor
2025	Aspermont	Shelbyville	Hill Country College Prep	Salado	Melissa	San Angelo Central
Journalism Team						
2024	Nazareth	Martins Mill	San Antonio Cole	Lindale	Mansfield Summit	Southlake Carroll
2025	Lasara	Martins Mill	White Oak	Dallas Sci. & Eng.	Cedar Park	Forney
Lincoln-Douglas Debate						
2024	Tyler UT Tyler Univ. Acad.	Saratoga West Hardin	Banquete	Salado	Nederland	San Antonio Johnson
2025	Savoy	Saratoga West Hardin	Banquete	Lindale	Argyle	Mansfield Legacy
Literary Criticism						
2024	Graford	Groveton	New Waverly	Sulphur Springs	Argyle	Waller
2025	Lasara	Graford	Holliday	Glen Rose	Pflugerville Hendrickson	Waller
Mathematics						
2024	Newcastle	Latexo	Mission Collegiate	Dallas Sci. & Eng.	Grapevine	Allen
2025	Knippa	Mart	Mission Collegiate	Dallas Sci. & Eng.	Grapevine	Fort Bend Elkins
News Writing						
2024	Lazbuddie	Martins Mill	Karnes City	Lindale	Denton Ryan	Southlake Carroll
2025	Lasara	Shelbyville	White Oak	Waco Connally	Nacogdoches	Cedar Park Vista Ridge
Number Sense						
2024	Jonesboro	Mart	Mission Collegiate	Dallas Sci. & Eng.	Grapevine	Fort Bend Clements
2025	Knippa	Shelbyville	Gladewater Sabine	Port Lavaca Calhoun	Hallsville	Fort Bend Clements
Persuasive Speaking						
2024	Aspermont	Saratoga West Hardin	Banquete	Salado	Pflugerville Hendrickson	Northside O'Connor
2025	Gail Borden County	Ore City	Bushland	Caddo Mills	Melissa	Plano West
Poetry Interpretation						
2024	Baird	Mason	Lexington	Seminole	Sharyland Pioneer	San Angelo Central
2025	Lometa	Abernathy	Lexington	Canyon Randall	Abilene Wylie	Humble Atascocita

YEAR	1A	2A	3A	4A	5A	6A
Prose Interpretation						
2024	Trinidad	Sudan	Lexington	CC Tuloso-Midway	Harlingen South	Converse Judson
2025	Trinidad	Ore City	Universal City Randolph	CC Tuloso-Midway	Harlingen South	Harlingen
Ready Writing						
2024	Iraan	Bartlett	Idalou	Sulphur Springs	San Antonio Wagner	Langham Creek
2025	Lenorah Grady	Shelbyville	Grandview	Sulphur Springs	Austin McCallum	Northside Clark
Science						
2024	Avery	Lockney	Canadian	Needville	Frisco Liberty	Dallas Highland Park
2025	Tiden McMullen County	Waco Meyer	Mansfield Frontier	Dallas Sci. & Eng.	Dallas Highland Park	Coppell
Social Studies						
2024	Moulton	Sabine Pass	GC Collegiate Acad. TCC NE	Sulphur Springs	Leander Rouse	Bridgeland
2025	Moulton	Spearman	CC Collegiate	Burnet	Boerne Champion	Katy Seven Lakes
Speech Team						
2024	Aspermont	Saratoga West Hardin	Banquete	Wimberley	Pflugerville Hendrickson	Katy Seven Lakes
2025	Gail Borden County	Shelbyville	Grandview	Lindale	College Station A&M Consolidated	Conroe Woodlands College Park
Spelling & Vocabulary						
2024	Moulton	Crawford	Henrietta	Burnet	Abilene Wylie	Katy Seven Lakes
2025	Imperial Buena Vista	Crawford	Henrietta	Needville	Abilene Wylie	Bridgeland
Spelling & Vocabulary Team						
2024	Moulton	Muenster	Henrietta	Sulphur Springs	CC Flour Bluff	Katy Seven Lakes
2025	Garden City	Sabine Pass	Henrietta	Sulphur Springs	Abilene Wylie	Bridgeland

PUBLICATIONS

YEAR	Yearbooks (Gold Awards)	Print Newspapers (Gold Awards)
2024	Aledo H.S., *Ledoian;* Gorzycki M.S., *The Roar;* Bowie H.S., *Lone Star;* Legacy H.S., *The Arena;* Marcus H.S., *The Maurader;* Pleasant Grove H.S., *The Hawk;* Richardson H.S., *The Eagle;* Round Rock H.S., *Dragon;* Thrall H.S., *The Tiger*	Episcopal School of Dallas, *Eagle Edition;* Bowie H. S., *The Dispatch;* McCallum H.S., *The Shield;* Pleasant Grove H.S., *The Edge;* St. Mark's School of Texas, *ReMarker*
2025	Aledo H.S., *Ledoian;* Hill Country Christian School, *The Bard;* Bowie H.S., *Lone Star;* Legacy H.S., *The Arena;* Marcus H.S., *The Marauder;* McKinney H.S., *The Lion;* Round Rock H.S., *Dragon;* Pleasant Grove H.S., *The Hawk;* Thrall H.S., *The Tiger*	Hebron H.S., *The Hawk Eye;* Bowie H.S., *Dispatch;* Kingwood Park H.S., *Kingwood Park Times;* McCallum H.S., *The Shield;* Pleasant Grove H.S., *The Edge;* St. Mark's School of Texas, *ReMarker*

MUSIC & THEATER

	1A	2A	3A	4A	5A	6A
One-Act Play						
2024	Guthrie	Shiner	Early	Zapata	Magnolia	Deer Park
2025	Ackerly Sands	Bogata Rivercrest	Lexington	Sunnyvale	Harlingen South	Keller
Marching Band						
2024	Menard HS	Rivercrest HS	Whitesboro HS	Celina HS	Cedar Park HS	Vandergrift HS
2025	Irion County HS	Sundown HS	Mineola HS	Celina HS	Cedar Park HS	Lewisville Hebron HS

STATE AND NATIONAL HISTORY DAY CONTESTS (2024 AND 2025)

Each year, thousands of students, encouraged by teachers and parents statewide, participate in the National History Day program in Texas. Texas History Day, an affiliate of NHD, is a highly regarded academic program for 6th through 12th grade students. Students that place first or second at the state contest earn the opportunity to compete at the national contest in Washington, D.C.

State History Day Winners 2024

Theme: Turning Points in History

	Junior	Senior
Documentaries		
Individual	**1st** *When Words Fail Music Speaks: Nina Simone's Social Reform for Civil Rights,* Otto M.S. (Plano)	**1st** *The Pakistan Movement: A South Asian Struggle for Self-Determination,* William B. Travis H.S. (Sugar Land)
	2nd *La Pasionaria: Emma Tenayuca and the Pecan Shellers Strike,* East Central Heritage M.S. (Converse)	**2nd** *The Salt March of 1930,* Austin Peace Academy
Group	**1st** *The Capture of Life: The Daguerreotype and its Impact on Art,* Sartartia M.S. (Sugar Land)	**1st** *Operation Mincemeat: Saving Lives from Beyond the Grave,* Plano East Senior H.S. (Parker)
	2nd *The Disaster That Changed the World,* Stell M.S. (Brownsville)	**2nd** *Treaty of Portsmouth,* Bellaire H.S. (Houston)
Exhibits		
Individual	**1st** *Through the Eyes of Nimitz- The Battle of Midway, A Turning Point in WW2,* Marathon ISD	**1st** *Panic on Wall Street: How the Stock Market Crash of 1929 Ignited a Turning Point in Texas' Economy,* Odyssey Academy - Bay Area (League City)
	2nd *No-Fault Divorce: Turning Point In American Matrimony,* Cedar Bayou (Baytown)	**2nd** *Turning the Page: The Sears Catalog's Impact On African Americans,* Lake Belton H.S.
Group	**1st** *From Sea to Shining Sea: The Transcontinental Railroad Redefines the Face of a Nation,* Edward "E.F." Green Junior School (Baytown)	**1st** *From Dust to Dust: How the Dust Bowl Revolutionized Agriculture and Society,* Midway H.S. (Hewitt)
	2nd *The Box That Changed The World,* Baytown	**2nd** *Exposed Wire Leads to Fire: How One Telegram Ignited America's Rise to Power,* Veterans Memorial Early College H.S. (Brownsville)
Performances		
Individual	**1st** *Nellie Bly: Her Story,* Garcia M.S. (Brownsville)	**1st** *Red Light! Gladys West the Global Positioning System,* Nimitz H.S. (Houston)
	2nd *The Discovery of the Double Helix: A Turning Point in Understanding the Structure of Deoxyribonucleic Acid (DNA),* Stillman M.S. (Brownsville)	**2nd** *Conspiracy – The Trial of the Chicago Eight and a Turning Point in American Law and Culture,* Odyssey Academy - Bay Area (Houston)
Group	**1st** *Reshaping the World: The Women's Rights Movement,* Garcia M.S. (Brownsville)	**1st** *Moses: How Harriet Tubman's Freedom Inspired a Legacy of Turning Points,* Princeton H.S.
	2nd *Winged Wonders: The Women's Air Force Service Pilots,* A&M Consolidated M.S. (College Station)	**2nd** *Mendez v Westminster: A Turning Point in Mexican American Civil Rights and the Segregation of Schools,* Veterans Memorial Early College H.S. (Brownsville)
Websites		
Individual	**1st** *Poisoned Pills: How the 1982 Tylenol Scare Became a Turning Point in Consumer Safety,* Dripping Springs M.S.	**1st** *Fueling Victory: How the Inch Pipelines Became a Turning Point in World War II,* Dripping H.S.
	2nd *The Digitalization of Film: A Turning Point in Modern Storytelling,* Young Women's Leadership Academy (San Antonio)	**2nd** *The Fight for the Right to Fight: Executive Order 9981 The Turning Point In Civil Rights,* Plano West Senior H.S.
Group	**1st** *Invention of the Smallpox Vaccine,* The Honor Roll School (Sugar Land)	**1st** *Where No Woman Has Gone Before: How Nichelle Nichols Launched a Turning Point in Diversity in NASA Programs,* Young Women's Leadership Academy (El Paso)
	2nd *The Creation of the Hydrogen Bomb: A Threatening Existence for Humanity,* Stell M.S. (Brownsville)	**2nd** *Edward Bernays: America's Pioneer of Modern Consumerism,* Plano East Senior H.S.
Papers		
Individual	**1st** *Black and White Love: How Loving v. Virginia became a Turning Point for Civil Rights, Interracial Couples, and Marriage, Forever Impacting America,* Edward "E.F." Green Junior School (Baytown)	**1st** *Taylored Politics: Progressivism and the Scientific Management of American Democracy,* Lasa H.S. (Austin)
	2nd *The Battle and Evacuation of Dunkirk in 1940; a Turning Point for the Allied War Effort for the Duration of World War II,* St. Patrick Cathedral School (Baytown)	**2nd** *Esther De Berdt Reed and The Ladies Association of Philadelphia,* Westlake H.S. (Austin)

National History Day 2024

2nd Place Senior Individual Performance	4th Place Junior Group Website	4th Place Junior Individual Website	4th Place Junior Group Exhibit
Red Light! Gladys West & the Global Positioning System, Nimitz H.S. (Houston)	*Invention of the Smallpox Vaccine: The Birth of Mass Vaccination,* The Honor Roll School (Sugar Land)	*Poisoned Pills: How the 1982 Tylenol Scare Became a Turning Point in Consumer Safety,* Dripping Springs M.S. (Dripping Springs)	*Exposed Wire Leads to Fire: How One Telegram Ignited America's Rise to Power,* Veterans Memorial Early College H.S. (Brownsville)

State History Day Winners 2025

Theme: Rights and Responsibilities in History

	Junior	Senior
Documentaries		
Individual	**1st:** *The Great IDEA: Speaking for Those Who Cannot Speak for Themselves,* Cedar Bayou Junior High (Baytown)	**1st:** *Church Rock Spill: Rights Denied, Responsibilities Neglected,* Dulles H.S. (Sugar Land)
	2nd: *Placing Out On the Orphan Trains: Balancing Rights and Responsibilities in an Early Child Welfare Program,* Cedar Bayou Junior High (Baytown)	**2nd:** *To Kill the Indian and Save the Man,* Impact Early H.S. (Baytown)
Group	**1st:** *Make Somebody Happy Today - Bake a Cake: Betty Crocker's Views on Women's Rights and Responsibilities in the Home,* Lake Belton M.S. (Temple)	**1st:** *The Pentagon Papers: War, Truth, and Press Freedom,* Bellaire H.S. (Houston)
	2nd: *The Destroyer of Worlds: How the Atomic Bomb Questioned Scientists' Rights and Responsibilities,* Lake Belton M.S. (Temple)	**2nd:** *The Major League Baseball Knocking Tobacco out of the Park,* New Caney H.S. (Splendora)
Exhibits		
Individual	**1st:** *Rights and Responsibilities of Women in Texas History,* East Central Heritage M.S. (Adkins)	**1st:** *Rx for Healthcare: Balancing Rights and Responsibilities within America's Medical System,* Odyssey Academy - Bay Area (League City)
	2nd: *Seltzer v. Green Day Inc. Where Rights and Fair Use Collide,* Incarnate Word Academy (Corpus Christi)	**2nd:** *Henrietta Lacks: How HeLa Cells Redefined Patient Rights and Scientist Responsibilities in Biomedical Research,* Plano East Senior H.S. (Plano)
Group	**1st:** *Set the Earth on Fire: Mining for Rights, Responsibilities and Equality during the Anthracite Coal Strike,* E.F. Green Junior School (Baytown)	**1st:** *Taming the Urban Jungle: The Fight for Public Health and the Passage of the Pure Food and Drug Act,* Blanson H.S. (Houston)
	2nd: *Exxon Valdez: Navigating The Tides Between Rights and Responsibilities,* Baytown Junior High (Baytown)	**2nd:** *The Shirtwaist Fire: A Spark for Labor's Rights,* MacArthur H.S. (Houston)
Performances		
Individual	**1st:** *Franklin on the Origins of the Fourth,* Gentry Junior High (Baytown)	**1st:** *Sharp as a Needle and Steady as the Hand Which Guides It: The ILGWU and the Fight for Workers' Rights,* Veterans Memorial Early College H.S. (Brownsville)
	2nd: *Playing Hardball: The Chavez Ravine Controversy,* Hutchinson M.S. (Lubbock)	**2nd:** *Bordering on Injustice: Environmental Struggles in the El Paso-Juarez Area,* Valle Verde Early College H.S. (El Paso)
Group	**1st:** *The United Farm Workers Association: Empowering Labor Rights and Social Justice,* Faulk M.S. (Brownsville)	**1st:** *Pennies and Pecans: How Chicano Women Raised Wages and Fought for Worker's Rights,* Travis B. Bryan H.S. (Bryan)
	2nd: *From Exclusion to Inclusion: How the Individuals with Disabilities Education Act (I.D.E.A.) Ensures Equal Access to Education,* Lanier M.S. (Houston)	**2nd:** *Bonnie and Clyde: Loss of Rights through Irresponsibility,* Hanna Early College H.S. (Brownsville)
Websites		
Individual	**1st:** *Beyond the Blast: The Texas City Disaster Sparks a Clash of Rights and Responsibilities,* Dripping Springs M.S. (Dripping Springs)	**1st:** *The Price of Patriotism: The Evolution of Rights and Responsibilities for World War I Veterans,* Dripping Springs H.S. (Dripping Springs)
	2nd: *The West Virginia Mine Wars: Justice in the Coal Field,* iUniversity Prep (Grapevine)	**2nd:** *Ethics on Trial: The Controversy of the Willowbrook Hepatitis Study,* Goose Creek Memorial (Baytown)
Group	**1st:** *The USPHS Experiment at Tuskegee: The Road to Informed Consent,* The Honor Roll School (Sugar Land)	**1st:** *America's Shining Women: How the Radium Girls Redefined Workers' Rights and Responsibilities,* Plano East Senior H.S. (Plano)
	2nd: *Loving in Color: Miscegenation vs. The Supreme Court,* Livingston Junior High (Livingston)	**2nd:** *The Price of Dissent: McCarthyism's Attack on Civil Rights,* Plano East Senior H.S. (Plano)
Papers		
Individual	**1st:** *The Montgomery Bus Boycott Empowering Rights, Embracing Responsibilities in a Journey Towards Equality, Justice, and Social Change for All,* E.F. Green Junior School (Baytown)	**1st:** *A Network of Incompatible Promises: How Britain Sowed the Seeds of Conflict in Mandatory Palestine,* Plano East Senior H.S. (Murphy)
	2nd: *HIPAA: The Intersection of Patient Rights and Healthcare Responsibilities,* Lake Belton M.S. (Temple)	**2nd:** *From Tribal Sovereignty to Corporate Personhood: Indians, Railroads, and the Fourteenth Amendment,* Lasa H.S. (Austin)

National History Day 2025

1st Place Junior Individual Documentary	1st Place Junior Individual Website	3rd Place Senior Group Documentary
The Great IDEA: Speaking for Those Who Cannot Speak for Themselves, Cedar Bayou Junior High (Baytown)	*The West Virginia Mine Wars: Justice in the Coal Field,* iUniversity Prep (Grapevine)	*The Pentagon Papers: War, Truth, and Press Freedom,* Bellaire High School (Bellaire)

COLLEGES & UNIVERSITIES

Enrollment in Texas public, independent, career, and private colleges and universities in Fall 2023 totaled 1,531,224 students, an increase of 35,212 students from the Fall 2022 enrollment of 1,496,012.

Enrollment in Fall 2023 in the 37 public universities was 676,467, a 1.52% increase from 2022's enrollment of 666,322. The state's public community colleges and Texas State Technical College System, which offer two-year degree programs, reported Fall 2023 enrollments totaling 695,673 students, an increase of 3.93% from enrollment of 669,354 reported in Fall 2022.

Enrollment for Fall 2023 at independent colleges and universities was 127,544 students, down slightly from the 127,741 students enrolled in Fall 2022.

Brief History of Higher Education in Texas

The first permanent institutions of higher education established in Texas were church-supported schools, although there were some earlier efforts.

Rutersville University was established in 1840 by Methodist minister Martin Ruter in Fayette County and was the predecessor of Southwestern University in Georgetown, which was established in 1843; Baylor University, now at Waco, was established in 1845 at Independence, in Washington County, by the Texas Union Baptist Association; and Austin College, now at Sherman, was founded in 1849 at Huntsville by the Brazos Presbytery of the Old School Presbyterian Church.

AddRan College, established in 1873 at Thorp Spring in Hood County was the predecessor of present-day Texas Christian University in Fort Worth.

Texas A&M University and The University of Texas

The Agricultural and Mechanical College of Texas (now Texas A&M University), authorized by the Texas Legislature in 1871, opened its doors in 1876 to become the first publicly supported institution of higher education in Texas.

In 1881, Texans established The University of Texas, setting up the Main University in Austin and the Medical Branch in Galveston. The Austin institution opened September 15, 1883, and the Galveston school opened in 1891.

First College for Women

In 1901, the 27th Legislature established the Girls Industrial College, which began classes at its campus in Denton in 1903. A campaign to establish a state industrial college for women was led by the State Grange and Patrons of Husbandry.

Cost of Public Higher Education in Texas

	2-Year Schools (75)		4-Year Schools (37)	
	2022	2023	2022	2023
Average Tuition and Fees	$2,877	$3,003	$10,075	$10,129
Average Debt	$15,664	$15,709	$24,527	$24,570
% of Students with Debt	26%	24.7%	52.5%	51%

Top 5 Undergrad Majors at Public Universities (2023)

1. Business, Management, Marketing, and Related Support Services (85,038 students)
2. Engineering (52,214 students)
3. Health Professions and Related Programs (44,302 students)
4. Biological and Biomedical Sciences (43,879 students)
5. Computer and Information Sciences and Support Services (33,740 students)

Source: Texas Public Higher Education Almanac 2023

UNSPLASH/MIKAEL KRISTENSON

Source: Texas Higher Education Coordinating Board.

A bill was signed into law on April 6, 1901, creating the college. It was charged with a dual mission, which continues to guide the university today: to provide a liberal arts education and to prepare young women with a specialized education "for the practical industries of the age."

In 1905, the name of the college was changed to the College of Industrial Arts. It was changed to Texas State College for Women in 1934.

Since 1957, the institution, which is now the largest university principally for women in the United States, has been the Texas Woman's University.

Historic, Primarily Black Colleges

A number of Texas schools were established primarily for Black people, although collegiate racial integration has long been the status quo. Title III of the Higher Education Act of 1965 established the term Historically Black College/University (HBCU), defined as a school of higher learning that was established and accredited before the 1964 Civil Rights Act and was dedicated to educating African Americans.

Today, there are nine HBCUs in Texas: state-supported Prairie View A&M University (originally established as Alta Vista Agricultural College in 1876, Prairie View); St. Philip's College (San Antonio); Texas Southern University (Houston); privately supported Huston-Tillotson University (Austin); Jarvis Christian College (Hawkins); Southwestern Christian College (Terrell); Wiley College (Marshall); Paul Quinn College (originally located in Waco, now in Dallas); and Texas College (Tyler).

Predominantly Black colleges that are important in the history of higher education in Texas, but which have ceased operations, include: Bishop College (established in Marshall in 1881, then moved to Dallas); Mary Allen College (established in Crockett in 1886); and Butler College (originally named the Texas Baptist Academy, in 1905 in Tyler).

Hispanic-Serving Institutions

Title V of the Higher Education Act of 2008 established grant programs for public colleges that qualify as Hispanic-Serving Institutions (HSIs). An HSI is defined as a not-for-profit institution of higher learning with a full-time equivalent undergraduate student enrollment that is at least 25% Hispanic.

According to the Hispanic Association of Colleges & Universities, Texas has 112 HSIs, including many community colleges, operating today.

HIGHER-EDUCATION SYSTEMS

System	Abbreviation	Location	Founded	Leader	Enrollment
					Fall Term, 2023
Alamo Colleges District	ACD	San Antonio	1978	Dr. Mike Flores	71,237
Howard County Junior College District	HCJCD	Big Spring	1946	Dr. Cheryl T. Sparks	3,116
Lone Star College System	LSC	The Woodlands	1973	Mario K. Castillo J.D.	76,389
Texas A&M University System	TAMUS	College Station	1948	Dr. John Sharp	112,109
Texas State University System	TSUS	Austin	1911	Dr. Brian McCall	61,633
Texas Tech University System	TTUS	Lubbock	1996	Dr. Tedd L. Mitchell	63,612
University of Houston System	UHS	Houston	1977	Dr. Renu Khator	58,795
University of North Texas System	UNTS	Dallas	1999	Dr. Michael R. Williams	50,522
University of Texas System	UTS	Austin	1883	Dr. James B. Milliken	181,203

Source: Texas Higher Education Coordinating Board.

PUBLIC UNIVERSITIES

Institution	System	Location	Founded	Leader	Enrollment Fall Term, 2023
Angelo State University	TTUS	San Angelo	1928	Lt. Gen. Ret. Ronnie D. Hawkins Jr.	10,885
Dallas College	—	Dallas	1966	Dr. Justin Lonon	61,536
East Texas A&M University	TAMUS	Commerce	1889	Dr. Mark J. Rudin	11,500
Lamar University	TSUS	Beaumont	1923	Dr. Jaime R. Taylor	16,919
Midwestern State University	TTUS	Wichita Falls	1922	Dr. Stacia Haynie	5,172
Prairie View A&M University	TAMUS	Prairie View	1876	Dr. Tomikia P. LeGrande	9,415
Sam Houston State University	TSUS	Huntsville	1879	Dr. Alisa White	20,761
Stephen F. Austin State University	UTS	Nacogdoches	1923	Dr. Neal Weaver	10,781
Sul Ross State University	TSUS	Alpine	1917	Dr. J. Carlos Hernández	1,449
Sul Ross State University Rio Grande College	TSUS	Del Rio	1973	Dr. J. Carlos Hernández	642
Tarleton State University	TAMUS	Stephenville	1899	Dr. James Hurley	14,513
Texas A&M International University	TAMUS	Laredo	1970	Christopher Maynard	8,256
Texas A&M University	TAMUS	College Station	1876	General (Ret.) Mark A. Welsh III	69,517
Texas A&M University–Central Texas	TAMUS	Killeen	2009	Dr. Richard Rhodes	2,251
Texas A&M University–Corpus Christi	TAMUS	Corpus Christi	1973	Dr. Kelly M. Miller	10,855
Texas A&M University at Galveston	TAMUS	Galveston	1962	Col. Michael E. Fossum	2,151
Texas A&M University–Kingsville	TAMUS	Kingsville	1925	Dr. Robert H. Vela Jr.	6,553
Texas A&M University–San Antonio	TAMUS	San Antonio	2009	Dr. Salvador Hector Ochoa	7,511
Texas A&M University–Texarkana	TAMUS	Texarkana	1971	Dr. Ross C. Alexander	2,056
Texas Southern University	—	Houston	1926	James W. Crawford III	8,469
Texas State University	TSUS	San Marcos	1903	Dr. Kelly R. Damphousse	38,723
Texas Tech University	TTUS	Lubbock	1923	Dr. Lawrence Schovanec	40,092
Texas Woman's University	—	Denton	1901	Dr. Carine M. Feyten	15,180
University of Houston	UHS	Houston	1927	Dr. Renu Khator	46,505
University of Houston–Clear Lake	UHS	Houston	1974	Dr. Richard Walker	8,210
University of Houston–Downtown	UHS	Houston	1948	Dr. Loren J. Blanchard	14,105
University of Houston–Victoria	UHS	Victoria	1973	Dr. Robert K. "Bob" Glenn	3,784
University of North Texas	UNTS	Denton	1890	Dr. Harrison Keller	46,724
University of North Texas at Dallas	UNTS	Dallas	2000	Dr. Warren von Eschenbach, Interim	3,798
University of Texas at Arlington, The	UTS	Arlington	1895	Dr. Jennifer Cowley	41,376
University of Texas at Austin, The	UTS	Austin	1883	Jim Davis	52,883
University of Texas at Dallas, The	UTS	Richardson	1961	Dr. Richard C. Benson	30,885
University of Texas at El Paso, The	UTS	El Paso	1913	Dr. Heather Wilson	24,351
University of Texas of the Permian Basin, The	UTS	Odessa	1969	Dr. Sandra K. Woodley	5,283
University of Texas Rio Grande Valley, The	UTS	Edinburg	1973	Dr. Guy Bailey	31,577
University of Texas at San Antonio, The	UTS	San Antonio	1969	Dr. Taylor Eighmy	34,864
University of Texas at Tyler, The	UTS	Tyler	1971	Dr. Julie V. Philley	9,442
West Texas A&M University	TAMUS	Canyon	1910	Dr. Walter Wendler	9,029

INDEPENDENT SENIOR COLLEGES OR UNIVERSITIES

Institution	Location	Founded	Affiliation	Leader	Enrollment Fall Term, 2023
Abilene Christian University	Abilene	1906	Church of Christ	Dr. Phil Schubert	5,950
Amberton University	Garland, Frisco	1971	Evangelical Christianity	Dr. Carol A. Palmer	758
Arlington Baptist University	Arlington	1939	Baptist	Dr. Clifton McDaniel	—
Austin College	Sherman	1849	Presbyterian USA	Dr. Steven P. O'Day	1,136
Baylor University	Waco	1845	Southern Baptist	Dr. Linda A. Livingstone	20,824
Concordia University Texas	Austin	1926	Lutheran Church–Missouri Synod	Dr. Kristi Kirk	1,659
Criswell College	Dallas	1971	Baptist	Dr. Barry Creamer	155
Dallas Baptist University	Dallas	1898	Baptist	Dr. Adam C. Wright	4,166
Dallas Christian College	Dallas	1950	Christian	Dr. Brian D. Smith	
East Texas Baptist University	Marshall	1913	Baptist	Dr. J. Blair Blackburn	1,955
Hardin-Simmons University	Abilene	1891	Southern Baptist	Eric I. Bruntmyer	1,655
Houston Christian University	Houston	1960	Baptist	Dr. Robert B. Sloan Jr.	4,182
Howard Payne University	Brown-wood	1889	Baptist	Dr. Cory Hines	832
Huston-Tillotson University	Austin	1952	United Church of Christ and United Methodist	Dr. Melva K. Williams	1,029
Jarvis Christian College	Hawkins	1912	Disciples of Christ	Dr. Glenell M. Lee-Pruitt	831
LeTourneau University	Longview	1946	Evangelical Christianity	Dr. Steven D. Mason	3,089
Lubbock Christian University	Lubbock	1957	Church of Christ	Dr. Scott McDowell	1,589
McMurry University	Abilene	1923	United Methodist	Dr. Lynne Murray	2,549
Our Lady of the Lake University of San Antonio	San Antonio	1895	Roman Catholic	Dr. Abel Antonio Chávez	2,096
Paul Quinn College	Dallas	1872	African Methodist Episcopal Church	Dr. Michael J. Sorrell	577
Rice University	Houston	1891	—	Dr. Reginald DesRoches	8,556
St. Edward's University	Austin	1885	Roman Catholic	Dr. Montserrat Fuentes	3,309
St. Mary's University of San Antonio	San Antonio	1852	Roman Catholic	Dr. Winston Erevelles	3,162
Schreiner University	Kerrville	1923	Presbyterian U.S.A.	Dr. Charlie McCormick	1,208
Southern Methodist University	Dallas	1911	United Methodist	Dr. Jay Hartzell	11,835
South Texas College of Law	Houston	1923	—	Reynaldo "Rey" Anaya Valencia	1,024
Southwestern Adventist University	Keene	1893	Seventh-Day Adventist	Ana Patterson	824
Southwestern Assemblies of God University	Waxahachie	1927	Assemblies of God	Dr. Kermit S. Bridges	1,461
Southwestern Christian College	Terrell	1948	Church of Christ	Dr. Ervin D. Seamster Jr.	103
Southwestern University	George-town	1840	United Methodist	Dr. Laura Skandera Trombley	1,454
Texas Christian University	Fort Worth	1873	Disciples of Christ	Daniel W. Pullin	12,731
Texas College	Tyler	1894	Christian Methodist Episcopal	Dr. Dwight J. Fennell	687
Texas Lutheran University	Seguin	1891	Evangelical Lutheran	Dr. Debbie Cottrell	1,354
Texas Wesleyan University	Fort Worth	1891	United Methodist	Dr. Emily W. Messer	2,666
Trinity University	San Antonio	1869	Presbyterian U.S.A.	Dr. Vanessa B. Beasley	2,733
University of Dallas	Irving	1956	Roman Catholic	Dr. Jonathan J. Sanford	2,182
University of the Incarnate Word	San Antonio	1881	Roman Catholic	Dr. Thomas M. Evans	6,614
University of Mary Hardin-Baylor	Belton	1845	Baptist	Dr. Randy O'Rear	3,520
University of St. Thomas	Houston	1947	Roman Catholic	Rob Vischer	3,781
Wayland Baptist University	Plainview	1910	Southern Baptist	Dr. Donna Hedgepath	2,150
Wiley College	Marshall	1873	United Methodist	Dr. Herman J. Felton Jr.	636

PUBLIC MEDICAL SCHOOL OR HEALTH SCIENCE CENTER

Institution	System	Location	Founded	Leader	Enrollment Fall Term, 2023
Sam Houston State University Medical School	—	Conroe	2019	Dr. Thomas Mohr	484
Texas A&M University Health Science Center	TAMUS	Bryan	1948	Dr. Jon Mogford	3,456
Texas Tech University Health Sciences Center	TTUS	Lubbock	1972	Dr. Lori Rice-Spearman	4,763
Texas Tech University Health Sciences Center El Paso	TTUS	El Paso	2013	Dr. Richard Lange	922
University of Houston Medical School	UHS	Houston	2019	Dr. Jonathan A. McCullers	171
University of North Texas Health Science Center at Fort Worth	UNTS	Fort Worth	1966	Dr. Kirk A. Calhoun, Interim	2,273
University of Texas at Austin Dell Medical School	UTS	Austin	2012	Dr. Claudia F. Lucchinetti	199
University of Texas Health Science Center at Houston, The	UTS	Houston	1972	Dr. Giuseppe N. Colasurdo	5,044
University of Texas Health Science Center at San Antonio, The	UTS	San Antonio	1968	Dr. Taylor Eighmy	3,616
University of Texas M.D. Anderson Cancer Center, The	UTS	Houston	1941	Dr. Peter W.T. Pisters	355
University of Texas Medical Branch at Galveston, The	UTS	Galveston	1891	Dr. Charles P. Mouton	3,214
University of Texas Rio Grande Valley Medical School	UTS	Edinburg	2013	Dr. Michael B. Hocker	287
University of Texas Southwestern Medical Center, The	UTS	Dallas	1943	Dr. Daniel K. Podolsky	2,501
University of Texas at Tyler Health Science Center, The	UTS	Tyler	1971	Dr. Julie V. Philley	125

INDEPENDENT MEDICAL, DENTAL, OR CHIROPRACTIC SCHOOL

Institution	Location	Founded	Leader	Enrollment Fall Term, 2023
Baylor College of Medicine	Houston	1903	Dr. Paul Klotman	1,667
Parker University	Dallas	1982	Dr. William E. Morgan	2,196
Texas Chiropractic College	Pasadena	1908	Dr. Sandra Hughes	267

PUBLIC COMMUNITY COLLEGES

Institution	System	Location	Founded	Leader	Enrollment Fall Term, 2023
Alamo Colleges—Northeast Lakeview College	ACD	Universal City	2007	Dr. Veronica Garcia	8,265
Alamo Colleges—Northwest Vista College	ACD	San Antonio	1995	Dr. Amy Bosley	18,808
Alamo Colleges—Palo Alto College	ACD	San Antonio	1983	Dr. Robert Garza	10,908
Alamo Colleges—St. Philip's College	ACD	San Antonio	1898	Dr. Adena Williams Loston	14,281
Alamo Colleges—San Antonio College	ACD	San Antonio	1925	Dr. Francisco Solis	18,975
Alvin Community College	—	Alvin	1949	Dr. Robert Exley	5,269
Amarillo College	—	Amarillo	1929	Dr. Jamelle J. Conner	9,170
Angelina College	—	Lufkin	1968	Dr. Michael J. Simon	3,890
Austin Community College	—	Austin	1972	Dr. Russell Lowery-Hart	32,994
Blinn College	—	Brenham	1883	Dr. Mary Hensley	18,301

Institution	System	Location	Founded	Leader	Enrollment Fall Term, 2023
Brazosport College	—	Lake Jackson	1967	Dr. Vincent R. Solis	4,100
Central Texas College	—	Killeen	1965	Dr. Michele J. Carter	6,379
Cisco College	—	Cisco	1909	Dr. Thad J. Anglin	3,012
Clarendon College	—	Clarendon	1898	Texas D. Buckhaults	1,369
Coastal Bend College	—	Beeville	1966	Dr. Justin Hoggard	3,981
College of the Mainland	—	Texas City	1967	Dr. Warren Nichols	4,961
Collin County Community College District	—	McKinney	1985	Dr. H. Neil Matkin	36,296
Del Mar College	—	Corpus Christi	1935	Dr. Mark Escamilla	9,720
El Paso Community College	—	El Paso	1969	Dr. William Serrata	24,683
Frank Phillips College	—	Borger	1948	Dr. Glendon Forgey	1,755
Galveston College	—	Galveston	1967	Dr. W. Myles Shelton	2,119
Grayson College	—	Denison	1963	Dr. Jeremy McMillen	4,146
Hill College	—	Hillsboro	1923	Dr. Thomas Mills	4,000
Houston Community College	—	Houston	1971	Dr. Margaret Ford Fisher	40,246
Howard College	HCJCD	Big Spring	1945	Dr. Cheryl T. Sparks	3,068
Kilgore College	—	Kilgore	1935	Dr. Brenda S. Kays	6,067
Lamar Institute of Technology	TSUS	Beaumont	1923	Dr. Sidney Valentine	5,261
Lamar State College–Orange	TSUS	Orange	1969	Dr. Thomas Johnson	3,154
Lamar State College–Port Arthur	TSUS	Port Arthur	1909	Dr. Betty J. Reynard	3,912
Laredo College	—	Laredo	1947	Dr. Minita Ramirez	10,166
Lee College	—	Baytown	1934	Dr. Lynda Villanueva	8,142
Lone Star College–CyFair	LSC	Houston	2003	Dr. Valerie Jones	20,703
Lone Star College–Houston North	LSC	The Woodlands	2017	Dr. Quentin Wright	2,422
Lone Star College–Kingwood	LSC	Humble	1984	Dr. Melissa N. Gonzalez	10,822
Lone Star College–Montgomery	LSC	Conroe	1995	Dr. De' Reese Reid-Hart	13,574
Lone Star College–North Harris	LSC	Houston	1973	Dr. Bennie Lambert	9,145
Lone Star College–Tomball	LSC	Tomball	1986	Dr. Lee Ann Nutt	6,449
Lone Star College–University Park	LSC	Houston	2012	Dr. Matthew Dempsey	9,599
McLennan Community College	—	Waco	1965	Dr. Johnette McKown	7,199
Midland College	—	Midland	1972	Dr. Damon Kennedy	5,251
Navarro College	—	Corsicana	1946	Dr. Kevin G. Fegan	6,421
North Central Texas College	—	Gainesville	1924	Dr. Brent Wallace	7,543
Northeast Texas Community College	—	Mount Pleasant	1984	Dr. Kevin Rose	2,919
Odessa College	—	Odessa	1946	Dr. Gregory Williams	8,677
Panola College	—	Carthage	1947	Dr. Jessica Pace	2,385
Paris Junior College	—	Paris	1924	Dr. Stephen Michael Benson	4,323
Ranger College	—	Ranger	1926	Derrick Worrells	2,479
San Jacinto College	—	Pasadena, La Porte, Houston	1961	Dr. Brenda Lang Hellyer	31,494
South Plains College	—	Levelland	1957	Dr. Robin Satterwhite	8,864
South Texas College	—	McAllen	1993	Dr. Ricardo Solis	5,964
Southwest Collegiate Institute for the Deaf	HCJCD	Big Spring	1979	Dr. Cheryl T. Sparks	48
Southwest Texas Junior College	—	Uvalde	1946	Dr. Hector Gonzales	5,964

Institution	System	Location	Founded	Leader	Enrollment Fall Term, 2023
Tarrant County College	—	Fort Worth	1965	Dr. Elva Concha LeBlanc	41,472
Temple College	—	Temple	1926	Dr. Christy Ponce	4,378
Texarkana College	—	Texarkana	1927	Dr. Jason Smith	3,652
Texas Southmost College	—	Brownsville	1926	Dr. Jesús Roberto Rodriguez	8,193
Texas State Technical College	—	Waco	1965	Dr. Michael L. Reeser	15,205
Trinity Valley Community College	—	Athens	1946	Dr. Jason Morrison	5,472
Tyler Junior College	—	Tyler	1926	Dr. Juan E. Mejia	11,956
Vernon College	—	Vernon	1970	Dr. Dusty R. Johnston	2,136
Victoria College	—	Victoria	1925	Dr. Jennifer Kent	3,161
Weatherford College	—	Weatherford	1869	Dr. Tod Allen Farmer	5,440
Western Texas College	—	Snyder	1969	Dr. Barbara Beebe	1,434
Wharton County Junior College	—	Wharton	1946	Dr. Betty A. McCrohan	5,687

INDEPENDENT JUNIOR COLLEGES

Institution	Location	Affiliation	Founded	Leader	Enrollment Fall Term, 2023
Jacksonville College	Jacksonville	Baptist Missionary Alliance	1899	Dr. David Erickson	522

UNSPLASH/ZABDIEL GONZALEZ

UNSPLASH/ZABDIEL GONZALEZ

Scottie Scheffler (Highland Park, UT) won two majors in 2025.

Texas SPORTS STARS

Victor Wembanyama (San Antonio Spurs)
NBA Rookie of the Year (2024)
NBA All-Star (2025)

Sha'Carri Richardson (Dallas) sprinted to gold in Paris.

Marcel Reed
Texas A&M QB
(2025)

Jose Altuve
(Houston Astros)
9-Time MLB All-Star

Kevin Durant (UT) captured his fourth Olympic gold medal in 2024.

Steve Sarkisian and the Texas Longhorns won the 2025 Peach Bowl.

Paige Bueckers (Dallas Wings) WNBA Rookie of the Year (2025)

Jamie Benn Dallas Stars Captain

Tara Davis-Woodhall (UT) took home gold in the long jump (2024).

Simone Biles (Spring) dazzled at the 2024 Olympics in Paris.

TEXAS STATE HIGH SCHOOL CHAMPIONSHIPS

The University Interscholastic League (UIL), which governs literary and athletic competition among public schools in Texas, was organized in 1910 as a division of the University of Texas extension service.

Initially, it sponsored forensic competition. By 1920, the UIL organized the structure of the high school football game in response to the growing popularity of the sport in Texas.

The Texas Association of Private and Parochial Schools (TAPPS) is the largest group of private schools in the state with more than 225 member institutions. The interscholastic competition began in 1978 and was significantly expanded when the Texas Christian Interscholastic League ceased to exist in 2000 and many of those schools moved into TAPPS.

Not represented are the Southwest Preparatory Conference (SPC), TAIAO (Texas Association of Independent Athletic Organizations), TCAL (Texas Christian Athletic League), or TCSAAL (Texas Charter School Academic & Athletic League).

Sources: The University Interscholastic League and the Texas Association of Private and Parochial Schools.

UNSPLASH/ANNA HECKER

Football

Year	Conference	Division	Champion	Runner-Up
2023-2024	UIL	1A Division I	Gordon 70	Westbrook 20
		1A Division II	Benjamin 82	Oglesby 34
		2A Division I	Timpson 49	Tolar 7
		2A Division II	Albany 28	Mart 10
		3A Division I	Malakoff 14	Franklin 7
		3A Division II	Gunter 30	El Maton Tidehaven 14
		4A Division I	Anna 26	Tyler Chapel Hill 0
		4A Division II	Gilmer 28	Belville 26
		5A Division I	Aledo 51	Comal Smithson Valley 8
		5A Division II	Port Neches-Groves 20	Dallas South Oak Cliff 17
		6A Division I	Duncanville 49	Galena Park North Shore 33
		6A Division II	DeSoto74	Humble Summer Creek 14
	TAPPS	Division I	Parish Episcopal School 40	St. Thomas High School 29
		Division II	Liberty Christian School 52	Regents School of Austin 10
		Division III	Dallas Christian School 28	Holy Cross of San Antonio 13
2024-2025	UIL	1A Division I	Gordon 70	Whiteface 24
		1A Division II	Jayton 54	Oakwood 8
		2A Division I	Ganado 30	Stamford 28
		2A Division II	Muenster 36	Shiner 29
		3A Division I	Columbus 48	Malakoff 14
		3A Division II	Gunter 28	Woodville 0
		4A Division I	Celina 55	Kilgore 21
		4A Division II	Carthage 28	Waco La Vega 14
		5A Division I	Comal Smithson Valley 32	Dallas Highland Park 20
		5A Division II	Richmond Randle 38	Dallas South Oak Cliff 35
		6A Division I	North Crowley 50	Austin Westlake 21
		6A Division II	Austin Vandegrift 24	Southlake Carroll 17
	TAPPS	**6-Man Football**		
		Division I	First Baptist Christian 76	Coram Deo Academy 36
		Division II	Covenant Classical (Fort Worth) 80	Alpha Omega Academy 32
		Division III	Wichita Christian 52	Heritage School (Fredericksburg) 12
		11-Man Football		
		Division I	Liberty Christian 45	Parish Episcopal 24
		Division II	All Saints Episcopal 21	Second Baptist School 3
		Division III	Dallas Christian School 21	Holy Cross of San Antonio 18
		Division IV	First Baptist 42	Brazos Christian 15

MADISEN SKINNER

XINHUA/ALAMY

Volleyball

Year	Conference	Division	Champion	Runner-Up
2023-2024	UIL	1A Division I	Blum 3	Harrold 1
		2A Division I	Iola 3	Crawford 1
		3A Division I	Bushland 3	Gunter 1
		4A Division I	Comal Davenport 3	Canyon Randall 2
		5A Division I	Lucas Lovejoy 3	Liberty Hill 0
		6A Division I	Conroe Grand Oaks 3	Katy Cinco Ranch 0
	TAPPS	1A Division I	Christ Academy Wichita Falls 3	Heritage School Fredericksburg 0
		2A Division I	Ovilla Christian School Red Oak 3	First Baptist Academy Dallas 0
		3A Division I	Keystone School San Antonio 3	Denton Calvary Academy 0
2024-2025	UIL	1A Division I	Harrold 3	Neches 1
		2A Division I	Johnson City LBJ 3	Wink 2
		2A Division II	Crawford 3	Iola 2
		3A Division I	Bushland 3	Goliad 1
		3A Division II	Stockdale 3	Boyd 1
		4A Division I	Decatur 3	Belville 1
		4A Division II	Wimberly 3	Canyon Randall 2
		5A Division I	Corpus Christi Flour Bluff 3	McKinney North 2
		5A Division II	Frisco Wakeland 3	Cedar Park 0
		6A Division I	Conroe Grand Oaks 3	Lamar Fulshear 1
		6A Division II	Northwest Nelson 3	Houston Stratford 0
	TAPPS	1A Division I	Christ Academy Wichita Falls 3	Hill Country Christian School 0
		2A Division I	Ovilla Christian School Red Oak 3	Faith West Academy 0
		3A Division I	Providence Classical School 3	Wylie Prepatory Academy 0

Boys Basketball

Year	Conference	Division	Champion	Runner-Up
2023-2024	UIL	1A Division I	Jayton 60	Benjamin 53
		2A Division I	Lipan 47	Shelbyville 36
		3A Division I	Hitchcock 53	Ponder 49
		4A Division I	Oak Cliff Faith Family Academy 80	Silsbee 66
		5A Division I	Lancaster 59	Kileen Ellison 30
		6A Division I	Plano East 53	Round Rock Stony Point 41
	TAPPS	1A Division I	Kingdom Collegiate Academy DeSoto 59	Cornerstone Christian San Antonio 58
		2A Division I	Bethseda Christian School Fort Worth 48	First Baptist Academy Dallas 33
		3A Division I	Lubbock Christian School 53	St. Francis Episcopal School Houston 61
		4A Division I	Grace Prep Academy Arlington 49	St. Thomas Episcopal School Houston 56
		5A Division I	Midland Christian High School 55	The Woodlands Christian Academy 37
		6A Division I	Parish Episcopal School Dallas 46	John Paul II High School Plano 42
2024-2025	UIL	1A Division I	Perrin-Whitt 65	Turkey Valley 46
		1A Division II	Jayton 70	Bryson 36
		2A Division I	Waco Meyer 53	Hearne 49
		2A Division II	Martin's Mill 55	Lipan 43
		3A Division I	Tatum 84	Columbus 49
		3A Division II	Kountze 67	Paradise 41
		4A Division I	Dallas Kimball 71	Houston Washington 48
		4A Division II	Kennedale 69	Houston Wheatley 65
		5A Division I	Beaumont West Brook 63	North Richland Hills Birdville 57
		5A Division II	Mansfield Summit 54	Fort Bend Marshall 47
		6A Division I	Duncanville 54	Houston Bellaire 52
		6A Division II	Denton Guyer 48	Katy Jordan 47
	TAPPS	1A Division I	Texoma Christian School 55	Divine Savior Academy 51
		2A Division I	O'Connell College Preparatory High School 49	Victory Christian Academy 35
		3A Division I	Akiba Yavneh Academy 55	Live Oak Classical School 45
		4A Division I	St. Francis Episcopal School 55	Lubbock Christian School 36
		5A Division I	Second Baptist School 65	Grace Preparatory Academy 47
		6A Division I	St. Michael's Catholic School 50	Parish Episcopal School 48

Girls Basketball

Year	Conference	Division	Champion	Runner-Up
2023-2024	UIL	1A Division I	Newcastle 48	Turkey Valley 32
		2A Division I	Martin's Mill 44	Nocona 42
		3A Division I	Shallowater 54	Huntington 49
		4A Division I	Waco La Vega 45	Canyon 36
		5A Division I	Frisco Liberty 60	Mansfield Timberview 51
		6A Division I	Duncanville 59	South Grand Prairie 41
	TAPPS	1A Division I	Harvest Christian Academy Edinburg 78	Texoma Christian School Sherman 27
		2A Division I	Covenant Christian School Conroe 50	Southcrest Christian School Lubbock 37
		3A Division I	Lubbock Christian School 64	Rosehill Christian School Tomball 59
		4A Division I	Lake Country Christian School Fort Worth 56	Bay Area Christian School League City 50
		5A Division I	Southwest Christian School Fort Worth 63	Second Baptist School Houston 58
		6A Division I	Bishop Lynch High School Dallas 56	Ursuline Academy Dallas 40
2024-2025	UIL	1A Division I	Broaddus 56	Clyde Eula 39
		1A Division II	Nazareth 53	Saltillo 31
		2A Division I	Nocona 54	San Saba 37
		2A Division II	Martin's Mill 43	Farwell 41
		3A Division I	Fairfield 50	Tuscola Jim Ned 44
		3A Division II	Kountze 69	Paradise 40
		4A Division I	Decatur 53	Waco La Vega 41
		4A Division II	Dallas Lincoln 60	Cuero 32
		5A Division I	Denton Ryan 58	San Antonio Wagner 47
		5A Division II	Lubbock Monterey 64	Liberty Hill 35
		6A Division I	Humble Summer Creek 52	Cedar Hill 49
		6A Division II	Fort Worth Boswell 51	Fort Bend Hightower 42
	TAPPS	1A Division I	Harvest Christian Academy Edinburg 57	Texoma Christian School Sherman 46
		2A Division I	First Baptist Academy 46	St. Joseph Catholic School 37
		3A Division I	Live Oak Classical School 47	Abilene Christian School 39
		4A Division I	Lubbock Christian School 43	Geneva School of Boerne 39
		5A Division I	Legacy Preparatory Christian Academy 53	Midland Christian School 64
		6A Division I	Prestonwood Christian Academy 54	Antonian College Prepatory High School 43

Boys Soccer

Year	Conference	Division	Champion	Runner-Up
2023-2024	UIL	4A Division I	San Elizario 1	Boerne 0
		5A Division I	Midlothian 3	Frisco Wakeland 1
		6A Division I	Katy Seven Lakes 2	Lewisville Flower Mound 1
	TAPPS	Division I	John Paul II (Plano) 2	Central Catholic (San Antonio) 1
		Division II	St. Joseph Academy (Brownsville) 1	St. Michael's (Austin) 0
		Division III	Brook Hill (Bullard) 1	British (Houston) 0
2024-2025	UIL	4A Division I	Salado 3	River Oaks Castleberry 2
		4A Division II	Austin Achieve 1	Gainesville 0
		5A Division I	Prosper Walnut Grove 3	San Antonio Southwest 2
		5A Division II	Liberty Hill 1	Dallas Southwest 0 (Forfeit)
		6A Division I	Klein Cain 1	Alief Elsik 0
		6A Division II	Austin Vandegrift 3	Mesquite 1
	TAPPS	Division I	Central Catholic 4	Parish Episcopal School 0
		Division II	The Brook Hill School 4	St. Joseph Academy 0
		Division III	The Covenant School 1	St. Thomas Episcopal School 1

Girls Soccer

Year	Conference	Division	Champion	Runner-Up
2023-2024	UIL	4A Division I	Celina 1	Boerne 0
		5A Division I	Frisco Wakeland 3	Colleyville Heritage 2
		6A Division I	Prosper 1	Austin Westlake 0
	TAPPS	Division I	Ursuline Academy (Dallas) 4	Bishop Lynch (Dallas) 0
		Division II	Grace Community (Tyler) 5	St. John XXIII (Katy) 3
		Division III	McKinney Christian Academy 3	Geneva (Boerne) 1
2024-2025	UIL	4A Division I	Celina 2	Comal Davenport 1
		4A Division II	Canyon Randall 3	Wimberley 2
		5A Division I	College Station A&M Consolidated 4	Colleyville Heritage 0
		5A Division II	Cedar Park 3	Frisco Wakeland 1
		6A Division I	Coppell 6	Austin Lake Travis 2
		6A Division II	Lewisville Marcus 1	Houston Strafford 0
	TAPPS	Division I	Ursuline Academy 2	St. Agnes Academy 0
		Division II	All Saints Episcopal School 2	Second Baptist School 1
		Division III	McKinney Christian Academy 3	The Atonement Catholic Academy 1

Baseball

Year	Conference	Division	Champion	Runner-Up
2023-2024	UIL	1A Division I	Ira 7	Fayetteville 6
		2A Division I	Collinsville 9	Hawley 0
		3A Division I	Franklin 7	Brock 4
		4A Division I	Texarkana Liberty-Eylau 3	Corpus Christi Calallen 1
		5A Division I	Grapevine 6	Lucas Lovejoy 5
		6A Division I	Tomball 4	Pearland 4
	TAPPS	Division I	Central Catholic San Antonio 3	Concordia Lutheran High School Tomball 2
		Division II	Second Baptist School Houston 10	Southwest Christian School Houston 7
		Division III	The Brook Hill School Bullard 9	Bay Area Christian School 2
		Division IV	First Baptist Christian Academy Pasadena 15	Covenant Classical Fort Worth 2
		Division V	St. Paul Catholic School Shiner 5	Christian Life School Prepatory Fort Worth 4
2024-2025	UIL	1A Division I	Fayetteville 4	Gordon 2
		2A Division I	Centerville 6	New Home 1
		2A Division II	Collinsville 12	Overton 0
		3A Division I	London (Corpus Christi) 4	Texarkana Liberty-Eylau 3
		3A Division II	Wall 14	Thrall 2
		4A Division I	Corpus Christi Calallen 5	Texarkana Pleasant Grove 3
		4A Division II	Longview Spring Hill 5	Wimberley 3
		5A Division I	Aledo 8	Spring Branch Smithson Valley 1
		5A Division II	Grapevine 9	Humble Kingwood Park 5
		6A Division I	Waco Midway 6	Humble Atascocita 2
		6A Division II	Humble Kingwood 5	Tomball 4
	TAPPS	Division I	Central Catholic San Antonio 2	Prestonwood Christian Academy 0
		Division II	Lutheran South Academy 11	Grapevine Faith Christian School 0
		Division III	McKinney Christian Academy 9	Northland Christian School 8
		Division IV	Alpha Omega Academy 13	Denton Calvary Academy 0
		Division V	Sacred Heart Catholic School 7	First Baptist Academy 3

Softball

Year	Conference	Division	Champion	Runner-Up
2023-2024	UIL	1A Division I	Jonesboro 3	Neches 1
		2A Division I	Shiner 10	Beckville 4
		3A Division I	Coahoma 3	Grandview 2
		4A Division I	Corpus Christi Calallen 2	Liberty 1
		5A Division I	Melissa 8	Harlingen South 0
		6A Division I	Weslaco 11	Waco Midway 9
	TAPPS	Division I	St. Agnes Academy 14	Antonian College Prep 10
		Division II	Grapevine Faith Christian School 2	St. Joseph High School Victoria 12
		Division III	The Brook Hill School 5	Cypress Christian School Houston 0
		Division IV	Sacred Heart Catholic School Hartletteville 5	Lubbock Christian School 0
2024-2025	UIL	1A Division I	Jonesboro 9	Brookland 1
		2A Division I	Ganado 5	Riesel 4
		2A Division II	Sundown 9	Shiner 3
		3A Division I	Grandview 9	Whiteboro 3
		3A Division II	Coahoma 6	Lexington 1
		4A Division I	Corpus Christi Calallen 9	Andrews 2
		4A Division II	Robinson 10	Aubrey 1
		5A Division I	Melissa 4	Barbers Hill 2
		5A Division II	Montgomery Lake Creek 12	Hallsville 1
		6A Division I	Waco Midway 9	Clear Springs 1
		6A Division II	Humble Kingwood 4	Forney 1
	TAPPS	Division I	John Paul II High School 12	Antonian College Prep 2
		Division II	Hyde Park High School 11	St. Joseph High School Victoria 10
		Division III	Dallas Christian School 6	Incarnate Word Academy 5
		Division IV	Sacred Heart Catholic School Hartletteville 16	Nazarene Christian Academy 2

UNSPLASH/ANDREW LOMAS

UIL STATE CHAMPIONS

YEAR	1A	2A	3A	4A	5A	6A
Cross Country Team, Boys						
2024	Slidell	Plains	SA Great Hearts Northern Oaks	Canyon	Lucas Lovejoy	Southlake Carroll
2025	Comstock	Plains	Lytle	Canyon	Lucas Lovejoy	Southlake Carroll
Cross Country Individual, Boys						
2024	Comstock	Wolfe City	Holliday	Fort Worth Diamond Hill-Jarvis	North Richland Hills Richland	Southlake Carroll
2025	Comstock	Waco Meyer	Holliday	Canyon	Anna	Southlake Carroll
Cross Country Team, Girls						
2024	Roby	Hamilton	Holliday	Canyon Randall	Lucas Lovejoy	Lewisville Flower Mound
2025	Tilden McMullen County	Hamilton	Holliday	Canyon	Comal Smithson Valley	Lewisville Flower Mound
Cross Country Individual, Girls						
2024	Earth Springlake	Shelbyville	Universal City Randolph	Canyon	Boerne Champion	Denton Braswell

YEAR	1A	2A	3A	4A	5A	6A
2025	Roby	Elysian Fields	Universal City Randolph	Canyon	Boerne Champion	Denton Braswell
Golf Team, Boys						
2024	Gail Borden County	Sonora	Lubbock Cooper Liberty	Bridgeport	Comal Smithson Valley	Austin Lake Travis
2025	Wildorado	Sonora	Wall	Bridgeport	Prosper Walnut Grove	Austin Westlake
Golf Individual, Boys						
2024	Iredell	Goldthwaite	Lubbock Cooper Liberty	Wimberley	Frisco Wakeland	Conroe The Woodlands
2025	Texline	Goldthwaite	Maypearl	Bridgeport	Frisco Wakeland	Conroe Grand Oaks
Golf Team, Girls						
2024	Garden City	Mason	Odessa Compass Academy	Andrews	San Antonio Alamo Heights	Austin Vandegrift
2025	Garden City	Mason	Odessa Compass Academy	Andrews	San Antonio Alamo Heights	Coppell
Golf Individual, Girls						
2024	Lenorah Grady	Mason	Odessa Compass Academy	Bullard	Frisco Centennial	Austin Vandegrift
2025	Lenorah Grady	Mason	Maypearl	Fort Worth Benbrook	Frisco Independence	Coppell
Tennis, Team						
2024	—	—	—	Wimberley	Frisco Centennial	Round Rock Westwood
2025	—	—	—	Canyon Randall	Frisco Centennial	Round Rock Westwood
Tennis, Boys Singles						
2024	Rising Star	Mason	Vernon	Lindale	Fort Bend Kempner	Katy Seven Lakes
2025	Lometa	Big Lake Reagan County	Henrietta	Frisco Panther Creek	Fort Bend Kempner	Round Rock Westwood
Tennis, Boys Doubles						
2024	Utopia	Quanah	Franklin	Burkburnett	Frisco Centennial	Round Rock Westwood
2025	Benjamin	Mason	Peaster	Wimberly	Prosper Walnut Grove	Round Rock Westwood
Tennis, Girls Singles						
2024	Lenorah Grady	Crawford	Clyde	Taylor	Argyle	Houston Memorial
2025	Runge	Crawford	Wall	Taylor	Abilene Wylie	Katy Tompkins
Tennis, Girls Doubles						
2024	Utopia	Mason	Peaster	Canyon Randall	Grapevine	Allen
2025	Knippa	Mason	Peaster	Canyon Randall	Grapevine	Roundrock Westwood
Tennis, Mixed Doubles						
2024	Barksdale Nueces Canyon	Mason	Wall	Canyon West Plains	Frisco Lebanon Trail	Plano West
2025	Utopia	Mason	Franklin	Cayon Randall	Frisco Lebanon Trail	Fort Bend Clements
Track & Field, Boys Team						
2024	Gordon	Refugio	Yoakum	Gilmer	Fort Band Marshall	Humble Atascocita
2025	Gordon	Tioga	Holliday	Lindale	Alvin Iowa Colony	Houston Lamar
Track & Field, Girls Team						
2024	Roby	Refugio	Universal City Randolph	Iowa Colony	Lancaster	Duncanville
2025	Gordon	Panhandle	Universal City Randolph	Brownwood	Fort Bend Marshall	Alvin Shadow Creek

Wrestling, Boys							
2024							
DIV	Weight Classes						
	106	113	120	126	132	138	144
5A	Cedar Park	Canyon Randall	Seguin	Burleson Centennial	Dumas	Midlothian	Amarillo Tascosa
6A	Southlake Carroll	Allen	Arlington Martin	Conroe Woodlands College Park	Katy Cinco Ranch	Katy Jordan	Arlington Martin
DIV	150	157	165	175	190	215	285
5A	Melissa	Dumas	Comal Smithson Valley	Melissa	Midlothian	Lubbock	Lucas Lovejoy
6A	Rockwall	Conroe Woodlands College Park	Arlington Martin	Arlington Martin	Klein	Dripping Springs	League City Clear Springs
2025							
DIV	106	113	120	126	132	138	144
5A	Midlothian	Cedar Park	Uvalde	Canyon Randall	Frisco Wakeland	Dumas	Amarillo Tascosa
6A	Southlake Carroll	Dripping Springs	Allen	Arlington Martin	Conroe Woodlands College Park	Southlake Carroll	Allen
DIV	150	157	165	175	190	215	285
5A	Comal Smithson Valley	Fort Worth Benbrook	Melissa	Canyon Randall	Amarillo Palo Duro	Dallas Highland Park	Amarillo Tascosa
6A	Conroe Woodlands College Park	Arlington Martin	Allen	Arlington Martin	Allen	Keller Timber Creek	Keller

Wrestling, Girls						
2024						
DIV	Weight Classes					
	100	107	114	120	126	132
5A	Amarillo Tascosa	Cedar Park	Lubbock	Azle	Killeen Chaparral	College Station A&M Consolidated
6A	Edinburg	Allen	Conroe The Woodlands	Allen	Arlington Martin	Northwest Eaton
DIV	138	145	152	165	185	235
5A	Lubbock Cooper	Burleson Centennial	El Paso Bel Air	Canyon Randall	Friendswood	Borger
6A	Arlington Martin	Prosper Rock Hill	Converse Judson	Allen	Klein Oak	El Paso Americas
2025						
DIV	100	107	114	120	126	132
5A	Azle	Anna	Azle	Corpus Christi Carroll	Melissa	Lubbock Cooper
6A	El Paso Eastwood	Katy	Conroe the Woodlands	Dripping Springs	Allen	Conroe Woodlands College Park
DIV	138	145	152	165	185	235
5A	Midlothian Heritage	Lubbock Cooper	El Paso Bel Air	Amarillo Palo Duro	Hereford	Borger
6A	Conroe Woodlands College Park	El Paso Eastwood	Prosper Rock Hill	Northwest Nelson	Haltom City Haltom	Euless Trinity

BIZ MACKEY

TEXAS SPORTS HALL OF FAME

The Texas Sports Hall of Fame was organized in 1951 by the Texas Sports Writers Association. Each year, the honorees are inducted into the Hall of Fame at a gala dinner.

The second such fête in 1952 was headlined by, "That filmland athlete, Ronald Reagan, and his actress wife, Nancy Davis," according to *The Dallas Morning News* on June 9, 1952.

The hall was originally in Grand Prairie in the Dallas-Fort Worth area. The Hall of Fame was closed in 1986 for financial reasons, but was reopened in Waco in 1991. In addition to memorabilia, the new location also houses archives.

Under the current selection process, dues-paying members of the Texas Sports Hall of Fame can nominate any number of individuals. (Anyone can become a member.)

The selection committee, chaired by Dave Campbell, founder of *Texas Football Magazine*, reviews all nominees and creates the "Official Voting Membership" ballot. Ballots are then mailed to the voting membership, former Texas Sports Hall of Fame inductees, and the media selection committee.

Year	Inductee	Sport	Texas Connection, Career
2025	Cedric Benson	Football	Houstonian; Robert E. Lee High School; UIL 5A rushing yard record; University of Texas (2001-2004); Doak Walker Award; All-American; NFL (2005-2012).
	Todd Dodge	Football	Port Arthur Jefferson High School; State record in passing yards; Hertz No. 1 state athlete; University of Texas (1982-1985); High School coach.
	Brittney Griner	Basketball	Nimitz High School; McDonald's All American; Top-rated high school player in the country; Baylor University (2009-2012); Three-time Big 12 Player of the Year; Four-time Big 12 Defensive Player of the Year; AP Player of the Year; Final Four Most Outstanding Player; ESPY for Best Female Athlete (2013); First-overall WNBA draft pick (2013); Olympic gold medalist (2016, 2020, 2024); 10-time WNBA All-Star; Two-time WNBA blocks-scoring champion; Two-time WNBA Defensive Player of the Year.
	Biz Mackey	Baseball	Eagle Pass-born; Five-time East-West All-Star Games; Two-time Negro World Series Championships; Record 18 seasons with the integrated California Winter League.
	Ed 'Too Tall' Jones	Football	Dallas Cowboys first-overall NFL draft pick (1974); First, and only, first pick from a Historically Black College; Team record for games played; Three-time Pro Bowls; All-Pro Honors (1982).
	Chris Plonsky	Administration	University of Texas women's athletics director (2001-2018); 64 conference championship wins, three national championships for women's teams; University of Texas Executive Senior Associate Athletics Director/Chief of Staff; University of Texas Senior Woman Administrator for Conference and NCAA governance; Served on the U.S. Olympic Collegiate Advisory Committee, USA Basketball Board of Directors, multiple NCAA comittees and Women's Basketball Hall of Fame Board of Trustees; Current Senior Woman Administrator for the Big 12 Conference.
	Richmond Webb	Football	Dallas-born; Texas A&M Atheletics Hall of Fame Inductee (2007); Team Captain; All-SWC Honors; Aggie Heart Award; First-round NFL draft pick (1990); Two-time All-Pro; Seven-time Pro Bowl selection; NFL 1990's All-Decade Team.
	Carla Overbeck	Soccer	Richardson High School; University of North Carolina; Won four consecutive national championships; U.S. Women's National Team (1988-2000); Three-time World Cup appearances; Captain in 1996 Olympic games, leading team to gold; WUSA league title; W-League Championship; Current Assistant Coach of Duke University women's soccer; 2017 ACC Championship title; Sports Illustrated Sportswoman of the Year (1999); National Soccer Hall of Fame Inductee (2006).

WIKIPEDIA

TEXAS SPORTS HALL OF FAME
WACO, TEXAS

Year	Inductee	Sport	Texas Connection, Career
2024	Jamaal Charles	Football	Port Arthur-born; Competed in the Special Olympics at 10 years old; Memorial High School; Two-time Willie Ray Smith Award for Southeast Texas Offensive MVP; University of Texas; Dual-sport athlete in track and football; Won the 100-meter dash in the Big 12 Championship (2006); Four-time All-American; National Championship Football Team (2005); NFL; Four-time Pro Bowler; Led the NFL in rushing touchdowns in 2013.
	Andy Cooper	Baseball	Paul Quinn College, Waco; Negro League All-Star Pitcher; Detroit Stars (1920-1927); Kansas City Monarchs (1928-1929, 1932-1939); Negro League career record for saves; Kansas City Monarchs Manager (1936-1940); Four consecutive wins in the Negro American League; National Baseball Hall of Fame Inductee (2006).
	Judge Roy Hofheinz	Administration	Mayor of Houston (1953-1956); Houston Sports Association (1959); Brought a national league baseball franchise to Houston the following year; Helped design Houston's Astrodome; Texas Baseball Hall of Fame inductee (2006); Houston Astros Hall of Fame (2021).
	Barbara Jacket	Track and Field	Prairie View A&M Women's Track and Field coach (1965-1991); 10-time National Association Intercollegiate Athletic titles; Led the men's track team to two SWAC Outdoor Conference titles; 23-time SWAC Coach of the Year; Five-time NAIA Coach of the Year; U.S. Women's team assistant coach in the 1979 Pan American Games; Women's team head coach at the 1975 University Games; Team USA head coach in the World Championships (1987, 1991); Team USA head coach in the 1992 Olympic games; International Women's Sports Hall of Fame (1995).
	Mike Leach	Football	Head Coach at Texas Tech University (2000-2009); Left the program with the record for most wins; 21-year coaching career with a 158-107 overall record; 17-time Bowl appearances; Two-time National Coach of the Year; Three-time Conference Coach of the Year; Credited for the NCAA "Air-Raid" offense.
	Colt McCoy	Football	Jim Ned High School; Two-time All-State Quarterback; 2A record for most yards by a quarterback; University of Texas (2005-2009); Set 47 school records, becoming one of the most decorated NCAA players; Walter Camp Award recipient (2008); Heisman Trophy Finalist (2009); Four-year Team MVP; 12 year NFL career.
	Jackie Sherill	Football	Texas A&M Coach (1982-1988); Walter Camp Coach of the Year Award (1981); Three-time Southwest Conference Coach of the Year Award; Brought back Aggie tradition of student body walk-on tryouts in 1983.
	Bubba Thornton	Track and Field	Keller-born; Texas Christian University; Dual-sport athlete in football and track and field; NFL (1969); Track and Field coach at Texas Christian University (1982-1995); University of Texas (1996-2013); Coached teams to 35 NCAA event titles, over 300 All-America honors and 161 conference championships; 11-time Big 12 Conference Championship Wins; SWC Men's Outdoor Championship (1996); USA World Junior Championship coach (1996); USA Olympic team Assistant Head Coach (2000); USA World Championship team Head Coach (2003); USA Olympic team Head Coach (2008); Ten-time Big 12 Coach of the Year; Two-time USTFCCCA South Central Region Indoor Coach of the Year; NCAA District VI Coach of the Year; Texas Track and Field Coaches Hall of Fame inductee (2015).
	Christa Williams	Softball	Pasadena-raised; Pitcher; University of Texas (1998-1999); Big 12 Newcomer of the Year; NCAA Regional Tournament MVP; Three-time NCAA All-American; Two-time Olympic gold medalist (1996, 2000); Two-time ISF World Champion; Gold-medalist at Pan-American Qualifier (1994); ISF Junior Women's World Championship (1995); Gold-medalist at ISF World Championships (1998).

WIKIMEDIA/MICHAEL BARERA

TEXAS OLYMPIC MEDALISTS

This is a list of athletes with Texas connections who have won medals in the Olympics, including the 2024 games in Paris. This list includes those born or who have lived in Texas, as well as U.S. team members who spent their collegiate careers at Texas universities.

Information included is: the athlete's name, the sport and the year, as well as the types of medals (G-Gold, S-Silver, B-Bronze). If the athlete won more than one of the same kind of medal in any one year, the number is noted before the letter code; e.g., 2G indicates that the athlete won two gold medals in the games that year.

The asterisk (*) signifies COVID-19 suspended the 2020 Olympics, which were held from July 23–August 8, 2021.

The symbol (†) following the medal code indicates that the athlete participated in preliminary contests only; the medal was awarded because of membership on a winning team. Years in which the athlete participated but did not win a medal are not included. Track indicates all track and field events except those noted separately.

Olympian	Sport	Year	Medal
Abbott, Monica	Softball	2020*	S
Abdallah, Nia Nicole	Taekwondo	2004	S
Adams, Rachel	Volleyball	2016	B
Allen, Chad	Baseball	1996	B
Alfred, Julien	T&F	2024	G,S
Allman, Valarie	T&F	2024	G,S
		2020*	G
Atkins, Ariel	Basketball	2020*	G
Armstrong, Lance	Cycling	2000	B**
Arnette, Jay Hoyland	Basketball	1960	G
Austin, Charles	T&F	1996	G
Baker, Walter Thane	T&F	1956	G,S,B
		1952	S
Baptiste, Kirk	T&F	1984	S
Barr, Beth	Swimming	1988	S
Bassham, Lanny Robert	Shooting	1976	G
		1972	S
Bates, Michael D.	T&F	1992	B
Baz, Shane	Baseball	2020*	S
Beamon, Bob	T&F	1968	G
Beck, Robert Lee	Pentathlon	1960	2B
Beckie, Janine	Soccer	2016	B
Bedforth, B.J.	Swimming	2000	G
Berens, Ricky	Swimming	2012	G,S
		2008	G
Berube, Ryan Thomas	Swimming	1996	G
Biles, Simone	Gymnastics	2024	3G,S
		2020*	S, B
		2016	4G,B
Bosh, Chris	Basketball	2008	G
Boudia, David	Diving	2016	S, B
		2012	G,B
Brew, Derrick K.	T&F	2004	G,B
Bridgewater, Brad	Swimming	1996	G
Brown, Earlene Dennis	T&F	1960	B
Browning, David (Skippy)	Diving	1952	G
Buckner, William Quinn	Basketball	1976	G
Buford-Bailey, Tonja	T&F	1996	B
Burrell, Leroy Russel	T&F	1992	G
Burrows, Brian	Shooting	2020*	B
Butler, Jimmy	Basketball	2016	G
Campbell, Jane	Soccer	2020*	B
Carey, Rick	Swimming	1984	3G
Carlisle, Daniel T.	Shooting	1984	B
Carter, Michael D.	Shotput	1984	S
Carter, Michelle	Shotput	2016	G

Olympian	Sport	Year	Medal
Cassell, Ollan	T&F	1964	G
Catchings, Tamika	Basketball	2016	G
		2012	G
Chiles, Jordan	Gymnastics	2024	G
		2020*	S
Clay, Bryan E.	Decathlon	2008	G
		2004	S
Clement, Kerron	T&F	2016	G
Clemons, Kyle	T&F	2016	G
Cline, Nancy Lieberman	Basketball	1976	S
Cohen, Tiffany	Swimming	1984	G
Conger, Jack	Swimming	2016	G
Cook, Cassidy	Diving	2024	S
Corbeau, Caspar	Swimming	2024	B
Corbelli, Laurie Flachmeier	Volleyball	1984	S
Cotton, John	Baseball	2000	G
Crocker, Ian	Swimming	2008	G
		2004	G,S,B
		2000	G
Cross-Battle, Tara	Volleyball	1992	B
Crouser, Ryan	Shotput	2024	G
		2020*	G
		2016	G
Daniels, Teahna	T&F	2020*	S
Davis, Clarissa G.	Basketball	1992	B
Davis, Jack Wells	T&F	1956	S
		1952	S
Davis, Josh C.	Swimming	2000	2S
		1996	3G
Davis, Tara Woodhall	T&F	2024	G
Davis, W.F. (Buddy)	High Jump	1952	G
Deadmon, Bryce	T&F	2024	G,S
		2020*	G,B
DeLoach, Joseph N. Jr.	T&F	1988	G
Dersch, Hans	Swimming	1992	G
Didrikson, Mildred (Babe)	T&F	1932	2G,S
Donie, Scott R.	Diving	1992	S
Drexler, Clyde	Basketball	1992	G
Dumais, Troy	Diving	2012	B
Durant, Kevin	Basketball	2024	G
		2020*	G
		2016	G
		2012	G
Dusing, Nate	Swimming	2004	B
		2000	S
Eller, Glenn	Shooting	2008	G

** In January 2013, the International Olympic Committee disqualified Lance Armstrong from the 2000 events he competed in after he was found to have used performance-enhancing drugs.

Source: United States Olympic Committee.

Olympian	Sport	Year	Medal
Eriksson, Agneta	Swimming	1980	S
Ethridge, Mary (Kamie)	Basketball	1988	G
Farmer-Patrick, Sandra	T&F	1992	S
Feigen, Jimmy	Swimming	2016	G
		2012	S†
Fields, Connor	Cycling	2016	G
Fink, Nic	Swimming	2024	G, 2S
Finn-Burrell, Michelle Bonae	T&F	1992	G
Foerster, Paul	Sailing	1992	S
		2000	S
		2004	G
Forbes, James Ricardo	Basketball	1972	S
Ford, Gilbert (Gib)	Basketball	1956	G
Foreman, George	Boxing	1968	G
Fortenberry, Joe Cephis	Basketball	1936	G
Foster, Carson	Swimming	2024	S,B
Francis, Phyllis	T&F	2016	G
Galloway, Jackie	Taekwondo	2016	B
Garrison, Zina	Tennis	1988	G,B
Gemmell, Erin	Swimming	2024	S
George, Chris	Baseball	2000	G
Manu Ginóbili	Basketball	2004	G
		2008	B
Gjertson, Doug	Swimming	1992	G,B
		1988	G
Glenesk, Dean William	Pentathlon	1984	S
Goldblatt, Scott	Swimming	2004	G
		2000	S
Gonzáles, Paul G. Jr.	Boxing	1984	G
Gordon, Chris-Ann	T&F	2016	S
Gray, Allisha	Basketball	2020*	G
Green, Josh	Basketball	2020*	B
Griner, Brittney	Basketball	2024	G
		2020*	G
		2016	G
Grosso, Julia	Soccer	2020*	G
Guidry, Carlette D.	T&F	1996	G†
		1992	G
Haas, Townley	Swimming	2016	G
Hall, Gary Jr.	Swimming	2004	G,B
		2000	2G,S,B
		1996	2G,2S
Hamm, Mia	Soccer	2004	G
		2000	S
		1996	G
		2024	G,B
Hancock-Benbrook, Vincent	Skeet Shooting	2020*	G
		2012	G
		2008	G
Hannan, Tommy	Swimming	2000	G
Hansen, Brendan	Swimming	2012	G,B
		2008	G
		2004	G,S,B
Hansen, Fred Morgan	T&F	1964	G
Hardee, Trey	T&F	2012	S
Harkrider, Kiplan P.	Baseball	1996	B
Harrison, Kendra	T&F	2020*	S
Hartwell, Erin Wesley	Cycling	1996	S
		1992	B
Hays, Todd	Bobsled	2002	S
Heath, Michael Steward	Swimming	1984	2G,S
Hedgepeth, Whitney L.	Swimming	1996	G,2S
Hedrick, Chad	Speed Skating	2010	S,B
		2006	G,S,B
Heidenreich, Jerry	Swimming	1972	2G,S,B
Henry, James Edward	Diving	1968	B
Hill, Denean E.	T&F	1992	S
		1988	S
		1984	G
Hill, Grant Henry	Basketball	1996	G
Hinds, Natalie	Swimming	2020*	B
Hobson, Luke	Swimming	2024	S, B
Hoffman, Sylvia	Bobsleigh	2022	B
Homfeld, Conrad E.	Equestrian	1984	G,S
Hong, Asher	Gymnastics	2024	B

Olympian	Sport	Year	Medal
Hooker, Destinee	Volleyball	2012	S
Hooper, Darrow	Shotput	1952	S
Horton, Jonathan	Gymnastics	2008	S
Howard, Sherri Francis	T&F	1988	S
		1984	G
Hurley, Kelley	Epee Fencing	2012	B
Hurley, Courtney	Epee Fencing	2012	B
Ilyina, Vera	Diving	2004	S
		2000	G
Jackson, Lucious Brown	Basketball	1964	G
Jacobs, Chris	Swimming	1988	2G,S
Jacobs, Lamont	T&F	2020*	2G
Jacoby, Lydia	Swimming	2020*	G,S
Johnson, Keldon	Basketball	2020*	G
Johnson, Michael	T&F	2000	2G
		1996	2G
		1992	G
Johnson, Rafer L.	Decathlon	1960	G
		1956	S
Jones, John Wesley (Lam)	T&F	1976	G
Jordan, DeAndre	Basketball	2016	G
Jordan, Shaun	Swimming	1992	G
		1988	G
Juarez, Ricardo Rocky	Boxing	2000	S
Julich, Robert William	Cycling	2004	B
Kaufhold, Casey	Archery	2024	B
Kazmir, Scott	Baseball	2020*	S
Keeler, Kathryn Elliott	Rowing	1984	G
Kerley, Fred	T&F	2024	B
		2020*	S
Kern, Douglas James	Sailing	1992	S
Kibbler, Drew	Swimming	2024	S
Kiefer, Adolph	Swimming	1936	G
Kimmons, Trell	T&F	2012	S
King, Judith Brown	T&F	1984	S
King, Matt	Swimming	2024	G
Kleine, Megan	Swimming	1992	G†
Knight, Bianca	T&F	2012	G
Krajicek, Austin	Tennis	2024	S
Kocian, Madison	Gymnastics	2016	G,S
Kolius, John Waldrip	Sailing	1976	S
Kos, Hubert	Swimming	2024	G
Lanne, Colleen	Swimming	2004	S
Langkop, Dorothy Franey	Speed Skating	1932	B
Leetch, Brian Joseph	Ice Hockey	2002	S
Lewis, F. (Carl) Carlton	T&F	1996	G
		1992	2G
		1988	2G,S
		1984	4G
Lienhard, William Barner	Basketball	1952	G
Lipinski, Tara K.	Figure Skating	1998	G
Little, Shamier	T&F	2024	S
Liukin, Nastia	Gymnastics	2008	G,3S,B
Lloyd, Andrea	Basketball	1988	G
Losey, Robert G. (Greg)	Pentathlon	1984	S
Lopez, Diana	Taekwondo	2008	B
Lopez, Mark	Taekwondo	2008	S
Lopez, Steven	Taekwondo	2008	B
		2004	G
		2000	G
Lowe, Sara Elizabeth	Swimming	2004	B
Magers, Rose Mary	Volleyball	1984	S
Malone, Jordan	Speed Skating	2014	S
		2010	B
Manuel, Simone	Swimming	2024	2S
		2020*	B
		2016	2G, 2S
Manzano, Leo	T&F	2012	S
Marsh, Michael L.	T&F	1996	S
		1992	2G
Marshall, Christine	Swimming	2008	B
Matson, James Randel (Randy)	Shotput	1968	G
		1964	G
Matson, Ollie G.	T&F	1952	S, B
McEwen, Shelby	T&F	2024	S
McFalls, Jennifer Yvonne	Softball	2000	G

Olympian	Sport	Year	Medal
McFarlane, Tracey	Swimming	1988	S
McKenzie, Kim	T&F	1984	B
McNeir, Forest	Shooting	1920	G
Meadows, Earle	T&F	1936	G
Meili, Katie	Swimming	2016	G, B
Mensah-Stock, Tamyra	Wrestling	2020*	G
Mewis, Kristie	Soccer	2020*	B
Middleton, Khris	Basketball	2020*	G
Mills, Ronald P.	Swimming	1968	B
Mitchell, Betsy	Swimming	1988	S
		1984	G, S
Moceanu, Dominique	Gymnastics	1996	G
Montgomery, James P.	Swimming	1976	3G, B
Moore, James Warren	Pentathlon	1964	S
Moore, Jasmine	T&F	2024	2B
Morrow, Bobby Joe	T&F	1956	3G
Mu, Athing	T&F	2020*	2G
Munoz, Felipe	Swimming	1968	G
Neilson-Bell, Sandy	Swimming	1972	3G
Nelson, Lianne Bennion	Rowing	2004	S
Neugebauer, Leo	Decathlon	2024	S
Newhouse, Frederick V.	T&F	1976	G, S
Nott/Cunningham, Tara Lee	Weightlifting	2004	G
Ogbogu, Chiaka	Volleyball	2024	S
		2020*	G
Okafor, Emeka	Basketball	2004	B
Okolo, Courtney	T&F	2016	G
Olajuwon, Hakeem	Basketball	1996	G
Olsen, Justin	Bobsled	2010	G
Osterman, Catherine (Cat)	Softball	2020*	S
		2008	S
		2004	G
Paddock, Charles W.	T&F	1924	S
		1920	2G, S
Patterson, Carly	Gymnastics	2004	G, 2S
Patton, Darvis	T&F	2004	S
Peirsol, Aaron	Swimming	2008	2G, S
		2004	3G
		2000	S
Perry, Nanceen L.	T&F	2000	B
Pesthy, Paul Karoly	Fencing	1964	S
Phenix, Erin	Swimming	2000	G
Pickrem, Sydney	Swimming	2020*	B
Pinder, Demetrius	T&F	2016	B
		2012	G
Postma, Joan Spillane	Swimming	1960	G
Potter, Cynthia Ann	Diving	1976	B
Prince, Conner	Shooting	2024	S
Rogers, Raevyn	T&F	2020*	S
Rambo, John Barnett	T&F	1964	B
Rauch, Jamie	Swimming	2000	S
Retton, Mary Lou	Gymnastics	1984	G,2S,2B
Richards, Robert E.	T&F	1956	G
		1952	G
		1948	B
Richards-Ross, Sanya	T&F	2012	2G
		2008	G, B
		2004	G
Richardson, Sha'Carri	T&F	2024	G
Ritter, Louise	T&F	1988	G
Rivera, Hezly	Gymnastics	2024	G
Roberts, Dave	T&F	1976	B
Roberts, Gil	T&F	2016	G
Robertson, Alvin Cyrrale	Basketball	1984	G
Robinson, David M.	Basketball	1996	G
		1992	G
		1988	B
Robinson, Moushaumi	T&F	2004	G
Robinson, Robert J.	Basketball	1948	G
Robinzine, Kevin B.	T&F	1988	G
Robles, Sarah	Weightlifting	2020*	B
		2016	B
Roe, Frederick	Polo	1924	S
Rogers, Raevyn	T&F	2020*	S
Russell, Douglas Albert	Swimming	1968	2G

Olympian	Sport	Year	Medal
Russell, John William	Equestrian	1952	B
Salmon, Riley	Volleyball	2008	G
Scheffler, Scottie	Golf	2024	G
Schneider, Marcus B.	Rowing	1996	B
Schooling, Joseph	Swimming	2016	G
Shaw, Jaedyn	Soccer	2024	G
Skinner, Avery	Volleyball	2024	S
Slay, Brandon Douglas	Wrestling	2000	G
Smith, Austen Jewell	Shooting	2024	S,B
Smith, Clark	Swimming	2016	G
Smith, Dean	T&F	1952	G
Smith, Lamont	T&F	1996	G
Smith, Owen Guinn	T&F	1948	G
Smith, Tommie C.	T&F	1968	G
Southern, S. Edward	T&F	1956	S
Spencer, Ashley	T&F	2016	B
Steinseifer, Carrie	Swimming	1984	2G
Sterkle, Jill Ann	Swimming	1988	2B
		1984	G
		1976	G
Stevenson, Toby	Pole Vault	2004	S
Stulce, Michael S.	Shotput	1992	G
Sullivan, Erica	Swimming	2020*	S
Swoopes, Sheryl Denise	Basketball	2004	G
		2000	G
		1996	G
Sykora, Stacy	Volleyball	2008	S
Tarmoh, Jeneba	T&F	2012	G
Taylor, Robert	T&F	1972	G, S
Teagarden, Taylor	Baseball	2008	B
Thomas, Gabby	T&F	2024	3G
		2020*	S, B
Tinsley, Michael	T&F	2012	S
Tisdale, Wayman L.	Basketball	1984	G
Valdez, Jesse	Boxing	1972	B
Van, Allen	Ice Hockey	1952	S
Van Lith, Hailey	Basketball	2024	B
Victor, Lindon	Decathlon	2024	B
Vollmer, Dana	Swimming	2016	G, S, B
		2012	3G
		2004	G
Walker, Laura Anne	Swimming	1988	B
Walker, Neil	Swimming	2004	G, B
		2000	G, S
Walters, Dave	Swimming	2008	G
Wariner, Jeremy	T&F	2008	G, S
		2004	2G
Watson, Sam	Climbing	2024	B
Weatherspoon, Teresa G.	Basketball	1992	B
		1988	G
Weber-Gale, Garrett	Swimming	2008	2G
Wells, Rhoshii S.	Boxing	1996	B
Wells, Wayne A.	Wrestling	1972	G
Whitfield, Malvin G.	T&F	1952	G, S
		1948	G, S
Wilkinson, Laura A.	Diving	2000	G
Williams, Christa L.	Softball	2000	G
		1996	G
Williams, Stacey Ann	T&F	2020*	B
Williamson, Darold	T&F	2004	G
Wilson, Craig Martin	Water Polo	1988	S
		1984	S
Wolfe, Rowland (Flip)	Gymnastics	1932	G
Woods-Richardson, Simeon	Baseball	2020*	S
Wrightson, Bernard C.	Diving	1968	G
Wylie, Paul Stanton	Figure Skating	1992	S
Young, Earl Verdelle	T&F	1960	2G
Zmeskal, Kim	Gymnastics	1992	B

UNSPLASH/MEGAN BUCKNALL

Texas

LAW ENFORCEMENT

UNSPLASH/BENJAMIN LEHMAN

CRIME IN TEXAS

The crime statistics in this chapter are from the **Uniform Crime Reporting (UCR)** programs used by law enforcement agencies in Texas and nationwide.

The first of these programs in the United States was the Committee on Uniform Crime Records — developed by the International Association of Chiefs of Police (IACP) in the 1920s.

The first IACP crime collection program, in 1930, was voluntary and gathered information from 400 police agencies in 43 states. The FBI was authorized as the national clearinghouse for the information collected by the program.

UCR programs collect data on a summary basis, which provides reliable information about crime, but has limitations.

In 1985, Texas began using the **Incident Based Reporting (IBR)** system, whereby crime data is collected electronically, and includes the circumstances of each incident. The national system is called NIBRS.

Texas first adopted the Uniform Crime Report in 1976, and the Department of Public Safety accepted the responsibility of collecting, validating, and tabulating reports from across the state. The Uniform Crime Reporting Section, created specifically for this purpose, is part of the Crime Records Service division of the department.

The state became certified to collect NIBRS data in 1998, and in 2015, House Bill 11 set a goal to transition all of Texas to NIBRS by September 1, 2019. About 550 agencies met that goal.

In 2023, the 88th Texas Legislature established amendments to Texas Government Code §411.054 making it a requirement for local law enforcement to implement a NIBRS compliant reporting system and using that system to submit data to the Texas UCR program. This mandate added 251 agencies reporting to the program.

Crime in Texas

In Texas, the Department of Public Safety collects data for the national UCR program from police, sheriff's offices, and its own officers. Data is estimated for non-reporting agencies and those that did not have 12 months of data. More than 1,400 agencies contributed to the UCR program in 2023.

Crime Rate by Offense

The 2023 violent crime rate decreased 7.2% from 2022, and the property crime rate decreased 3.3% from 2022.

The crime categories with the largest decreases were human trafficking (commercial sex acts) by 18.9% and human trafficking (involuntary servitude) by 13.2%. Motor vehicle theft had the largest increase (22.8%).

The estimated value of property stolen during the commission of index crimes in 2023 was more than $4.7 billion.

Non-Index Crimes

ARSON

The reported number of arsons committed in Texas in 2023 was 2,575, a decrease of 12.1% from 2022. Communities of more than 100,000 reported the highest volume of arson (1,892).

HATE CRIMES

There were 555 hate crime incidents reported in Texas in 2023. Broken down by bias motivation, 54.2% of incidents were motivated by race or ethnicity, 23.8% by sexual orientation, 14.8% by religion, and 2.6% by disability.

MASS SHOOTINGS

The 2023 crime report did not address mass shootings. According to the *Gun Violence Archive*, a nonprofit that documents gun violence and gun crime in the U.S., Texas had 65 mass shootings (defined as incidents where "four or more people are shot or killed in a single incident, not including the shooter") in 2023, resulting in 264 injuries and 81 deaths.

LAW ENFORCEMENT ASSAULTS AND DEATHS

Assaults on law enforcement personnel increased 19.8% in 2023 to 6,264 from 5,228 in 2022. Of those assaults, 45.3% resulted in personal injuries. The largest number of assaults occurred while officers were attempting other arrests.

Four law officers were killed in the line of duty in 2023.

Source: Texas Department of Public Safety, Austin.

UNSPLASH/MARISA TERUEL

Texas Crime Volume by Offense			
Crime	2023	2022	% Change
Aggravated Assault	86,254	92,001	-6.2
Robbery	21,068	21,269	-0.9
Rape	11,062	11,620	-4.8
Murder & Nonnegligent Manslaughter	1,847	2,069	-10.7
Human Trafficking - Commercial Sex Acts	326	394	-17.3
Human Trafficking - Commercial Involuntary Servitude	200	226	-11.5
VIOLENT CRIME TOTAL	**120,757**	**127,579**	**-5.3**
Larceny/Theft	473,190	499,119	-5.2
Motor Vehicle Theft	126,241	100,829	25.2
Burglary/Breaking & Entering	92,969	101,517	-8.4
Arson	2,575	2,931	-12.1
PROPERTY CRIME TOTAL	**694,975**	**704,396**	**-1.3**

Source: "2023 Crime in Texas," TDPS.

Crime Profile of Texas Counties (2023)											
	No. Agencies Reporting	Murder	Rape	Robbery	Aggravated Assault	Burglary	Larceny	Auto Theft	Arson	Human Trafficking	Total Index Crimes
Anderson	2	1	20	5	62	50	248	21	8	1	416
Andrews	2	0	7	0	47	30	239	38	1	0	362
Angelina	11	5	90	38	273	330	1,109	172	8	2	2,027
Aransas	3	1	35	10	117	113	384	54	3	4	721
Archer	3	0	0	0	2	8	2	2	0	0	14
Armstrong	1	0	0	0	2	1	9	1	0	0	13
Atascosa	7	9	5	5	99	139	612	144	2	14	1,029
Austin	5	0	9	3	54	47	141	48	1	0	303
Bailey	2	0	0	0	6	15	13	4	0	0	38
Bandera	2	3	1	4	20	54	97	14	2	0	195
Bastrop	5	3	65	19	282	238	798	242	9	1	1,657
Baylor	2	0	0	1	3	3	7	2	0	0	16
Bee	2	0	8	4	71	131	307	29	9	0	559
Bell	13	22	233	133	945	1,014	4,073	1,191	28	9	7,648
Bexar	33	177	1,641	2,020	8,111	10,226	61,619	21,689	254	21	105,758
Blanco	2	0	5	1	7	14	35	8	1	0	71
Borden	1	0	1	0	1	0	5	2	0	0	9
Bosque	6	0	8	0	20	22	29	3	1	0	83
Bowie	15	12	45	23	193	226	1,103	166	8	1	1,777
Brazoria	25	9	149	84	454	755	4,321	492	10	1	6,275
Brazos	7	4	72	24	163	266	1,818	263	3	3	2,616
Brewster	3	0	2	0	6	20	7	1	0	0	36
Briscoe	1	0	0	0	1	6	4	1	0	0	12
Brooks	2	0	2	0	14	3	8	5	1	0	33
Brown	4	3	25	11	102	115	574	44	5	0	879
Burleson	3	0	6	0	25	30	79	24	0	1	165
Burnet	9	1	27	1	86	88	283	35	3	0	524
Caldwell	4	0	18	4	55	158	210	80	0	0	525
Calhoun	5	1	16	3	37	36	121	19	1	0	234
Callahan	3	1	2	0	20	32	46	20	0	0	121
Cameron	21	15	121	206	1,164	1,054	6,389	814	39	13	9,815
Camp	2	0	6	0	23	22	52	23	3	0	129
Carson	2	1	5	0	5	10	19	4	1	0	45
Cass	6	0	3	0	16	95	116	30	4	0	264
Castro	2	0	1	2	5	16	10	3	0	0	37
Chambers	3	10	38	4	80	152	628	126	2	4	1,044
Cherokee	4	3	17	6	130	129	450	80	0	0	815
Childress	2	1	1	0	9	7	12	6	0	0	36
Clay	1	0	3	0	23	28	38	16	0	0	108
Cochran	1	0	0	0	5	9	9	3	0	0	26
Coke	1	0	0	0	3	9	2	1	0	0	15
Coleman	3	0	2	0	6	12	7	7	0	0	34
Collin	26	25	308	180	846	1,424	10,569	1,299	41	6	14,698
Collingsworth	1	0	1	0	1	1	1	0	0	0	4
Colorado	3	0	8	2	22	44	126	43	0	0	245
Comal	8	1	59	28	212	440	1,609	282	1	11	2,643
Comanche	3	3	10	1	16	23	112	14	4	0	183
Concho	1	0	0	0	0	3	8	1	0	0	12
Cooke	2	2	14	1	54	60	288	44	3	0	466
Coryell	3	3	78	11	102	138	684	92	6	1	1,115
Cottle	0	NR	NR	NR	NR	NR	NR	NR	NR	NR	NR

NR = Not Reported

Source: "2023 Crime in Texas," TDPS.

Crime Profile of Texas Counties (2023)

	No. Agencies Reporting	Murder	Rape	Robbery	Aggravated Assault	Burglary	Larceny	Auto Theft	Arson	Human Trafficking	Total Index Crimes
Crane	2	0	0	1	4	2	24	4	1	0	36
Crockett	1	0	1	0	5	20	10	4	0	0	40
Crosby	2	0	0	0	1	34	16	2	0	0	53
Culberson	0	NR	NR	NR	NR	NR	NR	NR	NR	NR	NR
Dallam	2	0	2	1	26	29	39	8	0	0	105
Dallas	39	307	1,027	2,889	8,785	10,140	53,191	26,295	223	56	102,913
Dawson	2	0	4	2	24	37	55	19	2	1	144
Deaf Smith	2	0	11	1	27	95	181	60	2	0	377
Delta	1	0	4	0	13	12	22	8	0	0	59
Denton	29	23	263	156	707	990	7,618	1,109	27	4	10,897
DeWitt	2	0	5	2	83	32	131	19	2	0	274
Dickens	0	NR	NR	NR	NR	NR	NR	NR	NR	NR	NR
Dimmit	1	1	9	0	14	33	63	26	4	0	150
Donley	1	0	0	0	8	4	7	5	0	0	24
Duval	2	0	4	2	30	23	38	17	3	0	117
Eastland	5	0	5	1	34	48	107	22	3	0	220
Ector	6	12	51	56	420	321	1,573	389	14	2	2,838
Edwards	1	0	0	0	6	8	10	7	1	0	32
Ellis	11	41	360	363	2,015	1,322	8,679	2,708	103	2	15,593
El Paso	13	3	50	25	237	239	1,685	241	7	0	2,487
Erath	4	1	26	0	55	56	241	18	0	0	397
Falls	3	0	4	3	26	26	18	9	1	0	87
Fannin	8	0	2	2	59	24	93	19	5	0	204
Fayette	4	0	18	2	36	35	167	36	0	0	294
Fisher	1	0	0	0	7	8	12	3	0	0	30
Floyd	3	0	3	0	15	18	31	4	1	0	72
Foard	2	0	0	0	0	0	0	0	0	0	0
Fort Bend	12	20	229	235	867	905	7,221	916	9	2	10,404
Franklin	2	1	5	0	11	17	31	6	0	0	71
Freestone	4	0	7	0	55	50	115	28	0	0	255
Frio	3	0	2	3	38	85	84	52	2	0	266
Gaines	2	1	3	0	24	27	90	19	1	0	165
Galveston	17	24	244	120	623	749	4,213	695	24	2	6,694
Garza	1	1	2	0	4	5	18	0	0	1	31
Gillespie	2	0	8	3	8	28	86	21	0	0	154
Glasscock	1	0	0	0	0	19	26	12	0	0	57
Goliad	1	0	1	0	12	15	42	7	0	0	77
Gonzales	9	1	12	2	148	57	161	27	2	0	410
Gray	2	1	12	1	71	80	281	27	3	0	476
Grayson	21	8	69	25	251	356	783	148	10	0	1,650
Gregg	7	10	61	45	333	411	2,061	292	1	0	3,214
Grimes	3	2	36	7	90	105	206	49	1	0	496
Guadalupe	4	5	46	19	152	195	1,081	157	7	27	1,689
Hale	4	0	14	6	50	67	302	42	1	0	482
Hall	3	1	0	0	1	6	2	1	0	0	11
Hamilton	4	1	0	0	12	8	22	3	0	0	46
Hansford	2	0	0	0	0	2	5	0	0	0	7
Hardeman	1	0	0	0	0	4	8	2	0	0	14
Hardin	7	1	19	5	61	86	236	77	3	1	489
Harris	45	484	2,801	9,126	25,118	22,103	115,410	32,506	697	142	208,387
Harrison	4	7	19	14	122	254	486	100	0	2	1,004

NR = Not Reported

Source: "2023 Crime in Texas," TDPS.

Crime Profile of Texas Counties (2023)

	No. Agencies Reporting	Murder	Rape	Robbery	Aggravated Assault	Burglary	Larceny	Auto Theft	Arson	Human Trafficking	Total Index Crimes
Hartley	1	0	0	0	3	0	11	3	0	0	17
Haskell	2	0	1	0	1	8	19	7	0	0	36
Hays	5	5	120	85	488	504	2,548	505	8	1	4,264
Hemphill	1	0	0	0	0	6	8	0	0	0	14
Henderson	14	3	71	14	162	273	567	161	3	0	1,254
Hidalgo	26	27	398	304	1,860	1,879	12,915	1,215	34	6	18,638
Hill	4	1	23	4	50	80	332	47	4	0	541
Hockley	3	1	5	4	68	70	128	27	2	0	305
Hood	3	8	19	3	84	88	586	55	1	0	844
Hopkins	2	1	15	2	23	17	119	21	1	0	199
Houston	4	1	3	4	32	56	147	30	0	0	273
Howard	2	6	21	9	196	156	585	90	3	0	1,066
Hudspeth	1	0	0	0	3	3	3	1	0	0	10
Hunt	12	5	62	15	227	221	789	143	7	0	1,469
Hutchinson	2	1	15	0	71	66	170	20	1	0	344
Irion	1	0	0	0	0	2	7	0	0	0	9
Jack	2	0	3	1	17	6	14	3	4	0	48
Jackson	3	2	6	0	22	23	41	14	3	0	111
Jasper	3	1	3	4	40	119	259	39	8	0	473
Jeff Davis	1	0	0	0	7	5	8	1	0	0	21
Jefferson	7	27	205	302	1,656	1,053	3,797	669	24	1	7,734
Jim Hogg	1	0	0	0	6	25	7	2	0	0	40
Jim Wells	3	2	27	13	168	211	425	77	10	5	938
Johnson	14	5	111	15	310	254	1,310	191	10	0	2,206
Jones	5	2	2	0	13	23	45	7	1	0	93
Karnes	3	0	1	2	12	74	70	15	4	0	178
Kaufman	10	10	56	38	273	308	1,253	301	6	0	2,245
Kendall	2	0	9	4	24	78	252	42	2	0	411
Kenedy	1	0	0	0	1	0	0	1	0	0	2
Kent	0	NR	NR	NR	NR	NR	NR	NR	NR	NR	NR
Kerr	4	2	19	6	59	88	245	43	0	3	465
Kimble	2	1	0	0	2	1	4	8	0	0	16
King	1	0	0	0	0	0	0	0	0	0	0
Kinney	1	0	0	0	1	1	2	2	0	0	6
Kleberg	2	13	7	67	91	460	35	0	0	673	
Knox	3	0	1	0	3	6	7	2	1	0	20
Lamar	2	0	0	0	2	1	4	7	0	0	14
Lamb	6	2	30	13	158	195	524	56	3	0	981
Lampasas	3	0	0	3	17	32	88	17	1	0	158
La Salle	3	3	9	1	28	21	205	14	1	0	282
Lavaca	5	2	9	1	24	34	67	13	0	0	150
Lee	3	1	12	0	24	64	109	12	0	0	222
Leon	3	1	3	1	17	66	94	22	2	0	206
Liberty	3	4	41	21	196	281	598	219	4	0	1,364
Limestone	3	1	25	5	68	94	160	22	2	0	377
Lipscomb	1	0	0	0	1	6	4	0	0	0	11
Live Oak	2	0	2	0	13	13	15	5	0	0	48
Llano	4	4	9	0	23	34	99	25	1	0	195
Loving	1	0	0	0	0	0	30	0	0	0	30
Lubbock	12	18	250	369	1,842	1,771	6,257	1,138	92	6	11,743
Lynn	2	1	2	1	10	10	12	3	1	0	40

NR = Not Reported

Source: "2023 Crime in Texas," TDPS.

Crime Profile of Texas Counties (2023)											
	No. Agencies Reporting	Murder	Rape	Robbery	Aggravated Assault	Burglary	Larceny	Auto Theft	Arson	Human Trafficking	Total Index Crimes
Madison	3	0	3	3	15	30	69	18	1	0	139
Marion	2	0	2	0	11	29	42	13	1	0	98
Martin	2	0	0	0	6	15	205	9	1	0	236
Mason	2	0	0	0	2	2	4	0	0	0	8
Matagorda	5	3	0	3	3	15	30	69	18	1	0
Maverick	2	6	8	14	117	291	657	128	5	0	1,226
McCulloch	2	0	2	0	10	31	31	6	3	0	83
McLennan	13	17	184	114	657	725	3,862	576	27	7	6,169
McMullen	1	0	0	0	0	0	3	0	0	0	3
Medina	5	2	9	4	83	94	328	112	3	0	635
Menard	1	0	0	0	0	0	0	0	0	0	0
Midland	4	10	113	52	604	485	2,356	521	7	0	4,148
Milam	4	0	3	1	45	79	84	26	3	0	241
Mills	1	0	0	0	12	9	11	2	0	0	34
Mitchell	1	1	0	0	6	23	37	10	0	0	77
Montague	2	1	5	1	23	97	104	13	2	0	246
Montgomery	18	14	340	154	1,081	1,303	5,765	1,065	19	12	9,753
Moore	5	0	14	0	51	36	301	34	0	0	436
Morris	4	0	1	2	32	38	80	9	1	0	163
Motley	1	0	1	0	0	15	2	0	0	0	18
Nacogdoches	6	4	38	14	70	109	560	65	1	0	861
Navarro	10	3	40	13	138	175	568	100	14	0	1,051
Newton	2	0	3	0	11	24	24	4	0	0	66
Nolan	4	1	5	4	51	47	93	18	0	0	219
Nueces	7	22	270	372	2,155	1,858	7,720	1,106	58	5	13,566
Ochiltree	2	0	7	0	25	12	47	2	0	0	93
Oldham	2	0	1	0	0	3	6	0	0	0	10
Orange	8	2	35	19	161	245	465	167	3	0	1,097
Palo Pinto	2	0	26	6	64	188	349	65	2	1	701
Panola	3	0	6	3	41	28	177	21	3	0	279
Parker	6	2	68	17	180	408	1,246	193	8	0	2,122
Parmer	4	0	3	0	5	9	15	6	0	0	38
Pecos	2	0	6	0	20	17	44	7	3	0	97
Polk	5	4	40	11	100	154	516	127	2	0	954
Potter	4	16	175	207	1,110	972	4,717	685	43	0	7,925
Presidio	3	0	1	0	4	0	0	3	0	0	8
Rains	2	0	5	1	14	11	14	1	0	0	46
Randall	3	1	8	0	64	38	154	26	2	1	294
Reagan	1	0	1	0	3	4	26	3	0	0	37
Real	1	0	0	0	2	7	19	6	1	0	35
Red River	4	1	2	0	15	16	35	6	0	0	75
Reeves	3	1	4	1	84	24	153	26	0	0	293
Refugio	3	0	2	0	11	23	35	13	1	0	85
Roberts	1	0	0	0	0	0	0	0	0	0	0
Robertson	5	0	3	2	41	55	78	20	2	0	201
Rockwall	5	1	29	17	111	113	1,088	99	0	1	1,459
Runnels	4	0	4	0	10	27	32	9	2	0	84
Rusk	7	2	16	11	94	148	457	74	3	0	805
Sabine	4	0	7	0	13	15	32	5	1	0	73
San Augustine	3	1	2	1	11	23	21	4	1	0	64
San Jacinto	3	8	2	0	8	47	98	25	1	0	189

NR = Not Reported

Source: "2023 Crime in Texas," TDPS.

Crime Profile of Texas Counties (2023)											
	No. Agencies Reporting	Murder	Rape	Robbery	Aggravated Assault	Burglary	Larceny	Auto Theft	Arson	Human Trafficking	Total Index Crimes
San Patricio	8	1	16	6	89	103	513	49	3	0	780
San Saba	1	0	2	0	1	0	5	0	1	0	9
Schleicher	1	0	0	0	3	1	4	1	0	0	9
Scurry	2	2	5	0	138	32	167	19	1	0	364
Shackelford	1	0	0	0	4	1	2	0	0	0	7
Shelby	4	0	4	2	40	51	149	14	1	4	265
Sherman	1	0	1	0	1	0	1	1	0	0	4
Smith	14	13	131	49	594	504	2,539	358	6	1	4,195
Somervell	1	1	1	0	3	16	46	1	0	0	68
Starr	6	2	12	10	105	137	404	60	5	0	735
Stephens	3	0	4	1	10	33	59	13	1	0	121
Sterling	1	0	0	1	1	1	1	4	0	0	8
Stonewall	1	0	0	0	0	0	0	0	0	0	0
Sutton	2	0	1	0	3	2	4	1	0	0	11
Swisher	2	0	5	2	17	25	68	9	0	0	126
Tarrant	44	123	1,286	1,127	5,755	6,702	35,486	8,424	143	54	59,100
Taylor	6	7	129	63	412	453	1,753	167	4	0	2,988
Terrell	1	0	0	0	0	0	0	0	0	0	0
Terry	2	0	2	1	33	39	102	18	0	0	195
Throckmorton	1	0	1	0	0	1	4	0	0	1	7
Titus	4	3	19	6	86	52	316	37	2	0	521
Tom Green	3	6	52	29	232	449	2,083	220	8	0	3,079
Travis	19	75	667	1,053	4,296	5,684	25,990	8,117	176	9	46,067
Trinity	2	0	3	0	18	40	58	10	1	0	130
Tyler	4	0	2	0	16	48	55	38	3	0	162
Upshur	7	3	16	5	44	104	215	30	3	5	425
Upton	1	0	3	0	1	6	11	2	0	0	23
Uvalde	3	0	16	4	46	99	261	57	2	0	485
Val Verde	2	1	34	7	58	193	453	43	4	0	793
Van Zandt	6	1	14	1	48	109	255	45	1	0	474
Victoria	2	5	57	25	227	329	1,212	109	5	0	1,969
Walker	4	9	53	23	214	211	769	153	5	1	1,438
Waller	8	4	29	14	109	182	493	144	4	1	980
Ward	2	1	12	3	33	53	190	28	3	0	323
Washington	3	1	12	7	69	49	333	30	1	0	502
Webb	5	10	143	88	906	470	2,830	346	39	64	4,896
Wharton	4	0	9	22	126	113	563	90	5	0	928
Wheeler	1	0	4	0	7	7	8	4	0	0	30
Wichita	11	6	112	63	381	484	2,053	227	17	0	3,343
Wilbarger	2	0	7	4	18	30	103	12	0	0	174
Willacy	4	4	5	3	55	85	188	24	3	0	367
Williamson	17	7	219	70	461	1,057	6,342	709	17	1	8,883
Wilson	5	1	21	6	52	89	364	73	4	0	610
Winkler	4	0	3	3	11	12	56	11	1	0	97
Wise	6	9	36	4	94	218	572	53	2	1	989
Wood	8	0	17	4	54	88	199	35	0	0	397
Yoakum	2	0	1	1	20	9	45	3	0	0	79
Young	3	0	8	1	10	10	86	9	0	0	124
Zapata	1	0	0	0	7	19	52	0	0	0	78
Zavala	2	0	4	2	32	27	22	14	1	0	102
TOTALS	1,234	1,851	14,873	21,019	85,398	92,366	461,629	12,4525	2,580	1,200	—

NR = Not Reported

Source: "2023 Crime in Texas," TDPS.

TEXAS JAILS AND PRISONS

The **Texas Board of Criminal Justice** is composed of nine non-salaried members who are appointed by the governor for staggered six-year terms. The board employs the **Texas Department of Criminal Justice** (TDCJ) executive director, sets rules and policies that guide the agency, and considers other agency actions at its meetings.

In addition, the board appoints an inspector general, a director of internal audits, a director of state counsel for offenders, an independent ombudsman, and a prison rape elimination act ombudsman.

Board members serve in a separate capacity as the Board of Trustees for the **Windham School District** by hiring a superintendent and providing similar oversight.

The Windham School District serves TDCJ inmates at over 80 sites, and offers both academic and career and technical programs. The school district is a separate entity primarily funded through the Texas Education Agency (TEA).

Texas Department of Criminal Justice

The TDCJ Executive Director is responsible for the administration and enforcement of statutes relative to the criminal justice system. In 2024, the agency restructured its departmental organization to better align with their project, 2023 Vision, which aims to address issues relating to the agency's staff, inmate population, and TCDJ's overall advancement.

Fifteen divisions are split under three officers: the Chief Programs Officer, Chief Operations Officer, and the Chief Financial Officer.

The six divisions under the Chief Operations Officer include:

- **Community Justice Assistance Division (CJAD):** responsible for the distribution of formula and grant funds; the development and enforcement of standards, including best-practice treatment standards; conducting program and fiscal audits; providing training and certification of community supervision officers; and more.
- **Correctional Institutions Division (CID):** responsible for the confinement of adult felony and state jail felony inmates sentenced to incarceration in Texas.
- **Parole Division:** supervises offenders released on parole or mandatory supervision, conducts release and transition planning, and verifies compliance with statutory provisions of release.
- **Health Services Division:** provides health care services to incarcerated offenders in the custody of TDCJ and conducts operational review audits of health services at TDCJ facilities.
- **Training and Leader Development Division:** trains employees through face to face programs and online educational content. The division evaluates employees through online assessments and identifies best practices for handling situations.
- **Human Resources Division:** creates programs related to staffing and employment, working to retain and train employees.

Programs under the Chief Programs Officer encompass five divisions: Rehabilitation and Reentry, Administrative Review and Risk Management, Victim Services, Chaplaincy and Volunteer Services, and Classification and Inmate Transportation.

The final four divisions operate in coordination with the TDCJ Chief Financial Officer: Business and Finance, Information Technology, Manufacturing, Agribusiness & Logistics, and Facilities.

Sources: Texas Department of Criminal Justice, Windham School District.

UNSPLASH/CASEY OLSEN

Texas Department of Criminal Justice Operating Budget (FY 2024)		
Budget Item	Total, All Funds* ($ in millions)	Percent of Total*
A. Provide Prison Diversions	$297.20	6.70%
B: Special Needs Inmates	$29.70	0.67%
C: Incarcerate Inmates	$3,741.40	84.90%
D: Board of Pardons and Paroles	$32.10	0.73%
E: Operate Parole System	$197.40	4.50%
F: Indirect Administration	$111.90	2.50%
TOTAL	$4,409.60	100%

* Figures are rounded and may not equal totals.
Source: TDCJ Annual Review for FYE 2024.

On-Hand Inmate Profile (Fiscal Year 2024)	
Sex	
Male: 92.1%	Female: 7.9%
Race	
Hispanic: 33.7%	Black: 32.5%
White: 33.3%	Other: 0.6%
Average Age	
Prison: 41.5	State jail: 39.2
Average Sentences	
Prison: 19.9	State jail: 1.2
Education	
Average IQ	89.6
Offense	
Violent: 61.5%	Drug: 14.7%
Property: 8.2%	Other: 15.5%

* Based on offenders released in FY 2024
Source: TDCJ Statistical Report FYE 2024.

CORRECTIONAL INSTITUTIONS DIVISION

In addition to the incarceration of offenders, the CID has support functions, including: classification and records; counsel substitute; laundry, food and supply; offender transportation; and correctional training and staff development.

As of May 2025, there were 103 state-operated facilities, including state prisons (66) and jails (16), psychiatric facilities (3), pre-release facilities (7), substance abuse felony punishment facilities (4), intermediate sanction facilities (3), a geriatric facility (1), medical facilities (2), and the Developmental Disability Program facility (1).

The table below lists all of the TDCJ correctional institutions in the state alphabetically by county. It includes both those operated by the CID as well as privately operated facilities.

The town listed is the nearest one to the facility, although the unit may actually be in another county. For instance, the Middleton Transfer Facility is in Jones County, but the nearest city is Abilene, which is in Taylor County.

On-Hand Population As of August 31, 2024	
Prisoners	
Prison	127,822
State Jails	3,258
SAFP (Substance Abuse)	3,084
TOTAL	**134,164**
Supervision	
Parole	76,055
Discretionary Mandatory Supervision	19,402
Mandatory Supervision	2,543
TOTAL	**98,000**
Probation	
Community Supervision Placements*	380,488

*Total adults on direct, indirect, and pretrial supervision, minus transfers
Source: TDCJ Statistical Report FYE 2024.

Correctional Institutions in Texas (2025)

County	Unit	Nearest Town	Max. Capacity, Gender	Employees	Type*/Operator**
Anderson	Beto	Tennessee Colony	3,471 (Male)	472	Prison (CID)
Anderson	Coffield	Tennessee Colony	4,139 (Male)	518	Prison (CID)
Anderson	Michael	Tennessee Colony	2,984 (Male)	504	Prison (CID)
Anderson	Gurney	Palestine	216 (Male)	434	Prisonn (CID)
Anderson	Powledge	Palestine	1,137 (Male)	290	Prison (CID)
Angelina	Diboll	Diboll	518 (Male)	136	Pre-Release (CID)
Angelina	Duncan	Diboll	530 (Male)	139	Geriatric Facility (CID)

* **Facility type abbreviations:** SAFPF (Substance Abuse Felony Punishment Facility); ISF (Intermediate Sanction Facility); DDP (Developmentally Disabled Program)
** **Operator abbreviations:** CID (TDCJ Correctional Institutions Division); MTC (Management and Training Corporation)
Source: TDCJ Unit Directory.

Correctional Institutions in Texas (2025)

County	Unit	Nearest Town	Max. Capacity, Gender	Employees	Type*/Operator**
Bee	Garza East	Beeville	1,928 (Male)	442	Prison (CID)
Bee	Garza West	Beeville	2,278 (Male)	401	Prison (CID)
Bee	McConnell	Beeville	2956 (Male)	473	Prison (CID)
Bexar	Dominguez	San Antonio	2,276 (Male)	382	State Jail (CID)
Bowie	Telford	New Boston	2,451 (Male)	449	Prison (CID)
Brazos	Hamilton	Bryan	1,166 (Male)	256	Pre-Release (CID)
Brazoria	Clemens	Brazoria	1,215 (Male)	348	Prison (CID)
Brazoria	Havins	Brownwood	596 (Male)	181	Pre-Release (CID)
Brazoria	Memorial	Rosharon	1,931 (Male)	567	Prison (CID)
Brazoria	Ramsey	Rosharon	1,865 (Male)	429	Prison (CID)
Brazoria	Stringfellow	Rosharon	1,212 (Male)	313	Prison (CID)
Brazoria	Terrell	Rosharon	1,603 (Male)	466	Prison (CID)
Burnet	Halbert	Burnet	612 (Female)	135	SAFPF (CID)
Caldwell	Coleman	Lockhart	1000 (Female)	204	Private Prison (MTC)
Cherokee	Hodge	Rusk	989 (Male)	333	DDP (CID)
Cherokee	Skyview	Rusk	562 (Co-gender)	318	Psychiatric (CID)
Childress	Roach	Childress	1,384 (Male)	289	Prison (CID)
Coryell	Crain	Gatesville	1,440 (Female)	711	Prison (CID)
Coryell	Hilltop	Gatesville	553 (Female)	268	Prison (CID)
Coryell	Hughes	Gatesville	2,552 (Male)	515	Prison (CID)
Coryell	Murray	Gatesville	1,264 (Female)	341	Prison (CID)
Coryell	O'Daniel	Gatesville	644 (Female)	300	Prison (CID)
Coryell	Woodman	Gatesville	900 (Female)	270	State Jail (CID)
Dallas	Hutchins	Dallas	2,276 (Male)	399	State Jail (CID)
Dawson	Smith	Lamesa	2,098 (Male)	252	Prison (CID)
DeWitt	Stevenson	Cuero	1,384 (Male)	272	Prison (CID)
Duvall	Glossbrenner	San Diego	612 (Male)	123	SAFPF (CID)
El Paso	Sanchez	El Paso	1,100 (Male)	287	State Jail (CID)
Falls	Hobby	Marlin	1,384 (Female)	299	Prison (CID)
Falls	Marlin	Marlin	606 (Female)	126	Prison (CID)
Fannin	Cole	Bonham	900 (Male)	226	State Jail (CID)
Fannin	[illegible]	Bonham	1,224 (Male)	245	Prison (CID)
Freestone	Boyd	Teague	1,372 (Male)	298	Prison (CID)
Frio	Briscoe	Dilley	1,132 (Male)	233	Prison (CID)
Fort Bend	Jester III	Richmond	1,185 (Male)	288	Prison (CID)
Fort Bend	Scott	Richmond	550 (Male)	433	Psychiatric (CID)
Fort Bend	Vance	Richmond	378 (Male)	116	Prison (CID)
Galveston	Hospital Galveston	Galveston	— (Co-Gender)	496	Medical (CID)
Galveston	Young	Dickinson	328 (Female)	302	Medical (CID)
Gray	Baten	Pampa	188 (Male)	29	ISF (CID)
Gray	Jordan	Pampa	1,152 (Male)	289	Prison (CID)
Grimes	Luther	Navasota	1,316 (Male)	323	Prison (CID)
Grimes	Pack	Navasota	1,426 (Male)	334	Prison (CID)
Hale	Formby	Plainview	1,100 (Male)	278	State Jail (CID)
Hale	Wheeler	Plainview	576 (Male)	127	State Jail (CID)
Harris	Kegans	Houston	657 (Male)	155	ISF (CID)

* **Facility type abbreviations:** SAFPF (Substance Abuse Felony Punishment Facility); ISF (Intermediate Sanction Facility); DDP (Developmentally Disabled Program)

** **Operator abbreviations:** CID (TDCJ Correctional Institutions Division); MTC (Management and Training Corporation)

Source: TDCJ Unit Directory.

Correctional Institutions in Texas (2025)					
County	Unit	Nearest Town	Max. Capacity, Gender	Employees	Type*/Operator**
Harris	Lychner	Humble	2,276 (Male)	413	State Jail (CID)
Hartley	Dalhart	Dalhart	780 (Male)	237	Prison (CID)
Hays	Kyle	Kyle	520 (Male)	117	Private Prison (MTC)
Hidalgo	Lopez	Edinburg	903 (Male)	257	State Jail (CID)
Hidalgo	Segovia	Edinburg	1,224 (Male)	233	Pre-Release (CID)
Houston	Wainwright	Lovelady	2,464 (Male)	423	Prison (CID)
Jack	Lindsey	Jacksboro	1,031 (Male)	202	Private State Jail (MTC)
Jasper	Goodman	Jasper	204 (Male)	155	Prison/ISF (CID)
Jefferson	LeBlanc	Beaumont	1,224 (Male)	248	Pre-Release (CID)
Jefferson	Gist	Beaumont	2,276 (Male)	368	State Jail (CID)
Jefferson	Stiles	Beaumont	3,367 (Male)	495	Prison (CID)
Johnson	Estes	Venus	1,040 (Male)	191	Pre-Release (CID)
Jones	Middleton	Abilene	2,128 (Male)	504	Prison (CID)
Jones	Robertson	Abilene	2,978 (Male)	513	Prison (CID)
Karnes	Connally	Kenedy	2,496 (Male)	354	Prison (CID)
La Salle	Cotulla	Cotulla	606 (Male)	99	Prison (CID)
Liberty	Bell	Cleveland	520 (Male)	134	Pre-Release (CID)
Liberty	Henley	Dayton	384 (Female)	124	State Jail (CID)
Liberty	Hightower	Dayton	1,384 (Male)	335	Prison (CID)
Liberty	Plane/Santa Maria Baby Bonding	Dayton	2,296 (Female)	418	State Jail (CID)
Lubbock	Montford/West Texas Hospital	Lubbock	950 (Male)	591	Psychiatric (CID)
Madison	Ferguson	Midway	2,417 (Male)	364	Prison (CID)
Medina	Ney	Hondo	576 (Male)	134	Prison (CID)
Medina	Torres	Hondo	1,384 (Male)	298	Prison (CID)
Mitchell	Wallace/San Angelo Work Camp	Colorado City	1,132 (Male)	255	Prison (CID)
Pecos	Fort Stockton	Fort Stockton	606 (Male)	114	Prison (CID)
Pecos	Lynaugh	Fort Stockton	1,416 (Male)	289	Prison (CID)
Polk	Polunsky	Livingston	2,984 (Male)	554	Prison (CID)
Potter	Clements	Amarillo	3,614 (Male)	590	Prison (CID)
Rusk	Bradshaw	Henderson	1,828 (Male)	266	Private State Jail (MTC)
Rusk	East Texas	Henderson	1,060 (Co-Gender)	493	Private Multi-Use (MTC)
Rusk	Moore, B.	Overton	500 (Male)	138	Private Prison (MTC)
San Saba	San Saba	San Saba	606 (Male)	135	Prison (CID)
Scurry	Daniel	Snyder	504 (Male)	224	Prison (CID)
Stephens	Sayle	Breckenridge	632 (Male)	146	SAFPF (CID)
Swisher	Mechler	Tulia	606 (Male)	117	Prison (CID)
Travis	Travis County	Austin	1,161 (Male)	264	State Jail (CID)
Tyler	Lewis	Woodville	2,380 (Male)	371	Prison (CID)
Walker	Byrd	Huntsville	1,341 (Male)	282	Prison (CID)
Walker	Ellis	Huntsville	2,482 (Male)	400	Prison (CID)
Walker	Estelle	Huntsville	3,460 (Male)	755	Prison (CID)
Walker	Goree	Huntsville	1,321 (Male)	315	Prison (CID)
Walker	Holliday	Huntsville	2,120 (Male)	435	Prison (CID)
Walker	Huntsville	Huntsville	1,090 (Male)	446	Prison (CID)

* **Facility type abbreviations:** SAFPF (Substance Abuse Felony Punishment Facility); ISF (Intermediate Sanction Facility); DDP (Developmentally Disabled Program)

** **Operator abbreviations:** CID (TDCJ Correctional Institutions Division); MTC (Management and Training Corporation)

Source: TDCJ Unit Directory.

Correctional Institutions in Texas (2025)					
County	Unit	Nearest Town	Max. Capacity, Gender	Employees	Type*/Operator**
Walker	Wynne	Huntsville	2,621 (Male)	480	Prison (CID)
Wichita	Allred	Iowa Park	4,438 (Male)	687	Prison (CID)
Willacy	Willacy County	Raymondville	1,069 (Male)	183	Private State Jail (MTC)
Williamson	Bartlett	Bartlett	1,049 (Male)	199	Prison (CID)
Wise	Bridgeport	Bridgeport	520 (Male)	117	Private Prison (MTC)
Wood	Johnston	Winnsboro	612 (Male)	160	SAFPF (CID)

* **Facility type abbreviations:** SAFPF (Substance Abuse Felony Punishment Facility); ISF (Intermediate Sanction Facility); DDP (Developmentally Disabled Program)

** **Operator abbreviations:** CID (TDCJ Correctional Institutions Division); MTC (Management and Training Corporation)

Source: TDCJ Unit Directory.

UNSPLASH/CARLES RABADA

FEDERAL PRISONS

The Federal Bureau of Prisons (BOP) operates 11 prisons and four offices in the state of Texas. Recent data shows 15,738 federal inmates confined to the following locations in Texas:

- Bastrop Federal Correction Institution
- Beaumont Federal Correction Complex
- Big Spring Federal Correction Institution
- Bryan Federal Prison Camp – Female
- Carswell Federal Medical Center – Female
- Fort Worth Federal Medical Center
- Houston Federal Detention Center – Female
- La Tuna Federal Correction Institution
- Seagoville Federal Correction Institution
- Texarkana Federal Correction Institution
- Three Rivers Federal Correction Institution

Currently, Texas is home to about 11% of the total 143,675 inmates in BOP-managed institutions nationwide.

Source: Federal Bureau of Prisons.

WIKIMEDIA COMMONS

Texas

ASTRONOMICAL CALENDAR

UNSPLASH/LEONARDO CORRAL

ASTRONOMICAL CALENDARS FOR 2026 & 2027

THE YEAR 2026

The year 2026 CE comprises the latter part of the 249th and the beginning of the 250th year of the independence of the United States of America.

The Seasons

Spring begins on Friday, March 20, at 9:46 a.m. (CDT)
Summer begins on Sunday, June 21, at 3:24 a.m. (CDT)
Autumn begins on Tuesday, Sept. 22, at 7:05 p.m. (CDT)
Winter begins on Monday, Dec. 21, at 2:50 p.m. (CST)

Eclipses 2026

Feb. 17: Solar (Annular) Visible in Antarctica, S. in Africa, S. in South America, Pacific Ocean, Atlantic Ocean, Indian Ocean

March 3: Lunar (Total) Visible in North America, Antarctica, E. in Europe, Asia, Australia, South America, Pacific Ocean, Atlantic Ocean, Arctic Ocean, Indian Ocean

Aug. 12: Solar (Total) Visible in North America, Europe, N. in Asia, N/W in Africa, Pacific Ocean, Atlantic Ocean, Arctic Ocean

Aug. 28: Lunar (Partial) Visible in North America, Europe, W. in Asia, Africa, South America, Antarctica, Pacific Ocean, Atlantic Ocean, Indian Ocean

Chronological Eras (2026)

Era	Year
Julian	3739
Byzantine	7535
Jewish (A.M.)*	5787
Chinese (bing wu)	—
Roman (A.U.C.)	2779
Nabonassar	2775
Japanese	2686
Seleucidæ (Grecian)	2338
Saka (Indian)	1948
Diocletian (Coptic)	1743
Islamic (Hegira)*	1448

**Year begins at sunset.*

Chronological Cycles (2026)

Dominical Letter	D	Golden Number (Lunar Cycle)	XIII
Epact	11		
Roman Indiction	4	Solar Cycle	19

THE YEAR 2027

The year 2027 CE comprises the latter part of the 250th and the beginning of the 251st year of the independence of the United States of America.

The Seasons

Spring begins on Saturday, March 20, at 3:25 p.m. (CDT)
Summer begins on Monday, June 21, at 9:11 a.m. (CDT)
Autumn begins on Thursday, Sept. 23, at 1:02 a.m. (CDT)
Winter begins on Tuesday, Dec. 21, at 8:42 p.m. (CST)

Eclipses 2027

Feb. 6: Solar (Annular) Visible in Antarctica, Africa, South America, Pacific Ocean, Atlantic Ocean

March 3: Lunar (Penumbral) Visible in North America, South America, Europe, Asia, N/W Australia, Africa, Antarctica, Pacific Ocean, Atlantic Ocean, Indian Ocean, Arctic Ocean

Aug. 2: Solar (Total) Visible in Europe, E. in North America, S/W Asia, Africa, Atlantic Ocean, Indian Ocean

Aug. 17: Lunar (Penumbral) Visible in North America, South America, W. in Europe, N. in Asia, Australia, N/W Africa, Antarctica, Pacific Ocean, Atlantic Ocean

Chronological Eras (2027)

Era	Year
Julian	3740
Byzantine	7536
Jewish (A.M.)*	5788
Chinese (gui mao)	—
Roman (A.U.C.)	2780
Nabonassar	2776
Japanese	2687
Seleucidæ (Grecian)	2339
Saka (Indian)	1949
Diocletian (Coptic)	1744
Islamic (Hegira)*	1449

**Year begins at sunset.*

Chronological Cycles (2027)

Dominical Letter	C	Golden Number (Lunar Cycle)	XIV
Epact	0		
Roman Indiction	5	Solar Cycle	20

Sources: McDonald Observatory; U.S. Naval Observatory's Astronomical Phenomena For The Year 2026; National Weather Service, Time and Date, Calendar Bede.

CLIMATIC DATA REGIONS OF TEXAS

See text for explanation of how to calculate sunrise, sunset, moonrise and moonset.

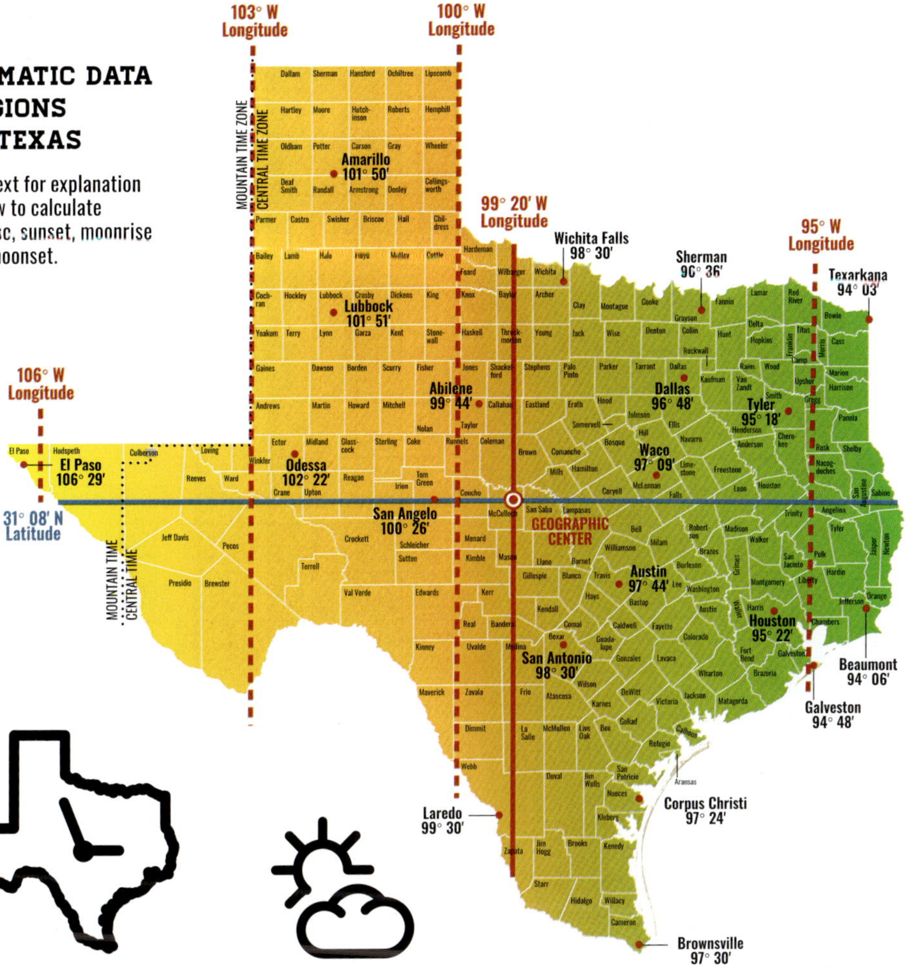

103° W Longitude
100° W Longitude
99° 20′ W Longitude
95° W Longitude
106° W Longitude
MOUNTAIN TIME ZONE
CENTRAL TIME ZONE
Amarillo 101° 50′
Lubbock 101° 51′
Wichita Falls 98° 30′
Sherman 96° 36′
Texarkana 94° 03′
Abilene 99° 44′
Dallas 96° 48′
Tyler 95° 18′
El Paso 106° 29′
Odessa 102° 22′
Waco 97° 09′
31° 08′ N Latitude
San Angelo 100° 26′
GEOGRAPHIC CENTER
Austin 97° 44′
Houston 95° 22′
San Antonio 98° 30′
Beaumont 94° 06′
Galveston 94° 48′
MOUNTAIN TIME
CENTRAL TIME
Laredo 99° 30′
Corpus Christi 97° 24′
Brownsville 97° 30′

AN EXPLANATION OF TEXAS TIME

Times listed here are **Central Standard Time**, except for the period from 2:00 a.m. on the second Sunday in March until 2:00 a.m. on the first Sunday in November, when **Daylight Saving Time**, which is one hour later than Central Standard Time, is in effect.

All of Texas is in the Central Time Zone, except El Paso and Hudspeth counties and the northwest corner of Culberson County, which observe **Mountain Time**. Mountain Time is one hour earlier than Central Time.

All times are calculated for the intersection of 97° 50′ west longitude and 30° 18′ north latitude. This point is the approximate geographical point of the state capital: Austin, Texas.

HOW TO ADJUST RISE & SET TIMES

To adjust the time of sunrise or sunset, moonrise or moonset for any point in Texas, apply the following rules:

- For each degree of longitude that the place lies **west** of the 99th meridian, **add four minutes** to the times given in the calendar.
- For each degree of longitude the place lies **east** of the 99th meridian, **subtract four minutes**.

At times there will be considerable variation for distances north and south of the line of 31° 08′ north latitude, but this formula will give sufficiently close results.

The map above shows the intersection for which all times given in this chapter are calculated, with some major cities and longitudes to aid in calculating times.

ASTRONOMICAL CALENDARS

The calendars on the following pages feature primary phases of the moon for 2026 and 2027 in the center columns.

2026 ASTRONOMICAL CALENDAR

Times are figured for the point **97° 50' west longitude and 30° 18' north latitude**, the geographical location for Austin, Texas.

1st Month — January 2026 — 31 Days

Day of Year	Day of Month	Day of Week	Primary Phases of Moon	Sunrise	Sunset	Moon-rise	Moon-set
1	1	Thu		7:28	5:42	3:50	5:44
2	2	Fri		7:28	5:43	4:57	6:54
3	3	Sat	Full Moon	7:28	5:43	6:09	7:55
4	4	Sun		7:28	5:44	7:21	8:46
5	5	Mon		7:28	5:45	8:29	9:28
6	6	Tues		7:28	5:46	9:33	10:03
7	7	Wed		7:28	5:46	10:33	10:34
8	8	Thu		7:28	5:47	11:30	11:02
9	9	Fri		7:28	5:48		11:29
10	10	Sat	Last Quarter	7:28	5:49	12:26	11:56
11	11	Sun		7:28	5:50	1:22	12:25
12	12	Mon		7:28	5:50	2:18	12:57
13	13	Tues		7:28	5:51	3:15	1:33
14	14	Wed		7:28	5:52	4:12	2:15
15	15	Thu		7:28	5:53	5:08	3:03
16	16	Fri		7:28	5:54	6:01	3:56
17	17	Sat		7:28	5:55	6:50	4:54
18	18	Sun	New Moon	7:27	5:56	7:34	5:54
19	19	Mon		7:27	5:56	8:13	6:56
20	20	Tues		7:27	5:57	8:47	7:56
21	21	Wed		7:27	5:58	9:18	8:57
22	22	Thu		7:26	5:59	9:47	9:57
23	23	Fri		7:26	6:00	10:16	10:58
24	24	Sat		7:26	6:01	10:47	
25	25	Sun		7:25	6:02	11:19	12:01
26	26	Mon	First Quarter Moon	7:25	6:03	11:57	1:07
27	27	Tues		7:24	6:03	12:42	2:16
28	28	Wed		7:24	6:04	1:35	3:27
29	29	Thu		7:23	6:05	2:37	4:36
30	30	Fri		7:23	6:06	3:45	5:39
31	31	Sat		7:22	6:07	4:57	6:33

2nd Month — February 2026 — 28 Days

Day of Year	Day of Month	Day of Week	Primary Phases of Moon	Sunrise	Sunset	Moon-rise	Moon-set
32	1	Sun	Full Moon	7:21	6:08	6:07	7:19
33	2	Mon		7:21	6:09	7:13	7:57
34	3	Tues		7:20	6:10	8:16	8:30
35	4	Wed		7:20	6:10	9:16	9:00
36	5	Thu		7:19	6:11	10:13	9:28
37	6	Fri		7:18	6:12	11:10	9:56
38	7	Sat		7:17	6:13		10:24
39	8	Sun		7:17	6:14	12:07	10:55
40	9	Mon	Last Quarter	7:16	6:15	1:04	11:30
41	10	Tues		7:15	6:15	2:02	12:09
42	11	Wed		7:14	6:16	2:58	12:54
43	12	Thu		7:13	6:17	3:53	1:46
44	13	Fri		7:13	6:18	4:43	2:42
45	14	Sat		7:12	6:19	5:29	3:42
46	15	Sun		7:11	6:19	6:10	4:43
47	16	Mon		7:10	6:20	6:46	5:45
48	17	Tues	New Moon	7:09	6:21	7:19	6:47
49	18	Wed		7:08	6:22	7:49	7:48
50	19	Thu		7:07	6:23	8:19	8:50
51	20	Fri		7:06	6:23	8:49	9:54
52	21	Sat		7:05	6:24	9:21	11:00
53	22	Sun		7:04	6:25	9:58	
54	23	Mon		7:03	6:26	10:40	12:08
55	24	Tues	First Quarter	7:02	6:26	11:29	1:18
56	25	Wed		7:01	6:27	12:27	2:26
57	26	Thu		7:00	6:28	1:32	3:30
58	27	Fri		6:59	6:28	2:40	4:26
59	28	Sat		6:58	6:29	3:49	5:13

3rd Month — March 2026 — 31 Days

Day of Year	Day of Month	Day of Week	Primary Phases of Moon	Sunrise	Sunset	Moon-rise	Moon-set
60	1	Sun		6:57	6:30	4:56	5:52
61	2	Mon		6:56	6:31	5:59	6:28
62	3	Tues	Full Moon	6:55	6:31	7:00	6:58
63	4	Wed		6:54	6:32	7:59	7:27
64	5	Thu		6:52	6:33	8:56	7:55
65	6	Fri		6:51	6:33	9:54	8:23
66	7	Sat		6:50	6:34	10:52	8:53
67	8	Sun		6:49	6:35	11:50	9:27
68	9	Mon		6:48	6:35		10:04
69	10	Tues		6:47	6:36	12:47	10:47
70	11	Wed	Last Quarter	6:45	6:37	1:43	11:35
71	12	Thu		6:44	6:37	235	12:29
72	13	Fri		6:43	6:38	3:22	1:27
73	14	Sat		6:42	6:39	4:05	2:27
74	15	Sun		6:41	6:39	4:42	3:29
75	16	Mon		6:39	6:40	5:16	4:31
76	17	Tues		6:38	6:41	5:48	5:33
77	18	Wed		6:37	6:41	6:16	6:36
78	19	Thu	New Moon	6:36	6:42	6:49	7:40
79	20	Fri		6:35	6:42	7:21	9:47
80	21	Sat		6:33	6:43	7:57	10:57
81	22	Sun		6:32	6:44	8:38	11:08
82	23	Mon		6:31	6:44	9:26	
83	24	Tues		6:30	6:45	10:22	12:18
84	25	Wed	First Quarter	6:28	6:46	11:25	1:24
85	26	Thu		6:27	6:46	12:32	2:22
86	27	Fri		6:26	6:47	1:40	3:11
87	28	Sat		6:25	6:47	2:46	3:53
88	29	Sun		6:24	6:48	3:49	4:28
89	30	Mon		6:22	6:49	4:49	4:59
90	31	Tues		6:21	6:49	5:47	5:28

Source: United States Naval Observatory.

2026 ASTRONOMICAL CALENDAR

Source: United States Naval Observatory.

4th Month — April 2026 — 30 Days

Day of Year	Day of Month	Day of Week	Primary Phases of Moon	Sunrise	Sunset	Moon-rise	Moon-set
91	1	Wed		6:20	6:50	6:45	5:56
92	2	Thu	Full Moon	6:19	6:50	7:42	6:24
93	3	Fri		6:18	6:51	8:40	6:53
94	4	Sat		6:16	6:52	9:38	7:25
95	5	Sun		6:15	6:52	10:36	8:01
96	6	Mon		6:14	6:52	11:33	8:42
97	7	Tues		6:13	6:53		9:28
98	8	Wed		6:12	6:54	12:26	10:19
99	9	Thu		6:10	6:54	1:15	11:15
100	10	Fri	Last Quarter	6:09	6:55	1:59	12:13
101	11	Sat		6:08	6:55	2:38	1:13
102	12	Sun		6:07	6:56	3:13	2:14
103	13	Mon		6:06	6:57	3:45	3:15
104	14	Tues		6:05	6:57	4:15	4:16
105	15	Wed		6:04	6:58	4:45	5:20
106	16	Thu		6:03	6:59	5:17	6:27
107	17	Fri	New Moon	6:01	7:00	5:51	8:37
108	18	Sat		6:00	7:00	6:31	9:49
109	19	Sun		5:59	7:01	7:18	10:03
110	20	Mon		5:58	7:02	8:12	11:13
111	21	Tues		5:57	7:02	9:15	
112	22	Wed		5:56	7:03	10:23	12:16
113	23	Thu		5:55	7:04	11:32	1:09
114	24	Fri	First Quarter	5:54	7:04	12:39	1:53
115	25	Sat		5:53	7:05	1:43	2:30
116	26	Sun		5:52	7:06	2:43	3:02
117	27	Mon		5:51	7:06	3:41	3:31
118	28	Tues		5:50	7:07	4:38	3:59
119	29	Wed		5:49	7:07	5:34	4:26
120	30	Thu		5:48	7:08	6:31	4:55

5th Month — May 2026 — 31 Days

Day of Year	Day of Month	Day of Week	Primary Phases of Moon	Sunrise	Sunset	Moon-rise	Moon-set
121	1	Fri	Full Moon	5:48	7:09	7:29	5:26
122	2	Sat		5:47	7:09	8:27	6:00
123	3	Sun		5:46	7:10	9:24	6:39
124	4	Mon		5:45	7:11	10:19	7:23
125	5	Tues		5:44	7:11	11:09	8:13
126	6	Wed		5:43	7:12	11:54	9:07
127	7	Thu		5:43	7:13		10:04
128	8	Fri		5:42	7:13	12:34	11:02
129	9	Sat	Last Quarter	5:41	7:14	1:10	12:01
130	10	Sun		5:40	7:15	1:42	1:00
131	11	Mon		5:40	7:15	2:13	2:00
132	12	Tues		5:39	7:16	2:42	3:01
133	13	Wed		5:38	7:17	3:12	4:04
134	14	Thu		5:38	7:17	3:45	5:12
135	15	Fri		5:37	7:18	4:22	6:24
136	16	Sat	New Moon	5:36	7:19	5:05	7:38
137	17	Sun		5:36	7:19	5:57	8:53
138	18	Mon		5:35	7:20	6:58	9:01
139	19	Tues		5:35	7:21	8:07	10:00
140	20	Wed		5:34	7:21	9:18	11:49
141	21	Thu		5:34	7:22	10:29	
142	22	Fri		5:33	7:22	11:35	12:30
143	23	Sat	First Quarter	5:33	7:23	12:37	1:04
144	24	Sun		5:32	7:24	1:36	1:34
145	25	Mon		5:32	7:24	2:33	2:02
146	26	Tues		5:31	7:25	3:30	2:30
147	27	Wed		5:31	7:25	4:26	2:58
148	28	Thu		5:31	7:26	5:23	3:28
149	29	Fri		5:30	7:27	6:20	4:01
150	30	Sat		5:30	7:27	7:18	4:38
151	31	Sun		5:30	7:28	8:13	5:21

6th Month — June 2026 — 30 Days

Day of Year	Day of Month	Day of Week	Primary Phases of Moon	Sunrise	Sunset	Moon-rise	Moon-set
152	1	Mon		5:30	7:28	9:05	6:09
153	2	Tues		5:29	7:29	9:52	7:02
154	3	Wed		5:29	7:29	10:33	7:58
155	4	Thu		5:29	7:30	11:10	8:55
156	5	Fri		5:29	7:30	11:43	9:54
157	6	Sat		5:29	7:31		10:51
158	7	Sun		5:29	7:31	12:13	11:49
159	8	Mon	Last Quarter	5:29	7:32	12:42	12:48
160	9	Tues		5:29	7:32	1:10	1:48
161	10	Wed		5:29	7:32	1:41	2:52
162	11	Thu		5:29	7:33	2:14	3:59
163	12	Fri		5:29	7:33	2:53	5:12
164	13	Sat		5:29	7:34	3:40	6:26
165	14	Sun		5:29	7:34	4:37	7:38
166	15	Mon	New Moon	5:29	7:34	5:43	8:43
167	16	Tues		5:29	7:35	6:56	9:38
168	17	Wed		5:29	7:35	8:09	10:24
169	18	Thu		5:29	7:35	9:20	11:02
170	19	Fri		5:29	7:35	10:26	11:35
171	20	Sat		5:30	7:36	11:28	
172	21	Sun	First Quarter	5:30	7:36	12:27	12:04
173	22	Mon		5:30	7:36	1:24	12:32
174	23	Tues		5:30	7:36	2:21	1:00
175	24	Wed		5:31	7:36	3:18	1:30
176	25	Thu		5:31	7:36	4:15	2:02
177	26	Fri		5:31	7:37	5:12	2:38
178	27	Sat		5:31	7:37	6:08	3:19
179	28	Sun		5:32	7:37	7:01	4:05
180	29	Mon	Full Moon	5:32	7:37	7:50	4:57
181	30	Tues		5:32	7:37	8:33	5:52

2026 ASTRONOMICAL CALENDAR

Times are figured for the point **97° 50' west longitude and 30° 18' north latitude**, the geographical location for Austin, Texas.

7th Month — July 2026 — 31 Days

Day of Year	Day of Month	Day of Week	Primary Phases of Moon	Sunrise	Sunset	Moon-rise	Moon-set
182	1	Wed		5:33	7:37	9:11	6:50
183	2	Thu		5:33	7:37	9:45	7:48
184	3	Fri		5:34	7:37	10:15	8:46
185	4	Sat		5:34	7:37	10:44	9:44
186	5	Sun		5:35	7:36	11:12	10:41
187	6	Mon		5:35	7:36	11:41	11:39
188	7	Tues	Last Quarter	5:35	7:36		12:40
189	8	Wed		5:36	7:36	12:12	1:44
190	9	Thu		5:36	7:36	12:47	2:52
191	10	Fri		5:37	7:36	1:29	4:03
192	11	Sat		5:37	7:35	2:20	5:15
193	12	Sun		5:38	7:35	3:30	6:23
194	13	Mon		5:39	7:35	4:29	7:23
195	14	Tues	New Moon	5:39	7:34	5:43	8:13
196	15	Wed		5:40	7:34	6:57	8:55
197	16	Thu		5:40	7:34	8:07	9:31
198	17	Fri		5:41	7:33	9:12	10:03
199	18	Sat		5:41	7:33	10:14	10:32
200	19	Sun		5:42	7:32	11:14	11:01
201	20	Mon		5:42	7:32	12:12	11:30
202	21	Tues	First Quarter	5:43	7:31	1:10	
203	22	Wed		5:44	7:31	2:08	12:02
204	23	Thu		5:44	7:30	3:05	12:37
205	24	Fri		5:45	7:30	4:02	1:16
206	25	Sat		5:45	7:29	4:56	2:01
207	26	Sun		5:46	7:29	5:46	2:51
208	27	Mon		5:47	7:28	6:31	3:45
209	28	Tues		5:47	7:27	7:11	4:43
210	29	Wed	Full Moon	5:48	7:27	7:47	5:41
211	30	Thu		5:48	7:26	8:18	6:40
212	31	Fri		5:49	7:25	8:48	7:38

8th Month — August 2026 — 31 Days

Day of Year	Day of Month	Day of Week	Primary Phases of Moon	Sunrise	Sunset	Moon-rise	Moon-set
213	1	Sat		5:50	7:25	9:16	8:36
214	2	Sun		5:50	7:24	9:44	9:34
215	3	Mon		5:51	7:23	10:14	10:34
216	4	Tues		5:51	7:22	10:47	11:35
217	5	Wed		5:52	7:21	11:25	12:41
218	6	Thu	Last Quarter	5:53	7:21		1:49
219	7	Fri		5:53	7:20	12:11	2:59
220	8	Sat		5:54	7:19	1:06	4:06
221	9	Sun		5:54	7:18	2:09	5:08
222	10	Mon		5:55	7:17	3:20	6:02
223	11	Tues		5:56	7:16	4:32	6:47
224	12	Wed	New Moon	5:56	7:15	5:44	7:26
225	13	Thu		5:57	7:14	6:52	7:59
226	14	Fri		5:57	7:13	7:57	8:30
227	15	Sat		5:58	7:12	8:59	9:26
228	16	Sun		5:59	7:11	9:59	9:29
229	17	Mon		5:59	7:10	10:58	10:00
230	18	Tues		6:00	7:09	11:57	10:34
231	19	Wed		6:00	7:08	12:56	11:12
232	20	Thu	First Quarter	6:01	7:07	1:53	11:55
233	21	Fri		6:02	7:06	2:49	
234	22	Sat		6:02	7:05	3:40	12:43
235	23	Sun		6:03	7:04	4:27	1:36
236	24	Mon		6:03	7:03	5:09	2:33
237	25	Tues		6:04	7:02	5:46	3:32
238	26	Wed		6:04	7:00	6:19	4:31
239	27	Thu		6:05	6:59	6:50	5:30
240	28	Fri	Full Moon	6:06	6:58	7:19	6:28
241	29	Sat		6:06	6:57	7:47	7:27
242	30	Sun		6:07	7:56	8:17	8:27
243	31	Mon		6:07	7:55	8:49	9:29

9th Month — September 2026 — 30 Days

Day of Year	Day of Month	Day of Week	Primary Phases of Moon	Sunrise	Sunset	Moon-rise	Moon-set
244	1	Tues		6:08	6:53	9:26	10:33
245	2	Wed		6:08	6:52	10:09	11:41
246	3	Thu		6:09	6:51	10:59	12:49
247	4	Fri	Last Quarter	6:09	6:50	11:59	1:57
248	5	Sat		6:10	6:49		2:59
249	6	Sun		6:11	6:47	1:05	3:54
250	7	Mon		6:11	6:46	2:15	4:41
251	8	Tues		6:12	6:45	3:25	5:21
252	9	Wed		6:12	6:44	4:34	5:56
253	10	Thu		6:13	6:42	5:39	6:28
254	11	Fri	New Moon	6:13	6:41	6:42	6:58
255	12	Sat		6:14	6:40	7:43	7:27
256	13	Sun		6:14	6:39	8:43	7:58
257	14	Mon		6:15	6:37	9:43	8:31
258	15	Tues		6:15	6:36	10:43	9:08
259	16	Wed		6:16	6:35	11:42	9:49
260	17	Thu		6:17	6:34	12:39	10:36
261	18	Fri	First Quarter	6:17	6:32	1:32	11:27
262	19	Sat		6:18	6:31	2:21	
263	20	Sun		6:18	6:30	3:05	12:22
264	21	Mon		6:19	6:29	3:43	1:19
265	22	Tues		6:19	6:27	4:18	2:18
266	23	Wed		6:20	6:26	4:49	3:17
267	24	Thu		6:20	6:25	5:19	4:16
268	25	Fri		6:21	6:24	5:48	5:15
269	26	Sat	Full Moon	6:22	6:22	5:18	6:15
270	27	Sun		6:22	6:21	6:50	7:18
271	28	Mon		6:23	6:20	7:26	8:23
272	29	Tues		6:23	6:19	8:07	9:31
273	30	Wed		6:24	6:17	8:56	10:40

Source: United States Naval Observatory.

2026 ASTRONOMICAL CALENDAR

Source: United States Naval Observatory.

10th Month — October 2026 — 31 Days

Day of Year	Day of Month	Day of Week	Primary Phases of Moon	Sunrise	Sunset	Moonrise	Moonset
274	1	Thu		6:24	6:16	9:53	11:49
275	2	Fri		6:25	6:15	10:57	12:53
276	3	Sat	Last Quarter	6:26	6:14		1:50
277	4	Sun		6:26	6:12	12:06	2:39
278	5	Mon		6:27	6:11	1:15	3:20
279	6	Tues		6:27	6:10	2:22	3:56
280	7	Wed		6:28	6:09	3:26	4:28
281	8	Thu		6:29	6:08	4:28	4:58
282	9	Fri		6:29	6:07	5:29	5:27
283	10	Sat	New Moon	6:30	6:05	6:29	5:57
284	11	Sun		6:31	6:04	7:29	6:29
285	12	Mon		6:31	6:03	8:29	7:05
286	13	Tues		6:32	6:02	9:29	7:44
287	14	Wed		6:32	6:01	10:27	8:29
288	15	Thu		6:33	6:00	11:22	9:18
289	16	Fri		6:34	5:59	12:13	10:12
290	17	Sat		6:34	5:58	12:59	11:08
291	18	Sun	First Quarter	6:35	5:57	1:39	
292	19	Mon		6:36	5:55	2:15	12:05
293	20	Tues		6:37	5:54	2:47	1:03
294	21	Wed		6:37	5:53	3:17	2:01
295	22	Thu		6:38	5:52	3:46	2:59
296	23	Fri		6:39	5:51	4:15	3:59
297	24	Sat		6:39	5:50	4:47	5:00
298	25	Sun		6:40	5:50	5:21	6:05
299	26	Mon	First Moon	6:41	5:49	6:01	7:13
300	27	Tues		6:42	5:48	6:49	8:24
301	28	Wed		6:42	5:47	7:45	9:36
302	29	Thu		6:43	5:46	8:49	10:44
303	30	Fri		6:44	5:45	9:57	11:45
304	31	Sat		6:45	5:44	11:07	12:37

11th Month — November 2026 — 30 Days

Day of Year	Day of Month	Day of Week	Primary Phases of Moon	Sunrise	Sunset	Moonrise	Moonset
305	1	Sun	Last Quarter	6:45	5:43		1:20
306	2	Mon		6:46	5:43	12:15	1:57
307	3	Tues		6:47	5:42	1:20	2:30
308	4	Wed		6:48	5:41	2:21	3:00
309	5	Thu		6:48	5:40	3:21	3:29
310	6	Fri		6:49	5:40	4:20	3:58
311	7	Sat		6:50	5:39	5:19	4:29
312	8	Sun		6:51	5:38	6:18	5:03
313	9	Mon	New Moon	6:52	5:38	7:18	5:41
314	10	Tues		6:52	5:37	8:16	6:24
315	11	Wed		6:53	5:36	9:13	7:11
316	12	Thu		6:54	5:36	10:06	8:04
317	13	Fri		6:55	5:35	10:53	8:59
318	14	Sat		6:56	5:35	11:35	9:55
319	15	Sun		6:57	5:34	12:12	10:52
320	16	Mon		6:57	5:34	12:45	11:49
321	17	Tues	First Quarter	6:58	5:33	1:15	
322	18	Wed		6:59	5:33	1:44	12:46
323	19	Thu		7:00	5:33	2:12	1:43
324	20	Fri		7:01	5:32	2:42	2:42
325	21	Sat		7:02	5:32	3:14	3:43
326	22	Sun		7:02	5:32	3:52	4:49
327	23	Mon		7:03	5:31	4:36	5:59
328	24	Tues	Full Moon	7:04	5:31	5:29	7:12
329	25	Wed		7:05	5:31	6:32	8:24
330	26	Thu		7:06	5:31	7:41	9:31
331	27	Fri		7:07	5:30	8:54	10:29
332	28	Sat		7:07	5:30	10:05	11:17
333	29	Sun		7:08	5:30	11:12	11:57
334	30	Mon		7:09	5:30		12:32

12th Month — December 2026 — 31 Days

Day of Year	Day of Month	Day of Week	Primary Phases of Moon	Sunrise	Sunset	Moonrise	Moonset
335	1	Tues	Last Quarter	7:10	5:30	12:16	1:03
336	2	Wed		7:11	5:30	1:16	1:32
337	3	Thu		7:11	5:30	2:15	2:01
338	4	Fri		7:12	5:30	3:13	2:31
339	5	Sat		7:13	5:30	4:11	3:03
340	6	Sun		7:14	5:30	5:10	3:40
341	7	Mon		7:14	5:30	6:09	4:21
342	8	Tues		7:15	5:31	7:06	5:07
343	9	Wed	New Moon	7:16	5:31	8:00	5:58
344	10	Thu		6:17	5:31	8:49	6:52
345	11	Fri		6:17	5:31	9:33	7:48
346	12	Sat		6:18	5:31	10:11	8:45
347	13	Sun		6:19	5:32	10:45	9:41
348	14	Mon		6:19	5:32	11:16	10:37
349	15	Tues		6:20	5:32	11:44	11:32
350	16	Wed		6:21	5:33	12:12	
351	17	Thu	First Quarter	6:21	5:33	12:40	12:29
352	18	Fri		6:22	5:34	1:09	1:27
353	19	Sat		6:22	5:34	1:43	2:28
354	20	Sun		6:23	5:34	2:23	3:34
355	21	Mon		6:23	5:35	3:10	4:44
356	22	Tues		6:24	5:35	4:08	5:57
357	23	Wed		6:24	5:36	5:15	7:07
358	24	Thu	Full Moon	6:25	5:37	6:29	8:11
359	25	Fri		6:25	5:37	7:43	9:05
360	26	Sat		6:26	5:38	8:55	9:51
361	27	Sun		6:26	5:38	10:03	10:29
362	28	Mon		6:26	5:39	11:07	11:03
363	29	Tues		6:27	5:40		11:33
364	30	Wed	Last Quarter	6:27	5:40	12:08	12:03
365	31	Thu		6:27	5:41	1:07	12:33

2027 ASTRONOMICAL CALENDAR

Times are figured for the point **97° 50' west longitude and 30° 18' north latitude**, the geographical location for Austin, Texas.

1st Month — January 2027 — 31 Days

Day of Year	Day of Month	Day of Week	Primary Phases of Moon	Sunrise	Sunset	Moon-rise	Moon-set
1	1	Fri		7:27	5:42	2:06	1:05
2	2	Sat		7:28	5:42	3:05	1:40
3	3	Sun		7:28	5:43	4:03	2:19
4	4	Mon		7:28	5:44	5:01	3:03
5	5	Tues		7:28	5:45	5:55	3:53
6	6	Wed		7:28	5:45	6:46	4:46
7	7	Thu	New Moon	7:28	5:46	7:31	5:42
8	8	Fri		7:28	5:47	8:11	6:39
9	9	Sat		7:28	5:48	8:47	7:36
10	10	Sun		7:28	5:49	9:18	8:32
11	11	Mon		7:28	5:49	9:47	9:27
12	12	Tues		7:28	5:50	10:14	10:22
13	13	Wed		7:28	5:51	10:41	11:18
14	14	Thu		7:28	5:52	11:10	
15	15	Fri	First Quarter	7:28	5:53	11:41	12:17
16	16	Sat		7:28	5:54	12:16	1:18
17	17	Sun		7:28	5:55	12:58	2:24
18	18	Mon		7:28	5:55	1:48	3:33
19	19	Tues		7:27	5:56	2:49	4:43
20	20	Wed		7:27	5:57	3:59	5:49
21	21	Thu		7:27	5:58	5:13	6:48
22	22	Fri	Full Moon	7:26	5:59	6:28	7:38
23	23	Sat		7:26	6:00	7:40	8:21
24	24	Sun		7:26	6:01	8:48	8:58
25	25	Mon		7:25	6:02	9:53	9:31
26	26	Tues		7:25	6:02	10:55	10:02
27	27	Wed		7:24	6:03	11:54	10:33
28	28	Thu		7:24	6:04		11:05
29	29	Fri	Last Quarter	7:23	6:05	12:56	11:39
30	30	Sat		7:23	6:06	1:56	12:17
31	31	Sun		7:22	6:07	2:54	1:00

2nd Month — February 2027 — 28 Days

Day of Year	Day of Month	Day of Week	Primary Phases of Moon	Sunrise	Sunset	Moon-rise	Moon-set
32	1	Mon		7:22	6:08	3:50	1:48
33	2	Tues		7:21	6:08	4:42	2:40
34	3	Wed		7:20	6:09	5:29	3:36
35	4	Thu		7:20	6:10	6:11	4:32
36	5	Fri		7:19	6:11	6:48	5:29
37	6	Sat	New Moon	7:18	6:12	7:21	6:26
38	7	Sun		7:18	6:13	7:50	7:22
39	8	Mon		7:17	6:14	8:18	8:17
40	9	Tues		7:16	6:14	8:45	9:13
41	10	Wed		7:15	6:15	9:13	10:11
42	11	Thu		7:15	6:16	9:43	11:11
43	12	Fri		7:14	6:17	10:16	
44	13	Sat		7:13	6:18	10:54	12:14
45	14	Sun	First Quarter	7:12	6:18	11:40	1:20
46	15	Mon		7:11	6:19	12:34	2:27
47	16	Tues		7:10	6:20	1:37	3:32
48	17	Wed		7:09	6:21	2:48	4:32
49	18	Thu		7:08	6:22	4:01	5:25
50	19	Fri		7:07	6:22	5:13	6:11
51	20	Sat	Full Moon	7:06	6:23	6:24	6:50
52	21	Sun		7:05	6:24	7:31	7:25
53	22	Mon		7:04	6:25	8:36	7:57
54	23	Tues		7:03	6:25	9:39	8:29
55	24	Wed		7:02	6:26	10:41	9:01
56	25	Thu		7:01	6:27	11:43	9:36
57	26	Fri		7:00	6:28		10:13
58	27	Sat		6:59	6:28	12:44	10:55
59	28	Sun	Last Quarter	6:58	6:29	1:42	11:42

3rd Month — March 2027 — 31 Days

Day of Year	Day of Month	Day of Week	Primary Phases of Moon	Sunrise	Sunset	Moon-rise	Moon-set
60	1	Mon		6:57	6:30	2:36	12:33
61	2	Tues		6:56	6:30	3:25	1:27
62	3	Wed		6:55	6:31	4:09	2:24
63	4	Thu		6:54	6:32	4:47	3:21
64	5	Fri		6:53	6:33	5:21	4:18
65	6	Sat		6:52	6:33	5:52	5:14
66	7	Sun		6:50	6:34	6:21	6:10
67	8	Mon	New Moon	6:49	6:35	6:49	7:07
68	9	Tues		6:48	6:35	7:17	8:05
69	10	Wed		6:47	6:36	7:46	9:04
70	11	Thu		6:46	6:37	8:18	10:07
71	12	Fri		6:45	6:37	8:55	11:12
72	13	Sat		6:43	6:38	9:38	
73	14	Sun		6:42	6:39	10:29	12:18
74	15	Mon	First Quarter	6:41	6:39	11:28	1:23
75	16	Tues		6:40	6:40	12:34	2:24
76	17	Wed		6:39	6:40	1:44	3:18
77	18	Thu		6:37	6:41	2:54	4:04
78	19	Fri		6:36	6:42	4:03	4:45
79	20	Sat		6:35	6:42	5:10	5:20
80	21	Sun		6:34	6:43	6:15	5:53
81	22	Mon	Full Moon	6:32	6:44	7:19	6:23
82	23	Tues		6:31	6:44	8:23	6:57
83	24	Wed		6:30	6:45	9:26	7:31
84	25	Thu		6:29	6:45	10:28	8:08
85	26	Fri		6:28	6:46	11:29	8:49
86	27	Sat		6:26	6:47		9:34
87	28	Sun		6:25	6:47	12:26	10:24
88	29	Mon		6:24	6:48	1:17	11:18
89	30	Tues	Last Quarter	6:23	6:48	2:04	12:14
90	31	Wed		6:21	6:49	2:44	1:11

Source: United States Naval Observatory.

2027 ASTRONOMICAL CALENDAR

Source: United States Naval Observatory.

4th Month — April 2027 — 30 Days

Day of Year	Day of Month	Day of Week	Primary Phases of Moon	Sunrise	Sunset	Moonrise	Moonset
91	1	Thu		6:20	6:50	3:20	2:07
92	2	Fri		6:19	6:50	3:52	3:03
93	3	Sat		6:18	6:51	4:21	4:00
94	4	Sun		6:17	6:52	4:49	4:56
95	5	Mon		6:15	6:52	5:17	5:54
96	6	Tues		6:14	6:53	5:47	6:54
97	7	Wed	New Moon	6:13	6:53	6:18	7:56
98	8	Thu		6:12	6:54	6:54	9:02
99	9	Fri		6:11	6:55	7:36	10:10
100	10	Sat		6:10	6:55	8:25	11:16
101	11	Sun		6:08	6:56	9:23	
102	12	Mon		6:07	6:57	10:27	12:19
103	13	Tues	First Quarter	6:06	6:57	11:35	1:14
104	14	Wed		6:05	6:58	12:44	2:02
105	15	Thu		6:04	6:58	1:52	2:43
106	16	Fri		6:03	6:59	2:57	3:20
107	17	Sat		6:02	7:00	4:01	3:53
108	18	Sun		6:01	7:00	5:04	4:24
109	19	Mon		6:00	7:01	6:06	4:55
110	20	Tues	Full Moon	5:59	7:02	7:09	5:28
111	21	Wed		5:57	7:02	8:12	6:03
112	22	Thu		5:56	7:03	9:14	6:42
113	23	Fri		5:55	7:03	10:13	7:26
114	24	Sat		5:54	7:04	11:08	8:15
115	25	Sun		5:53	7:05	11:56	9:08
116	26	Mon		5:52	7:05		10:03
117	27	Tues		5:51	7:06	12:39	11:0?
118	28	Wed	Last Quarter	5:51	7:07	1:17	11:57
119	29	Thu		5:50	7:07	1:50	12:52
120	30	Fri		5:49	7:08	2:20	1:43

5th Month — May 2027 — 31 Days

Day of Year	Day of Month	Day of Week	Primary Phases of Moon	Sunrise	Sunset	Moonrise	Moonset
121	1	Sat		5:48	7:09	2:49	2:43
122	2	Sun		5:47	7:09	3:17	3:40
123	3	Mon		5:46	7:10	3:45	4:39
124	4	Tues		5:45	7:11	4:16	5:40
125	5	Wed		5:44	7:11	4:50	6:46
126	6	Thu	New Moon	5:44	7:12	5:30	7:54
127	7	Fri		5:43	7:13	6:18	9:03
128	8	Sat		5:42	7:13	7:14	10:09
129	9	Sun		5:41	7L14	8:17	11:08
130	10	Mon		5:40	7:15	9:26	
131	11	Tues		5:40	7:15	10:36	12:00
132	12	Wed		5:39	7:16	11:45	12:43
133	13	Thu	First Quarter	5:38	7:17	12:51	1:21
134	14	Fri		5:38	7:17	1:54	1:54
135	15	Sat		5:37	7:18	2:56	2:26
136	16	Sun		5:36	7:18	3:57	2:56
137	17	Mon		5:36	7:19	4:58	3:28
138	18	Tues		5:35	7:20	6:00	4:02
139	19	Wed		5:35	7:20	7:02	4:39
140	20	Thu	Full Moon	5:34	7:21	8:02	5:21
141	21	Fri		5:34	7:22	8:58	6:07
142	22	Sat		5:33	7:22	9:49	6:59
143	23	Sun		5:33	7:23	10:35	7:54
144	24	Mon		5:32	7:23	11:14	8:50
145	25	Tues		5:32	7:24	11:49	9:47
146	26	Wed		5:32	7:25		10:43
147	27	Thu		5:31	7:25	12:20	11:38
148	28	Fri	Last Quarter	5:31	7:26	12:48	12:32
149	29	Sat		5:31	7:26	1:16	1:27
150	30	Sun		5:30	7:27	1:43	2:24
151	31	Mon		5:30	7:28	2:13	3:23

6th Month — June 2027 — 30 Days

Day of Year	Day of Month	Day of Week	Primary Phases of Moon	Sunrise	Sunset	Moonrise	Moonset
152	1	Tues		5:30	7:28	2:45	4:26
153	2	Wed		5:30	7:29	3:22	5:33
154	3	Thu		5:29	7:29	4:06	6:43
155	4	Fri	New Moon	5:29	7:30	4:59	7:51
156	5	Sat		5:29	7:30	6:01	8:56
157	6	Sun		5:29	7:31	7:10	9:52
158	7	Mon		5:29	7:31	8:22	10:40
159	8	Tues		5:29	7:31	9:34	11:20
160	9	Wed		5:29	7:32	10:42	11:56
161	10	Thu		5:29	7:32	11:48	
162	11	Fri	First Quarter	5:29	7:33	12:50	12:28
163	12	Sat		5:29	7:33	1:51	12:59
164	13	Sun		5:29	7:34	2:52	1:30
165	14	Mon		5:29	7:34	3:53	2:03
166	15	Tues		5:29	7:34	4:54	2:38
167	16	Wed		5:29	7:35	5:54	3:18
168	17	Thu		5:29	7:35	6:51	4:03
169	18	Fri		5:29	7:35	7:44	4:53
170	19	Sat	Full Moon	5:29	7:35	8:31	5:46
171	20	Sun		5:30	7:36	9:12	6:42
172	21	Mon		5:30	7:36	9:48	7:39
173	22	Tues		5:30	7:36	10:20	8:35
174	23	Wed		5:30	7:36	10:50	9:30
175	24	Thu		5:30	7:36	11:17	10:24
176	25	Fri		5:31	7:37	11:44	11:18
177	26	Sat		5:31	7:37		12:13
178	27	Sun	Last Quarter	5:31	7:37	12:12	1:10
179	28	Mon		5:32	7:37	12:41	2:09
180	29	Tues		5:32	7:37	1:15	3:13
181	30	Wed		5:32	7:37	1:55	4:20

2027 ASTRONOMICAL CALENDAR

Times are figured for the point **97° 50' west longitude and 30° 18' north latitude**, the geographical location for Austin, Texas.

7th Month — July 2027 — 31 Days

Day of Year	Day of Month	Day of Week	Primary Phases of Moon	Sunrise	Sunset	Moonrise	Moonset
182	1	Thu		5:33	7:37	2:43	5:29
183	2	Fri		5:33	7:37	3:40	6:36
184	3	Sat		5:34	7:37	4:46	7:37
185	4	Sun	New Moon	5:34	7:37	5:59	8:30
186	5	Mon		5:34	7:37	7:13	9:15
187	6	Tues		5:35	7:36	8:26	9:53
188	7	Wed		5:35	7:36	9:35	10:28
189	8	Thu		5:36	7:36	10:40	11:00
190	9	Fri		5:36	7:36	11:44	11:32
191	10	Sat	First Quarter	5:37	7:36	12:46	
192	11	Sun		5:37	7:35	1:47	12:04
193	12	Mon		5:38	7:35	2:48	12:39
194	13	Tues		5:38	7:35	3:48	1:18
195	14	Wed		5:39	7:35	4:46	2:01
196	15	Thu		5:39	7:34	5:40	2:48
197	16	Fri		5:40	7:34	6:29	3:41
198	17	Sat		5:41	7:33	7:12	4:36
199	18	Sun	Full Moon	5:41	7:33	7:49	5:33
200	19	Mon		5:42	7:33	8:22	6:29
201	20	Tues		5:42	7:32	8:52	7:25
202	21	Wed		5:43	7:32	9:20	8:19
203	22	Thu		5:43	7:31	9:47	9:13
204	23	Fri		5:44	7:31	10:14	10:07
205	24	Sat		5:45	7:30	10:42	11:02
206	25	Sun		5:45	7:29	11:13	11:59
207	26	Mon	Last Quarter	5:46	7:29	11:49	12:59
208	27	Tues		5:46	7:28		2:03
209	28	Wed		5:47	7:28	12:32	3:09
210	29	Thu		5:48	7:27	1:23	4:15
211	30	Fri		5:48	7:26	2:23	5:18
212	31	Sat		5:49	7:25	3:32	6:15

8th Month — August 2027 — 31 Days

Day of Year	Day of Month	Day of Week	Primary Phases of Moon	Sunrise	Sunset	Moonrise	Moonset
213	1	Sun		5:49	7:25	4:46	7:04
214	2	Mon	New Moon	5:50	7:24	6:00	7:46
215	3	Tues		5:51	7:23	7:13	8:23
216	4	Wed		5:51	7:22	8:22	8:58
217	5	Thu		5:52	7:22	9:28	9:30
218	6	Fri		5:53	7:21	10:33	10:04
219	7	Sat		5:53	7:20	11:37	10:38
220	8	Sun		5:54	7:19	12:40	11:16
221	9	Mon	First Quarter	5:54	7:18	1:41	11:58
222	10	Tues		5:55	7:17	2:40	
223	11	Wed		5:56	7:16	3:36	12:45
224	12	Thu		5:56	7:15	4:26	1:36
225	13	Fri		5:57	7:14	5:11	2:30
226	14	Sat		5:57	7:13	5:50	3:27
227	15	Sun		5:58	7:12	6:25	4:23
228	16	Mon		5:59	7:11	6:56	5:19
229	17	Tues	Full Moon	5:59	7:10	7:24	6:14
230	18	Wed		6:00	7:09	7:51	7:08
231	19	Thu		6:00	7:08	8:18	8:02
232	20	Fri		6:01	7:07	8:46	8:57
233	21	Sat		6:01	7:06	9:16	9:53
234	22	Sun		6:02	7:05	9:49	10:51
235	23	Mon		6:03	7:04	10:28	11:53
236	24	Tues		6:03	7:03	11:14	12:56
237	25	Wed		6:04	7:02		2:01
238	26	Thu	Last Quarter	6:04	7:01	12:09	3:03
239	27	Fri		6:05	7:00	1:12	4:01
240	28	Sat		6:05	6:58	2:22	4:52
241	29	Sun		6:06	6:57	3:35	5:37
242	30	Mon		6:07	6:56	4:47	6:16
243	31	Tues		6:07	6:55	5:58	6:52

9th Month — September 2027 — 30 Days

Day of Year	Day of Month	Day of Week	Primary Phases of Moon	Sunrise	Sunset	Moonrise	Moonset
244	1	Wed		6:08	6:54	7:06	7:26
245	2	Thu		6:08	6:52	8:13	8:00
246	3	Fri		6:09	6:51	9:19	8:35
247	4	Sat		6:09	6:50	10:25	9:12
248	5	Sun		6:10	6:49	11:29	9:54
249	6	Mon		6:10	6:48	12:30	10:40
250	7	Tues	First Quarter	6:11	6:46	1:28	11:30
251	8	Wed		6:12	6:45	2:21	
252	9	Thu		6:12	6:44	3:08	12:24
253	10	Fri		6:13	6:43	3:49	1:20
254	11	Sat		6:13	6:41	4:25	2:16
255	12	Sun		6:14	6:40	4:58	3:12
256	13	Mon		6:14	6:39	5:27	4:08
257	14	Tues		6:15	6:38	5:55	5:02
258	15	Wed	Full Moon	6:15	6:36	6:22	5:57
259	16	Thu		6:16	6:35	6:49	6:51
260	17	Fri		6:16	6:34	7:19	7:48
261	18	Sat		6:17	6:33	7:52	8:46
262	19	Sun		6:18	6:31	8:29	9:46
263	20	Mon		6:18	6:30	9:12	10:49
264	21	Tues		6:19	6:29	10:04	11:53
265	22	Wed		6:19	6:28	11:02	12:55
266	23	Thu	Last Quarter	6:20	6:26		1:53
267	24	Fri		6:20	6:25	12:08	2:45
268	25	Sat		6:21	6:24	1:17	3:30
269	26	Sun		6:21	6:23	2:27	4:10
270	27	Mon		6:22	6:21	3:36	4:47
271	28	Tues		6:23	6:20	4:44	5:21
272	29	Wed		6:23	6:19	5:51	5:54
273	30	Thu	New Moon	6:24	6:18	6:58	6:29

Source: United States Naval Observatory.

2027 ASTRONOMICAL CALENDAR

Source: United States Naval Observatory.

10th Month — October 2027 — 31 Days

Day of Year	Day of Month	Day of Week	Primary Phases of Moon	Sunrise	Sunset	Moonrise	Moonset
274	1	Fri		6:24	6:16	8:04	7:06
275	2	Sat		6:25	6:15	9:10	7:47
276	3	Sun		6:25	6:14	10:15	8:32
277	4	Mon		6:26	6:13	11:16	9:21
278	5	Tues		6:27	6:12	12:12	10:15
279	6	Wed		6:27	6:10	1:02	11:11
280	7	Thu	First Quarter	6:28	6:09	1:46	
281	8	Fri		6:29	6:08	2:24	12:07
282	9	Sat		6:29	6:07	2:57	1:04
283	10	Sun		6:30	6:06	3:28	1:59
284	11	Mon		6:30	6:04	3:56	2:54
285	12	Tues		6:31	6:03	4:23	3:48
286	13	Wed		6:32	6:02	4:51	4:43
287	14	Thu		6:32	6:01	5:20	5:39
288	15	Fri	Full Moon	6:33	6:00	5:52	6:37
289	16	Sat		6:34	5:59	6:29	7:38
290	17	Sun		6:34	5:58	7:11	8:41
291	18	Mon		6:35	5:57	8:01	9:45
292	19	Tues		6:36	5:56	8:58	10:49
293	20	Wed		6:36	5:55	10:01	11:48
294	21	Thu		6:37	5:54	11:08	12:41
295	22	Fri	Last Quarter	6:38	5:53		1:28
296	23	Sat		6:38	5:52	12:16	2:08
297	24	Sun		6:39	5:51	1:24	2:45
298	25	Mon		6:40	5:50	2:30	3:19
299	26	Tues		6:41	5:49	3:35	3:51
300	27	Wed		6:41	5:48	4:40	4:25
301	28	Thu		6:42	5:47	5:45	5:00
302	29	Fri	New Moon	6:43	5:46	6:51	5:39
303	30	Sat		6:44	5:45	7:56	6:22
304	31	Sun		6:44	5:44	8:59	7:11

11th Month — November 2027 — 30 Days

Day of Year	Day of Month	Day of Week	Primary Phases of Moon	Sunrise	Sunset	Moonrise	Moonset
305	1	Mon		6:45	5:44	9:59	8:03
306	2	Tues		6:46	5:43	10:52	8:59
307	3	Wed		6:47	5:42	11:39	9:57
308	4	Thu		6:47	5:41	12:20	10:54
309	5	Fri		6:48	5:40	12:55	11:49
310	6	Sat	First Quarter	6:49	5:40	1:27	
311	7	Sun		6:50	5:39	1:56	12:44
312	8	Mon		6:51	5:38	2:23	1:38
313	9	Tues		6:51	5:38	2:51	2:32
314	10	Wed		6:52	5:37	3:19	3:27
315	11	Thu		6:53	5:36	3:50	4:24
316	12	Fri		6:54	5:36	4:25	5:24
317	13	Sat		6:55	5:35	5:06	6:27
318	14	Sun	Full Moon	6:56	5:35	5:54	7:32
319	15	Mon		6:56	5:34	6:50	8:38
320	16	Tues		6:57	5:34	7:53	9:40
321	17	Wed		6:58	5:33	9:00	10:37
322	18	Thu		6:59	5:33	10:09	11:26
323	19	Fri		7:00	5:33	11:17	12:08
324	20	Sat		7:01	5:32		12:46
325	21	Sun	Last Quarter	7:01	5:32	12:23	1:20
326	22	Mon		7:02	5:32	1:27	1:52
327	23	Tues		7:03	5:31	2:30	2:24
328	24	Wed		7:04	5:31	3:33	2:58
329	25	Thu		7:05	5:31	4:37	3:35
330	26	Fri		7:06	5:31	5:41	4:15
331	27	Sat		7:06	5:30	6:44	5:01
332	28	Sun	New Moon	7:07	5:30	7:45	5:52
333	29	Mon		7:08	5:30	8:42	6:47
334	30	Tues		7:09	5:30	9:32	7:45

12th Month — December 2027 — 31 Days

Day of Year	Day of Month	Day of Week	Primary Phases of Moon	Sunrise	Sunset	Moonrise	Moonset
335	1	Wed		7:10	5:30	10:15	8:42
336	2	Thu		7:10	5:30	10:53	9:39
337	3	Fri		7:11	5:30	11:26	10:34
338	4	Sat		7:12	5:30	11:55	11:28
339	5	Sun		7:13	5:30	12:23	
340	6	Mon	First Quarter	7:14	5:30	12:50	12:21
341	7	Tues		7:14	5:30	1:18	1:15
342	8	Wed		7:15	5:30	1:47	2:10
343	9	Thu		7:16	5:31	2:19	3:08
344	10	Fri		7:16	5:31	2:57	4:08
345	11	Sat		7:17	5:31	3:42	5:13
346	12	Sun		7:18	5:31	4:35	6:19
347	13	Mon	Full Moon	7:18	5:32	5:36	7:24
348	14	Tues		7:19	5:32	6:44	8:25
349	15	Wed		7:20	5:32	7:55	9:19
350	16	Thu		7:20	5:33	9:06	10:05
351	17	Fri		7:21	5:33	10:14	10:46
352	18	Sat		7:22	5:33	11:20	11:21
353	19	Sun		7:22	5:34		11:54
354	20	Mon	Last Quarter	7:23	5:34	12:24	12:27
355	21	Tues		7:23	5:35	1:27	1:00
356	22	Wed		7:24	5:35	2:30	1:35
357	23	Thu		7:24	5:36	3:32	2:13
358	24	Fri		7:25	5:36	4:35	2:57
359	25	Sat		7:25	5:37	5:36	3:45
360	26	Sun		7:25	5:38	6:33	4:38
361	27	Mon	New Moon	7:26	5:38	7:25	5:35
362	28	Tues		7:26	5:39	8:11	6:32
363	29	Wed		7:27	5:39	8:50	7:29
364	30	Thu		7:27	5:40	9:25	8:25
365	31	Fri		7:27	5:41	9:56	10:20

Texas

APPENDIX

UNSPLASH/WLODZIMIERZ-JAWORSKI

SOURCES

"THE SPACE AGE IN TEXAS" SOURCES

The following list includes the sources used in Anthony Head's feature story on Pages 12-22.

ABC News.
ABI Research.
Academia.
AI LABS.
Air Force Technology.
Anderson (Indiana) Herald, 17 Jan. 2003.
Associated Press News.
Astronomers Without Borders.
Astronomy.
AST SpaceMobile.
Aviation Art Hangar.
Baseball Reference.
Baylor College of Medicine.
BBC News.
Biography.
Blue Origin.
Brazilian Space Agency.
Brownsville-Herald, 4 Apr. 1962, p. 10.
Built In.
Buzz Aldrin.
Cedar Park EDC.
Center for Space Research—The University of Texas at Austin.
China Academy.
China National Space Administration.
City of Bastrop.
City of Brownsville.
City of El Lago.
City of El Paso.
City of Hereford.
City of Midland.
City of San Marcos.
City of Seabrook.
City of Webster.
City of Van Horn.
CNN.
collectSPACE.
Congress.
Counterpoints, vol. 192, 2001, pp. 267–79.
Digital History.
Discover Magazine.
EBSCO Information Services, Inc.
Encyclopædia Britannica.
European Space Agency.
Federal Aviation Administration.
Firefly Aerospace.
GOV.UK.
Greater Big Bend International Dark Sky Reserve.
High Point Scientific.
History.com.
Hobby-Eberly Telescope | McDonald Observatory.
Houston Chronicle.
Houston Cougar, 11 Jan. 1962, p. 11.
Houston Cougar, 18 Sept. 1962, p. 4.
Houstonia Magazine.
IN.gov.
Indian Space Research Organisation.
International Astronautical Federation.
International Institute of Space Law.
Intuitive Machines.
ISS National Laboratory.
Japan Aerospace Exploration Agency.
JFK Library, 1961.
Johnson, Lyndon B. "The Vantage Point: Perspectives of the Presidency 1963-1969."
Johnson Space Center Facilities Map.
Lawrence (Kansas) Daily Journal World, 2 Oct. 1973, p. 2.
LBJ Library.
LeoLabs.
LiveScience.
Lunar and Planetary Institute.
McDonald Observatory.
McGregor Chamber of Commerce.
Morgan Lewis.
NASA.
National Air and Space Museum.
National Geographic.
National Oceanic and Atmospheric Administration.
National Parks Service, U.S. Department of the Interior.
NBA.
New Space Economy.
Northrop Grumman.
NPR.
NRG Park.
Office of Space Commerce.
Office of the Director of National Intelligence.
Office of the President | Rice University.
Orbital Today.
PeriscopeFilm, via YouTube (2025).
Polytechnique Insights.
Popular Mechanics.
Portree, David S. F., and Robert C. Treviño. "Walking to Olympus: An EVA Chronology."
PR Newswire.
Retro Space HD, via YouTube (2020).
Rice History Corner.
Rice Space Institute.
Rice University.
Richard Nixon Museum and Library.
Russia Beyond.
San Antonio Light, 15 June 1965.
Skylab's Untimely Fate.
Southern Methodist University.
Space.
Space Center Houston.
Space Daily.
Space Exploration Technologies.
Spaceflight Histories.

COURTESY OF CLARK CRENSHAW

Space Foundation.
Spaceline.
SpaceNews.
SpaceX.
Starlink.
STM Journals.
TechCrunch.
TelecomWorld101.
Texas A&M Foundation—Spirit Magazine.
Texas A&M University Space Institute.
Texas Aerospace Research and Space Economy Consortium.
Texas Almanac.
Texas Archive of the Moving Image.
Texas Beyond History.
Texas Monthly.
Texas Standard.
Texas State Historical Association.
The American Presidency Project.
The Atlantic.
The Boeing Company Official Website.
The Dallas Morning News.
The Independent.
The Library of Congress.
The New York Times Archive.
The Outer Space Treaty, 1966.
The Planetary Society.
The Portal to Texas History.
TheSkyLive.
The Space Review: LBJ's Space Race: What We Didn't Know Then (Part 2).
The Texas Space Commission.
The Texas Tribune.
The University of Texas.
U.S. Department of State.
U.S. Fish & Wildlife Service.
U.S. Senate.
United Nations Office for Outer Space Affairs.
United States Space Force.
University of Houston.
University of Houston—Sasakawa International Center for Space Architecture (SICSA).
University of Texas at Rio Grande Valley.
UPI.
UTEP.
Walla Walla Union-Bulletin. 1956, p. 17.
White House History.
William B. Hanson Center for Space Sciences.
Yahoo! Finance.

"OUT OF THIS WORLD TEXANS" SOURCES

The following list includes the sources used in Anthony Head's feature story on Pages 56-57.

AARP.
Apollo 13, Universal City Studios, Inc, 1995.
Astrodome Conservancy.
Austin Monthly Magazine.
Brinkley, Douglas. "American Moonshot: John F. Kennedy and the Great Space Race." HarperPerennial, 2019.
Carney, Emily, and Bruce McCandless. "Star Bound: A Beginner's Guide to the American Space Program, from Goddard's Rockets to Goldilocks Planets and Everything in Between." University of Nebraska Press, 2021.
Carter, Aline B. "Doubt Not the Dream." Naylor Co, 1968.
collectSPACE.
Dallas Observer.
Detour Film Production.
Discogs.
ESPN.
Fort Worth Star Telegram, 14 July 1975, p. 25.
Garrett T. Capps Rox.
Harrigan, Stephen. "Challenger Park." Ballantine Books, 2006.
Hernández, José M., and Emilio Estefan. "Reaching for the Stars: The Inspiring Story of a Migrant Farmworker Turned Astronaut." Center Street, 2012.
Houston Chronicle.
Janus Films.
Jemison, Mae. "Find Where the Wind Goes: Moments from My Life." Signal Hill Road Publishing, LLC, 2001.
Linklater, Richard, director. "Apollo 10½: A Space Age Childhood."
Los Conquistadores. "Corridos Y Tragedias Del Siglo 20." D.L.B. Records / Discos Norteño, c. 1965.
Maverick Carter House.
McDonald Observatory.
Mexico Historico.
Moving Sidewalks.
MTV.
NASA.
Public Broadcasting Service (PBS).
Ross-Nazzal, Jennifer M. "Making Space for Women: Stories from Trailblazing Women of NASA's Johnson Space Center." Texas A&M University Press, 2022.
Stephen Harrigan.
Steve Miller Band.
Steve Miller Band. "Space Cowboy." Brave New World, Capitol Records, 1969.
Steve Miller Band. "The Joker." The Joker, Capitol Records, 1973.
SWA Group.
Texas A&M University.
Texas A&M University Galveston Campus.
Texas Commission on the Arts.
Texas Monthly.
Texas Standard.
Texas State Historical Association.
Whitley Strieber's Unknown Country.
ZZ Top, Billy F. Gibbons, "Flyin' High." La Futura, Def Jam Recordings/ Universal Music Group, 2012., "Afterburner." Warner Bros. Records, 1985.

ARTS & CULTURE PHOTO GALLERY CREDITS

The following list includes the photography credits for Pages 38-41.

Microphone: *Unsplash/Israel Palacio*
Ruthie Foster: *Jody Domingue/ courtesy of The Press House*
Cody Johnson Leather album: *courtesy of codyjohnsonmusic.com*
Willie Nelson: *courtesy of Jax Music*
Kacey Musgraves Golden Hour album: *courtesy of kaceymusgraves.com*
Beyoncé: *courtesy of Parkwood Entertainment*
Post Malone: *dpa picture alliance/ Alamy*
Norah Jones: *courtesy of Chuffmedia*
Mixer: *Unsplash/Alexey Ruban*
Landman: *Album/Alamy*
Jennifer Garner: *Moviestore Collection Ltd/Alamy*
Woody Harrelson: *TT News Agency/Alamy*
Sadie Sink: *Album/Alamy*
Pedro Pascal: *FlixPix/Alamy*
Kevin Costner: *Pictorial Press Ltd/ Alamy*
Glen Powell: *FlixPix/Alamy*
Wes Anderson: *Everett Collection Inc/Alamy*

SPORTS PHOTO GALLERY CREDITS

The following list includes the photography credits for Pages 560-563.

Victor Wembanyama: *Sipa USA/ Alamy*
Scottie Scheffler: *PA Images/ Alamy*
Sha'Carri Richardson: *UPI/Alamy*
Jose Altuve: *Image of sport/Alamy*
Marcel Reed: *ZUMA Press, Inc./Alamy*
Kevin Durant: *Abaca Press/Alamy*
Texas Longhorns: *Cal Sport Media/Alamy*
Paige Bueckers: *SPP Sport Press Photo/Alamy*
Tara Davis-Woodhall: *Speed Media/Alamy*
Jamie Benn: *ZUMA Press, Inc./ Alamy*
Simone Biles: *PCN Photography/ Alamy*

PRONUNCIATION GUIDE

Texas' rich cultural diversity is reflected nowhere better than in the names of places. Standard pronunciation is used in many cases, but purely colloquial pronunciation often is used, too.

In the late 1940s, George Mitchel Stokes — a graduate student at Baylor University — developed a list of pronunciations of 2,300 place names across the state. Stokes earned his doctorate and eventually was the director of the speech division in the communications studies department at Baylor. He retired in 1983.

In the following list based on Stokes' longer list, pronunciation is by respelling and diacritical marking. Respelling is employed as follows: "ah" as in the exclamation, ah, or the "o" in tot; "ee" as in meet; "oo" as in moot; "yoo" as in use; "ow" as in cow; "oo" as in brood; "oi" as in oil; "uh" as in mud.

Note that ah, uh and the apostrophe(') are used for varying degrees of neutral vowel sounds, the apostrophe being used where the vowel is barely sounded. Diacritical markings are used as follows: bāle, bǎd, lět, rīse, rǐll, ōak, fŏŏt.

The stressed syllable is capitalized. Secondary stress is indicated by an underline as in Atascosa — ăt uhs KŌ suh.

A

Abbott — Ă buht
Abernathy — Ă ber nă thĭ
Abilene — ĂB uh leen
Acala — uh KĀ luh
Ackerly — ĂK er lĭ
Acme — ĂK mĭ
Acton — ĂK t'n
Acuff — Ā kuhf
Adamsville — Ă d'mz vĭl
Addicks — Ă dĭks
Addielou — ă dĭ LOO
Addison — A di s'n
Adkins — ĂT kĭnz
Adrian — Ā drĭ uhn
Afton — ĂF t'n
Agua Dulce — ah wuh DOOL sĭ
Agua Nueva — ah wuh noo Ā vuh
Aiken — Ā kĭn
Alamo — ĂL uh moh
Alamo Heights — ăl uh moh HĪTS
Alanreed — ĂL uhn reed
Alba — ĂL buh
Albany — AWL buh nĭ
Aledo — uh LEE doh
Alexander — ĕl ĭg ZĂN der
Alfred — ĂL frĕd
Algoa — ăl GŌ uh
Alice — Ă lĭs
Alief — Ā leef
Allen — Ă lĭn
Allenfarm — ălĭn FAHRM
Alleyton — Ă lĭ t'n
Allison — ĂL uh s'n
Alma — AHL muh
Alpine — ĂL pīn
Altair — awl TĂR
Alto — ĂL toh
Altoga — ăl TŌ guh
Alvarado — ăl vuh RĀ doh
Alvin — ĂL vĭn
Alvord — ĂL vord
Amarillo — ăm uh RĬL oh
Amherst — AM herst
Ammannsville — ĂM 'nz vĭl
Anahuac — ĂN uh wăk
Anderson — ĂN der s'n
Andice — ĂN dīs
Andrews — ĂN drooz
Angelina — ăn juh LEE nuh
Angleton — ĂNG g'l t'n
Annona — ă NŌ nuh
Anson — ĂN s'n
Anton — ĂNT n
Appleby — Ă p'l bĭ
Aquilla — uh KWĬL uh
Aransas — uh RĂN zuhs
Aransas Pass — uh răn zuhs PĂS
Arbala — ahr BĀ luh
Arcadia — ahr KĀ dĭ uh
Archer — AHR cher
Archer City — ahr cher SĬT ĭ
Arcola — ahr KŌ luh
Argo — AHR goh
Argyle — ahr GĪL
Arlington — AHR lĭng t'n
Arneckeville — AHR nĭ kĭ vĭl
Arnett — AHR nĭt
Arp — ahrp
Artesia Wells — ahr tee zh' WĔLZ
Arthur City — ahr ther SĬT ĭ
Asherton — ĂSH er t'n
Aspermont — ĂS per mahnt
Atascosa — ăt uhs KŌ suh
Athens — Ă thĕnz
Atlanta — ăt LĂN tuh
Atlas — ĂT l's
Attoyac — AT uh yăk
Aubrey — AW brĭ
Augusta — aw GUHS tuh
Austin — AWS t'n
Austonio — aws TŌ nĭ oh
Austwell — AWS wĕl
Avalon — ĂV uhl n
Avery — Ā vuh rĭ
Avinger — Ă vĭn jer
Avoca — uh VŌ kuh
Axtell — ĂKS t'l
Azle — Ā z'l

B

Bagwell — BĂG w'l
Bailey — BĀ lĭ
Baileyboro — BĀ lĭ ber ruh
Baileyville — BĀ lĭ vĭl
Baird — bărd
Bakersfield — BĀ kers feeld
Balch Springs — bawlch or bawlk SPRĬNGZ
Ballinger — BĂL ĭn jer
Balmorhea — băl muh RĀ
Bandera — băn DĔR uh
Banquete — băn KĔ tĭ
Barclay — BAHRK lĭ
Bardwell — BAHRD w'l
Barker — BAHR ker
Barksdale — BAHRKS dāl
Barnhart — BAHRN hahrt
Barnum — BAHR n'm
Barstow — BAHRS toh
Bartlett — BAHRT lĭt
Bassett — BĂ sĭt

Bastrop — BĂS trahp
Batesville — BĀTS v'l
Batson — BĂT s'n
Baxter — BĂKS ter
Bay City — ba SĬT ĭ
Baylor — BĀ ler
Bayside — BĀ sīd
Baytown — BĀ town
Beasley — BEEZ lĭ
Beaukiss — boh KĬS
Beaumont — BŌ mahnt
Beckville — BĔK v'l
Becton — BĔK t'n
Bedias — BEE dīs
Beehouse — BEE hows
Beeville — BEE vĭl
Belcherville — BĔL cher vĭl
Bellaire — bĕl ĂR
Bellevue — BĔL vyoo
Bellmead — bĕl MEED
Bellville — BĔL vĭl
Belmont — BĔL mahnt
Belton — BĔL t'n
Ben Arnold — bĕn AHR n'ld
Benavides — bĕn uh VEE d's
Ben Bolt — bĕn BŌLT
Benbrook — BĬN brook
Benchley — BĔNCH lĭ
Ben Franklin — bĕn FRĂNGk lĭn
Ben Hur — bĕn HER
Benjamin — BĔN juh m'n
Bennett — BĔN ĭt
Bentonville — BĔNT n vĭl
Ben Wheeler — bĭn HWEE ler
Berclair — ber KLĂR
Bertram — BERT r'm
Bessmay — bĕs MĀ
Bexar — BA är or băr
Beyersville — BĪRZ vĭl
Biardstown — BĂRDZ t'n
Bigfoot — BĬG foot
Big Lake — bĭg LĀK
Big Sandy — bĭg SĂN dĭ
Big Spring — bĭg SPRĬNG
Big Wells — bĭg WĔLZ
Birdville — BERD vĭl
Birome — bī RŌM
Birthright — BERTH rīt
Bishop — BĬ sh'p
Bivins — BĬ vĭnz
Blackfoot — BLĂK foot
Blackwell — BLĂK w'l
Blair — blăr
Blanchard — BLĂN cherd
Blanco — BLĂNG koh
Blanket — BLĂNG kĭt
Bleakwood — BLEEK wood
Bledsoe — BLĔD soh
Blessing — BLĔ sĭng
Blewett — BLOO ĭt
Blooming Grove — bloo mĭng GRŌV
Bloomington — BLOOM ĭng t'n
Blossom — BLAH s'm
Blue Grove — blyoo GRŌV
Blue Ridge — blyoo RĬJ
Bluff Dale — BLUHF dāl
Bluffton — BLUHF t'n
Blum — bluhm
Boerne — BER nĭ
Bogata — buh GŌ duh
Boling — BŌL ĭng
Bolivar — BAH lĭ ver
Bomarton — BŌ mer t'n
Bonham — BAH n'm
Bonita — boh NEE tuh
Bonney — BAH nĭ
Bonus — BŌ n's
Bon Wier — bahn WEER
Boonsville — BOONZ vĭl
Booth — booth
Borden — BAWRD n
Borger — BŌR ger
Bosque — BAHS kĭ
Boston — BAWS t'n
Bovina — boh VEE nuh
Bowie — BOO Ĭ
Boxelder — bahks ĔL der
Boyce — bawĭs
Boyd — boĭd
Brachfield — BRĂCH feeld
Bracken — BRĂ kĭn
Brackettville — BRĂ kĭt vĭl
Bradford — BRĂD ferd
Bradshaw — BRĂD shaw
Brady — BRĀ dĭ
Brandon — BRĂN d'n
Brashear — bruh SHĬR
Brazoria — bruh ZŌ rĭ uh
Brazos — BRĂZ uhs
Breckenridge — BRĔK uhn rĭj
Bremond — bree MAHND
Brenham — BRĒ n'm
Brewster — BROO ster
Brice — brīs
Bridgeport — BRĬJ pohrt
Briggs — brĭgz
Briscoe — BRĬS koh
Britton — BRĬT n
Broaddus — BRAW d's
Brock — brahk
Bronson — BRAHN s'n
Bronte — brahnt
Brookeland — BROOK l'nd
Brookesmith — BROOK smith
Brookshire — BROOK sher
Brookston — BROOKS t'n
Brown — brown
Browndel — brown DĔL
Brownfield — BROWN feeld
Brownsboro — BROWNZ buh ruh
Brownsville — BROWNZ vĭl
Brownwood — BROWN wood
Bruceville — BROOS v'l
Brundage — BRUHN dĭj
Bruni — BROO nĭ
Brushy Creek — bruh shĭ KREEK
Bryan — BRĪ uhn
Bryans Mill — brī 'nz MĬL
Bryarly — BRĪ er lĭ
Bryson — BRĪ s'n
Buchanan Dam — buhk hăn uhn DAM
Buckholts — BUHK hohlts
Buckhorn — BUHK hawrn
Buda — BYOO duh
Buena Vista — bwā nuh VEES tuh
Buffalo — BUHF uh loh
Buffalo Gap — buhf uh loh GĂP
Buffalo Springs — buhf uh loh SPRĬNGZ
Bula — BYOO luh
Bullard — BOOL erd
Bulverde — bool VER dĭ
Buna — BYOO nuh
Burkburnett — berk ber NET
Burkett — BER kĭt
Burkeville — BERK vĭl
Burleson — BER luh s'n
Burlington — BER lĭng t'n
Burnet — BER nĕt
Burton — BERT n
Bushland — BOOSH l'nd
Bustamante — buhs tuh MAHN tĭ
Butler — BUHT ler
Byers — BĪ erz
Bynum — BĪ n'm
Byrd — berd

C

Caddo Mills — kă doh MĬLZ
Calallen — kăl ĂL ĭn
Calaveras — kăl uh VĔR's
Caldwell — KAHL wĕl
Calhoun — kăl HOON
Call — kawl
Calliham — KĂL uh hăm
Callisburg — KĂ lĭs berg
Call Junction — kawl JUHNGK sh'n
Calvert — KĂL vert
Camden — KĂM dĭn
Cameron — KĂM uh r'n
Camilla — kuh MEEL yuh
Camp — kămp
Campbell — KĂM uhl
Campbellton — KĂM uhl t'n
Camp Wood — kămp WOOD
Canadian — kuh NĀ dĭ uhn
Candelaria — kăn duh LĒ rĭ uh

Canton — KĂNT n
Canyon — KĂN y'n
Caplen — KĂP lĭn
Caps — kăps
Caradan — KĂR uh dăn
Carbon — KAHR b'n
Carey — KĀ rĭ
Carlisle — KAHR līl
Carlsbad — KAHR uhlz băd
Carlton — KAHR uhl t'n
Carmine — kahr MEEN
Carmona — kahr MŌ nuh
Caro — KAH roh
Carrizo Springs — kuh ree zuh SPRĬNGZ
Carrollton — KĂR 'l t'n
Carson — KAHR s'n
Carthage — KAHR thĭj
Cash — kăsh
Cason — KĀ s'n
Cass — kăs
Castell — kăs TĔL
Castro — KĂS troh
Castroville — KĂS tro vĭl
Catarina — kăt uh REE nuh
Cat Spring — kăt SPRĬNG
Caviness — KĂ vĭ nĕs
Cayuga — kā YOO guh
Cedar Bayou — see der BĪ oh
Cedar Creek — see der KREEK
Cedar Hill — see der HĬL
Cedar Lake — see der LĀK
Cedar Lane — see der LĀN
Cedar Park — see der PAHRK
Cedar Valley — see der VA lĭ
Cee Vee — see VEE
Celeste — suh LĔST
Celina — suh LĪ nuh
Center — SENT er
Center City — sĕn ter SĬT ĭ
Center Point — sĕn ter POINT
Centerville — sĕn ter vĭl
Centralia — sĕn TRĀL yuh
Chalk — chawlk
Chalk Mountain — chawlk MOWNT n
Chambers — CHĀM berz
Chandler — CHĂND ler
Channelview — chăn uhl VYOO
Channing — CHĂN ĭng
Chapman Ranch — chăp m'n RĂNCH
Chappell Hill — chă p'l HĬL
Charco — CHAHR koh
Charleston — CHAHR uhls t'n
Charlie — CHAHR lĭ
Charlotte — SHAHR l't
Chatfield — CHĂT feeld
Cheapside — CHEEP sīd
Cherokee — CHĔR uh kee
Chester — CHĔS ter
Chico — CHEE koh
Chicota — chĭ KŌ tuh
Childress — CHĬL drĕs
Chillicothe — chĭl ĭ KAH thĭ
Chilton — CHĬL t'n
China — CHĪ nuh
China Spring — chī nuh SPRĬNG
Chireno — sh' REE noh
Chisholm — CHĬZ uhm
Chita — CHEE tuh
Chocolate Bayou — chah kuh lĭt BĪ oh
Choice — chois
Chriesman — KRĬS m'n
Christine — krĭs TEEN
Christoval — krĭs TŌ v'l
Cibolo — SEE boh loh
Circle Back — SER k'l băk
Circleville — SER k'l vĭl
Cisco — SĬS koh
Cistern — SĬS tern
Clairemont — KLĂR mahnt
Clairette — klăr ĭ ĔT
Clarendon — KLĂR ĭn d'n
Clareville — KLĂR vĭl
Clarksville — KLAHRKS vĭl
Clarkwood — KLAHRK wood
Claude — klawd
Clawson — KLAW s'n
Clay — klā
Clayton — KLĀT n
Clear Lake — KLĬR lăk
Clear Spring — klĭr SPRĬNG
Cleburne — KLEE bern
Clemville — KLĔM vĭl
Cleveland — KLEEV l'nd
Clifton — KLĬF t'n
Cline — klīn
Clodine — klaw DEEN
Clute — klyoot
Clyde — klīd
Coahoma — kuh HŌ muh
Cockrell Hill — kahk ruhl HĬL
Coke — kohk
Coldspring — KŌLD sprĭng
Coleman — KŌL m'n
Colfax — KAHL făks
Collegeport — kah lĭj PŌRT
College Station — kah lĭj STĀ sh'n
Collin — KAH lĭn
Collingsworth — KAH lĭnz werth
Collinsville — KAH lĭnz vĭl
Colmesneil — KŌL m's neel
Colorado — kahl uh RAH doh
Colorado City — kah luh rā duh or kah luh rah duh SĬT ĭ
Columbus — kuh LUHM b's
Comal — KŌ măl
Comanche — kuh MĂN chĭ
Combes — kohmz
Comfort — KUHM fert
Commerce — KAH mers
Como — KŌ moh
Comstock — KAHM stahk
Concan — KAHN kăn
Concepcion — kuhn sep sĭ ŌN
Concho — KAHN choh
Concord — KAHN kawrd
Concrete — kahn KREET
Cone — kohn
Conlen — KAHN lĭn
Conroe — KAHN roh
Converse — KAHN vers
Conway — KAHN wā
Cooke — kook
Cookville — KOOK vĭl
Coolidge — KOO lĭj
Copeville — KŌP v'l
Coppell — kahp pĕl or kuhp PĔL
Copperas Cove — kahp ruhs KŌV
Corbett — KAWR bĭt
Cordele — kawr DĔL
Corinth — KAH rĭnth
Corley — KAWR lĭ
Corpus Christi — kawr p's KRĬS tĭ
Corrigan — KAWR uh g'n
Corsicana — kawr sĭ KĂN uh
Coryell — koh rĭ ĔL
Cottle — KAH t'l
Cotton Center — kaht n SĔNT er
Cotton Gin — KAHT n jĭn
Cottonwood — KAHT n wood
Cotulla — kuh TOO luh
Coupland — KŌP l'n
Courtney — KŌRT nĭ
Covington — KUHV ĭng t'n
Coy City — koi SĬT ĭ
Craft — krăft
Crafton — KRĂF t'n
Crandall — KRĂN d'l
Crane — krān
Cranfills Gap — krăn f'lz GĂP
Crawford — KRAW ferd
Creedmoor — KREED mohr
Cresson — KRĔ s'n
Crockett — KRAH kĭt
Crosbyton — KRAWZ bĭ t'n
Cross Cut — KRAWS kuht
Cross Plains — kraws PLĀNZ
Cross Roads — KRAWS rohdz
Crowell — KRŌ uhl
Crowley — KROW li
Crystal City — krĭs t'l SĬT ĭ
Crystal Falls — krĭs t'l FAWLZ
Cuero — KWĔR o
Culberson — KUHL ber s'n
Cumby — KUHM bĭ
Cuney — KYOO nĭ
Cunningham — KUHN ĭng hăm

Currie — KER rĭ
Cushing — KOO shĭng
Cuthand — KUHT hănd

D

Dabney — DĂB nĭ
Dacosta — duh KAHS tuh
Dacus — DĂ k's
Daingerfield — DĀN jer feeld
Daisetta — dā ZĔT uh
Dalby Springs — dĂl bĭ SPRĬNGZ
Dalhart — DĂL hahrt
Dallam — DĂL uhm
Dallas — DĂ luhs
Damon — DĀ m'n
Danbury — DĂN bĕrĭ
Danciger — DĂN sĭ ger
Danevang — DĂN uh văng
Darrouzett — dăr uh ZĔT
Davilla — duh VĬL uh
Dawson — DAW s'n
Dayton — DĀT n
Deaf Smith — dĕf SMĬTH
Deanville — DEEN vĭl
DeBerry — duh BĔ rĭ
Decatur — dee KĀT er
De Kalb — dĭ KĂB
De Leon — da lee AHN
Del Rio — dĕl REE oh
Del Valle — dĕl VĂ lĭ
Delwin — DĔl wĭn
Denhawken — DĬN haw kĭn
Denison — DĔN uh s'n
Denning — DĔN ĭng
Denton — DĔNT n
Denver City — dĕn ver SĬT ĭ
Deport — DEE pohrt or dĭ PŌRT
Derby — DER bĭ
Desdemona — dĕz dĭ MŌ nuh
DeSoto — dĭ SŌ tuh
Detroit — dee TROIT
Devers — DĔ vers
Devine — duh VĪN
Dew — dyoo
Deweyville — DYOO ĭ vĭl
DeWitt — dĭ WĬT
Dewville — DYOO vĭl
Dexter — DĔKS ter
D'Hanis — duh HĂ nĭs
Dialville — DĪ uhl vil
Diboll — DĪ bawl
Dickens — DĬK ĭnz
Dickinson — DĬK ĭn s'n
Dike — dĭk
Dilley — DĬL i
Dilworth — DĬL werth
Dimebox — dīm BAHKS
Dimmit — DĬM ĭt
Dinero — dĭ NĔ roh
Direct — duh RĔKT
Dixon — DĬK s'n
Dobbin — DAH bĭn
Dobrowolski — dah bruh WAHL skĭ
Dodd City — dahd SĬT ĭ
Dodson — DAHD s'n
Donie — DŌ nĭ
Donley — DAHN lĭ
Doole — DOO lĭ
Dorchester — dawr CHĔS ter
Doucette — DOO sĕt
Dougherty — DAHR tĭ
Douglass — DUHG l's
Douglassville — DUHG lĭs vĭl
Downing — DOWN ĭng
Downsville — DOWNZ vĭl
Dozier — DŌ zher
Driftwood — DRĬFT wood
Dripping Springs — drĭp ĭng SPRĬNGZ
Driscoll — DRĬS k'l
Dryden — DRĪD n
Dublin — DUHB lĭn
Duffau — DUHF oh
Dumas — DOO m's
Dumont — DYOO mahnt
Dundee — DUHN dĭ
Dunlap — DUHN lăp
Dunlay — DUHN lĭ
Durango — duh RĂNG goh
Duval — DOO vawl

E

Eagle Lake — ee g'l LĀK
Eagle Pass — ee g'l PĂS
East Bernard — eest ber NAHRD
Easterly — EES ter lĭ
Eastland — EEST l'nd
Easton — EES t'n
Ector — ĔK ter
Edcouch — ĕd KOWCH
Eddy — E di
Eden — EED n
Edge — ĕj
Edgewood — ĔJ wood
Edinburg — ĔD n berg
Edmonson — ĔD m'n s'n
Edna — ED nuh
Edom — EE d'm
Edroy — ĔD roi
Egan — EE g'n
Egypt — EE juhpt
Elbert — ĔL bert
El Campo — ĕl KĂM poh
Eldorado — ĕl duh RĀ duh
Electra — ĭ LĔK truh
Elgin — ĔL gĭn
Eliasville — ee LĪ uhs vĭl
El Indio — ĕl ĬN dĭ oh
Elkhart — ĔLK hahrt
Ellinger — ĔL ĭn jer
Elliott — ĔL ĭ 't
Ellis — ĔL uhs
Elmendorf — ĔLM 'n dawrf
Elm Mott — ĕl MAHT
Elmo — ĔL moh
Eloise — ĔL o eez
Elsa — ĔL suh
Elysian Fields — uh lee zh'n FEELDZ
Emhouse — ĔM hows
Emory — ĔM uh rĭ
Encinal — ĕn suh NAHL
Encino — ĕn SEE noh
Energy — ĔN er jĭ
Engle — ĔN g'l
Enloe — ĔN loh
Ennis — ĔN ĭs
Enochs — EE nuhks
Eola — ee Ō luh
Era — EE ruh
Erath — EE răth
Esperanza — ĕs per RĂN zuh
Estelline — ĔS tuh leen
Etoile — ĭ TOIL
Etter — ĔT er
Eula — YOO luh
Euless — YOO lĭs
Eureka — yoo REE kuh
Eustace — YOOS t's
Evadale — EE vuh dāl
Evant — EE vănt
Everman — Ĕ ver m'n

F

Fabens — FĀ b'nz
Fairbanks — FĂR bangks
Fairfield — FĂR feeld
Fairlie — FĂR lee
Fair Play — făr PLĀ
Fairview — FĂR vyoo
Fairy — FĂ rĭ
Falfurrias — făl FYOO rĭ uhs
Falls City — fawlz SĬT ĭ
Fannett — fă NĔT
Fannin — FĂN ĭn
Fargo — FAHR goh
Farmers Branch — fahr merz BRĂNCH
Farmersville — FAHRM erz vĭl
Farnsworth — FAHRNZ werth
Farrar — FĂR uh
Farrsville — FAHRZ vĭl
Farwell — FAHR w'l
Fashing — FĂ shĭng
Fayette — fā ĔT
Fayetteville — FĀ uht vĭl
Fentress — FĔN trĭs

Ferris — FĔR ĭs
Field Creek — feeld KREEK
Fieldton — FEEL t'n
Fife — fīf
Fischer — FĬ sher
Fisher — FĬSH er
Flagg — flăg
Flatonia — flă TŌN yuh
Flomot — FLŌ maht
Florence — FLAH ruhns
Floresville — FLŌRZ vil
Florey — FLŌ ri
Floydada — floi DĀ duh
Fluvanna — flyoo VĂN uh
Flynn — flĭn
Foard — fohrd
Foard City — fohrd SĬT ĭ
Fodice — FŌ dĭs
Follett — fah LĔT
Fordtran — fohrd TRĂN
Forest — FAW rĕst
Forestburg — FAW rĕst berg
Forney — FAWR nĭ
Forreston — FAW rĕs t'n
Forsan — FŌR săn
Fort Bend — fohrt BĔND
Fort Chadbourne — fohrt CHĂD bern
Fort Davis — fohrt DĀ vĭs
Fort Griffin — fohrt GRĬF ĭn
Fort Hancock — fohrt HĂN kahk
Fort McKavett — fohrt muh KĂ vĕt
Fort Stockton — fohrt STAHK t'n
Fort Worth — fohrt WERTH
Fowlerton — FOW ler t'n
Francitas — frăn SEE t's
Franklin — FRĂNGK lĭn
Frankston — FRĂNGS t'n
Fred — frĕd
Fredericksburg — FRĔD er rĭks berg
Fredonia — free DŌN yuh
Freeport — FREE pohrt
Freer — FREE er
Freestone — FREE stohn
Frelsburg — FRĔLZ berg
Fresno — FRĔZ noh
Friday — FRĪ dĭ
Friendswood — FRĔNZ wood
Frio — FREE oh
Friona — free Ō nuh
Frisco — FRĬS koh
Fritch — frĭch
Fruitland — FROOT lănd
Fruitvale — FROOT vāl
Frydek — FRĪ dĕk
Fulbright — FOOL brīt
Fulshear — FUHL sher
Fulton — FOOL t'n

G

Gail — gāl
Gaines — gānz
Gainesville — GĀNZ vuhl
Galena Park — guh lee nuh PAHRK
Gallatin — GĂL uh t'n
Galveston — GĂL vĕs t'n
Ganado — guh NĀ doh
Garceno — gahr SĀ noh
Garciasville — gahr SEE uhs vĭl
Garden City — GAHRD n sĭt ĭ
Gardendale — GAHRD n dāl
Garden Valley — gahrd n VĂ lĭ
Garland — GAHR l'nd
Garner — GAHR ner
Garrett — GĂR ĭt
Garrison — GĂ rĭ s'n
Garwood — GAHR wood
Gary — GĔ rĭ
Garza — GAHR zuh
Gatesville — GĀTS vil
Gause — gawz
Gay Hill — gā HĬL
Geneva — juh NEE vuh
Georgetown — JAWRJ town
George West — jawrj WĔST
Geronimo — juh RAH nĭ moh
Giddings — GĬD ĭngz
Gillespie — guh LĔS pĭ
Gillett — juh LĔT
Gilliland — GĬL ĭ l'nd
Gilmer — GĬL mer
Ginger — JĬN jer
Girard — juh RAHRD
Girvin — GER vĭn
Gladewater — GLĀD wah ter
Glasscock — GLĂS kahk
Glazier — GLĀ zher
Glen Cove — glĕn KŌV
Glendale — GLĔN dāl
Glenfawn — glĕn FAWN
Glen Flora — glĕn FLŌ ruh
Glenn — glĕn
Glen Rose — GLĔN rohz
Glidden — GLĬD n
Gober — GŌ ber
Godley — GAHD lĭ
Golden — GŌL d'n
Goldfinch — GŌLD fĭnch
Goldsboro — GŌLZ buh ruh
Goldsmith — GŌL smith
Goldthwaite — GŌLTH wāt
Goliad — GŌ lĭ ăd
Golinda — goh LĬN duh
Gonzales — guhn ZAH l's
Goodland — GOOD l'n
Goodlett — GOOD lĕt
Goodnight — GOOD nīt
Goodrich — GOOD rĭch
Gordon — GAWRD n
Gordonville — GAWRD n vĭl
Goree — GŌ ree
Gorman — GAWR m'n
Gouldbusk — GOOLD buhsk
Graford — GRĀ ferd
Graham — GRĀ 'm
Granbury — GRĂN bĕ rĭ
Grandfalls — grănd FAWLZ
Grand Saline — grăn suh LEEN
Grandview — GRĂN vyoo
Granger — GRĀN jer
Grapeland — GRĀP l'nd
Grapevine — GRĀP vīn
Grassland — GRĂS l'nd
Grassyville — GRĂ sĭ vĭl
Gray — grā
Grayburg — GRĀ berg
Grayson — GRA s'n
Green — green
Greenville — GREEN v'l
Greenwood — GREEN wood
Gregg — grĕg
Gregory — GRĔG uh rĭ
Grimes — grīmz
Groesbeck — GRŌZ bĕk
Groom — gryoom
Groveton — GRŌV t'n
Gruene — green
Grulla — GROOL yuh
Gruver — GROO ver
Guadalupe — gwah duh LOO pĭ or gwah duh LOO pā
Guerra — GWĔ ruh
Gunter — GUHN ter
Gustine — GUHS teen
Guthrie — GUHTH rĭ
Guy — gī

H

Hackberry — HĂK bĕ rĭ
Hagansport — HĀ gĭnz pohrt
Hainesville — HĀNZ v'l
Hale — hāl
Hale Center — hāl SĔNT er
Hall — hawl
Hallettsville — HĂL ĕts vĭl
Hallsville — HAWLZ vĭl
Hamilton — HĂM uhl t'n
Hamlin — HĂM lĭn
Hammond — HĂM 'nd
Hamon — HĂ m'n
Hamshire — HĂM sher
Handley — HĂND lĭ
Hankamer — HĂN kăm er
Hansford — HĂNZ ferd
Happy — HĂ pĭ
Hardeman — HAHR duh m'n
Hardin — HAHRD n

Hare — hăr
Hargill — HAHR gĭl
Harleton — HAHR uhl t'n
Harlingen — HAHR lĭn juhn
Harper — HAHR per
Harrison — HĂ rĭ s'n
Harrold — HĂR 'ld
Hartburg — HAHRT berg
Hartley — HAHRT lĭ
Harwood — HAHR wood
Haskell — HĂS k'l
Haslam — HĂZ l'm
Haslet — HĂS lĕt
Hasse — HĂ sĭ
Hatchell — HĂ ch'l
Hawkins — HAW kĭnz
Hawley — HAW lĭ
Hearne — hern
Heath — heeth
Hebbronville — HĔB r'n vĭl
Hebron — HEE br'n
Hedley — HĔD lĭ
Heidenheimer — HĪD n hīmer
Helena — HĔL uh nuh
Helotes — hĕl Ō tĭs
Hemphill — HĔMP hĭl
Hempstead — HĔM stĕd
Henderson — HĔN der s'n
Henly — HĔN lĭ
Henrietta — hĕn rĭ Ĕ tuh
Hereford — HER ferd
Hermleigh — HER muh lee
Hewitt — HYOO ĭt
Hico — HĪ koh
Hidalgo — hĭ DĂL goh
Higgins — HĬ gĭnz
Highbank — HĪ băngk
High Island — hī Ī l'nd
Highlands — HĪ l'ndz
Hightower — HĪ tow er
Hillister — HĬL ĭs ter
Hillsboro — HĬLZ buh ruh
Hindes — hīndz
Hiram — HĪ r'm
Hitchcock — HĬCH kahk
Hitchland — HĬCH l'nd
Hobson — HAHB s'n
Hochheim — HŌ hīm
Hockley — HAHK lĭ
Holland — HAHL 'nd
Holliday — HAH luh dā
Hondo — HAHN doh
Honey Grove — HUHN ĭ grohv
Honey Island — huhn ĭ Ī l'nd
Honey Springs — huhn ĭ SPRĬNGZ
Hopkins — HAHP kĭnz
Houston — HYOOS t'n or YOOS t'n
Howard — HOW erd
Howe — how
Howland — HOW l'nd
Hubbard — HUH berd
Huckabay — HUHK uh bĭ
Hudspeth — HUHD sp'th
Huffman — HUHF m'n
Hufsmith — HUHF smĭth
Hughes Springs — hyooz SPRĬNGZ
Humble — UHM b'l
Hungerford — HUHNG ger ferd
Hunter — HUHNT er
Huntington — HUHNT ĭng t'n
Huntsville — HUHNTS v'l
Hurlwood — HERL wood
Hutchins — HUH chĭnz
Hutchinson — HUH chĭn s'n
Hutto — HUH toh
Hye — hī
Hylton — HĬL t'n

I

Iago — ī Ā goh
Idalou — Ī duh lyoo
Imperial — ĭm PĬR ĭ uhl
Inadale — Ī nuh dāl
Independence — ĭn duh PĔN d'ns
Indian Creek — ĭn dĭ uhn KREEK
Indian Gap — ĭn dĭ uhn GĂP
Industry — ĬN duhs trĭ
Inez — ī NĔZ
Ingleside — ĬNG g'l sīd
Ingram — ĬNG gr'm
Iola — ī Ō luh
Iowa Park — ī uh wuh PAHRK
Ira — Ī ruh
Iraan — ī ruh ĂN
Iredell — Ī ruh dĕl
Ireland — Ī rĭ l'nd
Irene — ī REEN
Irion — ĪR i uhn
Ironton — ĪRN t'n
Irving — ER vĭng
Italy — ĬT uh lĭ
Itasca — ī TĂS kuh
Ivan — Ī v'n
Ivanhoe — Ī v'n hoh

J

Jacksboro — JĂKS buh ruh
Jackson — JĂK s'n
Jacksonville — JĂK s'n vĭl
Jamestown — JĀMZ town
Jardin — JAHRD n
Jarrell — JĂR uhl
Jasper — JĂS per
Jayton — JĀT n
Jean — jeen
Jeddo — JĔ doh
Jeff Davis — jĕf DA vĭs
Jefferson — JĔF er s'n
Jericho — JĔ rĭ koh
Jermyn — JER m'n
Jewett — JOO ĭt
Jiba — HEE buh
Jim Hogg — jĭm HAWG
Jim Wells — jĭm WĔLZ
Joaquin — waw KEEN
Johnson — JAHN s'n
Johnson City — jahn s'n SĬT ĭ
Johntown — JAHN town
Johnsville — JAHNZ vĭl
Joinerville — JOI ner vĭl
Jolly — JAH lĭ
Jollyville — JAH lĭ vĭl
Jonah — JŌ nuh
Jones — johnz
Jonesboro — JŌNZ buh ruh
Jonesville — JŌNZ vĭl
Josephine — JŌ suh feen
Joshua — JAH sh' wa
Jourdanton — JERD n t'n
Joyce — jawĭs
Juliff — JOO lĭf
Junction — JUHNGK sh'n
Juno — JOO noh
Justiceburg — JUHS tĭs berg

K

Kalgary — KĂL gĕ rĭ
Kamay — KĀ ĭm ā
Kanawha — KAHN uh wah
Karnack — KAHR năk
Karnes — kahrnz
Karnes City — kahrnz SĬT ĭ
Katemcy — kuh TĔM sĭ
Katy — KĀ tĭ
Kaufman — KAWF m'n
Keechi — KEE chī
Keene — keen
Kellerville — KĔL er vĭl
Kemah — KEE muh
Kemp — kĕmp or kĭmp
Kemp City — kĕmp SĬT ĭ
Kempner — KĔMP ner
Kendalia — kĕn DĂL yuh
Kenedy — KĔN uh dĭ
Kennard — kuh NAHRD
Kennedale — KĔN uh dāl
Kerens — KER 'nz
Kermit — KER mĭt
Kerrville — KER vĭl
Kildare — KĬL dăr
Kilgore — KĬL gohr
Killeen — kuh LEEN
Kimble — KĬM b'l
Kingsbury — KĬNGZ bĕ rĭ
Kingsland — KĬNGZ l'nd
Kingsmill — kĭngz MĬL

Kingston — KĬNGZ t’n
Kingsville — KĬNGZ vĭl
Kinney — KĬN ĭ
Kirby — KER bĭ
Kirbyville — KER bĭ vĭl
Kirkland — KERK l’nd
Kirvin — KER vĭn
Kleberg — KLĀ berg
Klondike — KLAHN dīk
Knickerbocker — NĬK uh bah ker
Knippa — kuh NĬP uh
Knox — nahks
Knox City — nahks SĬT ĭ
Kosciusko — kuh SHOOS koh
Kosse — KAH sĭ
Kountze — kyoontz
Kurten — KER t’n

L

La Blanca — lah BLAHN kuh
La Coste — luh KAWST
Ladonia — luh DŌN yuh
LaFayette — lah fĭ ĔT
Laferia — luh FĔ rĭ uh
Lagarto — luh GAHR toh
La Gloria — lah GLŌ rĭ uh
La Grange — luh GRĀNJ
Laguna — luh GOO nuh
Laird Hill — lărd HĬL
La Joya — luh HŌ yuh
Lake Creek — lāk KREEK
Lake Dallas — lāk DĂL uhs
Lake Jackson — lāk JĂK s’n
Laketon — LĀK t’n
Lake Victor — lāk VĬK ter
Lakeview — LĀK vyoo
Lamar — luh MAHR
La Marque — luh MAHRK
Lamasco — luh MĂS koh
Lamb — lăm
Lamesa — luh MEE suh
Lamkin — LĂM kĭn
Lampasas — lăm PĂ s’s
Lancaster — LĂNG k’s ter
Laneville — LĀN vĭl
Langtry — LĂNG trĭ
Lanier — luh NĬR
La Paloma — lah puh LŌ muh
La Porte — luh PŌRT
La Pryor — luh PRĪ er
Laredo — luh RĀ doh
Lariat — LĂ ri uht
Larue — luh ROO
La Salle — luh SĂL
Lasara — luh SĔ ruh
Lassater — LĂ sĭ ter
Latch — lĂch
Latexo — luh TĔKS oh
Lavaca — luh VĂ kuh
La Vernia — luh VER nĭ uh
La Villa — lah VĬL uh
Lavon — luh VAHN
La Ward — luh WAWRD
Lawrence — LAH r’ns
Lazbuddie — LĂZ buh dĭ
League City — leeg SĬT ĭ
Leakey — LĀ kĭ
Leander — lee ĂN der
Leary — LĪ er ĭ
Ledbetter — LĔD bĕt er
Leesburg — LEEZ berg
Leesville — LEEZ vĭl
Lefors — lĭ FŌRZ
Leggett — LĔ gĭt
Leigh — lee
Lela — LEE luh
Lelia Lake — leel yuh LĀK
Leming — LĔ mĭng
Lenorah — lĕ NŌ ruh
Leon — lee AHN
Leona — lee Ō nuh
Leonard — LĔN erd
Leon Springs — lee ahn SPRĬNGZ
Leroy — LEE roi
Levelland — LĔ v’l lănd
Levita — luh VĪ tuh
Lewisville — LOO ĭs vĭl
Lexington — LĔKS ĭng t’n
Liberty — LĬB er tĭ
Liberty Hill — lĭ ber tĭ HĬL
Lillian — LĬL yuhn
Limestone — LĪM stohn
Lincoln — LĬNG k’n
Lindale — LĬN dāl
Linden — LĬN d’n
Lindenau — lĭn duh NOW
Lindsay — LĬN zĭ
Lingleville — LĬNG g’l vĭl
Linn — lĭn
Lipan — lī PĂN
Lipscomb — LĬPS k’m
Lissie — LĬ sĭ
Little Elm — lĭt l ĔLM
Littlefield — LĬT uhl feeld
Little River — lĭt uhl RĬV er
Live Oak — LĬV ohk
Liverpool — LĬ ver pyool
Livingston — LĬV ĭngz t’n
Llano — LĂ noh
Locker — LAH ker
Lockett — LAH kĭt
Lockhart — LAHK hahrt
Lockney — LAHK nĭ
Lodi — LŌ dī
Lohn — lahn
Lolita — loh LEE tuh
Loma Alto — loh muh ĂL toh
Lometa — loh MEE tuh
London — LUHN d’n
Lone Grove — lohn GRŌV
Lone Oak — LŌN ohk
Long Branch — lawng BRĂNCH
Long Mott — lawng MAHT
Longview — LAWNG vyoo
Longworth — LAWNG werth
Loop — loop
Lopeno — loh PEE noh
Loraine — loh RĀN
Lorena — loh REE nuh
Los Angeles — laws AN juh l’s
Los Ebanos — lohs ĔB uh nohs
Los Fresnos — lohs FRĔZ nohs
Los Indios — lohs ĬN dĭ ohs
Losoya — luh SAW yuh
Lott — laht
Louise — LOO eez
Lovelady — LUHV lā dĭ
Loving — LUH vĭng
Lowake — loh WĀ kĭ
Lubbock — LUH buhk or LUH b’k
Lueders — LOO derz
Luella — lyoo ĔL uh
Lufkin — LUHF kĭn
Luling — LOO lĭng
Lutie — LOO tĭ
Lyford — LĪ ferd
Lyons — LĪ ’nz
Lytton Springs — lĭt n SPRĬNGZ

M

Mabank — MĀ băngk
Macune — muh KOON
Madison — MĂ dĭ s’n
Madisonville — MĂ duh s’n vĭl
Magnolia — măg NŌL yuh
Magnolia Springs — măg nol yuh SPRĬNGZ
Malakoff — MĂL uh kawf
Malone — muh LŌN
Malta — MAWL tuh
Manchaca — MĂN shăk
Manchester — MĂN chĕs ter
Manheim — MĂN hīm
Mankins — MĂN kĭnz
Manor — MĀ ner
Mansfield — MĂNZ feeld
Manvel — MĂN v’l
Marathon — MĂR uh th’n
Marble Falls — mahr b’l FAWLZ
Marfa — MAHR fuh
Margaret — MAHR guh rĭt
Marietta — mĕ rĭ Ĕ tuh
Marion — MĔ rĭ uhn
Markham — MAHR k’m
Marlin — MAHR lĭn
Marquez — mahr KĀ
Marshall — MAHR sh’l
Martin — MAHRT n

Martindale — MAHRT n dāl
Martinsville — MAHRT nz vĭl
Maryneal — mā rĭ NEEL
Marysville — MĀ rĭz vĭl
Mason — MĀ s'n
Matador — MĂT uh dohr
Matagorda — măt uh GAWR duh
Mathis — MĂ thĭs
Maud — mawd
Mauriceville — maw REES vĭl
Maverick — MĂV rĭk
Maxey — MĂKS ĭ
Maxwell — MĂKS w'l
Maydell — MĀ dĕl
Maypearl — mā PERL
Maysfield — MĀZ feeld
McAdoo — MĂK uh dyoo
McAllen — măk ĂL ĭn
McCamey — muh KĀ mĭ
McCaulley — muh KAW lĭ
McCoy — muh KOI
McCulloch — muh KUH luhk
McFaddin — măk FĂD n
McGregor — muh GRĔ ger
McKinney — muh KĬN ĭ
McLean — muh KLĀN
McLennan — muhk LĔN uhn
McLeod — măk LOWD
McMahan — măk MĂN
McMullen — măk MUHL ĭn
McNary — măk NĂ rĭ
McNeil — măk NEEL
McQueeney — muh KWEE nĭ
Medicine Mound — mĕd uhs n MOWND
Medill — mĕ DĬL
Medina — muh DEE nuh
Megargel — muh GAHR g'l
Melissa — muh LĬS uh
Melrose — MĔL rohz
Melvin — MĔL vĭn
Memphis — MĔM fĭs
Menard — muh NAHRD
Mendoza — mĕn DŌ zuh
Mentone — mĕn TŌN
Mercedes — mer SĀ deez
Mercury — MER kyuh ri
Mereta — muh RĔT uh
Meridian — muh RĬ dĭ uhn
Merit — MĔR ĭt
Merkel — MER k'l
Mertens — mer TĔNZ
Mertzon — MERTS n
Mesquite — muhs KEET
Mexia — muh HĀ uh
Meyersville — MĪRZ vĭl
Miami — mī ĂM uh or mī ĂM ĭ
Mico — MEE koh
Middleton — MĬD uhl t'n
Midfields — MĬD feeldz
Midland — MĬD l'nd
Midlothian — mĭd LŌ thĭ n
Milam — MĪ l'm
Milano — mĭ LĂ noh
Mildred — MĬL drĕd
Miles — mīlz
Milford — MĬL ferd
Miller Grove — mĭl er GRŌV
Millersview — MĬL erz vyoo
Millett — MĬL ĭt
Millheim — MĬL hīm
Millican — MĬL uh kuhn
Mills — mĭlz
Millsap — MĬL săp
Minden — MĬN d'n
Mineola — mĭn ĭ Ō luh
Mineral — MĬN er uhl
Mineral Wells — mĭn er uhl WĔLZ
Minerva — mĭ NER vuh
Mingus — MĬNG guhs
Minter — MĬNT er
Mirando City — mĭ răn duh SĬT ĭ
Mission — MĬSH uhn
Mission Valley — mĭsh uhn VĂ lĭ
Missouri City — muh zoor uh SĬT ĭ
Mitchell — MĬ ch'l
Mobeetie — moh BEE tĭ
Moline — moh LEEN
Monahans — MAH nuh hănz
Monaville — MŌ nuh vĭl
Monkstown — MUHNGKS town
Monroe — MAHN roh
Monroe City — mahn roh SĬT ĭ
Montague — mahn TĀG
Montalba — mahnt ĂL buh
Mont Belvieu — mahnt BĔL vyoo
Montell — mahn TĔL
Montgomery — mahnt GUHM er ĭ
Monthalia — mahn THĀL yuh
Moore — mohr
Morales — muh RAH lĕs
Moran — moh RĂN
Morgan — MAWR g'n
Morgan Mill — mawr g'n MĬL
Morse — mawrs
Morton — MAWRT n
Moscow — MAHS kow
Mosheim — MŌ shīm
Moss Bluff — maws BLUHF
Motley — MAHT lĭ
Moulton — MŌL t'n
Mound — mownd
Mountain Home — mownt n HŌM
Mount Calm — mownt KAHM
Mount Enterprise — mownt ĔN ter prīz
Mount Pleasant — mownt PLĔ z'nt
Mount Selman — mownt SĔL m'n
Mount Sylvan — mownt SĬL v'n
Mount Vernon — mownt VER n'n
Muenster — MYOONS ter
Muldoon — muhl DOON
Muleshoe — MYOOL shyoo
Mullin — MUHL ĭn
Mumford — MUHM ferd
Munday — MUHN dĭ
Murchison — MER kuh s'n
Murphy — MER fĭ
Mykawa—mĭ KAH wuh
Myra — MĪ ruh
Myrtle Springs — mert l SPRĬNGZ

N

Nacogdoches — năk uh DŌ chĭs
Nada — NĀ duh
Naples — NĀ p'lz
Nash — năsh
Natalia — nuh TĂL yuh
Navarro — nuh VĂ roh
Navasota — năv uh SŌ tuh
Nazareth — NĂZ uh r'th
Neches — NĀ chĭs
Nederland — NEE der l'nd
Needville — NEED vĭl
Nelsonville — NĔL s'n vĭl
Neuville — NYOO v'l
Nevada — nuh VĀ duh
Newark — NOO erk
New Baden — nyoo BĀD n
New Berlin — nyoo BER lin
New Boston — nyoo BAWS t'n
New Braunfels — nyoo BRAHN f'ls or BROWN fĕlz
Newby — NYOO bĭ
New Caney — nyoo KĀ nĭ
Newcastle — NYOO kăs uhl
New Gulf — nyoo GUHLF
New Home — NYOO hohm
New Hope — nyoo HŌP
Newlin — NYOO lĭn
New London — nyoo LUHN d'n
Newman — NYOO m'n
Newport — NYOO pohrt
New Salem — nyoo SĀ l'm
Newsome — NYOO s'm
New Summerfield — nyoo SUHM er feeld
Newton — NYOOT n
New Ulm — nyoo UHLM
New Waverly — nyoo WĀ ver lĭ
New Willard — nyoo WĬL erd
Nimrod — NĬM rahd
Nineveh — NĬN uh vuh
Nixon — NĬKS uhn
Nocona — noh KŌ nuh
Nolan — NŌ l'n
Nolanville — NŌ l'n vĭl
Nome — nohm
Noonday — NOON dā

Nopal — NŌ păl
Nordheim — NAWRD hīm
Normandy — NAWR m'n dĭ
Normangee — NAWR m'n jee
Normanna — nawr MĂN uh
Northrup — NAWR thr'p
North Zulch — nawrth ZOOLCH
Norton — NAWRT n
Novice — NAH vĭs
Nueces — nyoo Ā sĭs
Nugent — NYOO j'nt

O

Oakalla — oh KĂL uh
Oakhurst — ŌK herst
Oakland — ŌK l'nd
Oakville — ŌK vĭl
Oakwood — ŌK wood
O'Brien — oh BRĪ uhn
Ochiltree — AH k'l tree
Odell — Ō dĕl or oh DĔL
Odem — Ō d'm
Odessa — oh DĔS uh
O'Donnell — oh DAH n'l
Oenaville — oh EEN uh v'l
Oglesby — Ō g'lz bĭ
Oilton — OIL t'n
Oklaunion — ohk luh YOON y'n
Olden — ŌL d'n
Oldenburg — ŌL dĭn berg
Oldham — ŌL d'm
Old Glory — ohld GLŌ rĭ
Olivia — oh LĬV ĭ uh
Olmito — awl MEE tuh
Olmos Park — ahl m's PAHRK
Olney — AHL nĭ
Olton — ŌL t'n
Omaha — Ō muh haw
Onalaska — uhn uh LĂS kuh
Oplin — AHP lĭn
Orange — AHR ĭnj
Orangefield — AHR ĭnj feeld
Orange Grove — AHR ĭnj GRŌV
Orchard — AWR cherd
Ore City — ohr SĬT ĭ
Osceola — oh sĭ Ō luh
Otey — Ō tĭ
Otis Chalk — oh tĭs CHAWLK
Ottine — ah TEEN
Otto — AH toh
Ovalo — oh VĂL uh
Overton — Ō ver t'n
Owens — Ō ĭnz
Ozona — oh ZŌ nuh

P

Paducah — puh DYOO kuh
Paige — pāj
Paint Rock — pānt RAHK
Palacios — puh LĂ sh's
Palestine — PAL uhs teen
Palito Blanco — p' lee to BLAHNG koh
Palmer — PAH mer
Palo Pinto — pă loh PĬN toh
Paluxy — puh LUHK sĭ
Pampa — PĂM puh
Pandora — păn DŌR uh
Panhandle — PĂN hăn d'l
Panna Maria — păn uh muh REE uh
Papalote — pah puh LŌ tĭ
Paradise — PĂR uh dīs
Parker — PAHR ker
Parmer — PAH mer
Parnell — pahr NĔL
Parsley Hill — pahrs lĭ HĬL
Pasadena — păs uh DEE nuh
Patricia — puh TRĬ shuh
Patroon — puh TROON
Pattison — PĂT uh s'n
Pattonville — PĂT n vĭl
Pawnee — paw NEE
Paxton — PĂKS t'n
Pearland — PĂR lănd
Pearsall — PEER sawl
Peaster — PEES ter
Pecan Gap — pĭ kahn GĂP
Pecos — PĀ k's
Penelope — puh NĔL uh pĭ
Peñitas — puh NEE t's
Pennington — PĔN ĭng t'n
Penwell — PĬN wĕl
Peoria — pee Ō rĭ uh
Percilla — per SĬL uh
Perrin — PĔR ĭn
Perry — PĔ rĭ
Perryton — PĔ rĭ t'n
Peters — PEET erz
Petersburg — PEET erz berg
Petrolia — puh TRŌL yuh
Petteway — PĔT uh wā
Pettit — PĔT ĭt
Pettus — PĔT uhs
Pflugerville — FLOO ger vĭl
Pharr — fahr
Phelps — fĕlps
Phillips — FĬL uhps
Pickton — PĬK t'n
Pidcoke — PĬD k6k
Piedmont — PEED mahnt
Pierce — PĪ ers
Pilot Point — pī l't POINT
Pine Forest — pīn FAW rĕst
Pinehurst — PĪN herst
Pineland — PĪN land
Pine Mills — pīn MĬLZ
Pine Springs — pīn SPRĬNGZ
Pioneer — pī uh NĬR
Pipecreek — pīp KREEK
Pittsburg — PĬTS berg
Placedo — PLĂS ĭ doh
Placid — PLĂ sĭd
Plainview — PLĀN vyoo
Plano — PLĀ noh
Plantersville — PLĂN terz vĭl
Plaska — PLĂS kuh
Plateau — plă TŌ
Pleasant Grove—plĕ z'nt GRŌV
Pleasanton — PLĔZ uhn t'n
Pledger — PLĔ jer
Pointblank — pint BLĂNGK
Pollock — PAHL uhk
Ponder — PAHN der
Ponta — pahn TĀ
Pontotoc — PAHNT uh tahk
Poolville — POOL vĭl
Port Aransas — pohrt uh RĂN zuhs
Port Arthur — pohrt AHR ther
Port Bolivar — pohrt BAH lĭ ver
Porter Springs — pohr ter SPRĬNGZ
Port Isabel — pohrt ĬZ uh bĕl
Portland — PŌRT l'nd
Port Lavaca — pohrt luh VĂ kuh
Port Neches — pohrt NĀ chĭs
Port O'Connor — pohrt oh KAH ner
Posey — PŌ zĭ
Post — pohst
Postoak — PŌST ohk
Poteet — poh TEET
Poth — pohth
Potosi — puh TŌ sĭ
Potter — PAHT er
Pottsboro — PAHTS buh ruh
Pottsville — PAHTS vĭl
Powderly — POW der lĭ
Powell — POW w'l
Poynor — POI ner
Prairie Dell — prĕr ĭ DĔL
Prairie Hill — prĕr ĭ HĬL
Prairie Lea — prĕr ĭ LEE
Prairie View — prĕr ĭ VYOO
Prairieville — PRĔR ĭ vĭl
Premont — PREE mahnt
Presidio — pruh SĬ dĭ oh
Priddy — PRĬ dĭ
Primera — pree MĔ ruh
Princeton — PRĬNS t'n
Pritchett — PRĬ chĭt
Proctor — PRAHK ter
Progreso — proh GRĔ soh
Prosper — PRAHS per
Purdon — PERD n
Purley — PER lĭ
Purmela — per MEE luh
Putnam — PUHT n'm
Pyote — PĪ oht

Q

Quanah — KWAH nuh
Queen City — kween SĬT ĭ
Quemado — kuh MAH doh
Quihi — KWEE hee
Quinlan — KWĬN l'n
Quintana — kwĭn TAH nuh
Quitaque — KĬT uh kwa
Quitman — KWĬT m'n

R

Ralls — rahlz
Randall — RĂN d'l
Randolph — RĂN dahlf
Ranger — RĀN jer
Rangerville — RĀN jer vĭl
Rankin — RĂNG kĭn
Ratcliff — RĂT klĭf
Ravenna — rĭ VĔN uh
Rayburn — RĀ bern
Raymondville — RĀ m'nd vĭl
Raywood — RĀ wood
Reagan — RĀ g'n
Real — REE awl
Realitos — ree uh LEE t's
Reeves — reevz
Refugio — rĕ FYOO rĭ oh
Reilly Springs — rī lĭ SPRĬNGZ
Reklaw — RĔK law
Reno — REE noh
Rhineland — RĪN l'nd
Rhome — rohm
Rhonesboro — RŌNZ buh ruh
Ricardo — rĭ KAHR doh
Richards — RĬCH erdz
Richardson — RĬCH erd s'n
Richland — RĬCH l'nd
Richland Springs — rĭch l'nd SPRĬNGZ
Richmond — RĬCH m'nd
Ridge — rĭj
Ridgeway — RĬJ wā
Riesel — REE s'l
Ringgold — RĬNG gohld
Rio Frio — ree oh FREE oh
Rio Grande City — ree oh grahn dĭ or ree oh grăn SĬT ĭ
Rio Hondo — ree oh HAHN doh
Riomedina — ree oh muh DEE nuh
Rios — REE ohs
Rio Vista — ree oh VĬS tuh
Rising Star — rī zĭng STAHR
River Oaks — rĭ ver ŌKS
Riverside — RĬ ver sīd
Riviera — ruh VĬR uh
Roane — rohn
Roanoke — RŌN ohk or RŌ uh nohk
Roans Prairie — rohnz PRĔR Ĭ
Roaring Springs — rohr ĭng SPRĬNGZ
Robert Lee — rah bert LEE
Roberts — RAH berts
Robertson — RAH bert s'n
Robinson — RAH bĭn s'n
Robstown — RAHBZ town
Rochelle — roh SHĔL
Rochester — RAH chĕs ter
Rockdale — RAHK dāl
Rock Island — rahk Ī l'nd
Rockland — RAHK l'nd
Rockport — rahk PŌRT
Rocksprings — rahk SPRĬNGZ
Rockwall — rahk WAWL
Rockwood — RAHK wood
Roganville — RŌ g'n vĭl
Rogers — RAH jerz
Romayor — roh MĀ er
Roosevelt — RŌ suh v'lt or ROO suh v'lt
Ropesville — RŌPS vĭl
Rosanky — roh ZĂNG kĭ
Roscoe — RAHS koh
Rosebud — RŌZ b'd
Rose Hill — rohz HĬL
Rosenberg — RŌZ n berg
Rosenthal — RŌZ uhn thawl
Rosewood — RŌZ wood
Rosharon — roh SHĔ r'n
Rosita — roh SEE tuh
Rosser — RAW ser
Rosston — RAWS t'n
Rossville — RAWS vĭl
Roswell — RAHZ w'l
Rotan — roh TĂN
Round Rock — ROWND rahk
Round Top — ROWN tahp
Rowena — roh EE nuh
Rowlett — ROW lĭt
Roxton — RAHKS t'n
Royalty — ROI uhl tĭ
Royse City — roi SĬT ĭ
Royston — ROIS t'n
Rugby — RUHG bĭ
Ruidosa — ree uh DŌ suh
Rule — ryool
Runge — RUHNG ĭ
Runnels — RUHN 'lz
Rural Shade — roor uhl SHĀD
Rutersville — ROO ter vĭl

S

Sabinal — SĂB uh năl
Sabine — suh BEEN
Sabine Pass — suh been PĂS
Sabinetown — suh been TOWN
Sachse — SĂK sĭ
Sacul — SĂ k'l
Sadler — SĂD ler
Sagerton — SĀ ger t'n
Saginaw — SĂ guh naw
Saint Jo — sānt JŌ
Saint Paul — sānt PAWL
Salado — suh LĀ doh
Salesville — SĀLZ vĭl
Salineno — suh LEEN yoh
Salmon — SĂL m'n
Saltillo — săl TĬL oh
Sam Fordyce — săm FOR dis
Samnorwood — săm NAWR wood
San Angelo — săn ĂN juh loh
San Antonio — săn ăn TŌ nĭ oh
San Augustine — săn AW g's teen
San Benito — săn buh NEE tuh
Sanderson — SĂN der s'n
Sandia — săn DEE uh
San Diego — săn dĭ Ā goh
Sandy Point — săn dĭ POINT
San Elizario — săn ĕl ĭ ZAH rĭ oh
San Felipe — săn fuh LEEP
Sanford — SĂN ferd
San Gabriel — săn GĀ brĭ uhl
Sanger — SĂNG er
San Jacinto — săn juh SĬN tuh or juh SĬN toh
San Juan — săn WAHN
San Marcos — săn MAHR k's
San Patricio — săn puh TRĬSH ĭ oh
San Perlita — săn per LEE tuh
San Saba — săn SĂ buh
Santa Anna — săn tuh ĂN uh
Santa Elena — săn tuh LEE nuh
Santa Maria — săn tuh muh REE uh
Santa Rosa — săn tuh RŌ suh
Santo — SĂN toh
San Ygnacio — săn ĭg NAH sĭ oh
Saragosa — sĕ ruh GŌ suh
Saratoga — sĕ ruh TŌ guh
Sargent — SAHR juhnt
Sarita — suh REE tuh
Saspamco — suh SPĂM koh
Savoy — suh VOI
Schattel — SHĂT uhl
Schertz — sherts
Schleicher — SHLĪ ker
Schroeder — SHRĀ der
Schulenburg — SHOO lĭn berg
Schwertner — SWERT ner
Scotland — SKAHT l'nd
Scottsville — SKAHTS vĭl
Scranton — SKRĂNT n
Scurry — SKUH rĭ
Scyene — sī EEN
Seabrook — SEE brook
Seadrift — SEE drĭft
Seagoville — SEE goh vĭl

Seagraves — SEE grāvz
Sebastopol — suh BĂS tuh pyool
Sebastian — suh BĂS tĭ 'n
Security — sĭ KYOOR ĭ tĭ
Segno — SĔG noh
Segovia — sĭ GŌ vĭ uh
Seguin — sĭ GEEN
Selma — SĔL muh
Seminole — SĔM uh nohl
Seymour — SEE mohr
Shackelford — SHĂK uhl ferd
Shady Grove — shā dĭ GRŌV
Shafter — SHĂF ter
Shallowater — SHĂL uh wah ter
Shamrock — SHĂM rahk
Shannon — SHĂN uhn
Sheffield — SHĔ feeld
Shelby — SHĔL bĭ
Shelbyville — SHĔL bĭ vĭl
Sheldon — SHĔL d'n
Shepherd — SHĔ perd
Sheridan — SHĔ rĭ dn
Sherman — SHER m'n
Sherwood — SHER wood
Shiner — SHĪ ner
Shiro — SHĪ roh
Shive — shīv
Sidney — SĬD nĭ
Sierra Blanca — sĭer ruh BLĂNG kuh
Siloam — suh LŌM
Silsbee — SĬLZ bĭ
Silver Lake — sĭl ver LĀK
Silverton — SĬL ver t'n
Silver Valley — sĭl ver VĂ lĭ
Simonton — SĪ m'n t'n
Singleton — SĬNG g'l t'n
Sinton — SĬNT n
Sipe Springs — SEEP sprĭngz
Sisterdale — SĬS ter dāl
Sivells Bend — sĭ v'lz BĔND
Skellytown — SKĔ lĭ town
Skidmore — SKĬD mohr
Slaton — SLĀT n
Slayden — SLĀD n
Slidell — slī DĔL
Slocum — SLŌ k'm
Smiley — SMĪ lĭ
Smith — smĭth
Smithfield — SMĬTH feeld
Smithland — SMĬTH l'nd
Smithson Valley — smĭth s'n VĂ lĭ
Smithville — SMĬTH vĭl
Smyer — SMĪ er
Snyder — SNĪ der
Somerset — SUH mer sĕt
Somervell — SUH mer vĕl
Somerville — SUH mer vĭl
Sonora — suh NŌ ruh
Sour Lake — sowr LĀK
South Bend — sowth BĔND
South Bosque — sowth BAHS kĭ
South Houston — sowth HYOOS t'n
Southland — SOWTH l'nd
Southmayd — sowth MĀD
South Plains — sowth PLĀNZ
Spanish Fort — spă nĭsh FŌRT
Sparenberg — SPĂR ĭn berg
Speaks — speeks
Spearman — SPĬR m'n
Spicewood — SPĪS wood
Splendora — splĕn DŌ ruh
Spofford — SPAH ferd
Springdale — SPRĬNG dāl
Springlake — sprĭng LĀK
Springtown — SPRĬNG town
Spurger — SPER ger
Stacy — STĀ sĭ
Stafford — STĂ ferd
Stamford — STĂM ferd
Stanton — STĂNT n
Staples — STĀ p'lz
Stephens — STEE vĕnz
Stephenville — STEEV n vĭl
Sterley — STER lĭ
Sterling — STER lĭng
Sterling City — ster lĭng SĬT ĭ
Stiles — stīlz
Stinnett — stĭ NĔT
Stockdale — STAHK dāl
Stoneburg — STŌN berg
Stoneham — STŌN uhm
Stone Point — stohn POINT
Stonewall — STŌN wawl
Stout — stowt
Stowell — STO w'l
Stranger — STRĀN jer
Stratford — STRĂT ferd
Strawn — strawn
Streeter — STREET er
Streetman — STREET m'n
Study Butte — styoo dĭ BYOOT
Sudan — SOO dăn
Sugar Land — SHOO ger lănd
Sullivan City — suh luh v'n SĬT ĭ
Sulphur Bluff — suhl fer BLUHF
Sulphur Springs — suhl fer SPRĬNGZ
Summerfield — SUHM er feeld
Sumner — SUHM ner
Sundown — SUHN down
Suniland — SUH nĭ lănd
Sunny Side — SUH nĭ sīd
Sunray — SUHN rā
Sunset — SUHN sĕt
Sutherland Springs — suh ther l'nd SPRĬNGZ
Sutton — SUHT n
Swan — swahn
Sweeny — SWEE nĭ
Sweet Home — sweet HŌM
Sweetwater — SWEET wah ter
Swenson — SWĔN s'n
Swift — swĭft
Swisher — SWĬ sher
Sylvester — sĭl VĔS ter

T

Tahoka — tuh HŌ kuh
Talco — TĂL koh
Talpa — TĂL puh
Tanglewood — TĂNG g'l wood
Tankersley — TĂNG kers lĭ
Tarrant — TAR uhnt
Tarzan — TAHR z'n
Tascosa — tăs KŌ suh
Tatum — TĀ t'm
Tavener — TĂV uh ner
Taylor — TĀ ler
Teague — teeg
Tehuacana — tuh WAW kuh nuh
Telferner — TĔLF ner
Tenaha — TĔN uh haw
Tennyson — TĔN uh s'n
Terlingua — TER lĭng guh
Terrell — TĔR uhl
Terrell Hills — ter uhl HILZ
Texarkana — tĕks ahr KĂN uh
Texas City — tĕks ĕz SĬT ĭ
Texhoma — tĕks Ō muh
Texline — TĔKS līn
Texon — tĕks AHN
Thalia — THĀL yuh
Thomaston — TAHM uhs t'n
Thompsons — TAHMP s'nz
Thorndale — THAWRN dāl
Thornton — THAWRN t'n
Thorp Spring — thawrp SPRĬNG
Three Rivers — three RĬ verz
Throckmorton — THRAHK mawrt n
Thurber — THER ber
Tilden — TĬL d'n
Timpson — TĬM s'n
Tioga — tī Ō guh
Tivoli — tī VŌ luh
Tokio — TŌ kĭ oh
Tolar — TŌ ler
Tolbert — TAHL bert
Tolosa — tuh LŌ suh
Tomball — TAHM bawl
Tom Bean — tahm BEEN
Tom Green — tahm GREEN
Topsey — TAHP sĭ
Tornillo — tawr NEE yoh
Toyah — TOI yuh
Toyahvale — TOI yuh vāl
Trawick — TRĀ wĭk
Travis — TRĂ vĭs
Trent — trĕnt

Trenton — TRĔNT n
Trickham — TRĬK uhm
Trinidad — TRĬN uh dăd
Trinity — TRĬN ĭ tĭ
Troup — tryoop
Truby — TROO bĭ
Trumbull — TRUHM b'l
Truscott — TRUHS k't
Tucker — TUHK er
Tuleta — tyoo LEE tuh
Tulia — TOOL yuh
Tulsita — tuhl SEE tuh
Tundra — TUHN druh
Tunis — TOO nĭs
Turkey — TER kĭ
Turlington — TER lĭng t'n
Turnersville — TER nerz vĭl
Turnertown — TER ner town
Turney — TER nĭ
Tuscola — tuhs KŌ luh
Twitty — TWĬ tĭ
Tyler — TĪ ler
Tynan — TĪ nuhn

U

Uhland — YOO l'nd
Umbarger — UHM bahr ger
Union — YOON y'n
Upshur — UHP sher
Upton — UHP t'n
Urbana — er BĂ nuh
Utley — YOOT lĭ
Uvalde — yoo VĂL dĭ

V

Valdasta — văl DĂS tuh
Valera — vuh LĪ ruh
Van Alstyne — văn AWLZ teen
Vancourt — VĂN kohrt
Vanderbilt — VĂN der bĭlt
Vanderpool — VĂN der pyool
Van Horn — văn hawrn
Van Vleck — văn VLĔK
Van Zandt — văn ZĂNT
Vashti — VĂSH tī
Vaughan — vawn
Vega — VĀ guh
Velasco — vuh LĂS koh
Vera — VĪ ruh
Veribest — VĔR ĭ bĕst
Verhalen — ver HĂ lĭn
Vickery — VĬK er ĭ
Vidor — VĪ der
Vienna — vee ĔN uh
Village Mills — vĭl ĭj MĬLZ
Vinegarone — vĭn er guh RŌN
Vineyard — VĬN yerd
Voca — VŌ kuh
Von Ormy — vahn AHR mĭ
Voss — vaws
Votaw — VŌ taw

W

Waco — WĀ koh
Wadsworth — WAHDZ werth
Waelder — WĔL der
Waka — WAH kuh
Walberg — WAWL berg
Waldeck — WAWL dek
Walker — WAWL ker
Waller — WAW ler
Wallis — WAH lĭs
Wallisville — WAH lĭs vĭl
Walnut Springs — wawl n't SPRĬNGZ
Walton — WAWL t'n
Warda — WAWR duh
Waring — WĂR ĭng
Warren — WAW rĭn
Warrenton — WAW rĭn t'n
Washburn — WAHSH bern
Washington — WAHSH ĭng t'n
Waskom — WAHS k'm
Wastella — wahs TĔL uh
Watauga — wuh TAW guh
Water Valley — wah ter VĂ lĭ
Waxahachie — wawks uh HĂ chĭ
Wayland — WĀ l'nd
Weatherford — WĔ ther ferd
Webberville — WĔ ber vĭl
Webster — WĔBS ter
Weches — WEE chĭz
Weesatche — WEE săch
Weimar — WĪ mer
Weinert — WĪ nert
Weir — weer
Weldon — WĔL d'n
Wellborn — WĔL bern
Wellington — WĔL ĭng t'n
Wellman — WĔL m'n
Weser — WEE zer
Weslaco — WĔS luh koh
Westbrook — WĔST brook
Westfield — WĔST feeld
Westhoff — WĔS tawf
Westminster — wĕst MĬN ster
Weston — WĔS t'n
Westover — WĔS toh ver
Westphalia — wĕst FĀL yuh
Wharton — HWAWRT n
Wheeler — HWEE ler
Wheelock — HWEE lahk
White Deer — HWĪT Deer
Whiteface — HWĪT fās
Whiteflat — hwīt FLĂT
Whitehouse — HWĪT hows
Whitesboro — HWĪTS buh ruh
Whitewright — HWĪT rīt
Whitharral — HWĬT hăr uhl
Whitsett — HWĬT sĭt
Whitson — HWĬT s'n
Whitt — hwĭt
Whon — hwahn
Wichita — WĬCH ĭ taw
Wichita Falls — wĭch ĭ taw FAWLZ
Wickett — WĬ kĭt
Wiergate — WEER gāt
Wilbarger — WĬL bahr ger
Wildorado — wĭl duh RĀ doh
Willacy — WĬL uh sĭ
Williamson — WĬL yuhm s'n
Wills Point — wĭlz POINT
Wilmer — WĬL mer
Wilson — WĬL s'n
Wimberley — WĬM ber lĭ
Winchester — WĬN ches ter
Windom — WĬN d'm
Windthorst — WĬN thr'st
Winfield — WĬN feeld
Wingate — WĬN gāt
Winkler — WĬNGK ler
Winnsboro — WĬNZ buh ruh
Winona — wī NŌ nuh
Winterhaven — WĬN ter hā v'n
Winters — WĬN terz
Woden — WŌD n
Wolfe City — woolf SĬT ĭ
Wolfforth — WOOL forth
Woodbine — WOOD bīn
Woodlake — wood LĀK
Woodland — WOOD l'nd
Woodlawn — wood LAWN
Woodrow — WOOD roh
Woodsboro — WOODZ buh ruh
Woodson — WOOD s'n
Woodville — WOOD v'l
Wortham — WERTH uhm
Wright City — rīt SĬT ĭ
Wrightsboro — RĪTS buh ruh
Wylie — WĪ lĭ

Y

Yancey — YĂN sĭ
Yantis — YĂN tĭs
Yoakum — YŌ k'm
Yorktown — YAWRK town
Youngsport — YUHNGZ pohrt
Ysleta — ĭs LĔT uh

Z

Zapata — zuh PAH tuh
Zavalla — zuh VĂL uh
Zephyr — ZĔF er
Zuehl — ZEE uhl

INDEX

Page numbers in *italics* refer to photographs and artwork and their captions.

F

I

J

Q

R

U

V

W

Y

Z

AD INDEX

Happy Trails